THE
BIRDS
OF
OHIO

THE BIRDS OF OHIO

□

by Bruce G. Peterjohn

Original Paintings
by William Zimmerman

INDIANA UNIVERSITY PRESS □ BLOOMINGTON & INDIANAPOLIS

MANUFACTURED IN JAPAN

Library of Congress Cataloging-in-Publication Data

Peterjohn, Bruce G.
The birds of Ohio / by Bruce G. Peterjohn ; original paintings by
William Zimmerman.
p.   cm.
Bibliography: p.
Includes index.
ISBN 0-253-34183-3
1. Birds—Ohio.   I. Zimmerman, William.   II. Title.
QL684.03P48   1989   89-45202
  598.29771—dc20   CIP
1 2 3 4 5 93 92 91 90 89

To Mary

CONTENTS

SPECIES
ACCOUNTS

1

Species are listed in taxonomic order
following the 1983 American Ornithologists'
Union Check-list and its supplements

ILLUSTRATIONS

PREFACE

Despite Ohio's reputation as a heavily urbanized state with extensive farmlands, it actually boasts a wide variety of habitats. This variety extends from the dry cedar barrens in Adams County near the Ohio River to the damp northeastern beech-maple forests in Ashtabula County and from the forested hillsides in the southeastern unglaciated counties to the Lake Erie marshes in the northwest. The diversity of habitats is attributable to Ohio's location at the point of transition between the Appalachian highlands to the east and the broad plains to the west. Not surprisingly, these diverse habitats attract a wide variety of migrant and resident birds to the state.

The composition of this avifauna has changed dramatically since the last comprehensive books describing the birds of Ohio were published in 1903. When William Dawson was writing his delightful volumes, birds such as Bewick's Wrens and Bachman's Sparrows were just beginning to invade Ohio. These species eventually established sizable populations, flourished for several decades, and mysteriously vanished. And when Lynds Jones's book was in preparation, heron populations had been decimated by the millinery trade, while waterfowl and shorebirds were suffering from market hunting. With adequate protection, these groups have recovered and some shorebirds may have become more numerous today than at any time in the past century. These examples are just a few of the many changes in Ohio's avifauna during the twentieth century, a pattern that has probably accelerated since 1940 as urban expansion and agricultural land-use practices continue to alter the state's habitats. Similar changes will undoubtedly occur in the future, and Ohio's avifauna of the twenty-first century will most likely be different from what we observe today.

This book is not intended to be a field guide. Instead, it was written to give an accounting of the present relative abundance and distribution of all species of birds that have been seen in Ohio and to provide some insight into their habitat preferences and breeding biology. In addition, I have chronicled the historical changes in abundance and distribution of many species since the late 1800s.

During the preparation of this book, I have relied on my own observations as well as the published and unpublished accounts of numerous observers. Interpretation of published and unpublished records is always a difficult process, especially when exceptionally large numbers, unseasonal dates, or difficult-to-identify species are reported without accompanying details. Although many of these records may be accurate, it is impossible to establish positively the veracity of undocumented sightings. When citing records in this book, I have admittedly taken a conservative stance and accepted only documented records or those reported by reputable observers and fitting established patterns of occurrence. The omission of published records does not necessarily imply that the birds were misidentified, only that they were supported by less than convincing details. My intention was to report the accurate records while putting the questionable sightings to rest. Today's birders should recognize the problems involved in the field identification of birds and strive to keep accurate and detailed records of their observations, including thorough descriptions of all unusual or unseasonal sightings. This information will prove invaluable for future researchers attempting to establish the veracity of sight records.

This book not only documents our knowledge of Ohio birds but also demonstrates areas of ignorance. New species are being discovered within our borders almost annually, and there is much still to be learned about many of the species that are regularly recorded from the state. It is hoped that this book will stimulate studies of the more poorly known species in order to fill in the gaps in our knowledge.

The relationship between habitat availability and the abundance of birds is obvious. Declining bird populations during the twentieth century are almost invariably caused by the loss of habitats. Habitat destruction has continued at an accelerated pace in recent decades, threatening to eliminate several vegetative communities and the wildlife associated with them. The issue of habitat preservation and wise use of our natural resources should be of the utmost importance to anyone interested in the welfare of birds. The maintenance of Ohio's diverse avifauna can be achieved only through the protection and conservation of all the state's natural habitats.

ACKNOWLEDGMENTS

This undertaking could not have been accomplished without the assistance of many birders and professional ornithologists throughout Ohio. Special thanks are due to the other members of the Ohio Bird Records Committee, Ray Hannikman, Jean Hoffman, Larry Rosche, and Elliot Tramer, whose previous review of innumerable sightings and research of historical records made this task much easier. I am also indebted to John Condit of the Ohio State University Museum of Zoology, Robert Kennedy of the Cincinnati Museum of Natural History, and Tim Matson of the Cleveland Museum of Natural History, who kindly allowed me to examine specimens at their respective museums. Ken Parkes of the Carnegie Museum of Natural History graciously provided information on specimens under his care. I am especially grateful to Dan Rice of the Ohio Department of Natural Resources, Division of Natural Areas and Preserves, for generously allowing me access, prior to publication, to some of the data obtained for the Ohio Breeding Bird Atlas. I am also grateful to the hundreds of birders who participated in this endeavor.

Most important, observers throughout Ohio contributed significant sightings, either through their regular reports submitted to the seasonal summaries published in *American Birds* or in other correspondence. These observers include Jon Ahlquist, J. Kirk Alexander, Matt Anderson, Ron Austing, Carole Babyak, Frank Bader, Robert Ball, H. Thomas Bartlett, Charles and Betty Berry, Kay Booth, W. William Brockner, Jerry Cairo, Lou Campbell, Cliff Cathers, Nancy Cherry, Bob Conlin, Dave Corbin (deceased), Joseph Croy, M. Owen Davies, Elinor Elder, F. W. Fais, Vic Fazio, Jim Fry, John Gallagher, Charles Gambill, Larry Gara, Bruce Glick, Robert Graham, Mary Gustafson, Ray Hannikman, Rob Harlan, Jim Haw, John Herman, Jim Hickman, Jim Hill, Chuck Hocevar, Jim Hoffman, Richard and Jean Hoffman, Judy Howard, James Ingold, Paula Jack, Tom Kemp, William and Nancy Klamm, Dennis Kline, Vernon Kline, Jean Knoblaugh, Tom LePage, Tony Leukering, Karl Maslowski, Charlotte Mathena, Jim McCormac, Steve McKee, Howard and Marcella Meahl, Dave Nolan, Reed Noss, Dave Osborne, Doug Overacker, J. Paul Perkins, A. Town Peterson, Dan Petit, Ken Petit, Ed Pierce, John Pogacnik, Worth Randle, Bill Reiner, Frank Renfrow, Dan Rice, Larry Rosche, Ed Schlabach, Mark Shieldcastle, John Shrader, Dave Smith, Bruce Stehling, Dave Styer, Ethel Surman (deceased), Bert Szabo, Jerry Talkington, Merrill Tawse, Tom Thomson, Elliot Tramer, Don Tumblin, Carol Tveekrem, Laurel Van Camp, Norm Walker, Pete Whan, and Art Wiseman. My thanks to all these people; their contributions are reflected in the wealth of information made available to me.

Other individuals provided assistance in the preparation of the manuscript. I am very grateful to Bill and Mary Baum, retired librarians at the Cleveland Museum of Natural History, who graciously allowed me access to all references under their care. Tom Bartlett, Dan Rice, and Jeff White also provided references that were not available from other sources. Dorothea Peterjohn spent many tedious hours entering most of the manuscript into the computer. Finally, Mary Gustafson provided invaluable assistance through the duration of the project, from providing references to entering manuscript to keeping me from destroying the computer after it scrambled a full disk of manuscript. In all likelihood, this book would never have been completed without her support.

I am also indebted to my parents, Dorothea and the late Alvin Peterjohn, who supported my interest in birds at an early age and tolerated it when it became an obsession. I must also express my deep appreciation to the late Evelyn Gordon, who had the patience to take me birding during my formative years and taught me the proper approach to the field identification of birds.

I wish to thank the staff at Indiana University Press for their advice and assistance throughout the preparation of the manuscript. John Gallman, Director of the Press, initiated the project and undertook the fund-raising that made it a reality. The manuscript benefited from the editing of Roberta L. Diehl and Kenneth Goodall. My thanks also go to the other staff members who contributed to the publication of this book.

BRUCE G. PETERJOHN

It would be impossible to list everyone who has assisted in the preparation of this book. I am particularly grateful, however, to the following individuals and companies who have purchased many of the paintings and without whom my part of this publication would have been impossible to complete: Mr. and Mrs. Jeffery Auer, Borden Incorporated, Mr. and Mrs. George Byers, Jr., Mr. and Mrs. Donald H. Clark, Mr. and Mrs. Steven L. Clark, Mr. and Mrs. Ralph Cobey, Mr. and Mrs. Thomas E. Donnelley II, Mrs. Elaine Ewing Fess, Dr. Stephen W. Fess, David and Libby Frey, Mr. Lawrence W. Friel, Jr., Mr. Daniel M. Galbreath, and Dr. and Mrs. G. E. Gustafson. Thanks also to Jay Shuler, for his constant support and advice; DeVere Burt, Director, and Robert S. Kennedy, Deputy Director, Collection and Research Division, for allowing me unlimited access to the bird collection at the Cincinnati Museum of Natural History; Jenny and Art Wiseman, for their assistance in selecting bird skins used; Willard L. Boyd, President, Scott M. Lanyon, Division Head and Assistant Curator of Birds, and David E. Willard, Collection Manager, for their ongoing willingness to loan me specimens from Chicago's Field Museum of Natural History; John A. Ruthven, for generously allowing us to use his beautiful painting of the Passenger Pigeon; and the employees of Indiana University Press for their assistance while this work was in progress and especially John Gallman, Director of the Press, for his untiring support and dedication from the project's conception. To my wife, Judy, and children, Martha and Matthew, for their sacrifices and assistance in the many tasks involved in the completion of this book, I dedicate the paintings.

WILLIAM ZIMMERMAN

It is fitting that a contemporary study of the birds of Ohio should include the Passenger Pigeon, a bird that flew the skies of Ohio in such countless numbers that they obscured the sun. In 1813 John James Audubon witnessed and recorded such flights. One hundred and one years later the last of the species, a female named Martha, died in the Cincinnati Zoo.

We destroyed the Passenger Pigeon for food, for feathers to decorate hats, and because we found it undesirable to cohabit with flocks of such incredible numbers. That is why I chose to paint a single bird to represent the once most abundant bird species on the face of the earth.

I am honored that my good friend Bill Zimmerman asked me to do this painting, and I dedicate it to the memory of Stanley Rowe, Sr., a man who loved nature and did so much to increase the public's awareness and appreciation of it.

JOHN A. RUTHVEN

John A. Ruthven

INTRODUCTION

An understanding of bird distribution patterns within Ohio requires knowledge of the state's physiography, vegetative communities, and climatology. People unfamiliar with Ohio may think of it as a state whose large urban areas are surrounded by extensive cornfields and few redeeming natural features. Admittedly, portions of Ohio are heavily urbanized and other areas are intensively farmed, but the state still supports thousands of acres of woodlands, successional fields, and wetlands that are inhabited by diverse and abundant avian communities.

The state of Ohio contains 41,263 square miles, extending approximately 210 miles north to south and 215 miles east to west. Elevations vary from 1550 feet above mean sea level near Bellefontaine in Logan County to 450 feet above mean sea level at the mouth of the Great Miami River in southwestern Hamilton County.

Ohio is exposed to a continental temperate climate. Precipitation is fairly evenly distributed, from mean annual levels of thirty-one to thirty-three inches in the northwestern counties near Lake Erie to forty-one to forty-four inches in northeastern Ohio and the south-central counties. Snowfall is greatest in the northeastern counties, particularly in the "snowbelt"

east of Cleveland, where it averages in excess of one hundred inches annually in Geauga County. Annual snowfall totals average more than fifty inches in other northeastern counties. In contrast, fewer than twenty inches of snow are expected each winter in the southern counties bordering the Ohio River. During winter, mean daily maximum temperatures approach or slightly exceed thirty-two degrees Fahrenheit. Periods of cold weather are frequent, and temperatures may drop below zero. The coldest temperature officially recorded was thirty-nine degrees below zero in Perry County on February 10, 1899. Summer temperatures normally peak during July, with mean daily maximums of eighty to eighty-two degrees in the northeastern counties and eighty-eight degrees in southern Ohio. Temperatures seldom exceed one hundred degrees but have been recorded as high as 113 in Gallia County on July 21, 1934.

Ohio is underlain by sedimentary rocks formed during the Paleozoic era 600 million to 200 million years ago.[47] The oldest formations are under the western half of the state—primarily limestones, dolomites, and shales. The eastern counties are underlain by younger sandstones, shales, limestones, and coals.

The existing topography is a result of a series of glacial invasions during the Pleistocene epoch. Within the past two million years, at least eight ice sheets have formed and covered portions of the state under as much as five thousand to eight thousand feet of ice. These ice sheets advanced slowly and covered the state for thousands of years, acting as giant bulldozers as they indelibly changed the landscape. Then they retreated. The most recent ice sheet, known as the Wisconsin glacier, melted only eleven thousand years ago, leaving the terrain that is visible today.[462] The western half of Ohio was covered by one or more ice sheets, creating flat to rolling terrain know as till plains. Similar till plains also characterize the northeastern counties. Unglaciated terrain is restricted to the southern and eastern counties, where the hilly countryside has local relief of one hundred to four hundred feet, and occasionally as high as eight hundred feet at bluffs overlooking the Ohio River.[126]

These topographic features and the natural vegetative communities form five distinct physiographic regions in Ohio. The avifauna of each region is different and, in combination, result in the diverse bird community that is known in the state. To better understand the reasons behind these bird distribution patterns, I will briefly describe the physiographic regions.

Unglaciated Allegheny Plateau. An important feature influencing bird distribution in Ohio is the glacial boundary. South of this boundary, the topography is very hilly with steep valleys dissected by small high-gradient streams. With its hilly terrain and relatively infertile soils, this portion of the Allegheny Plateau supports the most extensive woodlands in Ohio. Several woodland communities may be present depending upon exposure. In general, upland mixed oak forests are found along the upper slopes and ridges, dominated by various oaks and hickories. Mixed mesophytic forests occupy the lower protected slopes. These forests may be composed of beeches, oaks, elms, maples, tulip trees, cherries, and occasionally hemlocks. Lowland forests along streams also have a mixed composition, including sycamores, elms, ashes, maples, cottonwoods, and willows.[128]

Successional habitats are widely distributed where these forests have been cleared. Other habitats are relatively scarce within the rugged terrain on the unglaciated plateau. Farmlands tend to be small and are as likely to be devoted to pastures and hayfields as to cultivated crops. Wetlands are generally small and sparsely distributed except where they have been created as a result of strip mining. Open-water habitats are largely restricted to reservoirs and portions of the Scioto and Muskingum Rivers. Most counties are sparsely inhabited, with the largest cities scattered along the Ohio River and its major tributaries.

In portions of Harrison, Tuscarawas, Coshocton, Guernsey, Belmont, Muskingum, and Morgan Counties, these habitats have been greatly modified by strip mining. The forests, farmlands, and other habitats were destroyed and replaced by highly modified habitats. Old strip mines were not reclaimed and are presently reverting to various successional habitats. These strip mines frequently altered drainage patterns, creating wetlands in areas where such habitats were formerly absent. In contrast, recent strip mines are reclaimed to rolling terrain covered with extensive grasslands.

Glaciated Allegheny Plateau. The glaciated Allegheny Plateau extends from Ashtabula and Medina Counties south to Ross County. Since the glacier covered this portion of the plateau, the terrain is less hilly than that of the unglaciated counties.[126] This rolling terrain is more suitable for agriculture and urban development, and its natural habitats have been subjected to greater modification. Wooded habitats tend to be restricted to numerous isolated woodlots rather than the extensive forests characteristic of the unglaciated plateau.

Woodland communities are fairly similar to those on the unglaciated hillsides except within the northeastern counties, where beech-maple forests predominate.[128] Woodland, edge, and successional habitats are interspersed with farmlands and urban areas, producing the greatest diversity of terrestrial habitats of any of the state's physiographic regions. Wetlands are still widely distributed within the northeastern counties, although their acreage has greatly decreased as a result of drainage. These wetlands are found south to Holmes and Ashland Counties, including the marshes along the Killbuck Creek valley that constitute the largest remaining wetlands in the interior of Ohio. These habitats become sparsely distributed farther south along the glaciated plateau. Large reservoirs are generally restricted to the northeastern counties. Portions of Stark and Columbiana Counties have been modified by strip mining, but the glaciated plateau has not been subject to the severe modifications characteristic of portions of the unglaciated plateau.

Bluegrass Region. Our smallest physiographic region lies at the western edge of the Allegheny Plateau in portions of Adams and Brown Counties, an extension of the bluegrass region of Kentucky. Its terrain is similar to that of other unglaciated counties, but the area is underlain by limestone and shale bedrock rather than sandstone. In most aspects, the plant communities and prevailing land use are similar to those of the unglaciated plateau. The dry exposed hillsides, however, also support extensive red cedar barrens—abandoned fields overgrown with cedars—while supporting few other woody species.[128]

Lake Plain. A flat plain stretches along the south shore of Lake Erie. Only several miles wide from Ashtabula County west to Erie County, it eventually widens to cover most of northwestern Ohio. This plain was once the bottom of a larger lake formed during the retreat of the last glacier. As this glacial lake dried up, it left a plain with a slope of only two to three feet per mile, broken by a series of low sandy beach ridges.

With its flat terrain and poorly drained soils, this lake plain originally supported a vast wooded swamp known as the Great Black Swamp.[246] It covered approximately fifteen hundred square miles, beginning near Fort Wayne, Indiana, and paralleling the Maumee River to Lake Erie. This swamp supported an extensive elm-ash forest that was flooded during spring, was mostly mud through the summer and fall, and froze in winter.[128] Dry terrain was restricted to the beach ridges and narrow strips of land along the Maumee River and its larger tributaries. This inhospitable terrain was largely uninhabited until the mid-1800s when drainage projects were undertaken. Its destruction was very rapid, and virtually the entire swamp forest was converted to farmlands before 1900.[246]

Other habitats originally found along the lake plain in northwestern Ohio included extensive wet prairies that were flooded during spring and supported dense stands of grasses and other prairie vegetation later in the summer. Perhaps its most unique habitats were the Oak Openings west of Toledo in portions of Lucas and Fulton Counties. These openings occupy a ten-mile-wide strip of sandy land along a glacial beach ridge. They supported patchy open oak-hickory forests, interspersed with swamp forests, prairies, and marshes.[128]

Today the lake plain is probably the most highly modified of Ohio's physiographic regions. The Great Black Swamp has been transformed into some of the state's most productive and intensively cultivated lands. More than 90 percent of the land is farmed, with natural habitats restricted to isolated oak-hickory woodlots. In the northwestern counties, only the unproductive soils within the Oak Openings are not intensively farmed, and they support the most extensive remaining natural habitats. Most of the lake plain east from Huron has undergone extensive urbanization. Undeveloped lands are generally farmed, although some wooded habitats remain in portions of Lake and Ashtabula Counties.

Till Plains. The remainder of western Ohio is till plains created by the Wisconsin and Illinoian glaciers. These plains have a little more topographic relief than the lake plain, becoming rolling hills along end moraines. The Wisconsin till plain extends south to Butler, Warren, Clinton, and Highland Counties.[126] Farther south, the Illinoian till plain was only slightly modified by the ice sheet and the terrain becomes rather hilly.

Initially, these till plains supported extensive oak-hickory and beech-maple forests with a few prairie openings in central Ohio.[128] With their productive soils and relatively flat terrain, the till plains proved to be valuable farmlands. The forests were removed and replaced by cultivated fields, especially along the Wisconsin till plain where only isolated woodlots remain. While the original forests were also removed from the Illinois till plain, the hilly terrain and poorly drained soils are less suitable for agriculture. Second-growth forest, edge, and successional habitats are more widely distributed on this plain than in other counties in western Ohio. At one time, wetlands were widely scattered along the Wisconsin till plain, especially near the prairie openings. Similar habitats were scarce on the Illinois plain. These wetlands have largely been destroyed by drainage activities.

Lake Erie. No discussion of Ohio's physiography would be complete without mention of Lake Erie. Lake Erie is divided into three basins, two of which are associated with Ohio's waters. These basins have different physical characteristics that strongly influence the composition and relative abundance of their water-bird communities.

The Western Basin extends east to the Lake Erie islands and Cedar Point at the mouth of Sandusky Bay. The shallowest basin, the Western has an average depth of twenty-five to thirty-five feet with a maximum depth of sixty-two feet. At one time, this basin was bordered by extensive marshes. Each bay hosted abundant growths of aquatic and emergent vegetation, with the extent of this vegetation fluctuating in response to changes in water levels.[128] The nature of these wetlands has changed dramatically during the present century. Expanding lake levels and increased concentrations of suspended sediments have transformed these bays into large expanses of open water with little or no vegetation. During strong southerly winds or other periods with low water, extensive mudflats may be exposed within these bays. The wetlands have not entirely disappeared. Instead, most have been diked in order to maintain relatively constant water levels and vegetative communities.

The Central Basin of Lake Erie extends from the Lake Erie islands and Cedar Point east to Erie, Pennsylvania. This basin has an average depth of sixty-one feet and a maximum depth of eighty-four feet. In contrast to the Western Basin, the Central Basin is bordered by few sizable bays, wetlands, or exposed mudflats. Unlike the shores of the other Great Lakes, the south shore of Lake Erie does not have great quantities of sand and does not form extensive dune systems. Its beaches are narrow and include much gravel.

Of all features on the Ohio landscape, the lakefront makes the greatest single contribution to the overall diversity and abundance of the state's avifauna. Large numbers of waterfowl, shorebirds, gulls, terns, and other water birds visit Lake Erie each year. Among the flocks of expected species, small numbers of rarities are regularly detected. But the lake's influence extends beyond attracting large numbers of water birds. It serves as a migration corridor for hawks each spring, funneling them around both ends of the lake because many species are reluctant to pass over this large body of open water. Lake Erie also serves as the focal point of the annual songbird migrations.

Each spring, favorable winds produce phenomenal flights along the south shore, where songbirds gather to rest and feed before continuing their northward movements. Fall flights are generally not as spectacular, although sizable movements may be noted on northerly winds as flocks of migrant songbirds land on the south shore to rest after flying across the lake.

The habitats within Ohio have been extensively modified during historic times. These changes were exhaustively described by Trautman,[483,485] and I will only briefly summarize them. These changes are very important historically. Not only have they had a tremendous influence on the expansion of a number of species into the state; they have also affected the relative abundance of species that were already present.

The initial settlement of Ohio began during the eighteenth century. The settlers encountered a largely forested state. The primeval forest, Trautman reported, was composed of stately oaks, "many of them six feet and more in diameter, towering up royally fifty and sixty feet without a limb; the shellbark hickories, and the glowing maples, both with tops far aloft; the mild and moss-covered ash trees, some of them over four feet through; the elms and beeches, the great black walnuts, and the ghostly-robed sycamores, huge in limb and body, along the creek bottoms." Ohio was not uniformly forested. Even in the southern and eastern counties there were occasional openings produced by storms or cleared by Indians. The northwestern and central counties supported numerous prairie openings where grasses grew "as high as a horse's back" and woody vegetation was largely absent. At the beginning of the nineteenth century, Ohio was still largely undisturbed. An estimated forty-five thousand people inhabited the state in scattered settlements along large rivers and Lake Erie.

Ohio's human population expanded tremendously during the nineteenth century, to two million by 1850 and 4.1 million in 1900, according to Trautman. This population explosion greatly altered the face of the state. Most of the virgin forests disappeared before 1860 except within the Great Black Swamp; there, they were largely cleared during the 1870s and 1880s. The prairies also disappeared as their productive soils were converted to farmlands. Many wetlands were drained for agricultural purposes. By the late 1800s, most of Ohio was actively farmed with numerous small farm fields interspersed among brushy fencerows and occasional woodlots. Even in the hilly unglaciated counties, agricultural fields predominated.

Not surprisingly, the composition of Ohio's avifauna was radically altered during the nineteenth century. Species dependent on mature forests and other undisturbed habitats declined or disappeared. Other species benefited from these habitat changes, particularly birds occupying agricultural fields and shrubby edge habitats. A number of species invaded Ohio during the century, while others increased dramatically as suitable habitats became available.

The landscape continued to change during the twentieth century. Ohio's human population continued to expand and presently exceeds eleven million. Urban areas grew rapidly, converting farmlands and woodlands to residential areas. Agricultural practices became increasingly mechanized and dependent on pesticides, herbicides, and fertilizers to maintain production. These trends, particularly evident after 1940, resulted in greatly enlarged fields and the elimination of many shrubby fencerows and isolated woodlots. While agricultural fields formerly supported abundant and fairly diverse wildlife communities, today's habitats are relatively barren and occupied by few species of wildlife. Not all habitat changes have been adverse during this century. In the unglaciated counties, many small farms were abandoned and the land underwent successional changes and reverted to second-growth woods. Extensive forests presently exist where numerous small farm fields were formerly widespread.

Ohio's bird communities also continued to change during the present century. A few species expanded their ranges into the state, but their numbers were relatively small compared with the wholesale changes that occurred during the 1800s. Instead, bird populations changed in each portion of the state as patterns of habitat availability were altered. In urban areas and intensively farmed lands, many species substantially declined. Conversely, many woodland species prospered along the unglaciated Allegheny Plateau and adjacent counties as wooded acreages increased. Specific changes in the relative abundance and distribution of birds in Ohio during the twentieth century are described in the species accounts.

Given the immense magnitude of the changes to its landscape, Ohio is fortunate to have a fairly complete set of historical references describing its avifauna. While Ohio was visited in the early 1800s by the prominent ornithologists John James Audubon and Alexander Wilson, their coverage of the state was fragmentary and their writings contain many vague secondhand reports in addition to their personal observations. The first statewide investigation of the Ohio avifauna was performed by Dr. Jared Kirtland in the 1830s.[251] Kirtland became one of the prominent American naturalists of the mid-1800s, continuing his studies until his death in 1877. In the 1870s, Dr. J. M. Wheaton was Ohio's most prominent ornithologist. While his studies were largely restricted to central Ohio, his periodic observations from other areas along with reports by other reliable naturalists prompted him to publish the *Report on the Birds of Ohio* in 1882.[522]

After Wheaton's untimely death, William Dawson and Lynds Jones were recognized as the most authoritative ornithologists in Ohio. Jones largely confined his studies to northern Ohio, while Dawson was based in Columbus. The two men independently published their accounts of Ohio's avifauna in 1903.[102,236] Dawson left the state shortly after his book was published, but Jones actively contributed observations through the first decades of the twentieth century.

Surprisingly, there has not been a comprehensive statewide publication on Ohio's avifauna since 1903. Several annotated checklists briefly discussed statewide distribution patterns, most notably the lists produced by Borror in 1950,[45] Trautman and Trautman in 1968,[488] and Peterjohn et al. in 1987.[389] However, a number of regional publications thoroughly described the distribution and abundance of birds in various portions of the state. These publications were produced by the most prominent naturalists and ornithologists of the twentieth century.

In northwestern Ohio, Lou Campbell has extensively studied birds along western Lake Erie since the 1920s, producing au-

thoritative references on the birds of the Toledo area in 1940 and 1968.[86,89] These books were based on his own sightings and observations by Harold Mayfield, Milton Trautman, Laurel Van Camp, and other active naturalists. In contrast, the counties away from the lakefront have received relatively scant attention, except in Paulding and portions of adjacent counties where Homer Price was an active oologist into the 1930s and studied birds into the 1970s.[424,429] In west-central Ohio, most ornithological activity has been around Lake St. Mary's, where Clarence Clark regularly observed birds from the 1940s into the 1960s.[98]

The southwestern counties have been intensively studied throughout the twentieth century. Ben Blincoe contributed observations from the Dayton area between the 1920s and the 1960s. His sightings, along with more recent reports, were summarized by Mathena et al.[299] A number of naturalists have been active in the Cincinnati area since the 1930s. Emerson Kemsies was the most prominent ornithologist; he collaborated with Worth Randle to publish the only comprehensive book on the area's avifauna in 1953.[248] Other knowledgeable naturalists, including G. Ronald Austing, Woodrow Goodpaster, and Karl Maslowski, also significantly contributed to our understanding of southwestern Ohio bird distribution patterns.

For central Ohio, the classic reference on bird distribution is Milton Trautman's exhaustive study on the birds of Buckeye Lake during the 1920s and 1930s.[479] While there are no recent comprehensive references from the central Ohio area, observations by Donald Borror, myself, Edward Thomas, Tom Thomson, Milton and Mary Trautman, and other individuals have documented the changes in the area's avifauna since the 1940s. In northeastern Ohio, the Cleveland-Akron region has also been extensively studied since the 1920s, culminating in regional books produced by Arthur Williams in 1950[523] and Donald Newman in 1969.[335]

The unglaciated counties have traditionally received the poorest coverage with only sporadic reports from most counties. There is much to be learned about the patterns of bird distribution and abundance along the unglaciated plateau. The same situation applies to the north-central and northeastern counties away from the Cleveland-Akron area. With the exception of Jones's studies in Lorain and Erie Counties into the 1920s and Hicks's monograph on the breeding birds of Ashtabula County,[215] these areas have also been largely ignored during the twentieth century.

In addition to these regional publications, the distribution of breeding birds has been the subject of two statewide studies. As a part of his extensive travels through Ohio, Lawrence Hicks accumulated a wealth of breeding bird data during the late 1920s and 1930s. Much of this information appeared in his monograph on the breeding birds of Ohio published in 1935[220] and survey of the breeding birds in unglaciated Ohio published in 1937.[223] The Ohio breeding avifauna was largely ignored until 1982 when the Breeding Bird Atlas project was undertaken under the sponsorship of the Division of Natural Areas and Preserves within the Ohio Department of Natural Resources. This project continued through 1987, systematically surveying the breeding birds in every county of Ohio.[434]

REFERENCES

Obviously, any book describing the birds of Ohio relies on these regional and statewide references for information on the historical status, distribution, and relative abundance of the state's avifauna. In addition to these comprehensive references, numerous articles and notes appearing in various journals provide significant information. Another valuable source of distributional data on Ohio's birds is the seasonal summaries in the National Audubon Society's publications *Bird-Lore, Audubon Field Notes,* and *American Birds.* Beginning in the 1930s in *Bird-Lore,* these summaries have included the sightings of countless observers across the state, many of which were never published elsewhere. As the summaries became more sophisticated in later decades, the wealth of material on bird distribution and abundance in Ohio noticeably improved. All of these sources of material were reviewed for this book. All cited sources are included in the Bibliography. Many other articles and notes were reviewed but did not include material pertinent to this book.

Some unpublished information was also regularly utilized. Most unpublished material came from my personal records, which cover observations from every county during the past twenty-five years. Other unpublished sightings were obtained from reports submitted to the regional editors of *American Birds* since 1970.

A few sources of information were not utilized in the preparation of this book, particularly sightings published in the newsletters of local Audubon societies and natural history clubs. While most of these sightings may be accurate, they frequently lack supporting details and their veracity cannot be ascertained. In some instances, these newsletters include sightings from two states but do not provide adequate information to determine in which state the birds were actually observed. Similar problems plague recently published statewide bird journals, which include unreliable observations as well as numerous errors with regard to dates and locations. Material from the statewide publications was utilized only when it could be cross-referenced with other sources.

SPECIES ACCOUNTS

The species accounts in this book describe the abundance, distribution, and historic status of 390 species of birds positively recorded from Ohio as of June 30, 1988. As described in Peterjohn et al.,[389] species on the state list have been documented by specimens, identifiable photographs, or complete written descriptions prepared at the time of observation. Species lacking adequate documentation or thought to have escaped from captivity were excluded from the text.

To be consistent, the categories used to describe the status of Ohio's bird species are the same used by Peterjohn et al.:

Abundant. Requires no special effort to locate, widely distributed, and conspicuous when present.

Common. Present in lesser numbers than indicated by "abundant," but nearly always found when searched for in the appropriate habitat and season.

Fairly common. Not always found when searched for in the appropriate habitat, although frequently can be found with persistent effort.

Uncommon. Observed infrequently and found in small numbers, even in its preferred habitat.

Rare. Observed annually, but generally not more than once or twice a year despite diligent efforts to locate in appropriate habitat.

Casual. Not observed annually, but has established an apparent pattern of occurrence.

Accidental. Has single records or a very small number of scattered records without an established pattern of occurrence.

Extirpated. Formerly had established populations in Ohio that completely disappeared from the state. Extant populations are still present elsewhere in North America.

Use of these terms recognizes that abundance levels vary for the different groups of birds. Hence, songbirds might be considered "common" if 25–75 individuals are normally observed, while 5–10 hawks would constitue a "common" raptor.

Other terms used in the species accounts include:

Permanent resident. A species residing in Ohio throughout the year.

Summer resident. A species nesting in Ohio and present primarily during the breeding season.

Winter resident. A species appearing in Ohio throughout the winter months.

Summer visitor. A species appearing in Ohio during the summer months, but normally remaining for only a few days or weeks. These species do not normally breed in the state. Summer visitors do not include species that regularly migrate through Ohio during summer.

Winter visitor. A species only appearing for a few days or weeks during winter but not spending the entire season in the state. For example, species such as the House Wren that normally migrate during September and October but occasionally linger into December are treated as winter visitors since they normally disappear before the season is over. Birds that normally migrate during early winter are treated as migrants rather than winter visitors.

The calendar year was divided into the four seasons as follows: spring, March through May; summer, June and July; autumn, August through November; winter, December through February.

To facilitate discussion of avian distribution patterns, the state was subdivided into eight regions (see map, next page):

1 *Western Lake Erie.* The Western Basin of Lake Erie, extending east to the Lake Erie islands and the mouth of Sandusky Bay; includes all lands within two miles of the immediate lakefront.

2 *Central Lake Erie.* The Central Basin of Lake Erie, extending eastward from the Lake Erie islands and Cedar Point (Erie County); includes all lands within two miles of the lakefront.

3 *Northwestern counties.* All counties from the western border east to Erie, Huron, and Richland and from the northern

border south to Paulding, Putnam, Hancock, Wyandot, and Crawford.

4 *Northeastern counties*. All counties north of the glacial boundary and from Lorain and Ashland Counties east to the border.

5 *Unglaciated counties*. The southeastern portion of the state occupying the unglaciated Allegheny Plateau.

6 *Southwestern counties*. All counties from the southern border north to Preble, Montgomery, Greene, and Clinton Counties and west to the glacial boundary in Highland and Adams Counties.

7 *Central counties*. Franklin and Delaware Counties along with all contiguous counties and glaciated portions of Ross County.

8 *West-central counties*. All counties from Van Wert, Allen, and Hardin south through Darke, Miami, and Clark.

For some species, the state was divided into northern, central, and southern thirds. In these cases, *northern Ohio* refers to the northwestern and northeastern counties; *central Ohio* refers to the west-central and central counties and the unglaciated plateau south through Muskingum, Guernsey, and Belmont Counties; and *southern Ohio* refers to the southwestern counties and unglaciated plateau north through Perry, Morgan, Noble, and Monroe Counties.

For some species, the state was divided into western and eastern portions. In these cases, *western Ohio* refers to the northwestern, west-central, central, and southwestern counties and *eastern Ohio* refers to the northeastern and all unglaciated counties.

SPECIES
ACCOUNTS

□

RED-THROATED LOON

Gavia stellata (Pontoppidan)

Red-throated Loons, like many other water birds, have benefited from the building of reservoirs. Before 1955, these loons were casual to accidental migrants in Ohio, with most sightings from Lake Erie and the northern counties. The number of records increased during the late 1950s and early 1960s, mostly within the interior counties, where Red-throateds were repeatedly observed on new reservoirs. They have been annually reported since 1965. These increased sightings do not necessarily reflect expanding populations. They may only represent migrants that formerly flew over the state but presently rest and feed on the large lakes.

Red-throated Loons are casual to rare fall migrants on large lakes, with two to five sightings statewide most years. During the autumn of 1985, a small flight of at least 13 scattered individuals was reported.[380] Fall migrants are mostly individuals observed along central Lake Erie and on large reservoirs in the northern and glaciated central counties. They are inexplicably scarce in western Lake Erie and casual migrants through southwestern Ohio and the unglaciated counties. The validity of several late September sight records is questionable in the absence of supporting details. The earliest confirmed migrants returned between October 19 and 26. Most are reported during November, peaking between November 10 and 20 when as many as 3 Red-throateds have been reported. Many stop for an hour or two before continuing their journey; some may linger as long as a week. The last fall migrants normally depart by December 12–20.

Red-throated Loons have always been accidental midwinter visitors, with fewer than ten sightings between January and early March. Most winter records are along Lake Erie between Cleveland and Ashtabula, including a February 19, 1909, specimen at Ashtabula originally identified as a Pacific Loon.[45] In addition, there are inland winter records from Summit Lake in Akron during 1959 and 1965.[322,396] Most winter records are before 1966. The only recent visitor was recorded along Lake Erie at Oregon (Lucas County) on January 4, 1986.[381]

Spring Red-throated Loons have always been accidental to casual visitors to Ohio. They are reported once every two or three years, appearing between mid-March and mid-May and remaining as late as May 22–26. They are invariably solitary individuals, frequently in nonbreeding plumage and mostly at inland reservoirs. There are no summer records from Ohio.

PACIFIC LOON

Gavia pacifica (Lawrence)

Ohio's only confirmed Pacific Loon was discovered by Kirk Alexander, John Pogacnik, and Rick Counts on Lake Erie off Huron on December 7, 1985. This first-winter individual was studied by many observers through December 10.[381] Despite the absence of substantiating photographs, the described characteristics eliminate all similar species.

The Pacific Loon has recently been recognized as a distinct species. It is the North American counterpart of the Arctic Loon, whose range extends across Eurasia. Pacific Loons breed across the Arctic tundra from Hudson Bay west to Alaska. They normally winter along the Pacific Coast of North America.[5] They are also rare but regular migrants through the interior western states and have appeared casually east to the Great Lakes.

COMMON LOON

Gavia immer (Brünnich)

Few sounds are as enchanting as the calls of a Common Loon, which are mixtures of sharp cries, loud yells, and rolling laughter unlike the notes of any other bird. They add a mysterious if not supernatural quality to the north woods, especially on a calm moonlit night. In states such as Ohio where Common Loons do not breed, we have few chances to experience their magical charm, since these loons are normally silent during migration. Occasionally at sunset on a warm April day the laughter of a pair of loons may resound briefly across an Ohio reservoir.

Since breeding Common Loons are strikingly handsome, it is unfortunate they are in such a hurry to reach their nesting areas. While a few early migrants have appeared during the first half of March, they do not normally return until March 20–30. Breeding adults are noted first and generally depart by April 15–20. The drab immature loons are regularly observed through May 5–15 and a few may remain through the end of the month.

Spring Common Loons are uncommon to fairly common visitors to large lakes. They are surprisingly scarce along Lake

Erie, and greater numbers will be observed on inland reservoirs in the central and northern counties. Most spring migrants are encountered in groups of 12 or fewer; flocks of 25–50 are noteworthy. The largest concentrations were 112 at Findlay Reservoir (Hancock County) on April 10, 1974, and 75 in Lorain County on April 20, 1979.[273,417]

Nonbreeding Common Loons are accidental to casual visitors. They do not regularly appear at any location, but 1–4 are usually recorded each summer, generally on large lakes in the central and northern counties. Most summering loons are immatures, but a few nonbreeding adults have been observed. They are usually discovered during June; a few remain the entire summer.

Common Loons are most numerous in autumn. Early loons noted between August 25 and September 15 may represent nonbreeding summer visitors. The first migrants normally appear between October 5 and 15, while large flights are not expected until the last week of October. The largest movements are in November, when these loons may become locally abundant along Lake Erie and fairly common to common on large inland lakes.

Along Lake Erie during November, it is difficult to scan from any vantage point and not see a loon. When winds are southerly, only 5–25 loons may be observed daily. Following passage of a cold front, northwesterly winds may produce flights of 75–300+ loons along the lakefront between Huron and Cleveland. The largest counts were 638 at Cleveland on November 29, 1981, and 600 on November 23, 1978.[271,363] These flights begin at dawn. While some loons fly low over the water, most are high in the air, frequently in groups of 5–50+ heading south or east. They continue to pass overhead for an hour or two after sunrise.

Away from Lake Erie, 3–20 loons are expected on large lakes throughout the state. Sizable movements may also be noted as large flocks visiting inland lakes for a few hours or perhaps a day. These flights are most noticeable in the central and northern counties, usually producing flocks of 35–75 loons. Larger concentrations are possible: 300+ at Buckeye Lake on November 15, 1972;[471] 250 at Alum Creek Reservoir on November 11, 1979; and 200 at Senecaville Lake on November 18, 1983.[180] The largest flights in southwestern Ohio totaled 100–125.

During most years, numbers of Common Loons are greatly reduced by the first week of December. Most December sightings are of 1–8 loons. Large inland flights are still possible; there were central Ohio concentrations of 357 on December 1, 1986, and 170 on December 9, 1978.[272,384] Smaller flights have appeared in southwestern Ohio and along Lake Erie through December 17. Scattered loons may be expected until December 25–January 10, as long as open water is available.

Even during mild winters the last loons usually disappear by January 15–20. A few loons have attempted to overwinter, as indicated by February sightings at Cleveland, Columbus, Cincinnati, Youngstown, and Salem (Columbiana County). With the exception of 7 Commons at Cleveland on January 15, 1932,[523] all winter sightings have been of single loons.

PIED-BILLED GREBE

Podilymbus podiceps (Linnaeus)

Pied-billed Grebes are generally uncommon to common migrants on Ohio's lakes, ponds, rivers, and marshes, preferring the vegetated margins where suitable cover is readily available. Best known for their ability to dive quickly as danger approaches, Pied-billeds can instantly disappear under the water but take flight only with considerable difficulty.

Migrant Pied-billeds are uncommon to locally common and widely distributed each spring and fall. They are least numerous on Lake Erie and within counties lacking sizable lakes and marshes. The timing of their migratory movements is fairly uniform across the state.

The first spring migrants appear between February 20 and March 5 as the ice disappears from lakes and marshes. Peak numbers are usually attained between March 25 and April 20 when normally 10 or fewer grebes are observed daily. The largest flights are composed of 15–30 Pied-billeds, although Trautman[479] reported as many as 50 at Buckeye Lake on several dates before 1940. Smaller numbers may appear through May 10–20.

They are generally most numerous as fall migrants. The first fall Pied-billeds return during the last half of August; others pass through Ohio until freeze-up. The largest numbers are expected between September 25 and November 20. Fall flocks of 5–20 individuals account for most sightings and concentrations of 30–50 appear annually. The largest flight was composed of 100 Pied-billeds at Buckeye Lake on October 6, 1935.[26] There are exceptions to this migration pattern. During some years, the largest flocks appear before October 1. In other years, no more than 10–15 individuals may be noted at any location. Small influxes of 10–20+ are regularly noted in December, when cold weather forces lingering grebes to pass through the state in search of open water. Otherwise, Pied-billeds are usually noted in groups of 1–5 during December.

During relatively mild winters, Pied-billeds become rare winter residents across the state; though they are never numerous, 1–6 may be noted daily. Some spend the entire winter on one lake, others only a few days in January and February. Subfreezing temperatures normally force most Pied-billeds to leave Ohio by December 24–January 15. During harsh winters, 1–10 grebes are regularly encountered at localities retaining open water, including Summit Lake in Akron, hot-water outlets along Lake Erie, and the Great Miami, Scioto, and Ohio Rivers in southern Ohio.

Breeding Pied-billeds are restricted to large marshes where dense emergent vegetation is interspersed with small openings. Once nesting is under way, they become exceedingly shy and seldom stray from dense cover. Breeding grebes are surprisingly vocal and their presence is regularly detected by their distinctive loud calls. Their nests are constructed of decaying vegetation, as mats tied to stalks of cattails or floating through the marsh. While the earliest nest with eggs was discovered on May 3, downy young have been reported as early as May 18. Even along Lake Erie, young grebes are regularly observed by late May.[86] They may be fully grown by late June or early July. Unsuccessful adults will renest and some pairs may raise two broods. A number of nesting attempts have been discovered during July, and partially grown grebes have been reported as late as September 30, 1970, in Hancock County and November 1, 1972, at Magee Marsh Wildlife Area.[284,417]

Pied-billed Grebes have always been locally distributed summer residents in Ohio. The largest breeding population occupied the marshes bordering western Lake Erie, where Hicks[220] considered them common to abundant residents in the mid-1930s. Considerably fewer nested elsewhere. Nesting grebes were recorded from all northeastern counties, where they were generally rare and irregular residents but were locally common near Cleveland and Youngstown. Pied-billed Grebes were sporadic nesters in central Ohio with records from Buckeye Lake, Indian Lake, Lake Loramie, and Lake St. Mary's plus Delaware, Madison, Pickaway, and Franklin Counties.[220] In the unglaciated counties, grebes nested in Tuscarawas and Pike Counties.[193,223]

As a result of habitat destruction, numbers of breeding Pied-billed Grebes have declined since the 1930s. This decline is most apparent within the northeastern counties, where isolated pairs remain at only a few locations.[434] Along western Lake Erie, they became uncommon to fairly common residents. Elsewhere, Pied-billeds are accidental to rare and locally distributed summer residents in the western half of Ohio. As many as 5–10 pairs annually nest at Big Island Wildlife Area (Marion County), but grebes are irregular at other locations. Since 1970, nesting has been confirmed in Hancock, Seneca, Clark, Champaign, Delaware, Pickaway, Warren, and Butler Counties, while nonbreeders were detected at a few additional locations. Along the unglaciated Allegheny Plateau, Pied-billed Grebes are accidental to casual nonbreeding summer visitors; the only recent confirmed nest was discovered in Ross County in 1986.[434] While 100–200 pairs may reside along western Lake Erie, the inland population probably does not exceed 8–20 pairs.

HORNED GREBE

Podiceps auritus (Linnaeus)

Migrant Horned Grebes prefer sizable bodies of water; the greatest numbers appear on Lake Erie and large reservoirs. They are not restricted to these habitats, however, and may be found wherever water birds congregate. This species has a reputation as an irregular and unpredictable migrant, numerous some years and scarce in others with no apparent explanation for the fluctuations.

This irregular migratory behavior is most evident during spring. Some years these grebes are numerous throughout March and disappear by early April. In others, sizable numbers may not appear until mid-April, or they may completely bypass Ohio. The first Horned Grebes generally appear by February 25–March 5 and become widespread by March 15. Within the western half of Ohio, their northward movement usually peaks between March 15 and April 5. The largest flights in the eastern counties are usually noted during April. Most depart before April 25, although a few stragglers may remain through May 5–12.

Within the northeastern counties, Horned Grebes become fairly common to locally abundant migrants. Their appearance is irregular along central Lake Erie, where they are nearly absent some years and numerous in others. The largest spring lakefront concentrations totaled 486 Horned Grebes at Cleveland on April 4, 1970, and 467 on April 12, 1979.[273,410] Most sightings do not exceed 10–40. Larger flocks may appear on inland lakes, with maxima of 800 on Mosquito Creek Reservoir (Trumbull County) on April 16, 1977, and 606 on several lakes in Summit and Portage Counties on April 12–13, 1986.[266,382] Flocks of 100–300 Horned Grebes have also appeared at other northeastern locations, while daily totals normally are 10–25. These large flights have been recorded west to Lorain County (400 on April 9, 1979) and south to Carroll County (100 on May 1, 1955).[76,273]

Horned Grebes are generally uncommon to locally common migrants elsewhere. Spring totals normally are 5–20 within these counties. Larger flights are restricted to the northwestern and glaciated central counties, where 30–90 were counted on a few lakes.

These grebes are accidental nonbreeding summer visitors to the northern counties. Single June grebes were reported from Toledo and Lorain County; the only summering individual spent the entire summer of 1985 at Cleveland.[379]

Fall Horned Grebes are more predictable than spring migrants. Extremely early migrants appeared between August 16 and September 15. The first migrants frequently return by September 25–October 10 but are not regularly encountered until October 18–25. Their maximum abundance is achieved during November. Numbers decline during December, but small numbers remain as long as open water is available.

These grebes are most numerous along Lake Erie, where they become common to abundant along the entire lakefront. During most years, totals of 20–100+ develop during November. Larger flights are frequent and 150–500 are occasionally detected. The largest movements were noted at Cleveland: 958 on November 18, 1979, and 693 on November 26, 1978.[271,275] Periodically, fall Horned Grebes become inexplicably scarce and the largest flights total only 10–25.

They become uncommon to fairly common migrants on inland reservoirs. They are most numerous within the northern and glaciated central counties, where 5–30+ may be tallied and occasional flights of 50–90 have been reported. Fewer pass through the southern and unglaciated counties, where most fall totals are 20 or fewer.

The last fall migrants normally depart between December 20 and January 7. During some years, Horned Grebes are unreported after early January. In other years, a few scattered wintering grebes may be detected or small flights may be apparent during late January or early February.

In general, Horned Grebes are casual to rare winter visitors to hot-water outlets along central Lake Erie and accidental to casual visitors to all interior counties. All winter records are of 1–3 grebes. Most Horned Grebes appear for only a few days and are best characterized as temporary visitors rather than winter residents.

RED-NECKED GREBE

Podiceps grisegena (Boddaert)

Ohio lies just outside the established Red-necked Grebe migration corridor through the Great Lakes, and these grebes have always been rare visitors, most likely to be discovered along Lake Erie and within the northeastern counties. They prefer large lakes, frequently foraging far from shore, and are unlikely to be found in other habitats, except for migrants forced to land in fields after encountering inclement weather.

As fall migrants, Red-necked Grebes are casual to rare visitors along Lake Erie, mostly occurring within the Central Basin. They become casual migrants through the northern and glaciated central counties but are accidental elsewhere. These migrants are detected at one to four localities nearly every year but may be unrecorded during one or two autumns each decade. Most fall reports are of 1–2 grebes.

The earliest fall migrants returned to Lake Erie in Lucas County on September 9, 1978, and Cleveland on September 16, 1945.[271,523] There are few other sightings before October 20–30. They are most likely to appear during November and December. Late migrants usually depart by December 20–25 but may linger into January if open water remains available.

There are surprisingly few Red-necked Grebe sightings between January 7 and 25. They become accidental winter visitors during these weeks. However, these grebes fairly regularly appear in late winter, beginning during the last days of January and continuing through February. These late winter grebes are casual visitors along central Lake Erie and northeastern Ohio near Akron but are accidental elsewhere. They are normally detected during five to seven winters each decade with only one or two sightings in most years. Small flights are infrequent; 3 Red-neckeds were in the Toledo area during February 1934.[89]

Spring Red-neckeds are casual to rare migrants through the northeastern counties and along central Lake Erie but are generally accidental to casual elsewhere, least numerous along the unglaciated Allegheny Plateau. These migrants usually appear at four or fewer localities annually and are detected at a frequency of seven to nine years out of every decade. Most reports are of 1–2 grebes, although small flights include 6 breeding-plumaged grebes at Dayton on April 20, 1924;[299] 7 grebes scattered across Mahoning and Trumbull Counties between March 21 and April 10, 1959;[136] and at least 13 grebes reported from nine locations in northern and central Ohio, March 5–25, 1962.[130] These migrants are most frequently reported between March 20 and April 15. A few individuals lingered through May 11, 1913, at Cleveland and May 20, 1926, near Columbus.[45,523]

Red-necked Grebes are accidental summer visitors. The only acceptable record was provided by a molting male discovered at Lake St. Mary's on August 9, 1940. It remained through August 14, when it was collected.[95]

EARED GREBE

Podiceps nigricollis Brehm

Eared Grebes were unrecorded from Ohio until 1941, when an individual was discovered by B. P. Bole, Jr., at Holden Arboretum (Lake County) on April 21. This grebe was collected the following day.[125] Another Eared Grebe was collected on Lake Erie off South Bass Island on November 29, 1945.[480] In addition to these specimen records, there were a few sight records between 1941 and 1970. The number of sightings increased during the 1970s and Eared Grebes have been reported annually since 1980.

Within Ohio, Eared Grebes are mostly observed along Lake Erie, where they may associate with Horned Grebes. There are relatively few records from the interior counties, most from the western half of the state. There is only one undocumented sight record from the unglaciated counties.

Spring Eared Grebes are casual to accidental visitors throughout Ohio with confirmed sightings every two or three years since 1975. Their spring status is obscured by difficulties in separating them from the considerably more numerous Horned Grebes. Confirmed spring records total fewer than ten between March 18 and May 22 with most after April 15. All records are of single grebes.

Most Eared Grebes have been detected as fall migrants, with one to four documented sightings annually since 1980. They are apparently rare but regular migrants along the entire lakefront, usually as isolated individuals. Fall migrants are casual to accidental elsewhere, although small flocks with as many as five Eareds have appeared in the interior counties. An early Eared Grebe was noted near Akron between August 20 and 24, 1981,[363] and there have been two other sight records earlier than September 15. Most sightings are between November 1 and December 7 with a few stragglers remaining along Lake Erie through December 20–27.

A small flock of Eared Grebes has shown a remarkable fidelity to the C. J. Brown Reservoir near Springfield. In 1982, 4 Eared Grebes were discovered there on November 13, remaining into early December.[299] In subsequent years through 1987, 3–5 grebes returned to this lake. While the breeding and wintering areas of this flock remain a mystery, their ability to find this reservoir each fall is a testimony to avian navigation skills.

There is only one confirmed winter record from Ohio. An Eared Grebe discovered on December 25, 1955, at Summit Lake in Akron remained through February 26, 1956.[335] It was observed by many as it wintered on the lake.

WESTERN GREBE

Aechmophorus occidentalis (Lawrence)

Before 1985, the identification of Western Grebes was straightforward. In 1985, however, its two morphs were recognized as distinct species, presently known as Western Grebe (*Aech-*

mophorus occidentalis) and Clark's Grebe (A. clarkii).[6] These two species are very similar, requiring careful study to ensure correct identifications. Hence, all "Western Grebe" sightings earlier than 1985 required reevaluation to determine which species actually appeared in the state.

On the basis of this reevaluation, there are presently four unequivocal Western Grebe records from Ohio: single specimens collected at Youngstown, October 28–30, 1913,[118] and Columbus, April 25–May 13, 1964;[471] a Western Grebe photographed along Lake Erie at Bay Village (Cuyahoga County), November 24, 1985;[380] and a documented sight record along Lake Erie in Ottawa County, May 11, 1986.[382] Four additional reports of Aechmophorus grebes probably pertain to this species (although the sketchy details do not completely eliminate Clark's Grebe): from Pippin Lake (Portage County), March 30–April 5, 1959;[335] Clear Fork Reservoir, April 8–12, 1975;[259] Buckeye Lake, May 10, 1958;[471] and near Dayton, November 15–18, 1967.[299]

Of these two species, Western Grebes are more likely to appear in Ohio. They breed in western and central North America from Canada south into Mexico and east into the Dakotas and western Minnesota. They normally winter along the Pacific Coast.[5] As migrants, small numbers regularly pass through the Great Plains states but are accidental to casual visitors anywhere east of the Mississippi River. Most confirmed records of Aechmophorus grebes from eastern North America are Westerns.

BLACK-CAPPED PETREL

Pterodroma hasitata (Kuhl)

A storm along the Atlantic Coast in early October 1898 was thought to be responsible for the appearance of 3 Black-capped Petrels on the Ohio River near Cincinnati, October 4–5. While 1 of these petrels was recovered in Kentucky on October 4, 2 were found on the Ohio side of the river the next day. All were emaciated and died soon after their capture. One specimen is still preserved in the collection of the Cincinnati Museum of Natural History.[293] Since Black-capped Petrels nest on only a few islands in the Caribbean and spend the remainder of the year in the western Atlantic Ocean,[5] it is doubtful this accidental visitor will ever occur in Ohio again.

LEACH'S STORM-PETREL

Oceanodroma leucorhoa (Vieillot)

Like all storm-petrels, Leach's live on the open sea and normally come to shore only to nest. The presence of one in Ohio is a truly accidental event; Leach's have been found at only five locations in the interior of North America.[5] On May 16, 1929, a freshly killed Leach's Storm-Petrel was picked up from a Dayton street by a boy on his way to school. He gave this specimen to his teacher, Winifred Nutting, who had the foresight to ensure its preservation. It is deposited in the Ohio State University Museum of Zoology.[42] Its appearance in Ohio on this date is puzzling because there were no storms that might have blown it this far inland.

NORTHERN GANNET

Sula bassanus (Linnaeus)

Each spring Northern Gannets return by the thousands to their North Atlantic nesting colonies. After they fledge, most young gannets follow their parents to offshore feeding grounds. Occasional young gannets wander up the St. Lawrence River to the Great Lakes, continuing their journeys until they reach Lake Erie.

Ohio's first Northern Gannets were sighted near Cleveland on November 2, 1925, and November 10, 1929. The first specimen was collected at Cedar Point (Erie County) about November 15, 1931.[523] There were no additional records until December 1947, when a small flight produced 1–5 gannets daily at Cleveland between December 6 and January 13 and one record at Toledo.[89,523] Gannets also appeared at Cleveland during the winter of 1949–50.[310] There were substantiated reports in 1967, 1969, 1976, and 1978 and during six of eight years between 1980 and 1987. All confirmed records have been first-winter gannets during late fall and early winter; none of the spring and summer sightings of adults were supported by convincing details.

Northern Gannets are now casual late fall and early winter visitors to the Central Basin of Lake Erie. There are at least fourteen confirmed records between Huron and Cleveland. The earliest gannet appeared at Cleveland on November 2 but most sightings are between November 15 and December 15. These individuals usually wander along the lakefront and may appear at several locations over a period of several weeks. Most sightings are of single gannets, although multiple birds were detected during the winters of 1947–48, 1949–50, and 1982–83. If Lake Erie remains open, a few may remain through mid-January; one survived until February 18, 1950, at Cleveland.[310]

Northern Gannets are accidental visitors to western Lake Erie, with only three published records: single individuals noted between December 6 and January 2. They are also accidental visitors to the interior of Ohio. The only inland record was provided by a first-winter gannet intermittently observed at Cincinnati between December 7 and 24, 1967. Captured in a residential yard on the latter date, it had been banded at Bonaventure Island in the Gulf of St. Lawrence on September 9, 1967.[405]

The number of records from Ohio reflects the reproductive success of the North Atlantic nesting colonies. When these colonies were declining between the 1950s and the 1970s, very few gannets wandered inland. These colonies have increased during the 1980s, accounting for the increased sightings along the lakefront.

AMERICAN WHITE PELICAN

Pelecanus erythrorhynchos Gmelin

Within Ohio, White Pelicans were apparently "irregular but not infrequent" visitors between 1860 and 1910.[98,479] Although most early records are based on anecdotal accounts, reports of these distinctive birds are probably correct. Pelicans fairly regularly appeared at Lake St. Mary's and Buckeye Lake before 1910, and occasionally there were sightings elsewhere within the western half of the state.

As their continental populations declined after 1910, fewer pelicans were detected in Ohio. They became accidental visitors with only five published sightings between 1920 and 1940. Their status improved after 1940, especially along western Lake Erie, where Campbell[89] cited records during twelve years between 1940 and 1967. Pelicans remained accidental visitors to all other areas. This status was maintained through the 1970s but greater numbers have appeared during the 1980s. White Pelicans have been recorded annually since 1982, including a small flight involving at least 7 individuals during the fall of 1986. This recent increase corresponds with an expanding population in western North America.

White Pelicans are accidental spring visitors, averaging one to three sightings each decade. Before 1940, spring pelicans were only reported from Lake St. Mary's and Buckeye Lake. Since 1940, most records are along western Lake Erie in Ottawa and Lucas Counties. Recent spring sightings away from the lakefront are from Lake St. Mary's in 1956[98] and a flock of 8 pelicans near Canton on May 19–20, 1945, the only spring record from eastern Ohio.[38]

The earliest spring migrant was reported from Lake St. Mary's on March 16, 1909.[98] There are few other records earlier than mid-April. Pelicans are most likely to appear between April 20 and May 15 with a few late migrants through the end of the month. These sightings frequently are of single individuals, although small groups of 3–8 pelicans have been noted.

Pelicans are accidental nonbreeding summer visitors. There are at least seven summer records along western Lake Erie, two sightings at Buckeye Lake, and one sighting near Cincinnati. These pelicans appeared any time between mid-June and early August. Most remained for only one or two days, although individuals summered near Toledo during 1982 and 1983.[366,371] With the exception of 6 pelicans at Buckeye Lake on June 21, 1933,[471] all summer reports involve only 1–2 birds.

As fall migrants, White Pelicans are casual visitors along western Lake Erie, where they have been detected every two to four years since the early 1970s, and accidental migrants elsewhere. Away from western Lake Erie, fall pelicans are most likely to appear within the western half of Ohio, where there are at least fourteen scattered records. Fall sightings from the eastern counties are restricted to 2 pelicans at Cleveland on September 1, 1985,[380] and 2 at Lake Logan (Hocking County) and 1 at Athens on November 5, 1986.

Fall pelicans have returned to western Lake Erie by the last half of August and to other locations by September 1–8. While there are sightings throughout September and October, most pelicans have been reported between October 15 and November 10. Individuals have remained through November 17–18 at several locations and until November 29, 1975, at Deer Creek Reservoir.[261] All substantiated fall sightings involved 4 or fewer pelicans.

DOUBLE-CRESTED CORMORANT

Phalacrocorax auritus (Lesson)

In the early 1800s, Double-crested Cormorants were regular migrants only along Lake Erie. The creation of canal reservoirs provided additional habitats, and breeding populations were established at Buckeye Lake and Lake St. Mary's during the 1860s and 1870s.[98,479] Although "large numbers" nested at Lake St. Mary's, only 10–15 pairs made up the Buckeye Lake colony. Both colonies were subjected to indiscriminant hunting and egg collecting and disappeared by the early 1880s.

Their status did not change between 1900 and the 1940s. Migrant cormorants were most often observed along Lake Erie, where they were uncommon to fairly common during spring and fall. The largest flocks seldom exceeded 10–20 birds. While small numbers may have lingered into winter at Cleveland,[523] there were very few winter records elsewhere. At inland reservoirs, migrant cormorants were uncommonly encountered. As new reservoirs were constructed, they regularly appeared in areas where they were formerly absent.

During the 1950s, extensive use of DDT and other harmful pesticides proved disastrous for Double-crested Cormorants. The accumulation of pesticides in their tissues caused them to lay infertile or thin-shelled eggs. Relatively few young were produced, and populations significantly declined. Within Ohio, reduced numbers were not evident until the late 1950s. By 1965, cormorants became rare throughout the state with fewer than ten sightings annually of 1–5 individuals.

Even after use of these pesticides was banned, cormorants remained relatively rare during the 1970s. Most reports were of widely scattered individuals or small flocks. An exception was a remarkable concentration of 600 observed near North Bass Island (Ottawa County) on October 28, 1970.[90]

Their recovery during the 1980s was astounding. The first hint of this impending recovery was an autumn 1979 flock of 72 cormorants along Lake Erie. A flock of 24 over Hudson (Summit County) on April 13, 1980, provided an unusual inland total.[277] Their numbers improved in 1981, reaching a fall peak of 175 cormorants at East Harbor State Park (Ottawa County) on October 24.[363] These fall concentrations increased dramatically with 240–300 cormorants at two Lake Erie locations during 1982 and an incredible 1100 at East Harbor State Park on November 7, 1983.[368,372] Similar fall concentrations have been a regular occurrence along western Lake Erie in subsequent years. Increased numbers elsewhere indicate their populations are greater than ever.

Double-crested Cormorants are most numerous during autumn along western Lake Erie, a major staging area for the Great Lakes nesting population. During some years, most cormorants remain in Canadian waters and the largest Ohio flocks total 100–300. Large flocks congregate in Ohio waters during other years, producing concentrations of 500–2000 at Ottawa Wildlife Refuge, East Harbor State Park, and Sandusky Bay and around the Lake Erie islands. Smaller flocks are scattered elsewhere. The largest numbers occur between September 10 and November 15 and are usually counted at their evening roosts.

Cormorants are fairly common fall migrants along central Lake Erie but are normally observed in flocks of 10 or fewer with infrequent concentrations of 10–35+. Within the interior of Ohio, Double-crested Cormorants are uncommon to fairly common visitors to large lakes, least numerous in the southern and unglaciated counties. Most inland sightings are of 1–9 cormorants and few exceed 20–35. The largest inland flock totaled 95 at C. J. Brown Reservoir (Clark County) on October 11, 1987.[388]

Fall migration begins during the last half of August and migrants may be encountered throughout the state by September 3–10. Their numbers remain fairly constant through mid-November. By December, only scattered individuals remain except along western Lake Erie, where flocks of 20–30 have been noted. These cormorants normally depart by January 1.

Since 1980, Double-crested Cormorants have been casual winter visitors along Lake Erie. These winter records were of 1–2 cormorants lingering into February, mostly along the Cleveland-Lorain lakefront, although there are a few winter sightings from Toledo and one at Huron. Away from Lake Erie, cormorants overwintered only at Columbus during 1987–88.[388a] Additionally, a few cormorants have been noted in central and southern Ohio during February, but these sightings may represent very early migrants.

The first spring migrants normally return during the last week of March but are not regularly encountered until April 5–12. Spring migrants are common along Sandusky Bay and western Lake Erie, where the largest concentrations totaled 200–300 cormorants. Most sightings are of 50 or fewer. Elsewhere, Double-crested Cormorants are uncommon to fairly common migrants on all large lakes. These migrants are normally observed in flocks of 8 or fewer cormorants with occasional concentrations of 15–35. Their migration normally peaks between April 15 and May 7. Nonbreeders regularly remain until May 10–20 with scattered individuals lingering into June.

While Double-crested Cormorants are accidental to casual nonbreeding summer visitors to inland reservoirs, flocks of 20 or fewer are rare to uncommon visitors along western Lake Erie from colonies in Canadian waters. In 1987, 6 pairs of Double-crested Cormorants built nests on Ottawa Wildlife Refuge during June.[387] Several of these pairs apparently laid eggs, although none of the nests was successful. These cormorants provided the first Ohio nesting record of this century.

Despite these expanding populations, Great Lakes cormorants are experiencing some unexpected difficulties. At several colonies, thin-shelled eggs and deformed young indicate that toxic chemicals may be contaminating the adults. If these problems persist, the present abundance of cormorants may be short-lived.

ANHINGA

Anhinga anhinga (Linnaeus)

In November 1885, a specimen of this accidental visitor to Ohio was collected on the Muskingum River near the village of Lowell in Washington County.[238] The circumstances surrounding this specimen record were never disclosed. Anhingas are occupants of wetlands, lakes, and rivers in the southeastern United States and tend to disperse from their normal range after the breeding season.[5] The Ohio sighting was probably a result of this dispersal.

MAGNIFICENT FRIGATEBIRD

Fregata magnificens Mathews

This accidental visitor from tropical oceans has appeared in Ohio on three occasions. The first Magnificent Frigatebird was collected in Fairfield County during spring 1880 by Emmet Adcock.[488] This specimen is no longer extant and there is no additional information to substantiate this record. The other two frigatebirds were recorded on consecutive days in 1967. One was found dead in a suburb of Cincinnati on September 29. The other was discovered by Thomas Nye at Clear Fork Reservoir, Richland County, on September 30. When collected, it proved to be a greatly emaciated adult female in fresh fall plumage.[487]

With their ability to soar at high altitudes for long distances, Magnificent Frigatebirds occasionally wander far from their established range. They have been recorded along both coasts as far north as Alaska and Newfoundland and at a number of localities in the interior of North America.[5] These extralimital frigatebirds normally appear during summer and autumn and are frequently displaced by hurricanes.

AMERICAN BITTERN

Botaurus lentiginosus (Rackett)

At sunrise on a warm spring morning, a strange sound like a distant pump or a mallet driving a stake into the mud arises from a large marsh along western Lake Erie. It is instantly recognized as the territorial notes of an American Bittern, whose unique calls are not likely to be confused with any other noise coming from the marsh.

Nesting bitterns prefer large undisturbed wetlands whose dense vegetation is broken by scattered small pools. Occasionally they occupy bogs and large wet meadows. Their nests are platforms constructed of dead vegetation over shallow water. Within Ohio, nesting activities are initiated during May and nests with eggs are expected between mid-May and mid-June. Most clutches hatch during June and recently fledged young normally appear by late July.[52,89,423,523]

At one time, the American Bitterns' strange territorial calls were regularly heard in Ohio marshes. At the turn of the century, Jones[236] considered them local summer residents wherever suitable swamps and bogs were found. Their numbers were declining by the 1930s. Hicks[220] cited summer records from only the northern and central counties. Breeding American Bitterns were common within the extensive marshes bordering western Lake Erie. They were uncommon to rare in every northeastern county south to Wayne, Stark, and Columbiana, with scattered records elsewhere south to Guernsey, Perry, Franklin, Champaign, and Mercer Counties.

Of all factors responsible for this population loss, habitat destruction is undoubtedly the most important. Wetlands have been continuously drained and filled, especially within the interior counties. Remaining wetlands are mostly small, isolated areas or narrow strips of emergent vegetation, habitats unsuitable for nesting American Bitterns. Even where suitable marshes are available, spring and summer drawdowns are detrimental to breeding bitterns.

These factors adversely affected bittern populations in subsequent decades. At Lake St. Mary's, American Bitterns regularly summered through 1948, but all breeding habitat was eliminated by the early 1960s.[98] Similar declines were evident in the northeastern counties. Despite occasional breeding records at new sites, such as a Carroll County nest in 1956,[84] most nesting American Bitterns disappeared from interior Ohio by 1965. They also declined along western Lake Erie. Campbell[89] cited an abrupt decline during 1945 followed by substantially reduced numbers. Despite slight increases between 1969 and 1973,[90] numbers of breeding bitterns remained alarmingly low through the 1980s.

American Bitterns are now rare summer residents within the western Lake Erie marshes, where the total population probably does not exceed 10–20 pairs. They are also casual to rare summer residents within the northeastern counties. Since 1980, scattered reports from Geauga, Summit, Portage, and Trumbull Counties indicate that a small breeding population still remains, probably fewer than 10 pairs. The only other nesting American Bitterns sporadically reside at Big Island Wildlife Area (Marion County). Elsewhere American Bitterns are accidental to casual nonbreeding summer visitors, mostly within the northern half of the state, although there are several July sightings near Dayton.[299]

When their populations were larger, migrant bitterns were regularly encountered. As breeding populations declined throughout the Great Lakes region, the numbers of migrants have also significantly diminished.

In spring, the first American Bitterns are not usually encountered until April 5–12. They are mostly noted between April 15 and May 10 as uncommon migrants along western Lake Erie, rare visitors to the glaciated counties, and accidental to casual along the unglaciated Allegheny Plateau. When populations were larger, 4–20 could be observed daily at some inland marshes and along western Lake Erie.[89,479] Since 1960, spring sightings have been of only 1–4. Migrant bitterns are not found only in wetlands; they have been flushed from pastures, fallow fields, and other upland habitats. One of the first American Bitterns I ever observed was perched 15 feet high in a spruce tree, looking very out of place in a residential neighborhood.

American Bitterns were generally more numerous as fall migrants. Trautman[479] reported peaks of 25–37 daily within the marshes bordering Buckeye Lake during the 1920s and 1930s. Campbell[89] observed similar numbers along western Lake Erie before 1940. In recent years, only 1–2 bitterns have been observed daily. The present distribution and status of fall migrants are similar to those in spring. While migrants may appear by the last week of August, they are generally encountered between September 15 and October 10. Late bitterns may linger into November.

A few American Bitterns have attempted to overwinter in Ohio. Most winter sightings are from the western Lake Erie marshes, where they are casual visitors with at least thirteen records.[89,90] Some of these bitterns survived at least into February. Away from these marshes, American Bitterns are accidental early winter visitors with a single December record from Youngstown, two winter sightings in the Buckeye Lake–Newark area, and at least five December and January observations in the Cleveland area. Most of these winter sightings came before 1965.

LEAST BITTERN

Ixobrychus exilis (Gmelin)

At one time, Least Bitterns were locally common summer residents in Ohio. Bales[36] reported fourteen nests in one Pickaway County marsh in 1907, and similar numbers were distributed in other wetlands within the northern and central counties during the early 1900s. Extensive marshes supported larger populations. Trautman[479] considered Least Bitterns "the most numerous nesting heron" at Buckeye Lake during the 1920s and 1930s, estimating 40–90 nesting pairs annually. As many as 20 pairs nested at Lake St. Mary's and they were common in the marshes bordering western Lake Erie.[86,98] These numbers exhibited considerable annual variation, however.

By the mid-1930s, Least Bitterns were experiencing local declines, especially at inland marshes.[220] Despite these declines, they remained fairly common residents within western Lake Erie marshes. They were very locally distributed elsewhere, common at a few sites and rare within most counties south to Columbiana, Guernsey, Muskingum, Licking, Pickaway, Mercer, and Logan.[220,223] Their declines were most apparent between 1935 and 1965 when wetland drainage activities were prevalent. Least Bitterns disappeared from many counties and even sizable populations at Buckeye Lake and Lake St. Mary's declined substantially or were entirely eliminated. Nonetheless, breeding Least Bitterns spread into southwestern counties. Nesting pairs were first recorded in Montgomery County in 1935, Butler and Clermont Counties in 1938, and annually in Warren County since 1960.[248,299] Reduced numbers were also noted within the western Lake Erie marshes. This decline was obscured by annual fluctuations but reasonably stable levels were maintained into the early 1960s.[7,89] Campbell[90] noted declines between 1969 and 1973; additional reductions continued into the 1980s.

Least Bitterns are now uncommon residents of the western Lake Erie marshes with 1–10+ pairs occupying every wetland that has not been drawn down. Away from western Lake Erie, they are very locally distributed and generally rare summer residents south to Columbiana, Carroll, Licking, Warren, and Hamilton Counties.[434] As many as 11 males were counted in Mentor Marsh (Lake County),[382] and a few pairs are scattered within other northeastern counties. They are known from very widely scattered marshes elsewhere with only 1–4 breeding pairs at each site. These bitterns are absent along the unglaciated Allegheny Plateau except for a territorial male recorded in Ross County during 1986.

Least Bitterns normally remain hidden among dense vegetation and are unlikely to be seen except when one briefly flies over the cattails. On rare occasions, one may perch at the tops of cattails or quietly hunt at the edge of a small pool. Least Bitterns are not as vocal as their larger relative, the American Bittern, producing quiet cuckoolike notes at dawn or dusk.

The earliest Least Bittern returned to Dayton by April 11[299] but these birds do not normally appear until April 25–May 5. Most spring migrants and summer residents are noted during May, usually as 1–4 daily in recent years. When populations were larger, Trautman[479] observed 20–60 Leasts at Buckeye Lake in late May. Their northward migration continues into the first week of June.

Least Bitterns begin nesting shortly after returning to their territories. Nest construction has been noted by May 9 and continues into June.[479] Their nests are simple platforms of dried vegetation suspended between cattails 0.5 to 2.5 feet above water. They are rarely placed in dense buttonbush shrubs.[36] The first eggs are laid in mid-May and most clutches are complete by early June. Renesting efforts are responsible for nests with eggs through August 3.[215,479] Their young normally hatch by mid-June. These young may leave the nest platforms after only several weeks, but they remain dependent until late July or early August.

Fall migration begins in late July and apparently peaks between August 15 and September 10.[479] While these movements produced daily tallies of 5–25 bitterns before 1940, most recent fall sightings are of scattered individuals. The last migrants depart by October 3–7, except for a few stragglers into late October along western Lake Erie and in central Ohio. The latest Least Bitterns lingered in Ottawa and Lucas Counties through November 13, 1960, and December 27, 1970.[89,90]

The rare dark color phase known as "Cory's" Least Bittern has been substantiated only once in Ohio: a specimen collected at Toledo on May 25, 1907.[89] There are also several undocumented sight records of this color phase.

GREAT BLUE HERON

Ardea herodias Linnaeus

This stately heron is frequently observed along streams, lakes, and marshes. Foraging Great Blues are the epitome of patience as they stalk their aquatic prey. As described by Dawson:

While standing knee-deep in the water of some pond or stream, awaiting its customary prey of minnows or frogs, it may remain for an hour as motionless as a bronze statue; then with a movement like lightning, the head is drawn back and suddenly shot downward, and a wriggling fish is transfixed on the spear-like beak. A deft toss of the head puts the fish up and transfers it to the inside, and the bird moves with quiet, measured step to another station. . . .[102]

Observations of feeding Great Blue Herons are taken for granted today, but they have not always been numerous and widely distributed residents in Ohio. Their numbers were greatly diminished by the millinery trade during the 1800s. Repeated persecution caused their disappearance from portions of the state.[236] Complete protection allowed them to recover during the early twentieth century. By the mid-1930s, Hicks[220] cited breeding records from thirty-three counties and historic records from thirteen others. He estimated the statewide population at 1500–2000 pairs with heronries south through Warren, Franklin, Tuscarawas, and Trumbull Counties.

Great Blue Heron populations continued to expand during subsequent decades.[438] These herons are now abundant summer residents along western Lake Erie. The heronry on West Sister Island supports 1500–2000 pairs and other colonies number in the hundreds of pairs. Summer totals of 50–100+ individuals may be regularly observed. Considerably fewer herons breed elsewhere. Great Blues are fairly common to locally common summer residents throughout northern and central Ohio with colonies in most counties south to Belmont, Hocking, Ross, and Warren.[434] Most colonies have 10–75 pairs, while heronries with 100–200+ pairs are known from Buckeye Lake, Senecaville Reservoir (Noble County), and Ashtabula County. Summer totals are 5–30 herons daily within most interior counties. Summering Great Blues become uncommon in the southern counties bordering the Ohio River. A few colonies probably exist within these counties but their location has never been discovered. Our statewide breeding population is not precisely known but probably exceeds 5000 pairs.

Great Blue Herons may nest in tall trees near feeding areas but many inland colonies are in isolated woodlots several miles from streams or lakes. A large heronry is an exciting place. Early in their nesting cycle, courtship displays are repeated, nests are reconstructed, and territorial strife is evident as herons manuever for prime nest sites. Later in the season, activities are more sedate with the murmur of hungry young greeting each returning adult. Not all Great Blues nest in large colonies; some form heronries of 2–5 pairs. These small colonies generally exist for only a few years, in contrast with the large colonies, which may remain intact for more than forty years when undisturbed.

The first clutches are laid shortly after the nests have been refurnished. Incubating adults have been noted by March 12 in central Ohio and by the last week of the month along Lake Erie. Most pairs are incubating during April. Young herons normally hatch between late April and mid-May. Recently fledged young have been noted by June 23 but are most likely to appear during July. The last young herons may not leave the nest until mid-August.

Great Blue Herons return as soon as the ice melts from streams and lakes—by February 22–25 during warm seasons and mid-March in exceptionally cold years. Their northward movements peak between March 20 and April 15. Migrants may be noted through the first week of May. This migration seldom produces sizable movements. Along western Lake Erie, large concentrations may develop within drawdown marshes and 200–400+ have been counted in Ottawa and Lucas Counties.

Sizable concentrations are more likely to appear in late summer and autumn. Along western Lake Erie, fall flocks of 100–250 are observed annually, while as many as 400–1000+ have gathered in a single drawdown marsh. Similar concentrations do not normally develop elsewhere; most observations are of 40 or fewer herons with occasional flocks of 100–200.

Maximum abundance is normally attained between July 15 and September 30, although Great Blues remain fairly common to abundant until mid-October. Individuals and small flocks are regularly encountered through November 15–20. Subfreezing temperatures may force most herons to depart during December.

As winter residents, very few Great Blue Herons were reported before 1940. The few sightings were of widely scattered individuals or groups of 2–4. A report of 35 wintering Great Blues at Akron on January 20, 1935 was exceptional.[25] Their wintering numbers have noticeably increased since 1940. Great Blue Herons are now uncommon to rare winter residents within every county. Most sightings are of 1–10 herons. Their wintering numbers exhibit considerable annual variation. During extremely cold winters, they become casual to rare residents. Conversely, mild temperatures may tempt a number of Great Blues to overwinter. Midwinter concentrations are most likely in Ottawa and Lucas Counties, where 120 herons were counted at Winous Point on December 28, 1958, and flocks of 50–70 have appeared in other years.[89] Elsewhere, the largest wintering concentrations have not exceeded 15–20.

GREAT EGRET

Casmerodius albus (Linnaeus)

Watching an elegant Great Egret as it patiently forages in a marsh, quietly preens while standing on a muskrat house, or roosts in a tall dead tree, it is difficult to imagine that anybody could shoot one for its breeding plumes. Yet, breeding egrets were regularly persecuted in the late 1800s, nearly causing their demise in North America. Before 1880, Great Egrets were probably "rather common" late summer visitors to Ohio.[522] But as the plume trade flourished, fewer Great Egrets visited Ohio and their late summer flights ceased before 1895.[212] By the turn of the century, they were rare visitors, no longer observed annually.[236]

Great Egrets remained sporadic visitors into the early 1920s. Beginning in 1924, they regained their status as regular late summer visitors with four to fourteen sightings annually. These records were scattered across the state between mid-July and early December; only the western Lake Erie marshes hosted Great Egrets each year.[212]

In 1930, Ohio experienced its first Great Egret invasion of this century. This invasion produced sightings of 755 egrets from 110 localities in 45 counties.[212] The largest concentrations totaled 55 egrets in Portage County, 46 near Toledo, and flocks of 20–25 elsewhere. Late summer egrets were regularly reported throughout the 1930s, with invasions during 1933 and 1936. The 1933 movement brought a maximum of 190 egrets along western Lake Erie and 52 near Youngstown.[86,452] In 1936, their invasion was most noticeable in the western counties, with early August totals of 64 at Lake Loramie and 212 at Lake St. Mary's.[31]

These late summer movements normally commenced during mid-July. Largest concentrations were noted between the first week of August and the first week of September. Most departed by early October. Small numbers also appeared in spring, usually during the last half of April and May. A few remained through the summer.

The 1940s brought the first Great Egret breeding records. A single pair was discovered nesting within a Great Blue Heron colony along Sandusky Bay in Sandusky County during 1940.[88] In 1946, a colony of 25 pairs of Great Egrets was discovered on West Sister Island.[89] Away from western Lake Erie, 1–2 pairs nested at Lake St. Mary's between 1942 and 1944.[98] Their status was also changing as more egrets appeared during spring. However, they were still mostly known as late summer visitors, although the invasions of the 1930s were not repeated. Away from western Lake Erie, concentrations in excess of 15–20 were exceptional.

Similar trends continued through the 1950s and 1960s. The western Lake Erie breeding population slowly grew to an estimated 125 nests on West Sister Island in 1959.[89] As many as 25 pairs nested at Winous Point (Ottawa County) through 1959, although only one pair remained in 1960.[7] As this breeding population increased, Great Egrets became numerous summer residents throughout the western Lake Erie marshes. Large concentrations occasionally developed, including 255 near Toledo on September 25, 1959.[89] Elsewhere, small numbers regularly appeared throughout Ohio each spring, while the late summer movements were reduced to a trickle. Concentrations in excess of 10 egrets were exceptional away from western Lake Erie.

Great Egrets are now common to abundant summer residents in the marshes bordering western Lake Erie. The first migrants normally appear between March 20 and 25 and most breeding egrets return by April 20–25. Since 1970, at least 200 pairs of egrets have nested annually on West Sister Island.[434] Single pairs have occasionally nested in other Great Blue Heron colonies in Ottawa and Erie Counties. Great Egrets remain numerous until early October and decrease during the month. The last migrants usually depart by November 5–10.

Throughout the breeding season, daily totals of 30–60 Great Egrets are possible along western Lake Erie. Spring flocks of 100–200 egrets have developed in drawdown marshes. During August and September, flocks of 200–250 egrets have been noted on several occasions and 466 were counted at Ottawa Wildlife Refuge on September 21, 1978.[271]

Elsewhere along Lake Erie, Great Egrets are generally rare to uncommon migrants, slightly more numerous during autumn. Spring migrants normally appear between March 25 and May 15, fall migrants from mid-August through October 25. In recent years, most reports are of 1–5 egrets. They are also casual to rare nonbreeding summer visitors as scattered individuals along the Cleveland-Lorain lakefront.

Within the interior counties, Great Egrets are casual to uncommon migrants, most numerous in the central and northeastern counties. The timing of their inland migration is similar to their movements along central Lake Erie. Most inland reports consist of scattered individuals or flocks of 4–10 egrets. Nonbreeding egrets are casually noted at inland lakes and marshes during summer, generally as isolated individuals.

Great Egrets have always been accidental winter visitors to Ohio. Before 1970, the only published winter record was an egret observed near Peninsula (Summit County) on January 14, 1940.[507] Beginning in the 1970s, a few egrets have lingered in the western Lake Erie marshes until freeze-up. These late individuals normally disappear by early December. The mild winter of 1973–74 allowed one to remain at Magee Marsh Wildlife Area through January 4.[254] As many as 7 egrets remained into January in 1982, 1983, and 1987 and 1 successfully survived the winter of 1982–83 within these marshes.[364,369] The only recent winter record away from western Lake Erie was provided by a lingering egret in Holmes County through January 6, 1988.[388a]

SNOWY EGRET

Egretta thula (Molina)

The historic status of Snowy Egrets was obscured by the inability of early ornithologists to correctly identify small white herons. Jones[236] considered Snowy Egrets "rare and irregular" summer visitors during the nineteenth century, but others thought that many of the early sightings were probably of Little Blue Herons.[212] In all likelihood, Snowy Egrets were casual late summer visitors during the 1800s, although there are no extant specimens to substantiate this belief.

After the Snowy Egret population was decimated by plume hunters during the last decades of the nineteenth century, this species no longer visited Ohio during late summer. Between 1900 and 1929, the only published records were single Snowies at Buckeye Lake in 1901 and near Youngstown during 1924.[452,479]

During the 1930s, late summer invasions of southern herons produced a number of Snowy Egret sightings. These reports are plagued by misidentifications and their true status during this decade is uncertain. However, Snowies apparently appeared most years as visitors between late July and early October. Most confirmed reports were of scattered individuals, while a few flocks of 3–7 Snowies were also reported. These sightings were usually from the northern half of Ohio.

During the 1940s and early 1950s, Snowy Egrets sporadically appeared as scattered individuals or occasional flocks of 4–7. With the exception of a few spring sightings, they mostly appeared in late summer and early fall. In the mid-1950s, Snowy Egrets began to appear more regularly during spring while the number of fall records became progressively fewer. This trend continued into the 1960s as the number of sightings noticeably increased along western Lake Erie. Campbell[89] cited fifteen records from the Toledo area between 1962 and 1967. This increase was not apparent elsewhere.

Since 1970, the late summer movements of Snowy Egrets have been nonexistent while spring sightings have continued to accumulate. Small numbers also summered in the western

Lake Erie marshes as early as 1970–73.[90] In 1978, a Snowy was observed making regular visits to the heronry on West Sister Island but nesting was not established there until 1983, when two nests were discovered.[270,434] A small breeding population still occupies the island.

Snowy Egrets are now rare summer residents in the western Lake Erie marshes. While they occasionally return during the first half of April, the first Snowies are not usually encountered until April 25–May 7. Spring concentrations normally total 1–5 Snowies, although as many as 11 have been observed. Individuals or small flocks are occasionally observed throughout the summer. Their breeding activities normally commence during May and young fledge in late July or August. Once the young fledge, small flocks of 3–7 Snowies regularly appear and as many as 11–20 some years. These flocks usually remain until late September. A few late migrants have been noted through October 10–15.

Elsewhere, Snowy Egrets are accidental to casual spring visitors averaging one record annually of 1–2 egrets at widely scattered localities. While the earliest Snowy returned to Ashtabula County on March 31, 1962,[131] most records occur between April 20 and May 20. They are accidental summer and fall visitors away from western Lake Erie with only one or two sightings a decade since the mid-1960s.

LITTLE BLUE HERON

Egretta caerulea (Linnaeus)

A flock of Little Blue Herons roosting in a large dead tree silhouetted against an August sunset is a scene associated with the swamps of the southeastern United States. Yet it has also been observed in Ohio during periodic invasions of southern herons. No single factor adequately explains these mysterious irruptions of immature herons. While several species may be involved in these flights, the Little Blue Heron is one of the prominent components.

Little Blues have not always been regular visitors to Ohio. Although they visited the state during the nineteenth century, there are no specimen records to substantiate their presence. The millinery trade decimated the populations of Little Blue and other herons during the late 1800s, and all southern herons were virtually absent from Ohio after the early 1880s.

With protection of their nesting colonies, these herons recovered and the first Ohio specimen was collected along the Scioto River in Pike County during August 1901. Other Little Blues were observed in Butler County at the same time.[192,212] Between 1905 and 1920, they remained rare and very irregular visitors. During the 1920s, Little Blue Herons became regular late summer and early fall visitors, appearing in all portions of the state. Although their numbers fluctuated, there were as many as nineteen reports annually between 1924 and 1929.[212] They were most frequently encountered in flocks of 6 or fewer herons with a few reports of 11–13.

The 1930s were the decade of the southern heron, with immense movements during several years. Little Blues were the most frequently encountered southern invader, appearing in numbers that are almost inconceivable today. The largest invasion occurred between late July and early September 1930. Hicks[212] compiled reports from ninety-five localities in forty counties totaling 1185 individuals. They were encountered in all portions of the state. During August, the largest flocks included 85 in Lucas County, 77 at Buckeye Lake, 52 in Holmes County, 45 in Portage County, 28 in Butler County, and 26 in Columbiana County.[212,297] Another widespread movement occurred during 1934. While they were noted in all sections of the state, only a few large flocks developed, such as 62 at Youngstown and 37 at Dayton.[23,299] The last statewide movement occurred in 1939, but large concentrations developed only along western Lake Erie with a maximum of 35 in Lucas County.[86]

While Little Blues remained regular fall visitors during the 1940s, the massive invasions of the previous decade were not repeated. They were reported each year, mostly in groups of 6 or fewer. There were 20 in Hancock County in August 1949.[417] In addition, adult Little Blues began to appear as irregular spring visitors. During the 1950s, numbers of fall visitors gradually declined and large concentrations were unreported. Conversely, spring records continued to accumulate. These trends continued through the 1960s, except for small movements during July and August 1963, 1965, and 1966. These movements produced concentrations of 21 at Cincinnati and 6 at Dayton in late July 1965. Small numbers were reported throughout the state during late summer 1966.[398,401]

Since the mid-1960s, Little Blue Herons have not staged any noticeable fall movements. But despite declining populations elsewhere, they have become established as summer residents in Ohio. Since 1969, they have been rare summer residents in the western Lake Erie marshes, generally encountered in groups of 4 or fewer.[90] During June 1978, adults were observed making daily flights to the heronry on West Sister Island. No nests were discovered there until 1983, when 2 pairs were found breeding.[270,434] Similar numbers have nested on the island in subsequent years.

Elsewhere, Little Blues are accidental to casual spring visitors with one to four records annually. They are slightly less numerous during fall, with one or two sightings a season, although they may be unreported some years. Since 1970, all reports away from western Lake Erie were of only 1–2 herons. These spring and fall visitors are least numerous in the southeastern counties.

While an exceptionally early migrant returned to Columbus on March 19, 1978,[269] most spring arrivals are between April 20 and May 7. Except along western Lake Erie, spring Little Blues depart by May 20–27. Fall visitors may appear by mid-July with peak numbers between July 25 and August 30. Most depart by September 10–15 with occasional stragglers into early October.

TRICOLORED HERON

Egretta tricolor (Müller)

Tricolored Herons are primarily restricted to coastal marshes along the Gulf of Mexico and the Atlantic Coast north to south-

ern New England.[5] At one time, they rarely wandered even fifty miles inland. The appearance of Ohio's first record, a specimen collected in Ashtabula County on April 22, 1954, was astonishing because it represented one of the first Tricolored Herons ever noted in the Great Lakes region.[488] Since the late 1960s, these herons have demonstrated a greater tendency to wander from coastal marshes. While they remain among the rarest herons within the interior of eastern North America, they have become fairly regular visitors to the lower Great Lakes area.

Following Ohio's 1954 specimen, Tricolored Herons were unrecorded until 1971, when there were two sight records from marshes along western Lake Erie. Another was reported from these marshes during 1973.[90,471] There were single sight records elsewhere during 1976 and 1977. Beginning in 1979, this heron became a rare but regular nonbreeding summer visitor to the western Lake Erie marshes, where there were reports in every subsequent year except 1980.

While a Tricolored appeared along western Lake Erie as early as April 18, 1971,[90] these herons usually return during the second half of May. The latest fall records are during the second week of September. During 1979, a Tricolored Heron was observed making regular flights to the West Sister Island heronry but nesting could not be confirmed.[274] Another Tricolored visited this heronry during summer 1986 but neither a mate nor a nest could be located.[434]

Tricolored Herons are accidental visitors elsewhere. Other lakefront records are the Ashtabula County specimen plus three sight records at Cleveland. Inland sightings are limited to an undocumented record near Cincinnati on May 1, 1977,[266] and single Tricoloreds near Pickerington on April 28–30, 1981,[361] and near Barberton (Summit County) on May 5, 1987.[386] Of these seven records, five are during spring, including an early migrant at Cleveland on April 6, 1986,[382] while there are single Cleveland area sightings during July and August.

CATTLE EGRET

Bubulcus ibis (Linnaeus)

Few birds have undergone such a dramatic and widely publicized range expansion as Cattle Egrets. Formerly native to Africa, they colonized South America and quickly spread through Central America and the Caribbean region to occupy much of North America. Their North American range expansion was most noticeable from the 1950s to the 1970s. Populations have apparently stabilized, if not declined somewhat, during the 1980s.

Ohio's first Cattle Egret was discovered near Columbus on May 23, 1958.[352] The next appearance was along western Lake Erie, with several reports from Ottawa and Lucas Counties during summer 1960.[89,326] Spring 1961 produced a small flight along Lake Erie during May, including 5 at Toledo on May 6 and 3 at Conneaut (Ashtabula County) on May 1.[329] Cleveland's first Cattle Egret was recorded on April 27, 1962.[335] The first records from Dayton and Youngstown occurred in 1966,[152,299]

Lake St. Mary's in 1967,[403] and Marietta and Findlay in 1968.[154,417] During the 1960s, appearances were very sporadic except along western Lake Erie, where there were at least nine records.

During the 1970s, Cattle Egrets established a regular pattern of occurrence within Ohio. Most appeared during spring, particularly along western Lake Erie, where they were annually recorded. Spring Cattle Egrets were casual to rare visitors elsewhere, although they were fairly regularly observed in all portions of the state. After spring migration ended, they disappeared except along western Lake Erie, where breeding was confirmed in 1978 with twenty nests discovered on West Sister Island.[270] Fall migrants were regularly encountered along western Lake Erie, where flocks occasionally appeared after 1975. Elsewhere, small numbers were very infrequently reported during autumn.

Their status has not appreciably changed since 1980, although the number of sightings has slowly declined since 1983. The small breeding colony on West Sister Island numbered eight nests in 1987. A few pairs have also nested in a small Black-crowned Night-Heron colony near Sandusky (Erie County) since 1984.[434]

Cattle Egrets are now rare to uncommon spring migrants along western Lake Erie in Ottawa and Lucas Counties. Whereas spring flocks of 15–23 appeared during the 1970s and early 1980s, most sightings have been of 8 or fewer since 1984. Elsewhere, spring Cattle Egrets are accidental or casual visitors with one to three sightings annually since 1984. Most recent sightings are from the western half of the state and near Cleveland, normally 1–5 individuals with occasional flocks of 7–13. The first migrants have returned by the first week of April but are not normally encountered until April 15–25. Most spring sightings occur between April 25 and May 20.

Cattle Egrets are restricted to western Lake Erie during summer, where nesting activities are normally initiated by mid-May. They are very infrequently encountered away from their nesting islands during June and July. They are more likely to be observed during August after the young fledge. Summer reports invariably are of 6 or fewer.

During the last half of August and early September, the western Lake Erie population apparently congregates into one or two flocks to forage in fields along the Western Basin of the lake. These flocks have totaled 20–53 birds since 1976.[264] They normally depart by early October, but there are a number of November records and stragglers remained into the first week of December during 1982 and 1983.

Cattle Egrets are accidental or casual fall visitors away from western Lake Erie and are not reported annually. There are surprisingly few sightings during September and October. Most fall records have been lingering egrets during November or the first week of December, normally scattered individuals but including small flocks with as many as 7 egrets.

Foraging Cattle Egrets prefer upland fields over marshes. During spring they prefer wet meadows and pastures. Fall concentrations along western Lake Erie are found in dry grasslands or recently mowed fields where grasshoppers and other insects abound.

GREEN-BACKED HERON

Butorides striatus (Linnaeus)

While its common name was recently changed to Green-backed Heron, to many it will always be known as the Green Heron. Among our most widely distributed breeding herons, the diminutive Green-backeds are found along small streams, rivers, marshes, and the margins of ponds and lakes throughout Ohio. Breeding Green-backeds usually nest as isolated pairs and never frequent large colonies with other herons. Instead, they construct their loose platforms in dense bushes and small trees near water. If suitable low cover is unavailable, they place their nests at heights of forty to seventy-five feet in tall trees.[423,523] On rare occasions, Green-backeds nest in loose segregated colonies of 5–20+ pairs.[89,220]

Nest construction begins in late April and continues into May. Nests with eggs have been discovered by April 26 but are usually reported between May 10 and June 20.[479] A few late pairs were incubating eggs during July.[523] Young Green-backeds fledge before they can fly, clambering about woody cover as they await the return of their parents with food. These young herons have left their nests as early as June 12 but normally appear between late June and early August.[479]

At the turn of the century, Green-backed Herons were common summer residents throughout Ohio.[236] In the 1930s, Hicks[220] still described them as fairly common to abundant residents in every county. After 1940, wetland drainage and stream channelization significantly reduced their numbers, particularly in western Ohio. These declines continued through the 1980s.

Despite their declining numbers, Green-backed Herons remain uncommon to fairly common summer residents, most numerous within the northeastern counties and along western Lake Erie where summer totals are 4–8 herons daily. Nesting herons are least numerous within the intensively farmed western counties and along the unglaciated Allegheny Plateau; scattered pairs are infrequently observed. A few pairs nest along urban streams if undisturbed riparian habitats are available.

As spring migrants, a few Green-backed Herons have returned remarkably early: to Cleveland by March 12[523] and other localities by March 25–30. Most years, migrants are first observed between April 15 and 23 and are widely distributed by April 28–May 5. Spring Green-backeds are uncommon to fairly common migrants in most counties. Most spring totals are 8 or fewer daily; the largest movements total 15–20 individuals. A few migrants may be noted through the end of the month.

Greater numbers of Green-backed Herons pass through Ohio each autumn. Before 1965, fall concentrations of 30–50 were encountered within the northern and central counties each year. The last movement of this magnitude was 55 at Newtown (Hamilton County) on September 16, 1979.[275] During the 1980s, the largest fall movements totaled only 10–15 and even these concentrations have been scarce since 1984. In recent years, Green-backeds are fairly common to locally common fall migrants, with most sightings of 6 or fewer.

The first southward migrants are expected by July 20–30. In recent years, their maximum abundance has been attained during August with sharply reduced numbers by September 10–15. When populations were larger, sizable movements continued through mid-September. A few Green-backeds normally remain through October 1–5. Stragglers are not unusual and there are sightings through November 15. When the weather is relatively mild, a few Green-backeds survive into December, although they are accidental early winter visitors. One remained at Cleveland through January 1, 1942,[523] but this species is not known to have overwintered in Ohio.

BLACK-CROWNED NIGHT-HERON

Nycticorax nycticorax (Linnaeus)

Black-crowned Night-Herons have nested in Ohio since 1867, when the first colony was discovered at Lake St. Mary's.[98] During the remaining decades of the nineteenth century, they became locally common summer residents near the few colonies but were generally unreported elsewhere.[236] Unlike most other herons, Black-crowneds were not persecuted by the millinery trade and their numbers remained stable into the 1900s.

Their Ohio breeding population expanded between 1915 and 1935. Nesting night-herons became established along western Lake Erie by 1920. At the same time, a number of new colonies were scattered across the western half of the state. These colonies varied in size from a few pairs to several hundred; many were short-lived. Despite their constantly changing locations, Hicks[220] cited at least nineteen colonies in Ottawa, Lucas, Paulding, Madison, Franklin, Fairfield, Champaign, Mercer, Logan, Shelby, Hamilton, Butler, Warren, Greene, Montgomery, and Erie Counties. While there were numerous sightings from the northeastern counties, no breeding colonies were discovered. The largest colonies included 1000+ nests on West Sister Island, 500 nests at Lake Loramie (Shelby County), 300+ in Champaign and Greene Counties, and 200 near Cincinnati.[91,98,248,299]

These populations remained fairly stable through the 1940s and new colonies were reported from Hancock and Van Wert Counties.[417,429] The night-heron's status changed during the 1950s, particularly within the interior counties where every small colony and several large heronries disappeared. The only new colony was composed of several pairs at the Cleveland Zoo.[335] Trends of the western Lake Erie population were not apparent. The large heronry on West Sister Island remained intact, and another large heronry was established on North Bass Island.[349] Meanwhile, other small colonies in Ottawa and Lucas Counties disappeared. During the 1960s, the last colonies away from western Lake Erie disappeared. Breeding was last recorded in Cincinnati in 1963 and Cleveland in 1966.[335,393] In Ottawa and Lucas Counties, only the West Sister Island heronry remained intact with an estimated 1200 pairs.[89] Since 1970, numbers of Black-crowned Night-Herons reported throughout Ohio have remained fairly stable.

These herons are now common summer residents of the marshes bordering Lake Erie and Sandusky Bay. The first migrants normally return between March 22 and 27 but Black-crowneds do not become numerous until mid-April. Generally 10–40 are observed, although concentrations of 100+ may develop in favorable habitats. Larger flocks are expected during late summer and autumn when 100–300 may be encountered. Their numbers gradually decline during September and October with small flocks remaining through October 25–November 15.

Black-crowned Night-Herons presently breed at two colonies along western Lake Erie: at least 1300 pairs on West Sister Island and 100+ near Sandusky.[434] Black-crowneds usually nest in saplings, frequently at heights of less than twenty feet. Breeding activities are not necessarily synchronous. Some adults lay eggs as early as April 5, although most clutches are not initiated until late April or early May. Eggs may hatch by the first week of May and young may fledge before the end of the month.[89,119] Most young leave the nest during late June and July, while the latest remain until mid-August.

Although most Black-crowned Night-Herons spend the winter in the southern United States, the Caribbean islands, and Central America, some are very locally distributed but regular winter residents along western Lake Erie. Since the 1960s, a flock of Black-crowneds has wintered at the Acme power plant in Toledo. This flock is generally composed of 20–40+ night-herons, although 103 spent the winter of 1972–73. Wintering Black-crowneds are casually observed elsewhere along western Lake Erie, usually as isolated individuals, but small flocks of 5–10 have been reported.

Along central Lake Erie, Black-crowned Night-Herons are rare to uncommon spring migrants, with groups of 5 or fewer observed between March 25 and May 15. They are also rare nonbreeding summer visitors, usually isolated immatures during June and July. Beginning in late July and continuing into September, they become uncommon to fairly common fall migrants and may appear as individuals or groups of 2–12. These migrants normally depart around mid-October. Black-crowned Night-Herons are casual early winter visitors along central Lake Erie. Groups of 3 or fewer may remain as long as open water is available. A few have apparently overwintered at hot-water outlets of power plants, although they do not appear regularly each year.

Within the interior counties, Black-crowneds were once uncommon to locally common summer residents. Flocks of 10–25+ were regularly noted near their breeding colonies but were sporadically detected elsewhere. Migrants were frequently observed, including flocks of 40 in Summit County on April 19, 1947, and 150 on August 17, 1948.[523] Since the late 1960s, these herons have been accidental to rare migrants and nonbreeding summer visitors in most inland counties, least numerous in the unglaciated counties. Migrant groups of 6 or fewer are sporadically encountered, mostly between April 5 and May 15 and August 10 and September 30. Reports of 1–4 nonbreeding night-herons may occur during June and early July in the central, southwestern, and northeastern counties.

When their populations were larger, Black-crowneds were also accidental to casual winter visitors within the interior of Ohio. The winter records were widely scattered, mostly as individuals, with a maximum of 27 on the 1956 Dayton Christmas Bird Count. The last inland winter sightings were during the 1960s.

YELLOW-CROWNED NIGHT-HERON

Nycticorax violaceus (Linnaeus)

Yellow-crowned Night-Herons were unrecorded from Ohio until 1928, when a nesting pair was discovered in the heronry at Indian Lake (Logan County) on May 16.[495] While breeding adults returned to this colony through 1932,[220] the only other record before 1940 was provided by an adult encountered near Killbuck Creek in Wayne County on April 25, 1931.[82]

A northward range expansion became apparent during the 1940s when vagrant Yellow-crowneds began to appear regularly in Ohio. Most records were from the northern half of the state, including sightings at Toledo in 1940 and Cleveland in 1945,[89,523] usually single Yellow-crowneds appearing for a few days between early May and early September. The only nesting record was a pair along Flatrock Creek in Paulding County between 1943 and 1946.[429]

A permanent breeding population was established in the 1950s. While vagrant records continued to accumulate from the northern half of the state, nesting Yellow-crowneds were restricted to the southern and central counties. Small colonies were established at Cincinnati and Dayton in 1953 and Columbus in 1954.[11,299,345] Sightings in other southern counties suggested the presence of additional colonies.

This northward expansion apparently halted in the 1960s. Except for a nesting pair at Youngstown in 1967,[153] breeding Yellow-crowneds were restricted to traditional colonies at Columbus, Cincinnati, and Dayton. Regular observations in the Toledo area strongly suggested the possibility of a small breeding population.[89] By the late 1960s, the statewide population may have started to decline. The Cincinnati nesting colony disappeared and the number of vagrant sightings was markedly reduced. This trend continued into the 1970s. Except for Cleveland's first nesting record in 1978,[270] these herons were only infrequently encountered away from established colonies.

Since 1980, Yellow-crowned Night-Herons have been accidental to locally rare summer residents within the southern half of the state. The only known colonies at Dayton and Columbus support no more than 5–10 pairs. Another nest was reported at Lake Logan in 1980.[174] Other small colonies probably exist, as evidenced by summer records from Belmont, Morgan, Jackson, Ross, and Clinton Counties.[434] In the northern half of Ohio, Yellow-crowneds are accidental to casual summer residents with sightings restricted to the vicinity of Cleveland and the Toledo–western Lake Erie area. At Cleveland, a nesting pair remained through 1982, but only isolated nonbreeders have been recorded in subsequent years. In northwestern Ohio, summering Yellow-crowneds have been noted from Kelleys Island west to the Maumee River in Wood County, although the location of any colony has never been established.[434] The statewide breeding population is quite small, only 10–40 pairs.

Breeding Yellow-crowned Night-Herons are usually found along Ohio's shallow rocky streams, where they feed on crayfish and small fish. While these herons will nest in colonies with other herons, most Ohio nesting records are isolated pairs or small segregated colonies with 2–5 pairs. Their choice of nesting habitats varies from isolated woods and undisturbed parks to trees in residential yards. The urban colonies rank among the most stable. In fact, a Columbus colony in a residential neighborhood has been regularly occupied for more than twenty years.

Resident Yellow-crowned Night-Herons return fairly early, appearing near Oxford (Butler County) by March 16, 1980,[277] and traditionally returning to Columbus on April 1. The breeding adults return by April 20–25. Nesting activities begin shortly thereafter and complete clutches have been noted by the last week of April. Young normally hatch by late May or early June and fledge by early August. Small flocks of 8–13+ Yellow-crowneds have been detected at Columbus and Dayton in August. These herons normally depart during September, although a few occasionally remain into the first half of October. Yellow-crowneds are not hardy; the few December sight records most likely were misidentified immature Black-crowned Night-Herons.

Yellow-crowned Night-Herons are accidental visitors away from established and suspected colonies, averaging one or two sightings annually during the 1980s. These vagrant herons invariably occur as isolated individuals during late April and May or as postbreeding visitors in August and early September. Most recent records are along Lake Erie and within the southern counties.

WHITE IBIS

Eudocimus albus (Linnaeus)

Like most ibis and herons, postbreeding White Ibis tend to wander north of their established nesting range in the southern United States. These movements produced one record of this accidental visitor to Ohio: an immature White Ibis discovered by Ben Blincoe at Englewood Dam near Dayton on August 20, 1964. This cooperative bird remained at the dam through August 31, was viewed by many observers, and was photographed for the local newspapers.[299]

GLOSSY IBIS

Plegadis falcinellus (Linnaeus)

While *Plegadis* ibis are instantly recognized by their long decurved bills and distinctive plumages, separating Glossy and White-faced Ibis poses a serious challenge. Only adults in breeding plumage are readily identified in the field when they can be carefully studied under good viewing conditions. Field identification of immatures and nonbreeding adults is accomplished only under ideal conditions and most will never be satisfactorily identified. These identification problems have greatly obscured the status of both *Plegadis* ibis within Ohio. Most sightings are believed to pertain to Glossy Ibis, but two confirmed White-faced Ibis records indicate that the identification of all ibis should be proved and not assumed. Unfortunately, many sightings of *Plegadis* ibis are accompanied by insufficient details to positively eliminate either species and these sightings are best treated as unidentified ibis.

Ohio's first Glossy Ibis record was provided by two specimens collected at Cleveland in 1848 (one of them is still in the Cleveland Museum of Natural History).[523] They subsequently went unrecorded for nearly a century until 3 Glossies were discovered in Lucas County on May 30, 1943.[87] This sighting was followed by other Toledo area records in 1947 and 1952. Their status abruptly changed during the 1960s. Previously considered accidental visitors, they were reported almost annually during the 1960s with records from one to three localities most years. This pattern of regular sightings continued through 1976. The number of records has diminished since then, with only three confirmed sightings and five records of unidentified ibis that might pertain to this species.

The majority of Glossy Ibis were discovered along western Lake Erie in Ottawa and Lucas Counties. They are apparently casual visitors to this area with more than fifteen published records. They are accidental visitors elsewhere. There are at least four sightings in the Cleveland-Akron area, three records at Lake St. Mary's, three in the Columbus–Buckeye Lake region and single reports from Ashtabula County, Wayne County, and Hueston Woods State Park.

Most of these ibis appeared during spring. The earliest arrival was noted at Hueston Woods State Park on April 7, 1971,[280] while most sightings were during May. Most records are of 1–3 ibis. The largest concentration was 21 along western Lake Erie in Ottawa County on May 5, 1962.[131] Away from western Lake Erie, the largest flock was 5 ibis at Cleveland on May 14, 1973.[286]

All midsummer sightings are restricted to western Lake Erie, mostly single nonbreeding ibis briefly observed during June. However, 1–2 Glossy Ibis frequented the Black-crowned Night-Heron colony at North Bass Island between June 26 and July 5, 1963.[431] The breeding status of these ibis was never established.

There are very few autumn records of *Plegadis* ibis and most lack sufficient details for positive identification. The few fall reports are scattered between August and October, although a late ibis near Columbus, November 2–7, 1980, was conclusively identified as a Glossy. Three fall records along western Lake Erie and one at Cleveland may also pertain to this species.

WHITE-FACED IBIS

Plegadis chihi (Vieillot)

Western counterparts of Glossy Ibis, White-faced Ibis breed from the Great Plains and Great Basin south into Mexico. Wintering White-faced Ibis are largely restricted to the Pacific and Gulf Coasts.[5] They are presently accidental visitors east of the

Mississippi River, but their actual status is uncertain because of our inability to positively identify most immature *Plegadis* ibis in the field.

Within Ohio, White-faced Ibis have been positively identified on two occasions. The first was a specimen collected at Lake Grant in Brown County on October 1, 1949. According to Kemsies and Randle,[248] the identity of this immature ibis was established by Harry C. Oberholser. A recent examination of this skin indicates that bill, tarsi, and feet characteristics closely resemble a White-faced Ibis, but soft-part coloration was not recorded at the time of collection. The second record was an adult discovered by John Pogacnik at Magee Marsh Wildlife Area (Ottawa County) on May 18, 1985.[378] In full breeding plumage, it remained in the area through May 23.

ROSEATE SPOONBILL

Ajaia ajaja (Linnaeus)

Roseate Spoonbills only rarely wander from their established range during late summer and early autumn. Their North American populations are small and very locally distributed along the Gulf Coast, and the few extralimital sightings are usually from the southern states.[5] Spoonbills are accidental visitors elsewhere; hence, the appearance of a Roseate Spoonbill in Ohio is truly extraordinary. An immature spoonbill was discovered by Roger Emerling in a shallow pond near the Auglaize River in Defiance on September 24, 1986.[384] The bird was observed at close range by Emerling and several other persons as it spent most of the late afternoon sleeping along the edge of the pond.

WOOD STORK

Mycteria americana Linnaeus

Within the United States, Wood Storks nest in Florida, Georgia, and South Carolina. They also breed in Mexico and regularly wander north to Texas, Louisiana, and southern California during late summer and early fall.[5] On rare occasions, they have strayed as far north as New Brunswick, the lower Great Lakes states, and South Dakota. Most were immature storks discovered during summer and early autumn.

Wood Storks have always been accidental visitors to Ohio. The state's first confirmed visit was by an immature captured near Wilmington (Clinton County) on July 23, 1909.[244] Held in captivity "for some days," it died shortly after its release. The next Wood Stork was also discovered in the Wilmington area, an immature captured along Todd's Fork on May 5, 1946. Obviously weak, it died shortly after it was taken into captivity.[190] The only other confirmed record was of 2 Wood Storks discovered in an Ashtabula County field on July 1–2, 1955.[349] They were carefully observed during their brief visit. There were also unverified sightings in 1914 and 1964.

FULVOUS WHISTLING-DUCK

Dendrocygna bicolor (Vieillot)

Fulvous Whistling-Ducks have a North American breeding range restricted to Florida, coastal Texas, Louisiana, and very locally in southern California.[5] But they have wandered to many other states and Canadian provinces, appearing as individuals or small flocks any time between early spring and late autumn.

Ohio has at least eight valid records of Fulvous Whistling-Ducks, six between 1962 and 1969 and two in the mid-1970s. Three spring sightings were during April: 4 ducks in Butler County on April 11, 1974;[255] 1 near Amherst (Lorain County) on April 13, 1964;[335] and 9 near Carey (Wyandot County) on April 24–25, 1975.[259] The only summer record is of 2 Fulvous Whistling-Ducks spending June 1967 at Killdeer Plains Wildlife Area (Wyandot County).[471] Four fall records include Ohio's first specimen, collected by a hunter at Metzger Marsh Wildlife Area (Lucas County) on October 19, 1962. The next day, 9 Whistling-Ducks appeared at nearby Toussaint Wildlife Area (Ottawa County) and 3 were shot by hunters.[89] Other fall sightings: 6 near Ashland on November 21, 1963,[391] and a flock of 12 in flight over Buckeye Lake, November 24, 1969.[484]

TUNDRA SWAN

Cygnus columbianus (Ord)

The distant calls of Tundra Swans may resemble barking dogs or perhaps a flock of geese. As they come closer, their distinctive resonant calls can be recognized before the Tundras become visible. Eventually, a flock of these magnificent birds passes overhead and lands in a flooded field, providing the highlight of most March trips to western Lake Erie.

Ohio lies along the major migration corridor of Tundra Swans between their Arctic nesting grounds and wintering areas on the Atlantic Coast. During spring, this migration corridor crosses northern Ohio, covering the northeastern counties south to Wayne and Columbiana and extending to Erie, Sandusky, Ottawa, and Lucas Counties in the northwest. Spring Tundra Swans are mostly observed along western Lake Erie. The largest March concentrations totaled 5500 in 1962 and 5000 in 1930 in Ottawa and Lucas Counties.[89] During most years, however, the flocks may not exceed 50–600. Their appearance at other locations is more sporadic. Concentrations of 1000 at Lake Rockwell on March 27, 1981, 600 in Trumbull and Ashtabula Counties on March 12–13, 1966, and 400 in Wayne County on March 29, 1980, are exceptional.[150,277,361] Spring flocks usually total 20–100 in northeastern Ohio. Large flocks are observed only during unusually cold springs when most water remains frozen into March.

While Tundra Swans are uncommon to locally abundant spring migrants along their northern Ohio corridor, surprisingly few appear elsewhere. They are accidental to rare in other counties, least numerous in southern Ohio. They are usually detected in groups of 3–10 with occasional flocks of 24–45.

The first spring migrants may return by February 22–28. Their passage is relatively rapid, mostly between March 10 and 30. Their numbers are generally reduced by the first week of April, although flocks have been reported as late as April 21. Occasional stragglers after April 10–15 are normally nonbreeding immatures that may remain into May.

Despite these May sightings, Campbell[89] asserted that only "a few" June records came from the western Lake Erie marshes. There is one June observation from Cleveland. June swans normally remain for only a few days. The only summering record was provided by 2 Tundras at Cedar Point Wildlife Refuge (Lucas County) during 1943.[89]

Their fall migration is impressive across northern Ohio. Following a November cold front, large flocks fly eastward along Lake Erie, some passing over the shore while others are mere specks on the horizon. As evening approaches, these flocks move inland to settle on large lakes. Most rest only briefly, continuing their journey before dawn.

Although their numbers vary annually, Tundra Swans are generally more numerous in fall than in spring. This variability is most noticeable along western Lake Erie. Some years very few swans visit these marshes, but other years produce concentrations as large as 13,000 on November 23, 1985.[380] Elsewhere along Lake Erie, flights involving 1000–5000 are observed most years. Within the northeastern counties, flocks of 200–500+ swans may appear on inland lakes following November cold fronts; the largest inland concentration totaled 2000 near Youngstown on November 4–5, 1961.[143]

Tundra Swans are locally uncommon fall migrants through the northwestern and glaciated central counties. While flocks of 100–125 infrequently occur, Tundras are mostly encountered in flocks of 40 or fewer. These migrants are least numerous in the southern and unglaciated counties, where they are accidental to rare visitors, usually as groups of 10 or fewer with occasional flocks of 20–25.

A few early fall migrants return by the first week of October, but they do not normally appear until the last week of the month. Large flights normally occur between November 7 and 20. During some years, the entire Tundra Swan population may pass across Ohio during two or three days in November; in other years, defined movements may accompany each cold front throughout the month.

Most Tundra Swans usually depart by late November. Only small flocks and scattered individuals are reported later. Relatively mild weather may encourage swans to linger, and concentrations of 100–1200 have remained along western Lake Erie until freeze-up. The last migrants normally depart by December 15–25.

Wintering Tundra Swans were formerly exceptionally rare throughout Ohio. Beginning in the early 1960s, small numbers wintered in the western Lake Erie marshes during most years.[89] These wintering numbers vary from just a few swans to a flock of 130 during the winter of 1982–83.[369] They remain accidental to casual winter visitors away from western Lake Erie. There are usually one to four winter reports annually in the remainder of Ohio. They may appear wherever open water is available, usually in groups of fewer than 7 swans. While some have wintered at one locality, most remain for only a few days.

TRUMPETER SWAN

Cygnus buccinator Richardson

The former status of Trumpeter Swans is poorly understood. Anecdotal accounts by early naturalists provide sketchy information on their former abundance, their migrations, and other aspects of their life history. Much confusion stems from an inability to distinguish Trumpeters from Tundra Swans, causing the validity of many sight records to be questioned. While there are no extant specimens to document the Trumpeter's occurrence in Ohio, a specimen taken on the Ohio River near Cincinnati (technically in Kentucky) during December 1876 supports claims of Trumpeter Swans migrating through the state.[248] This specimen, along with the historical accounts, provides the justification for the Trumpeter's inclusion on the state list.[389]

Trumpeter Swans once nested across the northern United States east to northern Illinois.[39] Since their wintering grounds included the central Atlantic Coast, migrants certainly passed through Ohio. Trumpeters were early spring migrants and probably peaked during March and early April. Their return flight extended from late October until freeze-up. Some Trumpeters wintered along the Mississippi and lower Ohio Rivers upstream to southern Indiana. But despite assertions to the contrary,[236] there is no evidence to suggest that Trumpeters wintered in southwestern Ohio.

As a result of overhunting and habitat destruction, Trumpeter Swans rapidly declined throughout the eastern United States. While they were reported to be regular migrants through Ohio during the early 1800s, they were encountered only occasionally after 1860.[86,523] The last Ohio record was of a swan shot either April 18 or 19, 1900, near Wellston (Jackson County).[205] During the twentieth century, Trumpeter Swans have been restricted to small populations in western North America. The few Ohio sight records pertain to known escapes from captivity or swans of suspect origins.

MUTE SWAN

Cygnus olor (Gmelin)

With its curved neck and arched wings, the Mute Swan is the epitome of grace as it quietly swims along the edge of a small pond. Its elegance made this European swan a favorite among waterfowl fanciers on this continent. Some captive swans escaped or were intentionally released and established two feral populations in North America. The largest population is found along the Atlantic Coast from southern New England to North Carolina. The other is expanding in portions of Michigan, Ontario, Wisconsin, Illinois, and Indiana. These feral populations are normally resident, although Great Lakes swans undertake local winter movements to Ohio and adjacent states.

In Ohio, these swans were initially reported at Cleveland in 1936, Dayton in 1944, and Sandusky Bay in 1948.[89,299,451] They were irregular visitors along Lake Erie and at Youngstown dur-

ing the 1950s and have been regularly observed along the lakefront since 1962. They are now rare but regular winter visitors along Lake Erie. They may appear by late September but most are noted between November and early March. In November and early December, they are usually encountered along western Lake Erie and Sandusky Bay. When these marshes freeze, the swans move to hot-water outlets along the immediate lakefront. Spring thaws allow them to return to the Lake Erie marshes, and they depart by mid-April. Wintering Mutes are mostly observed in groups of 5 or fewer, although as many as 15 wintered at Oregon (Lucas County) during 1984–85.

Within the interior counties, Mute Swans are casual to accidental winter visitors, absent during milder winters but appearing at three to five locations when the weather is harsh. Most sightings are from the glaciated counties. There are only three records from the southeastern counties. They are mostly recorded between late December and February in groups of 7 or fewer.

The status of this feral population is obscured by Mute Swans that have escaped from captivity. These escapees may appear any month of the year but are most apparent in late spring and summer. They may be recognized by their tendency to remain at a locality for extended periods; the feral swans tend to be more mobile.

Feral Mute Swans began to nest in Ohio's western Lake Erie marshes in 1987.[434] Establishment of a breeding population should be discouraged. Wherever feral Mute Swan populations have become established, native waterfowl have suffered.

GREATER WHITE-FRONTED GOOSE

Anser albifrons (Scopoli)

During the nineteenth century, Greater White-fronted Geese were apparently rare but fairly regular visitors to Ohio. Anecdotal accounts indicated that they occasionally appeared within the western half of the state, and specimens were collected east to Fairfield County.[98,488,522] Overhunting greatly reduced their numbers during the late 1800s, and White-fronted Geese quit visiting Ohio.

A 1926 specimen from Lake St. Mary's was never substantiated and the first acceptable modern Ohio record was provided by a flock of 42 White-fronted Geese near Painesville (Lake County) on March 30, 1930.[96,523] White-fronted Geese did not reappear until 1945–49, when there were five sightings scattered across northern and western Ohio. They remained accidental during the 1950s, recorded on three occasions.

In the 1960s, Greater White-fronted Geese started to appear regularly east of the Mississippi River, producing increased sightings in Ohio. They were not annual visitors but were recorded nine times during this decade. An equal number of sightings was documented in the 1970s. Since 1980, these geese have been observed annually.

Greater White-fronted Geese are now rare but regular spring

visitors along western Lake Erie. There are normally one to three sightings each year of 4 or fewer geese, with infrequent flocks of 6–15. They are accidental to casual visitors elsewhere within the western half of Ohio from Cincinnati north to Lake St. Mary's and Killdeer Plains Wildlife Area (Wyandot County). These sightings usually total 6 or fewer geese, although a remarkable 97 White-fronteds appeared at Big Island Wildlife Area (Marion County) on March 16, 1985.[378] These geese are accidental spring migrants through eastern Ohio, with most sightings of 1–5 geese from the Cleveland area and flooded fields in southwestern Wayne County. The largest eastern Ohio flocks include the 1930 flock at Painesville, 62 geese in Wayne County on March 15, 1985, and 34 there on March 25–27, 1980.[277,378] The only spring sighting from the unglaciated plateau was a flock of 15 in Gallia County on March 8, 1986.[184] During some years, spring White-fronteds are unreported away from western Lake Erie, while in other years they appear at four or more inland locations. The earliest migrants return by February 25–28 but most records are during March. The last migrants disappear by April 10–15.

Fewer Greater White-fronted Geese appear as fall migrants, averaging one record every two or three years since 1980. These migrants are casual visitors to western Lake Erie and accidental elsewhere, with no reports from the unglaciated counties. Most fall records are of 1–4 geese. The only sizable flight comprised approximately 100 geese passing over Lake County on November 11, 1962.[335] These fall sightings occur between October 15 and December 15 with most during November.

As winter visitors, White-fronteds are casually encountered along western Lake Erie and accidental elsewhere. Since 1970, there have been a few records of 1–4 geese during December and the first half of January. Their status as winter residents has been greatly obscured by the presence of similar-appearing escaped geese. While wintering White-fronted Geese have been reported from several localities, some of these individuals have ultimately proven to be escapees.

SNOW GOOSE

Chen caerulescens (Linnaeus)

Large flocks of Snow Geese regularly migrate along the Mississippi River valley and the Atlantic Coast but unfortunately miss Ohio by several hundred miles. We must normally be content with isolated individuals and small flocks associated with Canada Geese. On rare occasions, however, strong winds displace migrating Snow Geese over Ohio, providing a marvelous spectacle for birders accustomed to observing these handsome geese in flocks of only 5–20 birds.

In the early 1900s, Snow Geese were rare migrants and not regularly detected in Ohio.[236] By the early 1930s, a few observers realized that flocks of Snow Geese occasionally flew over the state during their southward migration. These flocks were only briefly observed in passage, usually concentrated within a period of a few days.

The first substantial flight was recorded between October 13

and 24, 1939; more than 1000 Snow Geese were tallied at Toledo, and Hicks estimated at least 10,000 over Columbus on the evening of October 20.[86] Other flights were reported during the 1940s and early 1950s. Campbell[89] cited noticeable flights along western Lake Erie in 1940, 1945, 1946, 1948, and 1949. The 1948 movement was particularly strong, producing concentrations of 3200 geese at Toledo,[89] "several thousand" at Cincinnati,[248] 500 at Lake St. Mary's,[307] and "flocks" at Youngstown.[57] The October 1949 movement was only slightly less impressive. Perhaps the largest flight occurred in late October 1952, with "huge" numbers at Cleveland and an estimated 150,000 geese (95 percent "blue phase") over Meander Creek Reservoir (Mahoning County) during a two-hour period on October 25.[66,340] Surprisingly, this flight was not detected elsewhere. But just when these flights were becoming fairly regular, they abruptly stopped. Although Campbell[89] reported a flight along western Lake Erie in 1960 and another movement was apparent in northwestern and central Ohio during October 1969,[90,471] no sizable statewide movements have been subsequently reported.

Fall Snow Geese are now most frequently reported along western Lake Erie, where they are uncommon to fairly common migrants. Some years flock sizes are 150–250+, while in others they number fewer than 50. They casually appear in the unglaciated counties, where most reports are of 1–3 geese and the only flock totaled 55 at Senecaville Reservoir on November 28, 1973.[164] Elsewhere, Snow Geese are casual to locally uncommon fall migrants. Flocks of 1–6 Snow Geese are regularly detected at Killdeer Plains, Lake St. Mary's, and Mosquito Creek Wildlife Management Areas. Similar small flocks may appear at other western, central, and northeastern locations. Small movements are detected at two- to three-year intervals, producing scattered flocks of 30–200 in the western half of Ohio and along central Lake Erie. Most of these flocks pass over Ohio during a five- to ten-day period but are absent during the rest of autumn. Since 1960, the largest concentrations away from western Lake Erie were 620 Snows at Hoover Reservoir on October 21, 1969, and 600 at Findlay Reservoir on November 9–14, 1982.[368,471]

The earliest fall Snow Geese returned to Lake St. Mary's on September 5, 1964,[98] and Columbus by September 17–20. They do not normally appear until the first half of October. The largest flights are noted between October 15 and November 15, with the last migrants departing by December 15–25.

Most wintering Snow Geese are restricted to western Lake Erie, where they are rare to uncommon residents. Wintering numbers do not normally exceed 5–20. Flocks of 50–100 are exceptional, but 475 spent the winter of 1948–49 in Sandusky County.[89] Away from western Lake Erie, Snow Geese are accidental to casual winter visitors with very few records from the unglaciated counties. Sightings usually are of 1–5 Snows mixed among large flocks of Canada Geese. They are mostly detected at Killdeer Plains and Lake St. Mary's Wildlife Areas but could appear on any lake attracting flocks of wintering geese.

Their northward migration normally commences February 25–March 7. Most spring Snow Geese appear in March and depart by the first week of April. Only scattered immatures and nonbreeders remain after April 15–20, some through May 15–23, although none have attempted to summer in Ohio.

Spring Snow Geese are generally uncommon migrants along western Lake Erie, where most flocks are composed of 5–25 and no more than 150–200 have been noted. Snow Geese are casual to rare spring migrants elsewhere in western and central Ohio. Most reports are of 1–6 Snows at wildlife management areas with sporadic flocks of 10–25. Spring migrants are casually observed away from these wildlife areas, including a remarkable 3000 near Cincinnati on February 29, 1948.[306] Snow Geese are generally accidental or casual spring migrants through the eastern counties, becoming rare at Mosquito Creek Wildlife Area and in southwestern Wayne County. Most eastern Ohio sightings are of 1–3 geese, with a maximum of 40 in Holmes County on March 6, 1982.

ROSS' GOOSE

Chen rossii (Cassin)

Ross' Geese were formerly restricted to a limited breeding range in Arctic Canada. Migrants followed a narrow corridor through western North America to wintering grounds in California and southern Oregon. During the past twenty years, their populations substantially increased, new breeding colonies were established in the Arctic, and Ross' Geese became regular migrants through the Great Plains to wintering areas in Texas. Small numbers have been detected among large Snow Goose flocks in eastern North America as well.[5]

Given this recent range expansion, the appearance of a Ross' Goose in Ohio was expected. The only acceptable record was provided by one discovered at Ottawa Wildlife Refuge on March 18, 1982, by John Pogacnik and Bill Windnagel. It was observed on the refuge and nearby fields in Ottawa County through March 21.[365] Should their populations continue to increase, Ross' Geese may appear in Ohio periodically, although they will probably remain accidental visitors.

BRANT

Branta bernicla (Linnaeus)

During the first half of this century, Brant were accidental visitors to Ohio. There were only four published records, all during spring: a specimen taken at Indian Lake on March 29, 1905;[116] a flock of 20 in Lake County on March 23, 1930; 36 in Lake County on March 9, 1924;[523] and one at Buckeye Lake on May 30, 1902.[479]

Beginning in the early 1950s, Brant became casual visitors, mostly as fall migrants along Lake Erie. They were observed at two- to three-year intervals through the mid-1970s and every year but one since 1976. These increased sightings are partially the result of more observers along Lake Erie. However, the complete absence of fall sightings before 1949 indicates that their fall migration corridors shifted during the 1950s.

Brant are now rare but regular fall migrants along central Lake Erie but casual visitors to the Western Basin. While migrants have been reported as early as October 6,[89] most pass along the lakefront between October 29 and November 18. The latest migrants are noted through mid-December. These reports are mostly of 1–4 Brant flying along the lakefront or feeding near a breakwater. Fall flocks of 6–26 Brant are infrequently encountered. By far the largest flight occurred on November 11, 1985, when 290+ Brant flew past Vermilion (Erie County).[380] With the exception of 1985, when Brant were widely scattered along the lakefront, they have produced only one to four sightings annually since the late 1970s.

Brant are accidental fall migrants away from Lake Erie. There are at least four records from the Columbus area and single sightings at Evans Lake (Mahoning County), Findlay, and Gallia County. These inland records of 4 or fewer Brant coincide with the movements along Lake Erie.

Brant are accidental winter visitors, usually single individuals remaining for brief periods. There were sightings at Cleveland on January 23–25, 1960, and January 20, 1971, and at Magee Marsh Wildlife Area on January 22, 1983.[369,523] The only Brant to overwinter were singles sporadically observed at several Columbus area reservoirs during the winter of 1959–60 and at Lake St. Mary's between November 20, 1966, and March 14, 1967.[98]

They remain accidental spring migrants through Ohio. The only recent inland spring record was at Lake St. Mary's on May 9, 1958.[352] There are also four recent sightings along Lake Erie during May: singles at two locations in the Western Basin and flocks of 27 Brant at Ashtabula on May 20–25, 1956, and 28 at Crane Creek State Park on May 26, 1985.[378,471]

CANADA GOOSE

Branta canadensis (Linnaeus)

Initially, Canada Geese were primarily migrants passing through Ohio to and from their Arctic nesting range. Small numbers occasionally wintered within southern and central Ohio during relatively mild seasons.[236] As spring migrants, flocks were regularly encountered along western Lake Erie but made very brief appearances at other locations. Most spring flocks were composed of 50 or fewer and concentrations in excess of 100–200 were exceptional.[86,479] While larger numbers generally appeared each autumn, these movements lasted for only a few days. During some years, small flocks were detected along western Lake Erie and at a few inland lakes. In other years, sizable flights produced local concentrations of 500–1000 geese. Trautman's estimate[479] of 5000 Canadas at Buckeye Lake on October 21–22, 1925, was exceptional for that era.

These distribution patterns were maintained until the mid-1940s, when overhunting and poor reproductive success reduced Canada Goose populations to all-time low levels. Decisive action was necessary to prevent their disappearance. The first step was the establishment of refuges on their wintering grounds and along their migration corridors. Canada Geese quickly responded by changing their status within Ohio. Large flocks began to winter within the northern counties. For example, 2000 spent the winter of 1948–49 near Sandusky Bay in Sandusky County and an equal number wintered on Meander Creek Reservoir (Mahoning County) in 1949–50.[58,307] Similar flocks were reported during the 1950s. Numbers of migrants also increased dramatically. Canada Geese became numerous and widely distributed migrants and flocks of 500–1000 were frequently noted.

Concurrent with the establishment of refuges, the development of a locally nesting Canada Goose population was undertaken. This program has produced nesting pairs at Lake St. Mary's since 1953 and within the western Lake Erie marshes since 1955.[89,98] Initially, nesting geese were restricted to wildlife management areas. These populations spread throughout the state during the 1970s.

As a result of this intensive management, a semidomesticated resident population has become permanently established. But successful management was achieved with a price. Unlike their warier brethren, our resident geese are accustomed to people and readily adapt to disturbed habitats. No longer restricted to isolated marshes and lakes, they appear anywhere water is available. As this resident population expanded, it developed a reputation as a nuisance, befouling beaches and lawns and damaging corn and winter wheat crops. While the species still looks the same, its behavior is entirely different, and the noble character formerly associated with a skein of migrant geese passing overhead has been tarnished.

Canada Geese are still most numerous as migrants. During spring, their northward movements become apparent February 18–25 and peak during March. Small migrant flocks may be encountered through April 15–25. As fall migrants, a few Canadas appear during the first half of September. The first large flights are normally associated with strong cold fronts between September 15 and 25 and peak between October 20 and November 15. Migrants are noted until freeze-up in early January.

Canada Geese are fairly common to abundant migrants during spring and fall, more numerous during their southward migration. The largest concentrations appear along western Lake Erie, where 5000–20,000+ are expected each year. Sizable flocks also accumulate at Lake St. Mary's, Killdeer Plains, and Mosquito Creek Wildlife Management Areas, regularly attracting 1000–10,000+. Similar flocks generally do not appear elsewhere, although 100–500+ Canadas regularly visit most glaciated counties. Migrant Canadas are least numerous within the unglaciated counties. This status may change if an effort to establish a resident goose population in portions of Muskingum and Morgan Counties is successful.

Numbers of wintering Canada Geese fluctuate annually, but they are most numerous during mild seasons when open water is readily available. Canada Geese are locally abundant winter residents along western Lake Erie and at Lake St. Mary's, Killdeer Plains, and Mosquito Creek Wildlife Areas. Winter flocks of 1000–10,000+ Canadas are regularly noted at these locations. They are generally fairly common to common winter residents on large lakes and marshes within the glaciated counties. These winter flocks seldom exceed 200–500. Within the unglaciated counties, similar flocks regularly winter along the Ohio River and in Muskingum and Morgan Counties. Away from these locations, Canada Geese are generally rare to locally fairly common residents, mostly in flocks of 50 or fewer.

Canada Geese are least numerous during summer. They are locally common residents along western Lake Erie and at the wildlife areas where resident populations have been established. They are uncommon to fairly common summer residents in glaciated Ohio, where at least a few pairs are found in most counties.[434] They are generally rare to uncommon residents in unglaciated Ohio, except in Muskingum and Morgan Counties. The statewide population has rapidly expanded since 1970.

Breeding Canadas may be found on extensive marshes, large lakes, and farm ponds. They normally nest on the ground near water but readily accept "goose tubs" erected on ponds and marshes. Complete clutches are expected during the last half of March and downy young can be found by mid-April. Nesting activities normally peak in April and adult geese followed by a group of downy young are a familiar sight during May and June.

WOOD DUCK

Aix sponsa (Linnaeus)

Few ducks possess the beauty of a drake Wood Duck quietly perched on a log in a wooded swamp. This breathtaking sight is often taken for granted today, since Wood Ducks are numerous residents along streams, quiet backwaters of large lakes, wooded swamps, and marshes throughout Ohio. But they have not always been so numerous. In fact, they were protected during several decades of this century after their numbers were greatly reduced by overhunting.

By all accounts, sizable numbers of Wood Ducks graced the waterways of Ohio into the 1880s.[522] Their decline was fairly rapid; by 1900, Wood Ducks became rare at most localities.[89,193,479] Further reductions were apparent until 1910–15, when Wood Ducks essentially disappeared from most counties and the appearance of a small flock was noteworthy.

Their initial recovery was quite slow. By the mid-1930s, Wood Ducks remained uncommon to rare and very locally distributed summer residents. Hicks[220] cited breeding records from forty-seven counties. Only four of these counties were in the southern third of the state; Wood Ducks were very rare to absent along the unglaciated Allegheny Plateau.[223] While some improvement was evident after 1935, populations remained depressed because of a shortage of suitable nesting cavities.[86]

Beginning in the 1940s, the practice of providing nest boxes for Wood Ducks became widespread and their populations expanded. By the early 1960s, Wood Ducks regained their former abundance.[89,98] Their numbers continued to improve, reflecting significant increases throughout the eastern United States between 1965 and 1979.[438]

Wood Ducks are now the most widely distributed and numerous of our breeding waterfowl. They are fairly common to common summer residents in most counties, becoming locally uncommon within a few western counties. A canoe trip invariably will turn up three to ten broods of Wood Ducks during June and July, even along streams in urban areas if mature riparian corridors remain intact. The densest populations are noted in managed marshes where as many as ten to twenty broods may be observed.

Wood Ducks nest exclusively in cavities, including artificial ones built directly over water and natural ones at heights of fifty feet or more. While they prefer to nest close to water, they have nested more than half a mile from any stream or pond. Their nesting activities peak during May and the first half of June; nests with eggs have been reported through July 8.[345] A few pairs breed earlier; recently hatched young have been observed in central Ohio as early as April 18. The first broods are usually noted during the last half of May and most are detected between early June and mid-August. Late nesting attempts produce partially grown young through September 5–14. After their young become independent, Wood Ducks frequently accumulate in small flocks. These flocks gather at evening roosts, preferring isolated buttonbush swamps and quiet backwaters along rivers.

With such a substantial breeding population, the beginning of fall migration is difficult to determine. Trautman[479] reported southward movements by late August. In general, Wood Ducks remain fairly common to locally abundant fall migrants through October 15–25. Flocks of 15–35 may be encountered during the day, while 200–500+ may gather at evening roosts. Fall migrants are most numerous along Killbuck Creek in Wayne and Holmes Counties, where evening flights in excess of 1000 Wood Ducks can be witnessed during late September and early October. Their numbers noticeably diminish by early November. The last migrants usually depart by November 15.

At one time, Wood Ducks were accidental winter visitors. There were very few winter sightings before 1950, mostly near Toledo and Cleveland. As their breeding populations expanded, the number of winter records also increased, although they did not regularly overwinter until the early 1970s. Wood Ducks are now accidental to locally rare winter residents throughout Ohio. Within the northern counties, wintering ducks are normally restricted to two to four ponds and lakes that regularly host large numbers of waterfowl, mostly in the Cleveland-Akron area and occasionally at Castalia (Erie County). Most winter records are of 5 or fewer ducks with as many as 16–19 counted at Cleveland. Within the central and southern counties, a few wintering ducks are regularly found along the Scioto, Muskingum, Great Miami, and other large rivers. Small numbers may be mixed among flocks of wintering puddle ducks. Reports normally are of 5 or fewer Wood Ducks with occasional flocks of 6–12.

The first flocks of spring migrants are expected in southern and central Ohio by February 20–March 5. They may not appear in the northern counties until March 3–10. Wood Ducks are widely distributed by March 20–25. This movement usually comprises pairs and small flocks of 20 or fewer Wood Ducks. This northward migration continues into the last half of April, although late migrants are difficult to distinguish from residents.

GREEN-WINGED TEAL

Anas crecca Linnaeus

The first Green-winged Teal may appear during the last week of February but normally these spring migrants return by March 3–7. This movement peaks between March 10 and April 7. During these weeks, Green-wingeds are common to abundant migrants along western Lake Erie, where 50–200+ may be observed while larger concentrations are infrequently reported. Fewer Green-wingeds pass along central Lake Erie, where they become uncommon and flocks seldom exceed 10–20. Spring teal are uncommon to fairly common migrants within the northern and glaciated central counties, where daily totals of 5–50 are expected. These teal become locally abundant at preferred localities such as Big Island Wildlife Area (Marion County) and southwestern Wayne County, where flocks of 100–200+ may congregate. They are least numerous in the southern and unglaciated counties, becoming uncommon to rare migrants in flocks of 5–20. Numbers noticeably decline by mid-April. Green-wingeds largely depart from interior counties by April 25–30, although a few linger into the first week of May. Along western Lake Erie, small numbers regularly remain through May 15–22.

As summer residents, Green-winged Teal are largely restricted to marshes bordering western Lake Erie. Summering pairs were initially recorded there in 1934, and the first breeding attempt was confirmed in 1937.[86] Despite sporadic summer sightings, the next nesting record was not established until 1954.[89] Summering records became more frequent in the late 1950s. Breeding pairs were regularly noted at Magee Marsh Wildlife Area between 1962 and 1967[89] and their numbers slowly increased after 1970.

Green-winged Teal are now rare summer residents within the western Lake Erie marshes. A few breeding pairs are found in every extensive marsh and as many as 25–50 pairs may reside within Ohio some years. Away from western Lake Erie, Green-winged Teal are accidental summer residents. There are confirmed nesting records from Pymatuning Lake (Ashtabula County) in 1937 and possibly 1938,[499,502] Berlin Reservoir in Mahoning County in 1953,[69] near Pickerington in Franklin County in 1981,[362] and Barberton (Summit County) sporadically since 1985.[379]

Nesting teal are restricted to extensive wetlands where open water is interspersed with emergent vegetation. Their nests are placed on dikes or in grassy fields near these marshes. The few breeding records indicate that nesting activities begin in late April or early May. Most broods are observed in June or early July, although small young were discovered at Berlin Reservoir on August 2.[69]

While 125 Green-winged Teal were observed in Lucas County on July 1, 1983, this concentration comprised male teal returning to these marshes to molt. Similar "molt migrations" involving flocks of 20–40+ teal have been reported in other years. The beginning of fall migration is less well defined. Green-wingeds may appear along western Lake Erie and scattered inland localities between July 25 and August 7. By mid-August, fall Green-wingeds are regularly mixed among the migrant Blue-wingeds passing through the state.

Along western Lake Erie, 1500 teal were observed at Ottawa Wildlife Refuge on September 6, 1981, but they do not normally become common migrants until September 20–25. Fall Green-wingeds are most numerous during October and November. The largest concentrations include 3500 teal in Ottawa and Lucas Counties on October 5, 1986, and 1250 at Catawba Island (Ottawa County) on November 23, 1957.[89,384] Fall Green-wingeds are usually observed in groups of 50–250+. They normally depart during December as the marshes freeze, although as many as 75–250 teal have been counted through December 15–21.

Their inland passage peaks between October 5 and November 15. These migrants are generally rare to uncommon in most counties, becoming locally fairly common at a few preferred localities. Most fall totals are 5–40 Green-wingeds with infrequent concentrations of 50–100+ and a maximum of 200+ at Cincinnati in 1958.[321] Numbers of inland migrants noticeably decline during the last half of November.

Small numbers of Green-winged Teal are expected to linger until freeze-up in December or early January, appearing on several Christmas Bird Counts each year. Unlike most other puddle ducks, Green-wingeds do not regularly winter in the state; they become accidental to casual visitors after early January. While Trautman[479] reported small numbers of Green-wingeds regularly wintering at Buckeye Lake in the 1920s and 1930s, they have not been present in recent years. Wintering teal are most likely to be noted during mild years. They are most often reported from the western Lake Erie marshes but winter records are scattered across the state, invariably groups of 6 or fewer teal.

Most of our Green-winged Teal are members of the North American race, *A. c. carolinensis*. The European race, *A. c. crecca*, is an accidental visitor, including a specimen collected at New Bremen (Auglaize County) on March 18, 1910,[498] and documented males at Buckeye Lake on March 6, 1932,[479] and near Pickerington (Franklin County) March 18–30, 1976. Undocumented records near Youngstown during the springs of 1933, 1935, and 1938 could pertain to the same individual.[25,45,501]

AMERICAN BLACK DUCK

Anas rubripes Brewster

In every aspect of their life history, behavior, and habitat requirements, American Black Ducks are similar to Mallards. As a result of extensive hybridization of these two species, some ornithologists regard them as conspecific. Black Ducks have not fared well in competition with Mallards, declining throughout their entire range this century as Mallards increased.

This change is most apparent in their status as winter residents. Before 1940, Black Ducks were the most numerous wintering puddle ducks.[86,479] Their relative abundance began to change during the 1940s, and Mallards outnumbered Black Ducks at Buckeye Lake by the winter of 1952–53.[341] Similar trends were apparent at other localities and continued into the 1980s.

Despite declining populations, Black Ducks remain uncom-mon to abundant winter residents on large lakes, marshes, and streams throughout Ohio. Wintering Black Ducks are abundant residents along western Lake Erie, where totals of 500–2000 are frequent and larger concentrations are possible. Aerial surveys estimated populations in excess of 37,500 some winters.[90] The largest flocks are frequently noted between December 15 and January 15 but may be substantially reduced by February.

Elsewhere, the largest concentrations appear at reservoirs and wildlife management areas scattered across the northern and glaciated central counties, where flocks of 100–1000+ gather each year. Reservoirs within the southern and unglaciated counties normally host flocks of 50–250. Similar flocks regularly winter along central Lake Erie. In counties lacking large lakes, Black Ducks become uncommon and locally distributed along creeks and rivers and winter flocks are composed of only 5–30. These numbers represent a substantial decline from former wintering populations when flocks of 500–2500+ were regularly reported from the glaciated counties.

Spring migration begins during the last half of February and peaks in March. Along western Lake Erie, Black Ducks remain numerous through April 5–15 and small flocks are regularly observed into the first half of May. Elsewhere, small flocks are noted through April 7 and only scattered stragglers after April 10–20. These migrants are abundant along western Lake Erie, although totals have seldom surpassed 500–1000 during the 1980s. They become uncommon to locally abundant migrants elsewhere with occasional flocks of 50–250. They are least numerous within the unglaciated counties, where most flocks total 5–40.

In the mid-1930s, Black Ducks were common summer residents along western Lake Erie.[220] A few pairs nested within the northeastern counties, where they were rare to uncommon and locally distributed summer residents. Breeding Black Ducks were sporadically encountered elsewhere with scattered records south to Mercer, Shelby, Logan, Franklin, Fairfield, Guernsey, and Carroll Counties.[220,223]

Along western Lake Erie, this population remained stable into the 1960s.[9,89] Campbell[89] cited an average of 14 nesting pairs at Magee Marsh Wildlife Area with a maximum of 28 pairs in 1961. Anderson[7] estimated 20 pairs in the Winous Point marshes in 1960. Their numbers were declining elsewhere. A few pairs nested within the northeastern counties but they essentially disappeared from other counties except for nesting records in Butler County before 1953, Carroll County in 1962, and Jefferson County in 1974.[84,248]

American Black Ducks are now uncommon summer residents within the western Lake Erie marshes. Fewer than 100 pairs probably nest in these marshes and their numbers appear to be declining. Within northeastern Ohio, Black Ducks are accidental to casual nonbreeding summer visitors except for a small population of 5–10 pairs at Lake Rockwell (Portage County). Elsewhere, they are accidental summer visitors, with the only confirmed nesting record in Seneca County during 1984.[434]

Nesting Black Ducks are usually found in large marshes or isolated small ponds bordered by emergent vegetation. Their territorial activity starts by late March and peaks in mid-April when the first clutches are laid.[9] Most nests are located on dikes or in grasslands adjacent to marshes and are discovered during May. While downy young have been observed as early as May 5, most broods are noted in June and July.[89]

When populations were larger, Black Ducks regularly undertook a substantial molt migration into the western Lake Erie marshes and as many as 1000 were counted by the first week of August.[89] Similar flights have not been apparent in recent years, when their numbers have slowly accumulated during the last half of August and September. They do not normally become numerous until the first half of October. Peak concentrations are expected during November and the first half of December when 1000–10,000 may be tallied from the ground and aerial surveys may count more than 45,000.

Away from western Lake Erie, Black Ducks are casually encountered during August and the first half of September. The first migrants normally appear within the northern and central counties between September 15 and 25 but may not appear in southern Ohio until the first half of October. Peak concentrations are expected in November and the first half of December. Fall flocks of 200–5000+ are regularly reported in the northern and central counties. Flocks of 50–300+ may appear in the southern and unglaciated counties.

MALLARD

Anas platyrhynchos Linnaeus

At the turn of the century, Jones[236] described Mallards as "locally common migrants, but absent from many localities and mostly seen in small flocks." Breeding pairs were irregularly reported from the southern half of Ohio but were "more common and very local" elsewhere. While most puddle ducks declined after the early 1900s, the adaptable Mallard has substantially increased.

The expanding Mallard populations were evident during summer. In the mid-1930s, Hicks[220] considered Mallards common summer residents in the western Lake Erie marshes. They were uncommon to rare and very locally distributed elsewhere in the northern half of Ohio but were absent from the southern half. This population noticeably increased in the 1940s and 1950s as pairs expanded into the southern counties. Mallards released from game farms undoubtedly augmented the expanding populations. By the mid-1960s, nesting Mallards were found in most counties. They are probably still increasing.

Breeding Mallards are now fairly common to common summer residents within the marshes bordering western Lake Erie. Their relative abundance in these marshes was estimated at 20–25 pairs per square mile before 1952.[9] Similar densities are encountered today except in drawndown marshes. In addition, nonbreeders and molting males regularly form flocks of 50–500+ as early as the first half of June. Away from western Lake Erie, Mallards are uncommon to fairly common summer residents along rivers, creeks, ditches, marshes, large reservoirs, and ponds. They are generally most numerous in the northeastern counties but are locally distributed in southern and eastern Ohio, although a few pairs can be found in nearly every county.[434]

Breeding Mallards usually nest in upland grassy cover adjacent to ponds and marshes. A few nests are placed more than a mile from any stream or pond. They normally nest on the ground but some use tree cavities. Most pairs establish their territories in late March or early April. Nests have been discovered during the last week of March but first clutches are not normally laid until mid-April.[9] Renesting efforts are responsible for clutches through mid-June. The first broods have hatched by the last week of April, although most appear between May 15 and June 15. Partially grown young may be regularly observed through the first half of August.

Migrants are apparent along western Lake Erie by August 20–30, although flocks may not be encountered within the interior counties until the last half of September. Substantial movements may not occur until the first half of October. The largest numbers usually appear between October 25 and December 15. These flocks may remain until freeze-up in early January.

These migrants are most numerous along western Lake Erie, where flocks of 1000–5000+ may appear by early September. As many as 10,000–20,000 are expected on aerial surveys during mid-October with peak concentrations of 30,000–50,000+ in November and early December. From the ground, the largest flocks seldom exceed 5000–10,000. Their numbers decline during the last half of December, although 19,000–25,000 have been estimated through the first week of January.[89]

Fall migrants are common to abundant away from western Lake Erie, generally least numerous within the unglaciated counties. Inland flocks seldom exceed 100–500 Mallards during September and concentrations of 500–1000+ do not normally appear until mid-October. Peak numbers are expected between November 15 and December 15, producing local flocks of 3000–10,000 in the western half of the state but normally fewer than 1500 in the southeastern counties. The largest flocks frequently appear immediately before freeze-up and may remain into the first half of January.

Before 1940, wintering Mallards were outnumbered by Black Ducks throughout Ohio. Their status began to change in the late 1930s along western Lake Erie.[86] Increased numbers were apparent elsewhere during the 1940s and 1950s as Mallards became the most numerous wintering puddle ducks. Mallards are now generally fairly common to abundant winter residents, becoming locally uncommon in areas lacking large lakes and marshes. The largest concentrations are expected along western Lake Erie, where 3000–10,000 may winter in the marshes. Larger flocks are infrequent. Elsewhere, winter flocks of 500–4000+ may develop in the northern and glaciated central counties. In southern and unglaciated Ohio, winter totals seldom exceed 50–300.

Their spring migration begins during the first warm days of late February. These movements peak during March when they become fairly common to abundant migrants. Their numbers decline between April 5 and 15 with the last flocks departing by April 25–May 5. Spring concentrations of 300–1000+ may appear on large lakes, marshes, and flooded fields throughout Ohio. Larger concentrations are unusual, although flocks of 2500–4000+ may sporadically develop. Similar numbers are expected along western Lake Erie, where aerial surveys frequently produce estimates of 10,000–25,000+.

NORTHERN PINTAIL

Anas acuta Linnaeus

During the nineteenth and early twentieth centuries, Northern Pintails were the most numerous puddle ducks.[236,522] While precise counts are unavailable, anecdotal records indicate that they easily surpassed Mallards in abundance. Their numbers were already declining in the 1890s and pintails became less numerous than Mallards by the early 1920s.[479] This trend continued during subsequent decades.

Pintails remain fairly common to locally abundant spring migrants in most counties, becoming uncommon to rare in areas lacking sizable lakes and marshes. These migrants are most numerous along western Lake Erie, where flocks of 100–1000+ are regularly observed and as many as 5000 were reported during several years.[89] Fewer pintails migrate through central Lake Erie; concentrations seldom exceed 25–50. Inland migrants are most numerous in the northeastern and glaciated central counties. Pintails once gathered into local flocks of 400–1000+ and as many as 3000 were counted at Youngstown on March 24, 1934.[22] In recent years, pintails mostly appear in small flocks with occasional concentrations of 100–500. Smaller numbers migrate through other interior counties; concentrations of 100–300+ were formerly reported but flocks in excess of 50–75 are unusual today. The only other location where "hundreds" of pintails regularly congregate is the mouth of the Great Miami River (Hamilton County).

Pintails regularly appear by February 20–25 and become most numerous between March 7 and April 7. Away from western Lake Erie, their numbers noticeably decline by mid-April and very few stragglers remain after May 1. In the western Lake Erie marshes, small flocks are regularly observed through late April; late migrants frequently remain through May 10–20.

Northern Pintails were formerly irregular summer residents in the western Lake Erie marshes. Most early records were probably of nonbreeders, although nesting was confirmed in 1930 and 1937.[89,220] Between 1949 and 1952, approximately 2 percent of the ducks summering along western Lake Erie were pintails.[9] However, most were nonbreeders and there were few additional confirmed nesting attempts. Since 1960, pintails have been rare summer residents whose breeding population probably does not exceed 10–20 pairs. Most summer pintails are nonbreeders or ducks returning to the marshes to molt, producing summer flocks as large as 100.[7]

Breeding pintails prefer large undisturbed marshes. Their nests are located close to these wetlands. The few breeding records indicate that nesting activities are initiated during May; most family groups are observed in June.[89,220] Away from western Lake Erie, Northern Pintails are accidental summer visitors to the northern and central counties. Most are nonbreeders, although there are nesting records at Pymatuning Lake (Ashtabula County) during 1936 and 1937[31,499] and broods were discovered in Seneca County in 1984 and Killdeer Plains Wildlife Area in 1986.[375,383]

As fall migrants, pintails are decidedly most numerous in the western Lake Erie marshes. The first migrants usually return during the last half of August. They are commonly encountered by late September in flocks of 100–500+. The largest concentrations are discovered during November, including 13,325 counted during an aerial survey on November 11, 1960, and 6500 estimated from the ground on November 27, 1948.[89,90]

Fall pintails are much less numerous elsewhere. In recent years, most reports are of fewer than 50 pintails with infrequent concentrations of 100+. Earlier in this century, fall flocks of 100–400 were regularly noted in the central and northeastern counties. These migrants may appear during the last week of August, although they are not regularly observed until September 15–25. Most appear during the last half of October and November.

By mid-December, most pintails depart for their wintering grounds. Mild weather may allow flocks to linger; 200 have been reported along western Lake Erie through December 23.[89] But once the marshes and lakes freeze, they become rare to uncommon winter residents. Individuals and small flocks may be found among the large associations of Mallards and American Black Ducks. Numbers are generally small, usually fewer than 10 with occasional reports of 15–25.

BLUE-WINGED TEAL

Anas discors Linnaeus

These attractive ducks have always been among our more numerous migrant waterfowl. Regularly encountered in most counties, Blue-winged Teal generally avoid the open waters of large lakes in favor of sheltered backwaters, flooded fields, marshes, and small ponds. Unfortunately, wetland drainage and below-normal precipitation were responsible for substantially reduced populations during the 1980s.

Despite these recent declines, Blue-winged Teal remain fairly common to locally abundant spring migrants, least numerous along the unglaciated Allegheny Plateau. Local concentrations of 200–500+ may develop in any glaciated county but are most regularly encountered along western Lake Erie. Most spring reports total 25–150 teal. A few have appeared north to Lake Erie by February 22–23, but the first migrants do not normally appear until March 5–15. They do not become numerous until the last week of the month and their maximum abundance is normally attained during April. Small flocks and scattered pairs pass through most counties until May 20–25.

Breeding Blue-winged Teal were always most evident within the northern third of Ohio. In the mid-1930s, Hicks[220] considered them fairly common residents within the western Lake Erie marshes. They were rare and locally distributed elsewhere in northern Ohio with records from most northeastern counties and from Defiance, Huron, and Ashland Counties. The only other breeding teal were recorded at Lake St. Mary's and Indian Lake and in Holmes and Tuscarawas Counties. Of these inland sites, only Lake St. Mary's supported a sizable population.[98]

Their breeding range expanded in subsequent decades. The first Columbus broods were reported in 1942;[231] nesting was confirmed in Hamilton, Butler, and Brown Counties by 1953; and the first Dayton nest was discovered in 1963.[248,299] Nesting populations were also increasing along western Lake Erie, with 129 breeding pairs estimated at Magee Marsh Wildlife Area in 1966–67 and similar numbers in other marshes.[7,89] Population trends within the northeastern counties were uncertain. This range expansion ended during the 1970s and fewer breeding pairs have been evident since 1980.

Blue-winged Teal remain fairly common summer residents along western Lake Erie, where breeding pairs occupy all suitable marshes. They are casual to rare and locally distributed residents within the northeastern counties and accidental to casual summer visitors in other glaciated counties except at Big Island Wildlife Area (Marion County), where a small population is established.[434] Breeding teal are sporadic within the glaciated central and southern counties, where they are detected at two- to four-year intervals. They are accidental along the unglaciated Allegheny Plateau, where nesting has been confirmed only from Tuscarawas County.

Nesting Blue-wingeds prefer extensive marshes and large ponds bordered by dense emergent vegetation. Their nests are placed in upland grassy cover near these habitats. Most pairs do not establish territories until April 20–30.[9] Nests with eggs have been recorded as early as April 30–May 1, but most are discovered during May and early June. The first broods appear by June 15–25. Renesting attempts are responsible for clutches through July 31 and adults accompanied by partially grown young on August 25.[89,417]

These teal are the first waterfowl to begin their southward migration. Flocks frequently return by July 20–30 and are widely distributed by mid-August. This movement peaks between August 25 and September 30 but noticeably diminishes during the first half of October. Along western Lake Erie, small numbers regularly remain through November 3–10 with occasional stragglers later in the month. Elsewhere, Blue-wingeds normally depart by October 15–27 and there are few records after November 1.

Fall teal are common to abundant along western Lake Erie, where concentrations of 100–900+ regularly develop. They become uncommon to locally abundant migrants within the other glaciated counties. Local concentrations of 100–900+ may appear, although daily totals generally do not exceed 30–75. These migrants are rare to locally fairly common along the unglaciated Allegheny Plateau, mostly in flocks of 30 or fewer.

Although these teal normally depart long before the onset of winter weather, unusually mild weather has prompted a few to linger into early December. They become accidental visitors after December 5. The few confirmed winter records are invariably single teal, frequently birds crippled during the hunting season. There are only two reports of Blue-winged Teal overwintering during mild seasons. Trautman[479] reported one observed intermittently at Buckeye Lake throughout the winter of 1931–32, while another reportedly spent the winter of 1982–83 at Magee Marsh Wildlife Area.[369]

CINNAMON TEAL

Anas cyanoptera Vieillot

In North America, these attractive teal breed primarily on lakes and marshes in the western United States and Canada. Their winter range extends from California and the southwestern states into Mexico. Cinnamon Teal are most numerous west of the Rocky Mountains but regularly migrate through the Great Plains. They are generally accidental visitors east of the Mississippi River.

Cinnamon Teal are most conspicuous during spring. Four of Ohio's five confirmed records are distinctive breeding males that associated with Blue-winged Teal. The first Cinnamon Teal was collected at Buckeye Lake in Fairfield County on April 4, 1895.[479] Fifty-six years later, another appeared at Kellogg Pond near Cincinnati between March 20 and 31, 1951, and attempted to court several female Blue-wingeds.[248] Drake Cinnamons were also seen at Magee Marsh Wildlife Area on May 11, 1980, and Delaware Wildlife Area between April 19 and 26, 1986.[277,382]

As fall migrants, Cinnamon Teal retain their drab eclipse plumage and are very similar to Blue-wingeds. In addition, some Blue-wingeds become stained with iron oxides and superficially resemble breeding drake Cinnamon Teal. Given these identification problems, there is only one confirmed fall record from Ohio: a Cinnamon Teal shot by a hunter at Magee Marsh Wildlife Area on November 5, 1980. The specimen is on display at the wildlife area.

NORTHERN SHOVELER

Anas clypeata Linnaeus

Even in their obscure eclipse plumages, Northern Shovelers are instantly recognized by their oversized bills. These bills are very effective strainers of plant and animal matter from shallow water along the margins of ponds, wetlands, and flooded fields. While shovelers regularly associate with other puddle ducks, their unique feeding apparatus allows them to occupy a niche of their own.

A few early spring migrants return in late February, but Northern Shovelers are not expected until March 7–15. The largest concentrations appear between March 15 and April 15 and most depart by May 5–10. A few stragglers may linger into June, mostly along western Lake Erie.

Even though they are widely distributed, spring shovelers are seldom encountered in sizable flocks. They are most numerous along western Lake Erie, appearing as fairly common to common migrants in flocks of 5–25 with occasional concentrations of 50–300+. Elsewhere, migrant shovelers are generally uncommon, becoming locally fairly common in a few southwestern and central counties. These migrants are mostly observed in flocks of 20 or fewer with infrequent concentrations of 50–100+. The largest inland flocks totaled 275 in Butler County on April 6, 1950, and 200 in Shelby County on March 24, 1954.[248,299]

The first breeding shovelers were reported along western Lake Erie in the 1930s.[220] These nesting pairs were most evident in 1936 and 1937, probably displaced by drought from central North America.[86] Shovelers produced few summer sightings in the 1940s and early 1950s, but by the late 1950s summering Shovelers returned to western Lake Erie as part of an eastward range expansion.[104] They were considered "a definitely established nesting species" in the Winous Point marshes (Ottawa County) in 1960 and have summered annually in the Magee Marsh Wildlife Area–Ottawa Wildlife Refuge complex since 1960.[7,89]

Northern Shovelers are now rare but regular summer residents in marshes bordering western Lake Erie. Their population probably does not exceed 10–30 pairs. These summer shovelers are almost exclusively individuals or pairs. Small flocks have never been reported. The few confirmed breeding records indicate that clutches are laid during May and hatch by mid-June. Family groups remain intact until late July or early August.

Away from western Lake Erie, Northern Shovelers are accidental summer visitors in the northern and central counties. Confirmed breeding records are limited to a brood in Delaware Wildlife Area (Marion County) on June 22–23, 1956;[460] an unsuccessful nest at Killdeer Plains Wildlife Area (Wyandot County) during May 1984;[434] and a nest at Pymatuning Lake in 1936.[31] A pair may have nested at Big Island Wildlife Area (Marion County) during 1983.

Relatively few Northern Shovelers migrate through Ohio each autumn. These migrants are uncommon to fairly common within the western Lake Erie marshes but uncommon to rare elsewhere. Fall shovelers are mostly observed in flocks of 10 or fewer with occasional concentrations of 50–65 along western Lake Erie and 20–30 elsewhere.

The first few migrants may return during August within flocks of Blue-winged Teal. Shovelers regularly appear along western Lake Erie during the first half of September but are sporadically observed elsewhere until October. Most are reported between October 10 and November 20 with another small movement immediately before freeze-up in December. This late migration produced flocks of 50 at Hoover Reservoir (Delaware County) on December 2, 1978, and 12–17 along the Cleveland lakefront.

By early January, only a few wintering shovelers remain. These winter residents are regularly observed only at Castalia (Erie County), where 5–15 are found annually. They are casual to accidental winter residents elsewhere, mostly singles among large flocks of puddle ducks. Small shoveler flocks have wintered during mild seasons, including 33 at Buckeye Lake through the winter of 1931–32 and 50 at Magee Marsh Wildlife Area in 1982–83.[369,479]

GADWALL

Anas strepera Linnaeus

In the nineteenth century, Gadwalls were numerous migrants until their numbers were reduced by overhunting during the 1880s.[479] By 1900, Jones[236] considered them rare migrants. Their status did not improve until the 1930s and 1940s. As their populations increased during the 1960s and 1970s, their breeding range expanded eastward into the Great Lakes states.[104] These trends continued into the 1980s.

During spring, Gadwalls frequently associate with other puddle ducks in marshes, flooded fields, and the margins of large lakes. They are generally common along western Lake Erie and uncommon to fairly common elsewhere but locally rare in the unglaciated counties. Along western Lake Erie, 20–50 may be observed daily and flocks of 100–200+ are possible. Away from western Lake Erie, spring totals seldom exceed 10–30. The largest inland flocks totaled 200 at Youngstown and Cincinnati during the early 1950s.[62,248]

The first spring migrants return in late February but do not reach their peak abundance until March. Gadwalls are regularly encountered until mid-April but most depart from interior counties by April 20–30 with a few lingering into May. Along western Lake Erie, the last migrants depart by May 5–15.

Despite several anecdotal accounts, there were no confirmed Ohio summer records during the nineteenth century. The first summering Gadwalls were reported from Pymatuning Lake during 1938, although they were probably nonbreeders.[502] They also remained into June in northeastern Ohio during 1952.[65] Most summer records have been since 1960. Along western Lake Erie, 1–2 pairs summered at Magee Marsh Wildlife Area between 1962 and 1964 but nesting was not confirmed.[89] They did not regularly summer within Ottawa and Lucas Counties until the mid-1970s but have nested annually since 1979.[274] While breeding has not been confirmed at any inland location, Gadwalls remained into June at Killdeer Plains Wildlife Area (Wyandot County) during 1979 and Big Island Wildlife Area (Marion County) in 1984.[274,434]

While small flocks of 5–18 Gadwalls are infrequently reported along western Lake Erie during June and July, these flocks are probably nonbreeders and molting males. Some years, fewer than 10 pairs reside in the marshes; as many as 15–30 pairs may be present in other years. The few confirmed breeding records indicate that nesting is initiated in May, since most broods are reported during the last half of June and July.

The first fall migrants normally return to the western Lake Erie marshes by September 10–25 and become common by mid-October. While aerial surveys produced estimates of as many as 1700 Gadwalls on October 22, 1966,[90] these numbers are not apparent from the ground, where fall totals are comparable to spring. This status is maintained through mid-November with smaller numbers remaining until freeze-up.

Elsewhere, they are generally uncommon to locally rare fall migrants in flocks of 5–20 with occasional reports of 30–50. Along central Lake Erie, Gadwalls are relatively scarce until November or early December. In the interior counties, small numbers are mostly encountered between mid-October and early December.

Gadwalls were formerly rare winter residents before 1940. As their breeding populations expanded, wintering numbers increased. After freeze-up, Gadwalls are now uncommon to rare visitors among large flocks of wintering Mallards and Black Ducks. Flocks of 10–45 Gadwalls have congregated in the western Lake Erie marshes, Columbus, Dayton, Youngstown, and Castalia. Many of these flocks disappear by mid-January; others have overwintered. The largest winter concentration was 125 near Sandusky during February 1947.[303]

EURASIAN WIGEON

Anas penelope Linnaeus

Ohio's first Eurasian Wigeon was collected at Buckeye Lake on March 29, 1902.[236] Others were noted in the Sandusky Bay area between April 18 and 20, 1904.[103] By the 1920s, additional records indicated they were rare but fairly regular migrants through Ohio. In the mid-1940s, Hasbrouck[189] cited at least forty-two records, the most from any interior state. Thirty-nine were of spring migrants; only two were fall sightings and one was an early winter observation. Eurasian Wigeon were most frequently noted from the late 1930s to the early 1950s when they averaged two to six sightings annually. Since 1960, only one to three observations have occurred each year.

Eurasian Wigeon are now rare but regular spring migrants through the western Lake Erie marshes, producing one to three sightings annually of single males among flocks of American Wigeon. Eurasian Wigeon are accidental to casual spring migrants elsewhere, producing only three to six records each decade since 1960, mostly in the northeastern counties (twenty-five sightings) and central Ohio near Columbus (twenty). A few scattered records come from other northern counties, seven from Cincinnati-Dayton, three from the unglaciated counties, and one from Lake St. Mary's—mostly single males, although 4 Eurasians were noted in Canton on April 19, 1935, and 3 at Columbus on March 22, 1959.[27,322] A few Eurasians return by the last week of February and the first week of March but most are observed between March 15 and April 20. Stragglers lingered near Toledo through May 31, 1942, and at Cleveland until May 27, 1967.[89,117]

There are only ten records of this accidental fall visitor, eight in the northeastern counties and two along western Lake Erie. All single males molting into their distinctive breeding plumage, they appeared as early as September 13–15 at Lake Rockwell (Portage County) but most were noted during the last half of October and November.

Eurasian Wigeon are accidental winter visitors with only three records. A single male was observed at Buckeye Lake between December 30, 1938, and January 3, 1939, while others were noted at Castalia (Erie County) during the winters of 1947–48 and 1963-64.[89,479]

AMERICAN WIGEON

Anas americana Gmelin

As they pass overhead, American Wigeon are immediately recognized by their distinctive whistled calls. They are equally unmistakable on the ground. These wigeon readily join mixed flocks of puddle ducks or occasionally form large segregated flocks. They are likely to be observed wherever waterfowl congregate.

Early spring migrants, American Wigeon return with the first warm days of late February. Maximum abundance is attained between March 10 and April 7. Spring wigeon are abundant along western Lake Erie, where concentrations of 100–500 are not unusual. Flocks of 1000–2500+ may be encountered when waterfowl populations are relatively high. Larger concentrations are infrequent, although as many as 20,000 were estimated on March 18, 1971.[90] Along central Lake Erie and in most northern and glaciated central counties, wigeon are fairly common to common migrants but flocks seldom exceed 50–200. They become locally abundant at a few localities; at Big Island Wildlife Area (Marion County) and in southwestern Wayne County, concentrations of 400–1000+ may appear. Spring migrants are least numerous in the southern and unglaciated counties, where they are locally rare to fairly common. Flocks seldom exceed 20–75 except for occasional concentrations of 300–450 in southwestern Ohio.[248,299] Small flocks and individuals are regularly noted through the end of April. Most depart by May 5–10 except along western Lake Erie, where a few may remain into June.

American Wigeon are among the rarer summer residents within the western Lake Erie marshes. Small numbers have summered in these marshes since the 1930s, most of them nonbreeders. Before 1960, the only nesting attempt was confirmed in 1936.[89] Beginning in the early 1960s, wigeon expanded their breeding range eastward,[104] resulting in small numbers of breeding pairs along western Lake Erie since 1962.[89] They are now rare summer residents. This population probably does not exceed 5–15 nesting pairs. Nonbreeders are rare visitors, normally in groups of 1–6. Molt migrations may produce larger concentrations, including 50 at Cedar Point National Wildlife Refuge (Lucas County) on June 21, 1980.[278]

Elsewhere, American Wigeon are accidental to casual summer visitors in the northern half of Ohio. There are several summer records at Cleveland, and a pair nested there in 1967.[117] They also summered at Pymatuning Lake during 1938,[502] and isolated individuals have remained for a few days at scattered localities in the central counties.

During fall, the first American Wigeon return to western Lake Erie by August 25–September 5. Sizable concentrations may not be encountered until late September or early October. Although their numbers fluctuate annually, wigeon remain common to abundant migrants through early December. Some years the largest flocks are composed of 100–300. But there were 10,000 at East Harbor State Park on November 13, 1948, and 15,355 in an aerial survey along western Lake Erie on October 22, 1966.[89,90]

Away from western Lake Erie, American Wigeon do not normally return until September 15–25 and flocks may not appear until mid-October. These migrants are uncommon to fairly common in most counties. Fall concentrations are generally 25–100 with occasional flocks of 200–400 in the central and northeastern counties. Larger flocks are exceptional, although 2500 congregated at Pymatuning Lake during 1936 and 1938.[32,503]

Freezing temperatures during December force most wigeon to migrate. Small numbers regularly winter throughout Ohio as casual to rare and locally distributed residents. Their numbers have slowly increased since the early 1960s. Scattered individuals may join the large wintering flocks of Mallards and Black Ducks. Additionally, flocks of 15–40+ may develop at Columbus and Castalia.

COMMON LOON
Gavia immer

En route from the primordial freshwater lakes of the north where they make their summer home to the southern saltwater bays where they spend the winter, many Common Loons pass over the state. A few in brownish gray and white winter plumage linger until bad weather drives them on. In spring, when returning north, some have attained their full nuptial dress and look much like the birds shown here; many others are molting and are mottled with patches of brownish gray and white.

Adult in nuptial plumage
(sexes similar)

PIED-BILLED GREBE
Podilymbus podiceps

Compared with the elaborate and conspicuous displays of its cousin the Western Grebe, the Pied-billed's courtship might be considered rather subdued. However, courtship among grebes is always a formal affair. When Pied-billeds meet they face each other about a foot apart, stretch their necks high, cock their heads, and pivot in place to present the fluffy white feathers of their undertails, a ritual that they repeat several times before the encounter ends. The presumed male frequently carries a small piece of aquatic plant in its bill.

Adults in nuptial plumage
(sexes similar)

DOUBLE-CRESTED CORMORANT
Phalacrocorax auritus

The small Ohio population of cormorants disappeared prior to 1900 as a result of persecution. During the twentieth century, they were uncommon migrants through the 1940s, becoming quite rare between the 1950s and 1970s. Their numbers increased dramatically after 1975 and they are presently more numerous than they have ever been. A few pairs nested along Lake Erie in 1987.

Bluegill
(Lepomis macrochirus)

Adult
(sexes similar)

AMERICAN BITTERN
Botaurus lentiginosus

This well-camouflaged summer resident of cattail marshes is rarely seen except when it carelessly steps into a clearing or is driven to the edge of cover and forced to fly. More frequently its presence is revealed by its unusual pumplike call given in spring.

Adult
(sexes similar)

LITTLE BLUE HERON
Egretta caerulea

In late summer there is a postbreeding northward dispersal of Little Blue Herons that brings a few into the state. Most are immature birds dressed in white, a plumage they wear for at least a year before they molt into the blue and purple tones of adult birds.

Bigeye Chub
(Hybopsis amblops)

Adult
(sexes similar)   **Immature**

GREEN-BACKED HERON
Butorides striatus

BLACK-CROWNED NIGHT-HERON
Nycticorax nycticorax

The paths of the diurnal Green-backed Heron and the nocturnal Black-crowned Night-Heron frequently cross at the water's edge as they look for food when one's day is ending and the other's is about to begin.

Black-crowned Night-Heron
(sexes similar)

Green-backed Heron
(sexes similar)

TUNDRA SWAN
Cygnus columbianus

En route to and from their nesting grounds in the Arctic and their coastal winter resort on the Atlantic Coast around Chesapeake Bay, many Tundra Swans follow migration corridors that cross the state. Each winter, however, a few sometimes stay until all the available open water is covered by ice.

Adult
(sexes similar)

CANADA GOOSE
Branta canadensis

Through the efforts of conservationists a fairly strong breeding population of Canada Geese has been restored to the state. Nowadays, in early spring—on lakes, farm ponds, and just about anywhere there is water—it is not uncommon to see adult Canada Geese accompanied by their newly hatched brood.

Adult

(sexes similar)

Young

WOOD DUCK
Aix sponsa

In early spring even before the leaves appear, pairs of Wood Ducks can frequently be seen high up in the trees along our streams and lakes, investigating every old Pileated Woodpecker hole, natural cavity, or man-made box for a place to nest. After the selection has been made and the hen has laid her clutch of six to fourteen creamy white eggs and begun to incubate them, the male no longer visits the site. But the incubating female usually joins him whenever she leaves the nest to feed.

Adults

(male)

(female)

CANVASBACK

Aythya valisineria (Wilson)

In the early 1900s, the shallow bays along western Lake Erie supported abundant vegetation. Cattails formed dense patches over the exposed bars while deeper water supported extensive mats of pondweeds, eelgrass, and other aquatic vegetation. These bays provided abundant food for waterfowl and served as a major staging area during migration. The most notable migrant was the Canvasback, forming large rafts over the eelgrass beds. A sizable proportion of the Atlantic Coast wintering population of Canvasbacks passed through these marshes.

Conditions within these bays changed dramatically during the twentieth century. Most aquatic and emergent vegetation disappeared as a result of rising lake levels and increased suspended sediments in the water. As the food supply was reduced, waterfowl declined. Puddle ducks still abound in diked marshes along western Lake Erie, but these marshes are less suitable for diving ducks. They moved their staging grounds to Lake St. Clair and other locations where aquatic vegetation can be obtained.

Along western Lake Erie, large numbers of migrant Canvasbacks were observed into the 1930s, including concentrations of 11,000 on March 24, 1939; 7800 on March 21, 1937; and 5000 on November 7, 1936, and November 24, 1935.[33,89] Their decline became evident in the 1940s and continued into the 1980s. Deteriorating habitat quality on their breeding and wintering grounds contributed to this decline, which reduced Canvasbacks to a fraction of their former abundance.

Canvasbacks are early spring migrants, regularly appearing during late February. Migrant flocks may be regularly observed throughout March. Largest numbers appear during cold springs when open water is limited; warm March temperatures allow Canvasbacks to pass rapidly through the state.

Spring migrants are most numerous along western Lake Erie, where they are common to abundant. Peak concentrations of 400–700 are reported most years and flocks of 1000–2000+ are infrequently encountered. Elsewhere along the lakefront, Canvasbacks are fairly common to locally abundant migrants. When the lake is mostly ice covered, flocks of 200–600+ may appear at hot-water outlets from Huron eastward. Concentrations seldom exceed 50–200 once the ice disappears.

Away from Lake Erie, spring Canvasbacks are mostly reported from the northern half of Ohio, where they are uncommon to fairly common migrants and daily totals seldom exceed 50–150. While flocks of 300–600 occasionally form on northern and central lakes, large concentrations of 500–1000 are regularly noted only in southwestern Wayne County. Migrant Canvasbacks are uncommon in the southern half of Ohio, mostly reported in flocks of 10–50.

Most spring Canvasbacks depart during the first half of April. Stragglers may remain along western Lake Erie into early May, usually leaving these marshes by May 7–15.

Summering Canvasbacks are casually encountered along western Lake Erie but are accidental elsewhere. The few records are mostly during June and may represent very late migrants. Single birds have summered at Toledo and Cleveland and remained at Columbus through July 1, 1982.[89,117] There are no confirmed nesting records.

As fall migrants, Canvasbacks have been scarce throughout Ohio since the mid-1970s. They are presently uncommon to fairly common in the northern and central counties, even along western Lake Erie. They become rare to uncommon in southern Ohio. Daily totals are now generally fewer than 20 with occasional flocks in excess of 50. These migrants may return during the last half of October but most are encountered during November.

Along Lake Erie, Canvasbacks do not become fairly common to abundant visitors until mid-December. Severe weather during December has caused large numbers to appear in the Toledo area, including 10,206 on the 1976 Christmas Bird Count. Most years these concentrations do not develop until January or early February. Wintering Canvasbacks are most numerous at the mouth of Maumee Bay, where 1500–3000 regularly appear and as many as 8500 and 7500 during the winters of 1976–77 and 1984–85, respectively.[265,377] Smaller flocks are noted elsewhere along the lakefront wherever open water is available, usually 50–250 Canvasbacks with occasional concentrations of 500–1000+. These wintering Canvasbacks are almost exclusively adult males. In the interior counties, most Canvasbacks depart by December 10, although a few may remain as long as open water is available. They are accidental to casual winter visitors and do not regularly overwinter at any location. Most inland wintering reports come during mild seasons, invariably scattered individuals or flocks of fewer than 10.

REDHEAD

Aythya americana (Eyton)

Large flocks of Redheads once used Maumee and Sandusky Bays along western Lake Erie as migration staging areas, especially during spring. But most flocks shifted to other locations with the disappearance of aquatic vegetation from these bays. Redhead numbers also fluctuated in response to changing habitat conditions on their breeding and wintering grounds. Droughts during the 1930s and 1950s caused their numbers to plummet, but they recovered with the return of favorable water conditions. Populations have slowly declined since 1970 with the drainage of prairie wetlands and a series of dry years.

Redheads are among the first waterfowl initiating spring migration. The first thaw after February 18–25 usually prompts their return. Large flocks are normally present by the first week of March. They remain plentiful throughout the month and occasionally into early April. The last Redheads mostly depart by April 15–20 with stragglers into early May.

The largest concentrations develop during unusually cold seasons. In warm years, Redheads pass rapidly through Ohio and large flocks are only infrequently noted. These migrants are most numerous along western Lake Erie, where they are common to abundant during March. Daily totals of 100–500 Redheads are possible, with peak concentrations of 1000–2000. The largest flock totaled 7575 Redheads near Toledo on March

6, 1961.[90] Elsewhere, they are generally fairly common to common spring visitors to lakes and large marshes. Along central Lake Erie, flocks of 500–1000 may develop while the lake is frozen. Once the lake thaws, Redheads are mostly encountered in flocks of 200 or fewer. Inland reservoirs may host flocks of 50–600, and occasional concentrations of 800–1200 have appeared in the glaciated counties. These large flocks occurred in southwestern Ohio only after large reservoirs were constructed in the 1940s.[248,299]

Fall Redheads are considerably less numerous than spring migrants. They are uncommon to fairly common along Lake Erie and large inland lakes. In recent years, fall flocks mostly totaled fewer than 50 with occasional concentrations of 100–300. Late August Redheads may represent summering individuals, since the first fall migrants do not normally return until October 5–15. This migration normally peaks between October 20 and November 20. At inland reservoirs, numbers of migrants are considerably reduced by early December. December migrants are more frequently encountered along Lake Erie, although flocks seldom exceed 100 unless the lake becomes partially frozen.

Wintering Redheads are primarily restricted to Lake Erie, where they are uncommon to common residents, most numerous within the Central Basin. Their numbers are most plentiful when open water is restricted to hot-water outlets. Under these conditions, flocks of 200–800 Redheads may develop during January and February. When the lake does not freeze, only small flocks are scattered along the entire lakefront.

At inland localities, Redheads may linger until the reservoirs freeze over in early January. However, overwintering ducks are regularly observed only at Castalia (Erie County), where the flock does not exceed 10–12 individuals. Elsewhere, small numbers are casually encountered along the Scioto and Great Miami Rivers, but Redheads remain on large lakes only during mild seasons.

Nesting Redheads have recently expanded into the Great Lakes region.[104] This range expansion was responsible for Ohio summering records after the late 1930s. Breeding was not confirmed until 1961, when four nests were discovered at Magee Marsh Wildlife Area. As many as 11 pairs nested in this marsh through 1967.[89]

Redheads are now rare but regular summer residents in the western Lake Erie marshes. The size of this population probably does not exceed 6–15 pairs. Very little information is available on their nesting chronology. Most broods have been observed during late June and July. These nesting ducks prefer the extensive and deeper marshes where open water is interspersed with emergent vegetation.

Away from western Lake Erie, Redheads are accidental summer visitors. There are two inland breeding records: a pair that raised a brood in Seneca County during 1984 and several pairs that summered at Big Island Wildlife Area (Marion County) between 1983 and 1986 with breeding confirmed during the last year.[434] Nonbreeding summer visitors are mostly reported from the northern half of the state, including summering pairs at Pymatuning Lake during the late 1930s.[501] The only summer record from southern Ohio was one in Hamilton County on July 15, 1973.[252]

RING-NECKED DUCK

Aythya collaris (Donovan)

Unlike most diving ducks, Ring-neckeds prefer inland bodies of water. Spring migrants are considerably more numerous on reservoirs, ponds, and marshes than on Lake Erie. At the height of their spring movements, Ring-neckeds are fairly common to abundant through most inland counties, becoming locally uncommon in southern and unglaciated Ohio. Inland flocks of 50–500 are not unusual, and concentrations of 1000–1200+ are periodically reported from central and northern lakes. They are also common in the western Lake Erie marshes, where the largest flocks seldom exceed 250–400. On Lake Erie they are uncommon, normally observed in flocks of 50 or fewer.

The first migrants normally return in late February and early March. Large flocks usually appear by March 6–15. Ring-neckeds remain numerous until mid-April, while small flocks frequently linger through the end of the month. The last migrants generally depart by May 5–10.

A few nonbreeding Ring-neckeds have lingered at scattered localities, normally disappearing by June 15–25. Most summer records are of isolated individuals. Pairs were reported in the western Lake Erie marshes on June 27, 1934; at Pymatuning Lake in 1938; and in Portage County during June 1986.[89,383,501] Only the Portage County pair exhibited breeding behavior, although no nest was located. There are no confirmed nesting records from Ohio.

The preference for inland localities is more pronounced in autumn when Ring-neckeds are mostly observed on large reservoirs. Fall migrants are generally fairly common to abundant on inland lakes, mostly in flocks of 50–300. As many as 1000–1750 have been noted on several central and northeastern lakes. Ring-necked Ducks are uncommon fall migrants within the western Lake Erie marshes and along the entire lakefront, where flocks in excess of 50 are noteworthy.

A few fall Ring-neckeds return by the last week of September but the first migrants do not normally appear until October 1–10. The largest movements are mostly noted between October 15 and November 15, usually associated with cold fronts or a nearly full moon.[484] Small flocks remain through December 10–15 with a few scattered individuals lingering until freeze-up.

As winter residents, Ring-neckeds are rare and very locally distributed in the northern counties. Fewer than 15 annually overwinter at Castalia and individuals may appear at hot-water outlets along Lake Erie. They are accidental to casual visitors elsewhere. They may appear on large lakes during mild seasons; the largest flocks have totaled 10–15.

TUFTED DUCK

Aythya fuligula (Linnaeus)

A few Tufted Ducks have been detected in recent years among large flocks of scaup migrating and wintering along the Great Lakes and the Atlantic Coast. Since Tufted Ducks normally breed in Europe and northern Asia, it is generally assumed that these vagrants reach Alaska from Siberia and join the scaup in their transcontinental migrations. Sightings not fitting this pattern of vagrancy are usually dismissed as escapees, for Tufted Ducks are commonly kept in captivity.

Within Ohio, there is only one record generally accepted as a wild Tufted Duck: an adult male discovered by Tom LePage in the harbor at Lorain on March 3, 1980.[277] This duck, associated with a flock of 1000–2000 Greater Scaup, was seen intermittently through March 14.

GREATER SCAUP

Aythya marila (Linnaeus)

Identification of Greater Scaup posed an insurmountable challenge to most early ornithologists, who did not attempt to distinguish between the two scaup. These identification problems resulted in conflicting statements concerning their status. Trautman[477] cited only one specimen and "a few" reliable sight records of Greater Scaup; he considered them rare migrants that mostly passed north of Ohio. In contrast, Williams[523] described Greaters as uncommon winter visitors at Cleveland, citing flocks as large as 300–400. As the ability to correctly identify Greater Scaup improved, their distribution and relative abundance along Lake Erie became well established. They proved to be fairly numerous winter residents and may outnumber Lessers some years.

Greater Scaup are most numerous within central Lake Erie from Lorain eastward. While the first migrants may appear during the last week of October, they remain relatively scarce until mid-November. They are generally fairly common to common winter residents after mid-December, although large flocks may not appear until January. They are least numerous during warmer winters when daily totals seldom exceed 100–200. When the lake is mostly ice covered, flocks of 2000–3000+ Greaters have been reported from the Lorain–Avon Lake lakefront. Their spring migration is most pronounced when Lake Erie remains ice covered into March. Under these conditions, flocks of 1000–2500+ have appeared along the Cleveland-Lorain lakefront between March 5 and 20. When the lake is open, spring concentrations seldom exceed 50. Numbers noticeably decline by the last week of March. Only a few Greaters are encountered during April, although late migrants have been reported at Cleveland through mid-May.[117]

Greater Scaup are less numerous along western Lake Erie, where they are uncommon to rare migrants and winter residents. Most observations are of 15 or fewer individuals. The largest concentrations from Ottawa and Lucas Counties totaled 40–80.[89] Timing of their spring and fall movements coincides with their passage elsewhere along Lake Erie.

Greater Scaup are casual to rare migrants and winter visitors on large lakes throughout the state. Inland records invariably total 1–6 individuals. Fall migrants may appear by November 5 but most are noted between November 15 and January 15. They normally depart when the lakes become frozen. While there are scattered inland winter records, Greater Scaup do not regularly overwinter at any inland location. Spring migrants mostly appear before March 20 but depart by early April. There are very few reliable records after April 15, although one remained at Big Island Wildlife Area (Marion County) through May 18, 1985.

LESSER SCAUP

Aythya affinis (Eyton)

Lesser Scaup are among the most widely distributed of Ohio's diving ducks. Especially in spring, flocks of Lesser Scaup are fairly common to abundant visitors to small farm ponds, borrow pits, large reservoirs, and bays along Lake Erie.

Spring migrants are most numerous along western Lake Erie. Maumee Bay hosted flocks of 8000–10,000 annually during the 1920s and 1930s and a maximum of 20,000 on April 8, 1934.[86] As the aquatic vegetation disappeared, these flocks congregated elsewhere, but flocks of 300–2000+ are still encountered along western Lake Erie each spring. Lesser Scaup are also abundant spring migrants through central Lake Erie, most numerous during cold seasons when open water is limited; as many as 4000 have congregated along the Cleveland-Lorain lakefront. Warm spring weather allows these scaup to disperse along the entire lakefront, mostly in flocks of 200 or fewer.

Within the interior counties, spring Lesser Scaup are most numerous in northern and central Ohio, where flocks of 300–1000 are not unusual and 2000–2500 have concentrated at several locations. In the southern and unglaciated counties, flocks mostly total 100–500 with occasional reports of 750–1000.

Lesser Scaup begin returning in late February or early March. Large flocks appear by the second week of March and remain through mid-April. Small flocks are regularly observed through the first week of May. Most depart by May 12–18 except along western Lake Erie, where they may remain into early June. These late migrants normally are individuals, although a flock of 100 remained at Toledo as late as June 9.[89]

In the early 1900s, summering Lesser Scaup were regularly reported from inland lakes, sometimes "considerable numbers of both sexes."[236] Most were nonbreeders or cripples from spring hunting seasons. A few breeding records were established, including a Franklin County brood in 1919 and reports from Lorain, Summit, and Stark Counties.[220,236,250] Small numbers were also encountered along western Lake Erie, including an Erie County brood in 1907 and one near Toledo in 1918.[89,198]

Summering Lesser Scaup have declined on inland lakes with relatively few records since the 1920s. They are now accidental or casual summer visitors on large lakes and marshes. While Clark and Sipe[98] reported nest construction at Lake St. Mary's, no eggs were produced. The only recent inland nesting record was provided by a female with 10 young at Stony Lake in Carroll County during 1954.[72] Their status along western Lake Erie was uncertain. While Hicks[220] claimed a breeding population "was rather definitely established in Lucas, Ottawa, and Sandusky Counties," Campbell[86,89] thought these scaup were mostly nonbreeders and cited only one nesting record in 1937. This discrepancy was never resolved. In any event, numbers of summering scaup in the western Lake Erie marshes declined after 1940. They are presently casual nonbreeding summer visitors; there are no confirmed nesting records since 1937.

The few breeding reports provide little insight into their nesting ecology in Ohio. They apparently prefer large lakes and marshes with open water interspersed among emergent vegetation. The few broods were observed during June.

Fall migrants return to Lake Erie during the first week of October. Within the Western Basin, they become numerous by mid-October and remain common until early December. Most fall concentrations total 500 or fewer with occasional flocks of 1000–2000. In the Central Basin, they may not become abundant until mid-November or later when large flocks accumulate along the Cleveland-Lorain lakefront. These flocks continue to increase during early winter and may approach 500–2000+.

Within the interior counties, fall Lesser Scaup are mostly restricted to large lakes. The first return by October 5–12. As Trautman noted,[484] their peak movements are usually associated with clear nights and favorable winds immediately before a full moon. These flights may occur between mid-October and mid-November. Most scaup pass through the state in only two to five days. These flights produce flocks of 100–1000 on most reservoirs; as many as 2400 have been reported on one lake. Many more fly over Ohio than land on its lakes; Trautman[484] witnessed flights of 10,000+ Lesser Scaup over Buckeye Lake. Numbers of migrants noticeably decline by late November, although small flocks may remain until freeze-up.

Wintering Lesser Scaup are fairly common to abundant residents along Lake Erie. They are most numerous during cold winters when open water is restricted to hot-water outlets and flocks of 1000–5000 may develop along the Cleveland-Lorain lakefront. Milder winters allow these scaup to spread along the entire lakefront, normally in flocks of 100–200 or fewer. Still, concentrations of 1000–1500+ may be noted along the Western Basin during these warmer seasons.[89,90] Inland Lesser Scaup become accidental to locally rare residents after January 10–15. They are infrequently reported at open water throughout the state, usually scattered individuals or flocks of 15 or fewer.

COMMON EIDER

Somateria mollissima (Linnaeus)

Identification of female and immature eiders is difficult even for serious ornithologists. Because all eiders recorded from Ohio have been in these plumages, uncertainty over whether they were Common or King Eiders has obscured the status of both species. Unless specimens were collected, identification of sight records has always been viewed with considerable suspicion.

In recent years, better optical equipment and more detailed identification information have permitted the accurate identification of most eiders under good viewing conditions. If recent records accurately represent their status, then Common Eiders are accidental fall or early winter visitors to Ohio. There are no extant specimens. The only confirmed record is of one eider discovered by Jim Hoffman at the former White City Beach in Cleveland on October 9, 1978.[271] This bird was viewed by many other observers and diagnostic photographs were taken by Richard Hoffman.

There are a number of questionable unconfirmed records. A possible Common Eider was shot at Buckeye Lake on November 11, 1895; the specimen disappeared before its identity was confirmed.[479] Since 1947, there have been at least ten reports from the Cleveland-Lorain lakefront and two from Toledo, none of them accompanied by written descriptions or photographs conclusively establishing their identity. It is conceivable that most, if not all, of these records pertain to King Eiders.

KING EIDER

Somateria spectabilis (Linnaeus)

Since the late 1940s, King Eiders have been casual fall migrants along Lake Erie, most frequently recorded east from Huron. There are a few records during the first half of November, although the majority of eiders appear between November 15 and December 25. These sightings mostly are of 1–3 Kings with infrequent small flocks of 5–7, invariably females or first-winter males.

While most King Eiders eventually depart for the Atlantic Coast, they are accidental winter visitors to central Lake Erie with records from the Cleveland-Lorain lakefront during 1948–49, 1959–60, and 1981–82.[308,335,364] These winter sightings are of 1–3 eiders remaining into late January, although one survived until March 27, 1960, at Cleveland.

These eiders are also accidental spring visitors to Lake Erie. The four records probably pertain to individuals that wintered on the Great Lakes. These records are from Erie County eastward of single eiders observed between March 20 and April 20.

King Eiders have been observed more frequently in recent years, reflecting better coverage by birdwatchers along Lake Erie. Before the late 1940s, they were unknown except for a few anecdotal accounts. Between 1947 and 1979, these eiders averaged two to five sightings each decade. Since 1980, there have been one to four sightings annually but none in 1986.

King Eiders are accidental fall visitors away from Lake Erie. There are three records from central Ohio: 3 eiders at Buckeye Lake (Fairfield County) on December 2, 1926;[479] a Franklin County specimen collected November 26, 1960;[488] and an unspecified report on November 11, 1895.[45] The only other acceptable inland record is an eider shot along the Ohio River near Cincinnati on January 2, 1971.[471]

HARLEQUIN DUCK

Histrionicus histrionicus (Linnaeus)

In eastern North America, wintering Harlequin Ducks are normally found along rocky seacosts with a few regularly appearing on the Great Lakes. Since inland Harlequins seldom wander from the Great Lakes, Ohio's first sighting was unexpectedly from the Dayton area. An unmistakable adult male was discovered on the Great Miami River near West Carrollton (Montgomery County) on February 13, 1949. He was observed for more than an hour foraging within the river's swift currents.[299] There are only two other records from the interior of Ohio, both from the Springfield-Dayton area during winter: a female Harlequin frequenting Buck Creek in Springfield between December 27, 1980, and January 2, 1981, and an immature male below the dam at Eastwood Lake (Montgomery County) on December 18, 1983.[299] Along Lake Erie, the first record was a specimen collected in Ottawa County on November 2, 1951.[89] The first Cleveland sighting was in 1955.[335] Harlequins averaged one lakefront record every two or three years into the 1970s but were recorded annually after 1977.

Harlequin Ducks are now rare fall migrants along Lake Erie with one to three reports annually. Most sightings are from the Central Basin with relatively few detected in Ottawa and Lucas Counties. These fall records are distributed between October 29 and the first week of January but most occur between November 10 and December 15. They are apparently casual to accidental winter residents, most likely to appear during severe winters. These winter sightings are mostly from the Cleveland-Lorain area with at least seven records since 1954. Harlequin Ducks are accidental to casual spring migrants with an average of one record every two to three years. The few spring sightings are scattered between early March and mid-April. The only summer record was provided by a male originally discovered at Lorain on January 8, 1968. After wintering in the harbor, he never migrated and was last reported August 26, 1968.[117] All lakefront observations are of 1–3 Harlequins.

OLDSQUAW

Clangula hyemalis (Linnaeus)

Oldsquaw have always been irregular migrants and winter visitors to Ohio. They can be nearly absent some years but occur at widely scattered localities in other years, while sizable flights appear at rare intervals. Numbers of these handsome ducks have markedly declined since the early 1900s, perhaps reflecting a shift in their winter distribution or reduced populations throughout the Great Lakes.

In the early 1900s, Jones[236] thought their irregular appearance was governed by weather conditions, noting that Oldsquaw occasionally became "decidedly numerous anywhere along the lakefront and may venture well inland to the Ohio River." These movements were frequently followed by several years without any records. The only indication of the size of these movements is provided by Trautman's report[479] of "several hundred" Oldsquaw at Buckeye Lake during the spring of 1912. Within the past sixty years, only Ashtabula regularly hosted small flocks of Oldsquaw along Lake Erie. December flocks of 15–40+ were reported between the 1930s and 1950 but have not appeared in subsequent years.

Oldsquaw are now rare to locally uncommon fall migrants along Lake Erie, more numerous within the Central Basin. During most years, there are three to six sightings scattered along the lakefront, although small flights may produce ten or more reports. They become casual fall visitors to large lakes within the interior of Ohio, where the fewest records are from the southern and unglaciated counties. While they are not annually detected on any lake, there are usually up to three inland sightings each autumn. All recent fall records are invariably of 1–8 Oldsquaw.

The earliest fall Oldsquaw returned to Dayton on October 10, 1968, and Cleveland on October 12, 1941.[299,523] There are few other records before October 28–30. Most are observed between November 10 and December 7. This southward movement continues through January 5–15, but it is difficult to distinguish late migrants from winter visitors.

Wintering Oldsquaw are mostly restricted to Lake Erie, where they are casually recorded within the Western Basin and rare elsewhere. The number of winter lakefront records is variable with two to five reports most years and infrequent small flights producing ten or more sightings. Since the early 1950s, these winter records have mostly been of 8 or fewer Oldsquaw.

Away from Lake Erie, Oldsquaw are accidental to casual winter visitors. They may visit large lakes if open water is available but also frequent large rivers. These ducks usually remain for only a few days, although several have spent the entire winter.[248] Inland Oldsquaw are as likely to appear in the southern counties as in northern Ohio, with most reports of 3 or fewer. The largest winter flocks included 14 near Dayton on January 13, 1946;[299] 12 on the Maumee River near Toledo between February 10 and March 11, 1934;[86] and 9 specimens collected near Waverly (Pike County) between February 7 and 18, 1899.[193]

Spring Oldsquaw begin to move north during March but are mostly observed between March 25 and April 20. All flights have been detected during April. Stragglers remained through May 7 at Cincinnati and May 12–20 within the northern and central counties.

Spring Oldsquaw are normally accidental to casual migrants, as likely to appear on inland reservoirs as Lake Erie. During most years, there are one to five records of 6 or fewer Oldsquaw scattered across the state. Once or twice each decade, Oldsquaw stage a noticeable "flight." These movements may take the form of many individuals widely scattered across Ohio. In 1984, there were at least twenty-two sightings with fourteen records along Lake Erie and eight at inland lakes, mostly 1–5 individuals; the largest flock totaled 12. Other flights produce one or two large flocks but few records elsewhere. The 1986 flight was responsible for April 13 flocks of 24 in Summit and Portage Counties and 14 at Killdeer Plains Wildlife Area.[382] The largest spring flock in recent decades appeared at La Due Reservoir (Geauga County) on April 15, 1972, where 53 Oldsquaw presented an impressive sight.[471]

BLACK SCOTER

Melanitta nigra (Linnaeus)

The status and distribution of Black Scoters have dramatically changed within the present century. Before 1940, they were accidental visitors. The number of sightings increased during the 1940s, especially along Lake Erie. However, Black Scoters did not become annual visitors until the 1950s, usually as groups of 3 or fewer, although a "small flight" developed in Ottawa and Lucas Counties during 1952.[89] Most sightings were along Lake Erie; these scoters remained accidental visitors to inland lakes. This status was maintained through the 1970s.

Beginning in the early 1980s, numbers of Black Scoters noticeably increased. Along Lake Erie, small flocks appeared most autumns and an exceptional movement occurred during 1985. Small numbers were regularly detected on inland lakes. Two factors contributed to these increased sightings: greater numbers of birdwatchers along Lake Erie and at inland lakes discovered migrants that previously passed through the state undetected, and there may have been a shift in the scoters' migration corridor.

Black Scoters are now rare fall migrants along western Lake Erie in Ottawa and Lucas Counties but become uncommon visitors to the Central Basin. Most lakefront reports are of 1–6 individuals with occasional flocks of 10–20. Larger flights are occasionally encountered, including 60 Blacks flying past Vermilion (Erie County) on November 12, 1983.[372] The largest movement was noted during November 1985 when a remarkable 600 Blacks congregated in the Huron-Vermilion area on November 11 and flocks of 41–85 briefly appeared at other localities within the Central Basin.[380]

On inland reservoirs, Black Scoters are casual to rare fall migrants through the northern and glaciated central counties, producing one to five records annually. They are accidental fall migrants elsewhere. Sightings usually are of 5 or fewer individuals. The largest inland flock was composed of 15 on Bass Lake near Dayton on November 28, 1967.[299]

Fall Black Scoters have returned to Lake Erie by October 5 but do not normally appear until October 15–20. They are mostly observed between October 25 and November 15. At inland lakes, Black Scoters are generally detected between October 20 and November 20.

Winter Black Scoters are restricted to Lake Erie, where they are casually encountered through January 5–15. These scoters normally disappear when the lake freezes over and may represent very late fall migrants. A few individuals have attempted to overwinter along the Cleveland-Lorain lakefront, remaining into February.[335] All reliable winter records are of 3 or fewer Blacks, usually at hot-water outlets.

Considerably fewer Black Scoters pass through Ohio as spring migrants. They infrequently appear between February 25 and March 20 in association with large flocks of diving ducks. They are more likely to be detected during April and have remained as late as May 4, 1983, at Cleveland.[370] These migrants are accidental to casual visitors, as likely to appear on inland lakes as Lake Erie. There are sightings from all portions of the state except the unglaciated counties, invariably of 4 or fewer individuals. Spring Black Scoters are generally recorded during two to four years each decade.

SURF SCOTER

Melanitta perspicillata (Linnaeus)

Surf Scoters have undergone changes in status and distribution similar to those of Black Scoters during this century. They were accidental or casual visitors to Ohio before 1940 and were not annually reported until the 1950s. Small numbers were recorded each year through the 1970s, and the number of sightings has increased since 1980 but not as markedly as for Black Scoters.

Surf Scoters are casual to rare fall migrants along western Lake Erie and rare to uncommon through the Central Basin. Most sightings are of 1–6 with occasional flocks of 10–20 individuals. No large movements have been reliably reported. Away from Lake Erie, Surf Scoters are casual fall visitors to large lakes in the northern and glaciated central counties and accidental elsewhere. While they do not annually appear on any lake, these scoters are usually detected at one to four inland locations each autumn. These inland sightings are of groups of 6 or fewer scoters, frequently associated with mixed flocks of diving ducks.

The earliest fall migrant returned to Toledo on September 30, 1938.[89] Surf Scoters normally appear along the lakefront between October 7 and 17 and are mostly encountered between October 20 and November 15. They usually depart by November 25–December 5. On inland lakes, the earliest Surfs appear by October 5–12. The majority are detected between October 15 and November 15, while a few stragglers linger through December 7.

Their winter status has been obscured by difficulties in distinguishing Surfs from White-winged Scoters. Surf Scoters may remain along Lake Erie until freeze-up in early January. They become accidental visitors later in winter with only a few confirmed records along the lakefront at Cleveland-Lorain and Toledo. These acceptable records invariably are of single scoters, some remaining for only a few days while several were observed throughout the winter. There are presently no acceptable midwinter sightings away from Lake Erie.

Surf Scoters are accidental to casual spring visitors throughout the state, least numerous within the southern and unglaciated counties. These migrants are as likely to appear on inland lakes as on Lake Erie. Spring Surfs average three to six sightings each decade. These reports invariably are of 1–4 scoters. The earliest spring migrants appear during the last week of February and early March, but most are noted in April. The later migrants are frequently groups of 2–4 scoters, remaining for one day before continuing their journey. A few late Surf Scoters were detected in early May and 2 lingered through May 19, 1986, at Lake Rockwell (Portage County).[382] There are no confirmed summer records from the state.

WHITE-WINGED SCOTER

Melanitta fusca (Linnaeus)

At one time, White-wingeds were regarded as the most numerous scoters within Ohio. That is not necessarily true today. They are certainly our most numerous wintering scoters, but they may be outnumbered by other scoters during autumn flights. Their status and distribution have changed little in recent decades, with only a gradual decline since 1975.

As fall migrants, White-wingeds are rare to locally uncommon along Lake Erie, more frequently encountered within the Central Basin. They can be rather scarce some years and relatively numerous in others. Most fall reports are of 1–8 with infrequent flocks of 12–20 individuals. The only reliably reported fall flight totaled 55 at Cleveland on November 8, 1979.

White-winged Scoters are casual to locally rare fall visitors to large inland lakes across the state. Most records are from the northern and glaciated central counties, producing one to five reports most years. These records usually are of 6 or fewer with occasional flocks of 8–12 individuals. The largest reported inland flock was composed of 21 at Buckeye Lake.[479] Trautman[479] noted that they usually appeared after calm, clear, frosty nights.

While White-winged Scoters have returned to Cleveland by August 25, 1985, and September 2, 1944,[380,523] there are no other sightings before October 1. The first fall migrants do not normally appear until October 5–15 along Lake Erie and October 15–25 at inland lakes. There are generally two poorly defined peaks to their fall passage: between October 20 and November 10, when White-wingeds are most likely to visit inland lakes and small flocks appear along Lake Erie, and between November 25 and December 15, when greater numbers appear along Lake Erie but only scattered individuals inland. White-winged Scoters continue to pass through the state until December 25–January 10.

Small numbers of White-winged Scoters regularly spend the winter along Lake Erie. When the lake remains open, wintering scoters are scattered along the entire lakefront. Extended cold weather forces them to concentrate at hot-water outlets. White-wingeds are casual winter residents along the Western Basin but are rare to locally uncommon along central Lake Erie. Most winter reports are of 1–6 with occasional flocks of 8–12 individuals. The largest flock totaled 25 at Cleveland on February 5, 1949.[308]

Few White-wingeds overwinter away from the lakefront. They are accidental midwinter visitors to interior counties and have been recorded on several large rivers and Summit Lake in Akron. While small numbers regularly winter along the Ohio River, these scoters seldom venture into Ohio's limited portion of the river. Most midwinter records are of 1–2 appearing for only a few days. The only inland winter flock totaled 8 White-wingeds at Columbus on January 31, 1959.[322]

White-winged Scoters are casual to rare spring migrants along Lake Erie, most numerous within the Central Basin during March but with sightings distributed along the entire lakefront later in the season. The number of lakefront records exhibits marked annual variability, with only one or two sightings some springs and six to ten reports in others. Most reports are of 8 or fewer individuals. The only sizable flight totaled 36–50 White-wingeds in western Lake Erie on April 27–28, 1962.[89]

Inland White-winged Scoters are accidental to casual spring visitors to large lakes, producing one to three records most years in the northern and glaciated central counties. These records mostly are of 3 or fewer White-wingeds. Small flocks of 6–13 appear infrequently during April.

Their spring migration is fairly protracted. Small numbers may appear during the last half of February, but the majority of spring records are during March. However, White-wingeds also irregularly appear during April, mostly noted between April 10 and 30 and occasionally remaining into early May. A few stragglers have been noted through May 31, 1984, at Cleveland and June 4, 1940, off South Bass Island in western Lake Erie.[89,374]

COMMON GOLDENEYE

Bucephala clangula (Linnaeus)

Its tolerance for cold weather allows the Common Goldeneye to be one of our latest returning fall waterfowl. Along Lake Erie, unusually early migrants have appeared during September or early October but they are not normally noted until October 25–November 5. Their numbers gradually increase, although concentrations seldom exceed 20–100 during November. They do not become common until December. Relatively cold weather may produce large flocks by December 5–10, while warm temperatures may delay the arrival of sizable concentrations until January.

Away from Lake Erie, the first fall Common Goldeneyes appeared at Mogadore Reservoir (Portage County) on October 2, 1985, and Lake St. Mary's on October 10, 1945.[98,380] They do not normally return until the first half of November. They are generally most numerous in the northeastern counties, becoming fairly common to locally abundant between November 20 and December 20. Flocks of 50–200 are not unusual and larger concentrations, such as 1500 at Mosquito Creek Reservoir (Trumbull County) on December 1, 1984, have been infrequently encountered. Considerably fewer pass through the other counties, where they are uncommon to fairly common migrants and fall flocks seldom exceed 10–75. This inland migration continues until freeze-up.

Wintering Common Goldeneyes are common to abundant residents along Lake Erie. During mild winters, large concentrations do not normally develop and daily totals are 25–300 individuals. Harsh winter weather forces them to congregate at hot-water outlets, where 1000–2500+ are not unusual along the Cleveland-Lorain lakefront. The Western Basin normally supports smaller winter flocks, seldom exceeding 100–800 except at freeze-up when larger numbers congregate, such as 2325 near Toledo on December 22, 1940.[89]

These wintering numbers have substantially increased since 1900. At that time, Jones[236] thought Common Goldeneyes did not winter along Lake Erie. As late as the 1940s, only small flocks regularly wintered at Cleveland.[523] Improved wintering numbers since the 1950s probably result from the increased availability of gizzard shad and other small fish that form the bulk of the Common Goldeneye's diet.

Many Common Goldeneyes establish their pair bonds during the winter. Their courtship displays are a common sight in January and February, even in the harshest weather. It is not unusual to observe several males displaying before a single female, throwing their heads back, beating their wings, and producing a double-noted *beep* reminiscent of the call of a nighthawk.

Wintering Common Goldeneyes are rare to locally fairly common residents inland. Small numbers regularly winter throughout Ohio, usually 1–20 goldeneyes with occasional flocks of 30–60. The largest inland wintering concentrations totaled 100–300 in the Columbus area.

Their spring migration commences by February 15–25 regardless of weather conditions, producing flocks of 25–100+ on inland lakes and 100–1000+ along Lake Erie. Larger concentrations are infrequently observed: 350 near Cincinnati on February 27, 1937;[248] 1000 at Columbus on February 28, 1974;[471] and 6000 at Lorain on March 10, 1984.[374] These large flocks normally depart by March 15 from inland lakes and March 20–25 from Lake Erie. Smaller numbers are expected through April 1–5 within the interior counties and along Lake Erie until April 15. A few stragglers have remained into May.

Common Goldeneyes are accidental nonbreeding summer visitors. Summer records are limited to single individuals in the Toledo area in 1934 and 1937;[86] near Dayton on July 13, 1959; and at Cleveland on July 28, 1984.[299,375]

BARROW'S GOLDENEYE

Bucephala islandica (Gmelin)

Based on their status elsewhere along Lake Erie, Barrow's Goldeneyes are expected to be casual or accidental winter visitors and early spring migrants along the Ohio lakefront. Recent records conform to these expectations. Since 1980, there have been documented sightings of single Barrow's Goldeneyes at Lorain between January 7 and 10, 1984, and Eastlake on March 8–9, 1986; in Ottawa County on February 11, 1987; and at Lorain on February 20, 1988.[373,382,385,388a] The only sight record during the previous decade was an adult male at Avon Lake (Lorain County) between February 6 and 28, 1972.[283] Although details are unavailable, the bird was viewed by many observers and its identification is almost certainly correct.

Historic accounts include unsubstantiated sightings from the Cleveland-Lorain lakefront, western Lake Erie between Sandusky Bay and Port Clinton, and southern Ohio. Their veracity cannot be adequately assessed. Since female and immature Barrow's Goldeneyes are easily confused with the more numerous Common Goldeneyes, there is a strong possibility some of these birds were misidentified.

BUFFLEHEAD

Bucephala albeola (Linnaeus)

Buffleheads are feisty little ducks quite capable of successfully competing with larger waterfowl. Surprisingly hardy, they winter wherever open water is available, easily withstanding the midwinter rigors on Lake Erie. The handsome males have a distinctive black and white plumage with a small white crest they erect during nuptial displays before the plainer females. Like Common Goldeneyes, they do not let harsh winter weather deter them from their courtship displays.

Bufflehead sightings along Lake Erie during late August and early September probably pertain to nonbreeders.[335,372] The first fall migrants usually return to Lake Erie October 15–25 and to most inland lakes by the first week of November. They are generally fairly common to common migrants on large lakes during November and early December. The largest fall flocks totaled 275 Buffleheads at Toledo on November 24, 1935, and 65–75 on inland reservoirs.[89] Daily totals are usually 35 or fewer. Only wintering birds remain after early January.

Wintering Buffleheads are generally uncommon to fairly common residents along Lake Erie. During open winters, they are spread along the entire lakefront as small flocks of 10 or fewer ducks. Harsh weather forces them to congregate at hot-water outlets, and as many as 100 have been counted.

Buffleheads regularly linger on inland lakes as long as open water is available. During warm winters, they become casual to rare winter residents with 1–6 at widely scattered lakes. During most winters, Buffleheads are generally absent from the interior counties except at Castalia (Erie County) and Summit Lake in Akron, where a few individuals remain throughout the season. Spring Buffleheads are as likely to appear on small ponds and borrow pits as large lakes. They tend to be most numerous in northeastern Ohio, where several exceptionally large flights have been encountered, including 500 at Youngstown on April 19, 1932, and 658 in Summit and Portage Counties on April 13, 1986.[18,382] Spring totals of this fairly common to common migrant usually are 40 or fewer. Concentrations in excess of 100 are noteworthy away from northeastern Ohio. The first spring migrants appear as soon as open water is available. Largest numbers are normally reported between March 15 and April 15. Stragglers are regularly noted during the first half of May, particularly in the northern half of the state. There are very few records after May 20. Buffleheads lingering at Cleveland through June 1, 1941,[523] and Ottawa Wildlife Refuge through July 10, 1988,[388a] furnish the only summer records for Ohio.

HOODED MERGANSER

Lophodytes cucullatus (Linnaeus)

This exceptionally attractive duck is usually found on wooded ponds, swamps, streams, and lakes. On occasion the Hooded, our smallest merganser, joins other diving ducks resting on large lakes, but it is more likely to occur in small segregated flocks, where the brilliantly colored males are outnumbered by the somber females and immatures.

Spring Hooded Mergansers are generally uncommon to fairly common visitors, becoming locally rare on Lake Erie. Most records are of 10 or fewer with infrequent flocks of 15–30. Larger concentrations are exceptional; the maximum is 72 at Buckeye Lake on March 23, 1928.[479] This migration normally begins between February 20 and March 7 and is mostly restricted to March. Fewer migrants are detected through April 15–20 with stragglers lingering into the first week of May.

Small numbers of Hooded Mergansers nested in the northern half of Ohio during the nineteenth century.[98,479] This population was eliminated before 1900. There were very few summer records between 1900 and 1930. Beginning in 1930, individuals appeared on large lakes scattered across the northern and central counties. Hicks[231] cited totals of 2–14 Hooded Mergansers each summer after 1930. Many were nonbreeders, but nesting was documented at Pymatuning Lake, in Franklin County, and along western Lake Erie in Ottawa and Lucas Counties. In the early 1970s, the number of summer records began to increase. Hooded Mergansers became regular residents along western Lake Erie, while scattered individuals were detected elsewhere. Their breeding population slowly expanded during the 1980s.

Hooded Mergansers are now rare to uncommon summer residents in the western Lake Erie marshes, where as many as ten to twelve nests are discovered annually. They are casual to rare residents in northeastern Ohio, with scattered nesting attempts and summer records south to Trumbull and Wayne Counties.[434] Summering Hoodeds are accidental to casual residents within other glaciated counties. During the 1980s, nesting was confirmed at Killdeer Plains Wildlife Area and in Seneca and Butler Counties, while nonbreeders were detected at additional locations.[434] These mergansers are accidental nonbreeding visitors to the unglaciated counties, where there are no confirmed nesting records. This statewide breeding population probably numbers fewer than 40 pairs. Nonbreeding mergansers may appear at any time, but females with broods are mostly observed during May and June. Wandering family groups of 3–6 Hoodeds may appear during August and early September at locations where they did not nest.

Hooded Mergansers nest in cavities but also utilize Wood Duck boxes. In fact, most recent nests have been discovered in boxes and their use of these structures contributed to their expanding breeding population. Their nesting activities begin during April with most clutches hatching by mid-May.[89,231]

Hooded Mergansers attain their maximum abundance as fall migrants. They appear during the last half of October and gradually increase throughout November, peaking between November 10 and 25 when they are uncommon to locally abundant. While most localities support 30 or fewer, flocks of 50–150 visit inland lakes each autumn. Concentrations of 200–350+ Hoodeds have been reported from sheltered bays along Lake Erie in Ottawa and Erie Counties and from several lakes in northeastern and central Ohio. Subfreezing temperatures cause most Hooded Mergansers to depart by December 10–15 with a few stragglers until early January. Mild weather sometimes allows flocks of 20–150+ Hoodeds to remain until mid-January.

Hooded Mergansers are generally rare but regular winter residents at hot-water outlets along Lake Erie, where 1–3 may be observed among the mixed flocks of diving ducks. They are accidental to casual winter visitors elsewhere. A few Hoodeds may winter along the Scioto, Muskingum, and other large rivers. They have also wintered on large lakes, although no more than 2–4 have been reported from any location.

COMMON MERGANSER

Mergus merganser Linnaeus

Unfortunately, this handsome duck has declined in numbers throughout the present century. Clark and Sipe[98] reported a gradual reduction at Lake St. Mary's after 1910. In southwestern Ohio, Common Mergansers were common migrants at Dayton before 1950 and at Cincinnati until the early 1950s.[248,299] Flocks of 200–400 were reported from Dayton between 1943 and 1946 but have not appeared subsequently. In central Ohio, spring flocks of 100–200 were regularly observed and there were 1000 at O'Shaughnessy Reservoir (Delaware County) on March 11, 1940, and 2000 at Buckeye Lake on March 20, 1924.[479,508] Numbers declined during the 1950s and these mergansers have been scarce since 1962.[130] Within the northeastern counties, spring flocks of 200–400 were observed into the early 1950s but have not appeared since 1960.

Along Lake Erie, wintering and migrant Common Mergansers were regularly observed in considerable numbers through 1950. Then their appearance became erratic. For example, 10,000+ Commons wintered at Cleveland in 1951–52 but only 40 in 1954–55.[347]

Common Mergansers are now fairly common to common winter residents along Lake Erie, becoming locally abundant some years. The first may return by October 27–30 but are not expected until November 5–10. Flocks of 100+ Commons do not normally appear until December.

Along western Lake Erie, Common Mergansers are most numerous between December 20 and January 10. Concentrations of 9003 on December 23, 1979, and 5090 on December 26, 1949, are indicative of the large numbers that may congregate, although early winter flocks seldom exceed 200–1000.[89,471] Once the lake freezes over, flocks of 20–200 remain at isolated pockets of open water.

Along central Lake Erie, large flocks frequently appear between January 20 and February 15. The largest recent concentrations were noted during 1976–77 and 1977–78 with maxima of 7000–10,000 along the Cleveland-Lorain lakefront. In other years, winter flocks seldom exceed 200–1500 Commons.

Common Mergansers initiate their northward movements during the last half of February. Their largest lakefront concentrations are expected between February 25 and March 15, producing occasional flocks of 1000–2000 in the Central Basin and 1000+ along western Lake Erie. However, most flocks total 30–250. They usually depart from Lake Erie during the last half of March with small flocks remaining through April 7–15 and occasional stragglers into May.

Considerably fewer Common Mergansers visit inland lakes and large rivers, where their distribution and relative abundance are fairly uniform across the state. They normally return by November 5–15 but are not regularly observed until December, when they become uncommon migrants. Fall flocks are normally composed of 25 or fewer. Most depart by early January when the lakes freeze. As winter residents, inland Common Mergansers are rare to uncommon on large rivers within the southern half of Ohio. They are casual to rare on large lakes wherever open water is available. Winter flocks are composed of 5–20 individuals. Inland Common Mergansers are most numerous as spring migrants, becoming fairly common on large lakes between February 25 and March 15. The largest recent flocks have totaled 50–75 but most reports are of 10–30. These migrants normally depart by April 1–5 in the southern and central counties and April 15 in northern Ohio; a few have been reported into early May.

Common Mergansers are accidental nonbreeding summer visitors along western Lake Erie with reports in 1928, 1939, and 1984.[89,375] All sightings are of single mergansers, several of which apparently summered. The only inland record was provided by a Common Merganser summering at Buckeye Lake in 1925.[479]

RED-BREASTED MERGANSER

Mergus serrator Linnaeus

Fall flocks of Red-breasted Mergansers along Lake Erie can be awe-inspiring. Beginning at sunrise, these flocks fly low over the water, some days to the east and others to the west depending on wind direction. The greatest numbers are seen in early morning and late afternoon. I once witnessed an evening flight stretching across the entire horizon and continuing for more than ten minutes, easily exceeding 100,000 individuals, with additional flocks flying by as the sunlight disappeared from the sky. These flocks are usually composed of 20–500+ individuals but form rafts of 1000–15,000+ when actively feeding on gizzard shad in a frenzy of activity.

Despite careful observations from shore, our understanding of their movements is poor. As Red-breasted Mergansers fly along the lakefront at rates of 5000–20,000+ individuals per hour, many questions arise. Do they move from one Ohio locality to another, or do their movements extend around the entire western end of the lake? Are these movements only daily flights in search of food, or are they part of their seasonal migrations? While these questions cannot be answered, one point is clear. Each fall, Lake Erie hosts a sizable proportion of the North American population of Red-breasted Mergansers.

Fall Red-breasted Mergansers are most numerous between the Lake Erie islands and Cleveland; daily totals of 10,000–50,000+ are regularly observed there during November. They are also numerous east of Cleveland, although totals seldom exceed 1000–5000. West of the islands, they may be scarce some years and abundant in others. They may rival their status in central Lake Erie; an aerial survey estimated 210,000 mergansers within the Western Basin on November 29, 1985.[380]

These immense numbers have not always staged on Lake Erie. In the early 1900s, Jones[240] seldom observed flocks of more than 100–200 at Cedar Point (Erie County). Williams[523] reported only small flocks at Cleveland into the 1940s. Large numbers were regularly observed near the western Lake Erie islands by 1950,[346] but the huge flights within the Central Basin were not evident until the 1960s.

As fall concentrations increased along Lake Erie, fewer Red-breasted Mergansers appeared on inland reservoirs. While Trautman[479] regularly observed flocks of 200–500 on Buckeye Lake during the 1920s and 1930s, similar numbers have not been evident in recent decades. These mergansers are now uncommon to fairly common fall migrants on large reservoirs throughout Ohio. Most inland reports are of 20 or fewer with infrequent flocks of 50–200.

Along Lake Erie, the first migrants may appear by the last week of September but are usually noted between October 3 and 10. Maximum abundance is attained between October 22 and November 30. On inland reservoirs, the first migrants are expected by October 20–30 but most sightings are during November. The large Red-breasted Merganser flocks normally disappear between November 20 and December 7. When the weather is relatively mild, their departure is gradual and flocks of 1000–5000 may remain through December 15–20.

Numbers of wintering Red-breasted Mergansers fluctuate considerably along Lake Erie. They may be relatively scarce some winters with no more than 20–50 at any locality but numerous in other winters when concentrations of 1000–2000 may develop. These wintering mergansers are normally fairly common to abundant visitors within the Central Basin, particularly at hot-water outlets along the Lorain-Cleveland lakefront. Red-breasteds are rare to fairly common winter residents within the Western Basin, where the largest flocks may not exceed 30–50 individuals.

On inland reservoirs, small numbers of Red-breasted Mergansers may remain until December 20–January 10. During most winters, Red-breasted Mergansers are unreported from inland locations after early January. They become accidental to casual visitors during mild winters when the few records are of single mergansers.

Spring migration begins in late February or early March. While 192 mergansers were counted at Hueston Woods State Park in early February 1975,[258] flocks are unusual before March 15–20. The largest numbers are usually present between March 25 and April 25, although some linger through May 25–June 5, especially along Lake Erie.

While Red-breasted Mergansers are common to abundant spring migrants along Lake Erie, they do not appear in the immense numbers noted each autumn. The largest spring concentrations are composed of 1000–2500 and daily totals frequently do not exceed 50–500 individuals. They are uniformly distributed along the lakefront. Within the interior counties,

Red-breasted Mergansers are uncommon to locally common migrants on large reservoirs. Spring concentrations of 20–50+ appear on most lakes and flocks of 100–200 may develop. Larger concentrations are noteworthy: 1000 at Findlay Reservoir (Hancock County) on April 16, 1983, and 700 near Cincinnati during late March 1978.[269]

Red-breasted Mergansers are casual to rare summer visitors along Lake Erie with scattered reports of 1–3 individuals along the entire lakefront most years. While they frequently disappear by early July, some have survived into autumn. Summering Red-breasteds are accidental to casual nonbreeding visitors on inland reservoirs, mostly during June, although one successfully summered at Buckeye Lake in 1929.[479]

RUDDY DUCK

Oxyura jamaicensis (Gmelin)

For waterfowl, Ruddy Ducks are fairly late spring migrants, not normally appearing until March 5–15. Their movements normally peak between March 25 and April 15. Their numbers are diminished by April 20–25 and most depart by May 1–8.

Along western Lake Erie, spring Ruddies are common to abundant migrants. When their populations were larger, impressive flocks sometimes staged in Maumee Bay and elsewhere within the Western Basin: 20,000 estimated in Lucas County on April 19, 1951, and 26,660 tallied during an aerial survey in 1962.[89,313] But most reports before 1970 were of 300–2000 Ruddies. Since 1970, the largest flocks usually contain 100–500 while concentrations of 1000–1500 are exceptional.

Ruddy Ducks are common to abundant spring migrants within the northeastern counties, fairly common along central Lake Erie, and uncommon to fairly common on large lakes in other counties. Along central Lake Erie, most spring sightings are of 30–250 Ruddies. Within the inland northeastern counties before 1970, spring flocks of 1500–2000+ were occasionally noted at Youngstown and smaller flocks elsewhere. Similar flocks have not been evident since 1970, although concentrations of 50–500+ appear most years. Large spring concentrations are sporadically reported elsewhere. Ruddy Ducks like Findlay Reservoir (Hancock County); 1500 were estimated there on April 16, 1983, and smaller flocks appear most years.[370] A flock of 500 at Senecaville Reservoir on April 12, 1970, was exceptional for southeastern Ohio,[158] while no more than 250 have been reported from lakes near Columbus. Ruddy Ducks mostly pass through the southern and central counties in small flocks of 6–12, and daily totals seldom exceed 35–75.

Ohio's first nesting Ruddy Ducks were discovered at Pymatuning Lake in Ashtabula County in 1935.[220] One pair nested there in 1936 and summered in 1938, but this population eventually disappeared.[31,502] Except for occasional nonbreeding individuals, summer Ruddy Ducks were unrecorded until 1961 and 1962 when nesting pairs were discovered at Magee Marsh Wildlife Area.[89] Summering or nesting Ruddy Ducks have resided within the western Lake Erie marshes in subsequent years, part of an eastward range expansion.[104]

Ruddy Ducks are now rare but regular summer residents along western Lake Erie. This summering population includes small flocks of 5–12 nonbreeders as well as scattered nesting pairs, probably fewer than 20. Ruddy Ducks are accidental to casual summer visitors within other glaciated counties. While most records are of isolated nonbreeders, nesting was established in Hamilton County on July 15, 1973;[252] Big Island Wildlife Area (Marion County) on July 4, 1986;[383] and Cleveland on August 1, 1987.[387]

Nesting Ruddies normally prefer large undisturbed marshes where open water is interspersed among emergent vegetation. Their nests are placed within vegetation near water. The few confirmed breeding records indicate that nesting activities begin during May or early June. Most broods are observed during July when the young are already well developed.

Fall Ruddy Ducks are most numerous along western Lake Erie. As recently as the 1970s, flocks of 5000–7000 were noted off Lucas County and an aerial survey estimated 24,660 on November 30, 1962.[90] During the 1980s, the largest flocks have totaled 500–1000 Ruddies and daily totals are mostly 50–250. They are also common to abundant fall migrants through the inland northeastern counties. Large flocks were occasionally noted at Youngstown with 2000 on November 22, 1958, and 3000 on November 7, 1949.[58,79] In recent years, the largest flocks are composed of 500–900+, although most lakes support 30–200. They are fairly common to common migrants through central Lake Erie, where flocks of 30–200 are regularly noted and the largest concentrations are 500–1100. They become uncommmon to fairly common fall migrants elsewhere. The largest concentrations include flocks of 300–500 at Findlay Reservoir and 100–300 near Columbus. Sightings generally total 25–100 Ruddies in the northwestern and central counties and fewer than 30 in the southern and unglaciated counties.

The first fall migrants normally return to Lake Erie by September 25–October 2 and the inland lakes between October 3 and 10. Largest movements generally occur during the last half of October and November. Some years Ruddy Ducks remain numerous into the first half of December. Lakefront flocks of 600–1100 have been reported as late as December 19–23. Other years their numbers diminish by the last week of November. The last flocks normally disappear by December 25.

Few Ruddy Ducks winter within Ohio. They are rare but regular residents along Lake Erie, especially at the Cleveland-Lorain lakefront, where 1–8 regularly winter at hot-water outlets. They are accidental to casual winter residents at large inland lakes, with only a few reports during relatively mild seasons.

BLACK VULTURE

Coragyps atratus (Bechstein)

In the early 1800s, Black Vultures were residents of the southeastern United States. The northern edge of their range may have included southwestern Ohio. Audubon contended that they summered along the Ohio River at Cincinnati,[236] but he never substantiated his assertion and there were no corroborating sightings.

Beginning in the 1870s, Black Vultures underwent a northeastward range expansion into southern Ohio. Langdon[288] provided three Cincinnati area records, including the first specimen on January 1, 1877. They spread to Warren County by 1883, and the first Ohio breeding record was established there in 1891.[220,239] Their expansion into other southern counties apparently occurred by the early 1900s as evidenced by a specimen secured near Cadiz (Harrison County) on December 17, 1906.[239] By the mid-1930s, Hicks[220] considered Black Vultures "very local" residents in southern Ohio, nesting in twelve counties. He estimated the total breeding population at 100 or fewer pairs. Along the unglaciated Allegheny Plateau, their breeding range extended north to Hocking, Athens, and Washington Counties.[223] Though "fairly common" in Hocking County, they were rare elsewhere. Another range expansion was noted in the 1950s when a population became established in northeastern Licking County. First observed in 1952, they numbered as many as 90 in a roost there during the winter of 1957–58.[135,471]

Black Vultures remain very locally distributed in southern Ohio as small, fairly discrete breeding populations. Ten to fifteen pairs are present in Adams and eastern Brown Counties and from Chillicothe to the vicinity of Paint Creek Reservoir in Ross and Highland Counties. Breeding Black Vultures are most numerous in Hocking County and adjacent southern Fairfield County, where 35–50 pairs may nest. A population may still reside in northeastern Licking County; 23 Blacks were counted as recently as March 1, 1982. In southwestern Ohio, a few pairs regularly breed along the Little Miami River in Warren County. They have also sporadically nested at Hueston Woods State Park and in Hamilton County.[11,248,434] Based on these estimates, the known statewide nesting population is approximately 70–100 pairs.

Many Black Vultures appear to be permanent residents. Winter roosts with 90 Blacks in Licking County during 1957–58, 70 in Hocking County on February 7, 1982, and 20 in Highland County on January 28, 1984, are representative of the numbers that may be noted some years.[179,471] Wintering Blacks are generally observed in groups of 8 or fewer—reduced numbers that may indicate a southward migration by a portion of the breeding population. These seasonal movements are poorly understood.

Black Vultures may wander during the nonbreeding season. These local movements may extend twenty to more than fifty miles from known breeding locations; Black Vultures have casually appeared north to Dayton, Columbus, and Buckeye Lake and Belmont and Harrison Counties. Although there are a few winter sightings, Black Vultures are most likely to appear in these areas during March and April and from late August through October. Most extralimital sightings are of 1–5 Blacks, although 10 were counted in Delaware County on October 10, 1984.[376] Black Vultures are accidental visitors elsewhere. Singles appeared in Mahoning County on September 14, 1955, and July 20, 1950, and in Trumbull County on June 22, 1959.[60,77,80] The only other northeastern records are of 2 Blacks at Loudonville on April 9, 1951, and 1 at Hudson (Summit County) on May 30, 1966.[312,335] No migrant Black Vultures have been observed along western Lake Erie.

Black Vulture nests have been found within caves in sandstone cliffs, in large hollow logs, abandoned buildings, and bare ground surrounded by boulders. Most pairs lay their eggs in March, placing them on the ground. The young normally hatch during the last half of April after an incubation period of thirty-nine to forty-one days.[465] They remain in the nest for more than two months and are fed a diet of regurgitated food.[465] They normally leave the nest in July. Renesting attempts have been responsible for clutches during May and as late as July.[135]

TURKEY VULTURE

Cathartes aura (Linnaeus)

At sunrise, normally a time of peak avian activity, roosting Turkey Vultures have hardly stirred from their perches on tall dead trees. They remain at the roost until midmorning temperatures create the thermals needed to maintain their sustained flight. Masters at riding thermals, these vultures can soar effortlessly for many miles over fields, forests, rivers, and wetlands. Unlike Black Vultures, which locate food by sight, Turkey Vultures have a well-developed sense of smell, which they expertly use to locate decaying animals from considerable heights. During most years, warming temperatures and southerly winds in the last week of February bring the first returning Turkey Vultures. These migrants have appeared along western Lake Erie as early as February 14–23 but are not normally expected within the northern counties until March 7–12. Their arrival in the southern counties is approximately one week earlier. They become common to locally abundant migrants throughout Ohio by March 20–25. Sizable flights may occur along Lake Erie through April 20–25, while individuals and small flocks pass along the lakefront into the first week of June.

This migration is most noticeable along Lake Erie, particularly with strong southwesterly winds. Few migrants are detected with northerly winds. The largest lakefront flights total 200–250+ individuals along western Lake Erie and 100–200+ near Cleveland. Similar spring flights are not normally apparent away from Lake Erie. Inland spring totals normally are 10–50+ except at established roosts, where 100–200+ may gather.

Turkey Vultures have always been widely distributed summer residents. Hicks[220] indicated they almost certainly nested in all but two counties during the mid-1930s. They became locally uncommon in northern Ohio but were numerous elsewhere. He recorded 114 roosts in eighty-one counties and estimated a statewide population of 3650 vultures. Similar estimates are not available today, but there is no evidence to suggest their populations are declining. In fact, Turkey Vultures are expanding within the Great Lakes region,[104,438] resulting in increased numbers of breeding vultures within the northern counties since the 1930s.

Turkey Vultures are now fairly common to locally abundant summer residents except near urban areas, where they are normally absent. Breeding vultures are most numerous along the unglaciated Allegheny Plateau with daily totals of 30–50+.

They are least numerous within the intensively farmed western counties, where totals seldom exceed 3–10 except near roosts. Summer roosts may be encountered throughout Ohio, composed of nonbreeding vultures and breeding adults whose presence is not required at the nest. While the number varies from evening to evening, 20–100+ vultures may congregate at these roosts.

Breeding Turkey Vultures are quite timid around their nests and only occupy undisturbed areas. Within the western counties, breeding pairs inhabit large isolated woodlots. In southeastern Ohio, they prefer protected ledges or small caves on sheer rocky cliffs[100] but will also nest on the ground under rock ledges, in hollow logs, and in brush piles in extensive woodlands. They will also occupy abandoned buildings.[84,422] A few pairs have nested within large cavities in tall trees at heights of forty to sixty feet.[298,419] Nests with eggs have been discovered as early as April 8 but are mostly recorded between mid-April and late May with a few through mid-June. While some young vultures may remain at the nest into the first half of August, recently fledged young have appeared at roosts by the last week of June.[100,422,479,523]

Their fall migration apparently begins by September 15–25. The largest movements are generally noted through October 15. Fall Turkey Vultures do not congregate along Lake Erie. Instead, their southward movements are uniformly distributed. Fall totals of 10–50+ individuals are expected in most counties. At established roosts, as many as 100–270+ have been counted.

Turkey Vultures remain common to locally abundant fall migrants until October 20–25. Some years they may remain fairly widespread through the end of the month; in others, they are rare after October 25. The last migrant Turkey Vultures normally depart from the northern and central counties by October 25–November 5 and the southern counties by November 15. Stragglers may appear until mid-December. As their population expanded in recent years, the number of late sightings also increased and became an annual occurrence during the 1980s.

Wintering Turkey Vultures are locally fairly common near established roosts in southern Ohio. They regularly form mixed roosts with Black Vultures, and 30–100+ may be encountered in Adams, Hocking, and Morgan Counties. In addition, flocks of 20 or fewer have sporadically wintered in southwestern Ohio.[248] A large winter roost developed in northeastern Licking County during the 1950s and 1960s but has not been reported since 1982.[130,351] They are accidental midwinter visitors elsewhere.

OSPREY

Pandion haliaetus (Linnaeus)

For most people, their first encounter with an Osprey is a memorable experience. This large raptor suddenly appears over a lake or river, effortlessly riding the winds as it searches for food. It briefly hovers over a school of fish swimming near the surface of the water. By folding its wings, the Osprey drops out of the sky in a spectacular plunge as it attempts to catch its prey. It is usually unsuccessful and quickly rises from the water to resume its hunt. After repeating this sequence several times, the Osprey finally captures a fish, takes it to a perch, and consumes it.

Unfortunately, the experience of observing hunting Ospreys was almost eliminated from most of North America. Their populations were greatly reduced by pesticide contamination during the 1950s and 1960s. By the late 1960s, Ospreys were rare migrants with only four to eight sightings from Ohio during their annual migrations. This decline was reversed just in time. The use of harmful organochlorine pesticides was banned during the late 1960s while intensive management practices were undertaken to increase the breeding success of the remaining adults. Their recovery was widely apparent by the late 1970s, and numbers returned to normal by 1985.

Ospreys are now uncommon to fairly common migrants, becoming locally rare in the counties lacking sizable lakes and rivers. While the first spring Ospreys may return by March 27–30, they are not usually encountered until the first half of April. Their spring passage peaks between April 15 and May 15, when they are usually observed as isolated individuals on inland lakes and rivers or in small flights of 5–10 along western Lake Erie. The largest movements totaled 16 along Lake Erie on April 24, 1982, and 18 at East Liverpool (Columbiana County) on May 1, 1965.[148,365] Numbers decline during the last half of May, although nonbreeders may remain until June 3–8.

Ospreys are more widely reported during fall. Migrants may appear by August 3–10, mostly nonbreeders or unsuccessful adults, but are not normally encountered until August 25–September 7. They are most frequently observed between September 20 and October 10, usually as isolated individuals with occasional totals of 3–5. Most depart by the first week of November, but a few have lingered through November 20–26 and there are several reliable sight records during the first week of December.

During winter, Ospreys are normally scattered from the southern United States into South America.[5] Midwinter sightings from the Great Lakes region are generally dismissed as misidentifications. Within Ohio, there have been Osprey sight records during each month of winter. None of these records was substantiated by a specimen or photograph nor corroborated by multiple observers. Hence, these sightings are all questionable.

At one time, small numbers of Ospreys may have nested regularly within Ohio. During the nineteenth century, Kirtland[251] reported a nesting pair near Poland (Mahoning County). Small numbers regularly summered along Lake Erie, where a nest was claimed for Erie County.[220] They also may have nested at Buckeye Lake and Lake St. Mary's.[220,479]

In this century, a pair of Ospreys nested at Lake St. Mary's in 1913[203] but did not return in subsequent years. One pair reportedly summered along the Scioto River in Pike County between 1928 and 1930, although a nest was never discovered.[220] A pair constructed a nest at Buckeye Lake in 1941 but were shot before their eggs hatched. Another pair reportedly constructed a nest at Bur Oak State Park (Athens County) several years later.

In recent years, nonbreeding Ospreys have become casual to rare summer visitors to northern and central Ohio. Most appear at inland reservoirs, producing up to four sightings annually since 1980. These birds may remain for a few days or several weeks but do not normally exhibit territorial behavior. The only exception was an unmated Osprey in Belmont County that started to build nests during 1985 and 1986.[434]

AMERICAN SWALLOW-TAILED KITE

Elanoides forficatus (Linnaeus)

With their present North American breeding range restricted to the southeastern United States, it is difficult to imagine that these elegant raptors once resided in Ohio. Yet, accounts from early naturalists indicate that Swallow-tailed Kites probably nested in the state during the first half of the nineteenth century. Their distribution may have been decidedly local; there were reports from Portage, Stark, Crawford, Marion, Pickaway, Fayette, and Ross Counties.[220] These kites were described as "quite common" in Warren County and there is a specimen from Cincinnati.[248,299]

In all likelihood, Swallow-tailed Kites were disappearing from Ohio at the time of these initial sightings. Kirtland[251] found "considerable numbers" in Portage and Stark Counties during 1835 but none could be located in 1838. Kirkpatrick described them as "once numerous in Crawford County and still found occasionally" in 1858, a statement coinciding with Wheaton's belief that the kites disappeared as a "regularly occurring species" during the 1850s.[522] Kirtland speculated that cold summer weather during the 1830s may have been responsible for this decline. Habitat destruction and persecution of these kites may have eliminated local populations.

Following their disappearance as summer residents, Swallow-tailed Kites became accidental visitors. During the last half of the nineteenth century, confirmed reports are limited to specimens taken in Licking County on August 22, 1878, and Ross County on August 29, 1898.[220] There is only one sight record from the twentieth century. On May 26, 1975, Ted Hilty observed a Swallow-tailed Kite as it flew over fields east of Fremont.[259]

MISSISSIPPI KITE

Ictinia mississippiensis (Wilson)

In the eastern United States, Mississippi Kites are found across the Gulf Coast states and north along the Mississippi River to southern Missouri and southern Illinois.[5] This breeding range slowly expanded northward during the past twenty years, and the number of extralimital kites also increased. Small numbers of Mississippi Kites now regularly wander north to the Great Lakes and New England states during late spring and early summer.

Mississippi Kites are accidental late spring and early summer visitors to Ohio, with five confirmed sightings between May 11 and June 24, almost invariably immatures. Ohio's first Mississippi Kite was discovered by Frank Bader and Milton Rinehart on May 13, 1978, as it soared over Greenlawn Cemetery in Columbus.[471] Others were observed over Oak Openings (Lucas County) on May 16, 1982,[471] and along western Lake Erie in Lucas County on May 11, 1985.[378] The most recent sightings were during June 1987, when singles appeared at Ft. Loramie on June 4 and in Delaware County on June 23–24.[387]

BALD EAGLE

Haliaeetus leucocephalus (Linnaeus)

The south shore of Lake Erie has always supported a breeding Bald Eagle population. When Ohio was initially settled, breeding eagles were regularly spaced along the entire lakefront, but they began to disappear from the more populated sections during the nineteenth century. They have not nested in Cuyahoga County since the 1800s and the last lakefront nests in Lorain and Ashtabula Counties were reported during the 1930s.[215,220,523] Since the 1940s, this population has been restricted to Sandusky Bay and western Lake Erie.

Bald Eagles were always sporadic summer residents in the interior of the state. Trautman[479] cited anecdotal accounts of nesting at Buckeye Lake during the 1800s, although they have not nested there in the present century. At least one pair frequently nested at Lake St. Mary's through 1909 with occasional breeding attempts through 1925.[98,422] A pair also nested at Indian Lake in 1906.[115] The proliferation of reservoirs during the twentieth century encouraged a few additional attempts: at Lake Rockwell (Portage County) in 1935,[523] Charles Mill Reservoir in 1950,[311] and near Youngstown during 1954 and 1966.[71,150] A pair of eagles nested along Indian Creek in Butler County during 1953.[248]

Between 1955 and 1966, the Ohio Bald Eagle population remained stable with 11–15 pairs. However, very few young eagles were successfully fledged. The nesting pairs had become contaminated with the residues of DDT and other related pesticides that caused them to lay infertile eggs or eggs with thin shells that broke under the weight of an incubating adult. Since eagles are long-lived, the population did not decline immediately, but as the adults died, they were not replaced. This population declined to 4–5 pairs by 1979.[260,274] At this time, the Ohio Division of Wildlife began to intensively manage the remaining pairs by monitoring nests, protecting breeding adults from disturbance, and transplanting young eagles into the nests of sterile adults to supplement natural reproduction. The population increased to 12 pairs in 1988.[388a] In the interior counties, a pair has nested at Mosquito Creek Reservoir (Trumbull County) since 1981.

Most information on the nesting biology of Bald Eagles along Lake Erie was gathered by Francis Herrick in the 1920s.[207-10] Our breeding Bald Eagles remain within their territories throughout most of the year, sometimes abandoning them for brief periods during midwinter. Most of their activities are centered around their nests, immense structures maintained and reused for many years. Undoubtedly, the largest eyrie built in North America was near Vermilion. Initially constructed in 1891, it was used continually through 1925, when the tree it was in collapsed.[208] While some pairs maintain only one nest, others build several and use them in alternating years. Nest building usually occurs during fall and early spring through mid-March. While some nests are near the lakeshore, others are more than a mile from Lake Erie. These nests are generally fifty to eighty-five feet above the ground, although one pair reportedly attempted to nest on the ground.[263]

The first eggs may be laid by late February during advanced seasons or mid-March during relatively cold years. The young hatch by mid-April and the adults care for them for more than two months. By mid-June, adult eagles periodically provide food for the young, who are regularly exercising in preparation for their first flight. Fledging, described by Herrick,[211] normally occurs during the last week of June or first week of July.

Bald Eagles have fairly well-defined migrations along the lakefront during spring and fall. These movements were most pronounced before 1950. Along western Lake Erie, spring migrants are mostly observed between March 10 and April 15.[89] The largest flight totaled 14 near Toledo on March 31, 1948. Their fall migration extends between late August and early November. Since 1985, 5–10 eagles may be observed daily along western Lake Erie, although many may be resident adults and their young. Along central Lake Erie, Bald Eagles are casual to rare migrants, mostly isolated individuals appearing at the same time as along western Lake Erie. They are also casual to rare winter residents, periodically visiting hot-water outlets during January and February.

Within the interior counties, Bald Eagles may be encountered almost anywhere at any time of the year. Most reports are from the northeastern and central counties, where they are casual to rare visitors. In the unglaciated counties, they become accidental to casual visitors.

As winter visitors, inland Bald Eagles are mostly discovered along the Ohio River and its large tributaries. A few may also appear on reservoirs. This wintering population probably does not exceed 6–15 eagles during most years. Their spring migration has two poorly defined peaks. The first occurs between February 20 and March 20, and the second during May. While this migration produced concentrations of 5–6 eagles in central Ohio in the 1930s, only scattered individuals have been reported during the past thirty years. Away from Mosquito Creek Reservoir and Pymatuning Lake, Bald Eagles are casual to accidental nonbreeding summer visitors, with 2–5 reported most years. Their fall migration is poorly defined through the inland counties; most records are of scattered eagles during October and November.

NORTHERN HARRIER

Circus cyaneus (Linnaeus)

On a warm April morning, a male Northern Harrier catches a thermal and soars into the blue sky. He appears to be gaining altitude in order to continue his migration. All of a sudden he folds his wings and rockets toward the earth, only to pull up at the last second and give a loud call. This performance is repeated again and again, for it is the breeding season and this male is displaying for a female perched in a grassy field below.

At one time these displays were regularly observed between late March and early May in the northern two-thirds of Ohio, where these harriers were locally common summer residents.[220] They were most numerous in northwestern Ohio. Campbell[89] described them as "one of the more common breeding hawks" near Toledo, and Price[422] thought they "probably equaled the total number of all other hawks" in Paulding County. They were generally rare in most other counties, although local populations were found south to Montgomery, Fayette, Pickaway, Fairfield, Muskingum, Guernsey, Harrison, and Jefferson Counties. Harriers were absent from southern Ohio except for isolated nesting attempts in Jackson and Vinton Counties.[220,223]

Even in the mid-1930s this breeding population was declining. Hicks[220] noted their numbers were "much reduced," a result of habitat destruction and persecution. Additional declines were noted during the 1940s, especially near Toledo and in eastern Ohio.[84,89] By the mid-1950s, nesting harriers disappeared from most counties and became very scarce in northwestern Ohio.[89,417,429] Isolated pairs remained at only a few widely scattered locations.

Their status has not changed since the mid-1950s. While the Breeding Bird Atlas (1982–87) uncovered a few additional nesting pairs, Northern Harriers remain casual to rare and very locally distributed summer residents in northern and central Ohio.[434] Summering harriers are regularly observed along western Lake Erie and in the northeastern counties of Ashtabula, Trumbull, and Lake. Breeding pairs and summering harriers have appeared sporadically in Wyandot, Seneca, Wood, Henry, Madison, Clark, Clinton, Belmont, and Muskingum Counties. They resided occasionally in Clermont County as recently as 1976.[263] Harriers do not regularly nest at every location and many summer reports pertain to nonbreeders. Recent reports indicate that no more than 5–15 pairs may remain in Ohio.

Breeding harriers prefer wet meadows, wet prairies, and the grassy margins of wetlands.[89,479] As these habitats disappeared, they occupied upland pastures, hayfields, and reclaimed strip mines. Their nests are placed on the ground, often in the middle of rose tangles in wetlands. In upland grasslands, harriers prefer large undisturbed fields without woody cover. While nests with eggs were discovered as early as April 28,[523] most were reported during the last half of May with the young hatching by mid-June. The earliest fledglings were noted by July 1, although most appeared during the last half of July or early August.[89,479] Renesting attempts may produce clutches as late as July 5.

Northern Harriers disperse widely after the breeding season and begin to appear away from their nesting localities by July 25–August 20. Their fall migration is a gradual southward drift through Ohio. While they are most numerous in September and October, migrating harriers may be noted into the first half of January. Fall observations are usually 1–6 harriers daily; large fall movements have never been reported.

Numbers of wintering harriers also declined during this century. They were formerly one of the most numerous wintering hawks in central and northern Ohio.[89,479,523] This decline was gradual, reflecting changing land-use patterns and a significant reduction in breeding populations throughout eastern North America.[438] Since the 1940s, the conversion of grasslands to cultivated fields and the practice of fall plowing has contributed to further reductions in their populations.

Northern Harriers are now uncommon to locally common winter residents throughout Ohio, least numerous in the eastern counties, where most reports are of 1–4 daily. They become locally common in portions of central and western Ohio where habitats are more favorable. They congregate at Killdeer Plains Wildlife Area, Maumee Bay State Park (Lucas County), and the Ross-Pickaway county line, where 10–25+ may be observed. In other central and western counties, winter totals are 1–8 daily.

Numbers of wintering harriers reflect the abundance of their rodent prey. When rodents are scarce, even preferred wintering sites host only 3–8 harriers daily. Wintering harriers prefer open grasslands for foraging but regularly hunt over a variety of agricultural fields.[41] Unlike other raptors, harriers are as likely to hunt from the ground as from the wing.

Northern Harriers form communal roosts during winter in fallow fields where weeds and grasses provide protection from the harsh conditions. When their populations were larger, as many as 50–75 were counted at one roost. In recent years, the largest roosts hosted 20–30.

Spring migration is poorly defined. Within the interior counties, harriers simply depart quietly from their wintering sites. Inland totals are generally 8 or fewer through mid-April with very few after May 1. These movements are more apparent along Lake Erie, where the first migrants are noted by March 3–10 and others continue to move along the lakefront through May 10. The largest flights, between March 25 and April 18, may be composed of 25–50 harriers.

SHARP-SHINNED HAWK

Accipiter striatus Vieillot

As thermals develop during the midmorning hours, Sharp-shinned Hawks emerge from the woodlands where they spent the previous evening. Mostly as individuals but occasionally in groups of two or three, these migrant hawks soar higher and higher until they are hardly more than pinpoints in the sky. After attaining sufficient altitude, they take advantage of tail winds and continue their journey over Ohio.

Sharp-shinneds are normally most numerous during spring.

While their passage is generally associated with southerly winds, single migrants may be encountered under almost any condition except hard rains. Their northward migration begins with the first favorable winds after February 20 but they do not become widely distributed until March 10–20. The largest flights are most likely between April 23 and May 7. They normally depart by May 20 except along western Lake Erie, where nonbreeders may appear through June 5.

Spring Sharp-shinneds are fairly common to abundant along western Lake Erie. Favorable conditions produce flights of 30–60 and occasionally 100+. The largest flights totaled 400+ Sharp-shinneds over Lucas County on April 26–27, 1969, and 202 over Ottawa County on April 24, 1982.[90,365] With unfavorable conditions, fewer than 5 are noted daily. Along central Lake Erie, Sharp-shinneds are uncommon to fairly common migrants; most reports are of 10 or fewer. Favorable winds produce infrequent flights of 30–75 and the largest totaled 109 at Lorain on April 26, 1980, and 107 at Cleveland the following day.[277] These hawks are rare to uncommon migrants through every interior county, where most sightings are of 1–3 and the largest movements total 10–15.

Their southward migration is less conspicuous. Fall migrants are uncommon to rare in most areas, normally encountered as widely scattered individuals with occasional groups of 3–6. Defined movements are restricted to the western Lake Erie islands, where Sharp-shinneds become fairly common migrants. These hawks move south from Point Pelee in Canada, "island hopping" across the western end of the lake. Northerly winds may produce flights of 20–60 across the Bass Islands and Kelleys Island.

The earliest fall Sharp-shinneds return to northwestern Ohio by the last week of August but are not expected in most counties until September 10–20. These migrants are mostly observed between September 25 and October 20. This movement continues into November, but it is difficult to distinguish late migrants from wintering hawks.

At one time, Sharp-shinned Hawks were casual to rare winter residents throughout Ohio, mostly restricted to woodlands, wooded fencerows, and dense thickets. Given their secretive habits, their abundance may have been greater than the few reports indicated. Since the mid-1970s, wintering Sharp-shinneds have started visiting urban and rural residences to capture small songbirds at feeders. This behavior has resulted in increased numbers of sightings. Sharpies are presently rare to uncommon winter residents, invariably as scattered individuals.

Their status as summer residents has also fluctuated during the present century. In 1935, Hicks[220] considered breeding Sharp-shinneds rare and very locally distributed residents with records from forty-eight counties, mostly in the eastern half of Ohio. Recognizing their secretive behavior, he realized they might be more numerous than these sight records indicated. Beginning in the late 1940s, this population underwent a gradual decline that continued through the 1960s. This reduction was believed to be the result of pesticide contamination. By 1970, very few nesting pairs remained within Ohio, but after the harmful pesticides were banned, Sharp-shinned Hawks quickly recovered. Recent sightings indicate they have regained

COMMON GOLDENEYE
Bucephala clangula

This fast-flying hardy duck is a regular visitor from the north. Many flocks of Common Goldeneyes spend the winter throughout the state. Both these ducks and their cousins the Barrow's Goldeneyes are known as "whistlers," a name that refers to the particularly loud and musical whistling sound produced by their wings in flight. This sound has an extraordinary carrying power that announces their approach before they come into sight.

Adults

(male)

(female)

RED-BREASTED MERGANSER
Mergus serrator

The majority of Red-breasted Mergansers prefer to spend the winter months feeding on the animal life they can find along the coasts and in saltwater bays. Huge flights congregate on Lake Erie each autumn; some years they number in the tens of thousands.

Adults

(male)

(female)

RUDDY DUCK
Oxyura jamaicensis

About the time the new green leaves of the cattail (*Typha* sp.) are emerging at the edges of our ponds and lakes, Ruddy Ducks in full breeding plumage are passing through on the way to their nesting grounds on the northern plains. In the fall when these chunky little ducks are on their way south, males and females are dressed in a drab mottled brown. In this plumage, however, adult males can still be distinguished from their mates by the white patches on their cheeks that persist throughout the year.

Adults

(male)

(female)

TURKEY VULTURE
Cathartes aura

These ugly black birds of prey are miraculously transformed into soaring creatures of beauty when they take to the skies—an activity that roosting Turkey Vultures usually delay until the air has been warmed by the morning sun and the thermals have begun to rise. Frequently these vultures gather in small groups to feed and roost.

Adult
(sexes similar)

OSPREY
Pandion haliaetus

For years anglers have unjustly accused Ospreys of being a negative influence on the populations of many species of their favorite game fish. The fish in the talons of this Osprey is a Redhorse (*Moxostoma* sp.), one of several species of so-called "trash fish" upon which these fish hawks prey, but which few fishermen prize.

Adult
(sexes similar)

NORTHERN HARRIER
Circus cyaneus

It takes a male Northern Harrier up to three years to attain the pure silver-gray plumage of an adult bird. During this time, both the adult females and their young are dressed in shades of brown and rust. Consequently the chance of seeing an adult male in full gray plumage hunting on a windswept marsh can vary seasonally but is never more than about one in four.

Adult
*(male; female is brown—both have
the distinctive white rump)*

ROUGH-LEGGED HAWK
Buteo lagopus

These hawks of the Canadian tundra are only winter visitors to the state, and their highly variable plumage causes much confusion when they arrive. Some Rough-legged Hawks are dressed in black while others are very light trimmed in various shades of brown. Audubon once noted of a series of specimens he examined that no two were alike. The bird here is of the most common color phase. The winter diet of the Rough-legged Hawk is primarily voles (*Microtus*).

Adult
(sexes similar)

AMERICAN KESTREL
Falco sparverius

Silent most of the year, the American Kestrel becomes quite vocal and conspicuous in spring when courtship begins. Courtship includes a series of circling flights and dives performed by the male. These movements usually end in a graceful balancing act on the uppermost branch of a tree, where the female waits. The Kestrel is one of the few North American hawks that nest in cavities in trees.

Adults

(male)

(female)

RUFFED GROUSE
Bonasa umbellus

The drumming of the Ruffed Grouse has been heard every month of the year. In early spring, however, about the time the flowers of the Hepatica (*Hepatica acutiloba*) and Snow Trillium (*Trillium nivale*) appear, the male Ruffed Grouse's efforts to attract a mate begin in earnest as he displays and drums on a favorite resonant log.

Adult

(male; sexes similar)

their former abundance. Most summering Sharp-shinneds are discovered along the unglaciated Allegheny Plateau, where they are rare to locally uncommon residents.[434] They are rare but fairly regular summer residents in northeastern Ohio, but accidental to casual residents in most western counties. There are few confirmed breeding records from western Ohio since 1970, although nests near Cincinnati and Toledo indicate small local populations exist.

Nesting Sharp-shinned Hawks occupy wooded habitats varying from young second-growth woods to mature forests. They are seldom observed over open fields except in flight from one woodlot to another. They do not normally venture into residential areas. They prefer to nest in conifers but will also occupy large deciduous woodlots. Nests with eggs have been reported between mid-May and early June; an exceptionally late nest was found in Ashtabula County on July 12, 1928.[215] Recently fledged young have been reported during July.

COOPER'S HAWK

Accipiter cooperii (Bonaparte)

Stealthy hunters of birds and occasionally mammals, Cooper's Hawks are found wherever their prey congregates. These crow-sized accipiters prefer woodlands, wooded fencerows, and similar habitats where they adeptly pursue their prey through dense cover. Cooper's Hawks may also be observed pursuing blackbirds through their marshy roosts, Mourning Doves in cornfields, and songbirds at backyard feeders.

At the turn of the century, Cooper's Hawks were widespread residents.[236] Despite frequent persecution, they were among our more numerous breeding hawks. Campbell[86] considered them "second numerically only to Marsh Hawks" as summer residents at Toledo. Populations remained stable during the first decades of this century despite local declines resulting from habitat destruction.[479] In the mid-1930s, Hicks[220] considered Cooper's Hawks rare to common residents within every county, most numerous along the unglaciated Allegheny Plateau.

Their numbers began to decline during the 1940s, and breeding pairs disappeared from many localities during the 1950s.[84,89,98] By the early 1960s, these formerly widespread residents were reduced to scattered nesting pairs. While habitat destruction contributed to this decline, the major cause was eventually shown to be pesticide contamination of the adults. After use of the pesticides was banned, this decline was halted during the early 1970s.[438] Cooper's Hawks remained scarce through the end of the decade, but improved numbers became apparent between 1980 and 1983. By 1985, they once again became widely distributed residents and populations are still increasing.

Cooper's Hawks are now rare to uncommon summer residents within Ohio,[434] most numerous in the southern and eastern counties where wooded habitats are widely distributed. They become locally distributed within intensively farmed western and central counties.

Nesting Cooper's Hawks prefer pine plantations but also occupy second-growth deciduous woods.[332,427] Pairs will nest in small groves of trees if suitable dense cover is present. Their nests are placed at heights of twenty to fifty feet, frequently in the principal forks of large trees. Breeding pairs are most evident during their courtship displays in April. Pairs become secretive once their breeding activities begin. Nests are constructed in April or early May and clutches have been reported between April 21 and May 30.[523] Most young hatch during the last half of May and remain in the nest through late June or the first half of July.[89,479] Renesting attempts are responsible for small young in the nest through July 21.[215]

Wintering Cooper's Hawks are widely distributed in habitats varying from deciduous woods to rural farmlands and urban residential areas. They are uncommon to fairly common winter residents. Most reports are of 1–3 individuals, although 4–6 may be encountered daily at preferred localities.

The expansion of wintering Cooper's Hawks into urban areas is a phenomenon of the 1980s. Their stealth and hunting skills are useful in surprising songbirds at feeders, and urban Cooper's Hawks visit a number of feeders on a regular basis. The majority are immatures whose hunting skills may not be fully developed; the adults are more likely to be found in woodlands.

As a result of their substantial resident population, the migratory movements of Cooper's Hawks are poorly defined. These movements are most apparent during spring, especially along Lake Erie, where most migrants are noted between March 1 and April 15 with smaller numbers appearing through mid-May. The largest flights were reported before 1945; 100 were counted along western Lake Erie on March 19, 1942.[89] Since 1960, the largest movements have been composed of 10–20. Within the interior counties, migrant Cooper's Hawks are mostly noted as scattered singles during March and April.

The southward migration is mostly scattered individuals passing through each county; no sizable flights have been reported. This movement begins during the last half of September and is most apparent between September 25 and November 15. Smaller numbers may appear during December as the birds search for suitable winter territories.

NORTHERN GOSHAWK

Accipiter gentilis (Linnaeus)

This impressive raptor is a resident of northern coniferous and mixed forests whose eastern breeding range extends south to the upper Great Lakes and the mountains of Pennsylvania and northern New Jersey.[5] Remarkably wary, the Northern Goshawk is renowned for its stealth and hunting prowess. With perseverance, it may be viewed perched near the trunk of a tall tree, watching the surroundings for prey.

Goshawks were once considered accidental or casual winter visitors, with about one sighting every two or three years. Since 1968, there have been at least one or two reports every year, indicating that goshawks are rare winter visitors to northern Ohio and casual to accidental elsewhere. Undoubtedly, more of these wary birds occur within Ohio than are positively identified.

This species undertakes periodic movements away from its normal breeding range. These flights occur at ten-year intervals and are correlated with cyclical lows in its prey populations. The most pronounced flights were noted during the winters of 1972–73 and 1982–83. The latter flight produced at least sixteen winter sightings within Ohio and additional migrants during spring and fall. Smaller "echo" flights may appear during the winter following an invasion, but these flights normally produce fewer than six sightings. During invasions, a few goshawks were reliably reported as early as mid-October. They do not usually appear until November. All earlier sight records most likely are misidentifications.

As winter visitors, goshawks are mostly reported from the northern tier of counties and northeastern Ohio south to Akron and Youngstown. They usually wander farther south only during pronounced invasions, when there may be scattered sightings south to the Ohio River. Goshawks may appear anytime during winter. Most inhabit extensive woodlands but a few visit small woodlots, wooded parks within cities, and even backyard bird feeders.

Their spring migration is mostly evident along western Lake Erie, where 1 or 2 goshawks are reported during March of most years. Greater numbers pass along the lakefront following invasions, although no large flights have been recorded. Relatively few Goshawks are encountered within the interior counties. Spring records come mostly during March. The latest documented sight record was near Kent (Portage County) on April 28, 1981.[361]

HARRIS' HAWK

Parabuteo unicinctus (Temminck)

This accidental visitor from the southwestern United States has appeared in Ohio only once. About December 24, 1917, one of a pair of Harris' Hawks was collected in Pickaway County approximately four miles southwest of Harrisburg. T. M. Earl noted that these birds were "reported to be molesting poultry and had killed one or two." There was no indication they had been kept in captivity.[113] The specimen, an adult, is in the Ohio State University Museum of Zoology.

While all recent extralimital records of Harris' Hawks have been dismissed as birds that escaped from captivity,[5] the same explanation does not necessarily apply to the Ohio record. The sport of falconry was not as widely practiced in this country in 1917 as it is today, and captive birds were not as readily available. More important, Harris' Hawks are known to wander occasionally during late fall and early winter, the season when the pair appeared in Ohio. While the origins of this pair will never be conclusively proved, the evidence suggests the Ohio record represents truly wild birds.

RED-SHOULDERED HAWK

Buteo lineatus (Gmelin)

Without a doubt, the Red-shouldered Hawk is the most handsome of our resident buteos. A striking raptor with red underparts, rusty shoulders, and a black and white barred back, this hawk is equally impressive as it perches quietly in a tall tree or soars overhead. Unfortunately, encounters with this beautiful hawk have become too infrequent in recent decades.

In the early 1900s, Red-shouldereds were the most numerous large hawk within Ohio.[236] Breeding pairs were most frequently observed in the northern and central counties. Some were permanent residents but many migrated south each fall, producing an influx of wintering Red-shouldereds into southern Ohio. In the mid-1930s, Hicks[220] cited summer records from seventy counties, noting that they were most frequently observed in the northern third of the state and absent to very rare within most unglaciated and some southwestern counties. Their numbers were declining, however, since they were described as uncommon to rare and locally distributed. Trautman[479] recorded 22 nesting pairs at Buckeye Lake between 1922 and 1924 but only 4 pairs by 1933. Similar declines were evident throughout western Ohio.[422]

These declines continued during subsequent decades. At Toledo, Red-shouldereds were greatly reduced by the mid-1950s and only 2–3 pairs remained in 1968.[89] These hawks essentially disappeared from most northwestern and glaciated central counties by 1970. A sizable but declining population remained near Cincinnati. Surprisingly, populations remained stable in the northeastern counties,[335] and Red-shouldereds were increasing along the unglaciated Allegheny Plateau. These trends continued through the mid-1970s but have apparently stabilized since 1980.

Of all factors contributing to this decline, habitat destruction was most important. These hawks occupy mature lowland woods, hunting within these woods or along the margins of fields and wetlands for amphibians, reptiles, and birds during summer and mammals and birds in winter. Within the glaciated counties, most lowland forests were cleared during the past twenty to forty years, while many remaining forests are too small and disturbed to support nesting Red-shouldereds. Pesticide contamination may also have reduced breeding populations in suitable habitats.

Fortunately, some lowland forests remain intact and are occupied by breeding Red-shouldereds. These habitats are most prevalent in the northeastern counties and along the unglaciated Allegheny Plateau, where they are uncommon to locally rare residents as widely scattered pairs. They are scarce to absent near large cities and within extensively strip-mined areas from Tuscarawas, Harrison, and southern Jefferson Counties south to Perry, Morgan, and Washington Counties.[434] Red-shouldered Hawks are uncommon and locally distributed summer residents in the southwestern counties bordering the Ohio River and Warren County. They are accidental to locally rare within the northwestern and glaciated central counties, where the number of breeding pairs may not exceed 10–20.

Red-shouldered Hawks place their nests from forty to seventy-five feet high in large trees and may use these platforms for several years. Nest construction takes place during March and the first eggs may be laid during the last week of the month.[479,523] While most young hatch by late April or early May, nests with eggs have been reported as late as May 18.[53] The earliest fledglings are reported during the last week of May but normally appear in June or early July.

Wintering Red-shouldereds have also declined since the 1920s. As recently as the early 1960s, these wintering hawks were regularly detected in swamp forests and wooded riparian corridors throughout Ohio. By the mid-1960s, they disappeared from most northwestern and glaciated central counties. Small numbers were regularly observed elsewhere.

Red-shouldereds are now rare to locally uncommon winter residents in most southern and eastern counties. Most winter records consist of scattered hawks, although 3–5 may still be tallied on a few Christmas Bird Counts. Within the glaciated central and northwestern counties, these hawks are accidental or casual winter visitors averaging one or two sightings annually since 1970.

Their migratory movements are most noticeable in spring, when the first migrants may appear on strong southerly winds during the last half of February. Most migrants are detected during March, with smaller numbers through April 10–20 and scattered immatures passing along western Lake Erie through the last week of May.

This northward passage is most evident along western Lake Erie, where Red-shouldereds become fairly common to common migrants. On March days with strong southerly winds, kettles of 20+ adult Red-shouldereds can create quite a spectacle. Before 1950, sizable numbers appeared each spring and the largest flight totaled 800 near Toledo on March 19, 1942.[89] In recent years, as many as 50–80 Red-shouldereds have been counted in one day, while most reports are of 25 or fewer during March and only scattered singles after April 10–15. Red-shouldereds are rare to uncommon spring migrants away from western Lake Erie. Most reports are of scattered individuals, although flights of 10–15 have passed along central Lake Erie.

Their fall migration is very poorly defined. These migrants are casual to locally uncommon as scattered individuals. A few immature Red-shouldereds have appeared during August, but most fall migrants are detected between September 15 and November 7.

BROAD-WINGED HAWK

Buteo platypterus (Vieillot)

Broad-winged Hawks are renowned for their spectacular flights each spring and autumn as they move back and forth between their winter range in Central and South America and their breeding territories in the deciduous forests of eastern North America. Ohio is fortunate to share in this spectacle, although the appearance of sizable flocks in this state is not nearly as predictable as their movements elsewhere.

The first spring arrivals are resident pairs returning to the southern and eastern counties between April 5 and 15. A few migrants may appear elsewhere before April 15 but are not expected until April 15–20. Their northward migration peaks between April 20 and 30. Small numbers continue to appear until May 10–20 with stragglers along Lake Erie through June 7.

These spring movements are most pronounced along Lake Erie, where Broad-wingeds become fairly common to abundant migrants. Along the Western Basin, these hawks migrate around the western end of the lake. In the Cleveland area, their passage is predominantly eastward. During some years, the largest movements are composed of 100–250 Broad-wingeds. Other years produce moderate flights of 300–500. On rare occasions, immense flights appear, including 4500 on April 26–27, 1969, and 2000 on April 25, 1984 in Lucas County[89,374] and 1200 at Cleveland on April 24, 1961.[329] These flights occur on strong southwesterly winds; unfavorable winds produce only 3–20. Away from Lake Erie, Broad-wingeds are generally uncommon to fairly common migrants through most inland counties, where 1–6 are expected daily and the largest flights are composed of 10–39.

As summer residents, Broad-wingeds have gradually increased since 1900. In the mid-1930s, Hicks[220] reported that nesting pairs were largely restricted to the eastern counties, where they were locally distributed from Lake and Trumbull Counties south along the entire unglaciated plateau. More than a dozen pairs inhabited several counties, although most supported only a few pairs. Away from eastern Ohio, Hicks[220] cited nesting records only from Williams County, although a few pairs also resided at Cincinnati.[248] Their numbers gradually improved during subsequent years as the woodlands matured within the unglaciated counties. This expansion eventually resulted in scattered pairs in the glaciated central and northwestern counties during the 1970s.

Broad-winged Hawks are now uncommon to fairly common summer residents along the Allegheny Plateau, usually noted as scattered pairs. Their status is similar in northeastern Ohio but they are more locally distributed. Within southwestern Ohio, Broad-wingeds are uncommon residents in counties bordering the Ohio River and rare elsewhere. They are least numerous within the glaciated central and northwestern counties, where they are accidental to locally rare summer residents. A few pairs nest in Lucas, Fulton, and Williams Counties as well as in central Ohio near Columbus, but summering Broad-wingeds are absent from most of western Ohio.[434]

Nesting Broad-wingeds occupy extensive mature upland woods and frequently hunt in adjacent successional fields. Their nests are placed in the crotches of large trees at heights of thirty feet or more. Nest construction begins during the last half of April in southern Ohio but not until May near Lake Erie. Complete clutches are expected between early May and mid-June. Most young hatch in June and fledge by late July or early August.

In fall, large numbers of Broad-wingeds migrate around western Lake Erie, but after passing through southeastern Michigan they disperse in a broad front as they head toward Texas. Those hawks that pass around eastern Lake Erie migrate along the Appalachian Mountains and miss Ohio entirely. As in spring, these fall movements are quite variable. During some years, they miss Ohio. In other years, migrant Broad-wingeds become briefly numerous.

Fall Broad-wingeds are uncommon to locally abundant migrants through northwestern Ohio, where most sizable movements are reported from Toledo. The largest flight totaled 2000 over Oregon (Lucas County) on September 21, 1982.[368] Movements of 100–500 are detected most years.[89] Elsewhere within western Ohio, Broad-wingeds are rare to locally abundant migrants. Large kettles may appear in any county but are most frequently encountered near Cincinnati. These kettles usually total 35–200 individuals with occasional concentrations of 300–500+. Within the central third of the state, Broad-wingeds are casual to rare fall migrants. Small flocks are infrequently noted and the largest movement totaled 250 at Columbus on September 17, 1978.[471] Their status is similar within the eastern counties, although no sizable movements have been reported.

A few migrant Broad-wingeds are encountered during August, and the earliest kettle appeared in Ottawa County on August 28, 1957.[350] While a few migrants are observed between September 5 and 15, the largest flights almost invariably occur between September 15 and 25. October migrants are usually individuals or flocks of 6 or fewer; a flight of 100 at Cincinnati was exceptional on October 24, 1987.[388] The last fall migrants usually depart by October 10–15 with a few stragglers through the end of the month. There are no substantiated November sightings.

There have been a number of winter Broad-winged Hawk sightings, mostly on Christmas Bird Counts. These sightings are invariably misidentifications; there are no substantiated winter records. Since Broad-wingeds normally winter in Central and South America, it is very unlikely they would appear within Ohio during this season.

SWAINSON'S HAWK

Buteo swainsoni Bonaparte

Ohio has only one acceptable sight record of Swainson's Hawk.[389] An immature was discovered at Magee Marsh Wildlife Area in Lucas County on July 1, 1983, by Don Tumblin, Jim McCormac, and me. We observed it in flight for several minutes. It may also have been observed on several later dates.[371] None of the other sight records from Ohio is adequately documented.

Swainson's Hawk is a migratory raptor whose breeding range encompasses most of western North America. It nests east through the plains states, while a small disjunct population is located in northern Illinois.[5] In recent years, these hawks have proven to be very rare but regular migrants wherever large numbers of hawks congregate in eastern North America.

This species normally winters in Central and South America, although small numbers may occur in southern Florida and south Texas.[5] Winter records from other portions of North America are generally dismissed as misidentifications or hawks escaped from captivity.[81] Ohio has a winter record of an adult

Swainson's Hawk photographed in Ottawa County on February 14, 1984.[373] Based on its unseasonal occurrence and several broken primaries, this hawk may have escaped from captivity and does not constitute an acceptable record for Ohio.[389]

RED-TAILED HAWK

Buteo jamaicensis (Gmelin)

As it effortlessly rides the midday thermals, a Red-tailed Hawk surveys its territory below. For most Red-taileds, this territory consists of open farmlands, grassy roadside edges, and successional fields. Wooded habitats are essential, especially tall mature trees where they place their bulky nests. The Red-tailed may soar high in the sky, enjoying its free ride over the countryside, but most hunting is performed from perches closer to the ground.

The sight of soaring Red-tailed Hawks is now a fairly common occurrence in most counties. Although regularly encountered, they are never numerous and summer totals seldom exceed 3–10. They are least numerous along the wooded hillsides of southeastern Ohio and in urban areas.

Their nests are normally placed at heights of thirty feet or more in tall trees. These nests may be reused for several years, with fresh material added before each attempt. The oldest nests often become prominent features of barren winter woodlots throughout Ohio. Nest construction has been reported as early as January 24 and may continue into April.[89] The first clutches may be laid by March 11–17, although most are initiated in late March or early April. Most young hatch in May and fledge by late June, although early nesting attempts produce fledglings by May 23.[523] Red-taileds may renest if their first clutch fails, producing nests with eggs through May 31 and recently fledged young in early August.[89]

While Red-tailed Hawks are presently our most numerous breeding buteo, they have not always had that status. They were widely distributed before 1900 but their numbers were greatly reduced by persecution and habitat destruction during the first decades of this century. Their populations reached their lowest levels in the 1920s and 1930s when Red-taileds were uncommon in southeastern Ohio and rare to locally absent elsewhere.[220,223] Their numbers slowly improved during the 1940s, although they remained locally rare in western Ohio into the early 1950s.[248] Substantially greater numbers were apparent after the mid-1950s and continued to increase through the late 1970s.[438]

Most of our Red-tailed Hawks are permanent residents. Some migrate south for the winter but the proportion of migratory pairs appears to be small. These resident birds are joined by sizable numbers migrating south from Canada and the upper Great Lakes states. Their fall migration is poorly defined and no sizable movements have been reported. The first migrants are detected by mid-September.[479] Most appear between October 15 and November 15 with a second noticeable influx during December.

As winter residents, Red-tailed Hawks are fairly common to

common throughout Ohio. Except in the extreme northeastern counties, wintering numbers are generally greater than the breeding population. As many as 10–20 Red-taileds may be observed daily in most counties, while 30–40+ are possible at favored localities such as the Ross-Pickaway County Line Road area and Killdeer Plains Wildlife Area. Wintering Red-taileds occupy the same open fields they regularly hunt during summer. Fallow fields and corn stubble are preferred, especially if bordered by wooded fencerows or woodlots.[41] These wintering hawks are very beneficial since they prey mainly on rodents and other small mammals.

With the return of moderate temperatures in late February or early March, Red-taileds begin their northward passage through Ohio. Their wintering numbers noticeably diminish within the interior counties by mid-March as the Red-taileds take advantage of southerly tailwinds to pass northward. While their inland spring migration is poorly defined, large numbers regularly pass along western Lake Erie. The first lakefront migrants appear by February 20–25 and the largest flights normally occur between March 7 and April 15. With favorable winds, 50–250+ may pass along the lakefront; the maximum was 406 on March 23, 1982.[365] Smaller numbers pass along the Central Basin, where few counts exceed 30–75. Smaller numbers pass along Lake Erie through May 10–20, usually in totals of 40 or fewer. These later migrants are almost exclusively immatures.

ROUGH-LEGGED HAWK

Buteo lagopus (Pontoppidan)

The best Ohio location to observe and study these winter residents is the Ross-Pickaway County Line Road near the village of Kingston. The extensive farm fields there have hosted wintering Rough-leggeds throughout this century. The area's grassy hayfields and pastures with abundant rodent populations provide an ideal wintering habitat for these hawks. Unlike Red-taileds, which normally hunt from tall perches, Rough-leggeds are adept at hunting on the wing or from the tiny upper branches of young saplings.

Near this road, Rough-legged Hawks are fairly common winter residents with totals of 5–15 daily. Unfortunately, there are few other locations where this attractive raptor can be regularly observed. Rough-leggeds are also fairly common winter residents at Killdeer Plains Wildlife Area and in fields along western Lake Erie. Daily totals are generally fewer than 6 at these locations. Elsewhere, they are rare to uncommon winter residents with most reports of 1–3. Wintering Rough-leggeds are most frequently reported from the northern half of the state and are least numerous in the southeastern counties along the Ohio River.

These wintering numbers are variable, reflecting the cyclical fluctuations of prey populations on their Arctic breeding grounds and in their Ohio winter territories. The combination of large numbers of breeding Rough-leggeds and sizable winter rodent populations within Ohio have produced several pronounced "flights." The largest may have occurred during the winter of 1964–65 when 50 Rough-leggeds were observed between Magee Marsh Wildlife Area and Port Clinton in Ottawa County.[89] Flights during the winters of 1974–75 and 1975–76 produced Christmas Bird Count totals of 72 and 87 Rough-leggeds, respectively, in the vicinity of Kingston. Other smaller flights were reported during the winters of 1929–30, four winters during the 1930s, and the winter of 1944–45.[89,479] Conversely, small breeding populations combined with a scarcity of rodents can cause this species to be relatively rare throughout Ohio.

Rough-legged Hawks are the only eastern buteos to regularly exhibit melanism. The black Rough-leggeds with their silver underwings are particularly appealing. Unfortunately, they compose only 10–25 percent of our wintering population. This proportion may increase during pronounced "flights," when melanistic birds may outnumber light-phased individuals.

While fall Rough-leggeds have been reported as early as late August, these records are considered doubtful in the absence of substantiating details. A few have been reported from the northern counties between September 20 and 30, but these early migrants are extremely rare. The first Rough-leggeds do not normally return until October 20–November 10. Their fall migration is mostly individuals filtering through the state. The only detectable movement usually accompanies the onset of harsh winter weather during the first half of December. However, many of these hawks do not establish territories and move elsewhere. Hence, numbers of wintering Rough-leggeds decline by January 5–10.

Their spring migration is equally poorly defined. Unlike many other hawks, Rough-leggeds are not afraid to migrate over open water and readily fly across Lake Erie rather than around it. No large movements have been reported along western Lake Erie. The largest flight totaled 20 over Lake County on April 27, 1919.[523] Spring Rough-leggeds regularly remain until April 5–15. Most later individuals are recorded along Lake Erie, where they occasionally linger into early May. The latest documented migrant passed over Ottawa County on May 27, 1979.[273]

Rough-leggeds are accidental summer visitors with only three records. Campbell[89] reported a Rough-legged on West Sister Island in western Lake Erie on June 16, 1948, but did not mention whether it was healthy. Another Rough-legged was reported from Cleveland on July 26, 1978, while an injured hawk was captured at Cincinnati on July 25, 1981.[362]

GOLDEN EAGLE

Aquila chrysaetos (Linnaeus)

Golden Eagles have always ranked among the rarest hawks visiting Ohio. In North America, this magnificent raptor is largely confined to the western half of the continent, where breeding pairs are widely distributed from Alaska south into Mexico. Only a few nesting pairs are known from eastern North America, where they are primarily migrants and winter residents.

Their historic status is obscured by the inability of early

observers to distinguish between Golden Eagles and the more numerous Bald Eagles. While there are nineteenth-century specimens to support some reports, the confirmed records are too few to determine their status before 1900. After 1900, these eagles were accidental or casual visitors. Trautman's report[479] of 7 Ohio specimens between 1922 and 1933 may be indicative of their relative abundance before 1940. The number of records remained fairly constant through the 1970s with five to eight sightings per decade. Numbers of Golden Eagles have increased since 1980, reflecting increases throughout eastern North America. They now produce one to five records each year.

Before 1940, the number of Golden Eagle winter records was nearly equal to the observations of migrants. Since 1940, their winter records have been reduced to only one or two confirmed sightings each decade. They are presently accidental residents, appearing any time between the last half of December and mid-February. They prefer upland locations but may be found near large lakes. Winter records usually are of singles, although 2 may have spent the winter of 1947–48 near Toledo.[89] They have been reported from scattered localities with most sightings from the northern and central counties.

In recent years, Golden Eagles are most likely to appear as spring migrants. Spring Goldens are rare but regular migrants along western Lake Erie, producing one to four records annually. They are casual spring migrants along central Lake Erie and accidental through all interior counties with three to six records away from western Lake Erie each decade. All spring reports are of 1–2 eagles. Early migrants have passed along Lake Erie by February 19 but they are not expected until the last half of March. These migrants are most likely to appear between April 10 and May 5 with stragglers through May 20.

Autumn migrants are casual along western Lake Erie and accidental elsewhere, producing three to six records each decade. They have been reliably reported by October 12 but most sightings are during November. A few Goldens may pass through Ohio into the first half of December. All fall sightings have been of single eagles.

There have been a few Golden Eagle reports during July and August, but none of these summer records has been acceptably substantiated. They most likely pertain to misidentified Bald Eagles.

AMERICAN KESTREL

Falco sparverius Linnaeus

The adaptable American Kestrels have thrived despite Ohio's changing land-use patterns. They undoubtedly increased as the virgin forests were replaced by open farmlands and have been widely distributed ever since. Their populations fluctuated during the twentieth century, with local declines attributed to a reduction in suitable nest sites. As natural cavities were reduced, kestrels quickly took advantage of man-made structures and are the only hawks regularly found along urban freeways, the intensively farmed fields of western Ohio, and the mixed rural habitats of the unglaciated counties.

While some kestrels maintain their territories throughout the year, most do not. Their status as uncommon to locally common permanent residents hides a fairly complex pattern of seasonal movements within the state.

As summer residents, American Kestrels are widely distributed in every county.[434] They are slightly less numerous in intensively cultivated western Ohio, becoming locally uncommon residents. Kestrels are generally fairly common to common elsewhere. Summer totals seldom exceed 5–12 before the young fledge in midsummer. These populations have increased since the mid-1960s, a trend evident throughout eastern North America.[438]

American Kestrels are our only hawks to nest in cavities. When natural cavities are unavailable, they utilize other sites, including nest boxes, eaves of buildings, freeway signs, Purple Martin houses, church steeples, and a squirrel nest.[299,417,471] Their courtship displays are observed as soon as warm temperatures return in late February and early March. Clutches are normally produced in April, although renesting attempts have been recorded through the last week of May. Within the southern counties, recently fledged young may appear by May 25–June 5 but elsewhere they are not normally evident until the last half of June.[479,523] Late broods have been recorded through August 27.[86]

Wintering kestrels are presently widely distributed, but somewhat less numerous in the snowbelt of northeastern Ohio. They are fairly common to common winter residents with 5–15 daily in most counties, although 20–35+ may be tallied in favorable habitats. Their winter numbers are greatest during December and early January. February declines are attributable to harsh weather some years, but similar declines have been noted during mild seasons.

Wintering kestrels are most numerous in open farmlands where fence posts, telephone wires, or tall trees provide convenient perches. They regularly hunt near rural residences.[41] They also show an affinity for the grassy rights-of-way along interstate highways. Hovering kestrels are a familiar winter sight along urban and rural highways, invariably facing into the wind as they search the grassy strips for rodents.

Since breeding and wintering kestrels are so numerous, their migratory movements are difficult to discern. Spring migrants are most evident along western Lake Erie, where they regularly follow the lakeshore. The first migrants appear by March 5–15, and migrants have been noted as late as May 10–20. Kestrels normally trickle along the lakefront at a rate of 1–10 daily. Sizable movements total 20–30+ on late March or April days with southwesterly winds. Within the interior counties, their spring migration is mostly an influx of resident pairs between February 20 and March 20.

Their southward migration begins during September and continues into December. This movement is poorly defined in September and October, and the first noticeable influx is usually apparent between November 1 and 15. Another influx normally occurs between November 25 and December 15 and is largely composed of wintering individuals. Fall totals normally are fewer than 10 kestrels except during influxes, when 15–30+ may be recorded.

MERLIN

Falco columbarius Linnaeus

Slightly larger than kestrels but considerably more powerful and graceful in flight, Merlins look like miniature Peregrines as they deftly chase a flock of shorebirds over a mudflat. Migrant Merlins are occupants of open marshes, fields, and shorelines, usually providing unsatisfactory glimpses of small fleet falcons disappearing across the countryside. On rare occasions, they hunt from tall perches, warily scanning the terrain below for shorebirds, songbirds, or other suitable prey to be captured after a short but spectacular chase.

Merlins have always been rare migrants through Ohio. Along with several other hawks, their populations declined during the 1950s and 1960s as a result of pesticide contamination. Their populations rebounded after the pesticides were banned and returned to normal during the 1980s.

Merlins are now rare but regular spring migrants along Lake Erie, where there are usually one to four sightings each year. Away from the lakefront they are accidental to casual migrants, mostly encountered within the glaciated counties. These inland migrants are reliably reported during five to seven years each decade with no more than three sightings in any year. The earliest spring Merlins appeared between February 20 and 25 but there are relatively few records before March 10–20. They are mostly observed between March 20 and May 10. A few late migrants may linger, and Campbell[89] recorded a migrant along western Lake Erie on June 6, 1943. Most records are solitary Merlins, although 2–3 have been recorded along Lake Erie.

Fall Merlins are rare migrants along Lake Erie with one to five reports annually. They are accidental to casual visitors to the interior counties, least numerous along the unglaciated Allegheny Plateau. While they do not regularly appear at any inland location, Merlins normally produce one to four inland sightings each autumn. The earliest fall migrant was reported along western Lake Erie on August 23, 1942.[89] They do not normally return until September 7–15. These migrants are mostly detected between September 15 and October 20 with scattered records into the last half of November. All fall reports are of 1–2 Merlins.

Their winter status within Ohio is considerably obscured by many misidentifications on Christmas Bird Counts. The relatively few satisfactory records indicate that Merlins are accidental to casual winter visitors. These records, scattered across the glaciated counties, are invariably of single individuals. Most December Merlins are observed for only one or two days and subsequently disappear. They may be very late fall migrants. One Merlin spent the entire winter in the Cuyahoga Valley National Recreation Area (Summit County) in 1985–86.[381]

At one time, Ohio may have hosted a small breeding population within the extreme northeastern counties. Kirtland reported a nesting pair in Cuyahoga County before 1858, including specimens of 2 juveniles.[523] During the present century, summering Merlins were reported from the Rocky River gorge in Cuyahoga County in 1923 and 1934 and along the Grand River gorge in Lake and Ashtabula Counties and the Conneaut Creek gorge in Ashtabula County between 1928 and 1932.[215,220,523]

Few details are available for these sightings and the identifications may be questionable. Hicks[215] said there were fourteen summer records from Ashtabula County, including "an immature," but no nest was discovered. In fact, there are no indisputable breeding records from Ohio. No summering Merlins have been reported since 1934. If a small breeding population once existed, it apparently disappeared during the 1930s.

PEREGRINE FALCON

Falco peregrinus Tunstall

No other raptor produces the excitement generated by a hunting Peregrine. Its stoop is awe-inspiring, while its speed, maneuverability, and raw power are unrivaled as it pursues its intended victim over marsh or lake. Most birds are extremely wary of this fleet falcon, and its presence is frequently detected by the panic-stricken flight of waterfowl and shorebirds before the soaring Peregrine comes into view.

At one time, this magnificent raptor appeared doomed to extinction in North America. Its breeding populations were decimated by pesticide contamination between the 1940s and 1960s, resulting in the disappearance of the subspecies nesting in the eastern United States and southern Canada. This decline produced a substantial reduction in the numbers passing through Ohio. Campbell[89] cited fifty-two records from Toledo between 1927 and 1939 but only one record annually between 1940 and 1967. Fortunately, Peregrines slowly recovered after use of these pesticides was banned during the 1960s.

Migrant Peregrines have always been less numerous during spring. They are regularly observed along western Lake Erie as rare migrants, averaging three to six sightings annually during the 1980s. Peregrine Falcons are accidental to casual migrants elsewhere, least numerous in the southern and unglaciated counties. While migrants do not regularly appear at any central Lake Erie or inland site, usually 1–3 Peregrines are reported away from western Lake Erie each spring. All spring records have been of single falcons.

Before the eastern subspecies was extirpated, spring Peregrines were regularly recorded between February 25 and March 20.[479] With the disappearance of this subspecies, their migration tends to be later. Early migrants now appear during the last week of March, although they do not normally return until April 5–15. Most spring migrants are detected between April 20 and May 15 with a few lingering through the end of the month.

Peregrine Falcons have always been accidental summer visitors. Before 1940, the only summer record was provided by a Peregrine at Cedar Point Wildlife Refuge (Lucas County) on July 31, 1930.[89] There were no additional summer records until the mid-1980s when introduced Peregrines began to appear within the state.

Their fall migration timing also changed with the disappearance of the eastern subspecies. Before 1940, a few fall Peregrines appeared during the last half of August and they were regularly observed along Lake Erie by September 5–10.

In recent years, August sightings are nonexistent and very few Peregrines have been detected before September 15–20. Most fall migrants pass through Ohio between September 25 and October 20 with infrequent late Peregrines through mid-November.

These migrants are most numerous along Lake Erie, becoming rare within the Central Basin and rare to uncommon west of Huron. They average five to eight or more sightings annually, mostly of isolated individuals, although 2–3 are occasionally reported from the western Lake Erie marshes. Fall Peregrines are accidental to casual migrants through the interior counties, where they are most frequently noted at large reservoirs or marshes where waterfowl and shorebirds congregate. There are generally three to seven or more inland sightings each autumn, invariably of single falcons. These migrants are least numerous within the southern and unglaciated counties.

Peregrines are accidental visitors into December and early January within the glaciated counties. There are very few confirmed sightings after January 10. Virtually all substantiated wintering falcons were reported before 1940. Most were recorded in large cities, where they roosted on downtown buildings and subsisted on a diet of pigeons.[248]

Within the past decade, a number of eastern states have attempted to establish breeding Peregrine Falcons. No falcons were released in Ohio, but released Peregrines from adjacent states have been noted within our boundaries, frequently at unexpected dates when native Peregrines are not present. A few released Peregrines have established winter territories in large cities. A pair has resided in downtown Toledo since 1986 and raised two young in 1988. If Peregrines are reestablished in eastern North America, their status and distribution within Ohio may change considerably.

GYRFALCON

Falco rusticolus Linnaeus

Gyrfalcons are residents of the Arctic tundra across North America and Eurasia. While most stay there throughout the year, small numbers irregularly wander southward during winter. A few regularly appear in the upper Great Lakes states and Canada, occasionally wandering south to New England and the lower Great Lakes.[5]

Within Ohio, Gyrfalcons are casual winter visitors along western Lake Erie, where there are at least seven confirmed records since 1950 and an equal number of unconfirmed sightings. They prefer the western Lake Erie marshes with their open flat terrain and abundant waterfowl. They are accidental visitors elsewhere with substantiated records of specimens collected in Fayette County on January 30, 1907,[201] and Wood County on December 10, 1942,[89] and a sight record at Lorain on October 22, 1983.[372] There are also unverified sightings from Youngstown, Hamilton County, and near Coldwater (Mercer County). Most appear between November 20 and January 30.

There are few records of migrant Gyrfalcons from Ohio. Both fall sightings are during October: the one from Lorain and a

very early migrant in Lucas County on October 3, 1971.[90] The only spring records are singles observed along western Lake Erie March 14, 1982, and March 26, 1967.[89,365]

PRAIRIE FALCON

Falco mexicanus Schlegel

Prairie Falcons are normally associated with the vast open plains of western North America from southern Canada south into Mexico. In recent years, they have been rare but regular winter visitors east to Iowa, Missouri, and Illinois but accidental farther east.[5]

Ohio has one confirmed record that fits this established pattern of vagrancy. A wounded Prairie Falcon was recovered from the Rickenbacker Air Force Base in southern Franklin County on January 21, 1983.[369] It was captured and transported to the Ohio State University Veterinary School for rehabilitation, and its fresh plumage and antagonistic behavior toward people were indicative of a wild falcon.

There is one additional published sight record. A Prairie Falcon was discovered entangled in a fence and captured near Oberlin, Lorain County, on September 20, 1940.[245] The bird's plumage and behavior were not described, however, and whether or not this individual was correctly identified or had escaped from captivity cannot be ascertained.

GRAY PARTRIDGE

Perdix perdix (Linnaeus)

In the early 1900s, populations of native Ohio game birds were greatly reduced. Wild Turkeys and Greater Prairie-Chickens were extirpated, Ruffed Grouse were restricted to the southeastern counties, and Northern Bobwhite fluctuated erratically in response to severe winter weather. Only introduced Ring-necked Pheasants were thriving. Having succeeded with pheasant introductions, Ohio wildlife personnel introduced Gray Partridge to establish another game species in the state.

Approximately 2000 Gray Partridges were liberated statewide between 1909 and 1916. These partridges quickly disappeared from southern and eastern Ohio but thrived in the northwestern and west-central counties. Following a rapid increase, the first hunting season was declared in 1917.[517] Additional releases between 1924 and 1930 totaled 7000 partridges.[220] These releases resulted in increased numbers in western Ohio but did not establish sustained populations in southern and eastern Ohio.

Ohio Gray Partridges undoubtedly peaked during the early 1930s. Densities estimated at 25+ birds per square mile were recorded in portions of Fulton, Lucas, Defiance, Henry, Wood, Paulding, Putnam, Hancock, Van Wert, and Allen Counties.[220] Elsewhere in western Ohio, partridges were locally distributed and uncommon to rare in every county east to Erie, Crawford, and Delaware and south to Preble, Montgomery, Clinton, and Highland. These numbers were maintained through 1937 but noticeably decreased by 1940 despite additional releases of 8420 partridges in western Ohio. An estimated 110,000 remained in autumn 1939.[516]

Partridge populations declined rapidly during the 1940s. By 1948, they virtually disappeared from northwestern Ohio. Most remaining partridges were locally distributed in Madison, Fayette, Champaign, Clark, Miami, and Darke Counties.[517] These remnant populations quietly disappeared during the 1950s and early 1960s. Their disappearance is partially obscured by reintroduction efforts during the 1960s,[471] producing sightings near Utica (Licking County) through 1965 and at Lake St. Mary's in 1969. Elsewhere, the last partridges were reported from Toledo in 1962,[89] Dayton in 1966,[299] and Madison County in January 1968. Local landowners indicated they remained in Madison County into the early 1970s. Reports from west-central Ohio during the 1980s were of several birds released by landowners.[434] Barring further reintroductions, Gray Partridges have become extirpated within Ohio.

Gray Partridges were occupants of open farmlands, preferring flat or rolling terrain with sandy soils, numerous shrubby fencerows, and grasslands interspersed among small farm fields.[516] They tolerated severe winter weather as long as adequate food could be secured. Most nests were in pastures and hayfields. When suitable grasslands were unavailable, Gray Partridges nested along roadsides and ditches and in small fallow fields. Nesting normally began during the first half of May and most young hatched during the last half of June and early July. Their nesting success was generally low. Most nests in hayfields were destroyed by mowing and predation rates were high along roadsides.[516] Renesting attempts were frequent, resulting in nests with eggs as late as August 9.[31]

Why did Gray Partridges disappear from Ohio? Changing agricultural land-use patterns was the most prominent factor. The trend toward large fields devoted to corn and soybean monocultures largely eliminated their preferred habitat. Clay soils posed additional problems: following rains, clay particles frequently encased their feet in mud balls, reducing their mobility and producing excessive mortality of small chicks. Simply stated, Gray Partridges were not suited for Ohio's changing habitats during the twentieth century.

RING-NECKED PHEASANT

Phasianus colchicus Linnaeus

This gaudy game bird was introduced after populations of our native grouse, quail, and turkeys were severely depleted or extirpated during the late 1800s. The first Ring-necked Pheasants were released in 1896 and became established in ten counties by 1903.[236] In 1913, state agencies undertook an ambitious program to establish Ring-necked Pheasants throughout Ohio. Large numbers were liberated in all portions of the state, estimated at 10,000–25,000 each year between 1923 and 1935.[220,291] These releases established sizable populations in some counties but failed where suitable habitats were unavailable.

Ring-necked Pheasants peaked during the late 1930s and early 1940s.[291] They were common to abundant residents in western Ohio from Fulton, Lucas, and Ottawa Counties south to Hardin, Union, and Marion Counties. Estimates of 35,500 pheasants in Lucas County and 175,000+ in Wood County during 1939 provide an indication of their sizable populations.[86,89] They were generally common permanent residents east to Cuyahoga and Wayne Counties, and south to Preble, Greene, Fayette, and Pickaway Counties. Pheasants became uncommon to rare in other northeastern and southwestern counties.[291] Although they were also released within the unglaciated counties, permanent populations never became established. Hicks[223] considered them uncommon to fairly common residents in Coshocton, Tuscarawas, and Pike Counties. In other unglaciated counties, they were mostly observed only immediately following releases.

By the mid-1940s, pheasants were declining despite annual releases. Among the contributing factors, changing agricultural land-use practices was the most important. The trend toward large fields devoted to cultivated crops eliminated many pastures and hayfields occupied by nesting pheasants. Remaining hayfields were subject to more frequent mowing, increasing mortality of incubating females and destroying many nests. Fall plowing reduced the amount of food available during winter. These factors, combined with excessive mortality during the severe winters of the 1970s, reduced pheasants to a fraction of their former abundance.

Even though numbers are greatly reduced, the Ring-necked Pheasant's breeding range has not changed appreciably since the 1940s. They are presently uncommon to fairly common residents in northwestern and west-central Ohio and rare to locally uncommon in the northeastern and southwestern counties.[434] They are absent from the southwestern counties bordering the Ohio River. Daily totals seldom exceed 3–12 pheasants. Along the unglaciated Allegheny Plateau, small populations exist in portions of Coshocton, Holmes, Tuscarawas, Carroll, and Jefferson Counties, where pheasants are locally rare to uncommon. They are absent from other unglaciated counties.

Pheasants are most numerous in flat open farmlands where grassy fields and cultivated crops are interspersed with woodlots. They seldom enter wooded habitats except to find cover during severe winter weather. Pheasants are usually associated with grasslands and fallow fields. They regularly feed in harvested grainfields in autumn and winter but usually do not wander far from cover.

During winter, pheasants frequently associate in loose flocks composed of a few males and many females. When populations were larger, winter flocks of 25–50+ were not unusual in western Ohio. With the approach of spring, these flocks break up and breeding activities are initiated. The males attempt to mate with as many females as can be attracted by their courtship displays. After mating, the females search for suitable cover for their nests, preferring hayfields and lightly grazed pastures, although they also nest along roadsides, ditch banks, and fencerows and in wheatfields. The first clutches may be laid in late April but most are produced during the first half of May. These clutches normally hatch by mid-June and young pheasants remain with the hens into August. Their nesting success is fairly poor; many nests are lost to predators or mowing of hayfields and roadsides.[291] Females will renest, producing nests with eggs through August 4 and partially grown young through mid-September.[417]

Since Ring-necked Pheasants are still released each year, it is doubtful they will disappear from Ohio in the near future. In most counties, however, their outlook is not bright. Today's farmlands provide marginal habitats with critical shortages of suitable grasslands for nesting and cover and food for wintering pheasants. These trends are not irreversible, but it is doubtful that the immense populations of the 1930s and 1940s will ever be reestablished.

RUFFED GROUSE

Bonasa umbellus (Linnaeus)

"With the warm days of late March, small groups of grouse which have wintered together, disperse," F. B. Chapman and colleagues noted in 1952.

The males begin to drum and courtship is under way. The most spectacular event of courtship is the drumming by the cock Ruffed Grouse. Standing on a fallen log, rock, or other prominence, he beats the air rapidly with his wings with a forward and upward movement that produces a sound not unlike the "thump, thump, thump" of a far distant farm tractor. When approached by the female bird who has been attracted from her wintering territory not far away, the male bird often deserts the drumming log, and struts slowly and deliberately toward his prospective mate with tail spread fanwise and the black "ruffs" on the neck puffed out to the fullest extent.[93]

To experience these displays, one must visit the woodlands of eastern Ohio. Ruffed Grouse are locally rare to fairly common residents east of a line extending through eastern Cuyahoga, Medina, Wayne, Richland, Knox, Licking, Fairfield, Ross, Highland, Brown, and Clermont Counties.[461] In northeastern Ohio, grouse are most numerous in Geauga, Ashtabula, and Trumbull Counties but are rare and declining elsewhere. They are widely distributed along the unglaciated Allegheny Plateau except for areas extensively disturbed by strip mining. They become rare and very locally distributed in adjacent glaciated areas. The only recent expansion into glaciated Ohio was evident in portions of Adams, Brown, and southern Clermont Counties.[461]

Ruffed Grouse were not always restricted to eastern Ohio. When the state was initially settled, grouse were sparingly distributed throughout the mature virgin forests. After 1800, the transformation of these forests into younger woodlands was beneficial for grouse. Their populations increased dramatically and peaked between 1850 and 1875.[483] Habitat destruction and market hunting exacted a tremendous toll as their numbers sharply declined by 1885. After market hunting ceased, habitat destruction continued to decimate populations. Grouse disappeared from Lake St. Mary's prior to 1900,[98] Seneca County in 1892,[195] and Buckeye Lake and Lorain County

by 1900.[236,479] With their disappearance from Toledo by 1908,[89] grouse were virtually extirpated from glaciated western and central Ohio.

Grouse were scarce in eastern Ohio during the first decades of the twentieth century. In the 1920s and 1930s, many abandoned farms were reverting to brushy habitats and woodlands, allowing their populations to recover. By 1952, they were reestablished throughout their present range.[93] At the same time, small remnant populations in Butler and Warren Counties disappeared.[461]

In addition to this natural recovery, the Ohio Division of Wildlife attempted to reestablish grouse in northwestern Ohio. Small numbers were released in the Oak Openings of Lucas and Fulton Counties and on Kelleys Island during the 1950s. These releases produced regular sightings through the mid-1960s.[89] However, the absence of recent records indicates these introductions were not successful.

Since the early 1970s, grouse populations have been reasonably stable, although recent evidence suggests that Ohio grouse may be subject to cyclical fluctuations in abundance. Although long-term data are unavailable to conclusively establish these trends, indices of grouse abundance show relatively high numbers during the early 1970s and early 1980s followed by sharp declines in the mid-1970s and mid-1980s.[461] These cyclical fluctuations occur independently of hunting pressure and habitat changes.

Grouse are most numerous in young second-growth deciduous woods supporting dense bushes and tangles interspersed with scattered openings. They are seldom found more than a short flight from dense cover. In winter, grouse prefer woodlands with dense honeysuckle and greenbrier tangles and a few conifers.[93] Lower hillsides and valley slopes are preferred over dry ridges.

In mature woods or other marginal habitats, Ruffed Grouse are normally encountered as widely scattered individuals. In preferred habitats, totals of 15–20+ are possible. While they are mostly observed as individuals, small groups of 3–10 may be noted in prime cover during winter.

On calm mornings in mid-March, male grouse begin their courtship. The low thumps of drumming grouse vibrate across southeastern Ohio during late March and April and sometimes into early June. Most females mate during April. Full clutches have been reported as early as April 10, although most nests are initiated during late April and May. Most young hatch in June.[93] Reproductive success is greatest during warm dry summers; cool wet weather during June can cause extensive mortality of young grouse.

During fall, the family groups break up as the grouse move to their winter territories. Similar movements occur in spring when they wander in search of suitable breeding habitats. These birds seldom move more than two miles and are considered permanent residents. An occasional grouse may wander considerable distances and appear in unlikely places. There are at least two recent records from Cincinnati, Columbus, and Cleveland. One of the Columbus records was a grouse captured in a garage. In Cleveland, a grouse appeared in a small downtown park along the lakefront.[275]

GREATER PRAIRIE-CHICKEN

Tympanuchus cupido (Linnaeus)

No other native game bird matches the ritualistic spring court-ship displays of the Greater Prairie-Chicken. With the advent of warm weather in late March, groups of 10–30 males assemble on their display grounds, patches of bare soil and short grasses which these grassland grouse have used for decades. Their courtship antics are best described by Oberholser:

At dawn and dusk, males dance, boom, and spar. Frenzied birds space themselves about ten yards apart. Each cock inflates the golden air sacs on his neck, erects and spreads his tail, and raises the neck tufts as he stamps madly on the ground, booms loudly, springs, and whirls in the air, and intermittently charges his neighboring rivals. Usually one or two males mate with most of the hens which are attracted to the edge of the display ground.[356]

These displays were undoubtedly witnessed by the first set-tlers inhabiting prairie openings in Williams, Fulton, Lucas, and Wood Counties in northwestern Ohio and the scattered prairies in Erie, Crawford, Wyandot, Marion, Union, Madison, Fayette, and Pickaway Counties.[220] Anecdotal accounts from the southwestern and west-central counties are probably in-accurate. In the 1830s, these prairie-chickens were apparently numerous in the northwestern counties, although they were probably rare and very locally distributed in north-central and central Ohio.[251] Near Toledo, Campbell[89] cited historical ac-counts of "more than 500" and "thousands" of prairie-chick-ens, apparently during the 1830s, an indication of the sizable numbers in some northwestern counties.

Despite these substantial populations, there is virtually no information concerning their life history within Ohio. Greater Prairie-Chickens were permanent residents and undoubtedly nested, although no nests were ever described. Nesting was probably initiated during April and broods appeared during May and early June.

As their name implies, prairie-chickens were restricted to extensive grasslands, a habitat preference responsible for their demise within Ohio and perilous decline throughout most of their range. As the original prairies were converted to cultivated fields, the prairie-chickens disappeared. Their decline appar-ently occurred during a span of only several decades. The last Greater Prairie-Chicken in central Ohio was reported "seven miles west of Columbus" on November 16, 1868.[521] The pop-ulations in northern Ohio largely disappeared by the 1870s, with only a few isolated sightings as late as 1880.[89] This species was undoubtedly extirpated before 1900.

Beginning in 1925, scattered reports by hunters and local landowners indicated that prairie-chickens had returned to Ohio. The few documented reports included sightings from Ottawa County in 1928, Lucas County in 1932 and 1934, and Wood County in 1934,[89,478] apparently isolated and wandering individuals. The assertion by Hicks[220] of "reestablished pop-ulations in Fulton, Henry, and Wood Counties" is almost cer-tainly an exaggeration. These birds probably wandered south from Michigan, where prairie-chickens were still well estab-lished. This range expansion was short-lived; no Greater Prai-rie-Chickens were reported from northwestern Ohio after 1934. Reintroductions were attempted in Marion County during 1933 and nesting was reported in 1934 and 1935.[220] These birds disappeared by 1937 and no other reintroductions have been attempted.

WILD TURKEY

Meleagris gallopavo Linnaeus

"In all the United States," A. M. Wright[525] declared, "no state had more turkeys than Ohio and her neighbors." If anecdotal accounts by the first settlers are to be believed, a phenomenal number of Wild Turkeys must have inhabited Ohio during the eighteenth century. They were regularly encountered in flocks of 30–50+ during winter and as scattered individuals at other times of the year.

As soon as the first permanent settlers arrived, turkeys began to decline. Unrestricted harvests decimated populations; by 1822, turkeys were scarce near Chillicothe. Ten years later, none could be found near Mansfield.[525] Similar local extirpa-tions were apparent elsewhere. By the 1850s, habitat destruc-tion in combination with overharvesting resulted in the extir-pation of Wild Turkeys from most counties. They were already scarce in the Cleveland area by 1864 with very few reliable reports in subsequent years.[523] Turkeys were scarce in south-western Ohio after 1845, disappearing from Warren County in the early 1860s and Cincinnati before 1870.[289,299] In central Ohio, the last sightings from Buckeye Lake were between 1853 and 1870.[479] Despite their declining populations, no attempts were made to prevent their extirpation. The last northeastern Ohio records were from Ashtabula County about 1880.[215] In northwestern Ohio, they disappeared from Seneca County by 1880,[195] Paulding County about 1880–85,[424] and Toledo by 1892.[89] Their extirpation from the southern counties was poorly de-scribed, but Henninger[193] thought they disappeared from Scioto and Pike Counties before 1900. Wild Turkeys were almost cer-tainly extirpated from Ohio before 1900.

In an attempt to reestablish turkey populations, wild birds were transplanted into suitable habitats and protected until breeding populations developed. The first Wild Turkeys were released in southeastern Ohio in February 1956.[109] Similar re-leases were made in every subsequent year, and sizable pop-ulations were eventually established in the southeastern coun-ties.[110] Turkeys were also released within glaciated Ohio, initially in Ashtabula County with additional releases in central and western counties. Their eventual statewide distribution de-pends upon the ability of turkeys to succeed in rural farmlands of glaciated Ohio.

Wild Turkeys are presently established along the unglaciated Allegheny Plateau and very locally in northeastern Ohio. Within the southeastern counties, turkeys are rare to locally fairly com-mon residents north to Hocking, Perry, Morgan, and Athens

Counties. They are most numerous in portions of Hocking, Vinton, Ross, Pike, Adams, and Scioto Counties, where 3–10+ males are regularly heard on warm spring mornings and winter flocks of 15–40+ may be encountered. Turkeys are equally numerous near Mohican State Forest in portions of Ashland and Holmes Counties. They are generally rare to uncommon in other unglaciated counties, with spring totals of 1–3 males and winter flocks of 15 or fewer. In northeastern Ohio, Wild Turkeys are rare residents in southwestern Ashtabula County and adjacent portions of Geauga and Trumbull Counties. Based on surveys of gobbling males and estimates of their occupied range, Donohoe et al.[110] estimated that 7,677 turkeys resided in Ohio during 1982. Greater numbers are probably present today.

During winter, most turkeys congregate in flocks composed of several hens, their broods, and a number of adult males. These flocks roam across a territory of several square miles searching for food in woodlands, pastures, and harvested cornfields. When the weather is particularly severe, they may visit feedlots to feed among domestic livestock.

While some flocks remain intact through mid-April, most break apart by the last days of March. Male turkeys become intent on acquiring a harem, and dominant males are frequently surrounded by 5–8+ females. Most first-year males seldom, if ever, mate. The males maintain their breeding territories into May and are still gobbling on warm calm mornings through mid-May but normally fall silent before the end of the month.

During the breeding season, male turkeys are normally found within extensive woodlands. Females with their broods occupy deciduous woods but also visit woodland edges and occasionally pastures and other open fields. Most female turkeys are fertilized by April 15–25 and immediately lay eggs in nests located on the ground in dense cover, frequently at woodland edges. For such a large bird, their nests are surprisingly difficult to locate. Most clutches hatch in late May or early June and the young remain with the hen throughout summer and fall. Renesting attempts have produced recently hatched young through the last week of June. Like other gallinaceous birds, young turkeys acquire the ability to fly at an early age and can follow their mother into trees when necessary to avoid people or predators.

NORTHERN BOBWHITE

Colinus virginianus (Linnaeus)

Northern Bobwhites were probably absent from Ohio until the nineteenth century. The creation of open farmlands combined with a series of relatively mild winters allowed them to expand into the Great Lakes region during the 1840s and 1850s.[104] By the 1860s, bobwhites were established in most counties and their whistled calls were familiar sounds in Ohio's farmlands.

Their statewide population peaked between 1875 and 1900. Anecdotal accounts indicated that remarkable numbers inhabited most counties. Terms such as "very common" and "abundant" described bobwhites at Buckeye Lake and Lake St. Mary's,[98,479] while Campbell[89] cited 1000 at Toledo in 1893. This abundance resulted from very favorable land-use practices. Farm fields were small with interspersed grasslands and cultivated crops bordered by brushy fencerows and woodland edges, nearly ideal quail habitats.

Bobwhite populations fluctuated considerably during the first decades of the twentieth century. The first major decline was noted in 1912–13, followed by declines in the winters of 1917–18 and 1928–29.[249,479] These declines were largely the result of excessive mortality during severe winter weather. Unfavorable weather during the nesting season also reduced reproductive success. However, these declines generally lasted for only a few years.

Following the severe winter of 1928–29, bobwhites gradually increased and reached their "peak for the present century" in 1935. At that time, Hicks[220] described them as common to abundant residents in most counties, least numerous in extreme northeastern Ohio. He estimated their statewide abundance at 20 pairs per square mile, while winter totals of 50–100+ were frequently noted in southern and central Ohio.

Severe weather during the 1935–36 winter decimated quail populations, and such large densities have not been attained since then.[29] Cyclical fluctuations between "high" and "low" populations continued during the 1940s and 1950s, but each population peak was achieved at progressively smaller densities. As Trautman[479] predicted in 1940, declining numbers were inevitable as agricultural land use became more intensive. Increased field size, removal of fencerows, conversion of grasslands to cultivated crops, and fall plowing substantially reduced quail populations. Along the unglaciated Allegheny Plateau, secondary succession also contributed to this decline.

By 1960, Northern Bobwhites became uncommon and very locally distributed residents in northern Ohio.[89,335] They were common only within some southern counties. These populations continued to decline in the 1960s and early 1970s, especially in the western counties. Remaining quail populations were virtually eliminated by the harsh winters of 1976–78. Their numbers declined by more than 90 percent and bobwhites essentially disappeared except for small locally distributed populations in the southern and eastern counties. Fortunately, the following winters were not so severe and the population has slowly recovered.

Northern Bobwhites are now uncommon to fairly common residents of southern Ohio from Scioto and Pike Counties west to Hamilton and Butler Counties. Calling bobwhites are regularly heard during summer and 5–12+ may be counted daily in May and June. Coveys are regularly flushed during winter when daily totals of 20–30+ are possible. Bobwhites are also very locally distributed in eastern Ohio south of the snowbelt. They are generally rare in most eastern counties, becoming locally uncommon residents of Mahoning, Columbiana, Belmont, Monroe, Lawrence, and Meigs Counties. Throughout eastern Ohio, 1–8 may be tallied daily during summer. They are still largely absent from the remainder of Ohio, becoming locally rare in a few western and central counties where isolated pairs survive in favorable habitats.

Being sedentary, bobwhites cannot recover rapidly once

populations are reduced to extremely low levels. Moreover, they raise only one brood annually. Their nests are placed on the ground, usually in pastures, hayfields, and fallow fields. Most clutches are laid during May and early June. While recently hatched young have been reported as early as April 27,[523] they are expected between mid-June and mid-August. Bobwhites renest until they successfully hatch a brood. Nests with eggs are possible through the first half of August, and recently hatched young have been reported through mid-September. Extremely late broods were discovered on October 7 at Salem and November 1 at Dayton.[299,506]

What does the future hold for Northern Bobwhites in Ohio? As Kendeigh stated:

The whole problem of increasing the population of Bobwhite reduces down to the establishment and expansion of habitat areas containing suitable cover and food. . . . where given proper protection and habitat, and when the climate is favorable, the species is capable of rather rapidly increasing its numbers by natural reproduction. With the increase in abundance, the birds must of necessity expand their areas into new and favorable regions.[249]

Unless trends are reversed, bobwhites may be largely restricted to southern and eastern Ohio in future years.

YELLOW RAIL

Coturnicops noveboracensis (Gmelin)

Few birds are as elusive and secretive as Yellow Rails. Experts at hiding in grasses and sedges, they normally forage under dense vegetation and are rarely observed at the exposed edges of marshes. When disturbed, they would rather run than take flight and easily disappear under thick cover. Considerable luck is required to catch a glimpse of this shy bird as it vanishes into cover or flutters weakly over a marsh.

The status of Yellow Rails within Ohio is not precisely known. Given their wintering grounds along the Gulf Coast and breeding range extending from northern Michigan and Minnesota to Hudson Bay,[5] they undoubtedly pass through Ohio each spring and fall. However, only a small percentage of migrant rails will ever be detected.

Most migrant Yellow Rails are reported during spring, with an average of one to three sightings annually. They are accidental to casual visitors to most counties except unglaciated Ohio, where there are no published records. While migrants have been reported between March 31 and May 31,[98,117] they usually occur in two peaks. The first extends between April 15 and May 5 and may include birds in passage to more southerly nesting grounds. The second peak, May 15–30, may be rails breeding in northern Canada. Two factors are responsible for the preponderance of spring records. First, Yellow Rails are more likely to be calling during this season. Second, vegetation within their preferred wet meadows is not as dense and the rails are slightly more visible.

Yellow Rails average only one report every two to four years

during autumn. They probably return in August and depart by mid-October, although most records are during October. There are two November reports: an injured bird captured at Dayton on November 8, 1975, and a sight record from LaDue Reservoir (Geauga County) on November 11, 1979.[275,299] Their fall distribution pattern is similar to spring. Fall migrants occasionally appear in unlikely habitats. There are several records of Yellow Rails flushed from dry hayfields. During 1952 and 1954, they were also discovered in a cultivated cornfield near Oxford (Butler County).[340,346] As many as 7 Yellow Rails may have been present in this field during 1952.

At one time, Yellow Rails may have been very local and rare summer residents at several extensive sedge meadows, but their status cannot be accurately assessed from the few records. The only nest was collected in Pickaway County during 1909.[220] Breeding was indicated at the former Pymatuning Bog, where an adult was observed in July 1928 and a "half grown immature" on August 9, 1932.[215] An adult was killed in the former Huron Bog (Huron County) on July 16, 1928, but nesting was not confirmed.[220] The only recent summer record was provided by a calling rail in Lake County between June 25 and July 5, 1944.[523]

BLACK RAIL

Laterallus jamaicensis (Gmelin)

The smallest and most elusive of all rails, Black Rails are very seldom observed in the dense wetland vegetation where they prefer to live. They readily walk under matted grasses and easily disappear among cattails. While the males produce a distinctive kick-kee-doo quite unlike the calls of other rails, Blacks are vocal only at night. Even tape-recorded calls may not persuade them to venture away from dense cover.

There are few satisfactory sightings of Black Rails from Ohio, and thus their distribution and relative abundance have never been conclusively established. The first records were 7 specimens collected from Hamilton County between 1890 and 1893, all in May.[248] Twentieth-century records are of widely scattered individuals, averaging one to four reports each decade. These rails have been recorded from all portions of the state except the unglaciated counties and are accidental visitors throughout Ohio.

Most Black Rails are discovered during spring, with at least thirteen modern sightings in addition to the nineteenth-century specimens. The few confirmed spring Black Rails appear anytime during April and May without a defined pattern to their movements.

The only documented summer record is provided by a singing male in Lucas County June 15–23, 1980,[278] but sightings at Buckeye Lake on June 10, 1923, and Mentor Marsh (Lake County) on July 21, 1965, are also probably accurate.[335,479] Summer records from Lake St. Mary's in 1912 and 1915 are based on less than satisfactory evidence. These sightings are of single individuals and nesting has never been established. Nevertheless, Black Rails could conceivably breed within Ohio. At one time, a small and locally distributed summer population was established in several midwestern states.[5] Nesting Black Rails are most likely to be discovered in extensive wet meadows and wetlands dominated by grasses and sedges where standing water is only several inches deep. Attempts to locate this species should be limited to nighttime when Black Rails are most active and vocal.

Black Rails are least numerous as fall migrants. There are only three published sight records, two in the Toledo area and one in Paulding County;[89,426] all were single individuals observed between August 30 and October 1.

KING RAIL

Rallus elegans Audubon

The largest of our resident rails, Kings are as adept at hiding in marshlands as their smaller brethren. When undisturbed, they can be surprisingly tame and may forage at the edge of a marsh for many minutes. Except when they are nesting, King Rails are also very vocal; their deep hoarse calls formerly resonated across Ohio wetlands. As described by Trautman:

In the dusk of spring evenings the reiterated "umph-umph-umph" note could be heard coming from the swamps and marshes, and often the birds, presumably the males, could be seen uttering their calls. It was interesting to watch them as they stood in some small opening in the marsh or swamp, or under a rosebush or blackberry bush, and emphasized each "umph" with a grotesque jerk of the head.[479]

Although it is difficult to believe today, King Rails were once the most numerous nesting rails in many Ohio counties. In the mid-1930s, they were widely distributed within the western Lake Erie marshes, where Campbell[86] considered them common summer residents. In suitable inland marshes, King Rails became locally common. Trautman[479] estimated 45–50 pairs breeding at Buckeye Lake, while similar numbers were reported from Lake St. Mary's.[98] Elsewhere within the northern and central counties, they were rarely encountered as isolated pairs, with breeding records from forty-two counties south to Darke, Pickaway, Harrison, Guernsey, and Muskingum.[220,223] King Rails were accidental to casual summer residents in the southern counties, with isolated nesting attempts in Scioto, Adams, Butler, Warren, Hamilton, and Montgomery Counties.[220,248,299]

Nesting rails preferred cattail marshes but were also found in buttonbush swamps, wet prairies, marshy pools in swamp forests, and rose tangles in wet meadows.[479] They generally initiated their breeding activities slightly later than other resident rails.[8] Their nests were constructed during May, either on the ground or as a platform above standing water.[479] The earliest clutches were reported by May 10, although most nests with eggs were noted during the last half of May. Adults accompanied by small young were expected between late May and early August.

Their migrations were always poorly defined. Resident Kings occasionally returned during the first week of April but did not normally appear until April 16–25. Most returned in early May, although a few migrants were noted through the end of the month.[89,479] Spring Kings were apparently accidental to rare migrants away from known breeding sites. In autumn, most Kings quietly disappeared from their breeding territories during September. Small concentrations were sporadically encountered, including 21 at Lake St. Mary's on August 3, 1936, and 20 along western Lake Erie on September 3, 1948.[31,89] Most fall reports were of isolated Kings in their nesting marshes and as accidental to rare migrants elsewhere. They were fairly regularly observed through September 20–30 with infrequent stragglers into late October.

They were casually noted in the western Lake Erie marshes during winter. Campbell[89] cited records of 1–3 Kings during seven of thirty-nine winters, mostly in December and early January, although a few may have overwintered. Surprisingly, there were no winter records elsewhere.

During the 1930s, King Rails were noticeably declining. These declines were most apparent in inland counties where wetlands were rapidly disappearing.[479] These trends accelerated in subsequent years. Most isolated nesting pairs disappeared during the 1940s and the large populations at Lake St. Mary's and Buckeye Lake vanished by the 1950s. A few pairs remained in northeastern Ohio marshes with nesting at Youngstown in 1963 and Geauga County in 1965.[146,335]

Along western Lake Erie, they remained common summer residents through 1952 but then precipitously declined. By 1960, only a few pairs remained in these marshes.[7,89] This decline was partially the result of drought conditions during several summers as well as habitat destruction. However, they also inexplicably disappeared from suitable marshes.

Their status has not changed appreciably since the early 1960s. King Rails are now rare summer residents of western Lake Erie marshes in Ottawa and Lucas Counties. They may be found in only one to three marshes some years, but when water levels are favorable, 1–7 pairs have been reported from seven Lake Erie marshes.[434] This breeding population probably does not exceed 10–25 pairs. The inland King Rail population has virtually disappeared. Since 1970, the only confirmed summer records were at Big Island Wildlife Area (Marion County) during 1986 and 1987, and nesting was suspected.

Away from the nesting locations, King Rails are accidental to casual migrants. The timing of their migratory movements has not changed. All recent records are of single rails. They are strictly accidental winter visitors. The only recent winter records are a single King discovered on the Buckeye Lake Christmas Bird Count on December 27, 1965, and one banded in Ottawa County on January 1, 1980.[276]

VIRGINIA RAIL

Rallus limicola Vieillot

Unlike King Rails, which nest in a variety of wetlands, breeding Virginias prefer dense cattail marshes covering several acres.

Small openings are not essential, while water depths of 0.5 to 1.5 feet are preferred.[8] Virginias also occasionally occupy large wet meadows, but they avoid small wetlands and narrow fringes of cattails bordering ponds, except during migration.

Virginia Rails have always been locally distributed summer residents. Hicks[220] described them as "rather common" in the western Lake Erie marshes and at several unspecified inland reservoirs. They were rare and very locally distributed elsewhere, especially within the western counties. Their breeding range extended south to Columbiana, Carroll, Guernsey, Perry, Pickaway, and Butler Counties.

Like other marshland birds, Virginia Rails have declined in numbers as a result of habitat destruction. These declines are most apparent within the interior counties. In the large marshes along western Lake Erie and in the northeastern counties that still host sizable breeding populations, Virginias may be the most numerous resident rails. In eastern Ohio where strip mining has created some sizable marshes, Virginia Rails have recently increased. The breeding range has not changed substantially since the mid-1930s. Nesting Virginias are most numerous in the marshes bordering western Lake Erie, where they occupy every suitable wetland as uncommon to fairly common residents. Breeding Virginias are also uncommon residents within the northeastern counties south to Columbiana, Stark, and Wayne. In the remainder of northern Ohio, they become casual to rare and very locally distributed residents with the most reports from Richland and Ashland Counties.

Elsewhere, Virginia Rails are casual to rare and very locally distributed summer residents south to Belmont, Guernsey, Licking, Clark, Warren, and Butler Counties. They breed at no more than three localities in any central and southwestern county. With the exception of summering Virginias in a Jackson County marsh during the 1980s,[434] nesting rails are unknown from the remainder of southern and unglaciated Ohio.

Most Virginia Rail nests are expertly concealed among dense emergent vegetation, and many are placed over shallow water.[8] They may be domed structures on the ground or platforms 1.5 feet above the water.[523] Nest construction begins during the first half of May and most eggs are laid before the end of the month. The young normally hatch in June and remain with their parents until August.[8,523] A remarkably early nesting record was established by an adult Virginia Rail accompanied by a small downy chick at Spring Valley Wildlife Area on April 23, 1983.[299] Renesting attempts produce clutches as late as July 10.[89] While breeding rails are easily detected when they are establishing territories, they become surprisingly inconspicuous once the adults begin incubating. They remain silent and furtive until their young are fully grown.

They remain inconspicuous through autumn, and their fall migration is poorly defined. Migrants are occasionally flushed from upland fields and a few have appeared in cities, looking out of place among downtown office buildings.[248] Most fall migrants are detected in wetlands, where they are rare to uncommon throughout Ohio. Daily totals seldom exceed 1–4 Virginias. Their southward migration begins by the last week of August. Most depart by October 5–10, although stragglers are reported into November.[479]

A few have attempted to overwinter, producing at least twenty-five published sightings. Before 1960, wintering Virginias were only encountered once or twice a decade. They have been observed more frequently since 1960, averaging one record every two or three years. Virginias now appear to be casual winter residents along western Lake Erie and in the northeastern counties. They are accidental winter visitors elsewhere. These wintering rails are invariably scattered individuals, usually in cattail marshes and occasionally in wet meadows. They are mostly reported during December and early January; a few have overwintered within northern Ohio.

Migrant Virginias are most conspicuous each spring. Seldom numerous, they are generally uncommon to fairly common migrants across Ohio. Normally, 1–6 Virginias are noted daily and the largest flights produce concentrations of 15–20. Virginias are usually the first rails returning to Ohio. They have appeared as early as March 8 in Jackson County,[386] March 9 near Columbus,[370] and March 13 along western Lake Erie.[255] The first migrants regularly return by April 10–17. Spring migrants are most numerous between April 25 and May 10 and only summer residents remain after May 25.

SORA

Porzana carolina (Linnaeus)

Without a doubt, Soras are our most numerous migrant rails. Every cattail marsh, wet meadow, and pond margin host their share of Soras each spring and fall. While a few Soras may be observed as they lurk among the vegetation, their true abundance can only be ascertained by encouraging them to call. Tape-recorded calls, loud noises, and rocks thrown into the marsh prompt them to respond with their distinctive descending whinnies, whistled notes, or sharp *keeks*, revealing that the marsh is full of these secretive birds.

In spring, remarkably early Soras have appeared north to Lake Erie by March 20–30. They do not normally return until April 10–17 and are most numerous between April 27 and May 15. These migrants are common along western Lake Erie, where 25–50+ may be noted. They are uncommon to fairly common elsewhere, becoming locally common at a few large inland marshes. Daily totals of 3–10+ may be noted away from western Lake Erie with infrequent concentrations of 20–60 in central and northeastern Ohio. One hundred Soras at Mentor Marsh on May 1, 1976, were exceptional.[471] Numbers decline by May 20 and only summer residents remain by June 1.

The distribution of breeding Soras has not changed greatly since the 1930s. Hicks[220] described Soras as uncommon to rare residents within the western Lake Erie marshes. Small numbers were scattered across twenty-seven other northern and central counties south to Columbiana, Stark, Holmes, Licking, Pickaway, Champaign, and Mercer. Soras are still largely confined to this range, although there has been a slight southward expansion.[434] Isolated pairs nested or summered at Spring Valley Wildlife Area, at another Greene County marsh, and near Cincinnati in southwestern Ohio and in Carroll, Harrison, Tuscarawas, and Jackson Counties along the unglaciated Allegheny Plateau.[263,274,299,434]

While their breeding range remained fairly constant, their relative abundance was markedly altered. Along western Lake Erie, Hicks[220] considered Soras local and irregular summer residents, "greatly outnumbered" by other rails. As late as the 1960s, Campbell[89] cited reduced numbers of Soras in these marshes. Their status must have changed abruptly; he considered them "the most numerous of all rails" along western Lake Erie in the early 1970s.[90] Breeding Soras are presently fairly common residents in every extensive marsh in Ottawa, Lucas, Sandusky, and Erie Counties.

Similar improvements were not apparent elsewhere as inland breeding populations declined as a result of habitat destruction. Breeding Soras are rare to uncommon residents in northeastern Ohio. They are casual to rare and very locally distributed elsewhere in the northern and central counties.[434]

Breeding Soras occupy extensive marshes, usually the grass and sedge borders of cattail marshes.[8] Sora nests are placed on the ground in dense grassy cover. Their breeding activities begin during the first half of May and nests with eggs are mostly reported between May 13 and June 16.[479,523] Renesting attempts are responsible for clutches into early July. Young Soras may hatch during the last week of May but most broods are observed in June and July.

As soon as their young become independent, Soras initiate their southward migration. While a few migrants may appear by July 15–20, they do not become widely distributed until August 15–20. This movement largely takes place during September. The last migrants normally depart by October 10–15 with occasional stragglers through mid-November.

Numbers of fall Soras fluctuate considerably. These migrants are most numerous along western Lake Erie, where 184 were counted on October 4, 1983.[372] Peak fall counts usually total 10–40 daily. Away from western Lake Erie, Soras become uncommon to fairly common migrants in numbers similar to spring. The largest inland concentrations were 40–60. While most Soras pass through wetland habitats in autumn, a few have been found in upland fields.

Soras are accidental winter visitors. The first winter records were from Dayton on December 16, 1941, and December 10, 1948.[299] There was also a sighting at Youngstown during the winter of 1952–53.[67] After 1960, winter Soras were reported on four occasions along western Lake Erie and twice in southwestern Ohio. All winter sightings were single individuals noted through January 22.[89]

PURPLE GALLINULE

Porphyrula martinica (Linnaeus)

This colorful gallinule is largely restricted to the Gulf coastal plain with a few pairs nesting north to western Tennessee and Maryland.[5] However, Purple Gallinules have an uncanny knack for appearing at unexpected locations at unexpected times and may wander north to the Great Lakes and Canadian Maritime Provinces during any season.

The first Ohio specimen was collected near Circleville (Pick-away County) on May 10, 1877, a "flight year" that also produced four spring records from Cincinnati.[248,520] There were few records between the 1890s and 1950, but Purple Gallinules have averaged three to six sightings each decade since 1950.

Purple Gallinules are most likely to appear during spring, when they become accidental to casual visitors with at least twenty-four published records across Ohio. These sightings include eight records from Cincinnati (six in the 1800s); three reports each from Dayton, Cleveland, and Columbus; and single sightings from the Sandusky Bay area, Circleville, Washington Court House (Fayette County), Wayne County, Lorain, Seneca County, and Proctorville (Lawrence County). Most reports were of single gallinules, although 2 were noted in Lorain on April 18, 1980.[277] They have been noted as early as the last half of March but most appear between April 20 and May 20.

These extralimital gallinules are mostly detected in wetlands or small ponds bordered by emergent vegetation. They may also appear in unexpected locations. One of the 1980 Lorain gallinules was discovered swimming along the shore of Lake Erie and several have been found in residential areas miles from any water. While some remained for only one or two days, others have lingered for weeks.

Several lingered into summer, including 1 during June 1964 at Cincinnati and 1 through June 25, 1962, near Cleveland.[335,393] There are also several unconfirmed summer records from the western Lake Erie marshes. The most surprising summer record was the discovery of a pair on Baumgartner's Pond in southern Franklin County in May 1962. Their nest was discovered on June 15 and contained seven eggs on June 17. These eggs hatched between July 4 and 8 and the young gallinules were regularly observed into August.[486] This pair provided the only confirmed breeding record from Ohio.

Purple Gallinules are strictly accidental visitors at other seasons. The only fall record was a specimen found near Lake Erie in Erie County on September 2, 1894.[490] This species has also appeared once during winter. A Purple Gallinule was discovered at a Mansfield residence on February 21, 1983; it was alive when captured but died in captivity.[369]

COMMON MOORHEN

Gallinula chloropus (Linnaeus)

Common Moorhens suffered from the destruction of wetlands at Lake St. Mary's, Buckeye Lake, Indian Lake, and other inland marshes during the twentieth century. Substantial numbers of pairs nested there in the 1930s,[220] but they had largely disappeared by 1960.[98,479] Away from western Lake Erie, Common Moorhens are now rare and locally distributed summer residents of western and central Ohio. Fewer than 100 pairs reside south to Butler, Warren, and Licking Counties. Small populations occupy Big Island Wildlife Area (Marion County), Springville Marsh (Seneca County), and Spring Valley Wildlife Area. Scattered pairs are distributed in other suitable wetlands, although most counties lack breeding moorhens.[434]

Moorhens remain fairly common to common residents in

the marshes bordering western Lake Erie. Their numbers fluctuate considerably, from 6 or fewer reported daily in years of scarcity to 10–20+ in years of maximum abundance. In suitable marshes, densities of 4.6 pairs per hectare have been recorded and more than 60 pairs occupied a single marsh.[7,48] In marginal wetlands, breeding densities approach one pair in five hectares. While the present trends of this population are not known, Brackney and Bookhout[48] estimated approximately 1200 breeding pairs in 1978.

Moorhens are widely distributed within northeastern Ohio marshes south to northern Columbiana, Stark, and Holmes Counties. They are locally common residents in the wetlands bordering Killbuck Creek in Wayne and Holmes Counties but are generally uncommon to fairly common residents elsewhere. While 10–15+ individuals may be observed in large marshes, most wetlands support fewer than 5 pairs. The size of this population has never been estimated.

In the unglaciated counties, they were unknown as summer residents until strip-mining activities and an expanding beaver population recently created suitable wetlands. They have become accidental to casual summer residents, with summering individuals reported near Senecaville Lake in 1966 and in isolated marshes in Ross and Guernsey Counties after 1982.[152,434]

Moorhens breed in extensive marshes, where they furtively swim along the vegetated margins. At any disturbance, they immediately take cover. When undisturbed, they are readily observed swimming and picking food from the surface of the water. They prefer marshes with approximately 50 percent open water interspersed with cattails, bur reeds, and similar emergent vegetation.[48] Small numbers are also found in semipermanent marshes and shrub-dominated wetlands. Their nests are placed in dense vegetation near open water, either anchored to vegetation or floating.[479] Along western Lake Erie, clutches have been laid as early as May 2 with a peak during the last half of the month.[48] Renesting attempts have been recorded through July 10. Recently hatched young have been observed by June 7 but are most frequently noted during late June and July.[479] Most young become independent by mid-August. Renesting attempts produce small downy young as late as August 28 and reports of juveniles through October 21.[79]

Spring migrants are mostly resident pairs returning to their nesting territories. Moorhens become accidental or casual visitors away from breeding locations. Migrants have returned to western Lake Erie as early as March 20 but do not normally appear until April 15–20.[89] They attain their nesting densities during the first half of May.

Their southward movements largely occur during September. Their numbers are noticeably reduced by the first week of October and most depart by October 15–20. Occasional moorhens lingered through November 15, 1898, in Pike County; November 16, 1924, in central Ohio; and December 9, 1949, in the Cleveland area.[45,117,193]

On two occasions, Common Moorhens survived in northern Ohio into midwinter. One was discovered in Magee Marsh Wildlife Area on January 5, 1953.[89] Two were discovered near Cuyahoga Falls in late December 1959 and remained through February 28, 1960.[117,325]

AMERICAN COOT

Fulica americana Gmelin

No other native water birds receive as little respect as American Coots. Their relative abundance, plain plumage, and typically unwary behavior combine to make them invisible to most observers, who regularly encounter and ignore these slate-gray birds awkwardly swimming in tightly packed flocks across large lakes.

Coots certainly are common to abundant migrants. They are equally at home on large reservoirs, small ponds, and marshes, obtaining their food by feeding at the surface or with their peculiar brief dives. The first coots return during late February or early March as the ice melts from lakes and marshes. They become numerous by March 15–20 and remain conspicuous through May 3–7. Flocks of 50–500 coots are possible on all large lakes and marshes. Concentrations of 1000–2000+ may appear along western Lake Erie and within the northern and western counties. The largest spring flocks totaled 3500 along western Lake Erie and 10,000 at Buckeye Lake on April 17, 1936.[30,89] Fewer remain through May 12–15, while stragglers linger into early June.

Numbers of migrant coots have noticeably declined since the mid-1970s. This decline is largely attributed to poor wetland conditions and habitat destruction on coot breeding grounds in the prairies of central North America and on their coastal wintering range. Most spring flocks have totaled 500 or fewer since 1985.

During summer, nonbreeding coots are casually encountered on large lakes, small ponds, and isolated marshes throughout Ohio. Most are reported from the glaciated counties with very few summer records along the unglaciated Allegheny Plateau.

Ohio also supports a breeding coot population whose distribution has changed substantially during the present century. In the mid-1930s, American Coots were common summer residents within the western Lake Erie marshes. They nested in northeastern Ohio in Ashtabula, Stark, Wayne, Mahoning, and Columbiana Counties.[220] Breeding coots were also reported from Williams and Franklin Counties, Lake St. Mary's, Indian Lake, and Buckeye Lake. Of these latter locations, coots were "rather common" and regularly nested only at Lake St. Mary's.[98]

Breeding coots remained common along western Lake Erie into the early 1960s but reduced numbers were reported later in the decade.[89] Spring and summer drawdowns continued to reduce their numbers into the 1980s. Away from western Lake Erie, the breeding populations at Lake St. Mary's and in the northeastern counties largely disappeared during the 1950s and 1960s. But breeding coots were recorded from Hancock and Lake Counties in northern Ohio while a nest at Lake Grant (Brown County) on June 21, 1949, established the first southern Ohio breeding record.[248,417,523]

American Coots are now fairly common to locally common residents in the western Lake Erie marshes. They become rare, irregular, and locally distributed summer residents in other glaciated counties. In northeastern Ohio, a few pairs breed in Summit County but summering coots are only sporadically encountered elsewhere. Within the central counties, a small breeding population of 8–30+ pairs occupies Big Island Wildlife Area (Marion County). Isolated pairs occasionally nest in other central counties with records from Wyandot, Champaign, and Clark during the 1980s.[434] They are casual summer residents in the northwestern and southwestern counties, where recent nesting records are limited to nine broods discovered in Hamilton County in 1973 and a Seneca County nest and summering coots in Butler County during 1984.[252,434] There are no published nesting records along the unglaciated Allegheny Plateau.

Breeding coots prefer permanent marshes where open water is interspersed with emergent vegetation. Their nests are simple platforms constructed only a few inches above the water within dense cover. Some coots begin nesting in April; downy young have been observed by May 11 at Big Island Wildlife Area. Most pairs nest during May and June, while dependent young may be noted into early August. Late nesting attempts produced dependent young in Hancock County through August 26–27[417] and a chick in Mahoning County on September 19, 1978.

While a few early fall migrants return during late August and early September, the first coots do not normally appear until September 15–25. Their numbers peak between October 10 and November 25, when they become as numerous and conspicuous as during their spring migration. The largest fall concentrations occur along western Lake Erie, where 1000–5000+ may gather some years, and at central and northwestern Ohio reservoirs, where 1800–4000+ have been reported.[89,471,479] Elsewhere, flocks of 50–500+ may appear on large lakes and marshes. Numbers of fall migrants have noticeably declined since 1975 and few concentrations have been in excess of 500–700 since 1985.

Cold November weather causes most coots to migrate and only small flocks and individuals remain until freeze-up. Conversely, mild weather allows flocks of 100–500+ to linger into the last half of December. Subfreezing temperatures eventually force most coots to leave Ohio.

Most winters American Coots become rare and very locally distributed residents. Six or fewer are regularly observed at hot-water outlets along Lake Erie. Similar numbers regularly winter at Castalia and occasionally along large rivers in the southern half of the state. Relatively mild winters entice flocks to remain as long as open water is available. Trautman[479] observed 150–180 at Buckeye Lake through the winter of 1931–32. Flocks of 40–60 have wintered at other locations north to Lake Erie.

SANDHILL CRANE

Grus canadensis (Linnaeus)

In eastern North America, Sandhill Cranes nest from northern Ontario south to Michigan, Wisconsin, and Minnesota, with a few isolated pairs in northern Illinois and northeastern Indiana.[5] During fall migration, most of these cranes congregate at the Jasper-Pulaski Wildlife Area in northwestern Indiana; smaller numbers also accumulate at other staging areas in Indiana and southern Michigan. From these areas, they fly to their wintering grounds in Florida. They reverse this route each spring.[514] Ohio lies on the eastern edge of this migration corridor, and the number passing over the state depends on prevailing wind directions.

Most Sandhill Cranes are observed in passage over the state; relatively few are found on the ground. Since their loud guttural calls carry for miles, they may be heard long before they are seen. Their unmistakable trumpeting announces that a flock is about to pass overhead. These migrants may be mere specks soaring on midday thermals, or they may appear suddenly at low altitudes, necks and legs outstretched as they quickly proceed on shallow wing beats.

Until the extensive bogs and wetlands were converted to agricultural fields, small numbers of these cranes nested in northern Ohio. Campbell[89] cited accounts of 12–15 pairs breeding in the Oak Openings of Lucas and Fulton Counties around 1875. "Many juveniles" were reported from this area but no nests were discovered. This population disappeared around 1880. Other cranes nested in the bog that once covered much of southwestern Huron County. One or two pairs summered in this bog into the 1920s; Ohio's last nesting attempt was confirmed there during 1926. An unmated Sandhill remained in the area through 1931.[220] Summering Sandhills were also reported from Erie, Crawford, and Ashtabula Counties by Hicks,[220] although breeding was never confirmed.

The demise of Ohio's nesting population reflected the Sandhills' population trends throughout eastern North America during the nineteenth and early twentieth centuries as overhunting and habitat destruction significantly reduced their numbers. Even with complete protection, they did not begin to improve until the mid-1940s. Except for the Huron County breeding pairs, Sandhill Cranes were accidental visitors to Ohio between 1900 and 1940. They averaged one to three sightings a decade, mostly near Lake Erie with one fall record from Buckeye Lake.

Judging from numbers staging at the Jasper-Pulaski Wildlife Area, the Sandhill Crane population doubled between 1945 and 1955.[330] This increasing population produced additional records from Ohio. Cincinnati's first modern Sandhill Crane record was established in 1948 and the second central Ohio sighting was reported that year.[45,248] A flock of 28 flew over Toledo during October 1949,[89] but Sandhill Cranes remained casual visitors to the western half of Ohio through the 1950s. Their population expanded dramatically between 1955 and 1975 as evidenced by an exponential increase in numbers staging in Indiana,[330] producing greater numbers of sightings from Ohio.

Migrant Sandhills are now most frequently encountered in autumn with two to eight sightings annually. They are generally rare but regular migrants in southwestern Ohio north to Dayton and east through Clermont County as well as along western Lake Erie. These cranes are casually reported elsewhere in western Ohio. They normally appear in flocks of 20 or fewer with occasional groups of 50–75. Larger flocks are exceptional: 300 roosted at Indian Lake during November 1982;[368] 200 flew over Cincinnati on November 26, 1983;[372] and perhaps 500 were in northwestern Ohio during late November 1986. Fall Sandhills are casual to accidental migrants through central Ohio. The few reports include three flocks of 20–34 in the vicinity of Columbus since 1959 and a maximum of 94 over

Paint Creek Reservoir in Ross County on November 12, 1977.[267] They are accidental fall migrants in eastern Ohio, where the only records are of single birds in the northeastern counties.

A few fall migrants have appeared along western Lake Erie during early August, probably wandering nonbreeding cranes. The first migrants are not expected until the last week of October. The largest movements are usually between November 15 and December 7. The last fall migrants normally depart by December 15.

Before 1984, there was only one undocumented winter record from Ohio. In 1984, a Sandhill Crane was observed near Pickerington (Franklin County) during the first half of January.[373] There have been winter records in every subsequent year. A crane wintered in Ottawa County during 1984–85, while 4 appeared in Adams County between January 30 and February 9, 1985.[377] Three were noted near Cincinnati on January 12, 1986, and 1 wintered in Knox County during 1986–87.[381,385] The winter of 1987–88 produced a wintering crane at Mosquito Creek Wildlife Area (Trumbull County) and another near Ottawa National Wildlife Refuge into January. Despite these records, Sandhill Cranes remain accidental winter visitors.

The first spring migrants may return during the last week of February. Most are observed between March 5 and April 7. A few nonbreeders may appear during May, mostly along western Lake Erie. While spring sightings also average two to eight records annually, flock size seldom exceeds 15 cranes. The largest reported spring movement totaled 82 at Crane Creek State Park (Lucas County) on March 10, 1985.[378]

Spring migrants are rare but regular near Cincinnati and along western Lake Erie. They are casually observed elsewhere in western Ohio but become accidental in the central and northeastern counties. While 2 cranes were reported near Salem (Columbiana County) on April 30, 1932,[18] there are no spring records from the unglaciated counties.

After the breeding population disappeared, the only Ohio summer record was provided by a Sandhill Crane in Union County during 1954. This nonbreeding individual was discovered on June 21 and remained into August.[344] While a nonbreeding crane lingered near Big Island Wildlife Area through May 29, 1988, it did not summer there.

BLACK-BELLIED PLOVER

Pluvialis squatarola (Linnaeus)

As spring migrants, Black-bellied Plovers do not normally return until after they acquire their breeding plumage. Small flocks of these handsome plovers add a touch of class to flooded fields, drawndown marshes, and other habitats attracting shorebirds. These spring migrants are mostly encountered along western Lake Erie in Ottawa and Lucas Counties, where they are fairly common to common visitors. Flocks of 5–30+ are regularly observed, while smaller numbers may be evident when habitats are scarce. Favorable conditions attract large flocks; as many as 125–250 have been reported from a single field.

Similar numbers do not normally appear elsewhere. Along central Lake Erie, Black-bellied Plovers are rare to uncommon migrants and most reports are of 12 or fewer. Away from the lakefront, these plovers are casual to locally uncommon migrants through all glaciated counties. The largest flocks are most likely to be encountered in northern Ohio, where 75–95 have been noted in Wayne County on several occasions and 92 were reported from Seneca County. In the glaciated central and southwestern counties, 10–35 make up the largest flocks. Most inland sightings are of 15 or fewer. Along the unglaciated Allegheny Plateau, Black-bellies are accidental spring visitors with only a few reports of scattered individuals.

Late March sightings undoubtedly pertain to misidentified Lesser Golden-Plovers. The first Black-bellieds may return between April 17 and 25 but there are few sightings before May. They are most likely to be observed between May 7 and 23 with late migrants lingering into the first week of June.

Nonbreeding plovers have been reported only from western Lake Erie. They are casual summer visitors to Ottawa and Lucas Counties, where 1–6 are infrequently noted during June. Most remain for only several days, although a few lingered for a week or longer.[89]

The earliest fall migrants returned to western Lake Erie by July 5 but they are not expected along the lakefront until the last week of the month. Black-bellieds are most numerous along Lake Erie between August 5 and October 10. Most depart by October 20–30 with a few remaining into November. Away from the lakefront, Black-bellies do not appear until August 12–20 and are not widely distributed until September. Timing of their departure is similar to that of the Lake Erie migrants. Adult Black-bellieds predominate throughout August. Most depart by early September, although a few have been noted as late as September 25. A juvenile Black-bellied Plover along Lake Erie on August 4 was exceptionally early; they normally appear during the last week of August.

Black-bellied Plovers are uncommon to fairly common fall migrants along Lake Erie. They are rare to locally fairly common migrants at drawndown reservoirs in glaciated Ohio. Along the unglaciated Allegheny Plateau, they are mostly accidental or casual migrants, although they may become locally uncommon visitors to the few localities regularly attracting numbers of shorebirds. Along Lake Erie, most fall reports are of 20 or fewer with infrequent concentrations of 30–50. Flocks in excess of 100 are exceptional. At inland localities, only 10 or fewer make up most fall sightings and 15–22 compose the largest flocks.

The latest migrants normally disappear by November 10–20. Unusually mild weather allowed single plovers to linger into the first half of December at Toledo, Cleveland, Youngstown, and Columbus and late December in Columbiana County. These accidental early winter visitors invariably depart before January 1.

LESSER GOLDEN-PLOVER

Pluvialis dominica (Müller)

Lesser Golden-Plovers were numerous migrants in the nineteenth century until their populations were decimated by market hunting. At the turn of the century, these handsome plovers were reduced to "hardly more than casual visitors."[236] Their recovery started slowly, with the first increases evident by the 1920s.[479] Populations did not fully recover until the 1940s and 1950s.

Spring Lesser Golden-Plovers normally migrate through the central United States en route to their breeding territories on the Arctic tundra. These migrants are most numerous within the plains states and along the Mississippi River valley. The eastern edge of this migration corridor extends to western Ohio, where their appearance depends on weather conditions and other factors.

Spring plovers are most numerous in west-central and northwestern Ohio along a migration corridor extending east to Erie, Huron, Crawford, Marion, Union, and Madison Counties and south to Pickaway, Fayette, Clark, Miami, and Darke Counties. Golden-Plovers are generally fairly common to abundant spring migrants along western Lake Erie and uncommon to locally abundant within other counties. Flocks of 20–200 may be encountered throughout this corridor and concentrations of 500–1000 appear some years. Larger flocks are less frequently observed: 6000 near Bowling Green (Wood County) on May 10, 1940;[509] 5000 on May 2, 1950, and 4000 on April 24, 1954, in the Toledo area;[89] 3000 in Marion County on April 26, 1986; and 2500 in Pickaway County on April 2, 1967.

Golden-Plovers are uncommon to rare spring migrants through southwestern Ohio, where most reports are of 30 or fewer but flocks of 200–400 have appeared on several occasions.[248,299] Groups of 5–15 are locally rare to uncommon in southwestern Wayne County, the only location within eastern Ohio regularly hosting spring Golden-Plovers. They are accidental to casual visitors within all other eastern counties and along central Lake Erie.

Spring migrants prefer damp plowed fields and moist margins of flooded fields. The earliest Lesser Golden-Plovers returned to Dayton by March 4 and Lake St. Mary's by March 8.[98,299] There are few other sightings before March 20. The first flocks are normally detected by April 5–15 and maximum abundance is attained between April 20 and May 7. Their numbers diminish by May 15 and only a few late migrants remain along western Lake Erie through May 31.[89] There are no June records.

As fall migrants, most Golden-Plovers head toward the Atlantic Coast before initiating a transoceanic flight to South America. Hence, their fall distribution pattern is different than spring's. Fall Golden-Plovers are most numerous along Lake Erie, becoming uncommon to locally common migrants. Lakefront reports mostly total 20 or fewer with occasional flocks of 40–100. Larger concentrations are restricted to the Toledo area, where 800 were counted on October 3, 1976, and 500 on October 27, 1940.[89,471] They become uncommon to fairly common migrants within the northern and glaciated central counties, normally 15 or fewer daily with infrequent flocks of 20–50. Concentrations of 100–300 have appeared at several locations. These plovers are least numerous within the southern and unglaciated counties, becoming accidental to locally rare migrants. Fall flocks never exceed 6–10 within these counties.

These fall migrants regularly visit mudflats bordering drawndown reservoirs and dredge disposal sites along Lake Erie. They also frequently inhabit sod farms, mowed hayfields, pastures, grassy fields bordering airports, and harvested croplands. The earliest Golden-Plovers returned to Lake Erie by July 1–5. They do not normally appear along the lakefront until July 27–August 12 and become numerous by August 20–30. The largest flocks are expected during September and the first half of October. They normally depart by November 1. Most migrants are adults through September 1–7, and a few may remain as late as September 21–28. The first juveniles appear by the last week of August but do not become widespread until mid-September. Within the interior counties, there are few July sightings. The first migrants frequently return during the last half of August. Peak numbers are attained during September, and these migrants normally become scarce after October 7–12.

Their status as late fall migrants is obscured by the inability to distinguish Golden-Plovers from Black-bellieds. While Golden-Plovers have been confirmed during the first half of November, these individuals invariably depart by November 10–17. Later sight records are unsubstantiated. Any suspected Lesser Golden-Plover observed after November 15 should be very carefully identified and documented.

WILSON'S PLOVER

Charadrius wilsonia Ord

The only acceptable Ohio record for Wilson's Plover is a bird collected at the sandspit on Cedar Point (now the Cedar Point National Wildlife Refuge), Lucas County, on June 17, 1936. This adult male was "in good condition."[86] His appearance, not due to stormy weather conditions, was quite unexpected; there are very few confirmed inland records in the United States. The normal breeding range for Wilson's Plover is the Gulf and Atlantic Coasts north to Maryland.[5]

SEMIPALMATED PLOVER

Charadrius semipalmatus Bonaparte

This small plover is a regular visitor to mudflats, flooded fields, drawndown marshes, and other habitats attractive to shorebirds. It prefers damp mud and exposed gravel bars for feeding. Its presence may be detected by its distinctive plaintive call, easily recognized among the hoarse notes and sharp whistles produced by other shorebirds.

An incredibly early Semipalmated Plover was observed at Cleveland on March 18, 1986. The first spring migrants may return during the last week of April but are not expected until May 3–8. Their maximum abundance is normally attained between May 12 and 25. These migrants usually depart from inland counties by May 30 but frequently remain along Lake Erie through June 5–10.

These migrants are fairly common to common near western Lake Erie in Ottawa and Lucas Counties, where totals of 20–75+ are noted most years and 100–200+ may develop if conditions are favorable. Their appearance elsewhere is much more erratic. Spring Semipalmateds are uncommon to fairly common migrants along central Lake Erie and rare to locally fairly common within northern and glaciated central Ohio. They become accidental to uncommon migrants in the southwestern and unglaciated counties. Away from western Lake Erie, spring totals frequently are 1–10 daily with occasional flocks of 15–30. Larger concentrations are noteworthy: 50 in Wayne County on May 21, 1983; 74 at Cleveland on May 18, 1986; and 115 at Big Island Wildlife Area (Marion County) on May 18, 1987.

Nonbreeding Semipalmated Plovers are casual visitors along western Lake Erie. Campbell[86] cited six summer records in Ottawa and Lucas Counties between 1932 and 1937. In subsequent decades they have averaged one record every two to four years. These records are of single plovers, some remaining for only a few days while others lingered through June.

Along Lake Erie, fall migrants may appear during the first week of July but are not expected until July 8–12. Semipalmated Plovers become numerous by July 20–25. Their return to the interior counties is generally later; migrants may not appear there until July 25–August 15. Inland migrants are mostly observed during the last half of August and in September. Numbers of fall migrants diminish in all areas by the first week of October and most depart by October 10–20. A few individuals remained into early November; none were recorded after November 13.[89,523] Most fall migrants are adults through mid-August. A few adults remain into September, some as late as September 20–30. The first juvenile plovers returned to Lake Erie by August 9 but do not normally appear until August 15–22. By the last week of August, flocks are dominated by juveniles.

Fall Semipalmated Plovers become fairly common to common migrants along Lake Erie and uncommon to fairly common on mudflats bordering inland reservoirs. The largest fall concentrations appeared along western Lake Erie in Ottawa and Lucas Counties, where 354 were reported on September 5, 1979.[275] Flocks of 100–200+ have appeared on other dates, although daily totals normally are 5–40. Along central Lake Erie, fall totals seldom exceed 5–20 and flocks in excess of 100 are noteworthy. Inland locations seldom attract more than 3–30 Semipalmateds. The largest inland concentration was 200 at Lake St. Mary's on September 1, 1910.[202] A flock of 45 at Spring Valley Wildlife Area was remarkably late on October 25, 1987.[388]

PIPING PLOVER

Charadrius melodus Ord

Perhaps no bird is more symbolic of the Great Lakes beaches than this little plover. Its light brown and white plumage blends so well with the dry sand that it is nearly invisible until it scurries down the beach. And unfortunately, the plight of the Piping Plover reflects the deteriorating condition of the Great Lakes beaches. In recent years, high lake levels have eroded these beaches while the remaining areas are subjected to increased recreational use. These factors so reduced the Great Lakes Piping Plover population that it is now classified as endangered. Fewer than 20 pairs nest on the Great Lakes; the sighting of a Piping Plover has become a noteworthy event and its plaintive call is rapidly becoming only a memory.

Although nesting had been suspected for many years, the first Ohio breeding pairs were discovered at Cedar Point (Erie County) at the turn of the century.[236] Subsequently, breeding Piping Plovers were discovered in Lucas, Ottawa, Erie, Lorain, Lake, and Ashtabula Counties. This population peaked during the 1920s and early 1930s. Although their numbers fluctuated annually, as many as 26 pairs were estimated along the lakefront between 1925 and 1935.[227] This population was reduced to only 6 pairs by 1937 and the last documented nesting attempt occurred at Cedar Point National Wildlife Refuge (Lucas County) in 1942.[89]

Breeding Piping Plovers were restricted to large beaches and sand spits devoid of vegetation, with as many as 6 pairs nesting at a single location. Despite excellent camouflage of eggs and young and the constant attention of vigilant adults, their nesting attempts were frequently unsuccessful. Nests with eggs were mostly recorded between May 20 and late June with renesting attempts producing clutches through July 18. Adults with young were observed between June 16 and August 4.[86,89]

When Lake Erie supported a nesting population, Piping Plovers were regularly observed during migration. With the extirpation of this breeding population and substantial declines in other portions of the species' range, numbers passing along Lake Erie have noticeably declined since 1940. Piping Plovers are now casual to accidental spring migrants along the entire lakefront, averaging one sighting every two or three years. All recent records are single individuals noted between April 15 and May 15. Fall Piping Plovers were regularly reported into the early 1960s but became casual to rare migrants along Lake Erie within the past ten years. They presently average one to four sightings annually. Adult plovers may return by the second week of July and depart by early August. Juveniles generally appear during the last half of August and may be noted through September. Late migrants were noted at Toledo until November 5, 1966, and at Lorain until November 23, 1969.[89,408] Most recent fall sightings were single individuals, although a remarkable flock of 15 was reported from Lorain on August 24, 1963.[335]

Piping Plovers have always been accidental spring migrants and accidental to casual fall visitors in the interior of Ohio. The majority of inland sightings are from the central counties near Columbus, where they normally appear once or twice each decade. They are least numerous in southern Ohio, with no published records from the unglaciated Allegheny Plateau. All records were single individuals. The timing of their spring passage coincides with the migration along Lake Erie. Fall reports are almost exclusively of juvenile plovers during the last half of August and September.

KILLDEER

Charadrius vociferus Linnaeus

The first warming trend of late February produces the first returning Killdeers. These early arrivals rapidly spread across the state. They usually become common and widely distributed within the southern and central counties by March 5–12 and along Lake Erie by March 15. These migrants are mostly small flocks of 3–20 individuals, seldom producing daily totals exceeding 50–75. The largest flights totaled 100–225 in central Ohio and along Lake Erie.

The last migrants are usually detected during the first half of April. By that time, Killdeers become fairly common to common residents throughout Ohio. Since they prefer short-grass meadows, pastures, and edges of cultivated fields, Killdeers are most numerous within the intensively farmed western counties, where 10–30 are noted daily. In the more heavily forested southeastern counties, daily totals seldom exceed 5–15. Urban areas support the fewest nesting Killdeers, although pairs may be found in vacant lots, parks, and cemeteries. This adaptable plover has also nested on Lake Erie beaches, dikes in marshes, golf courses, and gravel-covered roofs.

Nesting begins early; nests with eggs have been reported by March 24 near Cincinnati, March 25 at Findlay, and March 31 at Cleveland.[254,417,523] First clutches are not normally laid until the last half of April. Some downy young may appear by the last week of April but most are encountered during the last half of May or early June. Killdeers may raise two broods each summer, although some late nests may be produced by adults unsuccessful in their initial breeding attempts. Many clutches are reported during June and the first week of July, while small young are repeatedly observed throughout July. Adults accompanied by partially grown young have been reported through August 19.

Breeding Killdeers have been widely distributed residents since the nineteenth century. Their populations are still increasing. Breeding Bird Surveys indicate significant increases throughout eastern and central North America since 1965 despite temporary reductions following severe winters.[438]

Small flocks of Killdeers may congregate during the last week of June or early July and their fall migration is under way by the middle of the month. These migrants are most numerous on exposed mudflats bordering lakes and marshes but flocks are also observed in dry agricultural fields. Fall migration normally peaks during August and September, when flocks of 30–250 are expected throughout Ohio. Larger concentrations are infrequent, but as many as 1500–1600 have been estimated from Buckeye Lake and Sandusky Bay.[475,479] They are regularly encountered until mid-November. While November concentrations are usually 30 or fewer, occasional large movements may produce flocks of 50–100 in the northeastern counties through November 18–21 and 200–300 at central Ohio reservoirs as late as November 22–26. Small numbers remain until the lakes and mudflats freeze. The last migrants may not depart until December 25–January 15. While most December sightings total 6 or fewer, as many as 20–60 have been noted into the second week of January during mild winters.

Killdeers are normally casual to accidental winter visitors after mid-January. Wintering birds are not regularly observed at any location, although 2–6 usually appear somewhere in the state each year, the majority in the southern and central counties. The largest reported wintering flock totaled 16 at Dayton on January 23, 1982.[299]

BLACK-NECKED STILT

Himantopus mexicanus (Müller)

During the nineteenth century, anecdotal accounts indicate that these distinctive shorebirds may have been fairly regular visitors to the lower Great Lakes area. Accounts from Ohio include assertions that "one or two were seen every year prior to 1900" at Lake St. Mary's and that Black-necked Stilts were "repeatedly taken" along Lake Erie.[98,523] The only specific records are a Cincinnati sighting in 1879 and a specimen taken in Cuyahoga County on October 24, 1881.[248,522] This specimen is no longer extant, and the other accounts are insufficiently substantiated to establish their accuracy.

Black-necked Stilts were decimated by overhunting during the late 1800s and became rare throughout the United States. While their populations recovered in the western states, eastern populations remained small and locally distributed along the Gulf and Atlantic Coasts north to Delaware.[5] They are accidental visitors elsewhere in eastern North America.

During this century, the only documented Black-necked Stilt was discovered by Chuck Hocevar and myself at Magee Marsh Wildlife Area on July 18, 1981.[362] We observed it foraging in a small pool in a drawdown marsh. Another stilt was reported from Lake St. Mary's on May 27, 1967.[403] Although details are unavailable, correspondence from Jim Hill and other observers indicates it was correctly identified. A road-killed stilt was reportedly found in Cleveland Heights (Cuyahoga County) on August 15, 1941.[523] The specimen was not preserved. Given its unlikely location in an urban area and the absence of supporting details, this record appears to be very questionable.

AMERICAN AVOCET

Recurvirostra americana Gmelin

The past status of American Avocets in Ohio is uncertain. They undoubtedly migrated through the state during the nineteenth century but were apparently rare and irregularly observed. There were only a few widely scattered records, with the last specimen collected at Lake St. Mary's in 1882.[224] Shortly thereafter, these avocets were decimated by market hunting and virtually disappeared from eastern North America.

During the first four decades of this century, American Avocets were accidental visitors to Ohio. Except for two vague records in 1907 and another in 1914, they were unrecorded until 1936, when one was observed near Toledo on September 6 and a specimen was collected at Ashtabula on September 21.[89,224] During the 1940s, only single avocets were discovered near Sandusky Bay in 1944 and 1946.[89,303] Their status improved in the 1950s, when they were detected with a frequency of one to three sightings every other year, producing the first recent records from Columbus, Dayton, Lake St. Mary's, and Pymatuning Lake. Avocets have been annually reported since 1963, including the first recent records from Cleveland and the unglaciated counties. During these years, they were as likely to appear at inland locations as along Lake Erie. In the 1970s, avocets established their present migration patterns.

Avocets are now erratic spring migrants. They are generally rare along western Lake Erie but accidental to casual elsewhere. The first migrants return by April 15 and most appear between April 20 and May 15. Late migrants may remain into the first week of June. They may be completely absent some years and appear as widely scattered individuals in others. Small flocks are sometimes discovered along western Lake Erie: 82 in Erie County on April 23, 1988;[388a] 42 near Sandusky on April 28, 1974;[471] and 32 at Oregon (Lucas County) on April 22, 1985.[378] Smaller flocks have appeared at interior locations: 40 at Athens on April 15, 1987, and 18 on April 23, 1970;[158,386] 16 in Fairfield County on May 3, 1980;[471] 14 at Paint Creek Reservoir on April 18, 1976;[262] 12 at Findlay on May 12, 1975;[259] and 10 in Licking County on April 21, 1974. Spring avocets are generally observed in groups of 6 or fewer, with reports from all parts of the state except the Cincinnati-Dayton area and interior northeastern counties.

American Avocets are accidental summer visitors. Most June records pertain to late spring or early fall migrants. However, an avocet in the Winous Point marshes (Ottawa County) on June 21, 1944, was considered a nonbreeding summer visitor.[89]

Fall avocets are rare to locally uncommon migrants along the entire lakefront, producing three to twelve sightings each fall since the late 1970s. Adult avocets normally appear between the first week of July and early August. Most reports are of individuals along the Western Basin and 1–12 in the Central Basin. Most juveniles pass along Lake Erie between August 10 and October 15, with a few remaining through November 7, usually in groups of 10 or fewer.

Within the interior counties, American Avocets are accidental to casual fall migrants. There may be no inland sightings during some years and two to four in others. A few adult avocets appear during July and early August but most inland records are juveniles in August and September. Late migrants may linger through October 25–November 11. Fall avocets have been detected in all portions of Ohio, usually as widely scattered individuals. The largest concentrations totaled 12 at Dayton on August 27, 1957;[299] 11 at Stonelick Lake (Clermont County) on August 12, 1977; and 11 at Killdeer Plains Wildlife Area on July 30, 1983.[371]

GREATER YELLOWLEGS

Tringa melanoleuca (Gmelin)

With their long legs and loud whistled calls, both species of yellowlegs can be immediately recognized among a mixed flock of shorebirds. Distinguishing between Greaters and Lessers is also easy when they are together, but identifying a single yellowlegs of either species is more difficult. Fortunately, both species are common migrants, allowing observers to become familiar with their diagnostic field marks.

As spring migrants, Greater Yellowlegs return slightly earlier than their smaller relatives. The earliest Greaters appeared in central Ohio by February 21, 1925, and along Lake Erie by the first week of March.[45] They are not normally observed until March 25–April 5. Their maximum abundance is expected between April 15 and May 7. Except for a few nonbreeders, the last Greaters depart by May 20–25.

Spring Greater Yellowlegs are widely distributed throughout Ohio. The largest flocks frequently form along western Lake Erie, where they are common migrants and 10–40 may be noted during late April and early May. Larger concentrations are unusual, although 250 gathered near Toledo on May 2, 1943.[89] Elsewhere, Greaters are uncommon to fairly common visitors to flooded fields, marshes, and pond margins. Their numbers fluctuate considerably in response to habitat availability. During some years, they are fairly scarce and mostly observed in flocks of 4–20. In other years, Greaters may be widely distributed with occasional flocks of 40–80.

While most Greater Yellowlegs breed in the boreal forests of Canada and Alaska, a few nonbreeders have summered in Ohio. These nonbreeders are casually encountered along Lake Erie, especially in the Western Basin and near Cleveland. Nonbreeding Greaters are accidental inland.

As fall migrants, Greater Yellowlegs are uncommon to fairly common visitors to mudflats bordering marshes and reservoirs within the interior counties. Inland Greaters are generally observed in flocks of 12 or fewer with occasional concentrations of 20–35. Along Lake Erie, Greaters become fairly common to common migrants. Flocks of 80–140 have been reported, although most fall observations total fewer than 30.

The first fall migrants return to Lake Erie by June 25–30 but are not expected until July 12–22. They become widely distributed by early August. Adult Greaters usually remain through August 15–25 when the first juveniles normally appear. These juveniles are regularly observed through late October. During most years, the last juveniles leave between November 5 and 15, although occasional stragglers linger until late November. Mild weather allowed a few Greaters to remain into December and they have been noted on several Christmas Bird Counts. There is only one January record of a single Greater near Cincinnati on January 15, 1951.[248]

LESSER YELLOWLEGS

Tringa flavipes (Gmelin)

Lesser Yellowlegs are among our more numerous and widely distributed shorebirds. Spring migrants prefer edges of marshes and ponds, flooded fields, and other shallow-water habitats. In autumn, they are mostly found on exposed mudflats bordering lakes, drawndown marshes, and gravel bars along large rivers. During both migrations, Lessers are considerably more numerous than their larger relatives.

Their spring arrival averages one or two weeks later than the Greaters'. Lessers were reported from Cincinnati in late February,[248] but few sightings come before March 15–20. Migrants frequently do not appear until April 1–5. The largest movements normally occur between April 20 and May 15. Most inland migrants depart by May 20–25, although small numbers linger along Lake Erie until June 3–7.

These spring migrants are generally fairly common to common in most counties, becoming locally abundant when habitats are plentiful. They are most numerous along western Lake Erie, where flocks of 20–100+ are regularly noted and occasional concentrations of 300–500 may develop. Elsewhere along Lake Erie and in the interior northern and glaciated central counties, flocks mostly contain 10–60 Lessers with infrequent groups of 100+. The largest concentration away from western Lake Erie totaled 400 at Buckeye Lake on April 26, 1928.[479] Spring Lessers are least numerous in the southern and unglaciated counties. Most reports there are of 5–30 with a maximum of 300 at Cincinnati on April 13, 1939.[504]

A few nonbreeders remain in Ohio throughout June. Most are observed along western Lake Erie, where Campbell[89] considered them regular visitors. There are very few mid-June records elsewhere.

Lesser Yellowlegs are among the first shorebirds migrating south each fall. Migrants frequently return to Lake Erie during the last week of June and are regularly observed by July 5–10 at inland locations. They become common along the lakefront by July 15 but large inland numbers may not appear until July 22–27. They remain fairly common to locally abundant migrants until mid-October. The last migrants normally depart by November 7. Unlike Greaters, which are regularly observed during November, there are very few sightings of Lessers after November 10–15. Singles have lingered as late as December 7, 1985, in Gallia County.[182] Adult Lessers comprise most fall migrants until mid-August and depart by August 22–27. Juveniles usually return during the first week of August but do not become numerous until August 15–20.

Fall migrants are most numerous along western Lake Erie, where 30–200 are regularly noted between mid-July and early September. The largest concentration totaled 1700 in Ottawa County on July 20, 1982.[366] Along the lake's Central Basin and within the central and northern counties, fall Lessers are mostly noted in groups of 50 or fewer, although concentrations of 100–200 may be observed. These migrants are least numerous in the southern and unglaciated counties, where most flocks total 10–25 and concentrations of 50–100 are exceptional.

SPOTTED REDSHANK

Tringa erythropus (Pallas)

Among the large numbers of shorebirds regularly migrating across Ohio, a few accidental Eurasian species have been detected in recent years. One, the Spotted Redshank, was discovered by Larry Rosche and Elinor Elder among a small flock of Lesser Yellowlegs at the dredge disposal basin in Huron (Erie County) on August 28, 1979.[275] This unmistakable wader was an adult retaining its breeding plumage. As frequently happens with migrant shorebirds along Lake Erie, this flock rested in the basin for only a few minutes before continuing its journey. There are no other acceptable sight records from Ohio.

Spotted Redshanks are accidental visitors in North America outside Alaska. The few extralimital records are primarily scattered along both coasts.[5]

SOLITARY SANDPIPER

Tringa solitaria Wilson

The Solitary Sandpiper is one of few shorebirds equally at home along a small rocky stream in Brown County and on a mudflat adjacent to Lake Erie. In fact, migrant Solitaries are more numerous through the interior counties than along the immediate lakefront. They prefer small shallow streams, quiet backwaters along large rivers, shallow marshes, and margins of small ponds, although they also visit mudflats with other shorebirds. Foraging Solitaries are mostly observed at the water's margin; they usually avoid dry mudflats.

During spring, Solitary Sandpipers may appear anywhere there is standing water, including shallow ditches and small vernal pools unattractive to any other shorebird. They are uncommon to fairly common migrants across the state. While a few overflights may appear between March 29 and April 5, Solitary Sandpipers do not normally return until mid-April. Peak numbers are encountered between April 20 and May 10. As their name implies, they are frequently observed as single individuals, but they also form small flocks. Spring totals are normally fewer than 10 daily with occasional flocks of 15–25. The largest movement occurred April 24, 1948, when an estimated 500 Solitaries flew over Buckeye Lake.[306] Most migrants depart by May 20.

Nonbreeding Solitaries occasionally linger into June, and fall migrants regularly return before the end of the month. These June records prompted early ornithologists to believe that Solitaries nested in Ohio, and one even claimed to have discovered a nest on the ground. This assertion was of course erroneous. Solitaries nest in the boreal forests of Canada and Alaska, exhibiting the surprising habit of laying their eggs in abandoned songbird nests in trees.

The first fall arrivals are expected June 25–30. Between mid-July and the first week of September, Solitaries become uncommon to common migrants in every county. While they are slightly more numerous than during spring, daily totals are usually fewer than 15 and seldom exceed 25. The largest concentrations totaled 40 at Dayton on August 23, 1959;[299] 53 at Columbus on July 21, 1941;[471] and 60 at Mosquito Creek Reservoir (Trumbull County) on July 10, 1954.[72] Fall migrants usually are adult Solitaries until the last week of July when the first juveniles appear. Juveniles predominate by mid-August. Numbers of migrants decline during the first half of September and only stragglers remain into October. There are two November records: November 5, 1930, in central Ohio and November 19, 1927, at Cleveland.[45,523]

WILLET

Catoptrophorus semipalmatus (Gmelin)

During the nineteenth century, Willets were regular migrants through Ohio, described as "local and regular in some numbers" along Lake Erie and "uncommon to rare" elsewhere.[226] Their numbers were drastically reduced by overhunting during the late 1800s. Between 1900 and 1937, Willets were reported every two or three years and Hicks[226] cited seventeen records of 32 individuals. Their status changed during the 1950s and Willets have been observed annually since 1959. Numbers of migrants steadily increased through the late 1970s but remained stable in subsequent years.

This large stocky shorebird with its distinctive wing pattern presents an unmistakable image as it lands on a mudflat to feed. Nevertheless, this species has been regularly misidentified. Undocumented reports of flocks during March and October seem very questionable when compared with known migration patterns, and unseasonable Willets should always be carefully identified.

Willets are now rare spring migrants along Lake Erie, averaging two to five reports annually. These migrants are mostly observed from Huron westward, with fewer sightings east to Cleveland. Most lakefront observations are of 1–2 Willets; flocks are unusual, although 18 appeared at Cleveland on May 2, 1987.[386] Spring Willets are accidental to casual migrants through the interior counties. They do not regularly appear at any locality, although there are usually one to four inland sightings most years of small flocks visiting a marsh or flooded field for a few hours or perhaps a day. The largest flocks totaled 18 at Dayton on May 1, 1983;[299] 14 at Lake St. Mary's on April 28, 1985; 12–15 near Columbus on several occasions; 12 near Barnesville (Belmont County) on April 30, 1966, and at Hueston Woods State Park on May 4, 1982;[471] and 10 at Barberton on May 2, 1987. These migrants mostly appear between April 25 and May 5 with smaller numbers returning by mid-April and others remaining into the first days of June.

Willets are rare to uncommon fall migrants along the entire lakefront. They may appear by June 20–25, although they are not normally encountered until the first week of July. Small flocks of migrant adults may be noted through July 15–18, mostly within the Central Basin, including reports of 10–24 from the Cleveland-Lorain lakefront. Fewer adult Willets are recorded later in July and are replaced by juveniles in early August. Three or fewer juveniles are normally detected during August, but occasionally large flocks appear, such as 50 at Cleveland on August 21, 1976.[264] Most depart by September 10. There are very few confirmed October and November records, although 2 remained at East Harbor State Park (Ottawa County) until November 12, 1949.[309]

Within the interior counties, Willets are accidental to casual fall migrants, detected every two or three years. There are very few records of adult Willets during July; a flock of 12 along the Little Miami River near Cincinnati on July 5, 1971, was exceptional.[281] Most inland sightings are of scattered juveniles during August and the first half of September, with occasional groups of 3–4. They are mostly observed in northeastern and

SPOTTED SANDPIPER

Actitis macularia (Linnaeus)

Anyone floating down an Ohio river or boating on its lakes has observed these small shorebirds. Spotted Sandpipers are mostly noted as they forage at the water's edge, preferring quiet backwaters, riprapped shorelines, and exposed gravel bars. Breeding adults are easily identified by their spotted underparts and their habit of constantly teetering as they walk along the shore. When flushed, Spotties emit their distinctive *peet-weet-weet* call notes as they fly with stiff fluttering wing beats just above the water.

Breeding Spotted Sandpipers are widely distributed in Ohio.[434] Pairs are most frequently observed along Lake Erie, where they are fairly common residents. Summer totals seldom exceed 5–12. They are more locally distributed within the interior counties, where nesting pairs are encountered on creeks, rivers, lakes, ponds, and gravel pits. These sandpipers are fairly common residents along every large river in numbers approaching those along Lake Erie. They are casual to uncommon elsewhere, least numerous in the southern counties, where most reports are of scattered pairs.

Their statewide distribution patterns have not appreciably changed during this century. In 1935, Hicks[220] recorded nesting pairs in every county. After 1960, local declines were evident on lakes receiving heavy recreational use and along some large rivers.

Spotted Sandpipers usually place their nests in herbaceous cover within fifty feet of water, although one pair nested on the face of a cliff overlooking Lake Erie.[523] Nests with eggs are mostly reported during the last half of May and June. Renesting attempts produced a few July clutches.[89,479,523] Adults with dependent young are expected between the last week of May and late July.

The earliest Spotted Sandpipers are overflights appearing in Cleveland by March 20, 1976, and other localities by March 27–30. The first migrants do not normally return until April 15–23. Their northward migration normally peaks between April 28 and May 20; small numbers may pass along Lake Erie through June 7. Spring Spotties are most numerous along Lake Erie, where they are locally common visitors. The largest flights total 75–80 but most reports are of 5–35. Within the interior counties, they are generally uncommon to fairly common migrants; the largest movements total 25–30 but most reports involve 10 or fewer.

Their southward passage begins by July 12–18. Fall migrants are most numerous between July 25 and August 25 with smaller numbers regularly noted through September. The last Spotted Sandpipers normally depart between October 15 and 27. A few stragglers have remained into November and there are two December sight records from the Cleveland-Lorain lakefront.

Fall Spotted Sandpipers are most numerous along Lake Erie.

Daily sightings of these fairly common to common migrants normally are of 5–20; the largest flights involved 75. They are uncommon to fairly common migrants through the interior counties. Most inland records total 3–15. Only Trautman[479] regularly reported as many as 40–60 at Buckeye Lake during the 1920s and 1930s.

UPLAND SANDPIPER

Bartramia longicauda (Bechstein)

Shortly after dawn on a mid-April morning, the grasslands bordering many Ohio airports come alive. Amid the cheerful whistles of meadowlarks and the lisping songs of Savannah Sparrows, a moderate-sized brown shorebird issues his distinctive whistle, proclaiming the surrounding grasslands as his breeding territory. As his name implies, the Upland Sandpiper is associated with grasslands, pastures, and prairies, preferring grasslands where the vegetation eventually reaches a height of one to two feet. Flat open terrain is favored, with fence posts, telephone poles, and tall trees serving as convenient sites for the male to declare his territory. Many generations of Upland Sandpipers have returned to Ohio, established territories on the same fence posts, and raised their young. But over the years, they have witnessed changes in land-use patterns detrimental to their survival.

When Ohio was initially settled, Upland Sandpipers were restricted to the prairie openings. Their populations expanded as the virgin forests were replaced with farmlands, and they became fairly common residents in many counties during the 1800s. They remained numerous until the last decades of the century when increased cultivation and market hunting considerably reduced their numbers.[479]

At the turn of the century, Jones[236] considered Upland Sandpipers fairly common residents in most counties, although they were "rather less common" along the southern border of Ohio. In the mid-1930s, Hicks[220] cited nesting records from seventy-six counties but noted that Uplands were absent or very rare in most southwestern counties and along the unglaciated Allegheny Plateau. Their most significant declines were apparent between 1940 and 1960; breeding sandpipers disappeared from many counties, although a few pairs spread into several southwestern counties.[357] Changing agricultural practices were responsible for these declines, especially the conversion of grasslands to cultivated crops. Remaining grasslands were frequently unsuitable; pastures were overgrazed and hayfields mowed too frequently. These declines continued into the 1970s but numbers have apparently stabilized since 1980.

In 1981, breeding Upland Sandpipers still occupied thirty counties, usually widely scattered pairs in the southwestern, central, and northeastern counties.[357] Very few remained in northwestern and west-central Ohio and they were absent along the unglaciated Allegheny Plateau. Nearly three-quarters of these sandpipers occupied grassy fields bordering airports with the remainder inhabiting meadows. Similar distributions and habitat preferences were evident in surveys for the Breeding Bird Atlas (1982–87).[434] While the size of the statewide breeding population has never been precisely estimated, recent sightings indicate that 100–200 pairs may remain in Ohio.

Upland Sandpipers begin nesting shortly after their territories are established. Their nests are shallow scrapes in the ground, expertly hidden among dense grasses. Most clutches are laid during the first half of May and hatch by early June. The young sandpipers remain with their parents into July.[89,479,523] A few pairs nested quite early, producing small young by May 7.[479] Renesting attempts produced nests with eggs through June 20.[429]

When their populations were larger, Upland Sandpipers exhibited well-defined migrations through Ohio. After the early 1960s, these migrants became scarce in most counties; Uplands are now seldom encountered away from nesting locations. The earliest Upland Sandpiper returned to Oxford (Butler County) on March 18, 1982.[365] There are few additional March sightings, mostly before 1940. Uplands do not normally return until April 8–15 in the central and southern counties and April 15–22 in northern Ohio. In recent years, the largest spring flocks are composed of 4–8 Uplands; concentrations of 20–30 were not unusual before 1940. Most Uplands return during April but a few may pass along Lake Erie until May 10–15.

After their young become independent, Upland Sandpipers form small flocks prior to their fall migration. These flocks are usually observed at airports and pastures. By mid-July, the first migrants are heading south and their distinctive *putty-put-put* call notes may be heard as they pass overhead. This migration mostly occurs between July 25 and August 20 with smaller numbers remaining through September 10–20. When populations were larger, a few migrants remained into October with sightings at Columbus on October 11, 1932;[45] Lake St. Mary's on October 16, 1953;[98] and in Pike County on October 23, 1898.[193]

At one time, a few migrant Uplands were usually heard each August evening; occasionally hundreds were counted.[479] Fall flocks were periodically encountered in grassy pastures, mowed clover fields, and harvested wheat fields. These flocks were composed of 20–50 Uplands and largely confined to the western half of the state, especially near western Lake Erie. A few flocks also congregated in the northeastern counties, including 31 in Lorain County on July 19, 1964, and 26 at Youngstown during July 1954.[72,394] The largest fall movement was 200 at Columbus on August 8, 1926.[475]

Since the mid-1960s, fall Uplands have become casual to rare migrants throughout Ohio and very few are heard as they pass overhead. Small flocks of 10–15 are infrequently encountered in grassy fields bordering airports in the western half of the state. Larger flights are limited to western Lake Erie in Ottawa and Lucas Counties, where 48 were counted on August 12, 1983, and a remarkable 96 on July 25, 1985.[372,379]

ESKIMO CURLEW

Numenius borealis (Forster)

During the last half of the nineteenth century, unrestricted market hunting had disastrous effects on every species of shorebird. Perhaps no species suffered greater losses than the Eskimo Curlew. This diminutive curlew was a common spring migrant through the Mississippi Valley and the plains states, and fall migrants congregated along the Atlantic Coast between New England and Newfoundland.[5] Nearly hunted to extinction before they received protection during the late 1800s, most other shorebirds eventually recovered. However, Eskimo Curlews remained inexplicably scarce. Only small flocks and scattered individuals were sporadically observed through the early 1960s. Since then, a few sightings by reputable observers indicate that Eskimo Curlews survive in very small numbers, but their prospects remain bleak.

The former status of Eskimo Curlews in Ohio is poorly known. While nineteenth-century accounts suggest that they may have been regular migrants, there is no specific information concerning numbers of individuals or the timing of their migrations. Given their known migration corridors, Eskimo Curlews probably were not regular spring migrants through Ohio. Their presence during spring was only mentioned by Wheaton,[522] who cited no specific records. If they occurred at all, Eskimo Curlews were probably casual or accidental spring visitors to the western counties.

Eskimo Curlews may have been regular fall migrants in Ohio, at least near Lake Erie from Sandusky Bay eastward. Winslow stated that they "were not rare" migrants in the Cleveland area during the mid-1800s, while Wheaton considered them to be "not common" fall migrants.[522,523] Most of these migrants appeared during September. Eskimo Curlews also occasionally visited the interior counties, where they were accidental or casual migrants. Inland records include a specimen (no longer extant) from Cincinnati during September 1878 and an unspecified sight record from Columbus.[248,522] The date of the last specimen or sight record from Ohio is unknown, but it undoubtedly was before 1900.

WHIMBREL

Numenius phaeopus (Linnaeus)

Whimbrels are readily recognized by their large size, long decurved bill, and well-marked head pattern on an otherwise nondescript plumage. While they occasionally visit mudflats and flooded fields with other shorebirds, they prefer upland grassy fields, drained marshes, and grassy dikes, where they readily blend into a background of dried vegetation.

Spring migration takes many Whimbrels from the Atlantic Coast across the Great Lakes to the tundra of Alaska and Canada. Though regularly observed along the north shore of Lake Erie, they are surprisingly scarce in Ohio. Whimbrels are casual spring visitors to the northeastern counties south to Mahoning, Summit, and Wayne and rare migrants along the entire lakefront. Since 1980, they have averaged one to five sightings annually, generally individuals or groups of 2–7. Large flocks are infrequently noted near Lake Erie: 80 at Ashtabula on May 23, 1959;[323] 42 at Cleveland on May 28, 1949;[308] and 80 in the Toledo area on May 20, 1934, and 75 on May 21, 1976.[89,471] A

few flocks have also been detected in the interior northeastern counties: 101 in Wayne County on May 26, 1984,[374] and 42 over Medina County on May 26, 1985.[378] Whimbrels are accidental visitors away from this corridor. There are only three reports from central Ohio and single sightings near Dayton and Findlay of single individuals, except for a flock of 12 at Findlay Reservoir on May 30, 1981.[361]

The earliest Whimbrel was reported from Dayton on April 19, 1980.[277] The first migrants do not normally appear until May 5–12 and most spring sightings are between May 20 and 30. Late migrants may remain into the first week of June.

Whimbrels are accidental nonbreeding summer visitors along western Lake Erie. Campbell[86] reported a summering Whimbrel between May 28 and June 24, 1933, and a group of 3–4 through June 15, 1935. The only recent summer record was provided by a Whimbrel periodically observed in Lucas County through July 5, 1985.[379]

As fall migrants, Whimbrels become rare to locally uncommon along the entire lakefront, averaging six to ten or more sightings annually. These migrants may return by June 27–July 7 but are not expected until July 15–25. All migrants are adults through the first half of August. Juveniles appear by the end of the month; most are noted between August 25 and September 20 with a few lingering into the second week of October. These migrants appear in groups of 10 or fewer. Fall Whimbrels are accidental visitors away from Lake Erie. Five reports from the eastern half of the state include three sightings from the northeastern counties and singles at Newcomerstown on October 16, 1977, and near Salem on October 16, 1981.[172,178] The only other inland fall records are 2 Whimbrels at Lake St. Mary's on August 27, 1955, and 1 at Hoover Reservoir on September 22, 1978.[98,271] With the exception of 1 in Wayne County on July 26, 1981,[362] all inland records have been after August 25.

Between July 10 and 18, 1988, a white-rumped Whimbrel was observed along the Maumee River near Toledo.[388a] Heavily barred underwings, breast streaking that extended to the legs, and the lightly barred rump were suggestive of the Siberian race *variegatus*, making it the first member of any Eurasian race of Whimbrel to establish a record from the Great Lakes region.

LONG-BILLED CURLEW

Numenius americanus Bechstein

The early status of Long-billed Curlews in Ohio is clouded with uncertainty. Anecdotal accounts provided by Kirtland, Wheaton, and others indicate they may have been rare migrants during the nineteenth century,[236] but no specimens or detailed descriptions are available. Because these observers had difficulty distinguishing Long-billed Curlews from Whimbrels, all nineteenth-century sightings are considered questionable.

Modern observers also have problems separating these two species, and most recent sightings of Long-billed Curlews proved to be Whimbrels. There are only two acceptable sight records, both from central Ohio during late May. The first Long-billed Curlew was discovered by Milton Trautman and others at O'Shaughnessy Reservoir in Delaware County on May 22, 1926.[479] The other was observed by Jim McCormac near Killdeer Plains Wildlife Area on May 25, 1983.[370] Both reports emphasized the bright cinnamon underwing coverts, the absence of crown stripes, and other characteristics of this species.

Long-billed Curlews nest on dry short grass prairies of the western United States and prairie provinces of Canada.[5] They migrate through the western states to wintering areas along the Pacific Coast and the Gulf Coast of Texas. In recent years, they have been very rare but regular migrants along the Atlantic Coast.

HUDSONIAN GODWIT

Limosa haemastica (Linnaeus)

Hudsonian Godwits were almost exterminated by market hunters during the nineteenth century. The few records from Ohio came before 1879 when their populations were still relatively large. Even after hunting ceased, their recovery was quite slow. There were only five Ohio sight records between 1900 and 1930. Slightly improved numbers during the 1930s included the first Hudsonians at Toledo and Youngstown in 1932.[89,449] This slowly increasing population produced very occasional sightings until the mid-1960s, when Hudsonians began to appear regularly along western Lake Erie, including a large flight during 1967. Dramatic improvements during the 1970s brought a pronounced flight along western Lake Erie in 1975 and increased sightings in the remainder of the state. Hudsonian Godwits retained their status as regular fall migrants during the 1980s.

During spring, Hudsonian Godwits are generally quite rare east of the Mississippi River and seldom wander as far east as Ohio. Since 1970, Hudsonians have been casual spring migrants along western Lake Erie, where they are reported once every three or four years. They are accidental spring visitors elsewhere with two sightings in central Ohio, two at Cincinnati, and single records at Lake St. Mary's, Cleveland, and Findlay. All spring records were of 1–3 Hudsonians observed between May 14 and June 6.

Many adult Hudsonian Godwits undertake a remarkable fall migration, flying directly from Canada to South America. Some juveniles undertake a similar nonstop migration but others stop in the Great Lakes states and along the Atlantic Coast during their southward passage.

Within Ohio, fall Hudsonian Godwits are mostly observed near western Lake Erie, where they are generally rare to uncommon migrants. There are relatively few records of adults, only occasional individuals during July and early August. Most migrants are juveniles appearing as early as the last week of August but most frequently between September 20 and October 15. The 1967 flight brought 63 Hudsonians to Ottawa Wildlife Refuge on October 7.[89] The largest movement occurred in 1975

when 143 were observed at Ottawa Wildlife Refuge on September 28 and 90 on October 5.[261] Smaller flights during 1974, 1976, 1983, and 1985 produced flocks of 30–40. During other years, Hudsonians are detected in flocks of 10 or fewer. While they normally depart by October 25–30, November records are not unexpected. In fact, 12 remained at Ottawa Wildlife Refuge through November 8, 1982.[368] One lingered along western Lake Erie until December 3, 1982.[369]

Hudsonian Godwits are casual to accidental fall migrants elsewhere in Ohio. They are most likely to appear along central Lake Erie, at large reservoirs near Columbus, and within the northeastern counties. Sightings are mostly of juveniles between late August and mid-October, either individuals or groups of 6 or fewer. The only flocks were 24 at Cleveland on September 10, 1984; 21 at C. J. Brown Reservoir (Clark County) on August 26, 1979;[299] and 12 at Hoover Reservoir (Delaware County) on September 30, 1967. A few remained as late as November 23–24 in Seneca County and Cleveland. None have been reported from the southwestern counties or the unglaciated Allegheny Plateau.

MARBLED GODWIT

Limosa fedoa (Linnaeus)

Marbled Godwits occasionally passed through Ohio during the nineteenth century, producing records from Cleveland, Columbus, Cincinnati, Buckeye Lake, and possibly other locations. After their populations were decimated by overhunting, they largely disappeared from eastern North America by the early 1880s.

This century's first Marbled Godwits were not recorded in Ohio until 1925, when 5 visited O'Shaughnessy Reservoir near Columbus.[479] They became accidental to casual visitors, averaging three to five sightings each decade through the mid-1960s. Most records were from western Lake Erie and large reservoirs in the northeastern counties. Their status improved in the late 1960s, especially along Lake Erie during autumn. They have been annually reported since 1971, attaining their maximum abundance between 1978 and 1983.

Marbled Godwits are now casual to rare spring migrants along western Lake Erie. They are unrecorded during dry seasons but produce one to three reports when habitats are abundant, usually of single godwits. Away from western Lake Erie, Marbled Godwits are strictly accidental spring migrants with single records from Lake St. Mary's, Butler County, Wayne County, Leetonia (Columbiana County), and Marietta and two sightings near Columbus and at Cleveland. Except for 2 godwits at Lake St. Mary's on May 27, 1955,[98] these records pertain to single individuals. Throughout Ohio, the earliest migrants appeared between April 19 and 21. Most are detected between April 28 and May 20 with a few late migrants remaining into early June.

Summering Marbled Godwits are accidental visitors along Lake Erie. Except for a single godwit at Cleveland on June 11–

12, 1978,[270] these records are restricted to Ottawa and Lucas Counties. As many as 3 Marbleds reportedly summered during 1981, 1982, and 1983 and remained through mid-June 1985. These summering godwits were presumably nonbreeders. While territorial behavior was reported in 1982, no nest was located.[366]

Marbled Godwits are mostly observed as fall migrants along Lake Erie. Within the Western Basin, they are generally rare to locally uncommon fall migrants, producing one to six reports annually. Most sightings are of 3 or fewer Marbleds with occasional flocks of 4–8. From Huron eastward along the lakefront, these godwits are rare visitors to dredge disposal basins with one to three records annually. Most reports are of 1–3 Marbleds. Small flocks are also possible and a remarkable 16 visited Cleveland on July 4, 1983.[371]

Away from Lake Erie, these godwits remain accidental fall migrants. Inland records are limited to reports from Mahoning and Trumbull Counties in 1931, 1948, 1949, and 1950; two records from Lake St. Mary's; and single sightings from Pymatuning Reservoir, Columbus, and Killdeer Plains Wildlife Area. All inland records involved single Marbled Godwits.

Along Lake Erie, the first fall migrants have appeared during the last days of June and are fairly regularly noted by July 3–12. They may be noted anytime during July, August, and September. Later migrants are restricted to western Lake Erie, where Marbleds occasionally linger through November 5–6. The few inland records have occurred between August 15 and October 25.

RUDDY TURNSTONE

Arenaria interpres (Linnaeus)

Ruddy Turnstones are not likely to be misidentified in their attractive breeding plumage. Even their somber juvenile plumage is not readily confused with any other shorebird in eastern North America. During both migrations, Ruddy Turnstones may occur anywhere shorebirds congregate, although they exhibit a preference for beaches, breakwaters, and mudflats along Lake Erie. Spring migrants also regularly visit flooded fields and drawndown marshes along western Lake Erie.

As spring migrants, these turnstones are normally among the later shorebirds passing through Ohio. While single turnstones were discovered along Lake Erie in Lorain County on March 31, 1912, and Cleveland on April 8, 1951,[117,243] these unusually early sightings may pertain to wintering individuals. There are very few records earlier than May 1. The first turnstones are not expected until May 5–10 with the largest movements between May 20 and June 5. The last migrants may not depart until June 10–15.

Although their numbers fluctuate annually, spring Ruddy Turnstones are most numerous along western Lake Erie in Ottawa and Lucas Counties. They are fairly common to common migrants, becoming locally abundant when flooded fields are widely distributed. Spring flocks of 15–50+ turnstones are

not unusual and 100–200 may be noted during their peak movements. Flocks of 350–800 have appeared during some years. Along central Lake Erie, they are generally uncommon migrants as flocks of 5–15. Within the interior counties, they may be completely absent some years but scattered across the state in small flocks other years. Spring Ruddy Turnstones are accidental to locally rare migrants through the northern and glaciated central counties, most numerous in northeastern Ohio. While most inland sightings are of 1–10 turnstones, an impressive 125 were discovered in Wayne County on May 17, 1978.[269] They become accidental to casual migrants within the southern and unglaciated counties, where the few reports are of 1–2 turnstones.

A few nonbreeding Ruddy Turnstones are accidental summer visitors along western Lake Erie in Ottawa and Lucas Counties.[86,89] They have not been reported anywhere else in the state.

The first fall Ruddy Turnstones normally return to Lake Erie between July 20 and 30 and are regularly observed by the first week of August. Adult turnstones appear through the last week of August. The first juveniles have been observed by August 18–23 but do not become numerous until September. Most depart by October 10–20; late migrants may remain into November.

Fall turnstones are distributed along the entire lakefront as uncommon to fairly common migrants. Most records total 10 or fewer, although small flocks of up to 20 may appear and there were 55 near Toledo on August 10, 1965.[89] Within the interior counties, relatively few adult turnstones are discovered during autumn. Most records are of juveniles seen between August 20 and October 15. These migrants are normally casual to rare at large reservoirs in the northern and glaciated central counties, becoming accidental to casual within southern and unglaciated Ohio. Inland records invariably are of 1–3 turnstones.

A few Ruddy Turnstones have lingered into winter along the Cleveland-Lorain lakefront. Single turnstones remained through December in 1974 and 1982 and as late as January 12, 1968, at Lorain.[405] The only wintering turnstone was regularly observed at Cleveland between December 25, 1974, and February 23, 1975; it disappeared with the onset of warmer temperatures.[258]

RED KNOT

Calidris canutus (Linnaeus)

Large flocks of Red Knots regularly gather along Delaware Bay each spring. As they head toward their Arctic nesting grounds, some regularly pass over the Great Lakes region. Although most fly directly to the tundra, a few visit locations in between.

Within Ohio, spring Red Knots are mostly observed near western Lake Erie in Ottawa and Lucas Counties as rare migrants, averaging three or fewer sightings annually. Most spring records are of individuals or groups of 2–8 knots. Larger flocks are exceptional: 150 at Bay Point (Ottawa County) on May 26,

1956;[89] 49 at Ottawa Wildlife Refuge on May 17, 1980;[277] and 15–35 on a few occasions.

Red Knots are casual spring migrants along the lake's Central Basin with a few records of single individuals from the Cleveland lakefront. They are accidental spring visitors to the interior counties with scattered records from northern Ohio west to Seneca County and from central Ohio near Columbus. Most inland sightings are 1 or 2 knots. The only sizable flocks were 60 in Wayne County on May 19, 1983, and 47 in Seneca County on May 18, 1984.[370,374]

The earliest spring knots appear by May 10–11 and most are observed between May 16 and 28. A few migrants are detected through the first week of June and infrequently as late as June 11–17.

Red Knots are accidental nonbreeding summer visitors along western Lake Erie. Individuals reported on June 26, 1954, and through July 1, 1985, were thought to be nonbreeding visitors rather than migrants.[89,379]

Red Knots are more likely to be observed within Ohio during autumn. These migrants are rare to uncommon along the entire lakefront. The first fall migrants may return by July 15–20 but are not regularly observed until August 5–15. They are mostly noted between August 20 and September 15 with smaller numbers through mid-October. They are very rare migrants after October 20 with a few November records along western Lake Erie and a late knot near Toledo on December 1, 1935.[89] Adult knots may pass along the lakefront through the last week of August. Juveniles normally appear during the last half of August and make up the whole migration after September 1.

Lakefront fall migrants can be scarce some years with fewer than six sightings of scattered individuals. In other years, knots become fairly regular migrants with ten to twenty or more records, mostly of 6 or fewer individuals with occasional concentrations of 8–13. A flock of 43 at Cleveland on September 9, 1984, was exceptional for autumn.[376]

Red Knots are generally accidental fall migrants to the interior counties, becoming casual visitors to Hoover Reservoir near Columbus and Lake St. Mary's. Fall records from the southern counties are limited to three sightings near Dayton[299] and one in Gallia County. Fall knots are usually detected at one to three inland localities each year, mostly as scattered individuals, although small flocks of 3–7 have been infrequently observed. The largest inland fall concentration totaled 21 at Lake St. Mary's on October 10, 1956.[98] While a few adult knots have been observed in August, most inland records are of juveniles between August 25 and October 15. Late migrants have lingered through November 3–10.

SANDERLING

Calidris alba (Pallas)

Renowned for their incessant chasing of waves on coastal beaches, Sanderlings are also familiar visitors to the Great Lake states. They are rare to uncommon spring migrants along Lake Erie, frequently mixed among flocks of Dunlins and Ruddy Turnstones. Sightings are of only 1–6 Sanderlings daily. Within the interior counties, they are accidental to casual migrants in groups of 3 or fewer. These inland spring records are equally distributed across the state. The earliest Sanderlings returned to Cleveland on March 27, 1988, and April 12, 1986. Other early arrivals were noted at lakefront sites and Columbus by April 22–23. They are not expected to appear until May 10–15. Most sightings are during the last half of May with a few through June 3–7.

Sanderlings are accidental nonbreeding summer visitors. The only midsummer record is of 2 at Toledo on June 17, 1933; they may have been very late spring migrants.[89]

Fall migrants are considerably more numerous. They become fairly common to common visitors along Lake Erie, most frequently noted in the Central Basin. Most fall reports are of 20 or fewer with occasional concentrations of 30–60. The largest fall flock was discovered on the Maumee River near Toledo: 225 on October 10, 1937.[89] Considerably fewer Sanderlings visit mudflats adjoining large reservoirs within the interior counties. They are uncommon to fairly common fall migrants through the northern and glaciated central counties, mostly observed in groups of 8 or fewer with occasional flocks of 15–20. The largest inland concentration was 50 at Lake St. Mary's on September 24, 1909.[98] Within the southern and unglaciated counties, fall Sanderlings are accidental to locally rare visitors. Most sightings are of 5 or fewer daily and the largest flocks totaled 8–11.

Along Lake Erie, the earliest fall migrants return by July 4–7 but do not normally appear until July 20–25. Their maximum abundance is usually attained between August 20 and October 10. Smaller numbers may remain through November 10–18. Adult Sanderlings make up this migration through mid-August, but they depart by the end of the month. The first juveniles arrive by August 9 but do not predominate until the first week of September. Within the interior counties, Sanderlings are unrecorded until August 8–15. They are mostly observed between August 28 and October 5 and normally depart by October 20–25. A few have lingered into November.

Sanderlings have survived along Lake Erie into early winter, producing at least five December records of single individuals. The latest individuals remained through January 11, 1979, at Lorain and January 2, 1960, at Ashtabula.[325]

SEMIPALMATED SANDPIPER

Calidris pusilla (Linnaeus)

For most birders, their first encounter with small sandpipers, or "peeps," is with an assemblage of look-alike species scattered across a mudflat in fall. Identifying these species is a challenge and a source of frustration, even for experienced observers. Separating them requires careful study, and the first step is to become familiar with the more common species. Among the most numerous of the "peeps" are the Semipalmated Sandpipers.

Semipalmated Sandpipers are found wherever shorebirds congregate. During spring, they are fairly late migrants and do not normally return until May 3–7. Maximum numbers are encountered between May 15 and 30 and small flocks are frequently observed during the first week of June. Last migrants depart by June 10–15, although occasional nonbreeders have summered along the lakefront.

Spring Semipalmateds are most numerous along western Lake Erie, where daily totals of 50–300+ may be noted during May. When suitable habitats are plentiful, concentrations of 700–1000+ have been reported. They are common visitors elsewhere along the lakefront, usually not exceeding 100 daily. Inland Semipalmateds are fairly common to common migrants through the northeastern counties, where most reports are of 50 or fewer and the largest flock totaled 1000 at Barberton on May 27, 1986.[382] They are rare to uncommon migrants in the southeastern counties and fairly common at other inland locations, although concentrations seldom exceed 15–50.

Fall migrants are generally more numerous. Maximum daily concentrations may reach 1000–1500 along western Lake Erie and 100–300 in the Central Basin. Inland migrants are rare to fairly common at most localities, least numerous in the unglaciated counties and southwestern Ohio. The largest inland flock totaled 900 at Lake St. Mary's on September 1, 1910.[202] Concentrations of 100–200 have appeared in central Ohio but seldom exceed 20–75 elsewhere.

Along Lake Erie, the first adult Semipalmateds return between July 7 and 15 but do not become numerous until the last week of the month. Juveniles arrive by August 3–10 but do not predominate until the last half of the month. Largest fall flocks normally appear between July 25 and September 7. Most depart before the end of September. Timing of the inland migration is similar except that adults are relatively scarce. Phillips[414] demonstrated that these sandpipers are early fall migrants, seldom remaining in the Great Lakes region past the first week of October. The latest Ohio specimen was collected in Lucas County on October 11, 1937. While a few migrants may linger into mid-October, later reports probably pertain to Western Sandpipers.

WESTERN SANDPIPER

Calidris mauri (Cabanis)

Ohio's first Western Sandpiper was a female reported August 10–11, 1914, near North Lima (Mahoning County).[526] By the 1920s and 1930s, Western Sandpipers were discovered to be rare but regular fall migrants, with most reports of 3 or fewer mixed among flocks of Semipalmated Sandpipers. Trautman's[479] observation of 12 Westerns at Buckeye Lake on September 4, 1929, was remarkable for that era. Their status remained unchanged until the 1970s when we found that Western Sandpipers were more numerous than previous records indicated.

Their spring status has been obscured by many misidentifications and their true abundance remains to be determined. Western Sandpipers are apparently casual spring migrants along western Lake Erie and accidental to casual elsewhere in northern and western Ohio. They are unrecorded from the remainder of the state. These migrants are mostly observed as individuals or groups of 2–4. The earliest Western returned to Lucas County on March 30, 1938.[89] Most early April records of Semipalmated Sandpipers probably pertain to Westerns. Most spring Westerns are reported during May. A few lingered into the first week of June but none have summered.

As fall migrants, adult Westerns are largely restricted to Lake Erie with very few sightings from the central and northeastern counties. A few adults return by July 2–7 but most are noted between July 15 and August 7. Most juvenile Westerns appear after August 15 and are widely distributed across the state. Their maximum abundance is normally attained between September 15 and October 15. Most depart by October 20–27. A few stragglers may remain into November; certainly all November sightings of Semipalmated Sandpipers are misidentified Westerns.[414] The latest Western remained at Cleveland through December 14, 1984.

Fall migrants are most numerous within the northern half of Ohio, particularly along Lake Erie from Huron westward and at a few reservoirs in the central counties. Westerns are rare to locally fairly common migrants. Most fall sightings are of 1–15. Along Lake Erie, the largest flocks totaled 75 at Ottawa Wildlife Refuge on September 21, 1986, and 40 at Huron on September 4, 1981.[363,384] Inland concentrations totaled 50 at Hoover Reservoir on September 18, 1982, and 30 at Lake St. Mary's on August 15, 1987.[368,388] Within the southern and unglaciated counties, they are casual to locally uncommon migrants in groups of 1–10.

RUFOUS-NECKED STINT

Calidris ruficollis (Pallas)

The appearance of this Old World sandpiper was one of the most remarkable sightings in Ohio. An adult Rufous-necked Stint in breeding plumage was discovered by Jon Ahlquist, Paul Savage, and Ralph Browning at Walnut Beach in Ashtabula on July 21, 1962. Along with a flock of about 50 Least and Semipalmated Sandpipers, it remained at the beach until the next day.[1] It was carefully studied and photographed. When compared with specimens at the National Museum in Washington, the photographs eliminated all similar sandpipers.

Rufous-necked Stints breed in Siberia and northwestern Alaska and normally winter from India east to New Zealand.[5] Outside Alaska, North American records of Rufous-necked Stints are limited to a small number of sightings along both coasts. This Ohio sighting provides the only record from the interior of the continent.

LEAST SANDPIPER

Calidris minutilla (Vieillot)

Our smallest "peeps" are also among the more numerous of the shorebirds passing through Ohio each spring and autumn. Least Sandpipers are found wherever shorebirds congregate, including flooded fields, drawndown marshes, and mudflats bordering large lakes.

The earliest spring migrant was reported on April 9, but the first Leasts normally appear between April 23 and 30. Their peak movements are expected May 5–18. Their numbers diminish by May 25 with a few stragglers lingering into early June along Lake Erie.

These migrants are most numerous along western Lake Erie, where they are common during May. Spring totals usually are 10–50 with occasional concentrations of 100–150+. Within the Central Basin, they are uncommon to fairly common migrants and daily totals seldom exceed 15–30.

Within the interior counties, spring migrants can be scarce during dry seasons and widely distributed in wet years. Spring Leasts are generally uncommon to fairly common migrants through the northern and glaciated central counties. Daily totals are usually 30 or fewer, although concentrations of 70–150+ are infrequently encountered. Least Sandpipers are normally accidental to rare along the unglaciated Allegheny Plateau and locally uncommon within southwestern Ohio. Most spring reports are of 10 or fewer, although 20–40+ may appear in the southwestern counties.

A few nonbreeders have spent the summer along Lake Erie, Buckeye Lake, and Lake St. Mary's.[89,98,479] They are casually reported along western Lake Erie and accidental elsewhere, mostly as individuals, although small groups of 2–6 have been noted near Toledo.[86]

Fall Least Sandpipers are fairly common to abundant migrants along Lake Erie and fairly common to common visitors to inland reservoirs in the northern and glaciated central counties. These migrants become rare to locally fairly common visitors in southern and unglaciated Ohio. Along Lake Erie, most fall reports are of 10–50 with occasional concentrations of 75–150. Larger flocks are restricted to the Western Basin, where 300–500 have infrequently congregated. Within the northern and glaciated central counties, most locations support 30 or fewer with occasional flocks of 50–75 Leasts. Larger concentrations include 100–150 near Columbus on several dates and 300 at Lake St. Mary's on September 1, 1910.[202] In southern and unglaciated Ohio, most fall flocks total 15 or fewer and the largest concentrations seldom exceed 30.

Along Lake Erie, fall Leasts invariably appear between June 25 and July 4 and become common by July 15–22. They remain numerous through October 5–15. The timing of their fall movement is similar at inland localities, where they may not become numerous until the last half of August. These flocks are dominated by adult Leasts through the first week of August. The first juveniles are expected between July 25 and August 3 and they make up the majority of fall migrants after August 10–15. Few adults have been found after August 20.

The last fall migrants normally depart between October 25 and November 10. During relatively mild autumns, scattered individuals and small flocks may linger through the end of November and occasionally into December and early January. Along Lake Erie, these early winter records are restricted to two sightings along the Western Basin during the first week of December. At inland locations, Leasts have been noted through December 13, 1953, at Youngstown;[70] December 27, 1957, at Tappan Lake (Harrison County);[78] and January 6, 1985, at C. J. Brown Reservoir (Clark County).[377] The only wintering record was also at C. J. Brown Reservoir, where 4 Leasts were noted on January 16, 1983, and 2 were regularly observed through February 13.[369]

WHITE-RUMPED SANDPIPER

Calidris fuscicollis (Vieillot)

White-rumpeds are among the last sandpipers passing through Ohio each spring. They may return during the first week of May but frequently do not appear until May 10–15. Their migration does not peak until May 18–June 7. Small flocks and individuals have been casually reported through June 20–July 5, but they could be nonbreeders rather than very late spring migrants.

Spring White-rumpeds are most numerous along western Lake Erie, where they become uncommon to fairly common in late May. They are mostly observed in flocks of 5–15 with occasional concentrations of 25+. The largest spring flight was noted in 1971 when 200 visited Magee Marsh Wildlife Area on May 23.[471] Considerably fewer pass along the Central Basin, where they are rare migrants in groups of 5 or fewer.

Within the interior counties, White-rumpeds may be absent during dry seasons, but when suitable habitats are plentiful they are rare to locally uncommon migrants in the northern and glaciated central counties. These migrants mostly appear in groups of 10 or fewer; occasional flocks of 15–25 have been reported. The largest inland concentration totaled 55 in Wayne County on May 17, 1978. These spring migrants are accidental to casual visitors to the southern and unglaciated counties, mostly in groups of 5 or fewer with a maximum of 15 in the Cincinnati area.

As fall migrants, the first adult White-rumpeds normally return in mid-July and may remain through August 5–15. There are relatively few sightings during the last half of August since juvenile White-rumpeds do not normally appear until September. Most juveniles are observed between September 10 and October 15. Stragglers have lingered into early November. One along Lake Erie near Huron until November 29, 1984, was exceptionally late.[376]

Fall White-rumpeds are rare to locally uncommon migrants along Lake Erie and within the northern and glaciated central counties. Adult White-rumpeds are mostly found along Lake Erie in groups of 5 or fewer. Juvenile White-rumpeds are evenly distributed in these counties, mostly in groups of 6 or fewer with occasional flocks of 8–25. The largest concentrations were detected in the northeastern counties: 40 at Mosquito Creek Reservoir (Trumbull County) on September 24, 1949, and near Youngstown on October 8, 1950.[58,62] Fall White-rumpeds are accidental to casual migrants in the southern and unglaciated counties, mostly in groups of 5 or fewer.

BAIRD'S SANDPIPER

Calidris bairdii (Coues)

Although Baird's Sandpipers will associate with mixed flocks of "peeps," they seldom join Leasts and Semipalmateds to forage on wet mud or in shallow water. Instead, Baird's prefer dry mud and exposed flats covered with short vegetation and may be found on sod farms, golf courses, and recently mowed hayfields far from mudflats.

Within Ohio, Baird's Sandpipers are almost exclusively fall migrants, most numerous along Lake Erie and at reservoirs within the glaciated central and northern counties. They become uncommon to locally fairly common migrants through these localities, mostly in groups of 6 or fewer, although small flocks of 10–15 have periodically appeared. Within the southern and unglaciated counties, they are accidental to locally rare migrants in groups of 4 or fewer.

Except for a few sightings of adults along Lake Erie during the last half of July, nearly all fall records are of juveniles. Along Lake Erie, Baird's Sandpipers are very sporadically encountered between July 16 and August 10. Their fall migration normally peaks between August 20 and September 20 and they become rare after October 5–10. Timing of their inland migration is similar, though there are few confirmed sightings before August 10.

Most Baird's Sandpipers depart by early October, but a few remain later into autumn. Jehl[235] contended that late fall and early winter records are most likely misidentifications, but growing evidence suggests that Baird's Sandpipers are capable of surviving until the mudflats freeze. Carefully identified Baird's lingered into November during six of eight years from 1980 through 1987. Combined with sight and specimen records from previous decades, these observations suggest that Baird's Sandpipers may be casual migrants during November as single individuals associating with other lingering shorebirds. Relatively mild weather allowed a few Baird's to remain into early winter. The latest confirmed records are a specimen collected at Cedar Point Wildlife Refuge (Lucas County) on December 16, 1939,[89] and single sandpipers photographed at Huron on December 11, 1979;[275] Alum Creek Reservoir on December 19–20, 1982; and C. J. Brown Reservoir through January 2, 1983.[369]

This species' status as a spring migrant has been obscured by numerous misidentifications. There are no spring records documented by specimens or photographs and very few acceptable sight records. Based on known distribution patterns, these sandpipers are expected to be accidental spring visitors and could appear anytime between the last days of March and mid-May. Whenever a spring Baird's Sandpiper is encountered, it should be thoroughly documented and photographed to help establish the spring status.

PECTORAL SANDPIPER

Calidris melanotos (Vieillot)

Pectoral Sandpipers are familiar and widely distributed migrants, as likely to appear on flooded farm fields and mudflats bordering inland reservoirs as along Lake Erie. Their spring numbers exhibit considerable annual fluctuations. Some years flocks are regularly encountered across the state, especially during relatively wet seasons when flooded fields are widely available. But spring migrants can become scarce in drier seasons.

Spring Pectorals are generally fairly common to locally abundant migrants except along central Lake Erie and the unglaciated Allegheny Plateau, where they become uncommon visitors. Within most counties, spring flocks are normally composed of 10–40 Pectorals with occasional flocks of 100–200. Larger concentrations mostly appear in southwestern Wayne County, where 1000–2000 are regularly noted. Along western Lake Erie, 300–800 Pectorals frequently congregate and flights of 1000+ have been encountered. Within the central and southwestern counties, the largest flights are composed of 300–500 Pectorals. Along central Lake Erie and the unglaciated counties, few flocks exceed 50.

The earliest spring migrant appeared along western Lake Erie on February 28, 1981,[360] but they are not expected to return until March 20–30. Their northward movements peak during April, although sizable flocks remain along western Lake Erie into the first week of May. The last Pectorals normally depart by May 7–15 with a few lingering through May 25–30.

A few nonbreeders have spent part of the summer within Ohio. These accidental visitors are restricted to western Lake Erie, where Campbell[89] reported "several" records—isolated nonbreeders noted for only a few days in mid-June and crippled birds remaining most of the summer.

Fall Pectoral Sandpipers are fairly common to locally abundant migrants along Lake Erie. Flocks of 20–50 are regularly noted with local concentrations of 100–200. Larger flocks are restricted to Ottawa and Lucas Counties, where 500–1000+ have occasionally congregated. Within the interior counties, Pectoral Sandpipers are fairly common to locally abundant visitors to lakes and fish hatcheries across Ohio, generally least numerous along the unglaciated Allegheny Plateau. They become uncommon to casual visitors to counties lacking these habitats; a few flocks may be found on golf courses, sod farms, and dry farm fields. Most inland reports are of 50 or fewer but 75–150 may be tallied at favorable habitats. The largest inland fall flocks totaled 225–350 at reservoirs near Dayton and Columbus.

Fall migrants have been noted along Lake Erie and a few inland sites during the first week of July. Along Lake Erie, they do not normally become numerous until July 15–22. They may not return to most inland areas until July 20–August 10. While sizable lakefront movements have been evident by late July, the largest statewide concentrations may not appear until September when juvenile Pectorals pass through Ohio. Small flocks are regularly noted through the end of October and the last migrants normally depart by November 10–15. Stragglers have remained to December 1.[45] There is also an undocumented Christmas Bird Count report from Wooster.

SHARP-TAILED SANDPIPER

Calidris acuminata (Horsfield)

Sharp-tailed Sandpipers nest in Siberia and migrate along the western Pacific Ocean to wintering areas in the Southern Hemisphere. Like several other Asian shorebirds, Sharp-tailed have appeared in North America, primarily disoriented juveniles in fall. These sandpipers regularly appear along the Pacific Coast of the United States and Canada and occasionally wander into interior North America. A handful of records come from the Great Lakes region and along the Atlantic Coast.[5] Ohio's only record of this accidental visitor fits this pattern of vagrancy. Larry Rosche discovered a juvenile Sharp-tailed in the Gordon Park impoundment at Cleveland on October 6, 1984. It was banded the following day and remained through October 23.[376]

PURPLE SANDPIPER

Calidris maritima (Brünnich)

To find these rare visitors to Ohio, one must visit jetties, breakwaters, or rocky shorelines along Lake Erie during late autumn and early winter. With perserverance, one may encounter them as they forage among moss-covered rocks at the water's edge. Because they are normally tame, they may even be closely approached. However, Purple Sandpipers are easily overlooked as they search for food among large boulders.

During the nineteenth century, Purple Sandpipers were considered accidental visitors with a few records from Ohio. During this century, they have proven to be rare but regular fall migrants along the south shore of Lake Erie. They are never numerous and average one to four sightings annually. Most records are from the Central Basin, especially the Lorain-Cleveland area, where they have been regularly observed since 1916.[523] In the Western Basin, they have been periodically encountered since 1943[89] with most sightings from rocky shores along the western Lake Erie islands.

The earliest migrant was a specimen collected at Cleveland on the exceptional date of September 11, 1883.[464] While a few Purple Sandpipers appear as early as mid-October, most pass through Ohio between November 5 and 25. Others may appear between December 15 and January 7, corresponding with the freeze-up of inshore habitats along the lake. The latest migrants normally depart by January 15. Most sightings are of 1–2 individuals, although small flocks of 4–6 are rarely encountered. Purple Sandpipers usually do not associate with other birds, but there are always exceptions. Certainly the most unusual behavior was exhibited by a Purple Sandpiper associating with a flock of starlings at Cleveland from December 31, 1977, to January 7, 1978. This sandpiper foraged with the starlings along the lakefront during the day and roosted with them on buildings at night.

Despite their annual appearance as fall migrants, few Purple Sandpipers winter in Ohio. They are accidentally encountered after mid-January with only four winter records since the 1940s along the Avon Lake-Cleveland lakefront. The only spring record was provided by an overwintering bird at Cleveland that was last observed March 21–22, 1949.[523]

There is only one documented inland record of a Purple Sandpiper from Ohio. This sandpiper was discovered by Dave Smith along the riprap-covered banks of Ferguson Reservoir near Lima on November 29, 1985.[380]

DUNLIN

Calidris alpina (Linnaeus)

A migrant flock of Dunlins presents an impressive spectacle as these sandpipers perform their aerial acrobatics over a flooded field near western Lake Erie. They twist and turn in unison, alternately exhibiting their reddish backs and black belly spots. These maneuvers are regularly observed along western Lake Erie, an important staging area for Dunlins in passage from the Atlantic Coast to nesting grounds on the Arctic tundra.

Along western Lake Erie, spring Dunlins return as early as the first week of April, although they do not normally appear until April 15–25. While flocks of 100 or more have been noted by April 20, the largest concentrations are normally encountered between May 5 and 25. When suitable flooded fields or drawndown marshes are available, spring migrants become abundant and concentrations of 1000–3000+ may be noted. When these habitats are scarce, the largest flocks are composed of 100–500. Their numbers are noticeably reduced by the last week of May, although flocks of 100 or more have remained into the first week of June.

These large spring Dunlin flocks do not normally visit other portions of the state. Dunlins are fairly common migrants in small numbers along central Lake Erie, but their appearance within the interior counties is irregular and dependent upon habitat availability. Spring migrants are generally casual to uncommon and locally distributed in the northern and glaciated central counties, becoming accidental to rare in southern and unglaciated Ohio. Away from western Lake Erie, spring Dunlins are normally observed in flocks of 25 or fewer with occasional concentrations of 35–50. An exceptional 500 appeared in Seneca County in 1984. Timing is similar to the movements along western Lake Erie.

A few nonbreeders may remain along the Great Lakes. These nonbreeders are casual to rare summer visitors along Lake Erie and may appear anytime between mid-June and mid-August.[89,335] The only inland summer Dunlins have been reported from Lake St. Mary's.[98]

Fall Dunlins are widely distributed along the entire lakefront and on mudflats bordering large reservoirs, generally as fairly common to locally abundant migrants. Concentrations of 1000–1500 have appeared along western Lake Erie. However, most fall flocks are composed of 50–250 in northern and central Ohio with occasional congregations of 300–500+. Smaller numbers visit reservoirs in the southern and unglaciated counties, where the largest flocks seldom exceed 25–75.

Dunlins are the last shorebirds returning to Ohio each fall. The first migrants do not normally appear along Lake Erie until September 18–25 or within the interior counties until September 25–October 2. Large flocks may be observed by mid-October. Most depart during the last half of November but flocks may infrequently remain into December. The latest flock totaled 225 at Ashtabula on December 27, 1952.[341] Occasional stragglers have lingered into the first week of January, and a few Dunlins have attempted to overwinter during relatively mild winters, including a successful attempt by 1–3 in the Toledo area during the winter of 1931–32.[89] Others remained through February 20, 1960, at Hoover Reservoir and February 13, 1983, at C. J. Brown Reservoir.[325,369]

CURLEW SANDPIPER

Calidris ferruginea (Pontoppidan)

Within North America, this Eurasian sandpiper is primarily a rare summer resident in Alaska and a rare migrant along both coasts. In recent years, a few Curlew Sandpipers have also been regularly observed as migrants through the upper Great Plains and Great Lakes regions.[5] Ohio's first Curlew Sandpiper was discovered by Tom Bartlett in Thompson Township, Seneca County, on May 16, 1984. The only other spring Curlew was discovered by John Pogacnik and myself in Carroll Township, Ottawa County, on May 7, 1985. This individual remained through May 12. A fall migrant was discovered by Jerry Talkington at Cleveland on July 15, 1984, and remained for four days.[389] All three were adults in breeding plumage. During spring migration, this species frequently associates with large flocks of Dunlins. Both Ohio spring Curlew Sandpipers were discovered in such flocks. Fall Curlew Sandpipers should pass through Ohio before the first Dunlins return.

STILT SANDPIPER

Calidris himantopus (Bonaparte)

Stilt Sandpipers, greatly reduced by overhunting during the nineteenth century, were very rare throughout Ohio in the early 1900s. With adequate protection, their numbers subsequently improved. By 1940, Stilts became fairly common fall migrants along western Lake Erie.[86] Elsewhere, they were regularly encountered at only a few localities in the central and northeastern counties. They did not become widespread fall migrants within the northern half of Ohio until the early 1960s. Their numbers steadily increased through the 1970s but have remained fairly constant during the 1980s.

Stilt Sandpipers normally pass through the central United States during spring migration. They are not annually recorded from Ohio but are usually observed three years out of four. Spring migrants are casually encountered along Lake Erie, mostly within Ottawa and Lucas Counties. They are also casual spring migrants in central Ohio near Columbus when suitable habitats are available. Spring Stilts are accidental elsewhere with fewer than five inland records from the eastern counties and none from southwestern Ohio. The earliest confirmed Stilt Sandpiper returned by April 20. Most are observed during the first three weeks of May and depart by May 25–30. These migrants are normally encountered in groups of 7 or fewer.

In most Ohio counties, Stilt Sandpipers are strictly fall migrants, appearing wherever shorebirds congregate. They usually forage in shallow water, wading belly deep and frequently immersing their heads and necks as they probe like dowitchers for invertebrates in the soft mud.

As fall migrants, their numbers vary from year to year, mostly in response to habitat availability. Fall Stilts are most numerous along western Lake Erie, where they are fairly common to common migrants. Although they are normally noted in groups of 30 or fewer, large concentrations may develop. Flocks in excess of 75 Stilts have appeared in most years since 1977, with a maximum of 157 on August 9, 1982.[368] They are uncommon to fairly common elsewhere along the lakefront. Concentrations of 40–60 are exceptional east of Sandusky Bay and most flocks are composed of 15 or fewer.

Within the interior of Ohio, Stilt Sandpipers are generally uncommon to fairly common migrants in the northern and glaciated central counties. They become casual to locally uncommon in the southwestern and unglaciated counties. Inland totals are normally 10 or fewer Stilts daily with occasional flocks of 20–30. By far the largest inland concentration was 150 at Killdeer Plains Wildlife Area between September 9 and 17, 1983.[372]

While the first fall migrants may return to western Lake Erie by July 1, they are not regularly encountered along the lakefront until July 10–17. The largest concentrations usually occur in August and early September. These migrants are largely adult Stilts through the first week of August; juveniles become prevalent by the third week of the month. At inland localities, adult Stilts are rarely encountered; most sightings are of juveniles after mid-August. Throughout Ohio, most Stilts depart by October 12–22, although 15 remained at Hoover Reservoir (Delaware County) through October 23, 1984. Occasional stragglers have lingered into the first week of November.

BUFF-BREASTED SANDPIPER

Tryngites subruficollis (Vieillot)

A highlight of the fall shorebird migration is the appearance of this attractive bird, which often acts more like a plover than a sandpiper. Buff-breasteds generally avoid the shoreline mudflats preferred by most other sandpipers in favor of dry fields, golf courses, sod farms, and dried mudflats covered with short vegetation. Their buff plumage provides surprisingly good camouflage against a background of dried mud or dead grasses, and Buff-breasteds are easily overlooked as they quietly forage in these habitats.

As fall migrants, Buff-breasted Sandpipers are generally rare in northern Ohio, most frequently recorded near Lake Erie. They are also rare but regular fall visitors to drawndown reservoirs near Columbus. They are casual migrants near large lakes in west-central Ohio and accidental visitors to the southwestern counties where there are fewer than ten records. There are no published sightings from the unglaciated counties.

The earliest fall migrants have been noted during the first half of August but these early arrivals are quite rare. Most Buff-breasted Sandpipers are juveniles appearing between the last week of August and late September. Only a few stragglers remain into the first week of October; an exceptionally late migrant lingered at Cleveland through October 24–28, 1981.[363]

Buff-breasteds are generally recorded at six or fewer localities most years, although they occasionally become locally uncommon migrants with twelve or more statewide sightings. Most reports are of 1–3 sandpipers with occasional flocks of 6–7. Flocks of 15–22 are very infrequent; most have been noted in northeastern Ohio. By far the largest flock totaled 78 in a mowed clover field in Ottawa County on September 12, 1985.[380]

Buff-breasteds have always been rare migrants. While they were fairly regularly recorded in northwestern Ohio during the 1920s and 1930s,[86] there were relatively few sightings elsewhere until the 1950s and 1960s. These greater numbers may reflect increased populations or increased efforts to locate this attractive shorebird during its southward journeys.

In spring, Buff-breasteds are normally restricted to a narrow migration corridor through the Great Plains. Relatively few stray from this corridor and they are accidental anywhere east of the Mississippi River. The only documented spring record from Ohio is provided by a flock of 7 discovered near Harpster (Wyandot County) on June 11, 1966.[416] They were observed at close range for nearly twenty minutes as they fed in a plowed field.

RUFF

Philomachus pugnax (Linnaeus)

Ohio's first record of this Eurasian shorebird was provided by a specimen taken at Buckeye Lake on November 10, 1872.[520] Another specimen was secured from the same area on April 28, 1878.[45] No other Ruffs were recorded until one appeared near Toledo on August 1, 1956.[89] This sighting signaled a change in their relative abundance, since there were at least five Ruff reports during the 1960s and eight records in the 1970s. Since 1980, there have been at least twelve acceptable Ruff sightings, although they are still not encountered annually. There have been similar increases elsewhere in North America, leading to speculation that a small breeding population exists on the continent.

The earliest spring Ruff was discovered in Pickaway County on April 2–3, 1972. There have been a few other April records but most northward migrants are detected during the first half of May. The latest migrants were noted through May 22–23. Of fifteen spring records, six are from Ottawa and Lucas Counties, where Ruffs have become casual visitors since 1980. They are accidental spring migrants elsewhere, with four records from central Ohio near Columbus, an equal number of sightings in Wayne County, and a single Seneca County report. Spring observations have been of single individuals except in 1985 when at least 3 Ruffs were discovered in Ottawa County between May 4 and 11.[378] The majority of these sightings have been of males in their distinctive breeding plumages.

The earliest fall Ruff returned to Killdeer Plains Wildlife Area on June 27, 1982.[366] Most fall migrants have been noted during August and September with only a single October record from Toledo and the November 10 specimen from Buckeye Lake. Ruffs are casual fall migrants along western Lake Erie east to

Huron with at least ten published records. They are accidental fall visitors elsewhere with single published records from Dayton, Buckeye Lake, and Killdeer Plains. All fall sightings have been of single individuals.

SHORT-BILLED DOWITCHER

Limnodromus griseus (Gmelin)

At one time, all dowitchers were classified as one species. Their identification was straightforward and their status well defined. The splitting of dowitchers into Short-billed and Long-billed species posed serious identification problems. As a result, there have been many misidentifications and the status of both species within Ohio was obscured. Only in the past ten to fifteen years has it been possible to accurately assess the status of both species.

Spring Short-billeds generally arrive later than Long-billeds. The earliest confirmed arrival was on April 23 but Short-billeds do not normally appear until the first week of May. This movement normally peaks between May 7 and 23. Most depart during the last week of May. While these dowitchers have remained along Lake Erie through June 10, none have summered within Ohio.

Spring Short-billeds are most numerous along western Lake Erie, where they are fairly common to abundant migrants. During some years, the largest flocks are composed of 30–40 dowitchers; 100–300+ may congregate in other springs. Short-billeds are rare to uncommon spring migrants along central Lake Erie, mostly as flocks of 15 or fewer. Their appearance within the interior counties is related to habitat availability with the largest numbers discovered during relatively wet seasons. They are casual to locally uncommon migrants through the northern and glaciated central counties. While most records are of 20 or fewer, flocks of 50–150 occasionally appear. In the southern and unglaciated counties, they are accidental to casual migrants. Most sightings are of 1–6, although as many as 40 have been reported near Cincinnati.

Fall migrants regularly appear along Lake Erie during the first week of July. By July 10–15, they are common to abundant along western Lake Erie and fairly common to common elsewhere along the lakefront. The largest concentrations appear in Ottawa and Lucas Counties with 6400 at Winous Point (Ottawa County) on July 20, 1982;[366] 1500 at Magee Marsh Wildlife Area on July 9, 1983;[371] and 1000 at Winous Point on July 5, 1972.[90] Most reports total 30–200 along western Lake Erie and 10–75+ within the Central Basin. July migrants are exclusively adults; they are replaced by juveniles during the first half of August. While Short-billeds remain fairly common to common migrants along Lake Erie through September 15, concentrations seldom exceed 50–300 along western Lake Erie and 5–40 within the Central Basin during August and September. Most depart by September 25–30, with a few lingering into early October.

Within the interior counties, adult Short-billed Dowitchers have appeared as early as June 30, but they are accidental to locally rare migrants until the first half of August when the juveniles normally appear. Inland Short-billeds are mostly observed between August 10 and September 15. A late Short-billed lingered at Lake St. Mary's through October 12, 1986,[384] but there are very few confirmed sightings after October 1. As along Lake Erie, inland October dowitchers are most likely Long-billeds.

Fall Short-billeds are rare to locally fairly common migrants through the northern and glaciated central counties. Most sightings are of 20 or fewer dowitchers, but 75 were at Barberton (Summit County) on July 26, 1985, and 136 at Hoover Reservoir on September 17, 1974.[471] They are accidental to locally uncommon fall migrants through the southern and unglaciated counties, mostly in groups of 12 or fewer.

LONG-BILLED DOWITCHER

Limnodromus scolopaceus (Say)

The status of Long-billed Dowitchers in Ohio was also obscured by identification problems. Within the past decade, our ability to distinguish them from Short-billed Dowitchers has improved tremendously. Recent records give a preliminary indication of the Long-billed's status, although it will take years to fully understand its distribution and migration patterns in every portion of the state.

Spring Long-billed Dowitchers tend to migrate earlier than Short-billeds, appearing as early as March 8, 1987, in Seneca County.[386] Most records are scattered between March 20 and April 30. A few Long-billeds have been reliably identified along Lake Erie as late as the first week of May. Hence, most Long-billeds depart before the Short-billeds arrive. There are presently no reliable mid-May Long-billed sightings from Ohio.

Spring Long-billeds are accidental to casual migrants throughout the state. They are not regularly observed at any locality but are usually detected at one to three locations most years. They are most likely to appear near Lake Erie but have been noted in all portions of Ohio except the unglaciated counties. Most spring reports are of 1–3 Long-billeds.

As fall migrants, Long-billed Dowitchers are considerably more numerous along western Lake Erie than in the remainder of the state. The first adults may return by July 20–30 but most appear in August. These adults are rare migrants, normally reported in groups of 3 or fewer. Juvenile Long-billeds have returned as early as August 28 but are not expected until September 7–15. A flock of 90 juvenile Long-billeds at Ottawa Wildlife Refuge on September 10, 1983, was exceptionally early. They do not normally become fairly common to common migrants until October when flocks of 100–200+ appear most years with a maximum of 370 in Lucas County on October 12, 1983.[372] These flocks are substantially reduced by November 15. The last Long-billeds usually depart by November 20–25 with late migrants through December 7.

Long-billed Dowitchers are rare fall migrants elsewhere along Lake Erie. There are very few records of adults during late July and August. Juveniles are generally rare between September

20 and November 7 in groups of 5 or fewer. A few late migrants have lingered into early December.

Away from Lake Erie, Long-billeds are accidental to locally rare fall migrants. Most sightings are of 1–5 juveniles in the western half of Ohio between September 20 and November 7. A few migrants remain later in the month. The largest inland flock totaled 16 at Big Island Wildlife Area (Marion County) on October 27, 1984.

COMMON SNIPE

Gallinago gallinago (Linnaeus)

Common Snipes occupy marshes, bogs, wet meadows, and ditches where they can readily take refuge in dense vegetation. Their subtly patterned plumage provides excellent camouflage as they quietly probe in the soft mud for worms and other invertebrates. When approached, snipes frequently crouch over the mud, relying on their cryptic coloration to hide them from predators. Should danger approach too closely, they flush with an explosive takeoff followed by a rapid zigzagging flight.

During spring migration, snipes are common to abundant within the marshes bordering western Lake Erie. Tallies of 20–50 daily are not unusual and flights of 75–100+ appear most years. The largest movements total 150–235. Their spring movements are more erratic elsewhere. Snipes are fairly common to locally abundant migrants through all glaciated counties. Spring totals are usually 5–25 daily with occasional concentrations of 40–75. Larger flights produced 100–125 snipes in several central Ohio counties and 150 estimated near Cincinnati on April 19, 1980.[277] Fewer pass through the unglaciated Allegheny Plateau, where they are uncommon to fairly common migrants and daily totals seldom exceed 5–20.

Throughout Ohio, the first spring migrants normally return between March 5 and 15. Common Snipes are most numerous between March 25 and April 30 and sizable movements may occur anytime during April. They depart from most interior counties by May 10–15. A few late migrants may linger along western Lake Erie through May 20–25.

While most Common Snipes silently pass through Ohio each spring, a few males undertake their spectacular courtship displays, flying in endless large circles high over a marsh. As they dive through the air, the wind vibrates their outer tail feathers to produce a diagnostic low booming sound. A single snipe may display for an hour or longer, providing a spectacular show that is witnessed too infrequently in Ohio.

On rare occasions, Common Snipes have summered and nested within the state's boundaries. The few nests with eggs have been reported between April 28 and May 30, and adults accompanied by partially grown chicks have been noted through July 11.[35,89,215] Common Snipes mostly establish their summer territories in marshes and wet meadows composed of grasses, sedges, and rushes. Except for the displaying males, snipes are exceptionally secretive during summer. Their nests are virtually impossible to find, cleverly concealed on the ground in dense cover.

A small summering population has always existed within northeastern Ohio. Hicks[215] recorded snipes from twelve Ashtabula County locations, including 16 pairs in the former Pymatuning Bog. Summering snipes were only sporadically encountered in Trumbull, Mahoning, and Portage Counties before 1935.[220] Habitat destruction reduced this population after the early 1930s. Common Snipes are presently casual to rare summer residents in Ashtabula, Lake, Geauga, and Trumbull Counties and accidental to casual elsewhere south to Columbiana County.[34,434] Only 1–3 pairs are reported from each county and the entire population may not exceed 10 pairs. Snipes are also rare summer residents within the marshes bordering western Lake Erie and a few pairs occupy wetlands in the Oak Openings.[90,434] This population probably does not exceed 5–8 pairs during most years. Snipes are accidental summer visitors within the remainder of northern Ohio, where nesting was confirmed in the Cleveland area in 1963 and Lorain County in 1967 and 1978.[117,404] They are accidental nonbreeding summer visitors within the central counties. They summered in Carroll County during 1948 and 1985 and nesting was suspected but never proved.[84,434] A few additional June records from other central counties may have been of migrants.

As fall migrants, snipes occupy the same wetlands favored during spring, although a few join other shorebirds on mudflats. Their southward migration may begin as early as July 7–10 within the northern and central counties. However, the first fall migrants are not expected until July 20–August 10. Their maximum abundance is normally attained between September 15 and October 25, although flocks may appear throughout November. These migrants are most numerous within the western Lake Erie marshes, where they are fairly common to locally abundant. Fall totals are usually 5–25 daily with periodic concentrations of 30–60. As many as 100–150+ have been rarely encountered. Elsewhere, snipes are generally uncommon to locally common migrants. Most reports are of 12 or fewer with infrequent concentrations of 30–55. These migrants are widely distributed within the glaciated counties but scarce along the unglaciated Allegheny Plateau.

Subfreezing temperatures eventually force most Common Snipes to depart for warmer climates. A few winter along ditches and at springs where open water is always available. Snipes are rare winter residents within the southern and central counties and casually recorded in northern Ohio. Most sightings are of scattered individuals with occasional groups of 2–6. Mild weather has enticed as many as 10–13 to remain in central Ohio into January.

EURASIAN WOODCOCK

Scolopax rusticola Linnaeus

This accidental visitor to North America is mostly known from nineteenth-century specimens from New England and eastern Canada. Outside this region, Eurasian Woodcocks have been reported only from Alabama and Ohio.[5] The Ohio record is one of very few during the twentieth century. On November 6, 1935, G. F. Dixon shot an unusually large woodcock along the banks of a stream in Newbury Township, Geauga County. John Aldrich of the Cleveland Museum of Natural History examined the remains and noted that the bird's total weight was ten ounces compared with five to seven ounces for a typical American Woodcock. After comparing the skeletal material with American Woodcock bones, Aldrich concluded that the bird was a Eurasian Woodcock.[3] This skeletal material was deposited in the Cleveland Museum of Natural History, but it is no longer in the museum's collections and its whereabouts is unknown.

AMERICAN WOODCOCK

Scolopax minor Gmelin

As darkness approaches each March evening, peenting noises are produced by unseen birds in abandoned fields, woodland edges, and other brushy habitats throughout Ohio. While the sound resembles the call of the nighthawk, March is much too early for that species. Instead, these noises are produced by courting male American Woodcocks. The peenting calls are associated with their courtship dance, performed on patches of short grass or bare soil. After the dance is completed, the male takes flight, spiraling upward in ever smaller circles with his stiff outer primaries producing a unique twittering sound. Higher and higher he flies until he passes from sight. After reaching his zenith, he quickly descends with his spiraling flight producing a different but equally diagnostic set of twittering notes as the wind rushes through his wings. He lands at the same location from which he departed, only to repeat these displays until darkness falls.

These courtship displays can be regularly witnessed, for American Woodcocks are fairly common to locally common spring migrants in most counties. These migrants are widely distributed in the eastern third of the state, especially the northeastern counties near Lake Erie, but become scarce in intensively cultivated western Ohio. Most reports are of 8 or fewer woodcocks with occasional concentrations of 12–18. Larger flights are unusual, although 40–50 have been reported near Columbus and 100+ in northeastern Ohio.

Spring woodcocks invariably return with the first warm days of late February and early March. This early migration is not without its risks. The return of deep snow cover and prolonged subfreezing temperatures can cause considerable mortality. Within the southern and central counties, the first migrants are expected between February 20 and March 5. In northern Ohio, most appear between March 5 and 12. Their numbers peak between March 15 and 30 and the last migrants depart by April 10–15.

The courtship displays are continued by resident males into May or June. A courting male was reported as late as July 14 at Cincinnati.[248] Their nesting activities begin by mid-March in central Ohio and late March within the northern counties.[479,523] These early nests are abandoned if inclement weather returns. Most woodcock nests have been discovered during

April; clutches through mid-June probably represent renesting attempts. Later clutches are restricted to Ashtabula County, where Hicks[215] cited three July records and hatching eggs on August 7, 1928. Downy young woodcocks have been discovered by the first week of April. Most appear between mid-April and mid-May.[479] The earliest broods may fledge by late June, but others have been noted into early August.

Breeding woodcocks normally prefer damp brushy fields, woodland edges, open moist woods, and the brushy edges of ponds. Their nests have also been reported from orchards, patches of grass between fences, steep grassy banks planted with pines, and oatfields.[51] They are normally located in small openings. Females rely on their cryptic plumage to avoid detection.

Woodcocks have been widely distributed summer residents since 1900 when Jones[236] regarded them as "fairly common" breeding birds in most counties. Hicks[220] cited summer records from eighty-four counties with the greatest number in northeastern, southeastern, and central Ohio. Woodcocks were very local in most western counties. Their breeding populations slowly declined in subsequent decades as a result of habitat loss.

Despite these declines, American Woodcocks remain widely distributed summer residents.[434] They are generally fairly common to locally common residents in the northeastern counties. They become uncommon to fairly common residents along the unglaciated Allegheny Plateau and in most southwestern and central counties. Breeding woodcocks are very locally distributed within west-central and northwestern Ohio. While they are fairly common in the Oak Openings of Lucas and Fulton Counties, they are generally rare to uncommon residents in the other counties. Summering woodcocks are never numerous; most reports are of 10 or fewer. Their movement patterns are fairly complex. Once the males abandon their territories, they may wander widely. Young woodcocks may also move considerable distances after fledging. Individuals may appear anytime during July or August at locations where they did not nest.

Woodcocks are less conspicuous during autumn and are more often encountered by hunters than birders. Southward migrants may appear by late August but are not widely noted until the last half of September.[479] The largest numbers are expected during October when woodcocks become uncommon to fairly common migrants, most numerous within the northeastern counties. Most fall reports are of 1–5 daily. Large flights are possible; Hicks[215] recorded 100+ individuals in Ashtabula County on twelve occasions during the 1920s and early 1930s. In recent years, the largest flight totaled 50 at Cincinnati on October 15, 1979.[275] They may be regularly observed through mid-November.

During December, a few woodcocks may remain until they are forced southward by extended subfreezing temperatures. There have been occasional sightings through December 15–25, but American Woodcocks are strictly accidental visitors after January 1. The few midwinter records include a courting male at Cincinnati on January 16;[11] 3 woodcocks in Adams County on February 6, 1986;[381] and 1 in Westerville (Franklin County) February 13–21, 1985.[377]

WILSON'S PHALAROPE

Phalaropus tricolor (Vieillot)

Wilson's Phalaropes have not always been regular migrants through Ohio. Their numbers were decimated during the 1880s and these phalaropes were exceptionally rare in the early 1900s.[236] Their status did not improve until the 1930s. Campbell[86] considered them "fairly regular but not numerous" migrants at Toledo with 14 recorded between 1931 and 1936. Away from western Lake Erie, they remained accidental migrants until the 1950s and 1960s, when single phalaropes were regularly encountered in most portions of Ohio during fall migration. Their numbers increased during the 1970s, reaching a peak between 1978 and 1983. This increase corresponded with an eastward expansion of their breeding range. Numbers of migrants have declined somewhat since 1983.

Spring Wilson's Phalaropes are now most numerous along western Lake Erie, where they are rare to uncommon migrants, usually in groups of 6 or fewer. An exceptional flight during 1978 produced 47 at Magee Marsh Wildlife Area on May 10.[269] Elsewhere in western and central Ohio, they are casual spring migrants in groups of 3 or fewer, although the 1978 flight produced 10 at Cincinnati on May 6–8. They become accidental spring migrants in eastern Ohio. The earliest spring migrant appeared by April 10 but there are few other April records. Most Wilson's are noted between May 7 and 21 with occasional stragglers in northwestern Ohio through June 3–7.

Fall Wilson's Phalaropes are also most numerous along western Lake Erie, where they are uncommon to fairly common migrants. Daily counts usually total 6 or fewer with maxima of 10–12. Between 1978 and 1983, concentrations of 20–35 occasionally frequented suitable mudflats in Ottawa and Lucas Counties. They are rare to uncommon migrants in groups of 6 or fewer along central Lake Erie. Along the entire lakeshore, adult Wilson's are normally noted between June 25 and July 20 but are replaced by juveniles during the last half of July. Largest concentrations develop between August 1 and September 7. The last migrants normally depart by September 25–October 7. Two exceptionally late phalaropes were documented from Toledo on November 20, 1987.[388]

At inland localities, Wilson's Phalaropes are rare but regular fall migrants in central Ohio but accidental to rare elsewhere and least numerous in the southeastern counties. They are normally encountered as scattered individuals, mostly juveniles between July 20 and September 25. The latest fall records include singles documented from Lake St. Mary's on November 7, 1982, and Pickerington (Franklin County) on December 4, 1981.[364,368]

Their recent eastward range expansion produced breeding records east to New England and was responsible for Ohio's only confirmed nesting records. During June 1980, 2 female and at least 2 male Wilson's Phalaropes attempted to nest at Magee Marsh Wildlife Area in Ottawa County. Mark Shieldcastle discovered a nest with four eggs on June 4, but these eggs disappeared from the nest by June 20. Another male and at least 2 young were located there on June 22.[445] One pair summered in the wildlife area during 1981 but nesting was not confirmed.[362] Another unsuccessful nest was reported from Ottawa National Wildlife Refuge during June 1988.[388a]

RED-NECKED PHALAROPE

Phalaropus lobatus (Linnaeus)

Numbers of Red-necked (formerly Northern) Phalaropes markedly increased during the present century. Before 1930, they were accidental visitors with no more than six sightings from the entire state.[85] The number of records increased during the 1930s and 1940s with sporadic appearances of widely scattered fall migrants. The first sizable fall movement was near Youngstown in 1949 with a maximum of 23 phalaropes on September 5.[58] This flight was not evident elsewhere and was not repeated during the next two decades. These phalaropes were relegated to the status of casual fall migrants during the 1950s and did not become annual visitors until the early 1960s. That decade produced regular observations of 1–6 phalaropes each autumn and occasional spring migrants. Additional increases were apparent in the 1970s and small flights were detected several autumns. Their status has not changed during the 1980s.

Red-necked Phalaropes are now rare spring migrants along western Lake Erie with one to three sightings most years, invariably of 1–5 individuals. They are accidental to casual spring visitors to the northern and glaciated central counties, producing four to seven records a decade. Most sightings involve 1 or 2 phalaropes with a maximum of 8 near Barberton (Summit County) between May 27 and June 1, 1986.[382] They are unrecorded from southern and unglaciated Ohio.

Their northward passage is normally quite rapid; many remain only a few minutes or hours. The earliest migrants appeared between May 7 and 10. They are most likely to be observed between May 15 and 25. Few linger into June, although there is a central Ohio record as late as June 11, 1938.[45]

As fall migrants, Red-necked Phalaropes can be scarce some years with only a few scattered individuals along Lake Erie and none inland. Other years may produce scattered records from across the state. Small flights occur during one to three years each decade, producing small flocks along Lake Erie and four to nine inland reports.

These migrants are rare to uncommon along Lake Erie, most numerous within the Western Basin. Most fall reports are of 1–6 individuals on exposed sandbars, dredge disposal areas, and drawndown marshes. Flights produced flocks of 26 at Ottawa National Wildlife Refuge on October 7, 1977; 22 there on September 28, 1986; and 10–11 at Cleveland.[267,384]

Away from Lake Erie, fall Red-neckeds are casual to rare visitors within the northern and glaciated central counties, most likely to appear near Columbus and at northeastern lakes. Except for the 1949 flight at Youngstown, the largest inland flocks totaled 11 at Mosquito Creek Reservoir on September 8, 1945, and 10 at Lima on August 29, 1974.[257,523] Most reports are of 3 or fewer. These phalaropes are accidental to casual visitors to the southwestern counties and along the unglaciated Allegheny Plateau with only two or three sightings each decade, mostly of single phalaropes, although 3–4 have been observed at several locations.

The earliest fall migrants returned to western Lake Erie during the last half of July. They usually appear between August 10 and 20 and most are observed through October 7. A few stragglers have been reliably reported into the first week of November; later reports most likely refer to misidentified Red Phalaropes. At inland localities, Red-neckeds return by August 10–15 but most are observed between August 25 and September 25. A few linger until October 15–20.

There are no acceptable winter Red-necked Phalarope records from Ohio. Reports of single Red-neckeds sighted at Toledo and Cleveland in January were accompanied by insufficient details to eliminate Red Phalaropes. Their appearance at this time of year is very unlikely. Any observation after early November should be carefully documented.

RED PHALAROPE

Phalaropus fulicaria (Linnaeus)

Along Lake Erie, Red Phalaropes are usually discovered in the relatively quiet waters along piers, breakwaters, and harbors. Few are found on the open waters of the lake where they are easily overlooked. At inland localities, Reds also occur mostly along shorelines rather than on the open waters of reservoirs.

Before 1940, Red Phalaropes were accidental visitors with only ten published records, all along Lake Erie and in the central counties near Columbus.[85,479] There were few additional records into the 1960s. Since 1965, this phalarope has been annually recorded, a result of more thorough coverage by birdwatchers along Lake Erie and at inland reservoirs during the late autumn months when this species is most likely to occur.

Red Phalaropes are now rare fall migrants along central Lake Erie and casual to rare visitors to the lake's Western Basin. During most years, there are two to four reports scattered along the lakefront. Once or twice each decade, small flights develop and as many as ten sightings may accumulate from Lake Erie. All substantiated reports are of 1–3 Reds; an undocumented flock of 30+ during mid-September seems very questionable. Exceptionally early fall Reds appeared at Cleveland on August 27, 1981, and September 3, 1982.[363,368] The first migrants do not normally appear until September 20–30. Individuals may be noted anytime during October and November but most are discovered between November 10 and 25. Their fall migration frequently continues into the first half of December.

Away from the lakefront, these phalaropes are casual fall visitors near Columbus, averaging two or three sightings each decade. They are accidental fall visitors elsewhere with at least three records from Lake St. Mary's, two sightings at northeastern Ohio reservoirs, and single sightings from C. J. Brown Reservoir (Clark County), Dayton, and Cincinnati. The only record from the unglaciated Allegheny Plateau is a specimen collected in Jefferson County on September 15, 1945.[83] Inland reports are usually of single phalaropes, although 3 appeared near Buckeye Lake on September 27, 1968.[471] Most are detected between September 12 and October 15 with a few stragglers through November 15.

While Reds are the hardiest of the phalaropes, most of them eventually depart for the Atlantic Ocean. The last sightings occur as the lake freezes between December 25 and January 7. There is only one record of an overwintering Red Phalarope: at Cleveland from January 1 through March 31, 1955.[335]

Red Phalaropes are strictly accidental spring visitors to Ohio. March records are limited to the overwintering phalarope at Cleveland and 1 at Mosquito Creek Wildlife Area (Trumbull County) on March 15, 1983. This phalarope was exceptionally early and may have overwintered in the Great Lakes area.[370] Other spring records are single Red Phalaropes at Wright-Patterson Air Force Base near Dayton May 2–6, 1953;[439] Bresler Reservoir near Lima on May 12, 1976;[263] and Cleveland on May 22, 1977.[266]

POMARINE JAEGER

Stercorarius pomarinus (Temminck)

Jaegers pose one of the most difficult identification challenges of all North American birds. While most adult jaegers can be safely identified, immatures of all three species exhibit considerable variability in their plumages. There are very few characteristics that consistently separate them. Even experts regularly disagree over the identity of immature jaegers and it is not unusual to have a single individual accused of being all three species.

Very few adult jaegers appear in Ohio. Sightings are mostly of immatures, many of whose identities are based on less than satisfactory evidence. The few specimen records provide only fragmentary data. Hence, our present understanding of their relative abundance is quite poor. As our ability to identify immature jaegers improves, observations may substantially alter our current understanding of their relative abundance in the state.

Pomarine Jaegers are believed to be accidental or casual fall migrants along Lake Erie, averaging three to five sightings each decade since 1960. These sightings are scattered along the entire lakefront, although the majority have been within the Central Basin. All confirmed records are of single jaegers. While they have been reported as early as September 8, Pomarines tend to migrate later than the other jaegers and are unlikely to appear before mid-October. Most reports have been during November and December.

Pomarine Jaegers are accidental winter visitors along the lakefront. The only confirmed winter record was of a closely studied adult at Cleveland on January 4, 1988, but there have been several other winter jaeger sightings from Lake Erie that may pertain to this species. Because Pomarines have the most northerly winter distribution of all the jaegers, they are the species most likely to appear on the Great Lakes after mid-December. However, any winter jaeger should be identified on the basis of its characteristics and not assumed to be a Pomarine.

Pomarines are accidental fall visitors away from Lake Erie.

The only confirmed inland record was of an immature collected at Lake St. Mary's on October 17, 1964.[98] Single Pomarines were reported from the same location on October 15, 1966, and at Lake Rockwell (Portage County) on September 30, 1973, but substantiating details are unconvincing.

PARASITIC JAEGER

Stercorarius parasiticus (Linnaeus)

If sight records were accurate, Parasitics would be the most numerous autumn jaegers along Lake Erie. It is not safe, however, to assume that any fall jaeger is a Parasitic. Instead, all jaegers should be carefully identified and documented to obtain an accurate understanding of the migration patterns and relative abundance of the three species.

Like many birds largely restricted to Lake Erie, Parasitic Jaegers have been more regularly observed since 1980 than during previous decades, probably a result of more thorough coverage by birdwatchers. Before 1980, Parasitics were considered accidental to casual fall migrants along the entire lakefront, averaging two to four sightings each decade. Campbell[89] cited six Toledo area records between 1931 and 1968. Williams[523] and Newman[335] reported a similar number from the Cleveland area, except in 1945 when up to 3 Parasitics were observed "almost daily" between October 2 and December 8.[523] The continuous sightings suggested that a considerable number of jaegers must have been involved in this flight.

Since 1980, Parasitic Jaegers have been observed annually along Lake Erie with one to three sightings every autumn. These sightings indicate that Parasitics are rare fall migrants through the Central Basin and casual visitors every two or three years in the Western Basin. All recent records have been of 1–3 jaegers, most of them briefly observed in migration. While migrants have been reported as early as July 26, these early sightings have not been adequately documented. The first confirmed Parasitics appeared during the last half of August; the majority of Lake Erie sight records have been in September with another peak during November. A few have remained through December 1–8, but their status later in December remains to be positively determined. They are accidental migrants away from Lake Erie. The only confirmed inland record is a specimen collected at Buckeye Lake on September 2, 1919.[479]

The only spring record is a specimen recovered from a field near Lebanon (Warren County) in late March or early April 1880 and now in the Cincinnati Museum of Natural History. Jones[236] said this jaeger appeared "after a week of stormy weather."

LONG-TAILED JAEGER

Stercorarius longicaudus Vieillot

By far the rarest jaegers to appear along the Great Lakes, Long-taileds are also the most difficult to identify. Immature Long-taileds can be quite similar to immature Parasitics and their positive identification requires careful study at close range, an opportunity one seldom gets with jaegers along Lake Erie. The Long-tailed's fall migration tends to be slightly earlier than the migrations of the other species, coming primarily in August and early September when few observers are searching for jaegers. Long-taileds are accidental visitors to Ohio with only three confirmed records, all of first-year birds in autumn. The first was collected at Buckeye Lake on September 5, 1928.[479] The second was an injured jaeger discovered along a rural road near Ashtabula on October 18, 1956; it died in captivity.[355] The third was a sick jaeger found in a residential yard in Parma (Cuyahoga County) on September 13, 1960. It too died in captivity.[335]

LAUGHING GULL

Larus atricilla Linnaeus

Laughing Gulls are very common and widely distributed residents along the Gulf of Mexico and the Atlantic Ocean north to Maine.[5] Before 1950, only a few wandered into the interior of North America, mostly storm-driven birds following hurricanes. Since then, stray gulls have occasionally visited the Great Lakes and other inland locations, where they have been regularly noted since the early 1970s.

Within Ohio, the status of Laughing Gulls has been obscured by difficulties separating them from Franklin's Gulls, especially during the 1950s and 1960s. Our ability to correctly identify Laughing Gulls has improved in recent years, allowing for a more accurate assessment of their present status.

Ohio's first Laughing Gull was collected along Lake Erie at Fairport Harbor (Lake County) on May 19, 1951.[335] The second was a juvenile collected at South Bass Island (Ottawa County) September 14, 1953.[481] In 1963 at least one Laughing Gull was at Lorain July 7–9.[335] Single gulls were in Lake County on May 24, 1964, and May 28, 1969.[335,407] One appeared near Toledo on July 9, 1972, and Laughing Gulls were reported along Lake Erie in every subsequent year. The first inland Laughing Gulls were confirmed in the 1970s. Only 1–3 Laughing Gulls were annually reported from Ohio during the 1970s. The number of sightings gradually increased after 1980 with five to ten reports most years.

Laughing Gulls are now rare spring visitors along Lake Erie. The earliest appeared at Oregon (Lucas County) on February 21, 1987;[385] this individual may have wintered somewhere on the Great Lakes. The first migrants may return by March 27–April 1 but few records are earlier than May 5. All sightings are of 1–2 gulls. They are accidental spring visitors to inland lakes with two sightings at Alum Creek Reservoir and single records at C. J. Brown Reservoir and in Gallia County.

Summering Laughing Gulls are restricted to Lake Erie, where they are casual to rare visitors. Both adults and immatures may be encountered as individuals or in groups of 2–3. The only indication of breeding was provided by a female Laughing Gull discovered in a large Ring-billed Gull colony at Oregon during 1984.[472] This unmated female built a nest and incubated eggs between May 21 and June 11. A female Ring-billed Gull also laid eggs in this nest. The Laughing Gull returned to the colony every year through 1987, never acquiring a mate but building nests and laying eggs each spring. None of her attempts is known to have been successful. However, a hybrid Laughing X Ring-billed Gull also appeared in this colony during 1986, leading to speculation that hybrid offspring may have been raised one year.[383]

As fall visitors, most Laughing Gulls are observed during August and September with a few scattered records through October 30. The latest Laughing Gulls were documented from the Cleveland-Lorain lakefront through December 6, 1986.[381,385] These migrants are casual to rare along Lake Erie. They are accidental to casual visitors to inland reservoirs with at least eight confirmed records since 1977 from Cincinnati, Lake St. Mary's, C. J. Brown Reservoir, Alum Creek Reservoir, and Hoover Reservoir (Delaware County).

While most fall sightings are of 1–2 gulls, an unprecedented influx produced flocks of 18 at Cleveland and 10 at Lorain on August 12, 1985, and smaller numbers scattered along the lakefront into October. This influx also produced 12 Laughing Gulls at C. J. Brown Reservoir and 1 at Lake St. Mary's on September 2.[380]

FRANKLIN'S GULL

Larus pipixcan Wagler

Ohio's first Franklin's Gull was collected at Buckeye Lake on October 15, 1906.[479] This specimen provided the only record until the late 1920s and 1930s when small numbers were discovered along western Lake Erie, where Campbell[86] considered them uncommon but regular migrants. They were described as rare and accidental at Cleveland.[523] The only inland record was near Columbus on October 10, 1937.

Fewer Franklin's Gulls were observed during the 1940s and 1950s, perhaps reflecting less intense coverage by birdwatchers. Their status gradually changed after 1960. As gulls dramatically increased along Lake Erie, a few Franklin's regularly associated with the large flocks of Bonaparte's and Ring-billeds. The number of inland records also increased, although inland Franklin's Gulls remained accidental through the mid-1970s.

Since 1975, Franklin's Gulls have been casual to rare spring migrants along Lake Erie from Cleveland westward and accidental visitors to the interior counties. There are thirteen spring records from the inland western and central counties but only one from eastern Ohio, at Senecaville Reservoir on April 23, 1981.[176] These migrants appear as early as mid-April but most are observed between May 5 and 25 in groups of 3 or fewer.

Nonbreeding Franklin's Gulls are casual to rare summer visitors along Lake Erie; one or two appear most years. These nonbreeders are mostly observed near Cleveland; surprisingly few are in the Western Basin. Most records come during July and early August, usually of immature gulls. Away from Lake

Erie, Franklin's Gulls are accidental summer visitors with only one sighting from Alum Creek Reservoir during 1978.[270]

As fall migrants, Franklin's Gulls are uncommon along Lake Erie between Toledo and Cleveland and rare farther east, producing only two to four reports some years and twelve or more in others. These migrants are recorded in groups of 7 or fewer, mostly immatures between September 20 and November 30. Away from Lake Erie, they are casual to rare fall migrants at reservoirs in the western and central counties. They average one to four inland sightings each year with most records of 1–3 immatures between September 25 and November 15. A few large flocks of adults have been observed, including 35 at Alum Creek Reservoir on October 28, 1984;[376] 18 at Hoover Reservoir on October 16, 1976; and 14 at Findlay on November 11, 1975. Within the eastern counties, Franklin's Gulls are accidental fall migrants with very few confirmed sightings.

Along Lake Erie, Franklin's Gulls are casual to rare early winter visitors, mostly scattered individuals along the Cleveland-Lorain lakefront. Although most depart during the first half of December, they occasionally remain through December 15–25. There are very few confirmed sightings after January 1, although one Franklin's Gull survived at Cleveland through late February of 1964.[392]

LITTLE GULL

Larus minutus Pallas

Our smallest gull is an immigrant from Europe, first reported in North America around the turn of the century. Little Gulls did not become regular visitors for several decades. Initially, they were winter residents, but as their numbers increased, they were noted throughout the year. Their first North American nesting records were established along the Great Lakes during the 1960s.

Ohio's first Little Gull was a thoroughly described adult discovered along Lake Erie at Fairport Harbor on December 24, 1923.[112] The next record came on December 23, 1947, when one was discovered along the lakefront in Ashtabula County.[45] Little Gulls also appeared in 1949, a wintering bird near Cleveland and a spring migrant visiting a reservoir near Columbus.[45,523] During the 1950s, Little Gulls became sporadic visitors along central Lake Erie. The first Toledo area record was furnished in 1960[89] and this species was annually reported from Lake Erie in subsequent years. Numbers peaked between 1975 and 1983.

Along Lake Erie, Little Gulls are mostly fall migrants and early winter visitors. Their fall migration exhibits two defined peaks, reflecting the movements of Bonaparte's Gulls, with whom they normally associate. The earliest Little Gulls appear between July 20 and September 10 with a few individuals remaining through the end of the month. There are few additional records until the last week of October when Little Gulls appear among the developing flocks of Bonaparte's. Little Gulls generally attain their maximum abundance during the last half of November and in December.

Within the Central Basin, these migrants are casually recorded before late October as scattered individuals. During November, they become rare to locally fairly common visitors, most frequently observed at river mouths. Most reports are of 5 or fewer; occasional groups of 8–13 were noted through 1983 but not subsequently. Along western Lake Erie, Little Gulls are casual migrants with most sightings of 1–3 during November.

During winter, Little Gulls are regularly observed as long as Lake Erie remains open and flocks of Bonaparte's Gulls frequent the lakefront. They normally leave the Western Basin before December 30 and the Central Basin between December 30 and January 15. Before January 15, this species is a casual to locally uncommon visitor in groups of 6 or fewer. They become casual visitors after January 15, although as many as 5–6 Little Gulls have overwintered during mild seasons.

As spring migrants, they are casual visitors within the Central Basin and accidental in Ottawa and Lucas Counties. Most sightings are of single gulls. A flock of 10 at Cleveland on March 20, 1983, was exceptional.[370] These migrants mostly appear between March 20 and April 25 with a few lingering through May 15–20.

Little Gulls are accidental nonbreeding summer visitors along Lake Erie. The few summer records are restricted to the Cleveland-Lorain lakefront, mostly immatures during the first half of June. Sightings during the first half of July may pertain to early fall migrants.

Away from Lake Erie, Little Gulls are accidental visitors. Four inland records were of single spring migrants at O'Shaughnessy Reservoir (Delaware County) on March 22, 1949;[470] along the Great Miami River in Hamilton County on March 30, 1978;[269] at Lake St. Mary's on May 14, 1984;[374] and at Lake Rockwell (Portage County) on April 13, 1986.[382] The only inland fall record was a specimen collected at Buckeye Lake on November 7, 1970.[489]

COMMON BLACK-HEADED GULL

Larus ridibundus Linneaus

This rare European visitor, like the Little Gull, associates with large flocks of Bonaparte's Gulls along Lake Erie; it has never been observed away from the lake in Ohio. But unlike Little Gulls, Common Black-headeds resemble Bonaparte's and are easily overlooked, especially when they are resting on the water.

Black-headed Gulls have a relatively brief history within the state. The first one was observed at Cleveland on December 13, 1965, and may have been the same gull noted at Lorain during the following month.[335] There were at least seven sight records between 1965 and 1974, and Black-headeds have been observed annually since 1978, producing one to four sightings each year. These increased sightings are correlated with increased numbers of Black-headed Gulls in eastern North America since the late 1970s and greater efforts to locate unusual gulls along Lake Erie.

Most Black-headed Gulls are encountered between mid-November and mid-January as casual to rare visitors to the Central

Basin and accidental within the Western Basin. They become accidental visitors later in winter with most records from the Central Basin. Spring migrants are accidental visitors along the entire lakefront between March 13 and April 6. The only confirmed summer record is from Cleveland between July 23 and August 4, 1978.[270] All sightings are of single gulls.

BONAPARTE'S GULL

Larus philadelphia (Ord)

Unlike the larger gulls with their loud raucous calls and aggressive behavior, the small Bonaparte's has a gentle and agreeable manner, much like a tern elegantly picking small fish off the surface of the water or capturing them with short plunges. The Bonaparte's flight pattern is graceful but deceptive; even gale-force winds do not deter its movements along the lakefront. Its aerial prowess allows it to make an honest living off fish. The Bonaparte's Gull is not a scavenger and avoids dumps and parking lots where its larger relatives congregate.

Bonaparte's Gulls have been common lakefront migrants throughout this century. Fall and early winter concentrations of 8,000–15,000 have been reported at Toledo and Cleveland since the 1930s.[89,523] Their populations underwent a dramatic increase during the 1960s. As early as 1967, 41,000 were reported on the Lorain Christmas Bird Count. Flocks numbering in the thousands are scattered along the lakefront each autumn, since the south shore of Lake Erie serves as a major staging area for Bonaparte's Gulls during fall migration. The largest reported flocks include an estimated 75,000 along the Cleveland lakefront during December 1984 and in excess of 100,000 frequenting the Cleveland-Lorain lakefront in November 1986.[377,384]

Fewer Bonaparte's Gulls pass through Ohio during spring. Along Lake Erie, the first migrants return between March 15 and 25 and are fairly common to common by the end of the month. They are most numerous during April, normally in flocks of 25–300. Large concentrations are infrequent and restricted to the Central Basin, where flocks of 1500–4500 have been reported. They remain locally common migrants until early May but most depart by May 15. Small numbers of nonbreeders linger through the end of the month.

Within the interior counties, spring migrants may be uncommonly encountered in flocks of only 5–15 some years but fairly common to locally common with flocks of 25–100+ gulls in other years. They are most numerous on large lakes in the northern and glaciated central counties; only small flocks are expected in southern and unglaciated Ohio. Timing is similar to the movements along Lake Erie but with fewer sightings after May 15.

Between late May and mid-July, nonbreeding Bonaparte's Gulls are rare visitors along Lake Erie, usually in groups of 10 or fewer but infrequently in larger flocks, such as 500 at Toledo on July 5, 1931, and 100 at Lorain on June 20, 1964.[89,394] They may remain for a few days or the entire summer. Summering Bonaparte's are accidental to casual visitors to inland reservoirs, invariably as isolated individuals.

Their fall migration is rather complex with two defined peaks corresponding with their movements elsewhere along Lake Erie.[40] During the last half of July, flocks of adult Bonaparte's Gulls accumulate along Lake Erie from Lorain eastward. Although their abundance and timing vary from year to year, flocks of 300–600 may appear by July 20–25 and remain into early September. The largest concentrations seldom exceed 1000–1500. This early migration may produce concentrations of 20–100 at Huron and 10–50 in the Western Basin. They remain accidental to casual visitors to inland reservoirs into September.

Along the Central Basin, numbers of Bonaparte's decline during late September, although flocks of 10–50 may be encountered. They do not become abundant again until November, when the size of their migration varies. During some years, the largest flocks total only 300–1000. In other years, more than 50,000 may congregate in one harbor. These numbers are maintained into December. Within the Western Basin, Bonaparte's increase during October and peak in November. Their numbers are generally smaller than farther east, with most reports of 200–2500 gulls. The largest concentrations total 10,000–15,000 Bonaparte's. These flocks normally depart during the last half of December. Sizable concentrations remain into January only during mild winters.

Inland, fall Bonaparte's Gulls are mostly observed between October 20 and December 10 with a peak during November. They are generally most numerous during the years they are least abundant along Lake Erie. During years of maximum abundance, most inland flocks total 25–75 with occasional concentrations of 300–500. Maximum flock size is only 15–50 during years when they are scarce. Their statewide distribution is similar to spring migration. These gulls depart inland reservoirs during the first half of December, although a few individuals and small flocks may remain until freeze-up. There are very few inland records after January 10. They overwinter on inland lakes only during exceptionally mild seasons, as was reported at Buckeye Lake and Senecaville Reservoir.[165,479]

Bonaparte's Gulls are casually observed along western Lake Erie after early January and are only expected during mild winters. These wintering Bonaparte's are normally observed as individuals or small flocks, although as many as 300 overwintered at Toledo during 1931–32.[86] The number wintering within the Central Basin is also related to the weather conditions. Most Bonaparte's depart when the lake freezes over, usually by mid-January, although a few stragglers may overwinter even when little open water is available. Large flocks may remain throughout mild seasons: 20,000 in winter 1982–83 at Cleveland[369] and as many as 35,000 there through January 24, 1987.[385]

HEERMANN'S GULL

Larus heermanni Cassin

The appearance of a Heermann's Gull in Ohio is one of those events that seemingly could never happen but did. A single individual was detected along Lake Erie near Detroit in winter 1979–80. It subsequently wandered into Ohio, where it was discovered at Lorain on February 12, 1980, by John Pogacnik and Jim Fry.[276] This distinctive gull was periodically observed through March 12, when it had assumed breeding plumage. The same individual returned to Lorain the following winter. Initially discovered on December 20, 1980, it was infrequently observed into February.[360] This sighting is unprecedented for eastern North America. Heermann's Gulls are normally restricted to the Pacific Coast from Mexico to southern British Columbia and seldom stray more than a mile or two inland.[5] The presence of a Heermann's in Ohio raises the intriguing questions of how it reached the Great Lakes and where it spent the breeding seasons.

MEW GULL

Larus canus Linnaeus

Mew Gulls are accidental visitors to Ohio and a prized species of the serious gull watcher. There are only two accepted records, both along Lake Erie in late autumn. A first-winter Mew Gull was discovered at Lorain on November 29, 1981, by myself, Larry Rosche, Ray Hannikman, and others.[363] Judging by its uniformly brown plumage, this individual was from the western North American population. The other Mew Gull was an adult found by John Pogacnik, Kirk Alexander, and Rick Counts at Huron on December 7, 1985. It was observed by many birders the following day.[381] Determination of this individual's race was not possible. In North America, Mew Gulls are mostly restricted to the Pacific Coast during winter. Their breeding range extends from Alaska south to British Columbia and northern Saskatchewan.[5] Other races are distributed across northern Eurasia.

RING-BILLED GULL

Larus delawarensis Ord

"I have searched for this gull in vain," mourned Lynds Jones[236] as he described the demise of Ring-billed Gulls during the late 1800s. The millinery trade nearly extirpated them from the Great Lakes between 1882 and 1900. At the turn of the century, they were "rare everywhere in the state,"[236] a status nearly impossible to imagine today.

Ring-billed Gulls were scarcely reported until the 1920s, when flocks of 5–30 visited Lake Erie and large inland lakes with infrequent concentrations of 100+ each spring and fall. The few wintering gulls were mostly restricted to Lake Erie. Summering Ring-billeds were unknown.[479,523] Between 1935 and 1940, immature Ring-billeds began to summer along Lake Erie, mostly near Toledo, where as many as 300 were regularly encountered.[86] Larger numbers congregated in August and Sep-

tember with occasional flocks of 1000+ at Toledo and Cleveland. Lakefront Christmas Bird Count totals gradually increased from 100+ in 1930 to 500+ by 1940. Similar increases were apparent at inland lakes, where they were mostly known as migrants and rare winter residents; summering gulls on inland lakes were not recorded until 1940.[509] These trends continued through the 1950s. Nonbreeding Ring-billeds were regular summer visitors along the lakefront but remained a novelty inland. Migrant flocks of 1000–5000 were commonplace along Lake Erie and would occasionally appear within the northeastern counties. Wintering numbers were also improving, although Ring-billeds were outnumbered by Herring Gulls on most Christmas Bird Counts.

Ring-billed Gull populations exploded along Lake Erie during the 1960s as the birds discovered new food sources at dumps, shopping centers, and cultivated fields, and also fed on a greatly expanded gizzard shad population in Lake Erie. As early as 1961, more than 30,000 Ring-billeds were estimated on the Lorain Christmas Bird Count. This number increased to 76,000 by 1965. Concentrations of 5000–20,000+ were encountered elsewhere within central Lake Erie each autumn and winter. Numbers of summering Ring-billeds also increased and resulted in the first two nests on a spoil island in Maumee Bay in 1966. This colony expanded to 50 pairs in 1967.[89] Away from Lake Erie, flocks of 50–500+ regularly appeared at large lakes across Ohio, although larger concentrations were exceptional. Small numbers of nonbreeding gulls remained at these lakes each summer. Similar increases continued through the 1970s.[108] The most dramatic expansion was in the nesting population. Only 6–55 pairs nested in Maumee Bay between 1968 and 1970; this small colony was subsequently abandoned.[90] Nesting gulls established another colony in Oregon (Lucas County) in 1975, expanding from 200 pairs in 1977 to 2000 in 1979.[274]

Ring-billed Gulls may still be increasing along Lake Erie or, perhaps, have finally stabilized as abundant residents. The most spectacular concentrations appear each autumn. Their numbers usually increase during the last half of July, producing flocks of 200–1000+ at scattered lakefront localities. They increase gradually between August and mid-October, but concentrations in excess of 2000–10,000+ are unusual during these months. Immense numbers do not usually appear until November, when 10,000–50,000+ may congregate near the mouths of bays and large rivers entering the lake. Their numbers normally peak between November 20 and December 25, when at least 100,000 Ring-billeds gather along the Cleveland-Lorain lakefront, 25,000+ at the mouth of Sandusky Bay, and 5000–20,000 elsewhere. These numbers decrease with the advent of winter weather in early January.

During mild winters, Ring-billed Gulls are scattered along the entire lakefront and are the most numerous gulls. Local concentrations of 10,000–50,000+ are possible, but daily totals frequently do not exceed 2000–5000+. When the lake freezes over, wintering Ring-billeds are restricted to hot-water outlets and are most numerous in the Central Basin. Flocks of 10,000–30,000+ may congregate around these outlets, but these immense concentrations may not remain intact throughout the winter. They are most prevalent in harsh weather with strong north winds but disperse on sunny days with south winds.

They can also vanish for several weeks in midwinter and their whereabouts becomes a mystery.

Their spring migration is unremarkable. The large winter concentrations usually disperse in late February and Ring-billeds become widely distributed by early March. Flocks of 500–2000+ may be expected during March but larger concentrations are unusual. Daily totals seldom exceed 500 after mid-April except near their nesting colony.

Breeding Ring-billed Gulls are restricted to the large colony at Oregon where 3600+ nests were estimated in 1984 and similar numbers still breed today.[375] Another small colony was briefly established near the mouth of Sandusky Bay in Ottawa County in 1983 but was not successful.[434] Nonbreeding gulls are fairly common to common residents along the lakefront, although summer concentrations mostly total fewer than 100–200.

Away from Lake Erie, Ring-billed Gulls are generally fairly common to common migrants along large rivers and reservoirs. The first fall migrants normally appear during the last half of August, but they do not become numerous until the first half of October. Peak concentrations are expected between October 20 and December 15. These migrants are least numerous in the southern and unglaciated counties, where flocks seldom exceed 100–250. Elsewhere, concentrations of 300–500 are regularly noted and flocks of 1000–2000+ may be encountered in northeastern Ohio. Similar numbers are expected each spring. Spring migrants usually appear in late February or early March and are prevalent between March 15 and April 20. Flocks of immatures may appear through the first half of May.

While Ring-billeds remain at inland lakes until they freeze over, relatively few of them winter within the interior of Ohio. They are fairly common to common winter residents only in the northeastern counties, where there is considerable interchange with birds wintering along Lake Erie. Small numbers regularly winter at Columbus, along the Great Miami River at Dayton, and along the entire Ohio River. They are casual winter visitors elsewhere except during mild winters when open water is readily available.

Nonbreeding Ring-billeds are presently increasing as summer residents on inland lakes. They are fairly common to locally common, most numerous in the northern and central counties. Summer flocks of 100–200 may occur in northeastern Ohio but usually total 30–100 elsewhere.

CALIFORNIA GULL

Larus californicus Lawrence

California Gulls normally reside in the western half of North America, breeding east to North Dakota and primarily wintering along the Pacific Coast.[5] In recent years, they have also regularly wandered eastward to the Great Lakes, where they associate with large flocks of Herring and Ring-billed Gulls. Within Ohio, the first acceptably documented record was provided by an adult at Huron on November 24–25, 1979.[275] There have been six additional sightings through 1987.

Of Ohio's seven records, two were in late autumn, between November 24 and 29. Three of the four winter records were in January and one in February. The only spring report was at Cleveland on April 29, 1987.[386] All sightings were of single gulls, mostly adults or third-year individuals with one acceptable record of a first-winter California. They were largely restricted to the Central Basin near Cleveland and Lorain. The only inland record was at Oberlin Reservoir (Lorain County) on November 29, 1985.[380]

This species is now an accidental visitor whose recent appearance reflects expanding gull populations along Lake Erie. As long as Ring-billed and Herring Gulls remain abundant, a few Californias may be expected to associate with them occasionally.

HERRING GULL

Larus argentatus Pontoppidan

The factors responsible for the incredible increase of Ring-billed Gulls along the Great Lakes also benefited Herring Gulls. Today, it is difficult to imagine that Herring Gulls were relatively scarce along Lake Erie only fifty years ago. Christmas Bird Counts in the early 1930s reported 100–300 Herring Gulls as compared with the tens of thousands encountered today. Even though they were relatively scarce, the first signs of their impending increase were already apparent.

Nesting Herring Gulls were initially recorded from western Lake Erie in 1926, when they were discovered on the Chicken Islands in Ontario.[523] Small colonies were established on other Canadian islands but did not appear in Ohio until 1945 when six nests were located on Starve Island.[89] This population rapidly expanded shortly thereafter. By the early 1950s, they spread to every suitable western Lake Erie island. They colonized Maumee Bay by the mid-1960s and eventually spread to other portions of the lake.

As this breeding population expanded, Herring Gulls underwent corresponding increases during other seasons. Concentrations in excess of 1000 were occasionally reported by the late 1930s with a maximum of 3250 on the 1939 Toledo Christmas Bird Count. During the 1940s, large concentrations were possible such as the "inestimable" numbers at Cleveland in January 1948.[523] As their populations exploded in the late 1950s and early 1960s, flocks of 5000–10,000+ appeared along the Cleveland-Lorain lakefront. This rapid expansion continued through the mid-1970s but numbers have remained fairly stable in subsequent years.[108]

Herring Gulls are now common to abundant permanent residents along the entire lakefront, most numerous during winter. Before freeze-up in December and January, they are distributed over the entire lakefront and concentrations of 500–5000+ are expected. Inclement weather may produce flocks of 10,000–20,000+.

Once Lake Erie freezes, their distribution patterns change. Most Herring Gulls leave the Western Basin and congregate at hot-water outlets near Cleveland and Lorain. Concentrations of 5,000–40,000+ may appear at these outlets during late January and February. Even when the lake is frozen, their movements are not readily explained. These large concentrations may be present for several weeks, then vanish overnight and fewer than 100 gulls may remain. During some years, they vanish and never come back while in others, they may be absent for a few weeks and just as mysteriously return. Where they go and the causes of these movements have never been explained. When the lake does not freeze, Herring Gulls are distributed along the entire lakefront, mostly in flocks of fewer than 2000.

With the advent of warming temperatures in late February and early March, the winter flocks rapidly disperse along the entire lakefront. By mid-April, they usually attain their summer distribution patterns. Flocks in excess of 500–2000 are unusual during spring.

As summer residents, Herring Gulls are most numerous near their nesting colonies in western Lake Erie. Except at these colonies, they are generally observed as flocks of fewer than 200 nonbreeders. Within the Western Basin, Herring Gulls presently nest at undisturbed sites on every Lake Erie island and the dredge disposal basin at Oregon. Colony size fluctuates annually; most colonies are composed of fewer than 200 pairs, although as many as 1000 pairs have gathered at a single colony. In addition to these nesting locations, Herring Gulls have developed the habit of breeding in artificial goose-nesting structures in the western Lake Erie marshes. This habit was first noted in the 1970s and has become increasingly common, with pairs scattered across most marshes. Within the Central Basin, a few isolated pairs nest on undisturbed breakwaters and dredge disposal basins east to Ashtabula, but this breeding population is quite small.

Herring Gulls return to their colonies by late March or early April and immediately claim a nest site. The first eggs are laid by mid-April, although some pairs may not begin nesting until early May. The first young hatch by mid-May and fledge in early July. Later young may not fledge until early August.

After the breeding season, Herring Gulls filter eastward into the Central Basin. Increased numbers are evident by August but flocks in excess of 1000 do not appear until mid-October. This gradual increase continues through November, although immense flocks do not normally appear until December.

While Herring Gulls were increasing along Lake Erie, numbers appearing on inland lakes have declined. At one time, they were the most numerous inland gulls and concentrations of 100–300 were widely reported except in the unglaciated counties.[299,479] These numbers gradually declined during the 1950s. Since the early 1960s, Ring-billed Gulls have outnumbered Herrings on inland lakes.

Their present abundance on inland lakes is directly related to the distance from Lake Erie. Inland Herring Gulls are most numerous in the northeastern counties near Cleveland, making daily flights from Lake Erie to lakes from southern Lorain County east to the Akron-Kent area. Concentrations of 100–200+ appear on many northeastern lakes and larger flocks visit bodies of water close to Lake Erie. Lakes and reservoirs in the northwestern and central counties seldom support more than 10–20 Herrings and smaller numbers are found in the southern and unglaciated counties. While occasional flights may produce flocks of 50–100+ in central and southern Ohio, these flights occur only once or twice a decade.

The largest inland spring movements, mostly adults, occur in late February and early March, coinciding with the thawing of reservoirs. Immatures migrate between March 20 and April 15 and depart by May 1.

Summering Herring Gulls were unusual in the interior of Ohio with very few published records before 1960. As the Great Lakes population expanded, inland nonbreeders also increased. They are presently rare but regular summer visitors throughout Ohio. Groups of 1–4 immatures may appear on any lake hosting flocks of summering gulls. In addition to nonbreeders, a few pairs attempted to breed on goose-nesting structures at several inland lakes. The first inland nesting attempt was at Lake Rockwell (Portage County) in 1981.[362] One or two pairs have nested there and at Mosquito Creek Reservoir (Trumbull County) since 1983. A pair may have nested at Lake St. Mary's in 1985.[434]

The first fall migrants may return to inland lakes by mid-August, although they do not normally appear until September. Fall Herring Gulls do not become widespread until mid-October and are regularly observed on these lakes until they freeze.

Once the lakes freeze, most wintering Herring Gulls are found in the northeastern counties at dumps, parking lots, and other foraging sites away from the lakefront. Numbers moving inland vary considerably depending on the conditions along Lake Erie. Some years, these inland movements easily total hundreds daily. Away from northeastern Ohio, Herring Gulls are casual to rare winter visitors with most records of 1–8 along large rivers and occasionally lakes.

THAYER'S GULL

Larus thayeri Brooks

Before 1973, this species was considered to be a race of the Herring Gull. Its distinguishing characteristics were poorly understood and the only Ohio record was provided by a first-winter specimen collected by Milton Trautman at South Bass Island on February 26, 1946.[89] In 1973, Thayer's Gull was elevated to the status of a full species. Several years passed before the subtle field marks distinguishing this species from Iceland and Herring Gulls were known. Once birders became familiar with the field marks, Thayer's Gulls were regularly observed among the large winter gull flocks along Lake Erie. The first sightings were during the winter of 1977–78.[268] They have been observed in every subsequent year, indicating they were probably overlooked during previous decades.

Thayer's Gulls are rare but regular winter residents along Lake Erie in association with large flocks of Herring Gulls. There are no acceptable inland records. They are only casually encountered during mild winters as isolated individuals. In contrast, they may become uncommon visitors to hot-water outlets along the Cleveland-Lorain lakefront during severe winters. As many as 6 Thayer's Gulls have been reported under these conditions. Most recent records are from Huron eastward, reflecting the normal midwinter distribution of gulls. There are surprisingly few sightings from the Western Basin.

The first Thayer's Gulls normally appear during November with a few records as early as the second week of the month. They are casually encountered until the lake freezes over. Thayer's Gulls are most likely to be observed between mid-January and mid-February. They quickly depart when the lake begins to thaw, usually during the latter half of February. Most leave by March 5–20, although immature Thayer's Gulls exhibit a tendency to linger into spring. Since 1980, there have been at least five May records with the latest individual remaining at Cleveland through May 19, 1985.[378]

ICELAND GULL

Larus glaucoides Meyer

Unlike Thayer's Gulls, Iceland Gulls have been known as winter residents along Lake Erie since the nineteenth century.[522] Between the 1880s and 1960s, they were among Ohio's rarest gulls with very infrequent sightings along the lakefront. Beginning in the early 1960s, however, Iceland Gulls have been fairly regular members of the lake's midwinter gull concentrations.

Their status along Lake Erie is similar to that of Thayer's Gulls except that Icelands are slightly less numerous. They are rare but regular winter residents from Lorain eastward but are only casually encountered within the Western Basin. Icelands are most numerous during cold winters when gulls are restricted to hot-water outlets. Under these conditions, generally 1–2 frequent each outlet; concentrations of 3–5 are unusual. During mild winters, Icelands are only casually encountered.

Iceland Gulls tend to arrive slightly later and depart earlier than Thayer's Gulls. While there are a few sightings during the first half of November, Icelands are accidental visitors during that month and are only casually encountered before early January. Most are observed between mid-January and the third week of February but disappear as soon as the lake begins to thaw. Unless winter ice conditions prevail into March, Iceland Gulls are casual visitors after the first week of the month. There are very few records of lingering Icelands, although one remained at Cleveland as late as May 6, 1984.[374] Midsummer and early fall sight records from Lake Erie have not been adequately substantiated; they may pertain to misidentified worn or leucistic Herring Gulls.

Iceland Gulls have been reported from the interior of Ohio on seven occasions, but only the sighting from Buckeye Lake between December 26, 1937, and January 1, 1938, was correctly identified. This second-winter Iceland was carefully studied and the description eliminates all similar species.[479]

LESSER BLACK-BACKED GULL

Larus fuscus Linnaeus

The Lesser Black-backed Gull is a Eurasian species regularly reported from North America since the 1960s. The North American population of these gulls has gradually increased and they have become regular visitors along portions of the Atlantic Coast and the eastern Great Lakes. They remain casual to accidental visitors elsewhere. While there are no confirmed North American breeding records, development of a breeding population seems likely as their numbers increase.

Ohio's first Lesser Black-backed Gull was discovered at Cleveland on January 20, 1977;[265] singles also appeared at Lorain and Eastlake that winter, and one wandering individual may have produced all three sightings. Lesser Black-backeds have been recorded in every subsequent year. Initially, they were discovered among the immense wintering flocks at hot-water outlets. By the early 1980s, individuals were also detected during autumn and spring. The first report of multiple Lessers was in November 1981 at Lorain.[363] Since these gulls wander along the entire lakefront, it is difficult to estimate precisely the number visiting Lake Erie, although as many as 7–10 may have been present some years.

Lesser Black-backed Gulls are accidental nonbreeding summer visitors. The confirmed sightings are of a single gull at Huron through July 31, 1988, and one photographed at Oregon (Lucas County) on August 7, 1981.[363,388a]

The first fall migrants appeared along the Cleveland lakefront by September 21–24, although there are few additional sightings before October 20. Lesser Black-backeds are casual to locally uncommon migrants along Lake Erie during November and the first half of December, with all reports of 4 or fewer. Their numbers generally diminish between December 20 and January 10.

Wintering Lesser Black-backeds are mostly observed along the Cleveland-Lorain lakefront at hot-water outlets. Most sightings are of single gulls, although 2–3 have occasionally been noted. They are accidental or casual winter visitors within the Western Basin, reflecting a shortage of open water and large gull concentrations during most years.

After the winter gull flocks disperse in late February or early March, Lesser Black-backeds become casual spring visitors along Lake Erie. They do not regularly appear at any location, although there are usually one to three sightings each spring. Spring Lessers have only been encountered as single individuals, primarily during March and early April with late migrants through April 28, 1984, at Cleveland and May 3, 1984, in Lucas County. They are accidental visitors away from Lake Erie with only one inland record, an adult at Summit Lake in Akron February 20–26, 1978. Its yellowish legs and other diagnostic field marks were described by Carol Tveekrem.

GLAUCOUS GULL

Larus hyperboreus Gunnerus

Early ornithologists did not record this species and its status during the nineteenth century is uncertain. Small numbers of Glaucous Gulls may always have wintered along Lake Erie. The first confirmed Ohio records were in the 1930s, when lakefront observers regularly noted small numbers, particularly near Toledo. Their numbers slowly increased through 1947.[89,301] They became inexplicably scarce after 1947 and there were relatively

WILD TURKEY
Meleagris gallopavo

Before conservationists restored the Wild Turkey to its former range, the largest of North America's upland game birds was extirpated from most midwestern states. Today it is again possible to see a turkey gobbler and one of his mates (he is polygamous) foraging in a patch of blooming Bloodroot (*Sanguinaria canadensis*) on the side of a hill.

Adults

(male)

(female)

NORTHERN BOBWHITE
Colinus virginianus

Those venturing into our remaining grassy fields may experience the heart-stopping explosion into flight of a covey of Bobwhites from beneath their feet. This tactic often leaves a predator unable to focus on a single victim and allows the entire covey to escape. Sometimes, in a flurry of rustling leaves and muttering musical chirps, the covey will choose to run a short distance before bursting into flight one or two at a time.

Adults

(male)

(female)

(male)

(female)

(female)

BLACK RAIL
Laterallus jamaicensis

VIRGINIA RAIL
Rallus limicola

The presence of the seldom-seen Black and Virginia Rails is frequently revealed only after danger has provoked one of them to call out an alarm, an action that usually stimulates answers from every corner of the marsh. Censuses of the calls of the different species of rails are sometimes the only way to evaluate a population.

Black Rail
(sexes similar)

Snapping Turtle
(Chelydra serpentina)

Virginia Rail
(sexes similar)

SANDHILL CRANE
Grus canadensis

In earlier days nesting Sandhill Cranes could be found foraging in remote, yet-undrained northern marshes. Here they fed on bulbs, tubers, seeds, and leaves of plants as well as a wide variety of insects, small reptiles, amphibians, mammals, and occasionally birds. Today the Sandhill Crane is considered to be mostly a migrant in the state. A few flocks are observed in spring and fall.

Adult
(sexes similar)

LESSER GOLDEN-PLOVER
Pluvialis dominica

KILLDEER
Charadrius vociferus

RUDDY TURNSTONE
Arenaria interpres

DUNLIN
Calidris alpina

During spring migration a wide variety of North American shorebirds pass through the state. Many stop to rest and feed but appear to be in a hurry to reach their Arctic nesting grounds. Having the same general requirements—mudflats and shorelines—many of these shorebirds are seen feeding with the Killdeer, a common resident of the state.

Killdeer
(sexes similar)

Ruddy Turnstone in nuptial plumage
(sexes similar)

Lesser Golden-Plover in nuptial plumage
(sexes similar)

Dunlin in nuptial plumage
(sexes similar)

BONAPARTE'S GULL
Larus philadelphia

FORSTER'S TERN
Sterna forsteri

Historically the status of these two birds has been somewhat ambiguous. The Bonaparte's Gull was considered America's smallest gull until 1962 when a small group of Little Gulls (*Larus minitus*), previously considered a straggler from Europe, were discovered nesting in Canada. The Forster's Tern was not recognized as a separate species from its cousin the Common Tern until 1831. Frequently traveling side by side, both species migrate overland to Lake Erie, stopping at large reservoirs along the way.

Bonaparte's Gull in nuptial plumage
(sexes similar)

Spottail Shiner
(Notropis hudsonius)

Forster's Tern in nuptial plumage
(sexes similar)

MOURNING DOVE
Zenaida macroura

Like so many other birds whose nests are vulnerable to predators, the Mourning Dove hides its nest among the thick foliage and thorny branches of a small tree or shrub such as the Wild Rose (*Rosa* sp.). These locations are usually revealed only by the activity of the adult birds, which increases and makes them more noticeable to the predator's watchful eye after the eggs have hatched.

Adults

(male)

(female)

BLACK-BILLED CUCKOO
Coccyzus erythropthalmus

YELLOW-BILLED CUCKOO
Coccyzus americanus

About the time the downturned deep brown-purple blossoms of the papaw (*Asimina triloba*) appear, Black- and Yellow-billed Cuckoos are returning to the state—an event that, because of the quiet, somewhat secretive nature of both species, is sometimes overlooked. Listening for the call of the bird farmers know as the rain crow is a good way to detect the presence of cuckoos.

Yellow-billed Cuckoo
(*sexes similar*)

Black-billed Cuckoo
(*sexes similar*)

COMMON BARN-OWL
Tyto alba

The facial disks that make up most of the Common Barn-Owl's heart-shaped face are in reality feather-covered flaps of skin that form the front of the enormous opening of their ear canal. Although these owls can see extremely well with very little light, their acute hearing allows them to hone in on their prey when it can only be detected by sound. The Barn-Owl's diet is primarily small rodents.

Adult
(*sexes similar*)

White-footed Mouse
(*Peromyscus leucopus*)

few sightings until the late 1950s. By the winter of 1959–60, winter gull populations were increasing rapidly along the entire lakefront. As birders sifted through the large flocks, they regularly encountered small numbers of Glaucous Gulls. As many as 2–8 were discovered on Christmas Bird Counts within the Central Basin that winter. When gull populations continued to expand during the 1960s and 1970s, Glaucous sightings underwent a corresponding increase. Their wintering numbers and distribution along Lake Erie have stabilized since 1980.

Like most birds wintering along the lakefront, Glaucous Gulls may be scarce during mild winters when the lake does not freeze but regularly observed during cold weather when open water is restricted to hot-water outlets. While there are a few sightings during September and early October, these gulls are accidental early fall visitors. The first winter residents do not normally return until the last half of November and most are observed between mid-December and mid-February. They may be regularly observed into March during unusually cold winters. The last gulls normally depart by March 25–April 7, although a few immatures casually remain through May 5–15. Glaucous Gulls are accidental summer visitors. Acceptable June records are limited to a specimen collected at Cedar Point Wildlife Refuge (Lucas County) on June 6, 1937, and an immature in Lucas County on June 22, 1983.[89,371]

Within the Western Basin, Glaucous Gulls are most prevalent immediately before freeze-up in December and early January and when the ice is breaking up during late February and early March. They are scarce in midwinter, especially during harsh weather when the lake is mostly frozen. They are casual to rare winter visitors in this basin and daily totals seldom exceed 1–4. In the Central Basin, they are most numerous between early January and late February when the lake is normally frozen. They become locally uncommon to fairly common winter residents during harsh winters, particularly along the Cleveland-Lorain lakefront, where as many as 10–20 have congregated at hot-water outlets. Fewer Glaucous Gulls are observed during mild winters, although 1–6 may be sporadically encountered.

Glaucous Gulls are accidental visitors away from Lake Erie. Single gulls were seen at Akron on February 8–9, 1959, and February 21, 1981;[322,360] in Seneca County on April 6–10, 1981;[361] on the Indian Lake Christmas Bird Count in 1966; at Lake St. Mary's on January 18, 1958;[98] and at Cincinnati on February 14–15, 1979.[272]

GREAT BLACK-BACKED GULL

Larus marinus Linnaeus

Great Black-backed Gulls benefited from changing conditions along the Great Lakes during the present century. In the 1800s, they were described as occasional visitors to Lake Erie with few specific records.[522] They were discovered with greater frequency in the 1920s but did not become annual winter visitors until 1935–39.[89,523] Winter populations slowly increased in the 1940s, when most sightings were of 1–4 Great Black-backeds and the largest winter flocks totaled 14–24.[301,523] In the 1960s,

Great Black-backeds increased dramatically along the Atlantic Coast and the eastern Great Lakes.[104] Midwinter concentrations in excess of 100 were no longer extraordinary and 350 were estimated at Toledo in December 1967.[89] These populations are still growing. Great Black-backed Gulls are now fairly common to locally abundant winter residents along Lake Erie, their distribution patterns differing in the Western and Central Basins.

The first fall migrants normally return to the Western Basin between August 20 and September 5, but flocks of more than 10–30 are unusual before early November. They markedly increase along western Lake Erie between November 15 and December 10. Their largest numbers are expected during December when the lake and Sandusky Bay begin to freeze. Daily totals of 25–100+ are expected and more than 1000 were reported on the 1986 Gypsum Christmas Bird Count. Once the Western Basin freezes, midwinter concentrations are normally 10–50 and flocks in excess of 75–100 are unusual. When western Lake Erie breaks up in late February or early March, large numbers of Great Black-backeds return to this basin. Their spring concentrations are restricted to March, seldom producing daily totals in excess of 30–100. Most depart from western Lake Erie by mid-April but small numbers of immatures are regularly encountered into May.

Within the Central Basin, Great Black-backed Gulls are casual visitors during August and September. They do not regularly appear until the last half of October. Their numbers remain small throughout November, usually no more than 5–10 daily. Large flocks do not appear until the harbors and bays begin to freeze. They are normally most numerous between early January and late February, especially after the lake freezes over, when flocks of 50–250+ congregate at hot-water outlets. As many as 500 gulls were counted at Cleveland on February 16, 1979, and 640 at Lorain on February 8, 1983.[272,369] During mild winters, the largest flocks are composed of 75–125+. Their numbers decrease when the ice breaks up and flocks in excess of 10–30 are unusual after early March. They mostly depart by late March with small numbers lingering into April.

Summering Great Black-backed Gulls were unknown along Lake Erie until single gulls appeared near Toledo in 1944 and at Cleveland in 1947.[89,523] There were few additional summer records until the mid-1960s, when small numbers of immatures appeared along western Lake Erie. They did not regularly summer there until the mid-1970s and are now rare but regular nonbreeding summer visitors. Within the Central Basin, they are only casually reported. Most summer sightings are of singles with as many as 3–6 along western Lake Erie; a report of 50 in 1983 was exceptional.[371] They are mostly immatures but a few nonbreeding adults have been noted.

Great Black-backed Gulls are accidental visitors away from the lakefront, even at reservoirs less than twenty miles inland. In northern Ohio, inland sightings are limited to 2 gulls at Lake Rockwell on December 24, 1982,[369] and singles near Youngstown during January 1961[141] and along the Maumee River in western Lucas County on February 18, 1934.[86] In the central counties, a documented immature was at Buckeye Lake on November 19, 1933,[479] and singles were at Columbus on November 17, 1962, and January 30–31, 1983.[369,471]

BLACK-LEGGED KITTIWAKE

Rissa tridactyla (Linnaeus)

Despite several anecdotal nineteenth-century accounts along Lake Erie, Ohio's first confirmed Black-legged Kittiwake was a specimen collected at Buckeye Lake on November 7, 1925.[474] This species then went unrecorded until single kittiwakes appeared at Cleveland in 1944 and 1947.[523] Since there were only two additional sight records through 1965, Trautman and Trautman[488] considered them accidental visitors to the state. Their status changed during the mid-1960s. Between 1966 and 1977, kittiwakes were observed in all but three years. They have been observed annually since 1977. More thorough coverage by birdwatchers along Lake Erie and expanding populations in the North Atlantic probably contributed to the increased numbers appearing in Ohio.

Black-legged Kittiwakes are now rare late fall visitors to central Lake Erie but casual migrants along the Western Basin. There are usually one to five sightings along the lakefront each autumn of 1–2 kittiwakes. The earliest confirmed fall kittiwakes appeared during the last week of October but most sightings are between November 10 and December 15. Kittiwakes are accidental late fall visitors away from the lakefront with two sightings from C. J. Brown Reservoir (Clark County), two from the Columbus area, and single kittiwakes at Buckeye Lake, Lake St. Mary's, Findlay, and Dayton. These inland kittiwakes were observed between October 25 and December 28.

Most kittiwakes disappear between December 30 and January 10. Wintering kittiwakes are casually encountered along the Cleveland-Lorain lakefront but are accidental elsewhere, including a possible January sighting from Dayton.[299] All winter records are of 1–2 individuals. Some remain for only a few days while others linger through the winter.

Spring kittiwakes are restricted to Lake Erie, where they are accidental visitors with one record in the 1970s and four since 1980. These records are mostly of single kittiwakes along the Cleveland-Lorain lakefront during March, although 1 remained through April 13, 1975.[259] They are most likely kittiwakes that wintered on the Great Lakes. The only spring record from western Lake Erie is of 4 kittiwakes discovered in Ottawa County on March 28, 1985, with 1 intermittently observed through May 2.[378]

No matter when these birds appeared, virtually all the satisfactory sightings were of first-year kittiwakes. There is only one acceptable record of an adult at Cleveland on November 15, 1986.[384]

SABINE'S GULL

Xema sabini (Sabine)

Sabine's Gulls are usually observed as individuals quietly migrating across open oceans or adults on their Arctic breeding grounds. For many years, these boldly patterned gulls appeared only accidentally in the interior of North America. Since the late 1960s, they have been rare but fairly regular fall migrants across the Great Lakes. Within Ohio, there were only four sightings before 1970 and three records between 1970 and 1979. But in the 1980s, there were observations during six of the first eight years. This increased number of sightings reflects expanded coverage by birdwatchers along the lakefront.

The best opportunity to observe a Sabine's Gull in Ohio comes during October storms along Lake Erie. A storm on October 3, 1987, produced 4 Sabine's Gulls at Vermilion and 3 in the Cleveland area.[388] However, not every movement of these gulls is associated with storms. The largest flock—1 adult and 7 immature gulls—was observed at Huron on September 15, 1984, an overcast day with light winds.[376]

Sabine's Gulls are casual to rare fall migrants along Lake Erie, principally from Huron eastward. Most sightings are of single individuals, primarily immatures. They may appear between mid-September and mid-November but most are noted between September 25 and October 20. Despite these gulls' distinctive characteristics, two undocumented Christmas Bird Count records along the lakefront have to be questioned because Sabine's Gulls are unknown anywhere in North America during early winter.

They are accidental fall migrants through the interior of Ohio. Three fall records are from central Ohio: Buckeye Lake on October 9, 1926;[479] Hoover Reservoir on October 4, 1970;[471] and Deer Creek Reservoir on October 11–12, 1987.[388] Other sightings come from Lake Milton (Mahoning County), September 21, 1940;[511] Lake St. Mary's, October 20, 1956;[98] and Hueston Woods State Park, November 3–13, 1985.[380]

IVORY GULL

Pagophila eburnea (Phipps)

Few North American birds can withstand the rigorous conditions favored by Ivory Gulls. They breed on a few barren islands high in the Arctic. During winter, they seldom wander away from the pack ice covering the northern oceans, although they occasionally appear along the Atlantic Coast south to New Jersey. They are accidental visitors to interior North America, where most sightings have been near the Great Lakes.[5] This species has wandered south to Ohio only once. An adult Ivory Gull was discovered by Jim Hoffman along the Cleveland lakefront on December 17, 1975. Apparently forced to shore by inclement weather, it associated with other gulls at the hot-water outlet of a power plant. It was closely studied and photographed through December 19 but departed as soon as weather conditions moderated.[389]

CASPIAN TERN

Sterna caspia Pallas

With loud rasping calls, Caspian Terns announce their presence as they fly along the shores of Lake Erie. The largest terns in the world, the breeding adults are impressive with their large crimson beaks and sharp black caps as they plunge into the lake in their quest for small fish. These birds are taken for granted today, but Caspian Terns have not always been regular visitors to Ohio. Decimated by the millinery trade during the nineteenth century, they were considered rare stragglers in the early 1900s.[236] Their numbers rebounded, and a flock of 200 was reported near Toledo by 1928.[89] Large flocks did not appear in the Central Basin until the 1970s.

Along Lake Erie, Caspian Terns are fairly common to locally common spring migrants. While the earliest returned to Sandusky Bay by March 13, 1982,[365] they do not usually appear until April 5–10. They are most numerous during the last half of April, frequently with flocks of 30–120 between Huron and Cleveland. The largest spring flock totaled 220 at Cleveland on April 21, 1984.[374] Twenty or fewer terns are normally observed elsewhere along the lakefront. Most depart by May 22–28, but an unusually late flock of 150 appeared at Oregon (Lucas County) on May 27, 1986.[382]

Within the interior counties, spring Caspians are rare to uncommon migrants at large lakes in the central and northern counties, becoming casual to rare in the southwestern and unglaciated counties. The largest inland flocks totaled 15–16 at Buckeye Lake and Lake St. Mary's[98,479] but most observations are of 6 or fewer. Their timing is similar to movements along Lake Erie with most sightings between April 12 and May 15. While Trautman[479] noted late May movements at Buckeye Lake before 1940, these movements have not been apparent in recent years.

Caspian Terns do not breed along Lake Erie, although colonies are established on the other Great Lakes. Nonbreeders are rarely encountered along the Ohio lakefront, usually in groups of 5 or fewer. Flocks with as many as 25 Caspians have occasionally appeared in late June. Nonbreeding Caspians are accidental to casual summer visitors in the interior counties. They are mostly observed in groups of 4 or fewer at large reservoirs in the northern half of the state with a few south to the Ohio River.

The first fall migrants return to Lake Erie by mid-July and are regularly noted after July 20. These migrants frequently include adults accompanied by dependent young; the shrill cries of begging Caspians become a familiar greeting for adults returning with a meal of small fish. Caspians are fairly common to locally abundant migrants along the lakefront. They are most numerous in August and the first half of September. In recent years, flocks of 50–250 regularly develop and the largest concentration totaled 450 at Huron on August 28, 1983.[372] Small numbers are regularly noted through October 20–25. There are few November records but Caspians have remained until November 18–20. The only December sight record is not accompanied by substantiating details.

In the interior counties, where Caspians are casual to locally uncommon fall migrants, they appear at the same time as the migrants that pass along Lake Erie. Most observations are of 1–8 during August and September with a maximum of 18 near Youngstown in August 1955.[74] The last inland migrants depart during October.

COMMON TERN

Sterna hirundo Linnaeus

Perhaps no bird attests to the health of the Great Lakes better than the Common Tern. A healthy tern population means healthy lakes, while environmental problems show up in declining numbers of terns. Unfortunately, people's impact on the Great Lakes has threatened Common Terns in ways we are only beginning to understand.

Common Terns were originally abundant summer residents along western Lake Erie, nesting on islands in Ohio and Canadian waters. Their numbers remained fairly constant until the late 1800s, when populations were reduced by the millinery trade. When this trade ended, terns recovered very quickly. By the early 1900s, Jones[240] estimated 3000 nesting pairs and 1500 nonbreeders on western Lake Erie islands in Ohio and Ontario.

Regular disturbance of some of these colonies forced Common Terns to expand to the mainland, where their first nests were located in 1928.[89] These mainland colonies suffered greater disturbance by egg collectors and mammalian predators and none achieved long-term success.[89,220] By 1939, 1000–2000 pairs nested on the western Lake Erie islands and 1000–5000 at mainland locations. Their reproductive success was poor and some years no young terns were raised.

Their status did not appreciably change in the 1940s. Mainland colonies were abandoned but large colonies remained on several islands. The expansion of nesting Herring Gulls within western Lake Erie proved disastrous for Common Terns. The gulls usurped the remaining tern colonies on Starve and Rattlesnake Islands in Ohio and the Chicken Islands in Ontario, where Common Terns have not nested since the mid-1950s.[89] Newly created dikes and dredge disposal sites in Maumee Bay provided temporary replacements for their lost colonies. Some of these colonies were fairly successful but all were short-lived. After several years, either nesting gulls or dense vegetation forced the terns to find new sites. These colonies moved around Maumee Bay during the 1950s and 1960s, and as many as 5000 nesting terns were still present in 1967.[89]

These colonies rapidly declined to 1250 nests in 1968 and 1000 in 1970.[90] Unusually high lake levels eliminated them in 1971. No terns nested until 1975, when a colony was established at a dredge disposal basin along Maumee Bay.[446] At least 350 pairs nested there, experiencing good success in 1975 and 1976 but raising few young between 1977 and 1979. Their last successful year was 1980, when 147 young were banded.[278] This colony subsequently declined and no nesting terns returned in 1983.[371] Common Terns did not reappear until 1986–88 but only as a few pairs at sites in Lucas and Erie Counties.[434]

Their inland status reflected their changing abundance along Lake Erie. During the 1920s and 1930s, migrants regularly visited every large lake. Trautman[479] observed as many as 600 at Buckeye Lake during spring while flocks of 100+ were not unusual in autumn. Smaller flocks were reported elsewhere, including concentrations of 50–75 in the Cincinnati-Dayton area during spring.[248,299] Numbers of migrant Commons declined in the 1940s and 1950s. Since 1960, inland flocks in excess of 30–40 have been very infrequently encountered.

While the first Common Terns have returned to Lake Erie and Youngstown by April 5, they do not normally appear until April 20–30. They are widely distributed by May 5–10. Spring migrants may be noted throughout May and occasionally into the first week of June. Common Terns are now uncommon to locally common spring migrants along Lake Erie. Before their populations declined, as many as 5000 assembled along western Lake Erie in May.[14] These large concentrations have not been reported since the 1940s. After 1970, the largest spring flocks were generally composed of 50–200. The 1500 Commons at Lorain on May 16, 1983, was exceptional for recent years.[370] Within the interior counties, spring Common Terns are mostly observed at large lakes but occasionally visit small ponds and borrow pits. They are presently casual to uncommon migrants, mostly noted in groups of 10 or fewer with infrequent concentrations of 20–25. The largest recent inland flock was an estimated 250–300 at Marietta on May 7, 1963.[145]

Breeding Common Terns are restricted to western Lake Erie in Ottawa, Lucas, and Erie Counties. Their colonies are mostly located on small islands, dredge disposal sites, dikes, and beaches, although they occasionally nest on muskrat houses in marshes.[86,89] Eggs are laid as early as May 7 and young may hatch by the first week of June.[89,446] If their first clutch is destroyed, Common Terns will renest and nests with eggs have been reported through August 4. These late nests rarely produce young. When the first clutches are successful, young Commons may appear with their parents along western Lake Erie during the last half of July.

Nonbreeding terns are casual to rare elsewhere along Lake Erie, mostly as scattered individuals. While nonbreeders once were observed regularly within the interior counties, the number of midsummer records has declined since the mid-1950s. Nonbreeding terns are presently accidental to casual visitors to all inland lakes.

Despite declining populations, Common Terns utilize the south shore of Lake Erie as a major staging area before their fall migration, remaining for several weeks to more than one month.[44] They do not remain at one location but move along the lakefront from Cleveland westward. The first fall migrants return to Lake Erie between July 15 and 25 and become locally abundant by August 7–10. Flocks of 500–2000 appear most years. The largest recent flocks totaled 3300 at Cleveland on September 21, 1969; 4000 at Ottawa National Wildlife Refuge on September 2, 1979; and an estimated 8000 there on September 4, 1974.[471] After October 15, flocks are usually composed of fewer than 100 terns, although a remarkable 500 appeared at Cleveland on November 15, 1960.[327] Most depart by November 5–15.

Since most Common Terns winter in oceans south of the United States,[5] their presence along Lake Erie in late November or early December may seem surprising. Given the numbers congregating along Lake Erie each fall, a few late migrants should be expected. Small flocks of 10–20 have been observed through November 24, but most late migrants are single terns, occasionally healthy adults but usually immatures in poor condition. Most stragglers disappear during the first half of December. When the weather is relatively mild, they may remain through December 15–25 and an adult specimen was taken at Lorain as late as December 30, 1892. Despite December sightings every two or three years, Common Terns have not been reported later than January 2.

Within the interior counties, Common Terns are casual to locally uncommon fall migrants at every large lake. Most recent records are of 1–10 terns with occasional flocks of 20–30. The largest recent inland fall concentration was 100 at Hoover Reservoir (Delaware County) on September 8, 1981. These migrants mostly appear between mid-August and late September with stragglers through October 15–20. The latest sighting was a small flock along the Scioto River at Waverly (Pike County) on November 11, 1898.[193]

The prospects for Common Terns along western Lake Erie remain bleak. Attempts to establish nesting colonies have not been successful. Elsewhere on the Great Lakes, Common Terns are experiencing high rates of infertile eggs and deformed embryos that point to contamination of adults with sublethal concentrations of toxic chemicals. Unless we quit polluting our streams and lakes with these toxic compounds, Common Terns may vanish from the Great Lakes.

ARCTIC TERN

Sterna paradisaea Pontoppidan

Few birds match the long-distance migrations of Arctic Terns. In North America, they breed across the tundra of Alaska and northern Canada and locally along the Atlantic Coast south to Massachusetts. Migrants normally occur well offshore of both coasts. These terns winter in southern oceans off Antarctica.[5] In recent years, small numbers have proved to be casual but fairly regular migrants through the Great Lakes. While most inland migrants are recorded during spring, Ohio's only sighting was an adult in its fall migration. This Arctic Tern was discovered along Lake Erie at the Huron pier on July 27, 1980, by myself and Don Tumblin. It was closely studied and photographed while resting among a flock of Common and Forster's Terns.[278] During this observation, a small earthquake startled both the terns and the observers, allowing us to compare its diagnostic wing pattern with the other species of terns.

FORSTER'S TERN

Sterna forsteri Nuttall

In the early 1900s, Forster's were apparently casual visitors, with very few substantiated records. The inability to distinguish Forster's from Common Terns undoubtedly contributed to the paucity of nineteenth-century records from Ohio.[236] Their status did not improve until the 1930s when observers became more adept at identifying terns. They began to discover Forster's along western Lake Erie. The first Toledo area records were in 1933 and they became regular fall migrants by the end of the decade with a maximum of 45 on October 18, 1937.[86] They remained accidental visitors elsewhere.

Their numbers gradually improved during the 1940s and

1950s in the western third of Ohio. Forster's Terns were regularly observed at Lake St. Mary's after 1940 and Cincinnati after 1948.[94,248] Along western Lake Erie, flocks of 100+ were noted during the 1950s with a maximum of 200 in 1958.[89] Surprisingly few terns were reported from central and eastern Ohio during these decades.

After the late 1960s, Forster's Terns became regular migrants along the lake's Central Basin, particularly in autumn. As many as 132 were counted at Lorain on August 24, 1987. For comparison, flocks of 200–400 regularly appear along western Lake Erie, where the largest concentration was 1000 in Sandusky Bay on September 15, 1968.[90] Within the interior counties, small numbers regularly pass through western and central Ohio but remain noteworthy in the eastern counties.

Forster's Terns are slightly earlier spring migrants than Commons. They returned to Lake St. Mary's by March 26, 1953,[98] but do not normally appear until April 10–17. Their largest numbers are expected between April 25 and May 15; they become scarce by May 22–25. Their spring status changed dramatically after 1980. Forster's Terns are presently uncommon to fairly common migrants along Lake Erie, most numerous from Huron westward and least numerous east of Cleveland; 15–40 terns comprise the largest flocks. Within the interior of Ohio, Forster's Terns are rare to uncommon spring migrants in the western and central counties but accidental to rare elsewhere. Most are detected on large lakes but they may also appear on ponds and borrow pits. Inland reports generally are of 5 or fewer with as many as 20 at Cincinnati.[248]

Forster's Terns do not breed in Ohio, although they nest as close as Lake St. Clair.[5] Nonbreeding terns are casual to rare summer visitors along the lakefront, mostly as scattered individuals from Huron westward. They are accidental summer visitors away from Lake Erie. The few inland sightings have been from western Ohio except for one Hocking County record.

As fall migrants, Forster's Terns are common to abundant along western Lake Erie. They associate with large flocks of Commons and concentrations of 200–400+ Forster's may appear east to Huron. Away from these concentrations, Forster's are mostly observed in flocks of 5–40. They are less numerous along the Central Basin, becoming uncommon east of Cleveland. Daily totals seldom exceed 10–30, although their numbers are presently increasing. Lakefront migrants usually appear between July 7 and 15 but may not become numerous until early August. Large flocks may be encountered by mid-July but are more likely between August 10 and October 7. Their numbers normally diminish by October 15–20 but as many as 200 remained near Toledo through November 5.[89] The last migrants usually depart by November 10–15; a few may linger into the first week of December. Within the interior counties, their fall status is similar to spring. They are usually encountered as individuals or pairs, although a flock of 30 was reported at C. J. Brown Reservoir on October 20, 1985. While they may appear between July 20 and October 25, inland Forster's are mostly observed August 10–September 20.

Although Forster's Terns are the hardiest of the North American terns, there are surprisingly few winter records from Ohio. The only documented sighting was of a single tern at Cleveland on January 6–8, 1983.[369]

LEAST TERN

Sterna antillarum (Lesson)

Within the interior United States, breeding Least Terns are normally associated with the Mississippi and Missouri River systems. Most nest along large rivers in the plains states from South Dakota to northern Texas. There are also many colonies scattered along the Mississippi River north to southern Illinois.[5] They infrequently nest along the lower Ohio River east to southwestern Indiana but are not expected to wander regularly into Ohio.

During this century, Least Terns were unrecorded from Ohio until 1924, when 5 appeared at Buckeye Lake on May 28.[479] The next record was from Toledo on September 16, 1934.[86] They averaged two to five sightings a decade through the late 1970s but have appeared in six of eight years since 1980. This recent increase is a result of more thorough coverage by birdwatchers.

Least Terns are accidental spring visitors with ten records scattered across Ohio. Two sightings were in April: 1 near Gallipolis on April 16, 1972, and 3 at Evans Lake (Mahoning County) on April 23, 1950.[60,160] The remaining records occurred between May 10 and 30: 1–5 Least Terns at Painesville, Lucas County, Lake St. Mary's, Logan County, Pickerington (Franklin County), Buckeye Lake, Marietta, and Cincinnati.

There is only one summer record, an adult discovered in Butler County on July 1, 1951.[248] It was probably a nonbreeder; there is no evidence that Leasts have nested in the state.

As fall migrants, Least Terns are casual visitors along Lake Erie. Since 1934, there have been at least twelve records along the lakefront, six in Ottawa and Lucas Counties and six in the Central Basin. All sightings were of single terns, two between July 11 and 17 and the remainder from August 14 to September 16. They are accidental fall migrants through the interior counties with only five records: 2 terns collected in Hamilton County in 1878 and singles reported at Lake St. Mary's in 1953 and 1965 and at reservoirs near Columbus in 1980 and 1987, mostly in late August and early September. A late adult was noted at Alum Creek Reservoir on September 23, 1980.[279]

Their status during the nineteenth century is uncertain. While there is only one published specimen record, both Jones[236] and Dawson[102] considered them rare migrants and implied that they had declined during recent decades. Least Terns were greatly reduced by the millinery trade, and their distribution and relative abundance may have been substantially different during the 1800s.

LARGE-BILLED TERN

Phaetusa simplex (Gmelin)

The appearance of a Large-billed Tern in Ohio is one of the most unlikely events in our ornithological history. This unmistakable tern was observed at Evans Lake in Mahoning County on May 29, 1954. It was discovered resting on a sandbar with Caspian and Common Terns by Vincent McLaughlin,

Evan Dressel, and William Findley.[317] This sighting provided only the second North American record.[5] Large-billed Terns are normally found along rivers and freshwater lakes in northern and central South America east of the Andes. They are partially migratory and wander to the coast during the austral winter.[5] Since extralimital sightings are few, both North American records have been questioned. However, this species is unknown in captivity and its appearance in Ohio corresponds with its seasonal movements in South America, providing justification for treating the Ohio sighting as a legitimate accidental visitor.

BLACK TERN

Chlidonias niger (Linnaeus)

No bird is a better indicator of the overall health of our wetlands than Black Terns. These handsome terns breed in only the most diverse and least disturbed wetlands. The adults gracefully forage over open water, hawking insects and capturing small fish for their young, which are found in nests placed on muskrat houses or piles of debris hidden among cattails. Adult Black Terns are very protective, aggressively attacking all intruders approaching too close to their eggs or broods.

Within the western Lake Erie marshes, Black Terns normally initiate their nesting activities during the last half of May. The first clutches are laid by May 20–June 10. Young terns mostly hatch by late June, although flying young have been reported as early as July 4.[86,89,198] Renesting attempts produce clutches through the first week of July but most are probably in vain.

Breeding Black Terns were formerly common residents in the marshes of Ottawa, Lucas, Erie, and Sandusky Counties and on North Bass, Middle Bass, and Kelleys Islands.[89,220] Through the early 1960s, nesting terns were expected in every large marsh with as many as 26 pairs in a single wetland.[7] They declined rapidly between 1965 and 1975.[90] By the late 1970s, breeding terns were restricted to only two or three marshes during some years and four to six in others depending upon habitat conditions. The total population has not exceeded 10–25 pairs during the 1980s. This decline was a result of habitat destruction and unfavorable management practices, especially midsummer drawdowns.

Black Terns have occasionally nested elsewhere in northern Ohio. Jones[243] reported breeding pairs in Lorain County around the turn of the century but provided little specific information. In Ashtabula County, Hicks[215] reported single nesting pairs during 1928 and 1932; they also nested at Pymatuning Lake in 1936.[31] The only Mahoning County breeding record was of two nests discovered during July 1959.[80] A small colony was established at Cleveland in 1958 when 14 pairs and three nests were noted. This colony had 20 pairs in 1959 but only 3 pairs and two nests in 1960.[335] There have been no nesting attempts away from western Lake Erie since 1960.

Nonbreeding Black Terns were once regularly encountered at inland reservoirs. Trautman[479] considered them uncommon summer visitors to Buckeye Lake in the 1920s and 1930s. Clark and Sipe[98] claimed they were fairly common nonbreeding visitors to Lake St. Mary's. Numbers of nonbreeders also declined after 1960. Black Terns are presently accidental or casual summer visitors away from western Lake Erie, usually observed as groups of 5 or fewer.

As their breeding populations declined, numbers of migrant Black Terns underwent a corresponding decrease, most noticeably during spring, when they were formerly common migrants. Trautman[479] reported 10–50 Black Terns daily at Buckeye Lake before 1940 with maxima of 300–700 during late May and early June. They were common migrants at Lake St. Mary's, where 200 were reported on May 18, 1952.[98] Kemsies and Randle[248] reported a large movement through western Ohio on May 12, 1951, with 100 in Butler County and flocks on most ponds and flooded fields north to Lake St. Mary's. Black Terns are now casual to uncommon spring migrants in most counties, usually in groups of 10 or fewer with occasional concentrations of 20–30. The first migrants may appear by the last week of April but they are mostly observed between May 10 and June 5.

As fall migrants, Black Terns frequently congregate along Lake Erie. Although these uncommon to fairly common migrants are normally observed in flocks of 20 or fewer, larger concentrations develop during most years. In the 1940s, the largest flocks formed in the Western Basin, where Campbell[89] reported 1500 Black Terns on July 19, 1941, and August 26, 1944. Since the mid-1970s, these concentrations mostly appeared between Huron and Cleveland. While 1000 terns were reported from Cleveland during August 1982, these flocks diminished to only 160 in August 1986.[368,384] No sizable flocks were detected during 1987, reflecting a precipitous decline in numbers of fall migrants passing along the lakefront. The first fall migrants appear in mid-July. Although large flocks may congregate by the end of the month, they are mostly present during August and the first week of September. Most depart by September 20–30. A few late migrants have remained through October 31–November 14.

Fall Black Terns have always been less numerous within the inland counties. Trautman[479] reported "generally less then 60 per day" at Buckeye Lake before 1940 with a maximum of 120. Smaller numbers were reported at other lakes, although they were generally regarded as fairly common to common migrants until the late 1950s. These migrants have subsequently declined, becoming casual to locally uncommon visitors to large lakes throughout Ohio. Recent sightings are limited to groups of 6 or fewer. They normally appear in August and early September with occasional stragglers through the end of the month.

THICK-BILLED MURRE

Uria lomvia (Linnaeus)

Except during the breeding season, Thick-billed Murres normally spend their lives on the northern oceans. On rare occasions, strong storms have produced dramatic inshore movements of these murres; some have even wandered considerable distances inland. The most famous flight of Thick-billed Murres followed an early December storm off New England in 1896. This storm scattered murres along the Atlantic Coast south to South Carolina and inland to Iowa. The first Ohio specimens were captured at Fairport Harbor on December 18 and Sandusky on December 19. By the end of the month, reports along Lake Erie totaled 4 murres in Lorain County, 3 in Erie County, 2 in Lake County, and 1 in Ashtabula County.[236] Similar circumstances produced a smaller flight during December 1907 that resulted in specimens taken at Sandusky on December 1 and inland near Jefferson (Ashtabula County) on December 22.[320,448] Moseley[320] also related accounts from Sandusky of 2 murres taken to taxidermists and of hunters shooting 4 others. The last Ohio record of this accidental visitor was not related to any storm. One was observed closely by Doolittle[111] on December 12, 1920, as it swam in Lake Erie at the entrance to Fairport Harbor.

ANCIENT MURRELET

Synthliboramphus antiquus (Gmelin)

Ancient Murrelets, normally occupants of the northern Pacific Ocean, have tended to wander into the interior of North America. There are a number of records east to the Great Lakes region,[5] primarily during late fall and early winter. The appearance of 2 of these accidental visitors in Ohio is not completely surprising, except that they provide one of very few spring records outside their normal range. On March 28, 1951, Herb Nielson noticed 2 small birds swimming in front of his commercial drag seine operating in Sandusky Bay near the Bay Bridge in Erie County. One flew away, but the other dove and drowned in the fishing net. The specimen was saved and deposited in the Ohio State University Museum of Zoology, establishing the only record for Ohio.[188]

ATLANTIC PUFFIN

Fratercula arctica (Linnaeus)

Atlantic Puffins normally nest along the Atlantic Coast south to Maine and spend the remainder of the year in the Atlantic Ocean. A specimen from the western end of Lake Erie represents the only report of this vagrant from the Great Lakes region. An immature puffin was discovered by Henry Kohler on the driveway of his residence in Oregon (Lucas County) on November 18, 1980. Emaciated and unable to fly, it was given to the Toledo zoo. Despite efforts to save it, the puffin died four days later.[279]

ROCK DOVE

Columba livia Gmelin

As a result of their close association with people, Rock Doves, or domestic pigeons, are among the most widely distributed birds in the world. Remarkably adaptable, they thrive wherever people have modified the surroundings. In this country, large flocks occupy every city, roosting on buildings and living off refuse discarded along streets. They are equally at home in farmlands, roosting on barns and feeding on waste grain in fields.

Since Rock Doves are largely ignored by most people, little information is available on their general biology in Ohio. The feral population was established from pigeons that escaped or were released from captivity. Timing of these releases was not documented, but feral pigeons were present in most large cities in the nineteenth century. They rapidly spread to small towns and rural farmlands. By the 1930s, Rock Doves were established residents throughout Ohio.[89,98,523]

Rock Doves are common to abundant permanent residents in most counties, becoming locally fairly common in rural southeastern Ohio. They are most numerous in large cities, where flocks of 100–200+ roost on buildings and more than 3000 have been counted on Christmas Bird Counts. Smaller flocks are found in rural farmlands, where 100–400+ may be tallied daily. In the southeastern counties, daily totals seldom exceed 10–60 except in cities. While persecution and clean farming practices have produced local declines, breeding populations have generally increased in North America since 1965.[438]

Although they are nonmigratory, Rock Doves undertake local movements. These movements are most noticeable in autumn when large flocks leave urban areas to feed in harvested farm fields. At Columbus, flocks may fly up to forty miles to find waste grain, leaving their urban roosts at dawn and returning at sunset.

The success of Rock Doves results from their fecundity. Pigeons breed throughout the year; nests with eggs or young are as likely in January as June. A pair may raise four or more broods annually. In urban areas, most nests are placed on buildings, although a few pairs breed in tree cavities.[413] Bridges, barns, and other farm buildings are also regularly utilized.

Despite their close association with people, a few pigeons have reverted to more natural habitats and behavior. In southeastern Ohio, they may occupy sheer rocky cliffs bordering steep ravines and highway cuts. Pairs nest in crevices on the cliffs and forage in nearby woods and fields, a life-style reminiscent of wild Rock Doves in Europe rather than our domesticated street-wise pigeons.

MOURNING DOVE

Zenaida macroura (Linnaeus)

Most people are familiar with Mourning Doves, either as visitors to backyard bird feeders, nesting pairs in residential shrubbery, or large winter flocks feeding in farm fields. Gentle and tame, these doves benefited from their close association with people. Mourning Doves expanded during the nineteenth century as the original forests were replaced by agricultural fields. Their breeding populations were well established by the late 1800s.[522] Hicks[220] described them as common to abundant summer residents in every county, a status that is applicable today. In fact, they are increasing throughout eastern and central North America.[438] These populations are subject to declines after unusually severe winter weather but quickly recover with the return of normal weather conditions.

Breeding Mourning Doves are most numerous near residences. Elsewhere, they are mostly found in edge habitats bordering open fields. Uniformly distributed across Ohio, totals of 50–100+ doves daily are expected during roadside surveys in early summer. They begin breeding with the first warm days of February and early March, although many early nests are abandoned if the weather turns sharply colder. Their breeding activities normally peak between mid-April and late July.[479,515] Most pairs make four or more nesting attempts annually and these activities may continue into autumn; recently fledged young have been noted through early November.[89] A few pairs have even produced clutches during December and January.[275,488] The nests are nothing more than a platform of loosely placed twigs. Nonetheless, doves successfully raise young in more than 50 percent of their attempts.[515] Their nests may be placed as high as forty feet but are usually less than twelve feet high. Conifers are their preferred nest sites, although other dense trees and shrubs will suffice. Ground nesting doves have been recorded in sphagnum bogs, dry cattail swamps, cutover woods, and red cedar–covered hillsides. They have also nested on limestone outcrops, eroding streambanks, bales of wire, buildings, squirrel nests, and abandoned robins' nests.[436,515]

While their summer status has not changed during this century, their winter numbers have increased dramatically. In the early 1900s, Mourning Doves were rather rare winter residents throughout northern Ohio.[236] In the central counties, they were uncommon residents and large flocks were only observed during warm winters.[479] Large numbers of wintering doves were only expected in southern Ohio. Their numbers gradually improved in the 1930s and 1940s, although wintering doves were mostly confined to cities in northern Ohio.[515] By the early 1960s, wintering Mourning Doves were established in every county. They are now fairly common to locally abundant winter residents, most numerous in the farmlands of western and central Ohio and near cities. Winter totals of 100–1000+ may be encountered in these areas. They are less numerous in eastern Ohio, where winter totals seldom exceed 25–100. Except for individuals visiting feeders, wintering Mourning Doves are normally encountered in flocks of 20–200+. These flocks usually feed on waste grain and weed seeds in farm fields. Mechanized crop harvesting leaves greater quantities of waste grain in these fields, contributing to their expanding winter populations.[191] Each evening, they gather at roosts in dense conifers, thick brush, and deciduous trees and on the ground in dense grassy cover.

While many Mourning Doves are permanent residents, others spend the winter in the southern United States. Their spring migration starts in late February and early March in southern Ohio and mid-March along Lake Erie.[515] This migration continues through April 15–25. Their fall migration begins in late July and peaks during August and September. The last migrants may not depart until early December. As their winter populations increased, these migratory movements became much less obvious and produced few detectable influxes.

PASSENGER PIGEON

Ectopistes migratorius (Linnaeus)

At one time, Passenger Pigeons were the most numerous of all North American birds. Their continental population was estimated at three to five billion individuals. As many as two billion may occasionally have congregated into a single flock.[43] Tales of their immense flocks filled the diaries of early settlers. As stated by Dawson:

During their passage the sun was darkened and the moon refused to give her light. The beating of their wings was like the voice of thunder, and their steady on-coming like the continuous roar of Niagara. Where they roosted great branches, and even trees two feet in diameter, were broken down beneath their weight, and where they nested a hundred square miles of timber groaned with the weight of their nests or lay buried in ordure.[102]

Passenger Pigeons were quite gregarious throughout the year. They nested, roosted, and migrated in large flocks, mostly feeding on the mast of oak, beech, and chestnut trees. Because mast production is quite unpredictable, these pigeons were nomadic in order to take advantage of available food supplies. Large flocks would fly hundreds of miles until they found an abundant mast crop, remaining in that area until the crop was depleted. This pattern of nomadic wanderings was most apparent during late summer and fall. As winter approached, many pigeons migrated to the southern states and continued their nomadic movements.[43]

Their colonial behavior was most pronounced on the nesting grounds. Millions of pairs normally congregated into huge colonies covering at least thirty square miles.[442] Perhaps fewer than a dozen large colonies existed in eastern North America with only scattered nesting attempts elsewhere. With their dependence upon suitable mast crops, the locations of these colonies varied annually. However, one enormous colony normally formed somewhere in Michigan or Wisconsin.[43] Their nesting activities were highly synchronous and most pairs laid their single egg on the same day. These activities were initiated in late March or early April and the young fledged by June.

Despite the radically changing landscape in eastern North America, Passenger Pigeons remained abundant through the mid-1800s. Their populations did not precipitously decline until 1871–80. Of the factors contributing to their eventual extinction, overhunting of the nesting colonies was probably the most important.[43] During this decade, better communication and transportation allowed market hunters to decimate every large pigeon colony. Within a single decade, these incredibly abundant birds were reduced to a mere fraction of their former numbers. Nesting success within the remaining small colonies was very poor, resulting in their extinction in the wild by 1900.

Anecdotal accounts indicate that Passenger Pigeons probably resided within Ohio throughout the year but were most numerous during spring and summer. Their spring movements were evident in late February and March. While nesting records were scattered across the state, a large colony regularly formed near Buckeye Lake into the 1850s. These pigeons spread out over the entire central Ohio area to feed during the day.[479] Nesting was also recorded from Fulton, Pickaway, Morrow, Wayne, Medina, Columbiana, Trumbull, Portage, Geauga, Ashtabula, Mercer, Darke, Highland, and Huron Counties.[215,220] The pigeons roosted at or near these colonies throughout summer and did not depart until September or October.[442] Their winter status was imprecisely known, although flocks were occasionally noted.

The Ohio breeding population noticeably declined during the 1850s. By the early 1870s, few nesting pigeons remained. Large migrant flocks still appeared during the 1860s and early 1870s with the last recorded large flight near Berkey (Lucas County) in 1876.[89,248] Their numbers were substantially reduced by 1880 and most counties recorded their last pigeons between 1880 and 1890. There were very few sightings during the 1890s and the last pigeon collected in the wild was shot near the Pike-Scioto county line on March 24, 1900.[220] This species became extinct when Martha, a captive Passenger Pigeon at the Cincinnati zoo, died on September 1, 1914.

CAROLINA PARAKEET

Conuropsis carolinensis (Linnaeus)

As the only native parrots in eastern North America, Carolina Parakeets were residents of primeval forests stretching from the Ohio River valley to the Gulf of Mexico. Although their exact abundance will never be known, Carolina Parakeets were widespread and regularly encountered during the eighteenth and early nineteenth centuries. Their demise closely paralleled the disappearance of these primeval forests. Because most of the limited information about these parakeets is gleaned from anecdotal accounts by early naturalists and settlers, it is difficult to separate fact from fiction concerning life history, behavior, and distribution.

During the early 1800s, Carolina Parakeets reportedly "occurred in numbers" in the southern Ohio counties bordering the Ohio River east to the Scioto River. They were most numerous near Cincinnati. Alexander Wilson traveled along the Ohio River during February and March 1811, observing flocks of parakeets at the mouths of the Great Miami and Little Miami Rivers.[522] McKinley,[316] however, believes that the resident population was relatively small and these sizable flocks only sporadically visited Ohio.

These parakeets frequented bottomland forests along large rivers. They roosted and presumably nested in large hollow trees. While historic accounts implied that Carolina Parakeets nested in Ohio, there is little supporting evidence other than a "former nesting tree" in Butler County shown to Dury and Langdon in the mid-1800s.[220] This tree was actually a roosting site and there are no indisputable nesting records from Ohio.[316] While these parakeets were apparently nomadic in their search for food, they resided within Ohio throughout the year. Severe winter weather took its toll. More than one early account described entire flocks perishing within their roosting trees during unusually harsh weather.[221]

Their former status is more conjectural elsewhere in Ohio. They probably resided within bottomland forests along Ohio River tributaries upstream to Chillicothe on the Scioto River and Piqua (Miami County) along the Great Miami River.[102,316] Small flocks occasionally wandered north to the Columbus area but were not regular residents. They seldom wandered into the southeastern counties, although flocks were reportedly observed at the mouth of the Little Hocking River (Athens County) and possibly Marietta.[316]

These parakeets may also have appeared infrequently in northern Ohio, but most of the records are based on less than satisfactory evidence. Audubon related an account of their occurrence near the mouth of the Maumee River shortly after 1800,[86] but this account was questioned by McKinley.[316] In northeastern Ohio, small numbers of parakeets may have resided in the Tuscarawas River basin. A sighting near Tallmadge (Summit County) is apparently valid, although the reported date of 1853 is probably erroneous. There are no other undisputed records from the northeastern counties; an 1863 specimen from Cleveland was most likely an escaped pet.[316]

Available evidence indicates that Carolina Parakeets were declining during the early nineteenth century. Audubon visited Cincinnati in 1831 and reported that numbers had "markedly decreased." Only a few scattered individuals remained.[220] In all likelihood, the resident population disappeared between 1835 and 1840 with only occasional visits by small flocks after 1840.[524] The last Ohio record of wild parakeets was a flock of 25–30 at Columbus during July 1862.[522] A parakeet collected at Newark on October 9, 1884, was believed to be an escaped cage bird.[316]

Carolina Parakeets normally fed on the fruits of hackberry, beech, oak, sycamore, and other trees as well as grape, cocklebur, and a variety of other natural foods.[524] They also fed in orchards and croplands, a habit that resulted in their widespread persecution. Moreover, these parakeets were regularly kept as pets and, in later years, became victims of the millinery trade. This widespread persecution combined with habitat destruction resulted in their eventual extinction. The last wild specimen was taken in Florida on March 12, 1913. The Cincinnati zoo kept the last captive specimen, which died on February 21, 1918.[5]

BLACK-BILLED CUCKOO

Coccyzus erythropthalmus (Wilson)

Within most Ohio counties, Black-billeds are the least numerous of our resident cuckoos. However, their status is somewhat obscured by difficulties distinguishing them from Yellow-billed Cuckoos. Although perched cuckoos at reasonable distances can be readily identified, many are observed only briefly in flight and their field marks are not discernible. Others are not observed at all; their identification is based solely on vocalizations, some of which are easily confused.

Breeding Black-billed Cuckoos are most numerous in northern Ohio. They are generally fairly common residents in the northeastern counties, where they usually outnumber Yellow-billeds. They are never numerous, and summer totals seldom exceed 4–6 Black-billeds daily within these counties. They are also locally fairly common summer residents near Toledo. Elsewhere in northwestern Ohio, they are uncommon to rare residents, least numerous within the intensively cultivated farmlands. They are generally uncommon and very locally distributed residents in every central county, becoming rare within many west-central counties. Central Ohio totals seldom exceed 1–3 daily. Nesting Black-billeds are rare residents throughout southern Ohio, mostly encountered as widely scattered pairs. Despite their relative scarcity in central and southern Ohio, breeding Black-billeds have been reported from most counties since 1982.[434] Both cuckoos exhibit rather marked annual fluctuations in abundance. Summering Black-billeds can be mostly restricted to the northern counties some years but more widely distributed in other years. The causes of these fluctuations have never been conclusively proved.

Statewide distribution of Black-billed Cuckoos has undergone considerable changes since the 1880s. Wheaton[522] considered them very common residents throughout Ohio. By the turn of the century, however, Jones[236] noted they were "decidedly less common than Yellow-billeds." In the mid-1930s, Hicks[220] cited summer records from eighty-four counties, noting that Black-billeds were locally distributed in most portions of the state and were most numerous within the eastern counties. They outnumbered Yellow-billeds along the Allegheny Plateau north to Washington, Morgan, and Hocking Counties.[223] The fewest summering Black-billeds were found in western Ohio.[220] Little information is available on their population trends during subsequent decades.

Nesting Black-billeds are mostly found in second-growth woods, woodland edges, and wooded riparian corridors. In Ashtabula County, Hicks[215] noted a preference for aspen thickets near swamps. While they are frequently found near water, Black-billeds also occupy upland woods. Their nests are placed at heights of two to six feet in dense shrubs and saplings. Most nests with eggs have been reported during the last half of May and June with young cuckoos fledging by late July or early August. Some late clutches have been reported through August 15.[89,523]

Spring Black-billeds may arrive slightly earlier than Yellow-billeds, although the northward movements of both species are frequently simultaneous. The earliest Black-billed returned to Oxford (Butler County) on April 19, 1982.[365] Other early migrants have been noted by April 25–30. They are not regularly observed until May 6–15 and are generally most numerous between May 15 and June 10. During some years, they may be virtually absent until the last half of May and their brief migration mostly occurs during June. Black-billed Cuckoos are normally uncommon to fairly common spring migrants across Ohio. Most reports are of 5 or fewer daily with maximums of 8–10.

Their fall migration is poorly defined. Black-billeds are uncommon to rare in every county; most sightings are of 1–6. This southward movement begins during the last half of August and continues through September. Late individuals may remain into the first half of October. Black-billeds are accidental after October 25. The only November records are of a single Black-billed at Canton on November 1, 1953, and 2 at Cleveland on November 13, 1954.[342,346]

YELLOW-BILLED CUCKOO

Coccyzus americanus (Linnaeus)

Few birds are as erratic in their seasonal migrations, relative abundance, and distribution patterns as Yellow-billed Cuckoos. During some years they may be quite plentiful, in others fairly scarce. Occasionally they do not appear in numbers until midsummer. The factors responsible for these fluctuations have never been satisfactorily established.

While spring overflights have appeared at Cleveland and Dayton as early as April 21–23,[299,378] Yellow-billed Cuckoos are traditionally late migrants with few records before May 2–7. Some years they can be fairly numerous by the second week of May. In other years, they are completely absent until May 18–24 and do not become widespread until June. In general, their northward passage peaks between May 20 and June 7. This migration probably continues through mid-June, although late migrants are difficult to distinguish from residents. Yellow-billeds are fairly common to common spring migrants across Ohio, normally totaling 1–8 daily with occasional flights of 10–20.

Yellow-billed Cuckoos are fairly shy and difficult to observe as they sit motionless in tall trees, concealed by the abundant foliage. They are mostly detected by their distinctive loud, throaty calls. Breeding Yellow-billeds occupy a variety of woodland edge and successional habitats. They prefer brushy woodland borders and shrubby corridors adjacent to streams and lakes but also inhabit open second-growth woods, roadside thickets, moist scrubby fields, and brushy fencerows.[479,523] Their nests are usually placed four to eight feet high in dense saplings and thickets. Most nests with eggs have been discovered during June and July with a few as early as May 28–30.[89,299] Late clutches have been occasionally reported during August. Most young fledge between mid-June and early August. Trautman[479] discovered a nest with eggs on September 20, 1929; the young did not fledge until October 3. Another late nest with young was noted near Dayton on September 19, 1925.[299]

Yellow-billed Cuckoos are widely distributed summer residents, fairly common to common in most counties but uncommon within northeastern Ohio.[434] They are most numerous in the southern and unglaciated counties, where 8–20+ may be counted daily. In contrast, daily totals seldom exceed 5–10 in the central and northwestern counties and 1–4 in northeastern Ohio. Despite considerable annual fluctuations in abundance, their breeding populations have remained fairly stable since 1965.[438] In fact, their breeding abundance and distribution have not appreciably changed since the early 1900s.[220,236]

Yellow-billed Cuckoos remain fairly conspicuous throughout August, the month their southward migration undoubtedly begins. In central and northwestern Ohio, they may attain their maximum fall abundance in August, regularly feeding on woolly bear caterpillars, which few other birds can digest. By the first week of September, their southward migration is well under way. These cuckoos become inconspicuous and many migrants are overlooked. Fall Yellow-billeds are generally uncommon to fairly common migrants across Ohio, most numerous along western Lake Erie, where as many as 10–20 may be observed daily. Fall totals seldom exceed 1–8 elsewhere. The last migrants usually depart by October 5–13. A few remain well into October and there are November sightings from all portions of the state. The latest cuckoos have been noted through November 11, 1931, at Columbus;[45] November 17, 1975, at Hueston Woods State Park;[261] November 19, 1972, at Toledo;[90] and November 24, 1985, at Cleveland.

GROOVE-BILLED ANI

Crotophaga sulcirostris Swainson

Although Groove-billed Anis are widely distributed in Central and South America, they have a limited breeding distribution in the United States. Nesting Groove-billeds are mostly confined to southern Texas with small numbers extending northward along the Gulf Coast to western Louisiana.[5] Despite this limited nesting range, these anis have exhibited a tendency to wander considerable distances during autumn, appearing north to the Great Lakes and in most eastern and southwestern states.

These anis are accidental fall visitors to Ohio, observed on four occasions. The first was discovered by Karl Bednarik, Laurel Van Camp, and Jack Brown at the Crane Creek State Park/Magee Marsh Wildlife Area in Ottawa and Lucas Counties on October 20, 1963. The bird, collected that day, furnished one of the first confirmed records from the Great Lakes region.[89] The second ani appeared at the Holmes County farm of Herman Kline in mid-October 1972. During its month-long visit, it became very tame and began to accept food from people. Eventually, its natural foods disappeared and the bird was fed a diet of thirty grasshoppers and one hundred mealworms daily.[284] It was taken into captivity on November 17 and given to the Cleveland zoo. Ohio's third ani was discovered by myself at Alum Creek Reservoir (Delaware County) on the early date of August 10, 1980.[279] The most recent ani subsisted on persimmons at the Arlene Brown farm near Owensville (Clermont County) during October 1981. It was regularly observed into early November and sporadically through the end of the month.[363]

COMMON BARN-OWL

Tyto alba (Scopoli)

Common Barn-Owls did not invade Ohio until the mid-1800s after the forested countryside was largely converted to farm fields. The first Ohio specimen was collected from the Cin-cinnati area around 1861.[289] There were few additional records before 1880, mostly in central Ohio between 1873 and 1878.[521] Wheaton[522] cited only six records, but these secretive owls were probably more numerous than these few records indicate.

Their population expanded considerably during the 1880s and 1890s, reaching Lake Erie by 1891.[240] At the turn of the century, Jones[236] considered them locally common residents in southern Ohio but generally rare elsewhere. They were probably most numerous along the lower Scioto River valley, where Henninger[193] described them as fairly common and well-established residents.

Breeding populations probably peaked in the 1930s and early 1940s. Hicks[220] recorded nesting Barn-Owls in eighty-four counties before 1935, describing them as rare to very common but locally distributed, least numerous in the northern tiers of counties. Their overall abundance is best summarized by his statement that Barn-Owls were the "second-most numerous owl in most of the state, rivaling Screech-Owls in a few counties."

Their decline was initially apparent in northern Ohio by the late 1940s. Campbell[89] noted a severe decline near Toledo in the 1950s; at the same time, considerably fewer Barn-Owls were observed at Cleveland.[335] Similar declines were under way in the central and southern counties. In the 1960s, Barn-Owls disappeared from a number of counties and became quite rare in many others. Local populations still survived; five nests produced 33 young in Ottawa and Lucas Counties in 1960, and 19 owls were banded at Cincinnati in 1964.[326,394] By the end of the decade, even these populations were declining or had disappeared.[11,89] During the 1970s, small populations remained in the Killbuck Creek valley in Wayne and Holmes Counties, the plains of the Ross-Pickaway County Line area, and the rolling grasslands in Mahoning and Columbiana Counties. Additional breeding pairs were occasionally reported from other locations.

Their fortunes and statewide distribution patterns have not changed during the 1980s. Common Barn-Owls are now casual to rare summer residents throughout Ohio. After 1981, nesting was confirmed or suspected in Wayne, Holmes, Tuscarawas, Fayette, Carroll, Pickaway, Ross, Ottawa, Mahoning, Highland, Guernsey, Geauga, Darke, Coshocton, Columbiana, Clinton, Lucas, Brown, and Morrow Counties. Given their nocturnal habits and secretive behavior, the size of our remaining Barn-Owl population is difficult to estimate but may not exceed 15–30 pairs.

Nesting Barn-Owls occupy undisturbed structures, including tree cavities, barns, silos, water towers, attics of houses, and church steeples. Their nests are usually placed within one mile of pastures, hayfields, and other grasslands where the adults capture rodents for themselves and their broods. Barn-Owls produce large clutches and raise as many young as they can feed. Their nesting activities frequently begin in mid-April and most clutches are complete by mid-May. Nests with young are mostly reported in June and July with young fledging by mid-August. Barn-Owls are opportunistic breeders and may nest during any month if rodents are plentiful. Nests with eggs have been reported between March 17 and September 3.[90,417] Later nesting attempts are indicated by November nests with young at Cleveland, Columbus, and Cincinnati and four-week-old young at Dayton on December 3, 1961.[299]

Most Barn-Owls are not permanent residents in Ohio. Their migratory movements were regularly noted before 1960 but have not been evident in recent years. As spring migrants, most Barn-Owls appear between March 15 and April 15. They are presently casual visitors to migrant traps along Lake Erie and near Columbus but there are few recent spring records elsewhere. Their fall migration apparently occurs in late September and October. These migrants are accidental visitors and do not regularly appear at any locality. Even when populations were larger, this migration was largely overlooked. During November 1917, however, many appeared in the southern half of the state and an estimated 200 were shot in central Ohio.[114]

A few Barn-Owls overwinter in Ohio, roosting in dense pines and abandoned buildings and hunting in grassy fields. These wintering owls are most numerous in southern and central Ohio, where they were rare to uncommon residents before 1960 but accidental to casual in recent years. They have always been accidental winter residents in northern Ohio. Wintering Barn-Owls are susceptible to considerable mortality caused by periods of snow cover and cold temperatures and may starve if they cannot obtain food after only three or four days.[459]

Of the factors contributing to their dramatic decline within Ohio, changing land-use patterns have been critical. Many grassy pastures and hayfields were converted to cultivated fields. Near urban areas, grasslands were turned into housing developments. Suitable nest sites were also lost when many abandoned buildings were torn down. However, other factors were probably involved because Barn-Owls also disappeared from areas where suitable habitats are still available.

EASTERN SCREECH-OWL

Otus asio (Linnaeus)

While their name evokes images of ear-piercing screams, Eastern Screech-Owls actually produce quiet tremulous whistles. With their unobtrusive habits and camouflaged plumage, their whistled calls may provide the only clues to their presence. Eastern Screech-Owls are polymorphic, occurring in both a gray and a red color phase. Intermediate phases are rare. The gray phase is most numerous throughout most of Ohio, although the red phase is equally abundant in the southern counties.[358] In northwestern Ohio, gray-phased owls make up 75 to 90 percent of the population.[492] This phase more readily survives the extended periods of cold weather and snow cover encountered at the northern edge of their range.

Screech-Owls are our most numerous resident owls. Concentrated efforts to locate them on Christmas Bird Counts provide an indication of their actual status, such as 112 on the Waterville-Whitehouse count on January 6, 1982. In most counties, these owls are fairly common to common permanent residents. They become uncommon only in the northeastern counties of Lake, Geauga, Ashtabula, and Trumbull, where they are subject to considerable mortality during the harsh winter weather.

Screech-Owl populations have remained fairly stable wherever suitable habitats exist. They experienced long-term declines only in some western and central counties where most woodlots were replaced by cultivated fields. In addition, Screech-Owls are subject to short-term fluctuations in response to unusually severe winter weather. The winters of 1976–78 reduced nesting populations by nearly 50 percent in Ottawa and Lucas Counties.[270] Similar declines were evident in other counties. Their numbers recovered by the early 1980s.

Screech-Owls are found anywhere suitable roosting and nesting cavities are available. In addition to deciduous woods, they regularly reside in orchards, wooded pastures, shaded residential areas, and wooded streambanks. While they occupy interiors of extensive forests, Screech-Owls prefer small woodlots (five to fifteen acres), wooded edges adjacent to fields, and open parklike habitats.[479] Most Screech-Owls nest in natural cavities, but they also use man-made structures. Along western Lake Erie, they regularly usurp nest boxes provided for Wood Ducks. An enterprising pair of Screech-Owls nested in a Purple Martin house in Carroll County, successfully raising a brood in 1944.[84]

Most life history information is provided by Van Camp and Henny,[492] who studied a Screech-Owl population in Ottawa and Lucas Counties for more than thirty years. Egg laying normally begins about March 15 with a few pairs nesting as early as March 5. Most clutches contain three to six eggs; a nest with ten eggs in 1967 was probably produced by two females. The first young normally hatch between April 11 and 20. Young Screech-Owls fledge in late May or early June. Approximately 86 percent of the nests successfully produce an average of three to four young. Breeding may begin slightly earlier in the southern counties. Screech-Owls may renest if their first attempt is unsuccessful. Renesting efforts produced nests with young through July 10 and adults with dependent young on August 18.[89,523]

Their diet varies seasonally depending on the availability of prey. In winter, Screech-Owls subsist on small mammals and occasional birds. During spring, nests with young Screech-Owls correspond with the peak passage of migrant songbirds through Ohio. Along western Lake Erie, nearly two-thirds of their spring diet is migratory birds. Food is most plentiful after the young have fledged. Insects and other invertebrates make up the bulk of the summer and autumn diet. In addition to terrestrial prey, small quantities of fish and crayfish are regularly taken throughout the year.[492]

Screech-Owls seldom wander from established territories. Banding studies indicate that most young owls remain within twenty miles of their birthplace.[492] A few wander considerable distances, however. A young Screech-Owl banded in northern Ohio in May 1957 was recovered in Michigan, 145 miles northwest of its banding site, the following December.

GREAT HORNED OWL

Bubo virginianus (Gmelin)

The most powerful of our predatory birds, Great Horned Owls readily capture prey as large as adult skunks. They have the advantage of striking silently and swiftly at night. Other raptors are not immune from their predation. Even Bald Eagles abandon their eyries to nesting Great Horneds rather than risk an injurious confrontation. These owls rank as the top predatory bird, fearing no other creatures except people.

Their reputation as fearless and ruthless hunters almost led to their extermination from Ohio. During the first decades of this century, Great Horned Owls were subject to intense persecution. Shot on sight, these fairly common residents became very rare in many areas. By the 1930s, they were eliminated near every city and were rare throughout the western half of Ohio. Great Horneds were uncommon only along the unglaciated Allegheny Plateau.[220]

Great Horneds received protection during the early 1940s and their populations immediately improved. These increases were first apparent in eastern Ohio, where more owls were noted in Carroll and Jefferson Counties by 1945 and in most northeastern counties by 1950.[84,523] Improved numbers were apparent at Toledo after 1948 and in the central counties during the 1950s.[89,349] They remained rare in the southwestern and west-central counties with only 2–3 pairs in the Cincinnati area during 1953 and very few Dayton area sightings before 1960.[248,299] Within these counties, their numbers did not improve until the early 1960s as exemplified by 56 Great Horneds tallied at Cincinnati in 1964.[394]

Since 1970, these owls have been uncommon to fairly common residents throughout Ohio. They are least numerous in the unglaciated counties, where they are largely restricted to riparian corridors and the vicinity of farms or other clearings. They are widely distributed elsewhere. As many as 1–6 may be recorded daily in most counties and Christmas Bird Count totals of 15–16 are occasionally tallied.

Great Horned Owls require undisturbed woodlots and riparian corridors with large trees for nesting and nearby open fields for hunting. They do not occupy extensive mature forests. Great Horneds have moved into residential areas, especially where parks or streams provide nest sites, and may hunt in residential yards from chimneys or large trees. Their preferred habitats remain the open farmlands of rural Ohio, where many woodlots are interspersed among agricultural fields.

Great Horned Owls are the first birds to begin nesting each year. Their territories are usually established in autumn and a duet of hooting owls frequently breaks the quiet of a cool October evening. Nesting activities are normally initiated by the last week of January and early February, even when the ground is snow covered and temperatures are well below freezing. They occupy suitable cavities if they are available but readily usurp Red-tailed Hawk and Great Blue Heron nests, even heron nests in trees in the middle of large lakes. The young hatch in late February and early March. By the last half of April, the young owls are sufficiently mobile to climb among the branches of trees, though they are unable to fly for several more weeks. In mid-May, most owlets are capable of flight but retain much of their down, looking like large fuzz balls among the vegetation. Like all owls, Great Horneds raise only one brood but will renest if the first clutch is unsuccessful. Renesting attempts produced nests with eggs as late as May 12.[422]

SNOWY OWL

Nyctea scandiaca (Linnaeus)

Wherever they appear, Snowy Owls are certain to attract attention. Mostly diurnal in their habits, they are likely to be observed during the midday hours as they hunt from low perches or the ground. These large owls are remarkably tame, normally inhabiting the Arctic tundra and infrequently encountering people. Although Snowies hunt over open fields, they regularly turn up in the middle of cities, perched on a large building and oblivious to the commotion on the street below.

Snowy Owls normally winter north of Ohio, where they subsist on lemmings and other rodents. Lemming populations undergo severe declines every three or four years, and then the owls move southward in search of food, producing sizable winter invasions into the Great Lakes region.

While Snowy Owls probably periodically invaded Ohio, the only reported nineteenth-century flight was in winter 1858–59 at Cleveland.[523] During the present century, the first reported flight occurred in the winter of 1926–27, producing at least 138 sightings across the state.[466] An invasion during the winter of 1930–31 produced 126 statewide sightings.[214] A smaller flight was noted in winter 1933–34. The 1941–42 winter produced 100–150 reports from the Cleveland area but lower numbers elsewhere.[523] The owl flight of 1945–46 was mostly limited to sixty-six records from the Toledo area.[89,456] Another flight during the 1949–50 winter resulted in at least thirty specimens from Cleveland and eleven sightings in Trumbull County.[59,310] Sizable numbers also appeared along western Lake Erie and south to Cincinnati.[248]

The first Snowies appeared in the last days of October and early November but the majority were not reported until December or January. Snowy Owls were first detected along Lake Erie with sizable numbers in the northwestern or northeastern counties depending upon the origin of the flight. After remaining along Lake Erie for a few days or weeks, they moved inland. Interior sightings were widely scattered with most from the northern and central counties. Their spring flight produced only scattered sightings during March and April and occasional stragglers into May.

Their winter distribution patterns have apparently changed since 1950. While these owls still undergo periodic invasions, the magnitude of their flights is considerably reduced. Defined movements in the winters of 1953–54, 1960–61, 1974–75, and 1980–81 produced twenty to thirty statewide sightings. Their appearance is no longer confined to these movements and "echo flights" the following winter. Instead, Snowy Owls annually appear in Ohio. During some years, reports are restricted to two or three sightings along Lake Erie; other years may produce five to seven lakefront reports and two or three inland.

Snowy Owls are now rare to uncommon winter visitors along Lake Erie. They may appear along the entire lakefront but prefer Burke Airport in Cleveland and the dredge disposal basin at Oregon (Lucas County). They are normally encountered as scattered individuals, although 2–3 owls may be observed. Larger numbers may appear during invasions; the largest tally was 20 along an eleven-mile drive across Ottawa County on February 20, 1950.[89] Wintering Snowies are casual to accidental visitors to the interior of Ohio, where sightings invariably are of single owls with the fewest reports from the unglaciated southeastern counties.

The timing of their movements has not changed in recent years. The earliest Snowy Owl returned by October 3, 1981, but they are not normally encountered until November or December.[363] Considerably fewer Snowies return north each spring, primarily between March 5 and April 10. Occasional stragglers linger into May with the latest confirmed sighting May 24, 1968, at Columbus.[471] There is one unconfirmed June record from Lake Erie.

Most of our Snowy Owls are immatures that have poorly developed hunting skills. Many cannot capture enough food to sustain themselves and perish during winter. One Snowy Owl provided a unique opportunity to observe its hunting techniques. During November 1980, it regularly visited Wildwood Park in Cleveland to feed on rats along the lakefront. Each evening, the rats boldly wandered around a lighted beach and parking lot as the owl hunted them from light poles, building roofs, and once from the hood of a birder's car. This young owl made a half-dozen or more strikes before eventually succeeding in capturing one.

NORTHERN HAWK-OWL

Surnia ulula (Linnaeus)

Northern Hawk-Owls are residents of boreal forests across Canada and Alaska. Like all northern owls, Hawk-Owls undergo periodic southward movements during winter in response to shortages of prey. Their movements are less predictable than the invasions of Snowy Owls and composed of considerably fewer individuals. Hawk-Owl movements are normally evident in southern Canada, the upper Great Lakes states, and northern New England but a few owls have accidentally wandered south to New Jersey, northern Ohio, and Iowa.[5] The only confirmed Northern Hawk-Owl record in Ohio is provided by a specimen collected at Pepper Pike (Cuyahoga County) on November 10, 1927.[523] This specimen is believed to be the unlabeled Hawk-Owl in the collection at the Cleveland Museum of Natural History. Four undocumented sight records from northern Ohio are believed to be correctly identified. These owls appeared at Northfield between December 24, 1940, and January 6, 1941; at Cleveland on March 2, 1957; at Lorain January 2–20,

1968;[335,405,523] and near Maumee (Lucas County) on January 16, 1978.[471] There are three additional published sightings from the northeastern counties and an anecdotal account from southeastern Ohio whose validity has been questioned.

BURROWING OWL

Athene cunicularia (Molina)

Most Burrowing Owls occupy open grasslands in central and western North America from southern Canada to Mexico. The eastern boundary of their range normally extends from the Dakotas south to Texas.[5] Like many migratory species, Burrowing Owls occasionally stray from this range and have wandered east to Ohio and southern Ontario. There are two sight records from Ohio. The first owl was discovered by Homer Price near Payne in Paulding County in early October 1944. While the details are sketchy, the bird's behavior leaves little doubt it was correctly identified. It was observed on four occasions as it roosted in a tile along the bare bank of a ditch. When flushed, it flew into a harvested soybean field, where it walked considerable distances and attempted to hide under clumps of soybean straw.[428] Another Burrowing Owl was closely studied by Sandra Zenser in Carroll Township, Ottawa County, on April 5–6, 1981.[361] It too was discovered roosting in a drainage tile along a ditch. It was fairly tame, allowing an examination of all diagnostic field marks. When approached, it was as likely to run into the adjacent fields as to take flight.

BARRED OWL

Strix varia Barton

Shortly after sunset on a calm evening in early March, the distinctive calls of a Barred Owl carry across a forested hillside in eastern Ohio. Its mate responds, initiating an eerie duet composed of traditional calls and various deep throaty notes, raucous shrieks, and other unusual sounds. These Barred Owls are courting and will shortly start the process of raising their young. Their nest site has already been selected, most likely a cavity within a large hollow tree. Nesting Barred Owls on rare occasions also use abandoned hawk, crow, or squirrel nests.[523] While nests with eggs have been reported during February in southwestern Ohio,[248] most clutches are laid in March and hatch by mid-April. Young Barred Owls have left the nest by April 23 but are most evident in the last half of May, and June.[479,523] Barred Owls require extensive mature woodlands with numerous hollow trees and large cavities for nesting and roosting. They prefer mesic habitats, especially wooded swamps, floodplain woods, large poorly drained woodlots, and protected hillsides. They are not likely to be found in other habitats, except during winter when they roost in pine groves.

Barred Owls were initially distributed throughout the virgin forests covering Ohio. As these forests were cleared, their numbers declined dramatically and they became locally rare by the mid-1800s. With the maturation of second-growth forests, their populations expanded during the last decades of the nineteenth century.[479] By the early 1900s, the Barred Owl was "the most common large owl" in most counties.[236] In the mid-1930s, Barred Owls were widely distributed. Hicks[220] cited breeding records from seventy-five counties, noting that they were absent only in some western counties where extensive mature woodlands were unavailable. Their relative abundance varied considerably depending upon the availability of suitable forests. They were locally rare in all portions of the state, even along the unglaciated Allegheny Plateau.[223] Their populations were also experiencing local declines, particularly in glaciated counties.[98,479]

Several factors contributed to their changing relative abundance in the past fifty years. Habitat destruction eliminated suitable woodlands, particularly within the intensively farmed western and central counties. Barred Owls are also unable to compete with expanding Great Horned Owl populations. Near most large cities and in many western and central counties, nesting Barred Owls were replaced by Great Horneds during the 1950s and early 1960s. Not every change has been detrimental for Barred Owls. The maturation of woodlands along the unglaciated Allegheny Plateau expanded their breeding populations.

Barred Owls are now uncommon to fairly common permanent residents throughout southern and eastern Ohio, becoming locally rare near large metropolitan areas. They are the most numerous large owls within the rural southeastern counties; 1–6 can be detected each evening, perhaps more if mature woodlands are extensively distributed and tapes are used to elicit responses. Barred Owls are uncommon residents within the central and northern counties bordering the unglaciated plateau. They become rare to absent in most west-central and northwestern counties.[434]

While Barred Owls reside within their territories throughout the year, some dispersal takes place between September and November when young Barred Owls search for suitable unoccupied territories. Some owls may also disperse in March; single Barreds have very infrequently appeared at migrant traps in central Ohio and along Lake Erie. There is no evidence to suggest regular migratory movements within Ohio.

GREAT GRAY OWL

Strix nebulosa Forster

Nocturnal visitors from Canadian boreal forests, Great Gray Owls undergo periodic southward invasions in response to food shortages. Most appear in the upper Great Lakes and northern New England states; on rare occasions, they have wandered south to Ohio and New Jersey.[5] Most Ohio Great Gray Owl reports were produced during the nineteenth century. Unfortunately, these records are anecdotal and do not even provide such basic information as specific locations and dates. Although two nineteenth-century specimens were sup-

posedly collected in Geauga and Clark Counties,[236,523] neither can be located today. None of these records adequately establishes the presence of Great Gray Owls in Ohio. During the present century, there is one sight record, a Great Gray discovered by Milton Trautman on Starve Island off the Marblehead Peninsula in Ottawa County on October 30, 1947. He carefully observed and described the owl as it perched in a tree, constantly harassed by Herring Gulls.[481]

LONG-EARED OWL

Asio otus (Linnaeus)

These secretive owls are mostly known as winter residents in Ohio. They spend the daylight hours roosting in dense cover, preferring conifers twenty-five to forty feet high. If pine plantations are unavailable, Long-eareds roost within young deciduous woodlots containing numerous grapevines or other tangles. They have also roosted in abandoned fields where groves of young hawthorn, Osage orange, or other trees provide dense cover. At night, Long-eareds hunt over open fields, capturing large numbers of rodents and a few birds.

As a result of their secretive behavior, their actual winter status has never been conclusively established. Many more owls are present than are ever discovered. Long-eareds are thought to be casual to rare and very locally distributed winter residents throughout Ohio. Most recent reports are from the glaciated counties. Winter roosts normally total 2–6 Long-eared Owls with occasional congregations of 10–20+. Their wintering numbers are subject to considerable fluctuations in response to prey availability. An example of this variability was provided by owls wintering in the Cincinnati area during 1949–50 and 1950–51. In the first winter, at least 50 Long-eareds wintered in eight roosts within a 177-square-mile area. Only 2 were discovered in the same area the following winter.[248,433] Five to twelve or more roosts may be discovered throughout Ohio during winters of relative abundance.

Their migratory movements are also poorly understood. Long-eareds are presently casual to rare migrants throughout Ohio during spring and fall. The only regular indication of these movements is provided by the appearance of small numbers of Long-eareds along Lake Erie and at a Columbus cemetery.

Based on the abandonment of their winter roosts, Long-eareds may initiate their northward migration during the last week of February. Most wintering owls disappear during March, when Long-eareds are most likely to appear at migrant traps. These migrant reports generally are of only 1–3 owls. A few migrants may appear through April 5–15 in every county. Sightings as late as April 20–30 are largely confined to Lake Erie. May records most likely pertain to summer residents rather than migrants.

Their fall migration is largely undetected. The few September sightings may apply to summering owls rather than migrants. The first migrants usually arrive during the last half of October, although most fall Long-eareds do not appear until November.

Their winter roosts normally develop between November 10 and 25 but may increase in size throughout December. Except at these roosts, most fall sightings are of solitary owls.

Their summer status has never been conclusively established and our knowledge of their distribution and relative abundance is fragmentary at best. Summer records indicate that Long-eareds are very sporadic and accidental to casual residents. Breeding pairs are not regularly reported from any locality. In the mid-1930s, Hicks[220] cited nesting records mostly from northern and central Ohio. Within the glaciated counties, breeding owls were reported from Williams, Ashtabula, Champaign, Paulding, Portage, Geauga, Erie, Huron, Lorain, Ashland, Van Wert, and Mercer Counties.[98,215,219,220] The only record from the unglaciated Allegheny Plateau was from Tuscarawas County.[220] Southern Ohio's only summer report was an anecdotal nineteenth-century account from Cincinnati.[220,248] There were relatively few summer records in subsequent decades, mostly from the Toledo area and near Youngstown.[89,153] During the 1980s, the few reports are confined to the northern half of the state with confirmed nests in Wayne, Wyandot, and Mahoning Counties and summer records from Seneca, Lucas, Geauga, and Portage Counties.[278,434] The only recent breeding record from the unglaciated plateau was in Jefferson County in 1967.[84] Within the southwestern counties, pairs were discovered nesting at Dayton during 1950 and 1962 and at Cincinnati in 1954 and 1960.[11,299]

Nesting Long-eareds utilize abandoned crow and hawk nests, preferably in pine plantations. Where suitable conifers are unavailable, Long-eareds will breed in young deciduous woodlots with dense woody vegetation and many grape tangles.[493] They normally breed in early spring; nests with eggs were reported between March 16 and April 19. The young may hatch during the last half of April and are usually observed in the nest during May. Only Hicks[215] reported nestlings as late as July 8. Most young owls leave the nest by early June.

SHORT-EARED OWL

Asio flammeus (Pontoppidan)

As sunset approaches on a calm January day, several harriers sail over a grassy field before settling into their winter roost. Their low flight flushes another raptor, which has spent the day roosting in this grassy cover. This second raptor, with its irregular flight pattern, is immediately recognized as a Short-eared Owl. The owl flies to a nearby fence post, where it remains for many minutes, swiveling its head as it scans the surrounding fields and occasionally produces a barklike yelp. As darkness falls, it takes flight over grasslands in pursuit of small rodents, which form the bulk of its diet.

Wintering Short-eareds are closely associated with open grasslands, especially farmlands, airports, and reclaimed strip mines. While Short-eareds are occasionally active during daylight hours, they are normally most active at sunrise and the last hour before sunset.

The interesting and frequently amusing behavior of this charismatic owl can be observed nightly at Killdeer Plains Wildlife Area, Maumee Bay State Park, the fields along Ross-Pickaway County Line Road, and other locales scattered across the state. Although these wintering owls are very locally distributed, they are generally rare to uncommon residents, least numerous in the northeastern counties and along the unglaciated plateau. Their wintering numbers exhibit marked annual fluctuations in response to prey availability. During some years, they are decidedly scarce with the largest roosts totaling only 5–10 owls. In other years, they are fairly numerous with scattered roosts of 10–20 in the southern counties and 15–35+ in central and northwestern Ohio. Large influxes produced roosts of 50 Short-eareds near Toledo in February 1965 and 100 at Killdeer Plains Wildlife Area on January 20, 1967.[89,471]

Based on early accounts,[36,236,479] their populations have substantially declined throughout western and central Ohio during this century. These declines resulted from the conversion of grasslands into cultivated fields. Conversely, wintering Short-eareds increased within the unglaciated counties, where reclaimed strip mines provided extensive new habitats.

In recent years, most Short-eareds are reported from wintering locations. There are very few records of migrants except along Lake Erie. Their northward migration is particularly inconspicuous. Wintering numbers diminish with the advent of warmer temperatures in late February and early March. Most depart during March, although small numbers may remain in the northern half of the state through mid-April. Sightings after April 20–28 may pertain to summer residents. Records of spring migrants invariably are of 5 or fewer owls.

Short-eareds have appeared in Brown County by August 23 and Toledo by September 7,[89,248] but these owls may have been wandering summer residents. The first fall Short-eareds do not normally return to Lake Erie until September 25–October 10 or to the central and southern counties until October 25–November 7. During some years, their numbers peak in early December and noticeably decline before the end of the month. In other years, large concentrations develop in early January and remain until spring.

Ohio lies at the southern edge of the Short-eared Owl nesting range in North America.[5] These owls have always been accidental to casual and very sporadic summer residents, averaging three to six sightings each decade since the 1920s. Many summer records are sightings of single owls whose breeding status is unknown. Confirmed nesting reports are exceptionally rare, usually at or near sites where they congregated during the previous winter. They rarely summer at any area for two consecutive years. Before 1940, nesting Short-eared Owls were reported from Paulding, Marion, Pickaway, Ross, Ashtabula, Mercer, and Van Wert Counties;[215,220] the Youngstown area;[19] Buckeye Lake;[479] and Huron County.[513] After 1960, breeding Short-eareds were only confirmed in Lucas, Wyandot, and Pickaway Counties; summering birds at Cleveland and in Holmes and Muskingum Counties were suspected of nesting.[121,434]

Breeding Short-eareds prefer extensive wet meadows but also nest in fallow fields and clover fields.[121,479] Price[429] reported a Paulding County nest in a mixed sedge meadow and brushy swamp. Their eggs are laid in shallow depressions on the ground, well concealed among the adjacent vegetation. Nests with eggs have been reported by April 3 and with small young by April 19.[422] However, most nests with eggs were discovered between mid-April and mid-May and young owls normally fledge in June and early July.

NORTHERN SAW-WHET OWL

Aegolius acadicus (Gmelin)

In a group renowned for inconspicuous behavior, the diminutive Northern Saw-whets easily achieve the distinction of being our most secretive owls. They are experts at choosing hiding places where they are not likely to be discovered, especially dense tangles and conifers. Hence, they rank as the least known of our migratory owls. Our understanding of their distribution, migratory patterns, and habitat preferences is fragmentary at best, and there is much to learn about every aspect of their life history.

Their fall migration is particularly poorly defined. These migrants are mostly detected along Lake Erie, where Saw-whets are casual to rare most years. They become accidental to casual fall migrants throughout the interior counties. While the earliest migrants have been discovered in northern and central Ohio by September 27–28, most are reported between October 15 and November 20. Their southward movement may continue into December. Fall sightings invariably are of 1–2 owls, although as many as 10 have been banded at Cincinnati during a single migration.[363]

While Saw-whet Owls winter throughout Ohio, they are casual to rare residents within the central and southwestern counties and accidental to casual elsewhere. The fewest records are from the northeastern and unglaciated counties. Wintering Saw-whets can be virtually absent during some years and widely distributed in others. This variability is most evident in banding studies undertaken by Ron Austing and others at Cincinnati. During some winters, only 1–2 Saw-whets are located despite extensive searches of suitable roosting sites. In other winters, as many as 24 have been banded.[325,364,433] In southwestern Ohio, wintering owls usually roost in pine trees but may be discovered in honeysuckle tangles and dense red cedars. They normally choose trees near the edges of groves or isolated trees slightly removed from large plantations, preferring upland sites and avoiding steep ravines.[433] Their diet is mostly *Peromyscus* mice, indicating that they hunt in woodland or wooded edge habitats.

These owls are most apparent during their northward migration. Spring migrants regularly appear at migrant traps near Lake Erie, where they become rare to locally uncommon most years. While records are normally of isolated individuals, small flights of 5–7 have been infrequently reported. While spring Saw-whets are rarely but regularly detected at Columbus, they are generally accidental to casual migrants elsewhere. Inland records are mostly of scattered individuals, although 3–5 have been discovered in a Columbus cemetery. A few early migrants

may appear by the first week of February, especially along Lake Erie. Most Saw-whets are observed between March 10 and April 7. Within the interior counties, there are very few records after mid-April. Occasional late migrants have been noted along Lake Erie through May 2–5.[89] Sightings later in May probably pertain to summering owls.

Most summering Saw-whets were recorded before 1940. Hicks[220] considered them locally distributed summer residents but regularly overlooked, citing records from Williams, Paulding, Licking, Portage, Geauga, Lake, Ashland, Knox, Holmes, Muskingum, Guernsey, Tuscarawas, and Mercer Counties and a May sighting near Cincinnati. Additional nesting owls were recorded from Franklin and Ashtabula Counties.[215,219] Most records are of isolated nesting attempts during a single year. Only Ashtabula County may have supported a regular breeding population; adult Saw-whets were recorded at seven locations between 1928 and 1932.[215] In recent decades, nesting Saw-whets sporadically appeared in the Cleveland area with confirmed nesting attempts in Lake and Cuyahoga Counties in 1946, 1964, and 1982.[335,366,523] They also nested at Toledo in 1966.[89] A pair occupied a nest box in the Oak Openings during early May 1978, although this box was removed before the owls could nest. The only other recent nesting record was at Youngstown in 1979.[173] While these few records indicate that Saw-whet Owls are accidental or casual summer residents in Ohio, their true status remains to be determined.

Summering owls have been found in mesic second-growth woods, especially where pines or hemlocks are mixed with deciduous vegetation, but most recent appearances have been in shaded residential areas. They normally breed in cavities but will occupy nest boxes. Their nesting activities probably begin during late March and April; recently fledged young have been reported as early as May 24 with most records in June or the first week of July.[219]

COMMON NIGHTHAWK

Chordeiles minor (Forster)

When Ohio was initially settled, Common Nighthawks were probably rather rare and locally distributed summer residents. A few pairs of these goatsuckers nested on gravel bars along large rivers, on exposed rock outcrops, and in prairie openings. But their habitat preferences dramatically changed during the nineteenth century. Breeding nighthawks readily adapted to the numerous flat roofs available in every city. Their breeding populations rapidly expanded and the *peenting* calls of these territorial nighthawks became a familiar evening sound.

Their status has not appreciably changed during the twentieth century. Hicks[220] cited summer records from 117 cities in seventy-four counties as well as "natural habitats" in Adams, Erie, and Ottawa Counties. Breeding pairs were unrecorded from scattered rural counties along the unglaciated Allegheny Plateau and locally in western Ohio. This distribution pattern is still applicable today.[434] These nighthawks are fairly common residents in every city but are largely absent from the rural countryside. The present trends of this population are uncertain, but local declines have been evident in several cities within the past ten years.

In their natural habitats, Common Nighthawks nest on the ground, relying on their cryptically colored plumage to hide them from predators. Urban nighthawks are decidedly more visible on their gravel-covered roofs, but the absence of predators allows them to successfully raise young. While nesting activities probably begin during late May in southern Ohio, most clutches have been reported between June 1 and July 17 with a few late attempts into the first week of August.[105,107,523] Young nighthawks fledge during July with late nests producing fledglings through August 19.

Their northward migration is largely resident nighthawks returning to their breeding territories. Most spring reports are of 10 or fewer individuals. The largest reported movements have totaled 15–25 in central Ohio and 45–50 along western Lake Erie.

While Common Nighthawks have been reported during the last half of March, none of these exceptionally early sightings has been adequately substantiated. The earliest confirmed nighthawks have returned between April 20 and 25. Territorial males are not widely distributed until May 10–20. They arrive slightly later in northern Ohio.

In contrast, Common Nighthawks stage a truly remarkable southward migration. The first fall migrants are normally solitary individuals during the last days of July and more frequently between August 5 and 15. During the last half of August, small flocks of 10–30 appear each evening. This movement invariably peaks between August 25 and September 7, when large flocks of 50–200+ nighthawks appear in the evening sky, occasionally mixing with Chimney Swifts and swallows. The large flights end abruptly and only small migrant flocks will be noted after September 12–15. The last migrants normally depart by October 5–15. While a few stragglers have lingered into the last half of October, none of the reported November sightings has been acceptably documented.

During late August and early September, nighthawks become fairly common to locally abundant migrants across Ohio. Most reports are of 10–100 nighthawks daily, while local movements of 200–600 have been occasionally encountered. Exceptionally large movements have produced estimates of 5000 nighthawks at Cincinnati, 3000 at Columbus, and 1000–2000 at Akron, Toledo, and Cleveland.

the distance, followed by the repetitive song of Whip-poor-wills. Finally, a Chuck-will's-widow adds its distinctive voice to the evening chorus.

Hearing a Chuck-will's-widow is not very difficult, since they are locally fairly common residents within this valley. Seeing one is a different story. With considerable luck, one may be discovered sitting on a county road, its eyes glowing a brilliant golden orange in the headlights of an approaching car.

Even though Chuck-will's-widows have resided in this valley for more than fifty years, surprisingly little information is available on their migration and breeding biology. The males establish territories by mid-May, preferring old fields overgrown with young red cedars. Nesting is probably initiated during the last half of May, judging from the few reports of adults accompanied by young during July. There are relatively few records after the males cease singing, but Chuck-will's-widows probably remain into September.

Ohio's first Chuck-will's-widows were discovered in Adams County on May 14, 1932. At least 8 males were recorded four days later.[467] A subsequent survey estimated 25–30 pairs along Ohio Brush Creek in Tiffin and Jefferson Townships in 1935.[220] The next systematic survey in 1985 counted at least 60 male Chuck-will's-widows in Adams County, most of them along Ohio Brush Creek north to Green and Meigs Townships with a few isolated males elsewhere.[434] Chucks also nested in Highland County during 1984 and Pike County in 1985 and have summered at two Scioto County locations since 1983.

Chuck-will's-widows now regularly reside only within this limited area of south-central Ohio. They are casual to accidental summer visitors in the southwestern counties, where specimens were collected near Dayton on May 1, 1933, and in Clermont County on May 20, 1945.[248,299] Other published records include a Hamilton County male in June 1954;[345] a female captured in Butler County on May 1, 1974;[255] a singing male at Charleston Falls Park near Dayton on May 20, 1982; and a territorial male returning to Germantown Reserve (Montgomery County) during the summers of 1981–83.[299]

Chuck-will's-widows are accidental visitors elsewhere. There are two published records from the central counties: a singing male in Franklin County on June 7, 1952, and a single Chuck observed at Greenlawn Cemetery in Columbus on May 2, 1983.[123,370] The only northwestern Ohio record was provided by a singing male at Maumee (Lucas County) on June 23, 1978.[270]

CHUCK-WILL'S-WIDOW

Caprimulgus carolinensis Gmelin

To record Chuck-will's-widow within Ohio, a visit to the lower Ohio Brush Creek valley in southern Adams County during May or June is a necessity. Drive the narrow county roads in this valley, looking for open vistas next to hillsides covered with young red cedars. After finding a suitable location, wait patiently for darkness to fall while listening to the evening sounds of rural southern Ohio. First, a nighthawk calls off in

WHIP-POOR-WILL

Caprimulgus vociferus Wilson

As the summer sun sets over the hills of southeastern Ohio, the evening songbird chorus gradually diminishes as most birds enter their nighttime roosts. When dusk turns into darkness, the silence is broken by the loud, repetitive calls of Whip-poor-wills echoing across the valleys. Shortly after they return to their breeding territories, a full moon may prompt them to sing for the entire evening, much to the dismay of anyone trying to sleep nearby. As summer progresses and hungry broods need to be fed, they may sing for only one or two minutes at dawn and dusk.

Breeding Whip-poor-wills reside within relatively young woods or along woodland edges bordering open fields. They occupy a variety of woodland communities, from mixed cedar-deciduous woods in southwestern Ohio to deciduous woods and pine-hemlock communities elsewhere.[299,523] Their nests are simple scrapes on the ground, normally placed close to woodland edges where ground cover is densest. Nesting activities must begin by late April within the southern counties, since recently fledged young have been reported as early as June 4.[54] Elsewhere, nests with eggs have been discovered between mid-May and July 1, while small young are mostly noted in June and early July.[89,299,523]

Their breeding populations have slowly declined throughout the twentieth century. In 1935, Hicks[220] noted greatly decreased numbers since 1900. Nevertheless, Whip-poor-wills were still recorded from seventy-four counties. They were most numerous along the Allegheny Plateau north to Washington, Athens, and Hocking Counties.[223] The fewest Whips were noted within west-central and northwestern Ohio.

Additional declines have been apparent throughout Ohio, beginning in the late 1940s and continuing into the 1980s. Summering Whip-poor-wills are still most numerous along the unglaciated Allegheny Plateau north to Hocking, Athens, and Washington Counties. They are generally fairly common to locally abundant along this portion of the plateau, where nightly totals of 5–40 singing males can still be encountered during May and June. Farther north along the plateau, Whips become uncommon to fairly common residents and nightly totals seldom exceed 2–8 individuals. Within the southwestern counties, they are rare to fairly common residents but very locally distributed. Most reports are of single males, although 5–10 Whips may be heard at a few localities. Whip-poor-wills are rare residents in northeastern Ohio, where only a few individuals remain. They have virtually disappeared from the glaciated central and northwestern counties except for a small population within the Oak Openings near Toledo.[434]

Whip-poor-wills are relatively early spring migrants; any goatsucker spotted in March is probably this species. The earliest migrant returned to Marietta by March 13, 1973, and migrants have appeared at several central localities by March 24–30.[163] The earliest overflight in northern Ohio is April 6. Spring Whips normally appear in the southern counties by April 15–25, although they are not expected along Lake Erie until the first week of May. Breeding populations are well established by May 15–20.

Observations of migrant Whip-poor-wills have noticeably declined since the 1950s and they are presently casual to rare spring visitors away from established breeding localities. These migrants are mostly detected between April 25 and May 15, usually as isolated individuals, although small flights of 3–8 Whips may be infrequently encountered along western Lake Erie.

Their southward migrations have always been poorly defined. Breeding Whip-poor-wills quietly depart during September and the last individuals are usually noted between Sep-

tember 15 and 25. Fall migrants are accidental to casual away from established nesting localities, with most records near Lake Erie. The latest records are October 15 at Dayton and several sightings between October 17 and 22 in the Cleveland area.[299]

CHIMNEY SWIFT

Chaetura pelagica (Linnaeus)

With their compact cigar-shaped bodies, short tails, and long narrow wings, Chimney Swifts are designed for sustained rapid flight. In fact, they spend virtually all the daylight hours on the wing. But while they rank among the strongest of all fliers, they are poorly adapted for a terrestrial existence. With their short weak legs, they are incapable of taking off from any horizontal surface and must roost by hanging onto the vertical sides of chimneys or hollow trees.

Chimney Swifts are normally very social birds, but the first ones returning in the spring are usually solitary individuals. The earliest swift appeared in Marietta on March 14, 1973.[163] During relatively mild springs, the first migrants may return by the first week of April. When spring temperatures are unusually cold, few swifts appear before April 15. They do not normally become widespread until April 20–25 and peak migratory movements are evident between April 25 and May 15.

Their northward migration is mostly resident birds returning to their nesting locations. While these migrants are common in every county, spring flocks are normally composed of only 10–50 swifts. The largest concentrations do not usually exceed 100–250, while a maximum of 1000+ has been estimated at Findlay, Toledo, and Cleveland during the first half of May.

Breeding Chimney Swifts are among the very few birds that are equally numerous in large cities, small villages, and the rural countryside. They are fairly common to locally abundant summer residents and daily totals of 15–75+ swifts are expected throughout Ohio. Chimney Swift populations have remained reasonably stable in recent decades. Data derived from breeding bird surveys have actually indicated slightly increased numbers within the Great Lakes states since 1965.[438]

As their name implies, Chimney Swifts now exhibit a strong preference for nesting in chimneys. During the present century, the only swifts known to be breeding in a natural cavity were using a large beech tree near Cincinnati on July 16, 1939.[505] Most available information on their nesting biology and behavior has been provided by Ralph Dexter's careful studies of breeding swifts at Kent (Portage County) over nearly forty years. Shortly after they return in early May, their courtship flights are commonly observed and most pair bonds are formed. Nest construction normally begins during the last half of May and continues through mid-June. These nests are simple platforms composed of small dead twigs held together and cemented to the chimney with the bird's saliva. Eggs are mostly laid during the last week of May and June with renesting efforts through mid-July. Young swifts have left the nest as early as June 20 but most fledge during the last half of July and early August.[106,523]

After the breeding season has ended, Chimney Swifts begin to gather into large evening roosts, invariably in large unused chimneys. At first these roosts may shelter several hundred swifts, predominantly resident adults and their offspring, but will expand as migrants appear from farther north. By early September, these roosts may contain 1000–2000 swifts.

Their evening descent into the chimney provides quite a spectacle. The birds begin to gather about an hour before sunset, first scattered individuals and then numerous small flocks. As darkness approaches, every roosting swift gathers overhead into a swirling mass of chattering birds, flying in large circles over the chimney. Initially, only individual swifts actually enter the roost. But as the sunlight fades, the swirling cloud of swifts rapidly descends. In only a few minutes, most have entered the chimney except for the inveterate straggler who quietly disappears as darkness falls.

In addition to these fall roosts, migrant flocks are widely distributed each autumn. Fall concentrations tend to be larger than during spring and 50–300+ swifts may be observed daily. Larger flights may produce flocks of 500–1000. The largest reported fall movement was of 5000 observed along the Scioto River valley in central and southern Ohio on September 30, 1939.[506]

The beginning of their southward migration is difficult to establish but migrant flocks may appear by August 5–15. This movement normally peaks during September and the first week of October. During most years, the large fall roosts normally disappear with the first strong cold front between October 5 and 12 while individuals and small flocks may remain through October 15–20. Even during relatively mild autumns, the last swifts depart by the last week of October. There are very few November sightings, although single swifts lingered through November 3, 1983, at Lorain[372] and November 7, 1979, at Columbus[275] while a flock of 12 was noted at Dayton on November 10, 1925.[299]

RUBY-THROATED HUMMINGBIRD

Archilochus colubris (Linnaeus)

Ruby-throated Hummingbirds do not normally return to Ohio until May, after the spring wildflowers become abundant and many insects have emerged. While overflights have appeared at Cincinnati by April 12 and Toledo by April 14,[89,248] these early arrivals face an inhospitable environment. Ruby-throateds do not normally arrive until April 25–May 2 in southern Ohio and May 5–12 along Lake Erie. Spring totals seldom exceed 1–6 birds daily and the only sizable movement totaled 35 along Lake Erie in Lake County on May 21, 1988. Spring migrants continue to arrive throughout May and these hummingbirds have been observed in passage over Lake Erie into the first week of June.

As summer residents, Ruby-throateds are found in woodlands, brushy fields, fallow fields, and residential gardens—wherever suitable flowers exist. While they forage in a variety of habitats, their nests are usually placed in woods or on woodland edges. As a result of these habitat preferences, breeding Ruby-throated Hummingbirds are widely distributed across Ohio. They are generally fairly common residents in the southern and eastern counties, where 3–10+ hummers may be observed daily. Ruby-throateds are decidedly less numerous elsewhere, becoming uncommon to locally rare residents in most northern and glaciated central counties, where summer totals seldom exceed 1–3 daily.

These breeding populations have apparently declined during this century. Jones[236] considered Ruby-throated Hummingbirds common residents throughout Ohio in the early 1900s. Their status was similar in the mid-1930s when Hicks[220] recorded Ruby-throateds as "fairly common to abundant but somewhat local" residents in every county. Their declining populations were most apparent within western Ohio after 1940. Habitat destruction has reduced hummingbird populations by at least 80 percent at Toledo and within most western counties.[90] Their population trends in eastern Ohio are less apparent, although breeding bird survey data indicate increased numbers between 1965 and 1979.[438]

Hummingbirds are polygamous and the males provide no assistance in raising the young. After mating, the females build tiny nests of lichens and spider webs, usually at heights of six to thirty feet on large tree limbs over streams, paths, or other woodland openings. Their first clutches are normally produced by late May in southern Ohio and mid-June elsewhere. These young fledge in July. Ruby-throateds may raise two broods annually, judging from the number of late nesting records. Nest construction has been noted through July 10 and nests with eggs through mid-August.[215,523] Young hummers have remained in the nest as late as September 8.[89]

Since they do not participate in nesting, male Ruby-throateds normally begin their southward migration before the females and young. Migrant males may appear during the last half of July and most depart by August 7. The fall migration of female and immature Ruby-throateds generally peaks between August 10 and September 7 when they become fairly common to locally common migrants throughout Ohio. Before the advent of hummingbird feeders, these migrants preferred patches of jewelweeds in wet woods or old fields where sunflowers, asters, and other flowers proliferated. Large concentrations were infrequently noted: 100 at Buckeye Lake on August 27, 1936;[32] 65–75 at Toledo on three dates between 1934 and 1940;[89] and 50 at Findlay on September 15, 1966.[417] With the recent proliferation of hummingbird feeders, fall migrants are as likely to appear in residential yards as in natural habitats. Fall totals of 3–10 Ruby-throateds are possible at most localities, with occasional concentrations of 18–25+.

Numbers of fall migrants noticeably diminish during the second week of September, although a few Ruby-throateds are regularly observed through the end of the month. The last migrants usually depart by October 5–12. There have been a few sight records during late October and even into November. While these late hummers were presumed to be Ruby-throateds, recent evidence indicates they may actually have been western strays.

RUFOUS HUMMINGBIRD

Selasphorus rufus (Gmelin)

This accidental visitor from western North America has been recorded in Ohio on three occasions. Fortunately, all sightings have been of adult males, which can be readily identified in the field. The first Rufous Hummingbird was discovered at the Westerville (Franklin County) feeders of Perry and Midge Van Sickle on August 15, 1985. It remained until August 18 and was viewed by more than 100 birders.[380] The other Rufous Hummingbirds appeared in 1987: single males at the William Hodgkiss feeder in Delightful (Trumbull County) on August 23–30 and at Muriel Cohen's feeder in Parma (Cuyahoga County) on November 5–10.[388]

Their appearance in Ohio was not unexpected. Rufous Hummingbirds are rare but regular fall visitors in eastern North America with a number of widely scattered records from many states. Small numbers also regularly winter along the Gulf Coast from southern Texas to western Florida.[5] Like most western strays, Rufous Hummingbirds are long-distance migrants that have demonstrated a tendency to wander from their normal migration routes.

BELTED KINGFISHER

Ceryle alcyon (Linnaeus)

A canoe trip down an Ohio stream or a walk along a streambank is a good way to become acquainted with Belted Kingfishers. With their distinctive plumage and characteristic rattling calls, they will be instantly recognized as they fly just above the surface of the water. As their name implies, kingfishers mostly subsist on minnows and other small fish, although they will also capture crayfish and other invertebrates. They normally hunt from perches bordering a stream, quietly scanning the waters below for signs of life. Most of their prey is captured near the surface of riffles and shallow pools, frequently in water only several inches deep.

During the summer months, kingfishers may feed in small ditches, creeks, and large rivers and along the margins of ponds and lakes. While they may forage over a large area, the number of nesting pairs is limited by the availability of suitable nest sites. Belted Kingfishers excavate their burrows in loose soil near the tops of steep eroding streambanks. These burrows extend several feet into the bank, ending in a small chamber where their eggs are normally laid during the last half of April or early May. The young kingfishers remain here until they fledge in June or early July. Kingfishers raise only one brood but will renest if their first clutch is destroyed. Renesting attempts have produced nests with eggs through July 4.[479]

Breeding kingfishers tend to be rather locally distributed. They are most likely to be found along moderate-sized creeks and large rivers, although pairs will also be scattered along small streams, reservoirs, and even Lake Erie. Belted Kingfishers are fairly common summer residents in most counties, becoming locally uncommon in some western counties where few nest sites are available. They are never numerous, and canoe trips will produce only 3–10 kingfishers daily, although counts of 15–20+ are possible along large rivers after the young have fledged.

Their status has remained fairly constant during this century. Hicks[220] considered kingfishers rare to abundant but locally distributed residents in every county during the 1930s. In subsequent years, kingfishers have experienced local declines only in some western counties.

After their young fledge, kingfishers disperse to small streams and lakes where suitable nest sites are unavailable. This dispersal, evident by the last half of July, marks the beginning of their fall migration. This southward movement is poorly defined as kingfishers gradually drift through the state. Fall kingfishers are most numerous between August 15 and October 10 but are regularly encountered well into November.

As winter residents, Belted Kingfishers are quite hardy. They are found wherever open water is available, normally along creeks and rivers, although a few regularly spend the winter at hot-water outlets along Lake Erie. Their wintering numbers fluctuate annually in response to weather conditions. Kingfishers may be fairly widespread during mild winters but quite scarce during seasons with long cold spells.

In general, Belted Kingfishers are rare and very locally distributed winter residents in the northern counties, where daily totals seldom exceed 1–3 individuals. They become uncommon to locally fairly common winter residents within the central and southern counties. While most winter counts total 1–5 individuals daily within these counties, a canoe trip down the Scioto River in Franklin and Pickaway Counties on February 18, 1985, produced at least 25 kingfishers along fifteen miles of the river.

Their northward migration is as inconspicuous as their autumn movements. Breeding kingfishers begin to appear on their territories by February 20–March 10. Most return by mid-April, although a few will continue to pass over Lake Erie into the first week of May. These migrants are mostly noted as scattered individuals.

RED-HEADED WOODPECKER

Melanerpes erythrocephalus (Linnaeus)

A summer drive through western Ohio farmlands invariably produces sightings of this unmistakable woodpecker. Red-headeds are most apparent in flight over open fields, their striking red, white, and black plumage quite unlike any other resident bird. When they are not in flight, their preferred perches are telephone poles and dead snags on tall isolated trees, giving them a commanding view of the surrounding countryside. Unlike most woodpeckers, Red-headeds seldom drill for burrowing insects. Instead, their summer diet is flying insects captured on the wing supplemented with acorns and other mast.

Their statewide breeding populations fluctuated dramatically during the past century. Numbers increased rapidly after 1860 when open farmlands with numerous fencerows and small woodlots provided nearly ideal habitats, and Red-headed Woodpeckers became one of Ohio's most numerous breeding birds.[236] This sizable population was short-lived. By the mid-1930s, Hicks[220] cited "decidedly reduced numbers" within most counties. They were common to abundant throughout the western half of the state, "less common" in the northeastern counties, and uncommon to rare and locally distributed along the unglaciated Allegheny Plateau.

A brief recovery was reported during the 1950s, most notably in the western counties. But this trend was reversed during the 1960s and Ohio breeding populations have experienced significant declines since 1965.[438] Breeding Red-headed Woodpeckers are still most numerous within the western half of Ohio, where they are presently fairly common to locally common residents.[434] In recent years, summer totals seldom exceeded 3–10 woodpeckers daily. They are uncommon to locally fairly common residents within the northeastern counties, somewhat more numerous near Lake Erie. Daily totals usually are 5 or fewer woodpeckers in these counties. Red-headeds are least numerous along the unglaciated Allegheny Plateau. They may be fairly common at a few localities, including the Killbuck Creek valley and portions of Carroll County.[84] However, these woodpeckers are casual to locally uncommon residents in most southeastern counties, usually as isolated pairs.

The ideal Red-headed Woodpecker nesting habitat is fields with scattered open woodlots dominated by oaks and hickories. Nesting usually begins during May and most nests with eggs have been reported between May 20 and June 15. Renesting efforts may continue into July. Recently fledged young have appeared by mid-June and may be noted through mid-August.[479,523]

The breeding population is largely migratory. Since Red-headeds are daytime migrants, their passage is conspicuous. At one time their migratory movements were a regular feature of each spring and autumn. But as their breeding populations have declined, migrant numbers have undergone a comparable decline.

Their spring migration is rather brief. Migrant Red-headeds usually appear during the last week of April and are most frequently observed between May 5 and 20. Spring flights may still produce tallies of 20–30+ along Lake Erie, although most recent spring reports are of 10 or fewer daily in the unglaciated counties.

As fall migrants, Red-headed Woodpeckers may leave their nesting territories by the last week of August. This movement normally peaks between September 10 and October 10, while smaller numbers are noted through November 10–15. The number and distribution of fall migrants are comparable to those in spring.

During winter, Red-headed Woodpeckers subsist entirely on acorns, beechnuts, and waste corn. Their distribution and relative abundance reflect the availability of these foods, particularly the mast crop. Hence, their winter distribution patterns are unpredictable and different each year, a pattern reminiscent of the food-related winter movements of most northern finches.[455] During the few winters with abundant mast, sizable influxes of woodpeckers from elsewhere in their range produced as many as 75–250+ on Christmas Bird Counts. Such influxes were periodically noted through 1962 but have not been apparent in recent years, perhaps reflecting a westward shift in their winter distribution.[455]

These woodpeckers are now uncommon to locally fairly common winter residents within the western half of Ohio and somewhat more numerous in the southern and central counties. During most winters, daily totals are 6 or fewer with local concentrations of 10–15. They become casual to locally uncommon winter residents elsewhere, generally least numerous along the unglaciated Allegheny Plateau. Most eastern winter reports involve only 1–4 Red-headeds and sizable winter influxes have never been reported.

Wintering Red-headeds are found within open woodlots dominated by oaks, beeches, and hickories. These woodpeckers infrequently visit bird feeders. They are very territorial and remain within a small area as long as food is available. On calm winter days, their distinctive rolling calls carry through open woods and Red-headeds are quite visible as they fly from tree to tree, defending their food supplies from competitors.

RED-BELLIED WOODPECKER

Melanerpes carolinus (Linnaeus)

With their loud calls and distinctive plumage, Red-bellied Woodpeckers are familiar residents of Ohio woodlands. Mature and second-growth woods invariably support resident pairs, as do extensive riparian corridors. They are not necessarily restricted to natural woodlands, however, and regularly inhabit parks, cemeteries, and shaded residential areas.

In the early 1900s, Jones[236] described Red-bellied Woodpeckers as fairly common residents in southern Ohio but less common in the northern counties. As late as the mid-1930s, breeding populations were not established in most northwestern counties and they remained very local and rare in northeastern Ohio.[220] Their populations increased throughout the state during the 1950s. They appeared at Findlay in 1956[417] but were not regularly reported at Toledo until 1960 and nesting was first recorded there in 1963.[89]

Red-bellied Woodpeckers today are generally fairly common to common permanent residents throughout Ohio, becoming locally uncommon in the northern tier of counties. They are never numerous and daily totals seldom exceed 1–6 in northern Ohio and 5–20 elsewhere. Although as many as 399 have been tallied on Cincinnati Christmas Bird Counts, such large numbers are not encountered by solitary birders.

Since their winter diet is mostly mast, Red-bellied Woodpeckers prefer oak-hickory and mixed oak forests where they can subsist on acorns. In northeastern Ohio where oak forests are scarce, they prefer beech-maple woods.[523] If adequate mast is not available, they will supplement their diet with regular visits to bird feeders or by obtaining insects and insect larvae in typical woodpecker fashion.

With the advent of warm weather in late March, male Red-bellieds become quite vocal as they establish their breeding territories. This conspicuous behavior lasts for only a few weeks until nesting activities are under way. Once the eggs are laid, usually during late April or early May, Red-bellieds become much less conspicuous until their young fledge in June or early July. Initiation of nesting activities depends on the weather and may begin earlier during unusually warm springs. Trautman[479] cited a nest with young as early as April 15, 1924, at Buckeye Lake. If the first clutches fail, Red-bellieds will renest and produce nests with eggs through June 8 and dependent young through mid-August.[54,479]

Red-bellied Woodpeckers are essentially permanent residents. Some movements may be evident in early spring when the birds are establishing their breeding territories. Greater dispersal is evident during fall as young Red-bellieds search for suitable unoccupied wintering sites.

YELLOW-BELLIED SAPSUCKER

Sphyrapicus varius (Linnaeus)

As their name implies, sapsuckers have a unique feeding behavior for North American woodpeckers. They drill rows of small holes into the bark of trees, then return later to these holes to feed on insects attracted to the sugary sap. While they drill into a variety of deciduous and coniferous trees, they prefer apples, cherries, and related species whose sap is particularly attractive to insects. Contrary to popular belief, their feeding does not harm the trees.

The northward migration of Yellow-bellied Sapsuckers is closely associated with sap production in trees. While a few early migrants appear by the first week of March, they are not expected until March 20–30 within the central and southern counties and March 28–April 5 along Lake Erie. Most sapsuckers pass through Ohio during April, becoming uncommon to fairly common migrants in most counties and locally common along Lake Erie. Spring totals of 1–5 sapsuckers daily are noted at most localities, with occasional movements of 8–15. Larger flights are infrequent and restricted to migrant traps along Lake Erie and near Columbus, where 20–35 sapsuckers have been noted on several occasions and as many as 50 on April 5, 1963.[471] Their numbers decrease by the last week of April and the last stragglers normally depart by May 5–10. A few late migrants have remained through May 18 in central Ohio,[479] May 19 at Dayton,[299] and May 25 at Toledo.[89]

While most sapsuckers breed in northern deciduous forests, Ohio apparently hosts a small nesting population. The distribution may once have been more widespread, since there are nesting records from Wayne County in 1891 and Lorain County in 1901 plus probable breeders near Toledo in 1907 and in Lorain County in 1897.[13,89,220] Since the 1930s, breeding sapsuckers have been restricted to the extreme northeastern counties. Hicks[220] cited isolated summer records from Trumbull and Geauga Counties but the only small population resided in Ashtabula County, where summering sapsuckers were "not uncommon" but locally distributed with records from twelve locations.[215]

During recent decades, there were very few reports of sum-

mering sapsuckers from northeastern Ohio, although sporadic sightings indicated that a small population remained. The existence of this population was confirmed during work on the Ohio Breeding Bird Atlas.[434] Summering and breeding sapsuckers were discovered in at least four sites in Ashtabula County and one in Geauga County, indicating that they remain rare and very locally distributed summer residents. The total size and present trends of this population have not been established.

Breeding sapsuckers are surprisingly secretive. Hence, there is relatively little information available on their nesting biology in Ohio. Most summering sapsuckers occupy wet deciduous woods or the margins of bogs where yellow birch, beech, and aspen are prevalent.[215] Their nesting activities begin during May and nests with young have been recorded between June 6 and July 1. Most young sapsuckers fledge in late June or early July.

Considerably fewer Yellow-bellied Sapsuckers are detected as fall migrants. These migrants usually return to the northern counties by September 10–17. While a few individuals may also appear in central and southern Ohio at this time, they are not expected until September 25–30. Their southward migration apparently peaks between September 25 and October 12 when they become fairly common migrants along Lake Erie and rare to uncommon through the interior counties. Fall sightings mostly are of 1–6 sapsuckers along Lake Erie and 3 or fewer inland. Larger flights are unusual and restricted to the lakefront, where concentrations of 13–30 sapsuckers have occasionally appeared during the first week of October. Numbers decrease during the last half of October, although scattered migrants may appear into the first half of November.

Before 1950, Yellow-bellied Sapsuckers were considered accidental winter visitors. Their winter status perceptibly changed in the 1950s and small numbers have regularly wintered since the early 1960s. Today they are rare to locally uncommon winter residents in southern Ohio. While most winter records are of single sapsuckers, groups of 3–6 may be occasionally encountered. They become casual to rare winter residents in other counties, where daily totals in excess of 1–2 individuals are unusual. While most wintering Yellow-bellieds are found in deciduous or mixed woods, they may also occupy parks and cemeteries.

DOWNY WOODPECKER

Picoides pubescens (Linnaeus)

As the most widespread and familiar of our woodpeckers, the Downy is an occupant of woodlands and a visitor to backyard bird feeders throughout Ohio. These woodpeckers thrive wherever there are trees, limited only by the availability of suitable nesting cavities. Being small, Downies generally forage along smaller limbs and branches than those frequented by the larger woodpeckers. The adaptable Downy also feeds on dead goldenrod stems in fallow fields or on dried cornstalks in unharvested cornfields, far from any woods.

Although they are generally considered fairly common to common permanent residents, Downy Woodpeckers are most conspicuous during winter. A full day's birding in suitable habitats might produce 20–45 during these months. Between November and early March, Downies band together with chickadees, titmice, nuthatches, and other gleaners to form the mixed-species foraging flocks characteristic of our winter woodlands. These flocks cover much larger areas than nesting birds, and Downies have been shown to "wander considerably" during this season.[89]

With the advent of warm weather in March, the mixed flocks disband and Downies establish their nesting territories. Territorial activity peaks in early April. While they normally declare their territories from knotty branches or dead limbs, Downies can become nuisances when they learn that gutters on houses provide equally suitable drumming sites. Their nesting chronology is fairly similar throughout the state. Nest excavation may begin as early as the middle of March and peaks in mid-April. As with most cavity nesters, breeding information is rather scanty but most clutches normally hatch in May. The young may fledge by the end of May, although fledglings are most evident during June. Renesting attempts have been responsible for nests with young through June 26 and adults with dependent young as late as September 4.[290]

Once their territorial activities subside, Downies are surprisingly inconspicuous between late April and early September. While as many as 20 Downies have been recorded during a single June day, midsummer counts generally total fewer than 10. Breeding Downies are most common in the eastern half of the state where suitable habitats are widespread but much less numerous in intensively cultivated sections of western Ohio. Since the mid-1960s, breeding bird survey data indicate the Ohio population is fairly stable.[438]

By early September, the adults have completed their annual molts and Downies are once again conspicuous. Although Downies are not known as a migratory species, some wander considerably during the fall months. Trautman[479] noted "distinct flights" in the Buckeye Lake area during late October and early November of several years, and single Downies occasionally appear at migrant traps along Lake Erie during fall. The exact nature of these autumn movements is poorly understood.

HAIRY WOODPECKER

Picoides villosus (Linnaeus)

While the adaptable Downy Woodpecker is familiar to people with only a passing interest in birds, Hairy Woodpeckers have more specific habitat requirements and are less likely to be encountered by the casual observer. Hairies require older, more mature trees for foraging and nest sites. They seemingly prefer extensive mature woodlands but will occupy wooded corridors along streams as well as residential areas if many large trees are present.

Hairy Woodpeckers are generally uncommon to fairly common permanent residents throughout Ohio. Summer totals seldom exceed 1–4 Hairies daily. They are most numerous in the eastern half of the state but can be rather locally distributed in intensively cultivated portions of western Ohio. They are outnumbered by Downies everywhere. The ratio of Downies to Hairies is greatest in the western counties, where it approaches ten or twelve to one; it is reduced to four to six Downies for every Hairy in eastern Ohio.

Like Downies, Hairy Woodpeckers are most conspicuous during winter, when as many as 10 may be recorded daily, although most reports are of 5 or fewer. Unlike Downies, Hairy Woodpeckers are very sedentary throughout the year and seldom stray from their established territories. In addition, Hairies do not normally associate with mixed-species foraging flocks.

Territorial behavior is initiated with the advent of warm weather in late February or March and reaches its peak in early April. Once this activity ceases, Hairies become inconspicuous among the emerging foliage. Their nests are generally placed in the trunks of dead trees at heights of fifteen to seventy-five feet. Most are excavated during March or early April and eggs are laid shortly after the nests have been completed. The first clutches normally hatch during May. Fledged young have been observed as early as May 22 but most appear during June.[479,523] If their first nesting attempt is unsuccessful, Hairies will renest. These renesting efforts account for nests with eggs as late as June 1, broods in the nest through June 26, and adults followed by dependent young well into July.[89,424]

In recent years, some concern has been expressed over the long-term trends of Hairy Woodpecker populations. But while Hairies may have declined in other states, their populations appear to be fairly stable in Ohio, especially within the eastern counties where suitable habitats remain plentiful. Local declines have been experienced in some northwestern and west-central counties where intensive agriculture has eliminated many suitable woodlots.

RED-COCKADED WOODPECKER

Picoides borealis (Vieillot)

Red-cockaded Woodpeckers are sedentary residents of mature pine woods in the southeastern United States whose present range extends north to southern Kentucky. They are locally distributed within this range, with few extralimital sightings.[5] Ohio's first record of this accidental visitor was provided by a specimen in the Ohio State University Museum of Zoology collected in Columbus on March 15, 1872. The collection label states that "it was in company with another of its own kind, two or three sapsuckers, nuthatches, etc., and shot from a high tree between the canal and Scioto River."[236]

Since this species' populations have seriously declined during this century, it was generally assumed that it would never be recorded from Ohio again. Surprisingly, another Red-cockaded Woodpecker was discovered by park naturalist Eddie Bower at Old Man's Cave State Park, Hocking County, on April 22, 1975. It was subsequently observed and photographed by many birders through May 4 as it fed among planted pines near the main parking lot.[469] These two records are the only acceptable reports for Ohio.

BLACK-BACKED WOODPECKER

Picoides arcticus (Swainson)

Black-backed Woodpeckers normally reside within the boreal forests of Canada and the extreme northern United States. While they are usually permanent residents in these forests, they periodically undertake defined movements southward. These invasions normally occur at intervals of seven to ten years and occasionally produce sightings south to the lower Great Lakes.[5]

Within Ohio, Black-backed Woodpeckers are accidental to casual visitors to the northern counties. Most records have been associated with noticeable southward incursions elsewhere in the Great Lakes region. The state's first Black-backed was discovered near Painesville (Lake County) on October 31, 1918.[523] Single Black-backeds were also detected in 1939 and 1940. Between 1957 and 1964, there were at least seven records from the Cleveland area.[335] In subsequent years, the only confirmed sighting was recorded in 1984.

There are currently eleven acceptable Black-backed Woodpecker sightings from Ohio. Ten are from the Cleveland area, mostly in Lake, Geauga, and eastern Cuyahoga Counties.[335,523] The other is from Toledo on January 8, 1939.[89] There is also an undocumented sighting from Columbiana County during December 1974 and several anecdotal accounts of nineteenth-century specimens from northeastern Ohio.

The earliest Black-backed Woodpecker was photographed at Lorain on September 27, 1984.[376] Most Ohio sightings have been during late fall and winter with six reports between November 13 and February 9. There are also three spring reports, with a single woodpecker remaining at Cleveland through April 20, 1957.[335] With the exception of 2 Black-backeds observed near Chardon (Geauga County) on March 10, 1940,[523] all acceptable records have been of single individuals.

NORTHERN FLICKER

Colaptes auratus (Linnaeus)

Flickers are widely distributed and conspicuous occupants of open habitats throughout Ohio. Even though they are classifed as woodpeckers, they are seldom encountered within extensive woodlands. Instead, they prefer grazed woodlots, woodland edges, parks, orchards, farmlands, and residential areas. This species is undoubtedly most conspicuous after dawn on spring and summer mornings when the males loudly proclaim their territories. Ascending to the tops of large dead trees or telephone poles, they produce sharp piercing calls while their constant drumming reminds other flickers to stay away.

Their territorial activities are most apparent during April, coinciding with the peculiar courtship displays by which they cement their pair bonds for the breeding season. Nesting activities follow shortly thereafter, beginning with nest construction in late April and early May. Flickers excavate their own cavities in trees, fence posts, and telephone poles, mostly at heights of ten to sixty feet.[89,479] Most clutches have been discovered between May 10 and June 15. The first fledglings have appeared by June 2 but most are noted during the last half of June and early July.[479,523] Renesting attempts have produced recently fledged young through early August.

Northern Flickers rank as one of the most widely distributed members of Ohio's summer avifauna.[434] They are fairly common to common residents within every county. They are never numerous, however, and summer totals are mostly 5–15 flickers daily, although fewer individuals may be recorded within some intensively farmed western counties.

Despite their present widespread distribution, Northern Flickers have noticeably declined during the twentieth century, largely because of competition with European Starlings for nesting cavities. There has also been extensive mortality caused by unusually severe winter weather, most notably following the harsh winters of the 1970s.[438]

While flickers are considered permanent residents throughout Ohio, they are most numerous during their seasonal migrations. Spring movements normally begin during the last half of March and peak between April 5 and 20. Flickers are fairly common to common spring migrants across the state, becoming locally abundant along Lake Erie. Lakefront movements of 75–150+ flickers daily were regularly reported before 1960, but within the past ten years most spring flights have involved only 15–50. By far the largest reported movement occurred April 15, 1972, when 1000 flickers were estimated in the vicinity of Crane Creek State Park/Magee Marsh Wildlife Area.[90] Within the interior counties, spring totals have mostly been 25 or fewer flickers in recent years. Larger inland movements were noted before 1960, producing local concentrations of 90–100 individuals in central Ohio near Columbus. Numbers of northward migrants noticeably diminish by late April, although a few individuals may appear along Lake Erie into the first week of May.

A similar southward movement is apparent each autumn. This migration begins between September 10 and 20 and normally peaks during October, producing numbers comparable to the spring migrations. It has mostly ended by November 1, although a few individuals may pass through Ohio until November 10–20.

As winter residents, Northern Flickers also occupy a wide variety of habitats. Some individuals may be found in mature woodlands, feasting on acorns and beechnuts, while others will regularly visit backyard bird feeders. But most wintering flickers prefer the same open habitats they occupy during summer, especially where harvested croplands provide food during bad weather.

Wintering numbers are generally greatest during December and early January but noticeably decline with the advent of sustained cold weather. In addition to seasonal fluctuations, these numbers exhibit considerable annual variability. Wintering flickers are least numerous within the northern counties, where they are normally rare to uncommon residents. Most winter reports are of only 1–5 flickers daily. Larger concentrations are unexpected, but a few locations have hosted as many as 20–30 during relatively mild winters. In the central and southern counties, flickers are generally uncommon to fairly common winter residents. While winter totals mostly are 1–8 daily, larger concentrations are not unexpected. Groups of 20–40 may congregate in favorable habitats. Trautman[479] noted as many as 100 at Buckeye Lake during some winters before 1940.

PILEATED WOODPECKER

Dryocopus pileatus (Linnaeus)

A singularly spectacular woodpecker, the Pileated is certain to impress even those people who pay little attention to birds. Nearly as large as a crow with a brilliant red crest and striking black and white wing pattern, Pileateds are usually observed in flight between woodlands within their territories. Despite their size, they are so wary that they are seldom closely observed as they forage among large trees. They are more often heard than seen and their loud flickerlike calls resound across the hills of southern and eastern Ohio throughout the year.

The status of Pileated Woodpeckers as occupants of extensive mature woodlands has changed tremendously within historic times. Their relative abundance reflects the changing health of Ohio's forests. When Ohio was initially settled, Pileateds undoubtedly roamed through the virgin forests across the state. As these forests were cleared and replaced by farmlands, the populations started to decline. The acceleration of these land-use trends during the last half of the nineteenth century caused the extirpation of Pileateds from many localities before 1900.

By the turn of the century, Pileateds had vanished from most counties except along the unglaciated Allegheny Plateau and extreme northeastern Ohio.[236] Even within these counties, they had become quite scarce and the sighting of a single Pileated or a nesting pair was noteworthy. Mature woodlands were still disappearing and Jones[236] felt their numbers were declining and in danger of extinction.

Their fortunes did not improve until the 1920s when abandoned farms in southeastern Ohio began to revert to woodlands. Their status was still improving in the mid-1930s when Hicks[220] described Pileateds as residents in every county east to Brown, Highland, Ross, Fairfield, Licking, Knox, Ashland, Medina, and Cuyahoga. They were generally rare in most southern and eastern counties but were locally common at a few places, especially in Muskingum County, where 46 adults and four nests were located in 1935.[220]

Pileated Woodpecker populations continued to increase and expand within eastern Ohio during the 1940s and 1950s. Except for a few strays at Cincinnati in 1937 and 1938, Dayton in 1949, Toledo in 1955 and 1958, and sporadically in the Columbus area,[89,248,299] their distribution did not appreciably change during these years.

Range expansions became apparent in the early 1960s and still continue as Pileateds attempt to reoccupy most of their former range. This expansion was first noted in the southwestern counties when these woodpeckers returned to Dayton and Butler County in 1960.[299,325] In 1962, 26 Pileateds were counted at Cincinnati, where they were absent only a few years earlier.[130] Their numbers also noticeably increased in the Columbus area during the 1960s. Expansion into the northwestern counties was not apparent until the 1970s, but this expansion has been quite slow because of a shortage of suitable woodlands within these intensively farmed counties.

Pileated Woodpeckers are now uncommon to fairly common residents in most southern and eastern counties. Only 1–5 individuals may be expected daily, although tallies of 6–10+ are possible in areas with extensive forests. They become uncommon residents in the central counties bordering the unglaciated Allegheny Plateau but are absent to rare in the remainder of the state.

While Pileateds are most numerous in extensive mature forests, they will also occupy second-growth woodlands and large isolated woodlots. Their breeding territories must include suitable large trees for nesting. Their nests are placed at heights of twenty to fifty-five feet in cavities constructed by the adults during April and early May. Nests with eggs have been reported between April 18 and May 21.[50,299] Their young usually hatch in early May. Most dependent young have been reported in late May or early June, although renesting attempts have produced fledglings during July.

Pileated Woodpeckers are normally quite sedentary. Despite their resident status, a few undertake local movements during spring and fall. These movements are hardly noticeable except when Pileateds appear at unexpected locations, such as migrant traps along Lake Erie. Their autumn movements, mostly noted in October and November, may be young birds searching for suitable territories. Their spring movements are not easily explained, but a few Pileateds have appeared along Lake Erie between March 25 and April 14.

IVORY-BILLED WOODPECKER

Campephilus principalis (Linnaeus)

The occurrence of this magnificent woodpecker within the state is based solely on archaeological evidence from southern Ohio. While the bill, head, and wings might be found almost anywhere since they were prized by Indians and actively traded between tribes, the presence of legs and other body parts is generally accepted as positive evidence of this woodpecker's natural occurrence in an area. It is considered unlikely that such a large bird would be carried great distances from the kill site.[331]

Within Ohio, archaeological evidence of Ivory-billed Woodpeckers has been obtained from sites in Ross, Scioto, and Muskingum Counties. Leg elements (tarsometatarsi) were recovered from each site.[331,518] Radiocarbon dating of material from the Muskingum site indicates that Ivory-billeds were present in Ohio between the twelfth and fourteenth centuries, while the Scioto County site may have been as recent as the fifteenth or sixteenth century. The date of their disappearance from the state is unknown. There is no evidence to substantiate their presence within Ohio during historic times.

OLIVE-SIDED FLYCATCHER

Contopus borealis (Swainson)

Sitting on dead branches at the top of a large oak, an Olive-sided Flycatcher quietly surveys the surrounding fields for large flying insects. With its keen eyesight, it can detect prey at distances of several hundred feet and is quickly off in pursuit. Whether the chase is successful or not, it will habitually return to the same perch to wait for more insects to fly by. Olive-sided Flycatchers are frequently found near water where insects are plentiful, but open fields, cemeteries, and parks are equally suitable if tall perches are available. Unfortunately, this behavior cannot be observed with any regularity as Olive-sided Flycatchers are normally rare migrants through Ohio, becoming locally uncommon along Lake Erie. They are least numerous in the unglaciated eastern counties where suitable habitats are plentiful and the few flycatchers are widely scattered.

Olive-sided Flycatchers are among our latest spring migrants. No reliable April records exist, although a few early individuals may return during the first week of May. They are most likely to be encountered during the last half of the month. They regularly linger through June 3–7 and sightings as late as June 10–14 are not unexpected. Migrants are normally encountered as individuals or pairs. However, small concentrations are occasionally noted in association with large flights along Lake Erie. By far the largest reported movement involved 30 Olive-sideds at Cedar Point (Erie County) on May 13, 1907.[241] In recent years, the largest concentrations have totaled 4–6.

In eastern North America, breeding Olive-sided Flycatchers occupy boreal forests in Canada, the northern United States, and very locally at high elevations along the Appalachian Mountains.[5] At one time, a very small population may have resided in extreme northeastern Ohio. Hicks[215] observed summering Olive-sideds at three Ashtabula County locations between 1925 and 1932. Of these locations, the former Pymatuning Bog hosted summering Olive-sideds during three years. An incubating adult was discovered within the bog on June 16, 1932, providing the only confirmed nesting record. With the bog's destruction, this summering population disappeared. Since the mid-1930s, nonbreeding Olive-sided Flycatchers have been casual summer visitors to the northeastern counties but are accidental elsewhere, producing two to four summer sightings during most decades.

Like most flycatchers, the Olive-sideds begin their fall migration quite early. Returning Olive-sideds may appear by the first week of August but most are observed between mid-August and mid-September. Most depart for wintering grounds in South and Central America by the end of September. The few October records include an October 11, 1908, specimen from Hamilton County[248] and a sighting in the Cleveland area on October 16, 1965.[117] Fall sightings are invariably of only 1–4 individuals.

EASTERN WOOD-PEWEE

Contopus virens (Linnaeus)

The first hint of dawn on a warm summer's morning will be greeted by the plaintive whistles of the Eastern Wood-Pewee, one of our more vocal woodland songbirds. The calls continue throughout the day, although they decrease in frequency during the warm midafternoon. Sunset produces another chorus that continues until the last sunlight vanishes from the evening sky.

During summer, most pewees are detected by their distinctive calls, since these drab flycatchers frequently choose to remain hidden among the foliage of tall trees. They are among Ohio's most numerous woodland flycatchers and are fairly common to common summer residents throughout the state. Their preferred habitats are mature woodlands, from small woodlots to extensive forests, but they also occupy riparian corridors, parks, and grazed woodlots.

Breeding pewees are most numerous in southern and eastern Ohio where mature woodlands are widely distributed. Between 12 and 20 pewees can be recorded during a June morning within these counties. They are least numerous in intensively cultivated western Ohio where few mature woodlots exist.[434] Within these counties, daily totals seldom exceed 2–8 except along extensive riparian corridors.

Pewee nests are usually located at heights of twenty-five to seventy-five feet along the outer branches of tall trees. Since these nests are inaccessible, there is a paucity of nesting data from Ohio. Most nests are initiated during May and nests with eggs have been reported as early as May 14.[523] First broods mostly fledge during the last half of June and July. Some pewees may raise two broods, as there are a number of nesting reports during August and early September. Nests with eggs have been reported as late as August 13–15; young have remained in nests through September 1, and adults have fed dependent young through September 13–16.[479,523]

Given their status as common summer residents, the initiation of their fall migration is difficult to detect. Records from lakefront migrant traps indicate that their passage begins during the last ten days of August. Eastern Wood-Pewees remain fairly common to common through the third week of September. Fall totals seldom exceed 5–10 pewees daily. Most depart by October 9–15 with the latest documented record on October 21, 1982.[368] While there are several November sight records, none is adequately documented and the identity of these individuals is uncertain.

Their spring status is also obscured by misidentifications, and all March sight records most likely pertain to phoebes. The earliest pewees have probably returned between April 18 and 25 as overflights along Lake Erie and very early returning residents to counties along the Ohio River. However, pewees normally do not return to southern and central Ohio until the first week of May. They arrive along Lake Erie approximately one week later and become fairly common to common throughout the state by May 15–20. The largest spring movements have involved 20–30 pewees daily along Lake Erie and in central Ohio. Migrant pewees may appear along Lake Erie through May 25–June 5.

Eastern Wood-Pewee populations have remained fairly stable since the 1800s. In recent years, however, their populations have suffered from the loss of mature woodlands in their North American breeding range and in the South American rain forests where they winter. This habitat loss has produced "slight but significant" declines in pewee populations across North America since the mid-1960s.[438]

YELLOW-BELLIED FLYCATCHER

Empidonax flaviventris (Baird & Baird)

Of all the songbirds in Ohio, *Empidonax* flycatchers are the most difficult species to identify positively in the field. All five species have greenish brown upperparts with a pair of wing-bars, grayish white underparts with varying amounts of yellowish wash on the belly and flanks, and an eye ring. Their plumage differences are subtle, and positive identification is frequently based on songs, call notes, or measurements in the hand. While Yellow-bellieds are probably the most distinctive member of this group, sight records are still subject to question, especially during fall when other species can have extensive yellowish wash on the underparts.

Yellow-bellied Flycatchers are rather late spring migrants. The earliest Yellow-bellieds may appear during the first week of May, although they do not normally arrive until May 10–15. They are most numerous during the last half of May, when they are rare to uncommon migrants through the interior of Ohio and uncommon to fairly common along Lake Erie. Daily totals are normally 3 or fewer individuals. Sizable passerine movements have produced as many as 10 Yellow-bellieds in central Ohio and 18–20 along Lake Erie. These migrants prefer dense woodlands and are frequently found near water. Yellow-bellieds normally depart by the first week of June but have lingered along Lake Erie through June 10–14.

These flycatchers normally breed in the boreal forests of Canada and the northern United States.[5] The only published summer sight record from Ohio is during late June in the Cleveland area.[523] Unfortunately, the details of this sighting were never provided and the acceptability of this record is debatable.

During fall, Yellow-bellied Flycatchers are rare to uncommon migrants throughout Ohio. In addition to mesic woodlands, they are found in drier wooded and edge habitats during this season. They are usually encountered as isolated individuals. The largest reported concentration is only 10 along Lake Erie.[89] Since Yellow-bellieds normally return to the north shore of Lake Erie during the last ten days of July,[233] they probably also appear in Ohio during this period. There are very few late July records from Ohio, however, probably because of their inconspicuous behavior and the absence of intensive bird-banding efforts along the lakefront. The first Yellow-bellieds are normally detected during the second week of August. Their fall migration usually extends through the third week of September. Only occasional stragglers remain into early October and the latest acceptable sighting is one banded at Cleveland on October 18, 1976.

ACADIAN FLYCATCHER

Empidonax virescens (Vieillot)

During summer, the various species of *Empidonax* flycatchers occupy distinctly different habitats, and that facilitates their identification. Acadian Flycatchers inhabit mature woodlands and are unlikely to be found anywhere else. Inconspicuous when they forage silently for insects within the understories of these forests, they are more likely to be detected by their diagnostic sharp loud calls.

While these plain flycatchers seemingly prefer mature beech-maple forests, they readily occupy other woodland communities. They require fairly open woodlands with well-defined understories, frequently with small creeks. Acadians become most numerous within extensive forests and normally avoid small isolated woodlots and narrow wooded corridors.

Their nests are usually placed at heights of eight to twenty feet, suspended between twigs on the branches of small trees. They are frequently placed over a small creek or ravine.[523] Nest construction normally begins during the last half of May and continues into mid-June. While complete clutches have been recorded by the first week of June, most are discovered between June 10 and July 2.[333,523] Recently fledged young may appear by the last week of June but most are noted during July.[479] Renesting attempts may produce fledglings as late as the first week of September.

As summer residents, Acadian Flycatchers have been widely distributed within Ohio during the present century. In 1903, Jones[236] considered them fairly common residents throughout the state. In 1935, Hicks[220] cited summer records from eighty-five counties, noting absences only in Putnam, Allen, and Hancock Counties. While these flycatchers were "infrequent and locally distributed" within most northwestern counties, they were fairly common to abundant elsewhere.

Their status did not change appreciably in subsequent decades. Since the mid-1960s, some increases have been evident at the northern edge of their range. Within Ohio, these increases have been apparent on breeding bird surveys within the southeastern counties and as expanding populations in several northwestern counties.[90,438]

Acadian Flycatchers are now fairly common to common summer residents throughout southern and eastern Ohio. They are most numerous along the unglaciated Allegheny Plateau, where 15–30+ individuals may be recorded daily; similar numbers may be locally distributed within southwestern and northeastern counties. These flycatchers are also widely distributed and fairly common residents within the central counties near Columbus, where daily totals seldom exceed 5–12. They are least numerous in west-central and northwestern Ohio. While they are locally fairly common residents at a few northwestern localities where 10–15 singing males may be recorded daily, they become uncommon to rare and locally distributed within most intensively cultivated counties.[434]

Acadian Flycatchers are relatively late spring migrants and the timing of their northward movements is fairly uniform across the state. The earliest arrivals have appeared by April 29–May 2 but they are not usually detected until May 5–10.

They do not become numerous until May 15–20; small numbers may continue to migrate into the first half of June. These migrants are mostly breeding birds returning to their territories. Spring Acadians are uncommon visitors to lakefront migrant traps, appearing mainly during the last half of May, when daily totals seldom exceed 1–3.

Their status as fall migrants is obscured by the inability to positively identify most silent *Empidonax* flycatchers. Our understanding of their relative distribution and abundance during autumn is thus incomplete. Most Acadians apparently depart quietly from their nesting territories and fall migrants are relatively uncommon throughout the state. All fall reports invariably are of 5 or fewer Acadians. Their numbers decline during the last half of August and the last Acadians normally disappear between September 10 and 20. Only a few stragglers remain later in the month. There have been several sight records into the first week of October.

ALDER FLYCATCHER

Empidonax alnorum Brewster

Until Alder Flycatchers were recognized as a distinct species in 1973, few birders paid any attention to them. Even after formal recognition, correctly identifying Alders proves to be a challenge. In the field, they are positively identified only by their vocalizations. Silent Alders cannot be identified in the field and frequently not even in the hand. Despite these identification problems, the status of Alder Flycatchers is becoming established within Ohio, although it will take some years of observation to fully understand their distribution and relative abundance.

Alder Flycatchers are the last migrants returning each spring. The earliest confirmed arrival is May 11; they do not normally appear until May 15–20. They pass through the state quite rapidly and most are observed between May 23 and June 7. These migrants are uncommon to fairly common along Lake Erie, where daily totals seldom exceed 1–6 individuals. Within the interior counties, Alders are casual to locally uncommon migrants, usually as scattered individuals. The last spring migrants may remain into the second week of June, especially along Lake Erie.

Summering Alder Flycatchers are most numerous in the northeastern counties of Ashtabula, northern Trumbull, Lake, Geauga, eastern Cuyahoga, and Portage, where they are locally uncommon summer residents. Territorial males are scattered throughout these counties, normally in groups of 4 or fewer Alders, although as many as 10 males have been reported from Gott Fen Nature Preserve in Portage County.[366] They are casual to rare and locally distributed summer residents in other northeastern counties. The southern edge of this breeding range barely extends onto the unglaciated Allegheny Plateau, with isolated summering males reported from Columbiana, Carroll, and Tuscarawas Counties.[434] Elsewhere in northern Ohio, Alder Flycatchers are accidental to locally rare summer residents and may regularly nest only in the northwestern counties of Lucas,

Fulton, and Williams. They are very locally distributed in these counties, usually as groups of 4 or fewer singing males. Additionally, Alders are accidental residents in the central counties. Single males have apparently summered in Champaign and Madison Counties.[383,434]

Marshes, bogs, and streambanks dominated by buttonbush, alders, dogwoods, and willows provide typical summer habitats for Alder Flycatchers—the same wet brushy swamps and thickets occupied by Willow Flycatchers. But unlike Willows, Alder Flycatchers avoid brushy successional habitats away from water. Very little information is available on their breeding biology in Ohio. The few confirmed breeding records indicate that nesting activities are initiated in early June and most young do not fledge until mid-July.

Their fall status is poorly understood. Alders appear to be fairly early migrants and most residents depart from their Ohio territories by mid-August. In addition, an influx of singing Alders is frequently noted between July 25 and August 10, perhaps migrant adults from farther north. As many as 8–9 have been reported from northeastern Ohio during this period. After the adults depart in mid-August, the very few confirmed records indicate that their migration continues into the last half of September.

WILLOW FLYCATCHER

Empidonax traillii (Audubon)

Willows are the most widely distributed *Empidonax* flycatchers of wet brushy habitats in Ohio. While they prefer shrubby swamps and thickets bordering streams, Willows also occupy brushy wet meadows and fallow fields. A few pairs may inhabit cattail wetlands if some brushy thickets are available. Their nests are usually placed within dense thickets at heights of two to twelve feet. While nests with eggs have been discovered as early as May 27,[523] most are noted between June 10 and 25 with a few as late as mid-July. Recently fledged Willows recorded on June 14 were exceptionally early; most young do not fledge until mid-July or early August.[479] Since their nesting efforts begin relatively late, there are few renesting attempts, although nests with young have been noted through August 17.[353]

Willow Flycatchers are widely distributed summer residents in most counties.[434] They are least numerous in southern Ohio, especially the Ohio River counties between Brown and Washington, where they are uncommon to locally fairly common residents. Summer totals seldom exceed 1–5 individuals daily within these counties. Elsewhere, Willow Flycatchers are fairly common to common summer residents, although they may be rather locally distributed within some southeastern and intensively cultivated western counties. As many as 5–25+ Willows may be reported daily away from the Ohio River. Larger concentrations of this semicolonial flycatcher are possible. Trautman[479] reported 218 Willows along one mile of brushy shoreline at Buckeye Lake on June 12, 1928.

Their breeding distribution was formerly more limited. At

the turn of the century, nesting Willows were mostly restricted to the northern half of Ohio.[236] Their expansion into southern Ohio occurred mainly during the first decades of this century but was poorly documented except for the first Cincinnati nesting record in 1931.[248] By the mid-1930s, Hicks[220] cited summer records from eighty counties. While Willows were widely distributed within glaciated Ohio, they remained rare and very local along the unglaciated Allegheny Plateau north to Vinton, Muskingum, and Carroll Counties.[223] Populations gradually increased within most southeastern counties during subsequent decades.

During spring, there is only one acceptable April record, an extraordinarily early singing male at Cleveland on April 18, 1976. A few Willows may return during the first week of May, although they do not normally arrive until May 10–15. Most of their spring passage occurs between May 20 and June 5. These migrants are fairly common to common, and 5–20 Willows may be observed daily in most counties.

Willow Flycatchers remain conspicuous until the males quit singing in mid-July. Their fall migration commences shortly after their young become independent. Southward migrants may appear at lakefront migrant traps during the first week of August; migration occurs principally between August 5 and 25. This migration is hardly noticeable except for the gradual disappearance of the resident flycatchers; August sightings seldom exceed 1–10 Willows daily. The last migrants normally depart by the first week of September. Late migrants are infrequently encountered into the first week of October, but none of the late October reports has been acceptably substantiated.

LEAST FLYCATCHER

Empidonax minimus (Baird & Baird)

Normally the first *Empidonax* flycatchers returning each spring, Leasts have appeared along Lake Erie by April 10 (in 1955 at Cleveland) and April 11 (in 1903 in Erie County).[117,241] These early records are exceptional. The first Leasts are not expected until April 25–30 in the southern and central counties and May 1–5 along Lake Erie. Their numbers increase rapidly, with most spring migrants appearing between May 7 and 23. The last migrants normally depart from interior counties before June 1, although a few stragglers may remain along Lake Erie into the first week of June.

Migrant Least Flycatchers prefer second-growth woods but are also found in parks, cemeteries, brushy fencerows, and thickets. They are widely distributed and fairly common to common spring migrants across Ohio. Between 2 and 10 Leasts are observed daily in most counties. Larger flights are fairly regular along Lake Erie, where concentrations of 25–50+ may appear. Similar flights are unusual within the interior counties; a remarkable 300 Leasts were estimated at Greenlawn Cemetery in Columbus on May 14, 1981.[471].

A small breeding population has always resided in northern Ohio. Hicks[220] cited summer records from Lucas, Fulton, Williams, Ashtabula, Lake, Geauga, Trumbull, and Cuyahoga Counties. Only a few pairs resided in most of these counties except Ashtabula, where they were recorded from twelve localities. Population trends were not apparent except in northwestern Ohio, where Campbell[86] cited declines resulting from habitat destruction.

Since the mid-1930s, this small breeding population has slowly expanded southward. In northeastern Ohio, increased numbers of summering Leasts were detected near Cleveland during the 1950s and 1960s.[335] They were noted south to Columbiana County by 1960.[140] This expansion was not apparent in the northwest except for isolated nesting records in a few additional counties.[417] By the mid-1970s, a few widely scattered summering Leasts also appeared in the central and southern counties.

Summering Least Flycatchers are now uncommon to fairly common residents in Ashtabula County, where 3–7 males can be recorded daily. They are less numerous in other northeastern counties. They become uncommon to rare in Lake, Geauga, Trumbull, and Portage Counties and are generally rare east to Cleveland and south to Wayne, Stark, and Columbiana Counties.[434] Elsewhere in northern Ohio, they are casual to rare summer residents south to Williams, Fulton, Lucas, Seneca, and Ashland Counties. Within these counties, most records are of isolated pairs, although small populations have become established at a few localities.

Away from the northern counties, Least Flycatchers are presently casual summer visitors to central Ohio, with records scattered from Belmont County on the unglaciated Allegheny Plateau to Logan County in the west. They become accidental summer visitors in southern Ohio; males summered in Butler County in 1982 and Muskingum County in 1986. Summer Leasts have briefly appeared within a few additional southern counties since 1980.[185,366,434] The only confirmed southern Ohio nesting attempt was in Vinton County in 1988.[388a]

Breeding Least Flycatchers may occupy a variety of woodland habitats from open groves and woodlots to extensive riparian corridors and young second-growth deciduous woodlands. Very little information is available on their nesting biology within Ohio. Most nests are apparently initiated during late May and June. While dependent young have been reported by June 24, some nests have contained young flycatchers as late as August 3.[417]

Since adult Least Flycatchers begin their southward movements shortly after their young become independent, they are among the first songbirds returning each autumn. Migrant Leasts may appear by July 20–25 in the northern and central counties and are regularly noted throughout the state during the first half of August. These migrants are most apparent between August 20 and September 15. Their numbers diminish during the last half of September, although a few may remain through October 3–7.

Least Flycatchers are generally uncommon to fairly common migrants throughout Ohio, most numerous along Lake Erie. Most fall reports total only 1–5 individuals daily. Sizable movements do not normally appear in autumn; only Trautman[479] reported as many as 25 daily at Buckeye Lake during the 1920s and 1930s.

EASTERN PHOEBE

Sayornis phoebe (Latham)

Before Ohio was settled, Eastern Phoebes were very locally distributed summer residents, restricted to wooded stream valleys bordered by rocky cliffs. As people altered this environment, the modified landscape proved quite acceptable for this adaptable flycatcher. Bridges over streams provided additional nest sites and populations expanded until nearly every bridge was occupied by its resident pair. Phoebes also adopted sheds, barns, abandoned houses, and other structures as nest sites. So successful was their adaptation to man-made habitats that Jones[236] considered them "almost a household bird" at the turn of the century.

They remained numerous through the 1930s. Hicks[220] described Eastern Phoebes as common to abundant summer residents in every county, most numerous along the unglaciated Allegheny Plateau. Considerable numbers of migrants also passed through the state. Trautman[479] reported spring peaks of 30–60 phoebes daily at Buckeye Lake during the 1920s and 1930s with fewer recorded in autumn.

Their populations declined during the 1940s, a trend that continued into the 1960s. Two factors contributed to this decline: in western Ohio, intensive agriculture eliminated many suitable nesting habitats, and periodic severe winters decimated phoebe populations throughout eastern North America. But populations have apparently stabilized since the mid-1960s. While phoebes experienced short-term declines following the severe winters of 1976–78, they fully recovered by the early 1980s.

Eastern Phoebes are now fairly common to common summer residents throughout southern Ohio and the unglaciated counties, where 5–20 individuals may be expected daily. They are generally fairly common residents in the central counties from Columbus eastward and in northeastern Ohio, becoming casual to rare within large urban areas and all intensively cultivated farmlands. Summer totals do not normally exceed 3–6 phoebes daily within these counties. Nesting phoebes are least numerous within the west-central and northwestern counties where few suitable breeding sites remain; they are rare to uncommon and locally distributed residents, usually encountered as isolated pairs.[434]

Breeding phoebes prefer small wooded streams but a few pairs nest under bridges over large rivers. Along the unglaciated plateau, they also regularly nest near upland wooded and edge habitats wherever outbuildings and abandoned houses provide suitable sites. They normally raise two broods annually. Nest construction frequently begins during the last week of March, even in northern Ohio. The first clutches are normally laid in April, as early as April 8 in the central and southern counties. These young have fledged by the first week of May but most are likely to appear after May 20.[479,523] Second clutches are laid during June with some noted through July 18. These young normally fledge by late July or early August.

Our hardiest flycatchers, phoebes may show up as early migrants with the first warm weather—in the southern and central counties by February 23–28 and along Lake Erie by March 2. They do not normally become widely distributed until mid-March and maximum abundance is attained between March 15 and April 10. During these weeks, they become fairly common to common migrants throughout Ohio. In recent years, most spring reports are of 1–8 phoebes daily with infrequent flights of 10–20. Few migrants are detected after April 20–25, even along Lake Erie.

Their southward migration is generally less conspicuous. Eastern Phoebes are uncommon to locally fairly common during autumn, most numerous along the unglaciated Allegheny Plateau. Most fall sightings are of 1–4 phoebes daily; movements of 10 or more are exceptional. Phoebes regularly appear at lakefront migrant traps by the first week of August; the disappearance of resident pairs during late July is also indicative of an early migration. Only small numbers of migrants are detected before September and their peak passage is expected between September 15 and October 10. Their numbers noticeably diminish after October 15, although a few phoebes may remain later in the southern counties.

Wintering phoebes are most likely to be discovered in southern Ohio, particularly the counties bordering the Ohio River, where they are accidental to casual residents producing one to five records annually. These phoebes are mostly observed before January 15 and usually disappear when extended subfreezing temperatures descend upon the state. A few phoebes have overwintered during relatively mild years. Elsewhere, Eastern Phoebes are accidental early winter visitors producing only one to three sightings per decade, mostly during December.

VERMILION FLYCATCHER

Pyrocephalus rubinus (Boddaert)

This handsome flycatcher is known primarily as a resident of riparian woodlands in arid regions from the southwestern United States into Central America. A disjunct population is also found in South America. While the Vermilion's North American breeding range normally extends north to southern California, southern Nevada, western Oklahoma, and central Texas, these flycatchers have exhibited a tendency to wander considerable distances from this established range. They are accidental visitors north to South Dakota, Minnesota, and the lower Great Lakes, while records extend east to the Atlantic Coast.[5]

Ohio's first Vermilion Flycatcher was discovered by William Porter, Jr., at Clark Lake Wildlife Area in Clark County on September 20, 1958. It was an immature male undergoing a pronounced molt. When collected the following day, he was found to be greatly emaciated.[488] There is also a spring sight record from northern Ohio: a male reported from Erie County on May 2, 1973.[286] This flycatcher apparently was studied closely by Allen Stickley, Jr., and subsequently by other birders as it caught insects along a rural road.

GREAT CRESTED FLYCATCHER

Myiarchus crinitus (Linnaeus)

Occupants of deciduous woodlands, Great Crested Flycatchers are more frequently detected by their loud hoarse calls than by their attractive plumage. Since they prefer to forage within the canopy of tall trees, silent birds are frequently overlooked. But with a little perseverance they can be observed as they quietly sit on a dead limb searching for prey or flash through the foliage in pursuit of a large insect.

While there are several unsubstantiated March sight records, the earliest confirmed Great Crested Flycatcher appeared at Akron on April 1, 1973. This extremely early flycatcher was observed and heard calling as it foraged within the branches of a large tree. The first spring migrants do not normally return to the southern and central counties until April 23–28 and along Lake Erie by May 1–5. Their numbers increase rapidly and Great Cresteds become fairly common to common migrants by May 10–12. They are seldom numerous, especially within the interior counties; daily totals of 5–20 individuals are expected. Sizable flights are infrequent along Lake Erie, where the largest movement totaled 50 Great Cresteds in Ottawa County on May 15, 1948.[89]

After returning to Ohio, Great Crested Flycatchers quickly establish their nesting territories. Mature deciduous woods are preferred but younger second-growth woodlands will be occupied if a few large trees are available. Nesting Great Crested Flycatchers are most numerous in eastern and southern Ohio. They are common summer residents in these counties, where 5–12 may be recorded daily during June. Similar numbers may also be noted in extensive woodlands elsewhere. However, Great Cresteds become locally uncommon residents within the intensively farmed western counties.[434] Daily totals seldom exceed 1–5 in any agricultural area with few woodlots. They have always been common and widely distributed residents in Ohio.[220,236] Their statewide population has remained fairly stable in recent decades,[438] though local populations have undoubtedly declined in western Ohio as a result of habitat destruction.

Unlike other eastern flycatchers, Great Cresteds normally nest in tree cavities. If suitable cavities are unavailable, they nest in telephone poles, bird boxes, and Purple Martin houses. Their nests are normally placed at heights of twenty to fifty feet but a few have been only five to seven feet above the ground. Nest construction normally begins during the last half of May. Great Cresteds have developed the curious and unexplained habit of lining their nests with snake skins. Since their nests are largely inaccessible, their nesting chronology is poorly documented. Most clutches are apparently laid during late May or early June. Dependent young have been observed by June 21 but most apparently fledge during July.[479,523]

Once their young fledge, adult Great Cresteds become silent. Even though their populations have been supplemented by numerous young, few of these inconspicuous flycatchers will be observed during July and early August. They become more visible in mid-August when their southward migration is initiated. This migration is poorly defined but most fall Great Cresteds are observed between August 25 and September 15. These uncommon migrants are mostly noted as scattered individuals and daily totals seldom exceed 3–6. The last migrants normally depart by September 25–30. Late migrants have rarely lingered into late October.

The phenomenon of reverse migration is not normally witnessed within Ohio during autumn. Once birds leave the state, they seldom return until the following spring. However, unusually warm temperatures and southerly winds may prompt some songbirds to migrate north during late October or early November. Hicks[213] witnessed a reverse migration along Alum Creek in southern Delaware County on the remarkably late date of November 16, 1931. Among the birds observed that day, he counted an incredible 9 Great Crested Flycatchers, one of which was collected.

WESTERN KINGBIRD

Tyrannus verticalis Say

Western Kingbirds are widely distributed summer residents from southern Canada through the western United States to the eastern edge of the Great Plains.[5] While most migrate through the western states to and from their wintering areas in Mexico and Central America, small numbers regularly migrate eastward each autumn and reach the Atlantic Coast. These eastward migrants undoubtedly pass through Ohio and other eastern states but relatively few are detected at inland localities as compared with the numbers appearing along the coast.

Within Ohio, the first Western Kingbird was discovered near Lake Erie in Lucas County on September 13, 1930.[86] In subsequent years, they averaged one to four published records each decade through the 1970s. The number of sightings has increased since 1980, probably reflecting greater numbers of observers rather than more Westerns passing through the state. There were published records every year but one between 1980 and 1987 with a maximum of two reports in 1986. Nevertheless, they are still considered accidental or casual fall migrants.

During autumn, Western Kingbirds have been detected as early as August 13 and as late as October 10.[248,282] Most are recorded between August 25 and September 20 with a decided peak during the first week of September. Approximately half of the Ohio records are from near Lake Erie, with at least nine sightings scattered between Toledo and Cleveland. The remaining sightings are widely scattered through the interior counties, with at least six published records from the Columbus area, two from Cincinnati, at least two in the Akron-Barberton area, and singles in Holmes County and near East Liverpool. With the exception of two Western Kingbirds in Hamilton County on August 13, 1938,[248] all sightings have been of single individuals.

Western Kingbirds are accidental spring migrants in most eastern states. There are only three published spring records from Ohio. Single Westerns were discovered at Cleveland on June 1, 1945; Holden Arboretum (Lake County) on May 11, 1959; and Columbus on May 13, 1964.[335,523]

GREAT HORNED OWL
Bubo virginianus

Few predators are willing to take on the powerfully protective spray of the striped skunk (*Mephitis mephitis*). The Great Horned Owl, however, appears to be one that will. In fact, the high number of recorded instances of its preying on skunks may indicate that it even relishes the skunk as a food item.

Adult
(sexes similar)

WHIP-POOR-WILL
Caprimulgus vociferus

In summer, these mysterious birds of the night sing for brief periods in the evening, and are then quiet as they search for food for their young; they sing incessantly only in the spring, when they arrive on their territories. Spring migrants have also been known to sing during flight. Their diet is predominantly moths, although they will eat other insects.

Adults

(male)

(female)

Luna moth
(Actias luna)

CHIMNEY SWIFT
Chaetura pelagica

Each evening for several weeks during fall migration, small bands of twittering, fast-flying Chimney Swifts gather in the air over the place where they plan to roost. As the light fades their numbers grow, until sometimes more than a hundred birds can be seen circling, criss-crossing, and then dropping into the chimney, where they will spend the night. Fall roosts regularly exceed 1000 swifts in some Ohio localities.

Adults
(sexes similar)

RUBY-THROATED HUMMINGBIRD
Archilochus colubris

In late summer after their young have fledged, Ruby-throated Hummingbirds gather where there are nectar-producing plants. A favorite that grows in low wet places, along streams, and in ditches along country roads is the Jewelweed (*Impatiens capensis*). Here these hummingbirds pass the summer days feeding, preening, and belligerently defending the choicest flowers.

Adults

(male)

(female)

BELTED KINGFISHER
Ceryle alcyon

The Belted Kingfisher is a conspicuous resident of the state, frequently announcing its presence with a harsh, clattery-rattling call. Kingfishers are particularly noisy during courtship. Much of their time is spent perched above water on a low-hanging branch waiting for an unsuspecting fish to swim into range. Sometimes they spot their prey by hovering almost motionless over a quiet pool.

Adults

Creek Chub *(female)*
(Semotilus atromaculatus)

(male)

DOWNY WOODPECKER
Picoides pubescens

PILEATED WOODPECKER
Dryocopus pileatus

The Downy and the Pileated, the smallest and the largest of our woodpeckers, occupy different ecological niches of the same woods. They usually come in close contact with each other only when a particularly attractive food item such as the wild grape (*Vitis* sp.) draws them to the same location.

Pileated Woodpecker
(male; female has less red on head)

Downy Woodpecker
(male; female has no red on head)

ACADIAN FLYCATCHER
Empidonax virescens

GREAT CRESTED FLYCATCHER
Myiarchus crinitus

When looking for a place to live, small mammals such as this Southern Flying Squirrel (*Glaucomys volans*) have no trouble competing with most cavity-nesting birds and might even make a meal of the displaced tenant's eggs and young when this takeover occurs. If a noisy dispute develops between the rival occupants, neighbors such as the Acadian Flycatcher come to see what the fuss is all about.

Great Crested Flycatcher
(sexes similar)

Acadian Flycatcher
(sexes similar)

HORNED LARK
Eremophila alpestris

WATER PIPIT
Anthus spinoletta

As the forests of the Midwest have been cut and transformed into open fields, the occurrence of both the Horned Lark and the Water Pipit has increased. During migration flocks of as many as a hundred birds of either species may be seen feeding in short-cropped or newly plowed fields. Because of their preference for barren conditions, the two species are often found side by side.

Horned Lark
*(male; female duller,
horns less prominent)*

Water Pipit
(sexes similar)

CLIFF SWALLOW
Hirundo pyrrhonota

BARN SWALLOW
Hirundo rustica

Where Barn Swallows and Cliff Swallows both nest, they can be seen together fluttering like butterflies at the edge of mud puddles in dirt roads or along the muddy banks of streams, gathering mouthfuls of the material they need to build their masonry nests.

Barn Swallow

(male)

(female)

Cliff Swallow
(sexes similar)

Breeding Western Kingbirds are regularly distributed along the western edge of Minnesota, Iowa, and Missouri with occasional nesting records east to the Mississippi River.[5] The appearance of a breeding pair in northwestern Ohio provides the easternmost nesting record in North America. Lou Campbell discovered a female Western Kingbird feeding three recently fledged juveniles on July 29, 1933, at Reno-by-the-Lake (Lucas County). The juveniles were incapable of sustained flight and undoubtedly had been raised in the area.[86]

There is only one additional documented summer record from Ohio. A single Western Kingbird was photographed in Adams County on June 22, 1984.[375] This individual could not be relocated and was presumably a wandering nonbreeder.

EASTERN KINGBIRD

Tyrannus tyrannus (Linnaeus)

Few birds are as relentless and aggressive in defense of their breeding territories as Eastern Kingbirds. Whenever a crow, hawk, or other potential predator comes into view, these kingbirds immediately take flight and attack the intruder long before it approaches their nest. Calling loudly throughout the encounter, they vigorously harass the intruder until it is driven from the area.

This territorial behavior can be regularly observed, since Eastern Kingbirds are widely distributed summer residents, a status they have maintained throughout the twentieth century.[220,434] While they breed in every county, summering Eastern Kingbirds are not uniformly distributed across the state. They are generally most numerous within the southern and eastern counties, where they are fairly common to common summer residents and 3–15 individuals may be noted daily. Breeding pairs are more locally distributed within the glaciated central and northwestern counties. They become fairly common to uncommon summer residents within these counties; daily totals seldom exceed 2–7 individuals.

Present population trends are uncertain. Within a number of western counties, nesting Eastern Kingbirds have noticeably declined since 1960. In many southern and eastern counties, however, populations have apparently remained fairly stable. Breeding bird survey data also indicated declining populations throughout North America until 1975, followed by a slight recovery between 1975 and 1979.[438]

Nesting Eastern Kingbirds exhibit a preference for wooded corridors bordering streams, marshes, and lakes. They prefer corridors with tall trees providing a commanding view of the surrounding countryside. Within most Ohio farmlands, breeding Eastern Kingbirds are seldom encountered away from these habitats. In the southern and eastern counties, however, they also occupy upland areas where open fields are bordered by woodlands and wooded fencerows.

Nests are normally placed on exposed branches high in tall trees but have also been located on telephone poles and fence posts and in bushes.[479,523] One pair constructed a nest on the boom of a dredge.[89] Nest construction normally begins during the last half of May. The first clutches are normally laid by May 20–30 within the southern counties and June 5–15 elsewhere. Replacement clutches have been noted through July 17.[479] The young hatch during June and the first fledglings may appear before the end of the month. Most fledglings are noted between July 10 and August 15.

In spring, a few overflights have appeared along Lake Erie by April 6–7.[89,523] These early migrants are exceptional; Eastern Kingbirds do not normally return to the southern counties until April 20–25 or along Lake Erie until April 28–May 3. They do not become numerous until the second week of May and their maximum abundance is attained between May 10 and 25. Smaller numbers may continue to pass along the lakefront into the first week of June. They are generally common along Lake Erie, where daily totals of 8–15+ individuals may be expected with occasional flights of 25–30. The largest spring flights were of 65 in the Toledo area on May 16, 1942, and 50+ at Euclid on May 11, 1986.[89,382] Similar movements are not apparent within the interior counties, where these kingbirds are generally fairly common migrants and spring totals seldom exceed 5–12 individuals.

Greater numbers of Eastern Kingbirds pass through Ohio each autumn. When breeding populations were larger, flights of 50–100+ individuals were detected along Lake Erie most years, especially near Toledo. Similar flights were more sporadic within the interior counties, although movements involving 50–80 individuals were reported from Dayton and Buckeye Lake.[299,479]

Numbers of fall migrants have noticeably diminished since 1965, although the Easterns remain fairly common to common throughout Ohio. In recent years, most fall totals are 3–12 individuals daily with occasional flights of 20–30. The only recent large movement was detected in 1983, when 62 individuals were counted at Lake Rockwell (Portage County) on September 3 and 50 at Ottawa Wildlife Refuge on September 4.[372]

During some years, their southward movements have begun by the first week of July, peaked in the middle of the month, and finished by early August.[342] Such early fall migrations are not typical. Generally, the first migrants are noted between August 3 and 7 and the largest movements between August 15 and September 5. The last migrants normally depart by September 14–23. Single Eastern Kingbirds at Magee Marsh Wildlife Area on November 4, 1985, Tiffin (Seneca County) on October 28, 1975, and Cleveland on October 24, 1976, were exceptionally late.[261,380]

SCISSOR-TAILED FLYCATCHER

Tyrannus forficatus (Gmelin)

The Scissor-tailed is an attractive, slender, medium-sized flycatcher with an extremely long tail. It is usually seen hawking insects over the fields and plains of the south-central United States. It nests north to southern Nebraska and east to southwestern Missouri[5] but frequently wanders considerable distances from this range, appearing along both coasts and in the Great Lakes region.

There are nine published records of Scissor-tailed Flycatchers from Ohio, including a male collected near Dunkinsville in Adams County on June 16, 1970,[489] and well-described birds near Jenera in Hancock County on May 17–18, 1962,[415] and in Wayne County on August 16, 1987.[388] None of the other records was substantiated by written descriptions or extant specimens. Given this species' unmistakable characteristics, however, these other sightings were most likely correctly identified. The first was recorded from Marietta on May 20, 1894; a specimen of a male, it is no longer extant.[236] Another was reportedly shot near Marysville during late May 1903; it too has been lost.[238] The third sighting was in Pickaway County on July 1, 1934,[45] while the other six records occurred between 1959 and 1987.

Of the nine records, five have been May sightings. In addition to the three already listed, single Scissor-taileds were sighted near Barberton (Summit County) on May 3, 1959, and in Adams County on May 8, 1966.[335,400] Summer records are limited to the Adams County specimen and the Pickaway County sighting. The two fall records are from Wayne County in 1987 and from near Cincinnati in 1970. The exact date was not provided for the latter sighting.[412]

HORNED LARK

Eremophila alpestris (Linnaeus)

Given the present abundance within Ohio of Horned Larks, it is difficult to imagine that they were not always widely distributed residents. Yet, like most prairie birds, Horned Larks started nesting in the state relatively recently. Before 1880, they were strictly migrants and winter visitors. Their status changed during the 1880s when the prairie race invaded Ohio from the west. This range expansion was fairly rapid. By 1900, they were common residents, most numerous in the northern and western counties.[236]

They have remained numerous permanent residents during this century, although their statewide distribution patterns changed in response to habitat availability. Hicks[220] cited breeding records from every county, noting they were abundant in some counties and rare and locally distributed in others.

Breeding Horned Larks are still found in every county.[434] However, they are common summer residents only within the northwestern and glaciated central counties, where 10–40 larks daily may be regularly observed. They are fairly common residents in southwestern Ohio, usually as 5–15 daily, although they become uncommon to rare and locally distributed in counties bordering the Ohio River. Within the northeastern counties, Horned Larks are locally rare to fairly common residents and their summer abundance rarely exceeds 5–15 daily. Breeding larks are least numerous along the unglaciated Allegheny Plateau. They are normally rare to uncommon residents along this plateau but become locally common on large reclaimed strip mines. Most daily totals are 1–5 larks except within reclaimed strip mines, where sizable populations may occur.

Horned Larks thrive in open and desolate habitats occupied by few other birds. Cultivated fields provide ideal nesting territories. Short-grass pastures, reclaimed strip mines, golf courses, quarries, even vacant lots in cities may support breeding pairs. These larks may be remarkably inconspicuous within these habitats, their plumage providing excellent camouflage against a background of bare soil. Their presence is readily detected by their sharp call notes and distinctive tinkling song, frequently delivered as they "skylark" overhead.

This species holds the distinction of being the first songbird to begin nesting each year. Any warm winter day prompts male larks to initiate their courtship flights. Most pairs establish their territories during late February or early March. Nests with eggs have been reported as early as March 11, although most first clutches are not laid until the last half of the month. These early nesting attempts are frequently interrupted by late winter snowstorms and more than one incubating female has kept her eggs warm while several inches of snow fell on top of her.[89,479] The first nests produce fledglings by April 5, although most appear later in the month. Horned Larks may raise two or more broods annually. Nests with eggs have been reported through June 24–30 and recently fledged young through July 20.[299,420] While most of our breeding population resides within Ohio throughout the year, their numbers are augmented by northern races migrating south for the winter. The first migrants may be heard passing overhead during the last week of September and this movement continues into the first half of December. These migrants are hardly noticeable among our breeding population and no sizable fall flights have been recorded. Fall flocks of 50–300+ individuals are largely composed of resident larks.

Horned Larks are most numerous during winter in the western half of Ohio. They may appear as scattered individuals or flocks of 50–250 individuals during mild seasons. Large flocks are most apparent during severe winters with extended snow cover; 100–500 larks may be noted daily and concentrations of as many as 1000–2000 individuals are infrequently observed. Larger flocks are exceptional; an incredible 50,000 Horned Larks were estimated near Cincinnati on January 12, 1982.[364]

Considerably fewer Horned Larks winter in eastern Ohio. They are normally uncommon to fairly common residents within the northeastern and unglaciated counties, where most sightings are of 50 or fewer larks. Inclement weather has forced 100–200+ larks to congregate into single flocks but these concentrations are relatively rare.

The first warm weather of February prompts Horned Larks to start moving northward. This movement is most pronounced through mid-March, although small migrant flocks may be observed through April 10–15. Migrant larks are mostly heard as they pass overhead and flocks on the ground seldom exceed 25–200 individuals.

PURPLE MARTIN

Progne subis (Linnaeus)

Purple Martins have been closely associated with people for centuries. Indians erected gourds to attract them to their settlements. The early settlers copied this practice by erecting nesting boxes near their residences. As the human population expanded, more nesting boxes were provided and Purple Martin populations increased. These martins became abundant by the mid-1800s and remained numerous until the 1880s, when their numbers declined as a result of competition with House Sparrows for nesting sites.[236] Purple Martins remained common to abundant summer residents in every county into the 1930s.[220]

In recent decades, Purple Martin populations have exhibited marked annual fluctuations that mask any long-term trends.[314] These fluctuations are mostly a result of their susceptibility to prolonged periods of cold wet weather. Unusually cold spring temperatures have caused considerable mortality of adults. Cold rainy weather when young are in the nest has been responsible for almost complete reproductive failure during some years. Extensive mortality in 1960, 1968, 1972, 1977, and 1978 noticeably reduced breeding populations in Ohio.[139,438] When weather conditions are favorable, populations can recover in two or three years.

Purple Martin populations expanded in portions of eastern and central North America after the mid-1960s,[438] but this trend has not been apparent within Ohio. In fact, the loss of nesting colonies and the reduced numbers gathering at autumn roosts indicate that these martins may have substantially declined since 1965. Purple Martins are presently fairly common to common summer residents throughout Ohio, though rather locally distributed depending upon the availability of nesting houses. Summer totals seldom exceed 5–40 individuals daily.

A few Purple Martins have returned quite early in spring, appearing at Cleveland by March 1 in 1929.[523] There are other records scattered across the state before March 20. These early arrivals are exceptional; Purple Martins do not regularly return to southern Ohio until March 25–30 and Lake Erie by the first week of April. They do not become numerous until April 20–May 5. This migration is fairly inconspicuous; large concentrations are rarely encountered. Trautman[479] reported spring movements of 700–800 individuals daily at Buckeye Lake during the 1920s and 1930s. Similar movements have not been apparent in recent years; spring concentrations have rarely exceeded 25–100.

The timing of their return varies from colony to colony. Nest construction usually begins in early May and requires three to four weeks since the adults work irregularly on these structures.[4] Eggs are normally laid in early June, although observations of dependent young during the first week of July indicate that some nests are initiated in May. Most young fledge during the last half of July. Purple Martins occasionally renest if their first clutch is destroyed. Nests with eggs have been reported through the first week of July and dependent young as late as August 20.[479]

During this century, Purple Martins have only been known to nest in houses provided by people. At one time they also nested in natural cavities. In 1882, Wheaton[522] cited nests in tree cavities, mostly in old woodpecker holes. At the turn of the century, Jones[236] observed their nests in stumps at Indian Lake.

As soon as the young fledge, Purple Martins abandon their breeding colonies. During daylight hours, they are widely scattered over the countryside foraging for insects. At night, these flocks may gather at traditional roosts. This roosting behavior presents an impressive spectacle. Langlois and Langlois[290] described the martin roost on South Bass Island:

The martins line up on telephone and power lines late each day and remain until the daylight begins to fade. Whenever one bird lands on a wire, others come to land there too, and the wire becomes covered with birds like a string of beads. . . . Occasionally the whole flock takes off and circles around for a while, then comes back to rest on the wires, but when darkness approaches, they leave the wires for good. They fly towards the roosting area, and the early birds come in quite low to the ground.

The would-be roosters do not go promptly into the thicket, but circle around and around above the area, and the size of the circling flock grows rapidly in the half-hour before dark. During this period, the flock rises progressively higher as if to stay in brighter light so as to be able to see each other better, and human eyes follow their movements with increasing difficulty. Presently, it seems as if there is a cloud-burst of fluttering leaves as some of the birds drop hoveringly down into the thicket, and after this occurs a few times, there is a mass descent in a beeline into the thicket. Within about ten minutes the entry into the thicket is complete, and the noise of birds settling such matters as who sits next to whom is deafening to cupped ears.

The South Bass Island roost was probably the largest; as many as 250,000 Purple Martins were estimated to congregate there.[89] Large numbers also roosted at the former state penitentiary in Columbus and at Akron, where 25,000–30,000 appeared each fall during the 1960s and early 1970s.[471] Smaller roosts were also reported near Cleveland, Cuyahoga Falls, Dayton, and Cincinnati. Most of these roosts disappeared during the 1960s and 1970s, but South Bass Island has been used consistently, although only 3000–8000 Purple Martins have been estimated there during this decade.[384] In addition, a roost of 3000+ was discovered near Dayton in 1987,[388] while 1000–1500 have occasionally roosted at Columbus and Cleveland. Away from these roosts, they become uncommon to fairly common migrants and daily totals seldom exceed 20–30 martins.

These roosts begin to form during the last half of July and normally reach their maximum size by mid-August. Many martins migrate south during the last half of August and their numbers noticeably decline by September 7. Smaller flocks may be noted through the third week of September. Late migrants are very infrequently observed during October, although a few martins have lingered quite late: through October 27, 1928, at Buckeye Lake;[479] October 30, 1977, at Senecaville Lake;[172] and November 11, 1931, at Cleveland.[523]

TREE SWALLOW

Tachycineta bicolor (Vieillot)

A remarkably hardy bird, the Tree Swallow invariably is the first swallow to appear in Ohio each spring. Overflights have returned to Dayton and western Lake Erie by February 13.[299,373] While these overflights must migrate south or perish, spring Tree Swallows regularly appear along western Lake Erie between March 7 and 15 and elsewhere by March 25–30.

During unusually warm springs, flocks of Tree Swallows have appeared before April 1, with as many as 450 individuals along western Lake Erie on March 29, 1981. Similar concentrations do not normally develop until April 10–20 most years. These flocks may be noted throughout Ohio until May 8–15. Tree Swallows are fairly common to locally abundant spring migrants, most numerous along Lake Erie. The largest concentrations normally develop within Ottawa and Lucas Counties where flocks of 300–1000+ individuals can be expected. Similar concentrations are less frequently encountered elsewhere along the lakefront; flights of 2000 at Euclid on April 14, 1983, and 1700 at Lorain on April 8, 1980, were exceptional.[277,370] Within the interior counties, flocks of 100–250+ may appear; the largest concentration was 1200 at Alum Creek Reservoir (Delaware County) on April 24, 1981.

After May 20, only resident pairs remain. Breeding Tree Swallows were formerly restricted to marshes, ponds, and lakes, where they nested in cavities within dead snags. Where dead snags were numerous, breeding Tree Swallows became abundant. During the nineteenth century, sizable populations nested at Buckeye Lake, Indian Lake, and Lake St. Mary's.[98,479] Only small numbers were distributed elsewhere in the northern half of Ohio.[236]

During the first decades of the twentieth century, Tree Swallows declined at these lakes as the dead snags decayed or were removed. By the mid-1930s, breeding pairs were very locally distributed within the northern half of Ohio south to Mercer, Pickaway, Fairfield, Guernsey, Tuscarawas, and Columbiana Counties. They were numerous only along western Lake Erie and locally within the northeastern counties.[220,223]

Their summer status remained unchanged until the late 1950s and early 1960s, when a southward range expansion became apparent. Tree Swallows increased within the central counties, finding suitable habitats at newly constructed reservoirs. Summering Tree Swallows also appeared near Dayton.[299] During the 1960s and 1970s, they became more flexible in their choice of nesting sites. In addition to natural cavities, they readily adopted Wood Duck boxes and occupied bluebird boxes miles from any body of water. This adaptability allowed their populations to rapidly expand. By 1980, resident pairs were found throughout the state.

Breeding Tree Swallows are now most numerous along western Lake Erie, where they are common to locally abundant and 25–100+ individuals may be noted daily. They are fairly common to locally common residents in the northeastern counties, where daily totals rarely exceed 20–30. They become uncommon to fairly common in other northern and central counties, with most summer reports involving 2–20. They are rare to locally uncommon in the southern third of the state, usually encountered as isolated pairs.[434]

Tree Swallows do not normally begin their nesting activities until late April or early May. Most clutches are laid between May 10 and June 5 and these young normally fledge between June 25 and July 10. Few nests with eggs have been reported after June 15, although nests with young into the last half of July are probably the result of renesting efforts.[479,523]

As soon as their young fledge, Tree Swallows congregate in large flocks. These flocks are most apparent between July 10

and August 15, comprising the first peak of a distinctly bimodal fall migration. This early movement is most apparent along western Lake Erie, where Tree Swallows become locally abundant migrants. As many as 3000 were tallied there on July 12, 1936, and August 15, 1931, although these concentrations have rarely exceeded 1000–1500 in recent years.[15,89] Decidedly fewer July migrants appear in the remainder of the state, where flocks of 50–100 are unusual before mid-August.

The second peak of their fall migration is apparent throughout Ohio except the northeastern counties. During most years, numbers peak between September 15 and October 20. In some years, large flocks have appeared by the last week of August; in others they may not develop until October. Tree Swallows become abundant migrants along western Lake Erie and fairly common to locally common elsewhere. This movement produced a concentration of 15,000 in Ottawa and Lucas Counties on September 30, 1934, although September and October concentrations have seldom exceeded 2000–2500+ since 1960.[89] Away from western Lake Erie, flocks of 50–500+ may develop and the largest inland concentration was 2000 at Lake St. Mary's on August 26, 1976.[264]

While most Tree Swallows depart by October 28–November 5, a few stragglers may linger well into November. Some have remained until harsh winter weather prevails, becoming accidental visitors after November 20. There are at least seven early winter sightings from Ohio: six records along western Lake Erie and one at Dayton. These records are of groups of 5 or fewer mostly during December, although one individual remained at Ottawa Wildlife Refuge through January 4, 1987.

NORTHERN ROUGH-WINGED SWALLOW

Stelgidopteryx serripennis (Audubon)

Uttering a hoarse *dirt-dirt-dirt*, several Rough-winged Swallows leave their perch on a dead snag along a stream and forage for insects low over the surface of the water. After feeding for several minutes, they fly to a nearby eroding streambank, enter a small burrow, and feed their brood of hungry young. The adults remain in the burrow just long enough to care for the young before emerging to secure more food. Even after the young have fledged, they remain dependent for several weeks, voraciously approaching the returning parents to obtain their share of the meal.

This behavior is a common sight along medium-sized and large streams throughout Ohio. Rough-winged Swallows prefer larger streams, which are more likely to be bordered by suitable eroding streambanks. They also commonly nest along small streams, but they avoid intermittent and channelized streams and ditches whose modified grass-covered banks are unsuitable for nesting. In the absence of eroding streambanks, the breeding adults may nest in bridge drainpipes, the ends of blocked field tiles, and boat pontoons. Frequently they nest far from water in the steep walls of gravel pits and quarries and the crevices of rocky cliffs next to highways and railroads. Some have nested in the overflow pipes of a swimming pool and openings in oil storage tanks.[92]

Given such adaptability, Rough-wingeds are fairly common to common and widely distributed summer residents. They become locally distributed only in intensively farmed western Ohio, where most streams are small and channelized. Daily totals are normally 5–25 individuals, although float trips down larger streams may produce summer counts of 30–50+. Totals in excess of 100 are possible along the Scioto, Muskingum, and other large rivers.

Since the mid-1960s, breeding populations have increased and expanded northward in eastern and central North America.[438] These increases have not been evident within Ohio, where breeding bird surveys indicate fairly stable populations since 1965. Rough-wingeds nest as isolated pairs or in loose colonies of 5–12 pairs. While they may be found near large Bank Swallow colonies, the two species generally do not form mixed colonies. The adults begin searching for suitable burrows immediately upon their return and have been observed entering cavities as early as March 30.[299] Most nest excavation occurs during late April and early May but has been reported as late as May 25.[479] The few nests with eggs have been noted between early May and early June. Most young apparently fledge between mid-June and mid-July.

Campbell[89] aptly described migrant Rough-wingeds as "unsocial," since they generally do not associate with other swallows. Their spring movements are not very pronounced; adults merely appear at nest sites. In the southern counties, the first adults normally return by April 1–5; along Lake Erie they appear one week later. Rough-wingeds are not widely encountered until April 18–24. Bad weather may occasionally produce concentrations of Rough-wingeds during late April or early May; the largest reported spring flocks have totaled 100–350 individuals.

Their fall migration is equally inconspicuous. As soon as the young become independent, family groups congregate into flocks along large rivers and other bodies of water. These local movements normally take place during the last half of July or early August. By mid-August, Rough-wingeds have quietly disappeared from their breeding sites and formed flocks of 100–300 scattered along large rivers throughout the state. Similar concentrations appear along Lake Erie near Huron (Erie County), at Lake St. Mary's, and occasionally at other large reservoirs. Away from these locations, Rough-wingeds are infrequently encountered. These autumn concentrations mostly depart by October 3–7. Small flocks have been noted through October 12–18 and a few stragglers into November, as late as November 15, 1972, at Magee Marsh Wildlife Area.[284]

BANK SWALLOW

Riparia riparia (Linnaeus)

Unlike Rough-winged Swallows, which normally nest in scattered aggregations of a dozen or fewer pairs, Bank Swallows breed only in well-defined colonies. While the smallest colonies may have only 20–30 pairs, most colonies support 50–100 nests with occasional congregations of 200–400 pairs. Larger colonies are unusual; the only report of a colony with 2000–3000 nests was from the Toledo area in 1933–34.[89]

Bank Swallows excavate their nest burrows in soft soil near the tops of eroding banks along streams and lakes, within sand and gravel quarries, and on abandoned high-walls in strip mines. A few small colonies have been reported at such unlikely spots as large piles of fly ash behind a power plant. Nest excavation may begin by April 19 but is most prevalent in May. Most nests contain eggs by late May or the first week of June and the first fledglings may appear from their burrows by June 28–30.[523] Unsuccessful nesting attempts are frequent and Bank Swallows will renest if their first clutch is destroyed. Renesting has produced recently fledged young as late as August 12.[510]

Instability of the nesting habitats causes frequent changes in colony location. Their colonies along lakes and rivers are particularly ephemeral, lasting only two to five years before they are eliminated by erosion. The most stable colonies are in quarries where constant excavation creates suitable nest sites each year.

Breeding Bank Swallows have always been locally distributed within Ohio. In general, they are most numerous in the northern third of the state but may appear wherever suitable nest sites are available. In the mid-1930s, for example, Hicks[220,223] cited breeding colonies from most northeastern counties, all the counties bordering Lake Erie and Sandusky Bay, and Williams and Fulton Counties. While they were locally common within these northern counties, they were rather rare and very locally distributed elsewhere, with scattered records south to Guernsey, Muskingum, Hocking, Franklin, Logan, and Mercer Counties and a few colonies along the Scioto and Ohio Rivers in Hamilton, Adams, Scioto, Lawrence, and Pike Counties.

Summer distribution has not appreciably changed in the past fifty years. Since colony locations change so frequently, population trends are difficult to determine, but there are indications of a decline since 1965.[438] Bank Swallows are now fairly common to locally common summer residents along Lake Erie and throughout the northeastern counties. They are uncommon and locally distributed elsewhere in northern Ohio and along the northern edge of the Allegheny Plateau in portions of Tuscarawas, Carroll, and adjacent counties. They are fairly common to locally common residents along the Scioto River south of Columbus and portions of the Ohio River but are absent to locally uncommon residents in all other central and southern counties.[434]

This species returns later in spring than most other swallows. The only March sightings are of single Banks in Wayne County on March 25, 1978, and near Dayton on March 30, 1980.[299] They do not normally appear in the southern and central counties until April 15–20 or along Lake Erie until April 18–25. Their northward migration normally peaks between May 5 and 20, although migrant flocks may appear through the end of the month. Most spring flocks total 30 or fewer swallows, although concentrations of 50–300+ Banks may develop. Like most swallows, migrant Banks may suffer substantial mortality when unusually cold weather persists during late April or early May.

In Ohio, Bank Swallows attain their maximum abundance as fall migrants. These migrants become common to abundant along western Lake Erie, where spectacular concentrations formerly developed each August. Flocks of 10,000+ Banks were regularly observed before 1940 and an incredible 1,000,000 were estimated at the present Cedar Point Wildlife Refuge (Lucas County) on August 8, 1931.[89] These concentrations have noticeably declined since 1940, although flocks of 2500–4000+ still appear in most years. Similar concentrations are not expected east of Sandusky Bay. Although Banks are generally common migrants along the lake's Central Basin, fall flights seldom have exceeded 100–250 in recent years. The largest reported movement totaled 3000 at Ashtabula July 20–22, 1962.[132]

Within the interior counties, Bank Swallows become uncommon to locally abundant fall migrants. Most inland reports are of 50 or fewer Banks, although as many as 200–500 may regularly appear at several localities each autumn. The largest recent concentration was 2500 at Barberton (Summit County) on July 27, 1988.[388a]

Bank Swallows are relatively early fall migrants; the first individuals may appear by June 28–July 5. Their southward movements are well under way by mid-July, normally peaking between July 20 and August 15. They remain fairly numerous through the end of August, but most depart by September 5–12. Only small numbers remain through the last week of September. The appearance of a Bank Swallow at Cleveland on November 12, 1955, was extraordinarily late.[117]

CLIFF SWALLOW

Hirundo pyrrhonota Vieillot

Cliff Swallows were initially restricted to the Great Plains and western North America, nesting on cliffs bordering large valleys and rivers. Their populations underwent a dramatic eastward range expansion during the nineteenth century, bringing them into close association with people. In fact, this expansion was a direct result of the early settlers' creation of open farmlands that proved suitable for foraging swallows. Since natural cliffs were unavailable, Cliff Swallows developed the habit of nesting under the eaves of barns or other outbuildings.

Within Ohio, the first Cliff Swallow colonies were discovered near Cincinnati around 1820. They had spread eastward to Columbiana County by 1838.[251] By midcentury they were common and generally distributed summer residents.[522] This expansion was relatively short-lived, however. A noticeable decline was apparent during the 1890s, and nesting Cliff Swallows disappeared from a number of localities shortly after the turn of the century.[89,102] Of all the factors contributing to this decline, competition with the rapidly expanding House Sparrow was probably most important. These aggressive sparrows regularly usurped Cliff Swallows' nests, evicting their eggs and young and seriously reducing their reproductive success.

The population decline continued during the twentieth century. By the mid-1930s, Hicks[220] recorded nesting Cliff Swallows from only 41 counties, mostly within southern and eastern Ohio. Most of these counties supported very small populations of fewer than six colonies and 100 pairs. These colonies were generally short-lived, existing for only two or three years before disappearing.

More declines occurred in subsequent decades. By the mid-1960s, Cliff Swallows were in danger of disappearing entirely from Ohio. The few sizable colonies were in Holmes and Wayne Counties, where Amish farmers encouraged their development and continued existence. But beginning in the mid-1970s their fortunes improved as new colonies became established. The majority were discovered on dams or highway bridges over large lakes where House Sparrows offered no competition. Once established, these new colonies have been regularly occupied. This expansion was not restricted to Ohio but happened throughout eastern North America.[438]

Nesting Cliff Swallows now are mostly encountered within the eastern half of Ohio and the southwestern counties.[434] They are very locally distributed throughout this range, varying from absent to locally fairly common summer residents. Their center of abundance is still the Amish farmlands in portions of Holmes, Wayne, Coshocton, and Tuscarawas Counties; there, colonies of 50–180+ pairs can be found under the eaves of barns. The newer colonies on dams and bridges tend to be smaller, seldom exceeding 20–40 pairs.

Surprisingly few Cliff Swallows breed within the northwestern and west-central counties, where they are absent to locally rare residents. A few small colonies are regularly reported along western Lake Erie, but they are largely absent from most of these counties.[434] Their absence is probably due to a shortage of suitable nest sites.

Cliff Swallows generally initiate their nesting activities shortly after they return in spring. Within southern Ohio, nest construction has been noted by the last week of April. These activities are not evident until mid-May along Lake Erie. Most clutches are laid by late May in the southern counties and during June elsewhere. The young normally fledge in late June or July. Nesting may begin somewhat later at newly established colonies and young may remain in the nest into the first half of August.

Migrant status is directly related to the size of the nesting populations. When numbers were exceptionally low during the 1960s and early 1970s, Cliff Swallows were rare migrants across Ohio. Since the mid-1970s, the expanding nesting populations have produced increased numbers of spring and fall migrants. These numbers may eventually approach the sizable concentrations reported during earlier decades.

As spring migrants, Cliff Swallows are presently rare to locally fairly common across Ohio. Most recent spring sightings have been of 10 or fewer individuals, although local concentrations of 10–20 may infrequently develop. Large spring movements have not been evident since the 1940s. When breeding populations were larger, sizable flights were periodically encountered, producing concentrations of 500 at Buckeye Lake on May 10, 1934, and Lake St. Mary's on May 14, 1947, and 150 near Toledo on May 26, 1949.[22,89,98]

These swallows do not normally return until the last half of April. The largest numbers are expected during May and detectable movements may appear as late as May 24–26. A few late migrants may remain into the first half of June.[479] Spring overflights are relatively unusual. March records are limited to single Cliffs at Dayton on March 25, 1980, and Ottawa Wildlife Refuge on March 31, 1979.[273,277]

The fall migration is not usually apparent until July 25–August 5. In general, these migrants are most prevalent between August 10 and September 6, with smaller numbers remaining through September 18–25. There are surprisingly few October records. The latest Cliff Swallows have remained only through October 9–10.

Fall Cliff Swallows are rare to locally fairly common migrants. Most sightings are of 10 or fewer Cliffs with occasional flocks of 15–30+. Sizable fall flocks were not apparent even when breeding populations were larger. The largest reported fall concentrations are 100+ individuals at lakes in Knox and Delaware Counties during August 1981 and 1982 and 75 near Dayton in 1936.

BARN SWALLOW

Hirundo rustica Linnaeus

The Barn Swallow is Ohio's most numerous and most familiar resident swallow. There is a near-universal familiarity with this bird owing to its close association with people. Most pairs nest in barns, sheds, and abandoned houses or under bridges, requiring only regular access to the nest sites and a minimum amount of disturbance. For the most part these active little birds are beneficial occupants of farmyards, since the adults consume quantities of insects in the process of raising their broods. They become a nuisance only when the young are in the nest and the adults stoutly defend them from all intruders, calling loudly and dive-bombing any creature approaching too close to their brood.

Barn Swallows nest as isolated pairs or in loosely defined colonies, normally raising two broods annually. Nest construction begins during May, and nests with eggs have been observed by the second week of the month. First broods have fledged as early as the first week of June, although most appear during the last half of June or early July. The second clutch is initiated while the adults are still feeding their first broods. These second nesting attempts have produced nests with eggs as late as August 10 and nests with young through August 26, although most second broods fledge by mid-August.[418,523]

As summer residents, Barn Swallows are common to abundant in every county. They are one of the few species that are as numerous in the intensively cultivated western counties as in the unglaciated southeastern counties. Summer totals are generally 30–60 individuals daily except in large urban areas, where they become locally scarce or absent.

This adaptable species rapidly expanded within Ohio during the eighteenth and nineteenth centuries. They became common summer residents by the mid-1800s.[522] While their numbers have declined periodically following unusually cold spring weather, they usually recover within one or two years. They may actually have increased within Ohio during the past twenty years, a trend apparent throughout much of North America.[438]

Except for occasional overflights as early as March 15, the first Barn Swallows return between March 28 and April 5. Most years they do not become numerous until April 15–22. Spring migrants are most evident during cold wet days in late April and early May when concentrations of 300–1000 may appear throughout the state. As many as 3000 were reported from central Ohio on May 8, 1960.[471] Large flights exceeding 5000 per hour have passed along Lake Erie during days with favorable southerly winds.[329] Their spring migration normally ends by May 20.

Like most swallows, Barn Swallows begin their fall passage rather early; migrants are usually evident by the third week of July. Their fall migration normally does not produce concentrations in excess of 30–100 individuals. The largest fall flights generally total 300–600; as many as 1400 have been reported along western Lake Erie.[384] Fall migrants remain common through mid-September, with most departing by September 25–October 5. Stragglers have lingered into late October and early November. The latest Barn Swallow appeared on the Toledo Christmas Bird Count on December 16, 1984.

BLUE JAY

Cyanocitta cristata (Linnaeus)

Since Blue Jays regularly occupy shaded residential yards, parks, cemeteries, and other wooded urban areas as well as forests, they are among the most familiar of Ohio's resident birds. During most of the year their loud and raucous calls announce their mischievous presence. In winter they regularly visit bird feeders, boldly chasing away the smaller songbirds as they voraciously fill their crops with sunflower seeds. These jays are inconspicuous only during the nesting season, when they are more intent on raising their young than on creating a ruckus.

While Blue Jays are considered fairly common to common permanent residents, this status hides a more complex pattern of occurrence. In fact, some Blue Jay populations are migratory, producing a fairly spectacular movement across the state.

Their migratory movements are most evident during spring, beginning between April 15 and 22 and continuing through June 3–10. On clear spring days with southerly winds, large silent flocks of migrant jays continuously pass along Lake Erie. The first flocks may appear by 7:30 A.M. They normally peak between 9:00 and 11:00, with smaller numbers continuing into early afternoon.[335] These flights usually occur at rates of 200–700+ jays per hour. With ideal conditions, flights of 1000–2000+ each hour have been reported at Cleveland and along western Lake Erie, with estimates of 5000–10,000 in a single day.

Similar spring movements are not normally apparent within the interior counties, where migrant jays are mostly observed in small flocks of 5–30. With favorable winds, a number of flocks may be noted in a single morning; 200–400+ jays can be tallied daily. By far the largest reported inland spring movement totaled 2000 jays at Lake St. Mary's on May 26, 1969.[407]

Along Lake Erie, their fall migration is not nearly so spectacular. These fall flights are restricted to the Western Basin and seldom exceed the numbers reported from inland counties. A flight of 4600 jays along western Lake Erie on September 28, 1985, was exceptional for autumn.[380]

Fall movements through the interior counties resemble the northward migration. They are most noticeable within the western counties, where flocks of 5–40 jays are regularly observed passing from fencerow to fencerow across the cultivated fields. With northerly winds, daily totals of 200–400 jays have been recorded. These movements are less noticeable within the eastern counties, where fall totals seldom exceed 30–60 jays daily. The first migrant flocks normally appear between September 10 and 20 and may be noted through the first half of November.

Blue Jays were formerly rather erratic winter residents within Ohio. Their abundance fluctuated with the size of the mast crop.[479] These fluctuations were most apparent within the northern and central counties but were also evident in the Dayton area.[86,299]

Their wintering numbers have noticeably increased since 1940. These wintering jays have been taking advantage of a regular food supply available at an ever-increasing number of bird feeders. Blue Jays are now fairly common to locally common winter residents throughout Ohio. While their wintering numbers are still somewhat variable, they do not exhibit the extreme fluctuations described by Trautman.[479] Within most counties, winter reports normally are of 8–25+ jays daily, while as many as 40–60 have been reported in years of peak abundance.

Blue Jays have always been widely distributed summer residents. Jones[236] considered them common residents at the turn of the century except within the southeastern counties. Hicks[220,223] noted a similar distribution in the 1930s. He described them as generally fairly common to abundant residents except in the southeastern counties bordering the West Virginia panhandle, where they became locally uncommon to rare.

Since the mid-1960s, nesting jays have significantly increased throughout eastern North America.[438] While they remain widely distributed summer residents and are regularly recorded within every Ohio county, they are still least numerous within the southeastern counties bordering the Ohio River. There they are uncommon to fairly common residents but are generally common elsewhere. As a result of their inconspicuous behavior during summer, they are never numerous and daily totals seldom exceed 5–15 jays.

Blue Jays normally place their nests in dense ornamental conifers in residential areas or tangles within woodlands. One pair nested in a mailbox.[195] Nest construction may begin during the last half of March although the first eggs have not been reported until mid-April.[299,479,523] Most clutches are discovered during late April or May with the young fledging during the first half of June. Some jays may raise two broods. Nests with eggs have been reported as late as June 30 and adults accompanied by dependent young through September 1.[511]

BLACK-BILLED MAGPIE

Pica pica (Linnaeus)

While Black-billed Magpies make their homes in the western half of North America, they tend to wander eastward during late fall and early winter. These wandering magpies have produced a number of extralimital records across the Great Lakes region into New England.[5] This vagrancy was more pronounced before the mid-1960s. The relatively few extralimital sightings in recent years reflect a significant decline in magpie numbers throughout western North America since 1965.[438] This vagrant tendency has also been obscured by magpies that have escaped or been released intentionally from captivity. A number of magpies were accidentally released in the Pittsburgh area in the late 1950s, producing scattered sightings within nearby states during the next few years. In general, escaped magpies may appear at any time of the year and frequently remain for a number of weeks or even months. Few of them exhibit evidence of previous captivity. An exception was the first magpie collected in Ohio (in Lucas County on May 9, 1937), described as a "female in good condition although primaries and tail feathers were badly worn."[86] This extreme feather wear and the unusual date strongly suggest that this individual was previously held in captivity.

Black-billed Magpies are accidental visitors to Ohio. There are only three acceptable winter records conforming to their established pattern of vagrancy. These records are of single magpies in Lucas County between January 29 and February 11, 1950, and on January 16, 1955, plus one near O'Shaughnessy Reservoir (Delaware County) on December 31, 1956.[89,471]

All other Ohio magpies have problematic origins. The records include three spring sightings from the Toledo area; two pairs attempting to nest near Sandusky between April 1 and May 10, 1973; a road-killed magpie found in a Columbus residential area during April 1960; and a pair remaining in the Canton area for nearly a year during 1961–62. In addition, a sight record from Lorain County during December 1972 was never adequately substantiated. Some of these records could pertain to genuine vagrants, but most were probably birds released or escaped from captivity.

AMERICAN CROW

Corvus brachyrhynchos Brehm

The sentiments of Dawson[102] about crows are still applicable:

The dusky bird is a notorious mischief-maker, but he is not quite so black as he has been painted. More than any other bird he has successfully matched his wits against those of man, and his frequent easy victories and consequent boastings are responsible in large measure for the unsavory reputation in which he is held. It is a familiar adage in ebony circles that the proper study of Crow-kind is man, and so well has he pursued this study that he may fairly be said to hold his own in spite of fierce and ingenious persecution. He rejoices in the name of outlaw, and ages of ill treatment have only served to sharpen his wits and intensify his cunning.

Crows have not always been widely distributed residents within Ohio. Their numbers substantially increased during the eighteenth and nineteenth centuries, coinciding with the clearing of the original forests and the spread of farmlands. By the early 1900s they were well established throughout the state, although the northern counties generally supported smaller populations.[236] Crows continued to increase during the 1900s, attaining their maximum abundance between the 1930s and 1950s. However, modern agricultural practices have been detrimental to crows, producing marked declines within the western half of the state since 1960.

While crows are considered permanent residents, their distribution patterns are fairly complex. Certainly the crows observed during summer are not necessarily the same individuals seen in our wintering flocks.

American Crows are least numerous during the breeding season. They are presently common residents throughout the eastern half of Ohio and the southwestern counties, where 15–50 crows may be observed daily and as many as 75–130+ may be noted. Breeding crows are more locally distributed within the northwestern and west-central counties. They are locally uncommon to common summer residents within these counties; daily totals normally are 20 or fewer crows.

Nesting crows are most numerous where woodlands, farm fields, successional fields, and residences are interspersed. Crows can also survive within intensively farmed lands by nesting in the few remaining woodlots. And they are regularly found in urban areas, nesting in parks, cemeteries, and backyards and finding a plentiful source of food in our refuse.

Crows prefer to nest in woodlands, especially pine plantations, although undisturbed deciduous forests are equally suitable. Nest construction is evident in March and early April. Within the southern counties, crows may have complete clutches by the last half of March. Elsewhere, nests with eggs have been reported between April 10 and May 10 with renesting attempts through June 15.[89,479,523] Young crows may fledge during the last half of May but most appear in June and early July.

Crows become common to abundant migrants throughout Ohio. Their spring movements begin with the first warm days of late winter, usually by February 15–25 but not until March if temperatures are unusually cold. The largest flights occur before March 20. Within the inland counties, few migrants are noted after April 1. The lakefront migration normally continues through April 10–20 with a few stragglers into the first week of May.

The largest spring movements pass along Lake Erie. Five thousand crows have been estimated at Toledo on several dates and 10,000 moved along the Cleveland lakefront on February 28, 1931.[89,523] Since 1970, 30–200 crows have comprised most daily observations and occasional flights totaled 500–1000. Smaller numbers migrate through the interior counties; there, only Trautman[479] reported flights of "several thousand" crows at Buckeye Lake and near Columbus during the 1920s and 1930s. Since the mid-1960s, most inland spring totals are 100 or fewer crows daily with infrequent flights involving 200–500.

Their autumn migration is less conspicuous. Along Lake Erie, fall sightings usually are of 100 or fewer crows with exceptional movements producing totals of 1000–2100+. These numbers have not significantly diminished since the 1950s. Within the interior counties, fall concentrations are comparable to those noted each spring. The only inland movement involving 1000 crows was reported by Trautman[479] at Buckeye Lake before 1940. These migrants may appear along Lake Erie by September 5–15.[89] The largest flights are not expected until October 20–December 10.

Before 1960, crows were common to abundant winter residents throughout Ohio. By day, flocks of 20–100+ crows were regularly encountered. Each evening these flocks returned to roosts, where several hundred to several thousand crows would gather. These roosts were scattered across the state, usually in young pine plantations or similar habitats providing dense cover. Most roosts supported fewer than 5000 crows but the largest hosted 10,000–25,000. As many as 100,000 crows were claimed at several northern Ohio roosts.

Since 1960, their wintering numbers have substantially declined within the intensively farmed western counties, where they became locally uncommon to fairly common winter residents and daily totals seldom exceed 15–25 crows. Wintering crows remain common to abundant residents in the eastern half of the state and southwestern counties. Winter totals of 20–50 crows are not unusual in these counties and flocks of 100–400+ individuals appear most years.

American Crows still congregate in winter roosts, although this behavior is less pronounced now than during the 1930s. In recent years, roosts have been maintained at Mansfield and Springfield and in Lucas County. These roosts generally support 1000–3000 crows; occasionally, as many as 5000–10,000 have been estimated.

COMMON RAVEN

Corvus corax Linnaeus

Although it is difficult to believe today, Common Ravens were probably the most numerous corvid (jays, magpies, crows) in Ohio when the state was first settled. As the human population increased and the primeval forests where the ravens resided were converted to farmlands, the species rapidly disappeared and ravens were replaced by the ubiquitous crows.

Specific information on the former abundance and distribution of ravens is difficult to find. Accounts indicate that they were common residents in the vicinity of Lake Erie, especially from Cleveland eastward. Jared Kirtland described them as common in the northeastern counties, a fact corroborated by Alexander Wilson during his visit to the area during the early 1800s.[523] They were said to be "undoubtedly present" in central Ohio, but the few records do not adequately establish their true status.[522] Ravens may also have resided in the southern counties, although no early naturalist specifically cited their presence.

Rapid destruction of the virgin forests extirpated ravens from the central and southern counties by the early nineteenth century. Nevertheless, ravens periodically wandered into these counties throughout the 1800s until the last central Ohio specimen was collected near Marysville (Union County) on September 3, 1879.[522] Raven populations fared slightly better in the northern counties. They were still frequently encountered near Cleveland during the 1850s but greatly declined by the late 1870s, when they were only rare winter visitors.[523] They probably disappeared from northeastern Ohio shortly thereafter. Their last stronghold was the extensive Black Swamp in northwestern Ohio. Anecdotal accounts indicate that ravens were still fairly common residents in Paulding County during 1880, outnumbering crows in winter.[424] Similar accounts tell of a nest in Fulton County during the late 1800s, but the details are quite vague.[220] This northwestern Ohio population apparently disappeared between 1900 and 1905.[236,424]

After the extirpation of this resident population, ravens became accidental visitors to Ohio. While there have been several unconfirmed sightings from eastern Ohio, only one raven has been reliably recorded since the early 1900s. It was carefully studied by Milton Trautman on ice-covered Lake Erie near South Bass Island on January 20, February 16, and March 6, 1946.[481] It was with a small flock of crows foraging for food around some ice shanties on the frozen lake.

BLACK-CAPPED CHICKADEE

Parus atricapillus Linnaeus

Identification problems have resulted in disparate and often inconsistent statements concerning the historic status of Black-capped Chickadees. Only the account of Wheaton,[522] published in 1882, is reasonably consistent with recent records, and it may provide a suitable basis for comparing historic changes in the distribution of this species. He stated that Black-capped Chickadees were resident south to central Ohio until the mid-1800s. Their breeding range gradually contracted northward during the last half of the nineteenth century as Black-cappeds were replaced by Carolinas. By the early 1900s, Black-cappeds were confined to northern Ohio and were only casual winter visitors to the central counties.[479]

The first complete account of Black-capped Chickadees' statewide distribution was provided by Hicks in the mid-1930s.[220] He described Black-cappeds as fairly common to abundant residents in northern Ohio, becoming locally rare within a few western counties. Their breeding range extended south to Mercer, Allen, Hancock, Wyandot, Crawford, Richland, Ashland, Wayne, Stark, and Columbiana Counties.

Their northward range contraction continued during subsequent decades. Black-capped Chickadees presently range south to Van Wert, Putnam, Hancock, Seneca, northern Ashland, northern Wayne, Summit, northern Stark, and Mahoning Counties.[434] A few isolated pairs may still be found slightly south of this range but are absent from central and southern Ohio except during periodic winter invasions.

Black-cappeds are common residents in the northeastern counties. Daily totals of 10–20+ individuals are noted during summer and 20–40+ in winter. These chickadees are more locally distributed west of Lorain and Medina Counties. They are uncommon to fairly common residents in most northwestern counties, becoming locally rare near Lake Erie and in intensively cultivated areas. Within these counties, Black-cappeds are found along mature wooded corridors bordering streams and in the few remaining extensive woodlands. Totals of 3–12+ individuals are reported during summer. Winter concentrations of 5–20+ are possible except near Lake Erie, where they are absent.

Chickadees normally nest in cavities at heights of two to sixty feet. If natural cavities are unavailable, they will nest in fence posts and bluebird boxes. Nest construction may begin during the last week of March but is mostly noted in April. Most nests contain eggs during May that normally hatch during the last half of the month. Young chickadees usually fledge in June.[89,523] Recently fledged young in the last half of July may represent successful renesting.[417]

While most Black-capped Chickadees are permanent residents, this species undertakes periodic winter invasions south of its established range. These invasions result from food shortages in forests in Canada and the upper Great Lakes states. Although these movements have probably occurred throughout historic times, the first noticeable southward invasion was in 1941. The largest movements were noted during the winters of 1951–52, 1954–55, 1959–60, 1961–62, and 1965–66.[89] For unknown reasons these movements have been less frequent since 1970. A sizable flight appeared in the winter of 1975–76, but no invasions were subsequently detected.

Away from their established range, Black-capped Chickadees are accidental to casual winter visitors. Their winter status in the central counties is directly related to the numbers of Black-cappeds moving southward. Small invasions produce only scattered individuals. During massive invasions they become fairly common or common winter residents and even outnumber the resident Carolinas. These large flights may result in as many as 10–30 Black-cappeds daily in central Ohio.

Black-capped Chickadees appear in the southern counties only during the largest invasions, usually as scattered individuals, although flocks of 5–10 were reported during the movements of the 1960s.[130] The southward extent of these invasions is verified by specimens collected in Athens, Morgan, and Vinton Counties. Their status in southwestern Ohio is less certain. A number of reports come from Dayton, including 43 on the Christmas Bird Count during the 1954–55 flight.[299] Recent records from Cincinnati were thought to be "of extremely doubtful validity."[248]

During the largest flights, the first individuals appear at lakefront migrant traps by October 5–12 and spread to the central counties before the end of the month. Smaller movements may not be apparent along Lake Erie until October 20–November 10. These migrations are most evident along Lake Erie, where Black-cappeds are normally very scarce or absent. Reports of 206 in one hour at Cleveland on October 23, 1954, and 507 in two and a half hours on October 8, 1959, are representative of lakefront totals during the largest movements.[324,346] Totals of 20–100 daily may occur in smaller movements. Similar flights have not been reported from the interior counties, where fall sightings are of 10 or fewer individuals.

Their northward movements are more poorly defined. In the central and southern counties, the last individuals depart by April 5–15. Their lakefront passage is most apparent in April, producing scattered flights of 75–175+, although most spring totals are fewer than 25 daily. The last spring migrants usually leave Lake Erie by the first week of May.

CAROLINA CHICKADEE

Parus carolinensis Audubon

While Carolina Chickadees were undoubtedly present in the southern and central counties during the nineteenth century, their status and distribution were the subjects of conflicting accounts. Wheaton[522] may be most accurate. In the 1880s, he described Carolinas as summer residents in central Ohio and said they migrated southward shortly after the breeding season. They were permanent residents within the southern counties.

Their status was better defined during the present century, although the Black-capped and Carolina Chickadees were regularly misidentified and many extralimital or unseasonal sightings were frequently in error. In any event, Carolina Chickadees were well-established permanent residents in southern and central Ohio by the early 1900s.[479] Their breeding range expanded northward during the 1920s and 1930s. This expansion was most apparent in eastern Ohio, where Carolinas eventually spread north to Columbiana, Stark, and Wayne Counties.[34,84,457] Their rate of expansion slowed in subsequent decades, although Carolinas still appear to be gradually spreading northward in Ohio.

Carolina Chickadees now breed north to southern Mahoning, Stark, Wayne, Ashland, Richland, Crawford, Wyandot, and Van Wert Counties.[434] Their distribution in western Ohio is poorly understood. They are generally permanent residents, although some may retreat from the northern boundary of this range during winter.

Carolina Chickadees are accidental visitors farther north. While a number of sight records come from these northern counties, most are not adequately substantiated. A few specimens were collected, however, to document the extralimital wanderings of a few Carolinas: one near Oberlin (Lorain County) on April 27, 1923; two females at Solon Bog (Portage County) on May 8, 1935; and two females east of Hudson (Portage County) on May 1, 1935.

Their habitat preferences and breeding biology are very similar to those of Black-cappeds. Carolina Chickadees are most numerous in mature woodlands and wooded riparian habitats. They will also occupy wooded fencerows, orchards, and shaded residential areas. They nest in cavities, usually at heights of two to fifteen feet. If suitable cavities are not present, a fence post or birdhouse will suffice. Most nest construction takes place in late March and early April. The first eggs are laid by mid-April and nests with young have been reported by the first week of May.[479] Fledglings have appeared by May 15 but most are noted in late May and early June. Renesting attempts may produce nests with eggs through June 5 and dependent young as late as July 22.[479]

Within their established range, Carolina Chickadees are generally fairly common to common permanent residents. They are least conspicuous during the breeding season, when the adults are busy raising broods and daily totals seldom exceed 5–15 individuals. Carolinas are most numerous in the southern and unglaciated eastern counties, where as many as 20–50 may be observed daily during winter. They are least numerous in intensively cultivated western Ohio. There, winter totals seldom exceed 4–12.

This species also responds to the periodic Black-capped Chickadee invasions, which produce marked southward movements of Carolinas between mid-October and December. These movements are poorly described but have produced some noteworthy concentrations: 400 Carolinas on November 18, 1961, and 200 during the first week of October 1963 along the Scioto River in Pickaway County.[391,482] Following these movements, Carolinas are observed in reduced wintering numbers in central and southern Ohio. During the largest Black-capped invasions, Carolinas have virtually disappeared from the central counties.[130,482] While Carolinas undoubtedly undertake spring movements following these invasions, no sizable concentrations have been encountered.

BOREAL CHICKADEE

Parus hudsonicus Forster

Normally residents of boreal forests in Canada and the extreme northern United States, Boreal Chickadees tend to wander south of this range during late fall and winter. These periodic movements, triggered by food shortages, are normally associated with massive southward flights of Black-capped Chickadees. Wandering Boreals may spread southward through New England and the lower Great Lakes. Eleven records exist from northern Ohio, where Boreals are accidental late fall and winter visitors.

Ohio's first Boreal Chickadee was collected on Turtle Island in western Lake Erie on November 6, 1943.[302] The next Boreals were associated with Black-capped Chickadee invasions during the 1950s: three northwestern Ohio records in 1951 and single 1954 sightings from Ottawa County and Ashtabula.[89,347] The winter of 1963–64 produced three Boreal Chickadee records from the Cleveland area.[335] The most recent, during the winter of 1972–73, were single sightings from Toledo and Cleveland.[90,285]

With one exception, these sightings have occurred between November 6 and January 1. The exception was a Boreal Chickadee visiting a Columbia Station feeder between March 7 and April 2, 1964.[335] They are most likely to be encountered on the western Lake Erie islands or close to the lakeshore, having wandered inland to the village of Holgate (Henry County) on November 17, 1951.[89] Most records are of single individuals, although as many as 4 have been reported from South Bass Island.

TUFTED TITMOUSE

Parus bicolor Linnaeus

Fairly common to common residents of woodlands throughout Ohio, Tufted Titmice join chickadees and other gleaners in mixed-species foraging flocks during the nonbreeding season. Their hoarse calls and loud ringing songs are regularly heard throughout the year, frequently providing the first indication that a flock is in the area.

As woodland residents, Tufted Titmice were well established

in every county by the early 1900s,[236] although their numbers in northern Ohio may have increased somewhat during the first decades of this century. Their populations have remained relatively stable since the 1930s except for fluctuations produced by severe winter weather. Like all gleaners, titmice suffer substantial mortality during ice storms and extreme temperatures. A single severe storm may significantly reduce their populations, as was widely noted following the winter of 1977–78.[438] However, they recover quickly given one or two mild winters.

Tufted Titmice generally prefer mature woodlands and wooded riparian corridors; they are unlikely to be found in small open woodlots and brushy thickets except during winter.[479] Small numbers occupy orchards and shaded residential areas. Given these habitat preferences, Tufted Titmice are most numerous in the southern and unglaciated eastern counties, where daily totals of 5–15 individuals are regularly noted in summer and 20–40+ during winter. While similar numbers may be locally encountered elsewhere, titmice are generally least numerous in the intensively cultivated western counties and northern tier of counties. They become locally uncommon in these areas; summer totals normally are 1–6 titmice daily and winter reports seldom exceed 5–15.

Rather sedentary birds, most titmice spend their entire lives within an area of only several square miles. A few may wander and appear at lakefront migrant traps during spring and fall. These individuals may merely be searching for suitable nesting or wintering habitats rather than being true migrants.

Their breeding chronology is very similar to that of chickadees. They form pairs during mid-March and begin searching for suitable nesting cavities. While they will nest in fence posts and occasionally in birdhouses, most titmice choose natural cavities at heights of five to forty feet. Their eggs may be laid by mid-April in the southern counties and during May in northern Ohio. Renesting attempts have produced clutches as late as June 10.[479] Most young fledge during the last half of May and June, although some fledglings will accompany their parents through early July.[89,417]

RED-BREASTED NUTHATCH

Sitta canadensis Linnaeus

These attractive little nuthatches normally reside in coniferous forests of Canada, the northern United States, and the higher elevations of the western mountains. Food availability greatly influences their seasonal movements, just as it does with other residents of these forests. When food is plentiful, most Red-breasted Nuthatches remain in these forests and do not migrate south. But virtually all of them will desert these forests when food is scarce, producing a massive invasion of states to the south. These movements are frequently associated with invasions of Pine Siskins and Evening Grosbeaks. Southward flights were sporadic during the first half of the nineteenth century but have generally occurred at intervals of two to three years since the 1950s.

Timing of their autumn migration varies with the size of the southward flight. During sizable invasions, the first Red-breasted Nuthatches may appear along Lake Erie by August 20–25 and within the southern counties between August 23 and 30. The migration normally peaks between September 10 and October 15. Their numbers decline during the last half of October and few migrants are detected after November 3–10. Their fall movements are later during "noninvasion" years, when the first nuthatches return during September 10–20. A defined peak is not apparent, with only scattered sightings through late October.

Fall Red-breasted Nuthatches are most numerous along Lake Erie. During flight years, they become fairly common to locally common migrants and concentrations of 10–30 individuals may develop. In nonflight years, these nuthatches are uncommon lakefront migrants with most reports of 1–5 individuals. Their fall distribution is fairly uniform across the interior counties; they become uncommon to fairly common migrants during flight years and casual to rare at other times. Even during flight years most reports are of only 1–5 individuals.

Wintering Red-breasted Nuthatches are most numerous within pine plantations and mixed woodlands throughout the unglaciated Allegheny Plateau and northeastern counties. They are normally uncommon to fairly common residents within these counties, usually in groups of 2–8. They become locally common following sizable invasions, when daily totals of 15–25+ are possible. Elsewhere these nuthatches are very erratic winter residents and may be completely absent some years, casual to rare in others, and rare to locally fairly common following sizable invasions. Winter totals normally are only 1–5 individuals daily, with local concentrations of 5–10 during invasion years.

The size of their spring movements is directly related to the number migrating south the previous autumn. The largest spring movements follow sizable fall invasions. Timing of their northward movements is reasonably consistent. Spring migrants are normally apparent by mid-April and peak between April 22 and May 15. The last migrants usually depart from the interior counties by May 20 and Lake Erie by May 25–June 5.

These nuthatches are uncommon to fairly common spring migrants along Lake Erie, where most sightings are of 10 or fewer daily. Spring flights seldom exceed 20 Red-breasteds, even during invasion years. Within the interior counties, spring nuthatches are normally rare to uncommon, becoming locally fairly common in flight years. Most inland spring records are of 1–5 individuals with occasional concentrations of 6–20. A report of 45 Red-breasteds at Columbus on April 23, 1981 was exceptional.[471]

In earlier days, Red-breasted Nuthatches were very sporadic summer residents in Ohio. The first breeding records were from two Ashtabula County locations, where Hicks[215] discovered an adult with dependent young on July 18, 1929, and located a nest on June 13, 1931. The only other summer sightings were also from northeastern Ohio. The July 17, 1931, record from Headlands State Park (Lake County) may have been an unusually early migrant.[16] However, two pairs summering on Little Mountain in 1938 may have nested.[523]

This pattern of sporadic nesting records from the northeastern counties continued through the 1970s, averaging one to three summer sightings each decade. These records invariably followed sizable winter invasions. Since 1980, summering Red-breasted Nuthatches have been recorded annually. Most recent records are from the northern counties where they are accidental to casual residents. Nesting Red-breasteds have been confirmed from two locations in Portage County and from Findley State Park (Lorain County), Tiffin, and the Oak Openings of Lucas County. Summering individuals have been encountered at additional scattered locations.[278,362,434] They are accidental summer visitors elsewhere, with the only confirmed nest at Cincinnati during 1982.[365] They have also summered in Hocking and Miami Counties and at Dayton.[278,299,434] These summering Red-breasteds normally remain for only one or two years and then disappear.

Most summering Red-breasteds are found in residential areas, occupying conifers and regularly visiting bird feeders. A few inhabit pine plantations in rural areas. The few breeding records indicate that nesting activities are initiated in late April or early May with the young fledging by mid-June. Ashtabula County records by Hicks[215] are late and may represent renesting attempts.

WHITE-BREASTED NUTHATCH

Sitta carolinensis Latham

This nuthatch is a familiar resident of deciduous woods, mature riparian corridors, parks, cemeteries, and shaded residential areas throughout Ohio. Its territories center on mature deciduous trees providing cavities for nesting and roosting. Perhaps their most distinctive trait is their peculiar method of foraging for food. Unlike woodpeckers and creepers, which steadily move up tree trunks and branches, White-breasted Nuthatches normally walk head first down the trunks or around branches.

As breeding birds, White-breasted Nuthatches are fairly common to common residents in most counties, although they become locally uncommon in intensively farmed western Ohio. These breeding populations have increased slightly since 1965, a trend noted throughout eastern and central North America.[438]

White-breasted Nuthatches are fairly conspicuous during spring, especially in late March and early April when their territorial and courtship activities peak. They become surprisingly inconspicuous later in the breeding season, when daily totals seldom exceed 10 individuals. Nest building commences in April. Their cavities may be located ten to sixty feet high, usually in live deciduous trees. Nesting records indicate most eggs are laid during the last half of April and early in May, although nests with young have been reported as early as May 1.[523] Recently fledged young have been observed as early as May 22 with most appearing during June.[479] Young nuthatches observed as late as August 15 are probably the result of renesting attempts.[523]

Although they are normally sedentary, White-breasted Nuthatches periodically undertake noticeable fall movements. These influxes are most apparent at lakefront migrant traps, where the White-breasted is usually absent. During the largest movements, as many as 10–15 individuals may appear daily

during late September and October. These movements are poorly understood but usually coincide with southward invasions of Black-capped Chickadees.

During winter, White-breasted Nuthatches are important members of the mixed-species flocks foraging within deciduous woods. Their nasal calls are readily recognized above the chatter produced by these flocks. Although their numbers are subject to annual fluctuations, White-breasted Nuthatches are fairly common to common winter residents throughout Ohio. Winter sightings usually total 4–15 individuals daily. As many as 60 have been recorded during years of peak abundance.[479] Several factors are responsible for these fluctuating winter populations. Influxes from farther north may raise populations to their highest levels. Conversely, winter storms may cause their numbers to decline.

While fall influxes are apparent along the lakefront, the return flights are normally very small. Spring movements occur in April but seldom produce more than 5 individuals daily at lakefront migrant traps.

BROWN CREEPER

Certhia americana Bonaparte

The least conspicuous members of Ohio's mixed-species flocks of wintering birds, Brown Creepers are easily overlooked as they move from tree to tree in search of food hidden in crevices in the bark. With their upperparts serving as camouflage, motionless creepers disappear against the bark of most deciduous trees. But creepers call persistently, and their presence is announced by their high-pitched calls long before they are observed.

Brown Creepers are primarily migrants and winter residents. A few individuals have appeared at scattered localities during August, some as early as the first week. In all likelihood, these early creepers are wandering nonbreeders or postbreeding adults. In general, the first southward migrants appear along Lake Erie between September 10 and 17 and in the central and southern counties by September 20–October 5. This movement is most pronounced during October but continues through the first half of November.

Fall creepers are uncommon to locally common visitors, with the largest numbers appearing along Lake Erie. They are seldom numerous; fall totals mostly are 8 or fewer creepers daily. The few sizable fall movements, restricted to Lake Erie, produce local concentrations of 25–30 creepers. Perhaps the largest fall movement occurred on October 14, 1928, when "scores" of creepers were grounded at Bay Point (Ottawa County), where they were observed on the ground catching insects among the dune grasses.[89]

Most wintering Brown Creepers inhabit woodlands, although a few reside in parks and cemeteries. They are most numerous in floodplain woods but also occupy upland forests and isolated woodlots.

While they are widely distributed, wintering creepers are slightly more numerous within the central and southern counties, where they are normally fairly common residents. In northern Ohio, creepers become uncommon to locally fairly common residents. Most winter reports are of 1–6 creepers daily with occasional concentrations of 8–12. These numbers exhibit considerable annual fluctuations. Years of peak abundance may produce Christmas Bird Count totals of 40+ creepers in northern Ohio and 100–140+ in the central and southwestern counties.

Winter populations have remained fairly stable during the twentieth century. The largest reported concentrations occurred after 1950, perhaps indicating gradually improving numbers. Increased numbers are to be expected because the Great Lakes breeding population has been expanding since the mid-1960s.[438]

The beginning of their spring migration probably occurs during the last half of March. Their northward movements normally peak in April, when creepers become fairly common to locally common visitors in most counties. Most spring totals are 8 or fewer creepers daily with occasional concentrations of 20–35+ individuals in central Ohio and along Lake Erie. By far the largest spring movement was encountered on April 19, 1964, when "hundreds" of creepers visited the Toledo area.[89] Most creepers depart by April 20–30 with the last migrants remaining through May 7–10 along Lake Erie.

At one time, Brown Creepers were unknown as summer residents within Ohio. The first nesting records were from Ashtabula County, where Hicks[215] recorded summering pairs at only two locations between 1928 and 1931. The only other northeastern Ohio summer records before 1950 were of a Geauga County nest and summering birds in Lorain and Cuyahoga Counties.[305,523]

Their status changed in the 1960s, when summering creepers became rare but fairly regular residents in northeastern Ohio. This increase was first noticed in the Cleveland area, where breeding pairs have been regularly recorded since 1964.[335] During the 1970s, summering creepers began to appear elsewhere. Nesting was recorded in Carroll and Jefferson Counties in 1972, while a singing male was recorded near Dayton in 1974.[84,256] This range expansion continued into the 1980s, producing additional summer records from Ohio.

Brown Creepers are now rare to locally uncommon summer residents in northeastern Ohio. They are most frequently encountered near Cleveland, where as many as 9 males have been recorded from a single locality, and in Ashtabula County.[434] Scattered pairs have been located in most other northeastern counties south to Columbiana and Wayne. Creepers are accidental to casual summer residents elsewhere, with a few widely scattered records from all portions of the state except the northwestern and west-central counties. Surprisingly, most recent sightings have been from the southwestern counties, including nests in Hamilton County in 1982 and Montgomery County in 1985 and as many as 4 creepers in a Dayton park in 1984.[299,434] Along the unglaciated Allegheny Plateau, summering creepers have been recorded south to Hocking County.[471] These summering creepers can be remarkably inconspicuous and easily overlooked, especially after the males quit singing in early June.

Breeding creepers occupy a variety of second-growth and mature woodland habitats, preferring mesic woods and swamp forests. Their nests are cleverly hidden under the loose bark of dead trees. The few documented nesting attempts indicate that construction normally begins in early May, and all clutches have been discovered during that month. Recently fledged young may be expected by mid-June.[215,523]

ROCK WREN

Salpinctes obsoletus (Say)

Rock Wrens are widespread summer residents in western North America from southern Canada into Mexico but retreat from northern portions of their range during winter. Since they undertake fairly lengthy migrations, a few disoriented Rock Wrens wander east of their established range, appearing at scattered localities in central and eastern North America.[5] Ohio's only record of this accidental visitor was provided by a Rock Wren discovered at Edgewater Park in Cleveland on December 7, 1963. It remained through December 14, foraging for insects among the rocks along the breakwall and occasionally visiting weeds, scattered bushes, and rubble in an adjoining parking lot and field.[335] It was closely studied by many observers and photographed by William Klamm.

CAROLINA WREN

Thryothorus ludovicianus (Latham)

Like most wrens, Carolinas are unobtrusive, spending most of their lives skulking through brushy thickets, dense undergrowth, and shrubbery. Among our most vocal songbirds, they sing throughout the year. Their loud rolling song resounds through the otherwise silent woodlands in early February before most other birds are declaring their territories and in August after most quit singing.

Carolina Wrens are common and widespread residents in the southeastern United States. They reach the northern edge of their range in the Great Lakes and New England states, where they underwent considerable expansions after the 1880s.[104] While these wrens always resided in the southern half of Ohio, their historic status in the northern counties is problematic. A few may have been present prior to 1880, but their numbers increased during the last decades of the nineteenth century.[236]

Their status has not appreciably changed during this century except in response to severe winter weather. Prolonged deep snow cover is detrimental to Carolina Wrens, since it buries most of their available food. When combined with subzero temperatures, this condition can cause declines of 50–90 percent in our wren populations.

Exceptionally severe weather during three winters produced the most dramatic declines. Although the available information is scanty, the winter of 1917–18 apparently eliminated Carolina Wrens from most of Ohio.[479] Their populations did not recover until 1922 at Buckeye Lake and later in more northerly locations. While smaller declines were noted in subsequent decades, the general trend was toward increasing populations through the 1950s and 1960s. They peaked in the early 1970s as evidenced by an incredible 1801 Carolina Wrens on the 1974 Cincinnati Christmas Bird Count.

These all-time high populations were decimated by the unusually brutal winters of 1976–77 and 1977–78.[438] Following the second severe winter, Carolina Wrens were reduced by more than 90 percent and eliminated from many localities. The few remaining wrens were mostly found in the extreme southern counties. With these individuals forming the nucleus, Carolina Wrens have gradually recovered during the 1980s. They are presently widely distributed in the southern half of the state, but only scattered wrens are reported from the northern counties. These populations are still less than the extraordinary numbers of the early 1970s.

As permanent residents, Carolina Wrens are most numerous in the southwestern counties north to Butler, Warren, and Highland and along the unglaciated Allegheny Plateau north to Muskingum, Guernsey, and Belmont Counties. Most years they are fairly common to locally abundant residents, and daily totals of 15–35 are not unusual. Following severe winters, they become uncommon to locally rare residents with no more than 6–8 daily.

Elsewhere along the Allegheny Plateau and in the central counties adjacent to Columbus, Carolina Wrens are normally uncommon to fairly common residents, although daily totals seldom exceed 3–8. They become casual to rare within these counties following severe winters. They are generally rare to uncommon residents in the west-central counties, normally encountered as isolated pairs, although concentrations of 6–8 individuals may be found along riparian corridors. Carolina Wrens are least numerous in the northern third of Ohio, where they are casual to locally uncommon residents following mild winters and casually observed after severe winters. They are mostly observed as isolated pairs, least numerous in the northeastern counties of Ashtabula, Lake, Geauga, and Trumbull and the northwestern counties of Williams, Fulton, and Defiance.

Carolina Wrens exhibit no defined spring or fall migrations. Individuals that appear between August and November at localities where they do not normally breed probably are wandering in search of mates and suitable unoccupied habitats. Unless a territory is established, these individuals normally disappear after a few days or several weeks.

The primary habitat requirement of Carolina Wrens is thick undergrowth and dense tangles. They may be found wherever such a habitat is available: woodlots, wooded ravines, riparian corridors, roadside edges, fencerows, and residential areas. Normally associated with edges, they are not encountered in forest interiors.

Carolina Wrens nest on or near the ground in brush piles, cavities, roots of fallen trees, and similar situations. While they rarely occupy birdboxes, they frequently nest in buildings. Their nests have been found in hanging flower baskets, mailboxes, and junk left in isolated corners of outbuildings. One pair attempted to nest in a garden tractor. Most pairs raise at least two broods. Nest construction normally begins during the last

half of March or early April and the first clutches are laid by mid-April. While fledglings have been reported by the last week of April, most first broods fledge during May.[299,479] Second clutches are initiated during June or early July. These young fledge by mid-August, although late attempts may produce young wrens through the first week of September.

BEWICK'S WREN

Thryomanes bewickii (Audubon)

According to Trautman,[479] Ohio's first Bewick's Wren was discovered in 1879. The initial records were from the southern and central counties, where numbers increased dramatically in the next twenty years. By the turn of the century, Bewick's Wrens were common summer residents throughout southern Ohio and the central counties "nearly to Columbus."[193,236] Scattered individuals were observed north to Lake Erie, although breeding populations were not established in the northern half of the state. Range expansion continued into the first decades of the twentieth century but at a slower rate.

Bewick's Wrens apparently peaked between 1925 and 1940. During this period, they regularly nested in every county north to Mercer, Shelby, Logan, Union, Morrow, Knox, Wayne, Stark, and Columbiana.[220] Only a few isolated records came from the northern counties. As summer residents, they were fairly common to very common along the unglaciated plateau north to Muskingum, Noble, and Washington Counties.[223] They were uncommon to rare elsewhere along this plateau as well as in most glaciated southern and central counties. Additional range expansion was hardly evident except for the first Trumbull County nest in 1932.[450]

Populations declined during the 1940s, although this trend was not obvious until the end of the decade. During the late 1940s and early 1950s, populations were subject to marked annual fluctuations.[69] Most remaining pairs inhabited the unglaciated southeastern counties, with small numbers regularly appearing in southwestern Ohio.[248]

Beginning in the mid-1950s, the remnant Bewick's Wren population underwent a rapid decline. Most of these wrens disappeared by 1960–65, although a few isolated pairs were still reported every year through 1970. Despite these declines, a few Bewick's Wrens appeared in the northern counties. The first Cleveland area nest was established at Kent (Portage County) in 1949 and nesting wrens were also recorded in 1952 and 1957 in Summit and Cuyahoga Counties.[335,523] In the Toledo area, Campbell[89] recorded summering males in 1956, 1957, and 1961. A nesting pair was also reported from South Bass Island in western Lake Erie in 1950.[290]

During the 1970s, Bewick's Wrens were no longer annually observed within Ohio. A few pairs were occasionally discovered and nesting attempts were reported from Cuyahoga, Muskingum, Belmont, Athens, and Hocking Counties. Even fewer Bewick's Wrens have been noted in the 1980s. A pair successfully raised young in Brown County in 1980 and two pairs were reported from Hamilton County during May 1983, although nesting was not confirmed.[278,370] In 1986, single pairs nested in Pike and Scioto Counties.[434] The Pike County pair returned in 1987 and successfully raised two broods. There have been few additional sight records, and Bewick's Wrens are presently accidental to casual summer residents in the southern counties and strictly accidental elsewhere.

Competition from an expanding House Wren population may have been the primary cause of their disappearance. Whenever territories overlapped, conflicts between these species were inevitable. As witnessed by Newman[334] in Cuyahoga County, Bewick's Wrens invariably disappear after repeated conflicts with the more aggressive House Wrens. But other factors were also involved, since Bewick's Wrens vanished from areas where House Wrens were scarce or absent.[454]

As summer residents, Bewick's Wrens preferred rural homesteads—typically, a small unkempt residence surrounded by trash piles, open outbuildings, and brushy fencerows. They also infrequently occupied orchards and shrubby edge habitats.

Most pairs apparently raised two broods each summer.[200] Nest construction was recorded as early as the last week of March, but most first clutches were produced between mid-April and mid-May. These broods normally fledged by mid-June. Second clutches were initiated in late June or July and adults with dependent young were observed into late August. Bewick's Wrens exhibited a typical adaptability in their choice of nest sites: birdboxes, natural cavities, trash piles, and a wide variety of objects, including old hats, coffee cups, and tin cans placed in undisturbed corners of outbuildings.

The majority of Bewick's Wrens were summer residents. Most appeared between March 15 and April 20. Scattered sightings along Lake Erie indicated that their spring migration continued until May 10–20. Spring overflights were casual to accidental north of their established range. Their fall migration was poorly defined as most wrens simply disappeared from the state. The few records indicated that the bulk of this migration occurred during September and early October.

While most Bewick's Wrens wintered in the southern United States, small numbers apparently remained within Ohio. Although there are few specific records, these wrens were described as rare winter residents in southern Ohio during the 1920s and 1930s.[479] They were casual to accidental winter visitors away from the unglaciated southeastern counties, where the few winter records included single wrens at Cleveland in 1960 and near Toledo in 1962.[89,335]

HOUSE WREN

Troglodytes aedon Vieillot

Of all wrens found in Ohio, House Wrens have most successfully adapted to edge habitats available near rural and urban residences. As their name implies, these plain wrens regularly occupy any suitable house erected for them, assuming adequate foraging sites are present.

The distribution of House Wrens greatly expanded after Ohio was settled. They became common summer residents in most counties by the mid-1800s.[522] Their populations declined during the latter decades of the nineteenth century. Langdon[289] attributed this decline to competition with growing numbers of House Sparrows at Cincinnati. However, sizable wren populations coexisted with House Sparrows elsewhere, so other factors were probably responsible for the reduced numbers. By the turn of the century, breeding House Wrens largely disappeared from southern Ohio and were common only in the northern counties.[193,236]

These reduced populations were short-lived. In fact, increased numbers were evident during the first decades of this century. By 1935, Hicks[220] considered them fairly common to very abundant summer residents in every county but least numerous in southern Ohio. Along the unglaciated Allegheny Plateau, House Wrens were rare residents in Adams and Lawrence Counties and rather rare to uncommon in other counties north to Hocking, Athens, and Washington.[223]

Their populations generally increased in subsequent decades despite brief declines. They are probably still increasing today. House Wrens are presently fairly common to abundant summer residents in most counties. They are most numerous in the northeastern counties and locally in central and western Ohio, especially along streams bordered by mature wooded corridors. While 10–30+ individuals daily are regularly noted in most glaciated counties, totals of 50–75+ may be tallied in locally favorable habitats. These wrens are least numerous in southern Ohio from Adams and Pike Counties east to Washington and Morgan Counties. They are fairly common to locally uncommon residents in these counties and daily totals seldom exceed 3–10.

House Wrens thrive within wooded edge habitats, especially wooded fencerows, woodland edges and openings, orchards, riparian corridors, and shrubby thickets near residences. In addition to birdhouses, House Wrens regularly nest in natural cavities. If these sites are unavailable, breeding pairs may choose pants left on a clothesline, the eaves of buildings, tin cans, clothespin bags, pipes, and mail boxes. House Wrens normally raise two broods. The first nests are initiated in early May and these young fledge by late June. Second nesting attempts begin in early July and these young normally leave the nest in August. A few late nests produced dependent young into early September.[523]

During their spring migration, a few early House Wrens return during the last week of March, but these overflights are unexpected. The first migrants do not normally appear within the central and southern counties until April 12–20 and along Lake Erie by the last week of the month. They become numerous by the first week of May. Spring migrants are mostly individuals returning to their breeding territories, but large flights may develop during the first half of May. These flights are most noticeable along western Lake Erie, where 200 individuals were counted near Toledo on May 14, 1949.[89] Spring concentrations of 40–75 have appeared in other areas.

House Wrens are regularly detected until the males quit singing in late July or early August. They become surprisingly inconspicuous late in the summer. As a result, their fall migration is poorly defined. It apparently begins in early September, marked by the gradual disappearance of resident wrens.[479] Fall totals of these uncommon to fairly common migrants seldom exceed 1–8 individuals. House Wrens are regularly observed through October 5–15. The last migrants occasionally remain until late October or the first week of November.

When weather conditions are favorable, lingering House Wrens may survive into early winter. They are accidental to casual visitors during December, averaging one acceptable sighting every two to four years. These early winter records are scattered across Ohio but are more likely in the central and southern counties. Virtually all of these wrens succumb to the rigors of a typical Ohio winter. The only confirmed sighting after the first week of January was furnished by a House Wren overwintering in Hamilton County during 1949–50.[248]

WINTER WREN

Troglodytes troglodytes (Linnaeus)

One cannot help but be enchanted by these tiny energetic wrens. Hardly more than small balls of brown feathers with short wings and virtually no tails, Winter Wrens actively forage close to the ground within deciduous woods. At times they are frustrating to observe as they fly from thicket to thicket and immediately disappear into dense tangles. On other occasions they are inquisitive and react to the presence of an observer by hopping on a log, bouncing up and down on their short legs, and repeatedly scolding with their sharp call notes.

Despite their size, Winter Wrens are not daunted by a normal Ohio winter. They spend the winter in underbrush, tangles, piles of debris, and other cover in woodlands and wooded stream valleys. They are seldom found away from woody cover, although Campbell[89] observed them in herbaceous cover at the edge of marshes.

Their winter status fluctuates in response to weather conditions. Numbers are decreased following severe winters but gradually improve during successive mild seasons. In addition to these weather-induced fluctuations, their wintering numbers have experienced gradual long-term declines. These declines are most apparent in the central and southern counties, where these wrens were formerly regular residents and 3–8+ individuals were observed daily before 1950.

Winter Wrens are presently uncommon winter residents in the southern and unglaciated eastern counties, where 1–5 may be observed daily. They are generally absent from the northeastern snow-belt counties of Lake, Geauga, and Ashtabula. Elsewhere, they are casual to rare residents as widely scattered individuals. Even during the mildest seasons, their numbers are greatest before January 15 and noticeably decline by mid-February.

Winter Wrens are normally most numerous as migrants. They prefer brushy woodlands but are also found in shrubbery in parks, cemeteries, and residential areas; fallow fields with scattered bushes; and barren riprap along dams. As spring migrants, the earliest Winter Wrens may appear during the first half of March, although they do not normally return until March 25–30. Their northward movement peaks between April

5 and 22. These migrants normally depart from the interior counties by the end of April, but small numbers remain along Lake Erie until May 7–15.

In spring these wrens are most numerous along Lake Erie, where they are fairly common to common migrants. While 3–10 individuals are observed along the lakefront during most days, larger flights may produce tallies of 20–30. A remarkable flight concentrated 200 at Magee Marsh Wildlife Area on April 15, 1972.[90] Fewer pass through the interior counties, where they are uncommon to fairly common migrants. Spring totals seldom exceed 1–6 daily at most inland sites. Larger flights are restricted to central Ohio, where Trautman[479] reported a maximum of 50 at Buckeye Lake and 60 appeared at Columbus on April 18, 1975.[259]

The first fall migrants are usually detected along Lake Erie, occasionally during the first week of September but frequently not until September 15–22. They are not expected in the southern counties until September 27–October 5. Peak numbers may pass along Lake Erie between October 1 and 10 but are more likely within the interior counties during the last half of the month. A few migrants appear throughout November and may continue until the first sizable December snowstorm.[479]

Fall migrants are also most numerous along Lake Erie, where Winter Wrens become fairly common in October. Daily totals of 3–10 are expected along the lakefront. Following strong cold fronts, flights may produce concentrations of 20–35+ and as many as 75 have been reported in one day. They are uncommon fall migrants in most interior counties, where 1–5 may be observed daily. The largest inland fall flights have involved totals of only 10–12.

In recent years, a small breeding population has been discovered in northeastern Ohio. Summering Winter Wrens are largely restricted to the hemlock gorges along the Chagrin River watershed in Lake, Geauga, and Cuyahoga Counties. They were initially recorded there in 1926; territorial males also appeared in 1938, 1947, and 1948.[523] These wrens were believed to be unmated. Ohio's first nesting record was established in 1964 when adults accompanied by two dependent young were noted at Bedford Reservation (Cuyahoga County) on July 11.[335] Since 1969, a few pairs presumably nested in hemlock woods at Stebbins Gulch and Little Mountain. They have also sporadically appeared in eastern Cuyahoga County. This population does not normally exceed 3–8 pairs.

Away from northeastern Ohio, Winter Wrens are accidental summer residents. The only confirmed nesting attempt was established at Conkles Hollow Nature Preserve (Hocking County) in 1974. Winter Wrens also summered in Mohican State Forest (Ashland County) in 1981 and Hocking County in 1982.[177,367] These males were believed to be unmated. Winter Wrens have reportedly summered in deciduous woodlots near western Lake Erie but were undoubtedly nonbreeders.

Breeding Winter Wrens are restricted to cool mesic ravines where hemlocks predominate or are mixed with deciduous trees. They prefer areas with dense underbrush, overturned trees, and similar cover. Their nests are placed on the ground, frequently hidden among tree roots or fallen logs. The few confirmed Ohio breeding attempts have been initiated in May, with the young fledging in June or early July.

SEDGE WREN

Cistothorus platensis (Latham)

The Sedge Wren has a reputation as an erratic summer resident whose movements frequently defy logical explanation. Breeding pairs are as likely to appear in mid-July as mid-May, and they seldom occupy the same nesting territories for two consecutive years. These erratic movements became even more noticeable in recent decades as this wren's populations declined. Since Ohio lies near the eastern edge of their range, Sedge Wrens were always locally distributed and relatively rare summer residents. In the mid-1930s, Hicks[220] cited summer records from thirty-five counties. Sedge Wrens were usually noted at only one to three localities in each county, mostly 5 or fewer males, although a few "colonies" of 10–30 males also existed. The largest and most dependable populations occupied the Oak Openings and former Pymatuning Bog, where 20–25 males were recorded most years.[2,89] They were accidental to rare within the southern counties and along the unglaciated Allegheny Plateau, usually as isolated males, although colonies of 9 and 26 singing males were reported from Muskingum County in 1934.[222]

These populations declined in subsequent decades. In the Oak Openings, numbers of singing males were reduced to 10 by 1941 and 1 in 1947. They completely disappeared by 1950.[89] The declines were equally dramatic within the northeastern counties, where every colony disappeared prior to 1940.[2] Elsewhere, summering Sedge Wrens repeatedly failed to appear in most counties. In subsequent decades, occasional "flights" produced a flurry of sightings during some years, but these movements never resulted in permanent breeding populations.

Sedge Wrens are presently rare but regular summer residents within wetlands bordering Lake Erie and Sandusky Bay in Ottawa and Lucas Counties. They are usually detected at one to four localities each year, mostly as groups of 4 or fewer territorial males and a total population of no more than 3–15 males. Elsewhere, Sedge Wrens are accidental to casual summer residents within the northern and western counties, where they are usually discovered at one to five locations each year but do not consistently appear at any site.[434] Most reports are of 5 or fewer males and the total population is less than 15 pairs. Sedge Wrens are accidental summer residents elsewhere.

As their name implies, Sedge Wrens are occupants of sedge meadows, wet prairies, and grassy borders of wetlands. They prefer areas with damp soils or even rather dry upland fields. Their nests are globular structures located close to the ground in dense vegetation. They begin nesting in late May or early June with the young fledging by July. After this brood is raised, they frequently shift breeding locations. These shifts may only be from one wet meadow to an adjacent one. At other times, small "flights" apparently move into Ohio from nearby states. Their second nesting attempts are initiated in late July and the young may not fledge until September 15–20.

Their spring migration is poorly defined. While overflights appeared at Cleveland by March 24–April 7,[117,523] the first migrants have not returned to other locations until the last week of April. Most spring Sedge Wrens are detected between May 5 and 22. These migrants are casual to rare along Lake Erie, with most sightings of 1–4 individuals. They are accidental to casual elsewhere, with three or fewer reports annually. When their breeding populations were larger, spring Sedge Wrens were generally casual to uncommon migrants and daily totals seldom exceeded 6 individuals.[479,523]

Sedge Wrens are slightly more numerous as fall migrants. These migrants are also most frequently observed along Lake Erie, where they are presently casual to locally uncommon in totals of 1–5. They become accidental to locally rare migrants through the interior counties, mostly within the western half of the state. Even when the breeding populations were larger, their fall status was similar. These migrants are most likely to appear between September 15 and October 15, with a few remaining through the end of October. They become accidental visitors after November 5. Migrant Sedge Wrens prefer wet meadows and grassy habitats, but are also observed in dry weedy fields, especially along Lake Erie.

Sedge Wrens have always been accidental winter visitors. There are only two published December records: single wrens in Lucas County on December 24, 1939, and near Dayton on December 28, 1940.[89,299] A Jackson County specimen collected on March 10, 1932, apparently overwintered.[476]

MARSH WREN

Cistothorus palustris (Wilson)

Marsh Wrens might also be known as "cattail wrens" since they nest only in cattail marshes in Ohio. An aggressive and vocal bird, this wren produces a distinctive, rollicking song that carries across the marsh while the singer remains hidden in dense vegetation.

Like most of Ohio's wetland avifauna, Marsh Wrens substantially declined in numbers during this century. In the early 1900s, Jones[236] considered them abundant residents in most large marshes, recognizing that they were locally distributed and absent from areas lacking suitable wetlands. Their statewide distribution was better defined by Hicks.[220] In the mid-1930s, these wrens were numerous in the western Lake Erie marshes and were regularly encountered in most northeastern counties. They were locally distributed elsewhere, with nesting records from forty-three counties south to Columbiana, Carroll, Guernsey, Muskingum, Perry, Fairfield, Pickaway, Champaign, Mercer, and Shelby.

Despite declining populations, statewide totals were substantial. For example, Trautman[479] estimated at least 200 males at Buckeye Lake in the 1920s and 1930s. Similar numbers were probably present at Lake St. Mary's.[98] Campbell[86] estimated 150 males in the Cedar Point marshes (Lucas County) on July 18, 1936, and remarked that summering Marsh Wrens were encountered "wherever there is a patch of cattails of any size."

The inland population substantially declined between 1940 and 1960. At Buckeye Lake, only a few pairs remained by the early 1960s. Marsh Wrens were common at Lake St. Mary's through 1950 but virtually disappeared during the next ten years.[98] As these populations were declining, Marsh Wrens expanded into the southwestern counties. They have annually nested at Spring Valley Wildlife Area (Warren County) since 1952 and sporadically appeared near Cincinnati.[248]

Populations remained stable in northern Ohio marshes into the 1960s. Marsh Wrens were widely distributed within the northeastern counties and numerous along western Lake Erie, where Anderson[7] estimated 100 males in the Winous Point marshes (Ottawa County) in 1960. These populations declined after 1970[90] and may still be declining.

Marsh Wrens are now fairly common to common summer residents in the marshes bordering Sandusky Bay and western Lake Erie. Most marshes support only 2–6 males, although 10–20+ individuals still inhabit large undisturbed wetlands. They are generally uncommon and locally distributed summer residents in northeastern Ohio, with small numbers scattered within most counties south to Columbiana, Stark, and Wayne. They are casual to rare and very locally distributed residents elsewhere south to Belmont, Licking, Madison, Clark, and Warren Counties.[434] While as many as 25 males may reside at Spring Valley Wildlife Area, most inland colonies have 1–5 males. Breeding Marsh Wrens are generally absent elsewhere except for a nesting record at Senecaville Reservoir in 1977.[171]

Male Marsh Wrens are polygamous, frequently building "dummy nests" as they attempt to attract several females into their territories. Nesting activities are usually initiated by mid-May. First clutches are mostly noted between May 20 and June 15, while later clutches may be laid through August 4.[89,479] Nests with young may be discovered by May 25 and recently fledged young may appear between early June and mid-August.

In recent years, spring migrations mostly include birds returning to their breeding territories. While the first Marsh Wrens may arrive between April 20 and 30, they are not normally encountered until May 5–10. This migration continues through May 25–30. These migrants are casual to rare within marshes in the southern and eastern counties where they do not breed, appearing mostly as scattered singles.

When populations were larger, their northward movements were impressive. Trautman[479] regularly observed "hundreds" of Marsh Wrens daily at Buckeye Lake during the 1920s and 1930s; peak movements between May 8 and 20 produced flights of "thousands." While similar numbers were not reported elsewhere, large numbers also must have accumulated along western Lake Erie. Spring movements were slightly earlier then, with individuals regularly appearing throughout Ohio by April 20–25.

Their southward migration was always less conspicuous. Even when their breeding populations were larger, no sizable fall flights were reported. Presently, 3–10 individuals are observed daily during autumn in the marshes where they regularly breed. Away from their established breeding range, Marsh Wrens are accidental to rare fall migrants with most sightings consisting of single wrens. According to Trautman,[479] their southward passage normally peaks during the last three weeks of September. Smaller numbers may be regularly observed through October 10–20, while occasional late migrants remain into November. Fall Marsh Wrens may be found far from wetlands. Small numbers regularly appear in weedy fields along Lake Erie. Within the interior counties, they have been observed in fallow fields and brushy edge habitats.

As early as the 1930s, Trautman[476] believed "a few individuals winter practically every year in the Lake Erie marshes." While Campbell[89] cited only fourteen winter records from the Toledo area through 1968, winter Marsh Wrens have been observed almost annually in subsequent years, confirming Trautman's belief. These wrens are presently casual to rare winter residents along western Lake Erie, averaging one to two sightings annually. While most were discovered during December and the first half of January, a few have survived until spring. Elsewhere, the number of winter records has declined as breeding populations disappeared. Wintering Marsh Wrens are accidental to casual visitors away from western Lake Erie, averaging one record every two or three years. These records are fairly well distributed, although there are no recent winter sightings along the unglaciated Allegheny Plateau.

GOLDEN-CROWNED KINGLET

Regulus satrapa Lichtenstein

A midwinter's walk through a cold Ohio woodlot is always enlivened by the appearance of tiny Golden-crowned Kinglets nervously moving through the bare trees. Their greenish plumage with the male's brilliant orange crown or the female's yellow crown provides a touch of color to an otherwise drab landscape. Golden-crowned Kinglets frequently associate with woodpeckers, chickadees, titmice, and other birds in mixed-species flocks foraging for insect eggs and pupae among dead leaves and barren branches. These kinglets are a bundle of energy, constantly flicking their wings and actively flitting from branch to branch in their search for food.

Golden-crowned Kinglets are uncommon to fairly common winter residents of pine plantations, hemlock groves, and ornamental conifers throughout Ohio. If conifers are absent, they will occupy dense shrubby thickets and brushy woodlots. Wintering Golden-crowned Kinglets are widely distributed, a status they have maintained since the 1800s.[236] While they tend to be slightly less numerous in the northern counties, they are locally common winter residents in the cedar thickets on the western Lake Erie islands. Most locations support only 1–5 individuals, although flocks of 10–15 may occupy extensive groves of conifers. Daily totals seldom exceed 10–30.

Their wintering numbers are subject to dramatic fluctuations in response to severe weather. Prolonged cold temperatures and ice storms can take a considerable toll of these diminutive birds, and they can become rather scarce during February and March in severe winters. In particular, the extremely harsh winters of 1976–78 decimated populations throughout eastern North America.[438]

The largest numbers of Golden-crowneds occur during fall, especially along Lake Erie, where they may become abundant migrants. They normally return to the lakefront by September 15–22. Substantial movements may occur during the first week of October. By far the largest flight ever recorded produced an estimated 25,000–50,000 on South Bass Island on October 7, 1954.[89] Other pronounced flights have produced 100–500+ during October. Numbers of migrants are greatly diminished during November.

While a Golden-crowned Kinglet appeared at Cincinnati as early as September 11, 1985,[380] the first migrants normally appear during the last days of September. The peak occurs by mid-October. These fall migrants are fairly common to locally common in most counties, normally producing daily totals of 5–30 individuals. The largest inland flight totaled only 70 in central Ohio.[479]

As a result of winter mortality, fewer Golden-crowneds appear each spring, although they are still fairly common to common migrants. Most observations are of 20 or fewer, with occasional flights of 50–150 reported from central Ohio and along Lake Erie. The first migrants normally appear by March 20–30, with the largest concentrations reported during the first three weeks of April. They usually depart from all inland locations by the end of April, but a few linger along Lake Erie through May 7–10. They become quite rare later in the month but have remained through May 27, 1983, at Dayton[299] and May 30, 1954, at Cleveland.[117]

They are accidental summer visitors to Ohio, with one July and one mid-August sighting from the Cleveland area.[117,335] These kinglets were presumably nonbreeders.

RUBY-CROWNED KINGLET

Regulus calendula (Linnaeus)

Unlike Golden-crowneds, Ruby-crowned Kinglets are mostly known as migrants through Ohio. Since they primarily spend the winter months in the southeastern United States, the numbers appearing each spring reflect the severity of the preceding winter in that region. Unusually severe winters such as those of 1976–78 can cause extensive mortality among Ruby-crowneds and sharply reduce the number of migrants.[438]

Their spring arrival is announced by the loud and remarkably complex songs produced by the spritely little males. Migrant Ruby-crowneds frequently associate with Golden-crowneds, forming small flocks actively foraging through woodlands, wooded edges, parks, and shaded residential areas. Unlike Golden-crowneds, they do not show a strong preference for conifers. The majority of Ruby-crowneds are found in brushy thickets or dense saplings, although they will also forage in the upper branches of tall trees.

While the first migrants may return during the last days of March, they are not usually encountered until the first week of April. They are most numerous between April 15 and May 10, when they become fairly common to common migrants across Ohio. Daily totals are generally 10–25 individuals, with large flights occasionally producing concentrations of 40–60. The largest reported spring flight was of 120 at Columbus on April 26, 1959.[471] Numbers of migrants noticeably decline during the second week of May. Most depart from the interior counties by May 16–18, although they have been recorded as late as May 27, 1983, at Dayton and May 31, 1925, near Columbus.[45,370] Late May stragglers are more frequently reported along Lake Erie, where a few have lingered through June 7.

Ruby-crowneds are accidental nonbreeding summer visitors to Ohio; the few summer records have been during June. A Ruby-crowned at Wooster (Wayne County) on June 6, 1971, was most likely a very late migrant. One reported from Old Mans Cave State Park in Hocking County on June 13, 1974, was described by Worth Randle as a male in full song. He was found within a hemlock woods and may have been on territory but could not be subsequently relocated. The latest Ruby-crowned remained in the Cleveland area through June 28, 1954.[117]

A remarkably early fall migrant Ruby-crowned returned to Cleveland by August 16, 1953, and a few may occasionally accompany large flights of warblers and vireos during the last days of the month.[117] Early migrants also returned to central Ohio by August 22, 1931, and Cincinnati by August 30, 1936.[45,248] Their migration does not normally begin until the last half of September. Fall migrants are most numerous along Lake Erie, where they become common to locally abundant between September 25 and October 20. The largest flights produced 400 Ruby-crowneds at Ottawa Wildlife Refuge on October 5, 1986, and several other reports of 100–200+.[384] Daily totals normally are 5–40 along the lakefront. Fall migrants are decidedly less numerous through the interior counties. They are fairly common during the first three weeks of October, with generally 3–12 individuals daily. The largest inland fall flights have totaled only 20–30 Ruby-crowneds. Their numbers decline rapidly during late October and the last migrants are normally observed between November 3 and 10.

Ruby-crowned Kinglets were formerly accidental winter visitors to Ohio, with very few records before 1940. Numbers of winter sightings have noticeably increased during the past thirty years and Ruby-crowneds have become casual to rare but regular early winter visitors. There are usually four to ten winter records annually, the majority in the southern and central counties. Most reports are of isolated individuals, although as many as 8 were noted on the Dayton Christmas Bird Count in 1949.[299] Winter Ruby-crowneds are mostly discovered within dense shrubby woodland thickets or shrub-dominated successional habitats. Most winter records are during December or the first half of January. However, a few have survived the rigors of an Ohio winter.

BLUE-GRAY GNATCATCHER

Polioptila caerulea (Linnaeus)

Blue-gray Gnatcatchers can be remarkably early spring migrants, frequently returning before there are many gnats to catch. The earliest arrivals have been noted between March 25 and 31, mostly as overflights along Lake Erie, while small numbers of migrants regularly return to the southern counties by the first week of April.

Within the central and northern counties, gnatcatchers normally return by April 10–16. Their maximum abundance is attained between April 20 and May 5. Spring gnatcatchers are fairly common to common migrants throughout the southern and unglaciated eastern counties, where daily totals of 10–20 individuals are not unusual and as many as 30–40 may be observed. These totals include resident pairs and migrants. They are uncommon to locally common migrants through the glaciated central counties, where 3–12+ gnatcatchers may be observed daily. Their spring status within the northern counties has greatly improved since 1970. Blue-gray Gnatcatchers are presently uncommon to locally common migrants in most northern counties. While as many as 10–20+ have been observed along Lake Erie, similar concentrations are not expected away from the lakefront, where only 1–5 individuals are normally detected. The last migrants depart lakefront migrant traps by May 15–20.

Breeding gnatcatchers occupy mature woodlands with many tall trees. They exhibit a preference for swamp forests but will also inhabit upland woods and mature riparian corridors. Their nests are mostly placed at heights of twenty to sixty feet, anchored to fairly stout limbs. These compact structures are composed of lichens and spider webs, although other material is gathered for their lining. Within the southern counties, nest construction begins during the last half of April and clutches are completed by early May. Fledglings may appear by the last week of the month but are mostly noted in June. Their nesting activities are delayed by two to three weeks in the northern counties, where the earliest clutches have been discovered by mid-May and fledglings are not expected until the last half of June.[479,523] Renesting attempts and second clutches have produced nests with young well into July.

As summer residents, gnatcatchers have been increasing during this century. In the mid-1930s, Hicks[220] considered them uncommon to abundant residents in the southern two-thirds of Ohio, with the largest numbers along the unglaciated Allegheny Plateau. They were rare to absent and very locally distributed within the northern counties.

Their northward expansion was most apparent after 1960, a trend noted throughout eastern North America.[438] Blue-gray Gnatcatchers are now fairly common to common summer residents throughout the southern counties and the unglaciated Allegheny Plateau. Since they become inconspicuous once nesting is under way, summer totals seldom exceed 5–15 gnatcatchers daily within these counties. Gnatcatchers have become fairly common residents in the central counties and northeastern Ohio, where 3–8 individuals may be detected daily. Breeding pairs are least numerous in the intensively farmed west-central and northwestern counties, where gnatcatchers are locally rare to fairly common summer residents.[434] Most reports are of 5 or fewer gnatcatchers within these western counties.

Their southward migration has always been poorly defined. This movement normally begins during the first half of August and continues through mid-September. The last fall migrants are usually recorded between September 20 and 30 with very few sightings in October. A migrant at Headlands State Park (Lake County) on November 1–3, 1987, was exceptionally late.[388] Fall gnatcatchers are most evident within the southern and unglaciated eastern counties, where they are uncommon to fairly common migrants. They are generally uncommon in the glaciated central counties and rare to uncommon in northern Ohio. Most fall sightings are of individuals or groups of 2–4.

Blue-gray Gnatcatchers are accidental early winter visitors to Ohio. There have been at least five December records of single gnatcatchers at Buckeye Lake, Tiffin, Ottawa County, Lowell (Washington County), and near Cincinnati. The latest records were provided by gnatcatchers at Lowell on December 24, 1971,[159] and Mariemont (Hamilton County) on December 27–28, 1987. It is unlikely that this insectivorous species could survive an Ohio winter.

NORTHERN WHEATEAR

Oenanthe oenanthe (Linnaeus)

These members of the thrush family breed from Greenland across Eurasia to Alaska and the Yukon Territories in western North America.[5] They normally spend the winter months in Africa and southern Asia. Migrant Northern Wheatears are very rare but fairly regular visitors to eastern North America, primarily along the Atlantic Coast in autumn. Small numbers have also been detected as spring migrants, but there are exceptionally few winter records from our continent.

Hence, the appearance of a wintering Northern Wheatear in Ohio was completely unexpected. This individual was discovered by Mark Shieldcastle on January 4, 1988, in a frozen marsh adjacent to a marina near Lake Erie in Ottawa County. It roosted in the marsh and apparently was subsisting on spiders and insects captured on the boat docks. It was banded on January 17 and viewed by a number of observers through January 21. Plumage characteristics indicated that it was not an adult male. Its measurements suggested that it was a member of one of the Eurasian races or a small representative of the Greenland race.

EASTERN BLUEBIRD

Sialia sialis (Linnaeus)

Dawson[102] eloquently described the first spring flocks of Eastern Bluebirds:

How the waiting countryside thrills with joy when Bluebird brings us the first word of returning spring. . . . The cruel north wind may sweep down again and all the ugly signs of winter return, but Bluebird has kindled in our hearts the fires of an inextinguishable confidence. . . . Surely there is nothing in nature more heartening than the resolute courage and sublime good cheer of this dauntless bird. Reflecting heaven from his back and the ground from his breast, he floats between sky and earth like the winged voice of Hope.

Bluebirds may be expected during the last half of February except along Lake Erie, where they may not appear until the first week of March. Their northward movements normally peak between March 10 and April 5, although occasional bluebirds may be heard passing overhead through the first week of May. The appearance of bluebirds at Cleveland lakefront migrant traps as late as May 27 is perplexing but may only represent extraordinarily late spring migrants.[382]

Spring bluebirds are normally observed as pairs returning to their breeding territories or as small flocks. Most spring sightings are of 30 or fewer bluebirds. Large flights are unusual, although movements of 65–120 individuals have been reported from central and northern Ohio.[89,479]

Breeding bluebirds prefer open habitats, especially grassy fields and roadsides with scattered trees, fencerows, and telephone wires. They regularly nest near rural residences but avoid developed residential areas. The most critical component of their territory is a suitable cavity for nesting, within a tree, a fencepost, or a birdbox. Most territories are established during March, but nesting activities do not normally begin until the last week of the month within the southern counties and the first half of April elsewhere. Eastern Bluebirds normally raise two or three broods annually. While a complete clutch has been reported by March 11, most first clutches are noted after April 10. These young fledge during the last half of May or early June. Additional nesting attempts may produce clutches through mid-July and dependent young well into August.[479,523]

Ohio's bluebird population undoubtedly expanded during the nineteenth century and became widely distributed by the late 1800s.[522] During the past 100 years, their populations have dramatically fluctuated in response to severe weather and intense interspecific competition for nesting cavities. Prolonged cold and snow cover can cause extensive mortality of both wintering bluebirds and recently returned migrants. The most famous episode occurred during the spring of 1895 when the sudden return of winter weather nearly eliminated bluebirds from the Great Lakes states and New England.[102] Marked declines also followed the severe winters of 1958–60 and 1976–78.[438] After unusually harsh weather, breeding bluebirds may become quite scarce, with only a few scattered pairs where they would normally be numerous. Their populations usually quickly recover, although complete recovery may require three to six years after the most severe declines.

Breeding Eastern Bluebirds are now most numerous in the southern and unglaciated eastern counties. As common summer residents within these counties, 10–30+ bluebirds may be expected daily during years of normal abundance. They become fairly common to locally common residents within the central and northeastern counties, where summer totals seldom exceed 5–15 bluebirds daily except along established nest box "trails." They are least numerous within the intensively farmed northwestern and west-central counties, where most natural cavities have been eliminated.[434] Bluebirds are generally uncommon summer residents within these counties, becoming common only where nest boxes are provided.

Their fall migration normally begins during the last half of September; the nearly invisible bluebirds are detected by their call notes as they pass overhead. This southward movement peaks in October, when bluebirds become fairly common to common migrants across Ohio. Fall totals seldom exceed 30 bluebirds daily. Larger flights are more apparent in autumn, and movements of 60–120 have been detected in most portions of the state. The largest flights were of 200+ near Utica (Licking County) on October 8, 1957, and a similar number near Dayton

on October 14, 1932.[299,350] While their numbers diminish by early November, some southward movement may still be detected into the last half of December.

Numbers of wintering bluebirds fluctuate with weather conditions. They are most numerous and widely distributed during milder winters but will mostly vacate Ohio when the weather is unusually harsh. During most years, Eastern Bluebirds are fairly common to locally common winter residents within the southern and eastern counties, where 10–35+ individuals may be encountered daily. They are decidedly less numerous elsewhere, becoming uncommon to rare winter residents in the central counties near Columbus and casual to rare residents in the northern and west-central counties. After early January, daily totals seldom exceed 3–8 bluebirds away from southern and eastern Ohio. Wintering bluebirds occupy habitats similar to those of the summer residents but prefer areas with brushy fencerows, thickets, or other cover. Some may even visit woodlands. Since they largely subsist on berries, their abundance and winter movements are dictated by the availability of these foods.

TOWNSEND'S SOLITAIRE

Myadestes townsendi (Audubon)

Townsend's Solitaires are occupants of the western mountains, breeding from Alaska south into Mexico. The northern populations generally retreat into the western United States and Mexico during winter.[5] Like other migratory birds from these mountains, Townsend's Solitaires have demonstrated a tendency to wander east of this range. Small numbers regularly appear from the northern plains across the upper Great Lakes to New England and the Maritime Provinces during winter.

Ohio's first record of this accidental visitor fits this pattern of vagrancy. A Townsend's Solitaire was discovered on December 26, 1938, in Sylvania Township, Lucas County, during the Toledo Christmas Bird Count. It was initially reported by a group led by F. R. Flickinger and was intermittently viewed through January 14, 1939.[86]

The second Townsend's Solitaire was an unexpected discovery at Magee Marsh Wildlife Area. It was discovered by Milton and Mary Trautman, Evelyn Gordon, and Avis Newell on the exceptional date of May 24, 1970. This individual was collected the following day, proving to be an emaciated female in "wretched plumage."[489]

VEERY

Catharus fuscescens (Stephens)

As summer residents, Veeries prefer young moist deciduous woods dominated by dense saplings and shrubby thickets. They easily hide among the dense woody cover and are seldom observed during summer. Their presence is readily detected, however, by their beautiful descending song, cascading from these young woodlands in the early morning and evening hours of late May and June.

The nests of this thrush are difficult to discover in the dense woods, and very little information is available on the Veeries' breeding biology in Ohio. Within the northeastern counties, nest construction has been reported by May 13, although most nests probably are not built until late May or early June.[523] Nests with eggs have been reported between May 18 and June 17 and young have remained in the nest through July 18.[89,523] Most fledglings appear in late June and July.

Breeding Veeries have been gradually expanding their summer range southward. Jones[236] reported only "small numbers" of summering Veeries within the northern counties and alluded to summer records elsewhere in the state in 1903. By the mid-1930s, Hicks[220] considered Veeries local summer residents in northern Ohio, citing records from twenty-four counties south to Paulding, Fulton, Lucas, Seneca, Huron, Ashland, Wayne, Stark, and Columbiana. They were common residents in Ashtabula County and the Oak Openings of Lucas County.[86,215] Elsewhere, they were very locally distributed and generally uncommon residents in the northeastern counties and rare in northwestern Ohio.[220,523]

During subsequent decades, Veeries have noticeably increased within the northern counties and small numbers have expanded into the southern half of Ohio. Today they are fairly common to common summer residents in every northeastern county. As many as 10–20 summering Veeries may be counted daily in portions of Ashtabula, Lake, Geauga, Trumbull, and Portage Counties, although reports seldom exceed 6–10 Veeries in other northeastern counties. In northwestern Ohio, their breeding range is mostly limited to Williams, Fulton, and Lucas Counties plus scattered records south to Seneca County.[434] Veeries remain common residents in the Oak Openings area, where 12–25+ may be noted during June. In other northwestern counties, they are rare to uncommon residents and daily totals mostly are 1–5 Veeries.

Within central Ohio, Veeries have been casual to rare but fairly regular summer residents since the mid-1970s. Records usually are of widely scattered pairs, mostly in counties near Columbus. Along the unglaciated Allegheny Plateau, Veeries are rare residents in portions of Carroll, Jefferson, and Tuscarawas Counties.[434] They are generally absent elsewhere on the plateau except for a few pairs breeding in the Clear Creek Valley of Hocking and Fairfield Counties since 1982.[366] In southwestern Ohio, they are accidental to casual summer residents. There have been sporadic nesting records in Montgomery County since 1958,[299] a Hamilton County summer record in 1964 and a nest in 1966,[394,401] and a summering Veery at Hueston Woods State Park in 1987.[434]

Migrant Veeries are most evident during their northward passage. While they have been reported as early as March 31–April 5 along Lake Erie, there are no substantiated Ohio records until April 13–15. Spring Veeries usually return to the southern and central counties by April 22–28 but are not expected along the lakefront until the first week of May. Spring Veeries are most numerous between May 7 and 21. Small numbers may remain into the first week of June.

These migrants are most numerous along Lake Erie, where they become fairly common to common. Concentrations of 20–40+ Veeries may appear during large flights, with totals of 3–8+ on other days. These thrushes are normally uncommon to locally common migrants elsewhere in the northern and glaciated central counties. Spring totals usually are 1–8 Veeries daily within these counties, although flights have produced as many as 43 at Columbus on May 14, 1981.[471] They are least numerous in the southern and unglaciated eastern counties, where spring Veeries are regarded as uncommon migrants. Except for a remarkable flight of 100 Veeries daily at Cincinnati between April 20 and 24, 1982,[365] most spring records are of fewer than 5.

Veeries are much less conspicuous during their autumn migration. They migrate slightly earlier than the other thrushes, and the first migrants can be expected during the last half of August. Most fall Veeries are reported between August 25 and September 20, with small numbers lingering into the first week of October. There are no substantiated sightings after October 10–18. Fall Veeries are generally uncommon to locally rare migrants across Ohio. Relatively few are detected as night migrants passing over the state. Most fall records are of only 1–5 Veeries.

GRAY-CHEEKED THRUSH

Catharus minimus (Lafresnaye)

At the turn of the century, Gray-cheeked Thrushes were considered rare migrants throughout Ohio.[236] Their nondescript plumage and similarity to the more numerous Swainson's Thrush posed a field identification problem for the early ornithologists. With the advent of better field guides and optical equipment, however, Gray-cheekeds have proven to be more numerous than previously thought, although they are still generally regarded to be the least numerous of the migrant thrushes.

Gray-cheekeds are normally the last thrushes returning to Ohio each spring. Except for an occasional overflight in mid-April, the first arrivals may be encounterd during the last week of April in mild springs and the first week of May during most years. Peak numbers occur between May 12 and 25, when they are uncommon to fairly common migrants along Lake Erie and uncommon elsewhere. Fewer than 10 individuals daily are normally observed along the lakefront and 5 inland. Larger concentrations will occasionally develop, such as the exceptional flight of 45 at Buckeye Lake on May 15, 1932.[479] Only occasional stragglers are encountered in the first week of June.

During fall, Gray-cheekeds are most readily detected at night when migrants utter their distinctive hoarse *quee-ah* call notes as they pass overhead. Largest flights over Westerville (Franklin County) have produced counts in excess of 100 Gray-cheekeds per hour, although rates of 25–50 per hour are more typical.

These movements are not evident to daytime birders, who regard Gray-cheekeds as uncommon to fairly common fall migrants, most numerous along Lake Erie. Daily counts seldom exceed 10 and no sizable concentrations have ever been reported on the ground.

The first fall migrants frequently return during the last week of August. Gray-cheekeds are distributed throughout Ohio by the first week of September, and the largest nighttime flights normally occur during the last three weeks of the month. Numbers are diminished by the first week of October, although large evening movements may still occur in early October. Flights in excess of 50 Gray-cheekeds per hour have been recorded over Westerville as late as October 4. Gray-cheekeds normally depart by mid-October, with a late migrant banded at Cleveland on November 13, 1971.

Their winter range normally is within the rain forests of South America; a few records come from Central America and several Caribbean Islands.[5] There are also a few winter sight records from North America, but most are considered to be misidentifications. One legitimate winter record is a specimen collected in Clermont County on December 28, 1947. It provides the only acceptable winter record from Ohio.[248] While exceptionally late birds are frequently injured, this individual appeared to be healthy.

SWAINSON'S THRUSH

Catharus ustulatus (Nuttall)

The most numerous of the migrant spotted thrushes, Swainson's are found wherever trees and dense shrubbery are available. They abound in young woodlands and swamp forests with dense shrub layers and understories. Smaller numbers are regularly encountered in riparian corridors, parks, cemeteries, and shaded residential areas.

During spring, a few overflights have appeared in central and northern Ohio as early as April 6. The first migrants do not normally return to the southern half of the state until April 22–27 or to Lake Erie by May 1. Their spring arrival is fairly erratic, however, and Swainson's Thrushes may be completely absent until the first week of May and then become widespread overnight. Spring migrants are most numerous between May 10 and 25 when they are fairly common to locally abundant throughout Ohio. Spring reports mostly are of 5–40 individuals daily, although large flights may produce concentrations of 300–400 in central Ohio and along Lake Erie.[89,471,479] Their numbers noticeably decline during the last week of May and a few late migrants regularly linger until June 3–7. The last migrants have occasionally remained along Lake Erie into the second week of June.

Since they are relatively late spring migrants, it is not unusual to hear male Swainson's Thrushes singing during early June. Such observations have led to reports of breeding Swainson's Thrushes in Ohio, reports that have never been adequately verified. No nests have been discovered, and the only record of a "recently fledged juvenile" lacked adequate details to eliminate similar species. A Swainson's Thrush reported from Cleveland during July 1958 was probably a nonbreeding summer visitor, while another apparently summered at Magee Marsh Wildlife Area during 1985.[117,379]

As fall migrants, a few Swainson's Thrushes have returned to northern Ohio by July 25–August 10, although they do not normally appear along the lakefront until the first cold front following August 20. They may not be detected in the southern and central counties until August 27–September 5. This movement peaks between September 10 and October 5 when they become fairly common to locally abundant migrants in every county. Numbers of fall migrants normally decline by October 10 and the last Swainson's Thrushes depart by October 15–20.

Fall Swainson's Thrushes are as numerous as the spring migrants. Fall totals seldom exceed 5–40 individuals daily, although large flights have produced concentrations of 300+ in central Ohio and along Lake Erie.[380,479] Their fall abundance is subject to considerable annual variation, and migrants can be scarce during some years.

Numbers observed on the ground represent a fraction of the population passing over Ohio each fall. Swainson's Thrushes normally are the most numerous songbirds recorded as nighttime migrants. Following the passage of a September cold front, the loud calls of migrant Swainson's are regularly heard from dusk to dawn and counts of 100–300 per hour are not unusual in central Ohio. The largest flights have produced estimates of nearly 1000 per hour.

A few Swainson's Thrushes have lingered quite late into autumn. There are a number of sightings during the last days of October and early November with specimen records through November 13, 1976, at Cincinnati.[264] While Swainson's Thrushes occasionally have been reported during December and January, most of these winter records are believed to be misidentifications. The only documented winter sighting was at Cleveland on December 20, 1980.[360] All winter Swainson's Thrushes should be carefully identified and documented to eliminate the similar Hermit Thrush, which regularly winters in Ohio.

HERMIT THRUSH

Catharus guttatus (Pallas)

In a family renowned for its beautiful songs, no other North American thrush can match this inconspicuous species. Delivered from a perch near the top of a tall conifer, the Hermit Thrush's song begins innocently with several short introductory notes, followed by a brief pause and then a cascade of clear flutelike notes eloquently descending the musical scale. Each repetition produces a remarkably complex yet perceptibly different song, providing an enchanting serenade for all occupants of the cool coniferous forests preferred by Hermit Thrushes.

The presence of breeding Hermit Thrushes is unexpected in Ohio because the state is removed from established populations in Ontario, northern Michigan, and the higher elevations of the Appalachian Mountains.[5] But they have found suitable nesting sites at a few Ohio localities closely resembling their preferred northern coniferous woodlands. Despite anecdotal nineteenth-century nesting accounts at Cincinnati and Cleveland, breeding Hermit Thrushes were initially confirmed at the former Pymatuning Bog in Ashtabula County by Lawrence Hicks.[215,220] Summering birds were noted in 1928, 1930,

1932, and 1933, with nests discovered in the latter two years. The bog's destruction in the mid-1930s eliminated this small isolated population. Summering Hermit Thrushes then went unrecorded until 1953, when two males summered at Conkles Hollow Nature Preserve in Hocking County.[69] Nesting was not confirmed that summer. Worth Randle revisited this site and other hemlock ravines in Hocking County during the 1960s and 1970s. Breeding Hermit Thrushes were discovered at Conkles Hollow only in 1966 and 1976, indicating they were not regular summer residents during those years.[401]

Very small breeding populations are now established at two isolated localities in eastern Ohio. Nesting Hermit Thrushes were initially discovered at Mohican State Forest in Ashland County in 1979 and near Old Man's Cave State Park (Hocking County) in 1982. Three to five pairs annually reside at both sites. A pair also nested in the Cuyahoga Valley Recreation Area (Summit County) during 1983 and 1984. Occasional unmated males have briefly established territories at several other eastern Ohio hemlock ravines.[434] To date, their nesting chronology has been poorly documented. Nest construction has been observed between late April and early June; fledged young are expected in June or early July.

Most observers recognize Hermit Thrushes as familiar migrants, more numerous during spring. They are generally considered fairly common or common spring migrants, but their numbers are subject to considerable fluctuations. Hermits are the first "brown thrushes" returning to Ohio. They appear in the southern counties by March 20–30 and along Lake Erie by the first week of April. Peak numbers, normally encountered between April 15 and 30, produce daily counts of 5–30 individuals along the lakefront and occasional flights involving as many as 250 on April 29, 1934, and 300 on April 15, 1972, near Toledo.[86,90] Inland Hermits are normally encountered as daily totals of 3–15 with peaks of 25–4 10. While Trautman[479] reported spring counts of 200 at Buckeye Lake during the 1920s and 1930s, similar flights have not been reported recently. Most migrants depart from inland localities by May 5–10, although a few linger along Lake Erie through May 15–20.

As fall migrants, Hermit Thrushes are generally uncommon or fairly common visitors. Daily totals seldom exceed 3–20 individuals. Largest concentrations totaled 75–95 at Buckeye Lake before 1940 and along Lake Erie.[89,479] Like the spring migrants, fall Hermits are most numerous near the lakefront. The earliest migrants return to northern Ohio during the first half of September, but most arrive between September 20 and 27 along Lake Erie and by October 1–5 elsewhere. Fall migration peaks during the first three weeks of October, and small numbers regularly remain through mid-November.

While most Hermit Thrushes winter in the southeastern United States, small numbers are regular winter residents in Ohio. Their winter status is poorly documented since they are inconspicuous and difficult to locate. The only indication of their presence may be a sharp *chuck* note uttered from dense cover. Hermit Thrushes are known as locally uncommon winter residents of southeastern Ohio woodlands, where as many as 1–6 individuals may be tallied. They are generally less numerous elsewhere, usually casually or rarely encountered as isolated individuals. Surprisingly, the largest wintering con-

centration occurs on Kelleys Island in western Lake Erie where dense red cedar and dogwood thickets provide abundant food and cover. Only a small proportion of these wintering Hermit Thrushes are detected, but as many as 39 have been recorded in early December.[377]

WOOD THRUSH

Hylocichla mustelina (Gmelin)

The woodlands are remarkably peaceful as another calm, warm June day approaches dusk. In the distance, the silence is broken by the clear flutelike phrases of a Wood Thrush. At this time of day, he seems to be the only living bird as his song echoes through the still woods. His serenade continues until dark, when a series of sharp call notes signals the end of another summer day. The next morning, when these woods are alive with the chorus of a multitude of birds, the Wood Thrush will briefly join the chorus, but usually only as a background voice lost amid the clamor. He saves his prime vocalizations for the evening hours when they can be fully appreciated.

Persons who appreciate high-quality bird songs will be glad to know that Wood Thrushes are fairly common to common summer residents of woodlands throughout Ohio. While they prefer mesic woods with well-defined understories, they are found in most any woods that have a complete canopy and are not heavily grazed or recently cutover. They are at home in hemlock forests but avoid uniform pine plantations and seldom reside in shaded residential areas.

Like other woodland occupants, summering Wood Thrushes are most numerous within the southern and eastern counties, where they are common and widely distributed. They are least numerous in the west-central and northwestern counties, where they remain common only along extensive riparian corridors or woodland preserves such as the Oak Openings of Lucas County. Within the most intensively cultivated counties, they become fairly common or even locally uncommon summer residents.[434] Generally 10–20 Wood Thrushes are counted daily in southern and eastern Ohio, although daily tallies seldom exceed 2–8 in the western counties. While Wood Thrush populations remain fairly stable in eastern Ohio, numbers are slowly declining elsewhere as breeding habitats are destroyed. This habitat destruction, along with the loss of wintering areas in Central America, may be responsible for declines in their continental populations since 1965.[438]

The earliest spring migrants return as overflights along Lake Erie. There is only one late March sighting, but several migrants have appeared during the first week of April. The first migrants normally return to southern Ohio by April 15–20 and are regularly encountered throughout the southern half of the state by April 25–30. Wood Thrushes are expected along Lake Erie by May 1–5. Their spring migration is mostly individuals returning to their territories. Spring totals seldom exceed 5–20 daily; the largest reported concentration was only 35. The last migrants normally depart from lakefront migrant traps by May 20–25.

Upon their return, Wood Thrushes immediately initiate the process of raising their broods. Nest construction begins during the first half of May and nests with eggs have been reported as early as May 16–18 in central and northern Ohio.[479,523] Adults accompanied by young have been reported as early as the first week of June.[299,479] Some adults may raise two broods. Later breeding attempts are responsible for nest construction during the first week of July and nests with young as late as August 28.[523]

Once they cease singing, Wood Thrushes become very inconspicuous and considerably fewer are detected after August 1. Their fall migration is very poorly defined. The largest fall concentration is only 18 and fall totals seldom exceed 1–5 daily. Wood Thrushes are regularly encountered through the third week of September; most depart by the end of the month. Small numbers remain into October, a few into November. There are at least two confirmed December records from Ohio and several undocumented records. One Wood Thrush survived at a Willoughby feeder through January 10, 1975.

AMERICAN ROBIN

Turdus migratorius Linnaeus

Our most familiar native songbirds, Robins can be seen almost any summer day quietly gathering worms on residential lawns in suburban and rural Ohio. Few native species have adapted so successfully to man-made habitats as the American Robin; its density may reach one pair per acre on large mowed lawns with scattered shade trees.[523] Robins are also at home in parks, cemeteries, and similar habitats. A few pairs prefer open second-growth woodlands. Unlike the suburban Robins, which are tame and easily observed, woodland nesting pairs are remarkably furtive and only provide fleeting glimpses as they disappear into the foliage.

Their true abundance is apparent at dawn, when virtually every male Robin greets the new day with a brief chorus. Robins are common to abundant summer residents in every county. Generally 40–100+ individuals are detected daily, with larger numbers in most urban areas.

When the state was initially settled, Robins were probably rather rare inhabitants of the younger woods and woodland edges. Their populations exploded during the nineteenth century as forests were cleared. They have been common to abundant summer residents since the mid-1800s.[522] However, their populations have fluctuated. Declines are apparent following unusually harsh winters. Robin populations were decimated by the widespread use of harmful pesticides during the 1950s and 1960s. Once these pesticides were banned, their numbers significantly increased.[438]

Their nesting habits are very well known. Their mud and grass nests are normally placed in trees but in rare instances are located on the ground. An adaptable species, Robins have nested on bridges, buildings, porch lights, and fence posts, inside barns, and even in tree cavities.[417,458] They normally raise two or three broods each summer. Nest construction begins during late March or early April and the first nests with eggs are expected between March 31 and April 15. Recently

fledged young have appeared by April 18 but are most apparent during the last half of May.[479] Second clutches are mostly reported between May 25 and June 30 with fledging in late July and early August. A few late pairs may feed dependent young through Sepember 20.[89] An exceptionally late pair was incubating eggs in Columbiana County on November 10–11, 1933.[21] There have even been two winter nesting records. In Columbus, a pair started nest construction on December 12, 1965, and hatched their eggs January 6–7 but abandoned the nest two days later because of cold temperatures and the absence of food.[287] Another winter Robin's nest with eggs was reported from Cincinnati on January 17, 1955.[347]

Robins become even more numerous during their seasonal migrations. Their northward movements begin with the advent of warming temperatures, normally in the last half of February. These movements usually peak during March when as many as 100–500 Robins may be observed daily and flights of 1000–2000+ have been reported. Smaller numbers continue to pass northward through the first half of April.

Robins begin to retire to woodland habitats during late July and August. By early September, most Robins abandon residential yards in favor of woodlands, where roosts of 100–1000+ individuals may be encountered. Their southward movements usually begin by mid-September. These migrants are most visible during October; flocks may still pass through the state until mid-November.

Before 1940, winter Robins were regularly encountered in southern Ohio, becoming uncommon in the central counties and rather rare along Lake Erie.[86,236,479] Sizable winter roosts were only reported from the southern counties.[193] The largest central Ohio winter flocks totaled 100–300 Robins, while most northern sightings were of 25 or fewer.

Since 1950, their wintering numbers have dramatically increased. With their dependence on fruit-producing trees, the size and distribution of these wintering flocks fluctuate annually. These flocks are frequently nomadic, remaining at any locality only as long as fruits are available and then traveling considerable distances in search of food. Hence, sizable influxes during January and early February are regular occurrences in all portions of the state.

American Robins are now generally uncommon to fairly common winter residents, becoming common in southwestern Ohio near Cincinnati. Most winter sightings are of 50 or fewer Robins with occasional concentrations of 100–250. On rare occasions, sizable winter roosts develop in association with starlings and blackbirds. These roosts have formed throughout the state but are most regularly reported from the Cincinnati area. Most are composed of 2000 or fewer Robins. The largest roosts have included 3000 Robins at Painesville, 5500+ at Lorain, 6000 at Utica (Licking County), and a remarkable 15,000+ at Cincinnati during the winters of 1958–59 and 1964–65.[322,396]

VARIED THRUSH

Ixoreus naevius (Gmelin)

Varied Thrushes normally breed in mature coniferous forests of the Pacific Northwest from Alaska to northwestern California. Wintering members of the species generally extend along the Pacific Coast from southern Alaska to Mexico.[5] For many years, however, they were also known as rare but regular winter visitors to eastern North America. These eastern winter records were mostly concentrated in the upper Great Lakes and New England states. Since the mid-1970s, they have been fairly regular winter visitors around the lower Great Lakes as well.

Ohio's first Varied Thrush appeared at a Mentor (Lake County) feeder on December 18, 1977. This individual was observed and photographed through January 5, 1978.[268] The next sightings occurred during the winter of 1979–80 when single Varied Thrushes appeared at three widely scattered locations. Subsequently, 1–3 have been recorded during five of eight winters through 1987–88. They are presently considered accidental to casual winter visitors with at least twelve documented sightings. These records are widely scattered except within the unglaciated counties: three sightings from the Cleveland area, two from the Columbus area, and singles at Cincinnati, Dayton, Mansfield, Lima, Bluffton (Allen County), Findley State Park (Lorain County), and Ottawa County. All have appeared at bird feeders. The earliest were noted during mid-December and a few have remained until late March.

GRAY CATBIRD

Dumetella carolinensis (Linnaeus)

Gray Catbirds are unobtrusive occupants of dense shrubbery, their plain gray plumage allowing them to disappear into the vegetation. Their mewing call notes may provide the first clue to their presence, but Catbirds are usually very inquisitive and easily coaxed into the open. They are most conspicuous during spring and early summer, when male Catbirds provide an almost nonstop chorus of disjointed notes. Unlike mockingbirds and Brown Thrashers, Catbirds seldom imitate the songs of other birds.

The first spring migrants usually return to the southern counties between April 15 and 20 and Catbirds are widely encountered within these counties by the end of the month. Their migration along Lake Erie is approximately one week later, not becoming numerous until the first week of May. During advanced springs, however, they may be common migrants throughout Ohio by the last week of April. Their spring migration normally peaks between May 7 and 18, when daily totals of 10–30 Catbirds are possible. The largest spring flights have produced concentrations of 50–60 along Lake Erie and in central Ohio. The last migrants usually depart from lakefront migrant traps by May 25.

Gray Catbirds are fairly common to common summer residents throughout Ohio, a status that has prevailed since the mid-1800s.[220,522] Breeding bird survey data since 1965 indicate their numbers have remained fairly stable.[438] Catbirds are most numerous in the eastern half of Ohio where shrubby edge and successional habitats are widely available. Daily totals of 15–30 Catbirds are expected during late May and June. Numbers are generally reduced in the western half of the state where suitable shrubby habitats are more restricted. Summer reports

seldom exceed 5–15 Catbirds daily in extensively cultivated western Ohio. Larger numbers may be noted along extensive riparian corridors and in successional habitats within the southwestern counties and the Oak Openings of Lucas County.[89,248]

This species normally raises two broods annually.[339] Their nests are usually placed at heights of three to eight feet in dense shrubbery. Nest construction is normally under way in central and southern Ohio by the second week of May and nests with eggs may be expected throughout the state by the end of the month.[479,523] These young normally fledge during the last half of June or early July. Second clutches are produced during July and nests with young have been reported as late as August 20–29.[89,339,511]

Their southward migration is less conspicuous. Trautman[479] reported migrants at Buckeye Lake as early as late August but the bulk of their migration occurs during September and the first week of October. Fall totals are generally 5–15 Catbirds daily with occasional concentrations of 25–35. Their numbers noticeably diminish by the second week of October and only occasional stragglers are encountered after October 20.

While Gray Catbirds normally winter in the southeastern United States, a few regularly linger into winter as far north as Ohio. Generally one to three wintering Catbirds are reported each year. They may appear at any locality, although the majority of the sightings are from the southern and central counties. Most wintering Catbirds are discovered in the shrubby habitats where they spend the summer, although a few become regular visitors to bird feeders. Most disappear following the onset of extended snow cover and cold temperatures, usually by the middle of January. Only a few have overwintered, usually in the southern counties during relatively mild seasons.

NORTHERN MOCKINGBIRD

Mimus polyglottos (Linnaeus)

Northern Mockingbirds are sure to catch the attention of anybody residing within the domain of these distinctive backyard birds. Their drab grayish plumage flashes diagnostic white patches in the wings and tail as they move from perch to perch. An aggressive species, mockers are not afraid to chase birds considerably larger than themselves or even small dogs and cats. Their ability to mimic bird songs is legendary, and many mockers regularly repeat the songs of twenty or more species. Persistent singers, they may repeat their repertoire throughout the day and most calm, moonlit spring nights, much to the chagrin of anybody trying to sleep in the neighborhood.

Mockingbirds have not always resided in the state. They initially appeared within Ohio during the mid-1800s, mostly as widely scattered individuals. By the 1870s, they were established as rare residents in the southern counties but were virtually unknown elsewhere.[289,522] At the turn of the century, Jones[236] considered them rare residents north to Columbus but felt that the few northern Ohio records may have pertained to escapes. They were numerous at only a few localities as exemplified by 20 tallied in Morgan County in 1896.

Mockingbird populations noticeably expanded during the first decades of this century. By 1910, they became sporadic visitors to northern Ohio and nesting populations were established in the Columbus area.[36,241] They were firmly entrenched in central Ohio during the 1920s.[479] They did not invade the extreme northeastern counties until the 1930s; there were very few confirmed northern Ohio nesting records before 1940.[86,523]

In the mid-1930s, Northern Mockingbirds were considered "regular residents" within the southern half of Ohio; they were locally distributed except in Adams, Lawrence, Guernsey, Muskingum, and Morgan Counties, where they became "fairly common to very common."[220,223] They remained rare and very locally distributed in the northern half of the state. These numbers exhibited considerable annual variation.

During the 1940s and 1950s, the widespread introduction of multiflora rose greatly benefited mockingbirds. They became widely distributed throughout the southern half of Ohio. Within the northern counties, small local breeding populations were established north to Lake Erie and mockingbirds appeared at a number of localities where they were formerly absent. Nesting pairs were missing only from the extreme northeastern counties.

Numbers probably peaked during the late 1960s and early 1970s. Mockingbirds became common residents in southern Ohio, especially the southwestern counties near Cincinnati, where more than 400 were tallied on Christmas Bird Counts. Similar numbers were not reported from other southern counties, although 15–30 mockers could be expected daily in most counties bordering the Ohio River. Even at Columbus, as many as 10–20 mockingbirds were observed at a few localities. Numbers remained low within the northern counties, although 3–5 individuals could be locally encountered.

The severe winters of 1976–78 decimated mockingbird populations, and their numbers have never fully recovered. Moreover, multiflora rose hedgerows are no longer popular and many have been removed. This habitat loss prevented mockers from returning to some counties.

Northern Mockingbirds are now fairly common to locally common residents in southern Ohio north to southern Preble, Montgomery, Clinton, Ross, Vinton, Athens, and Washington Counties. As many as 5–20 individuals may be recorded daily within these counties. They are uncommon to locally fairly common residents north to Darke, Logan, southern Morrow, Coshocton, and Jefferson Counties. Daily totals seldom exceed 3–10 mockers in these central counties. They remain accidental to rare and very locally distributed residents in the northern counties, usually as widely scattered pairs.[434]

While mockingbirds are mostly permanent residents, a few undertake seasonal movements. Wandering mockers are most likely to appear in March or April as they search for mates and suitable breeding territories. Trautman and Trautman[488] reported occasional daytime migrants over western Lake Erie during April, and strays have appeared at lakefront migrant traps through May 11. Their fall movements are less well defined. The few lakefront migrants are mostly noted in September; other wandering mockingbirds may appear during October and November as they search for suitable winter territories.

Breeding mockingbirds are fairly numerous in urban areas, residing in ornamental plantings surrounding residences, parks, and cemeteries. They are equally at home within hedgerows bordering rural residences. Mockingbirds will also inhabit brushy pastures, especially where hawthorns, rosebushes, and similar tangles are present. If multiflora rose hedges are available, they may even be found in extensively cultivated areas. Their nests are usually placed in dense shrubs at heights of two to seven feet. Mockingbirds are multibrooded and may raise three broods in the southern counties, where their nesting activities commence in April. Most young fledge between late May and August, although dependent young have been reported as late as November 16.[402]

BROWN THRASHER

Toxostoma rufum (Linnaeus)

Brown Thrashers are most apparent during their spring migration when the males perch on bushes or small saplings and sing incessantly. These migrants appear along fencerows, woodland edges, and upland brushy fields but also visit wooded migrant traps along Lake Erie. The first migrants normally return to the southern counties during the last week of March but are not expected in central and northern Ohio until April 3–8. Their maximum abundance is normally between April 15 and May 5, and a few migrants may remain along Lake Erie through May 15–20.

Spring thrashers are fairly common to common migrants throughout Ohio. They are seldom numerous, however, and only 3–12 will be observed during most days. Larger flights are infrequently encountered but have produced concentrations of 75 thrashers at the Oak Openings (Lucas County) on May 2, 1936, and 30–40 in central Ohio on several dates.[89]

Breeding thrashers occupy dry and dense shrubby cover; fencerows and other brushy corridors are as suitable as extensive overgrown fields. They are generally fairly common to common residents in the southern and eastern counties but are only fairly common residents elsewhere, becoming locally uncommon in the intensively farmed western and central counties. While 10–25 thrashers may be counted in the southern and eastern counties, daily totals seldom exceed 4–10 elsewhere.

These populations have remained reasonably stable throughout this century. Both Jones[236] and Hicks[220] considered thrashers fairly common or common residents statewide, and breeding bird survey data indicate essentially stable populations since 1965.[438] However, local declines have occurred within some western and central counties where agriculture eliminated most suitable brushy cover.

Nesting activities may be initiated by late April in the southern counties, and nests with eggs have been reported as early as April 30 near Youngstown.[435] Most pairs have complete clutches by mid-May. These young fledge by mid-June, although some early attempts have produced dependent young by the last week of May in southern and central Ohio. Brown

Thrashers apparently raise two broods annually as indicated by nests with eggs into mid-July and adults accompanied by young through August 20.[479]

Most thrashers nest in thorny shrubs, thickets, and other dense cover. Their first nests are normally placed on or near the ground; subsequent nests may be up to fourteen feet high.[89,479] A few thrashers constructed nests in unusual locations. Phillips[417] cited a Hancock County nest placed in a can in a juniper bush, and I discovered a pair nesting among riprap along a dam, far from any brushy cover.

By late July, most thrashers have finished nesting and become remarkably inconspicuous. They remain secretive throughout autumn. Their southward migration is poorly defined. A few thrashers may migrate early; some have appeared along Lake Erie by the first half of August. Most of their migration apparently occurs between September 15 and October 5. The last thrashers normally depart by October 10–20. Fall observations mostly are of 1–4 thrashers daily.

Before 1940, Brown Thrashers were accidental or casual winter visitors, with the few records scattered across the state at two- to four-year intervals. Campbell[86] cited only three winter records from the Toledo area and Trautman[479] only three from Buckeye Lake. Numbers increased during the 1940s and 1950s, and thrashers have been reported each winter since the 1960s.

Brown Thrashers are now casual winter visitors in northern and central Ohio and casual to rare in the southern counties. As many as 5–12 thrashers may be reported from the state during some winters. Given their secretive behavior, a number of wintering thrashers are probably overlooked. Most reports are of isolated individuals, although 3–4 have been reported on southern Ohio Christmas Bird Counts. They are normally found in the same brushy habitats where they nest, although a few regularly visit feeders. While many thrashers disappear after early January, a number have overwintered.

WATER PIPIT

Anthus spinoletta (Linnaeus)

As spring migrants, Water Pipits prefer farm fields where they can slowly pursue insects and other invertebrates along the ground. Neither shy nor wary, they frequent barren plowed fields, grassy pastures, and flooded fields, relying on their somber plumage to hide them from predators. This plumage provides them with surprisingly good camouflage against bare soil; more than once I have carefully scanned a field and found only 5–10 pipits on the ground but then counted 100–200 as they flew away.

Given these habitat preferences, spring Water Pipits are uncommon to fairly common migrants in western and central Ohio but rare to uncommon within the eastern third of the state. They are erratic migrants, however, and large spring flocks might appear anywhere. Their erratic migratory behavior also results in considerable annual variability in abundance.

The first spring migrants may return during the last week of February, but they are not regularly encountered until mid-March. Their spring passage has two fairly distinct peaks. Large flights are observed between March 20 and April 15, most prominently after early spring snowstorms. Smaller flights are occasionally encountered around the first week of May, mostly in the northern counties and rarely elsewhere. These migrants are usually observed as flocks of 50 or fewer individuals; the largest flights have produced flocks of 200–800. The last spring migrants normally depart from the southern half of the state by May 10–15 and Lake Erie by May 20 with stragglers remaining through May 27–28.[45,117]

Fall Water Pipits frequent open fields but are also found along the exposed margins of large rivers and reservoirs. These migrants are uncommon to fairly common in most counties. While Water Pipits have returned to northern and central Ohio by September 3–10, they are not expected until September 22–October 5. Most fall Water Pipits appear between mid-October and mid-November in numbers comparable to spring. The largest flights have been composed of 300–800 individuals.[479] Their numbers decline during the last half of November and the last migrants normally depart by December 5–10.

Water Pipits can be surprisingly hardy. In the northern counties, they are accidental to casual winter visitors as lingering individuals or flocks of 10 or fewer. Most sightings occur before January 15–20. Winter Water Pipits are casual to rare in central and southern Ohio through early January. Small flocks may remain until the first winter storm forces them south; late concentrations include flocks of 60 on December 19, 1971, and 75 on January 6, 1983, in Pickaway County[369,471] and 40 on January 8, 1917, in Mercer County.[198] Water Pipits become accidental visitors in central and southern Ohio after January 15, although a few have overwintered.

SPRAGUE'S PIPIT

Anthus spragueii (Audubon)

Sprague's Pipits occupy grasslands and are unlikely to be found elsewhere. As migrants, they are quite shy and furtive, preferring to remain hidden among the grasses; they take flight only when flushed underfoot. These pipits are normally found within central North America, breeding in the prairies of southern Canada and the northern United States and wintering in Texas and Mexico.[5] They are accidental visitors anywhere east of the Mississippi River.

While there have been a handful of Sprague's Pipit records from Ohio, most of these sightings are undoubtedly misidentifications. There are only two acceptable records of this accidental visitor. Ohio's first Sprague's Pipit was collected by Jay Sheppard at the Oxford airport in Butler County on November 15, 1958.[444] It was with three other Sprague's Pipits, one of which was banded on November 25. This small flock occupied the grassy border of the airport in an area where the grass was dead or burned out. The other acceptably documented sighting was provided by a single Sprague's Pipit flushed by Jim Hoffman from grasses and weeds at a lakefront landfill in Cleveland on October 31, 1974.[257]

BOHEMIAN WAXWING

Bombycilla garrulus (Linnaeus)

In the first half of the nineteenth century, Bohemian Waxwings were apparently fairly regular winter visitors to Ohio. The accounts of Kirtland and Read cited the frequent presence of winter flocks of these wanderers from western North America. Their status noticeably changed during the latter half of the century and their visits became much more sporadic.[522,523]

Their sporadic winter visits continued into the present century. During most winters, these waxwings were completely absent; in others, only widely scattered individuals or small flocks were observed. Defined flights were exceptionally rare. Probably the largest flight of this century occurred in the winter of 1919–20 with smaller movements in spring 1944 and winter 1961–62. This status was maintained through the mid-1960s with two to eight sightings per decade. Since 1967, there have been only two acceptable records, both of single Bohemians in the Toledo area, on March 11–12, 1978, and December 20, 1981.[269,389]

The earliest acceptable winter visitor was recorded on November 29, but these visitors did not normally appear until the last half of December. Reports of wintering Bohemian Waxwings were distributed throughout January and February. Their numbers were generally diminished during March, although a few remained through March 20–April 4. An exceptionally late Bohemian was reported from Cleveland on May 11, 1920.[523]

During the present century, most reports have been of 1–10 Bohemian Waxwings. While single individuals may be associated with flocks of Cedar Waxwings, the Bohemian flocks have been mostly segregated from their more numerous brethren. The largest flocks are most likely to appear within the northeastern counties: 75 at Painesville on January 27, 1920; 32 in Ashtabula County on December 22, 1919; 30 in Lake County on January 2, 1963; and 30 at Cleveland on March 8, 1944.[335,519,523] The largest flocks from other portions of Ohio totaled about 20 Bohemians in New Bremen (Auglaize County) on January 18–22, 1910, and 15 at Findlay on March 15, 1962.[199,417]

Since 1900, the majority of Ohio's twenty-eight acceptable sightings have been from the northern counties: twelve from the Cleveland area, four from Toledo, two from Findlay and Youngstown, and one each from Ashtabula County, Lorain County, Bowling Green (Wood County), and Canton. The four other sightings were of single Bohemians from Cincinnati in 1961 and 1963,[130,391] the New Bremen flock in 1910, and a single Bohemian near Quincy (Logan County) on December 31, 1930.[101]

CEDAR WAXWING

Bombycilla cedrorum Vieillot

Belying their elegant appearance, Cedar Waxwings are voracious feeders. When a winter flock descends upon a hawthorn, crabapple, or other fruit tree, these birds move from branch to branch, eating until their crops bulge and they look as if they were about to burst. Depending on the flock size and the amount of fruit on a tree, Cedar Waxwings can completely strip a tree in a few hours or days. Then the flock moves on in search of another fruit-laden tree.

This nomadic behavior explains the erratic winter status of Cedar Waxwings throughout Ohio. Some years they may be virtually absent from the entire state. In other winters, they may be locally distributed within only a few counties. Even during periodic flights, they become uncommon and very locally distributed winter residents as they follow their customary feeding pattern. While wintering Cedar Waxwings may be observed in small groups of 10 or fewer birds, they are mostly encountered in flocks of 20–50. During winters when they are fairly numerous, flocks of 75–100 are not unusual. By far the largest reported winter concentration was an estimated 1600 at Toledo on January 6, 1985.[377]

Given their erratic winter status, Cedar Waxwings are also rather erratic migrants through Ohio. Actually, they exhibit a fairly complex migration pattern with two distinct peaks during both spring and fall.

The first spring peak occurs between February 15 and March 15. Where these waxwings come from and where they are going has never been conclusively established. The size of this movement is quite variable from year to year and locality to locality. During some years, it is not evident anywhere. In other years, it may produce locally distributed flocks of 15–50 individuals or occasional large concentrations: 400 in the Ross-Pickaway county line area on March 13, 1968, and 175 in Ottawa County on February 28, 1959.[322,471]

A second and decidedly larger spring movement occurs during May—some years by the first week of the month, other years not until after May 15. During the last half of May, Cedar Waxwings usually become common to locally abundant migrants throughout the state. They are mostly observed in flocks of 30–75; daily totals of 200–400+ individuals are possible in every county. These migrants are most plentiful along Lake Erie, where 1000–2000+ can be counted daily as they pass along the lakefront. The last migrant flocks may remain along Lake Erie through June 8–12.

As summer residents, Cedar Waxwings formerly fluctuated considerably in numbers each year. These fluctuations were most noticeable in central and southern Ohio, where these waxwings might be locally absent some years and uncommon in others.[248,479] They regularly resided only within the northern counties, where they were uncommon to common.

In recent years, their populations have apparently increased within Ohio, a trend evident throughout eastern North America since 1965.[438] Their summer status has also become less variable. Cedar Waxwings now are generally fairly common to common and widely distributed summer residents, perhaps slightly less numerous in the southern counties bordering the Ohio River.[434] They are normally encountered as pairs or small groups, and summer totals seldom exceed 10–25 individuals daily in most counties.

Breeding Cedar Waxwings reach their greatest densities in mature wooded corridors bordering streams and lakes, although they will also regularly occupy orchards, parks, roadsides, and shaded residential areas. Breeders add large quantities of insects to the usual waxwing diet of fruits.

Their breeding biology was studied in great detail by Putnam.[430] Cedar Waxwings are already mated upon arrival on their territories. Their territories are quite small: a nest, a guarding perch, and between 225 and 1100 square yards of space. Waxwings do not defend feeding territories. Nest construction begins by early June. Eggs are usually laid by mid-June and the female performs all of the incubation. While the eggs normally hatch in late June or early July, nests with young have been reported by June 20 and recently fledged young as early as June 26.[417,479] The males care for the fledglings while the females start the process of raising another brood. These second nesting attempts have produced nests with eggs through September 3 and a nest with young on October 26, 1981, near Dayton.[219,299]

Flocks of Cedar Waxwings begin to develop in late July or early August. By mid-August, their fall migration has begun. These migrants exhibit a first peak in numbers between August 20 and September 30, when flocks of 30–100 individuals are scattered across the state. Larger concentrations, such as 1800 on South Bass Island on September 13, 1985,[380] are exceptional.

A second migration peak between October 15 and November 7 is normally less pronounced than the first, although flocks of 30–50 may still be regularly encountered. The report of "several thousand" along the Little Miami River in southwestern Ohio on October 23, 1983, is exceptional for late fall.[372] These flocks may linger into early November, but only erratic and nomadic wintering Cedar Waxwings will remain by the end of the month.

NORTHERN SHRIKE

Lanius excubitor Linnaeus

The status of Northern Shrikes has been obscured by frequent misidentifications, generating a number of questionable records especially of unseasonal and extralimital shrikes. In recent years, however, careful observations have apparently established their actual winter status.

Northern Shrikes are apparently rare but fairly regular winter visitors to northern Ohio. Their normal winter range extends south to Trumbull, Portage, Medina, Seneca, and Defiance Counties. They occasionally wander slightly farther south in northeastern Ohio with documented sightings from northern Columbiana, Wayne, and central Richland Counties. They are accidental winter visitors elsewhere, and any Northern Shrike away from this established range should be carefully identified and documented. While there are a number of sight records scattered across central and southern Ohio, most are unsubstantiated. The only confirmed records are provided by specimens collected near Buckeye Lake in Perry County on December 26, 1954, and in Hamilton County on November 3, 1883.

The earliest confirmed Northern Shrikes returned between October 25 and November 7. Most Northerns do not appear until November 20–December 15. As winter residents, a few Northerns are nomadic but most establish defined territories.

These territories frequently include successional fields, brushy pastures, and wooded fencerows bordering cultivated fields. These shrikes are most visible on calm, sunny days when they hunt from exposed perches on treetops or shrubs, pursuing rodents and small birds.

Wintering Northern Shrikes remain until the advent of warm weather in late February or early March. Most depart by March 15–20, although a few may remain along Lake Erie until the end of the month. Late migrants have lingered through mid-April, as evidenced by one photographed at Mentor Marsh Nature Preserve (Lake County) on April 14, 1979.

Like most northern predatory birds, wintering Northern Shrikes vary considerably in numbers from year to year. During most winters, they are relatively rare, with two to six sightings from the northern counties. However, they will occasionally stage southward incursions in response to food shortages within their Canadian winter range. Perhaps their largest winter invasions occurred during the mid-1950s. Unprecedented numbers appeared throughout the Great Lakes area during the winter of 1953–54, although unusual numbers were not reported from Ohio.[343] A flight the following winter produced at least 10 Northerns in the Toledo area as well as the only central Ohio specimen.[89,347] A smaller movement the next winter produced 8 Northerns on the Ashtabula Christmas Bird Count. In subsequent decades, the only substantial movement was noted in the winter of 1981–82 when shrikes were detected at fourteen locations in the northern counties.[364]

LOGGERHEAD SHRIKE

Lanius ludovicianus Linnaeus

When Ohio was initially settled, the virgin forests with few scattered openings did not support Loggerhead Shrikes. As these forests were cleared and replaced by open farmlands, Loggerheads quickly took advantage of the newly created habitats. They apparently invaded during the mid-1800s, becoming widely distributed before the turn of the century.[522]

During the first decades of the twentieth century, land-use practices produced ideal Loggerhead Shrike habitats. Farm fields were small and included considerable acreages of grassy pastures where Loggerheads hunted for insects, mice, and other prey. These fields were bordered by brushy fencerows and Osage orange hedgerows whose dense thorny vegetation provided nest sites. Shrikes thrived within these habitats and the largest statewide populations were present between 1900 and 1930.

During the mid-1930s, Loggerhead Shrikes were rare to very common and locally distributed summer residents.[220] They were most frequently encountered in the central third of the state and were least numerous in the eastern counties bordering West Virginia. Breeding shrikes were never abundant. Trautman's report[479] of 10–19 pairs nesting around Buckeye Lake and Jones's estimate[241] of "about 12 pairs in each township" in Erie County may be representative of their densities during these decades.

Beginning in the 1930s, land-use practices dramatically changed in the central and western counties. The trend toward intensive agricultural production eliminated most Osage orange hedgerows and shrubby fencerows, converted most pastures to cultivated crops, and greatly enlarged the size of farm fields. The ideal shrike habitats eventually disappeared and their populations plummeted.

These declines were evident as early as the mid-1930s in Paulding County.[424] Widespread declines were not noticeable until the late 1940s at Findlay and Cleveland.[417,523] Campbell[89] reported a marked decrease near Toledo during 1949. Populations continued to shrink throughout the 1950s and 1960s. By 1970, only a few widely scattered pairs remained.

Numbers of breeding pairs have continued to decline, a trend noted throughout most of North America.[438] Since 1980, Loggerheads have been accidental to rare summer residents with most records from the western half of the state. Nesting pairs were discovered in Brown, Adams, Clark, Fayette, Highland, Warren, Hamilton, Wood, Pickaway, and Madison Counties as well as Ottawa Wildlife Refuge. Additional summering birds appeared in Seneca, Hardin, Crawford, Erie, Scioto, and Columbiana Counties, although nesting was not confirmed. Estimating their population is quite difficult. No more than 7 nesting pairs have been located during any year, and the total statewide population probably does not exceed 20–25 pairs.

Loggerhead Shrikes begin their breeding activities as soon as they establish territories in late March or early April. Their nests are placed four to fifteen feet high in thorny trees or bushes. Their first clutches are normally laid during the last half of April or early May. While adults with dependent young have been noted as early as May 17, most young do not fledge until June.[523] Shrikes raise only one brood but will renest if their first attempt is unsuccessful. These renesting efforts are responsible for nests with young as late as July 31 and observations of recently fledged young during late July and early August.[299]

Even when their populations were larger, most Loggerheads were only summer residents in Ohio. Their migratory movements were better defined during the early 1900s but have not been apparent in recent years, when Loggerheads became accidental to rare migrants throughout the state.

Their spring migration was formerly fairly conspicuous. The first migrants normally appeared in mid-March and the migration continued through the third week of April. They were most numerous between March 25 and April 15, when as many as 15 shrikes daily were recorded during the largest flights.[479]

In contrast, their fall movements were poorly defined. Loggerheads became very inconspicuous after the young fledged and quietly disappeared from their breeding territories. Trautman[479] claimed their fall migration was evident by July 23 and peaked in mid-August. Small numbers continued to pass through Ohio until late September.

During winter, Loggerhead Shrikes have always been accidental to casual residents in the northern counties and casual to rare in central and southern Ohio. Not surprisingly, numbers of wintering Loggerheads have also declined during the past forty years. Although they do not regularly winter at any location, they have been reported at a frequency of one to six sightings annually since the late 1960s. Most recent winter records are from the southern half of Ohio, with very few confirmed sightings from the northern counties.

Wintering Loggerhead Shrikes are not necessarily the same individuals that breed in Ohio, since Loggerheads do not maintain their nesting territories throughout the year. In winter the Loggerheads are rather nomadic and establish defined feeding territories for only a few days or several weeks. They mostly appear during November or December with considerably fewer sightings after mid-January.

EUROPEAN STARLING

Sturnus vulgaris Linnaeus

The introduction of European Starlings into North America was a blunder whose disastrous consequences even surpass those associated with the introduction of House Sparrows. Starlings' adaptability allowed the species to rapidly expand across the continent wherever man has substantially altered the natural surroundings. Pugnacious and quarrelsome pests, starlings normally dominate our native birds when securing food and nest sites.

Starlings were initially released along the Atlantic Coast in 1890 and rapidly spread westward. Their expansion across Ohio was described by Hicks.[216] Ohio's first starling was reported from West Lafayette (Coshocton County) during January 1916. The next sightings were from Ashtabula County in 1918 and Knox County in 1919. In 1920, the first nest was discovered near Belleville in Richland County on May 11; flocks of 18–38 starlings in Knox County during August indicated that they were also nesting at other locations.[216,220] Their numbers literally exploded between 1921 and 1925 when individuals or breeding pairs "had certainly appeared in every Ohio county."[216] Sizable flocks formed in early autumn, including 1800+ starlings in Knox County on August 14, 1924. By the end of the decade, starlings became common to abundant residents throughout Ohio and fall flocks of 1000–5000+ were not unusual. Their numbers increased during the 1930s and large roosts composed of 100,000+ starlings were discovered at Buckeye Lake as early as the winter of 1935–36.[479]

Starlings are now abundant permanent residents in every county. As many as 100–500+ individuals may be observed daily during summer. Based on breeding bird survey data, Ohio has the unfortunate distinction of supporting the largest nesting population in North America.[438]

Breeding starlings are normally closely associated with people. They are equally at home in Ohio's cities, in the intensively farmed fields of western Ohio, and at rural homesteads in the unglaciated southeastern counties. While they may prefer urban and residential areas, nesting starlings also occupy parks, woodland clearings, riparian corridors, and wooded fencerows. They nest in natural cavities but also utilize birdhouses and holes under the eaves of buildings. They normally raise two broods annually. Nest construction has been observed as early as March 28 but most first clutches are laid between April 15

BLUE JAY
Cyanocitta cristata

Blue Jays eat a variety of foods and can frequently be seen foraging through the woods in pursuit of fruits, nuts, insects, and sometimes baby birds and eggs. In the fall their diet becomes almost exclusively fruits and nuts. Nothing is more striking than the brilliant plumage of this beautiful bird contrasted with the foliage of the persimmon (*Diospyros virginiana*), one of the trees that provide it with food.

Adult
(sexes similar)

EASTERN SCREECH-OWL
Otus asio

CAROLINA CHICKADEE
Parus carolinensis

TUFTED TITMOUSE
Parus bicolor

RED-BREASTED NUTHATCH
Sitta canadensis

WHITE-BREASTED NUTHATCH
Sitta carolinensis

The presence of the Eastern Screech-Owl is frequently only revealed at dusk by the nervous scolding of a band of woodland birds. Along with a wide variety of other prey, the Screech-Owl preys on small birds.

Tufted Titmouse
(sexes similar)

Carolina Chickadee
(sexes similar) **Red-breasted Nuthatch**
(male; female duller)

Eastern Screech-Owl **White-breasted Nuthatch**
(sexes similar) *(male; female has gray*
on crown)

BROWN CREEPER
Certhia americana

CAROLINA WREN
Thryothorus ludovicianus

Both of these small brown birds can be found in our winter woods. Carolina Wrens flit from branch to branch and along the ground, looking for insects hidden in rolled-up leaves, clusters of seeds, and other protected places. Brown Creepers most often forage by flying from the top of one tree to the base of another, then spiraling up the trunk searching for hidden food in the cracks and crevices of the bark.

Carolina Wren
(sexes similar)

Brown Creeper
(sexes similar)

GOLDEN-CROWNED KINGLET
Regulus satrapa

RUBY-CROWNED KINGLET
Regulus calendula

BLUE-GRAY GNATCATCHER
Polioptila caerulea

The paths of the three species of Old World warblers that occur in the state cross about the time the blooms of the Serviceberry (*Amelanchier arborea*) appear. Golden-crowned Kinglets are still lingering here on their wintering grounds. Ruby-crowned Kinglets are passing through en route from the south, and Blue-gray Gnatcatchers are just beginning to arrive and will stay to nest.

Blue-gray Gnatcatcher
(male; female lacks eyebrow)

Golden-crowned Kinglet

(male)

(female)

Ruby-crowned Kinglet
(male; female lacks red crown)

EASTERN BLUEBIRD
Sialia sialis

HERMIT THRUSH
Catharus guttatus

The ripening of the fruit of the Black Gum (*Nyssa sylvatica*) seems to coincide with the fall migration of thrushes. I have seen all seven species of thrushes that commonly occur in the state, including the Eastern Bluebird and the Hermit Thrush, feeding on the same heavily fruited gum tree during the same autumn.

Eastern Bluebird
(male)

(female)

Hermit Thrush
(sexes similar)

and May 7.[89,417] First broods normally fledge in late May or early June. Their second clutches are laid during June and these broods fledge in July.

As soon as the first broods fledge, juvenile starlings accumulate into small flocks. These flocks are evident by mid-June and continue to grow as more young are produced. Concentrations of 300–1000+ starlings may be regularly observed in farm fields and along roadsides by early August.

Their fall migration is not well defined. It probably begins in late August but the largest concentrations are normally apparent between late September and mid-November. Immense numbers may appear, frequently mixed with blackbirds, and fall roosts of 10,000–100,000+ starlings are not unusual. These roosts are frequently located in cattail marshes during August and September but shift to pine plantations, dense deciduous woods, and even buildings as the weather turns colder.

Starlings remain abundant winter residents throughout Ohio. They are most numerous in cities and farmlands, where 500–2000+ birds can be observed daily. Fewer are found in the rural southeastern counties; there, daily totals infrequently exceed 200–500. They also form large winter roosts, frequently in association with blackbirds. If undisturbed, winter roosts may be occupied for many years and attract concentrations of 10,000-25,000+ starlings each evening. Larger roosts occasionally develop. For example, Dayton roosts supported an estimated 449,000 starlings in 1977 and 607,000 in 1952.[299]

With the return of warmer temperatures in late February or early March, starlings begin their northward migration. They rapidly move through the state, primarily during March, when flocks of 500–5000 are regularly observed. Large roosts will also be formed—an estimated 150,000 starlings were reported at Columbus on March 12, 1972—but spring roosts are normally of short duration.[471] Numbers of migrants are sharply reduced by April 7, although small flocks may still pass along Lake Erie until April 15–20.

WHITE-EYED VIREO

Vireo griseus (Boddaert)

White-eyed Vireos were largely restricted to the southern counties at the turn of the century. They may have been rather numerous near Cincinnati but were generally rare and locally distributed in other southern counties.[194] Elsewhere, these vireos were known only as spring migrants, regularly appearing in central Ohio and very rarely wandering north to Lake Erie.

Their breeding range slowly expanded northward. By the mid-1930s, Hicks[220] cited breeding records from thirty-five southern and eastern counties north to Butler, Warren, Clinton, Fayette, Pickaway, Franklin, Licking, Coshocton, Tuscarawas, and Jefferson. Along the unglaciated plateau, White-eyeds were numerous north to Hocking, Vinton, Jackson, and Meigs Counties.[223] They remained rare elsewhere on the plateau.[479] Outside this breeding range, these vireos were fairly regular spring migrants within the eastern half of Ohio but accidental in the west-central and northwestern counties.

By the 1950s, White-eyed Vireos spread northward along the entire unglaciated plateau and were regularly found nesting at Youngstown and Columbus. Their expansion into the Dayton area was evident by the early 1960s.[299] Within the northern counties, these vireos were regularly noted as spring migrants during the 1960s and there were a few scattered summer records without conclusive evidence of nesting.[89,335] The first confirmed breeding records near Lake Erie were not established until the mid-1970s. This expansion corresponded with a marked population increase throughout eastern North America.[438]

White-eyed Vireos are now fairly common to locally common summer residents throughout southern and unglaciated eastern Ohio. Seldom very numerous, summer vireos do not normally exceed 5–15 daily within these counties. They remain fairly common residents within the central counties bordering the Allegheny Plateau but become uncommon within the intensively farmed west-central counties.[434] Only 2–6 daily are expected within these counties. Nesting White-eyeds are least numerous in northern Ohio, where they are generally rare to locally uncommon residents, becoming casual within most intensively cultivated northwestern counties. Most northern reports are of widely scattered pairs and singing males.

Breeding White-eyed Vireos occupy brushy successional habitats, especially mesic areas along stream valleys. They may also inhabit dry hillsides, roadside thickets, woodland clearings, and the brushy borders of woods. Their nests are placed fairly low in dense shrubs. Within the southern counties, their nesting activities are initiated in early May and clutches may be discovered by mid-month. Nests with young have been noted by June 1 and these young will fledge before the end of the month. Their nesting chronology is normally delayed by at least two weeks in northern Ohio, where young vireos may not fledge until July. In southern Ohio, reports of fledglings in early August might pertain to second nesting attempts.

Their spring migration largely comprises resident vireos returning to their nesting territories. Away from known breeding locations, White-eyeds are generally uncommon spring visitors to the central counties and rare to locally uncommon migrants in northern Ohio with most reports of 1–3 individuals.

The earliest spring migrants returned to Dayton by March 30, 1986, and Pickaway County by April 1, 1950.[311,382] Lake Erie's earliest overflights have been noted by April 17–19. White-eyed Vireos do not normally return to the southern counties until April 20–25. In northern Ohio, they are not expected until the first week of May; they may appear along the lakefront through May 20–25.

Most fall sightings are of resident vireos, with the only sizable movement totaling 25 White-eyeds at Cincinnati on September 13, 1981.[363] Resident White-eyeds are regularly detected through September 20–25. In northern Ohio, they normally depart by October 1 but may remain through October 7–10 in the southern and central counties. Away from their breeding territories, these vireos are casual to rare fall migrants, mostly scattered individuals during September.

A few may linger well after their normal departure dates. Exceptionally late vireos have been reported only from northern Ohio: at least two November sightings from western Lake

Erie near Toledo and three in the vicinity of Cleveland. Single vireos have survived into December, with documented records from Lorain on December 18, 1982, and Seneca County on December 16, 1984.

BELL'S VIREO

Vireo bellii Audubon

In the past few decades, Bell's Vireo gradually expanded its breeding range eastward through the lower Great Lakes states. First moving through Illinois and then Indiana, this nondescript vireo with its distinctive rolling song did not appear in Ohio until 1962. Although it has been more regularly observed in the 1980s, its status is still evolving. Its eastward range expansion is somewhat surprising in view of its declining populations within the central United States.[438] Ohio's first confirmed Bell's Vireo was a cooperative male discovered in Whetstone Park in Columbus on May 26–27, 1962. He was widely observed and more than thirty-five minutes of his song was recorded on tape.[46] The next Bell's Vireo also appeared in Columbus, another male whose songs were recorded at Greenlawn Cemetery on May 19, 1966.[46] In 1968, a pair was discovered nesting near Cincinnati.[406] This attempt was unsuccessful since the nest and eggs were collected.

Bell's Vireos remained accidental visitors through the 1970s. There was a confirmed sighting every two or three years in the western half of the state. With the exception of a summering male in Franklin County during 1972, all confirmed records were of spring migrants, mostly singing males. The number of Bell's Vireo sightings has increased since 1980, reflecting its continued expansion into Ohio. Isolated nesting pairs have been discovered each summer except 1983.

Bell's Vireos are now accidental to casual spring migrants through the western half of Ohio, averaging one to three sightings annually. While the majority of these sightings have been near Toledo and Columbus, the remainder are widely scattered. The earliest Bell's Vireos were reported during the last week of April but most have been observed between May 7 and 25. All records have been of only 1–2 individuals. Bell's Vireos are accidental spring visitors to the eastern counties, where the only published records are of single vireos in Holmes County on June 1–2, 1981; Headlands State Park (Lake County) on May 26, 1984; and Wayne County during May 1988.[362,374,388a]

As summer residents, Bell's Vireos have been recorded from Irwin Prairie Nature Preserve (Lucas County) between 1980 and 1982,[471] Resthaven Wildlife Area (Erie County) in 1984, Columbus in 1985, and Buck Creek State Park (Clark County) in 1986–88.[434] Territorial males were also reported from Stark, Lucas, and Franklin Counties between 1985 and 1987, although they were believed to be unmated.

Nesting Bell's Vireos occupy successional habitats dominated by shrubs and saplings but may also nest in small openings covered with weeds and grasses. They exhibit a preference for dry fields. The first clue to their presence is the male's distinctive song, which may be delivered from the middle of thick cover or an exposed perch.

Their nests are normally placed in dense shrubs, usually at heights of less than eight feet. Their nesting activities normally begin in late May or early June with the young fledging by early July. A later attempt produced a nest with eggs through July 12–16+ and the young did not fledge until August 1.

Once they quit singing, Bell's Vireos become nearly impossible to observe among the dense shrubbery. Additionally, they can be difficult to separate from immature White-eyeds. Hence, their fall status is poorly understood. There are fewer than six acceptable fall records, mostly during August and early September of single vireos at scattered locations in the western half of the state.

SOLITARY VIREO

Vireo solitarius (Wilson)

While Solitary Vireos are primarily migrants through Ohio, their status appears to be changing. Their breeding range has been expanding throughout the Appalachian region since the early 1950s,[65,438] resulting in increased numbers of summering Solitary Vireos in Ohio.

Ohio's first nesting Solitary Vireos were discovered in Ashtabula County by Hicks.[215] Between 1928 and 1931, he observed summering vireos at four sites and located two nests. Williams[523] cited 1–3 pairs at Little Mountain (Lake and Geauga Counties) after 1937 and a similar number at Stebbins Gulch (Geauga County) beginning in 1947. Along the unglaciated Allegheny Plateau, breeding Solitaries were unrecorded until 1961, when Randle[432] observed males at two Hocking County locations. He noted 5 males at these sites in 1962, the same year a summering Solitary Vireo was reported from Columbiana County.[144] Additional summering Solitaries have been discovered in the eastern counties since the 1970s.

Solitary Vireos are now rare and locally distributed summer residents in eastern Ohio. In the northeastern counties, 1–5 breeding pairs annually occupy scattered locations in Ashtabula, Lake, Geauga, Portage, Cuyahoga, and Summit Counties. Summering Solitaries are also occasionally encountered in Medina and Lorain Counties.[434] Along the unglaciated Allegheny Plateau, similar numbers are scattered along the Little Beaver Creek watershed in Columbiana County and the Mohican River in Ashland, Holmes, and Knox Counties. Breeding Solitaries are probably most numerous in the hemlock ravines of Hocking County, where 2–9 pairs regularly nest at six or more locations.[367] Scattered nesting pairs have also been observed in Jackson and Scioto Counties. While the known breeding population may not presently exceed 100 pairs, this population is still expanding.

In northwestern Ohio, summering Solitary Vireos have only been reported from the vicinity of Toledo. The first records were of nonbreeders during 1940 and 1973.[89,90] Beginning in 1983, a few pairs have summered annually in the Oak Openings area, and nesting was confirmed in 1986.[383]

Initially, breeding Solitary Vireos were restricted to cool mesic hemlock forests. As their population expanded, these vireos spread into pine plantations in northern Ohio and mixed pine-deciduous woods along the dry ridges of Hocking and Scioto Counties. These breeding vireos generally forage within the understory and lower branches of tall trees and are seldom found in the canopy. Their nests are placed in saplings or small trees, usually at heights of less than twenty feet. Nest construction has been observed during late May and early June. Nests with eggs have been reported between June 12 and July 11.[215,367]

Nesting Solitaries return before the arrival of most spring migrants. In the southeastern counties, the first resident Solitaries may appear by April 5–10, although they may not return to northeastern Ohio until April 15–22. Even though the females may appear one or two weeks later, established pairs may occupy their territories for nearly one month before nesting activities are initiated.

A few overflights of spring migrants have been discovered, at Columbus on April 1, 1982, and the Cleveland area by April 4, 1946.[365,523] However, migrant Solitaries do not normally return to southern and central Ohio until the last week of April and along Lake Erie by May 1–5. Most Solitaries are observed between April 30 and May 15, when they become rare to uncommon migrants through the interior counties and uncommon to fairly common along Lake Erie. They are never numerous and generally 1–5 Solitaries are noted daily. The largest flights have produced only 10–12 in central Ohio and along Lake Erie. Most migrants depart between May 20 and 25, although a few linger through the end of the month.

The first fall migrants normally return to northern and central counties by mid-September but may not appear in southern Ohio until September 23–28. They are mostly observed between September 25 and October 15, becoming uncommon migrants along Lake Erie and rare to uncommon within the interior counties. These migrants are mostly observed as 1–3 vireos with a maximum of 10 at Buckeye Lake.[479] While they normally depart by October 20–25, Solitaries occasionally remain through November 3–11. An exceptionally late Solitary was discovered at Euclid (Cuyahoga County) on November 22, 1985.[380] There are no acceptable December records.

YELLOW-THROATED VIREO

Vireo flavifrons Vieillot

With their colorful plumage, Yellow-throated Vireos have a reputation as our most attractive vireos. But they can be remarkably difficult to observe, preferring the upper branches of tall trees and seldom appearing anywhere else. The first spring migrants frequently return when vegetation is still budding, offering little concealment for these brightly plumaged vireos. As soon as the vegetation becomes fully developed, these vireos easily hide among the abundant foliage. Fortunately, Yellow-throateds are quite vocal and most identifications will be by means of their vocalizations after early May.

Spring overflights have appeared along Lake Erie as early as April 7, 1947, near Toledo.[89] Within the southern counties,

breeding Yellow-throateds regularly return by April 15–20 and become fairly common before the end of the month. In contrast, there are relatively few April records from the northern counties, where they do not normally return until the first week of May. These vireos become uncommon to fairly common spring migrants except within some western counties where they are locally rare. These migrants are never numerous; spring totals rarely exceed 1–10 daily. Most residents return by May 15–20, although occasional Yellow-throateds appear at lakefront migrant traps into the first week of June.

Breeding Yellow-throated Vireos are found almost exclusively in extensive mature woodlands. While they may prefer large oaks and maples, they are found in a variety of wooded habitats from floodplain forests to woodlands covering dry ridges. Since they nest in the tops of tall trees, relatively little information is available on their nesting biology. Nest construction has been noted by the first week of May at Cincinnati.[248] While most nests are probably constructed during mid-May in the northern counties, nests with young have been reported as early as May 22 in the Cleveland area.[523] Within the southern counties, the first fledglings may appear by June 5–15, although they do not normally fledge until late June or early July elsewhere. These vireos apparently raise two broods, since nests with young have been reported through August 9 and dependent young as late as August 28.[89,479]

As summer residents, Yellow-throated Vireos have always been widely distributed. Hicks[220] cited breeding records from seventy-nine counties, noting that these breeders were often locally distributed or absent in some western counties. Breeding vireos underwent a substantial increase in the Cincinnati area after 1947.[248] Similar increases have not been evident elsewhere. In fact, summer populations have significantly declined throughout Ohio since 1965.[438]

Despite declining populations, the statewide breeding distribution has not appreciably changed since the 1930s.[434] Yellow-throated Vireos now are fairly common summer residents throughout southern and eastern Ohio, most numerous along the unglaciated Allegheny Plateau. Summer totals seldom exceed 3–12 individuals daily in these counties. These vireos become uncommon to fairly common summer residents in most central and northern counties adjacent to the plateau; in these counties, 2–5 Yellow-throateds are noted daily. They are least numerous within the west-central and northwestern counties, becoming uncommon to locally rare residents. Although a few pairs reside in every county, breeding Yellow-throated Vireos become very locally distributed where few extensive mature woodlots remain.[434]

These vireos are regularly detected into the first half of July but become inconspicuous after the males quit singing. Relatively few are noted in August. They become more conspicuous during September when the males begin to sing again. Their fall migration is poorly defined. The last fall Yellow-throateds normally depart from northern Ohio by September 15–20, although they remain in the southern counties until September 23–28. There are very few records after the first week of October and none have been later than October 17–19. Most fall records are of only 1–3 individuals daily.

WARBLING VIREO

Vireo gilvus (Vieillot)

Unremarkable in their green and white plumage, foraging Warbling Vireos are virtually impossible to detect as they silently move along the outer branches of cottonwoods, sycamores, and other tall trees. Once their distinctive song is learned, however, Warbling Vireos will be regularly detected in mature wooded corridors bordering streams and lakes throughout Ohio.

While the earliest overflight was discovered near Dayton on April 4, 1986,[382] the first Warbling Vireos do not normally appear in the southern and central counties until April 22–30 or along Lake Erie until the first days of May. They become fairly common migrants by May 5–10. Spring Warbling Vireos are seldom numerous; most reports are of 6–20 individuals daily. Their northward migration apparently continues through May 20–25, but late migrants are difficult to distinguish from residents.

As summer residents, Warbling Vireos have always been widely distributed. Hicks[220] recorded them from every county but noted that they were "less frequent" in portions of southern and southeastern Ohio. He later described them as uncommon to fairly common residents along the entire unglaciated Allegheny Plateau.[223] Their status has not substantially changed during subsequent decades.[438] Warbling Vireos are now generally fairly common to common summer residents, becoming locally uncommon in some southeastern counties. They are least numerous from Hocking and Athens Counties south to Adams County.

When males are most vocal in June, as many as 15–35 individuals may be tallied during a morning's canoe trip down a large river. Such counts are exceptional, however; summer totals seldom exceed 5–12 in most areas. Warbling Vireos are decidedly less numerous in other habitats. In recent years, only a few pairs have been recorded in shade trees, orchards, and wooded groves, although they may have been "common" in these habitats at the turn of the century.[236]

Within riparian habitats, their nests are usually placed at heights of thirty to fifty feet along inaccessible outer branches of tall trees.[479] They may be placed lower in other habitats and have been recorded only six feet off the ground in an apple orchard.[424] Nest construction has been reported as early as April 25 but is mostly noted in May.[523] The first clutches are normally laid in the last half of May and these young fledge in late June or early July. Later nesting attempts have been responsible for clutches through July 15 and adults accompanied by young through August 7.[89,479]

By mid-July, the males quit singing and Warbling Vireos become quite inconspicuous. They are seldom observed until late August, when the first migrants appear and resident males begin singing again. Their fall migration is rather poorly defined. Warbling Vireos are generally uncommon to fairly common migrants throughout Ohio until September 20–25. These migrants are mostly noted in groups of 5 or fewer. The largest reported fall concentrations have totaled 10–15 along Lake Erie. Most Warbling Vireos depart by October 1–5 but a few have remained through October 12–15. The latest fall migrant was noted at Akron on October 31, 1987.

PHILADELPHIA VIREO

Vireo philadelphicus (Cassin)

During spring, migrating Philadelphia Vireos are uncommon to fairly common along Lake Erie and rare to uncommon within the interior counties. Daily totals seldom exceed 3 individuals inland and 6 along the lakefront. Only Jones[241] reported concentrations exceeding 10, including "uncountable numbers" associated with an exceptional May 13, 1907, flight at Cedar Point (Erie County). While a Philadelphia Vireo returned as early as April 22, 1981, to Hueston Woods State Park,[361] there are very few April sightings of these normally late migrants. They generally arrive during the first week of May and most reports are between May 12 and 25. Only occasional stragglers remain into the first week of June.

Their status during fall migration is more obscure, in part because of difficulties distinguishing Philadelphias from other vireos and even several warblers. Sightings during early August are especially suspect and most proved to be Warbling Vireos, which can have extensive yellowish underparts in fresh fall plumage. While fall Philadelphia Vireos may appear within the northern and central counties by August 25–30, they do not normally return until September 6–10. They are fairly regularly encountered into the first week of October and depart by October 10–15. There are relatively few sightings of lingering Philadelphias, and the only November records have been along western Lake Erie through November 10, 1983.[372] Fall migrants are more frequently encountered along the lakefront, where they are uncommon to fairly common. Their inland status is the same as during spring migration. No autumn concentrations in excess of 6 individuals have been reported; they are normally encountered as singles.

RED-EYED VIREO

Vireo olivaceus (Linnaeus)

Few woodland birds can match the Red-eyed Vireos' reputation as persistent vocalists. Their song is a monotonous series of Robinlike phrases endlessly repeated throughout even the hottest summer day. A single male may sing several thousand phrases daily, but his songs are easily lost in the varied chorus produced by Ohio's woodland avifauna. While silent Red-eyeds are easily overlooked, a careful count of singing males indicates that this species ranks among the most numerous occupants of Ohio's woods.

Breeding Red-eyed Vireos may occupy the canopies of younger forests but most dwell within the understories of more mature woods. They inhabit all woodland communities varying in size from several-acre oak-hickory woodlots to extensive deciduous forests and eastern Ohio's hemlock woods. Small numbers may nest in shaded residential areas, although they avoid open parklike habitats with scattered trees.

During summer, Red-eyed Vireos are generally common and widely distributed residents. Totals of 25–30 Red-eyeds are frequently tallied within wooded habitats throughout the state.

They become locally abundant in the southeastern counties, where daily counts in excess of 50 singing males are possible. Breeding Red-eyeds are least numerous in intensively cultivated western Ohio, where they are fairly common residents and daily totals seldom exceed 5–10 except along extensive riparian corridors. Their population trends are not uniform across Ohio. The maturation of eastern Ohio forests has produced increases in some counties. Conversely, agricultural activities have reduced populations in most western counties.

Their breeding biology was extensively studied in the mid-1940s by Norberg[354] on South Bass Island in western Lake Erie. Their average territory size was approximately one acre but could be as small as three-tenths of an acre. Nests were usually placed along slender limbs near the periphery of young trees at an average height of fifteen feet. Some nests have been reported as high as eighty feet.[479] Red-eyed Vireos normally raise two broods. Nest construction begins by mid-May and the first clutches appear as early as May 22. Adults accompanied by young have been reported by June 9, although the first broods normally fledge during late June or early July.[479] Second broods are normally initiated during July and are responsible for nests with eggs as late as August 16 and fledglings into late August.[523]

The first spring records of Red-eyed Vireos are of overflights encountered along Lake Erie on April 5 at Toledo and April 8 at Cleveland.[89,523] During their normal migration, spring Red-eyed Vireos may return to southern Ohio by the third week of April and can be fairly numerous by the end of the month. They frequently return to the central counties during the last week of April but are not regularly encountered until the first week of May. Spring migrants do not reach Lake Erie in numbers until May 5–10. These migrants are not particularly numerous; large flights along Lake Erie seldom produce totals in excess of 25–35 individuals. While as many as 140 Red-eyeds have been reported from central Ohio during spring,[479] these reports undoubtedly include many residents. The end of their spring migration is poorly defined, but Red-eyeds are regularly observed at Lake Erie migrant traps through May 25-June 3.

Fall Red-eyed Vireos generally peak during September. Most of these silent Red-eyeds remain hidden by the vegetation, and fall migrants are uncommon to fairly common throughout the state. Fall totals seldom exceed 8–20 daily. The largest reported concentration was 42 along western Lake Erie on August 31, 1980.[471] Most Red-eyeds depart by the first week of October with only occasional stragglers after October 15. There are three published November sight records, including a remarkably late Red-eyed in the Cleveland area on November 25, 1931.[523]

BLUE-WINGED WARBLER

Vermivora pinus (Linnaeus)

The earliest Blue-winged Warblers have appeared by April 13–17 but these overflights are infrequent. Territorial males do not usually return to the southern counties until April 22–27 or along Lake Erie until the first week of May. Their northward migration is fairly short and virtually all residents return by May 15–20.

Since their breeding range extends just barely north of Ohio, this spring migration mostly comprises residents returning to their nesting territories. These warblers are uncommon to rare spring visitors to migrant traps across the state, mostly appearing between April 25 and May 15. Most sightings of migrant Blue-wingeds are of single individuals, although small groups of 4–6 may appear. The largest movement was of 12 at Buckeye Lake on May 8, 1928.[479]

Nesting Blue-winged Warblers prefer damp shrub-dominated habitats, including successional fields, woodland edges, and clearings. Since they occupy successional habitats, these attractive warblers invariably disappear when the shrubs are replaced by trees.

Nests are placed on or near the ground, usually expertly concealed within dense herbaceous vegetation. Nest construction may begin during the first half of May and continue into early June. Most clutches are noted between mid-May and mid-June. Dependent young may appear by June 12–20, especially within southern Ohio, but most fledglings are expected in late June or July.[89,523] Blue-wingeds raise only one brood but will renest if their first clutch is destroyed.

At one time, Blue-winged Warblers were predominantly a southern species whose breeding range extended only into southern and central Ohio. This range slowly expanded northward, mostly during the nineteenth century, since nesting Blue-wingeds were widely distributed by the early 1900s.[236] Range expansions during the twentieth century were restricted to the Toledo area, where they did not become numerous until the 1920s and 1930s.[86]

In the mid-1930s, Hicks[220] considered Blue-wingeds uncommon to rare and locally distributed summer residents, although he cited records from eighty counties. They were most numerous within southern Ohio and along the unglaciated Allegheny Plateau north to Hocking and Athens Counties.[223] These warblers were only locally common elsewhere in eastern Ohio. They were decidedly less numerous in western Ohio, where suitable successional habitats were scarce, and were unrecorded from a number of northwestern counties.

In subsequent decades, their breeding populations have increased within portions of the state, most notably in eastern Ohio. Blue-wingeds are presently regularly distributed along the entire unglaciated Allegheny Plateau and in most northeastern counties.[434] Conversely, their numbers declined within many western counties where most shrubby habitats have disappeared.

Blue-wingeds are now fairly common to common residents throughout southern and eastern Ohio, somewhat less numerous within southwestern Ohio. Summer totals of 5–18+ individuals daily may be expected in most of these counties. They become uncommon and locally distributed residents of the central counties near Columbus; in these counties, 1–7 Blue-wingeds may be observed daily. Breeding Blue-wingeds are least numerous within the west-central and northwestern counties; while they are locally uncommon to fairly common near Toledo, they are generally casual to rare elsewhere and are absent from intensively cultivated areas.[434] Once the males quit singing in early July, Blue-winged Warblers are infrequently encountered. Their inconspicuous behavior continues into autumn and their fall migration is very poorly defined.

They become casual to locally uncommon fall migrants throughout Ohio with all sightings consisting of 1–4 individuals. Their southward migration apparently begins by mid-August. The last Blue-wingeds are normally observed between September 10 and 20. While a few individuals have lingered into the first half of October, a Blue-winged Warbler at Cleveland on November 14, 1948, was extraordinarily late.[523]

Blue-winged Warblers frequently interbreed with Golden-wingeds, producing recognizable hybrid offspring known as "Brewster's" and "Lawrence's" Warblers. When both species regularly nested within Ohio, "Brewster's" Warblers were rare but regular summer residents. In recent years, they have become accidental to casual summer residents with sightings every two or three years. Small numbers of "Brewster's" Warblers regularly pass through Ohio each year, mostly as widely scattered spring migrants. They are casual to locally rare spring migrants along Lake Erie but are generally accidental within most interior counties. They become accidental to casual migrants throughout Ohio during autumn.

"Lawrence's" Warblers have always been considerably less numerous than "Brewster's." "Lawrence's" are presently accidental to casual migrants and summer residents throughout Ohio and are not reported annually. The migration patterns, habitat preferences, and nesting biology of these hybrids are identical to those of the parental species. It is not unusual to find mixed pairs of hybrids mated to either parental species or occasionally with another hybrid.

GOLDEN-WINGED WARBLER

Vermivora chrysoptera (Linnaeus)

Despite dissimilar appearances, Golden-winged and Blue-winged Warblers are actually closely related. In fact, regular hybridization between these two species has prompted a number of ornithologists to conclude that they are morphs of a single species. This hybridization has significantly altered the distribution of nesting Golden-wingeds within North America. Wherever Blue-winged Warblers expand into the breeding range of Golden-wingeds, the latter species invariably declines and disappears.[124]

An expanding Blue-winged Warbler population has largely replaced Ohio's locally distributed pairs of nesting Golden-wingeds. These pairs were never very numerous. The only substantial Golden-winged population existed in the Oak Openings of Lucas County, where Campbell[89] reported 37 males in 1932. Ashtabula County may also have supported a small population; pairs were recorded at eight locations between 1928 and 1932.[215] Elsewhere, breeding pairs were rare and very sporadically encountered during the 1920s and 1930s. Hicks[220] cited nesting records from only fifteen counties scattered across the state except for southwestern Ohio. These records were mostly of single pairs breeding for only one or two years. A few additional pairs were discovered along the unglaciated Allegheny Plateau before 1937.[223]

In all likelihood, breeding Golden-wingeds were declining by the 1930s. In the Oak Openings, only 14 males were reported between 1937 and 1939. This number was reduced to 10 by 1945.[89] Nesting Golden-wingeds essentially disappeared from the remainder of the state except for occasional summering males or pairs at widely scattered northern and eastern localities. Between 1950 and 1968, only 1–3 males were recorded annually in the Oak Openings.[89,90] A small population was established in Columbiana County during the 1960s but disappeared before the end of the decade.[144,146] After 1968, the Oak Openings population vanished except for sporadic territorial males.

Golden-winged Warblers are now casual summer residents in the Oak Openings, where 1–3 males are reported at two- to three-year intervals. They are accidental to casual summer residents elsewhere. Since 1982, singing males have been detected in Trumbull, Delaware, Franklin, Summit, and Coshocton Counties and the Dayton area.[434] Many of these males briefly established territories during the first half of June but disappeared without nesting. This population appears to be on the verge of extirpation.

Nesting Golden-winged Warblers occupy the same brushy habitats preferred by Blue-wingeds. Their breeding biology is also similar. Golden-winged nests are placed on or near the ground in dense cover. Nests with eggs were reported between May 30 and June 21. The first fledglings appeared during the last half of June but were mostly noted in the first half of July.[86]

Golden-winged Warblers have always been scarce migrants through Ohio. Each spring, they are casually to rarely observed at most localities, becoming locally uncommon at a few migrant traps along Lake Erie. These sightings are mostly of scattered individuals with infrequent reports of 3–6 Golden-wingeds daily. The earliest arrivals appeared between April 26 and 30. Spring Golden-wingeds are mostly observed between May 5 and 15 with very few migrants after May 22.

Fewer Golden-wingeds are detected in autumn, when they become rare migrants along Lake Erie and accidental to casual inland. All fall reports have been of only 1–3 individuals. They mostly pass through the state during August, before the main movements of other warblers. The last fall migrants are normally observed between September 7 and 15 with only a few records through October 1. Remarkably late Golden-wingeds lingered at Cleveland through October 21, 1978, and near Toledo until November 21, 1987.[388]

TENNESSEE WARBLER

Vermivora peregrina (Wilson)

A warm morning in mid-May will invariably be greeted by the loud ringing song of Tennessee Warblers. Seemingly every woodlot, park, and shaded residential area resounds with this distinctive song. Vibrant songs are usually produced by rather unremarkable birds, and this bird is no exception: the Tennessee is one of our plainest warblers. Its plumage of various shades of green and gray renders it quite difficult to observe in the emerging foliage.

While Tennessees are among our most numerous migrant warblers, their numbers are subject to considerable annual fluctuations. The causes of these fluctuations are poorly understood. However, relatively high numbers since the mid-1960s may reflect population increases produced by spruce budworm outbreaks within their nesting range.[438]

While overflights have appeared in the Toledo area as early as April 20,[89] these warblers do not return during late April except in the warmest seasons. They normally appear during the first week of May throughout Ohio. Peak numbers are encountered between May 10 and 25, normally totaling fewer than 40 individuals daily in the southern and central counties and 25–100 in northern Ohio. The largest flights have produced estimates of 200–250 Tennessees in the Toledo area and at Buckeye Lake.[89,479] Most depart by June 1–3 except for occasional stragglers along Lake Erie.

During the breeding season, Tennessee Warblers normally occupy boreal coniferous habitats across Canada and the extreme northern United States.[5] While they do not nest near Ohio, single singing males have been noted along western Lake Erie on July 2, 1939, and July 6, 1980.[89,278] Both are believed to be nonbreeding birds, providing the only summer records for the state.

Each autumn, Tennessees are fairly common to common migrants. During the past twenty years, peak concentrations have seldom exceeded 20–40 daily, well below the fall maxima of 100 reported from the Toledo area by Campbell[89] and 1000 from Buckeye Lake by Trautman.[479] Tennessee Warblers normally return rather early, particularly along Lake Erie, where they have appeared by July 31.[380] They are not expected until the last half of August. Away from Lake Erie, the first migrants normally appear by August 25–September 5. This warbler is widely distributed throughout September and the first week of October with most recent reports of 15 or fewer Tennessees daily. They normally depart between October 7 and 14 with a few stragglers through November 1–4.

ORANGE-CROWNED WARBLER

Vermivora celata (Say)

Despite the absence of distinctive field marks, the Orange-crowned is a rather attractive warbler. Its plumage is a mixture of greens and grays with indistinct streaks on the breast. The male's orange crown is normally concealed except when he is extremely agitated.

During spring migration, most Orange-crowneds are encountered in brushy thickets, tangles, and dense saplings; they seldom venture to the tops of tall trees. They are most frequently observed along Lake Erie, where they become uncommon migrants, mostly in groups of 1–3 individuals. A concentration of 32 Orange-crowneds at South Bass Island (Ottawa County) on May 16, 1948, was exceptional.[89] Away from the lakefront, they are casual to rare spring migrants, least numerous in the unglaciated counties. Most inland sightings are of scattered individuals. The earliest migrants may appear by

April 15 but do not normally return until April 25–May 2. They are mostly observed between May 5 and 15 and the last migrants depart by May 20–23.

Confusion with Tennessee Warblers has greatly obscured the fall status of Orange-crowneds. They are actually among the last warblers returning to Ohio; reports during August and early September are most likely misidentifications. The first migrants may appear along Lake Erie between September 18 and 23 but are not expected in the interior counties until September 25–October 5. They are mostly observed during the first three weeks of October, when they become uncommon migrants along Lake Erie and casual to rare inland. As in spring, most fall sightings are of scattered individuals, although as many as 6 have been reported along Lake Erie. Fall migrants also prefer brushy thickets and tangles, although they may be found in weedy fields dominated by ragweeds. The last fall migrants normally depart by October 20–25 with a few stragglers into November.

Orange-crowneds are accidental early winter visitors. A few sightings along Lake Erie between December 3 and 14 may be of very late migrants. Other December records include an Orange-crowned in the Cleveland area through December 24, 1964, and near Youngstown through December 27, 1953.[71,117] Later sightings are limited to single Orange-crowneds lingering at Cincinnati through January 6, 1980, and at Toledo on January 26, 1958.[89,276] An Orange-crowned attempting to overwinter at Greenlawn Cemetery in Columbus was discovered on December 26, 1926. It was regularly observed through February 10, 1927,[494] but then disappeared.

NASHVILLE WARBLER

Vermivora ruficapilla (Wilson)

Since Nashville Warblers retain their distinctive plumage throughout the year, they are among our more easily identified warblers. With their gray heads, white eyerings, green backs, and yellow underparts, Nashvilles are not likely to be confused with any other warbler foraging among the branches of small or large trees.

Nashvilles are widely distributed spring migrants. An overflight at Cleveland on April 8, 1945, was exceptionally early.[523] During most years, the first migrants appear in the southern counties by April 20–25 and along Lake Erie by April 27–30. They become fairly common to common migrants between May 5 and 15, when 5–20 Nashvilles may be observed daily. Large flights yielded concentrations of 40–80 in central Ohio. Along western Lake Erie, the largest movement produced 150 Nashvilles on May 13, 1961.[471] Their numbers sharply diminish after May 15 and most depart by May 20–25. A few stragglers remain along the lakefront into early June.

A small breeding population may once have resided in Ashtabula County. Hicks[215] cited summering Nashvilles in Monroe and Wayne Townships, although these birds may have been unmated. The only confirmed breeding record was provided by an adult feeding a fledgling in the former Pymatuning Bog on June 15, 1931. Summering Nashvilles were not recorded in Ashtabula County after the 1930s.

Elsewhere in northern Ohio, Nashville Warblers are accidental summer visitors. Sightings through June 13 at Cleveland could pertain to late spring migrants. Single individuals summered near Canton during 1936 and in Lorain County during 1982, but they were probably unmated.[31,366] In addition, a pair reportedly nested in Stebbins Gulch (Geauga County) in 1969.

While early Nashville Warblers returned to Lake Erie by the first week of August, fall migrants do not normally appear along the lakefront until the first strong cold front after August 20. They do not arrive within the interior counties until the first week of September. Most Nashvilles pass through Ohio between September 15 and October 10 and the last migrants normally depart by October 18–25. A few individuals lingered as late as November 19, 1974, at Columbus[257] and through December 1, 1980 at Cleveland.

Fall Nashville Warblers were formerly considered to be as numerous as spring migrants. September totals of 10 or more daily were not unusual. The largest reported concentrations were of 60 Nashvilles along western Lake Erie and 100 at Buckeye Lake.[89,479] Similar numbers have not been apparent during the past twenty years. Nashvilles are now uncommon to fairly common fall migrants throughout Ohio, where daily totals seldom exceed 2–8 individuals. These fall migrants also prefer woodlands, although a few frequent weedy fields devoid of woody vegetation.

NORTHERN PARULA

Parula americana (Linnaeus)

It is unfortunate that this beautiful little warbler is such an uncommon migrant. The Northern Parula is observed all too infrequently, mostly in fleeting glimpses as a small bird flits through the canopy of a tall tree. Despite this uncooperative behavior, the species' presence is frequently detected by the male's distinctive buzzy song.

While the earliest Northern Parulas returned during the first week of April, these overflights are unexpected. The first spring migrants are normally breeding warblers returning to their territories in the southern and eastern counties by April 15–20. These resident parulas establish their territories by the first week of May, the same time migrants are passing through the remainder of the state. These migrants are uncommon in most counties, becoming rare in the west-central and northwestern counties away from Lake Erie. Fewer than 3 parulas are usually observed daily and the largest flights produced tallies of 8–12. Their spring migration normally continues through May 20–25.

As summer residents, Northern Parulas prefer hemlock forests along the unglaciated Allegheny Plateau. They are very locally distributed from eastern Adams County north to southern Fairfield, Muskingum, and Belmont Counties, with isolated populations along Little Beaver Creek in Columbiana County and Mohican River in Ashland County.[220,434] Parulas are casual to rare in most counties, usually encountered as scattered pairs or groups of 2–4 territorial males. They are most numerous in Hocking County, becoming uncommon to locally fairly common residents. This county probably supports 75–100 pairs, more than all other counties combined.

Since the late 1950s, summering parulas have expanded into mature sycamore-oak riparian woodlands in southwestern Ohio. The first Cincinnati area nest was discovered in 1958.[353] In subsequent years, they spread north to Montgomery and western Ross Counties. They are locally distributed and rare in most of these counties, usually encountered as isolated pairs or territorial males, although as many as 11 males were counted along the Little Miami River in Warren County.[434]

A small breeding population formerly occupied hemlock woods in the northeastern counties. Hicks[215,220] cited summering birds at seven locations in Ashtabula County and at isolated sites in Lake and Mahoning Counties during the 1930s. They disappeared shortly thereafter. While occasional territorial males may still be found in northeastern Ohio, there is no evidence that a breeding population exists in these counties.

Since their nests are normally placed at inaccessible locations in tall trees, little information is available on their breeding biology in Ohio. Parulas build unique nests of mosses, probably during late April and May. The few breeding records indicate that eggs are normally laid during the last half of May and the young fledge by late June.

As fall migrants, Northern Parulas become casual to rare across Ohio. These migrants are mostly observed as scattered individuals with infrequent groups of 3–6 along Lake Erie and in the central counties. The first fall migrants return to Lake Erie by the last week of August but most do not appear until September. They are most likely to be observed between September 15 and October 7. A few migrants may remain later. The only November records are from the Cleveland area: single parulas on November 5, 1977, and November 20, 1976.

YELLOW WARBLER

Dendroica petechia (Linnaeus)

This common and widely distributed species is one of our most numerous resident warblers. While they have appeared in southern Ohio as early as April 5,[193] the first migrants are not normally encountered in these counties until April 13–18. Occasional overflights have been observed along Lake Erie at the same time. Yellow Warblers normally return to the central counties by April 22–26 and northern Ohio between April 28 and May 2. By the first week of May, they become common migrants in brushy thickets, shrubby old fields, woodland edges, and the brushy margins bordering ponds and streams.

Spring migrants are most numerous along western Lake Erie, where large flights produced concentrations of 1500 Yellows on May 15, 1948; 1000 on May 22, 1943; and 800 on May 7, 1983.[89,370] These large movements are not representative, however, and daily totals of 25–75 Yellows are expected during May. While Trautman[479] alluded to large flights at Buckeye Lake during the 1920s and 1930s, these flights have not been evident in recent decades. Away from western Lake Erie, 15–30 Yellows are normally observed daily with occasional movements of 50+. These migrants may pass through the interior counties until May 15–20 and remain at lakefront migrant traps until May 20–25.

Breeding Yellow Warblers prefer unshaded shrubby thickets near lakes and wetlands and willow saplings along streams. While they are most numerous near water, they also occupy brushy old fields and abandoned orchards. Their nests are usually placed at heights of one to ten feet in shrubs and saplings, although Trautman[479] described one nest placed fifty feet high in a sycamore. Nest construction begins during the first half of May. Nests with eggs have been reported by May 12–13 in central and northern Ohio, although earlier dates are probable in the southern counties. While most eggs are laid during the last half of May and hatch in mid-June, nests with young have been noted by May 18 and recently fledged young by May 25.[479] Most dependent young are observed during late June or early July. Nests with young as late as July 17 are probably the result of renesting attempts.

Yellow Warblers are fairly common to common and widely distributed summer residents. Breeding warblers are most numerous in northern Ohio, especially in Lucas, Ottawa, Sandusky and Erie Counties. As many as 30–75 Yellows may be counted daily during June. Similar numbers may also be encountered in Ashtabula, Trumbull, Lake, Geauga, and Portage Counties. Fewer breeding Yellows are found in the central and southern counties, where daily totals seldom exceed 5–25. They are least numerous in the southern counties bordering the Ohio River, especially southwestern Ohio, where only 1–10 may be observed daily.

While continental populations have remained stable since the mid-1960s,[438] local populations have experienced noticeable declines. Within Ohio, these declines are most apparent in every intensively farmed county where most habitats have been eliminated. Populations in eastern Ohio have also suffered local declines as preferred brushy habitats underwent succession into second-growth woods.

Yellow Warblers are among the first songbirds to begin their fall migration. The first fall migrants may appear along Lake Erie by mid-July and their southward movements are very noticeable by the last week of the month. This migration normally peaks during the first half of August. These migrants are most numerous along Lake Erie, where 5–20 are noted daily and the largest flights have been composed of 100–225. Smaller numbers pass through the interior counties, where fall totals seldom exceed 5–15 daily. Most Yellows depart by September 10–17 with stragglers through early October. Despite this early migration, a few Yellows have appeared remarkably late. They have been observed on November 1 in the Toledo area and at Headlands State Park, while an incredibly late Yellow Warbler was carefully identified during a snow squall at Cleveland on December 7, 1983.[89,372,388]

CHESTNUT-SIDED WARBLER

Dendroica pensylvanica (Linnaeus)

Lynds Jones expressed affection for this attractive warbler:

It is not easy for me to tell why Chestnut-sided Warbler impresses me as an exquisite. Perhaps it is on account of his small size and close-knit form, or his willingness to have me approach within speaking distance. His colors are not so bright, nor their pattern in either the contrast or harmony that may be found with other warblers, but there seems to be something about the bird which makes the day brighter, the wearing field work easier and the hours of parting forgotten when he flits into view.[102]

Jones's affection is shared by many who become acquainted with Chestnut-sideds as they pass through Ohio each year. These migrants are frequently encountered in brushy woods but are also regularly noted in parks, cemeteries, and shaded residential areas.

While overflights have been detected along Lake Erie as early as April 13,[90] Chestnut-sideds do not become widespread until the first week of May. Their numbers peak between May 10 and 22, and they become fairly common to common migrants in most counties. Spring Chestnut-sideds are most numerous along western Lake Erie, where flights of 200 warblers were detected on May 13, 1961, and May 7, 1983.[370,471] Lakefront totals of 8–20+ Chestnut-sideds may be noted during most mid-May days. Away from Lake Erie, spring totals are usually 1–8 daily with occasional reports of 10–20. The largest inland movement produced 75 at Buckeye Lake on May 11, 1929.[479] Most spring Chestnut-sideds depart from the interior counties during the last week of May but a few linger along Lake Erie through June 3–7.

A small nesting population exists within Ohio. Breeding Chestnut-sideds are most apparent in Ashtabula County, where the first nest was located in 1907.[447] Hicks[215] described them as "very local but sometimes common" residents in this county between 1929 and 1932 with observations from 32 localities. A small population also occupies the Oak Openings of Lucas County, where 13 males were counted in 1932 but only 5–6 males in subsequent years.[86] Except at these two localities, Chestnut-sided Warblers were rare and sporadic summer residents of northern Ohio during the mid-1930s with records from Paulding, Defiance, Williams, Fulton, Wayne, Lake, Geauga, Cuyahoga, and Trumbull Counties.[220]

This population has slowly expanded in subsequent decades. Chestnut-sided Warblers are now uncommon to rare summer residents in northeastern Ohio, with summering males regularly recorded south to Columbiana, Wayne, Ashland, and Richland Counties.[434] A similar status is attained in the Oak Openings of Lucas and Fulton Counties. Chestnut-sideds are casual to rare and very locally distributed elsewhere in northwestern Ohio. Summering Chestnut-sideds are casual visitors to central Ohio near Columbus, where they are discovered at two- to four-year intervals. They are generally accidental summer visitors along the unglaciated Allegheny Plateau, although a few pairs have resided along the Clear Creek valley in Hocking and Fairfield Counties during the 1980s.[471]

Breeding Chestnut-sided Warblers are encountered within brushy clearings in recently timbered woodlots, shrubby woodland edges, and dense overgrown fields.[318,447,523] Their nests are located near the ground in dense shrubs and herbaceous vegetation. Breeding activities normally begin during the last half of May. While fledglings have been reported as early as June 4,[89] these early nesting attempts are exceptional. Most nests with eggs have been discovered between June 11 and July

20 and the young usually fledge during July and the first half of August.[86,89,523]

Chestnut-sided Warblers have returned to Youngstown by August 8 and regularly appear along Lake Erie between August 15 and 23.[20] The first southward migrants do not normally appear in the central and southern counties until August 25–September 2. These migrants are mostly observed during the first three weeks of September. Fall Chestnut-sideds are generally fairly common migrants along Lake Erie but uncommon inland; daily totals seldom exceed 1–8 individuals anywhere in Ohio and the largest reported flights have totaled only 20. The last migrants normally depart by October 5. The latest fall Chestnut-sideds lingered until October 18 at Hancock County and October 19 at Cleveland.[417]

MAGNOLIA WARBLER

Dendroica magnolia (Wilson)

The Magnolia Warbler is another occupant of northern coniferous woodlands that is also a rare but regular summer resident of hemlock forests in eastern Ohio. The first Ohio breeding records were provided by Hicks[215] from Ashtabula County, citing summer records from eight locations into the early 1930s. With the destruction of the former Pymatuning Bog and with logging activities in other hemlock woods, this small population apparently disappeared before 1940.

Breeding Magnolias were also discovered at Stebbins Gulch in Geauga County during 1947.[523] As many as four pairs nested at this location during subsequent years. A similar number regularly occupied nearby Little Mountain (Lake and Geauga Counties). Isolated males and breeding pairs have periodically inhabited other hemlock-dominated ravines in Lake, Cuyahoga, Medina, and Lorain Counties. Despite annual fluctuations, breeding Magnolias in northeastern Ohio probably total 5–15 pairs most years.

Within the unglaciated southeastern counties, Magnolia Warblers regularly breed only at Mohican State Forest in Ashland County, where 3–6 singing males have been present since the late 1970s. These warblers also reside within Hocking County hemlock ravines, although they may not be reported annually. Worth Randle discovered the first Hocking County breeding pair at Conkle's Hollow Nature Preserve in 1966. One or two pairs have intermittently nested in Clear Creek Valley since 1970.[411] Small numbers of summering males have appeared at other Hocking County locations during the 1980s.[367]

Away from the eastern counties, breeding Magnolia Warblers have been reported only from the Toledo area.[89] This northwestern Ohio breeding record is of a summering pair near Sylvania (Lucas County) during 1965; a nest with young was discovered on July 12.

Within hemlock woodlands, breeding Magnolias prefer steep ravines and woodland edges where the understory and shrub layers are densest. Their nests are usually placed relatively low in small trees within dense cover. The few breeding records indicate most nests are initiated during late May and early June

with the young fledging by early July. An exceptionally early nesting attempt was reported by Hicks[215] in Ashtabula County; adults were feeding dependent young on June 10, 1931.

This attractive warbler is fortunately a common migrant through the state. With the exception of occasional overflights during mid-April, the first Magnolia Warblers usually return to the southern half of Ohio by May 1–4 and Lake Erie by May 3–7. They become common spring migrants between May 10 and 24. Daily totals are generally 5–20 within the interior counties and 10–30 along Lake Erie. Large flights produce concentrations of 40–75 within the central counties and 100+ along western Lake Erie.[374,479] Numbers of migrants decline during the last week of May. A few linger within the interior counties into the first week of June and along Lake Erie through June 18.[89]

The first fall migrants occasionally return to Lake Erie between July 19 and 28.[89,523] These early migrants probably are nonbreeders or unsuccessful adults, since Magnolias do not normally appear along the lakefront until August 20–25. Fall migrants may become common along Lake Erie by the last week of August but do not become common within the interior counties until the first week of September. Normally, 5–20 Magnolias are observed daily, while infrequent flights have produced concentrations of 50–125+.[89,479] Most Magnolias depart by the first week of October. Only occasional stragglers remain after October 10–16 with scattered sightings as late as November 15, 1957, at Toledo and November 19, 1972, at Cleveland.[89]

CAPE MAY WARBLER

Dendroica tigrina (Gmelin)

Within Ohio, Cape May Warblers are primarily migrants in passage to and from their breeding range in the coniferous forests of northern New England and eastern Canada. Numbers of most warblers nesting within these forests, including Cape Mays, fluctuate considerably in response to food availability. During spruce budworm outbreaks, the Cape May population increases dramatically and this species ranks among our most numerous migrant warblers. At other times, only relatively small numbers may be observed.

While a few early spring migrants may return during the last week of April, Cape Mays are not normally encountered until the first week of May. Most pass through the state between May 5 and 22. These spring migrants are most numerous along Lake Erie, where they are normally fairly common to common visitors. Generally, 20 or fewer individuals are observed daily along the lakefront, although large flights have produced totals of 30–60+. They are normally uncommon migrants within the interior counties but may become fairly common during years of peak abundance. Inland totals seldom exceed 3–12 daily, although as many as 40 have been reported from Buckeye Lake.[479] Most Cape Mays depart during the last week of May with stragglers remaining in northern Ohio through June 6–9.

While Cape May Warblers have returned as early as July

25–30,[362] the first fall migrants do not normally appear along Lake Erie until August 20–25. They may become fairly numerous along the lakefront during the last week of August but are not expected in the inland counties until August 28–September 5. They remain fairly common to common migrants along Lake Erie throughout September, producing daily reports of 5–25 individuals and occasional flights of 50–100+. Fall migrants are less numerous within the interior counties, where they are generally uncommon visitors. Inland totals are normally 1–8 daily and the largest reported flights have totaled 15–20. The last migrants normally depart by October 7–15.

Cape May Warblers are surprisingly hardy for a species that usually winters in the West Indies.[5] In addition to a few late migrants during November, Cape Mays are accidental early winter visitors. There are at least ten published sight records during December and January: four in the Cleveland area, two at Youngstown, and singles at Belpre, Zanesville, Buckeye Lake, and Cincinnati. Most wintering Cape Mays disappeared before January 20. However, one individual overwintered at a Cincinnati area feeder during January and February 1980.[276]

BLACK-THROATED BLUE WARBLER

Dendroica caerulescens (Gmelin)

Black-throated Blues are among our most easily identified warblers. Their distinctive plumages are identical in spring and fall, allowing for their immediate recognition as they forage within shrubs and small saplings at relatively low heights. They mostly occur within young deciduous woodlands but may also appear in parks and cemeteries.

In spring, overflights have appeared in the Cleveland area as early as April 14, 1959,[117] but there are very few additional records before May 1. Black-throated Blues normally appear during the first week of May and their spring movement peaks between May 10–20. The last migrants depart before the end of the month.

These spring migrants are most numerous along Lake Erie, where they are generally fairly common, although daily totals seldom exceed 3–10 individuals. Large flights in excess of 15–25 Black-throated Blues are exceptional. The largest reported flight totaled 200 in Lake County on May 4, 1936.[523] Fewer Black-throated Blues are observed within the interior counties. They are generally uncommon migrants in northern and glaciated central Ohio, becoming rare to uncommon in the southern and unglaciated counties. These inland migrants are mostly encountered as individuals or groups of 2–4, although as many as 10–15 were reported from Buckeye Lake.[479]

At one time, a few Black-throated Blues may have regularly nested in Ashtabula County. Hicks[215] observed summering birds in Wayne Township in 1928 and 1929 and the former Pymatuning Bog during 1931. Breeding was established at both sites; a nest with eggs was discovered on June 11, 1931, and adults accompanied by dependent young were observed on July 7,

1928. Since then, habitat destruction eliminated these locations, and breeding Black-throated Blues have not been observed in the county.

With the disappearance of these breeding pairs, Black-throated Blues became accidental nonbreeding summer visitors. Most nonbreeders have been detected in the hemlock ravines within the Chagrin River watershed in eastern Cuyahoga, Lake, and Geauga Counties. Males have irregularly appeared within these ravines since the mid-1960s but without any evidence of nesting. Other recent summer records are limited to two territorial males at Mohican State Forest (Ashland County) during 1981 and single nonterritorial individuals in northwestern and southeastern Ohio during 1987.[177,434]

While a few Black-throated Blues may return to northern Ohio during the last week of August, they do not normally appear until September 1–5. They may not be noted in the central and southern counties until September 5–10. Black-throated Blues trickle through the state during September and the first week of October, while the last migrants usually depart between October 10 and 17. A few migrants may remain later, but the only November records are of warblers at Cincinnati on November 8, 1975, and a central Ohio specimen collected November 11, 1944.[45,261]

Fall migrants are generally uncommon to fairly common along Lake Erie, where they are usually observed in groups of 5 or fewer. Fall Black-throated Blues are rare to locally uncommon within the interior counties and least numerous in southwestern Ohio. These migrants are mostly noted in groups of 3 or fewer, although as many as 15 were reported from Buckeye Lake.[479]

YELLOW-RUMPED WARBLER

Dendroica coronata (Linnaeus)

While other warblers spend the winter in warm tropical climates, one regularly survives the harsh Ohio winters. The hardy Yellow-rumped Warbler overwinters in woodlands throughout the state, subsisting on berries. It prefers poison ivy berries, but it also eats dogwood and other small berries. Its numbers, like those of all birds subsisting on fruit, fluctuate considerably in response to food availability.

Numbers of wintering Yellow-rumped Warblers have become more plentiful in recent years. Before 1940, they were accidental to casual winter visitors throughout Ohio and were not reported annually. Their numbers gradually improved during the 1940s and 1950s, and they have been regularly encountered since 1960.

Yellow-rumped Warblers are normally casual to rare winter residents in northern Ohio, where they are mostly observed as individuals or small flocks of 3–11.[523] They are surprisingly plentiful within red cedar groves on Kelleys Island (Erie County). At least 30–50 regularly winter in these groves and 300 were counted on December 5, 1984.[377] In the central counties, Yellow-rumped Warblers are normally rare winter residents. During most winters, they are encountered as scattered individuals. Small flocks may be observed when fruit is abundant; as many as 118 individuals were tallied on the 1979 Columbus Christmas Bird Count and 117 on the 1968 Buckeye Lake Christmas Bird Count. These warblers become locally uncommon in southern Ohio. They are usually observed in groups of 6 or fewer, but larger concentrations are possible as evidenced by 100+ in the Forestville area (Hamilton County) during the winter of 1950–51.[248]

During relatively warm springs, the first migrants may return by the last days of March. In other years, they may not appear until mid-April. Yellow-rumpeds are undoubtedly our most numerous migrant warbler, becoming common to abundant between April 25 and May 10. Their numbers decline precipitously after May 15 and the last migrants normally depart from the central and southern counties by May 22–25. A few linger along Lake Erie through June 1–2.[273]

These spring migrants regularly occur in woodlands, parks, cemeteries, and other wooded habitats. During some years, only 15–40 Yellow-rumpeds are observed daily and the largest lakefront flights are composed of 100–150. In other years, their numbers can be astounding and daily totals of 100+ Yellow-rumpeds may be encountered throughout the state. The largest inland flights have been composed of 500 at Dayton and 200–500 at Buckeye Lake.[479] These numbers are dwarfed by the largest flights along western Lake Erie: 5000 warblers on May 6, 1972, and 2000 on May 7, 1983.[90,370]

While early fall Yellow-rumpeds have been noted along Lake Erie by August 21–23, they do not normally return there until September 10–15. They are not expected in the central and southern counties until September 20–27. The largest lakefront flights are noted between September 27 and October 20, while inland flights are usually about one week later. The southward migration continues through November 10–20.

Migrating Yellow-rumped Warblers are as numerous in fall as in spring. Daily totals of 25–100 along Lake Erie and 10–50 inland are expected during October. Occasional large flights have been encountered, including an estimated 7500 Yellow-rumpeds at Crane Creek State Park–Magee Marsh Wildlife Refuge complex on October 5, 1985, and 1000–1200+ at Buckeye Lake on several October dates during the 1920s and 1930s.[380,479]

Most Ohio records are of the eastern "Myrtle Warbler" race. However, the western "Audubon's" race has been observed on at least two occasions. Adult male "Audubon's" were documented from the Cleveland area at Shaker Lakes April 30–May 3, 1931, and at Richmond Heights on October 5, 1941.[523]

BLACK-THROATED
GRAY WARBLER

Dendroica nigrescens (Townsend)

An accidental visitor to Ohio, the first substantiated Black-throated Gray Warbler was collected on the Ohio State University campus in Columbus on November 15, 1950. This warbler was initially discovered by Gene Rea and Edward Thomas

earlier in the day as it foraged with a small flock of juncos and Ruby-crowned Kinglets.[468] Ohio's only other substantiated record was provided by a warbler discovered near Athens on November 19, 1969. It was photographed during its daily visits to a suet feeder through December 16.[157]

There are at least eleven spring sightings from the Cleveland area, but only the Black-throated Gray discovered at Cleveland on April 25–26, 1967, and studied by many birders appears to be correctly identified.[335] The other records lack documentation or verification by knowledgeable observers.

Black-throated Gray Warblers normally breed in the mountains of western North America from southern Canada to southeastern Arizona and northern Baja California.[5] They mostly winter in Mexico, with small numbers in southern Texas, southern Arizona, and southern California. This western warbler has proven to be an accidental but regular vagrant to eastern North America, primarily during late fall and early winter.

TOWNSEND'S WARBLER

Dendroica townsendi (Townsend)

As occupants of mountain coniferous forests, Townsend's Warblers breed in western North America from Alaska to northern Oregon and Wyoming. Their winter range normally extends from California south to Costa Rica.[5] Like many other long-distance migrants, a few of these warblers wander from this established range and become accidental visitors elsewhere in North America.

There is one accepted record of this accidental visitor to Ohio. A male Townsend's Warbler was discovered along the bird trail at Magee Marsh Wildlife Area, Lucas County, on April 7, 1973, by Elliot Tramer and members of his ornithology class from Toledo University.[286] The bird was closely studied, carefully described, and its distinctive song heard on several occasions. It was observed for twenty minutes as it foraged with several Yellow-rumped Warblers in the leafless box elders along the trail.

BLACK-THROATED
GREEN WARBLER

Dendroica virens (Gmelin)

The first spring Black-throated Green Warblers are normally resident males returning to their territories within the southeastern counties. These males may appear during the first week of April and are regularly encountered by April 10–16. They occasionally overfly their nesting range and have been detected at Dayton by April 1 and Findlay, Lima, Cleveland, and Lucas County by April 4–8. The first spring migrants are not expected outside their breeding range until April 20–27 within the southern and central counties and April 25–May 2 along Lake Erie. Their northward migration peaks between May 5 and 20. Stragglers may remain along the lakefront through the first week of June.

Black-throated Greens are fairly common to common spring migrants within woods, riparian corridors, parks, cemeteries, and shaded residential areas across Ohio. These migrants are most numerous along Lake Erie, where 10–30 may be observed daily and flights of 50–100 are not surprising. Larger movements have produced as many as 400 at Magee Marsh Wildlife Area (Lucas County) on May 7, 1983.[370] Similar numbers are not normally apparent within the interior counties, where daily totals are 15 or fewer. Spring flights may produce local inland concentrations of 20–40, but only Trautman[479] reported as many as 50–125 daily at Buckeye Lake during the 1920s and 1930s.

Ohio has always supported a small breeding population of Black-throated Green Warblers. Initially, breeding pairs were restricted to the northern counties, especially northeastern Ohio east of Cleveland.[523] A few pairs also occasionally summered and probably nested in Lorain County.[13,241] By the mid-1930s, nesting warblers were very locally distributed in Ashtabula, Lake, Geauga, Cuyahoga, and Mahoning Counties.[215,220] They were rare to uncommon in every county except within the Chagrin River watershed, where 10–19 pairs were counted at Little Mountain between 1933 and 1938.[523] Along the unglaciated Allegheny Plateau, Black-throated Greens were uncommon residents within the Shawnee State Forest in Scioto County, but only a few pairs were also known from Adams, Jackson, Hocking, Lawrence, Fairfield, and Knox Counties.[220,223] The only other breeding Black-throated Greens were in Ashland County, while summering males were infrequently reported from Williams and Lucas Counties in northwestern Ohio.[89,220]

Breeding populations have slowly expanded along the unglaciated Allegheny Plateau, where breeding Black-throated Greens moved northward through the hemlock forests, appearing in Columbiana County by the early 1960s.[144] Similar expansions were not apparent elsewhere.

Black-throated Green Warblers are now locally distributed summer residents along the entire Allegheny Plateau, including the glaciated northeastern counties. They are fairly common to locally common residents throughout Hocking County, along the Mohican River in Ashland County, and within the Chagrin River watershed in portions of Cuyahoga, Lake, and Geauga Counties.[434] As many as 10–20 males can be counted daily at these localities. These warblers are casual to locally uncommon residents elsewhere within the eastern third of the state with scattered records from Adams and Scioto Counties north to Ashtabula County. Summering Black-throated Greens are accidental in the remainder of Ohio. During the 1980s, a few unmated males have very sporadically appeared at widely scattered locations within the northwestern counties.[434]

Breeding Black-throated Green Warblers are mostly restricted to hemlock or mixed hemlock-deciduous forests. A few males have also been found within mixed deciduous-pine woodlands. Relatively little information is available on their nesting biology in Ohio. Within the southeastern counties, their breeding activities probably begin by late April or early May and fledglings may be observed by mid-June. These ac-

tivities are delayed by one to two weeks within the northeastern counties, where young may not appear until the last week of June or July.

Black-throated Greens have a protracted fall migration. Early migrants have returned to the Toledo area by August 2 and Cincinnati by August 7.[89,363] During most years, they do not appear along the lakefront until August 25–September 2 or within the interior counties until the first week of September. Their southward movements peak between September 15 and October 8. The last migrants normally depart by October 12–18, although stragglers will occasionally remain into November with at least four records as late as November 8 at Findlay and November 18 at Cleveland.[417,523]

These fall warblers are also fairly common to common migrants throughout Ohio. They are most numerous along Lake Erie, where 5–20 Black-throated Greens may be observed daily. Large flights are less frequent than in spring, although as many as 200 individuals were reported from the Toledo area on September 23, 1944.[89] Inland fall totals are 5–15 individuals daily with occasional flights of 20–30. The only larger flights were reported by Trautman[479] at Buckeye Lake, where up to 100 individuals were tallied daily in late September.

BLACKBURNIAN WARBLER

Dendroica fusca (Müller)

For those who enjoy birds for their attractive plumages, this species becomes an immediate favorite. Few birds can match the visual impact made by a male Blackburnian Warbler in full sunlight against the bare branches of a budding tree. His vivid orange and black face pattern adds sparks of brilliant color to a somber landscape, a sure sign that spring has arrived. It is difficult to believe that such a colorful bird could be difficult to observe. Yet, once the trees have fully acquired their leaves, a male may be virtually impossible to discover as he sings from a perch within the canopy of a large tree.

This attractive warbler is a widely distributed and fairly common spring migrant throughout the state. Daily totals seldom exceed 5–12 individuals. While large flights have produced occasional concentrations of 30–50 in central and northern Ohio, the largest reported movement totaled 100 in the Toledo area on May 24, 1947.[89] The first migrants normally return to the southern half of Ohio during the last week of April. Overflights have appeared along Lake Erie by April 19, 1942,[523] but these warblers do not normally return to the lakefront until the first week of May. Their maximum abundance is attained between May 7 and 20. Smaller numbers remain through the end of the month with lingering males along Lake Erie through June 7–15.

Fewer Blackburnian Warblers are observed during autumn. They are uncommon to fairly common fall migrants throughout Ohio; daily totals seldom exceed 3–10 individuals. By far the largest fall flight totaled 60 Blackburnians at Buckeye Lake on September 26, 1925.[479] They are relatively early fall migrants and have returned to Lake Erie by July 31. However, the first fall migrants do not normally return to the lakefront until August 18–25 or to the interior counties until the last week of August. Their passage through Ohio is mostly completed by September 25–30; only a few warblers remain into the first week of October. The latest migrants have been reported through October 20–22. While there is one December sight record, it lacks supporting details.

Blackburnian Warblers were unknown as summer residents in Ohio until 1931, when males were discovered in Ashtabula County at the former Pymatuning Bog and in Kingsville Township. A nest was discovered at the latter site during 1932.[215] During 1933 and 1934, one or two pairs summered at Little Mountain on the Lake-Geauga county line.[523] These records established Blackburnian Warblers as casual or accidental summer residents in extreme northeastern Ohio, a status they have maintained. While none has been reported from Ashtabula County since the 1930s, one or two pairs have sporadically appeared at Little Mountain and nearby Stebbin's Gulch (Geauga County) as recently as 1980. In addition, a pair nested at Lake Rockwell in Portage County between 1984 and 1986.[434] A few nonbreeders have been reported from several other locations.

In 1954, a summering Blackburnian Warbler was discovered by Worth Randle at Old Man's Cave–Cedar Falls State Parks in Hocking County. Annual June surveys of this location between 1960 and 1975 recorded at least one male each year with a maximum of six in 1961. They disappeared during 1976.[367] During the 1980s, a few Blackburnians have been occasionally reported from southeastern Ohio during June but they appear to be wandering males. The only territorial male was discovered by Brian Gara at Lake Hope State Park in Vinton County during June 1985.[434] Hence, Blackburnian Warblers are presently accidental summer residents within the unglaciated southeastern counties.

Most summering Blackburnians have been found within Ohio's mature hemlock forests. The only exception is at Lake Rockwell, where a nesting pair occupied an extensive stand of planted pines. There are fewer than six confirmed nesting records and very little information on their nesting chronology. The few records indicate that breeding begins during late May; adults have been observed carrying food to nestlings during the last half of June.

YELLOW-THROATED WARBLER

Dendroica dominica (Linnaeus)

In the nineteenth century, Yellow-throated Warblers were regarded as widely distributed summer residents, regularly encountered north to Lake Erie.[522] Their numbers rapidly diminished during the late 1800s, and breeding warblers disappeared from most counties.[236] Habitat availability was not a factor in this decline, but the causes were never established. By the early 1900s, these warblers had largely disappeared except for small numbers in Scioto and adjacent southern counties.[194]

By the mid-1920s, nesting pairs could be located along the Scioto River north to Circleville (Pickaway County) and there

was a nesting attempt in Columbus during 1925.[497] This expansion was not apparent elsewhere. In the 1930s, Hicks[220,223] described Yellow-throated Warblers as very local summer residents in southern Ohio, with records from every county along the unglaciated Allegheny Plateau north to Hocking and Athens. In southwestern Ohio, he cited records from Hamilton, Clermont, and Brown Counties although these sightings were disputed by others.[248] These warblers were rare in every county except Pike and Scioto, where 50–100 pairs may have been present. They were accidental spring visitors to the remainder of the state.

This population slowly spread northward along the unglaciated Allegheny Plateau after 1940. In southwestern Ohio, the first breeding pairs were recorded at Cincinnati and Dayton during the 1950s, although they did not become widely distributed until the late 1960s.[248,299] Nesting pairs reappeared in central Ohio during the 1960s. Within the northern counties, spring migrants were not regularly reported until the 1970s and summering pairs have been present since 1975.

Yellow-throated Warblers are now fairly common to locally common summer residents throughout southern Ohio. Most reports are of 3–10 Yellow-throateds daily with local concentrations of 12–20. They become uncommon to fairly common residents in the central counties, most numerous in eastern Ohio but rather locally distributed in the west-central counties. Summer totals seldom exceed 1–5 individuals daily in all central counties. These warblers are presently accidental to locally rare residents in northern Ohio, where a few pairs regularly reside from Erie County east to Cleveland and in Seneca, Wood, and Henry Counties.[434]

Breeding Yellow-throated Warblers exhibit a decided preference for large sycamores bordering creeks and rivers. They are not exclusively restricted to these habitats, however, and occasional pairs will occupy upland mixed deciduous-pine woods.

Since they normally nest at considerable heights, relatively little information is available on their breeding chronology in Ohio. Within the southern counties, nesting activities are probably initiated during the last half of April, although nest construction has been reported into early June. The few nests have been discovered during May and early June, while recently fledged young have appeared between June 7–10 and August 11.[497] Their breeding activities are probably delayed by one or two weeks in northern Ohio.

Their spring migration is mostly resident warblers returning to their territories. Away from nesting locations, Yellow-throated Warblers are presently casual to rare spring visitors, invariably occurring as scattered individuals. Spring overflights regularly appear north to Lake Erie, where there are two to five sightings during most years. The earliest spring migrant returned to Pike County on April 2, 1940.[508] A few migrants have appeared at other southern locations by April 5–8, but they do not normally return until April 12–18. Breeding pairs are widely distributed in all southern counties by April 22–25. In northern Ohio, the earliest migrants have been detected between April 14 and 20, but most spring Yellow-throateds are noted between April 25 and May 15 with only a few stragglers later in the month.

Like many of our resident warblers, Yellow-throateds become very inconspicuous once the males quit singing in early

July. Hence, their fall migration patterns are poorly understood. These warblers begin moving southward during the last half of August. The last migrants normally depart between September 22 and 27. Fall Yellow-throated Warblers are uncommonly reported in southern Ohio but are rare elsewhere in their nesting range. These records mostly are of single warblers. They are accidental fall visitors away from known summering locations. Published fall records from northern Ohio are limited to single sightings at Cleveland, Lucas County, and Portage County.

This species is an accidental early winter visitor. Ohio's only record is provided by a Yellow-throated Warbler visiting a Mansfield feeder between December 6, 1981 and January 10, 1982.[364] It disappeared during an extended period of severe weather.

PINE WARBLER

Dendroica pinus (Wilson)

As their name implies, breeding Pine Warblers are found only in tracts of mature pines. Their preferred habitats are dry ridges where tall pines are interspersed with younger deciduous trees, but they will also occupy uniform pine plantations. Within these habitats, they can be surprisingly inconspicuous as they forage among the outer branches of the tall pines. Only singing males are readily detected.

At one time, Pine Warblers were among the least known of our resident warblers. Hicks[220] considered them "extremely rare and local" summer residents in eastern Ohio. Scioto County hosted the largest breeding population, with an estimated 40–50 pairs. Scattered pairs and summering warblers were also known from Jackson, Hocking, Fairfield, Knox, Ashland, Lake, and Ashtabula Counties.

Breeding Pine Warbler populations have generally increased within eastern North America since 1965.[438] These expanding populations have also been apparent in Ohio. Along the unglaciated Allegheny Plateau, Pine Warblers have become uncommon to fairly common but locally distributed summer residents north to Ross, Hocking, and Athens Counties.[434] Daily totals seldom exceed 3–5 individuals except in preferred areas, where 6–10 males can be regularly counted. Elsewhere along this plateau, these warblers are casual to rare residents north to Ashland County, usually encountered as groups of 3 or fewer singing males.

Away from the unglaciated counties, Pine Warblers are very rare and locally distributed summer residents in the northern counties. Within northeastern Ohio, they are known to nest regularly only near Lake Rockwell in Portage County. In northwestern Ohio, extensive pine plantations are present only within the Oak Openings, where Pine Warblers have summered since 1983 and nesting was confirmed in 1987.[434]

Surprisingly little information is available on their nesting biology in Ohio. Pine Warblers place their nests in the outer branches of tall pines. In southern Ohio, nest construction frequently begins in mid-April. Eggs may be laid by late April and the young fledge by late May or early June. These warblers could raise two broods annually but later nesting attempts have never been reported. Nesting activities begin several weeks later in northern Ohio, where nest construction is initiated during the first half of May, eggs are laid by late May, and the young fledge in late June or July.

The Pine Warbler is the first resident warbler returning to Ohio each year. The first territorial males appear in the southern counties by March 12–18 and become widespread by March 25-April 5. These early migrants are not apparent at the northern edge of the Allegheny Plateau or in the northern counties, where they do not normally return until the last half of April.

Away from their breeding range, Pine Warblers are normally rare to locally uncommon spring migrants. Overflights have appeared as early as March 6, 1961, at Columbus and March 15, 1986, along western Lake Erie.[329,382] These overflights normally are of single Pines, although 15+ appeared at Cincinnati on March 13–14, 1977.[266] Most migrant Pine Warblers pass through Ohio between April 15 and May 7, usually in groups of 4 or fewer. The last spring migrants depart by May 15. Unlike the resident warblers, migrant Pines are regularly observed in deciduous woods.

Their status as fall migrants is poorly understood. Other fall warblers are regularly misidentified as Pines and many sight records have proven to be incorrect. Fall Pine Warblers are generally rare throughout Ohio and are usually encountered as scattered individuals. They tend to be rather late migrants with few confirmed sightings before mid-September. Most migrants appear between September 15 and October 10 with a few sightings later in the month.

Most Pine Warblers spend the winter months in the southeastern United States. They are relatively hardy warblers, however, and a few may regularly overwinter as far north as southern Missouri and southern Kentucky. They could even overwinter in southern Ohio. Pine Warblers are casual early winter visitors to southeastern Ohio with at least eight published records since the mid-1950s. These records are of 1–2 individuals in pine woods, mostly during December. They are accidental winter visitors elsewhere in Ohio, where sightings include at least two records at Dayton, Columbus, Toledo, and Findlay and single reports from Cleveland and Akron. While most were reported during December, several overwintered with the assistance of food obtained from bird feeders.

KIRTLAND'S WARBLER

Dendroica kirtlandii (Baird)

Kirtland's Warbler was first described from a specimen collected by Charles Pease in Lakewood (Cuyahoga County) on May 13, 1851.[523] Pease presented the specimen to Dr. Jared Kirtland, who sent it to Spencer Baird at the National Museum in Washington. Baird named the species in Kirtland's honor, recognizing his significant contributions to our understanding of the natural history of the Ohio and Mississippi River valleys.

This warbler was known only as a very rare migrant until its limited breeding range was discovered within young jack pine woods in the northern lower peninsula of Michigan. These warblers apparently winter in the Bahamas and adjacent islands.[5] Their migration corridor crosses Ohio, and the entire population probably passes over the state each spring and autumn.

Kirtland's Warblers are the rarest of the eastern wood warblers regularly appearing in Ohio. There are at least forty reports from the state, some of which are based on specimens, photographs, and thoroughly prepared descriptions. Others are undocumented and their identification is questionable.

Most Kirtland's Warblers are detected during spring when they are accidental visitors. Mayfield[315] reported at least thirty sightings, mostly from the northern half of Ohio. However, there are very few records from the northeastern counties after 1900. These spring records are of 1–2 individuals normally appearing between May 10 and 25. The only confirmed April record was at Tiffin on April 30, 1975.[259]

Considerably fewer Kirtland's Warblers are observed as fall migrants. Mayfield[315] cites only nine fall records widely scattered across the state. These accidental fall migrants have been reported between the last week of August and early October, but all confirmed sightings are during September.

More Kirtland's Warblers were detected before 1970 than after. This species averaged one Ohio record every two or three years during each decade through the 1960s. In the 1970s, published sightings were restricted to the April Kirtland's photographed at Tiffin and a specimen recovered at Cincinnati on September 27, 1975.[261] The 1980s produced a documented fall record at Marietta on September 12, 1980, and two singles at Magee Marsh Wildlife Area (Lucas County): a female banded on May 21, 1980, and a male photographed on May 9, 1987.[277,386]

PRAIRIE WARBLER

Dendroica discolor (Vieillot)

This occupant of abandoned fields overgrown with shrubs and saplings has gradually extended its breeding range northward during the twentieth century. In the late 1800s, Prairie Warblers were rare spring visitors throughout Ohio.[236] The first summer residents were recorded from Scioto County, where Prairies were considered "not common" in 1905 and the first nest was discovered in 1908.[194,196]

Their initial northward expansion was restricted to the unglaciated Allegheny Plateau. By the mid-1930s, breeding Prairie Warblers were found in every county north to Muskingum, Morgan, and Washington.[220,223] They were locally numerous in Hocking, Jackson, and Vinton Counties but were rather rare elsewhere. This population eventually spread into other unglaciated counties. By 1960, summering Prairies reached the northern edge of the plateau.

Prairie Warblers also expanded into glaciated Ohio. Breeding Prairies initially appeared in the southwestern counties at Cincinnati in 1958 and Dayton in 1961.[299,353] Few nonbreeding summer visitors were reported from the glaciated central and northern counties until the late 1960s. Territorial males were initially recorded at Toledo in 1968 and Cleveland in 1976, although nesting was not established at either area for several years.[90,263] This gradual range expansion continued into the 1980s.

Breeding Prairie Warblers are now most numerous within the red cedar–covered hillsides of Adams County, where they are common to abundant residents. Daily totals of 25–75+ individuals are possible throughout the county. Elsewhere along the unglaciated Allegheny Plateau, these warblers are fairly common residents north to Muskingum, Guernsey, and Belmont Counties, where 3–10 Prairies may be noted daily. They become uncommon residents along the remainder of the unglaciated plateau, where most reports are of 5 or fewer daily. In southwestern Ohio, they are fairly common residents in Highland and Brown Counties but are uncommon to rare and locally distributed elsewhere. Most summer sightings are of 4 or fewer individuals within these counties. The fewest resident Prairies inhabit the glaciated central and northern counties, where they become accidental to locally rare residents. Scattered males and pairs are regularly observed near Columbus, the Oak Openings near Toledo, several sites near Cleveland, and north to Lorain and Ashtabula Counties.[434]

Prairie Warblers nest in dry brushy fields studded with small pines, red cedars, and deciduous saplings. They are generally found in fields where the trees are less than ten feet high. With their preference for these successional habitats, Prairies normally disappear when the woody vegetation becomes too dense and tall. Nesting activities begin during May. Most clutches are reported between May 15 and June 15 and nests with young have been discovered by the last week of May.[54,497] Fledgling warblers are expected by mid-June with late clutches producing young into July. Their breeding chronology is delayed by several weeks in northern Ohio, where the first clutches are not laid until early June and the young fledge during mid-July.

As spring migrants, the earliest Prairies appear by April 12–16. In southern and unglaciated Ohio, Prairie Warblers are regularly encountered by April 20–25 and all return by May 10–15. This movement largely comprises residents arriving on their breeding territories. Elsewhere, Prairie Warblers are casual to rare spring migrants, normally encountered as single individuals. These migrants mostly appear between April 25 and May 15 with stragglers along Lake Erie into the last half of May.

Prairies become inconspicuous once the males stop singing in early July. There are remarkably few fall records. Fall Prairie Warblers are normally rare to uncommon along the unglaciated plateau and accidental elsewhere. Records mostly are of single warblers. Their southward movements may peak between August 15 and September 15 with stragglers through October 2–9 at Buckeye Lake and Cleveland and in Scioto County. The latest sighting was at Cincinnati on November 8, 1975.[261]

PALM WARBLER

Dendroica palmarum (Gmelin)

During migrations, Palm Warblers are mostly encountered on or near the ground in brushy thickets, wooded fencerows, woodland edges, and other shrubby habitats. They also occur in weedy fields during fall. Most prefer fairly open habitats, such as shrubs along Lake Erie beaches and bushes scattered within cemeteries and parks.

While their numbers fluctuate considerably from year to year, Palm Warblers are generally most numerous during spring. Overflights have been reported from Toledo as early as March 24, 1941,[89] and there are sightings from other locations during the first week of April. They do not normally return until April 20–28. Palm Warblers are most numerous during the first two weeks of May, when they become fairly common to common migrants along Lake Erie but uncommon to fairly common inland. Daily lakefront totals are normally 5–25 Palms, but large flights along western Lake Erie have produced estimates of 200 on May 6, 1934, and May 7, 1983.[89,370] Fewer than 10 daily are noted at most interior locations, although flights may produce as many as 25–50 in central Ohio.[479] Most Palms depart between May 17 and 23 with occasional stragglers through the end of the month along Lake Erie.

The earliest fall Palm Warbler returned to Buckeye Lake by August 9, 1933, but even late August records are quite rare.[479] These warblers normally appear between September 8 and 15. Most fall Palms pass through Ohio between September 20 and October 10. They are generally fairly common migrants along Lake Erie and uncommon inland. Daily totals seldom exceed 10 and the largest concentrations total only 25–30. Most migrants depart by the third week of October with small numbers lingering into November.

Our Palm Warblers are normally of the western race characterized by mostly grayish underparts. The eastern race has entirely yellow underparts and is a very rare migrant, mostly along Lake Erie during spring days with strong northeasterly winds.

Palm Warblers are casual early winter visitors; there are more than thirty published records. These records are scattered throughout Ohio; the greatest number come from the southwestern counties. They are mostly encountered as individuals with occasional flocks of 3–5, normally during December and early January. Most disappear by January 15 and very few have overwintered. One survived the winter of 1926–27 at Greenlawn Cemetery in Columbus by feeding on the ground under dense evergreens and shrubs.[494] Other February records are limited to single warblers at Columbus through February 3, 1947, and at Buckeye Lake on February 28, 1925.[304,479]

BAY-BREASTED WARBLER

Dendroica castanea (Wilson)

Bay-breasted Warblers are occupants of northern coniferous forests across northern New England and eastern Canada.[5] Although they nest in conifers, spring Bay-breasteds are found in all types of woodlands. A few overflights have appeared as early as April 20–21. However, they are not normally encountered until the first week of May. Their numbers reach a decided peak during the third week of May when they become fairly common to common migrants. Spring totals are generally 3–20 Bay-breasteds daily, although large flights produced con-

centrations of 150 on May 18, 1984, at Magee Marsh Wildlife Area and 100 on May 24, 1973, at Columbus.[374,471] Most migrants depart by May 25–31 with small numbers occasionally lingering into early June. While the latest migrants remained at Toledo through June 13, 1948, and Cleveland until June 14, 1964, this species has not summered in Ohio.[89,117]

As fall migrants, Bay-breasteds are among our most numerous warblers. They frequently make up a sizable proportion of the mixed-species warbler flocks visiting woodland, edge, and shrubby habitats. While the earliest Bay-breasted Warbler returned to Cleveland by July 17,[117] there are very few additional records before August 10. They are expected to return to Lake Erie by August 18–22 and can be fairly numerous by August 25. They do not regularly appear in the interior counties until the first week of September. Fall Bay-breasteds are most numerous during September, when they are common statewide migrants. Daily totals of 10–40 are not unusual and as many as 100–150 have been reported along Lake Erie and in central Ohio. Most depart by October 7–12. Only occasional stragglers are noted during the last half of October and there are no published records after October 30.

Their numbers are subject to considerable annual fluctuations, mostly the result of periodic outbreaks of the spruce budworm caterpillars within their boreal forest breeding range. When the caterpillars are abundant, warbler populations exhibit substantial increases. These high population levels are maintained for several years, followed by a rapid decline to more typical numbers.

BLACKPOLL WARBLER

Dendroica striata (Forster)

The status and distribution of Blackpoll Warblers are remarkably similar to those of the Bay-breasteds. Both warblers are relatively late spring migrants en route to their boreal forest breeding grounds. Both are subject to substantial population fluctuations in response to spruce budworm outbreaks. Moreover, they are both considerably more numerous during fall migration than in spring. Even their fall plumages are very similar.

Blackpoll Warblers undergo a truly incredible fall migration. They are among the very few songbirds who fly directly from North America to their wintering grounds in South America. The initial stages of this migration are a series of relatively short flights from their breeding grounds to the Atlantic Coast. During these flights, the Blackpolls accumulate considerable fat deposits that will eventually fuel their several-thousand-mile transoceanic flight.

Blackpoll Warblers are generally fairly common to common fall migrants, although they are locally uncommon in the southwestern counties. These migrants are most numerous along Lake Erie, where daily totals of 8–35 are not unusual. Large flights may produce 50–100 daily; there were as many as 200 at Toledo on September 25, 1943.[89] Within the interior counties, daily totals seldom exceed 3–20. Only Trautman[479] reported substantial inland movements with as many as 150 individuals daily at Buckeye Lake during the 1920s and 1930s. While the first fall migrants returned to western Lake Erie by July 25–31, they do not regularly appear along the lakefront until the last half of August. Within the interior counties, there are very few late August records and these warblers normally appear between September 5 and 10. Fall Blackpolls are regularly encountered through October 5–12. Only occasional stragglers remain until late October or early November.

Blackpolls are uncommon to fairly common spring migrants throughout Ohio. Daily spring totals seldom exceed 5–10 individuals. The largest spring flights produced concentrations of only 30–40. Unusually early overflights include an April 16, 1875, specimen from central Ohio and an April 17, 1982, sighting from Lucas County.[45,365] However, the first migrants do not normally appear until the first week of May. Their peak spring movement occurs between May 15 and 25. Most depart before May 30 with only a few stragglers into June.

While migrant Blackpolls have lingered along Lake Erie into the second week of June, there is only one midsummer record from Ohio. An unmated male remained at Magee Marsh Wildlife Area into early July 1985.[379]

CERULEAN WARBLER

Dendroica cerulea (Wilson)

When the first Cerulean Warblers return each spring, the budding vegetation is just beginning to emerge and these attractive warblers may be forced to feed relatively close to the ground. They normally return to the southern counties by April 25–30 but are not expected along Lake Erie until the first week of May. Most resident Ceruleans appear by May 12–17 and very few migrants are detected after May 20. This northward migration is mostly resident warblers returning to their breeding territories. They are decidedly uncommon spring migrants elsewhere, mostly appearing as scattered individuals, although as many as 10–15 Ceruleans have been reported along Lake Erie.

As soon as the vegetation is fully developed, Cerulean Warblers retreat to the canopies of tall trees where they remain throughout the summer. Breeding Cerulean Warblers occupy only mature deciduous woodlands. While they may prefer upland oak-hickory and beech forests, Ceruleans also readily occupy mesic beech-maple woodlands and mixed riparian corridors.

Their historic status and distribution within Ohio reflect their dependence on mature wooded habitats. In the late 1800s, Jones[236] considered them "not uncommon" summer residents throughout Ohio. During the twentieth century, their fortunes have undoubtedly improved in most southern and eastern counties where extensive mature woodlands have developed. By the mid-1930s, Ceruleans were among the most numerous woodland warblers along the Allegheny Plateau.[220] They have remained fairly common to common residents within these counties. In contrast, their numbers have steadily declined in many west-central and northwestern counties since the 1930s.[89]

Cerulean Warblers are now fairly common to common summer residents in southern and eastern Ohio west to the glacial boundary and Cuyahoga, Medina, and Ashland Counties. In southwestern Ohio, they are generally fairly common residents north to southern Preble, Montgomery, and Greene Counties. Daily totals of 5–12 Ceruleans may be noted in most southern and eastern counties, with 15–25 warblers in extensively wooded areas. In the remainder of Ohio, Cerulean Warblers are generally uncommon residents in Pickaway, Franklin, Delaware, Morrow, and Richland Counties but become casual to rare and very locally distributed in most west-central and northwestern counties.[434] Most locations support only 1–3 territorial males, although they may be more numerous where habitats are particularly suitable.

Since their nests are located at heights of thirty to 100 feet in the canopies of tall trees, relatively little information is available on their breeding biology within Ohio. Nest construction probably begins during the first half of May and continues through early June. The few nests with eggs have been reported in June. Recently fledged young may appear by June 18 but are mostly noted during July.[523]

Once the males quit singing, Cerulean Warblers become remarkably inconspicuous. Even within the southern and eastern counties they are rarely and very sporadically observed after July 15. The fall migration apparently begins in August and peaks before September 15.[479] These migrants are invariably observed as widely scattered individuals. Most depart before September 25 with very few sightings as late as October 9, 1960, at Ashtabula.[327]

BLACK-AND-WHITE WARBLER

Mniotilta varia (Linnaeus)

Readily recognized by their distinctive plumages and nuthatch-like behavior, Black-and-white Warblers are familiar migrants throughout Ohio. The earliest acceptable spring migrants are Lake Erie overflights noted between April 2 and 8. They do not normally return to the southern counties until April 15–20 or elsewhere before April 25–30. Their northward migration normally peaks between May 3 and 18 with smaller numbers appearing through May 25–28. Along Lake Erie, a few stragglers have remained into the first week of June.

These migrants are generally fairly common to common along Lake Erie, where 3–10 are observed daily. They are seldom abundant; sizable songbird flights produce concentrations of 25–50 Black-and-whites. Away from the lakefront, similar numbers are encountered within some southeastern counties, where migrants are augmented by breeding pairs. Elsewhere, Black-and-whites are generally fairly common migrants with 1–6 individuals daily. In recent years, few inland flights have exceeded 10–15 individuals, although Trautman[479] reported as many as 42 from Buckeye Lake.

Breeding Black-and-white Warblers are fairly common residents along the unglaciated Allegheny Plateau north to Hocking, Perry, Morgan, and Washington Counties.[434] Most localities support 5 or fewer daily, although as many as 6–12 may be tallied within favorable habitats in Hocking, Scioto, Vinton, and Ross Counties. Farther north along the unglaciated plateau, they become uncommon to rare summer residents and are mostly encountered as widely scattered pairs. Within glaciated Ohio, Black-and-white Warblers are casual to rare summer residents within the southwestern, central, and northeastern counties.[434] They are largely absent from the west-central and northwestern counties, although a few males occupy woodlands near western Lake Erie.

Their distribution and relative abundance have not appreciably changed since the mid-1930s except for the disappearance of a small breeding population in northwestern Ohio.[89,220] But nesting Black-and-whites were more widely distributed during the nineteenth century. Langdon[289] considered them common summer residents in the 1870s at Cincinnati, where there have been few summer records in the present century.[248] Jones[241] regularly observed a few breeding pairs in Lorain and Erie Counties around the turn of the century. This decline was probably related to the destruction of mature woodlands.

Nesting Black-and-white Warblers normally prefer extensive woodlands with dense understories and shrub layers. In southeastern Ohio, they are mostly found on dry wooded hillsides. The former population in the northwestern counties occupied swamp forests. But these warblers are not necessarily restricted to extensive woods. Several pairs occupy young wooded corridors only 100–150 feet wide along the Scioto River in Ross County.

Their nests are expertly hidden on the ground, usually at the base of a tree or shrub. In the southeastern counties, nesting activities probably begin in late April or early May, since fledglings have been reported by the second week of June.[37] These activities probably begin one or two weeks later elsewhere. Nests with eggs have been discovered between May 29 and June 14 in northern Ohio, while recently fledged young have appeared during the first half of July.[89,215]

Black-and-white Warblers are remarkably early fall migrants. Campbell[89] reports probable migrants at Toledo by July 7 and they occasionally appear within the northern and central counties before the end of the month. Their southward movement normally begins between August 5 and 15 and continues through September 22–30. The last migrants usually depart by October 7–10 but stragglers have remained into November, with at least three sightings from the Cleveland area and one at Columbus. An exceptionally late migrant was noted at Kent on December 16, 1979.[276]

Fewer Black-and-whites are detected as fall migrants, a result of their less conspicuous behavior during this season. They are generally fairly common migrants along Lake Erie, where most fall sightings are of 6 or fewer individuals. These migrants are uncommon to fairly common in most inland counties, with 1–4 observed daily. The largest inland movements involved 10–12 individuals.

AMERICAN REDSTART

Setophaga ruticilla (Linnaeus)

This distinctive warbler is one of our more numerous migrants. American Redstarts visit all types of woodlands, from swamp forests and second-growth woods to parks, cemeteries, and shaded residential areas. Feeding in low shrubs or high in the canopy, they are certain to be noticed as they actively flit from branch to branch.

American Redstarts are relatively late spring migrants. While the earliest lakefront overflight was detected on April 22, 1945,[523] redstarts seldom appear in southern Ohio during April. Spring migrants are not expected until the first week of May. Their numbers normally peak between May 10 and 25, and frequently they become the most numerous migrant warbler during the last half of May. Numbers noticeably diminish by May 30, although a few stragglers regularly remain into the first week of June.

Spring American Redstarts are most numerous along Lake Erie, where they are common to abundant migrants. At most localities, 15–30 are encountered daily, while sizable flights produce concentrations of 50–100+. This species is a fairly common to locally common spring migrant in most inland counties, where daily totals normally are 5–15. Sizable movements involve only 20–40 individuals.

Their status as summer residents has undergone considerable change within the past century. In the late 1800s, American Redstarts were considered common residents throughout Ohio.[236] But in 1935 Hicks[220] recorded breeding redstarts from only 68 counties. They were most numerous within the eastern third of the state and the swamp forests of northwestern Ohio but were very locally distributed or absent elsewhere. Even in eastern Ohio, nesting redstarts were not uniformly distributed. They were most numerous in the northeastern counties and within Lawrence, Scioto, and Adams Counties but were uncommon to rare elsewhere.[220,223]

Redstarts declined in subsequent decades. Near Toledo, they remained numerous until 1940 but have been rare since 1950.[89] Similar reductions were locally apparent in eastern Ohio. The only indication of range expansion was noted at Cincinnati, where a few summering individuals have been intermittently noted since the 1940s.

American Redstarts are now uncommon to fairly common summer residents in eastern Ohio, becoming rare near major urban areas. Summer totals seldom exceed 2–12 individuals daily. They are generally casual to locally uncommon residents elsewhere, although they are absent from most intensively farmed western counties.[434] Nesting redstarts are locally distributed. While they frequently occur as isolated pairs, nesters also form loose associations. It is not unusual to find 5–10+ pairs nesting at one locality, yet they are completely absent from nearby woods.

Breeding redstarts normally occupy young woods with dense understories and shrub layers, utilizing them until they mature and become more open underneath. Nesters prefer swamp forests or mesic woods along streams. Nest construction is initiated by May 15–25 and continues into June. The first clutches are laid by May 19–28 but most are discovered in early June. Renesting attempts may produce clutches into the first week of July.[463,479] Recently fledged young may appear by June 12 but are more likely to be detected in late June and July.

American Redstarts have a fairly protracted fall migration. The first arrivals may return to Lake Erie by the last week of July but do not normally appear until August 10–20. Fall migrants are expected within most interior counties by August 25–30. They are generally numerous throughout September. Small numbers regularly remain into early October but normally depart by October 10–15. Stragglers produced two November records from Cleveland and one from Cincinnati, while an exceptionally late redstart was discovered at Cleveland on December 8, 1973.

Along Lake Erie, American Redstarts are fairly common to common fall visitors, with most reports of 25 or fewer individuals daily. A few large flights produced concentrations of 75–110 near Toledo.[89] They become uncommon to fairly common fall migrants within the inland counties. Most September totals are 10 or fewer individuals daily with occasional concentrations of 15–25.

PROTHONOTARY WARBLER

Protonotaria citrea (Boddaert)

Perched on a dead snag in a wooded swamp, a male Prothonotary Warbler looks like a golden-orange jewel in the morning sunlight. One of the most stunning of our warblers, he is not reticent about showing off his exquisite plumage as he forages along the margins of the swamp, nor about declaring his territory from an exposed perch. His loud song rings through the swamp, a distinctive *sweet-sweet-sweet-sweet* on one pitch.

Prothonotary Warblers are normally associated with wooded swamps in the southern United States. But they find suitable breeding habitats within Ohio, even though relatively few shrubby swamps remain. Fairly adaptable, the Prothonotaries also reside along the wooded margins of reservoirs, large rivers, quiet backwaters, and ponds.

Prothonotary Warblers have always been locally distributed summer residents. Hicks[220] cited breeding records from twenty-nine counties south to Montgomery, Pickaway, Muskingum, and Guernsey and the Buckeye Lake area plus isolated records from Washington County. While these warblers were generally rare summer residents, many pairs were concentrated at the ''canal lakes'' of Buckeye, St. Mary's, Loramie (Shelby County), and Indian and the Muskingum River near Ellis Dam. Trautman[479] estimated 50–80 nesting pairs at Buckeye Lake between 1922 and 1924 but only 25–45 pairs by 1933. Similar populations were found at other lakes, while 15 pairs were counted near Ellis Dam in Muskingum County during 1934–35.[222]

Their statewide distribution has changed considerably since the mid-1930s. The sizable populations at most ''canal lakes'' have largely disappeared. However, Indian Lake and Lake St. Mary's still host 10–15 pairs. Prothonotaries discovered a number of breeding locations at newly constructed reservoirs and along large rivers. Their range has also spread southward throughout Ohio.

Prothonotary Warblers are now very locally distributed summer residents with recent records from more than forty counties.[434] They are least numerous in the western counties, where suitable habitats are particularly scarce. Breeding Prothonotaries are rare in many counties, with only 5 or fewer pairs at one to three locations. Where habitats are suitable, they may become locally fairly common summer residents. The largest population resides within the Killbuck Creek valley in Wayne, Holmes, and Coshocton Counties, where 10–20+ males are noted daily. Other sizable populations are scattered along the Scioto River south of Circleville, the Little Miami River in Warren County, and the western Lake Erie marshes. Daily totals of 5–15 individuals are possible at these locations.

Breeding Prothonotaries prefer natural cavities over standing water. If natural cavities are unavailable, they readily occupy birdhouses or other nest sites, including crevices in buildings, coffee cans, paper bags, minnow buckets, and even a mailbox.[89,479] Their nesting activities are initiated during the first half of May in the southern and central counties but not until late May along Lake Erie. Nests with eggs have been reported between May 15 and June 28.[319,479] While some young have left the nest by June 5, they do not normally fledge until late June or early July. Nests with young reported through July 11–14 and dependent young observed between August 8 and 15 probably represent renesting attempts.[479,523]

Unusually early spring Prothonotaries returned to Columbus by April 6, 1947, and East Liverpool (Columbiana County) on April 7, 1969.[45,156] The first migrants do not normally appear within the southern counties until April 20–27 or along Lake Erie before the first week of May. Most summer residents return by May 20. Their spring migration is largely made up of residents arriving on their breeding territories. Prothonotaries are accidental to casual migrants away from established breeding sites.

Their southward movements are equally inconspicuous. According to Trautman,[479] fall Prothonotaries are most numerous between August 10 and 20, when he tallied as many as 50 daily at Buckeye Lake. The sizable breeding population comprised most of his August concentrations. Elsewhere, only 1–5 individuals compose most fall sightings. The last migrants normally depart by September 15–20. Since there are only two October sight records, the appearance of a Prothonotary at Columbus on November 11, 1963, was extraordinarily late.[391]

WORM-EATING WARBLER

Helmitheros vermivorus (Gmelin)

As summer residents, Worm-eating Warblers have particularly strict habitat requirements. They occupy only the understory and shrub layers within the interior of extensive mature forests. Unobtrusive, they are frequently overlooked as they forage within the underbrush. Only singing males are fairly conspicuous, delivering their dry buzzing rattle from a tall perch, frequently as high as forty to fifty feet, near the canopy.

Breeding Worm-eating Warblers have always been most numerous along the unglaciated Allegheny Plateau. Summering warblers are uncommon to fairly common residents along this plateau north to Ross, Hocking, Morgan, and Washington Counties, becoming uncommon to rare and locally distributed elsewhere north to Columbiana, Holmes, and southern Ashland Counties.[434] They are most numerous in Hocking, Ross, Vinton, Pike, Scioto, and Adams Counties, where 10–15 may be recorded daily. Summer totals seldom exceed 1–6 in other unglaciated counties.

Within southwestern Ohio, Worm-eating Warblers are rare and very locally distributed summer residents north to Butler, Montgomery, and Highland Counties. This population is small, composed of scattered pairs and singing males within parks or along steep wooded valleys bordering large rivers.[248,299]

Breeding Worm-eating Warblers have never been confirmed elsewhere. There are no summer records from the glaciated central counties. In northern Ohio, anecdotal nineteenth-century nesting records from Cuyahoga and Ashtabula Counties are not considered valid.[236] In recent years, single summering males have been located in Geauga County during 1984 and the Cuyahoga River National Recreation Area since 1985.[375,434] At Toledo, the only summer record was furnished by a non-breeder observed on June 16, 1930.[86]

There is surprisingly little information on their breeding biology within Ohio. Worm-eating Warblers nest on the ground, frequently near the base of small saplings. Nest construction apparently begins in May and the first clutches are laid during the last half of the month or early June. Recently fledged young may appear by late June or July.

Worm-eating Warblers become difficult to locate after early July. Although their fall migration is poorly defined, these movements apparently begin by August 20–25 and continue through September 15–20. Outside their established breeding range, Worm-eating Warblers are accidental fall visitors. There are eight published fall records from central Ohio, two from the Toledo area, and one from Cleveland. Most of these records are within the normal migration period, although a late individual was noted near Toledo on October 9, 1963.[89] The only later record was provided by a specimen washed onto the Ohio River shore near the Clermont-Hamilton county line on November 1, 1947.[248]

Their spring migration is better defined. The first males normally return to their territories between April 18 and 25 in southern Ohio. Most breeding birds return by May 10–15.

Small numbers of Worm-eating Warblers regularly appear north of their established breeding range each spring. These overflights are most apparent along Lake Erie, where they have been reported as early as April 6, 1947, near Toledo.[89] They are rarely encountered along the entire lakefront, with fewer than six sightings some years and as many as twelve to fifteen reports in others. Most are of scattered individuals, with a maximum of 7 reported from Magee Marsh Wildlife Area on April 28, 1974.[471] Spring overflights are casual to rare near Columbus and the northeastern counties but there are very few sightings from the west-central counties and northwestern Ohio away from Lake Erie. These inland overflights are also mostly scattered individuals, although a remarkable group of 12 was reported from Akron following a thunderstorm on May 6, 1975.[471] Most overflights appear between April 28 and May 12 with a few late migrants noted through May 25–June 1.

SWAINSON'S WARBLER

Limnothlypis swainsonii (Audubon)

Swainson's Warbler is an uncommon and locally distributed occupant of woodlands with dense shrub layers in the southeastern United States. While these warblers breed in cane thickets within swamp forests along the Mississippi River valley, their preferred habitats along the Appalachian Mountains are rhododendron hollows or similar impenetrable thickets in damp woods. Their breeding range normally extends north to eastern Kentucky and central West Virginia.[5]

Ohio's first Swainson's Warbler was discovered near the village of Chesapeake in Lawrence County on May 4, 1947. This singing male was intermittently observed through June 21, when it was collected. It was believed to be unmated and did not occupy typical breeding habitat, frequenting a steep stream valley supporting honeysuckle, Virginia creeper, crossvine, and blackberry tangles but few trees.[134] Its appearance corresponded with a northward range expansion in West Virginia during the 1940s and 1950s.[68]

In addition to the Lawrence County specimen, summering Swainson's Warblers were reported from Jefferson County during 1964, 1966, 1970, and 1971 and Columbiana County in 1976.[84,170] These sightings are not supported by substantiating details and their validity is difficult to determine. Although a pair was reported from Columbiana County, all the other records were of isolated singing males. No nesting attempts were established. Despite claims to the contrary,[5] there are no confirmed Swainson's Warbler nesting records from Ohio.

During the 1980s, Swainson's Warblers have apparently declined in West Virginia and eastern Kentucky. The only reported Ohio summer record during this decade was of a singing male in Jackson County between May 18 and 25, 1987.[434] This male also occupied atypical breeding habitat: a cutover hillside supporting an impenetrable thicket of shrubs and saplings but no large trees. In all likelihood, he too was unmated.

Swainson's do not regularly overfly their breeding range and there are relatively few extralimital spring sightings. They are accidental spring visitors to Ohio, where the only confirmed Swainson's Warbler was photographed at Greenlawn Cemetery in Columbus on April 27–28, 1985.[378] Another warbler was closely observed near Dayton on April 22, 1961, but could not be relocated.[299] Other details are unavailable and the validity of this sighting is difficult to judge. There are four undocumented spring records from the Cleveland-Akron area and one at Steubenville. Without supporting details, the validity of these sightings is questionable.

OVENBIRD

Seiurus aurocapillus (Linnaeus)

Ovenbirds were named for the domed nests resembling Dutch ovens that they cleverly hide in leaf litter on the forest floor. Through a small entrance on the side, the adults easily slip in and out of these nests without revealing their location. These nests are usually discovered only by accident when an adult flushes at an observer's feet. Cowbirds, however, seem to have little trouble locating Ovenbird nests and regularly parasitize them.

Since the Ovenbirds' nests are so difficult to locate, there is relatively little information on their breeding biology. Within the southern counties, Ovenbirds begin their nesting activities by late April or early May and recently fledged young may appear by June 14–19. These pairs may raise two broods annually, since fledglings will be recorded through early August. Their nesting activities commence several weeks later in northern Ohio, where nest construction begins in mid-May and nests with eggs have been reported between May 20 and July 4.[89,417] These young normally fledge during late June or July.[523]

Breeding Ovenbirds occupy mature woods with open understories and a forest floor covered with considerable leaf litter. They are equally at home on the dry wooded hillsides of southeastern Ohio and in the swamp forests of the northwestern counties. Inhabitants of extensive woodlands, they will be found only within shaded forest interiors, shying away from brushy cover along woodland edges.

The relative abundance of breeding Ovenbirds reflects the distribution of these wooded habitats. Throughout eastern and unglaciated Ohio, these warblers are fairly common to locally abundant summer residents. Summer totals frequently are 5–18 Ovenbirds daily, while as many as 30–50 may be counted within the heavily wooded southeastern counties. They are decidedly less numerous in other portions of the state. Ovenbirds are locally rare to fairly common residents in most southwestern, glaciated central, and northwestern counties, where summer totals seldom exceed 3–5 individuals daily. They are least numerous within intensively farmed northwestern and west-central Ohio where breeding pairs are absent from a number of counties.[434] They become locally common at only a few western Ohio locations; in the Oak Openings of Lucas County, as many as 50 males have been counted in one day.[89]

These breeding populations have remained fairly stable during the present century. Since the 1930s, declines have been apparent only in western Ohio where wooded habitats have been extensively converted to farmlands. Populations within the eastern counties have not appreciably changed.

As spring migrants, the earliest Ovenbirds have appeared at Dayton by March 29–30 and along Lake Erie by April 14–19. These early migrants are the exception rather than the rule. Within the southern counties, the first resident males normally return by April 14–18 and are widely distributed by April 25–30. In northern Ohio, Ovenbirds usually return by April 25–May 2 and become numerous by May 10. Along Lake Erie, their northward movement peaks between May 5 and 20; scattered individuals may appear into the first week of June.

Within the interior counties, most spring reports are of resident Ovenbirds returning to their nesting territories. Away from breeding locations, they become uncommon to fairly common migrants with only 1–6 individuals observed daily. The only sizable inland movement totaled 50 migrant Ovenbirds at Buckeye Lake on May 11, 1929.[479] Along Lake Erie, they become fairly common spring migrants. Most lakefront reports are of 10 or fewer Ovenbirds daily. Sizable songbird movements have occasionally produced concentrations of 50+ individuals.

Given the inconspicuous behavior of silent Ovenbirds, their southward migration is normally rather poorly defined. It apparently begins during the last half of August. Small numbers of fall migrants may be detected throughout September, but they normally depart October 5–15. Stragglers have lingered into mid-November at a few localities. During autumn, Ovenbirds are locally rare to fairly common migrants throughout Ohio. They are seldom numerous, even within the eastern counties. Most fall sightings are of 5 or fewer individuals daily, although Trautman[479] occasionally noted 15–25 at Buckeye Lake during the 1920s and 1930s.

Ovenbirds normally winter in Central America and the Caribbean region. A few may remain in North America.[5] They are accidental winter visitors in Ohio with at least six records since 1966: four at Cincinnati and single birds at Dayton and Toledo. Surprisingly, these birds have mostly visited bird feeders, although the Dayton individual was discovered in a pine grove.[299] The Cincinnati Ovenbirds apparently overwintered.

NORTHERN WATERTHRUSH

Seiurus noveboracensis (Gmelin)

As their name implies, waterthrushes are invariably found along small streams, quiet backwaters, ponds, and wooded swamps. They are not thrushes but large warblers, immediately recognized by their plain brown upperparts, striped underparts, and distinctive habit of teetering like Spotted Sandpipers. While recognizing a waterthrush is no problem, distinguishing between the two species, Northern and Louisiana, is a challenge. Singing males can be readily separated, but silent individuals require careful study. Northern Waterthrushes are mostly known as transients through Ohio. Unlike our resident Louisiana Waterthrushes, Northerns generally prefer quieter water, including wooded swamps, brushy margins of small ponds, and backwaters along large creeks and rivers.

During their northward migration, a few Northern Waterthrushes have returned by April 12–16. These mid-April sightings are quite unusual and all earlier sight records most likely pertain to misidentified Louisianas. The first Northerns are not normally encountered until April 23–30 in the central and southern counties and April 28–May 5 along Lake Erie. Most pass through the state between May 5 and 20. Only a few stragglers have remained along western Lake Erie into the first week of June.

These waterthrushes are most numerous along Lake Erie, where they become locally fairly common migrants and 6–12 Northerns may be observed daily. They are seldom abundant, and daily totals in excess of 20–25 Northerns are noteworthy. Fewer Northerns are detected within the interior counties, where they are normally uncommon to locally rare migrants. In recent years, most inland spring sightings have been of 1–5 individuals and daily totals of 10–15 are exceptional.

A small breeding population exists in northeastern Ohio. This population was undoubtedly larger in the 1920s and 1930s when suitable breeding habitats were more widely distributed. While Hicks[220] cited nesting records from Lake, Geauga, Trumbull, and Ashtabula Counties, only Geauga and Ashtabula regularly supported nesting pairs. Ashtabula County hosted by far the largest number of breeding Northerns; they were known from eleven locations, and 22 pairs were counted at the former Pymatuning Bog in 1932.[215] Summering Northerns also regularly appeared at five Geauga County sites.[523] Away from these northeastern counties, the only summering Northern Waterthrushes were reported from a Huron County bog.[220]

Destruction of the Pymatuning Bog and other northeastern Ohio wetlands has apparently reduced this population. Within the past decade, summering Northerns have been recorded from only two to four locations in Portage, Geauga, and Ashtabula Counties, mostly as widely scattered pairs. This known breeding population probably does not exceed 10–15 pairs.[434] However, the status of this resident population is imperfectly known and additional nesting pairs are likely.

Within Ohio, breeding Northern Waterthrushes prefer bogs where buttonbush, dogwood, alder, and poison sumac thickets provide dense cover along shallow water. Red maple–yellow birch swamp forests with dense shrub layers are equally suitable.[2,219] Northern Waterthrushes nest on the ground within dense cover. The few confirmed breeding records indicate that nests are normally constructed in late May and early June. Nests with eggs have been reported between May 17 and June 15; young do not normally fledge until late June or early July.[220,523]

Their status as fall migrants is obscured by identification problems. A few have been reported during the last half of July, but the first fall Northerns do not normally appear along Lake Erie until August 10–20 or within the central and southern counties until the last week of the month. Migrants may be expected through September 25–30. The last Northerns normally depart by October 5–15, although a few late migrants have lingered into early November. Considerably fewer Northerns are reported in fall than in spring. They are rare to uncommon in all counties but tend to be most numerous near Lake Erie. Most fall sightings are of 1–4 waterthrushes daily, although as many as 10–12 have been reported from the lakefront and central Ohio.

Northern Waterthrushes are accidental early winter visitors. There have been at least four winter sightings, all on Christmas Bird Counts since 1963: two at Dayton and one each at Ashland and Magee Marsh Wildlife Area. All sightings have been of single birds, the latest at Magee Marsh on January 1, 1971.[90]

LOUISIANA WATERTHRUSH

Seiurus motacilla (Vieillot)

By far the more widely distributed of our resident waterthrushes, Louisianas reside along small rocky streams flowing through mature woodlands. Nesting Louisianas are not particular about the woodland communities surrounding these high gradient streams as long as the trees are mature and the streams mostly shaded. Nesters are as numerous along the hemlock-dominated headwaters of the Chagrin River in Geauga County as along southeastern Ohio streams bordered by deciduous woods.

Louisiana Waterthrush nests are placed on the ground, usually under tree roots or among herbaceous vegetation fairly close to the stream. Their nesting activities are normally initiated during the last half of April. Nests with eggs are expected during May, although renesting attempts may result in clutches through the first week of June.[523] In southern Ohio, fledglings may appear by the last days of May or first week of June. They do not normally appear until mid-June within the northern counties, while late nesting attempts may produce young into July.

Nesting Louisiana Waterthrushes are most numerous along the unglaciated Allegheny Plateau where forested stream valleys are widely distributed. They are generally common residents along this plateau north to Hocking, Athens, and Washington Counties, becoming fairly common elsewhere within the unglaciated counties.[434] From 3 to 15 individuals may be encountered daily in most southeastern counties. Within southwestern Ohio, Louisiana Waterthrushes are generally fairly common residents in the counties bordering the Ohio River but become uncommon and locally distributed elsewhere north to southern Preble, Montgomery, and Greene Counties. They are also uncommon to fairly common but locally distributed residents in northeastern Ohio west to Lorain, Medina, and Richland Counties. They become rare and very locally distributed residents in central Ohio from Morrow, Delaware, Franklin, and Pickaway Counties east to the Allegheny Plateau. Nesters are largely absent from the remainder of Ohio.[434] In west-central Ohio, nesters are restricted to isolated pairs along small streams in Miami and Logan Counties. The only nesting record from northwestern Ohio was established in Lucas County in 1934, although territorial males were also noted near Toledo in 1971 and 1978.[89,90,270] Populations have been stable during recent decades.[438] In fact, the Ohio breeding distribution has not substantially changed since 1900.

While overflight Louisianas have appeared in southeastern Ohio by March 7, 1946, and Lorain County by March 16, 1983,[45,370] the first migrants normally appear between March 25 and April 2 in the southern counties and April 5–10 in northeastern Ohio. Their migration largely takes place in April and is normally concluded by April 20–25. This movement is mostly of residents returning to their nesting territories. Away from their breeding sites, Louisiana Waterthrushes are casual to rare spring migrants with all confirmed sightings during late March and April, usually of single individuals. While there are innumerable May sight records of migrant Louisianas, these reports undoubtedly pertain to misidentified Northerns.

Their fall status has also been greatly obscured by apparent misidentifications. Louisiana Waterthrushes are actually very early fall migrants. They quietly disappear from their breeding territories during the last half of July and most have departed by August 15–22. They are accidental migrants away from their established nesting locations. While a few Louisianas might linger into the first week of September, all later sight records are almost certainly misidentified Northern Waterthrushes.

KENTUCKY WARBLER

Oporornis formosus (Wilson)

As summer residents, Kentucky Warblers reside exclusively within mature deciduous woodlands. They are equally numerous in dry upland woods and more mesic communities but normally avoid swamp forests. Occupants of shrub and understory habitats, Kentuckies prefer forest interiors and usually avoid woodland edges. Hence, they are only found in extensive woodlands and large woodlots, avoiding regularly timbered forests and small woodlots of only a few acres.

Kentucky Warblers nest on the ground, typically at the base of a sapling or small shrub. Their expertly concealed nests are rather bulky and mostly composed of dead leaves and grasses. In southern Ohio, clutches are laid by mid-May. The young usually fledge during the last half of June. Their nesting chronology is delayed by two or three weeks in the northern counties, where young warblers may not fledge until July. Renesting attempts may produce July broods in the southern counties.[479]

Their statewide distribution has been gradually expanding northward during this century. In the early 1900s, Jones[236] considered Kentucky Warblers fairly common summer residents in the southern third of Ohio, although this status was disputed by Henninger.[193] They were unrecorded from the remainder of the state. Their breeding range expanded northward along the unglaciated Allegheny Plateau between 1910 and the early 1930s.

By 1935, Hicks[220] recorded breeding Kentucky Warblers in every southern and eastern county north to Butler, Montgomery, Clinton, Ross, Fairfield, Licking, Knox, Ashland, Wayne, Stark, and Columbiana. They were locally distributed and uncommon at the northern edge of this range and fairly common to common only along the Allegheny Plateau north to Coshocton, Guernsey, and Monroe Counties.[223]

This range expansion continued in subsequent decades. By the 1940s, Kentuckies became rather common residents in Carroll and Jefferson Counties but remained "very infrequent" north of the glacial boundary.[84] Nesting Kentuckies were detected at Youngstown by 1950[60] and in the Toledo area in 1958 and 1963.[89] A summering male appeared near Cleveland in 1960.[335] This expansion is still producing new breeding records from the glaciated counties.

Kentucky Warblers are now fairly common to common summer residents in southern and eastern Ohio north to Preble, Montgomery, Clinton, Highland, Ross, Licking, Knox, Richland, Ashland, Wayne, Stark, and Columbiana Counties.[434] Where extensive mature woodlands are prevalent, 15–20+ individuals can be noted daily. At the northern and western boundaries of this range, daily totals seldom exceed 1–6. In the central counties adjacent to Columbus, they become uncommon residents with only 1–4 daily. Kentuckies remain casual to rare and very locally distributed residents elsewhere,

with records from all but seven scattered counties.[434] Most of these sightings are of isolated pairs and summering males.

The first spring Kentuckies appear in the southern counties by April 18–25 and northern Ohio by May 5–10. Most breeding warblers return by May 15–20. This migration, which is poorly defined, normally consists of Kentuckies returning to their breeding territories.

Away from known breeding locations, Kentucky Warblers are casual to rare spring migrants. They are usually detected at lakefront migrant traps, where there are five to ten reports during most years. The earliest extralimital Kentucky appeared at Tiffin on April 19, 1976, but most are observed between May 8 and 25.[262]

Like most woodland warblers, Kentuckies become inconspicuous once the males quit singing in early July. There are relatively few records after July 15. Most resident Kentuckies quietly leave Ohio between the last half of August and September 10–20. They are accidental to casual fall migrants away from their established nesting range, even along Lake Erie; only one fall record comes from Toledo and several from the Cleveland area.[89,335] Most of these extralimital fall sightings are before September 20 but include two October reports, the latest at Cleveland on October 17, 1958.[117]

CONNECTICUT WARBLER

Oporornis agilis (Wilson)

This elusive skulker of woodland thickets is one of the rarest warblers regularly migrating through Ohio. Discovering a Connecticut Warbler is noteworthy during either fall or spring migration, and obtaining a satisfactory view of it requires considerable patience and perseverance. Even singing males are quite adept at remaining hidden. With a little luck, foraging Connecticuts will occasionally come into view—always near the ground or in dense tangles no more than six or eight feet high.

As spring migrants, Connecticuts are among the last warblers returning to Ohio. There are probably no valid sightings before the second week of May. The first migrants normally appear around May 15; most are recorded between May 18 and 28. Connecticuts are regarded as rare to uncommon spring migrants along Lake Erie and casual to rare inland. They are generally encountered as scattered individuals, with occasional totals of 3–6 daily. The spring of 1929 brought unprecedented numbers to Buckeye Lake, where 15–25 Connecticuts were recorded daily between May 22 and 25.[479] Most depart by June 1–5 with a few stragglers into the second week of the month.

Fall migrants may inhabit weedy and brushy fields in addition to woodland thickets. They silently hide in the abundant vegetation, and their status is further obscured by the difficulty of separating Connecticuts from the similar Mourning Warblers. Fall Connecticuts are generally casual to rare migrants, normally encountered as scattered individuals. Most migrants are overlooked, and Trautman's report of 19 Connecticuts, including 14 specimens, on South Bass Island during September

1950 may be representative of the numbers actually passing through the state.[89] The first migrants are not expected until the last week of August. They are most frequently observed between September 10 and October 5 but depart shortly thereafter. The latest Ohio fall sighting is only October 16.

MOURNING WARBLER

Oporornis philadelphia (Wilson)

The behavior and migrations of the Mourning Warbler, another skulker through shrubs and other low woodland cover, are similar to those of the Connecticut Warbler. Both species rank among the last migrants returning each spring. A few early Mournings have appeared during the first week of May but they do not normally return until May 10–15. Most migrate between May 18 and June 3. The last migrants may linger along Lake Erie until June 5–10 and occasionally through June 15.

These spring migrants are most numerous along Lake Erie, where they become uncommon to locally fairly common in late May. As many as 1–6 Mournings can be observed daily and concentrations of 8–12 are possible. They become rare to locally uncommon migrants within the interior counties and daily totals seldom exceed 1–4. Their spring status varies somewhat from year to year. Occasional large flights have been reported, perhaps the largest in 1929 when Trautman[479] observed 15–50 daily at Buckeye Lake between May 22 and 25.

At one time, a small summering population of Mourning Warblers existed in the Oak Openings of Lucas County. During the 1930s, Campbell[86] considered them uncommon summer residents with 4–7 pairs annually. Although nesting was suspected most years, a nest was discovered only in 1932. These summering Mournings remained through 1941 but were only intermittently observed in subsequent years, averaging one record every four years.[89] Most of these later males were probably unmated. The last summering males were reported in 1960. Hicks[220] also cited unspecified summer records in northeastern Ohio but provided no evidence of confirmed nesting attempts.

Between 1960 and 1980, Mourning Warblers were unrecorded as summer residents and the small Ohio breeding population was presumably extirpated. Intensive surveys for the Breeding Bird Atlas proved otherwise, beginning in 1983 when a territorial male summered in Geauga County.[434] The following year, nesting behavior was exhibited by pairs in Summit and Geauga Counties, while a male summered in Clinton County. The Geauga County pair returned in subsequent years, and territorial males were reported from the Maumee State Forest and Ashtabula and Williams Counties. These sightings indicate that Mournings are casual to rare and very locally distributed summer residents in the extreme northeastern and northwestern counties. They are accidental summer residents elsewhere.

Breeding Mourning Warblers prefer dense brushy habitats with a few scattered trees. Extensive cutover areas are ideal, although woodland clearings and edges may also be occupied. Their nests are cleverly hidden near the ground in dense shrubbery. The few Ohio breeding records indicate that nesting activities begin in early June and the young fledge by mid-July.

As fall migrants, a few early Mournings have been reported along Lake Erie during the first half of August; however, they do not normally return until August 20–25. Most fall Mournings pass through Ohio during September and depart by October 4–8. While there have been several unsubstantiated sight records later in October, the latest documented fall Mourning was an immature female carefully studied at Euclid (Cuyahoga County) on November 2, 1985.[380]

Fall Mourning Warblers are generally rare migrants in every county, although many are undoubtedly overlooked as they skulk through the dense underbrush. They are mostly observed as scattered individuals with no more than 3 noted daily, even along Lake Erie.

COMMON YELLOWTHROAT

Geothlypis trichas (Linnaeus)

Among our most numerous resident warblers, Common Yellowthroats are found wherever suitable edge and successional habitats are available. They are numerous along the shrubby margins of ponds, streams, ditches, and wetlands but are also commonly recorded in brushy fields, fallow fields, fencerows, woodland edges, and young open woodlots. The distinctive males frequently sing from exposed perches. Their song, a repetitive *witchety-witchety-witchety*, is among the first songs learned by most birders.

As summer residents, yellowthroats have been widely distributed ever since the virgin forests were cleared. Breeding bird surveys since 1965 indicate slightly increased numbers in the Great Lakes region.[438] They are least numerous in intensively farmed western Ohio where edge and successional habitats are relatively scarce. Yellowthroats are fairly common to common residents in Wood, Henry, Defiance, Paulding, Van Wert, Putnam, Madison, Fayette, and Clinton Counties, where daily totals seldom exceed 8–15 except along extensive riparian corridors. They are common to abundant summer residents in other counties, where 25–80 may be recorded daily. Campbell's report[89] of 300 in the Oak Openings of Lucas County on July 18, 1936, probably included many young raised that summer.

While observing Common Yellowthroats is fairly easy, discovering their nests is difficult (although cowbirds seemingly find them with great regularity). These nests are usually well concealed by herbaceous vegetation, on or within six inches of the ground. Nest construction is initiated by mid-May, while the first clutches are completed by the end of the month or early June. The first broods may fledge by June 10–20 but are most frequently noted during early July. Second broods or renesting attempts are responsible for nests with young through July 28 and adults accompanied by young through August 22.[479]

The first Common Yellowthroats normally return to southern Ohio during the third week of April and are commonly encountered by May 1. While a few overflights have returned to Lake Erie by April 15–18, yellowthroats do not usually appear in northern Ohio until April 27–30 and are not common until May 5–9. Spring totals seldom exceed 10–50 daily, although as many as 200 were reported from Buckeye Lake during the 1920s and 1930s.[479] Yellowthroats may still frequent lakefront migrant traps through May 22–27.

Fall yellowthroats are difficult to locate until their distinctive harsh call notes are learned; then they become numerous fall migrants. No sizable fall concentrations have been reported, but daily totals of 10–30 yellowthroats are not unusual. While their southward movement may begin during the last days of August, most yellowthroats apparently pass through Ohio in September. Their numbers diminish by the first week of October, although a few may be found through October 15–20. Stragglers linger into November.

Common Yellowthroats normally spend the winter months in the southern United States, Central America, and the Caribbean region, although they are occasionally found north to the lower Great Lakes.[5] Within Ohio, there was only one published winter record before 1940. The number of winter sightings began to accumulate in the 1940s and 1950s. Wintering yellowthroats have been reported nearly every year since the mid-1960s. This increased number of sightings may reflect greater numbers of observers as well as more yellowthroats attempting to overwinter.

Wintering yellowthroats are now casual to accidental visitors, averaging one to four reports annually. While they are not regularly detected at any location, most records are from the western Lake Erie marshes and the southern half of Ohio, predominantly of isolated individuals, although as many as 3 have been reported on Christmas Bird Counts. These records are mostly during December and first half of January. Many yellowthroats do not survive the rigors of a typical Ohio winter, although a few early March sightings may represent overwintering individuals.

HOODED WARBLER

Wilsonia citrina (Boddaert)

An exquisite combination of greenish upperparts, golden yellow underparts, and a bright yellow face surrounded by a jet black hood, male Hooded Warblers look like feathered jewels as they flit through the understory of mature woods. Like most occupants of understory habitats, however, these bright warblers become remarkably inconspicuous once the foliage is fully developed, and their presence is mostly detected by their loud rolling song.

Breeding Hooded Warblers only occupy extensive mature woods, remaining within the forest interiors and seldom wandering to the edges. They prefer mesic woodlands, especially beech-maple communities. Their nests are placed in saplings, grape tangles, or similar cover, usually at heights of less than four feet.[523] Within the southern counties, clutches are produced before the end of May. These young fledge by late June. Their breeding chronology is delayed by one or two weeks in

northern Ohio, where the first nests are not normally discovered until the first week of June and the young fledge during July. Renesting attempts may produce nests with eggs through July 4 and young into early August.[497,523]

Nesting Hooded Warblers are decidedly more numerous within the eastern third of Ohio.[434] Along the unglaciated Allegheny Plateau, they are generally fairly common to locally common residents north to Hocking, Morgan, and southern Belmont Counties, where 4–15 may be noted daily. They become less numerous along the remainder of the plateau, mostly uncommon to fairly common residents with daily totals seldom exceeding 4–6 individuals. Within the northeastern counties, Hoodeds are rare to locally common summer residents, most numerous within the mature forests along the Chagrin River watershed, where they approach the numbers found in southeastern Ohio. In other northeastern locations, summer reports normally are of 3 or fewer Hoodeds.

Considerably fewer nesting Hoodeds are found elsewhere. They are rare and very locally distributed summer residents in the central counties near Columbus and southwestern Ohio, where most reports involve only 1–2 pairs. Even fewer reside in the west-central and northwestern counties; they are absent from most of these counties and accidental to locally rare elsewhere.[434]

Their breeding distribution has not changed appreciably during this century. Jones[236] noted that Hooded Warblers were most numerous within the extreme northeastern and southeastern counties. Hicks[220] cited breeding records from twenty-nine counties, mostly within southern and northeastern Ohio, although the records from the Cincinnati area were disputed by Kemsies and Randle.[248] Numbers have been slowly increasing along the unglaciated Allegheny Plateau since the 1930s. The first confirmed Cincinnati nesting record was in 1958, while their appearance at most other western localities has been since 1960.

As spring migrants, Hooded Warblers are mostly known as residents returning to their breeding territories. Away from their nesting sites, Hooded Warblers are generally casual to locally uncommon migrants, most likely to appear at migrant traps along Lake Erie and near Columbus. These migrants are mostly scattered individuals with occasional groups of 2–5.

The earliest Hooded Warblers appeared during the unprecedented overflight between March 28 and April 2, 1950, producing sightings at Toledo and at least three records from Columbus.[89,311] There are few other records before April 18–24, when the first residents normally return to the southern counties. There, most residents have returned by May 10–12. Elsewhere, migrant Hoodeds are most likely to appear between April 25 and May 20.

After the males quit singing, Hooded Warblers become inconspicuous, with surprisingly few records after mid-July. Most Hoodeds quietly disappear during the last half of August through September 20–25. Occasional warblers linger until October 5–12. Exceptionally late Hoodeds were reported from Cleveland on October 31, 1949, and Toledo between November 25 and 29, 1961.[89,117] These fall migrants are casual to locally uncommon, most numerous within the eastern counties. Fall sightings normally involve only 1–3 individuals.

WILSON'S WARBLER

Wilsonia pusilla (Wilson)

During their passage through Ohio, these handsome warblers are most likely to be found in brushy woods, willow thickets, and other habitats dominated by shrubs and saplings. Although they occupy upland habitats, Wilson's Warblers are especially fond of dense shrubby thickets near water. They are not particularly shy and can be readily observed as they forage within the low bushes.

Wilson's Warblers rank among the later spring migrants. There are surprisingly few records during late April, even though the first migrants normally appear by the first week of May. They attain their maximum abundance between May 12 and 24. At that time, they become fairly common to common migrants along Lake Erie, where daily totals of 10–20 individuals are not unusual. The largest reported flight was of 50 Wilson's near Toledo on May 21, 1939.[89] Within central and northern Ohio, Wilson's Warblers are uncommon to fairly common spring migrants. While as many as 25 have been reported from Buckeye Lake,[479] most observations are of 6 or fewer daily. These warblers are remarkably scarce spring migrants through southern Ohio, particularly the unglaciated southeastern counties, where they are rarely encountered. Most southern sightings involve isolated individuals, although as many as 6–8 have been noted at Dayton.[299] While the last migrants normally depart from Lake Erie by early June, they have remained in the Cleveland area as late as June 10–14.[117]

Breeding Wilson's Warblers occupy bogs and damp willow thickets across Alaska and Canada south to northern New England, the upper Great Lakes, and the western mountains.[5] There are no confirmed summer records from Ohio after the last migrants depart by mid-June.

The initiation of fall migration is somewhat uncertain, since sight records during the first days of August frequently represent misidentifications of similar warblers. The first confirmed fall migrants have appeared along Lake Erie during the third week of August and are regularly encountered by September 1. Inland migrants are not normally detected until the first week of September. Fall Wilson's become fairly common to common migrants along Lake Erie and rare to uncommon inland. Fall concentrations seldom exceed 10 daily with infrequent reports of 15–20 along Lake Erie and in the central counties. Wilson's Warblers may be observed through the first week of October but become quite scarce later in the month. The latest confirmed record is October 31, 1974, at Columbus.[257] There is also an undocumented January sight record from eastern Ohio.

CANADA WARBLER

Wilsonia canadensis (Linnaeus)

One of our later spring migrants, the Canada Warbler is exceptional during April, although overflights have appeared at Cleveland and central Ohio by April 20–21.[117,390] The first migrants do not normally return until May 5–10 and Canadas are not regularly encountered until May 15–18. These migrants are mostly observed in young woods with dense shrub layers, especially swamp forests or woodlands near water. Spring migration is fairly rapid and most depart by May 25–June 1. While a few late migrants may pass along Lake Erie through June 8–13, early June migrants are unusual away from the lakefront.

Spring Canadas are most numerous along Lake Erie, where they become common migrants during the last half of May. As many as 10–20 individuals daily may be observed and occasional flights of 30–40+ have been reported. They are uncommon to fairly common migrants through the central and northern counties, becoming uncommon to locally rare in southern and unglaciated eastern Ohio. Inland spring totals seldom exceed 3–10 Canadas. Only Trautman[479] reported a sizable inland flight, with 25–55 daily at Buckeye Lake between May 22 and 25, 1929.

At one time, nesting Canadas were largely restricted to Ashtabula County. Hicks[215] regularly observed summering pairs in the former Pymatuning Bog and cited eight records from five other locations before 1933. The only other summer Canadas sporadically appeared in the Oak Openings of Lucas County, where Campbell[89] cited records during seven years between 1931 and 1946, including a successful nest in 1937.

In 1947, Canada Warblers initiated an expansion into Ohio's hemlock forests. This expansion was first apparent in the northeastern counties, where a territorial male was detected at Little Mountain (Lake County) on June 20, 1947.[523] In subsequent years, as many as 4–6 pairs regularly appeared at that location, at Stebbins Gulch, and in other hemlock ravines in Geauga, Lake, and Cuyahoga Counties.[335] Summering Canadas were first recorded from southeastern Ohio in 1963 when Worth Randle discovered a male in Hocking County. The next summering warbler was recorded from this county in 1968, and they have regularly nested there since 1970.[411]

Canada Warblers are now casual to rare and very locally distributed summer residents within hemlock forests in eastern Ohio. They are most numerous along the Chagrin River watershed in Lake, Geauga, and Cuyahoga Counties, where 3–10 pairs regularly nest at seven or more sites. As many as 6–12 pairs also nest along the Mohican River in Ashland, Knox, and Holmes Counties. Only 1–3 pairs regularly breed along the Clear Creek valley in Hocking County, although scattered pairs and summering males may be found in other Hocking County hemlock forests. Isolated pairs have also appeared in Summit, Jackson, and Vinton Counties.[434] This breeding population exhibits marked annual fluctuations in abundance. Even when they are most numerous, the population probably does not exceed 40–60 singing males, some unmated. Causes for these fluctuations are not readily apparent.

While summering Canada Warblers in the Oak Openings occupied second-growth deciduous woods,[89] all other summer records have been from hemlock forests. Breeding warblers prefer openings where the shrub layer and ground cover is relatively dense, especially along small streams and springs. Nesting activities begin during the last half of May and most pairs have complete clutches by the first week of June. Adults accompanied by dependent young have been recorded between June 27 and July 28.

Canadas are among the first warblers returning to Ohio each autumn. Southward migrants appear along Lake Erie during the first half of August and return to most interior counties by August 15–20. This passage peaks between August 23 and September 15. Fall Canadas are rare to uncommon migrants in every county, mostly as scattered individuals, although as many as 7–10 have been observed. Most depart by September 22–27. October sightings are very unusual, but Canadas have reportedly remained through October 22–26 at several locations.

PAINTED REDSTART

Myioborus pictus (Swainson)

Ohio's only record of this accidental visitor was provided by a Painted Redstart in Middleburg Heights, Cuyahoga County, between November 15 and 22, 1970.[412] This distinctive warbler was observed by numerous individuals and photographed during its periodic visits to a feeder at the residence of Dr. and Mrs. Joseph Hadden. Since Painted Redstarts normally nest in the southwestern United States,[5] the appearance in Ohio was quite unexpected. These warblers have subsequently proven to wander occasionally during late fall and early winter, producing a few other records from eastern North America.

YELLOW-BREASTED CHAT

Icteria virens (Linnaeus)

"If there is a feathered oddity in America, it is the Yellow-breasted Chat," Dawson[102] wrote,

and when you listen to his quaint medley of calls, caws, squawks, pipings, and objurations, you almost feel that the scientists must be as queer as himself for having placed him among the warblers. Structurally he does belong to this family, but his vocal performances are about as far from warbling as midnight is from midday.

Dawson's sentiments have been echoed by many others who are amused by the antics of these large handsome warblers. The breeding male's outlandish vocalizations and strange territorial displays are quite unlike those of any other North American warbler. Yet, a foraging chat appears shy, if not reclusive, and allows only brief views before disappearing into cover.

Yellow-breasted Chats are occupants of dense thickets and tangles found in abandoned fields and woodland clearings. The red cedar–covered hillsides in southwestern Ohio provide ideal habitats, as do blackberry and rose tangles dominating clearcuts and fallow fields in the southeastern counties. They are not found along fencerows or other narrow shrubby corridors. With their preference for successional habitats, chats invariably disappear when the shrubby tangles are replaced by small trees.

Their statewide distribution reflects the availability of these successional habitats. Chats have always been locally distributed within the west-central and northwestern counties where extensive brushy fields are scarce. Moreover, Ohio lies near the northern boundary of their range and there is a noticeable decrease in abundance from the southern to the northern counties.

Hicks[220] provided the first detailed account of the chat's summer distribution. He cited records from eighty-one counties, noting their absence from seven northwestern counties. Chats were common to abundant throughout southern Ohio, gradually declining to uncommon to rare and very locally distributed residents within the northern counties. Along the unglaciated Allegheny Plateau, they were most numerous north to Muskingum, Guernsey, and Monroe Counties.[223] In subsequent decades, Campbell[89] described an abrupt decrease in abundance at Toledo after 1948. Elsewhere, breeding bird surveys have indicated a negative trend in Ohio populations since 1965, a tendency repeated throughout eastern and central North America.[438]

Despite these declines, chat distribution patterns have not appreciably changed since the 1930s.[434] Chats remain fairly common to locally abundant residents throughout southern Ohio and along the unglaciated Allegheny Plateau north to Muskingum, Guernsey, and Belmont Counties. Daily totals of 8–15+ are possible within most of these counties, while as many as 30–50 have been tallied at a few localities. They become fairly common to locally common residents elsewhere along the unglaciated plateau, although summer totals seldom exceed 5–12 chats daily. Within the glaciated central counties, chats become locally distributed and uncommon to fairly common residents, with most reports of 1–6 individuals. They are least numerous within northern Ohio, generally being casual to locally uncommon residents, although they may be absent from intensively farmed northwestern counties. While Campbell[89] counted 20–35 chats daily in the Oak Openings near Toledo, similar numbers have not been evident since 1950. In recent years, most northern reports have been of only 1–4 chats daily.

For a "southern warbler," the Yellow-breasted Chat is a relatively late migrant. The earliest chats have returned to the southern counties by April 21–25, although they do not normally appear until April 28–May 3. They are expected within central and northern Ohio by May 5–10. Their spring migration is brief and few migrants are noted after May 20–25. This movement mostly consists of resident chats returning to their territories.

Along Lake Erie, spring chats are generally rare visitors to lakefront migrant traps. These migrants mostly appear during May, but a few late individuals have been observed at Cleveland through June 10–11. These sightings invariably are of only 1–3 chats daily.

The male's conspicuous territorial displays belie a secretive bird whose nests are difficult to locate, generally placed at heights of two to four feet in dense thickets. Within the southern counties, most chats have complete clutches by the last half of May. These activities are delayed in northern Ohio, where nests are mostly reported during June.[89,523] Recently fledged young have been noted as early as June 2 at Buckeye Lake but most appear in late June or early July.[479] Renesting attempts may produce young into early August.

After the males quit singing in early July, Yellow-breasted Chats become remarkably inconspicuous. There are relatively few records after July 15, although chats are undoubtedly more numerous than these sightings indicate. They are casual to rare fall migrants across Ohio, invariably observed as single individuals. This migration apparently begins in August and is mostly completed by September 15–25. A few late chats have remained through October 20–25.

Yellow-breasted Chats are accidental early winter visitors with three published December sightings. These records are of single chats in Ottawa County, near Buckeye Lake, and at Brecksville (Cuyahoga County). The Brecksville chat managed to survive until December 22 but was found dead a few days later.[343]

SUMMER TANAGER

Piranga rubra (Linnaeus)

Summer Tanagers have always had a limited distribution, primarily restricted to the southern and unglaciated eastern counties. In the mid-1930s, Hicks[220] described their breeding range as extending north to Butler, Montgomery, Greene, Madison, Franklin, Licking, Coshocton, Tuscarawas, Carroll, and Columbiana Counties. Summer Tanagers were accidentally observed north of this range. They were common only within Adams, Scioto, and Lawrence Counties and regularly encountered along the Allegheny Plateau north to Muskingum, Guernsey, and Washington Counties.[223] Breeding Summer Tanagers were rare and locally distributed elsewhere.

While nesting populations have apparently remained fairly stable,[438] evidence suggests that Summer Tanagers are slowly expanding their breeding range northward within Ohio. Along the unglaciated Allegheny Plateau, Summer Tanagers are most numerous in Adams, Pike, Scioto, and Lawrence Counties and portions of adjacent counties. As many as 5–10 Summer Tanagers may be observed daily in these counties. Summer Tanagers are fairly common and regularly observed elsewhere along the plateau north to Coshocton, Tuscarawas, southern Carroll, and Jefferson Counties, although daily totals seldom exceed 1–5 individuals. Breeding Summer Tanagers are presently uncommon and locally distributed residents along the northern edge of the unglaciated plateau.[434] They remain fairly common residents near Cincinnati but are rare to uncommon and locally distributed in other southwestern counties north to Preble, Montgomery, and Greene.[299,434] Their expanding populations have been apparent in central Ohio near Columbus. They have become rare but regular residents within Franklin and adjacent counties as locally distributed pairs and singing males.[434]

Beginning in the 1950s, breeding Summer Tanagers appeared in northern Ohio. The first nesting records were reported at Youngstown in 1950,[61] Akron in 1956–58,[335] and Toledo, where nesting was suspected in 1955 and confirmed at two sites be-

tween 1957 and 1961.[89] Despite these few breeding records, they remain accidental to casual summer residents. Most records are of isolated males or pairs observed for only one or two years before they disappear.[434]

Breeding Summer Tanagers exhibit a preference for upland woods. While they may occupy mature woodlands, they will also be found in open, disturbed woods and woodland edges. Summer Tanagers normally remain within the canopy. However, singing males can be regularly detected by their clear robinlike song, which lacks the hoarse notes characteristic of Scarlet Tanagers. Nesting activities are under way by the last half of May within the southern and eastern counties but may not begin until early June in northern Ohio. The young normally fledge by late June or July.

While resident Summer Tanagers may return to southern Ohio by April 25–30, they are not normally encountered until the first week of May. Their breeding populations are generally well established by May 15–20. This northward movement largely comprises tanagers returning to their territories.

Small numbers of Summer Tanagers regularly overshoot their normal breeding range each spring. These overflights are rare along Lake Erie and near Columbus but are accidental to casual elsewhere. The number of overflights varies considerably, with only two to four sightings some years and six to ten or more in others. These records invariably are of single tanagers, mostly observed between May 5 and 24, although a few have appeared through June 7.

Their southward migration is poorly defined. Summer Tanagers normally depart from the northern edge of their breeding range by September 14–18 but may remain in the southern counties through September 22–27. Only occasional individuals linger into the first week of October. Fall records are mostly of 1–3 individuals daily. Summer Tanagers are accidental to casual fall visitors throughout the northern and glaciated central counties. The few extralimital fall records are mostly during September, although a late Summer Tanager appeared in the Toledo area on October 13, 1984.

SCARLET TANAGER

Piranga olivacea (Gmelin)

For most people captivated by birds, spring migration is made memorable by multitudes of brightly colored songbirds flitting among the branches of flowering trees. Perhaps no songbird presents such an unforgettable image as a brilliant male Scarlet Tanager. As Dawson described it:

Never shall I forget the day, when in treading an overgrown path by the riverside I came suddenly upon four males on a single limb not twenty feet away. The vision smote me like a blinding flash. The two oldest of the group were certainly among the most magnificent birds ever seen in Northern latitudes. Their coats were red-dyed to the point of scarlet saturation, and as they moved off slowly, the memory of the bird-man received an indelible image of these most beautiful four.[102]

Fortunately, Scarlet Tanagers are uncommon to locally common spring migrants and summer residents throughout Ohio. An exceptionally early male was reported from the Cleveland area on March 29, 1977, but there are no other sightings before mid-April. The first Scarlet Tanagers normally return to the southern counties by April 20–25 but may not appear along Lake Erie until the first week of May. During advanced seasons, the males can be surprisingly inconspicuous among the abundant vegetation. They are much more visible during late springs, as Dawson noted:

Those who haunt the woods in maying time are almost sure to see a vision of scarlet and black revealing itself for a moment in the higher tree tops, but swallowed up again all too soon by the consuming green. If, however, the leaves are not fully sprung the Tanager will move about quietly or sit rather stupidly in the middle branches, as tho bored by the lack of green and at a loss what to do with his brightness.[102]

Spring migration lasts only a few weeks. Most resident Scarlet Tanagers have returned by mid-May and the last migrants depart lakefront migrant traps by May 25. The largest lakefront and inland flights have produced counts of only 20–30 individuals and spring totals seldom exceed 4–12 daily at most localities.

As summer residents, Scarlet Tanagers are most numerous in extensive mature woodlands and riparian corridors where they reside within the canopy. They may also occupy second-growth woods if some large trees remain. Breeding Scarlet Tanagers are most numerous in the eastern and southern counties, where they are generally fairly common to common residents. As many as 20–30 males may be counted daily in heavily wooded areas. They are normally fairly common residents elsewhere but become uncommon and locally distributed in intensively cultivated counties in central and western Ohio.[434] Summer totals seldom exceed 4–8 individuals daily away from southern and eastern Ohio. In recent decades, Scarlet Tanagers undoubtedly declined in most western counties as woodlands were converted to agricultural fields and residential areas. Conversely, populations increased in many southern and eastern counties where woodlands are maturing. The net result has been a gradually increasing statewide populations on breeding bird surveys since 1965.[438]

Their nests are normally placed at heights of twenty feet or more in tall trees. Nest construction has been noted during the last half of May but probably begins earlier in the southern counties. Eggs are normally laid by late May, although recently fledged young have been reported as early as June 8.[523] Most young Scarlet Tanagers fledge in late June or early July. Second broods or renesting attempts are responsible for nests with eggs through August 3 and a nest with young on August 9.[479,523] Scarlet Tanagers are regularly detected as long as the males continue to sing. Once singing ceases, usually during the first half of July, they become very inconspicuous, although a few can be located by their distinctive *chip-burr* call notes.

Their southward migration is poorly defined. Fall Scarlet Tanagers are fairly common in the unglaciated counties but uncommon elsewhere. Most depart by October 1. Occasional stragglers have lingered as late as October 21, 1956, at Cleveland.[117] Most fall observations are of 4 or fewer individuals.

WESTERN TANAGER

Piranga ludoviciana (Wilson)

Breeding Western Tanagers are widely distributed throughout western North America from southeastern Alaska to southern Arizona.[5] They normally winter in Mexico and Central America. In eastern North America, these tanagers are primarily known as accidental vagrants during late fall or early winter. These wandering individuals are frequently discovered at bird feeders, usually at localities near the Atlantic and Gulf Coasts.

There is only one confirmed record of this accidental visitor to Ohio. A Western Tanager was observed and photographed by John Pogacnik at East Harbor State Park in Ottawa County on November 20, 1982.[368] In addition, there are three undocumented sight records that fit this species' known pattern of vagrancy: one bird at Mayfield Heights (Cuyahoga County) on November 24, 1962; one visiting a Mentor (Lake County) feeder between December 1 and 28, 1963; and another at Mentor between December 21, 1971, and January 3, 1972.[335,471] The two at Mentor were reportedly observed by a number of individuals.

During spring, there are very few confirmed records of Western Tanagers from eastern North America. Most sight records have proven to be aberrant Scarlet Tanagers. While there have been four published spring and early summer sight records from Ohio, these sightings are either undocumented or supported by inconclusive details.

NORTHERN CARDINAL

Cardinalis cardinalis (Linnaeus)

January thaws provide brief respites from the rigors of winter, melting the accumulated snows and encouraging the male Cardinal to cheerfully proclaim the beginning of spring. A snowstorm several days later sends him back to the cover of brushy thickets to await the return of more favorable weather. As the days increase in length, the urge to proclaim his territory becomes stronger and the male Cardinal sings every morning, even in the middle of a March blizzard. The Cardinal will eventually be correct and spring will return, but our affection for this handsome backyard visitor extends beyond his optimistic song during a January morning. As simply stated by Dawson, "Not merely for the splendor of his plumage, but for the gentle boldness of his comradeship and the daily heartening of his stirring song, the Cardinal is beloved of all who know him."[102]

Cardinals rank among our most familiar native songbirds because of their preference for shrubbery in residential yards and their frequent visits to backyard bird feeders. In addition to urban areas, they are found wherever shrubby cover is available, including brushy fields, thickets, fencerows, and woodland edges. These permanent residents are most numerous during winter, when they are fairly common to locally abundant in every county. Wintering Cardinals frequently congregate into flocks of as many as 60 birds, and 6–10 males may be observed adorning a single shrub. A winter day's birding usually produces 20–80 Cardinals, and totals in excess of 100 are not extraordinary. They are most numerous in the southwestern counties, especially at Cincinnati, where Christmas Bird Count totals frequently exceed 2000 Cardinals.

During late February and March, the winter flocks of Cardinals disband as pairs establish their territories for the breeding season. As a result of this dispersal and winter mortality, Cardinals become less numerous in summer, although they remain fairly common to common residents throughout the state. Summer totals normally are 10–20 Cardinals in intensively cultivated western Ohio and 30–50 daily elsewhere. Their nesting activities begin fairly early, normally during the first half of April. Their nests are usually placed in shrubs and vines at heights of three to eight feet, although some are as high as twenty to thirty-eight feet in trees.[24,479] Nests with eggs have been reported as early as April 7 at Dayton,[299] but first clutches are normally laid during late April and early May. First broods fledge by mid-June. Subsequent nesting attempts produce young throughout the summer months, and nests with eggs have been reported as late as September 1.[24] Adults with dependent young may be observed through the first week of October.

While they are permanent residents, some Cardinals exhibit migratory behavior. These movements are poorly understood, since migrants are difficult to distinguish from residents. Migrants are most apparent over western Lake Erie, where Trautman and Trautman[488] reported spring movements during April and May and fall migrants in September and October.

Cardinals have not always been common residents throughout Ohio. In fact, when Ohio was initially settled, they were restricted to the southern half of the state. They expanded into northern Ohio during the last half of the nineteenth century.[104] At the turn of the century, Cardinals occupied most counties, although they were still rather rare near Lake Erie.[89,236] Their northern Ohio populations continued to increase into the 1920s and 1930s, when present levels were achieved.

ROSE-BREASTED GROSBEAK

Pheucticus ludovicianus (Linnaeus)

Each spring the first male Rose-breasted Grosbeaks normally return when the vegetation is still budding. These attractive males are readily observed as they forage among the bare branches of tall trees. Unfortunately, by the time the rest of these grosbeaks return, the foliage is well developed. Like most colorful songbirds, Rose-breasted Grosbeaks remain hidden among the dense vegetation; most later migrants are detected only by their robinlike songs or sharp call notes.

While overflights have appeared in the Cleveland area as early as April 5–8,[117,523] the first Rose-breasted Grosbeaks do not normally return until April 25–30 in the southern and central counties and May 1–5 along Lake Erie. Their northward migration peaks between May 7 and 24, when they become fairly common to common migrants across the northern and central counties and uncommon to fairly common in southern Ohio. These grosbeaks are seldom numerous and only 3–10 individuals are noted most days. In the central and northern counties, concentrations of 15–30+ are not unusual. The largest spring movements totaled 81 individuals at Columbus on May 13, 1975, and 40–60+ along Lake Erie.[471] The last spring migrants pass through lakefront migrant traps into the first week of June.

When Ohio was initially settled, Rose-breasted Grosbeaks may have been summer residents throughout the state. Audubon claimed he found nests in the Cincinnati area, and there were nineteenth-century summer records from Columbus.[236,248] The southerly populations disappeared by the mid-1930s, when Hicks[220] cited summer records south to Paulding, Wood, Seneca, Ashland, Holmes, Tuscarawas, Stark, and Columbiana Counties. These breeding grosbeaks were generally uncommon to locally common and widely distributed throughout the northeastern counties. They were very locally distributed elsewhere and common at only a few localities.

Their breeding range has been expanding southward during the past three decades. Dayton's first summer record came in 1962, and isolated sightings were reported from the central counties in the 1960s.[299] Cincinnati's first recent nesting record came in 1975, and there were a number of other sightings from the central and southwestern counties in that decade.[260] Additional range expansion was apparent in the 1980s.

Rose-breasted Grosbeaks are now fairly common to common and widely distributed summer residents throughout northeastern Ohio, where 3–10+ individuals may be recorded daily. While they are also widely distributed in the northwestern counties, they are generally uncommon to locally common residents, least numerous in all intensively farmed counties. Summer totals seldom exceed 2–5 individuals daily within these counties. In central Ohio, Rose-breasted Grosbeaks are generally uncommon residents, regularly encountered as 1–4 individuals daily south to Darke, Clark, Pickaway, Fairfield, Perry, Muskingum, Tuscarawas, Harrison, and Jefferson Counties.[434] They remain rare and very locally distributed summer residents within southwestern Ohio. Breeding Rose-breasteds are largely rare to absent along the unglaciated Allegheny Plateau from Belmont, Guernsey, Morgan, Hocking, and Ross Counties south to the Ohio River.

Breeders prefer young second-growth deciduous woods and woodland edges. They are usually found along riparian corridors, in mesic woods, and occasionally in swamp forests. Their nests are normally placed at heights of ten to twenty-five feet in young trees but have been recorded at greater heights. Nesting activities are initiated during the last half of May and nests with eggs have been discovered through late June. While recently fledged young have appeared by May 25, they are not expected until the last half of June and July.[89,523]

Their southward migration begins during the last half of August in the northern counties and by the first week of September along the Ohio River. This movement continues throughout September. Fall migrants are generally fairly common to common in northern Ohio, most numerous along Lake Erie, and uncommon to fairly common elsewhere. Most fall records are of 10 or fewer individuals daily. Larger flights are restricted to Lake Erie, where concentrations of 30–38 have been reported. Most depart by October 5–10. A few stragglers have lingered as late as mid-November.

Most Rose-breasted Grosbeaks spend the winter in tropical climates. Some are accidental winter visitors in North America. These wintering Rose-breasteds are invariably found at bird feeders. Within Ohio, they are accidental winter visitors with at least five acceptable records from Cleveland, Columbus, Toledo, and Oxford (Butler County) and several unsubstantiated sightings. While these wintering grosbeaks are more likely to appear in December and early January, several have survived into February and March.

BLACK-HEADED GROSBEAK

Pheucticus melanocephalus (Swainson)

Western counterparts of our familiar Rose-breasted Grosbeaks, Black-headeds are accidental visitors in most states and provinces east of the Great Plains. Despite their accidental status, a few Black-headeds normally turn up somewhere in eastern North America each year, frequently visiting bird feeders during winter.

Black-headed Grosbeaks are accidental visitors to Ohio. Their actual status is obscured by the inability to accurately distinguish Black-headeds from the considerably more numerous Rose-breasted Grosbeaks. Female and immature grosbeaks are particularly difficult to identify, and even adult male grosbeaks can be confusing.

Within Ohio, there are two indisputable records of Black-headed Grosbeaks. A male visited an Akron feeder between January 1 and April 5, 1975, and photos taken by Robert Graham clearly established its identity.[389] Another was photographed by Karl Maslowski at a Milford (Clermont County) feeder between April 10 and 13, 1969.[407] A Black-headed studied by Jerry Cairo, Don Tumblin, and Karen Zanders at Rising Park in Lancaster on May 6, 1978, also appears to be correctly identified. There are several other reports of Black-headed Grosbeaks visiting Ohio feeders in winter and early spring, including single grosbeaks at Cincinnati between January and March 1976[471] and an immature male at Sylvania (Lucas County) March 3–15, 1965.[89] Unfortunately, these grosbeaks were not photographed and written descriptions are not available. Hence, the accuracy of their identifications cannot be assessed.

BLUE GROSBEAK

Guiraca caerulea (Linnaeus)

The historic status of Blue Grosbeaks in Ohio is clouded with uncertainty. While there were many reports during the late 1800s and first decades of this century, these sightings were undocumented or supported by details suggesting the birds were misidentified. If these grosbeaks occurred in the state, they were undoubtedly accidental visitors.

Ohio's first confirmed Blue Grosbeak records were provided by Hicks.[229] He discovered males in Adams County on June 9 and 30, 1940. In 1941, a pair was regularly observed between June 8 and 22. While the female was noted carrying food, no nest was discovered. Breeding was established in 1942 when a nest with eggs was discovered along Beasley Fork in Monroe Township, Adams County, on June 6. An adult accompanied by dependent young was observed on June 21. A permanent population did not become established in this county, however, since Blue Grosbeaks could not be relocated later in the decade.

Between 1945 and the early 1970s, this species once again became an accidental visitor. As before 1940, most sightings during these years were either undocumented or supported by inconclusive details. However, Blue Grosbeak populations were gradually expanding northward, a trend particularly evident since 1965.[438] As they expanded northward, the likelihood of occasional stray Blue Grosbeaks reaching Ohio increased. Hence, some sightings during the 1960s and early 1970s may have been correct, constituting the vanguard of its eventual expansion into the state.

This range expansion resulted in a nesting pair of Blue Grosbeaks discovered in Vinton County during 1975.[169] In 1976, a pair probably nested near Cincinnati, while 1977 produced nesting records from Vinton and Meigs Counties.[171,263] Breeding pairs were recorded during every subsequent year and their numbers have been gradually expanding throughout the 1980s.

Breeding Blue Grosbeaks are now primarily restricted to southern Ohio. They are uncommon summer residents in Adams County. Nesting Blue Grosbeaks become rare to locally uncommon residents in portions of Pike, Scioto, Lawrence, Gallia, and Meigs Counties but are generally casual to rare elsewhere north to Butler, Ross, and Noble Counties.[434] Blue Grosbeaks are accidental summer visitors in central and northern Ohio, where there are a few widely scattered sightings of unmated males.[434] The only confirmed nest away from southern Ohio was an unsuccessful attempt at the Oak Openings in Lucas County during 1988.[388a]

Breeding Blue Grosbeaks are occupants of brushy successional habitats and dense thickets along fencerows and roadsides. Singing males are fairly conspicuous, delivering their rich warbling song from telephone wires, treetops, and other exposed perches. Their nests are placed in dense cover, usually at heights of three to ten feet. Nesting activities probably begin during the last half of May, but the few nests with eggs have been discovered in early June. Dependent young have been observed during the last half of June and July.

Their migratory patterns are poorly understood. In southern Ohio, resident pairs may appear during the first week of May but most return between May 10 and 22. Spring overflights are accidental within the central and northern counties, although they are reported more frequently as the breeding population expands. These overflights include a singing male in Holmes County in 1979 plus one Dayton and two Cleveland sightings

BROWN THRASHER
Toxostoma rufum

Occasionally a Brown Thrasher will be found spending the winter in the state. The majority, however, winter to the south. Together with the first blooms of the violet (*Viola* sp.) and unfurling fronds of the Christmas fern (*Polystichum acrostichoides*), this thrasher's return is one of the earliest signs of spring. The vigorous tossing of leaf litter about with their bills is the activity for which the thrasher family is named.

Adults
(sexes similar)

BOHEMIAN WAXWING
Bombycilla garrulus

CEDAR WAXWING
Bombycilla cedrorum

During fall and winter, flocks of Cedar Waxwings wander the state in search of fruit-bearing trees and shrubs, which they frequently pick clean. Over the years a few of their grayer and larger cousins, Bohemian Waxwings, have been sighted. Because of their social nature, the rare Bohemians when seen are often with flocks of Cedar Waxwings.

Bohemian Waxwing
(sexes similar)

Cedar Waxwing
Cedar Waxwing

Cedar Waxwing
(sexes similar)

LOGGERHEAD SHRIKE
Lanius ludovicianus

Because shrikes impale excess prey on the thorny branches of trees, the Loggerhead and other members of this family are frequently called butcher-birds. In some years grasshoppers and other insects such as the Seventeen-year Cicada (*Magicicada septendecim*) emerge in numbers so large that nothing could possibly consume them all. The shrike's unusual method of storing food can be handy when the supply is abundant. Since shrikes don't have sharp talons like most birds of prey, they also utilize the thorns of trees to hold their prey in place while they tear it apart.

Adult
(sexes similar)

SOLITARY VIREO
Vireo solitarius

YELLOW-THROATED VIREO
Vireo flavifrons

The Yellow-throated Vireo is a summer resident that spends much of its time in the upper two-thirds of our largest trees. Its cousin the Solitary Vireo seems to prefer the smaller trees and shrubs that make up the understory of our woods. Their paths occasionally cross where the preferred habitat of these two birds overlaps.

Yellow-throated Vireo
(sexes similar)

Solitary Vireo
(sexes similar)

MAGNOLIA WARBLER
Dendroica magnolia

BLACK-THROATED GREEN WARBLER
Dendroica virens

BLACKBURNIAN WARBLER
Dendroica fusca

YELLOW-THROATED WARBLER
Dendroica dominica

BAY-BREASTED WARBLER
Dendroica castanea

BLACKPOLL WARBLER
Dendroica striata

In May, along with the warm balmy weather fronts pushing up from the south, come waves of migrating wood warblers. On a good day a lucky birder might find four or five species in a single tree, all flitting and chasing about in pursuit of caterpillars that are feeding on the newly emerging leaves.

Blackburnian Warbler *(male)*

Yellow-throated Warbler *(sexes similar)*

Blackburnian Warbler *(female)*   **Bay-breasted Warbler** *(female)*

Bay-breasted Warbler *(male)*

Blackpoll Warbler *(female)*

Black-throated Green Warbler

(male; female has less black on throat)   **Blackpoll Warbler** *(male)*

Magnolia Warbler
(male; female has less black on breast and white on wings)

SUMMER TANAGER
Piranga rubra

SCARLET TANAGER
Piranga olivacea

NORTHERN ORIOLE
Icterus galbula

In late June the fruit of the Wild Cherry (*Prunus serotina*) is one of the earliest to ripen in our woods. Scattered throughout the hardwood forest, Wild Cherry trees provide a welcome summer treat for a wide variety of birds, many of which, being territorial, are much less tolerant of intruders of their own kind than they are of the other species that come to feed. That may explain why several species can be found in the same tree feeding side by side.

Scarlet Tanager
(male)
(female)

Summer Tanager
(male)
(female)

Northern Oriole
(female)
(male)

NORTHERN CARDINAL
Cardinalis cardinalis

RUFOUS-SIDED TOWHEE
Pipilo erythrophthalmus

AMERICAN TREE SPARROW
Spizella arborea

FOX SPARROW
Passerella iliaca

SONG SPARROW
Melospiza melodia

SWAMP SPARROW
Melospiza georgiana

WHITE-THROATED SPARROW
Zonotrichia albicollis

DARK-EYED JUNCO
Junco hyemalis

EVENING GROSBEAK
Coccothraustes vespertinus

In late winter when the fields, fencerows, and woods are filled with drifts of snow, many species of seedeaters gather together in overgrown tangles of weeds where food and shelter can be found. On particularly stormy days, if food is plentiful and easy to obtain, the birds seem reluctant to stir from the spot where they spent the night.

Evening Grosbeak
(male)
    (female)

Song Sparrow
(sexes similar)

American Tree Sparrow
Northern Cardinal   *(sexes similar)*
(female)
(male)

White-throated Sparrow
(sexes similar)

Fox Sparrow
(sexes similar)

Dark-eyed Junco
(male) **Swamp Sparrow**
   (sexes similar)
(female)

Rufous-sided Towhee
(female)
(male)

RED-WINGED BLACKBIRD
Agelaius phoeniceus

RUSTY BLACKBIRD
Euphagus carolinus

COMMON GRACKLE
Quiscalus quiscula

Every fall, enormous mixed flocks of noisy blackbirds pass through the state. When they roost, their large concentrations can become quite a nuisance if they are located near buildings. Many towns and cities have resorted to drastic action when migrating blackbirds have chosen to roost in trees within their municipalities.

Red-winged Blackbird *(male)*

Rusty Blackbird *(male)*
Rusty Blackbird *(female)*

Red-winged Blackbird *(female)*

Common Grackle
(male; female smaller and duller)

since 1985. All overflights were single Blues observed between May 10 and 25.

There are few records from southern Ohio after the males quit singing in early July. In all likelihood, Blue Grosbeaks begin their southward migration during the last half of August with very few remaining after mid-September. There are no confirmed fall records away from the southern counties.

INDIGO BUNTING

Passerina cyanea (Linnaeus)

Indigo Buntings are a prime example of the saying "familiarity breeds contempt." As they perch on a telephone wire or small tree in the sunlight of a summer morning, male Indigos are actually quite beautiful, surpassed by few other songbirds. If they were rare, their beauty would be appreciated by anybody having the opportunity to observe one. But Indigo Buntings are common to abundant summer residents, and singing males are hardly ever noticed except by those who appreciate birds for their aesthetic qualities.

Except for a few mid-April overflights along Lake Erie, the first Indigo Buntings normally return to southern Ohio by April 20–25. They may not appear in the central and northern counties until the first days of May. Their spring movement is poorly defined within the interior counties, where it mostly consists of returning residents. Sizable spring movements may appear along Lake Erie. Migrant flocks of 20–40+ individuals may pass along the lakefront and more than 200 may be observed daily during the largest flights. Their movements peak in mid-May, while the last lakefront migrants are noted through May 23–27.

As summer residents, Indigo Buntings are widely distributed within every county, and the male's repetitive song resounds throughout the rural countryside. Indigo Buntings are found wherever brushy habitats are available, including woodland edges and openings, fencerows, roadsides, and riparian corridors. They are most numerous along the red cedar–covered hillsides in southern Ohio, where 200+ may be tallied daily. They are also quite plentiful throughout southern and eastern Ohio, where daily totals of 100+ are possible. They are less numerous in intensively farmed central and western Ohio, where 30–50 may be noted daily. If suitable brushy habitats are available, Indigo Buntings become abundant in these counties as well. For example, Campbell[89] counted 150 in the Oak Openings in a single June day. While they have been abundant in Ohio throughout this century, their populations have undergone a slight but steady increase since 1965.[438]

Male Indigo Buntings are persistent singers whose song is heard long after most other birds become silent. Once they quit singing, Indigos become rather inconspicuous and the adults undergo their postnuptial molt. After mid-August, daily totals seldom exceed 3–15 individuals except when flocks are encountered and 30–40 may be observed. By far the largest fall concentration was 300 Indigos in the Toledo area on September 6, 1941.[89] These buntings are regularly recorded throughout September, but their numbers noticeably decline by the first week of October. The last migrants usually depart by October 10–17. A few individuals have infrequently lingered into late October or the first week of November.

Most Indigo Buntings spend the winter months well south of the United States. A few attempt to overwinter as far north as the lower Great Lakes—probably buntings that have been injured or are otherwise unable to complete their normal migration. Most are found at bird feeders. Indigo Buntings are accidental winter visitors in Ohio. There were single Indigos at Barnesville (Belmont County) on December 17, 1959, and Columbus on December 25, 1924.[10,138] Another Indigo lingered in the Cincinnati area through January 29, 1960, and may have overwintered.[325] Still another at Lake St. Mary's on March 18, 1944, was more likely a wintering bird than an exceptionally early migrant.[98]

DICKCISSEL

Spiza americana (Gmelin)

The status of Dickcissels in Ohio reflects their erratically fluctuating populations. Fretwell[120] and others theorized that food availability on their Central and South American wintering grounds may be responsible for the dramatic variation in the numbers returning to North America each summer. In Ohio, at the eastern edge of their breeding range,[5] their fluctuating numbers are quite apparent.

Dickcissels spread eastward from the Great Plains during the nineteenth century, entering Ohio during the mid-1800s.[522] By the 1880s, they became locally abundant summer residents in some central and southern counties. At the turn of the century, their populations were fairly well established in the western half of the state but they remained quite rare in the east.[236] Their relative abundance has fluctuated considerably over the decades. Sizable breeding populations are infrequent, with only two well-defined peaks since 1900: in the western and central counties between 1932 and 1934, when single fields supported 150 in Lucas County and 50 in the Newark area,[23,89] and between 1983 and 1988, when as many as 100 were reported from a single Butler County field.[371] During these peak years, they become uncommon to locally common residents in the western and central counties, with most reports of 1–6 males. These sizable breeding populations are normally followed by precipitous declines. Populations may then remain low for ten to fifteen or more years. Even so, a few pairs or singing males are discovered in the central and western counties, although the total statewide population may not exceed 10–30+ males. But their summer status is not completely boom or bust. Moderate numbers were recorded in the mid-1950s and mid-1960s, including a few colonies of 5–15+ and widely scattered males in many western and central counties.

Breeding Dickcissels are most likely to appear in the western half of the state east to Scioto, Pike, Ross, Pickaway, Fairfield, Licking, Knox, Richland, Huron, and Erie Counties.[220,434] They are generally most numerous in the tier of counties bordering

Indiana. Dickcissels have always been accidental to rare and very irregular summer residents in the eastern half of Ohio. Along the unglaciated Allegheny Plateau, summering Dickcissels were discovered in Morgan County in 1967.[153] They did not appear again until the 1980s, when small isolated populations were discovered on reclaimed strip mines in Coshocton, Tuscarawas, Muskingum, and Gallia Counties.[434] Within the northeastern counties, the few records include nests in Lake and Columbiana Counties[23,523] and summer sightings from Ashtabula, Mahoning, and Geauga Counties.[146,220,434]

Breeding Dickcissels prefer clover and alfalfa hayfields but also occupy timothy fields, the grassy borders of marshes, wet prairies, and weedy fallow fields.[89,479] On reclaimed strip mines, they are found in areas supporting mixed grasses and sweet clovers. Males attempt to mate with several females but do not help rear the young. The females build their nests on or near the ground in dense grassy cover. Most nests are apparently constructed in early June with the young fledging in July or early August.[479]

Migratory movements are not very apparent within Ohio. Spring migration is largely made up of birds appearing on their territories. The few March records most likely pertain to wintering individuals. Earliest spring migrants have appeared during the last half of April but there are very few sightings before May 3–8. Most summering birds return during the last half of May and early June. Spring Dickcissels are mostly recorded from the western half of Ohio; they are accidental in the eastern counties.

After the males quit singing in July, Dickcissels become quite inconspicuous. Most fall migrants are detected by their distinctive buzzy call notes as they pass overhead. Casual throughout Ohio, most Dickcissels depart during August and the first half of September. Relatively few migrants are detected through October 5–15.

While most Dickcissels migrate to tropical climates for the winter, a few elect to overwinter within Ohio. These accidental to casual winter visitors are mostly detected at bird feeders, frequently in urban areas. There are at least fifteen winter records, from Conneaut (Ashtabula County), Cleveland, and Toledo in the northern counties to Columbus, Marietta, and Cincinnati. Some Dickcissels appear for only a few days in late November or early December, while others remain for the entire winter. Most winter sightings are of single individuals, although 2 appeared at Findley State Park (Lorain County) during the winter of 1979–80.[276]

GREEN-TAILED TOWHEE

Pipilo chlorurus (Audubon)

Green-tailed Towhees are inhabitants of the western mountains that regularly wander east. There are reports from many states and provinces in eastern North America, mostly in the Great Lakes region and the Northeast.[5] Most were discovered at feeders during winter.

The three confirmed records of Green-tailed Towhees from Ohio fit this established pattern of vagrancy. The first was discovered in the Columbus area during late December 1963. It remained at a feeder through the following February,[392] but no photographs or written descriptions are available. The second wintered in Hamilton County between December 12, 1969, and March 31, 1970. It was widely observed and photographed by Karl Maslowski as it regularly visited a bird feeder.[409] The third was a fall migrant discovered near Lake Erie in Saybrook Township, Ashtabula County, on September 24, 1964. It was captured by Howard and Marcella Meahl, banded and photographed, and then released.[395]

RUFOUS-SIDED TOWHEE

Pipilo erythrophthalmus (Linnaeus)

With their distinctive plumages and characteristic calls, Rufous-sided Towhees rank among our most familiar occupants of brushy habitats. They are found in successional fields, small woodlots, and woodland edges and are particularly fond of red cedar–covered hillsides in southern Ohio. They also occupy dense hedgerows if successional fields are nearby, but they avoid shrubby fencerows surrounded by cultivated fields.

These towhees normally raise two broods annually. Their first nests are placed on the ground, with construction beginning during the last half of April in southern Ohio and early May in the northern counties. These broods usually fledge in late May or June. Their second nests are mostly placed in low dense shrubs and tangles but have been reported as high as twelve feet in red cedars.[54] These second nests are constructed during June or early July, with the last young fledging in August.[417,479]

Rufous-sided Towhees are generally fairly common to common summer residents. They are most numerous in the southern and eastern counties, where 8–40+ individuals may be counted daily during summer. Similar numbers may be encountered locally in central and western Ohio. Smaller numbers generally summer in glaciated Ohio north of Butler, Warren, Clinton, Highland, and Ross Counties, where daily totals seldom exceed 2–12. They are uncommon to locally rare summer residents in the intensively cultivated western counties where successional habitats are quite scarce.[434]

Since the mid-1960s, breeding Rufous-sided Towhee populations have declined significantly in Ohio and eastern North America.[438] Several factors contributed to this decline, most notably the loss of suitable shrubby habitats through secondary succession and conversion into cultivated fields. Populations were also reduced by the severe winters of 1976–78 and did not recover until the 1980s.

Most of these towhees do not permanently reside in Ohio but spend the winter months in the southeastern United States. Fall migrants are uncommon to fairly common producing daily totals of 3–15 individuals. The first fall migrants appear at lakefront migrant traps by September 18–25 and most migration occurs between October 1 and 21. The last migrants normally depart by the first week of November.

Migrant Rufous-sideds are quite noticeable during spring. A few may arrive in late February but they do not normally appear until mid-March. They are regularly encountered during the last half of March, becoming fairly common to common between April 15 and May 8. Spring totals are usually 3–10 daily. Large flights produce local concentrations of 15–40 and as many as 125–150 at Columbus and the Oak Openings.[89,471] The latest spring migrants usually depart from Lake Erie by May 15.

As winter residents, Rufous-sided Towhees are casual to rare in northern Ohio, rare to uncommon in the glaciated central counties, and uncommon to fairly common in southern and unglaciated eastern Ohio. They may be relatively scarce some years, with very few sightings from the northern half of the state and only scattered individuals or flocks of 8 or fewer in the southern counties. During other years, they may be fairly numerous and small flocks may appear in any county. The largest reported winter concentrations included 18 at Cleveland on January 28, 1961, and 75 in the Salem area (Columbiana County) during the winter of 1931–32,[17,328] plus Christmas Bird Count totals of 30 at Cleveland, 74 at Oxford (Butler County), and 118–214 at Cincinnati. Wintering Rufous-sided Towhees occupy the same shrubby habitats where they are found during summer, although a few may also visit backyard bird feeders.

BACHMAN'S SPARROW

Aimophila aestivalis (Lichtenstein)

Bachman's Sparrow was first recorded from Ohio on August 18, 1890, when a specimen was secured at Columbus.[236] These sparrows were only sporadically reported during the 1890s, although spring migrants appeared as far north as Lake Erie at Cedar Point (Erie County) on May 14–17, 1900.[241] Most of their range expansion apparently occurred between 1900 and 1915 when Bachman's Sparrows were initially recorded from many locations in southern and eastern Ohio. The first nests were reported from Highland County in 1898 and Fairfield County in 1903. Nesting populations were firmly established by 1910.[55,437]

Their populations apparently peaked between 1915 and 1922 but may have declined by the 1930s.[55] In 1935, summering Bachman's Sparrows were recorded from every county north to Butler, Montgomery, Greene, Fayette, Franklin, Knox, Ashland, Wayne, Tuscarawas, and Belmont.[55,220] Only a few spring overflights were reported north of these counties. These summering sparrows were generally rare to uncommon and irregularly reported from the southwestern counties. Along the Allegheny Plateau, they were rare in most counties, becoming uncommon in Vinton County and fairly common in Hocking County.[223]

Breeding Bachman's Sparrows were frequently encountered on the dry upper slopes of hillsides. These hillsides were generally eroded and covered with sparse herbaceous vegetation invariably including some blackberry tangles; the gullies were covered with trees, shrubs, and vines.[55] Despite these fairly open habitats, these sparrows were shy and difficult to observe, since they mostly skulked along the ground. Only singing males were obvious, and their beautiful songs carried considerable distances on a calm summer evening. They nested on the ground under weeds and grasses and their nests were difficult to discover. Their first nesting attempts were normally initiated during May with the broods fledging in late June and early July. They may have raised two broods, since nests with eggs were recorded as late as August 6.[295]

As spring migrants, the earliest Bachman's Sparrow returned to Portsmouth by April 2. Most males appeared on their breeding territories between April 18 and 30.[55] Spring migration apparently continued through mid-May, based on the few extralimital sightings near Lake Erie. Singing males were regularly located into early July but there were relatively few records once singing ceased. Their fall migration was poorly documented. Most sparrows apparently departed during August and early September. The latest reported fall sighting was only September 17.[45]

Breeding populations underwent another brief expansion between the mid-1940s and early 1950s. This expansion was most evident in northern Ohio, where the first Cleveland area records occurred in 1944 and 1949 while Toledo's first Bachman's Sparrow was noted in 1948.[89,523] Increased populations were not evident within the southern and eastern counties during these years.

Their final decline apparently began during the late 1950s. Bachman's Sparrows just quietly disappeared from Ohio. These sparrows were last recorded at East Liverpool in 1963 and at Utica and Dayton in 1964.[146,299,393] By the mid-1960s, remnant populations remained near Cincinnati and very locally in the southeastern counties.[11] These populations disappeared by the late 1960s and only isolated pairs remained. Surprisingly, the last confirmed sightings were from locations outside their normal range. Male Bachman's Sparrows summered in the Oak Openings of Lucas County in 1968, 1971, and 1972, although breeding was never established.[90] Single birds were recorded from Trumbull County and the Youngstown area during 1972.[161] The last recorded territorial male summered at Highbanks Metropolitan Park in Delaware County in 1974.

Their disappearance is perplexing; there are no apparent reasons for their decline. Suitable habitats seem to be available throughout the southeastern counties, and no species is known to compete directly with Bachman's Sparrows. But for whatever reasons, they are presently accidental visitors to Ohio. The last reported sighting was from Scioto County on September 6, 1978, and there have been no confirmed records during the 1980s.[271]

AMERICAN TREE SPARROW

Spizella arborea (Wilson)

During the waning days of October, a strong cold front encourages most migrant songbirds to depart for warmer climates. This cold weather also prompts the return of a few winter residents, including the American Tree Sparrow, a resident of the arctic tundra well suited to withstand an Ohio winter. While the earliest Tree Sparrows have returned to Lake Erie by September 25 and central Ohio by September 27,[45,117] they do not normally appear in northern Ohio until the last week of October. The first migrants may not reach the southern counties until the first week of November. Their numbers increase rapidly and flocks of 12–100+ may appear by late November. As winter residents, Tree Sparrows inhabit weedy fields, roadsides, wetlands, brushy thickets, and edges of woodlots. They seldom wander into residential neighborhoods but will visit rural bird feeders.

Tree Sparrows were formerly among our most numerous wintering birds. During the 1920s and 1930s, daily field trips in central Ohio regularly produced totals of 200–700 individuals.[483] Similar numbers were encountered elsewhere, while as many as 1000+ might be tallied under favorable circumstances. Their numbers declined in the 1940s, a trend continuing into the 1980s. This decline was attributed to the loss of successional habitats.[483]

Tree Sparrows remain fairly numerous winter residents, although their numbers fluctuate from year to year. Their abundance is frequently correlated with winter weather conditions. Influxes are usually associated with severe weather in Canada and the upper Great Lakes that forces birds into Ohio. Prolonged severe weather in Ohio may cause them to migrate farther south.

Wintering Tree Sparrows are generally most numerous in the central and northern counties, where they are normally common to locally abundant residents. As many as 30–100 may be recorded most days and totals of 150–300 are not unusual. Christmas Bird Counts may produce tallies of 1000–2000+ during years of maximum abundance. Tree Sparrows are fairly common to common residents in the southwestern counties. While daily totals seldom exceed 25–75, concentrations of 500–800 are occasionally reported. They are least numerous in the unglaciated southeastern counties, especially those bordering the Ohio River, where daily totals seldom exceed 10–50.

A warm sunny March day may prompt male Tree Sparrows to produce their beautiful clear whistled song. This song is not regularly heard within Ohio, since most Tree Sparrows begin their northward migration as soon as the weather begins to moderate. They depart from the southern and central counties by late March, although they are regularly encountered along Lake Erie through the first week of April. The last migrants are usually recorded between April 10 and 18. A few late migrants have lingered through May 7 at Dayton[299] and at Cleveland and Toledo until May 22–30.[89,117,523]

CHIPPING SPARROW

Spizella passerina (Bechstein)

These handsome little sparrows are summer residents familiar to many Ohioans as a result of a preference for nesting in shrubbery around residences. They prefer large mowed lawns surrounding suburban and rural residences where they can forage for insects and seeds among the short grasses. They also occupy orchards and pine plantations or, in densely populated urban areas, parks and cemeteries.

Given these habitat preferences, Chipping Sparrows are fairly common to common summer residents throughout Ohio. They are most numerous in the southern and unglaciated counties, where summer roadside censuses readily produce 20–40 Chipping Sparrows daily. Similar numbers may be encountered within suburban and rural areas bordering large cities in the remainder of the state. Fewer Chipping Sparrows are found in the intensively farmed western and central counties, where daily totals seldom exceed 5–15.

Their long-term population trends apparently differ in the various sections of Ohio. Chipping Sparrows reportedly declined in the Toledo area after the early 1900s, a trend continuing into the 1970s.[89,90] Similar declines were evident in other central and western counties where intensive farming practices have eliminated suitable habitats. These locally declining populations are not apparent elsewhere, and breeding bird surveys indicate increasing populations in every Great Lakes state since 1965.[438]

As spring migrants, the first Chipping Sparrows normally return to the southern counties during the last week of March, when overflights may appear north to Lake Erie. They are not commonly encountered throughout Ohio until April 10–20. Their spring migration is mostly composed of resident sparrows returning to their territories. Small flights of 15–50 are occasionally encountered along Lake Erie and in central Ohio. The last migrants normally depart lakefront migrant traps by May 15–20.

Nest construction has been reported as early as April 7 and a nest with eggs by April 16, although most first clutches are not normally laid until late April or May.[479] The first broods may fledge during the last half of May but most are observed in June. Chipping Sparrows raise two broods annually; nests with eggs are reported through August 1, while adults accompanied by dependent young are regularly noted well into August.[49,89]

Chipping Sparrows become less conspicuous once the males quit singing; fewer individuals are detected after early August. The summer residents leave their breeding territories and form flocks of 5–15, which may be regularly observed throughout September. The largest fall concentrations have totaled 50 individuals along Lake Erie. Their numbers noticeably decline between October 5 and 15 but small numbers may remain through the end of the month. Stragglers linger into November.

They normally spend the winter months in the southern United States and Mexico.[5] While wintering Chipping Sparrows are reported annually on Christmas Bird Counts, these sightings are generally considered misidentifications. Chipping Sparrows are actually accidental winter visitors to Ohio. The few confirmed reports have been of isolated individuals, frequently visiting bird feeders. During the past fifteen years, wintering Chipping Sparrows have been documented from Pickaway County, Lorain County, Ottawa County, Wilmington, Lima, Cleveland, and Kent, averaging one sighting every two or three years.

CLAY-COLORED SPARROW

Spizella pallida (Swainson)

Before 1920, Clay-colored Sparrows were restricted to the northern Great Plains states and adjacent Canadian provinces, migrating through the central United States to wintering areas in Mexico. The 1920s marked the initiation of a gradual eastward range expansion through Ontario, Minnesota, Wisconsin, and Michigan.[104] These sparrows became firmly established around the upper Great Lakes by the mid-1960s. This range expansion continued, and they presently breed across southern Ontario to southwestern Quebec and occasionally western New York.[5]

The appearance of Clay-colored Sparrows in Ohio and the evolution of their status are correlated with this range expansion. Ohio's first Clay-colored Sparrow was collected by Charles Walker at South Bass Island (Ottawa County) on May 12, 1940.[512] Another was sighted in Ottawa County on May 16, 1948.[89] There were no sight records during the 1950s and only three in the 1960s. Once a breeding population became established in southern Ontario, they became fairly regular migrants through Ohio. On the average, Clay-coloreds have been recorded in two of every three years since 1976.

Most Ohio records are of spring migrants with at least thirteen sightings through 1988, all of single sparrows between April 25 and May 22. Clay-colored Sparrows are now casual but fairly regular spring migrants along Lake Erie, with most records in Ottawa and Lucas Counties and near Cleveland. They are accidental migrants through the interior counties, where the only confirmed records are of a Clay-colored on the Ohio State University campus at Columbus on May 15, 1969; one banded at Oxford (Butler County) on May 1, 1981;[361] and one banded at Spring Valley Wildlife Area on May 7, 1988.[388a]

Although Clay-colored Sparrows should also pass through Ohio during their fall migration, there are few fall records. Two factors may be responsible for this paucity: Clay-colored Sparrows are more difficult to identify during this season, being easily confused with two related sparrows; and fall Clay-coloreds cannot be located and identified by their distinctive buzzy songs. The only acceptable records of this accidental fall migrant are one observed at Kent (Portage County) on September 14, 1980, and one banded at Cleveland on October 4, 1986.[279,384]

There are no confirmed winter records from Ohio. One Clay-colored reportedly was banded in Miami County during December 1961, but no details are available to support this record.

FIELD SPARROW

Spizella pusilla (Wilson)

Occupants of brushy successional habitats, Field Sparrows are most numerous in fallow fields where tangles, shrubs, and saplings are scattered among the weeds and grasses. Breeding densities may approach one pair per acre in ideal habitats.[523] In addition to fallow fields, smaller numbers inhabit brushy pastures, shrubby woodland edges, fencerows, and brushy borders of streams and swamps.

Breeding Field Sparrows are generally most numerous in the southern and eastern counties. They are abundant on the red cedar–covered hillsides in Adams and Brown Counties, where 100+ individuals can be tallied daily. While they are less numerous in other successional habitats, 25–50+ may be counted in other eastern and southern counties. Similar numbers may be locally encountered in suitable habitats elsewhere, including the Oak Openings near Toledo. In intensively farmed central and western Ohio, Field Sparrows are only fairly common summer residents; daily totals seldom exceed 12–20. They become scarce within large urban areas.

Field Sparrows undoubtedly increased in numbers after Ohio's virgin forests were replaced by younger successional habitats. They became common summer residents by the late nineteenth century.[522] Their populations may be slowly declining. Habitat loss, along with severe winter weather during the late 1970s, contributed to this decline, which has been apparent in central and eastern North America since 1965.[438]

Their nesting activities begin by late April in southern and central Ohio and early May farther north. Their nests are built on the ground or in shrubs and saplings to heights of fourteen feet. First clutches are normally laid by May 5–15, although unusually early nests have produced dependent young by May 14.[479] The first fledglings are not normally observed until June. Field Sparrows raise two broods annually. Nests with eggs have been discovered as late as August 26 at Cleveland.[523] Extraordinarily late fledglings were reported from Cincinnati on October 10, 1937.[500]

Most Field Sparrows spend the winter months in the southeastern United States. Since these sparrows are common summer residents, the beginning of their fall migration is difficult to determine. The bulk of this migration apparently occurs between September 20 and October 20, with the last migrants departing by November 15. These migrants are mostly observed in flocks of 10–60.

Before 1940, Field Sparrows were rather unusual winter residents in Ohio. Since then their numbers have markedly increased. Today, winter Field Sparrows are most numerous in southern Ohio, especially near Cincinnati. They are generally uncommon to fairly common residents in these counties. Winter totals normally are 5–30 individuals daily. These numbers are subject to considerable annual fluctuations. During years of peak abundance, more than 200 Field Sparrows have been reported on several southwestern Ohio Christmas Bird Counts.

Wintering Field Sparrows are much less numerous in central Ohio, where they are rare to locally uncommon residents, mostly as scattered individuals or flocks of 10 or fewer. They are least numerous in northern Ohio, where they are rare winter residents, becoming casual in the extreme northeastern counties. Most northern Ohio winter records are of only 1–3 individuals.

The first spring migrants appear in the southern counties in mid-March and along Lake Erie before the end of the month. Their migration peaks during April. While the largest flights formerly produced totals of 300–400,[89,479] these large movements have not been apparent since the 1960s. In recent years, the largest spring flights seldom exceed 20–100. Their spring migration normally ends by April 20–25, although a few migrants may remain along Lake Erie into the first week of May.

VESPER SPARROW

Pooecetes gramineus (Gmelin)

Few birds benefited more from the clearing of Ohio's virgin forests than the Vesper Sparrow. These forests were replaced by small cultivated fields, pastures, and hayfields bordered by brushy fencerows—nearly ideal habitats for this occupant of open farmlands. Numbers of Vesper Sparrows increased considerably during the nineteenth century; in its latter decades, Vesper Sparrows became abundant summer residents throughout the state. Migrants were also quite plentiful, especially in spring, when Jones[236] found Vespers "swarming over fields and pastures" in considerable numbers.

Their sizable populations were maintained into the first decades of the present century. Hicks[220] considered Vespers common to abundant residents in every county, somewhat less numerous and locally distributed in extreme southern Ohio. Impressive numbers of migrants also appeared each spring and autumn. Peak spring flights frequently produced concentrations of 100–160 individuals.[89,479] Larger numbers appeared each autumn, at least near Buckeye Lake, where Trautman[479] regularly encountered flocks of 100–300 and as many as 500 could be observed daily.

By the 1930s, changing land-use practices were already causing noticeable declines in Vesper Sparrow breeding populations.[424] Farm fields were becoming larger, grasslands were converted to cultivated crops, and fencerows were disappearing. In the southeastern counties, Vesper Sparrows were also losing breeding habitats to successional changes. These factors reduced Vesper Sparrow breeding populations during subsequent decades. Their numbers were substantially reduced in most counties by 1960.[471]

Despite their reduced populations, Vesper Sparrows remain fairly common to common summer residents within farmlands east through Huron, Richland, Knox, Licking, Pickaway, Ross, Highland, and Brown Counties.[434] Daily totals of 5–20 individuals are possible within most of these counties, although they are less numerous in southwestern Ohio and near large cities. Vesper Sparrows are uncommon to fairly common summer residents in northeastern Ohio and along the unglaciated Allegheny Plateau south to Coshocton, northern Guernsey, and northern Belmont Counties. While they may become locally common in extensive reclaimed strip mines, generally 1–6 Vespers will be recorded daily within most of these counties. Elsewhere along the Allegheny Plateau, Vesper Sparrows are presently casual to rare residents, with a few pairs occupying farm fields near the boundary of the plateau and small populations inhabiting reclaimed strip mines.

Their nests are placed on the ground, usually under a clump of grasses. Nests with eggs have been reported by the last week of April, although most first clutches are usually laid in mid-

May.[479,523] While fledglings have been detected by May 17, they are not normally expected until mid-June. Vesper Sparrows apparently raise two broods annually. Second clutches may be noted through mid-July and adults accompanied by fledglings through August 13.[425,479]

As spring migrants, Vesper Sparrows no longer swarm over fields and pastures. In fact, their northward migration is mostly residents returning to their territories. Small flights occasionally appear along Lake Erie, producing local concentrations of 20–35+ individuals. Within unglaciated southeastern Ohio, these migrants become uncommon, with no more than 1–5 daily. While the first migrants may appear as early as the first week of March, they do not normally return until March 20–30. Most Vespers return during April and few migrants are detected after April 25.

Their fall migration has become poorly defined in recent years. After the males quit singing in July, Vesper Sparrows become inconspicuous. Most resident Vespers quietly depart between September 15 and October 20 with the last migrants lingering until November 1. When their populations were larger, a few Vespers would remain well into November, but these late migrants have become very rare since 1960. Fall Vespers are generally uncommon to rare migrants at most localities, usually reported as scattered individuals. The largest recent fall flocks have been composed of 20–25 Vespers. Fall concentrations in excess of 100 have not been reported since the 1930s.

Vesper Sparrows have always been accidental to casual winter visitors in Ohio. Most are discovered before January 15, although a few have overwintered. While they have been reported throughout Ohio, they are not regularly noted at any location and there are relatively few winter records from the northeastern counties. These wintering Vespers are almost invariably isolated individuals inhabiting brushy fencerows and woodland edges near farm fields. The number of winter records has not declined in recent years, averaging one sighting every two years since the mid-1960s.

LARK SPARROW

Chondestes grammacus (Say)

Lark Sparrows expanded into Ohio during the nineteenth century as the state's land use became predominantly agricultural. They were first recorded in 1861 and appeared east to the Scioto River and north to central Ohio by 1882.[522] Small numbers expanded into northern Ohio during the 1890s. Their populations probably peaked between 1900 and 1910. In that decade, small numbers were regularly encountered in northern Ohio, particularly near Toledo, Oberlin, and Cleveland.[89,236] They were also "rather common" summer residents near Buckeye Lake.[479] Lark Sparrows were widely distributed elsewhere except for the eastern third of the state.[236]

By 1935, Lark Sparrows had declined, and the center of their distribution shifted to the south-central and southeastern counties.[220,223] Along the unglaciated Allegheny Plateau, they were very locally distributed and generally very rare or rare in every county north to Coshocton, Guernsey, and Belmont. Larger populations were noted only in Adams County, where as many as 25 pairs summered during some years, and Muskingum County, where 14 pairs were located in 1935.[56] Numbers were variable and Lark Sparrows seldom remained at any locality for more than a few years. Within the remainder of Ohio, breeding or summering Lark Sparrows were reported from four southwestern counties, twelve central and west-central counties, and six counties in the northern third of the state. While nesting Lark Sparrows were regularly encountered near Toledo and in Butler County,[89,248] their appearance in the other counties was very sporadic.

Their breeding population continued to decline. This decline was poorly documented, partly as a result of their fluctuating numbers and sporadic appearance even at traditional nesting locations. This variability produced short-lived increases during the 1950s and 1960s.[349,397] Lark Sparrows then quietly disappeared from most counties. By the late 1960s, breeding Lark Sparrows were restricted to isolated populations in the Oak Openings of Lucas County and southern Adams County. Only infrequent individuals were encountered elsewhere, primarily in southeastern Ohio.

Their status has not changed appreciably during the past twenty years. Intensive surveys between 1982 and 1987 produced few additional summer records.[434] As many as 5 pairs annually nest in the Oak Openings and a few additional pairs may reside in adjacent portions of Fulton County. Sporadic observations indicate that a few Lark Sparrows remain in southwestern Adams County, but the size of this remnant population is not known. The only other recent summer records are of breeding pairs in Hamilton and Auglaize Counties. Lark Sparrows now rank among the rarest of our breeding birds; their total population may not exceed 12 pairs.

Lark Sparrows prefer to nest in disturbed open habitats characterized by short vegetation interspersed with open soil where there are a few boulders, fenceposts, small trees, and telephone poles that can be used by singing males. Rocky overgrazed hillside pastures are preferred in southeastern Ohio, while the Oak Openings Lark Sparrows occupy sparse weedy and shrubby fields along sandy beach ridges. Nesting pairs have also inhabited abandoned quarries. Their nesting activities normally commence during the last half of May, although adults accompanied by young have been observed as early as June 12.[89] Second broods may be represented by nests with eggs through July 15 and fledglings through July 27.[90,122]

These summer residents normally disappear shortly after their young fledge. Breeding adults are seldom encountered after early August. They are accidental fall migrants throughout Ohio, with only one to three reports each decade. These few fall records are mostly single sparrows observed in the vicinity of Lake Erie between the last week of August and mid-October. There is one undocumented winter record of a Lark Sparrow at the North Chagrin Reservation in Cuyahoga County on January 25–27, 1964.[335]

As spring migrants, most Lark Sparrows are noted between April 20 and May 15. Since the mid-1960s, this movement has been made up chiefly of the few resident pairs returning to their territories. These sparrows are accidental spring migrants away from established nesting locations, producing three to six records each decade. Most extralimital spring Lark Sparrows are discovered within the western half of Ohio, although one was discovered in Holmes County on April 28, 1986.[382]

Their disappearance is perplexing; there are no obvious factors responsible. Suitable habitats are seemingly available. While Lark Sparrows are susceptible to nest parasitism by Brown-headed Cowbirds, their decline started long before cowbirds were as numerous as they are today. However, Brooks[56] noted that these sparrows occupied markedly different habitats within the Ohio River valley than elsewhere in their range. Perhaps these habitats are marginal for Lark Sparrows and their reproductive success was insufficient to maintain their populations.

BLACK-THROATED SPARROW

Amphispiza bilineata (Cassin)

As occupants of deserts and dry shrublands, Black-throated Sparrows are widely distributed in Mexico and the western United States north to southern Oregon, southern Wyoming, and western Oklahoma. They withdraw from the northern edge of this range during winter. Black-throated Sparrows have also demonstrated a tendency to wander into central and eastern North America.[5] Most appear during late fall and winter at bird feeders.

Ohio's first record of this accidental visitor fits this established pattern of vagrancy. A Black-throated Sparrow visited the feeder of Helen Stump in Conneaut (Ashtabula County) daily between November 5 and December 9, 1961. It was carefully studied by Mrs. Stump and its identification corroborated by J. Paul Perkins and Paul Savage.[440]

The only other Black-throated Sparrow was discovered by Andy Fondryk at the Hambden Orchard Wildlife Area (Geauga County) on June 3, 1988. This singing male established a territory and was observed through August 1.[388a] His unexpected appearance in northeastern Ohio may represent the first summer record anywhere in eastern North America.

LARK BUNTING

Calamospiza melanocorys Stejneger

Lark Buntings are widespread occupants of short-grass prairies throughout central North America. Their breeding range extends from the southern Canadian Prairie Provinces to northern New Mexico and Texas. Most wintering Lark Buntings are found in the southwestern United States and Mexico.[5] They also wander and have appeared outside their normal range in all seasons. Ohio's eight acceptable records of this accidental visitor consist of four sightings during summer, two in spring, one in fall, and one in winter. Several additional sightings lack sufficient information to constitute acceptable records.

Ohio's first Lark Buntings were reported during the 1930s. Lawrence Hicks noted a flock of 7 males along the Maumee River near Napoleon (Henry County) on July 28, 1930, and a flock of 3 Lark Buntings in Jerusalem Township, Henry County, on August 9, 1937.[232] These sight records were supported by sketchy details suggesting that these distinctive birds were correctly identified. These appearances may have been associated with the extended droughts on the North American prairies during that decade.

The first specimens were secured during the 1940s. An immature Lark Bunting was collected by M. B. Skaggs in South Euclid (Cuyahoga County) on September 6, 1944.[453] Another Lark Bunting was collected by Lawrence Hicks near the village of Deshler (Henry County) on August 7, 1945.[232] It was discovered the previous day in association with a second bunting.

Lark Buntings then went unrecorded until 1962, when a female was discovered near Columbus on April 28.[471] The remaining records were produced during the 1970s. A singing male was discovered near Conneaut (Ashtabula County) on June 28, 1970. This unmistakable Lark Bunting was studied by several observers, although few other details are available. A male appeared at a feeder in the village of Thurston (Licking County) during January 1971. It remained at this feeder through May 8 and was closely studied as it molted into its breeding plumage.[471] The most recent record was provided by two females that I discovered along a county road in Scioto Township, Pickaway County, on April 24, 1977. These birds were carefully observed on the ground and in flight as they foraged along the edge of cultivated fields. There are no acceptable sightings during the 1980s.

SAVANNAH SPARROW

Passerculus sandwichensis (Gmelin)

Savannah Sparrows rank among the more numerous summer residents of Ohio's remaining grasslands. Their buzzy high-pitched songs are heard wherever suitable habitats exist. While breeding pairs presently reside in most counties, they are not uniformly distributed across the state.[434] Savannahs are most numerous within the northern and glaciated central counties, where they are fairly common to common summer residents. Summer totals of 5–20+ individuals daily are noted in most counties except near large urban areas. Within the southwestern counties, they become uncommon to rare and rather locally distributed residents, least numerous near the Ohio River. Most summer sightings are of 10 or fewer daily, although local concentrations may develop. For example, 160 Savannahs were estimated in a single Clinton County field during 1984.[375] Along the unglaciated Allegheny Plateau, Savannah Sparrows are presently fairly common residents south through Belmont, Guernsey, and Muskingum Counties in numbers comparable to other portions of the state. They become uncommon to rare and locally distributed along the remainder of the plateau, most likely to be encountered on reclaimed strip mines.

They have not always been widely distributed summer res-

idents. In fact, they were strictly migrants through Ohio during the nineteenth century.[236] The first breeding populations were reported in several northern counties in the 1920s.[86] By the mid-1930s, Hicks[220] cited summer records from thirty-two counties south to Defiance, Wyandot, Franklin, Licking, Wayne, Stark, and Columbiana.

This expansion continued during subsequent decades, with nesting pairs reaching Dayton and Cincinnati by 1952.[248,299] Their southward expansion along the unglaciated Allegheny Plateau continued into the early 1970s. Their statewide breeding populations have apparently stabilized within the past decade.

Savannah Sparrows breed in pastures and hayfields composed of grasses, clovers, and alfalfa. They prefer lightly grazed pastures with tall grasses but also reside in hayfields mowed once or twice a year. Their nests, expertly concealed on the ground under clumps of grasses, are usually discovered by accident. Nesting activities begin during May and nests with eggs have been reported between May 10 and July 18.[523] Recently fledged young have appeared by June 5 but are mostly noted during late June and July.

The spring migration of Savannah Sparrows is fairly well defined by the passage of singing males. While a few early migrants have returned during the first half of March, especially when temperatures are relatively mild, the first Savannahs are not expected until March 23–April 3. They become widely distributed by April 8–12 and remain numerous into the first week of May. A few migrants are noted through May 20–25.

Spring Savannahs are generally uncommon to locally common migrants, most numerous within the glaciated counties. Daily totals are mostly 3–25 individuals during April. Larger flights are occasionally encountered, producing concentrations of 60–80 at several localities and flights of 103 at Cleveland on April 14, 1981, and 150 in Pickaway County on April 15, 1956.[361,471] The largest movement occurred on April 22, 1951, when Trautman[481] noted "hundreds" on South Bass Island in western Lake Erie.

Their status as fall migrants is not so thoroughly understood. When an effort is made to locate fall Savannahs, greater numbers are found than were reported during spring. For example, Trautman[479] regularly noted 15–50 Savannahs daily at Buckeye Lake during the 1920s and 1930s and frequently noted as many as 60–180. Campbell[89] also reported flights involving 100+ in the Toledo area. If such totals are applicable to the entire state, Savannah Sparrows may be fairly common to common fall migrants through most northern and central counties. They may be locally uncommon along the unglaciated Allegheny Plateau where suitable habitats are scarce.

The first fall migrants appear by September 10–15 but they do not become widespread until the last half of the month. Their maximum abundance is normally attained between September 25 and October 20. They usually depart by November 7–10, with a few stragglers later in the month.

While Savannah Sparrows are considered accidental or casual winter visitors within Ohio, they may not be as rare as the few records indicate. During the 1980s, small numbers of wintering Savannahs have been regularly flushed from grassy fields along the Ross-Pickaway County Line Road in central Ohio.

No more than 1–6 Savannahs have been flushed from any field, but their regular presence indicates the existence of a wintering population. If similar fields were systematically searched elsewhere within the southern half of Ohio, other populations would probably be discovered. These observations indicate that Savannah Sparrows may be rare and locally distributed winter residents in the southern and central counties, becoming accidental to casual within the northern counties.

BAIRD'S SPARROW

Ammodramus bairdii (Audubon)

On April 22, 1951, the passage of a cold front produced a spectacular movement of migrating birds along the south shore of Lake Erie. As Milton Trautman surveyed this movement on South Bass Island in Ottawa County, he noticed an unusual sparrow among the multitudes of common sparrows. It was similar to a Savannah but had an ochraceous central crown stripe and face pattern, while the streaking on its underparts was finer than the Savannah's, with only a narrow band of streaks across the upper breast.[481] After carefully studying and describing the bird, Dr. Trautman concluded that it was a Baird's Sparrow. His sighting provides the only acceptable record of this accidental visitor to Ohio and one of very few extralimital records from the eastern United States. Baird's Sparrows inhabit grasslands in central North America. They breed in the Dakotas, Montana, and adjacent southern Canada and winter in the southwestern United States and nearby Mexico.[5]

GRASSHOPPER SPARROW

Ammodramus savannarum (Gmelin)

Named for their high-pitched insectlike song, Grasshopper Sparrows are inconspicuous, more likely to be heard than seen. Males may be observed, since they regularly sing from the tops of weeds and grasses, but silent Grasshoppers remain hidden amid dense grassy cover and are observed only when flushed underfoot.

Grasshopper Sparrows reside only in grassy hayfields, pastures, clover fields, and occasionally weedy fallow fields.[479,523] Their distribution is closely related to the availability of these habitats. Breeding Grasshoppers underwent a tremendous expansion during the nineteenth century, becoming widely distributed by the late 1800s. At the turn of the century, Jones[236] considered them fairly common but locally distributed residents. Their numbers probably peaked in the 1920s and 1930s. At Buckeye Lake, for example, Trautman[479] estimated 100–200 breeding pairs. In 1935, Hicks[220] described Grasshoppers as common to extremely abundant summer residents, with records from every county. He later noted they were locally rare to uncommon within a few southeastern counties.[223]

Numbers of breeding Grasshoppers declined in the 1940s and have continued to decrease.[438,483] Factors contributing to this decline include conversion of grasslands and clover fields into cultivated crops and frequent mowing of the remaining hayfields, which greatly reduces these sparrows' breeding success and increases the mortalilty of nesting adults. However, not all changes in land-use patterns have been detrimental. Within several eastern counties, reclaimed strip mines created abundant grasslands.

Breeding Grasshopper Sparrows still occupy every Ohio county, although their relative abundance varies considerably across the state.[434] They are least numerous within the extreme northeastern counties, becoming rare to uncommon and very locally distributed across Lake, Geauga, Ashtabula, and Trumbull Counties. In other northern and glaciated central counties, Grasshoppers are uncommon to fairly common residents. Daily totals of 3–10 individuals can be noted in most of these counties. Larger concentrations are unusual, although at least 100 males were counted within a reclaimed strip mine in Stark County.[379] Grasshopper Sparrows become fairly common to locally abundant summer residents in the southern and unglaciated eastern counties. While 3–12 may be encountered daily in most areas, sizable colonies may develop in fallow fields in southwestern Ohio and in reclaimed strip mines in the eastern counties. These strip mines may support 40–100+ singing males, while as many as 120 Grasshoppers were estimated from a fallow field in Clinton County in 1984.[375,434]

Relatively little information is available on their breeding biology in Ohio. First clutches are generally laid during the last half of May and early June. While fledglings have been reported by June 5,[479] most are observed in late June or early July. Second nesting attempts produce clutches through mid-July. These young may not fledge until the first half of August.[89,421,424]

The spring migration is mostly Grasshopper Sparrows returning to their territories. The earliest overflights appeared at Cleveland by March 23 and at other localities during the first half of April.[523] The first sparrows are not normally detected until April 20–27 in the southern and central counties or April 25–May 3 along Lake Erie. Their numbers increase rapidly and little migration is evident after May 15–20.

Once the males quit singing, Grasshopper Sparrows become very inconspicuous. There are very few fall records after the first half of August. This paucity prompted Campbell[89] to speculate that their southward movement is primarily during August. However, scattered sightings in September and October may be indicative of a southward movement corresponding with the migrations of most other sparrows. These migrants may be noted into the first half of October, with a few late sightings through early November.

Grasshopper Sparrows are apparently accidental winter visitors to Ohio but are easily overlooked. There are at least four confirmed winter records and several undocumented sightings that may be correct. These records are scattered across the state, including one banded in Ottawa County on December 14, 1983.[373] Most winter reports are of single sparrows during December and early January. A Grasshoper Sparrow in Butler County on February 5, 1983, probably overwintered.[369]

HENSLOW'S SPARROW

Ammodramus henslowii (Audubon)

Most sparrows are drab brown birds that occupy obscure habitats and have few admirers. Nevertheless, they possess a certain charm. I have a particular affection for Henslow's Sparrows, partly because of their obscurity and partly because of their attractive appearance. In fresh plumage, their olive faces, chestnut wings, and purplish brown backs are quite colorful. Unfortunately, they usually remain hidden in vegetation rather than exhibiting this plumage. Even when they sing their distinctive song—which is really more like a hiccup—they are as likely to be perched within vegetation as on an exposed branch.

The distribution and abundance of Henslow's Sparrows have been almost constantly changing within Ohio. Some of these changes reflect our increased ability to locate this species but most are the direct result of habitat availability. Nesting Henslow's Sparrows are restricted to early successional communities. Their typical breeding habitat is a grassy or weedy overgrown field with a few scattered saplings and shrubs. They are equally at home in hillside grasslands dominated by broomsedge and in reclaimed strip mines with extensive grasslands mixed with sweet clovers. In northwestern Ohio, they prefer wet prairies dominated by sedges with scattered shrubs.[234] Breeding Henslow's have also inhabited cranberry bogs, timothy pastures, and clover hayfields.[496]

As with most other obscure birds, there is considerable confusion about the historic status of these sparrows. Audubon collected the first Henslow's Sparrow known to science in Kentucky, across the Ohio River from Cincinnati, in 1820. He later described the species as an accidental visitor to Ohio but provided no basis for this claim.[234] The first Ohio specimen was not collected until 1872 at Buckeye Lake.[479] Henslow's were sporadically observed during the 1890s, with records from Hamilton, Lorain, and Erie Counties.[248,496] Breeding was not confirmed until 1904, when a nest was discovered in Seneca County.[197] However, they were not regularly reported until the 1920s.

Henslow's Sparrows greatly expanded their range and populations during the 1920s and 1930s. By the mid-1930s, Hicks[220] cited summer records from forty-six counties, primarily in northern and central Ohio. He noted records from "every county north of Paulding, Henry, Wood, Seneca, Wyandot, Marion, Delaware, Franklin, Fairfield, Hocking, Perry, Muskingum, Coshocton, Tuscarawas, Stark, and Columbiana," claiming they were "locally abundant" in many counties. The only other records were from Champaign, Greene, Madison, and Jackson Counties.

Populations probably peaked in central and northern Ohio during the 1930s when early successional habitats were most prevalent. Declines were evident in the 1940s and continued through the 1950s, mostly the result of changing land-use practices. In the late 1960s, they became quite rare at Toledo and uncommon at Cleveland.[89,335]

While Henslow's Sparrows were declining in glaciated northern and central Ohio, they were expanding into the southern and unglaciated counties. This expansion was poorly documented during the 1940s and 1950s with the first records east of the Flushing Escarpment in Carroll and Jefferson Counties in 1944.[84] These birds largely took advantage of successional habitats available in abandoned farmlands.

Henslow's Sparrows became firmly established in the southern and unglaciated counties, where they are presently uncommon to locally abundant summer residents. They nest in most counties southeast from Clermont, Highland, Ross, Pickaway, Licking, Knox, Richland, Stark, and Columbiana. They are most numerous along the entire edge of the Allegheny Plateau where early successional habitats and suitable grassy hayfields are most widely distributed. They are less frequently encountered elsewhere on the plateau but become locally abundant on extensive reclaimed strip mines in Belmont, Harrison, Guernsey, and eastern Muskingum Counties. The largest colonies are composed of 50–100 singing males in fields near Paint Creek Reservoir in Highland and Ross Counties, Salt Fork Reservoir (Guernsey County), and East Fork Reservoir in Clermont County. Colonies in abandoned fields last for only a few years before the habitats become unsuitable. Daily totals usually are 3–15 individuals away from large colonies. Populations have declined elsewhere, and these sparrows have become accidental to rare summer residents in glaciated central and northern Ohio, with small numbers very locally distributed.

Relatively few Henslow's Sparrows are detected as spring migrants; most simply appear at their breeding territories. While they have returned as early as March 18,[248] they are quite rare before mid-April. Most return between April 20 and May 15. The only sizable migration occurred on April 22, 1951, when "many dozens" of Henslow's were reported among an immense movement of sparrows on South Bass Island.[481]

As summer residents, Henslow's Sparrows are among the few birds known to regularly switch locations between broods. Some of these movements are in response to mowing of hayfields, but this behavior has also been reported from undisturbed fields. Relatively little information is available on the nesting chronology of grassland sparrows, including Henslow's. Nests are located on the ground and are very difficult to discover. The few reports of Henslow's nests indicate that first clutches may be laid during late May, while second clutches have been noted as late as August 8. The first broods usually fledge during the last half of June or early July, the second in August. Dependent young have been observed as late as September 24.[89]

Henslow's Sparrows become quite difficult to detect once the males cease singing. There are relatively few records after early August. The few records indicate that migrants are most likely to appear during October, although they may remain into the first week of November at Cincinnati.[248] While there are two published December sight records, neither is accompanied by details sufficient to constitute an acceptable winter record.

LE CONTE'S SPARROW

Ammodramus leconteii (Audubon)

The most elusive of our grassland sparrows, migrant Le Conte's are secretive skulkers through dense herbaceous vegetation bordering marshes, bogs, and mudflats. Frustrating the birder's desire to get a good look, Le Conte's do not normally respond to any form of attraction. Instead, they remain hidden in vegetation until they are flushed at the observer's feet. Their flights are short, and they barely go above the top of the vegetation before dropping into dense cover. With considerable perseverance, a Le Conte's Sparrow may eventually be observed closely; it will prove to be one of the most handsome of all sparrows.

The status of Le Conte's Sparrow is very poorly understood. The first record was provided by a specimen collected in Hamilton County on April 5, 1880.[248] There were no additional records for fifty-two years until one Le Conte's was observed near Toledo on September 3, 1932.[86]

The 1936 fall migration featured an unbelievable invasion for a species that had been recorded only twice previously. This movement was most noticeable in Lucas County, where the first Le Conte's appeared on August 30. Relatively few were detected during September but the October movement was substantial. The largest numbers appeared in Jerusalem Township, Lucas County; 53 were counted in a single wet meadow on October 25 and several hundred were thought to be present.[89] Six Le Conte's were also collected in Clermont County between October 11 and 25,[127] while groups of 6 or fewer were reported from Wood, Franklin, Delaware, and Licking Counties.[225] Small numbers lingered through November 22–23 in Licking County.

That flight has never been repeated. Le Conte's Sparrows remained accidental visitors, with only one to four sightings per decade between 1940 and 1979. Between 1980 and 1987, greater observer activity produced six documented records of this secretive sparrow.

Le Conte's Sparrows are now accidental to casual spring visitors to northern Ohio, where there are at least ten published sightings, most of them near Lake Erie. Spring Le Conte's are accidental migrants elsewhere, with only two records from the Cincinnati area.[248] These migrants were encountered as scattered individuals. They have returned in March but most records are between April 15 and May 7. The latest spring Le Conte's was noted at Toledo on May 12, 1945.[89]

Le Conte's Sparrows are more likely to appear as fall migrants. They are apparently casual migrants along Lake Erie, averaging one sighting every two or three years. They are accidental elsewhere. After the 1936 invasion, the only inland records have been of single sparrows near Cincinnati on October 29, 1960;[327] Pickaway County on October 9, 1978; and Big Island Wildlife Area (Marion County) on September 29, 1984.[376] All recent fall records have been of single Le Conte's Sparrows. While there are two August sightings, most fall reports are between September 25 and October 25. The latest Le Conte's was collected in Lorain County on December 19, 1962.[335]

SHARP-TAILED SPARROW

Ammodramus caudacutus (Gmelin)

The behavior and habitat preferences of Le Conte's Sparrows are shared by this reclusive species. Migrant Sharp-tailed Sparrows prefer sedge meadows, wet pastures, grassy marsh borders, depressions, and wet fields dominated by dense herbaceous vegetation. These brightly colored sparrows normally remain hidden within dense vegetation. Even spring migrants are unlikely to be detected, since Sharp-taileds seldom sing away from their nesting range. Unlike Le Conte's Sparrows, which seldom offer satisfactory views, Sharp-taileds are somewhat more obliging and will respond to various forms of attraction by emerging from dense cover.

Sharp-tailed Sparrows undoubtedly pass through Ohio each spring and autumn. Before 1960, these regular migrations went largely undetected. The majority of Ohio sightings have been reported since 1960, reflecting greater efforts to locate these sparrows rather than a shift in their migration corridors.

Sharp-tailed Sparrows are generally late spring migrants. While there are a few April sightings, none of these records is adequately substantiated. The earliest spring specimen was collected May 8, 1890, near Cincinnati.[248] Most spring Sharp-taileds are detected between May 15 and 27. These migrants are accidental to casual along Lake Erie with at least twelve records, mostly along the Central Basin. They are accidental spring migrants through the interior counties with three reports from central Ohio near Columbus, two Cincinnati area sightings, and single records in Trumbull and Wyandot Counties. All spring reports involve 1–3 individuals. These few records probably represent only a fraction of the numbers passing through Ohio each spring.

Their fall migration patterns are more thoroughly understood. The first southward migrants appear between September 11 and 15 and are most likely to be observed between September 20 and October 10. Only a few stragglers remain as late as October 20–26. These migrants are rare to locally uncommon along the entire lakefront with most sightings of 1–5 individuals. Within the interior counties, they become accidental to casual fall migrants through the glaciated counties. There are presently no fall sightings from the unglaciated counties. Most inland records are of 5 or fewer sparrows, although as many as 10 were flushed near Findlay on October 8, 1961.[417]

During two years, Sharp-tailed Sparrows staged pronounced invasions. In late September 1953, flocks of these sparrows were reported from the Cincinnati area. Few specific details were provided, but this movement coincided with a "substantial" invasion elsewhere in the Midwest.[342] A similar invasion was noted along western Lake Erie during autumn 1964. This movement was most apparent in the Winous Point marshes (Ottawa County), where 75 were counted September 30–October 1 and at least 200 were believed to be present.[89,395]

These sparrows are accidental winter visitors with only one acceptable record. Three were discovered at Cleveland on December 4, 1952. They were regularly observed through February 1, 1953.[117,341] Their subsequent disappearance may indicate that these sparrows did not overwinter.

FOX SPARROW

Passerella iliaca (Merrem)

Fox Sparrows are among our earliest spring migrants, returning to brushy fields, dense fencerows, and shrubby woodlots with the first warm days. Their beautiful whistled song, too infrequently heard, is a welcome signal of the approaching spring. A few early migrants may appear during the last week of February, and it is not unusual to spot Fox Sparrows in the southern and central counties between March 3 and 10 or along Lake Erie by March 10–15. This migration peaks between March 20 and April 15; they normally depart by April 23–25. A few stragglers have lingered through May 15, 1983, at Spring Valley Wildlife Area near Dayton;[370] May 16–21 along Lake Erie;[89,523] May 20, 1922, in central Ohio;[45] and May 28 at Findlay.[417]

Relative abundance varies considerably from year to year. During most springs, Fox Sparrows are fairly common to common migrants along Lake Erie, where concentrations of 25–50+ individuals may develop. Fewer migrants are detected inland, where they become uncommon to fairly common migrants and daily totals seldom exceed 5–25. Fox Sparrows have staged sizable spring movements, becoming fairly common to common migrants in most counties. These movements produced flocks of 75 at Buckeye Lake in the 1920s and 1930s and 100 along Lake Erie at Magee Marsh Wildlife Area on April 15, 1972.[90,479] They can also be remarkably scarce with no more than 2–10 at any locality.

Fewer Fox Sparrows are observed during their fall migration. They become uncommon to fairly common migrants along the lakefront but are generally rare to uncommon within the interior counties. Most fall sightings are of 6 or fewer individuals; the largest concentrations have totaled only 8–25. While migrants have appeared at Ashtabula and Cleveland by August 21–22,[324,523] these sightings were exceptionally early. They are not expected along Lake Erie until September 18–25. A Fox Sparrow in Hocking County on September 16, 1965,[149] was quite early for the southern counties, where they may not appear until mid-October. Fall migrants are mostly observed between October 10 and November 10 with relatively few after November 15.

While most Fox Sparrows winter in the southern United States, small numbers regularly remain north to the Great Lakes. Within Ohio, they are rare but fairly regular winter residents within the southern counties, especially near Cincinnati. Most southern Ohio winter records are of 1–2 individuals, although small flocks of 8–10 may develop. A December 1987 concentration of approximately 100 near Cincinnati was remarkable; they may have been very late migrants. Elsewhere, wintering Fox Sparrows are casual to rare residents within the central counties and accidental to casual in northern Ohio. As many as 5 wintering sparrows have been reported from the central counties, but virtually all northern reports are of scattered individuals. Winter Fox Sparrow records have noticeably increased since 1940, as have records for most other half-hardy birds.

SONG SPARROW

Melospiza melodia (Wilson)

Few songbirds have been as extensively studied as Song Sparrows, whose life history became the subject of Margaret Morse Nice's classic studies.[336,338] At a small area within the present city limits of Columbus, Nice carefully examined all aspects of their behavior and daily activities throughout the year. In addition to providing a wealth of information on this common species, her studies serve as a model for all other research into the life histories of songbirds.

As winter residents, Song Sparrows are common to locally abundant, generally most numerous within the southern half of the state. Their numbers fluctuate in response to food and cover availability as well as weather conditions. During years of maximum abundance, daily totals of 40–200 Song Sparrows may be encountered within the central and southern counties, while northern Ohio totals seldom exceed 30–75 daily. When they are relatively scarce, 20–40 or fewer will be observed most days. These wintering sparrows occupy all types of edge and successional habitats. The majority are males; approximately half are permanent residents within Ohio, while the remainder are migrants from farther north.[336]

Although they are classified as permanent residents, Song Sparrows undergo definite migrations each spring and fall. Their spring migration begins during late February or early March. The earliest migrants are mostly males.[336] The largest movements occur between March 10 and 25, when most females return and many sparrows are in passage to more northerly breeding locations. These movements may produce daily totals of 50–100+ Song Sparrows in most counties and flights of 100–500 along Lake Erie. The last migrants depart from northern Ohio by April 10–15.

Well before this spring migration is under way, the resident males establish their breeding territories. Any warm weather during late January or early February will prompt these males to start singing, each producing a variable song that is distinctly different from his neighbor. As described by Nice:[338]

The songs of each male are entirely distinct; as a rule they sound pleasant and "cheerful" to human ears, yet a few are disagreeable while still others are of great beauty. Many individuals have no specially distinctive songs, while some have one or two songs which are unforgettable to an attentive observer. The same individual may have songs of all degrees of quality: harsh, typical, and especially musical.

Breeding activities begin shortly after the females arrive. The nests are built solely by the females and construction may begin by the last week of March. The first nests are almost invariably placed on the ground.[336] As the season progresses, their nests will be placed at increasingly greater heights; by midsummer, the majority of nests will be two to three feet above ground. The first eggs have been laid as early as April 10 but most first clutches are initiated between April 17 and 30. Nests with young have been noted by April 21, and most first broods hatch between May 5 and 18. Recently fledged young have appeared as early as April 25; most first broods fledge during the last half of May.[336,479] The second broods normally fledge during the last half of June or July.[336] The latest breeding attempts have included nest construction through August 10 and nests with young as late as September 7.[299,510]

During summer, Song Sparrows are common residents throughout Ohio, occupying an array of habitats from residential yards to fallow fields, roadside thickets, brushy fencerows, woodland edges, and the margins of wetlands. Daily totals of 50–100+ Song Sparrows are expected in most counties except the intensively cultivated western counties and large urban areas, where only 10–40 will be recorded. Data from breeding bird surveys indicate that Ohio supports one of the largest Song Sparrow populations in North America.[438] This population has remained fairly constant throughout this century.

Their fall migration coincides with the movements of other sparrows. The first migrants are normally apparent during the last week of September but their main passage is in October. Fall migrants are as numerous as spring migrants, producing movements of 50–500 daily along Lake Erie and 25–200 within the interior counties. The last lakefront migrants depart by November 10–15, while local movements may continue into early December within the interior counties.

LINCOLN'S SPARROW

Melospiza lincolnii (Audubon)

This retiring species may be more abundant than our sightings indicate. As a spring migrant, Lincoln's Sparrow is a skulker through dense brushy tangles, thickets, and woodland edges. It must be coaxed from the underbrush by pishing or by imitating a screech-owl's whistle. Identification problems also have partially obscured its status, and most unseasonal records likely pertain to misidentified Song Sparrows.

A few Lincoln's Sparrows may return during the last week of April, although they are not expected until the first week of May. Most spring migrants are reported between May 8 and 22, when they become uncommon to fairly common along Lake Erie but are rare to uncommon inland. While inland totals seldom exceed 1–6 individuals daily, larger flights along Lake Erie have produced concentrations of 15–25 at lakefront migrant traps; the largest flight totaled 100 at Euclid on May 11, 1984.[374] Only 1–8 may be expected along Lake Erie on nonflight days. Most depart by May 25–30 with occasional stragglers along the lakefront as late as June 12, 1986, at Euclid.[383]

Greater numbers of Lincoln's Sparrows pass through Ohio each autumn. These migrants also prefer dense brushy cover but will be found in weeds and grasses in fallow fields. They too are secretive but are especially responsive to imitated screech-owl whistles.

The first Lincoln's Sparrows usually return to Lake Erie by September 12–20 but may not appear in southern Ohio until the last days of the month. Most fall migrants are recorded between September 28 and October 20 as they become fairly

common along Lake Erie and uncommon through most inland counties. Autumn totals of 1–8 Lincoln's Sparrows may be expected inland and 1–10 along Lake Erie during most days. Larger flights are infrequent but have produced as many as 42 Lincoln's in one thicket and 200 daily at Buckeye Lake during the late 1920s and 1930s and 100+ at Cleveland on October 4, 1986.[384,479] Only occasional late migrants remain into November.

Most Lincoln's Sparrows winter from the southern United States south into Central America.[5] While there have been a number of early winter sight records from Ohio, especially on Christmas Bird Counts, most of them are questionable. Observers should be aware that Lincoln's Sparrows are accidental throughout Ohio during December; all early winter sightings should be accompanied by thorough details. A few Lincoln's Sparrows have been positively identified as late as December 15–25, and one overwintered in downtown Cleveland during 1987–88 with the assistance of food provided by several thoughtful birders.

SWAMP SPARROW

Melospiza georgiana (Latham)

As their name implies, Swamp Sparrows are restricted to wetlands during the breeding season. Nesting pairs occupy a variety of habitats, including cattail marshes; grassy wet meadows; shrubby vegetation bordering ponds, bogs, and lakes; and even birch-maple swamp forests.[523] Their nests are placed low in the herbaceous cover. Construction begins by late April or early May. Some clutches may be laid during the last half of April, since fledged young have been reported by May 30.[479] However, most nests with eggs have been noted between May 13 and June 25 and fledglings are not expected until the last half of June or July.[523]

Breeding Swamp Sparrows are most numerous within northeastern Ohio south to the glacial boundary and west to Wayne and Medina Counties.[434] They are widely distributed in these counties and are uncommon to locally common residents. Summer totals normally are 3–10 individuals daily, although favorable habitats may support 15–20+ territorial males. They are also uncommon to fairly common residents within the marshes bordering Sandusky Bay and western Lake Erie, where daily totals seldom exceed 3–8. Nesting Swamp Sparrows are uncommon and locally distributed within wetlands scattered across Ashland, Richland, Holmes, Huron, Knox, and northern Morrow Counties, mostly as scattered pairs or as groups of 2–12 males. Away from Lake Erie, they have mostly disappeared from the northwestern counties except for a few pairs within the Oak Openings of Lucas County and in Williams County.[434]

Along the unglaciated Allegheny Plateau, they are generally rare to uncommon and very locally distributed in Carroll and Tuscarawas Counties, while a few scattered pairs have been noted south to Guernsey County.[434] Most records are of 1–6 territorial males. They are presently accidental to rare residents within the glaciated central counties with summer records south to Clark, Pickaway, and Licking Counties. While small populations reside at Knox Lake (Knox County) and Indian Lake (Logan County), resident males are only sporadically encountered elsewhere. Nesting Swamp Sparrows have never been confirmed in southern Ohio, although a few singing males have lingered into the first week of June.

Their statewide distribution and relative abundance have not appreciably changed during this century.[220,434] The only noticeable decline has been in northwestern Ohio, especially near Toledo, where Campbell[89,90] reported reduced numbers in the western Lake Erie marshes and the Oak Openings.

As migrants, Swamp Sparrows are most numerous within marshes and wet meadows, but they frequent other habitats, including fallow fields, brushy thickets, shrubby woodland borders, parks, and cemeteries. Swamp Sparrows begin their northward movements during the last week of March. Their maximum abundance is frequently attained between April 10 and May 7 and the last migrants depart by May 18–23. Spring Swamp Sparrows are most numerous along western Lake Erie and in northeastern Ohio. They are fairly common to common visitors to the marshes; 10–30 may be recorded daily and concentrations of 50–60 are possible. Similar concentrations may develop locally elsewhere in northern and central Ohio but have not been reported from the southern counties. Away from wetlands, spring Swamp Sparrows are uncommon to fairly common migrants and most reports are of 1–10.

The first fall migrants may return by September 5–10 but are not expected until September 15–22. The largest southward movements occur during October. Only wintering Swamp Sparrows remain after mid-November. Distribution in fall is similar to that in spring but fall Swamp Sparrows are generally more numerous. These migrants become common to abundant along western Lake Erie, where 20–50 may be observed daily and flights of 100–200 regularly appear in late October.[89] The largest reported fall movement totaled 532 Swamp Sparrows in Ottawa County on October 5, 1979.[275] They are also common migrants through northeastern Ohio, although fall totals seldom exceed 10–50. Within the remainder of Ohio, Swamp Sparrows become locally common migrants through preferred wetlands in the northern and central counties, where as many as 30–80 individuals may be counted during the largest flights. Away from these wetlands, they become uncommon to fairly common migrants with only 3–10 daily.

Wintering Swamp Sparrows are also most numerous within wetland habitats but are regularly found in weedy fields, brushy thickets, and woodland tangles. While they have wintered regularly in Ohio during the present century, their numbers have noticeably increased since the 1950s.

Swamp Sparrows are now fairly common winter residents within the southern counties, where 3–10 individuals may be expected daily and as many as 20–40 may congregate in favorable habitats. They attain a similar status within the western Lake Erie marshes. Within the central and interior northwestern counties, Swamp Sparrows become locally rare to fairly common winter residents; daily totals are usually 6 or fewer individuals. Local concentrations may develop, at least in central Ohio near Columbus, where as many as 50–60 Swamp Sparrows have been tallied. Wintering Swamp Sparrows are

least numerous within northeastern Ohio, where they are rare to locally uncommon residents and most sightings are of only 1–3 individuals. Numbers noticeably diminish during winter and they may become fairly scarce by February, especially when the weather has been unusually harsh.

WHITE-THROATED SPARROW

Zonotrichia albicollis (Gmelin)

White-throated Sparrows are found wherever migrant birds congregate, most frequently brushy fields, dense thickets, and shrubby woodland edges but also woodlands, parks, and cemeteries. They spend most of their time on the ground, scratching through the leaf litter. As they forage among vegetation or hide in thick cover, their presence is readily detected by their distinctive call notes.

Their northward migration begins as early as the last week of March in the southern and central counties. They do not become widely distributed until April 10–17 and their maximum abundance is normally attained between April 22 and May 10. At that time, White-throated Sparrows become fairly common to common migrants in most counties and locally abundant along Lake Erie. Daily totals of 10–50 individuals are noted at most localities, while larger movements produce concentrations of 50–100+. Sizable flights produce phenomenal numbers, such as 800 estimated at Columbus on May 6, 1975. Along Lake Erie, concentrations of 500+ are infrequently recorded and more than 1200 were estimated at Magee Marsh Wildlife Area on May 11, 1980.[471] The last migrants normally depart from interior counties by May 25, although a few linger along the lakefront into the first half of June. The only central Ohio June record is provided by a White-throated near Columbus on June 11, 1948.[45]

A few White-throated Sparrows summer in northern Ohio. Most are nonbreeders that appear any time during June, July, or August, remaining for several days and subsequently disappearing. However, there are breeding records from the Marblehead Peninsula (Ottawa County) in 1913 and Cleveland in 1929.[89,523] A small population may have existed in Ashtabula County, where Hicks[215] discovered pairs in Wayne Township and the former Pymatuning Bog between 1928 and 1932. The Ashtabula County pairs occupied young swamp forests, nesting on the ground among dense herbaceous vegetation.[217] Several nests contained eggs or young by June 14–15, while adults accompanied by dependent young were noted through July 6–16.[215]

Nesting White-throated Sparrows have not been recorded since 1932. In subsequent decades, they became accidental and very sporadic nonbreeding summer visitors to the northern counties. Except for several late migrants, the only summer records during the 1980s were July sightings at Cleveland and Kelleys Island (Erie County) and a singing male in Ashtabula County on June 6, 1986.[434] The Ashtabula County male occupied young woodlands adjacent to a bog and may have been on territory. Its breeding status could not be determined.

White-throated Sparrows are fairly common to locally abundant fall migrants. A few very early migrants appeared along Lake Erie by August 22–23. However, their southward movement does not normally begin until September 10–15 along the lakefront and September 22–30 within the central and southern counties. Most White-throateds pass through the state during October. Their numbers diminish by the first week of November, with the last migrant flocks departing by November 15.

Fall White-throateds are also fairly common to locally abundant migrants, most numerous along Lake Erie. Most fall sightings are of 10–50 individuals daily; sizable movements may produce concentrations of 100–200. The largest fall flights totaled 300–500, but these movements have been restricted to the lakefront.

Before 1940, wintering White-throated Sparrows were rare in northern and central Ohio. For example, Campbell[86] cited only one winter record in the Toledo area, while Trautman[479] encountered only one winter flock at Buckeye Lake. They were regularly encountered only within the southern counties, where they became uncommon to locally fairly common winter visitors, with most flocks totaling fewer than 10 individuals. Wintering populations increased during the 1940s, resulting in additional records from central and northern Ohio. They did not become regular residents in these counties until the 1950s. Statewide wintering numbers substantially increased during the 1960s and 1970s. These increases were most apparent on Christmas Bird Counts. At Cincinnati, for example, the largest total on any count before 1952 was 124 individuals; by 1977, more than 1000 were tallied on this count. Their winter populations have apparently stablized since 1980.

White-throated Sparrows are now generally fairly common to locally common winter residents throughout southern Ohio; 5–25 may be observed daily and concentrations of 30–50+ may be encountered, especially near Cincinnati. They become uncommon to fairly common residents in the central counties, where most reports are of 25 or fewer daily. Within northern Ohio, wintering White-throateds are generally uncommon residents, becoming rare in northeastern counties and fairly common at favored localities. More than 100 winter within the red cedar thickets on Kelleys Island. Similar totals are remarkable elsewhere in northern Ohio, where most sightings are of 12 or fewer individuals. These winter numbers, greatest during December, may be reduced by late January during years with severe weather.

WHITE-CROWNED SPARROW

Zonotrichia leucophrys (Forster)

As migrants, White-crowned Sparrows are regularly found along brushy fencerows, woodland edges, weedy old fields, and pastures supporting hawthorn and multiflora rose tangles. Smaller numbers also visit parks, cemeteries, and residential yards during migration.

Spring White-crowneds appear during the first half of April but do not become widely distributed until April 15–22. The largest movements normally occur between April 28 and May 12. At this time, White-crowneds become fairly common to common migrants along Lake Erie and uncommon to fairly common through the interior counties. Spring totals seldom exceed 10–20 individuals, with the largest flights involving 25–100 along Lake Erie but no more than 30 inland. During some years, White-crowneds are scarce and the largest flocks are composed of only 3–10. At most localities, the last spring migrants depart by May 20–25, although stragglers may remain through the end of the month.

White-crowneds appear in greater numbers in autumn. The first migrants return to Lake Erie by September 20–25 and most interior counties by the first week of October. Their maximum abundance is attained between October 7 and 25, with smaller numbers remaining through mid-November. Fall White-crowneds are most numerous along Lake Erie, where they become fairly common to locally abundant migrants. While fall totals mostly are 5–25 individuals daily, sizable movements are detected almost annually, producing concentrations of 100–250+. Within the interior counties, they are uncommon to locally common migrants, generally observed in flocks of 15 or fewer individuals. Large flights are less frequently noted, although as many as 100 White-crowneds were tallied at Buckeye Lake during several autumns[479] and a remarkable 300+ at Spring Valley Wildlife Area on October 24–27, 1987.[388]

Wintering White-crowned Sparrows were unrecorded until the 1930s and did not become widely distributed until the 1950s. Their numbers increased dramatically during the 1960s, peaked in the 1970s, and declined after 1980. These changes are related to the presence of multiflora rose hedges, with which wintering White-crowneds are frequently associated, especially where croplands, weedy fields, and grassy pastures are nearby. Multiflora rose was widely planted from the 1930s to the 1960s. In recent years, however, it has been labeled a nuisance and is being eradicated. Disappearance of these hedgerows has contributed to the declining winter populations of White-crowneds during the 1980s.

They are now most numerous within the southwestern and glaciated central counties, where they are rare to locally common winter residents. At most localities, winter concentrations seldom exceed 3–15 individuals daily, although as many as 50–110 have been counted in areas supporting plentiful multiflora rose hedgerows. They become casual to uncommon winter residents within the northwestern counties, where daily totals normally are 10 or fewer. Larger tallies have been reported on Christmas Bird Counts, with as many as 95 counted at Toledo during the early 1970s.[90] Wintering White-crowneds are generally uncommon to fairly common along the unglaciated Allegheny Plateau. Most reports are of only 3–15 daily. White-crowneds are least numerous in northeastern Ohio, where they are casual to rare residents and no more than 1–5 are observed daily.

White-crowneds can be scarce one winter and fairly numerous the next, even in areas with relatively stable habitat conditions. Moreover, populations are generally larger during December than later in the winter. In fact, December reports of 100+ White-crowneds may pertain to very late migrants, since similar concentrations have never been noted during January and February.

White-crowned Sparrows have always been accidental non-breeding summer visitors. The few summer records are restricted to Lake Erie, including single sparrows lingering in Lucas County through July 3, 1937, and July 11, 1983,[89,371] and Cleveland area sightings on June 23, 1945, and August 20, 1961.[117,523]

HARRIS' SPARROW

Zonotrichia querula (Nuttall)

These large sparrows normally reside in central North America, breeding in the taiga forests of Canada and migrating through the Great Plains to a winter range extending from Nebraska to Texas.[5] Harris' Sparrows also regularly stray to the states and provinces bordering their established range, while fewer individuals wander toward the two coasts.

Within Ohio, the first Harris' Sparrow was collected at Columbus on April 29, 1889. This individual was reportedly taken from a flock of 3–5 sparrows.[236] The next sighting was not recorded until 1921, but this species was observed fairly regularly in subsequent years. Between 1920 and 1980, Harris' Sparrows were observed from three to nine times each decade, with the largest number of sightings during the 1920s, 1950s, and 1960s. The number of reports has markedly declined in the 1980s; the only substantiated sighting was provided by a single sparrow in Lucas County on October 11, 1985.[380]

Most Harris' Sparrows have been reported as migrants, invariably within flocks of White-crowned and White-throated Sparrows. Harris' Sparrows also visit bird feeders during winter. Wandering Harris' Sparrows are most likely to occur within the western half of Ohio and along Lake Erie, while very few have been confirmed from the eastern counties.

Harris' Sparrows are now accidental to casual migrants throughout Ohio. There have been at least fifteen fall records, mostly of single individuals, with a maximum of 3 at Toledo on October 21, 1928.[89] These migrants have been noted between October 9 and November 12, although one at Akron on November 25, 1974, may have been a late migrant.[167] Spring Harris' Sparrows have been reported on twenty occasions. These migrants have appeared as early as April 1 but most are noted between April 20 and May 15. The latest migrant remained at Cleveland through May 24, 1960.[117] Spring records, like those in fall, are mostly of single individuals, although 2–5 Harris' Sparrows have appeared at a few locations. Small "flights" may develop when this species produces three or four scattered records during a single season.

Wintering Harris' Sparrows are accidental visitors. There are at least eight confirmed winter sightings and a number of unconfirmed records, mostly scattered across the southern half of the state; the only acceptable report from the northern counties was provided by one at North Canton (Stark County) throughout the winter of 1974–75.[168] All substantiated winter records have been of single sparrows.

DARK-EYED JUNCO

Junco hyemalis (Linnaeus)

Anyone who feeds birds during winter has hosted Dark-eyed Juncos. Formerly known as Slate-colored Juncos for their handsome gray and white plumage, these sparrows are likely to occur wherever adequate food and shrubby cover are available. They prefer brushy thickets, fencerows, and woodland edges bordering fields. In recent years, they have taken advantage of bird feeders and are as likely to occur in suburban backyards as in the rural countryside.

Dark-eyed Juncos are fairly common to common winter residents throughout Ohio. During some years, they may be relatively scarce until late January or February, when sizable numbers are driven south in search of food. In other years, they may be widely distributed until prolonged snow cover forces them to leave Ohio.

Wintering juncos are widely distributed through the southern and eastern counties. Between 20 and 60 may be observed daily during most winters. They are more locally distributed in the west-central and northwestern counties, especially in intensively farmed areas. Winter totals there seldom exceed 5–30 daily.

These wintering numbers represent a marked decline from their populations of twenty to fifty years ago. Trautman[479] regularly observed 30–300 juncos daily at Buckeye Lake during the 1920s and 1930s. On Christmas Bird Counts, reports of 700–2500+ were not unusual through the early 1970s but have seldom exceeded 300–800 since 1980. These declining numbers reflect a significant reduction in their eastern North American breeding populations since 1965.[438]

Most of our wintering juncos are of the eastern "Slate-colored" race. However, two western races have also appeared in Ohio. The "Oregon" race is generally an accidental to casual winter visitor. Scattered "Oregons" may be discovered wherever large numbers of juncos congregate. The "Gray-headed" race is an accidental visitor with single sightings from Adams and Lorain Counties.

The first fall migrants are expected along Lake Erie by September 15–25. While they have also appeared near Columbus as early as September 15,[45] they do not normally return to the central and southern counties until the first week of October. Their numbers gradually increase through November. Most recent fall reports are of 50 or fewer juncos, with occasional concentrations of 100–300+. Even when populations were larger, the largest reported fall flocks were composed of 200–400 juncos.[89,479]

In contrast, their spring migration regularly produces sizable concentrations. This migration may begin in late February or early March but the largest movements are mostly noted between March 25 and April 25. Within the interior counties, these movements may produce concentrations of 100–500 juncos. Larger flights may occur along Lake Erie, producing "thousands" of juncos at South Bass Island on April 22, 1951;[481] 2000 at Magee Marsh Wildlife Area on April 15, 1972;[90] and 1500 at Cleveland on April 15, 1985.[378] But spring totals usually are 25–

75 juncos daily. They usually depart from the central and southern counties by May 1–5 and Lake Erie by May 10. Juncos occasionally remain quite late, with reports through May 27–30 at Columbus and Dayton and along Lake Erie.[45,299]

During summer, juncos reside in the coniferous forests of the northern United States, Canada, and the western mountains. Most people are surprised to learn that a small breeding population also exists in Ohio—a remnant of a formerly sizable summer population. Kirtland[251] described "great numbers" of Dark-eyed Juncos breeding in the Cleveland area during the 1830s. They were apparently widely distributed, although there are few factual accounts describing their status. As the mature beech-maple forests were cleared during the 1800s, this population largely disappeared. By 1935, breeding juncos were restricted to Lake, Geauga, Trumbull, and Ashtabula Counties.[220] Only Ashtabula County supported a sizable population, with summer records from twelve locations and a maximum of 50 pairs in eastern Monroe Township through 1930.[215] Most of these breeding juncos disappeared before 1932 and the last pairs were displaced by the destruction of Pymatuning Bog.

Breeding Dark-eyed Juncos are now restricted to scattered pairs within the Chagrin River watershed in portions of Geauga, Lake, and Cuyahoga Counties. They are rare and very locally distributed in cool hemlock ravines and mature beech-maple forests, mostly as isolated pairs with groups of 4–8 territorial males at preferred habitats such as Stebbins Gulch, Little Mountain, and North Chagrin Reservation. The size of this population probably does not exceed 20–30 pairs.

Breeding juncos choose areas with dense shrub layers and ground cover, frequently placing their nests on the ground at bases of overturned trees or in clumps of ferns. Nests with eggs have been discovered as early as April 9 and adults with dependent young are observed by late May. Later attempts have produced nests with eggs through August 21 and adults with young on September 10.[217,262]

Dark-eyed Juncos are accidental summer visitors elsewhere in northern Ohio. There are several scattered Cleveland area sightings of nonbreeding juncos, and summering juncos were noted in the Toledo area in 1934 and 1942.[89]

LAPLAND LONGSPUR

Calcarius lapponicus (Linnaeus)

After spending the summer on the arctic tundra, Lapland Longspurs migrate south to winter in the open fields of Canada and the United States. Along Lake Erie, the first fall Laplands may appear by September 20–30 but are not regularly observed until October. This southward passage is made up mostly of infrequent small flocks scattered along the lakefront. These flocks normally total 20 or fewer Laplands, although concentrations in excess of 100 have been reported along western Lake Erie. They remain rare to uncommon migrants along the lakefront into the first half of December but eventually move into the interior of Ohio.

Fall Laplands are accidental to rare migrants away from Lake Erie, least numerous in the southern and unglaciated eastern counties. Fall records are of single individuals or flocks of 10 or fewer. While a fall migrant appeared near Columbus as early as September 26,[275] there are very few inland records before the first week of November. Their inland movements are poorly understood, since these migrants are inconspicuous occupants of large farm fields, which are seldom visited by birders during this season.

Wintering Lapland Longspurs inhabit farmlands, where they usually associate with mixed flocks of Horned Larks and Snow Buntings. When snow covers the ground, these flocks may wander considerable distances before congregating in fields where manure has been recently spread. The absence of snow cover allows them to disperse throughout the farmlands.

Modern agricultural practices are detrimental to wintering Laplands. Clean farming techniques and fall plowing eliminate most food from farm fields and are responsible for a marked decline in the numbers of wintering Laplands during the past fifty years. Campbell[86] often encountered winter flocks of 200–400 in the Toledo area during the 1930s, while concentrations of 100–300 were regularly reported from central Ohio.[479] Even in the northeastern counties, flocks of 75–200 were occasionally noted.[523]

Similar flocks may still occur today but they are certainly an exception rather than the rule. Lapland Longspurs are presently rare to locally uncommon winter residents in the northern, central, and southwestern counties, becoming accidental to casual along the unglaciated Allegheny Plateau. They are most plentiful during cold snowy winters, when flocks of 3–15 may be scattered across the state. Sizable flocks are most likely to be encountered under these conditions. Since 1960, the largest winter flocks are generally composed of 50–100 individuals. Concentrations of 400 Laplands in Marion County on January 8, 1984, and 1176 on the 1961 Tiffin Christmas Bird Count are exceptional for recent years. In contrast, Laplands may be very scarce during mild winters, although most are undoubtedly overlooked.

While spring Laplands are generally most numerous during March, migrant flocks may appear anytime between the last half of February and first week of May. A few stragglers have remained as late as May 17–18. These migrants are most apparent as small flocks moving along western Lake Erie, where they are uncommonly observed. Elsewhere, they are rare to locally uncommon spring migrants through western and central Ohio, becoming accidental to casual within the northeastern and unglaciated counties. Most spring flocks are composed of 15–40 Laplands, flying low overhead and producing their characteristic dry rattling call notes. Sizable spring concentrations are infrequent: an estimated 10,000 Laplands in Lucas County on May 1, 1949, and 2600 near Celeryville (Huron County) on March 25, 1939.[89,504] Flocks of 625 in Mercer County on April 13, 1986,[382] 400 in Greene County on March 31, 1940,[299] and 75 near Salem (Columbiana County) between March 26 and April 9, 1933,[20] were noteworthy for those locations.

SMITH'S LONGSPUR

Calcarius pictus (Swainson)

Smith's Longspurs are enigmatic birds within Ohio. Even their initial status is clouded with uncertainty. The first published account was provided by two specimens reportedly collected in Portage County on January 29, 1888.[247] These specimens are no longer extant. Since these longspurs were described as feeding on ragweeds, a very unlikely behavior for this species, in all likelihood they were not correctly identified. Additional sight records from the Cleveland area during May 1924 were also from unlikely habitats.[523] In the absence of specimens and written descriptions, these records are also considered very questionable.

Ohio's first confirmed record of Smith's Longspur was furnished by a specimen collected at Lake St. Mary's on October 23, 1944.[97] More specimens were taken near Oxford (Butler County) in 1949.[247] When observers became familiar with this species' habitat preferences, they discovered that Smith's Longspurs were actually fairly regular migrants in portions of western and central Ohio.

They were observed during most years between 1950 and the early 1970s, when they were casual to rare spring migrants through the southwestern, west-central, and central counties. They became locally uncommon at preferred sites, including the grassy fields bordering the Oxford airport in Butler County and several pastures in Madison County. Surprisingly, there were no published records from the northwestern counties. Four sightings from the Cleveland area were the only records along Lake Erie.[335] Other than these lakefront records, Smith's Longspurs were unrecorded from eastern Ohio.

While these spring migrants appeared as early as March 6,[471] they were mostly recorded between March 20 and April 15. A few late migrants remained into the first week of May. They were usually observed in small flocks of fewer than 30 individuals. Larger concentrations were occasionally encountered: 150 near Oxford on March 31, 1962;[131] 200 in Madison County on April 20, 1965;[397] and 250 in the Ross-Pickaway county line area on April 15, 1956.[471] They were frequently discovered in segregated flocks, although some were with Lapland Longspurs. They exhibited a preference for large open fields covered with short grasses or grasses mixed with clovers.

Relatively few Smith's Longspurs were recorded as fall migrants. They were apparently accidental or casual migrants through the southwestern, west-central, and central counties, with most sightings during late October and November. The few published sightings include 12 Smith's at Lake St. Mary's on October 23, 1944;[97] 13 near Oxford on November 15, 1958;[444] and 2 in Madison County on November 30, 1968.[294]

Their winter status in Ohio is problematic. Trautman and Trautman[488] described Smith's Longspurs as accidental to rare winter visitors. There are no specimens or documented sight records to substantiate this claim. There is an undocumented record of one Smith's in Madison County on January 7, 1968.[294] Since Ohio is removed from their established winter range in the south-central United States,[5] it is very doubtful that Smith's Longspurs were ever regular winter residents within the state.

Despite nearly annual records through the early 1970s, Smith's Longspurs have mysteriously vanished from Ohio in subsequent years. During the 1980s there have been only three sight records. These sightings were of spring migrants along Lake Erie: two in Cleveland and one in Ottawa County. Their disappearance is partly explained by habitat changes. Several preferred pastures and hayfields have been converted to cultivated crops. But they also no longer appear at the Oxford airport where adjacent fields have not been visibly altered. The absence of recent Ohio sightings may reflect a shift in migration routes. It is also conceivable that Smith's Longspurs still regularly pass through the state but are overlooked by observers unfamiliar with their habitat preferences.

SNOW BUNTING

Plectrophenax nivalis (Linnaeus)

Long before winter storms bring snow and cold temperatures, Snow Buntings return to Ohio. They first appear along Lake Erie, usually in small compact flocks flying low over the water. These buntings are immediately recognized by the flash of their white wing coverts against the lake's dark waters, creating the impression of a small group of snowflakes blown ashore by the November winds.

The earliest Snow Buntings returned to Ashtabula on September 21, 1936,[32] but fall migrants are quite rare before mid-October. Small flocks are regularly observed along Lake Erie by October 25–30, the same time they arrive at inland localities in northern Ohio. While Snow Buntings have appeared near Cincinnati as early as October 31, 1953,[342] they do not normally arrive in central Ohio until the first week of November or the southern counties until the last half of the month. Their lakefront passage is largely completed by December 3–10, with a few stragglers and small flocks through December 20–25.

Fall flocks are widespread along the entire lakefront, becoming fairly common during November with daily totals of 20–200 and occasional flights of 500 or more individuals. A concentration of 5000 Snow Buntings near Toledo on October 25, 1945, was remarkably early.[89] These migrants are very locally distributed within the interior counties, usually detected on mudflats and riprap bordering large reservoirs. They are casual to locally fairly common migrants in the northern half of Ohio, becoming accidental to rare within the southern counties. Inland flocks are normally composed of 50 or fewer individuals; the largest have totaled 75–100.

As winter residents, Snow Buntings occupy barren agricultural fields, frequently in association with Horned Larks and Lapland Longspurs. They also form large segregated flocks. Their relative abundance exhibits considerable annual variation, with occasional pronounced movements. However, their detectability is directly related to the extent of snow cover; the largest flocks are usually reported during cold snowy weather. Throughout winter, Snow Buntings wander widely in search of food and large flocks tend to move southward as the season progresses.

Their complex winter distribution patterns are related to land use. Snow Buntings are most numerous in the extensive agricultural fields of northwestern Ohio. When the fields become snow covered, these buntings become fairly common to common winter residents. They are normally encountered in flocks of 25–300; concentrations in excess of 500 are fairly frequent. The largest reported flocks occurred during the last week of January, with an estimated 5500 near Toledo in 1943 and 5000 in Hancock County in 1977.[89,417]

Wintering Snow Buntings are less numerous in northeastern Ohio, where they are generally uncommon residents in flocks of 5–50 individuals. Larger concentrations have included 1000+ near Youngstown on several dates, 2000 near Chardon (Geauga County) on December 25, 1930, and an estimated 5000 near Wooster (Wayne County) during the winter of 1981–82.[179,523]

Large wintering flocks do not normally wander into central Ohio, although concentrations of 1000–2000 individuals may appear south to Lake St. Mary's and Killdeer Plains Wildlife Area. Elsewhere in central and west-central Ohio, Snow Buntings are uncommon winter residents, usually observed in flocks of 20 or fewer individuals. Flocks of 50–300 are rarely noted near Columbus.

In the southwestern counties, they are casual to rare residents; midwinter sightings normally total 6 or fewer with occasional flocks of 10–50 individuals. Their largest movement occurred during the winter of 1980–81 when as many as 400 individuals appeared near Dayton and 100 near Cincinnati.[360] They are least numerous in the unglaciated counties, where they are casual visitors, usually encountered as scattered individuals or flocks of 6–12.

Throughout the year, Snow Buntings make a comfortable living in rather inhospitable surroundings. On a cold January morning, they quietly forage in open fields oblivious of the subzero temperatures and biting winds. Only extreme weather conditions force them out of these habitats. The great blizzard of the 1977–78 winter caused many Snow Buntings to seek refuge at bird feeders. A few even appeared in residential areas in Columbus, unprecedented behavior for this hardy little bird.

The first migrants appear along Lake Erie during mid-February. Their spring passage begins in earnest with the first late February thaw and continues into the last half of March. The last migrants usually depart from southern and central Ohio by the first week of March and along Lake Erie by the first week of April. Lingering Snow Buntings have remained through March 26, 1930, in Hamilton County and May 2, 1955, at Cleveland.[117,248]

This migration is poorly defined, especially inland, where Snow Buntings are casual to rare migrants in small numbers. Spring migrants are not uniformly distributed along Lake Erie but congregate in Lucas, Ottawa, and Erie Counties; they are decidedly rare farther east. Along western Lake Erie, Snow Buntings are uncommon to locally fairly common migrants, usually in flocks of 30 or fewer with occasional groups of 75–100. The largest spring movements have produced estimates of 1000–2500 Snow Buntings along western Lake Erie.

BOBOLINK

Dolichonyx oryzivorus (Linnaeus)

Distinctive and conspicuous, Bobolinks are certain to be noticed when they arrive. Breeding males are unique, with brightly colored upperparts and uniformly black underparts. The value of this plumage pattern is not apparent until they are observed quietly perched on the tops of grasses and their upperparts are seen to closely resemble the scattered flowers in the pastures and hayfields where they reside. These blackbirds are seldom quiet for long, and males frequently declare their territories with a distinctive loud bubbly song.

An exceptionally early spring migrant Bobolink was noted at Cleveland on March 28, 1965.[117] The first flocks do not normally appear until April 23–30. Bobolinks become widely distributed by May 5–10. This northward movement is relatively brief, ending by May 20–23 within the interior counties but continuing through May 27–30 along Lake Erie.

These spring migrants are widely distributed but seldom numerous. In recent years, they are fairly common within the northern and glaciated central counties, with most sightings of 20 or fewer individuals daily and occasional flocks of 30–50+. While Trautman[479] reported spring flights of 100–250 at Buckeye Lake during the 1920s and 1930s, similar movements have not been apparent in recent decades. Fewer spring migrants appear within the southern and unglaciated counties, where they are presently uncommon to fairly common visitors. Daily totals seldom exceed 10 Bobolinks within these counties and the largest recent flocks are composed of 15–25 individuals. Larger flights were occasionally encountered in earlier decades; Kemsies and Randle[248] reported flocks of 100–150 Bobolinks at Cincinnati into the early 1950s.

Like most grassland birds, Bobolinks expanded into Ohio during the nineteenth century. Breeding populations were well established by the mid-1800s.[522] Bobolinks remained reasonably numerous through the mid-1930s. At that time, Hicks[220] considered them usually common to abundant but locally distributed summer residents in every county south to Butler, Montgomery, Greene, Madison, Pickaway, Fairfield, Perry, Muskingum, Guernsey, Harrison, and Jefferson. Breeding pairs were essentially absent from other southern and eastern counties, although they were rarely recorded from Hocking County.[223]

Their numbers markedly decreased in most counties after 1940. This trend continued unabated into the 1980s, a pattern apparent throughout the species' entire breeding range.[438] Habitat destruction was largely responsible for this decline. The more frequent mowing of hayfields has also contributed to reduced populations.

Despite their declining fortunes, their range has expanded slightly south to Brown, Highland, Ross, Hocking, Morgan, Noble, and Monroe Counties. A few pairs may also reside in extensive reclaimed strip mines in other southeastern counties.[434] They are most numerous in northeastern Ohio, where they are fairly common to locally common summer residents and 5–20 individuals are detected daily. They become uncommon to fairly common residents in most other northern and central counties, where summer reports normally are of 10 or fewer Bobolinks daily. In the southern counties, these blackbirds are generally casual to rare summer residents and very locally distributed. Nonetheless, large numbers may gather in suitable habitats; there were 100+ in a Clinton County field during 1984 and 50 near Dayton in 1985.[434]

Nesting Bobolinks are restricted to large grassy fields and clover-alfalfa hayfields. Their nests are located on the ground, expertly concealed among the vegetation. Nest construction begins during the last half of May and continues into June. Nests with eggs have been reported between May 26 and July 4 and young may remain in the nest through mid-July. Dependent young have been observed by June 12–15 but are most likely to appear during late June, July, or possibly the first week of August.[241,479,523]

Beginning in the last half of July and continuing through August, Bobolinks accumulate into flocks within grasslands, weedy fields, and the edges of marshes. Between July 20 and August 5, they begin their southward migration. While these migrants are inconspicuous on the ground, they are regularly detected as they pass overhead, uttering their distinctive call notes. Their fall migration peaks between August 10 and September 10. Their numbers diminish during the last half of September and the last migrants usually depart by October 5–12. Occasional stragglers linger into November.

When their breeding populations were larger, 100–500 individuals were observed daily in the central and northern counties, while 25–75 Bobolinks might appear in the southern counties. Larger flights produced occasional concentrations of 500–2000 Bobolinks in central and northwestern Ohio and 100–200 individuals in the southern counties. By far the largest reported fall concentration totaled 7500 Bobolinks at Toledo on August 8, 1936.[31]

Similar numbers have not been apparent since 1960. Bobolinks are presently fairly common to common fall migrants through the glaciated counties, where 5–30 individuals may be detected daily with occasional movements of 50–300. Along the unglaciated Allegheny Plateau, they become uncommon to fairly common migrants, mostly in flocks of 25 or fewer individuals.

Bobolinks are accidental early winter visitors anywhere in North America. Within Ohio, the latest Bobolinks lingered at Toledo through November 28, 1953,[89] and into December on Christmas Bird Counts at Cincinnati and Ashland. These late migrants were studied at close range and carefully identified.

RED-WINGED BLACKBIRD

Agelaius phoeniceus (Linnaeus)

The first hint of moderating temperatures is invariably accompanied by the return of Red-winged Blackbirds. The male Red-wingeds quickly spread across the state, establishing their territories in wetlands and old fields and along roadsides. While these territorial activities may be temporarily suspended during inclement weather, they are quickly reinitiated as soon as the sun appears, only to intensify when the females return later in the season.

Except during unusually cold years, the first migrants are expected between February 18 and 25 and are widely distributed by the first week of March. This passage usually peaks during March. At that time, Red-wingeds become abundant migrants in every county. Daily totals of 100–1000+ individuals are frequent, while 10,000+ may congregate into evening roosts. Immense roosts are not normally reported during spring, although there were estimates of 500,000+ roosting near Columbus and more than 1,000,000 at Toledo during the 1960s and 1970s.[89,471] By the first week of April, most migrants have passed through Ohio. Small flocks of female Red-wingeds may be noted through April 15–20.

At one time, nesting Red-wingeds were confined to cattail marshes and shrubby swamps. As their populations expanded and wetlands were drained, breeding pairs spread to upland habitats. They are now as likely to occupy weedy old fields, clover hayfields, and highway rights-of-way as marshes. Red-wingeds are abundant summer residents, ranking among our most numerous breeding birds. Summer totals of 50–200 daily are noted in most localities.

Their breeding populations have increased throughout the twentieth century, most obviously between 1950 and 1975.[438] This trend has apparently been reversed within the past ten years, perhaps reflecting the effects of several severe winters and efforts to eliminate some large winter roosts.

Nesting activities begin as soon as the females arrive. Nests with eggs have been reported by April 16 in central Ohio, although most clutches are not produced until early May.[479] The earliest clutches hatch by April 28 and fledge by May 16. Most young Red-wingeds appear during the first half of June. The second clutches are laid as soon as these young fledge. Nests with eggs are regularly noted through the first week of July and the young may not fledge until early August.[479,523] A nest with eggs in Clermont County on July 31, 1938, was very late.[503] Most nests are placed at heights of two to four feet within herbaceous vegetation. One nest was found 30 feet high in a large conifer and another in a hole in a stump.[89,417]

Even before many pairs have finished nesting, Red-winged Blackbirds accumulate into large flocks. These flocks have been reported during the last half of June but are more prevalent during July. By August, the entire population gathers into evening roosts. As a result of their substantial breeding populations and their habit of forming large evening roosts, fall migratory patterns are not particularly evident. Trautman[479] reported fall peaks between mid-September and late October. Flocks of hundreds are regularly observed in every county, while evening roosts supporting 10,000–50,000+ individuals are not unusual. Numbers decline during the first half of November and relatively few large flocks are encountered after November 20–25.

Before 1940, wintering Red-wingeds were infrequently noted as scattered individuals or flocks of 20 or fewer.[86,248,523] Only Trautman[479] reported winter flocks of 100–200+ blackbirds at Buckeye Lake. As the breeding populations expanded during the 1950s and 1960s, their wintering numbers experienced a corresponding increase. These winter populations apparently stabilized during the 1970s.

Red-winged Blackbirds are presently uncommon to locally fairly common winter residents within the southern and central counties. Most sightings are of 20 or fewer individuals and occasional flocks of 30–75. Large roosts are quite rare, but flocks of 500–10,000+ may develop. Within the northern counties, Red-wingeds become uncommon to rare residents except along western Lake Erie, where they are fairly common or common each year. Most of these sightings are of 20 or fewer with infrequent concentrations of 30–100+ individuals. Large roosts are expected only along western Lake Erie, where as many as 5000 Red-wingeds were reported during the winter of 1965–66.[89]

EASTERN MEADOWLARK

Sturnella magna (Linnaeus)

On a warm spring day, male Eastern Meadowlarks are likely to pass most hours perched on fence posts, telephone wires, or tall trees, loudly proclaiming their territories. With their distinctive yellow and black breast pattern, they are readily identified and regularly observed along highways throughout the rural countryside. As their name implies, meadowlarks exhibit a decided preference for grasslands. Pastures, hayfields, fallow fields, and highway rights-of-way provide their preferred nesting habitats, although they have also been found in grain fields and grassy woodland clearings.[479]

Small numbers of Eastern Meadowlarks originally inhabited prairie openings within western Ohio. As the virgin forests were replaced by small farm fields, they rapidly expanded across the state. They became common to abundant summer residents by the mid-1800s and retained that status through the first decades of this century.[236,479,522] Changing land-use practices during the late 1930s and 1940s converted grasslands into cultivated crops. The constant loss of suitable habitats produced a steady decline during subsequent decades.[438] Other factors contributed to this decline: more frequent mowing of hayfields significantly reduced these birds' reproductive success and unusually severe winter weather during the 1970s depressed breeding populations throughout eastern North America.[438]

Despite declining populations, Eastern Meadowlarks remain fairly common to common summer residents throughout Ohio. Perhaps the largest populations occupy extensive reclaimed strip mines in the eastern counties, where 40–75+ Easterns may be counted daily. While similar numbers are locally encountered in other southern and eastern locations, daily totals in the more intensively cultivated central and western counties seldom exceed 15–30.

Meadowlarks nest on the ground, building domed structures cleverly hidden among the grasses. Nesting activities begin by mid-April in the southern and central counties, but most northern Ohio clutches are noted in early May.[479,523] Recently fledged young have been reported as early as May 16 but most do not appear until June. Some meadowlarks may raise two broods, since nests with eggs have been discovered through July 10

and adults were still feeding dependent young as late as August 26.[417]

After their young become independent, meadowlarks form small flocks and unobtrusively forage through grasslands and harvested fields. When their populations were greater, their fall migration was quite evident. Trautman[479] regularly observed "many thousands" daily at Buckeye Lake during the 1920s and 1930s. His observations seem almost inconceivable today, when fall meadowlarks are uncommon to fairly common migrants as flocks of 20 or fewer individuals. According to Trautman,[479] this migration begins during the first week of September and peaks between September 15 and October 25. The last migrants depart by mid-November.

Numbers of wintering Eastern Meadowlarks have remained fairly constant during this century. They are least numerous in the northern counties, where they are generally rare but regular residents, becoming casual in the northeastern counties. They are usually observed as individuals or flocks of 10 or fewer. A total of 119 on the 1960 Toledo Christmas Count represents an exceptional winter number for northern Ohio. They become uncommon winter residents in the central counties. While they are locally distributed, flocks of 20–30 may be encountered and concentrations of 100–210 have been flushed from a single field. They are most numerous in the southern counties, where they become uncommon to fairly common residents. They are more widely distributed there than in central Ohio, although their flock size is similar.

The advent of warming temperatures during late February and early March initiates their spring migration. The first returning migrants are solitary males rapidly spreading across the state. They are followed by migrant flocks. We may never again witness the movements of "several hundred" meadowlarks daily that were reported earlier in this century.[479] Flights of 30–50 may still be noted, primarily on days with southerly winds between March 15 and April 10. These movements are most noticeable along western Lake Erie, where meadowlarks migrate around the lake rather than across it. This migration may continue through April 20–May 5, mostly as individuals along the lakefront.

WESTERN MEADOWLARK

Sturnella neglecta Audubon

While Western Meadowlarks are readily identified by their distinctive songs and call notes, separating the Western and Eastern Meadowlarks when they are silent is a difficult challenge. No single plumage characteristic safely identifies all individuals. Hence, our understanding of Western Meadowlark distribution and relative abundance is based almost entirely on observations of singing males.

Ohio's first Western Meadowlark record was provided by a specimen collected in Lakewood (Cuyahoga County) on April 8, 1880.[523] This individual was undoubtedly a vagrant, since there were no other records for fifty years.

Beginning in the 1920s, Western Meadowlarks underwent

an eastward expansion of their breeding range.[104] Moving eastward from the Mississippi River valley, this expansion reached Ohio by 1930. During 1930 and 1931, at least 11 Westerns were discovered in Henry, Fulton, and Wood Counties, including a pair feeding fledglings in the latter county during 1930.[86,228] By 1937, Hicks[228] reported at least twenty-six records involving eighteen individuals within eight counties, mostly in northwestern Ohio. Isolated males were also noted in Logan and Muskingum Counties. The majority of these records pertained to unmated males, but two unspecified nesting attempts were also cited.

Between the late 1930s and 1950s, small numbers regularly appeared within the northwestern counties, including annual records from Toledo after 1946,[89] but Western Meadowlarks were only accidentally encountered elsewhere. The few records included singing males at Cleveland in 1938 and Youngstown in 1939,[504,523] a possible nesting pair at Bath (Summit County) in 1945 and 1946,[523] and records from Columbus in 1946 and Cincinnati in 1959.[45,323]

The western Ohio population underwent a brief expansion during the 1960s. Summering Western Meadowlarks were regularly encountered within the northwestern and west-central counties, including a "colony" of 26 males in Oregon and Jerusalem Townships of Lucas County on May 13, 1962, and a smaller "colony" reported from Lake St. Mary's in 1964.[89,394] A pair nested at Cleveland in 1960, while males were reported from two other Cleveland area locations during the 1960s.[335] Their statewide population trends were then reversed and fewer Westerns have been observed since 1970.

Western Meadowlarks are now casual to rare and very locally distributed summer residents within northwestern and west-central Ohio. Between 1 and 4 males regularly summer at Maumee Bay State Park (Lucas County) and 1–2 males at Killdeer Plains Wildlife Area in Wyandot County. Widely scattered males and pairs are sporadically encountered south to Darke and Union and east to Marion and Erie Counties.[434] Western Meadowlarks become accidental summer visitors elsewhere with summer records from Holmes, Stark, and Muskingum Counties during the 1980s.[362,434] Since 1982, the statewide population has been 5–15 males annually.

Western Meadowlarks occupy the same grassy fields and pastures as Easterns. There are very few reports of pairs of Western Meadowlarks and even fewer confirmed breeding attempts. These nesting records are restricted to the northwestern counties, including the Toledo area and Paulding, Seneca, Defiance, and Henry Counties.[434,471] Based on these few reports, most nests are established during May and June and fledged young appear by the last half of June or July.

As spring migrants, Western Meadowlarks are casual to rare within the northwestern and west-central counties but accidental elsewhere. Spring reports invariably are of single Westerns except near established summering sites. The earliest Westerns may appear by February 25–March 10, although they do not normally return until the last half of March. Most are recorded during April and the first half of May. During the 1980s, spring Westerns have been discovered away from established summering locations in only three years. Numbers of spring records were greater during the 1960s.

There are very few confirmed records of Western Meadowlarks after the males quit singing during July. In all likelihood, the territorial males and pairs remain at or near their summering locations into autumn. Their fall migration probably coincides with the southward movements of Easterns. Most Westerns probably depart during October.

Their winter status remains a mystery. While there have been a few winter sight records from northwestern Ohio, none was adequately confirmed. Moreover, there are no winter specimen records from the state.

YELLOW-HEADED BLACKBIRD

Xanthocephalus xanthocephalus (Bonaparte)

This distinctive blackbird was initially recorded in 1873 when a pair summered near the village of Groveport in southern Franklin County.[522] Yellow-headed Blackbirds remained accidental visitors in the late 1800s and early 1900s, with only eight acceptable records before 1930.[230]

Their status changed abruptly in the 1930s, a result of the extended drought in the prairie states. As the wetlands in these states dried up, Yellow-headed Blackbirds were displaced from their normal breeding range. They were recorded from Ohio every year between 1931 and 1947, mostly as migrants during spring and fall. While most sightings were of only 1–3 individuals, small flocks were occasionally noted: 22 at Lake St. Mary's on March 8, 1936; 21 at Bay Bridge (Erie County) on March 28, 1939; 9 in Marion County on March 11, 1942; and 25 in western Lucas County on October 22, 1947.[89,230] Most of the twenty-three or more reports during these years were from the western half of Ohio except for single sightings at Cleveland and Pymatuning Reservoir.[206]

A few pairs found suitable summer territories in the western Lake Erie marshes. The first territorial males were reported near Sandusky (Erie County) in 1934 and at Magee Marsh Wildlife Area in 1936, although these birds were apparently unmated.[230,441] Nesting was established at Metzger Marsh Wildlife Area (Lucas County) in 1938, when dependent young were observed during July, and again in 1940, with a nest discovered on May 18.[89,230] This pair returned in 1941 but not subsequently.

With the return of normal water conditions in the prairie states during the mid-1940s, Yellow-headed Blackbirds quit visiting Ohio. There were no published records between 1948 and 1956. Single Yellow-headeds appeared near Barberton (Summit County) and Hebron (Licking County) in 1957 and in Ashtabula County during 1959.[206] They returned to the western Lake Erie marshes in 1960 and have been recorded annually in subsequent years.[89] These records reflect a recent range expansion into the lower Great Lakes region.[438]

Since 1960, Yellow-headed Blackbirds have become rare but regular residents in the western Lake Erie marshes of Ottawa, Lucas, and Sandusky Counties. Away from these marshes, they are accidental to casual visitors and may appear anywhere at any time in habitats varying from cattail marshes to agricultural fields and residential feeders. They are frequently found in mixed flocks with other blackbirds. There have been at least forty-five records scattered across Ohio,[206] mostly in the western half of the state and along Lake Erie east to Cleveland. All recent sightings are of single individuals or of 2–5.

As spring migrants, a few Yellow-headeds return in late February and early March. These early migrants are unusual. Most are detected between April 20 and May 15, coinciding with their arrival in the western Lake Erie marshes.

Summering Yellow-headed Blackbirds are rare residents along western Lake Erie. During some years, only one male may be located at a single location, while in others they may appear in two or three marshes. A small colony of 7 males and at least 1 female was established at Cedar Point Wildlife Refuge (Lucas County) in 1979.[206] Many of the territorial males are unmated and there are no recent confirmed nesting records. These summering blackbirds prefer extensive marshes with large patches of cattails interspersed with open water. Away from western Lake Erie, Yellow-headed Blackbirds are accidental summer residents. Records are limited to 2 males in Hancock County during June 1946[417] and single males at Cleveland during 1960 and 1961 and at Big Island Wildlife Area (Marion County) during May 1986.[335,382] All of these males were unmated.

Few Yellow-headeds are observed during fall. Five at Gnadenhutten (Tuscarawas County) on July 25–26, 1964, probably were early migrants.[206] Most other fall records are distributed between late August and early December. Fall migrants are most frequently observed near Lake Erie.

While Yellow-headed Blackbirds do not regularly overwinter at any location, there has been at least one record each winter since 1978–79. They were detected in the Ottawa–Lucas County area during six winters, mixed among the wintering blackbird flocks in the marshes. Wintering Yellow-headeds have also been reported from the Columbus area (four records), the Dayton area (at least three records), and the Cleveland area (at least two records), and there were single sightings at Nelsonville, Austintown (Mahoning County), Mansfield, and Tiffin, frequently at bird feeders.

RUSTY BLACKBIRD

Euphagus carolinus (Müller)

Migrant Rusty Blackbirds are most frequently observed along damp wooded corridors bordering streams, lakes, and wetlands and in flooded woodlots. They are gregarious, however, and will also associate with mixed flocks of blackbirds foraging in farm fields far from any water.

While the earliest fall migrant returned to Toledo by August 23, 1931,[89] Rusty Blackbirds do not normally appear along Lake Erie until September 20–30. They are not expected in the central and southern counties until October 5–15. Their maximum abundance is attained between October 15 and November 15, when they become uncommon to locally common migrants throughout Ohio. Rusties are more locally distributed in fall than in spring. Sizable concentrations may develop in suitable habitats, and flocks of 1000–2000 Rusties have been reported from the northern half of the state. Most fall flocks are composed of 50 or fewer except along western Lake Erie, where 100–400 Rusties regularly congregate. Their migration is completed by the first week of December.

Before 1950, Rusty Blackbirds were casual winter visitors, with most records comprising individuals or small flocks in the southern half of the state. As other wintering blackbirds increased in numbers during the 1950s and 1960s, Rusties underwent a similar increase. The first sizable winter roosts totaled 3000 Rusties at Dayton during December 1952 and 2500 near O'Shaughnessy Reservoir (Delaware County) during the winter of 1953–54.[299,343] Similar roosts have periodically appeared in subsequent years with a maximum of 5000 Rusties at Buckeye Lake during December 1979.[471] These winter roosts have been restricted to the western two-thirds of Ohio.

Rusty Blackbirds are now rare and rather irregular winter visitors throughout Ohio. Most winter sightings are of scattered individuals or flocks of 20 or fewer, generally during December and the first half of January. Some Rusties have overwintered where adequate food is available. Wintering Rusties are mostly encountered in agricultural areas, where they obtain waste grain from harvested fields.

The first spring Rusties normally return between March 5 and 12. The largest concentrations are frequently encountered between March 18 and April 15. Spring Rusties are widely distributed and fairly common to locally abundant migrants. Most spring reports are of 75 or fewer Rusties and flocks of 100–250 may appear in suitable habitats. Large roosts of 1000–3000 are occasionally discovered, while the largest reported flock totaled 10,000 near Dayton on March 18, 1967.[299] They usually depart by the first week of May, with a few stragglers later in the month, generally along Lake Erie. Ohio's latest spring record was provided by a central Ohio specimen collected May 31, 1941.[45]

BREWER'S BLACKBIRD

Euphagus cyanocephalus (Wagler)

Formerly restricted to the western half of North America, nesting Brewer's Blackbirds moved eastward into the upper Great Lakes area during the 1930s. By the 1950s, breeding populations were established east to northern Michigan and adjacent portions of Ontario.[5,104] At the same time, wintering Brewer's Blackbirds became regular residents in the southeastern United States. In subsequent years, however, additional range expansion has not been apparent.

Their status within Ohio reflects this eastward range expansion. Brewer's Blackbirds were unrecorded until April 12, 1936, when Lou Campbell discovered a flock of 5 in Spencer Township, Lucas County.[86] At first they were known only from sporadic records in the northwestern counties. They did not appear in other portions of the state until the 1950s and early 1960s. They have been annually reported since 1960.

Two factors have obscured their status within Ohio. Brewer's Blackbirds are fairly difficult to distinguish from Rusty Blackbirds and many reports have proven to be misidentifications. Moreover, many observers hold a bias against all blackbirds and seldom examine large flocks in search of the few Brewer's mixed in with the thousands of other blackbirds. Hence, our understanding of their distribution and relative abundance may not accurately represent their status.

Brewer's Blackbirds are apparently rare but regular spring migrants near western Lake Erie in Ottawa and Lucas Counties, averaging one to three sightings annually in the 1980s. Most of these reports are of 10 or fewer individuals. Larger concentrations are exceptional: 55 on April 3, 1938, and an incredible 300 on April 6, 1963, in Lucas County.[89] They are apparently accidental to casual spring migrants through other western counties and strictly accidental within central and eastern Ohio. Reliable spring sightings away from western Lake Erie are almost invariably of only 1–5 individuals. Their spring migration usually comes slightly later than the northward passage of Rusties. Most reliable records are during April and the first half of May.

Within Michigan, the breeding range of these blackbirds extends south to Saginaw Bay and Berrien County, with only one nesting record from the southeastern counties.[359] Barring additional range expansions, Brewer's Blackbirds are unlikely to occur within Ohio during summer.

Considerably fewer Brewer's Blackbirds are detected as migrants in fall than in spring. They are apparently accidental to casual visitors within the western half of the state, becoming strictly accidental in the eastern half. The few fall sightings are mostly scattered between mid-October and early November, usually as flocks of 10 or fewer individuals. The largest reliable fall concentrations have been several flocks of 20 Brewer's along western Lake Erie near Toledo and 32 at Killdeer Plains Wildlife Area (Wyandot County) on November 8, 1987.[388]

Their status as winter residents is poorly understood. Within Ohio, wintering Brewer's Blackbirds are found almost exclusively near large feedlots. They are accidental to casual winter residents in the western half of Ohio, averaging one confirmed sighting every two or three years, and accidental in the eastern half of the state. Most reliable winter records are of only 1–5 individuals, although small flocks occasionally develop. Campbell[89] reported winter flocks of 14–15 Brewer's near Toledo in 1963 and 1966, and as many as 24 were counted at a feedlot in Ross County during the winter of 1987–88.

GREAT-TAILED GRACKLE

Quiscalus mexicanus (Gmelin)

Great-tailed Grackles were formerly restricted to Central and South America and the extreme southwestern United States. During this century, their nesting range has expanded quite rapidly and they presently breed north to southern California and southern Colorado and locally in the midwestern states to Nebraska, Iowa, and western Missouri.[5] Some birds occasionally wander as far north as Washington and east to Illinois and Ohio. Ohio's only record of this accidental visitor was provided by a male discovered by J. Kirk Alexander in Carroll Township, Ottawa County, on May 6, 1985. This Great-tailed Grackle was relocated at the same site and photographed the following day.[378]

COMMON GRACKLE

Quiscalus quiscula (Linnaeus)

Few native birds have so successfully adapted to man-made habitats as Common Grackles. From the western Ohio farmlands to rural roadsides of the southeastern counties and urban areas throughout the state, these grackles are abundant summer residents, seen by the hundreds each day. Smaller numbers also occupy wetlands, wooded edges, and open successional fields. Only extensive mature woodlands do not support nesting grackles.

Not surprisingly, Common Grackle populations have increased tremendously during the twentieth century. These increases were particularly evident in the 1940s and 1950s and continued into the 1970s.[438] Populations may have stabilized during the 1980s.

Their spring migration coincides with the early movements of other blackbirds. Warm weather during the last half of February will invariably be accompanied by the first returning flocks. They quickly spread across the entire state. Their northward movements peak during March, when flocks numbering in the thousands of individuals are commonly observed. Larger roosts have hosted as many as an estimated 500,000 Common Grackles, but these immense flocks are unusual. Their spring passage is rapid and few migrant flocks are encountered after the first week of April.

Common Grackles begin breeding activities immediately upon arrival. Their displays are familiar sights on residential lawns and in shade trees during March and April. As described by Dawson:[102]

His love-making antics, too, are all the more ridiculous for being earnest. Perched upon the tip-top of an evergreen he thrusts his wings out, spreads his tail and ruffles all his feathers, and then throws his head forward like a person about to obtain relief from seasickness. The outcome of all this effect is a sound by no means ravishing. . . .

Nest construction has been reported as early as mid-March. There is considerable variability in nesting behavior among pairs, however, and some nests are not constructed until mid-May.[300] Common Grackles nest as isolated pairs but may also breed in aggregations of 3–25 pairs. Large conifers near residences provide preferred nest sites, although other dense trees, shrubs, and bridge girders are regularly utilized. If these sites are unavailable, Common Grackles have nested in cattail wetlands, buttonbush swamps, orchards, Wood Duck boxes, and Purple Martin houses.[89] One pair nested in a woodpecker cavity enlarged by decay and excavation.[296]

The first clutches are normally laid during the last half of April or early May, and nests with young have been reported as early as April 23.[479] Fledged young normally appear by mid-May and are regularly encountered through late June. Renesting efforts have produced nests with young through June 30 and adults accompanied by dependent young through August 3.

As soon as the young become independent, Common Grackles congregate in large foraging flocks and form evening roosts. Flocks of 100 or more may be encountered during the last half of June or early July. These concentrations steadily grow through the summer and autumn, their numbers swelled by migrants during September and October. By day these flocks spread over the countryside, feeding on grain and weed seeds in farm fields and refuse or other available food in urban areas. At night they return to the roost in groves of trees or cattail swamps, where 10,000 to more than 100,000 may spend the night. Some roosts have supported an estimated 1,000,000 Common Grackles. Most of them usually migrate south during late October and early November, although some roosts remain intact into December.

At one time, Common Grackles were rare winter residents within Ohio. Their numbers increased after 1900, corresponding with their expanding breeding populations. Between 1920 and 1940, they were still casual to uncommon winter residents, usually in groups of 12 or fewer with occasional flocks of 100–400 individuals. By the 1950s, they became regular winter residents and periodically formed sizable roosts. Their winter status has not changed appreciably in subsequent years.

Common Grackles are generally rare to uncommon winter residents in northern Ohio and uncommon to fairly common elsewhere. These wintering grackles are normally observed in small flocks of 25 or fewer individuals with occasional concentrations of 100–1000. While large winter roosts have appeared in all portions of the state, they do not form every year. As many as 20,000 to 83,000 Common Grackles have been estimated at these roosts, making them locally common to abundant winter residents at some localities.

BROWN-HEADED COWBIRD

Molothrus ater (Boddaert)

Brown-headed Cowbirds are brood parasites. Female cowbirds, virtual egg-laying machines, produce an egg nearly every day during the breeding season, but rather than building their own nests, they lay their eggs in the nests of other songbirds. These songbirds dutifully incubate the cowbird eggs along with their own. The cowbird eggs hatch first, bringing forth young that are larger and more aggressive than the rightful nestlings. The cowbirds invariably thrive while the other young frequently die of starvation. Female cowbirds prefer to parasitize the nests of the smaller songbirds, particularly Red-eyed Vireos, Yellow Warblers, Common Yellowthroats, Indigo Buntings, Chipping Sparrows, and Song Sparrows. Hence, as cowbirds have expanded within Ohio, their success has been achieved at the expense of the parasitized species. This habit has given the Brown-headed Cowbird the distinction of being the most despised of all native songbirds.

Cowbirds are native to the Great Plains region and did not expand into Ohio until 1840.[104] Their expansion through the state was rapid and they became common and widely distributed summer residents by the late 1800s.[522] Their populations remained fairly stable through the 1930s, when Hicks [220] described them as common to abundant residents in every county, but substantially increased during the 1950s and 1960s and continued to increase in subsequent years.

Cowbirds are now common to abundant summer residents throughout Ohio, equally numerous in woodlands, successional fields, farmlands, and urban areas. Between 25 and 100+ cowbirds are observed daily, mostly as groups of 1–6 individuals, although flocks of 20–60+ nonbreeding males may be encountered. Female cowbirds begin laying eggs during the last half of April; this activity normally peaks between May 10 and June 20. A few females produce eggs through late July.[523] The first fledgling cowbirds are reported by early June and are regularly noted into early August.

Like most other blackbirds, cowbirds accumulate into flocks shortly after the end of the breeding season. Congregations of 100–200+ cowbirds may be encountered by mid-July and flock size increases as the season progresses. Their southward migration apparently begins during the last half of August, peaking between mid-September and early November.[479] These migrants are fairly common to locally abundant throughout Ohio, most numerous around feedlots and farm fields. The largest fall concentrations normally contain 500–2000+ cowbirds.

As late as the early 1900s, Jones[236] cited no winter records from the state. The number of winter sightings accumulated very slowly. By 1940, cowbirds were generally casual to rare and sporadically observed winter residents within the central and southern counties.[248,479] They remained accidental visitors in northern Ohio.[86,523] Their status changed dramatically during the 1950s and 1960s as wintering cowbirds were discovered throughout Ohio. As early as the winter of 1953–54, 40,000 cowbirds were estimated at a roost near O'Shaughnessy Reservoir in Delaware County.[343] These large roosts remain exceptional, although as many as 80,000 cowbirds may have congregated at Dayton during the winter of 1980–81.[299] Most winter roosts contain 500–5000 cowbirds.

Brown-headed Cowbirds are presently uncommon to locally abundant winter residents. They are abundant only at their roosts, near large cities. Away from these roosts, they are encountered most frequently within the farmlands of western Ohio. They can be rather scarce along the unglaciated Allegheny Plateau. Most winter sightings are of flocks of 5–100 cowbirds except at large roosts.

Timing of their spring migration normally coincides with the movements of other blackbirds. The first migrants are expected during the first warm days of late February and early March. This movement normally peaks between March 10 and April 10, with very few migrants after April 20. Spring cowbirds are common to abundant migrants across the state. Most spring reports are of 50–1000 cowbirds daily with occasional flocks of 2000–5000+. Large roosts may briefly form; as many as 25,000 cowbirds have been estimated at a mixed blackbird roost near Columbus.[471]

ORCHARD ORIOLE

Icterus spurius (Linnaeus)

While Orchard Orioles are not as brightly colored as the more familiar Northern Orioles, they are still quite welcome additions to our breeding avifauna. Adult male Orchards are very handsome in their mixed black and chestnut-orange plumage—quite unlike the females and second-year males, whose hues are predominantly bright yellows and greens. These sprightly little orioles produce a distinctive song, an outburst of whistles and harsh chatter unlikely to be confused with the loud clear whistles repeated by Northerns.

As summer residents, most Orchard Orioles are encountered in young wooded riparian corridors, shade trees near rural residences, fencerows, roadside thickets, parks, orchards, pastures, and fallow fields with scattered small trees. They are equally numerous along streams and in upland habitats.

Their nests are normally placed at heights of less than twenty feet in small trees. Within the southern counties, nesting activities are initiated by mid-May and adults may be feeding young in the nest by the first week of June. The first fledglings have been noted by mid-June. Breeding activities are delayed by one to two weeks in the northern counties, where young Orchards are not expected out of the nest until the last week of June or early July.[54,299,523] A very late nest with eggs discovered near Toledo on July 27, 1935, certainly represented a renesting attempt.[89]

Their statewide distribution has repeatedly expanded and contracted during the twentieth century. In the early 1900s, Orchard Orioles were apparently expanding northward. This expansion was mostly noted in the northern counties, particularly near Lake Erie in Lorain and Erie Counties, where they nearly became as numerous as Northern Orioles.[236,241] This expansion was short-lived and their breeding range was markedly reduced by the mid-1930s. Hicks[220] considered Orchard Orioles uncommon to rare and very locally distributed summer residents, citing records from fifty-one counties, mostly within the eastern half of the state. Breeding Orchards were most numerous within Muskingum, Morgan, Athens, Hocking, Jackson, and Scioto Counties.

Their most recent range expansion began in 1945, when increased numbers were apparent at Cincinnati and along the unglaciated Allegheny Plateau.[84,248] Until the early 1960s, this expansion was mostly restricted to the southern and unglaciated eastern counties. By the mid-1960s, however, increasing populations were apparent throughout the western half of the state and some northeastern counties. This expansion continued into the 1980s.

Orchard Orioles presently breed within every county.[434] They are least numerous in northeastern Ohio, where they are uncommon and locally distributed as scattered pairs. Elsewhere in northern Ohio and the central counties, they are fairly common to locally uncommon residents, least numerous within the intensively farmed northwestern and west-central counties. Most summer reports are of 1–5 Orchards daily, although as many as 6–13 have been detected at a few localities. Nesting Orchards are most numerous in southern Ohio, where they

are fairly common to common residents. Within the counties bordering the Ohio River, 10–20+ Orchards may be noted daily, but totals seldom exceed 5–12 Orchards in other southern counties.

While an exceptionally early Orchard Oriole returned to Utica (Licking County) on March 31, 1965,[397] they do not normally appear in the southern counties until April 17–25 or central Ohio until April 27–May 3. They may not return to Lake Erie until the second week of May. Breeding populations are established within the southern counties by May 15, but the last pairs may not appear along Lake Erie until June 2–5. This migration mostly includes resident orioles returning to their territories. At migrant traps along Lake Erie and other locations where they do not nest, Orchard Orioles are uncommon to rare spring migrants, mostly noted as scattered individuals.

Orchard Orioles are among the earliest songbirds to begin their fall migration. Migrant Orchards have appeared along Lake Erie by July 10 but most are reported between July 25 and August 15. They are rare to uncommon in most counties, with no more than 1–5 daily. The latest migrants usually depart by September 2–5. An Orchard Oriole at Toledo on September 24, 1938, was exceptionally late.[89]

NORTHERN ORIOLE

Icterus galbula (Linnaeus)

With a sharp loud whistle and a flash of brilliant orange and black, a male Northern Oriole announces his presence from the top of a large flowering oak. His return is a sure sign spring has arrived. While spring overflights have appeared along Lake Erie by the first week of April, the first Northerns normally return to southern and central Ohio during the last week of April and Lake Erie by May 1–5.

The greater part of this spring migration occurs between May 7 and 20. During these brief weeks, the countryside and wooded residential areas come alive with the Northerns' loud calls and colorful plumage. These migrants are fairly common to common across Ohio; 5–25 may be observed daily. Large flights along Lake Erie have produced as many as 100 in the Toledo area on May 14, 1948.[89] The number of migrants sharply declines after May 20, with a few passing through Lake Erie migrant traps until May 27–30.

As summer residents, Northern Orioles have been fairly common to common and widely distributed residents throughout most of Ohio during this century. Nesting Northerns are slightly less numerous in extreme southern Ohio, especially Adams, Scioto, and Lawrence Counties, where they are presently locally uncommon to fairly common residents. While their populations have experienced local fluctuations during this century, overall trends have remained fairly stable in Ohio since the mid-1960s—at the same time that increases have been evident elsewhere.[438]

Nesting Northerns favor wooded riparian corridors, forest edges, and large shade trees in parks or near residences. They were formerly familiar summer residents in most large cities and regularly built their nests in the large elms that provided shade for urban streets. The disappearance of most elms substantially reduced the numbers of orioles nesting in urban areas. They are now most numerous along wooded corridors bordering creeks and rivers. A canoe trip down any stream bordered by large sycamores and cottonwoods may produce 15–30 Northerns daily, and as many as 52 have been tallied in a single day.[471] Summer totals generally are 3–12 daily in other habitats.

Northern Orioles are renowned for their nests, which hang down from the outer branches of tall trees. These nests may be fairly well concealed during summer but become quite obvious after the leaves fall. Nest construction begins shortly after their return and has been noted by April 25.[523] Nests with eggs have been reported between May 18 and June 20 and most nests contain young during the last half of June. Recently fledged young mostly appear in late June or early July but renesting attempts have produced fledglings in early August.[479]

Once the males quit singing in early July, Northern Orioles become surprisingly difficult to locate. Their inconspicuous behavior continues through their fall migration, when they become uncommon to fairly common in every county. Most fall reports are of 1–8 Northerns daily with occasional flights of 10–30. The first fall migrants are apparent by August 3–8. They are most frequently noted between August 15 and September 5, with the last migrants normally departing by September 10–17.

A surprising number of Northern Orioles have lingered quite late into autumn, with late October and November sightings scattered across the state and an equal number during early winter. Most winter records are of Northerns visiting bird feeders during December and the first half of January, although a few individuals have overwintered. Winter records include at least eight sightings from the Cleveland-Akron area, four at Cincinnati, three at Toledo, three at Columbus, single records from Youngstown, Oxford, and Buckeye Lake, and an unspecified number at Dayton. Perhaps most noteworthy was a female oriole of the western "Bullock's" race that overwintered at a Columbus feeder during 1974–75 and returned the following winter. She was carefully studied by many observers and established Ohio's only documented record of this race.

BRAMBLING

Fringilla montifringilla Linnaeus

Snowstorms during late March or early April can exasperate anyone anxious for the arrival of spring. But they can be productive for birding, causing birds to congregate at feeders and allowing migrants to be observed that otherwise would be missed. Such was the case in the appearance of Ohio's only Brambling, which was first observed on March 31, 1987, at the Bath (Summit County) feeder of Horace and Helen Harger after a snowstorm had blanketed northern Ohio. Although the bird was a male acquiring its breeding plumage, its identity was not confirmed until April 5. On its very irregular visits to the Hargers' feeder, this attractive finch was viewed by many observers through April 7.[386] Bramblings are Eurasian finches whose breeding range extends from Siberia to Scandinavia. In winter they are found south to the Mediterranean region, India, and China.[5] They are accidental winter visitors to North America.

ROSY FINCH

Leucosticte arctoa (Pallas)

This accidental visitor from the western mountains has been detected in Ohio on two occasions. The first Rosy Finch frequented a feeder at the Norman Hazen residence in Conneaut on April 5–6, 1971. Detailed descriptions provided by the Hazens and J. Paul Perkins indicated that this individual was of the "Black" race. Ohio's second Rosy Finch briefly visited the Joseph Croy residence near Whitehouse (Lucas County) on February 6–7, 1984. Photographs taken by the Croys clearly establish its identity as a "Gray-crowned" Rosy Finch.[373] These finches normally occupy alpine tundra in the western mountains, although they move to lower elevations during winter. Periodic food shortages result in movements outside this range. While Rosy Finches seldom wander east of the plains, vagrants have appeared as far east as Maine.[5]

PINE GROSBEAK

Pinicola enucleator (Linnaeus)

This visitor from boreal coniferous forests has always been very erratic in its movements into Ohio. Most winters, Pine Grosbeaks remain in the northern forests. Periodic food shortages prompt them to move southward, and they infrequently penetrate the northern borders of the state.

There were few nineteenth-century records of Pine Grosbeaks from Ohio. The first noticeable movement occurred in the winter of 1903–4, producing sightings along the entire lakefront.[237,241] These finches were infrequently reported from northern Ohio in subsequent years until the winter of 1933–34, when a large movement into the northeastern United States produced multiple observations at Toledo and Cleveland.[89,523]

Their winter movements were most apparent between 1950 and the early 1970s. An "unprecedented flight" of Pine Grosbeaks appeared in the winter of 1951–52.[64] The largest numbers were noted during December, with flocks of 10–20 scattered south to Wooster (Wayne County) and Youngstown. An adult male provided the first Cincinnati area record as it remained there between December 20 and January 27.[248] A smaller flight was reported during the winter of 1954–55, while scattered Pine Grosbeaks were noted somewhere in northern Ohio during most winters of that decade.

Their largest invasion of this century was noted in the winter of 1961–62. These grosbeaks appeared during late November and remained in numbers throughout the winter. There were flocks of 100 at Iradale and 60 at Akron on February 7.[129,130] Smaller flocks of 15–40 were noted south to Youngstown and Mohican State Forest (Ashland County). This flight also produced the first Columbus area record and a second sighting from Cincinnati. A smaller movement recorded during the winter of 1965–66 was limited to the counties bordering Lake Erie.

The last defined flight was apparent only in the Cleveland area. The winter of 1972–73 produced multiple records, including several flocks of 10–16.[285] In subsequent years, Pine Grosbeaks became very sporadic winter visitors, averaging one record every two to four winters and restricted to northern Ohio. Small flocks were reported only from the Toledo area, while other sightings were of isolated individuals.

The earliest fall arrivals have appeared by November 2, but they are not normally detected until the last half of the month or in December. During flight years, largest numbers usually appear in December or early January. Pine Grosbeaks frequently become less numerous in February. Their spring movements are poorly defined, with only sporadic encounters in March, April, and as late as mid-May. As winter visitors, they are casually observed within the lakefront counties and northeastern Ohio south to Youngstown and Akron. Pine Grosbeaks are accidental winter visitors elsewhere, with several sightings at Findlay and the Mansfield-Wooster area, three central Ohio records, and three reports from Cincinnati.

PURPLE FINCH

Carpodacus purpureus (Gmelin)

Purple Finches share the erratic movements of other members of their family. They appear annually in Ohio but may be fairly scarce one year and rather numerous the next depending upon food availability elsewhere within their range. Whenever they appear, Purple Finches are always welcomed at backyard bird feeders. The brightly colored males are particularly pleasing during winter when most other birds are in somber plumages.

Purple Finches breed in portions of Ohio, and the population has steadily increased during this century. Nesting Purple Finches were first recorded at Cleveland in 1925 and they have regularly nested there in subsequent years.[523] By the mid-1930s, small numbers were scattered across Cuyahoga, Lake, Geauga, Trumbull, and Ashtabula Counties.[220] A southward and westward range extension became apparent in the 1950s, producing the first Youngstown nesting record in 1954 and an East Liverpool (Columbiana County) record by 1960.[72,140] The first Toledo nesting attempt was reported in 1955 and summering Purple Finches were noted in Mansfield by 1970.[89,411] This range extension continued into the 1980s, producing nesting records in other northern counties and a few attempts in central Ohio. Breeding Purple Finches are now uncommon to fairly common throughout northeastern Ohio. They are never numerous, but 1–8 individuals may be recorded daily in counties east of Cleveland and south to Columbiana, Stark, and Wayne.[434] Small numbers also reside in Carroll and Jefferson Counties at the northern edge of the unglaciated plateau. They become accidental to locally rare summer residents in other northern counties, with most records from Toledo, Mansfield, Lorain, Findlay, and Tiffin.

These finches are accidental to casual summer residents in central Ohio. The only confirmed breeding attempts are from Columbus, where the first nest was located in 1972.[471] They have summered at Springfield, where nesting was suspected but never established. A few scattered Purple Finches have briefly appeared at several other central locations during June but were probably nonbreeders. There are no confirmed summer records from the southern counties.

Within Ohio, the first nesting pairs were discovered in hemlock ravines, bogs, and tall conifers in residential areas.[215,523] As the nesting population expanded, they exhibited a preference for ornamental conifers in urban areas and rural Christmas tree farms. Purple Finch nests have been recorded as high as thirty-one feet in a tall spruce, but most are placed at heights of less than fifteen feet.[89,523] The few breeding records indicate that most nests are initiated in May. The young normally hatch during the first half of June and fledge by early July. A few pairs have nested later in the season, and a nest with hatching young has been observed as late as July 7.[89]

A few Purple Finches begin their fall migration quite early, having appeared at several northern locations by August 28–29 and in the Columbus area by September 1. The first migrants are not normally reported until September 25–October 5. Most of these finches apparently pass through Ohio during October. Despite annual fluctuations, 1–8 Purple Finches may be observed most days with occasional flocks of 15–25. Flocks of 50–120+ are exceptional in autumn. These migrants are uncommon to fairly common in deciduous woods and occasionally in weedy fields throughout Ohio. The last migrants normally depart during the first week of November, although stragglers may be noted into early December.

The distribution and abundance of wintering Purple Finches vary considerably from year to year. On rare occasions, they may be virtually absent from the entire state. But at least a few are detected during most winters. They infrequently stage pronounced movements and become widely distributed. These winter invasions have occurred once or twice per decade since the 1950s. Perhaps the largest recent movements were in the winters of 1959–60 and 1982–83, when flocks of 25–150+ were reported from a number of locations.

Their winter movement patterns may be fairly complex. During some years, Purple Finches remain throughout the winter. In others, they may be numerous only in December and become quite scarce by late January and February. But if they are scarce in December, they will probably remain scarce throughout the season; late winter influxes have not been reported.

Wintering Purple Finches are normally most numerous in the southwestern counties near Cincinnati, where they are uncommon to fairly common residents. They are mostly observed in groups of 3–15 with occasional flocks of 25–50+. During influxes, as many as 165 Purple Finches have been counted in one tree.[369] Small numbers also regularly winter along the un-glaciated Allegheny Plateau, especially south from Hocking, Perry, and Belmont Counties. They are uncommon winter residents, generally noted as individuals or flocks of 12 or fewer. Larger flocks are noted during influxes; 25–40+ may be observed daily.

Considerably fewer Purple Finches normally winter in the remainder of Ohio except on Kelleys Island (Erie County), where December flocks of 30–60+ are regular and as many as 193 were counted on December 8, 1982.[369] Away from this island, Purple Finches are casual to rare winter residents in the central and northern counties, mostly observed as individuals or small flocks during December. They regularly remain the entire winter only during influxes, when flocks of 5–25+ may appear. Larger concentrations are infrequent but have included as many as 250 individuals at Toledo on December 27, 1959,[89] and 186 on the 1956 O'Shaughnessy Reservoir Christmas Bird Count.[471]

As spring migrants, they may be numerous some years and almost absent in others. Sizable winter influxes are frequently followed by strong spring movements, but large migrations may follow winters with relatively few residents. When they are most plentiful, spring migrants appear in late March and peak between April 15 and May 5, when 10–50+ may be observed daily and tallies of 100+ are possible.[479] During a "normal" spring, the timing of their migration is similar but daily totals seldom exceed 5–20. When they are scarce, Purple Finches may not appear until April 15–20 and are usually observed in groups of 10 or fewer. These migrants depart by May 15–20.

Despite a slowly expanding breeding population, their future is uncertain. In recent years, these native finches have faced greatly increased competition from House Finches for breeding sites and winter food supplies. Since House Finches are more aggressive, they could displace Purple Finches from portions of their established range, though there is no information suggesting such a displacement is presently taking place.

HOUSE FINCH

Carpodacus mexicanus (Müller)

The story behind the introduction and spread of House Finches through eastern North America has been widely repeated. From a handful of finches liberated from a New York pet store in the 1940s, they rapidly spread westward. Their populations, which averaged a 21 percent annual increase between 1966 and 1979, are still expanding in every eastern state and province.[438]

Ohio's first House Finches appeared at Holden Arboretum near Cleveland on January 5, 1964.[335] As many as 4 were reported at or near this locality throughout the winter.[392] By the end of 1965, they had appeared at four Cleveland area locations.[335] Small numbers were sporadically reported from this area in subsequent years, but none was recorded elsewhere until October 29, 1972, when one was detected at Marietta.[162] These finches appeared at Dayton in 1973, East Liverpool and

Columbus in 1974, Wayne County in 1975, Mansfield in 1976, the Toledo area in 1978, and Cincinnati in 1979.[166,259,471] The first records were mostly of finches visiting urban feeders during winter and spring.

Establishment of a breeding population involved a more orderly but rapid westward expansion across Ohio. Breeding finches were initially restricted to the larger cities and towns. In eastern Ohio, nesting was strongly suspected or confirmed at several localities from Cleveland south to Belmont County in 1976 and 1977. By 1978, a few pairs were nesting at Columbus. Breeding populations were not established in the Cincinnati-Dayton area or at Toledo until 1981 and 1982.

Through the mid-1970s, most reports were of only 1–5 individuals at each locality. Large concentrations were initially reported from the Cleveland-Lorain-Akron metropolitan area. The first sizable flock at Cleveland totaled 125 House Finches on January 2, 1978, an exceptional concentration at that time.[268] At other northeastern locations, the largest reported flocks were composed of 5–12 finches in the winter of 1977–78, 15–25 in the winter of 1978–79, and 40–80 in the winter of 1979–80. A maximum of 200 House Finches was reported from Lorain during the fall of 1980 and similar concentrations have been present in subsequent years.[279]

Elsewhere, House Finches were mostly reported as groups of 15 or fewer individuals until the autumn of 1980, when 40 were counted at Columbus.[279] Their populations expanded rapidly in the next few years. For example, 100 were counted in Butler County on January 7, 1983, while flocks of 30–45 were reported from Cincinnati and Toledo that year.[369]

As their populations increased within large metropolitan areas, House Finches also spread to smaller towns and eventually to rural residences. By 1984 and 1985, they were established in every city, and singing males were regularly heard in most rural counties.

House Finches are now fairly common to common summer residents throughout Ohio, breeding in every county.[434] They are most numerous within large metropolitan areas, where 15–100+ individuals are noted daily. In rural areas, House Finches are widely distributed in the eastern counties but are still rather local in western Ohio near the Indiana border. While 5–15+ may be observed daily in rural eastern Ohio, daily totals seldom exceed 1–8 in the western counties.

Breeding House Finches are closely associated with residences. While their nests may be located in various sites, most nesters prefer ornamental shrubbery or young conifers. Their nesting activities begin in March or early April. Most clutches are laid in April or the first half of May. While adults with dependent young have been reported by April 15–25, most fledglings appear in May and the first half of June. Some pairs raise more than one brood. House Finches have constructed nests through the first week of July and dependent young have accompanied their parents as late as August 25.

House Finches are also fairly common to locally abundant winter residents throughout Ohio, forming flocks of 15–50+ individuals at bird feeders. Larger concentrations frequently develop, and flocks of 100–200+ are reported most years. In addition to individuals found at feeders, some forage for seeds in fallow fields and harvested croplands. Presently, winter concentrations in excess of 300–400 are unusual, although the largest reported flock was composed of at least 2000 House Finches feeding in a sunflower field near Ashville (Pickaway County) on December 8, 1985.[381]

Not all House Finches are permanent residents. There are definite migrations each spring and autumn, but their migratory patterns remain to be precisely established. These migrants are most evident at Lake Erie as flocks passing along the lakefront. Their fall migration apparently peaks between September 25 and November 10, with smaller numbers moving southward into December. Most spring migrants are detected between March 15 and April 15, with a few noted through the first week of May.

The recent spread of House Finches raises some perplexing questions. Most important, how will their expanding populations affect the status and distribution of our native winter finches? It is hoped that the answer will not be that the accidental introduction of House Finches produced disastrous consequences similar to those that followed the spread of European Starlings and House Sparrows across North America.

RED CROSSBILL

Loxia curvirostra Linnaeus

Renowned for their erratic movements, Red Crossbills invariably appear as a result of food shortages within their traditional range. But the origin of these flocks is as unpredictable as their presence within the state. Invading Red Crossbills are as likely to have wandered east from the Rocky Mountains as south from Canada. Hence, their statewide distribution varies from flight to flight. During some years, they may be restricted to western counties; in other years, flocks may only appear along Lake Erie. A statewide movement is rare, usually part of a massive invasion throughout the lower Great Lakes. Their movements are most erratic in autumn. During the phenomenal invasion of 1972–73, the first flocks were detected in the last half of August and Red Crossbills were fairly numerous by mid-September. This early fall migration was exceptional; there are few records earlier than October. The first fall migrants normally appear during November and their movements may continue into January.

Their fall abundance depends upon the size of the invasion. Red Crossbills may be completely absent some years. They are normally casual and sporadic fall visitors to most counties, usually as individuals or flocks of 10 or fewer. During small invasions, they may become locally rare fall migrants within the northern counties but casual elsewhere. Only during infrequent massive invasions do they become rare to locally fairly common migrants throughout Ohio and flocks of 20–50+ may appear in any county.

Red Crossbills do not appear each year but are unrecorded in approximately one out of every four winters. During most years, wintering flocks appear at one to three scattered localities. These flocks are casual visitors to the northern counties, especially near Toledo and Cleveland, but may also occupy pine plantations along the Allegheny Plateau. Wintering Red Crossbills are generally accidental elsewhere. Following major fall invasions, they become rare to locally fairly common winter residents in northern and eastern Ohio but casual to locally uncommon elsewhere. Most winter flocks are composed of 10 or fewer individuals; concentrations of 30–50+ are restricted to the large invasions.

Their winter behavior is also unpredictable. Some flocks may spend the entire winter within a cemetery or small park. Other flocks visit a location for only an hour or a day, then mysteriously disappear. Wintering flocks are most likely to appear within pine plantations or ornamental conifers planted in parks, cemeteries, and residential areas. A few crossbills have subsisted on sunflower seeds at bird feeders. When food is widely available, Red Crossbills may spend the entire winter within Ohio. If pine cone production was poor, wintering numbers may diminish by late January or February.

As spring migrants, their distribution and relative abundance are usually related to the size of the previous autumn's flight. On a few occasions, however, they have staged detectable spring movements into the state. Spring Red Crossbills are normally casual migrants but may become rare to locally fairly common following invasions. Most of these flocks are composed of 10 or fewer individuals with groups of 20–40+ during flight years. Their northward movements are also very erratic but are generally most pronounced between March 15 and May 10. Many flocks have lingered into late May, especially after large winter movements.

Red Crossbills are accidental summer visitors, usually following major flights. Most of them have been recorded during June, although there are July sightings from Cleveland and Canton in 1970.[411] These summer reports may be of scattered individuals or flocks of 5–40. Most summering Red Crossbills have been encountered within northern Ohio, especially near Cleveland. There are also June records from Columbus and Hocking County.[45,252] These summering crossbills are normally assumed to be nonbreeders, an assumption that is not necessarily valid. Crossbills nest any time food is abundant, even in the middle of winter. They will also attempt to nest outside their normal range when food is plentiful. Within Ohio, there is only one confirmed nesting record, following the invasion of 1972–73. An incubating pair was discovered by Al Staffan at Tar Hollow State Forest in Ross County during April 1973.[471] This nest was subsequently abandoned. There is a probable breeding record from Cleveland, where two juveniles were reported along the Rocky River on July 12–13, 1970.[411]

The pattern of erratic Red Crossbill flights has been apparent since the nineteenth century. Jones[236] considered these crossbills "irregular" winter visitors with "considerable flights sometimes during winter or early spring, followed abruptly by total disappearance." Nineteenth-century flights were indicated during the winters of 1868–69 and 1874–75, but additional movements almost certainly occurred.[248]

During the twentieth century, major winter invasions have generally followed a ten- to eleven-year cycle. Sizable flights occurred during the winters of 1920–21, 1931–32, and 1940–41, with only sporadic encounters during intervening years.[89,523] This pattern changed in the 1950s when the only substantial movement was noted in the winter of 1954–55.[75] Their flights became more frequent during the 1960s and 1970s. The flight in 1972–73 may have produced the largest numbers of Red Crossbills ever recorded from Ohio.[285] Surprisingly, there have been no widespread Red Crossbill movements during the 1980s, only sporadic visits by small flocks to a few localities.

WHITE-WINGED CROSSBILL

Loxia leucoptera Gmelin

A series of harsh call notes similar to those of redpolls announces the presence of a small flock of White-winged Crossbills as they descend upon the upper branches of a tall hemlock tree. White-wingeds prefer conifers with relatively small cones, exhibiting a decided preference for hemlock cones in Ohio. If these trees are unavailable, they may feed on pine cones or the seeds of deciduous trees such as sweet gums, alders, and sycamores.

White-winged Crossbills are very sporadic and casual winter visitors, just like the Reds, but White-wingeds tend to be less frequently reported. Their movements into Ohio are also a result of food shortages within the northern coniferous forests where they normally reside. Since the two crossbills have different food preferences, the southward movements of the two species are normally unrelated. While a few White-wingeds may associate with large flights of Reds, the largest White-winged movements usually are accompanied by relatively few Reds.

The first major White-winged flight was noted during the winter of 1868–69, but little information is available concerning the magnitude of this movement. A smaller flight was reported during the winter of 1901–2.[236] Except for a small movement during the winter of 1919–20, only isolated individuals and small flocks were irregularly noted until the winter of 1940–41, when a number of flocks appeared in the Cleveland area.[523] Additional small flights were noted during the winters of 1948–49, 1954–55, and 1958–59. The next defined movement occurred in 1963–64, when "unprecedented numbers" appeared in eastern Ohio and small flocks were scattered throughout the state.[147] A similar statewide invasion was detected during the winter of 1965–66.[150,399] Small movements were reported during the winters of 1971–72, 1975–76, and 1977–78. The most recent flights occurred during the winters of 1980–81 and 1981–82, but only one White-winged has been reported from Ohio since the winter of 1982–83.[360,364]

The largest concentrations have been reported during invasion years, including flocks of 50–100 individuals near Cleveland and Youngstown, 75 at Cincinnati, and 20–30 elsewhere.[147,523] Most flocks contain 15 or fewer White-wingeds. During noninvasion years, these crossbills are noted as individuals or flocks of 5 or fewer. While White-wingeds have returned as early as September 5, 1977, to Genoa (Ottawa County),[267] the first migrants normally return during November. Flocks may appear anytime during winter and some sizable movements were not evident until the last half of Feb-

ruary. Most spring migrants depart by mid-April, but a few may linger into May. The latest White-wingeds include one at East Liverpool (Columbiana County) through May 20, 1966; another at Cincinnati through May 27, 1955; and two at Lorain through June 9, 1981.[151,348,362]

COMMON REDPOLL

Carduelis flammea (Linnaeus)

The first returning Common Redpolls are normally encountered as small flocks with hoarse rattling call notes in migration along Lake Erie. These flocks may land in fallow fields where they consort with goldfinches and feed on sunflowers, evening primrose, and other weeds. They may also join goldfinches and Pine Siskins as they devour the seeds of alder, birch, sweet gum, and sycamore. If natural foods are not available, these redpolls readily accept food supplied at bird feeders.

Like all northern finches, Common Redpolls are erratic and unpredictable winter visitors. They may be quite rare and restricted to northern Ohio during some years but almost abundant and widely distributed in others. Common Redpolls may be numerous by late November during some flights but may not appear until February or even March in other movements. The timing of their appearance is largely a function of the distance traveled to reach the state. Some flights originate in arctic Canada directly to our north. But some Common Redpolls banded in Ohio have been recaptured in Alaska, indicating a northwestward migration after leaving the state. Other flights have included small numbers of "Greater" Redpolls migrating from Greenland.

In the northern counties, their relative abundance generally follows a two-year cycle of fairly high numbers one winter followed by relatively few the next.[335,523] During winters when they are scarce, these redpolls are encountered as individuals or flocks of 10 or fewer near Lake Erie. When they are fairly numerous, flocks of 10–50+ may be uncommonly observed along the lakefront with smaller numbers filtering inland. During periodic invasions, they become fairly common to locally abundant migrants with 20–350 individuals appearing along the lakefront and in most northern counties south to Youngstown and Findlay.[417,471]

While Common Redpolls have returned to Toledo by October 20,[89] they normally appear along Lake Erie between November 10 and December 15. Early flights produced 1000 migrants at Cleveland on November 8, 1980, and 200 at Youngstown on November 1, 1959.[137,279] During some years, these redpolls inexplicably disappear after early January; in others, flocks may be periodically encountered throughout winter. Common Redpolls normally depart during the first half of March, with occasional stragglers lingering into April. Following massive invasions, they were noted through May 11, 1978, at Findlay and May 13, 1978, at Cleveland.[417]

In central and southern Ohio, Common Redpolls are accidental to casual winter visitors except during periodic invasions. Only a few sizable flights were reported during the nineteenth century, most notably in the winters of 1836–37 and 1868–69.[248,523] Another major movement occurred in the winter of 1906–7, but most substantial flights were noted after 1930. Sizable influxes were noted during the winters of 1933–34, 1935–36, 1943–44, and 1946–47.[89,304] The winter of 1959–60 witnessed the "heaviest invasion in recent years,"[138] and large flights have subsequently appeared at a frequency of every three to seven years. The largest recent invasions were reported during the winters of 1961–62, 1965–66, 1969–70, 1977–78, and 1981–82.[129,399]

During some years, Common Redpolls may not wander south of Columbus. In other years, flocks may appear south to the Ohio River. Probably the largest recorded movement occurred during the winter of 1981–82, with flocks of 100–150 near Columbus, 113 at Dayton, and 54 at Cincinnati.[364]

Within these counties, the earliest fall migrants have been noted during the last half of November, although small flocks do not normally appear until mid-December. The largest numbers are usually encountered during late January or February. Most Common Redpolls depart by early March, but may remain later following strong invasions: until April 12, 1982, at Dayton and April 25, 1969, at East Liverpool.[156,299]

HOARY REDPOLL

Carduelis hornemanni (Holböll)

Hoary Redpolls are occupants of the arctic tundra in Alaska and Canada, normally remaining there throughout the year. Periodic food shortages prompt southward movements during some winters, invariably in association with massive invasions of Common Redpolls. While Hoaries are presently accidental winter visitors to Ohio, they may eventually prove to be slightly more regular visitors than the few existing sightings indicate.

Their true status will always be obscured by the inability to positively identify most Hoary Redpolls in the field. Only typical frosty-appearing males can be safely identified on sight; these males are a small proportion of the population. Identity of all other Hoaries can only be confirmed in the hand. Moreover, Hoaries readily hybridize with Commons and many redpolls with Hoary characteristics have proven to be hybrids.

Ohio's first Hoary Redpoll was collected in Lucas County on March 16, 1931.[218] The species then went unrecorded until the redpoll invasions during the 1960s. Other redpoll movements during the winters of 1977–78 and 1981–82 produced a few additional Hoary sightings. Confirmed records do not exceed ten, with sightings from Cleveland, Lorain, Akron, Toledo, and Columbus. Hoary Redpolls were recorded between December 19 and March 22, mostly as visitors to bird feeders. There have also been a number of unconfirmed sight records from the northern half of Ohio, mostly near Lake Erie.

PINE SISKIN

Carduelis pinus (Wilson)

Before 1950, wintering Pine Siskins were regularly recorded only within the northern counties, mostly as scattered individuals and small flocks.[89,523] Sizable flocks were irregularly encountered during periodic invasions. They only sporadically appeared within the central counties, usually as small flocks when the northern counties experienced noticeable invasions.[10,479] Wintering siskins were almost unknown within the southern counties; Kemsies and Randle[248] cited no Cincinnati records between 1869 and 1947.

Beginning in the 1950s, Pine Siskins initiated a pattern of regular invasions of the Midwest. These invasions were frequently noted at two- or three-year intervals, although there were occasional flights during successive winters. These pronounced invasions, evident throughout Ohio, were frequently associated with movements of Evening Grosbeaks. During nonflight years, most reports were of scattered siskins within the northern counties. This pattern of periodic winter invasions continued into the 1980s. During some invasions, a few siskins appear along Lake Erie in September and flocks are reported throughout the state during the first half of October. Other invasions have been characterized by movements beginning in mid-October with sizable numbers appearing in November. Nonflight years produce only scattered sightings during October and November. Their fall movements may continue through mid-December during sustained invasions. During noticeable flights, flocks of 15–100+ may appear as they become fairly common to common fall migrants across Ohio. Nonflight years produce only scattered individuals and flocks of 5–20; they become uncommon within the northern counties and casual to uncommon elsewhere.

Pine Siskins are uncommon and locally distributed winter residents throughout the northern and unglaciated counties during nonflight years. They are normally encountered as flocks of 20 or fewer individuals, usually visiting bird feeders or frequenting parks, cemeteries, and coniferous woodlands. They are casual to locally rare residents elsewhere, infrequently appearing in small flocks. During invasion years, Pine Siskins become uncommon to locally abundant winter residents within the northern and unglaciated counties, where favored localities may support flocks of 50–200+. These large flocks are unusual; only 8–30+ are observed at most locations. Elsewhere, they become rare to locally common winter visitors. While flocks of 100+ siskins have wintered at Columbus and Cincinnati, winter totals mostly consist of 20 or fewer in the southwestern and glaciated central counties.

Spring Pine Siskins also undertake erratic movements. During some years, large flocks may appear in March and disappear by mid-April. In other years, siskins may be virtually absent until late April and early May. Spring siskins are generally most apparent between April 15 and May 15. Small numbers may remain into the last half of May and occasionally early June.

Numbers of spring migrants are directly related to the size

of the previous autumn movement. During nonflight years, Pine Siskins become rare to locally fairly common migrants, most numerous along Lake Erie. Most reports are of only 1–20 individuals. Following sizable winter invasions, siskins become uncommon to locally abundant spring migrants. Flocks of 50–200+ siskins may appear in late April and early May. A report of 500 siskins at Youngstown on May 7, 1961, is indicative of the numbers that may accumulate under favorable conditions.[142] Even during these flights, most spring sightings are of fewer than 50 siskins.

Pine Siskins are opportunistic breeders and will nest south of their traditional range when food is plentiful. These southerly breeding records normally follow massive winter invasions. Initially, Ohio breeding records followed this pattern of very sporadic breeding attempts. Hicks[215] indicated Pine Siskins "almost certainly" nested within the former Pymatuning Bog in Ashtabula County between 1928 and 1930, but breeding was not confirmed before the bog was destroyed. Kemsies and Randle[248] recorded courtship behavior at Cincinnati in April 1953, but a nest was not located. The first published nesting attempt followed the winter invasion of 1972–73. This unsuccessful nesting attempt was noted at Columbus.[471] Nesting attempts were recorded following every large flight during the 1970s, producing records from Toledo, Cincinnati, and Cleveland and midsummer sightings at other localities.

Their status as breeding birds noticeably changed following the sizable invasion of the 1977–78 winter. This invasion produced nesting records from Toledo, Cincinnati, and Columbus. Siskins have nested during every year but one since 1978. Nests have been located near Ohio's four largest cities and at scattered locations in Lorain and Portage Counties.[434] Summering siskins have been reported from other locations where breeding was suspected. They are presently accidental to casual and very erratic summer residents, usually noted before June 20 with very few reports during July and August. The few confirmed nesting attempts have been located in ornamental conifers within parks, cemeteries, and residential areas. These attempts are mostly initiated in April. While their success has been quite low, a few pairs have produced young as evidenced by fledglings observed between April 12 and May 9.

AMERICAN GOLDFINCH

Carduelis tristis (Linnaeus)

Dawson expressed great admiration for these attractive finches:

One is at a loss to decide whether nature awarded the Goldfinch his suit of fine clothes in recognition of his dauntless cheer or whether he is only happy because of his panoply of jet and gold. At any rate he is the bird of sunshine the year around, happy, careless, free. Rollicking companies of them rove the countryside, now searching the heads of last year's mullein stalks and enlivening their quest with much pleasant chatter, now scattering in obedience to some whimsical command and sowing the air with their laughter.[102]

Dawson's admiration is shared by all who come in contact with them. Fortunately, American Goldfinches rank among our more numerous and widely distributed residents, equally well known to the ornithologist and the backyard birder.

As summer residents, American Goldfinches are generally common to abundant in every county. Daily totals of 30–75+ individuals are observed in most areas except the intensively cultivated western counties, where 15–40+ are noted. They have remained fairly stable throughout this century; both Jones[236] and Hicks[220] described them as among our most abundant nesting birds. But breeding bird surveys indicated a significant decline throughout eastern and central North America after 1965.[438] This decline may have been caused partly by the severe winters of 1976–78, from which their populations did not completely recover until the 1980s.

Breeding American Goldfinches inhabit abandoned fields dominated by weeds and brush, weedy fencerows, woodland edges, and cutover woods with open canopies. In intensively farmed areas, they mostly occupy weedy rights-of-way along highways and railroads, ditch banks, wooded riparian corridors, and the edges of isolated woodlots.

American Goldfinches begin the task of raising young at a time when most other songbirds have completed nesting. Surprisingly, these goldfinches begin forming pairs as early as the last week of April, although this process continues into June. While nest construction has been reported as early as May 30, serious construction is not expected until mid-July.[337] Trautman[479] reported nests with eggs by June 19 and dependent young by July 12 at Buckeye Lake, but these early nesting efforts are exceptional. Most clutches are discovered between July 20 and August 15 with renesting attempts as late as September 14.[479,523] Their young generally fledge between mid-August and mid-September, a few as late as the first week of October.

At one time, most American Goldfinches migrated south after the breeding season. Wintering numbers exhibited considerable variability. During extended inclement weather, these goldfinches became rare visitors within most counties. Conversely, relatively warm weather and plentiful food encouraged flocks to winter throughout the state. During some winters, flocks of 100–200 individuals occurred north to Lake Erie, although these concentrations were unusual.[86,479]

Their winter status has gradually changed since the 1940s. American Goldfinches have become fairly common to common winter residents. Winter flocks of 5–30 are regularly encountered with occasional concentrations of 50–300 individuals. These numbers remain reasonably constant throughout winter, although some decreases may be evident following extended inclement weather. Increased food availability at bird feeders is largely responsible for their changing winter distribution patterns.

American Goldfinches undertake regular migrations each spring and autumn, but these movements are no longer particularly evident. Their northward movements generally begin by April 10–20 and peak between April 28 and May 18. This migration continues through May 25–30 along Lake Erie. In recent years, their spring migration is most apparent along western Lake Erie. During the first half of May, concentrations of 100–300 goldfinches are encountered daily, while as many as 1000–1500 have been estimated during sizable flights. A report by Campbell[89] of 2000 goldfinches passing near Toledo during three hours on May 1, 1954, is indicative of the huge numbers migrating along western Lake Erie. Similar numbers are not evident elsewhere. Along the lake's Central Basin, the largest spring concentrations seldom exceed 100–250. Away from the lakefront, few spring flocks in excess of 100 have been reported in recent years.

Before the recent increases in the wintering population, sizable flocks of American Goldfinches migrated through the interior of Ohio. Trautman[479] observed 25–250 individuals daily and occasional movements of 500 at Buckeye Lake, indicative of the numbers passing through most counties before 1940.

Their fall migration has always been less apparent. It produces totals of 30–60 daily at most localities with occasional movements involving 100–200. While a few migrants have been noted along Lake Erie by the first week of September, the largest numbers are observed between October 10 and November 5. Their southward movements are largely terminated by mid-November.

EVENING GROSBEAK

Coccothraustes vespertinus (Cooper)

Before 1900, breeding Evening Grosbeaks were restricted to western North America and their winter movements seldom extended east of the Mississippi River. They were accidental visitors to Ohio. The only reports were from the Cleveland-Lorain area in 1860 and during a small incursion in the winter of 1890–91.[523] Another small flight developed in the winter of 1910–11, producing several sightings from northeastern Ohio and the first records from the northwestern, southwestern, and central counties.[242]

During the first decades of this century, Evening Grosbeaks expanded their breeding range across Canada, eventually reaching the Maritime Provinces and New England.[104] As they spread eastward, wintering Evening Grosbeaks appeared more frequently within Ohio. Between 1910 and 1930, they were reported at two- to four-year intervals, mostly from the northern and central counties, as small flocks or scattered individuals. More records accumulated during the 1930s. Wintering Evening Grosbeaks became fairly regular visitors to Toledo and Cleveland and produced scattered sightings elsewhere. However, they were not detected annually.[89,523]

By the early 1940s, Evening Grosbeaks developed a regular pattern of winter movements into the lower Great Lakes states.[104] These movements constituted sizable invasions at two- to three-year intervals with smaller numbers during other winters. The incursion during the 1945–46 winter produced scattered sightings across Ohio with a maximum of 125 at Cleveland.[523] Similar numbers appeared in the 1949–50 and 1951–52 invasions, while the movement of 1954–55 produced many flocks totaling 75–195 individuals in the northeastern counties. The winter of 1959–60 produced the first sizable in-

vasion of the southeastern counties.[138,443] These flights continued at two- to three-year intervals during the 1960s, producing local concentrations of 200+ individuals at scattered northern and eastern locations and smaller numbers from other counties. Periodic invasions have highlighted winters in the 1970s and 1980s. While the largest concentrations increased to 300–500 individuals at several northern and eastern locations, the magnitude of these winter movements has remained fairly constant since 1970.

In nonflight years, Evening Grosbeaks become casual to rare in northwestern Ohio near Toledo, in the northeastern counties east of Cleveland, and along the entire unglaciated Allegheny Plateau. They are absent from the remainder of the state. Sightings usually are of scattered individuals or flocks of 20 or fewer.

During invasions, wintering Evening Grosbeaks generally produce two types of distribution patterns. During some invasions, they are fairly common to locally abundant residents only along the unglaciated Allegheny Plateau, where flocks of 50–200+ may be widespread. They become rare to uncommon visitors in northern Ohio and casual to rare in the glaciated central and southwestern counties. Most reports are of 15–30 or fewer individuals away from the unglaciated counties. During other invasions, these grosbeaks may be fairly common to common residents near Toledo, within the northeastern counties, along the unglaciated plateau, and locally near Cincinnati. Concentrations of 100–500 may appear in the northern and southeastern counties but seldom exceed 50 individuals near Cincinnati. Elsewhere, they remain casual to rare winter visitors, usually in small flocks of 15 or fewer.

Initially, wintering Evening Grosbeaks resided in deciduous woods, exhibiting a preference for box elder, ash, and maple seeds. During the past ten to fifteen years, they have seldom been encountered away from bird feeders, where they eagerly devour large quantities of sunflower seeds.

Their migrations are equally unpredictable, especially in autumn. During some years, the largest movements occur in October and early November; in other years, large numbers may not appear until late November or December. Flocks may even pass into Ohio during January and February.

The earliest fall migrants have returned to Lake Erie by September 8–10. These early sightings are exceptional and there are relatively few northern Ohio records before the first week of October. During flight years, flocks of 15–40 individuals frequently appear in northern Ohio by October 5–15 and in the southern counties during the last half of the month. Their fall movements frequently show a bimodal pattern, with one peak between October 10 and November 15 and another in December. During large flights, migrants become uncommon to locally common across the state. In nonflight years, fall migrants are uncommon to rare along Lake Erie and eastern Ohio, becoming casual elsewhere.

In spring, migrants may appear during the last half of March but most are noted between April 5 and May 10. Following sizable fall flights, Evening Grosbeaks become rare to fairly common spring migrants, most numerous along Lake Erie and the eastern counties in scattered flocks of 10–50+ individuals. Following winters when these grosbeaks are relatively scarce, spring migrants are generally casual to rare and few flocks are composed of more than 10–15 individuals. Most depart by May 10–20, although scattered individuals have remained until May 27, 1976, at Tiffin;[262] June 8, 1911, at Cincinnati;[248] and June 24, 1962, at Toledo.[89] An unmated female was seen building a nest at Mineral Ridge (Trumbull County) during the first week of April 1979, but she disappeared before completing it.[273]

HOUSE SPARROW

Passer domesticus (Linnaeus)

Dawson accurately summarized the attitude of most people toward this Eurasian native:

> Without question the most deplorable event in the history of American ornithology was the introduction of the English Sparrow. The extinction of the Great Auk, the passing of the Wild Pigeon and the Turkey,—sad as these are, they are trifles compared to the wholesale reduction of our smaller birds which is due to the invasion of that wretched foreigner, the English Sparrow.[102]

According to Hicks,[220] House Sparrows were initially released in Cleveland, Cincinnati, and Warren in 1869. They were also released at Marietta in 1870, Coshocton and Portsmouth in 1874, Steubenville in 1880–81, and Wapakoneta in 1882. They rapidly spread throughout the state. They were common and widely distributed residents by the turn of the century,[236] and their numbers were still increasing,

Their rapid expansion resulted from their close association with people. During the 1800s, House Sparrows thrived on refuse in cities, waste grain in farm fields, and grain from horse manure. Moreover, they are aggressive and readily dominate our native songbirds, usurping nesting locations and food sources.

Throughout eastern North America, their populations peaked between 1900 and 1920. Small declines were noted during the 1920s as populations stabilized. These sparrows also lost an important food source when horses were replaced by cars and mechanized farm machinery. Their populations slowly declined in subsequent decades, a result of the "clean farming" practices that have been so harmful to most wildlife.

Since 1965, House Sparrows have continuously declined throughout eastern North America.[438] These declines reflected the effects not only of unfavorable farming practices but also of severe winter weather. During the 1980s, House Sparrows have also had competition from another introduced and aggressive occupant of residential habitats, the House Finch.

Despite their reduced populations, House Sparrows remain common to abundant permanent residents. In fact, Ohio supports one of the largest populations of any state.[438] They are most numerous in cities, villages, and farmlands, where 200–1000+ individuals can be counted daily—if one should desire to do so. Fewer House Sparrows are encountered in the unglaciated southeastern counties, where daily totals of 50–200 are expected, although larger numbers are present within cities.

House Sparrows may nest as isolated pairs or semicolonially. As described by Dawson:

> The Sparrow exhibits a most cosmopolitan taste in the matter of nesting sites. The normal half-bushel ball of trash in the tree-top is still adhered to by some builders, but the cavity left by a missing brick, a Woodpecker's hole . . . will do as well. Of late the choicest rural sites have been appropriated, and the cliffs once sacred to the gentle Swallow, now resound with the vulgar bletherings and maudlin mirth of this avian blot on nature.[102]

These nests are normally placed near residences, but House Sparrows will also nest far from any home. One pair built a nest at the base of a large Bald Eagle eyrie.[89]

Nest construction has been observed as early as January 7 but does not normally begin until March.[89] These sparrows produce multiple broods and are almost constantly incubating eggs or raising young. Nests with eggs have been reported by March 8 and young accompanying adults by April 10. Fledgling House Sparrows have been noted as late as September 23.[89,523]

As soon as the young fledge, these sparrows form small flocks. This postbreeding behavior was described by Trautman:

> At first the flocks consisted principally of young, but as June advanced the percentage of adults increased and by mid-July the flocks averaged about 60 percent young and 40 percent adults. Throughout the last two-thirds of July and all of August flocks of 15 to 200 individuals could be found in grain fields and along roads.[479]

The largest roosts occur in winter. While 20,000 House Sparrows congregated at Dayton during the winter of 1953–54,[299] similar flocks have not plagued other communities.

Although House Sparrows are considered permanent residents, Trautman and Trautman[488] reported visible migrations over western Lake Erie. These movements are poorly understood, but small flocks were noted passing over the lake during March and April and again in September and October.

BIBLIOGRAPHY

1. Ahlquist, J. 1964. Rufous-necked Sandpiper, *Erolia ruficollis,* in northeastern Ohio. Auk 81:432–33.

2. Aldrich, J. W. 1934. Observations on a few breeding birds in northeastern Ohio. Wilson Bulletin 46:96–103.

3. ———. 1936. European Woodcock (*Scolopax rusticola rusticola*) in Ohio. Auk 53:329–30.

4. Allen, R. W., and M. M. Nice. 1952. A study of the breeding biology of the Purple Martin. American Midland Naturalist 47:606–65.

5. American Ornithologists' Union. 1983. Check-list of North American birds. 6th ed. Allen Press, Lawrence, Kansas. 877 pp.

6. ———. 1985. Thirty-fifth supplement to the American Ornithologists' Union Check-list of North American birds. Auk 102:680–86.

7. Anderson, J. M. 1960. Summer birds of Winous Point in 1880, 1930, and 1960. 21 pp. (mimeo).

8. Andrews, D. A. 1973. Habitat utilization by Sora, Virginia Rails, and King Rails near southwestern Lake Erie. M.S. thesis, Ohio State University, Columbus. 112 pp.

9. Andrews, R. 1952. A study of waterfowl nesting on a Lake Erie marsh. M.S. thesis, Ohio State University, Columbus. 153 pp.

10. Anonymous. (Thomas, E. S., C. F. Walker, and M. B. Trautman). 1928. The winter birds of central Ohio. Ohio State Museum of Science Bulletin 1:24–28.

11. Austing, G. R., and D. A. Imbrogno. 1976. Birds of the Hamilton County Park District and southwestern Ohio. Hamilton County Park District, Cincinnati. 52 pp.

12. Averbach, B. F. 1925. Hudsonian Curlew near Youngstown, Ohio. Auk 42:580.

13. Baird, R. L. 1905. Bird migration at Oberlin, Ohio. Wilson Bulletin 17:75–83.

14. ———. 1931a. Oberlin Region. Bird-Lore 33(4):268–70.

15. ———. 1931b. Oberlin Region. Bird-Lore 33(5):335–37.

16. ———. 1932a. Oberlin Region. Bird-Lore 34(1):14–16.

17. ———. 1932b. Oberlin Region. Bird-Lore 34(2):140–42.

18. ———. 1932c. Oberlin Region. Bird-Lore 34(4):275–76.

19. ———. 1932d. Oberlin Region. Bird-Lore 34(5):343–44.

20. ———. 1933. Oberlin Region. Bird-Lore 35(6):330–31.

21. ———. 1934a. Oberlin Region. Bird-Lore 36(2):115–16.

22. ———. 1934b. Oberlin Region. Bird-Lore 36(3):183–84.

23. ———. 1934c. Oberlin Region. Bird-Lore 36(5):310–11.

24. ———. 1934d. Oberlin Region. Bird-Lore 36(6):372–73.

25. ———. 1935a. Oberlin Region. Bird-Lore 37(2):141–42.

26. ———. 1935b. Oberlin Region. Bird-Lore 37(3):224–25.

27. ———. 1935c. Oberlin Region. Bird-Lore 37(4):291–92.

28. ———. 1935d. Oberlin Region. Bird-Lore 37(6):468–69.

29. ———. 1936a. Oberlin Region. Bird-Lore 38(3):245–46.

30. ———. 1936b. Oberlin Region. Bird-Lore 38(4):275–76.

31. ———. 1936c. Oberlin Region. Bird-Lore 38(5):388–89.

32. ———. 1936d. Oberlin Region. Bird-Lore 38(6):468–70.

33. ———. 1937. Oberlin Region. Bird-Lore 39(3):169–70.

34. Baker, W. C. 1933. Some sight records from Ohio. Wilson Bulletin 45:35–36.

35. ———. 1946. Notes on summer resident Wilson's Snipe in Columbiana County, Ohio. Auk 63:446–48.

36. Bales, B. R. 1911a. Some notes from Pickaway County, Ohio. Wilson Bulletin 23:43–48.

37. ———. 1911b. An Ohio nest of the Black-and-white Warbler. Wilson Bulletin 23:55–56.

38. Ball, R. E. 1946. White Pelicans in northeastern Ohio. Auk 63:104.

39. Banko, W. E. 1960. The Trumpeter Swan, its history, habits, and population in the United States. U.S. Fish and Wildlife Service, North American Fauna No. 63. 214 pp.

40. Beardslee, C. S. 1944. Bonaparte's Gull on the Niagara River and eastern Lake Erie. Wilson Bulletin 56:9–14.

41. Bildstein, K. L. 1987. Behavioral ecology of Red-tailed Hawks (*Buteo jamaicensis*), Rough-legged Hawks (*Buteo lagopus*), Northern Harriers (*Circus cyaneus*) and American Kestrels (*Falco sparverius*) in south central Ohio. Ohio Biological Survey, Biological Notes No. 18. 53 pp.

42. Blincoe, B. J. 1930. Leach's Petrel in Ohio. Auk 47:72.

43. Blockstein, D. E., and H. B. Tordoff. 1985. Gone forever—a contemporary look at the extinction of the Passenger Pigeon. American Birds 39:845–51.

44. Blokpoel, H., G. D. Tessier, and A. Harfenist. 1987. Distribution during post-breeding dispersal, migration and overwintering of Common Terns color-marked on the lower Great Lakes. Journal of Field Ornithology 58:206–17.

45. Borror, D. J. 1950. A checklist of the birds of Ohio with the migration dates for the birds of central Ohio. Ohio Journal of Science 50:1–32.

46. ———. 1970. Tape recordings as evidence of a bird's occurrence in an area. Wheaton Club Bulletin No. 15.

47. Bownocker, J. A. 1965. Geologic map of Ohio. Ohio Geological Survey, Columbus.

48. Brackney, A. W., and T. A. Bookhout. 1982. Population ecology of Common Gallinules in southwestern Lake Erie marshes. Ohio Journal of Science 82:229–37.

49. Braund, F. W. 1938a. Nesting records for Ohio birds: June 1–September 1, 1937. Oologist 55:81–83.

50. ———. 1938b. Status of the Northern Pileated Woodpecker in Ashtabula County, Ohio. Oologist 55:128–30.

51. ———. 1939a. The versatile nesting habitats of the American Woodcock. Oologist 56:69–70.

52. ———. 1939b. Breeding records of Ohio birds, March 1–October 1, 1939. Oologist 56:110–112.

53. ———. 1940a. Nesting records for Ohio birds: January 1–September 1, 1940. Oologist 57:134–35.

54. ———. 1940b. The birds of Smoky Creek valley, Adams County, Ohio. Oologist 57:62–72.

55. Brooks, M. 1938a. Bachman's Sparrow in the north-central portion of its range. Wilson Bulletin 50:86–109.

56. ———. 1938b. The Eastern Lark Sparrow in the Upper Ohio Valley. Cardinal 4(8):181–200.

57. ———. 1949. Appalachian Region. Audubon Field Notes 3(1):14–15.

58. ———. 1950a. Appalachian Region. Audubon Field Notes 4(1):14–15.

59. ———. 1950b. Appalachian Region. Audubon Field Notes 4(3):200–202.

60. ———. 1950c. Appalachian Region. Audubon Field Notes 4(4):240–42.

61. ———. 1950d. Appalachian Region. Audubon Field Notes 4(5):274–76.

62. ———. 1951a. Appalachian Region. Audubon Field Notes 5(3):203–5.

63. ———. 1951b. Appalachian Region. Audubon Field Notes 5(5):287–89.

64. ———. 1952a. Appalachian Region. Audubon Field Notes 6(3):194–96.

65. ———. 1952b. Appalachian Region. Audubon Field Notes 6(5):280–82.

66. ———. 1953a. Appalachian Region. Audubon Field Notes 7(1):15–17.

67. ———. 1953b. Appalachian Region. Audubon Field Notes 7(3):212–13.

68. ———. 1953c. Appalachian Region. Audubon Field Notes 7(4)272–73.

69. ———. 1953d. Appalachian Region. Audubon Field Notes 7(5):307–9.

70. ———. 1954a. Appalachian Region. Audubon Field Notes 8(1):17–19.

71. ———. 1954b. Appalachian Region. Audubon Field Notes 8(3):250–52.

72. ———. 1954c. Appalachian Region. Audubon Field Notes 8(4):344–45.

73. Not used.

74. ———. 1955a. Appalachian Region. Audubon Field Notes 9(1):24–26.

75. ———. 1955b. Appalachian Region. Audubon Field Notes 9(3):256–59.

76. ———. 1955c. Appalachian Region. Audubon Field Notes 9(4):329–32.

77. ———. 1956. Appalachian Region. Audubon Field Notes 10(1):22–25.

78. ———. 1958. Appalachian Region. Audubon Field Notes 12(3):278–80.

79. ———. 1959a. Appalachian Region. Audubon Field Notes 13(1):28–30.

80. ———. 1959b. Appalachian Region. Audubon Field Notes 13(4):429–31.

81. Browning, M. R. 1974. Comments on the winter distribution of Swainson's Hawk (*Buteo swainsoni*) in North America. American Birds 28:865–67.

82. Bruce, J. 1931. Yellow-crowned Night-Heron in Ohio. Auk 48:593–94.

83. Buchanan, F. W. 1937. Red Phalarope in eastern Ohio. Wilson Bulletin 59:36.

84. ———. 1980. The breeding birds of Carroll and northern Jefferson Counties, Ohio, with notes on selected vascular plants and animal species. Ohio Biological Survey, Biological Notes No. 12. 50 pp.

85. Campbell, L. W. 1938. Phalaropes of the western Lake Erie region. Auk 55:89–94.

86. ———. 1940. Birds of Lucas County. Toledo Museum of Science Bulletin 1(1):1–225.

87. ———. 1944. Glossy Ibis near Toledo, Ohio. Auk 61:471.

88. ———. 1947. American Egrets nesting on West Sister Island in Lake Erie. Auk 64:461–62.

89. ———. 1968. Birds of the Toledo area. Toledo Blade Company, Toledo. 330 pp.

90. ———. 1973. Additions to the birds of the Toledo area for years 1968 through November 1973. Toledo Naturalists Association Yearbook, pp. 13–45.

91. Chapman, F. B. 1931. An Ohio heron colony. Bird-Lore 33:256–57.

92. ———. 1938. An unusual nesting site of the Rough-winged Swallow. Wilson Bulletin 50:203.

93. ———, H. Bezdek, and E. H. Dustman. 1952. The Ruffed Grouse and its management in Ohio. Ohio Department of Natural Resources, Division of Wildlife Conservation Bulletin No. 6. 24 pp.

94. Clark, C. F. 1944a. Forster's Tern in central-western Ohio. Auk: 61:474.

95. ———. 1944b. Summer occurrence of Holboell's Grebe in Ohio. Wilson Bulletin 56:169.

96. ———. 1946. Rare birds in west-central Ohio. Auk 63:594.

97. ———. 1964. Bird records from the vicinity of Lake St. Mary's, Mercer and Auglaize Counties, Ohio. Ohio Journal of Science 64:25–26.

98. ———, and J. P. Sipe. 1970. Birds of the Lake St. Mary's area. Ohio Department of Natural Resources, Division of Wildlife Publication No. 350. 93 pp.

99. Coale, H. K. 1915. The present status of the Trumpeter Swan (*Olor buccinator*). Auk 32:82–90.

100. Coles, V. 1944. Nesting of the Turkey Vulture in Ohio caves. Auk 61:219–28.

101. Curl, A. L. 1932. The Bohemian Waxwing in Ohio. Auk 49:225.

102. Dawson, W. L. 1903. The birds of Ohio. Wheaton Publishing Company, Columbus, Ohio. 2 vols. 671 pp.

103. Deane, R. 1905. Two additional records of the European Widgeon (*Mareca penelope*). Auk 22:206.

104. DeVos, A. 1964. Range changes of birds in the Great Lakes region. American Midland Naturalist 71:489–502.

105. Dexter, R. W. 1956a. Further banding and nesting studies of the Eastern Nighthawk. Bird-Banding 27:9–15.

106. ———. 1956b. Ten-year life history of a banded Chimney Swift. Auk 73:276–80.

107. ———. 1961. Further studies on nesting of the Common Nighthawk. Bird-Banding 32:79–85.

108. Dolbeer, R. A., and G. E. Bernhardt. 1986. Early-winter population trends of gulls on western Lake Erie, 1950–1984. American Birds 40(4):1097–1102.

109. Donohoe, R. W., and C. E. McKibben. 1973. History of the Wild Turkey (*Meleagris gallopavo*) transplants in the Ohio hill country. Ohio Journal of Science 73:96–102.

110. ———, W. P. Parker, M. W. McClain, and C. E. McKibben. 1983. Distribution and population estimates of Ohio Wild Turkeys (*Meleagris gallopavo*), 1981–82. Ohio Journal of Science 83:188–90.

111. Doolittle, E. A. 1924a. Record of Brunnich's Murre for Lake County, Ohio. Auk 41:148.

112. ———. 1924b. Little Gull at Lake County, Ohio. Wilson Bulletin 36:62–63.

113. Earl, T. M. 1918. Harris' Hawks in Ohio. Wilson Bulletin 30:15–16.

114. ———. 1934. Observations on owls in Ohio. Wilson Bulletin 46:137–42.

115. Fisher, G. C. 1907a. Bald Eagle's nest at Lewistown Reservoir. Wilson Bulletin 19:13–16.

116. ———. 1907b. A Brant at the Lewistown Reservoir. Wilson Bulletin 19:33.

117. Flanigan, A. B. 1968. Early and late dates for birds of the Cleveland region. 7 pp. (mimeo).

118. Fordyce, G. L. 1914. The Western Grebe in Ohio. Auk 31:243.

119. Franks, R. W. 1928. A Champaign County heronry. Ohio State Museum of Science Bulletin 1:36–39.

120. Fretwell, S. 1977. Is the Dickcissel a threatened species? American Birds 31(5):923–32.

121. Gibbons, M. 1966. Short-eared Owl nesting in northwestern Pickaway County. Wheaton Club Bulletin 11:36–37.

122. Gier, H. T. 1949. Lark Sparrow nesting in southeastern Ohio. Auk 66:209–10.

123. Gilbert, W. N. 1953. Chuck-will's-widow in central Ohio. Wilson Bulletin 65:43.

124. Gill, F. B. 1980. Historical aspects of hybridization between Blue-winged and Golden-winged Warblers. Auk 97:1–18.

125. Godfrey, W. E. 1943. Eared Grebe in Ohio. Auk 60:452.

126. Goldthwait, R. P., G. W. White, and J. L. Forsyth. 1961. Glacial map of Ohio. U.S. Geological Survey Miscellaneous Geologic Investigations Map I-316.

127. Goodpaster, W., and K. H. Maslowski. 1937. Le Conte's Sparrow in Clermont County, Ohio. Auk 54:397.

128. Gordon, R. B. 1969. The natural vegetation of Ohio in pioneer days. Ohio Biological Survey New Series Bulletin 3:1–109.

129. Graber, R. R. 1962a. Middlewestern Prairie Region. Audubon Field Notes 16(1):35–37, 41–43.

130. ———. 1962b. Middlewestern Prairie Region. Audubon Field Notes 16(3):332–36.

131. ———. 1962c. Middlewestern Prairie Region. Audubon Field Notes 16(4):413, 417–420.

132. ———. 1962d. Middlewestern Prairie Region. Audubon Field Notes 16(5):478–80.

133. Not used.

134. Green, N. B. 1947. Swainson's Warbler in southern Ohio. Wilson Bulletin 59:211.

135. Greider, M., and E. S. Wagner. 1960. Black Vulture extends breeding range northward. Wilson Bulletin 72:291.

136. Hall, G. A. 1959. Appalachian Region. Audubon Field Notes 13(3):292–94.

137. ———. 1960a. Appalachian Region. Audubon Field Notes 14(1):35–38.

138. ———. 1960b. Appalachian Region. Audubon Field Notes 14(3):309–11.

139. ———. 1960c. Appalachian Region. Audubon Field Notes 14(4):386–88.

140. ———. 1960d. Appalachian Region. Audubon Field Notes 14(5):448–51.

141. ———. 1961a. Appalachian Region. Audubon Field Notes 15(3):328–31.

142. ———. 1961b. Appalachian Region. Audubon Field Notes 15(4):409–12.

143. ———. 1962a. Appalachian Region. Audubon Field Notes 16(1):31–34.

144. ———. 1962b. Appalachian Region. Audubon Field Notes 16(5):475–77.

145. ———. 1963a. Appalachian Region. Audubon Field Notes 17(4):401–4.

146. ———. 1963b. Appalachian Region. Audubon Field Notes 17(5):459–61.

147. ———. 1964. Appalachian Region. Audubon Field Notes 18(3):353–56.

148. ———. 1965. Appalachian Region. Audubon Field Notes 19(4):470–73.

149. ———. 1966a. Appalachian Region. Audubon Field Notes 20(1):41–45.

150. ———. 1966b. Appalachian Region. Audubon Field Notes 20(3):422–25.

151. ———. 1966c. Appalachian Region. Audubon Field Notes 20(4):506–11.

152. ———. 1966d. Appalachian Region. Audubon Field Notes 20(5):568–70.

153. ———. 1967. Appalachian Region. Audubon Field Notes 21(4):506–10.

154. ———. 1968a. Appalachian Region. Audubon Field Notes 22(4):525–28.

155. ———. 1968b. Appalachian Region. Audubon Field Notes 22(5):606–9.

156. ———. 1969. Appalachian Region. Audubon Field Notes 23(4):589–92.

157. ———. 1970a. Appalachian Region. Audubon Field Notes 24(1):47–51.

158. ———. 1970b. Appalachian Region. Audubon Field Notes 24(4):601–4.

159. ———. 1972a. Appalachian Region. American Birds 26(3):604–7.

160. ———. 1972b. Appalachian Region. American Birds 26(4):760–63.

161. ———. 1972c. Appalachian Region. American Birds 26(5):857–60.

162. ———. 1973a. Appalachian Region. American Birds 27(1):59–63.

163. ———. 1973b. Appalachian Region. American Birds 27(3):614–17.

164. ———. 1974a. Appalachian Region. American Birds 28(1):52–56.

165. ———. 1974b. Appalachian Region. American Birds 28(3):638–41.

166. ———. 1974c. Appalachian Region. American Birds 28(4):800–804.

167. ———. 1975a. Appalachian Region. American Birds 29(1):57–61.

168. ———. 1975b. Appalachian Region. American Birds 29(3):690–93.

169. ———. 1976a. Appalachian Region. American Birds 30(1):67–71.

170. ———. 1976b. Appalachian Region. American Birds 30(4):841–44.

171. ———. 1977. Appalachian Region. American Birds 31(6):1138–42.

172. ———. 1978. Appalachian Region. American Birds 32(2):203–6.

173. ———. 1979. Appalachian Region. American Birds 33(6):862–64.

174. ———. 1980. Appalachian Region. American Birds 34(6):894–96.

175. ———. 1981a. Appalachian Region. American Birds 35(3):299–301.

176. ———. 1981b. Appalachian Region. American Birds 35(5):822–25.

177. ———. 1981c. Appalachian Region. American Birds 35(6):938–40.

178. ———. 1982a. Appalachian Region. American Birds 36(2):176–79.

179. ———. 1982b. Appalachian Region. American Birds 36(3):293–95.

180. ———. 1984a. Appalachian Region. American Birds 38(2):200–204.

181. ———. 1984b. Appalachian Region. American Birds 38(3):316–18.

182. ———. 1986a. Appalachian Region. American Birds 40(1):111–14.

183. ———. 1986b. Appalachian Region. American Birds 40(2):279–82.

184. ———. 1986c. Appalachian Region. American Birds 40(3):469–72.

185. ———. 1986d. Appalachian Region. American Birds 40(5):1202–5.

186. ———. 1987a. Appalachian Region. American Birds 41(2):281–84.

187. ———. 1987b. Appalachian Region. American Birds 41(3):430–33.

188. Handley, D. 1953. Ancient Murrelet (*Synthliboramphus antiquus*) taken in Erie County, Ohio. Auk 70:206–7.

189. Hasbrouck, E. M. 1944. Apparent status of the European Widgeon in North America. Auk 61:93–104.

190. Hazard, F. O. 1947. An Ohio record for the Wood Ibis. Wilson Bulletin 59:110.

191. Hennessy, T. E., and L. Van Camp. 1963. Wintering Mourning Doves in northern Ohio. Journal of Wildlife Management 27:367-73.

192. Henninger, W. F. 1901. A new bird for the state of Ohio—*Ardea caerulea*. Auk 18:392.

193. ———. 1902. A preliminary list of the birds of middle-southern Ohio. Wilson Bulletin 14:77–93.

194. ———. 1905. Further notes on the birds of middle-southern Ohio. Wilson Bulletin 17:89–93.

195. ———. 1906. Notes on the birds of Seneca County, Ohio. Wilson Bulletin 20:57–60.

196. ———. 1908. Nesting of the Prairie Warbler in Ohio. Wilson Bulletin 20:213.

197. ———. 1910a. Henslow's Sparrow nesting in Ohio. Wilson Bulletin 22:125.

198. ———. 1910b. Notes on some Ohio birds. Auk 27:66–68.

199. ———. 1910c. Horned Lark and Bohemian Waxwing in middle-western Ohio. Wilson Bulletin 22:55.

200. ———. 1910d. Notes on the nesting of Bewick's Wren. Wilson Bulletin 22:57.

201. ———. 1911a. *Falco rusticolus* in Ohio. Wilson Bulletin 23:58.

202. ———. 1911b. Records from the Tri-Reservoir region in Ohio in 1910. Wilson Bulletin 23:61–62.

203. ———. 1916. Notes on some Ohio birds. Wilson Bulletin 28:86–88.

204. ———. 1918. Notes on some Ohio birds. Wilson Bulletin 30:19–21.

205. ———. 1919. An overlooked record of the Trumpeter Swan. Auk 36:564–65.

206. Herman, J. 1981. Ohio records of the Yellow-headed Blackbird (*Xanthocephalus xanthocephalus*). Ohio Cardinal 3(4):31-34.

207. Herrick, F. H. 1924a. An eagle observatory. Auk 41:89–105.

208. ———. 1924b. Nest and nesting habits of the American Eagle. Auk 41:213–31.

209. ———. 1924c. The daily life of the American Eagle: late phase. Auk 41:389–422.

210. ———. 1924d. The daily life of the American Eagle: late phase (concluded). Auk 41:517–43.

211. ———. 1927. The American Eagle at Vermilion, Ohio. Western Reserve University, Cleveland, Ohio. 34 pp.

212. Hicks, L. E. 1931. The American Egret and the Little Blue Heron in Ohio during the summer of 1930. Wilson Bulletin 43:268-81.

213. ———. 1932a. Crested Flycatchers in Ohio in mid-November. Auk 49:222.

214. ———. 1932b. The Snowy Owl invasion of Ohio in 1930-1931. Wilson Bulletin 44:221–26.

215. ———. 1933a. The breeding birds of Ashtabula County, Ohio. Wilson Bulletin 45:168–95.

216. ———. 1933b. The first appearance and spread of the breeding range of the European Starling (*Sturnus vulgaris*) in Ohio. Auk 50:317–22.

217. ———. 1933c. Some breeding records for Ohio. Auk 50:448-49.

218. ———. 1934a. The Hoary Redpoll in Ohio. Auk 51:244–45.

219. ———. 1934b. Some additional Ohio breeding records. Wilson Bulletin 46:201–2.

220. ———. 1935a. Distribution of the breeding birds of Ohio. Ohio Biological Survey, Bulletin No. 32, 6(3):125–90.

221. ———. 1935b. The Louisiana Paroquet in Ohio, Kentucky, and Indiana. Wilson Bulletin 47:76–77.

222. ———. 1936. Notes on the breeding birds of southeastern Ohio. Wilson Bulletin 46:96–103.

223. ———. 1937a. Breeding birds of unglaciated Ohio. Cardinal 4(6):125–41.

224. ———. 1937b. Avocet taken in Ohio. Auk 54:538.

225. ———. 1937c. An Ohio invasion of Le Conte's Sparrow. Auk 54:545–46.

226. ———. 1937d. Western Willet in Ohio. Auk 54:536–37.

227. ———. 1938a. Piping Plover taken in central Ohio. Wilson Bulletin 50:141.

228. ———. 1938b. The Western Meadowlark in Ohio. Auk 55:544-45.

229. ———. 1945a. Blue Grosbeak breeding in Ohio. Auk 62:314.

230. ———. 1945b. Yellow-headed Blackbird breeding in Ohio. Auk 62:314–15.

231. ———. 1945c. Hooded Merganser breeding in Ohio. Auk 62:315–16.

232. ———. 1946. Lark Bunting records for Ohio. Auk 63:256-57.

233. Hussell, D. J. T. 1982. The timing of fall migration in Yellow-bellied Flycatchers. Journal of Field Ornithology 53:1–6.

234. Hyde, A. S. 1939. The life history of Henslow's Sparrow, *Passerherbulus henslowi* (Audubon). University of Michigan Museum of Zoology Miscellaneous Publication No. 41. 72 pp.

235. Jehl, J. R., Jr. 1979. The autumnal migration of Baird's Sandpiper. In F. A. Pitelka, ed. Shorebirds in marine environments. Studies in Avian Biology No. 2., pp. 55–68.

236. Jones, L. 1903. The birds of Ohio, a revised catalogue. Ohio State Academy of Science, Special Papers No. 6. 241 pp.

237. ———. 1904. Additional records of Ohio birds. Ohio Naturalist 4:112–13.

238. ———. 1905. Additions to the birds of Ohio. Wilson Bulletin 17:64.

239. ———. 1907. *Catharista atrata,* Black Vulture, in Harrison County, Ohio. Wilson Bulletin 19:33–34.

240. ———. 1909. The birds of Cedar Point and vicinity. Wilson Bulletin 21:55–76, 114–31, 187–204.

241. ———. 1910. The birds of Cedar Point and vicinity. Wilson Bulletin 22:25–41, 97–115, 172–82.

242. ———. 1911. Exceptional Ohio records. Wilson Bulletin 23:60–61.

243. ———. 1914. Nineteen years of bird migration at Oberlin, Ohio. Wilson Bulletin 26:198–205.

244. ———. 1918. Some Ohio records and notes. Wilson Bulletin 30:120–21.

245. ———. 1941. Prairie Falcon at Oberlin, Ohio. Wilson Bulletin 53:123.

246. Kaatz, M. R. 1955. The Black Swamp: a study in historical geography. Annals of the Association of American Geographers 45:1–35.

247. Kemsies, E., and G. R. Austing. 1950. Smith's Longspur in Ohio. Wilson Bulletin 62:37.

248. Kemsies, E., and W. Randle. 1953. Birds of southwestern Ohio. No publisher listed, Ann Arbor, Michigan. 74 pp.

249. Kendeigh, S. C. 1933. Abundance and conservation of the Bobwhite in Ohio. Ohio Journal of Science 33:1–18.

250. Kimes, E. D. 1912. A few Stark County, Ohio, notes. Wilson Bulletin 24:156–57.

251. Kirtland, J. P. 1838. Report on the zoology of Ohio. Second Annual Report, Geologic Survey of Ohio, pp. 157–77.

252. Kleen, V. M. 1973. Middlewestern Prairie Region. American Birds 27(5):874–78.

253. ———. 1974a. Middlewestern Prairie Region. American Birds 28(1):58–63.

254. ———. 1974b. Middlewestern Prairie Region. American Birds 28(3):645–49.

255. ———. 1974c. Middlewestern Prairie Region. American Birds 28(4):807–10.

256. ———. 1974d. Middlewestern Prairie Region. American Birds 28(5):908–11.

257. ———. 1975a. Middlewestern Prairie Region. American Birds 29(1):64–68.

258. ———. 1975b. Middlewestern Prairie Region. American Birds 29(3):696–700.

259. ———. 1975c. Middlewestern Prairie Region. American Birds 29(4):858–62.

260. ———. 1975d. Middlewestern Prairie Region. American Birds 29(5):978–82.

261. ———. 1976a. Middlewestern Prairie Region. American Birds 30(1):77–82.

262. ———. 1976b. Middlewestern Prairie Region. American Birds 30(4):846–50.

263. ———. 1976c. Middlewestern Prairie Region. American Birds 30(5):961–65.

264. ———. 1977a. Middlewestern Prairie Region. American Birds 31(2):182–86.

265. ———. 1977b. Middlewestern Prairie Region. American Birds 31(3):336–39.

266. ———. 1977c. Middlewestern Prairie Region. American Birds 31(5):1006–10.

267. ———. 1978a. Middlewestern Prairie Region. American Birds 32(2):210–15.

268. ———. 1978b. Middlewestern Prairie Region. American Birds 32(3):357–61.

269. ———. 1978c. Middlewestern Prairie Region. American Birds 32(5):1012–17.

270. ———. 1978d. Middlewestern Prairie Region. American Birds 32(6):1166–71.

271. ———. 1979a. Middlewestern Prairie Region. American Birds 33(2):181–85.

272. ———. 1979b. Middlewestern Prairie Region. American Birds 33(3):285–87.

273. ———. 1979c. Middlewestern Prairie Region. American Birds 33(5):775–78.

274. ———. 1979d. Middlewestern Prairie Region. American Birds 33(6):866–69.

275. ———. 1980a. Middlewestern Prairie Region. American Birds 34(2):166–69.

276. ———. 1980b. Middlewestern Prairie Region. American Birds 34(3):277–79.

277. ———. 1980c. Middlewestern Prairie Region. American Birds 34(5):781–85.

278. ———. 1980d. Middlewestern Prairie Region. American Birds 34(6):898–902.

279. ———. 1981. Middlewestern Prairie Region. American Birds 35(2):187–91.

280. ———, and L. Bush. 1971a. Middlewestern Prairie Region. American Birds 25(4):750–53.

281. ———. 1971b. Middlewestern Prairie Region. American Birds 25(5):862–65.

282. ———. 1972a. Middlewestern Prairie Region. American Birds 26(1):70–73.

283. ———. 1972b. Middlewestern Prairie Region. American Birds 26(3):610–14.

284. ———. 1973a. Middlewestern Prairie Region. American Birds 27(1):66–70.

285. ———. 1973b. Middlewestern Prairie Region. American Birds 27(3):622–25.

286. ———. 1973c. Middlewestern Prairie Region. American Birds 27(4):777–81.

287. Kress, S. W. 1967. A robin nests in winter. Wilson Bulletin 79:245–46.

288. Langdon, F. W. 1877. Occurrence of the Black Vulture, or Carrion Crow, in Ohio. Bulletin of Nuttall Ornithological Club 2:109.

289. ———. 1879. A revised list of Cincinnati birds. Cincinnati Society of Natural History Bulletin 1:167–93.

290. Langlois, T. H., and M. H. Langlois. 1964. Annotated list of the birds of South Bass Island, Lake Erie. Wheaton Club Bulletin 9:29–55.

291. Leedy, D. L., and W. B. Hendershot. 1947. The Ring-necked Pheasant and its management in Ohio. Ohio Division of Wildlife Conservation Bulletin No. 1. 16 pp.

292. Leopold, A. 1947. On a monument to the pigeon. In Silent wings—memorial to the Passenger Pigeon, Wisconsin Society for Ornithology, pp. 3–5.

293. Lindahl, J. 1899. The Black-capped Petrel (*Aestrelata hasitata*) on the Ohio River at Cincinnati. Auk 16:75.

294. Little, R. S. 1969. Field observations of the Wheaton Club. Wheaton Club Bulletin 14.

295. Lloyd, C. K. 1931. Nesting of Bachman's Sparrow in Butler County, Ohio. Wilson Bulletin 43:145.

296. ———. 1943. An unusual nest of the Bronzed Grackle. Wilson Bulletin 55:56.

297. Marshall, R. O. 1931. Birds observed in eastern Ohio, 1930. Oologist 48:43.

298. Maslowski, K. H. 1934. An aerial nest of the Turkey Vulture (*Cathartes aura septentrionalis*). Auk 51:229–30.

299. Mathena, C., J. Hickman, J. Hill, R. Mercer, C. and B. Berry, N. Cherry, and P. Flynn. 1984. The birds of Dayton. Landfall Press, Dayton. 189 pp.

300. Maxwell II, G. R. 1970. Pair formation, nest building and egg laying of the Common Grackle in northern Ohio. Ohio Journal of Science 70:284–91.

301. Mayfield, H. 1943. Glaucous and Great Black-backed Gulls at the western end of Lake Erie. Wilson Bulletin 55:129–30.

302. ———. 1944. First Hudsonian Chickadee for Ohio. Wilson Bulletin 56:46.

303. ———. 1947a. Ohio-Michigan Region. Audubon Field Notes 1(1):7–8.

304. ———. 1947b. Ohio-Michigan Region. Audubon Field Notes 1(3):131, 135.

305. ———. 1947c. Ohio-Michigan Region. Audubon Field Notes 1(5):176–77.

306. ———. 1948. Ohio Region. Audubon Field Notes 2(4):179–80.

307. ———. 1949a. Middlewestern Prairie Region. Audubon Field Notes 3(1):17–19.

308. ———. 1949b. Middlewestern Prairie Region. Audubon Field Notes 3(3):171–72.

309. ———. 1950a. Middlewestern Prairie Region. Audubon Field Notes 4(1):17–19.

310. ———. 1950b. Middlewestern Prairie Region. Audubon Field Notes 4(3):203–5.

311. ———. 1950c. Middlewestern Prairie Region. Audubon Field Notes 4(4):243–45.

312. ———. 1951a. Middlewestern Prairie Region. Audubon Field Notes 5(3):207–8.

313. ———. 1951b. Middlewestern Prairie Region. Audubon Field Notes 5(4):257–59.

314. ———. 1964. Yearly fluctuations in a population of Purple Martins. Auk 81:274–80.

315. ———. 1988. Do Kirtland's Warblers migrate in one hop? Auk 105:204–5.

316. McKinley, D. 1977. Records of the Carolina Parakeet in Ohio. Ohio Journal of Science 77(1):3–9.

317. McLaughlin, V. P. 1979. Occurrence of Large-billed Tern (*Phaetusa simplex*) in Ohio. American Birds 33:727.

318. Miller, L. 1930. The Chestnut-sided and other warblers nesting in Geauga County, Ohio. Wilson Bulletin 42:56–57.

319. Morse, H. G. 1914. Nesting of Prothonotary Warbler near Huron, Ohio. Wilson Bulletin 26:212.

320. Moseley, E. L. 1908. Brunnich's Murre on Lake Erie, 1907. Wilson Bulletin 20:104.

321. Mumford, R. E. 1959a. Middlewestern Prairie Region. Audubon Field Notes 13(1):33–37.

322. ———. 1959b. Middlewestern Prairie Region. Audubon Field Notes 13(3):295–98.

323. ———. 1959c. Middlewestern Prairie Region. Audubon Field Notes 13(4):373–76.

324. ———. 1960a. Middlewestern Prairie Region. Audubon Field Notes 14(1):38–41.

325. ———. 1960b. Middlewestern Prairie Region. Audubon Field Notes 14(3):312–14.

326. ———. 1960c. Middlewestern Prairie Region. Audubon Field Notes 14(5):452–54.

327. ———. 1961a. Middlewestern Prairie Region. Audubon Field Notes 15(1):44–46.

328. ———. 1961b. Middlewestern Prairie Region. Audubon Field Notes 15(3):332–34.

329. ———. 1961c. Middlewestern Prairie Region. Audubon Field Notes 15(4):413–16.

330. ———, and C. E. Keller. 1984. The Birds of Indiana. Indiana University Press, Bloomington. 376 pp.

331. Murphy, J. L., and J. Farrand, Jr. 1979. Prehistoric occurrence of the Ivory-billed Woodpecker (*Campephilus principalis*), Muskingum County, Ohio. Ohio Journal of Science 79:22–23.

332. Mutter, D., D. Nolan, and A. Shartle. 1984. Raptor populations on selected park reserves in Montgomery County, Ohio. Ohio Journal of Science 84:29–32.

333. Newman, D. L. 1958. A nesting of the Acadian Flycatcher. Wilson Bulletin 70:130–44.

334. ———. 1961. House Wren and Bewick's Wren in northern Ohio. Wilson Bulletin 73:84–86.

335. ———. 1969. A field book of the birds of the Cleveland region. Cleveland Museum of Natural History, Cleveland. 46 pp.

336. Nice, M. M. 1937. Studies in the life history of the Song Sparrow. Vol. 1: A population study of the Song Sparrow. Transactions of Linnaean Society of New York, vol. 4. 246 pp.

337. ———. 1939. "Territorial song" and non-territorial behavior of Goldfinches in Ohio. Wilson Bulletin 51:123.

338. ———. 1943. Studies in the life history of the Song Sparrow. Vol. 2: The behavior of the Song Sparrow and other passerines. Transactions of Linnaean Society of New York, vol. 6. 328 pp.

339. Nickell, W. P. 1965. Habitats, territory and nesting of the Catbird. American Midland Naturalist 73:433–78.

340. Nolan, V., Jr. 1953a. Middlewestern Prairie Region. Audubon Field Notes 7(1):18–20.

341. ———. 1953b. Middlewestern Prairie Region. Audubon Field Notes 7(3). 215–16.

342. ———. 1954a. Middlewestern Prairie Region. Audubon Field Notes 8(1):21–23.

343. ———. 1954b. Middlewestern Prairie Region. Audubon Field Notes 8(3):254–56.

344. ———. 1954c. Middlewestern Prairie Region. Audubon Field Notes 8(4):314–16.

345. ———. 1954d. Middlewestern Prairie Region. Audubon Field Notes 8(5):347–49.

346. ———. 1955a. Middlewestern Prairie Region. Audubon Field Notes 9(1):28–31.

347. ———. 1955b. Middlewestern Prairie Region. Audubon Field Notes 9(3):261–62.

348. ———. 1955c. Middlewestern Prairie Region. Audubon Field Notes 9(4):333–35.

349. ———. 1955d. Middlewestern Prairie Region. Audubon Field Notes 9(5):380–82.

350. ———. 1958a. Middlewestern Prairie Region. Audubon Field Notes 12(1):33–36.

351. ———. 1958b. Middlewestern Prairie Region. Audubon Field Notes 12(3):282–84.

352. ———. 1958c. Middlewestern Prairie Region. Audubon Field Notes 12(4):356–58.

353. ———. 1958d. Middlewestern Prairie Region. Audubon Field Notes 12(5):415–17.

354. Norberg, A. H. 1945. The nesting cycle and behavior of the Red-eyed Vireo. M.S. thesis, Ohio State University, Columbus. 48 pp.

355. Novotny, E. 1961. Long-tailed Jaeger in Ohio. Wilson Bulletin 73:280–81.

356. Oberholser, H. C. 1974. The bird life of Texas. Vol. 1. University of Texas Press, Austin. 266 pp.

357. Osborne, D. R., and A. T. Peterson. 1984. Decline of the Upland Sandpiper (*Bartramia longicauda*) in Ohio: an endangered species. Ohio Journal of Science 84:8–10.

358. Owen, D. F. 1963. Polymorphism in the Screech-Owl in eastern North America. Wilson Bulletin 75:183–90.

359. Payne, R. B. 1983. A distributional checklist of the birds of Michigan. University of Michigan Museum of Zoology Miscellaneous Publication No. 164. 71 pp.

360. Peterjohn, B. G. 1981a. Middlewestern Prairie Region. American Birds 35(3):304–7.

361. ———. 1981b. Middlewestern Prairie Region. American Birds 35(5): 828–32.

362. ———. 1981c. Middlewestern Prairie Region. American Birds 35(6):943–47.

363. ———. 1982a. Middlewestern Prairie Region. American Birds 36(2):182–86.

364. ———. 1982b. Middlewestern Prairie Region. American Birds 36(3):298–301.

365. ———. 1982c. Middlewestern Prairie Region. American Birds 36(5):857–61.

366. ———. 1982d. Middlewestern Prairie Region. American Birds 36(6):981–85.

367. ———. 1982e. Breeding avifauna of the South Bloomingville Quadrangle, Hocking County, Ohio. Report submitted to Ohio Department of Natural Resources, Division of Natural Areas and Preserves. 34 pp.

368. ———. 1983a. Middlewestern Prairie Region. American Birds 37(2):185–89.

369. ———. 1983b. Middlewestern Prairie Region. American Birds 37(3): 306–9.

370. ———. 1983c. Middlewestern Prairie Region. American Birds 37(5):874–78.

371. ———. 1983d. Middlewestern Prairie Region. American Birds 37(6):992–95.

372. ———. 1984a. Middlewestern Prairie Region. American Birds 38(2):207–11.

373. ———. 1984b. Middlewestern Prairie Region. American Birds 38(3):322–25.

374. ———. 1984c. Middlewestern Prairie Region. American Birds 38(5):916–20.

375. ———. 1984d. Middlewestern Prairie Region. American Birds 38(6):1024–28.

376. ———. 1985a. Middlewestern Prairie Region. American Birds 39(1):59–63.

377. ———. 1985b. Middlewestern Prairie Region. American Birds 39(2):171–74.

378. ———. 1985c. Middlewestern Prairie Region. American Birds 39(3):305–10.

379. ———. 1985d. Middlewestern Prairie Region. American Birds 39(5):917–20.

380. ———. 1986a. Middlewestern Prairie Region. American Birds 40(1):118–23.

381. ———. 1986b. Middlewestern Prairie Region. American Birds 40(2):285–89.

382. ———. 1986c. Middlewestern Prairie Region. American Birds 40(3):476–81.

383. ———. 1986d. Middlewestern Prairie Region. American Birds 40(5):1208–12.

384. ———. 1987a. Middlewestern Prairie Region. American Birds 41(1):93–99.

385. ———. 1987b. Middlewestern Prairie Region. American Birds 41(2):286–90.

386. ———. 1987c. Middlewestern Prairie Region. American Birds 41(3):437–41.

387. ———. 1987d. Middlewestern Prairie Region. American Birds 41(5):1440–44.

388. ———. 1988a. Middlewestern Prairie Region. American Birds 42(1):80–85.

388a. ———. 1988b. Middlewestern Prairie Region. American Birds 42(2):270–74, 42(3):440–44, 42(5):1293–98.

389. ———, R. L. Hannikman, J. M. Hoffman, and E. J. Tramer. 1987. Abundance and distribution of the birds of Ohio. Ohio Biological Survey, Biological Notes No. 19. 52 pp.

390. Petersen, P. C., Jr. 1963. Middlewestern Prairie Region. Audubon Field Notes 17(4):407–9.

391. ———. 1964a. Middlewestern Prairie Region. Audubon Field Notes 18(1):42–44.

392. ———. 1964b. Middlewestern Prairie Region. Audubon Field Notes 18(3):359–60.

393. ———. 1964c. Middlewestern Prairie Region. Audubon Field Notes 18(4):454–56.

394. ———. 1964d. Middlewestern Prairie Region. Audubon Field Notes 18(5):511–12.

395. ———. 1965a. Middlewestern Prairie Region. Audubon Field Notes 19(1):44–46.

396. ———. 1965b. Middlewestern Prairie Region. Audubon Field Notes 19(3):383–85.

397. ———. 1965c. Middlewestern Prairie Region. Audubon Field Notes 19(4):480–82.

398. ———. 1965d. Middlewestern Prairie Region. Audubon Field Notes 19(5):551–52.

399. ———. 1966a. Middlewestern Prairie Region. Audubon Field Notes 20(3):429–31.

400. ———. 1966b. Middlewestern Prairie Region. Audubon Field Notes 20(4):513–15.

401. ———. 1966c. Middlewestern Prairie Region. Audubon Field Notes 20(5):574–75.

402. ———. 1967a. Middlewestern Prairie Region. Audubon Field Notes 21(1):44–45.

403. ———. 1967b. Middlewestern Prairie Region. Audubon Field Notes 21(4):513–14.

404. ———. 1967c. Middlewestern Prairie Region. Audubon Field Notes 21(5):577–78.

405. ———. 1968a. Middlewestern Prairie Region. Audubon Field Notes 22(3):443–45.

406. ———. 1968b. Middlewestern Prairie Region. Audubon Field Notes 22(5):612–14.

407. ———. 1969. Middlewestern Prairie Region. Audubon Field Notes 23(4):596–97.

408. ———. 1970a. Middlewestern Prairie Region. Audubon Field Notes 24(1):54–55.

409. ———. 1970b. Middlewestern Prairie Region. Audubon Field Notes 24(3):509–11.

410. ———. 1970c. Middlewestern Prairie Region. Audubon Field Notes 24(4):608, 613–15.

411. ———. 1970d. Middlewestern Prairie Region. Audubon Field Notes 24(5):689–91.

412. ———. 1971. Middlewestern Prairie Region. Audubon Field Notes 25(1):64–66.

413. Peterson, A. T. 1986. Rock Doves nesting in trees. Wilson Bulletin 98:168–69.

414. Phillips, A. S. 1975. Semipalmated Sandpiper: identification, migrations, summer and winter ranges. American Birds 29(4):799–806.

415. Phillips, R. S. 1963. Scissor-tailed Flycatcher in Ohio. Wilson Bulletin 75:273–74.

416. ———. 1967. Buff-breasted Sandpiper in northwestern Ohio. Wilson Bulletin 79:340.

417. ———. 1980. Birds of the Hancock County, Ohio, area. Findlay College, Findlay. 154 pp.

418. Price, H. F. 1928a. Late nesting of Barn Swallow. Oologist 45:11.

419. ———. 1928b. Notes on the Turkey Vulture. Oologist 45:62–63.

420. ———. 1931. Persistence in nesting of the Prairie Horned Lark. Oologist 48:146.

421. ———. 1932. Destruction of birds' nests on two Ohio farms. Oologist 49:102.

422. ———. 1934a. The hawks, eagles, and vultures of northwestern Ohio. Oologist 51:29–35.

423. ———. 1934b. Herons and bitterns of northwestern Ohio. Oologist 51:77–79.

424. ———. 1935. The summer birds of northwestern Ohio. Oologist 52:26–36.

425. ———. 1940a. Some Ohio and Indiana nesting dates for 1940. Oologist 57:98–101.

426. ———. 1940b. Notes on a Black Rail. Oologist 57:54.

427. ———. 1941. Nests and eggs of the Cooper's Hawk. Oologist 58:26–27.

428. ———. 1946. Burrowing Owl in Ohio. Auk 63:450–51.

429. ———. 1972. The nesting birds of northwestern Ohio. Wheaton Club Bulletin (New Series) 17.

430. Putnam, L. S. 1949. The life history of the Cedar Waxwing. Wilson Bulletin 61:141–82.

431. ———, G. Maxwell, and S. Tilley. 1964. Sight record of the

Glossy Ibis for the Bass Islands, Lake Erie, Ohio. Wilson Bulletin 76:98.

432. Randle, W. 1963. Solitary Vireo found nesting in south-central Ohio's Hocking County. Wilson Bulletin 75:277–78.

433. ———, and R. Austing. 1952. Ecological notes on Long-eared and Saw-whet Owls in southwestern Ohio. Ecology 33:422–26.

434. Rice, D., and B. Peterjohn. Ohio breeding bird atlas. Ohio Department of Natural Resources, Division of Natural Areas and Preserves. In preparation.

435. Richter, G. W. 1939. Ohio nesting dates for 1938. Oologist 56:40–41.

436. Roads, M. K. 1931. Doves use an old robin's nest. Auk 48:265.

437. ———. 1936. An early Ohio record of the Bachman's Sparrow. Wilson Bulletin 48:310.

438. Robbins, C. S., D. Bystrak, and P. H. Geissler. 1986. The breeding bird survey: its first fifteen years, 1965–1979. U.S. Fish and Wildlife Service Resource Publication No. 157. 196 pp.

439. Rogers, G. T. 1955. Red Phalarope in Ohio. Wilson Bulletin 67:63–64.

440. Savage, P. H. 1962. Black-throated Sparrow (*Amphispiza bilineata*) occurrence in northern Ohio. Redstart 29:75.

441. Sawyer, E. 1934. Yellow-headed Blackbird (*Xanthocephalus xanthocephalus*) in Ohio. Auk 51:527.

442. Schorger, A. W. 1955. The Passenger Pigeon, its natural history and extinction. University of Wisconsin Press, Madison. 424 pp.

443. Shaub, M. S. 1963. Evening Grosbeak winter invasions—1958–59, 1959–60, 1960–61. Bird-Banding 34:1–22.

444. Sheppard, J. M. 1959. Sprague's Pipit and Smith's Longspur in Ohio. Auk 76:362–63.

445. Shieldcastle, M. C. 1980. First state nesting record of Wilson's Phalarope. Ohio Cardinal 3(2):1–2.

446. Shields, M. A., and T. W. Townsend. 1985. Nesting success of Ohio's endangered Common Tern. Ohio Journal of Science 85:45–49.

447. Sim, R. J. 1907. The Chestnut-sided Warbler nesting at Jefferson, Ashtabula County, Ohio. Ohio Naturalist 8:209–10.

448. ———. 1908. Another Brunnich's Murre record for Ohio. Wilson Bulletin 20:54.

449. Skaggs, M. B. 1932. Rare bird visitors at Youngstown, Ohio. Bird-Lore 34:389.

450. ———. 1934. A study of the Bewick's Wren in northeastern Ohio. Bird-Lore 36:301–2.

451. ———. 1936a. The Mute Swan and European Wigeon in Ohio. Wilson Bulletin 48:131.

452. ———. 1936b. The occurrence of white herons in the Youngstown, Ohio, region. Wilson Bulletin 48:269–72.

453. ———. 1945. First Ohio record of the Lark Bunting. Auk 62:313.

454. Smith, J. L. 1980. Decline of the Bewick's Wren. Redstart 47:77–82.

455. Smith, K. G. 1986. Winter bird population dynamics of three species of mast-eating birds in the eastern United States. Wilson Bulletin 98:407–18.

456. Snyder, L. L. 1947. The Snowy Owl migration of 1945–46. Wilson Bulletin 59:74–78.

457. Stevenson, J. 1928. Additional notes from Wayne County, Ohio. Auk 45:226–27.

458. Stewart, P. A. 1931. Cavity nesting robins. Wilson Bulletin 43:59.

459. ———. 1952. Winter mortality of Barn Owls in central Ohio. Wilson Bulletin 64:164–66.

460. ———. 1957. Nesting of the Shoveller (*Spatula clypeata*) in central Ohio. Wilson Bulletin 69:280.

461. Stoll, R. J., Jr., and M. W. McClain. 1986. Distribution and relative abundance of the Ruffed Grouse in Ohio. Ohio Journal of Science 86:182–85.

462. Stout, W., K. Ver Steeg, and G. F. Lamb. 1943. Geology of water in Ohio. Ohio Geological Survey Bulletin 44. 694 pp.

463. Sturm, L. 1945. A study of the nesting activities of the American Redstart. Auk 62:189–206.

464. Swales, B. H. 1918. The Purple Sandpiper at Cleveland, Ohio. Occasional Papers, University of Michigan Museum of Zoology No. 57. 2 pp.

465. Thomas, E. S. 1928a. Nesting of the Black Vulture in Hocking County, Ohio. Ohio State Museum of Science Bulletin 1:29-35.

466. ———. 1928b. The Snowy Owl invasion of 1926–1927. Ohio State Museum of Science Bulletin 1:64–69.

467. ———. 1932. Chuck-will's-widow, a new bird for Ohio. Auk 49:479.

468. ———. 1951. Black-throated Gray Warbler in Ohio. Wilson Bulletin 63:206.

469. ———. 1980. Rare woodpecker at OSU Museum. Ohio Cardinal 3(4):4–5.

470. Thomas, M. W., and E. P. Hengst. 1949. Little Gull at Columbus, Ohio. Wilson Bulletin 61:236.

471. Thomson, T. 1983. Birding in Ohio. Indiana University Press, Bloomington. 256 pp.

472. Tramer, E. J., and L. W. Campbell. 1986. Laughing Gull nesting attempt on Lake Erie. Wilson Bulletin 98:170–71.

473. Transeau, E. N. 1935. The prairie peninsula. Ecology 16:423–37.

474. Trautman, M. B. 1926. Kittiwake in Ohio. Auk 43:228.

475. ———. 1928. Notes on Ohio shorebirds. Ohio State Museum of Science Bulletin 1:40–44.

476. ———. 1933. Some recent Ohio records. Auk 50:234–36.

477. ———. 1935a. Notes on some Ohio birds. Auk 52:201–2.

478. ———. 1935b. Additional notes on some Ohio birds. Auk 52:321–23.

479. ———. 1940. The birds of Buckeye Lake, Ohio. University of Michigan Museum of Zoology Miscellaneous Publication No. 44. 466 pp.

480. ———. 1946. A second Ohio record for the Eared Grebe. Wilson Bulletin 58:216.

481. ———. 1956. Unusual bird records for Ohio. Auk 73:272–76.

482. ———. 1962. The 39th Buckeye Lake Audubon Christmas Bird Count and notes concerning the Black-capped Chickadee invasion of 1961–62. Wheaton Club Bulletin 6:14–17.

483. ———. 1977. The Ohio country from 1750 to 1977: a naturalist's view. Ohio Biological Survey, Biological Notes No. 10. 25 pp.

484. ———. 1978. Autumn migrations of selected species of ducks at Buckeye Lake, Ohio. Ohio Biological Survey, Biological Notes No. 11. 10 pp.

485. ———. 1981. The fishes of Ohio. Ohio State University Press, Columbus. 782 pp.

486. ———, and S. J. Glines. 1964. A nesting of the Purple Gallinule (*Porphyrula martinica*) in Ohio. Auk 81:224–26.

487. Trautman, M. B., and T. W. Nye. 1968. An Ohio record of the Magnificent Frigatebird (*Fregata magnificens*). Wilson Bulletin 80:487–88.

488. Trautman, M. B., and M. A. Trautman. 1968. Annotated list of the birds of Ohio. Ohio Journal of Science 68:257–332.

489. ———. 1971. Three additions to the "Annotated list of the birds of Ohio." Ohio Journal of Science 71:216.

490. Tuttle, C. 1895. Some uncommon and rare birds of Erie County, Ohio. Auk 12:190–91.

491. Van Camp, L. 1974. The Bald Eagle. Toledo Naturalists Association 1974 Yearbook, pp. 11–17.

492. ———, and C. J. Henny. 1975. The Screech Owl: its life history and population ecology in northern Ohio. U.S. Fish and Wildlife Service, North American Fauna No. 71. 65 pp.

493. Van Camp, L., and H. Mayfield. 1943. Two Long-eared Owl nests near Toledo, Ohio. Wilson Bulletin 55:54–55.

494. Walker, C. F. 1928a. Wintering Mniotiltidae in central Ohio. Auk 45:231–33.

495. ———. 1928b. The Yellow-crowned Night-Heron nesting in Logan County, Ohio. Auk 45:370.

496. ———. 1928c. Henslow's Sparrow in Ohio. Ohio State Museum of Science Bulletin 1:45–46.

497. ———. 1928d. Notes on the breeding warblers of central Ohio. Ohio State Museum of Science Bulletin 1:53–58.

498. ———. 1931. An Ohio record for the European Teal. Wilson Bulletin 43:69.

499. ———. 1937a. Dayton Region. Bird-Lore 39(5):395–96.

500. ———. 1937b. Dayton Region. Bird-Lore 39(6):472–73.

501. ———. 1938a. Dayton Region. Bird-Lore 40(3):222–23.

502. ———. 1938b. Dayton Region. Bird-Lore 40(4):289–90.

503. ———. 1938c. Put-in-Bay Region. Bird-Lore 40(6):462–63.

504. ———. 1939a. Dayton Region. Bird-Lore 41(3):188–89.

505. ———. 1939b. Put-in-Bay Region. Bird-Lore 41(5):7–8 (supplement).

506. ———. 1939c. Put-in-Bay Region. Bird-Lore 41(6):7–9 (supplement).

507. ———. 1940a. Put-in-Bay Region. Bird-Lore 42(2):217–18.

508. ———. 1940b. Put-in-Bay Region. Bird-Lore 42(3):304–5.

509. ———. 1940c. Put-in-Bay Region. Bird-Lore 42(4):385–86.

510. ———. 1940d. Ohio Region. Bird-Lore 42(5):464–65.

511. ———. 1940e. Ohio Region. Bird-Lore 42(6):575–76.

512. ———. 1941. Clay-colored Sparrow in Ohio. Wilson Bulletin 53:46.

513. ———, and R. W. Franks. 1928. Birds of an Ohio cranberry bog. Ohio State Museum Science Bulletin 1:59–63.

514. Walkinshaw, L. H. 1960. Migration of the Sandhill Crane east of the Mississippi River. Wilson Bulletin 72:358–84.

515. Webb, L. G. 1949. The life history of the Mourning Dove, *Zenaidura macroura carolinensis* (Linnaeus), in Ohio. Ph.D. thesis, Ohio State University, Columbus. 147 pp.

516. Westerkov, K. E. 1949. A comparative study of the ecology and management of the European Partridge (*Perdix perdix*) in Ohio and Denmark. M.S. thesis, Ohio State University, Columbus. 339 pp.

517. ———. 1956. History and distribution of the Hungarian Partridge in Ohio. Ohio Journal of Science 56:65–70.

518. Wetmore, A. 1943. Evidence of the former occurrence of the Ivory-billed Woodpecker in Ohio. Wilson Bulletin 55:55.

519. Wharram, S. V. 1921. Notes from Ashtabula County, Ohio. Wilson Bulletin 33:146–47.

520. Wheaton, J. M. 1877. The Ruff and Purple Gallinule in Ohio. Bulletin of Nuttall Ornithological Club 2:83.

521. ———. 1879. Occurrence of birds rare to the vicinity of Columbus, Ohio. Bulletin of Nuttall Ornithological Club 4:62–63.

522. ———. 1882. Report on the birds of Ohio. Ohio Geologic Survey Bulletin 4:187–628.

523. Williams, A. B. 1950. Birds of the Cleveland Region. Kirtland Society Bulletin No. 2. Cleveland Museum of Natural History, Cleveland. 215 pp.

524. Wright, A. M. 1912. Early records of the Carolina Paroquet. Auk 29:343–63.

525. ———. 1915. Early records of the Wild Turkey, part 4. Auk 32:207–24.

526. Young, J. P. 1914. A flight of shorebirds near Youngstown, Ohio. Wilson Bulletin 26:193–95.

INDEX

EDITOR: Kenneth Goodall
DESIGNER: Matt Williamson
MANAGING EDITOR: Roberta L. Diehl
PRODUCTION COORDINATOR: Harriet Curry
TYPEFACE: Linotron Berkeley with Centaur display
COMPOSITOR: Impressions, Inc.
PRINTER & BINDER: Toppan

DICTIONARY
OF
AMERICAN HISTORY

DICTIONARY
OF
AMERICAN
HISTORY

SUPPLEMENT

Robert H. Ferrell and Joan Hoff, Senior Editors

PART 2
MacArthur Foundation—Zoology

Charles Scribner's Sons Reference Books
MACMILLAN LIBRARY REFERENCE USA
SIMON & SCHUSTER MACMILLAN
NEW YORK

SIMON & SCHUSTER AND PRENTICE HALL INTERNATIONAL
LONDON • MEXICO CITY • NEW DELHI • SINGAPORE • SYDNEY • TORONTO

Library of Congress Cataloging-in-Publication Data
Dictionary of American history. Supplement / Robert H. Ferrell and
  Joan Hoff, editors.
      p.   cm.
    Includes bibliographical references and index.
    Contents: pt. 1. AARP–Lyme Disease — pt. 2. MacArthur Foundation–Zoology.
    ISBN 0-684-19579-8 (set : alk. paper). — ISBN 0-684-80464-6 (pt.
  1). — ISBN 0-684-80465-4 (pt. 2)
    1. United States—History—Dictionaries.   I. Ferrell, Robert H.
  II. Hoff, Joan, 1939–   .
  E174.D52 1976 Suppl
  973'.03—dc20   96-7844
                                                                    CIP

            1 3 5 7 9 11 13 15 17 19 20 18 16 14 12 10 8 6 4 2

DICTIONARY
OF
AMERICAN HISTORY

MacArthur Foundation–Zoology

M

MacARTHUR FOUNDATION "GENIUS" AWARDS. Launched in 1981, the fellowship program of the John D. and Catherine T. MacArthur Foundation of Chicago annually awards "no-strings" grants of between $150,000 and $375,000 to creative individuals in all fields and supports them for five-year periods. Although the awards became popularly known as "genius grants," that is not a term encouraged by the foundation. The nomination process is secret but criteria include creativity, the person's contribution to society, and the potential effect on the recipient's career. The foundation was created by the billionaire founder of Bankers Life and Casualty, John D. MacArthur (1897–1978) and instituted upon his death. As of 1991 it was the fifth largest foundation in the United States. Of the 350 awards distributed between 1981 and 1991, 109 were in the sciences, 81 in the arts, 70 in the humanities, 53 in public affairs, and 37 in the social sciences.

[Anne Matthews, "The MacArthur Truffle Hunt," *New York Times Magazine* (June 7, 1992); Denise G. Shekerjian, *Uncommon Genius* (New York, 1990).]

JEFFREY M. MERRON

MAGAZINES. Following World War II specialization became the route to success, or at least survival, for magazines. In the 1990s general interest weeklies such as the *Saturday Evening Post* were gone, but magazine racks groaned beneath the weight of new ventures, most of which quickly sank. Weeklies such as *Sports Illustrated* and *Money* attracted upscale readers that advertisers wanted to reach, as did such monthlies as *Bride's* and *Yachting*. *Time* and other giants changed ads and copy on selected pages in each weekly edition, and thus delivered issues customized geographically and according to readers' interests. For example, a college student's issue could differ from the one delivered that same week to his or her parents.

A few regional magazines prospered, notably *Sunset*, a home magazine for readers in the West, and *Southern Living*. Although most city magazines concentrated on listing restaurants and entertainment, a few, such as *Philadelphia Magazine*, won national reporting awards. Many specialized publications, such as *Engineering News-Record*, boasted large but controlled circulations, that is, they were mailed free to every individual in the defined field but others could not even buy a copy. Again, this served the advertisers who want to reach only their best prospects. Magazines for African Americans multiplied and also specialized. *Ebony* prospered as a general monthly, while other publications targeted black young women (*Essence*), businessmen (*Black Enterprise*), and scholars (*Black Scholar*).

As the number of newsstands began to diminish after World War II, retail stores, especially supermarkets, became major magazine outlets. Although supermarket tabloids look like newspapers, the Audit Bureau of Circulations classified them as magazines. In 1994 the six largest sold a total of 10 million copies a week, with the *National Enquirer* having the largest circulation. Comic books, many intended for adults, made a comeback in the 1980s. Illustration and text became more diverse in men's magazines. *Playboy*'s pages contained not only pictures of nude women and cartoons but also works by leading authors. Another showplace for writing was *Esquire*, whose contributors were at the center of the so-called "new journalism," in which writers immersed themselves in topics to convey the "true essence" to readers, even if it required invented dialogue and composite characters. Literary magazines, mostly quarterlies affiliated with universities, continued to publish fiction and poetry.

Reader's Digest continued to lead all general magazines in circulation, with a paid circulation in 1993 of more than 16 million copies. Although *Modern Maturity* had a larger circulation, it is tied to a membership organization, the American Association of Retired Persons. At the same time, *TV Guide* was the leading weekly. Women's magazines (*Better Homes and Gardens, Family Circle, Good Housekeeping*) were among the top ten magazines in 1993. *Time* continued to outsell other newsmagazines by more than 1 million copies, and its 1993 circulation of 4.1 million was followed on the list of leading magazines by *People,* with 3.4 million copies. Magazines in the 1990s were increasingly being published on CD-ROM for access by computers.

[Michael Emery and Edwin Emery, *The Press and America* (Englewood Cliffs, N.J., 1988).]

JOHN D. STEVENS

MAGNETIC RESONANCE IMAGING (MRI), first used for medical purposes in 1976, is based on the phenomenon of nuclear magnetic resonance reported in 1946 by Felix Bloch of Stanford University and Edward Purcell of Harvard University, physicists awarded the Nobel Prize in 1952. Using complicated equipment to measure resonating frequencies emitted by tissue components, images of those tissues are constructed in much the same way as in CAT (computerized axial tomography) scanning. Information can be obtained about the soft tissues of the body, such as the brain, spinal cord, heart, kidneys, and liver, but not bone. MRI does not involve ionizing radiations and is noninvasive.

[Joseph K. T. Lee, Stuart S. Sagel, and Robert J. Stanley, eds., *Computed Body Tomography with MRI Correlation* (New York, 1989).]

PETER H. WRIGHT

See also **SUPP:** Computerized Axial Tomography.

MAGNET SCHOOLS. *See* **Schools, Magnet.**

MAIL-ORDER INDUSTRY. The techniques for promoting, selling, and distributing products through the mail or private delivery services have become increasingly diverse and sophisticated since the 1970s. In addition to continued growth of established mail-order companies, many new ventures started as small businesses or as offshoots of larger businesses. L. L. Bean is perhaps the best-known example of a traditional company that grew into a successful national mail-order retailer. The Sharper Image is one of a new generation of mail-order retailers, specializing in unusual, upscale items. Mail-order hence became more important to many retailers whose businesses were primarily based on in-store sales. Social and economic trends such as the increased number of working couples with less time to shop stimulated mail-order sales. Business buyers began to rely on mail-order vendors when they purchased equipment and supplies. The proliferation of credit cards and other types of financing and introduction of toll-free long-distance 800 numbers made buying faster and easier.

Promotional mailings and advertising targeted demographic groups. Development of complex computer databases, comprehensive mailing lists, and other information technology allowed merchandisers to pinpoint the most likely buyers for their products based on income, past purchases, and personal interest. The comprehensive information-gathering methods and pervasive nature of the new forms of direct marketing raised some concern about individual privacy. One sign of the shift from mass merchandising to more specific approaches was the decision by two of the original mail-order giants—Sears (in 1993) and Montgomery Ward (in 1985)—to discontinue their large general catalogs. They formed partnerships with other firms to produce smaller, more specialized catalogs at lower costs.

Printed catalogs and order forms continued to be a mainstay of mail-order marketing, but other marketing techniques became important as postal rates and other mailing costs increased. Television became a powerful direct-sales tool. The Home Shopping Network pioneered this approach in 1985 with continual on-air sales pitches for products that viewers ordered directly by telephone. The distinction between commercials and other programming had not always been clear in the early days of television. Sponsors produced entertainment shows in which their products were prominently featured in the name of and during the show, such as Texaco's sponsorship of Milton Berle's variety hour. In the late 1950s and the 1960s regulations and industry standard brought more clear-cut separations between commercials and programming, but this changed in the mid-1980s, when program-length commercials, known as "infomercials," began to appear on cable networks and later on broadcast channels. Infomercials are often made to resemble newscasts, talk shows, or other programming but are actually half-hour commercials. Unlike earlier sponsor-identified shows that also provided entertainment, the sole purpose of infomercials is to sell specific products.

Computers emerged as a vehicle for direct marketing. On-line services (telephone-based commercial networks that link computer users) began to feature "electronic malls" with descriptions of products that people could order on their computers. Merchants began to experiment with electronic multimedia catalogs, with products presented on CD computer disks or videocassettes. Another form of direct sales was telemarketing, in which salespeople (or automated recordings) made unsolicited and often irritating sales pitches to potential customers by telephone. The growth of direct marketing slowed with the recession of the late 1980s and early 1990s, when some of the new companies using innovative marketing failed. Renewal of economic growth persuaded survivors to press on.

[Ed Burnett, *The Complete Direct Mail List Handbook* (Englewood Cliffs, N.J., 1988); Cecil C. Hoge, *The Electronic Marketing Manual* (New York, 1993); Erik Larson, *The Naked Consumer* (New York, 1992).]

JOHN TOWNES

See also **SUPP:** Advertising; Credit Cards; Direct Mail; Home Shopping Networks.

MAINE began to change in the 1970s in ways that by the end of the twentieth century necessitated a new image for a state with a heritage of community, friendliness, and independence. For a while, the economic scene was troublesome. The closing of many mills and other industries during the recession of the 1970s forced workers to accept lesser positions or unemployment checks. Many left the state. Cutbacks in defense spending forced layoffs at the Bath Iron Works and the Portsmouth Naval Shipyard in Kittery. Since 1985, however, people looking for a better way of life and a safe place to raise children moved into the state. Low bank-loan rates encouraged residential construction, providing many jobs for skilled workers. The cities of Maine saw many changes in the 1980s. Shopping malls expanded, forcing downtown retailers to close their doors. Community-supported arts flourished. Portland, Bangor, and Lewiston-Auburn drew visitors and local residents to art museums, a wide range of musical events, theater arts, and dance company performances. Maine experienced a striking increase in tourism, especially to such ski resorts as Sugarloaf U.S.A.

Maine's population in 1990 was 1,233,223, and changing demographics had exacerbated social and economic divisions, giving rise to the terms "the two Maines" or "the other Maine." Many parts of the state remained economically undeveloped, with rural poverty in farming and seasonal employment in the tourist industry. Maine remained a nearly white state, with a minority population of 2.5 percent that included African Americans, Native Americans, and a slightly rising number of Asians and Hispanics clustering in the major cities. With the economic expansion in southern Maine, something of a north-south split evolved. Census information from 1989 indicated a substantial difference in median household incomes between York County in the southern part of the state ($32,432) and Washington County in the north ($19,993). For all their differences, most Maine residents remained committed to the preservation of the environment and the natural beauty and resources of the state. A significant portion of the economy continued to be based on the natural resources of land, rivers, and the sea. Access to wilderness areas for recreation and sport was a priority, even when economic development opportunities were in conflict. Education was also a high priority for the people of Maine, as state residents realized that quality public education and technical schools attracted businesses to the state, which created jobs for Maine in the competitive global economy. In the late twentieth century commercial fishing was still a vital part of the economic stability of the state. In 1989 commercial fishing produced a catch valued at more than $132 million, including $60 million from lobstering. Inland, the Maine forest industry provided a livelihood for more than 100,000 residents. Timber was harvested primarily for paper (1.3 million cords in 1989).

Politically, the once staunchly Republican state saw a rise in Democratic representation. In 1978 Maine voters elected Democrat Joseph Brennan as governor to succeed an independent, James Longley, who had promised to serve only one term. Without raising taxes, Governor Brennan restored many public services diminished during previous years. He was succeeded for two terms by John McKernan, the first Republican governor in twenty years. Appointed by Brennan to the U.S. Senate to fill the term of Edmund Muskie, George Mitchell went on to be elected Senate majority leader in 1988. His decision to leave the Senate in 1994 dramatically affected Maine politics, widening the pool of candidates seeking office, bringing new voices and ideas to lead Maine into the twenty-first century. Looking for new direction and the promise of broad-based nonpartisan leadership, the citizens of Maine rejected "politics as usual" in November 1994 and elected another independent, Angus King, as governor.

Property taxes rose dramatically in Maine from the 1970s to the 1990s, partly as a result of economic growth and reduced federal assistance. In 1988 the state legislature enacted a program that offered direct financial assistance for low- and moderate-income households and increased municipal revenue-sharing from sales tax and income tax collections. Middle-income property owners assumed most of the tax burden. In 1974 a state lottery began, and in 1994 proposals were presented for gambling casinos run by Native Americans.

[Richard Barringer, *Changing Maine* (Portland, Maine, 1990); Joseph McGonigle, *Maine's Changing Face* (Augusta, Maine, 1989); Neil Rolde, *Maine* (Gardiner, Maine, 1990).]

GAIL S. THOMPSON

MALLS, SHOPPING, have their predecessors in the covered bazaars of the Middle East, the arcades of Victorian England, and the skylighted galleries of Italy. The first shopping centers in the United States were located in the downtown sections of suburban areas, near major intersections, with free off-street parking. The Country Club Plaza, built in 1922 in Kansas City, is a Spanish-motif extravaganza extending over several city blocks that is still in operation. The first truly regional shopping center (which attracts consumers from a twenty-mile radius) was Northgate on the outskirts of Seattle (1950), with a long open-air pedestrian walkway and a large anchor department store surrounded by smaller shops. This was followed by the first completely enclosed shopping center, Southdale, in Edina, Minn., built in 1956. The 1970s and 1980s witnessed expanded construction of shopping centers, such as the Galleria in Houston and Woodfield near Chicago. Shopping malls proliferated from the mid-1970s until by the end of 1992, according to the National Research Bureau, there were 38,966 across the country, of which 1,835 were large regional malls.

Due to overbuilding and undue competition, shopping malls began to experience an economic downturn in the late 1980s. Pressed for time and short of money, exhausted consumers lost interest in leisure shopping and turned to factory-outlet centers such as Sawgrass Mills in Sunrise, Fla., which covers 120 acres and is the world's largest outlet mall. Catalog purchasing, home shopping networks on television, and specialty stores such as Home Depot and Price Club also diminished mall shopping. Mall builders soon realized that new marketing was necessary and started a bread-and-circuses approach, in some instances attempting to make malls into virtual tourist attractions. Malls such as that in Las Vegas, Nevada, have become popular vacation spots. They are esteemed for the variety of activities, number of stores, and quality of entertainment provided. These huge malls are true urban centers with post offices, hotels, and even amusement parks and schools in a weather-proof, safe, clean environment. They have became social centers where young people meet their friends and socialize rather than shop. Elderly people walk the malls for exercise, not merchandise. The mega-malls offer visitors such diversions as theme parks, miniature golf, bungee jumping, and water slides.

The Mall of America, which opened in the summer of 1992 on seventy-eight acres in Bloomington, Minn., is the largest enclosed shopping center in the United States. It is enormous—five times larger than Red Square in Moscow and twenty times larger than Saint Peter's Basilica in Rome—and covers 4.2 million square feet and cost $625 million to construct. It is a successful prototype of futuristic shopping, attracting 130,000 visitors a day, each of whom spends an average of four hours in the mall. Families and international tourists patronize restaurants, theaters, and fine stores and can go on amusement rides in the seven-acre Knott's Camp Snoopy, the nation's largest indoor theme park, with a carousel, log flume ride, and one-half-mile-long roller coaster.

[Joel Garreau, *Edge City: Life on the New Frontier* (New York, 1991).]

JOHN J. BYRNE

See also **SUPP:** Advertising; Home Shopping Networks; Mail-Order Industry; Retailing Industry.

MANNERS, as described in Edith Wharton's *The Age of Innocence* (1920) and Emily Post's *Etiquette* (1922), reflected a sense of propriety that was expected of everyone. Critics of the late twentieth century claimed that since then incivility has become more common than politeness. The alleged breakdown of family, church, and neighborhood led to a more individualized society, because of the protest spirit of the 1960s, which preached freedom for the individual from the constraints of societal conformity and which resulted in free love and the hippie movement. Responsibilities to the community, the critics said, were abandoned. In a time when presidents are called by their first names (Jimmy, Ron, Bill), or even by their nicknames ("Bubba"), and when sneakers have become the footwear of choice in workplaces, increasing casualness may be leading to widespread vulgarity. A 1993 poll by *Reader's Digest* revealed that both men and women swear an average of sixteen times a day. At home, preschoolers often adopt rude behavior and language, not realizing the consequences of their remarks. By emphasizing self-expression over manners, parents often do not train children early in politeness and courtesy. In business, managers claim they are too busy to be polite. Workers interested in career development are told they must adapt to the corporate culture with a take-charge attitude that often conflicts with good manners.

Nevertheless, people are social animals, and codes of conduct do exist in modern society. Business etiquette dictates a hierarchical seating at meetings, appropriate dress styles, and gifts to business associates and clients at holiday seasons. Restaurant etiquette requires that people cancel reservations that will not be kept, that they avoid inappropriate conversation and excessive noise, and that they dress appropriately. It is considered tacky to use a calculator to figure out a waiter's tip. Now that fitness centers have ceased to be dating facilities, gym manners have emerged, ranging from taboos on ridiculous dress to monopolizing mirrors. An unspoken hierarchy exists that dictates the closer one stands to the instructor, the fitter and more expert one must be. Advances in communications have required rules of etiquette regarding telephone call-waiting, cellular phones, television remote controls, answering machines, and electronic mail. Even to chat by computer, users need etiquette spelled out in an electronic rule book. Users of electronic bulletin boards must observe rules of behavior that include greeting the crowd upon "entering the room," reading before "speaking," avoiding defamatory statements and obscenities, and avoiding using all capital letters or "shouting." Camcorder users are expected not to block other people's views and always to ask permission before videotaping.

Technological advances also raised such questions of manners as where and when is it appropriate to wear beepers or Walkmans. Traditional rules of conduct may no longer apply, however, due to the changing mores. How does one congratulate an unmarried pregnant woman? What does one say to someone who has had plastic surgery? Must one ask if dinner guests are vegetarians? Such situations, which developed in the last quarter of the twentieth century, were addressed by etiquette author and columnist Miss Manners (Judith Martin), who wrote on subjects that did not exist in Emily Post's time, such as "significant others" and political correctness.

[David J. Knowles, *Etiquette of American Society* (Pittsburgh, 1993).]

JOHN J. BYRNE

See also **SUPP:** Fashion and Style; Political Correctness.

MANUFACTURING. During the late 1970s many economists and political leaders argued that U.S. manufacturing had lost its dominant position in the nation's and the world's economy. While others argued that U.S. manufacturers remained the world's leaders, the period from 1975 to 1995 showed two unmistakable trends: U.S. manufacturers needed fewer workers to maintain or improve output, while foreign manufacturers—especially companies based in Japan or Germany—either increased their ownership of U.S. manufacturers or built their own plants and factories in the United States. These trends, which many Americans felt personally with the closing of auto plants and steel mills in the Northeast and Great Lakes region, initiated a prolonged debate about whether the U.S. economy had declined, how to respond to foreign competition, and whether the government had a responsibility to help workers who lost jobs as manufacturers closed shop during the 1970s and 1980s.

According to the Bureau of Labor Statistics, in 1950 almost 34 percent of the nation's 45 million workers were engaged in some type of manufacturing; in 1970 manufacturing's share of that year's 71 million workers was 27.3 percent; by 1990, when the United States had almost 118 million workers, manufacturing claimed only 17.4 percent of the total. Moreover, between 1979 and 1992 U.S. manufacturing output annually grew 1.1 percent but employment fell 1.2 percent, with 3 million manufacturing jobs eliminated during that period. It is generally agreed that the jobs lost between 1970 and 1990—losses accelerated by economic recessions—provided good pay and benefits for unskilled and semiskilled workers and were jobs that had helped propel the booming U.S. economy during the first six decades of the twentieth century. Hardest hit during the decline were manufacturers that had produced most of that economic growth: steel and textile producers, automobile companies, and manufacturers of appliances, televisions, and radios. Makers of paper, chemicals, industrial and analytical instruments, production machinery, and metalworking equipment also suffered.

Many of the problems faced by these companies came from overseas competition. Japan used lower-cost labor and heavy investment in plant and equipment to produce higher-quality goods at more productive rates. By the 1980s overseas advances, coupled with changes in the tastes of U.S. consumers, allowed Japan, West Germany, Brazil, South Korea, and other countries to make significant headway in the sales of automobiles, steel, and televisions and other electronic equipment. Some economists, businessmen, and politicians, however, said manufacturing's problems in the 1970s and 1980s went deeper than foreign competition. They maintained that poor economic policies, such as an overvalued dollar, credit business cycles that disrupted capital formation needed for plant and equipment modernization, and tax and regulatory policies that rewarded consumption instead of production, had wounded U.S. manufacturing just as deeply. Other economists maintained that the nation was not deindustrializing but rather that production was moving to the southern and western United States, where nonunion labor (meaning lower wages and benefits) was available. Still other observers downplayed any decline in manufacturing. They argued that the country merely was going through a transition from an industrial society to an economy organized around information and services. Companies and workers ready to exploit the new economy would prosper as had the old-line manufacturers.

The burgeoning services sector did provide higher-paying jobs in such areas as law, accounting, and the medical professions. In addition, thanks to a postwar push toward higher education, some workers who in the past might have been consigned to factory jobs took advantage of new opportunities offered in the 1970s and 1980s by the professions. On the other hand, the growing services sector—12 percent of the 45 million jobs in the United States in 1950 and 19.1 percent of the 118 million jobs in 1990—was more often typified by low-paying, low-benefit jobs in restaurants, retail stores, and other service-oriented businesses. For workers with few skills and educational opportunities—workers who once found family-supporting wages at steel mills or auto plants—the change was ominous, even if the new work was safer.

By 1982 a withering recession brought on by high interest rates used to extinguish double-digit inflation, aggravated manufacturing's problems. Chemical plants reported operating at 67 percent of capacity, while machinery plants, which supplied manufacturers with equipment, slashed their workforces by about 30 percent. Steel mills were in the worst shape. They operated at 30 percent of capacity and 60 percent of the workforce was unemployed. Several mills appeared close to asking the courts for protection from creditors as the industry's financial losses ran close to $2.5 billion for 1982.

U.S. manufacturers did report success stories during the period. One study, comparing manufacturing in 1970–1972 and 1980–1982, showed that production of electronic products rose 19 percent; plastic products, 125 percent; office equipment, 87 percent; synthetic materials, 77 percent; chemical products, 63 percent; and communications equipment, 59 percent. These manufacturers were emblematic of the higher-tech companies—both in terms of the goods being produced and the way they were being produced—that were becoming successful as steel mills and textile plants closed. High-tech manufacturers, however, often had different work needs. They relied on higher-skilled workers with better reading and math skills and automated many processes that had previously been staffed by unskilled and semiskilled workers. One important sector of high-tech manufacturing—computer equipment manufacturers—suffered from foreign and domestic competition as well.

As the crisis in manufacturing became apparent in the early 1980s, manufacturers tried to alleviate their problems. They slashed costs, laid off workers, closed unproductive or outdated plants and renegotiated union contracts. They looked at how foreign competitors, especially the Japanese, organized production. New management techniques and theories flooded the workplace, such as just-in-time inventories, statistical process control, lean production, continuous improvement, and total quality management. Success stories cropped up. The Ford Motor Company, considered almost dead in the early 1980s, sprang back to life in 1985 with a popular line of new cars and trucks that competed effectively against imports. Specialty steelmakers built smaller, more efficient plants to compete against imports from Brazil, Spain, and South Korea.

By the early 1990s many U.S. manufacturers reported a much better economic climate. Overall, U.S. manufacturing production climbed 26 percent during a fifteen-year period. Output per employee improved 37 percent. Productivity in the early 1990s showed average increases of 3 percent per year. By 1994 the Big Three automakers—General Motors, Ford, and

Chrysler—showed improved market share and better profits. The automakers, which many had dismissed as incompetent and incapable of adjusting to rapidly shifting markets, rededicated themselves to producing better-quality cars and trucks and began reaping benefits from the new focus. In the final quarter of 1993, for example, Chrysler, which had tried to sell itself to the Italian automaker Fiat three years earlier, reported earnings of $777 million, its highest-ever quarterly profit. Automaking provided an interesting example of how manufacturing was changing in the United States. U.S. automakers increasingly shifted production to such foreign countries as Mexico while foreign automakers, especially the Japanese, began producing cars in the United States. Honda, for example, produced its Accord sedans at an Ohio plant.

The productivity and profitability increases for U.S. manufacturers, combined with never-ending competition from foreign and domestic manufacturers, meant that there would be no return to the employment levels that defined manufacturing from the beginning of the twentieth century to the 1970s. Bureau of Labor Statistics data showed what had happened—manufacturers could make more with less and production generally was cheaper. By the mid-1990s a new manufacturing industry had taken shape, with economists predicting that computer manufacturing would become increasingly important. Other durable-goods manufacturers were expected to prosper, such as electronics, transportation, and instruments. The fastest-growing areas of nondurables manufacturing included paper and allied products, printing and publishing, chemicals and related products, and rubber.

Although U.S. manufacturers rejoiced over their improved conditions in many areas, they still lagged behind their foreign competition, especially Japan. Despite financial and economic problems in Japan in the mid-1990s, its manufacturers still led their U.S. counterparts in such areas as output per employed person, output per hour, and unit labor costs. Moreover, the average Japanese worker in manufacturing was taking home much more real compensation than U.S. workers, while Japan's manufacturing employment continued to grow. Meanwhile, U.S. high-tech companies entered into joint ventures with the Japanese that called for the manufacturing of products in Japan. In 1992 Intel and three other U.S. producers of "flash" memory chip semiconductors announced joint ventures, and the following year IBM and Toshiba entered into a billion-dollar venture to build flat-panel computer displays.

[Robert W. Crandall, *Manufacturing on the Move* (Washington, D.C., 1993); *DRI Report on U.S. Manufacturing Industries* (New York, 1984); Paul Ingrassia and Joseph B. White, *The Fall and Rise of the American Automobile Industry* (New York, 1994).]

THOMAS G. GRESS

See also **SUPP:** Automobile Industry; Computer Industry; Foreign Investment in the United States; Labor Unions; Rustbelt; Unemployment.

MARATHONS. The long-distance foot race known as the marathon is named after the celebrated Athenian victory over Persian invaders near the Bay of Marathon in Greece in 490 B.C. It commemorates the fact that a Greek soldier ran the twenty-five miles from the battlefield to Athens with tidings of the victory, only to die of exhaustion. A marathon was incorporated into the Olympic Games when the modern series began in Athens in 1896 and has retained an important place in them. The first victor was a Greek, Spiridon Loues, who won in 2 hours, 58 minutes, and 50 seconds. A year later the Boston Marathon was established and is held annually on Patriots' Day; by the 1990s it was attracting 10,000 competitors. The New York Marathon, founded in 1970 by Fred Lebow, head of the New York Road Runners Club, draws about 25,000 entrants each year. The length of the marathon was fixed at 26 miles, 385 yards in 1908 when the British Olympic Committee determined that the race should commence at Windsor Castle and finish in front of the royal box at Shepherds Bush in London. Although no official records of marathons are kept because the courses are of varied difficulty, by 1995 the fastest recorded times were about two hours and seven minutes for a man and about two hours and twenty minutes for a woman. Violet Percy of Great Britain became the first woman to officially enter a marathon, the London Marathon, in 1926. In 1970 the Road Runners Club of America organized the first championship marathon for women, although it was not until 1984 that a women's race was included in the Olympic Games. In 1970 two women in the New York Marathon became the first to break three hours. Marathons grew in popularity in the United States after Frank Shorter won the marathon in the 1972 Olympic Games. The New York Marathon began to be televised in 1979, and the following year, after fraudulent finishes in both Boston and New York by Rosie Ruiz, videotaping became routine. Triathlons, such as the Ironman Triathlon World Championship held on the Kona coast of Hawaii, which began in 1978, incorporate a marathon, a 2.4-mile swim, and a 112-mile bicycle race. A related sporting challenge is the endurance marathon, in which the length of uninterrupted participation is the determining factor in any number of activities, from tiddlywinks to trampolining.

ROBERT GARLAND

See also **DAH** and **SUPP:** Olympics.

MARINE LIFE. *See* **Fish and Marine Life; Marine Sanctuaries.**

MARINE SANCTUARIES were created by Title III of the Marine Protection, Research, and Sanctuaries Act of 1972. Twenty years later the National Marine Sanctuary System, administered by the National Oceanic and Atmospheric Administration, included fourteen designated and proposed unique and threatened coastal locations. Designated sanctuaries included Monitor in Virginia, Gray's Reef in Georgia, the Florida Keys, Flower Garden Banks in Texas, the Cordell Bank, Gulf of the Farallones, and Channel Islands off California, and Fagetele Bay of American Samoa. Proposed sanctuaries include Thunder Bay (Great Lakes), Stellwagen Bank (Mass.), Norfolk Canyon (Va.), Northern Puget Sound and Olympic Coast (Wash.), Monterey Bay (Calif.), and Kahoolawe (Hawaii). The environmental movement prompted Congress to enact laws for environmental protection. Books such as *The Sea Around Us* (1951, rev. 1961) by Rachel Carson and television documentaries by the French undersea explorer Jacques Cousteau enchanted a wide popular audience with descriptions of marine organisms. Their works carried the message that human impacts on marine ecosystems affect human health. The 1972 legislation not only provided the mechanism for protecting the ecosystems of the U.S. coast through ocean sanctuaries but also mandated a federal marine research program and enabled the Environmental Protection Agency to regulate industrial and municipal disposal of wastes at sea.

[Samuel P. Hays, *Beauty, Health, and Permanence: Environmental Politics in the United States, 1955–1985* (Cambridge, Mass., 1987).]

DENNIS WILLIAMS

See also: **SUPP:** Environmental Protection; Fish and Marine Life; Wildlife Refuges and Sanctuaries.

MARRIAGE AND DIVORCE. Twentieth-century family trends in the United States, as in other industrialized countries, have been on a seesaw. In the nineteenth century and the first third of the twentieth century, average age at marriage increased, family size declined, and divorce became easier to obtain. After the Depression of the 1930s, however, all three of these trends turned around—the median marriage age for women dropped to near twenty, there was a "baby boom" in which the birth rate increased by 60 percent, and the divorce rate fell. By the late 1960s the seesaw reverted to its former position as the habits of previous decades reemerged. The baby boom now looked like an aberration, a reaction to the deprivations and disruptions of the Great Depression and World War II, when many could not plan on a stable future. The abrupt return to an older age at marriage, a decline in fertility, and rise in the divorce rate created a "crisis" atmosphere, leading many to fear the "end" of the family.

This decline in the centrality of marriage in adult lives reflected socioeconomic and demographic changes in American society beginning in the late 1960s, but the causal relationship between those changes and the decline was difficult to pinpoint. It may have been that many adults in the United States did in fact celebrate romance but at the same time placed a high value on personal freedom, particularly as the U.S. economy made that freedom possible. It was no longer necessary to find oneself trapped in an unhappy marriage. Another possibility was that the necessity for both partners to work to support themselves and their children in a way they deemed satisfactory, and the emphasis on commitment that characterized many occupations, led women and men to have little time for family life. The growth of organized leisure, sports, and other recreation provided many adults with absorbing alternatives to family life as well.

Perhaps two more phenomena account for the reduced importance of marriage in the lives of adults. First, changes in gender roles made marriages difficult to negotiate and maintain. In the nineteenth century industrialization took men away from the family to work, which deprived them of involvement with children and left the tasks and reward of child rearing to women. The result was that men were far less likely than women to see children either as a source of personal meaning, happiness, stability, or as a source of adult status in the community. As more and more women entered the workforce, people became confused about what the division of labor inside marriage should be. Some opted to form other relationships, cohabiting with others (of the same or opposite sex) or living alone.

The growth in the number of people living alone was another force influencing change in family life. The living arrangements of unmarried adults changed dramatically after World War II, with the result that in 1990 more than one-quarter of U.S. households contained only one person, compared with only 10 percent in 1940. Much of this increase reflected a decline in family extension among the unmarried, as those who once lived with available family members (parents, adult children, or other kin) were able to afford homes of their own. This change, however, meant that young adults no longer had to marry to leave their parents, and those contemplating ending a marriage had alternatives that preserved their privacy, autonomy, and adult status.

One result of the increase in the divorce rate has been the impoverishment of women. Professional women suffered inequalities of divorce settlements to be sure, but poor women suffered more, especially after the introduction of no-fault divorce in the late 1960s. The reason for impoverishment was in part visible in a statistic of the 1980s, namely, that less than 4 percent of divorced women received alimony, and only half of all women awarded child support received the full amount, with women receiving $2,500 annually on average.

The decline in marriage and remarriage has also meant that many children are raised by and often born into one-parent families. In 1991 the median family income of female-headed households with children was only 30 percent the level of income of households where both parents were living with children. In other industrialized countries, child poverty rates were a third or less than in the United States, because either the divorce rate was still low, as in Japan and southern Europe, or welfare programs supporting children were substantial. Children in the poorest U.S. communities have disproportionately suffered from these trends in poverty and family dislocation. Marriage declined dramatically in African-American communities. By 1990 more than half of all black children lived in one-parent families, compared with less than one-quarter of white or Hispanic children. About one-third of white children living with one parent were poor, while this was the case for nearly two-thirds of minority children.

By the 1990s many novelties accompanied the return of the marriage-trend seesaw. As divorces increased to nearly one of every two marriages so did remarriages. Although more than 70 percent of divorced men and women remarried, it was predicted 60 percent of those remarriages would fail, resulting in 1 million remarriages every year and leading to the practice known as "serial monogamy." Remarried couples suffer from more stress than those couples marrying for the first time, including greater financial problems, stepparenting, and dealing with former spouses. About 40 percent of remarriages in the 1990s involved stepchildren, and those couples experienced a higher divorce rate than childless remarried couples.

Another novel aspect of the post–baby boom era has been the increasing frequency of detailed contracts along with the general contract of marriage itself. Beginning in the colonial period, wealthy women tried to protect themselves with prenuptial agreements. These contracts fell into disuse, only to reappear and became quite common in the 1980s, as couples attempted to transform a relationship of love, or perhaps reinforce it, by resorting to economics. An economic agreement, it was believed, would protect both sides of a marriage. By 1995 all fifty states permitted such contracts, although only thirty recognized them as legal instruments.

Conservative commentators often urge that a return to the family patterns and gender roles of the 1950s, that is, yet another swing of the seesaw, is needed to preserve the family. Others argue that marriage and family life will need to continue to change to reflect the new realities of men's and women's lives. An altogether new equilibrium, centered on a family-friendly workplace in which men and women build long-term relationships around children, home, and community, is theoretically possible, although the complexities of the late twentieth century made the likelihood of its achievement uncertain.

[Andrew J. Cherlin, *Marriage, Divorce and Remarriage,* rev. ed. (Cambridge, Mass., 1992); Frances K. Goldscheider and Linda Waite, *New Families, No Families? The Transformation of the American Home* (Berkeley, Calif., 1991); David Popenoe, *Disturbing the Nest: Family Change and Decline in Modern Societies* (New York, 1988); Lenore J. Weitzman, *The Divorce Revolution: The Unexpected Social and Economic Consequences for Women and Children in America* (New York, 1985).]

FRANCES K. GOLDSCHEIDER

See also **SUPP:** Family.

MARYLAND, one of the smallest states in size, by the 1990s was one of the most divided. Since the 1970s urban Baltimore, once so dominant, rapidly declined in influence and increasingly became blue-collar. The five western counties were egalitarian and contentious. The twelve eastern and southern counties around Chesapeake Bay were hierarchical and conservative. The six counties of suburban Washington and Baltimore, surged in size and power with prosperous and mobile populations. The accommodation of such differences within one state gave Maryland a certain representativeness in the United States. Suburbanization characterized the state's post–World War II history. In the late 1940s the suburban population doubled, often with low-cost tract housing. In the 1950s and 1960s it doubled again as jobs and freeways extended and shopping centers developed. Split-level houses, cookouts, and station wagons became suburban symbols. Since 1970 the suburban population has doubled once more, bringing malls, office parks, and a demographic mix. By 1990 almost two-thirds of the state's population lived in the six suburban counties. Newcomers to the suburbs were usually young, upwardly mobile, liberal, eager for zoning and good schools, and often politically independent. Even with legislative reapportionment in the 1960s, their voices in state affairs were fewer than their numbers. It was not until the 1970s that they gained control of their counties from the old organizations of large landowners and developers.

The clash of the old politics of patronage and favors with the new politics of innocence and issues invited corruption, for which the state was briefly renowned. Spiro T. Agnew, elected in 1966 as a reform governor, was the first suburban representative to serve in that office, but he was unable to distinguish between campaign contributions and bribery. He was elected vice president of the United States in 1968, remaining a symbol of suburban probity until forced to resign for accepting a quarter of a million dollars from developers in return for favors. Agnew was succeeded as governor by Marven Mandel, an old-style machine politician from Baltimore, one of the ablest administrators the state ever had, progressive, and efficient. He took care of his friends as had his predecessors until he was convicted and imprisoned for violating the new conflict-of-interest laws he had championed. During the 1970s, a U.S. senator from Maryland, two congressmen, nine state legislators, and a score of lesser officials were convicted of crimes. For most of the United States, including Maryland, the 1970s was a discordant time, with Watergate, urban riots, and Vietnam protests. Maryland emerged from the 1970s with its innocence lost and its political machines broken but with some of the strongest laws governing political ethics in the country.

Along with the move to the suburbs came the transformation of an agricultural and manufacturing economy into a service economy. By the 1990s approximately 60 percent of the state's workers were employed by government or engaged in service work (including finance and transportation), 23 percent were engaged in trade, 10 percent in manufacturing or farming, and 6 percent in construction or other activities. Numerous federal agencies had offices throughout the state, including main offices of the Social Security Administration, the Bureau of the Census, the Bureau of Standards, the National Institutes of Health, and the National Archives.

One of the burgeoning new government services was environmental management. During the 1960s Maryland emphasized preservation of natural resources, soil conservation, halting strip mining, control of beach erosion, and rescue of the collapsing oyster fisheries. In the 1970s attention shifted toward appreciation of nature—expansion of state parks and forests, wildlife preserves, and care of waterfowl and endangered species. By the 1980s environmentalists were most concerned with pollution—control of industrial waste spewed into the air and waterways, toxic waste, sewage treatment, farm run-off, and recycling. The 1990s produced multistate agreements for control of Chesapeake Bay and state-sponsored research into marine life and biotechnology. Maryland was usually near the forefront of the environmental movement, and by most measures the environment was cleaner in the 1990s than in earlier decades.

During the 1980s incomes rose and political tensions lessened. Governor Harry Hughes was an appropriate symbol for the decade, clean cut and quiet spoken, neither liberal nor conservative, judiciously managing the legislature's expansion of health and welfare services, transportation, and schools and colleges. The real-estate boom of the early 1980s tempted the state's poorly regulated savings and loan associations to overexpand and by mid-decade some faced bankruptcy. The state froze assets, sent miscreants to jail, and established controls and depositor insurance, and the episode passed without lasting damage.

Prosperity encouraged the multiplication of cultural and recreational facilities. The Morris Mechanic Theater and the Meyerhoff Symphony Hall came to Baltimore and a major performing arts center to the University of Maryland; the Baltimore Museum of Art, the Walters Art Gallery, and many private galleries expanded; the Maryland Historical Society and the Hall of Records moved into splendid new facilities; the Maryland Arts Council and the Maryland Humanities Council took their activities into every county; and there were hundreds of historical restorations and reenactments of historical events. Ethnic pride increased and ethnic restaurants multiplied. In 1984 the state celebrated the 350th anniversary of its colonial founding. The Baltimore Colts football team left Maryland, but the state built a magnificent new stadium for the Baltimore Orioles baseball team and planned one for the Washington Redskins. Boating on the Chesapeake, hiking in the Appalachians, and sunning at Ocean City reached new peaks of popularity.

As Maryland suburbs soared, and suburban spillover allowed the western and eastern counties to hold their own, Baltimore declined despite valiant efforts at renewal. The city's population fell from 47 percent of the state population in 1940 to 23 percent in 1970 and 12 percent in 1994. As prosperous residents departed for the suburbs, urban tax revenues declined and the poor were left behind. William Donald Schaefer served as governor of Maryland from 1987 to 1995, mainly as a spokesman of economic development. He expanded the state's subsidy for Baltimore with a light-rail system to tie it to the suburbs, new stadiums for its harbor, and funds for schools, police, libraries, and parks. Convinced that universities were engines of economic growth, he combined the University of Maryland, with eleven state colleges, into a single system, hoping that unification would reduce costs and bring research into closer collaboration with business. The state also offered land and tax benefits to entice new businesses and, like the rest of the country, wrestled inconclusively with the problems of abortion, gun control, drunk driving, prostitution, the death penalty, and the right to die. In 1994 the Democratic candidate Parris Glendening, with a program similar to that of Schaefer, won a hairbreadth victory over a conservative Republican candidate.

[Robert J. Brugger, *Maryland* (Baltimore, 1988); George H. Callcott, *Maryland and America, 1940 to 1980* (Baltimore, 1985).]

GEORGE H. CALLCOTT

See also **SUPP:** Baltimore.

MASSACHUSETTS. One of the oldest settlements in British North America in the eighteenth century, the colony most associated with the American Revolution, and later the state most closely associated with the movement to abolish slavery, Massachusetts in the late twentieth century continued to be a national leader in business, politics, education, and the arts and sciences. The state's population grew moderately during the 1970s and 1980s, reaching 6,016,425 in 1990, when Massachusetts ranked sixth among the states in numbers of foreign-born residents and seventh in households with languages other than English. Immigration has continued from the Caribbean, Canada, Britain, Ireland, Italy, Portugal, the Cape Verde Islands, Poland, Russia, and Southeast Asia. African Americans constituted 5 percent of the state's population, Hispanics 4.8 percent, and Asians 2.4 percent. The state ranked third in population living in urban areas (84.3 percent) and sixth in median household income ($36,558). It was first in percentage of the population possessing college degrees.

With its highly concentrated population, Massachusetts nonetheless developed an awkward division between a predominantly white, financially comfortable, highly educated populace in urban and suburban areas, and a poor and much less educated population in the older manufacturing cities and former mill towns. This division may be the most important development in the state since the 1970s. Massachusetts has in effect two separate and unequal societies, one marked by people with excellent housing, schools, and libraries, surrounded by modern office buildings and laboratories, and the other in the older cities and towns plagued by poor housing, dismal schools, and all the economic and social problems that stem from them. Economic trends prior to World War II continued after 1970. There was continuing decline of the textile, shoe, machinery, and food-processing industries. High costs associated with lack of fossil fuels, cold winters, and a location distant from national markets and raw materials, together with unionized workers, made competition with Sunbelt states and newly industrial nations difficult. Most of the traditional manufacturing operations left the state and were replaced by high technology and service industries, which were crucial to the state's late twentieth-century prosperity.

During the recessions of the early 1970s and the late 1980s, state government was plagued by unbalanced budgets, high unemployment, and large increases in public assistance. The subsequent recovery has been called the "Massachusetts miracle." High technology began in the 1960s, supported by military research and breakthroughs in electronics and miniaturization, producing the economic turnaround. Expansion of architecture and engineering firms and centers for medical treatment and research also helped. Unemployment soared to 11.2 percent in 1975 but dropped to 3.2 percent in 1987. New office and hotel towers were built in Boston's business district, matched by office buildings, hotels, factories, and warehouses at almost every interchange of the state's metropolitan highway, Route 128, one of the highest concentrations of high-tech industries in the United States. The early 1990s were marked by cutbacks in military contracts and computer orders, and statewide unemployment reached 9 percent in 1991, but the downturn quickly came to an end. Highly important in the revival was the scientific and technological excellence of the state's universities, especially the Massachusetts Institute of Technology (MIT). Government-sponsored research conducted at MIT during World War II and the cold war decades produced many military breakthroughs with civilian applications. Another contribution was the region's skilled manpower, especially in machine tools, which provided an abundance of trained technicians.

State government may have been antiquated, burdened by patronage, and unable to plan continued economic development, but the Massachusetts Port Authority developed Logan Airport into one of the nation's most important. In the mid-1990s the Massachusetts Bay Transportation Authority operated four subway lines and had expanded rail and boat commuter lines and many bus routes in and around Boston. The state undertook the nation's most costly highway project, rebuilding Boston's Central Artery underground, together with construction of a third harbor tunnel, neither completed as of 1996. On the national political scene, Massachusetts' history of voting for Democrats gave it a reputation for liberalism. Although President Ronald Reagan carried the state with thin majorities in 1980 and 1984, Clinton's majority over George Bush in 1992 was larger than in any other state. In 1990 the state's entire delegation to Congress comprised liberal Democrats. The party held overwhelming majorities in both houses of the state legislature. Massachusetts Representative Thomas P. (Tip) O'Neill served as speaker of the U.S. House of Representatives from 1977 to 1987. All incumbent Massachusetts Democrats in the House were unseated, however, in the November 1994 election.

Republicans and conservative Democrats had remarkable successes in the last quarter of the twentieth century in winning state and local offices. In 1978 a conservative Democrat, Edward J. King, was elected governor. He was closely associated with Proposition 2½, which severely limited the powers of cities and towns to raise taxes on real estate and motor vehicles. A startling change in political sentiments was the downfall of Governor Michael S. Dukakis. His loss of the 1988 presidential election to Bush was attributed to his failure to respond to the Bush campaign's racist and jingoist tactics. For this Dukakis lost the respect of large sectors of a public that had elected him governor three times, and he served as a near powerless "lame duck" during his last two years in office. A Republican, William Weld, was elected governor in 1990, defeating the conservative John Silber, president of Boston University. Democratic leaders in both houses of the state legislature frequently were described as conservative. Conservatives have been notably successful in the state's nonpartisan local elections. Party loyalty weakened in Massachusetts because of an unusual ballot form that scatters party nominees almost at random across the ballot. Nonpartisan local elections deprived parties of support in odd-numbered years.

Culturally, Massachusetts continued to dominate New England in the late twentieth century. A 1971 addition to the Boston Public Library was followed by renovation of its magnificent 1887 building. New wings were added to Boston's Museum of Fine Arts, School of Art, Museum of Science, and the Clark Museum in Williamstown. The Boston Symphony Orchestra gained a new summer hall at Tanglewood in the Berkshires. The State Archives and Museum relocated from the State House in Boston to Columbia Point in Dorchester, joining the John F. Kennedy Library. Boston's Children's Museum relocated to an abandoned waterside warehouse, which it shared successively with the Museum of Transportation and the Computer Museum. In the 1980s community planning was barely mentioned, but a variety of planning proposals appeared in the 1990s. The most successful was the creation of the Cape Cod Commission, established to guide development of one of the state's most popular regions. To counter the continuing rise in automobile use and congestion, three rail transportation improvements were discussed during 1994. One, a rail connection between Boston's North and South Stations, would permit interstate trains to proceed across the city. A circumferential ring just outside downtown Boston would connect two medical centers, three universities, and Logan Airport with South Boston, Roxbury, and Chelsea. A third rail proposal looked to reconstruction of existing freight lines to accommodate passenger rail traffic and connect suburban towns in an arc eighteen to twenty miles west of Boston.

[Michael S. Dukakis and Rosabeth Moss Kanter, *Creating the Future* (New York, 1988); *Encyclopedia of Massachusetts* (New York, 1984); Lawrence W. Kennedy, *Planning the City upon a Hill* (Amherst, Mass., 1992);

David Lampe, ed., *The Massachusetts Miracle* (Cambridge, Mass., 1988); Richard Wilkie et al., *Historical Atlas of Massachusetts* (Amherst, Mass., 1991).]

ROGER FEINSTEIN

See also **SUPP:** Boston.

MEDICARE AND MEDICAID. In most industrialized countries, virtually everyone is covered by governmentally insured health care. The uniquely expensive U.S. medical system, however, consigns most citizens to private health insurance or to none at all. Medicare (government health insurance for the elderly and seriously disabled) and Medicaid (health coverage for the poor under welfare) stand as notable exceptions, accounting for almost one of every three dollars spent on health care in the early 1990s. Since the 1910s major government reform of the U.S. health care system has often seemed to be just around the corner, but, despite overwhelming public support, it has usually foundered on pressures from the medical establishment, crippling charges of socialized medicine, and predictions of greater expense and intrusive, impersonal bureaucracy. President Franklin D. Roosevelt thus omitted health insurance from his Social Security proposals in the 1930s, and President Harry S. Truman's plan in 1945 for national health insurance succumbed to conservative partisanship and an attack from the American Medical Association. With the vast expansion of private health insurance, particularly union-negotiated medical plans, in the 1940s, government plans seemed doomed, but in the 1950s key officials in the Social Security Administration, a group commonly at the core of U.S. welfare state expansion, shifted strategy. To make government health insurance more politically marketable, they proposed that it be confined to the elderly and tied to the increasingly popular old-age insurance program. After all, older Americans, who had to stretch incomes half the national average to cover medical expenses three times as great, could not easily be cast as unworthy welfare cheats. By the late 1950s Medicare was backed by organized labor and many Democrats, including candidate and future president John F. Kennedy. Kennedy never was able to push the program through either house of Congress, and even the legendary legislative skills of his successor, Lyndon B. Johnson, at first could only secure Senate passage. In 1965, however, Kennedy's martyred legacy combined with a strong economy and the overwhelming Democratic congressional majority elected on the coattails of Johnson's 1964 landslide to allow passage of the Social Security Act Amendments of 1965, which established both Medicaid and Medicare as part of Johnson's Great Society.

Medicaid's success came less controversially. Medical interests saw some virtue in the government picking up the tab for hospital or doctor bills of "charity cases," and confining government-funded health care to the poor was a common fall-back position for opponents of more wide-ranging plans. As early as 1950 states had been allowed to make payments under federally subsidized welfare programs directly to hospitals, nursing homes, and doctors. An amendment to the Social Security Act in 1960 (the Kerr-Mills program) beefed up these so-called "vendor payments" for the elderly poor while adding coverage of the "medically indigent" elderly, whose health care expenses would otherwise leave them impoverished. In 1965 a new medical assistance program (Medicaid) extended this coverage of the elderly poor's medical costs to low-income people of all ages who qualified under any federally subsidized, state-administered welfare program.

The Medicaid program had a marked impact. It allowed the poor to receive much more care from doctors and hospitals than previously, when they had often postponed treatment until they required emergency-room care. While two-thirds of its recipients by the mid-1990s were low-income women and children, half of its outlays went to nursing home and other long-term institutional services for the elderly, the disabled, and AIDS patients. It became, in short, a safety net for the American medical system, assisting in coverage ranging from the elderly poor's Medicare premiums and copayments to long-term institutional services for the developmentally disabled and AIDS patients. Medicaid, however, carried the stigma of welfare, and wide disparities among state programs assured that many who needed medical treatment would receive inadequate coverage or none at all. Medicare, by contrast, was a federally administered, contributory, social insurance program, provided to almost all Americans aged sixty-five and over as a right that they had purportedly earned through previous payments. Medicare opponents sought to limit government's role by proposing the alternative of government-subsidized voluntary private insurance that, they noted, would cover a wider range of medical services, including doctor bills, than the original Medicare plan. Wilbur Mills, chairman of the House Ways and Means Committee, cannily adapted this alternative into a new Part B of Medicare. Thus, Medicare Part A, financed by payroll taxes on employers and employees, reimbursed recipients for hospital and limited post-hospitalization home health care and nursing-home costs, while Part B offered older Americans cut-rate insurance policies (made possible by a 75 percent subsidy taken from government general-revenue funds) covering doctor bills, ambulance charges, and certain lab tests.

Despite, or perhaps because of, the gap between the perception of Medicare as an earned benefit and the reality that most of its costs had not been paid by the elderly themselves, the program became very popular, but it was also much more expensive than advocates had anticipated, even though the Social Security Administration's overhead to administer the program was gratifyingly low. To gain the acquiescence of medical interests, Medicare had no cost-control provisions to speak of. Guaranteed reimbursement of all customary or reasonable fees, hospitals and doctors cashed in, pushing up medical prices far faster than general inflation, and provided medical services, lab tests, and technologies that a more cost-conscious system might have precluded. Medicaid reimbursement rates soon became less generous, enough so that many doctors refused to participate. Even so, Medicaid expenditures also rocketed, fueled less by sensational cases of provider fraud than by a combination of greater use of medical services and a 700 percent increase in the number of recipients over the program's first fifteen years—a boon, to be sure, for the health of the poor, but an increasingly resented bust for state budgets. Facing mounting costs, Medicare kept increasing payroll taxes, deductibles, and copayments, and in 1983 and 1992 established systems to limit allowable charges by hospitals and doctors. By the mid-1990s Medicare, Medicaid, and medical costs in general approached financial crisis, assuring further reform.

[Edward D. Berkowitz, *America's Welfare State* (Baltimore, 1991); Sheri I. David, *With Dignity: The Search for Medicare and Medicaid* (Westport, Conn., 1985).]

MARK H. LEFF

See also **SUPP:** Health Care; Social Security; Welfare.

MEDICINE. In the United States as elsewhere, scientific medicine came of age in the twentieth century. Since its improvised colonial beginnings, medicine in America has evolved into an imposing system of skills and technology capable of delivering strikingly successful therapies, but its successes are increasingly powered by a large and complex scientific, commercial, and governmental establishment that many observers criticize as bureaucratic, depersonalizing, and unaffordable. Not coincidentally, the final decades of the twentieth century witnessed important transformations in the way in which medical care was delivered, who delivered it, and how it was financed.

Equally significant changes occurred in the nature of the diseases that affect us and the rate at which they occur. Some of these changes are also the paradoxical legacy of contemporary medicine's successes. As people live longer, the resulting increase in the number of aging Americans has led to a dramatic increase in the degenerative diseases of old age—cancer, heart and kidney disease, dementia, and stroke. Changing social realities have required that matters not previously considered medical, such as the use of tobacco products, become public health issues. A rapidly increasing alcohol- and drug-addicted population became a major public health concern, as did the shocking escalation in the number of injuries and deaths from firearms.

Acquired immune deficiency syndrome (AIDS), a disease first reported in 1981, quickly assumed epidemic proportions, particularly among gay men and intravenous drug users, but fifteen years later AIDS was spreading more rapidly among heterosexual women. By 1995 more than a quarter of a million people with AIDS had died in the United States, and about a million more were infected with the lethal virus, for which no immunization or cure has been discovered. Despite an impressive rate of improvement through use of new antipsychotic and antidepressant drugs, many people required care for mental illness.

Perhaps the most significant advance in medicine in the last quarter of the twentieth century was the burgeoning ability to study human genetic diseases, a breakthrough made possible by the development of recombinant DNA technology. The investigation of a number of devastating genetic diseases, including sickle-cell anemia, Down's syndrome, Huntington's disease, cystic fibrosis, and muscular dystrophy, was made possible by this technology. Historically, disease was dealt with by treating its overt symptoms. It appeared likely that the next advance would be the revolutionary ability to treat disease at its molecular level by introducing normal copies of defective genes into the existing, abnormal genetic structure. In the mid-1990s clinical trials were under way employing gene therapy in the treatment of rheumatoid arthritis, hemophilia, and some types of cancer, as well as sickle-cell anemia, cystic fibrosis, muscular dystrophy, and other conditions.

Important developments also took place in neurology and psychoneuroimmunology, with the discovery that the normal release of chemicals in the brain has an extremely far-reaching effect that influences most of the body's systems, nerve functioning, and emotional behavior. The development of medications that enhance or inhibit the production of serotonin, dopamine, and other neurotransmitters mitigated the debilitating neurological and psychological symptoms of disorders such as Parkinson's disease, Huntington's disease, and depression.

Other major advances occurred at the juncture of recombinant gene therapy, immunology, and virology. In 1994 vaccines were licensed for chicken pox and hepatitis A. A hepatitis B vaccine was licensed a decade earlier. The rapidly mutating influenza virus has defeated all efforts to bring it under effective control, but a global network of laboratories, led by the World Health Organization, began collaborating to identify new strains of influenza as they appear, saving many lives by minimizing the time between the beginning of epidemics and the production and distribution of appropriate vaccines. Although neither immunization nor a cure had been found for AIDS, the duration and quality of the lives of HIV and AIDS patients improved dramatically with the development of a number of drugs that inhibit reproduction of the virus at various stages of the disease.

A substantial number of the major breakthroughs in contemporary medicine were technological. Extremely sophisticated diagnostic techniques were developed, including nuclear medicine scanning tests and imaging devices such as magnetic resonance imaging (MRI) and computerized axial tomography (CAT scans), which provide images of the brain, heart, gastrointestinal tract, and other soft tissues. Advances in Doppler echo and other ultrasound technology provided a noninvasive technique for determining blood flow velocity in various locations in the body. This technology affords the opportunity for noninvasive anatomical evaluation in many fields, including obstetrics, gastroenterology, and urology. DNA science now permits replication of human genes and their transfer to products that can be used for therapeutic purposes. Furthermore, its diagnostic, predictive, and forensic uses have become increasingly refined. Equally sophisticated therapeutic and surgical procedures also rely on complex, advanced technology, such as organ transplantation.

One totally nontechnological field that came to the fore as an important part of medical intercession was prevention. Since the 1970s much emphasis is placed on educational programs designed to teach people proper nutrition and exercise in order to avoid illness. Nutrition and exercise were recognized as important in the prevention and control of heart disease, hypertension, diabetes, and other chronic diseases and in promoting health generally. Nonetheless, technology is central to contemporary medicine and is very costly. Reliance upon elaborate equipment and procedures resulted in a growing number of people receiving outpatient examination, testing, and treatment in hospitals rather than in doctors' offices or at home. The greatest increase in the cost of medical care since the 1960s was in hospital care. The enormous medical establishment that evolved in the last third of the twentieth century included pharmaceutical and medical equipment manufacturers, insurance carriers, and an abundantly supported research community, as well as federal, state, and local government.

The federal government is involved in important ways in the furnishing of health care. On the civilian side, through the Department of Veterans Affairs, it operates approximately 900 hospitals, nursing homes, ambulatory care clinics, and veterans counseling centers. It also directs the Indian Health Service, which provides comprehensive health care services to Native Americans. Through the Public Health Service, the federal government administers the Centers for Disease Control and Prevention (CDC) and the National Institutes of Health (NIH). The CDC is the federal agency charged with providing leadership and direction in the prevention and control of diseases and responding to public health emergencies. The NIH is the principal biomedical research agency of the federal government. Both were intimately involved in virtually all of the significant advances since the mid-1960s. The medical contributions of the military are not limited to the health services commands of the armed forces. Ultrasound technology, adapted from military sonar, is an example of an important military contribution to the health of the population as a whole.

Beginning in the 1970s, the trend among physicians toward specialization was reversed and more family practitioners, general pediatricians, and internists entered practice. Increasingly, too, physician assistants, nurse-practitioners, and nurse-midwives—often referred to as physician extenders—performed many procedures traditionally reserved to physicians.

Ethical issues have always been critical in medicine because they deal with matters of life and death, but the medical technology developed in the late twentieth century gave new urgency to ethical questions. The ability to prolong life for months and even years after a person's heart or lungs have failed recasts the question of what life is and when death occurs. Organ transplantation and human medical experiments generate great debate, and DNA science has raised a new world of ethical concerns.

[James H. Cassedy, *Medicine in America: A Short History* (Baltimore, 1991); Lester S. King, *Transformations in American Medicine* (Baltimore, 1991); Jeff Lyon and Peter Gorner, *Altered Fates: Gene Therapy and the Retooling of Human Life* (New York, 1995); Paul Starr, *The Social Transformation of American Medicine* (New York, 1982).]

JACK HANDLER

See also **SUPP:** Acquired Immune Deficiency Syndrome; Cardiovascular Disease; Centers for Disease Control and Prevention; Clinical Research; Computerized Axial Tomography; Euthanasia; Genetic Engineering; Health and Human Services, Department of; Health Care; Health Maintenance Organizations; Magnetic Resonance Imaging; Medicaid and Medicare; Medicine, Alternative; National Institutes of Health; Patients' Rights; Physician Assistants; Public Health Service; Surgery; Transplants and Organ Donation; Women's Health.

MEDICINE, ALTERNATIVE. In seeking to understand and treat their illnesses, Americans have always had recourse to a great variety of healing practices. Conventional physicians have had to compete with a wide range of alternatives, including folk healing, prayer, popular health manuals, midwifery, patent medicines, osteopathy, Christian Science, homeopathy, herbalism, water cure, and more recently Chinese medicine, Ayurveda, meditation, yoga, and an assortment of New Age practices. The list of available and emergent alternatives could be expanded indefinitely. Healing in America can take place in a clinic, home, community center, church, and temple. Despite the efforts of organized medicine to regulate access to health care providers, the medical marketplace in the late twentieth century remained as diverse and as crowded as ever.

When suffering from illness, people generally are pragmatic in seeking care. They might initially try self-treatment or ask advice from friends, family, and neighbors. Depending on the character, severity, and duration of the complaint, and in accordance with past experiences and trusted advice, they may then visit one or more health care providers, following an implicit hierarchy of resort. Most people do not use only one sort of health care for all the ailments they may suffer; for a chronic condition, a person will often seek out a variety of explanations and treatments. In practice, then, alternative medicine is more accurately described as complementary medicine. Since the 1980s surveys have shown that those with the most resources—the better educated and those with access to information networks—are more likely than the poor and less educated to use alternative medicine. The search for explanations and therapeutic experimentation are strongly associated with having the confidence and the knowledge to assert control over one's state of health.

There is no fixed definition of conventional scientific medicine. Indeed, some practices and theories, such as autointoxication, that once were impeccably conventional came to appear quite unconventional, while many previously alternative modalities, such as acupuncture, gradually gained biomedical validation. No medical intervention is inherently or self-evidently conventional or alternative. Accordingly, the best definitions of conventional medicine are those derived from its organizational or social features. A practice is conventional if it is taught in medical schools and is acceptable to the organized medical profession—in this context, the American Medical Association (AMA) and specialist groups.

Between the 1830s, when most states repealed medical licensing laws, and the 1870s, when licensure was gradually reintroduced, the medical profession was remarkably open. Orthodox physicians competed equally with nonorthodox or "sectarian" doctors; proprietary medical schools proliferated, often providing only perfunctory training; and many new healing practices were imported from Europe or were formulated locally. During this period orthodox physicians tried to develop a coherent and stable professional identity in order to distinguish themselves from sectarians. Orthodox medical training began to include more formal scientific education, often in universities rather than proprietary schools, and state medical associations made sure their members did not later stray onto the sectarian path. The AMA, established in 1847, campaigned vigorously against nonscientific competitors. By 1900 the organized medical profession could demand that anyone wanting to practice medicine show a diploma from a recognized medical school. Those who could not were deemed "quacks," a term that once had been applied to self-promoters and frauds of all persuasions (including those making fanciful claims for conventional therapies). When a healing practice could not be suppressed, many of its practitioners could be assimilated; thus, in 1903 the AMA welcomed into its ranks those homeopaths and herbalists willing to forsake their "speculations" for "science." Once the most liberal of medical marketplaces, the United States, after the orthodox backlash, began to restrict alternative medicine with a rigor rarely observed in comparable societies, such as Australia, Great Britain, and the rest of Europe.

Folk medicine has always been one of the more popular resources for understanding and treating disease in America. Unlike many modern alternatives, access to folk methods usually requires a long-standing and broad allegiance to a specific cultural group. Long before Europeans arrived with their folk medicines (and a more cosmopolitan elite medicine based on classical texts), Native Americans had developed their own healing traditions, which emphasized spiritual well-being and ecological integration, including the use of local botanical remedies. Over the past 300 and more years African Americans have constructed out of African and Christian traditions socially potent blends of herbal and spiritual healing, sometimes called hoodoo or rootwork. Like most folk medicine, this healing system gives its adherents an understanding and a sense of control of the community, the environment, and the spiritual world. Similarly, Hispanic folk medicine, which derives from indigenous herbal knowledge and Spanish humoral theories, has worked for many centuries as an adaptable and intellectually satisfying explanatory model of disease. Health, in this nonmedical model, is a state of balance between the four humors; if disturbed by a "cold" or a "hot" disease, the balance can be restored by using food or medicine with an opposing character. These are some examples of the more vigorous folk traditions. Every family and community in the United States retains elements of their folk medical heritage—even if only to "feed a cold and starve a fever."

Belief in miraculous, divine healing frequently has offered an alternative to the materialism of modern conventional medicine. Religious healing—oriented toward worship and devotion—finds expression in individual prayer, the Catholic tradition of pilgrimage, and the evangelical laying on of hands. In the late nineteenth century, Mary Baker Eddy drew on New England transcendentalism to fashion a belief system, Christian Science, that depended on religious faith to cure all disease. A form of radical idealism, Christian Science requires its followers to regard the body, disease, and death as illusions; any materialist preoccupation, such as an interest in conventional medical explanation, is assumed to impede spiritual healing. The great majority of alternative therapies, however, are not so exclusive.

One of the earlier semi-institutionalized alternatives to orthodox medical practices was botanical medicine, the systematic use of roots, herbs, and barks by lay healers. Formulated by Samuel Thomson in the early nineteenth century, this mild, herbal regime became a popular alternative to conventional "heroic" therapeutics, especially in rural areas of the West and South. By the 1840s botanical physicians had begun to form medical societies and issue diplomas, but the movement soon divided into factions and faded away at the end of the century. A more lasting challenge to conventional therapeutics came from homeopathy, the doctrine that disease could be cured only by very small doses of the drugs that produced in a healthy person the symptoms found in the sick. In other words, like cures like, using infinitesimal amounts. Derived from the experimental pharmacology of Samuel Hahnemann, homeopathy became popular among the urban elite in the northeastern United States soon after its introduction in the 1820s. By the 1880s most large cities had a homeopathic college, and in the 1890s examining boards were set up to license homeopathic physicians. Although most homeopathic institutions converted to conventional teaching in the early twentieth century, since the 1970s there has been a revival of interest in homeopathic principles.

In the twentieth century, osteopathy was the most significant institutionalized alternative to conventional medicine. When Andrew Taylor Still, a frontier physician, became dissatisfied with conventional "drugging" methods, he speculated that the underlying cause of illness was an obstruction to the flow of electricity through the body, leading to an imbalance of vital force that could be fixed only through spinal manipulation. By merging magnetic healing and the older technique of bonesetting and expressing his findings in religious language, Still attracted thousands of patients to his clinic in Kirksville, Mo., during the 1890s. In the twentieth century osteopathic medicine managed to maintain its schools, hospitals, specialty boards, and journals, although doctors of osteopathy increasingly provided the same services as medical doctors, with manipulation having only a small part in their repertoire. Chiropractics, which was developed by Daniel D. Palmer a few years after Still announced his new doctrine, has remained more focused on spinal manipulation but has not yet enjoyed the same institutional success as osteopathy.

In the late twentieth century, an interest in Asian healing systems emerged in the United States. Acupuncture has probably attracted more popular and scientific attention than any other recent introduction. Part of traditional Chinese medicine—along with acupressure, herbology, moxibustion, and dietetic regimes—the insertion of needles at certain acupuncture points is supposed to rebalance or unblock the flow of life energy (*chi*), which normally circulates through the body along the acupuncture meridians. According to this theory, illness develops from an obstruction of *chi* along one of the twelve double meridians. In the 1980s scientists began to try to provide more conventional explanations for the physiological changes observed in acupuncture.

Since the 1970s an eclectic holistic health movement promoted a broader health consciousness, drawing on a vast array of old and new alternative practices, including (but not limited to) naturopathy, meditation, yoga, acupuncture, "bodywork," biofeedback, flower essences, and exercise. The emphasis of this middle-class health reform movement was on the individual's responsibility for finding the right idiosyncratic mixture of holistic practices. Health was viewed as a positive physical and spiritual state, not just the absence of disease. This social movement had its information networks, metaphysical bookstores, health-food shops, informal groups, and journals, but unlike many nineteenth-century alternatives, it was not based itself on a conventional medical model.

[Norman Gevitz, ed., *Other Healers: Unorthodox Medicine in America* (Baltimore, 1988); Wayland D. Hand, ed., *American Folk Medicine: A Symposium* (Berkeley, Calif., 1976).]

WARWICK ANDERSON

See also **DAH:** Folk Medicine; Homeopathy; Indian Medicine; Medicine and Surgery; Osteopathy; **SUPP:** Medicine.

MEGALOPOLIS, a term coined from the name of a settlement in Peloponnese Greece meaning "great city," was first employed by the urbanist Lewis Mumford in *The Culture of Cities* (1938) as a metaphor for unnaturally large urban development. Such inorganic trends, he maintained, reflected "not a new kind of city on a supermetropolitan scale" but rather an "anti-city." Likened to one big "atomized container," megalopolitan areas, he warned, would produce "massive monotony" and result in "an increasingly homogenized urbanoid mass that lacks the complex social and cultural attributes of the city." With no nucleus, no organic nature, no essence of city, this process both "denatures the countryside and mechanically scatters fragments of the city over the whole landscape."

In contrast, the American physicist J. Robert Oppenheimer and the French geographer Jean Gottmann contended in 1950 that the megalopolis should be seen more positively. In *Megalopolis* (1961), Gottmann challenged Mumford's gloomy forecast, saying that a continuous network of urban communities, such as that stretching from Boston to Washington, D.C., represented the blueprint for the future. He argued that this region constitutes one of the world's largest industrial belts and "the greatest financial and political hubs on earth." With a population exceeding 40 million in 1995, more the size of a nation than a metropolis, the Northeast corridor of the United States contains the world's most highly developed concentration of large urban centers, with an increasingly suburban, white-collar population.

In addition to this prototype there are eight other megalopolises around the globe with more than 25 million people each, the second largest being located in the "Tokaido" region of Japan stretching from the conurbation of Tokyo-Yokohama to Osaka-Kōbe. Others include the Great Lakes megalopolis, extending from Quebec City to Milwaukee; the urban constellation of Shanghai; the area of northwestern Europe from Amsterdam and the Ruhr to Lille; the English urban sprawl from Dover to Merseyside; the Italian plain of the Po River to the Mediterranean, from Genoa to Marseilles and Pisa; Rio de Janeiro to São Paulo; California from the Mexico border to the San Francisco Bay area, and, most recently, a megalopolitan region in India.

[Jean Gottmann, *Megalopolis: The Urbanized Seaboard of the United States* (New York, 1961); Jean Gottmann and Robert A. Harper, eds., *Since Megalopolis: The Urban Writings of Jean Gottmann* (Baltimore, 1990); Lewis Mumford, *The Urban Prospect* (New York, 1968).]

TIMOTHY C. COOGAN

See also **DAH:** Cities, Growth of; City Planning; Urban Structure; **SUPP:** Demographic Changes; Suburban Living; Urban Living.

MEMPHIS, the largest city in Tennessee and the eighteenth largest in the United States, experienced an economic and cultural resurgence from the late 1970s to the mid-1990s. A thriving port city because of its location on the east bank of the Mississippi River, Memphis languished during the 1970s but rebounded in the 1980s. It established itself as a major distribution center, especially as the central terminal of the delivery service Federal Express in the 1970s. During the 1980s the city's downtown area prospered. The historic Peabody Hotel was renovated, and the city spent $63 million constructing a museum on Mud Island, near the downtown area, that included a five-block-long model of the Mississippi River. Along the river itself, old cotton shippers' offices were restored, and the architecturally striking thirty-two-story Pyramid entertainment and sports arena was built. In 1991 the National Civil Rights Museum opened, occupying the shell of the Loran Motel, the site of the assassination in 1968 of Martin Luther King, Jr. Following the death of Elvis Presley at his Graceland estate on Aug. 16, 1977, Graceland became the most visited house in the United States, with 750,000 tourists in 1994. During Elvis International Tribute Week, held annually in mid-August, dozens of events attract 50,000 tourists. Memphis has retained its dominance in cotton marketing and hardwood lumber trading. By the early 1990s its largest industry was health care, with treatment, education, and research bringing $2.5 billion per year to the city's economy. The 1990 population of Memphis was 610,337, 54.8 percent of which were African Americans.

JEFFREY M. MERRON

See also **SUPP:** Tennessee.

MENTAL ILLNESS, a common reference for disorders of thought, mood, or conduct, including schizophrenia, which affects about 1 percent of the U.S. population at some time in their lives; bipolar disorder (or manic-depressive illness), which affects 1 to 2 percent; and major depression, which strikes about 5 percent. These disorders are considered major because when untreated they have devastating consequences. They can take a considerable economic and social toll and cause great personal suffering. The ability to work or to have stable relationships and families is often lost or severely impaired. Rates of suicide are very high (10 to 20 percent) in people with these diagnoses and early death is the norm. Treatment often requires hospitalization. Other important diagnoses associated with disability or suicide include borderline personality disorder, panic disorder, and obsessive-compulsive disorder. Alcoholism and drug abuse often are included among major psychiatric diagnoses. In the United States, 10 percent of the population meet the definition for alcohol abuse or dependence at some time in their lives and almost 6 percent for other drugs.

In the last third of the twentieth century, ways to define mental illness sharpened and led to widespread belief that some of the most important disorders are diseases. Although patterns of symptoms had long been recognized, such as "schizophrenia" or "manic-depressive illness," there was uncertainty as to whether a psychiatric condition was an "illness" or an understandable response to a disturbed familial and social environment. Three developments made these disorders appear as illnesses. First, as drug treatment developed, mental disorders responded to them. It became clear that tranquilizers are not just sedatives. They help schizophrenics organize their thoughts and behaviors and suppress or eliminate hallucinations. These drugs, commonly called neuroleptics, were introduced in the 1950s. Twenty years later lithium (a mineral) came into use as an aid to stabilizing mood swings of bipolar disorder. Research results on the response to these medications showed that people with schizophrenia and bipolar disorder are biologically different from each other, even though in the acute phase of illness they are not easy to tell apart. Second, the risk of developing one or the other of these diseases appears to be inherited. Epidemiological research conducted since the 1950s shows that there is a genetic component to these illnesses, although environmental influences, such as toxic exposures, may function as triggers. It is also apparent that psychological stressors initiate episodes of illness. Third, research in the neurosciences provided evidence that mental illnesses are associated with abnormalities in the brain. As imaging methods developed it became possible to demonstrate subtle structural damage in the brains of schizophrenics. Bipolar disorder, however, is associated with biochemical abnormalities.

The emerging belief that mental illnesses are specific disorders, often with a basis in biology, supported a shift in psychiatry. Whereas assignment to a diagnostic category often included inferences about the psychological processes of the patient, psychiatrists turned to a descriptive approach, using observable behavior and the course of the illness to establish a diagnosis. This change now appears in the *Diagnostic and Statistical Manual of Mental Disorders,* published by the American Psychiatric Association. The first two editions, 1952 and 1968, maintained a "process" orientation, whereas the third and fourth, in 1980 and 1994, emphasized a descriptive approach. These books, known as *DSM-III* or *DSM-IV,* have enormous influence on mental health practice. Insurance reimbursement usually requires a *DSM* diagnosis. Examinations to certify psychiatrists rely on familiarity with *DSM* criteria.

Years ago there were two avenues to treat major mental disorders. A "cure" could be attempted through restructuring the patient's experience, chiefly with psychotherapy or milieu treatment in an institution. If unavailing and the illness did not remit of its own accord the alternative was prolonged institutional care. The dichotomy between cure or custody was superseded by both medical and social approaches. Medication helped keep the mentally ill out of hospitals, often called "deinstitutionalization." The community mental health movement, originally focused on efforts to prevent mental illness, evolved in part into a philosophy of rehabilitation. The environment of a mental hospital itself produces dependency and disorganization. Allowing patients to live in the least restrictive environment compatible with their well-being proved more effective. There is evidence that people with chronic mental illness prefer being able to live outside a hospital, although deinstitutionalization has deprived many people of care and led to increased homelessness. Such was the case in the last quarter of the twentieth century in large cities, where political and economic exigencies (for example, overcrowding of institutions) rather than social or bureaucratic munificence prompted the emptying out of mental hospitals.

Although drugs for psychiatric disorders can have serious side effects, they can improve the quality of life for people with schizophrenia, major depression, or manic-depressive illness as well as anxiety disorders, obsessive-compulsive disorder, and other conditions, such as premenstrual dysphoric disorder (commonly referred to as PMS). The most important innovation in drug treatment since the late 1980s is the increasingly widespread use of clozapine (trade name Clozaril), a unique antipsychotic drug once thought to be too dangerous because of its ability to cause a dramatic and even lethal lowering of white blood cells. Research shows that clozapine benefits one-third of people with schizophrenia resistant to treatment with other medications. The drug requires a blood test every week.

Meanwhile there was a shift in ethical and legal attitudes. Individual autonomy increasingly received attention, even if the person's choice would not be seen by most people as in his or her own best interest. The right of a competent person to refuse medical treatment of any kind, even if it is life-saving, became established. Definitions of competence changed and many people with impairment due to mental ill-

ness are now considered competent to manage some of their affairs and particularly to refuse psychiatric treatment unless symptoms are so severe as to put life (their own or another's) at risk. Many more people with disturbing symptoms are now living independently, often in public view, rather than confined to hospitals.

[Michael J. Dear and Jennifer R. Wolch, *Landscapes of Despair: From Deinstitutionalization to Homelessness* (Princeton, N.J., 1987); James H. Kocsis et al., *Diagnosis and Treatment of Chronic Depression* (New York, 1995); Christian L. Shriqui and Henry A. Nasrallah, eds., *Contemporary Issues in the Treatment of Schizophrenia* (Washington, D.C., 1995); J. Mark G. Williams, *The Psychological Treatment of Depression,* 2nd ed. (New York, 1992).]

WILLIAM IRA BENNETT

See also **SUPP:** Psychiatry; Psychology; Substance Abuse.

MERCHANT MARINE, and to a lesser extent the seagoing shipping of other nations, underwent enormous change beginning in the second half of the twentieth century, including a veritable revolution in handling freight. Over the centuries, merchandise carried overseas went in break-bulk, that is, divided into parcels of varying size. Such handling continued during the age of steam and the diesel engine. Terminal activities in this scheme of moving goods were labor intensive. Cargoes should have been handled at a low cost with care and speed, but often this was not the case. Collective-bargaining agreements between shippers and unions increased longshoremen's hours for specific jobs. Work stoppages occurred on the docks. Moreover, break-bulk items were frequently damaged or lost due to poor handling or theft.

All this came to an end with the introduction of the container system, created by Malcolm McLean, a former truck driver and founder of McLean Trucking who knew little about shipping. (A container is a box up to forty feet long and eight feet wide and is transported on land by the use of a chassis that is pulled by a truck; containers are double stacked without a chassis when hauled by train.) McLean sought an inexpensive way to return containers from New York to Texas and fitted two tankers with platforms above the decks for carrying thirty-five-foot boxes. He purchased Pan-Atlantic Steamship Corporation and Waterman Steamship in 1955. In April of the next year, Pan Atlantic's *Ideal X*, the world's first container ship, sailed from Port Newark, N.J., to Houston. Pan-Atlantic announced that it would convert other ships into container ships. When these vessels went to sea, McLean told their captains not to bother him with nautical nonsense; they were ship drivers at sea. The first fully containerized vessel, *Gateway City*, began regular service between New York, Florida, and Texas in 1957. Pan-Atlantic Steamship Corporation changed its name to Sea-Land in 1960. In sending freight across the oceans, the container revolution proved as influential as the shift from sail to steam. In one brilliant leap McLean produced an entirely different type of ship. The *Gateway City* had a capacity for 226 thirty-five-foot containers. It could be turned around in one day by two shore-based gantry cranes. With break-bulk, this would have taken weeks. Once the system came into full operation, damage and pilferage decreased dramatically. Matson Navigation helped to make containerization a familiar word in the shipping industry; the company developed a gantry crane that could handle 520 containers every twenty-four hours.

Other developments quickly followed. During the early 1960s a division of American President Lines known as Pacific Far East Line (PFEL) transported military supplies to Vietnam. No one knew how long that war would last, and it seemed unwise to consider building docks and erecting gantry cranes at Cam Ranh Bay in South Vietnam. PFEL used a lighter aboard ship (LASH) system. Sea-Land, the original innovator, then introduced another novelty, this time in the pattern of trade employed by container ships voyaging to East Asia. Because Sea-Land ships were returning to Oakland, Calif., with empty containers, the company therefore sought business in Japan, and without waiting for cooperation from the Japanese government, it arranged gantry cranes and other container equipment in a Japanese port, thereby giving Sea-Land a profitable back haul. The result was worldwide competition. After Sea-Land's move in Japan, local shipping firms installed U.S. equipment. In a short time Japanese companies built container ships and were competing with U.S. companies. British shippers also moved to develop container capability.

McLean eventually overreached himself in attempting to create a worldwide line specializing in container ship commerce. After selling Sea-Land in May 1969 to the R. J. Reynolds Tobacco Company, which was seeking to diversify, McLean acquired the United States Lines and purchased another old American line, Moore McCormack. He signed contracts in 1983 for twelve new container ships, to be built in the huge Daewoo yards in South Korea. The $570 million order represented the largest single

peacetime shipbuilding contract and the largest expansion of the U.S. Merchant Marine in its entire history. McLean conceived of a remarkable commerce, in which a Daewoo-built ship would depart an East Asian port for the Panama Canal, and after transit calls at East Coast ports, sail to Western Europe. After leaving the Mediterranean, passing through the Suez Canal, and calling at Middle Eastern ports, the ship would move on to the East Asian port of origin, thus completing a worldwide loop. He described the proposed route as his Sea Bridge. He would reach all areas of the world with the Sea Bridge except for West Africa, Australia, and New Zealand. The Sea Bridge operation began in December 1984, but after a few months of operation, McLean's venture turned into bankruptcy, with a loss of nearly $100 million in a single quarter. In 1987 the Econships, as they were known, were sold, then began operating under U.S. flag and Sea-Land ownership.

U.S. container ships continued to carry much world commerce. From 1985 to 1995 the volume of exports of containerized cargo from New York harbor alone jumped by 53 percent, from 2.68 million long tons to 4.1 million (a long ton, the traditional measure of shipping, is 2,240 pounds). The value of this shipping rose from $9.59 billion to $17.14 billion, a 32 percent increase after factoring in inflation. The Port Authority of New York and New Jersey estimated that it handled $56.31 billion in cargo in 1993, generating 180,800 jobs. Part of the Port Authority's increase in business was caused by modernization, including new railway links, crucial because containers go directly from freighters onto trucks and trains, all the while tracked by computers. Labor relations in the Port of New York area have improved, but the principal reason for the resurgence of the New York–New Jersey area has been the sheer efficiency of the container ships.

The leading U.S. ports on the East Coast are New York–New Jersey, with 38 percent of the North Atlantic trade, mostly containerized cargo, followed by Norfolk, Va., Philadelphia, and Baltimore. In the Gulf of Mexico, the principal port is Houston. New Orleans leads on the Mississippi. On the West Coast the leading ports are Seattle-Tacoma, San Francisco (including Oakland), Long Beach, and Los Angeles. The tonnage carried by the U.S. Merchant Marine has risen because of container ships. In the 1940s construction of mass-produced Liberty and Victory ships raised tonnage spectacularly, and as late as 1960 the Merchant Marine under U.S. registry stood at almost 25 billion gross tons. Twenty years later it had dropped to nearly 18.5 billion, but by 1993 it had reached the remarkable figure of almost 22.5 billion gross tons.

[René De La Pedraja, *The Rise and Decline of U.S. Merchant Shipping in the Twentieth Century* (New York, 1992); John Niven, *The American President Line* (Newark, Del., 1986).]

CHARLES V. REYNOLDS, JR.

MERCY KILLING. *See* **Euthanasia.**

MERGERS AND ACQUISITIONS. *See* **Leveraged Buyouts.**

MERITOR SAVINGS BANK V. MECHELLE VINSON, 477 U.S. 57 (1986), a Supreme Court decision that attempted for the first time to define what standard a court should use to determine sexual harassment under Title VII of the Civil Rights Act of 1964. The two main issues were whether a plaintiff's claim of sexual harassment could succeed if based on psychological aspects without tangible loss of an economic character, and whether employers are absolutely liable in cases of sexual harassment by supervisors. Mechelle Vinson was an employee at Meritor Savings Bank under the supervision of the vice president and branch manager, Sidney Taylor, and Vinson had earned various promotions on the basis of merit. Vinson testified that Taylor invited her to dinner, repeatedly proposed sexual relations, leading to forty or fifty occasions of intercourse, fondled her in front of employees, followed her into the women's restroom, exposed himself to her, and raped her on several occasions. At first Vinson resisted but ceased to do so out of fear of losing her job. She testified she never reported the incidents or used the bank's complaint procedure out of fear and because she would have to make the claim directly to her supervisor, Taylor. He stopped sexually harassing her when Vinson began dating someone steadily. She was fired for taking an excessive leave of absence.

Subsequently, she filed a sexual harassment claim for violations of Title VII. Both the bank and Taylor denied Vinson's accusations and insisted that the claim arose from a business-related dispute. The bank asserted that if Vinson's claims were true, the supervisor's activities were unknown to the bank's executive managers and engaged in without its consent. The federal district court held that for a sexual harassment claim to prevail the plaintiff had to demonstrate a tangible economic loss. The court also held that the bank was not liable for the misconduct of its supervisors. On both counts the circuit court reversed in favor of Vinson. The bank appealed to the Supreme Court, which in a unanimous decision decided for Vinson on the first point, but held that employers were not automatically liable for sexual harassment by supervisors. Similarly, however, absence of notice to an employer did not insulate the business from liability for the acts of supervisors. In such cases the issue was one of fact, which required meeting a burden of proof. The case placed sexual harassment resulting from a hostile work environment on an equal footing with sexual harassment resulting in the loss of job or promotion. The case put employers on notice that they must review supervisors' conduct because mere absence of notice of improper conduct is no longer a defense.

TONY FREYER

See also **SUPP: Sexual Harassment.**

MEXICAN AMERICANS represent both an old and a new ethnic group in the United States. Some can trace their backgrounds to the early Spanish-Indian encounters in both Mexico and the U.S. Southwest. Others migrated to the United States from Mexico in the twentieth century. It is this combination of old and new, past and present, that gives the history of Mexican Americans its character. Spain's conquest of Mexico and the Aztec empire in 1521 led to development of a mixed or mestizo people consisting of Indians and Spaniards. This encounter became the basis for the colonial missions and settlements that stretched from Texas to California. A Spanish-Mexican cultural presence was implanted that is visible today in the names of southwestern locations. These Spanish-Mexican settlements, however, were coveted by the United States following independence from Great Britain. The United States undertook an expansionist drive after the Louisiana Purchase (1803) from France placed the young nation in direct proximity to Spain's northern frontier. After Mexico's own independence from Spain in 1821, it came under increased U.S. pressure to cede its inherited northern borderlands. In 1836 Texas, under control of U.S. immigrants, established its independence, and in 1845 it was annexed by the United States. Coveting additional Mexican territory, the United States successfully waged war against Mexico in 1846–1848. The subsequent Treaty of Guadalupe Hidalgo provided for transfer of the balance of Mexico's northern lands, which included the present-day states of Colorado, Nevada, Utah, California, and most of Arizona and New Mexico. The resident Mexican population became U.S. citizens.

The period following the Mexican War marked a dark era in Mexican-American history. U.S. rule led to pressures on Mexican-American landowners resulting in loss of property to squatters, litigation, taxes, and market pressures. In addition, Mexican Americans were treated like second-class citizens. Mexican Americans might have become a footnote in U.S. history had it not been for a subsequent mass migration from Mexico. Pushed out of their own country by both poverty and the Mexican Revolution that began in 1910, immigrants were drawn into the United States because of the need for labor for U.S. railroads, mines, and farms. More than a million crossed the border between 1900 and 1930. They expanded older settlements in the Southwest, established new barrios, and renewed the Mexican-American cultural presence in the United States. The Great Depression stopped this migration and generated pressure to deport immigrants. In response, U.S.-born Mexicans launched a civil rights movement focusing on discrimination in education, jobs, wages, housing, political representation, and racial and cultural stereotyping. They sought integration in U.S. society. The move was vastly assisted by the involvement of thousands of Mexican Americans in World War II, in which many were awarded citations for bravery, including the Medal of Honor.

A new generation, that of Chicano Americans, appeared in the 1960s. Composed of children or grandchildren of immigrants, this generation of activists defiantly called themselves Chicanos (a working-class barrio term) and advocated cultural pride. Influenced by the struggle of farm workers led by Cesar Chavez, they brought pressure on schools to institute Chicano studies and bilingual education. They instituted a cultural and artistic resurgence centered on Chicano identity. There was a Chicano anti–Vietnam War movement and the beginning of a Chicano feminist movement. They established a Chicano political party (La Raza Unida). The most widespread Mexican-American protest movement in history, the Chicano movement brought the plight and aspirations of Mexican Americans to national and international attention. The Chicano movement of the 1960s and 1970s defeated some but by no means all forms of discrimination. The emergence of a more conservative U.S. political climate in the 1980s and 1990s made civil rights struggles more difficult. Still, Mexi-

can Americans continued to integrate into U.S. society while asserting their identity in a pluralistic nation, partly because of their and other Hispanics' growing numbers in the United States. By 1990 Mexican Americans constituted three-fifths of the twenty-two million Hispanics in the United States.

While Mexican Americans have constituted a permanent and settled part of the U.S. population for some time, immigration from Mexico has continued to reinforce this population and remains a key factor in Mexican-American life. During World War II, for example, thousands of braceros (contract workers) were imported into the United States from Mexico to work, especially in agriculture. The Bracero Program was maintained from 1942 to 1964. Many braceros did not return to Mexico at the prescribed time and remained in the United States without proper documentation. Moreover, the Bracero Program helped stimulate an increase in undocumented immigration; many who did not qualify for the program crossed the border illegally and undocumented immigration continued to escalate after the program ended. To deal with the impact of illegal immigration, Congress in 1986 passed the Immigration Reform and Control Act, which provided amnesty for those who could prove they had been working in the United States for a number of years.

[Mario T. Garcia, *Desert Immigrants: The Mexicans of El Paso, 1880–1920* (New Haven, Conn., 1981), and *Mexican Americans: Leadership, Ideology, and Identity, 1930–1960* (New Haven, Conn., 1989); Peter Skerry, *Mexican Americans: The Ambivalent Minority* (New York, 1993).]

MARIO T. GARCIA

See also **DAH:** Guadalupe Hidalgo, Treaty of; Mexican War; Texas; **DAH** and **SUPP:** Immigration; Mexico, Relations with.

MEXICO, RELATIONS WITH. U.S. relations with Mexico in the second half of the twentieth century were complicated, principally because the two nations, despite strikingly different cultures and often conflicting political agendas in the international arena, nonetheless created economic bonds of lasting importance. The modern relationship between Mexico and the United States took form during and after World War II, when Washington's need for strategic resources and cheap Mexican labor coincided with Mexican determination to achieve U.S. approval of its revolutionary agenda and to modernize its economy. The half century after World War II witnessed volatile political exchanges between Washington and Mexico City over cold war issues (such as the Cuban and Nicaraguan revolutions), immigration, trade, U.S. business in Mexico, debts, drugs, and political corruption—but the intertwining of the two economies continued. The approval of the North American Free Trade Agreement (NAFTA) in 1993 merely formalized this unequal economic union, particularly along the 2,000-mile border. By the year 2000, some observers believe, the 100-mile-wide swath on either side of the legal demarcation may be the most populated region in North America and will be filled with factories. Unlike its Canadian-U.S. counterpart, however, the Mexican-U.S. border embodies the anticipated social, cultural, and political dysfunctions that accompany the meshing of a postindustrial with a putative Third World economy.

Since the early 1970s the border industrialization program, which was designed to create jobs in Mexico and thus retard the flow of illegal entries into the United States, has instead exacerbated the problem. Confronting a financial crisis brought on by overspending and a $100 billion foreign debt, Mexican President José López Portillo nationalized his country's banks. The Mexican standard of living, particularly for the middle class, fell sharply. After more than a decade of debate, in 1986 the U.S. Congress passed the Immigration Reform and Control Act, establishing sanctions against U.S. employers who knowingly employ undocumented workers. Two years later, after a bitterly fought campaign laced with charges of fraud, Harvard-educated Carlos Salinas de Gortari, candidate of the ruling Institutional Revolutionary Party, became president of Mexico. Salinas committed his administration to a revival of the Mexican economy through strengthened economic ties with the United States. A decade earlier, a more bombastic Mexican leader had defied the United States, condemning its intervention in Central America and proclaiming Mexico as a leader in the Third World. Weathering the inevitable charges hurled at him by nationalists, Salinas endorsed an economic union with the United States and Canada.

President George Bush pushed hard for NAFTA and President Bill Clinton expended considerable political energy getting the measure through the U.S. Congress, despite opposition from environmentalists and organized labor. Unlike the European Economic Community, now the Economic Union of Nations, NAFTA does not erase national boundaries or create a common currency; rather, it represents the formalization of the symbiotic economic relationship that began during World War II. Continued charges of po-

litical corruption and socioeconomic injustice on the part of the Mexican government, which was unable to put down a revolt of Indians in the state of Chiapas in 1994, belie the positive image projected of Mexico during the NAFTA debates.

[Lester D. Langley, *Mexico and the United States* (Boston, 1991); Robert A. Pastor, *Integration with Mexico* (New York, 1993).]

LESTER D. LANGLEY

See also **SUPP:** El Paso; Mexican Americans; North American Free Trade Agreement.

MIAMI, city in southeastern Florida, was founded in 1896 by railroad and hotel baron Henry M. Flagler as a tourist destination at the terminus of Flagler's Florida East Coast Railway. Miami possesses sunshine, seashore, and a subtropical climate, and these amenities attracted vacationers by the hundreds of thousands as early as the 1920s. The Florida real estate boom of the 1920s helped push Miami's population to 110,000 by 1930, while stimulating the growth of such nearby communities as Miami Beach, Coral Gables, and Hialeah. Despite the Great Depression, the Miami area's permanent and visitor population continued on an upward spiral; between 1920 and 1940, Miami was one of the fastest-growing metropolitan areas in the nation. Implanted in the public consciousness by 1940, Miami's image was that of a glamorous resort catering to the rich and famous: business tycoons and movie stars, labor leaders and politicians, presidents and gangsters.

World War II had an important impact on the city. The establishment of military training facilities and numerous air and naval bases boosted the local economy during the war. More than one hundred hotels housed military trainees, providing year-round income to their owners. The big military payroll also stimulated the building and service trades, attracting civilian workers to south Florida. In addition, the war led Miamians to a greater appreciation of the importance of air travel, and from this period local boosters touted Miami as the aviation capital of the Americas and the "Gateway to Latin America." Miami experienced dynamic growth in the postwar era. The local economy became more diverse as construction, services, and light manufacturing complemented the tourist industry. The population of metropolitan Miami grew rapidly to 495,000 in 1950 and 935,000 in 1960. Developers subdivided the periphery to house residents and retirees from the Northeast and Midwest. Miami's population became more affluent and more liberal on political and social issues. Jewish migrants helped form the Miami chapter of the Congress of Racial Equality and joined with black activists in lunch-counter sit-ins, bringing civil rights issues to south Florida. In the late 1950s, urban reformers addressed the area's fragmented government, introducing the nation's first two-tiered, metropolitan or "metro" government in 1957.

The Cuban revolution of 1959 led by Fidel Castro initiated a massive exodus of Cuban exiles to the United States, totaling 900,000 by 1990. Most Cubans settled in metropolitan Miami, where they dramatically altered the city's character. Several hundred thousand exiles from other Caribbean nations and from Central and South America, added to the Cubans, constituted half of metropolitan Miami's 1990 population of 2 million people; according to the 1990 census, some 70 percent of Miami's population was foreign born. This demographic revolution made Miami a bilingual, multicultural city. Demographic patterns turned Miami into the economic and cultural capital of the entire Caribbean basin. International trade and banking surged beginning in the 1970s, as did foreign investment in Miami real estate. In the late twentieth century Latin American tourists mingled with northern vacationers. Although Miami came to be recognized for its new skyscraper skyline, there was a darker side to the city's history in the late twentieth century. Ethnic conflicts and economic disparities led to polarization, pitting Hispanics, blacks, and native-born whites against each other. Miami experienced four major race riots in 1980–1992, suggesting deep underlying tensions. Crime and murder damaged Miami's image, as did a persistent illegal drug trade. Rapid development of the urban periphery, especially along the fringes of the ecologically sensitive Everglades, has posed environmental dangers. Nevertheless, Miami still displayed the vitality that can accompany growth, change, and cultural diversity.

[Raymond A. Mohl, "Miami: The Ethnic Cauldron," in *Sunbelt Cities: Politics and Growth Since World War II,* edited by Richard M. Bernard and Bradley R. Rice (Austin, Tex., 1983); Nicholas N. Patricios, *Building Marvelous Miami* (Gainesville, Fla., 1994); Alejandro Portes and Alex Stepick, *City on the Edge: The Transformation of Miami* (Berkeley, Calif., 1993).]

RAYMOND A. MOHL

See also **SUPP:** Caribbean Policy; Cuban Americans; Florida; Hispanic Americans; Tourism.

MIAs. *See* **Prisoners of War and Missing in Action.**

MICHIGAN. During the 1970s the state endured a threefold increase in violent crime and the erosion of urban centers, the effects of which were most evident in industrial cities such as Detroit and Flint. Relocation of automotive plants and their suppliers from the cities to suburban areas and other states, combined with a decline in employment resulting from increased automation and advances in production techniques, created high unemployment, with nearly 50 percent of inner-city black youths jobless. Neighborhoods deteriorated and houses and shops became vacant. By the end of the decade, Detroit, which derisively had been dubbed "murder city" because of its 44.5 homicides for every 100,000 residents in 1975, had undergone a transformation. Under the leadership of its first black mayor, Coleman Young, elected in 1973, a business-hotel complex aptly named the Renaissance Center and the Joe Louis Sports Arena were erected and later showcased when Detroit hosted the 1980 Republican National Convention. Neighborhood revitalization was encouraged, and many young middle-class people returned to live in the city. Detroit's revitalization program served as an important model for a state with an urban population of 81.3 percent in 1980. Other communities followed Detroit's lead and by 1980 Michigan was making widespread efforts at urban renewal.

Another problem facing the state in the 1970s was the economic devastation caused by the October 1973 embargo on oil from the Middle East. Gasoline shortages, combined with threats of rationing, led to a reduction in new car sales. In addition, Michigan's billion-dollar-a-year tourist industry, especially critical to the economy of the upper peninsula, was crippled as concern over the availability of gasoline kept many travelers at home. By 1978 automobile production and sales had recovered, but the message of the 1970s was evident. If Michigan persisted in relying on the automobile industry, it would face stagnation or decline.

Two popular political leaders became prominent during the 1970s. William G. Milliken moved up from his post as lieutenant governor when Governor George Romney resigned in 1969 to become a member of President Richard Nixon's cabinet. A moderate Republican, Milliken held office for fourteen years. In 1976 liberal Democrat Philip Hart ended eighteen years of service in the U.S. Senate, where he had helped shape virtually every piece of legislation favoring civil rights, consumer protection, and regulation of big business. Michiganians also were proud of

Gerald R. Ford, who, after twenty-five years in Congress, became the first Michigan resident to serve as president of the United States.

The 1980s began on a sour note as spiraling inflation and soaring interest rates thrust the automobile industry into another nosedive. By mid-1980 more than 620,000 auto workers were jobless, the most since the Great Depression. As sales plunged and unemployment rose, state revenues plummeted, while demands for state assistance for the needy increased at a record pace. In 1982 Democrats took advantage of Michigan's having the highest unemployment rate in the nation (16 percent), Milliken's retirement, and a split in the Republican party to elect a Detroit congressman, James Blanchard, as their party's first governor in twenty years. The new governor inherited a $200 million deficit. Because the state constitution mandated a balanced budget, he proposed a temporary 38 percent increase in the state income tax, as well as additional cuts in state-supported programs. With this change in administration Michigan started on yet another slow road to recovery. Bond ratings were upgraded, funding for state services and education increased, and the Michigan Youth Corps was formed to offer temporary summer employment to more than 60,000 young people. Car sales, aided by a federal import quota on foreign automobiles, began to rise, unemployment declined to 14 percent, and Michigan was hailed as one of the nation's "comeback states." Refusing to ignore the lessons of the past, Blanchard outlined a program of economic strategies stressing diversification of industry, retraining of workers for high-technology jobs, and regional cooperation among the Great Lakes states to attract new industry. His ability to achieve these goals was hindered by an electorate angered by the tax increase. After an unsuccessful recall campaign against the governor, voters returned control of the state senate in 1983 to the more fiscally conservative Republicans. Blanchard was reelected in 1986, primarily because of another division within the Republican party, but his second term was marred before it even began. Two days after his reelection General Motors announced that it was closing seven plants in Michigan and laying off nearly 18,000 workers, an action that Blanchard had told voters would not occur.

The 1980s also saw a decline in the number of residents engaged in the state's third largest industry—agriculture. Farms declined during the decade from 66,000 to 55,000, and cultivated acreage fell from 11.4 million to 10.8 million. One of the state's major contributions during the decade was the creation of the Michigan Educational Trust Fund, which allowed parents to invest $3,000 per child and in return receive assurance that the child would receive a four-year education at any of Michigan's fifteen state-supported colleges beginning in the year 2005. This program was in the best tradition of Michigan's commitment to educational excellence. In 1980, 60 percent of Michigan's residents were high school graduates, and 14.3 percent had completed at least four years of college. Between 70 and 80 percent of Michigan's college students attend public, rather than private, institutions, a rate nearly 20 percent above the national average. The trust fund met the future needs of a population fearful of the spiraling costs of higher education.

In 1990, plagued by yet another decline in the automobile industry and facing charges that he had not done enough to remedy problems of inner-city minorities, Blanchard lost his bid for a third term to Republican State Senator John Engler by 17,000 votes. The new governor inherited a $1.8 billion deficit, which he sought to reduce through a program of cost-cutting and reorganization. In 1993 Michigan had the most robust economic growth of all industrial states. A record 4.35 million workers were employed, an increase of nearly 400,000 since 1991; unemployment was at its lowest level in fifteen years; and growth in personal income was nearly three times the national average. Michigan's turnaround was based on three factors. The first, welfare reform, was aimed at ending dependency on the state, and in 1991 general assistance welfare payments stopped for 83,000 single, able-bodied adults. Retraining programs and community service alternatives were instituted. The retraining worked so well that Michigan in 1993 led the nation in the number of welfare recipients employed and moving toward self-sufficiency. Second, a tax relief program, including a property tax freeze, a cut in the state small business tax, and elimination of inheritance taxes helped produce a $312 million surplus in 1993. Third, the state embarked on partnerships with private industries and privatized state services. Partnership with a pharmaceutical company made it possible to supply free vaccines to nearly all of the state's children, and Michigan contracted with the Salvation Army to provide shelter for 5,000 homeless persons. Education continued to be a popular program in the 1990s and was spared from budget cuts, receiving increases of more than $500 million over four years. In a bold move, Governor Engler in 1993 called for ending reliance on property taxes for school funding, and in 1994 he signed a bill establishing the most sweeping charter school act in the nation.

Despite its economic vicissitudes and political changes, Michigan continued to support cultural organizations and events. The Interlochen Center for the Arts maintained its status as one of the nation's premier music training centers, while art fairs and summer stock theater developed into summer showcases throughout the state. Two living history museums, Greenfield Village in Dearborn and Crossroads Village in Flint, enable visitors to experience life in pre-twentieth-century Michigan, and Detroit's Afro-American Museum and Holocaust Museum serve as reminders of the struggles of blacks and Jews everywhere. Ethnic cultural contributions are evident in events such as the Holland Tulip Festival, Frankenmuth's Oktoberfest, and Detroit's summer-long series of ethnic festivals.

[Richard J. Hathaway, ed., *Michigan: Visions of Our Past* (East Lansing, Mich., 1989); Bruce A. Rubenstein and Lawrence C. Ziewacz, *Michigan: A History of the Great Lakes State* (Arlington Heights, Ill., 1981).]

BRUCE A. RUBENSTEIN

See also **SUPP:** Detroit.

MICROBIOLOGY. During the last quarter of the twentieth century the biological sciences achieved a wealth of benefits from progress in microbiology, the study of living organisms invisible to the naked eye. Sophisticated electron microscopes, improved staining, cloning, sequencing, and the availability of computer graphics enabled scientists in the United States and elsewhere to learn more about the structure and composition of viruses, fungi, protozoa, bacteria, and other members of the microbial world. Such enlightenment contributed to efforts aimed at preventing, ameliorating, and curing certain diseases. Studies of microorganisms in the late twentieth century opened new areas of research in cell physiology, biochemistry, and genetics. Microbiological research enhanced molecular biology by leading to a more precise means of investigating the structure and functions of nucleic acids and proteins. The focus on the arrangement of genetic materials, including the nature of genes and mechanisms controlling their functions, also helped develop molecular genetics.

Microbiology research aided in clarifying the causes of diseases that drew national attention in the 1970s and 1980s, including Legionnaire's disease, a mysterious respiratory disease that struck 182 members of the American Legion at a convention in Phila-

delphia in 1976. By 1978 microbiologists at the Centers for Disease Control had isolated the *legionella* bacteria. Subsequent studies of the bacteria assisted health officials in identifying sources and victims. Research also helped scientists at the National Institutes of Health (NIH), the federal government's largest biomedical research center, identify certain microbes responsible for other human illnesses. In 1980 Robert Gallo and his team at the National Cancer Institute linked cancer to a virus. In 1982 Willy Burgdorfer of the NIH Rocky Mountain Laboratories in Hamilton, Mont., observed the spiral-shaped spirochete from a tick that caused Lyme disease. Burgdorfer's find led to more accurate diagnoses and treatment and to research for a vaccine.

One of the more notable advances was the use of the colon bacterium *Escherichia coli* (*E. coli*), especially for biotechnology. Because of the work of several Nobel Prize winners and their colleagues, including Marshall Nirenberg of the National Heart, Lung, and Blood Institute of NIH and Walter Gilbert of Harvard University, researchers recognized that strains of *E. coli* could house a variety of genes for testing. Scientists found that strains of *E. coli* could help develop processes for producing human insulin and possibly protective materials with the strength, resistance, and light weight of spider webs. Additional efforts resulted in the isolation of hepatitis viruses previously unrecognized, identification of an acquired immunodeficiency syndrome (AIDS) virus, and reconstruction of a major histocompatibility complex protein involved in immune responses to infection—studies that, among other improvements, contributed to the development of tests to make blood transfusions safer.

[Ronald M. Atlas, *Microbiology: Fundamentals and Applications* (New York, 1984); Wolfgang K. Joklik et al., eds., *Zinsser Microbiology* (Norwalk, Conn., 1992).]

RUTH ROY HARRIS

See also **SUPP:** Acquired Immune Deficiency Syndrome; Bacteriology and Virology; Legionnaire's Disease; Lyme Disease; Medicine; Toxic Shock Syndrome.

MIDDLE EAST, RELATIONS WITH. Prior to World War I the United States had few diplomatic relations with the Middle East. Only in major capitals such as Istanbul, Cairo, and Tehran was there a continuous U.S. diplomatic presence. Private citizens, archaeologists, a few businessmen, and, most important, Protestant missionaries and educators acted as unofficial representatives of the United States. Although few in number the latter exerted influence through their educational institutions, such as the American University of Beirut, Robert College in Istanbul, and Damavand College in Tehran, where they trained many future Mideast leaders. These U.S. citizens had political contacts in Washington and when occasion demanded could call upon the assistance of their government. In the early 1880s the missionary community of Iran prevailed upon President Chester A. Arthur to send a permanent diplomatic representative to Tehran. As in East Asia, missionaries often served as consuls in cities where there was no permanent U.S. representative in residence. In the years following World War I, U.S. oil companies became interested in regional resources. European companies had discovered oil in Iraq and neighboring Iran and arranged to keep control for themselves. Successive Republican administrations helped to open the door for U.S. capital, but the heyday of the nation's economic penetration would come after World War II, with the discovery that much of the region adjacent to the Persian Gulf was floating on a sea of oil.

World War II served as a catalyst for U.S. involvement in the Middle East. The administration of President Franklin D. Roosevelt helped to maintain a bridge to victory for the Allies from 1942, channeling military supplies through Iran to the Soviet Union. In 1943 important Allied meetings took place at Casablanca, Cairo, and Tehran, where leaders worked out strategies for defeating the Axis powers. As a sign of changing times Roosevelt met with King Abd al-Aziz Ibn Saud of oil-rich Saudi Arabia on his way back from the Yalta Conference in 1945. After the war the U.S. government would have been content to let Great Britain and France continue to represent Western diplomatic interests in the Middle East. Faced with the rising force of nationalism and demands for independence, however, the European colonial powers had neither the resources nor the energy to reimpose their domination. Great Britain withdrew from Palestine (now Israel, the West Bank, and Gaza) in 1948, Egypt in 1954, Aden (later the People's Republic of Yemen and now part of Yemen) in 1967, and the Persian Gulf in 1971. France withdrew from Lebanon in 1943, Syria in 1946, Morocco and Tunisia in 1956, and finally Algeria after a bloody struggle that raged from 1954 to 1962.

As the cold war with the Soviet Union intensified, only the United States had the power to oppose communist penetration of the region. Until the end of this struggle in the late 1980s, the two principles of U.S. Middle East policy were to contain the Soviets and guarantee regional oil supplies for the West. Many historians believe the cold war began in the Middle East, where the two superpowers openly disagreed over the issue of Soviet troop withdrawals from postwar Iran in 1945–1946. Then Great Britain, plagued by deficits, withdrew from Greece, where a civil war raged. President Harry S. Truman, believing that the Russians had instigated the turmoil there and that they also threatened neighboring Turkey, in 1947 announced the Truman Doctrine of economic and military assistance for the two states. In 1952 Greece and Turkey became members of the North Atlantic Treaty Organization (NATO), anchoring the eastern flank of the alliance.

Step by step the United States entered more deeply into regional affairs. No undertaking would be more decisive than Truman's support in 1948 of an independent Jewish state in the former British mandate of Palestine. A combination of factors inspired the president: sympathy for survivors of the Holocaust, lobbying by Zionists (supporters of a Jewish state) in the United States, a desire to thwart Soviet moves to befriend the Jewish settlers in Palestine, and a wish to nurture a stable, democratic, pro-Western state in the region. Although historians differ on the importance of these factors, they agree that the issue divided the Truman administration. Officials who opposed recognition feared it would antagonize the Arabs and push them into closer contact with the Soviets.

Since 1948, Arab hostility toward the United States, Israel's staunchest ally, has at times become intense and threatened to undermine U.S. goals in the region. Egyptian president Gamal Abdul Nasser tried to buy arms from Washington after an Israeli attack into the Egyptian-controlled Gaza Strip in February 1955. When President Dwight D. Eisenhower refused, Nasser purchased them instead from Soviet-controlled Czechoslovakia, inaugurating years of Soviet-Egyptian collaboration. Secretary of State John Foster Dulles decided to teach Nasser a lesson and withdrew U.S. support for the project to build a higher dam at Aswan on the Nile River. Nasser in turn nationalized the Suez Canal and contracted with the Soviet Union to complete the dam project. Great Britain, France, and Israel joined in a war against Nasser in October 1956. Eisenhower pressed them to withdraw. His action produced a surge of pro-U.S. sentiment throughout the Middle East but worsened relations with Washington's two European allies and Israel.

When the United States supported Israel in its June 1967 preemptive war against Egypt and Syria, many Arab states broke diplomatic relations. In the October 1973 Yom Kippur War, Nasser's successor, Anwar as-Sadat, sent Egyptian forces across the Suez Canal, taking Israeli defenders by surprise. Sadat wanted to regain the Sinai Peninsula, occupied by Israel since 1967. Arab states criticized President Richard M. Nixon's decisions in the middle of the war to release military supplies to Israel and to announce a large loan for Tel Aviv. This time the Arab states, led by Saudi Arabia, imposed an oil boycott on the United States, sending gasoline prices skyrocketing.

The United States tried repeatedly to work out a compromise that would reconcile the Arabs to the existence of Israel but the barriers were formidable and each initiative fell short of its goal. Democratic administrations, especially those of Truman, John F. Kennedy, and Lyndon B. Johnson, tended to look more favorably on the Jewish state than did Republican ones, in particular those of Eisenhower, Gerald R. Ford, and George Bush. Whenever the United States attempted negotiations the fate of the Palestinian Arabs proved the hardest issue to resolve. Displaced in the 1948 and 1967 wars, they had become part of a great diaspora; many lived in primitive refugee camps in states bordering Israel. In 1968 they selected the activist Yasir Arafat, founder of the guerrilla group Fatah, to lead the Palestine Liberation Organization (PLO). Rival Palestinian factions began to target Israeli and U.S. citizens in an effort to draw attention to their cause. Airliners and airports came under terrorist attack. For years the U.S. government refused all contact with the PLO, even after members of the League of Arab States recognized the organization as the sole legitimate representative of the Palestinian people. Washington was bound by a 1975 agreement with Israel not to negotiate with the PLO as long as the latter refused to recognize the existence of Israel. Secretary of State Henry Kissinger, renowned for his shuttle (airport-to-airport) diplomacy after the October War, had agreed to this demand to secure a partial Israeli withdrawal from the Sinai.

Only in 1988, as the Palestinian Intifada (uprising) raged in the Israeli-occupied West Bank and Gaza Strip, did the United States open talks with Arafat. Initiated by the Ronald Reagan administration and continued by President Bush and his secretary of state, James Baker, the talks resulted in a peace conference in Madrid and the September 1993 signing of an interim Palestinian-Israeli peace accord at a ceremony in Washington hosted by President Bill Clinton.

Despite early optimism in the United States, however, Israelis and Palestinians were far from a just and lasting peace. Much earlier the United States had achieved an important breakthrough with the Camp David Accords. In September 1978 President Jimmy Carter helped negotiate a treaty establishing peace and diplomatic relations between Egypt and Israel. Egypt thus became the first Arab state to recognize Israel. The agreement came at a high price for the United States, which consented to increase dramatically its economic and military assistance to the two signees. Thereafter they received more than half of all U.S. foreign aid. The Arab world ostracized Egypt for breaking ranks and Cairo consequently moved closer to Washington.

From the early post–World War II years the United States looked for friends in the region. As elsewhere in the world, it often found them in the ranks of conservative nations headed by hereditary rulers, such as Iran, Libya, and Saudi Arabia. This policy, which incidentally guaranteed access to vast oil reserves, often placed the United States in the position of supporting the status quo. Critics accused Washington of ignoring regional problems in pursuit of a global strategy of winning the cold war. The pro-Western king of Libya was overthrown in September 1969. Colonel Mu'ammar al-Gadhafi, a young, militant Arab nationalist, replaced him as leader of the oil-rich state and immediately pressed the United States to evacuate its Wheelus Air Force Base. The crisis in U.S.-Libyan relations, however, came much later, during the Reagan administration. Gadhafi supported liberation movements around the world and reportedly had ties to the terrorist bombing of a West Berlin disco in April 1986 at which two U.S. soldiers were killed and many others were injured. Reagan, pursuing a tough policy on terrorism, ordered a massive retaliatory raid on Gadhafi's compound in Tripoli. The Libyan leader narrowly escaped, but U.S. bombs killed an adopted daughter and wounded two of his sons. After this attack, which received strong support in the United States but considerable criticism from U.S. allies in Europe and the Middle East, both nations pulled back from the brink of open hostilities.

In 1951 a crisis developed in Iran over the rights of the Anglo-Iranian Oil Company to monopolize production and sale of petroleum. An elderly nationalist leader, Mohammad Mosaddeq, ignited popular enthusiasm for nationalizing the company's holdings. Becoming prime minister in May of that year, he waged a two-year struggle to force the British, who had initiated a worldwide blockade of Iranian oil, to accept the takeover. At first the United States sympathized with Mosaddeq and urged Great Britain to compromise, but as the prime minister's internal support weakened and the local communist party, the Tudeh, seemed to gain ground, the new Eisenhower administration turned against him. The Central Intelligence Agency (CIA) plotted with groups of dissident Iranians to undermine the regime and restore Shah Mohammad Reza Pahlavi to power. After a coup d'état in August 1953, the United States consistently supported the increasingly dictatorial shah.

Many Iranians came to view the shah as Washington's puppet—which he decidedly was not—and their disillusionment with him and the United States increased. Opposition to the shah passed into the hands of the religious class, many of whom rejected the increasing secularization of the Pahlavi state. Ayatollah Ruholla Khomeini, an exile since 1964, organized his forces from afar to destroy the shah's regime. Suffering secretly from a terminal illness, the shah vacillated and the opposition took heart. After a series of blunders and with mixed signals from the Carter administration, which was divided on the issue, the shah fled the country in January 1979. Khomeini returned to establish an Islamic republic with himself as final arbiter. The U.S. government had few ties with the new Iranian leadership and officials in Washington were again divided over whether to adopt a hard-line or a conciliatory approach. When President Carter allowed the ailing shah to enter the United States in October 1979 for medical treatment, Iranians, remembering the events of 1953, feared a conspiracy to restore the ousted monarch. On Nov. 4, 1979, militant students seized the U.S. embassy in Tehran and took its occupants hostage. The ensuing crisis lasted until the end of Carter's term, helping to deny him reelection.

After 1981 the United States had several brushes with the prickly revolutionaries in Tehran. Diplomatic relations languished. U.S. officials feared the spread of militant Islam to neighboring states. Their concern brought closer ties with Iran's only Arab neighbor, Iraq. U.S.-Iraq relations have resembled the dips and rises of a roller coaster. Washington worked closely with the monarchy to establish the anti-Soviet Baghdad Pact in 1955 (Iraq, Iran, Turkey, Pakistan, and Great Britain), but three years later revolutionary forces overwhelmed the conservative, pro-Western regime of King Faisal II and Premier Nuri al-Said. At the same time Jordan's King Hussein faced increasing challenges. It seemed the royal dominoes were falling. Acting under the Eisenhower Doctrine announced in 1957 to block communist aggression in the region, the United States sent marines into Lebanon to strengthen its pro-Western president, who had come under attack. This also served as a gesture of support to other friendly regimes in the region. The crisis passed quickly and the marines soon went home but the U.S. action (and similar British steps in Jordan) left many Arabs bitter. Ostensibly the move was to thwart communists but the real threat, as Eisenhower knew, came from supporters of Egypt's Nasser, who preached a pan-Arab union, which they believed would restore past glories.

Ties with Iraq were never again as cordial as they had been prior to 1958. Baghdad broke relations in 1967 and they were only restored in 1984 during the Iran-Iraq War. Washington saw the Iraqi leader, Saddam Hussein, as a barrier to the spread of revolutionary ideas from Iran. The Reagan and Bush administrations overlooked the brutal, authoritarian character of the regime, seeing it as the cork in the Iranian bottle. Iraq also offered a lucrative market for U.S. business. The 1989 collapse of the Soviet Union, a longtime ally of Iraq, removed a restraining influence on Saddam Hussein. The United States seemed to offer no opposition to his hints of annexing tiny neighboring Kuwait, over which he had long claimed sovereignty. The U.S. message had been ambiguous, but once Iraq's army poured into Kuwait in August 1990, President Bush left no doubt about his policy. He condemned Iraq and rushed to organize an international coalition to force its withdrawal. In the ensuing Gulf War of 1991 the Iraqi army suffered near-total defeat. Kuwait was restored and Iraq was forced to accept a series of United Nations resolutions. President Bush stopped short of removing Saddam Hussein; he restricted U.S. ground forces to a zone in southern Iraq far from Baghdad. He did this because his Arab coalition partners disagreed and because of fears that removal might trigger a power struggle during which surrounding states, including Iran, would seek territorial gains at Iraq's expense. The success of the Gulf War gave impulse to plans to resolve the Palestinian-Israeli conflict. With the end of the cold war, Israel lost some of its leverage as a bastion of anticommunism in the region. One reason the United States moved with such speed against Iraq was the threat it posed to the oil-rich Gulf states adjacent to Kuwait. Despite attempts in the 1970s to lower imports of foreign oil and to develop energy alternatives, the 1980s saw increasing consumption of Middle Eastern petroleum. The United States had a vested interest in maintaining stability in the Persian Gulf.

After the cold war, President Bush and his successor, Bill Clinton, spoke of a new world order, but no one knew what was envisioned for the United States in this part of the world. As pressures for change built throughout the region, it was unclear how conservative regimes like Saudi Arabia would adjust. In states such as Egypt and Algeria the United States aligned itself with the status quo against Islamic activists. Some observers questioned whether these corrupt and inefficient regimes would be able to introduce much-needed reform. The United States risked being identified with governments that many believed served the interests of only a minority of their citizens.

[James A. Bill, *The Eagle and the Lion* (New Haven, Conn., 1988); John A. DeNovo, *American Interests and Policies in the Middle East, 1900–1939* (Minneapolis, 1963); George Lenczowski, *American Presidents and the Middle East* (Durham, N.C., 1990); William B. Quandt, *Decade of Decisions: American Policy Toward the Arab-Israeli Conflict, 1967–1976* (Berkeley, Calif., 1977); Barry M. Rubin, *Paved With Good Intentions: The American Experience and Iran* (New York, 1980); Steven L. Spiegel, *The Other Arab-Israeli Conflict* (Chicago, 1985); Robert W. Stookey, *America and the Arab States* (New York, 1975); Seth P. Tillman, *The United States in the Middle East* (Bloomington, Ind., 1982).]

JAMES F. GOODE

See also **DAH:** Arab-American Relations; **SUPP:** Arab Americans; Beirut Bombing; Foreign Aid; Gulf War of 1991; Hostage Crises; Iran-Contra Affair; Iranian Americans; Iran-Iraq War; Iraq-gate; Iraqi Americans; Israel-Palestine Peace Accords; Lebanon; Oil Crises; Palestinian Americans; West Berlin Disco Bombing.

MIDDLE EAST HOSTAGES. *See* **Hostage Crises.**

MIDWIFERY. *See* **Childbirth.**

MILITARY BASE CLOSINGS. By the late 1980s the United States had approximately 3,800 military installations within its borders, including army forts, navy and air force bases, supply depots, and building and repair facilities. Their locations had sometimes been a matter of national politics, because members of Congress regarded the establishment of a military base as a way of bringing federal money and jobs to their state or district as well as of creating additional employment for servicing the base's population. In the late 1980s this protective attitude toward bases started to change. The conclusion of the cold war with the collapse of the Warsaw Pact and the Soviet Union ended a major threat to U.S. national security. A mounting federal budget deficit and a desire to redirect federal spending into domestic programs reinforced arguments to cut national defense spending. As a consequence, military base closings began, along with reductions in military personnel and weapons. Congress chose neither to allow the president or the Department of Defense to decide which bases to close nor to make such decisions itself. Instead, it voted in 1988 to create an independent, bipartisan advisory commission to the Pentagon to propose lists of bases for closure. The secretary of defense would announce the proposed list, and, provided Congress did not reject it within forty-five legislative days, the schedule for closings would become official. Three subsequent defense base closure and realignment commissions were established to act in 1991, 1993, and 1995. While some bases were shut down, others actually grew through realignment or the shifting of personnel and functions among installations.

Secretary of Defense Frank Carlucci announced, and Congress accepted, the first commission's list in 1989. Eighty-six bases were to be closed, five were to be partially closed, and fifty-four were to undergo realignment. The bases had at least four years advance notice, except for Pease Air Force Base in New Hampshire, which closed in 1991. In 1990 Secretary of Defense Richard Cheney announced a second list of proposed base closings without relying on a commission. This caused an outcry in Congress, where the Democratic majority thought the list contained too many bases in states or districts represented by Democrats. The chair of the House Armed Services Committee, Les Aspin of Wisconsin, recommended that a second commission propose another list. In October 1990 Congress approved the commission's creation. In 1991 the commission presented its list, which called for the closure of thirty-four bases and the realignment of another forty-eight. Congress accepted these recommendations.

Even though Congress had created the commission format, some senators and representatives were concerned about the impact of these closures on state and local economies. Legislators from the Philadelphia area, opposed to the closing of that city's naval shipyard, turned to the federal courts to determine whether base closure decisions should be subject to judicial review, but in May 1994 the Supreme Court unanimously ruled against this. Also, in approving closings Congress stated that the secretary of defense must consider closing overseas bases. The 1993 commission faced similar difficulties. Concerned about the loss of jobs and the economic impact on communities and states, Congress closely scrutinized the proposed list. Aspin, now secretary of defense, rebutted allegations that some of the closings were politically motivated. The third list affected 175 military installations, with some 30 major U.S. bases to be closed, 12 other major bases subject to realignment, and additional smaller bases being closed, realigned, or relocated. Congress accepted the list in 1993. In June 1995 the commission recommended closing 79 bases and realigning 26 others. Although President Bill Clinton expressed strong concern about the economic impact of base closings in Texas and California, he approved the recommendations in July. Later that month the House National Security Committee rejected proposed legislation that would have overturned the recommendations.

Base closings in themselves did not substantially reduce the annual defense budget. For example, closures announced in 1991 would save about $1.5 billion annually after 1997, and the 1993 list would save about $2.3 billion annually after 1999. It was more difficult to estimate the effect of base closings on local economies. States such as California, with more than 300,000 people employed at sixty-seven bases in 1991, felt the loss of jobs and income disproportionately. Including all base closures through the 1995 recommendations, Senator Diane Feinstein of California estimated that 108,900 Californians employed at these bases would lose their jobs. Evidence suggested, however, that base closings did not affect communities as seriously as layoffs in the defense industry. Military bases tended not to be as integrated into local economies as defense manufacturing. Many communities even hoped to benefit by acquiring the land once occupied by bases, although federal regulations often slowed up this process. A greater problem in this regard was perhaps the serious environmental hazards at military installations resulting from use of machinery and storage of solvents, fuels, and explosives. In the 1990s the cleanup of such hazards depended on the availability of federal funding.

[Andrew C. Mayer and George H. Siehl, *Military Base Closures: Issues for the 104th Congress* (Washington, D.C., 1995); U.S. Congress, Office of Technology Assessment, *After the Cold War: Living with Lower Defense Spending*, OTA-ITE-524 (Washington, D.C., 1992).]

KENNETH B. MOSS

See also **SUPP:** Defense, Department of.

MILITARY SERVICE, WOMEN IN. *See* **Women in Military Service.**

MILITIAS. Modern, private, citizen-organized militias have their roots in the post–World War II right-wing Patriot movement. Militia members and Patriots share a fear of a tyrannical federal government and domination of the United States by a global conspiracy controlled by the United Nations. While the majority of Patriots have historically sought to reverse these perceived trends through political organization and social movements, militia participants believe an armed citizenry is the only real defense against despotism. The bombing of the Oklahoma City federal building in April 1995 and the arrest of suspects and militia members Timothy McVeigh and Terry Nichols brought notoriety and public attention to the militia movement, but civilian paramilitary groups have been active in the United States at least as far back as the first Ku Klux Klan, formed just after the Civil War. Several armed groupings emerged in the late 1970s and 1980s, mostly identified with the racist, anti-Semitic far right. The FBI uncovered and disbanded the white supremacist Order, or Silent Brotherhood, after the group committed armed robbery, counterfeited currency, and murdered radio talk-show host Alan Berg, a Jewish liberal, in 1984.

In the mid-1990s white supremacy continued to have a profound impact on paramilitary groups, but the more recent militia movement has a broader base, resulting from two events. The first concerned the armed confrontation between federal agents and white supremacist Randy Weaver at Ruby Ridge, Idaho, in 1992 after he failed to appear for trial on weapons violations. In the resulting standoff a federal marshal, as well as Weaver's son and wife, were killed. Although Weaver was acquitted of the federal marshal's murder, his case became for many Patriots a symbol of governmental excess. In 1995 the Justice Department agreed to pay the Weaver family $3.1 million in damages without admitting wrongdoing. In the aftermath of Ruby Ridge, former Green Beret and right-wing Populist party presidential candidate James "Bo" Gritz mobilized supporters to form militias to defend their social status and constitutional rights. Those answering his call included farmers facing foreclosure, displaced industrial workers, gun-rights advocates, anti–income tax protesters, Christian millennialists, adherents of the confrontational wing of the pro-life movement, militant antienvironmentalists, states' rights advocates, and people who believe that the county is the highest acceptable level of government. While most members are white males, some local militias include African-American and female participants. The largest of the local paramilitary groups is John Trochman's Militia of Montana.

The second event spurring militia participation was the April 1993 siege of the Branch Davidian compound in Waco, Texas, by agents of the Bureau of Alcohol, Tobacco and Firearms, culminating in the deaths of cult leader David Koresh and seventy-seven of his followers. For many militia members and potential recruits, the Waco siege appeared to be a trial run by the federal government for imposition of national martial law. Gun control legislation was viewed as a part of the plot. In 1995 the estimated militia membership was between 10,000 and 40,000, with organizing activity probably occurring in every state.

[Michael Barkun, *Religion and the Racist Right* (Chapel Hill, N.C., 1994); Chip Berlet and Matthew N. Lyons, "Militia Nation," *The Progressive* (June 1995), and *Too Close for Comfort: Rightwing Populism, Scapegoating, and Fascist Potentials in U.S. Politics* (Boston, 1996); Daniel Junas, "Angry White Guys with Guns: Rise of Citizen Militias," *Covert Action Quarterly* (Spring 1995).]

ELLEN A. SLATKIN

See also **SUPP:** Fundamentalism; Gun Control; Oklahoma City Bombing; Vigilantes; Waco Siege; White Supremacists.

MILLENARIANISM, or millennialism, focuses on a thousand-year period of unprecedented peace and righteousness that some Christians believe will either precede or follow the return of Christ to earth, marking the end of history. In the twentieth century the most militant millenarians have been premillennialists—people who expect Christ to return and preside over the millennium. Some believers set dates for Christ's coming, as in Harold Camping's *1994?* (1992) or Edgar Whisenant's *Eighty-eight Reasons Why the Rapture Will Be in 1988* (1988). Inspired especially by events in the Middle East since the creation of the state of Israel in 1948, premillennialism has produced a vast literature speculating about current events and the end of history. The all-time best-seller was Hal Lindsey's *The Late Great Planet Earth* (1970). At the popular level, postmillennialism is perhaps most visible in advocates of reconstructionism, or ushering in the millennium through natural means by Christianizing the social and cultural institutions as well as humankind. Amillennialism assigns spiritual importance to one thousand years and empha-

sizes conforming the individual Christian's life to the rule of Christ within the heart.

[Timothy P. Weber, *Living in the Shadow of the Second Coming* (Chicago, 1987).]

EDITH BLUMHOFER

See also **SUPP:** Fundamentalism.

MILWAUKEE, the largest city in Wisconsin and the seventeenth largest in the United States, experienced a marked change of demographics since World War II. It began with a white exodus from the city's core areas in the years after the war. This exit accelerated following 1967 demonstrations over fair housing and race rioting; by 1985 Milwaukee was the nation's most segregated city, with 90 percent of its African-American population residing in the downtown core. The population declined from 717,000 in 1970 to 636,000 in 1980 and 628,000 in 1990, but the metropolitan area increased from 1,397,000 in 1980 to 1,432,000 in 1990. Milwaukee's traditional European image has altered in the last two decades, with the establishment of Hmong, Vietnamese, Hispanic, and Arab communities. These groups, along with the more established German, Italian, Polish, Irish, Native American, and African-American communities, celebrate their heritage annually in a series of ethnic galas, earning Milwaukee the title City of Festivals. For the city and metropolitan area, industry continued to be important and included production of machinery, fabricated metal products, and electrical and electronic equipment. Breweries, which once had made the city famous, were of lesser importance, although three remained. Milwaukee hosts the annual Great Circus Parade and is home to major league baseball and basketball teams. The city boasts two universities and is ranked high for housing affordability and quality of life. Municipal elections in Milwaukee are officially nonpartisan, but candidates usually represent moderate to liberal Democratic positions.

[Harry H. Anderson and Frederick I. Olson, *Milwaukee* (Tulsa, Okla., 1981).]

KATHLEEN FOSS-MOLLAN

See also **SUPP:** Wisconsin.

MINNEAPOLIS, a city located in southeastern Minnesota, derived its identity before World War II from milling and food processing (Pillsbury, General Mills) and its predominant German-Scandinavian-Lutheran-New England population mix. Since then, the population has become more mixed and less European. In 1980 the population was 87 percent white, 7.7 percent African American, 2.4 percent Native American, and 1.1 percent Asian; in 1990 the figures were 78 percent white, 13 percent African American, 3.3 percent Native American, and 4.3 percent Asian. Minneapolis's population decreased from 370,951 in 1980 to 368,383 in 1990; its county, however, has grown. Light manufacturing (Munsingwear, for example) declined, while the computer and financial services industries, medicine, and entertainment expanded. A downtown revival included renovation of the Orpheum and State Theaters and construction of the Jeune Lune Theatre, Orchestra Hall, new night spots, and the elimination of several unattractive buildings. The changes are highlighted on the landscape, dominated until 1973 by the Art Deco Foshay Tower, and in 1995 by a half-dozen pastel and glassed office buildings, the Humphrey Metrodome (home of baseball's Minnesota Twins and football's Minnesota Vikings), the Target Center (home of professional basketball's Timberwolves), and the Sculpture Garden. Ethnic and class differences have long marked Minneapolis's neighborhoods. "Nordeast" is predominantly eastern and southern European, while Kenwood is well-to-do; Native Americans increasingly moved to the area around the American Indian Center on Franklin Avenue; African Americans resided in south Minneapolis; gays and lesbians grouped around Loring Park; and middle-class whites lived in the suburbs. Magnet schools and the many lakes and parks reflect the city's aspirations. In 1993 Minneapolis elected Mayor Sharon Sayles Belton, the city's first female mayor and first African-American political leader, signaling a demographic change and growing liberalism.

[Larry Millett, *Lost Twin Cities* (Saint Paul, Minn., 1992).]

ANNETTE ATKINS

See also **DAH:** Twin Cities; **SUPP:** Minnesota.

MINNESOTA. Machinery Hill has been a farm-implement mecca at the Minnesota State Fair for nearly one hundred years, but at the 1993 fair, snowblowers and garden tractors replaced combines, harrows, and field tractors. Butter sculptures, Hardanger embroidery, and prize lambs still drew crowds, but bungee jumping, the midway, minidoughnuts, and the Beach Boys captured more fairgoers' attention. The fair draws more than 1.5 million visitors annually because, while catering to current tastes, it holds out images of an older Minnesota. Minnesotans make many claims

to the good life. On average they live two years longer than other Americans. They passed the trend-setting Clean Indoor Air Act in 1976. They point to the Mayo Clinic, the University of Minnesota Hospitals, the large number of doctors and dentists, pacemaker production (Medtronic), and pathbreaking work in open-heart surgery as examples of Minnesota's advantages. They cite the "Minnesota method" of addiction treatment pioneered at the Hazelden Institute. The state's crime rate has risen but remains low (forty-seventh nationally in 1970; thirty-sixth in 1990). Minnesotans even take a perverse pleasure in winter—ice fishing, cross-country skiing, and inventing and elaborating indoor shopping malls (Southdale in Edina was the first, built in 1956; Mall of America in Bloomington is the largest in the United States).

Governor Rudy Perpich (1977–1978, 1982–1990) called Minnesota the "brain-power state," and many take pride in the state's commitment to education. Minnesota ranks seventh in per capita funding of all education. In 1971 the state shifted from property-tax-based to income-tax-based school funding, thus equalizing school expenditures across school districts (at least through the 1970s). In the mid-1990s Minnesota supported forty-six state, community, and private colleges and universities and thirty-four technical colleges. Standardized test scores consistently ranked the state's students among the top five states in the nation. The computer-to-pupil ratio was third nationally. Of the state's over-twenty-five population, 85 percent were high school graduates.

Minnesota's economy in the nineteenth and early twentieth centuries depended on food, wood, and iron ore. The late-twentieth-century economy still did but had changed radically since World War II, when the state responded to the demand for weapons and defense systems. Minnesota businesses—Honeywell, Control Data, Cray Research, National Computer Systems—have pioneered in high tech and computer products and services. Minnesota also has strong service companies: Dayton Hudson, Ecolab, Lutheran Brotherhood, and the St. Paul Companies. More recently, the music industry has boomed in Minnesota, including such independent recording companies as Twin Tone Records and Red House Records, Minnesota Public Radio, and American Public Radio. This diversification made the economy partially recession-proof, but there were some casualties: high unemployment on the Iron Range; the decline of small towns; a bitter and protracted 1986 strike against the Hormel Company in Austin; and layoffs to make companies more competitive. These changes fractured lives, sometimes created less congenial workplaces, and bruised a state that has prided itself on corporate generosity and the family quality of its farms and businesses.

Minnesotans continued to struggle to define the proper relation between business and government. In the nineteenth century many viewed big business as a danger and government as a force for good. This suspicion and faith nourished a liberal tradition that in the twentieth century produced such nationally known politicians as Hubert Humphrey, Walter Mondale, Orville Freeman, Harold Stassen, Eugene McCarthy, and Paul Wellstone. In the 1990s many Minnesotans advocated an activist government, but others worried that the state's tax structure, workers' compensation, and generous state programs had created a chilly business climate. Minnesota politicians have worked since the 1970s to reduce taxes and tap the research and development talents of the University of Minnesota. They instituted the Minnesota Department of Trade and Economic Development and created regional initiative funds, enterprise zones, and business tax credits. The result of thirty years of focusing on the business climate (and arguing about it) was relatively high personal income taxes (but not the highest in the nation) and good state services.

Minnesota's political parties—Democratic Farmer-Labor (DFL) and Independent Republican (IR)—traditionally formed two coalitions: labor, Catholic, ethnic, farm people (DFL) and Protestant, business, small town (IR). In the mid-1970s the two parties underwent a major realignment when issues of abortion, feminism, and homosexual rights led to factional division and drove many religious conservatives from the DFL to the IR. In 1978 the IR candidates defeated their DFL opponents for the governor's seat (Albert Quie) and both senate seats (David Durenberger and Rudy Boschwitz). In the 1980s and 1990s women also became increasingly active in politics: Joan Growe was elected secretary of state continuously beginning in 1974; Dee Long took office as speaker of the house in 1992; Marlene Johnson was lieutenant governor from 1982 to 1990 and Joanell Drystad took over that office in 1992; and Sharon Sayles Belton became mayor of Minneapolis in 1994.

Minnesota was populated in the nineteenth century by Scandinavians, Germans, and Irish in farm and urban areas, and southern and eastern Europeans settled on the Iron Range and northern Minnesota. The largest groups of immigrants were Asians, Hmong people in particular, who, it was estimated, would outnumber the African-American population by the end of the twentieth century. Minnesota's 1990 population of 4,375,099 was 2.2 percent African American, 1.8 percent Asian, 1.2 percent Hispanic, and 1.1 percent Native American. Minnesota has held steady in the ranking of state populations since 1970 (nineteenth in 1970, twenty-first in 1980, and twentieth in 1990). Ojibwa and Dakota peoples originally populated the territory and near the end of the twentieth century were spread across eleven reservations-communities. Minneapolis has the largest urban population of Native Americans in the United States, perhaps accounting for the birth there of the American Indian Movement (AIM) in the 1970s. Poverty is the most immediate problem facing Native Americans, a problem in the midst of change as native groups opened casinos (eighteen in 1994) that attracted thousands of visitors and billions of dollars. Racism continued to be a problem in a state so predominantly white, although the first Urban Coalition chapter was founded in Minnesota following the1966 and 1967 riots, and in 1993 Minneapolis elected as mayor an African-American women.

Minnesota's Twin Cities—Saint Paul and Minneapolis—are not identical. Minneapolis, the more Protestant, African American, and Native American, is the home of the University of Minnesota's main campus, the Lake Harriet Rose Garden, the Minnesota Orchestra (known until 1968 as the Minnesota Symphony), and many lakes. Its skyline, once dominated by the Foshay Tower, now shows off the IDS Tower, the First Bank Place, and the Norwest Center buildings, all housing financial services companies. Saint Paul, which is more Catholic, Jewish, and Hispanic, is home of the University of Minnesota agricultural campus, the State Fairgrounds, the Ordway Theater, and the Como Conservatory. The Minnesota capitol, Saint Paul Cathedral, Minnesota History Center, and Saint Paul Companies dominate the Saint Paul skyline. Bloomington, the state's third largest city and a Twin Cities suburb, sports mostly hotels, service companies, shopping centers, and the Mall of America. Duluth, which is more working class and is located on Lake Superior, supports itself with shipping and tourism, having weathered, if not recovered from, a near economic collapse that began in the 1970s. Its decline in relative size, from third to fourth in the state according to the 1990 census, signaled larger population shifts in the state toward the Twin Cities and their suburbs.

In the late twentieth century, audiences supported more than thirty theater companies, as different from each other as the Guthrie Theater Company, the Jeune Lune Theatre, the Heart of the Beast Puppet Theatre, Mixed Blood Theater, and the Children's Theater Company. Minnesota was also home to several small publishers (West, Graywolf, and Milkweed Editions, for example) and a variety of authors, including Jon Hassler, Louise Erdrich, Fred Manfred, Patricia Hampl, J. F. Powers, LaVyrle Spencer, Robert Bly, Peg Meier, and, perhaps best known, Garrison Keillor.

[Jo Blatti, *Women's History in Minnesota* (Saint Paul, 1993); Theodore C. Blegen, *Minnesota* (Minneapolis, 1975); Clifford E. Clark, Jr., ed., *Minnesota in a Century of Change* (Saint Paul, 1989); Elizabeth Ebbott, *Indians in Minnesota*, 4th ed. (Minneapolis, 1985); June Drenning Holmquist, ed., *They Chose Minnesota* (Saint Paul, 1980); Ramedo J. Saucedo, ed., *Mexican Americans in Minnesota* (Saint Paul, 1977); Barbara Stuhler and Gretchen Kreuter, eds., *Women of Minnesota* (Saint Paul, 1977); David Vassar Taylor, ed., *Blacks in Minnesota* (Saint Paul, 1976).]

ANNETTE ATKINS

See also **SUPP:** Minneapolis.

MINORITY BUSINESS. Enterprises owned or operated by members of racial and ethnic minority groups have historically been a distinctive element of U.S. business. The nature and role of minority businesses have evolved with changing social and political circumstances. Business activity among African Americans has been traditionally concentrated in small retail and personal-service firms serving a black clientele and usually located in inner-city ghettos. Most were less capitalized than white-owned firms operating in the same areas. As a result of the civil rights movement of the 1960s, the federal government began programs to actively encourage black business enterprise. In 1965 the Small Business Administration began to channel loans to minority businesses. In 1969 the Office of Minority Business Enterprise (OMBE) was created within the Department of Commerce to coordinate public and private initiatives in the development of minority business. Critics charged that the enthusiasm of politicians for black capitalism masked a lessening commitment to alleviating urban poverty through public employment and job training. They pointed out that the initial appropriation for the OMBE came from funds transferred out of the budget of the Office for Economic Opportunity. Nevertheless, independent surveys in 1981 by *Nuestro Business Review* and *Black Enterprise* showed that 45 of the top 100 Latino businesses had been formed between 1969 and 1976 and that 56 of the top 100 black firms had been established between 1969 and

1976, 30 of them between 1969 and 1971. In 1985, 1,000 African-American businesspersons gave a testimonial dinner praising the establishment of OMBE (now the Minority Business Development Agency).

While the traditional small retail business still accounts for more than half of black enterprises, in the 1970s and 1980s blacks established or expanded firms in construction, engineering, and business and professional services. Beginning with the administration of President Richard M. Nixon (1969–1974), their efforts were aided by minority set-aside programs of local, state, and federal governments that mandated a certain percentage of public contracts for minority firms. These set asides were justified as ways to overcome past racial discrimination, but in 1989, in *City of Richmond* v. *J. A. Croson Company,* the Supreme Court struck down such a program and ruled that public officials would have to offer evidence of past discrimination to justify such policies.

The law establishing the OMBE in 1969 also designated Hispanics, Native Americans, Asians, Aleuts, and Eskimos as minority groups eligible for assistance in business development. Small business entrepreneurship has often been associated with ethnic groups that are recent immigrants. Since the most recent period of large-scale immigration to the United States began in 1965, Koreans, Chinese, and Cubans have shown high levels of entrepreneurial activity. Using family members and relatives as employees and drawing on financial resources inside and outside the United States, they have been successful in retail and wholesale trade in urban areas where supermarkets and other stores belonging to regional and national corporations have departed. In some instances these businesses thrive by serving an ethnic clientele.

Since the 1960s small business in general has reversed an earlier decline and benefited from the shift away from manufacturing in industrial nations. Different racial and ethnic groups, however, have varying levels of success in business. Recent Asian immigrants, especially Koreans and Chinese, have percentages of population engaged in small business at levels higher than the national average, while the percentage is below the average for Mexican Americans and blacks. Participation and success in small business enterprise have depended on education, access to credit, and management experience. Blacks have historically lagged behind various Asian and European immigrant groups in each of these areas. One study conducted in 1989 found that banks loaned black-owned businesses located in minority neighborhoods an average of $40,000 less than black-owned businesses in predominantly white areas. The record shows that with more education and affluence, later generations of ethnic immigrant groups move out of small-business ownership and into higher-paying managerial and professional occupations.

[Timothy Bates, *Banking on Black Enterprise* (Washington, D.C., 1993); Roger Waldinger, *Ethnic Entrepreneurs: Immigrant Business in Industrial Societies* (Newbury Park, Calif., 1990).]

JOHN B. WEAVER

See also **SUPP:** African Americans; Chinese Americans; Cuban Americans; Korean Americans; Set-Asides.

MISSILES, MILITARY. *See* **Defense, Department of.**

MISSING IN ACTION. *See* **Prisoners of War and Missing in Action.**

MISSISSIPPI. The history of Mississippi during the last quarter of the twentieth century was dominated by two themes—racial change and economic progress. In the mid-1960s Mississippi was still a firm bastion—perhaps the firmest—of racial segregation, and many civil rights battles were fought out in the state, including the crisis in 1962 over James Meredith's admission to the University of Mississippi; the murder of civil rights leader Medgar Evers in 1963; and the violent resistance to voter registration drives in 1964. Segregation depended on an agrarian economy, and as Mississippi's civil rights battles were occurring, socioeconomic change was beginning, represented by the rise of an urban, industrial, and commercial culture that fundamentally altered Mississippi's institutions.

Mississippi was a one-party state from the end of Reconstruction until well after World War II. Loyalty to the Democratic party was almost universal among Mississippi's whites, while almost all blacks were denied the right to vote or to run for office. In the 1990s the state elected the first Republican governor (Kirk Fordice) and lieutenant governor (Eddie Briggs) since 1875. By the mid-1990s it also had two Republican senators (Thad Cochran and Trent Lott) and one Republican congressmen (Roger Wicker). Republican candidates have carried the state in every presidential election starting with 1980. Similarly, large-scale black voter registration in the 1960s changed Mississippi's politics. In 1971 Charles Evers became the first black to wage a vigorous, although unsuccessful, campaign for governor. Since that time

blacks have held positions as mayors, state legislators, and U.S. representatives. Mississippi Congressman Mike Espy served as secretary of agriculture in President Bill Clinton's administration.

After World War II, Mississippi's economy shifted from a one-crop cotton economy to a more diversified agricultural and industrial system. Tenancy and sharecropping disappeared, and agriculture became not only diversified but mechanized. Soybeans, rice, livestock, poultry, and fish farming replaced the old dependency on cotton. Individuals employed in agriculture dropped from 43 percent in 1950 to only 2.7 percent in 1990. Employment in manufacturing, trade, and government soared. In 1990, 24 percent of Mississippians were employed in manufacturing, 42 percent in trade, and 23 percent in government.

Mississippi has made important contributions to the nation's music and literature. Before World War II such blues musicians from the Mississippi Delta as "Big Bill" Broonzy and Charley Patton began a virtual revolution in American music that soon spread over the world. Similarly, Mississippi writers such as William Faulkner, Richard Wright, and Eudora Welty created a body of literature of unparalleled volume and power. Scholars still wonder how such an outpouring could come from so small and isolated a state. The influence of these writers continues in the work of such authors as Shelby Foote, Ellen Douglas, Ellen Gilchrist, and Beth Henley. Like Faulkner and Welty, the stories of this new generation of writers are rooted in the people and history of Mississippi.

In the years before World War II, Mississippi's schools suffered from segregation, poor funding, and rural isolation. During the 1950s and 1960s, the state's schools were wracked by confrontations over integration. By 1970 public schools and colleges alike were integrated, and remain so today. While Mississippi still ranks near the bottom among the states in total expenditures for education, it ranks near the top in per capita tax burden for education, and 45 percent of the state's budget goes for that purpose. Similarly, consolidation of rural schools, begun in the 1920s, has steadily eliminated the small schools and created larger ones with more diverse offerings. Colleges and universities admittedly have undergone less consolidation than the public schools. Three comprehensive universities—the University of Mississippi (Ole Miss), Mississippi State University, and the University of Southern Mississippi—are at the top of the educational hierarchy. Mississippi has five smaller regional universities with more limited offerings: Mississippi University for Women, Delta

State, Alcorn, Jackson State, and Mississippi Valley. The latter three are historically black colleges whose enrollments were still predominantly black in the 1990s. The state has thirteen public community college systems, which offer technical and vocational courses and the first two years of college courses. Enrollments in the public universities totaled 57,602 in the fall of 1994, and enrollment in community colleges totaled 76,900. In addition to the public colleges and universities, Mississippi has four-year and two-year denominational colleges, the largest of which are Mississippi College at Clinton (Baptist) and Millsaps College at Jackson (Methodist).

The state's population rose only modestly from 2,178,000 in 1960 to 2,573,000 in 1990. Mississippi always was and remains a rural state. In 1970 only 45 percent of Mississippians lived in towns and cities; by 1990 that figure had risen just slightly to 47 percent. Only three states—Vermont, West Virginia, and Maine—had smaller urban populations. These figures, however, must be qualified by two population trends. First, a great number of rural dwellers, perhaps as many as half, commuted daily to work in nearby towns and cities. Second, three metropolitan areas, Jackson, the Gulf Coast, and the Mississippi suburbs of Memphis contained 64 percent of Mississippi's urban population.

[Richard A. McLemore, ed., *A History of Mississippi*, 2 vols. (Hattiesburg, Miss., 1973); John R. Skates, *Mississippi: A Bicentennial History* (New York, 1979).]

JOHN R. SKATES

MISSOURI, the Show Me State, is centrally located and defined by its rivers, especially the mighty Mississippi along its eastern border and the Missouri, which flows west to east, cutting the 69,697-square-mile state in half. The topography varies from the rugged Ozarks in the south to rolling farm land in the north. In the last quarter of the twentieth century the state did fairly well economically, although not markedly so. In agriculture the cotton-producing Bootheel, jutting into Arkansas, had much in common with the lower South. In northern Missouri agricultural pursuits resembled those in neighboring Iowa and Nebraska, with soybeans the most important crop. The cost of machinery forced consolidation of some farms, and 10 percent of Missouri's farms accounted for 60 percent of sales in the 1990s, although the state's 107,000 farms were second in number only to Texas. Factories were located primarily in the state's two largest metropolitan areas, Saint Louis in the east and Kansas City in the west, and the principle manufactures were for transportation—motor

vehicles, railroad cars, and aircraft. Food processing, primarily dairy products, flour, and beer, and chemicals were next in importance in manufactures.

The state's two metropolitan areas were sizable; in 1992 Saint Louis had 2,518,528 residents and Kansas City had 1,616,930. Both metropolitan areas spill over into neighboring states, respectively, East Saint Louis, Ill., and Kansas City, Kans. Both Saint Louis and Kansas City have large international airports, and the huge Kansas City airport in the 1970s replaced a downtown airport with runways almost too short for jet aircraft. The state's smaller cities were hardly comparable to Saint Louis and Kansas City; Missouri's third- and fourth-largest cities, Springfield and Independence, had populations in 1990 of 140,593 and 112,301, respectively. Independence, an eastern suburb of Kansas City, grew notably, doubling and tripling from the earlier rural town.

Politically, in the 1970s, 1980s, and early 1990s, Missouri continued to display the same rural-urban antagonisms that had marked the state's history since statehood in 1821. With its two major metropolitan areas having more than 4 million residents in a state that contained a 1990 population of 5,117,073, the state government seemed incapable of bridging the rural-urban gap. It did not seem to matter much if governors were Republicans or Democrats. Starting in 1977 there was a Democratic governor, followed by two Republicans, then a Democrat; rural-urban antagonisms continued. The building of interstate highways, which promised to tie rural areas to metropolises, only accentuated the division in Missouri. While interstate highways ran through the middle of the state and along the eastern and western boundaries, large parts of the state remained without four-lane roads in the 1990s.

Environmental problems began to appear in the 1970s, caused by both city and rural practices, including the dumping of solid wastes (garbage) and the use of farm chemicals. The solid waste problem became massive, and the more than 100 landfills in the state were expected to be filled by the end of the twentieth century. Meanwhile, massive concentrations of the chemical dioxin were discovered at Times Beach and thirty other sites in the state in 1982. The problem was attacked at a cost of many millions of dollars, but in 1988 the state had twenty-one sites on the federal Superfund list of abandoned hazardous waste sites. Rural streams were badly polluted by acid runoff from abandoned coal mines. The Missouri and Mississippi rivers were also badly polluted.

Race relations in Saint Louis and Kansas City improved after desegregation in the 1950s and 1960s, but there were continuing problems. A significant school desegregation controversy arose in Kansas City in 1987. A federal judge ordered an increase in the city property tax and a surcharge on the state income tax, in order to provide money for Kansas City district schools. A federal appeals court upheld the property tax increase and authorized the district school board to set the tax rate but overturned the income tax surcharge. The Supreme Court upheld the appeals court in 1990, on the principle that constitutionally judges cannot set tax rates, although they can order local government bodies, in this instance the district school board, to do so.

In the mid-1990s Missouri continued to take an interest in its historical heritage, and the state attracts about 40 million tourists each year, which contributes approximately $6 billion per year to state revenues. The spectacular Gateway Arch at Saint Louis announces that city's historical role as the gateway to the West, and the city developed its Mississippi riverfront as part of the Jefferson National Expansion Memorial. On the western side of the state, the National Park Service developed a site near the Harry S. Truman Library and Museum in Independence that includes the president's house and the farmhouse where Truman once lived, now encircled by the Kansas City suburb of Grandview. In celebration of the state's most famous citizen, Northeast Missouri State University, located in the rural "outstate" town of Kirksville, became Truman State University in 1996.

[William E. Foley, *The Genesis of Missouri: From Wilderness Outpost to Statehood* (Columbia, Mo., 1989); William E. Parrish, ed., *A History of Missouri,* 5 vols. (Columbia, Mo., 1971–1986); William E. Parrish, Charles T. Jones, Jr., and Lawrence O. Christensen, *Missouri,* 2nd ed. (Arlington Heights, Ill., 1992).]

LAWRENCE H. LARSEN

See also **SUPP:** Branson; Kansas City; Saint Louis; Times Beach.

MONTANA, the fourth-largest state in area, remained lightly populated in 1970 with only 694,409 people. At that time its citizens began actively to explore how to balance economic growth with protection of their environment, a goal that was partly fulfilled in the decade that followed only to be dashed in the 1980s. The Montana of the 1990s was a state somber, cautious, and perhaps wiser for the experience. Economic, social, and political forces combined during the late 1960s and early 1970s to produce a popular revolution in Montana. Increasing numbers of the state's people recognized the consequences of a con-

tinued headlong depletion of the state's land. They supported the national movement to establish wilderness areas and preserve wild and scenic rivers and joined in a statewide effort to protect both the land and land-dependent employment. Politics embraced the popular sentiment. The state's 1972 constitution—containing significant changes from its 1889 predecessor—was noteworthy for protection of the environment. Two legislatures supported the environmental revolution, passing the Strip Mining and Reclamation Act (1973), the Water Use Act (1973), the Major Facility Siting Act (1975), and the Coal Severance Tax (1975). Suddenly Montana became a national leader on environmental and consumer protection issues.

Despite public support Montana's traditional, natural-resource extractive industries have stumbled or fallen since 1970. Hardrock mining, timber, petroleum, coal, and agriculture all experienced the downside of Montana's cyclical boom-and-bust economy. The 1980s proved particularly devastating. Reacting to national and international forces, Montana suffered from foreign economic fluctuations, reduced industrial demands, and rapidly changing technology. The state's major employer throughout the century—the Anaconda Copper Mining Company—departed during the 1970s. Its successor, the Atlantic Richfield Company (ARCO), closed its smelters and then terminated all operations in 1983, devastating such old mining towns as Butte. Champion International purchased the Anaconda Company's massive timber holdings, only to endure the national lumber market's disintegration through the 1970s and into the 1990s. These years marked the deindustrialization of Montana. Impressive petroleum discoveries in the 1970s and 1980s and a bituminous-coal boom in the early 1970s turned Billings, on the Yellowstone River, into Montana's largest and most affluent city. Despite drastic declines in the petroleum market and a reduction in coal production, Montana's energy reserves offer promise for development. Montana's future rests on the ability to handle such challenges as replacing traditional natural-resource-extractive industries and increasing per capita income. The latter in 1948 was 16 percent above the national average but by 1986 had dropped to 77 percent of the national average; by 1993 it had increased only to 84 percent, still far below what it once had been.

In the mid-1990s agriculture remained Montana's most lucrative basic industry. Farmers and ranchers adapted to technology, to special crops and breeds, to new farming and livestock techniques, and to international markets. Montana continued to rely on the wheat-beef-barley triumvirate but was quick to embrace such specialty crops as canola. In the 1970s a wet cycle and huge wheat sales to the Soviet Union produced an agricultural boom across the state, while the 1980s brought plummeting prices and the severe, lingering drought of 1985–1990. Agriculture continued to withstand the boom-and-bust cycle.

The constant in Montana through the 1970–1995 period was land, the state's ultimate natural resource. Montana offered the inhabitants of an increasingly pressurized nation its clean, quiet, open spaces, varied recreational opportunities, and scenic beauty. The realization by Montanans that open space represented a financial asset was a novelty in the 1990s. The new attitudes about Montana's land sustained the state's tourism. In 1970 nonresident visitors spent $75 million; in 1992 they contributed $930 million to the state's economy. Yellowstone National Park and Glacier National Park drew the most tourists, but other destination resorts, especially those for skiing, hunting, and fishing, extended tourism's bounties.

With a 1994 population of 856,000, Montana remained "a small city with very long streets connecting its neighborhoods." Increasingly both natives and newcomers have settled in the western Rocky Mountains, "yuppifying" Livingston and Bozeman on the borders of Paradise Valley and depopulating the eastern high plains. Despite vast space, few people, and no sales tax, Montana supported a diverse educational system. The state also became a haven for the arts, ranging from Western painting, photography, and regional literature to Hollywood film. With the withdrawal of the Anaconda Company from Montana politics, the few remaining large corporations had to share power with trade unions, consumer advocates, and single-issue coalitions. In the 1970–1995 period Montana tended to elect conservatives to state and local offices while sending liberal Democrats to Congress, including Mike Mansfield, Lee Metcalf, John Melcher, Max Baucus, and Pat Williams. The exception was Conrad Burns, a conservative who in 1994 became the only Montana Republican ever reelected to the Senate. Despite the state's slight increases in population, it lost one of its two seats in the House of Representatives in 1990.

[Harry W. Fritz, *Montana: Land of Contrast* (Woodland Hills, Calif., 1984); Michael P. Malone, Richard B. Roeder, and William L. Lang, *Montana: A History of Two Centuries* (Seattle, 1991); K. Ross Toole, *Montana: An Uncommon Land* (Norman, Okla., 1959).]

DAVID A. WALTER

See also **SUPP:** Butte.

MORMONS. *See* **Latter-day Saints, Church of Jesus Christ of; Reorganized Church of Jesus Christ of Latter-day Saints.**

MOTION PICTURES. *See* **Movies.**

MOUNT ST. HELENS, a stratovolcanic peak composed of alternating layers of lava and ash, in southwest Washington State, forty miles northeast of Portland, Oreg. Dormant since 1857, Mount St. Helens erupted on May 18, 1980. The eruption was triggered by a series of earthquakes below the volcano's peak and resulted in the release of a mushroom cloud of gases 63,000 feet high, carrying superheated ash and core particles. A lavalike mixture of glass, gas, and ash swept down the mountainside at speeds up to 100 miles per hour. The natural disaster killed 60 people, decimated several native animal populations, and destroyed $500 million worth of timber; economic losses to the region totaled $3 billion. Subsequent minor eruptions occurred on May 25, 1980, and April 11, 1981. In 1982 Mount St. Helens was declared a national volcano monument.

[Caroline D. Harnly and David A. Tyckoson, *Mount St. Helens, The 1980 Eruptions: An Annotated Bibliography* (Metuchen, N.J., 1984).]

CAROLYN BRONSTEIN

See also **SUPP:** Washington State.

MOVIES. Historians place the beginning of projected images in the mid-seventeenth century, when two Germans, Athanasius Kirschner and Johannes Zahn, first mounted figures on glass slides inside a rotating cylinder. Such "magic lanterns," lacking as they were in pliable celluloid film, electromotive force, and, not unimportantly, urban crowds large enough to support this machine-driven form of communication, could hardly be called motion pictures in any contemporary sense, but the optical principles that made Kirschner and Zahn's work possible pointed toward a future that included commercial movies made for mass audiences. Tinkerers and inventors of several European nations, along with several Americans, carried on their experiments. In 1877 Leland Stanford, the American railroad entrepreneur, commissioned an eccentric researcher, Eadweard Muybridge, to settle a bet on the question of whether or not the hooves of a galloping horse ever simultaneously left the ground; the issue was resolved in the affirmative when Muybridge caught the horse at full gallop by means of a row of cameras linked to trip wires over which the horse raced. By 1890 George Eastman had patented a reel of flexible celluloid that made possible exposing film in sequential frames, and beginning in 1896 movies were projected onto screens for audiences at Koster and Bial's Music Hall in New York City.

Inventor Thomas Edison managed to synthesize much research by engaging the scientist William Kennedy Laurie Dickson and by buying up patents for ancillary inventions filed by Thomas Armat, Woodville Latham, and others. At first Edison's firm focused only on his Kinetoscope, a hand-cranked device through which a single viewer peered at a few moments of motion—Annie Oakley firing a rifle, shots of the daily lives of Western Indians, and other fleeting vignettes. Patented in 1891, demonstrated at the Columbian Exposition of 1893 in Chicago, shown to a paying public in the spring of 1894 in New York City, the Kinetoscope peep shows quickly gave way to projected images, again invented by Edison, only two years later at Koster and Bial's. In 1902 Thomas L. Tally opened his Electric Theatre in Los Angeles, a debut soon followed by theater owners in McKeesport and New Castle, Pa., and eventually in every major city. These new theaters—Nickel Odeons, as they were called—helped establish movies as a medium distinct from performance theater, such as vaudeville. Movies soon began to appear in a complex national network of chain theaters supplied by distribution centers called "exchanges." Studios anticipated the Hollywood system of vertically integrated, script-to-screen enterprise.

To a great extent the early system of making and distributing movies was held in place by a patent pool, the Motion Picture Patents Company, led by Edison and other patent holders who used licensing fees as a means of restraining competition. Oddly, these inventive entrepreneurs were aesthetically conservative to the point that few of them thought audiences could tolerate feature-length movies. By 1913 the rivals of the pool had begun to make inroads into its market. Carl Laemmle moved his studio from the Midwest to southern California, where he could get 200 sunny shooting days per year, cheap real estate, and a haven remote from lawyers of the Patents Company. The pioneers included Samuel Goldwyn, Jesse L. Lasky, and Cecil B. DeMille, who together made one of the first features in Hollywood, *The Squaw Man* (1914). Parallel to this westward movement, other movie innovators, such as George Kleine and Adolph Zukor, imported lengthier and more presti-

gious films, with Zukor bringing in *Queen Elizabeth* (1912) with Sarah Bernhardt. The campaign against the patents trust was also assisted by the success of D. W. Griffith, J. Stuart Blackton, and others. They synthesized an emerging canon of cinematic techniques—narrative editing, expressive closeups, and mobile cameras—into an aesthetic that made possible the evolution of feature-length films. Moviemaking by 1915 had been transformed into the Hollywood system by circumstances seemingly unrelated. Griffith completed *The Birth of a Nation* (1915), his famous (and racist) jeremiad against Reconstruction, which demonstrated the political power of the medium and expanded its capacity for advertisement. Gradually the rebels against the mainly Anglo-Saxon patents trust evolved into a Jewish elite whose recent arrival in the United States inspired a broad synthesis of America that harmonized old and new, immigrant and settler, working class and middle class.

World War I stifled European moviemaking so much that American studios, by filling the void, assumed a dominant place in the international marketplace. By the time the United States entered the war in 1917, movies dominated popular culture and movie "stars" were engaged to sell millions of dollars worth of war bonds. By war's end the Hollywood system had become institutionalized, with power in the hands of such producers as Irving Thalberg of Metro-Goldwyn-Mayer. The movie business eventually generated 600 movies each year (some of which grossed millions of dollars), built 5,000 new theaters, raised capital totaling $2 billion, and dominated the world's markets. "The film is to America what the flag was once to Britain," warned the *London Post* in 1925. "By its means, Uncle Sam may hope some day . . . to Americanize the world." "Movies in the age of innocence" described the era when Hollywood's reach seemed limitless and its style universal. Westerns grew into vast epics, such as *The Iron Horse* (1924) and *Covered Wagon* (1923). *The Thief of Baghdad* (1924), *The Phantom of the Opera* (1925), and *The Hunchback of Notre Dame* (1923) filled screens with exotically romantic eras and places. The demimonde appeared in *Broken Blossoms* (1919) and *Beggars of Life* (1928). Racial tensions strained the fabric of *Showboat* (1929) and *Uncle Tom's Cabin* (1927). Social dramas played out in *Manslaughter* (1922) and *Male and Female* (1919). The Judeo-Christian Bible came vividly to life in *The King of Kings* (1927) and other spectacles. The system gradually stifled the artistic impulses of directors—Erich von Stroheim's movies were edited into miniatures and Griffith made his last film in 1931—all this in the name of profitability.

The coming into theaters of sound-on-films is more accurately explained by studio connections with brokers and bankers than by the old legend of a fiscally shaky Warner Brothers gambling everything on sound films as if on a last throw of the dice. Sound film had existed for years but proved usable only when accompanied by the wherewithal to wire thousands of theaters. Between 1926 and 1929, sound film came in the form of *Don Juan* (1926); Al Jolson in *The Jazz Singer* (1927); the first all-talkie, *Lights of New York* (1928), and the first attempts at depicting African-American life on film, all in 1929—*Hallelujah!*, *Hearts in Dixie,* and Bessie Smith's short film by Dudley Murphy, *The St. Louis Blues.* The quick success of sound film encouraged studios to try Herbert Kalmus's long-simmering Technicolor process. From the first Technicolor short, *La Cucaracha* (1934), to David O. Selznick's epochal *Gone with the Wind* (1939), color changed from a costly adventure in research and development into an increasingly common element in movie aesthetics. Here is another innovation best explained by a symbiosis between scientists and investors rather than by a romantic legend of bold moguls saving their studios.

With the coming of the Great Depression, Hollywood studios sought to move against the tide, and some actually made a profit. Only Paramount, overextended in theatrical realty, brushed against bankruptcy. Indeed, as sound film became conventional the studios extended their range into whole new genres. As the American theatrical stage became more naturalistic, its best works, such as Eugene O'Neill's *Anna Christie* and Sidney Kingsley's *Dead End*, came to the screen in 1930 and 1937, respectively, along with movie versions of such American novels as Sinclair Lewis's *Dodsworth* in 1936, Ernest Hemingway's *A Farewell to Arms* in 1932, and John Steinbeck's *The Grapes of Wrath* in 1940. At the same time, DeMille and other makers of movie epics adapted their silent movie styles to sound film in such works as *Cleopatra* (1934), *The Crusades* (1935), and *Union Pacific* (1939). Biographies from Abraham Lincoln to Lillian Russell emerged from every studio, especially Twentieth Century–Fox. The "star system" flourished, again particularly at Fox, in such Shirley Temple films as *The Little Colonel* (1934), *The Littlest Rebel* (1936), *Wee Willie Winkie* (1937), and a score of others. Will Rogers had his own genre of local color in such movies as *David Harum* (1934), *Judge Priest* (1934), and *The County Chairman* (1935).

Crime dramas that portrayed a dark underside of urban culture—*Scarface* (1932), *Bullets or Ballots* (1936), and *Public Enemy* (1931), to name but a few—became vehicles by which moviemakers addressed social dysfunctions brought about by the Great Depression. Even such musicals as *The Gold Diggers of 1933* (1933) served not only as escapist fare but as ideologically optimistic responses to the economic crisis. The Hollywood system reached an apogee of sorts in 1939, the year of *Gone with the Wind, The Wizard of Oz, Stagecoach, Wuthering Heights, Juarez,* and *Goodbye Mr. Chips.*

During this heady era, Hollywood studios reached a complex level of corporate structure. Each maintained a close affiliation with bankers and brokers on both the East and West coasts, a system of producer units on each lot, sales departments that presented their products to the world, stables of contractual stars and directors, adversarial links to many craft guilds, and influential links to movie fan magazines. Most compelling in defining the Hollywood product, however, was the Hays Office of the Motion Picture Producers and Distributors of America (MPPDA) (after 1945 known as the Motion Picture Association of America, or MPAA). Hollywood created the MPPDA in 1922 in response to scandals involving movie stars. Will H. Hays became its first president. When critics continued to charge that moviegoing caused moral and social decay, the movie industry adopted a production code in 1930. Heavily moral in emphasis but also politically conservative, the code was largely the work of a Jesuit priest, Daniel A. Lord. The ability of Hays and the MPPDA to enforce the code was strengthened in 1934 with the creation of the Production Code Administration (an arm of the Hays Office) and the Roman Catholic Legion of Decency (independent of Hays), which could organize some 8 million Catholics to boycott offensive movies. Thenceforth, evildoers met bad ends and virtue was rewarded on theater screens.

The movie industry entered World War II with considerable concern, generated by the prospect of federal interference. A newly minted Office of War Information (OWI) sought to prescribe Hollywood's contribution to the war effort. Even before the war, a Senate committee had investigated Hollywood's alleged "warmongering," and a House committee had probed a presumed infiltration of the movie industry by the Communist party. As it turned out, the OWI proved an accommodating monitor, and the congressional committees put aside their curiosity for the duration of the war. Furthermore, Hollywood's craft guilds, like most other trade unions, deferred strikes. Within their familiar formulas the studios produced simply phrased war movies, and satisfied audiences provided studios with their greatest profits ever. War movies typically ranged over a wide field to influence Anglophobes, draftees in search of war aims, African Americans in need of a reason to fight despite their oppression at home, and civilians who felt the loss of their men under arms. These movies also sometimes served the country simply by offering diversions from the stresses imposed by war. *Sergeant York* (1941) defined the notion of a "just war" in folkish terms; *Sundown* (1941) contained an implicit promise that a victorious Britain would find a way out of colonialism; *Sahara* (1943) and *Lifeboat* (1944) dramatized the virtues of allying against fascism; *Mrs. Miniver* (1942) and *In Which We Serve* (1942) revealed a Britain unified across class lines; *Bataan* (1943) and *Crashdive* (1943) placed black Americans in the military ranks; *Casablanca* (1943) traced the conversion of an American in Morocco from isolationism to action against the Germans; and *Since You Went Away* (1944) and *Gangway for Tomorrow* (1943) brought the war to civilians. At the same time, outside the circle of Hollywood studios the war stimulated a movement of documentary filmmakers toward a cinema of social advocacy. Responding to requirements of the Signal Corps, OWI, and other agencies, filmmakers turned out a sweeping range of propaganda movies, such as *The Negro Soldier* (1944), *The Battle of Midway* (1942), *With the Marines at Tarawa* (1943), and *The Memphis Belle* (1944). After the war these same filmmakers brought their training to bear on U.S. political and social issues in such films as *The Quiet One* (1947) and a generation of television documentaries such as *The Twentieth Century* (1957–1966).

Unfortunately for the Hollywood that America had come to know, the era of peace brought an irresistible assault of pent-up social forces. Simmering labor disputes produced strife at the studio gates, resulting in soaring labor costs; wartime savings led consumers on a binge of leisure-time spending, seemingly on everything but moviegoing, that brought a period of inflation, which meant another boost in moviemaking costs; Congress, freed from wartime pressures for unity, revived its inquiry into communism in Hollywood, this time with a vengeance that trampled on the civil rights of its victims; the Supreme Court, which had muted its opposition to trusts, handed down the 1948 *Paramount* decision that obliged studios to dismantle the vertical integration of the sys-

tem that had brought each movie from script to screen; and finally, the shaken system was first threatened, then dominated by the new medium of network television. Such innovations as stereophonic sound and widescreen processes, like CinemaScope, only momentarily gave movies an edge in the face of TV's popularity. In the twenty-five years after World War II, Hollywood lost hundreds of millions of dollars. Hollywood recovered, but at the price of transforming its very nature. Its will to survive drove it into the arms of television, first selling off its vast libraries of feature films and, second, becoming the principal producer of the thousands of hours of broadcast time that television required. The made-for-television movie and the miniseries became staples of the old studios, while hour-length serial dramas and "sitcoms" assumed the role of older, cheaply made B-movies.

The mainstream fare, with its undemanding embrace of middle American values, was challenged during the 1960s by theatrical movies that brought to the screen occasionally revolutionary ideas and images that could find no place on the TV schedule. *Bonnie and Clyde* (1967) celebrated the lives of two murderous bank robbers of the Depression era. *Easy Rider* (1969) sympathetically portrayed the romantic rebels known as "flower children." *Sweet Sweetback's Baadasssss Song* (1971) offered a violent depiction of a black assault on white oppressors personified in a sadistically brutal Los Angeles police force.

Accompanying this sectoring of the audience into interest groups of television viewers and newly selective and politically aware audiences, was an opening of the nation's screens to foreign films, often played in "art houses" set apart from the increasingly unused downtown "picture palaces." At their best they included psychologically and socially sophisticated fare from Europe, some of them—such as Jules Dassin's *Never on Sunday* (1960)—running for more than a year in a single art house. Some, like *La Chinoise* (1967), were highly charged leftist films, while others paid homage to older American forms, much as *Tirez sur le Pianiste* (1960) echoed American gangster movies and the bleak postwar detective movies that came to be known as film noir. Still other imports, such as *Rashomon* (1950) and *Pather Panchali* (1955), came from Japan and India, respectively. Each in its way undercut the market for American movies and all but drove Hollywood into other areas of entertainment, as in the case of MGM's hotels and casinos. In the 1970s a few studios recovered by reaching for a newly discovered audience, a disaffected, urban, black youth that embraced the violence of so-called "blaxploitation" movies, such as Gordon Parks's *Shaft* (1971), which simultaneously recast the private detective into black terms and saved MGM from closure.

In the Hollywood that survived, several trends marked off the new generation from the old. Directors and writers such as Martin Scorsese and Steven Spielberg came to Hollywood from university film schools rather than up through the studio hierarchies. Some came willing to take risks, as in the case of George Lucas, who used computer-generated techniques in *Star Wars* (1977). Both in television and movies, the makers embraced a strategy of betting resources on hoped-for "blockbusters"—impressively expensive theatrical films that earned hundreds of millions—or television miniseries during "sweeps weeks," when audience-sampling firms provided the networks with data on the nation's viewing habits upon which advertising rates were based. Because audiences were ever younger, the movie year took on a rhythm grounded in the hiatuses of the academic year. Prospective blockbusters opened in summer and at Christmas, while offbeat movies such as Spike Lee's *She's Gotta Have It* (1986) opened in the new off-seasons of fall and spring. By the 1990s Hollywood had taken on the traits of conglomeration, an international trend in corporate enterprise, so that studios often came to be owned by foreign firms such as Sony, energy firms such as Gulf and Western, and soft-drink companies such as Coca-Cola. Accompanying this trend toward conglomeration, however, there was also a small growth of independent cinema that offered hope for ethnic minorities and cinematic innovators.

[Robert C. Allen and Douglas Gomery, *Film History* (New York, 1985); David Bordwell, Janet Staiger, and Kristin Thompson, *The Classical Hollywood Cinema* (New York, 1985); Thomas Cripps, *Slow Fade to Black: The Negro in American Film* (New York, 1977); Douglas Gomery, *Movie History* (Belmont, Calif., 1991); Garth Jowett, *Film: The Democratic Art* (Boston, 1976); Robert Sklar, *Movie-Made America* (New York, 1975).]

THOMAS CRIPPS

See also **DAH:** Motion Pictures; **SUPP:** Television.

MRI. *See* **Magnetic Resonance Imaging.**

MTV. *See* **MUSIC TELEVISION.**

MULTICULTURALISM. In the 1990s multiculturalism dominated interpretive and curricular debates about history in schools and universities. The idea responds in part to the diversity of students, especially in urban areas, increasingly from African-, Hispanic-, and Asian-American backgrounds. Taken together, minority groups are nearing a majority in such major cities as New York and Los Angeles and in states including California, Texas, Florida, and New York. By the year 2000 non-European ethnic minorities are expected to make up one-fourth of the nation's population. State and federal education officials, test designers, and educational publishers are concerned by these changes. Since demonstrations at Stanford University in 1988, educators on campuses across the country have debated the extent to which a history curriculum should be Eurocentric, that is, be based on classical Western texts, take a triumphal view of national settlement or expansion by Europeans, or emphasize the history of U.S. political and economic elites. Some multiculturalists claim that white Americans of European heritage have unjustly tried to impose ethnocentric values on nonwhite Americans. They hold that the school-based imposition of Western history, literature, ideas, institutions, and values on children of non-European backgrounds is unjust and culturally biased. Other scholars assert that the nation's political institutions, language, cultural ideals, and economic system derive mainly from Europe, notably from England.

Multiculturalism emphasizes the recognition and study of national diversity, especially along lines of ethnicity and gender. Both pluralists and group separatists claim its philosophical foundations: Multiculturalism may acknowledge qualities of U.S. culture and politics that transcend group differences, or it may contend that racial, ethnic, sexual, religious, and other human characteristics create "separate realities" and "multiple cultural perspectives" of learning. Many multiculturalists reject the idea of a common culture, including older ethnic melting-pot ideals and the idea of pluralism. The multicultural concept is often linked to self-esteem training used to advance the self-image of minorities and women. Some educators envision multiculturalism as a tool to change the educational environment so that students from various groups and social classes will experience equal educational opportunity. According to a 1991 New York City Board of Education declaration, "Multicultural education is an interdisciplinary approach to education designed to foster intergroup knowledge and understanding, to engender greater self-esteem within the entire school community, and to equip students to function effectively in a global society." Some philosophers distinguish between multiculturalism and pluralism in that the former "repudiates the idea of national identity and the emotion of national pride." They worry that such a repudiation, if standard in history and government, invites social fragmentation and civil disorder, whereby students will identify with groups rather than through bonds of citizenship, language, and law.

GILBERT T. SEWALL

See also **SUPP:** Curriculum; Pluralism; Political Correctness; Women's Studies.

MUSEUMS. Although museums in the United States date back to the late eighteenth century, the great age of museum building occurred in the 1870s with the founding of such institutions as the Metropolitan Museum of Art and the American Museum of Natural History, both in New York City, the Art Institute of Chicago, and the Boston Museum of Fine Arts. These grand public buildings emphasized rare and exemplary objects of great beauty, technical importance, or historical relevance, chiefly from cultures abroad, past and present. By the early twentieth century, however, U.S. museums began to respond to broad reform currents with a greater emphasis on U.S. culture itself. John Cotton Dana's work at the Newark Museum, for example, attempted to reach out to recent immigrants. A new interest in ordinary objects, on period rooms and contextual display, on historic houses, and on U.S. arts and crafts manifested itself. The era saw the emergence of such specialized art museums as the Museum of Modern Art, the Whitney Museum of American Art, and the Boston Institute of Contemporary Art.

The focus on U.S. history and culture was taken a step further in the 1920s with the development of the outdoor museum. Colonial Williamsburg in Virginia and the Henry Ford Museum and Greenfield Village in Michigan were the most visible and the best financed. Such museums brought a history focused in part around the daily lives of ordinary people and sought to teach a common past to a population that had become heterogeneous. As collections of buildings brought together to form a single site, Williamsburg and Greenfield Village served as models for such later museums as Old Sturbridge in Massachusetts and Old World Wisconsin. During these years the New York State Historical Association, under Dixon Ryan Fox, also began to play a leadership role that extended into the second half of the century, fostering ties between museum and university historians, exploring further the history of ordinary Americans,

and eventually playing an important role in the development of history exhibitions and graduate education.

The 1930s brought several changes in museum management. The reorganization of the National Park Service in 1933 greatly expanded its responsibility for historic interpretation and preservation and marked the beginning of a larger role for the federal government in support of museum development. The Chicago Museum of Science and Industry opened in 1933, inaugurating a more interactive form of science education and leading to the development of science centers, many supported and programmed directly by business. The decade was marked by calls to make museums instruments of social change and by a deepening interest in the U.S. past, especially in its folk and populist roots.

After World War II collectors and philanthropists founded museums devoted to neglected areas of national culture. Among the most important were Electra Havemeyer Webb's collection of Americana at the Shelburne Museum in Shelburne, Vt., and the Henry Francis du Pont Winterthur Museum in Delaware. Museums of business and industry emerged in these years, including the Hagley Museum and Library in Wilmington, Del., the Slater Historic Site in Pawtucket, R.I., and the Saugus Iron Works National Historic Site in Saugus, Mass.

Since the 1960s there have been several new trends. The federal government assumed an even larger role, and the National Park Service began to operate visitor centers with museum-quality displays, the Department of Defense supported a large network of military museums, and the National Endowment for the Humanities, the National Endowment for the Arts, and the Institute for Museum Services have served not just as financial supporters but as standard setters for museums. With public funding came a stronger commitment to education and access as well as greater scrutiny. The increasingly public face of museums enhanced the roles of museum educators, exhibition designers, and visitor survey specialists. Museums also became more specialized. Museums of sports, of broadcasting, and of labor have taken their places alongside museums of art, history, and science. There has been a substantial growth in small, community-based museums, and the social movements of the 1960s have led traditional museums to be more inclusive of the U.S. populace in their showings. Among the most innovative new museums are the Exploratorium, the science teaching center in San Francisco; the imaginative and well-designed aquariums in Baltimore and Monterey, Calif.; the Holocaust Museum in Washington, D.C., the first major institution devoted to the understanding of human tragedy; and Manhattan's Lower East Side Tenement Museum, a new kind of historic-house museum. The growing movement of museums devoted to ethnic groups was given legitimacy by creation of the Museum of the American Indian, planned for the last open space on the Mall in Washington, D.C.

For art museums the 1970s and early 1980s marked an era of big and expensive loan exhibitions. Blockbuster shows on British country houses, impressionism, and Egyptian culture, among others, attracted huge crowds but strained museum resources. Smaller shows relying on in-house collections became the norm in the 1990s as museums struggled with lowered budgets. Venerable historical societies and urban history museums transformed themselves and their exhibitions in the 1980s in Pittsburgh, Richmond, and Minneapolis in an effort to reach a broader public. Not every such effort worked. The New-York Historical Society came close to failure as costs outran income. At the same time, however, natural history museums, among the most traditional and predictable of museums, put a renewed emphasis on education and imaginative exhibitions. Chicago's Field Museum was among the leaders. Far more than in the past, museums have become places of great controversy. Heated public debates in Madison, Wisc., accompanied the development of Old World Wisconsin. An exhibition of Robert Mapplethorpe's photographs in Cincinnati elicited a lawsuit for obscenity, and the funding practices of the National Endowment for the Arts came under harsh attack. The Smithsonian Institution's efforts to interpret the art of the American West and, through its Air and Space Museum, the bombing of Hiroshima and Nagasaki, produced intense public controversy.

[Warren Leon and Roy Rosenzweig, eds., *History Museums in the U.S.* (Urbana, Ill., 1989); Joel J. Orosz, *Curators and Culture* (Tuscaloosa, Ala., 1990); Michael Steven Shapiro, ed., *The Museum: A Reference Guide* (New York, 1990).]

GARY KULIK

See also **SUPP:** National Endowment for the Arts; National Endowment for the Humanities; Park Service, National; National Trust for Historic Preservation; Science Museums.

MUSEUMS, SCIENCE. *See* **Science Museums.**

MUSIC, BLUEGRASS, is a form of country music that emerged in the 1940s and 1950s from a group known as the Blue Grass Boys headed by Grand Ole Opry star Bill Monroe, who came to be known as "the father of bluegrass." The music in its definitive form was first heard in Nashville, Tenn. Early bluegrass was distinctively flavored by Appalachia, where such groups as the Stanley Brothers and their Clinch Mountain Boys and Lester Flatt, Earl Scruggs, and the Foggy Mountain Boys performed on radio station WCYB in Bristol on the Tennessee-Virginia border. Several characteristics define bluegrass style. A typical band consists of four to seven players and singers who use acoustic rather than electrical instruments. Bluegrass is pitched high and requires more than one voice to sing something other than harmony parts. The guitar, mandolin, banjo, string bass, and fiddle play both melody and provide rhythm and background for vocal soloists. Through recordings, television, tours, and festivals, bluegrass performers have gained a national and even international constituency. An establishment consisting of several recording companies (Country, Rebel, Rounder, Sugar Hill, and others), clubs, and magazines, such as *Bluegrass Unlimited*, developed as the bluegrass festival movement spread in the 1960s. In the 1970s performances departed from the traditional form with "new grass," using rock repertoire and techniques.

[Neil V. Rosenberg, *Bluegrass: A History* (Chicago, 1985).]

CHARLES A. WEEKS

MUSIC, CLASSICAL, encompasses instrumental and vocal music written by trained composers. It expresses more fully the artistic values of composers than music of an essentially commercial nature (popular) or music that develops anonymously and is transmitted aurally (folk). In the United States classical music has appealed to fewer people than popular or folk music. In the eighteenth century, classical music could be heard in Boston, Philadelphia, New York, Williamsburg, Charleston, and New Orleans and elsewhere in the houses of the well-to-do. Composers such as William Billings, Francis Hopkinson, and Alexander Reinagle produced hymns, songs, instrumental music, and opera similar in style to that of European contemporaries but noteworthy for a degree of originality. None of these composers could make a living from compositions; Billings died penniless. Much of their best music went unpublished in their lifetimes, as was the case with a Reinagle piano sonata that was not published until 1978. The music of such Europeans as George Handel, Antonio Vivaldi, Arcangelo Corelli, Luigi Boccherini, Jean-Philippe

Rameau, and Joseph Haydn was probably better known and more often played in these coastal cities and in the houses of talented amateur musicians, such as Robert Carter and Thomas Jefferson, both of Virginia.

Composition of American classical music in the nineteenth century was dominated by a group of people eager to emulate the European masters, particularly those in the Germanic tradition. Many studied with teachers in Germany and did not deviate from what they learned. John Knowles Paine, the first musician to hold a professorship in a university (Harvard), became the prototype of the academic composer and, along with Dudley Buck, Edward MacDowell, Horatio Parker, Amy Cheney Beach, and George Whitefield Chadwick, wrote symphonies, concertos, songs, and choral music in the style of European contemporaries. Some African-American composers, beginning with Harry Thacker Burleigh, practiced more compositional diversity in an effort to express their African-American heritage. A significant result of this endeavor was William Grant Still's "Afro-American Symphony" of 1930.

Audiences, performing venues, and important musical organizations emerged in the nineteenth century. The predecessor of the New York Philharmonic, the Philharmonic Society, gave its first concert in 1842. Orchestras were established in Boston (1881), Chicago (1891), St. Louis (1893), and Cincinnati (1895). As early as the 1790s operas were performed in New Orleans and Philadelphia. In New York City opera was performed in theaters and the Academy of Music. The Metropolitan Opera House opened in 1883 and in 1910 transmitted a radio broadcast. Performers went on tour, the most famous being the Swedish singer Jenny Lind, promoted by the greatest of all entertainment entrepreneurs of the century, Phineas T. Barnum. Very little music, however, by native composers was performed.

In the twentieth century, opera flourished in the United States. An early work, *Treemonisha*, by composer and popularizer of ragtime Scott Joplin, received a limited production in 1915, and George Gershwin's *Porgy and Bess* was first heard in 1935. A new Metropolitan Opera House opened in 1966 with a production of *Antony and Cleopatra*, written by Samuel Barber in the tradition of European grand opera. In 1957 Barber had composed *Vanessa*, which was performed at the Metropolitan and elsewhere. Other composers of opera were Marc Blitzstein (*Regina*, 1949), Leonard Bernstein (*Trouble in Tahiti*, 1952), Douglas Moore (*The Ballad of Baby Doe*,

1956), Gian Carlo Menotti (*The Medium*, 1945; *The Consul*, 1949; *Amahl and the Night Visitors*, composed for television in 1951), Virgil Thomson (*Four Saints in Three Acts*, 1934), Philip Glass (*Einstein on the Beach*, 1975; *Satyagraha*, 1981; *The Voyage*, 1992), John Adams (*Nixon in China*, 1987; *Death of Klinghofer*, 1991), John Corigliano (*The Ghosts of Versailles*, 1991), and Hugo Weisgall (*Six Characters in Search of an Author*, 1956; *Esther*, 1987).

American composers produced a wealth of instrumental music over the course of the twentieth century. Some sought to innovate; others enriched European tradition. Most taught at universities or such conservatories as Juilliard (established 1905), the Eastman School of Music (1919), and the New England Conservatory (1867). The giant of American innovative composers was Charles Ives, whose music had to wait until after his death in 1951 for full recognition, as did that of Charles Tomlinson Griffes, who died in 1920, and Carl Ruggles, who died in 1971. French-born Edgar Varèse took up residence in the United States in 1915 and influenced native composers, notably Henry Cowell and Harry Partch, to write music to unsettle, shock, disturb. Two other innovators were John Cage and Milton Babbitt, whose 1989 work "Transfigured Notes" was unplayable because of limited rehearsal time by the Philadelphia Orchestra. Leonard Bernstein and Aaron Copland, who many have characterized as the dean of American composers, stand out because of the quantity and variety of their compositions and because of their roles as performers and advocates of music.

Among the best representatives of postromantic and expressionist music are Roger Sessions, called the greatest of American symphonists; Roy Harris; Howard Hanson; Peter Mennin; Walter Piston; and David Diamond. Leslie Bassett and Elliott Carter might also be placed in the expressionist tradition. Harris, composer of fourteen symphonies, and Robert Palmer wrote music showing the influence of central European nationalism. Barber and Hanson, who for forty years headed the Eastman School of Music, sustained an Italian, Scandinavian, and Russian romanticism. The career of George Rochberg encompassed experiments with atonality, but most of his output is expressionistic and romantic.

Much American classical music found audiences because of the large numbers of American symphony orchestras—1,400 by the late twentieth century. Radio and television disseminated music, as illustrated by the Metropolitan Opera's Saturday afternoon radio broadcasts beginning in 1940 and such public television series as *Great Performances* and *Live from Lincoln Center*. New halls and cultural centers opened in New York, Washington, Atlanta, San Francisco, Los Angeles, Dallas, and other cities; older halls, including former movie theaters, were renovated and restored in Detroit, Pittsburgh, Oakland, and St. Louis.

Despite observations suggesting trouble in the world of classical music (the recital and symphony orchestra dead or dying, for example), enrollment in conservatories and music schools and attendance at a growing number of summer music festivals increased. Many orchestras expanded seasons, encouraged new music through composer-in-residence programs, and showed a remarkable ability to innovate in programming and format. Classical music at the end of the twentieth century remained a vital part of the musical culture of the United States.

[Gilbert Chase, *America's Music: From the Pilgrims to the Present*, 3rd rev. ed. (Chicago, 1992); Richard Crawford, *The American Musical Landscape* (Berkeley, Calif., 1993); John Dizikes, *Opera in America: A Cultural History* (New Haven, Conn., 1993); Monroe Levin, *Clues to American Music* (Washington, D.C., 1992); Stanley Sadie and H. Wiley Hitchcock, eds., *The New Grove Dictionary of American Music*, 4 vols. (New York, 1986).]

CHARLES A. WEEKS

MUSIC, COUNTRY AND WESTERN, often referred to just as country music, eludes precise definition because of its many sources and varieties. It can best be understood as a style of popular music that originated in the folk culture of the rural South, a culture of European and African origin. Fiddlers, banjo players, string bands, balladeers, and gospel singers drew upon existing music to develop materials suitable for performance at family and community events. As southerners migrated to northern cities in the early twentieth century, their music went with them; and, beginning in the 1920s, radio and recordings did much to popularize and diversify this music. Musicians from Texas, Louisiana, and Oklahoma were especially innovative with regard to developing and promoting this essentially rural form of entertainment. In 1934, when a radio hillbilly singer from Texas named Orvon Gene Autry went to Hollywood, the era of the great cowboy singer in the movies began. The Grand Ole Opry in Nashville, beginning in the 1940s, made that city a mecca for country music fans, many of whom listened religiously to its performances on the radio. The popularity of rock and roll through the revolution in popular music begun by Elvis Presley in the mid-1950s posed a challenge to country music, but it was countered in part by development of a new style known as country pop or the Nashville Sound. By the 1990s country and western music had an international following.

[Bill C. Malone, *Country Music, U.S.A.: A Fifty-year History*, rev. ed. (New York, 1985).]

CHARLES A. WEEKS

See also **SUPP:** Music, Bluegrass; Music, Rock and Roll.

MUSIC, JAZZ, is characterized by improvisation, bent pitches or blues notes, syncopation, and polyrhythms. It first appeared in the southern part of the United States during the late nineteenth century, blossomed in New Orleans at the turn of the century, and spread to other cities between 1890 and 1920, as dance halls, cabarets, restaurants, and theaters proliferated to satisfy a growing demand by Americans for pleasure and self-expression. The first jazz recording was made in New Orleans by the Original Dixieland Jazz Band in 1917, and during the 1920s jazz and jazz-influenced dance music became the popular music of the United States. F. Scott Fitzgerald entitled a collection of his short stories *Tales of the Jazz Age* (1922), and the phrase became part of the lexicon of the decade. In the next two decades the success of jazz was assured by the big swing bands. By the end of World War II, bebop, which originated in the practice of vocalizing or singing instrumental lines and was played by small groups of three to six members, was becoming popular among musicians who disliked the size and formality of the swing bands. Another style, cool jazz, emerged at the same time. By the 1960s rock and rock-based styles had displaced jazz as the popular music of the United States. Since the 1970s many styles have flourished, including modal jazz, an avant-garde free jazz, and jazz rock or fusion. Beginning in the 1980s a movement emerged to preserve a purer or classical jazz against attempts to fuse it with rock or rhythm and blues.

[Frank Tirro, *Jazz: A History*, 2nd ed. (New York, 1993).]

JOSHUA L. COX
CHARLES A. WEEKS

MUSIC, NEW, in the most comprehensive sense, is music produced each time a composer puts notes to paper. Music can, however, stand out because of its departure from norms. Creators of such music may be responding to new social and economic conditions or they may simply set out to invent something not heard before. Prior to the twentieth century, religious and ethnic groups constituted important sources of new music. African Americans adapted the music they brought with them to serve new needs and produced a distinctive dance and vocal music. Some of this music evolved into the spirituals of the nineteenth century and the blues, ragtime, jazz, and soul music of the twentieth century. Beginning with the Second Awakening, the great religious revival of the early nineteenth century, evangelical religion, with its camp and revival meetings, produced revival hymns and spiritual songs. Southern and midwestern rural singers, tunebook compilers, and singing-school teachers developed a system of notation, the shape note, that designated a body of semifolk music and a style of singing known as fasola-folk or sacred-harp singing, after the most widely used shape-note tunebook, *The Sacred Harp* (1844).

Technology and social changes in the twentieth century created a time of ferment and encouragement in the production of new music. Recordings, radio, television, movies, and electronics all influenced the composition and performance of music. In the first two decades of the twentieth century such composers as Charles Ives, Carl Ruggles, Wallingford Riegger, Ruth Crawford Seeger, and Henry Cowell began employing atonality, the absence of a tonal center, with little or no knowledge of similar experiments in Europe. Ives experimented freely with tonality and rhythm, taking a cue from his father, who believed there were no rules in music. Cowell emerged as a major advocate of the unorthodox in music; his *New Music Quarterly* championed the music of Ruggles, Seeger, and other innovators.

Jazz emerged in the first three decades of the twentieth century from the dance and vocal music of nineteenth-century African Americans and entered into the composition of operas. Scott Joplin, the ragtime composer, published the opera *Treemonisha* in 1911, but it was almost forgotten until its revival in the 1970s. George Gershwin's opera *Porgy and Bess* (1935) similarly departed from European models by incorporating native materials. Beginning in the 1920s Gershwin, and later Richard Rodgers, Harold Rome, Jerome Kern, Cole Porter, Frank Loesser, Leonard Bernstein, Stephen Sondheim, and others, made music theater a part of cultural life in the United States.

Experimentation and innovation continued in the late 1940s and 1950s, to include electronic music, that is, music composed or altered by electronic apparatus. The tape recorder was the first device employed for this novel purpose. By the 1960s the synthesizer and similar instruments expanded possi-

bilities, as illustrated by the Columbia-Princeton Electronic Music Center headed by composer Milton Babbitt, a rigorous exponent of serial music and its disregard for tonality. After World War II Harry Partch and John Cage experimented similarly with chance or aleatoric music. In popular music, another innovation of the 1950s was rock and roll, popularized by singer Elvis Presley.

While many of these experimental traditions continued into the last quarter of the century, new music became a conservative reaction against atonality, serialism, and chance music. In 1964 "In C" by Terry Riley heralded the advent of minimalism, music characterized by repetitions of a motif or group of motifs coupled with strict adherence to tonality. The best-known composers of this genre, in addition to Riley, were La Monte Young, Steve Reich, and Philip Glass. In popular music perhaps the most significant innovation of the 1980s was rap music, an urban African-American form said to be as important to its period as jazz was to an earlier time. Innovation continued in the music of Pulitzer Prize–winning classical composers Elliott Carter, Dominick Argento, Ned Rorem, Joseph Schwantner, David Del Tredici, Ellen Taaffe Zwilich, and William Bolcom. In their work one can note a preference for tonality and form, perhaps complementing a conservatism found in politics, religion, architecture, and the visual arts. Musical styles of the late twentieth century thus showed a distinct preference for earlier aesthetics.

[Gilbert Chase, *America's Music: From the Pilgrims to the Present,* 3rd ed. (Urbana, Ill., 1992); David H. Cope, *New Directions in Music,* 6th ed. (Madison, Wis., 1993); Paul Griffiths, *Modern Music: A Concise History from Debussy to Boulez* (New York, 1978); Joan Peyser, *The New Music: The Sense Behind the Sound* (New York, 1971); John Rockwell, *All American Music: Composition in the Late Twentieth Century* (New York, 1983).]

CHARLES A. WEEKS

See also **DAH:** Awakening, Second; Camp Meetings; Hymns; Music; Music, Afro-American; Singing Schools; **SUPP:** Music, Classical; Music, Jazz; Music, Rock and Roll; Music Festivals.

MUSIC, RHYTHM AND BLUES. The term "rhythm and blues" was first used by the popular music magazine *Billboard* in 1949 to replace its category of "race records." By then and continuing into the 1950s, blues artists, who drew on a musical heritage that originated in the rural South, were incorporating the rhythms of jazz to produce a commercial urbanized music. It drew styles and performers from the big bands, such as Count Basie and His Orchestra; pop groups, such as the Inkspots; and blues men, such as Joe Turner, Jimmy Rushing, B. B. King, and Bobby Bland. It also produced such major stars as Ray Charles, who used jazz instrumentation and urbanized blues and gospel idioms, and such balladeers as Percy Mayfield and Ruth and Charles Brown. Promoters and recording entrepreneurs Phil Spector and Jerry Wexler promoted markets for these styles, and through the 1960s such groups as the Clovers, Orioles, and Jackson Five penetrated mass markets. As with other popular music idioms, rhythm and blues blurred in the 1960s as its elements merged with other commercial art forms and as new urban social systems and values developed. Even by the mid-1950s such rhythm and blues performers as Fats Domino and Little Richard had crossed over to rock and roll, which was initially a country music–based genre. Memphis Minnie, a rhythm and blues artist, had a profound influence on Elvis Presley. By the 1970s the term "rhythm and blues" had lost its original meaning and was retained only to indicate commercial music by African-American performers.

[Peter Grammond, *The Oxford Companion to Popular Music* (New York, 1991); L. E. McCutcheon, *Rhythm and Blues: An Experience and Adventure in Its Origins and Developments* (Arlington, Va., 1971).]

JOHN DAVIS

See also **SUPP:** Music, Jazz; Music, Rock and Roll.

MUSIC, ROCK AND ROLL, reflected youth and social change in post–World War II America. It integrated musically blacks and whites in the mid-1950s, was pivotal in the youth counterculture and protest movements of the mid-1960s through the early 1970s, and reflected societal divisions from the 1970s through the 1990s. Elvis Presley helped create rock and roll with "That's Alright Mama" (1954), "Mystery Train" (1955), and other recordings for Memphis-based Sun Records, which also produced the Jerry Lee Lewis classics "Whole Lot of Shakin' Going On (1957) and "Great Balls of Fire" (1957). Presley's blend of blues and country smashed the color barrier between black and white musical styles, triggering a musical revolution that was amplified by Chuck Berry, a black guitarist who drew heavily from white country music when writing such enduring standards as "Johnny B. Goode" (1958). White youths increasingly embraced black music, from the smooth harmonies of the Drifters to the hyperkinetic screams of Little Richard (Richard Penniman), whose "Tutti Frutti" (1965) stunned unprepared listeners. By 1956,

when Presley began to enjoy massive national popularity, black and white music were achieving an integration rare in the larger society.

The early 1960s heard the Beach Boys harmonizing about a mythic California; Phil Spector's "wall of sound," which exploded with the Crystals epic "Then He Kissed Me" (1963); the Ventures' influential instrumental rock, and the emergence of such Motown Records stars as Smokey Robinson and Marvin Gaye. It was the Beatles, however, who defined rock and roll in a way no act has before or since. They not only dominated the American popular music charts (beginning with their 1964 hit "I Want to Hold Your Hand") but also helped lead the music's expansion from simple adolescent love songs to complex aggressions that could reflect the social and political changes sweeping the United States. Bob Dylan's stunning *Highway 61 Revisited* (1965) and *Blonde on Blonde* (1966) were pivotal albums in this transformation, which was accelerated by other albums, such as the Beatles' *Rubber Soul* (1965) and *Sgt. Pepper's Lonely Hearts Club Band* (1967) and the Rolling Stones' *Aftermath* (1966) and *Let It Bleed* (1969). Despite growing diversity, rock and roll did not seem fragmented at the end of the 1960s. The Woodstock music festival (1969) was able to encompass Jimi Hendrix's guitar explosions, the Grateful Dead's folk-rock, Sly Stone's eclectic funk, Credence Clearwater Revival's straightforward rock, Janis Joplin's anguished blues, the Who's furious intellectualism, and much more.

By the 1970s, however, rock's fault lines grew. The disco music of Donna Summer and others was reviled by the heavy metal fans of Led Zeppelin, while devotees of such introspective singer-songwriters as Paul Simon or Joni Mitchell were at best puzzled by the Sex Pistols, Patti Smith, Television, and other pioneering punk rockers. New-wave bands, such as the Talking Heads, expanded rock's musical vocabulary, but they too spoke to one part of what had once seemed a unified audience.

In the 1980s Madonna (Madonna Louise Ciccone) combined sexual provocation and steely business acumen to win huge commercial success, while rap music restored distinctly black music to a central place in rock. Although such rappers as Run-DMC developed an interracial appeal, other hip hop artists seemed to encourage an animosity toward whites that was unknown to such earlier black music exemplars as Aretha Franklin and James Brown, and many whites remained hostile to rap. Rock artistry thrived in the 1990s, from Prince's (Prince Rogers Nelson) infectious fusion of musical styles to Nirvana's incendiary mix of punk and heavy metal, but no one could rejoin the splintered rock audience. Such top acts as Michael Jackson and REM spoke to different musical worlds, while Bruce Springsteen, one of the most popular and important artists of the 1980s, sang only to that fraction of listeners eager to hear him. The music that had grown out of the integration power of Elvis and had reached its mythic unifying peak at Woodstock was deeply divided as the United States faced a new millennium.

[Greil Marcus, *Mystery Train: Images of America in Rock 'n' Roll Music,* rev. ed. (New York, 1982); Ed Ward et al., eds., *Rock of Ages: The "Rolling Stone" History of Rock & Roll* (New York, 1986).]

ANDREW L. AOKI

See also **SUPP:** Music, Rhythm and Blues.

MUSIC EVENTS. *See* **Benefit Concerts; Music Festivals.**

MUSIC FESTIVALS commemorate anniversaries, celebrate religious or ethnic traditions, or offer music of a composer, period, or type; they can range from a single event to many events encompassing days or even a season. The earliest festivals in the United States date from the eighteenth century and had religious, social, or pedagogical functions. The first were associated with singing schools, to promote the singing of psalms according to established rules and order. Folk music began in the eighteenth century in the form of fiddlers' contests, many expanding to several days and involved instrumental music and community audiences. Several large events took place beginning in the middle of the nineteenth century. In 1856 the Boston Handel and Haydn Society presented three major choral works—Haydn's *The Seasons*, Handel's *Messiah*, and Mendelssohn's *Elijah*. In 1869 the bandmaster Patrick S. Gilmore arranged a National Peace Jubilee in Boston comprising 20,000 instrumentalists. During the 1876 centennial of independence, Philadelphia sponsored a major music festival. Worcester, Mass., in 1858 and Cincinnati, Ohio, in 1873 inaugurated festivals that have continued to the present day. Four festivals that came out of the tradition of singing schools continued into the twentieth century: the Messiah Festival in Lindsborg, Kans. (1882), the Big Singing Day in Benton, Ky. (1884), the Ann Arbor May Festival (1894), and the Bethlehem, Pa., Bach Festival (1900).

Festivals proliferated in the twentieth century. Many occur in rural settings during summer months and feature classical music, jazz, folk, bluegrass, country, cajun, and light or pops. Commercial motives and entrepreneurial talent have been a significant force in their promotion. Major symphony orchestras that employ musicians year-round include summer seasons that have become virtual festivals. Beginning in 1936 the Chicago Symphony Orchestra has played in Ravinia Park north of Chicago. Tanglewood, in the Berkshire Hills of western Massachusetts, has been the summer home of the Boston Symphony Orchestra since 1936; in 1940 its former music director, Serge Koussevitzky, opened the Tanglewood Music Center. Meadowbrook became the summer home of Detroit's orchestra in 1964; the Blossom Music Center between Cleveland and Akron became the summer residence of the Cleveland Orchestra in 1968. The Philadelphia Orchestra has given free concerts at the Mann Music Center in Philadelphia and since 1966 has performed at Saratoga Springs, N.Y. In that year the annual Mostly Mozart Festival became a major offering of the Lincoln Center for the Performing Arts in New York City. Many of these summer centers have expanded to offer jazz, folk, and rock music. Smaller festivals have grown out of centers that specialize in the study of particular styles of music. The Marlboro School in Vermont has stressed chamber music since 1950. The National Music Camp at Interlochen, Mich., has offered a variety of musical programs since 1928. The Brevard Music Center in western North Carolina has sponsored festivals since 1936. A number of festivals center on opera. Since 1920 the Cincinnati Summer Opera Festival has offered a series of productions, while Santa Fe (1957) has featured little-known operas. Beginning in 1975 the Seattle Opera offered Richard Wagner's *Ring Cycle*, first in German, then in English, in an event that has become the Pacific Northwest Festival. Contemporary or new music is offered in programs in California—Ojai since 1947 and Cabrillo since 1963. New Music Across America began as a festival in New York in 1979 and has emphasized works by composers using new techniques and new instruments; in 1992 the festival took place simultaneously in many sites across the country.

Festivals of indigenous or folk music have similarly increased in the twentieth century. Building on the tradition of fiddlers' contests, the Old Time Fiddler's Convention began in North Carolina in 1924. The National Folk Festival first took place in St. Louis in 1934 and in 1971 moved to Wolf Trap Farm Park southwest of Washington, D.C. The Kool Jazz Festival, founded in 1954 as the Newport Jazz Festival in Rhode Island, moved to New York City in

1972, and, on the Pacific coast, the Monterey Jazz Festival began in 1958. Rock music promoters staged big events in the 1960s, notably the 1967 Monterey International Pop Festival in California and the Woodstock, N.Y., Music and Arts Fair in 1969, which was the biggest rock concert ever organized, attracting about 400,000 representatives of the counterculture of the decade. The Woodstock event took on iconic status for many and was commemorated in 1994 by a second concert.

[Robin Carol Price, *Music Festivals in America,* 4th ed. (New York, 1990).]

CHARLES A. WEEKS

See also **DAH:** Fiddlers and Fiddle Tunes; Singing Schools; **SUPP:** Woodstock.

MUSIC INDUSTRY, the business of selling music, in the nineteenth century was often the domain of composers, who assumed the role of entrepreneur to ensure dissemination of their music. In the twentieth century the business became more specialized and organized. What eventually emerged was a complex musical culture of composer, performer, marketer, consumer and writer. In 1896 the American Federation of Musicians brought performers together in the first union. In 1914 artists helped found the American Society of Composers, Authors, and Performers (ASCAP), a performing rights organization. Broadcast Music Inc. (BMI) was established in 1940 for the same purpose. A recording industry defined in the 1920s and 1930s by such major companies as Victor and Columbia and a large number of smaller firms by the 1980s provided a significant outlet for music. Talent representatives and organizations, such as Community Concerts and Columbia Artists, established by Arthur Judson in 1928 and 1931, respectively, promoted the performance of music in communities throughout the country. Beginning in the 1920s radio, movies, and television provided other outlets for music, often influencing its character. From the 1960s onward, cultural centers in large cities, notably Lincoln Center in New York, provided new venues for performance, achieving national scope when assisted by radio and television. While universities, conservatories, private persons, and government have supported in the twentieth century a significant amount of financial and artistic autonomy for composers and performers, music in the United States continues to be influenced significantly by the opportunities and pressures of the market.

[Richard Crawford, *The American Musical Landscape* (Berkeley, Calif., 1993); Harvey Rachlin, *The Encyclopedia of the Music Business* (New York, 1981).]

JOSHUA L. COX
CHARLES A. WEEKS

MUSIC TELEVISION (MTV), the first all-music television network, began broadcasting on Aug. 1, 1981, and targeted an audience aged twelve to thirty-four. The network's programming comprised back-to-back videos created by record companies to promote their artists. MTV was troubled in its early years by accusations of racism, concerning failure to broadcast videos by black artists. The founders, among them Robert Pittman, prescribed a policy of "narrowcasting" drawn from radio, which aired only a restricted range of music. British "new pop" acts such as Duran Duran and the Thompson Twins were so heavily programmed that observers credited MTV with launching a second "British invasion" (the first being the Beatles in the 1960s) of the U.S. music marketplace. Because music videos are primarily advertisements for recording artists, MTV has been frequently criticized for commercialism. It was also criticized by women's groups for sexism. Following the sale of MTV from Warner-Amex to Viacom International in 1986, the network diversified its output, expanding into nonmusic programming and encompassing a broader range of music. Heavy metal was for some years the staple, and following the success of *Yo! MTV Raps* in 1989 (for some time the most popular show on the network), many rap artists concluded that MTV was responsible for introducing this form to Middle America. In 1987 MTV launched MTV Europe and began a period of world expansion. By 1994 it was available in fifty-eight countries to a potential audience of 240 million households. It continued to expand nonmusic programming (notably with its highest-rated show, the controversial cartoon *Beavis and Butt-head*) and was credited with mainstreaming the "grunge" rock of Nirvana, Pearl Jam, and Soundgarden. News coverage on MTV stressed social and political issues relevant to young people. In 1992 MTV's "Rock the Vote" campaign was credited by President Bill Clinton with helping increase the youth vote.

[Andrew Goodwin, *Dancing in the Distraction Factory* (Minneapolis, 1992).]

ANDREW GOODWIN

See also **SUPP:** Music, New; Music, Rock and Roll; Music Industry; Television.

NAACP. *See* **National Association for the Advancement of Colored People.**

NADER'S RAIDERS. *See* **Consumer Protection.**

NAFTA. *See* **North American Free Trade Agreement.**

NAMING. American personal names typically include a given name, middle name, surname, and occasionally suffixes. Anglo-American surnames can be traced back to the English adoption of surnames after the Crusades in the thirteenth century. Traditionally, American surnames are transmitted along the male line, and at marriage women usually assume husbands' surnames, although many women retain their natal surnames after marriage or hyphenate their surname with that of their husband. Middle names appeared in the United States and Great Britain at the end of the eighteenth century. By the end of the nineteenth century most Americans received middle names, and by the end of the twentieth century, fewer than 5 percent of Anglo-American children lacked such names. Middle names and suffixes were first popular among the elite and later were adopted generally.

Most twentieth-century American given names trace to three sources: a small stock of traditional Anglo-Saxon names popular in England before the Norman Conquest in 1066, a stock of Norman names introduced following the Conquest, and a stock of biblical names from both the Old and New Testaments. Throughout the nineteenth century the stock of American given names continued to grow as names were introduced by immigrant groups (especially German and Scotch-Irish), surnames occasionally were used as given names, masculine names were transformed to feminine forms (Roberta, Michelle), and many new names were coined. In the twentieth century the pool of American given names greatly expanded, especially since the 1970s. While many traditional names continued in popularity, especially among religious groups who preferred biblical names or those of saints, names gained and lost popularity with increasing speed. In the 1990s the ten most popular names for men and women were given to 20 to 30 percent of children, down from 50 percent or more two centuries ago. There were two notable trends in naming in the late twentieth century. First, while parents continued to name children after relatives (especially sons after fathers), family names were more often used as middle names and less often as first names. Second, Americans increasingly selected names that express identification with or pride in ethnic, racial, or religious groups. African Americans, for example, after a century of preference for traditional given names, began to draw names from a wider variety of sources and to coin new names.

[Richard D. Alford, *Naming and Identity: A Cross-Cultural Study of Personal Naming Practices* (New Haven, Conn., 1988); George R. Stewart, *American Given Names* (New York, 1979).]

RICHARD D. ALFORD

NASHVILLE. Speculators settled Nashville in 1779 on the Cumberland River in central Tennessee. Principally a place of commerce, it grew slowly, despite becoming the state capital in 1843. Indeed, throughout the nineteenth century it was a traditional southern town. Matters changed during the Great Depression of the 1930s with an infusion of federal money for the Tennessee Valley Authority. The end of segregation in the 1960s also gave the city a lift, what with removal of uneconomic hiring practices and thereby new livelihoods for many of its citizens. Nashville technically became Nashville-Davidson after the creation of a metropolitan government in 1963, with a mayor, vice mayor, and a forty-member metropolitan council. Thereafter the city boomed. In some ways development had an ironic twist, because as the boom spread throughout the entire South, Nashville lost some of its former stature to other cities, but the local boom was undeniable, and in 1990 the city's population reached 488,374, the Nashville-Davidson area 985,026. Nashville's reputation steadily increased, for the city was the site of the Grand Ole Opry, a household name known worldwide for country music. In this respect Nashville rivaled Los Angeles and New York in music recording, publishing, distribution, and production. In the years before the Civil War, Nashville had become known for its political figures—Andrew Jackson, James Polk, and Sam Houston. In the 1990s, because of country music, the well-known names were Dolly Parton, Chet Atkins, Loretta Lynn, Hank Williams, and Johnny Cash.

The city's economy in 1990 was primarily service oriented, with 28 percent of the workforce so employed. Retail-wholesale trade was not far behind, at 25 percent of the workforce. Manufacturing industries employed 17 percent of the population and the government 12 percent. In a 1992 survey of top U.S. cities for business, Nashville ranked second for pro-business attitude and race relations, third for labor-management relations, and ninth for vocational training of workers. Its central location helped, having brought into the vicinity two large automobile plants. The diverse economy of the metropolitan area included banking, health care, and a large religious publishing and printing industry.

[Anita Shafer Goodstein, *Nashville, 1780–1860: From Frontier to City* (Gainesville, Fla., 1989).]

LAWRENCE H. LARSEN

See also **SUPP:** Tennessee.

NATIONAL AERONAUTICS AND SPACE ADMINISTRATION (NASA). *See* **Space Program.**

NATIONAL ASSOCIATION FOR THE ADVANCEMENT OF COLORED PEOPLE (NAACP). Since 1975 the NAACP has continued to fight for equal rights for African Americans but internal divisions

and lack of funding have stifled its progress. Although the NAACP's victories historically came through litigation in the courts, the organization found it increasingly difficult to sustain such activity in the 1970s and 1980s. Much of this resulted from a rift between the NAACP and the independent NAACP Legal Defense and Educational Fund (LDF). Disagreement became so intense that in May 1982 the NAACP sued the LDF in an effort to control the LDF's activities. The split shifted the NAACP's focus from legal action to lobbying against federal policies that threatened existing civil rights legislation and affirmative action programs.

In 1993 the NAACP's longtime executive director, Benjamin Hooks, retired and was succeeded by Benjamin F. Chavis. An aggressive civil rights activist and head of the United Church of Christ's Commission for Racial Justice, Chavis in 1982 coined the term "environmental racism," to describe the tendency of manufacturing and other companies to dump toxic waste in or near areas where racial minorities resided. Chavis promised to revamp the NAACP by developing a marketing plan targeted at the younger generation through music videos, by promoting health care reform, and by embracing issues of global human rights. When Chavis took office the NAACP had shown little growth since the 1970s and had only 500,000 members with about 2,000 chapters nationwide. He was determined to recruit not only more African Americans, but Latinos, Asian Americans, and people of color around the world.

Chavis immediately ran into criticism for embracing Louis Farrakhan, minister of the Nation of Islam; for producing a deficit of $3 million; and for his lobbying efforts on behalf of corporations attempting to avoid paying for toxic waste cleanup. He was fired in 1994 for not informing the NAACP board of directors that he had agreed to pay more than $300,000 in NAACP funds to a former female employee who had charged him with sexual harassment. William F. Gibson, chair of the NAACP board of directors since 1985, supported Chavis until his ouster, only to find himself under investigation for excessive spending. With the future of the NAACP in doubt, Myrlie Evers-Williams, civil rights activist and widow of Medgar Evers, unseated Gibson as chair by one vote in February 1995. She faced the challenge of a $4.5 million deficit, falling contributions because of the perceived state of disarray within the organization, and the task of finding a new executive director. In February 1996 Democratic Congressman Kweisi Mfume of Maryland resigned his seat in the House to take over the executive directorship of the NAACP.

Mfume, former leader of the congressional black caucus, promised to rehabilitate the NAACP and unite it for aggressive action and embarked immediately on a voter registration drive.

[Lynne Duke, "What Is Happening to the NAACP?," *Washington Post National Weekly Edition* (Jan. 16–22, 1995); Kenneth Goings, *The NAACP Comes of Age* (Bloomington, Ind., 1990); Matthew S. Scott, "Chavis to Lead NAACP into New Era," *Black Enterprise* (July 1993); Hanes Walton, Jr., *When the Marching Stopped: The Politics of Civil Rights Regulatory Agencies* (Albany, N.Y., 1988).]

JILL WATTS

See also **SUPP:** Affirmative Action; African Americans; Civil Rights Movement.

NATIONAL ENDOWMENT FOR THE ARTS (NEA), an independent agency of the federal government created in 1965 along with the National Endowment for the Humanities. The NEA began with a budget of $2.5 million, and support rose to $175 million in 1991, before cutbacks to $167.6 in 1994. Although the NEA has had critics throughout its existence, it became a center of controversy in the late 1980s as questions arose over grants for controversial works and the propriety, in general, of federal financial support for the arts. The NEA funds an array of works and activities, including music, theater, and visual and performance arts. It also distributes funds to smaller organizations, which grant them to individual artists and organizations. Proponents argue that the NEA is essential because grants provide "seed money" necessary for raising private donations. NEA officials estimate that recipients are able to generate $11 to $26 in private money for every dollar given by the NEA. Critics claim that the NEA is an unfair tax on the many to support the tastes of a few, and that although grants for controversial works admittedly make up only a tiny portion of total NEA funding, they remain an inappropriate use of taxpayer money.

Controversy came to a boil in 1989 as opponents focused on works of art they termed obscene and immoral. These included a photograph by Andres Serrano, entitled *Piss Christ,* that showed a plastic crucifix immersed in a jar of the artist's urine; a display by art student Scott Tyler, entitled *What Is the Proper Way to Display a U.S. Flag?,* which allowed people to comment on the question while stepping on an American flag placed on the gallery floor; and a series of photographs by Robert Mapplethorpe that contained sadomasochistic and homoerotic images, as well as pictures of nude children. Some members of Congress, most notably Republican Senator Jesse Helms of North Carolina and Republican Representative Dana Rohrabacher of California, used the controversy to attack NEA funding. Some conservative legislators and activist right-wing Christian groups endorsed moves to cut funding or attach content restrictions to grants, measures that were opposed by artists, arts organizations, and gay and lesbian alliances.

The NEA changed its procedures in response to congressional pressure. One of the most disputed reforms involved an "obscenity pledge," requiring grant recipients to sign a statement promising their work would not be obscene. John Frohnmayer, named NEA chairman by President George Bush in 1989, drew fire from artists and arts organizations for denying certain grants recommended by NEA panels. Critics accused Frohnmayer of using political criteria in denying the funding. In 1990 Dennis Barrie, director of Cincinnati's Contemporary Art Center, was arrested and tried on obscenity charges for exhibiting Mapplethorpe's work. Organization of the touring exhibition had been partially supported by an NEA grant. The acquittal of Barrie and his center later that year brought to a close the arguments about the obscenity of Mapplethorpe's work, but congressional interest in NEA grants did not wane.

Senator Helms continued to introduce bills and amendments to limit grants for works that were sexually oriented or that denigrated religion. In 1990 the House and Senate passed a three-year reauthorization of the NEA that eliminated restrictions on the sort of art the endowment might fund, but Congress required "general standards of decency and respect for the diverse beliefs and values of the American public." The NEA then eliminated its obscenity pledge. A few organizations, artists, and panel members continued to protest by declining to accept endowment funding.

In 1994 Congress renewed its attack on the NEA. The endowment already received a 2 percent targeted budget cut, from $171 million to $167.6 million, because of an NEA grant to a performance artist, Ron Athey, who at the Walker Art Center in Minneapolis carved a pattern on another artist's back, wiped the blood with paper towels, and hung the latter on a clothesline over the audience. Although only $150 of NEA money went to support the performance, many lawmakers were outraged. The budget cut was in visual arts, theater, performance art, and photography. In 1995 the head of the NEA, Jane Alexander, testifying before a Senate committee, stressed how the NEA benefited the nation. She estimated that the per capita contribution was sixty-four cents and that without such support arts organizations would be less able to raise private money. Opponents argued that the endowment needed to monitor funds and refuse grants for works that depict controversial issues or endorse controversial views. Other proposals included supporting the NEA for a limited time until it could become a private corporation or support itself from copyright fees.

[Livingston Biddle, *Our Government and the Arts* (New York, 1988); Richard Bolton, ed., *Culture Wars: Documents from the Recent Controversies in the Arts* (New York, 1992).]

KATHLEEN B. CULVER

See also **SUPP:** National Endowment for the Humanities; Philanthropy.

NATIONAL ENDOWMENT FOR THE HUMANITIES (NEH), established by Congress in 1965, provides funds for research, education, and public programs to such individuals, groups, and institutions as schools, museums, and libraries. It is headed by a chairperson appointed by the president. Chairs since 1965 have been Barnaby C. Keeney (administrations of Lyndon B. Jackson and Richard M. Nixon), Ronald Berman (Nixon administration), Joseph D. Duffey (Jimmy Carter administration), William J. Bennett (Ronald Reagan administration), Lynne V. Cheney (Reagan and George Bush administrations), and former University of Pennsylvania President Sheldon Hackney (Bill Clinton administration). The NEH is directed by a twenty-six person council whose members are appointed to rotating six-year terms by the president. It is often confused with the National Endowment for the Arts, a separate institution. During the 1993 fiscal year the NEH distributed $132 million in grants, fellowships, honoraria, and awards. Of this amount $28 million went to state programs, $25 million to public programs, $18 million to fellowships and seminars, $21 million to education programs, and $17.8 million to research programs.

The two most prestigious annual awards by the NEH are the Jefferson Lecture, established in 1972, and the Charles Frankel Award, established in 1988. The lecture, which carries a $10,000 honorarium and is the highest award that the U.S. government confers in the humanities, recognizes an intellectual leader who combines the virtues of thinker, scholar, and citizen in the tradition of Thomas Jefferson. The Charles Frankel Award honors individuals who have made outstanding contributions to public understanding of history, literature, and philosophy. Recipients of the Jefferson Lecture award include poets, historians,

novelists, philosophers, and social critics. Women received five of the twenty-three awards made between 1972 and 1994. Recipients were Lionel Trilling (1972), Erik Erikson (1973), Robert Penn Warren (1974), Paul A. Freund (1975), John Hope Franklin (1976), Saul Bellow (1977), C. Vann Woodward (1978), Edward Shils (1979), Barbara Tuchman (1980), Gerald Holton (1981), Emily Townsend Vermeule (1982), Jaroslav Pelikan (1983), Sidney Hook (1984), Cleanth Brooks (1985), Leszek Kolakowski (1986), Forrest McDonald (1987), Robert Nisbet (1988), Walker Percy (1989), Bernard Lewis (1990), Gertrude Himmelfarb (1991), Bernard M. W. Knox (1992), Robert Conquest (1993), and Gwendolyn Brooks (1994). Thirty individuals, including nine women, received the Charles Frankel Award between 1989 and 1994: Patricia L. Bates, Daniel J. Boorstin, Willard L. Boyd, Clay S. Jenkinson, and Américo Paredes (1989); Mortimer J. Adler, Henry Hampton, Bernard M. W. Knox, David Van Tassel, and Ethyle R. Wolfe (1990); Winton Blount, Ken Burns, Louise Cowan, Karl Haas, and John Tchen (1991); Allan Bloom, Shelby Foote, Richard Rodriguez, Harold K. Skramstad, Jr., and Eudora Welty (1992); Ricardo Alegría, John Hope Franklin, Hanna Holborn Gray, Andrew Heiskell, Laurel Thatcher Ulrich (1993); Ernest L. Boyer, William Kittredge, Peggy Whitman Prenshaw, Sharon Percy Rockefeller, and Dorothy Porter Wesley (1994).

ELIZABETH V. BURT

NATIONAL INSTITUTES OF HEALTH (NIH) has changed since the mid-1970s, although its objective has remained constant—to recruit high-quality biomedical researchers in the service of health for Americans—and two new funding programs were created to achieve this objective. The intramural program supports research in NIH laboratories on the Bethesda, Md., campus, and the extramural program distributes grants to university investigators across the United States and makes collaborative arrangements with researchers in other countries. The NIH annual budget in the early 1990s was more than $8 billion, and personnel on the Bethesda campus numbered more than 16,000. In 1993 Congress directed the NIH to include more women in research designs and analysis instead of continuing to concentrate on studies involving only men. Other changes since the mid-1970s include organizational shifts of the different institutes, centers, divisions, and offices that comprise the NIH. In 1994 the NIH consisted of seventeen institutes (Aging; Alcohol Abuse and Alcoholism; Allergy and Infectious Diseases; Arthritis and Musculoskeletal and Skin Diseases; Cancer; Child Health and Human Development; Deafness and Other Communication Disorders; Dental Research; Diabetes and Digestive and Kidney Diseases; Drug Abuse; Environmental Health Sciences; Eye; General Medical Sciences; Heart, Lung, and Blood; Mental Health; Neurological Disorders and Stroke; and Nursing Research); two divisions (Computer Research and Technology and Research Grants); four centers (Center for Research Resources; John E. Fogarty International Center; National Center for Human Genome Research; and Warren Grant Magnuson Clinical Center); three offices (Women's Health; Alternative Medicine; and Minority Health); the National Library of Medicine; and the Children's Inn at NIH. The NIH also funds three field units (the Gerontology Research Center in Baltimore, Md.; the Rocky Mountain Laboratories in Hamilton, Mont.; and the NIH Animal Center in Poolesville, Md.). NIH has joined with other agencies to advance biomedical research. In one of the larger projects, NIH and the Howard Hughes Medical Institute launched a multimillion-dollar cooperative program to encourage physicians to enter research.

As of 1995 there had been four Nobel Prize laureates among NIH researchers who were intramural scientists as well as seventy-one laureates whose projects were supported by NIH grants. Much intramural research includes bench research, which takes place in laboratories on campus. Such research has resulted in prominent scientific advances. In 1984 National Cancer Institute scientists headed by Dr. Robert Gallo, Jr., uncovered evidence that variants of a human cancer virus (called HTLV-III) are the primary cause of acquired immunodeficiency syndrome (AIDS). Beyond bench research NIH supports clinical research, including patient studies and experimental treatments. A landmark treatment took place in 1991, when cancer patients were treated with the first human-gene therapy. Much clinical research takes place in the Warren Grant Magnuson Clinical Center involving surgery, outpatient clinics, diagnostic radiology, clinical pathology, and nuclear medicine.

[Edward H. Ahrens, Jr., *The Crisis in Clinical Research* (New York, 1992); William N. Kelley et al., *Emerging Policies for Biomedical Research* (Washington, D.C., 1993); U.S. Department of Health, Education, and Welfare, Public Health Service, National Institutes of Health, *NIH Almanac* (Washington, D.C., 1992).]

CHERI L. WIGGS

See also **SUPP:** Acquired Immune Deficiency Syndrome; Health and Human Services, Department of; Public Health Service.

NATIONAL ORGANIZATION FOR WOMEN. *See* **Women's Movement.**

NATIONAL PARKS. *See* **Parks, National; Park Service, National.**

NATIONAL PUBLIC RADIO (NPR) is a private, nonprofit corporation serving more than 470 member radio stations throughout the United States. Founded in 1970, NPR initially served primarily as a producer and distributor of programs for public radio stations. It won critical acclaim for its thoughtful, in-depth news programming, such as the evening news magazine *All Things Considered,* which debuted in 1971. In the late 1970s NPR began serving the broader needs of its member stations, providing them with program promotion, training, and management assistance. It has been in the forefront of technological innovation, for example, setting up a satellite system for program distribution in 1979 and producing or distributing radio dramas, live concert performances, and even a humorous program focusing on automobile repair. By the early 1990s NPR's member stations reached more than 14 million listeners each week. Headquartered in Washington, D.C., NPR was formed in response to the Public Broadcasting Act of 1967, which authorized federal financing of public television and radio. Republican administrations, beginning with that of Richard M. Nixon in 1969, often questioned such funding, but no administration has succeeded in its elimination.

From their beginnings, many of the nation's public radio stations were affiliated with colleges and universities. They filled a small but important niche by providing educational programming (such as on-air classes for rural populations), news, and classical music. Federal funds allowed NPR to expand the role of public radio—an alternative to commercial radio fare, most of which by the early 1970s consisted of disc-jockey programs and brief newscasts. NPR established a reputation with news and information programming. *All Things Considered* combined news headlines with reports from NPR staff members and part-time correspondents. The program included incisive and often decidedly offbeat features. Reporters did lengthy profiles of prominent newsmakers and ventured afield to cover such topics as Appalachian folkways, the ravages of drug addiction, and life on an Iowa farm, bringing about a new style of radio reporting—one that relied on sound, not just narrative, to tell stories. Many of the NPR reporters credited the influence of Edward R. Murrow, the noted CBS correspondent of earlier years. As a radio reporter during World War II, Murrow had placed his microphone in the street to let his audience hear the sounds of the bombing of London. Murrow's style of reporting had disappeared from commercial radio, where tight formats discouraged long stories. It was revived and refined at NPR, first on *All Things Considered,* then on *Morning Edition,* a program launched in 1979. By the 1990s NPR had news bureaus in Chicago, New York, Los Angeles, London, and Moscow, and a corps of part-time correspondents in nearly every corner of the world. In the 1980s and 1990s NPR focused on innovative cultural and information programming, in part mirroring the nation's ethnic and racial diversity, as well as reaching younger listeners. Public radio's traditional focus on classical music was augmented by NPR programming featuring jazz, blues, and contemporary African music. *Car Talk,* hosted by the Magliozzi brothers of Cambridge, Mass., invited listeners to phone in their questions about auto repair. NPR documentaries and talk shows in the 1990s placed attention on contemporary social concerns, particularly environmental protection.

Besides producing its own programming, NPR distributes programs produced by its member stations and independent producers. In 1992 NPR launched its Hothouse Project, which provides money and technical assistance for development of new radio programming. The project's first undertaking was a program about the sacred music traditions of African Americans. From 1983 to 1986 NPR withstood a severe financial crisis—a deficit of several million dollars—that was widely blamed on poor management and nearly bankrupted the organization. In order to survive NPR dismissed more than 100 employees and instituted tough financial controls. The crisis also prompted a fundamental change in the financing of public radio in the United States. The Corporation for Public Broadcasting (CPB), an agency of the federal government, granted a loan to NPR and later began funneling public money to individual public radio stations, rather than to NPR. The stations used the money to acquire national programming. The move was intended to give public stations a greater voice in the governance of NPR and other program suppliers. Since the early 1980s public radio as a whole has relied less on government support and more on contributions.

[Mary Collins, Murray Bognovitz, and Jerome Liebling, *National Public Radio: The Cast of Characters* (Washington, D.C., 1993); Mel G. Grinspan, ed., *News and Views from National Public Radio* (Memphis, 1987); Susan Stamberg, *Talk: NPR's Susan Stamberg Considers All Things* (New York, 1993).]

James Kates

See also **SUPP:** Radio.

NATIONAL RIFLE ASSOCIATION (NRA) was founded in 1871 to encourage marksmanship and is the largest organization in the United States opposed to gun control. The NRA lobbies to protect the rights of gun owners and to oppose more stringent gun controls through its Institute for Legislative Action and its literal interpretation of the Second Amendment to the U.S. Constitution ("the right of the people to keep and bear Arms, shall not be infringed"), contrary to the Supreme Court interpretation of the amendment. The organization has its largest following in small town and rural areas. For many years the NRA was considered one of the most powerful lobbying groups in Washington, but its failure to prevent passage of the Brady Handgun Violence Prevention Act (Brady Bill) in 1993 and the federal Crime Bill in 1994 was seen by many observers as evidence that the NRA's influence had diminished, while public concerns about crime had increased.

[Osha Gray Davidson, *Under Fire: The NRA and the Battle for Gun Control* (New York, 1993); Gary Kleck, *Point Blank: Guns and Violence in America* (Hawthorne, N.Y., 1991); James D. Wright, Peter H. Rossi, and Kathleen Daly, *Under the Gun* (Hawthorne, N.Y., 1983).]

James D. Wright

See also **SUPP:** Brady Bill; Gun Control.

NATIONAL SCIENCE FOUNDATION. Establishment of the National Science Foundation (NSF) in 1950 resulted from concern during and after World II about the role of the U.S. government in supporting scientific research and a science policy that would answer the needs of national security, industry, and the general concerns of U.S. scientists. Led by a presidentially appointed director, who works with a twenty-four-member National Science Board, the NSF concentrates on supporting basic research rather than applied research, which seeks a particular application of the findings. Because universities are the setting for most basic research in the United States, the NSF is especially important to those institutions. Although the NSF provided only 3 percent of the governments research and development funding in the mid-1990s, that figure represented nearly one-fourth of the government's support of university research. More than 2,000 colleges, universities, and research institutions in the United States have received grants or contracts from the NSF. None of the laboratories administered by the federal government is operated by the NSF, but it does support national research centers, often located at major universities, and some Antarctic research stations and oceanographic vessels. NSF's focus remains basic research, but in 1968 Congress changed its charter to enable support of applied research and in 1986 added engineering to NSF's mission.

Such changes reflected the growing concern in the United States about its ability to compete against Japanese and European industry in particular and the growing conviction in Congress during the 1980s and early 1990s that the government should act through more funding and changes in laws to strengthen research and development that could benefit U.S. industry. Thus, even during the administration of President George Bush (1989–1993), who was not a strong advocate of a government industrial policy, the NSF was supporting research in high performance computing and communications, which, after Bill Clinton became president in 1993, was part of the attempt to create a national information infrastructure—the so-called information highway. NSF was also supporting research in new manufacturing technologies, robotics, and advanced materials and actively studying the state of U.S. education in science and math in order to make recommendations on how to improve the curricula. Clinton placed far more emphasis on government support for industry. Nevertheless, NSF money still backed significant basic scientific research at universities and other centers. For example, ongoing efforts to determine the origins, age, and size of the universe depended in part on NSF funds, as did research attempting to assess the extent and implications of global environmental change. By the late 1990s, however, pressure to reduce significantly the size of government, as well as the level of funding for it, and a simultaneous debate over the role and means by which government should aid science and industry, created questions about the future course of NSF. Although not targeted for elimination, NSF could not forecast how much money it would have in the future and the degree to which it could support basic research at universities and applied research and engineering.

[George T. Mazuzan, *The National Science Foundation* (Washington, D.C., 1988); National Science Board, *Science and Engineering Indicators, 1993* (Washington, D.C., 1993); Bruce L. R. Smith, *American Science Policy Since World War II* (Washington, D.C., 1990).]

KENNETH B. MOSS

See also **SUPP:** Research Laboratories.

NATIONAL TRUST FOR HISTORIC PRESERVATION. Since its founding by Congress in 1949 as a private, nonprofit organization, the trust has acquired eighteen historic properties that it maintains as house museums, including Decatur House, its Washington, D.C., headquarters. To continue to carry out its goal of preserving the historical and cultural foundations of the nation, the trust established its Main Street program in 1980. The program has involved more than 800 communities in forty-five states, which have invested nearly $3 billion in historic business districts. As a result, there have been 21,000 building rehabilitations and the creation of 51,700 jobs and 14,800 new businesses. The trust's budget ($33 million in 1994) comes principally from private sources, including dues from 250,000 members, corporate and foundation grants, endowment income, and merchandise sales. Congress contributes about one-fifth of the trust's income in the form of matching grants through the Department of the Interior.

[David E. Finley, *History of the National Trust for Historic Preservation, 1947–1963* (Washington, D.C., 1965); Elizabeth D. Mulloy, *The History of the National Trust for Historic Preservation, 1963–1973* (Washington, D.C., 1976).]

EDWIN C. BEARSS

NATIONAL WEATHER SERVICE. *See* **Weather Service, National.**

NATION OF ISLAM. *See* **African-American Religions and Sects; Islam.**

NATIVE AMERICAN CHURCH has continued to provide religious experience and community to hundreds of thousands of American Indians through the ritual ingestion of peyote since its incorporation in 1918. Peyotism's legal standing, however, met a serious challenge in 1990. In 1984 Al Smith was fired in Oregon when his employer learned of his participation in Native American Church rituals and enforced its policy that employees be drug free. Although twenty-three states and national law protected peyote use in the Native American Church, Oregon law barred the use of peyote without exceptions. When

Smith sought unemployment benefits, the state refused them. Upon appeal the U.S. Supreme Court decreed in *Employment Division* v. *Smith* (1990) that the free exercise clause of the First Amendment did not exempt Smith from a neutral, generally applicable criminal law. The decision placed minority religions in jeopardy. In response, Oregon passed a 1991 law permitting the sacramental use of peyote by American Indians in the state, and Congress passed the Religious Freedom Restoration Act in 1993, which required the government to demonstrate a compelling state interest to justify any measure restricting religious practices.

[Christopher Vecsey, *Handbook of American Indian Religious Freedom* (New York, 1991); Christopher Vecsey and Omer C. Stewart, *Peyote Religion* (Norman, Okla., 1987).]

CHRISTOPHER VECSEY

See also **SUPP:** Freedom of Religion; Native Americans.

NATIVE AMERICANS. The U.S. census of 1990 enumerated some 2 million Native Americans, a more than 40 percent increase over 1980, making them one of the fastest-growing ethnic groups in the country, although they constitute less than 1 percent of the total U.S. population. The Cherokee (308,000) and Navajo (219,000) are the largest tribal groups. More than 60 percent of Native Americans live in such cities as Los Angeles, Chicago, and New York. The urban environment fosters contacts and cultural exchange through such institutions as the American Indian Community House in New York City. Native Americans generally return home to reservations each year, and some attempt to relocate to home reservations at some time in their lives.

Reservation environments, always fragile, have felt the impact of industrialization. Oil wells, coal mines, and the extraction of natural gas and uranium have disrupted environments from the Navajo and Hopi reservations in the Southwest to Inuit communities at the edge of the Arctic Sea. Hydroelectric projects have decimated fish populations in the Northwest, and pollution has had a deleterious effect on reservation ecologies. The expanding U.S. population in the Southwest has placed severe constrictions on water use, and Indians have had to sue for their water rights, sometimes successfully. The Clean Air Act of 1977 made it possible for the Northern Cheyenne to shut down or alter the operations of factories polluting their territories. The Exxon Corporation agreed to pay $20 million when the Exxon *Valdez* oil spill in 1989 ruined Alaskan hunting and fishing grounds at least in the short run. In some communities people were contaminated by nuclear radiation as a result of mining operations, particularly the Navajo. Others, such as the Chickasaw, offered to store nuclear waste to make money from government contracts, much to the dismay of local environmentalists and some tribal members.

Since the 1970s the past generation of Native Americans has attempted to revive such religious rituals as pipe ceremonies, spirit dances, sweats, and vision quests. Programs have sprung up to record and pass down tribal languages. Nonetheless, various forms of Christianity have become "traditional" in virtually every community, and perhaps only 100 of the 300 or so aboriginal languages are still spoken, many only by a handful of elders. At most, one of three Native Americans speaks a native language. Traditions are always in danger, especially when half of marriages are to non-Indians.

In 1977 the American Indian Policy Review Commission recommended that the United States recognize greater Native American sovereignty. The next two decades witnessed a marked growth in Indian sovereignty, despite congressional reluctance to accept the commission's report. Tribes possess the right to determine membership; 147 tribal courts have power not only over members but nonmembers in their territories. Tribal governments possess a right to tax their members. Reservation businesses have an exemption from state sales taxes. By 1995 federally recognized tribes had increased to 547, an increase of 22 since the federal acknowledgment process began in 1978. In the mid-1990s more than 100 other groups were seeking recognition. In 1994 President Bill Clinton issued a directive to federal agencies to treat the tribes with the same deference given to state governments.

Based on the Indian Claims Commission (ICC) Act (1946), tribes have pressed suits against the United States and individual states for recompense or return of lands taken illegally. In 1978 the ICC expired, after hearing 670 cases, with another 80 cases appealed. It had awarded $774 million to claimants. In the next decade the courts awarded another $487 million. From the Penobscot in Maine to the Puyallup in Washington, tribes have received substantial payments. Some tribes, such as the Sioux in South Dakota, have refused cash settlements, holding out for return of lands. Award money has helped tribes establish investment schemes and social service systems.

Titles to lands have increased, so that 4 percent of U.S. land in 1995 was held by tribes on 267 reservations. Some 140 of the total 287 reservations in the United States are entirely tribally owned.

The Indian Gaming Regulatory Act of 1988 encouraged Indian nations to establish gambling casinos, with the approval of and regulation by individual states. By 1995 seventy-four tribes had opened casinos, none more successful than the 300-member Mashantucket Pequot, who earned $600 million in profits in 1993 alone and who provide $80 million from these earnings each year as a "gift" (technically not a tax) to the state of Connecticut. Their $10 million bequest to the Smithsonian Institution (to help create the National Museum of the American Indian) was the largest donation ever received by the Smithsonian. By the mid-1990s Native American gaming was a $6 billion industry. Gambling is not the only form of economic enterprise on reservations. The Mescalero Apache maintain resorts; the Ak-Chin Pima and Maricopa grow cotton; the Choctaw assemble wire devices for automobiles; the Skagit make decorative boxes and sell salmon; and the Turtle Mountain Chippewa build house trailers. The Passamaquoddy hired investment bankers who helped boost the tribe's portfolio to $100 million. The Cherokee produce parts for military contractors. Native American art earns $500 million a year, protected from forgeries by the 1990 Indian Arts and Crafts Act.

Since the mid-1970s public and governmental sympathy for Native American culture has been growing, and the American Indian Religious Freedom Act (1978) attempted to direct governmental agencies to protect Indian spiritual interests, such as sacred sites. In 1992 the Columbus Quincentenary was marked by a debunking of Columbus's accomplishments, as tribes asserted the value of their ways of life. When the film *Dances with Wolves* played to packed movie houses in 1990, audiences applauded the deaths of white soldiers at the hands of the noble Lakota Sioux. Not everyone applauds Indian commerce. The Interstate Congress for Equal Rights and Responsibilities has attempted many times since its founding in 1976 to abrogate Native American treaties and hence destroy the underpinnings of recognition and sovereignty. The landmark decision in *United States* v. *Washington* (1979) gave half of the salmon catch in the state of Washington to Native Americans based upon treaty rights, which not only helped Northwest Indian economies but aroused the fury of non–Native American fishermen from Washington to Wisconsin.

Since the 1970s there has sometimes been violence within Indian communities, such as among the Mohawk at Akwesasne, N.Y. Several times in the 1970s and 1990s fighting broke out, and violence occurred in 1990 over the issue of gambling. Alcoholism continued to plague Native American communities throughout North America, with rates three times those in U.S. society as a whole. Suicides, accidental deaths, and arrest rates are connected to alcohol, and fetal-alcohol-syndrome births were distressingly high, as many as one-fourth of all births on some reservations.

Indians are the poorest population group in the United States, with 31 percent living in poverty in 1990. On reservations the median household income per annum was $13,000, per capita income was under $5,000, and unemployment was as high as 80 percent. The poorest county in the United States (Shannon, S.Dak.) was that of the Pine Ridge Lakota Sioux Reservation, where two-thirds of the population lived below the poverty line and per capita income was $3,000. In 1978 Congress passed the Tribally Controlled Community College Assistance Act; in 1995 there were twenty-six Native American–run colleges or junior colleges from the state of Washington to Michigan, most of them on the northern Great Plains. Only three are four-year institutions, including Sinte Gleska University in Rosebud, S.Dak. About 13,000 students attend these colleges. Tribal colleges emphasize Native American values and traditions, as well as training Indians for jobs in the modern world.

[Mary B. Davis, ed., *Native America in the Twentieth Century: An Encyclopedia* (New York, 1994); Marlita A. Reddy, ed., *Statistical Record of Native North Americans* (Detroit, 1993).]

CHRISTOPHER VECSEY

See also **DAH:** Indians, American, of the 1970s; **SUPP:** *Exxon Valdez;* Gambling; Native American Church; Poverty.

NATO. *See* **North Atlantic Treaty Organization.**

NEA. *See* **National Endowment for the Arts.**

NEBRASKA, bordered on the east by the Missouri River, on the south by Kansas and Colorado, on the west by Colorado and Wyoming, and on the north by South Dakota, has led some commentators to assert that the state, with only the Missouri River as a natural boundary, has had trouble gaining an identity.

Several factors, however, have created a sense of community. Almost all of the state's 77,227 square miles are on the Great Plains, sloping upward and westward from the Missouri. The state's severe winters and hot summers, with an average mean rainfall of roughly 32 inches in the east to 15 inches in the west, have led to an economy dominated by grain and livestock production. Population stabilized during the twentieth century, standing at 1,192,214 in 1910 and moving slowly ahead to 1,325,510 in 1950 and 1,578,385 in 1990. Lincoln, the state capital, and Omaha grew moderately, remaining the state's principal cities and having the only metropolitan areas in Nebraska. Omaha's population in 1990 was 335,795, with the metropolitan area at 618,262; Lincoln's city and metropolitan populations were 191,972 and 213,641, respectively. The next largest city is Grand Island, with a population in 1990 of 39,386. Because of the huge rural area to the west of the two principal cities, Nebraska as a whole had a population of 20 persons per square mile.

Agriculture has dominated the state, as evidenced by the fact that 95 percent of the state's total acreage is devoted to agricultural use, including the extensive production of cattle. The state ranked second in cattle ranching in 1990, and nearly half the state's acreage was grassland. Farmland throughout the state occupied 45 million acres, of which one-third is cropland. The principal farm crop is corn, followed by sorghum, soybeans, and wheat. Farm supports have ensured acceptable prices for producers. In keeping with national trends, single-family farms declined, replaced by huge corporate farms that are regulated by computers, connected with market information by radio and television, and farmed by employees. A small number of farms—fewer than 1,300 of the state's total of 56,000—account for 40 percent of farm income. The concentration of farms led to passage by the state legislature and approval by referendum of the Family Farm Preservation Act in 1982, which permits the acquisition of additional farmland only by Nebraska family-farm corporations. Local opinion has differed over the act's success, with some Nebraskans celebrating the limiting of farm corporations and others believing that the state's land values have been harmed.

While most of the state's industry is in services of one sort or another, agriculture accounts for 11 percent of the state's gross product, and much of that product has been related to the processing of food, especially the processing of corn for livestock feed. Manufacturing also made some advances, notably in printing and publishing and the manufacture of machinery. By the early 1990s Omaha had become a center for the manufacture of telecommunications equipment, surpassing meat-packing in employment. Nebraska is the only state in which all electric utilities are publicly owned and operated. Nuclear power supplies 35 percent of the state's electrical power. Transportation has long relied on the Missouri River, with bulk products passing down to Saint Louis. As in all states, Nebraska has seen a decline in railroad trackage, which stood at 4,150 miles in 1989. Roads have accounted for some of the decline, with the state having 92,405 miles of road in the 1990s, including 482 miles of interstate highways.

The politics of Nebraska have been predominantly Republican, with that party filling most state offices and congressional seats, although from the late 1970s to the early 1990s Democrats have primarily filled the governor's seat and those of the U.S. Senate. Nebraska is the only unicameral state legislature in the United States and elections to that body are officially nonpartisan. As might be expected in an agricultural state, the Nebraska environment has had its ups and downs, mostly the latter. More than 80 percent of Nebraskans drink groundwater, and almost half of it is contaminated by pesticides. More than 2,100 miles of streams are contaminated by agricultural pollutants. Only 9 percent of solid waste is recycled, and several hundred small municipal landfills have been exempted from state regulation since 1972. In the mid-1990s six hazardous waste sites were on the federal Superfund list. The state's important libraries are at the University of Nebraska campuses at Lincoln and at Omaha, where that city also maintains a large public library. The two cities maintain noted museums and symphony orchestras, and Omaha has an opera company. The state's largest festival is the annual state fair at the capital in Lincoln, and an important attraction is the greatly upgraded Omaha Zoo. The most important unifying factor among state residents is the University of Nebraska's football team (the Cornhuskers), which won the national championship in 1995.

[Robert W. Cherny, *Populism, Progressivism, and the Transformation of American Politics, 1885–1915* (Lincoln, Nebr., 1991); Lawrence H. Larsen and Barbara J. Cottrell, *The Gate City: A History of Omaha* (Boulder, Colo., 1982).]

LAWRENCE H. LARSEN

See also **SUPP:** Omaha.

NEH. *See* **National Endowment for the Humanities.**

NEO-ISOLATIONISM, a belief that grew out of disillusionment with the Vietnam War, is marked by a reluctance toward large-scale U.S. involvement in security matters involving foreign countries that could be costly in lives, equipment, and dollars. The term is often used in derision by those who favor a particular intervention opposed by others. Advocates of a more cautious policy prefer such labels as "interest-based policies," "strategic disengagement," "strategic independence," or "national strategy." Neoisolationism can include repudiation of "universal containment" and "indiscriminate globalism"; withdrawal from alliance systems, security agreements, and international organizations; and limiting defense to the Western Hemisphere. Advocates frequently differ but seldom repudiate U.S. trade relations, military aid, economic sanctions, or even combat forces. Because of neoisolationism's specific opposition to the intervention in Vietnam in the 1960s and 1970s and the opposition of conservatives in the 1980s to U.S. intervention in Haiti, Somalia, and Bosnia, it has little if any connection with U.S. isolationism of the nineteenth century or between World Wars I and II.

[Wayne S. Cole, "United States Isolation in the 1990s?," *International Journal* 48 (Winter 1992–1993); Earl C. Ravenal, *Never Again: Learning from America's Foreign Policy Failures* (Philadelphia, 1978); Robert W. Tucker, *A New Isolationism* (New York, 1972).]

JUSTUS DOENECKE

NEVADA. Since the 1960s Nevada's two principal urban centers, Las Vegas and Reno, have grown at an astounding pace. Despite this, the state's politics revolve around the use and ownership of Nevada's vast nonurban areas. With 82.9 percent (fiscal 1991) of the state's land owned by the federal government, primarily military installations and three areas administered by the National Park Service, numerous conflicts have erupted between state officials and federal agencies concerning the use and ownership of that land. Although economic diversification has long been the state's professed goal, in the mid-1990s Nevada remained heavily dependent on tourism and gambling as well as on the federal government's large military presence. Because Nevada's population increased so dramatically beginning in the 1950s, a relatively small percentage of residents are native to the state. Between 1980 and 1990 the state's population increased by 50.1 percent to 1,201,833, the highest increase recorded by any state in that period. By the late 1980s Nevada's urban population outnumbered its rural population by nine to one. According

to the 1980 census, a majority of Nevada's residents lived in southern Clark County, where the Las Vegas Metropolitan Statistical Area is located; the state legislature was reapportioned in 1981 to reflect this fact, giving Clark County a majority in both houses. The concentration of the state's population in and around Las Vegas and on the eastern slopes of the northern Sierra, where both Reno and the state capital, Carson City, are situated, left much of the remainder of the state open to ranching and mining. A significant portion of Nevada's rural lands was used by the Department of Energy and by the air force and the navy for testing weapons and training pilots. Despite the absence of settlement, little of Nevada's sagebrush desert remained unaffected by human projects.

Nevada has struggled to make the best of its close relation to the federal government. In 1977 Nevada took the lead among western states, in what was known as the Sagebrush Rebellion, to weaken the Bureau of Land Management's control over land within their borders. The movement faltered in 1981 when attempts failed to prove the bureau's control over western lands was unconstitutional. The Sagebrush Rebellion lost political steam, but many Nevadans continued to resent the bureau's presence. Nevada in the early 1990s found itself pitted against the federal government over whether the Department of Energy would continue with its plans to open a high-level nuclear waste repository at Yucca Mountain, seventy miles northwest of Las Vegas. Although Nevada has the right to veto construction of a repository within its boundaries, its veto can be overridden by a simple majority in the U.S. Senate. Extensive excavations began at the site in April 1993, but it was expected that safety tests would not be completed until 1998. An overwhelming majority of Nevadans opposed the project, although a vocal minority of residents who lived close to the site supported it because of the potential economic boost. Nevada's conflicts with the federal government are best understood as expressions of a state political culture that emphasizes local control and limited government. Brothels, for example, are permitted in Nevada by county option. The state's legislature is still confined to biennial sessions, despite the considerable difficulty of fashioning a biennial budget for a state that has been growing so rapidly.

In 1988 voters, by an overwhelming margin of four to one, approved a constitutional amendment prohibiting a state income tax. Nevada's economy, therefore, continued to be dominated by tourism and the casino industry, with the great majority of Nevada's workforce employed in casino or casino-related service jobs. The increased gambling revenue collected by the state, although considerable (more than half the state's annual general-fund revenue), threatened to be outstripped by the growing population's need for services. The military is a significant employer in some areas of Nevada, notably at Nellis Air Force Base, northeast of Las Vegas, and at the Fallon Naval Air Station, east of Reno. The Department of Energy's Nevada Test Site, northwest of Las Vegas, is a major employer for southern Nevadans. In addition, Nevada's mining industry, which appeared to be dying in the first half of the twentieth century, experienced a boom in the 1980s, especially in gold and silver mining, but the industry accounted for a meager 3 percent of Nevada's jobs in 1990. Nevertheless, the industry's growth had a dramatic influence on northeastern towns such as Elko, whose population almost doubled between 1980 and 1990 to 33,530. Despite its rapid population growth, Nevada remained overwhelmingly white. According to the 1990 census, 84.3 percent of Nevadans were white, 6.5 percent were African American, and 10.1 percent were Hispanic. Despite the presence of four reservations in the state, Native Americans made up only 1.7 percent of the population. At the same time Nevada had a small but visible Basque population.

[James W. Hulse, *The Silver State: Nevada's Heritage Reinterpreted* (Reno, 1991); Wilbur S. Shepperson, ed., *East of Eden, West of Zion: Essays on Nevada* (Reno, 1989).]

EMILY HAUPTMANN

See also **SUPP:** Las Vegas.

NEW AGE MOVEMENT, an international social movement that began in the late 1960s when Eastern religions became popular in the United States. It combined earlier metaphysical beliefs such as Swedenborgianism, mesmerism, transcendentalism, and theosophy. As expressed by Baba Ram Dass (born Richard Alpert), its first recognized national exponent, the New Age movement believes in the totality of the human body, mind, and spirit. The movement may be defined by its experience of transformation through rebirthing, meditation, possessing a crystal, or receiving a healing. Projecting from the concept of personal transformation, New Agers envision a new era that will witness a universal religion placing emphasis on mystical self-knowledge and belief in a pantheistic god as the ultimate unifying principle. The New Age movement is perhaps best known for its emphasis on holistic health, which emphasizes the need to treat patients as persons and offers alternative methods of curing, including chronobiological diet, naturopathy, vegetarianism, and a belief in the healing process of crystals and their vibrations, which restore the balance of bodily energy. New Age techniques include reflexology, which involves foot massage; acupuncture; herbalism; shiatsu, a form of massage; and Rolfing, a technique named after Ida P. Rolf, the originator of structural integration, in which deep massage aims to create a structurally well-balanced human being. Music is also used as therapy and as a form of meditation. While the term "New Age music" in the mid-1990s was a marketing slogan that included almost any type of music, true New Age music carries no message and has no specific form because its major use is as background for meditation.

[J. Gordon Melton et al., *New Age Encyclopedia* (Detroit, 1990).]

JOHN J. BYRNE

See also **SUPP:** Medicine, Alternative.

NEWARK, New Jersey's largest city, in the last quarter of the twentieth century tried to erase the stigma of being the nation's worst and unhealthiest city. Commenting on Newark's spreading black ghetto, one city official declared in 1970 that "wherever American cities are going, Newark will get there first." That haunting image confronted Kenneth Allen Gibson, Newark's first black mayor (1970–1986), as he fervently tried to resuscitate the racially torn, financially strapped, and socially bankrupt city, while bitterly fighting the economic retrenchment policies of the state capital at Trenton and the federal government. Defeated in the 1986 mayoral election by black Councilman Sharpe James, Gibson helped Mayor James launch and oversee the "new Newark." The city's massive restructuring of its downtown involved the investment of hundreds of millions of dollars to develop the Gateway–Penn Station area, Newark International Airport, the College of Medicine and Dentistry, Rutgers University's Newark campus, New Community Corporation properties, and an industrial parks program. The city's metamorphosis and urban "renaissance" earned Newark an All-American Cities Award, especially because it was selected as the site for a $300 million cultural complex, to be funded by the state, and for such strategic corporations as Prudential. Newark's administrators carefully crafted their policies to fit an urban population that had declined nearly 30 percent between 1967 and 1990, from 390,000 to 275,221. In 1990 Newark reported 78,771 whites, 160,885 blacks, 71,761 Hispanics, and a foreign-born population of 18.7 percent.

[Gordon Bishop, *Greater Newark* (Chatsworth, Calif., 1989); John T. Cunningham, *Newark,* rev. ed. (Newark, 1988); Stuart Galishoff, *Newark* (New Brunswick, N.J., 1988); Clement Alexander Price, "Newark and the Rhetoric of Optimism," in Gary Jardim, ed., *Blue Newark Culture* (Orange, N.J., 1993).]

TIMOTHY C. COOGAN

See also **SUPP:** New Jersey.

NEW HAMPSHIRE. Dramatic population and economic growth in the 1970s and 1980s, followed by reversals in the early 1990s, are the most striking features of New Hampshire's history since 1976. In 1990 the population rose for the first time to more than one million. Between 1980 and 1990 the state experienced the sixth highest rate of population growth, 20.5 percent, of any state, which was also the highest in the Northeast, but there was a slight decline in the early 1990s. One feature of New Hampshire's growth in the 1980s was a marked increase in the Asian, Hispanic, and African-American populations. Although none of these groups exceeded 1 percent of the total population in the 1990s, and although New Hampshire had the third highest concentration of non-Hispanic whites of any state, the rate of growth among ethnic minorities far exceeded that of whites and was among the fastest in the United States. Because the population boom resulted mainly from migration across the southern border with Massachusetts, the greatest social and demographic changes were concentrated in the south-central and southeastern parts of New Hampshire, the so-called "golden triangle." Clustered within this area were most of the newer electronics firms, other high-technology industries, suppliers of components for products ranging from computers to automobiles, and other manufacturing and service industries that for a time supported an almost fully employed and well-paid population. The abrupt transition in this part of New Hampshire, which is connected handily by highway with metropolitan Boston, led some Massachusetts émigrés to use their new homes in southern New Hampshire as part of the commuting suburbs, which gave rise to the "two New Hampshires" theory. According to that theory, the "golden triangle" differed not only socioeconomically but also in its orientation toward greater Boston and potentially in political attitudes from the more rural, less prosperous, and traditionally Yankee northern and western parts of the state.

These underlying economic and demographic tendencies, combined with nationwide concerns over energy and the environment, account for two especially dramatic controversies over further industrial development during the last quarter of the twentieth century. In 1974 the residents of Durham protested angrily against a plan by Greek tycoon Aristotle Onassis to build the world's largest oil refinery in their coastal town. Against the backing of Republican Governor Meldrim Thomson, Jr., and the powerful *Manchester Union Leader,* the state legislature voted down by more than two to one a bill that would have allowed the state to override local preference on such matters, and the refinery plan collapsed. This assertion of traditional home rule, however, was not enough to defeat the protracted construction of a nuclear power plant in the coastal town of Seabrook, from 1976 to 1986; the plant began generating electricity in 1990. The long construction process was marked by frequent interruptions, mass protests and mass arrests, conflict over the question whether consumers should pay construction costs while the work was still in progress, an interstate battle over the project between New Hampshire Governor John Sununu and Massachusetts Governor Michael S. Dukakis, court actions over the decisions of federal agencies, and the bankruptcy in 1988 of the Public Service Company of New Hampshire, the sponsoring power company. The economic downturn of the late 1980s was exacerbated by the closing in 1990 of Pease Air Force Base in Portsmouth and Newington, one of the first major military base closings of the post–cold war era. Much study and debate have gone into the problem of how to convert this large military facility to civilian uses, in order to revive the economy in southeastern New Hampshire.

Between 1976 and 1994 New Hampshire voters seldom strayed from their traditional Republican preferences. Democrat Hugh J. Gallen was elected governor in 1978, partly by opposing the proposed consumer charges for construction works in progress at Seabrook. He was reelected in 1980 but lost the 1982 election to Republican Sununu, a strong supporter of the Seabrook project and opponent of new state taxes. Gallen died at the end of December, leaving State Senate President Vesta Roy to fill in as governor until Sununu took office in January 1983. After serving three terms and playing a prominent role in the presidential campaign of George Bush in 1988,

Sununu became chief of staff in the Bush White House. In 1990 President Bush appointed David H. Souter, a respected New Hampshire jurist little known outside his own state, to the U.S. Supreme Court. In 1992 the New Hampshire spring presidential primary, which the legislature had repeatedly moved to earlier dates in order to retain its claim of being the first in the nation, lost some of its cachet as an election forecaster. Since the state's first presidential primary in 1952, no candidate had been elected president without first having won his party's primary election in New Hampshire, but the Democratic winner in New Hampshire in 1992 was not Bill Clinton, who won his party's nomination and the presidency, but Senator Paul E. Tsongas of Massachusetts. Tsongas remained a familiar figure in the state through his association with former New Hampshire Republican Senator Warren Rudman in the "Concord Coalition," a movement against federal budget deficits.

Questions of public finance were also high on New Hampshire's internal agenda in the mid-1990s. With the soaring costs of public education, the state's heavy reliance on local real estate taxes for school funding prompted taxpayer revolts in some communities and a lawsuit demanding greater state contributions to school costs. In late 1993 the New Hampshire Supreme Court ruled that the state bore a constitutional duty to assure adequate and equal schools for every community. The overwhelming reelection of Governor Stephen Merrill and heavy Republican legislative gains in the 1994 election nevertheless appeared to endorse New Hampshire's historic opposition to any form of broad-based state tax.

[Henry F. Bedford, *Seabrook Station: Citizen Politics and Nuclear Power* (Amherst, Mass., 1990); Nancy Caffey Heffernan and Ann Page Stecker, *New Hampshire: Crosscurrents in Its Development* (Grantham, N.H., 1986).]

CHARLES E. CLARK

NEW JERSEY. Ranked eighth nationally in 1978 with 7.5 million people, New Jersey had already become America's most urbanized state (even though 42 percent of its land remained forested and it still had 8,000 farms). By decade's end New Jersey had also developed into four distinct topographical areas: the Hudson-to-Trenton manufacturing hub, with its heavy concentration of chemical and pharmaceutical companies (New Jersey ranked first in the nation in both industries), petroleum, apparel, and glass industries; the Atlantic coastal region (from New York harbor to Atlantic City and Cape May), the state's vaca-

tionland; the Pinelands; and southern, western, and northern regions, composed primarily of farms, forests, and expanding wealthy suburbs.

The removal, relocation, and decentralization of the state's old manufacturing plants, away from older areas in or near the major cities, caused dramatic shifts in New Jersey's industrial economy, forcing the legislature in Trenton to adopt new policies toward wholesale, retail, service, transportation, utilities, and finance sectors. Although urban populations have declined since World War II (Camden, 13.4 percent; Jersey City, 6.7 percent; and Newark, 7.4 percent), commercial activities in the state's tertiary sector provided jobs for an even larger share of the labor force than industry. Hudson County (Jersey City) suffered the heaviest job loss (it grew by just 2.1 percent in the 1980s and projections suggested a mere doubling of that figure in the 1990s). Only two major cities experienced growth during these years—Paterson by 2.8 percent and Elizabeth by 6.3 percent. An equally severe drop in population was predicted for the 1990s in the largest cities: Camden, Newark, Hoboken, Jersey City, Bayonne, Trenton, Passaic, and Paterson. These changes, along with decreasing fertility rates, a reduced movement of jobs into New Jersey from New York City and Philadelphia, a marked decline of jobs in the Middle Atlantic states, and the state's transient status, should assure only modest population growth in the near future. During the 1980s New Jersey's population increased only 5 percent, from 7,365,011 to 7,730,188.

While cities lost population from the 1970s to the 1990s, New Jersey also developed into the nation's most suburbanized state. In 1990 it ranked ninth nationally, with nearly 90 percent of the population classified as living in urban areas. New Jersey had the seventh highest population density, an unemployment rate of just 5 percent, and a per capita personal income second only to Connecticut. The state's largest ethnic group remained Italian Americans, while African Americans constituted 13.4 percent and Hispanics 9.7 percent of the population. Manufacturing employed one-third of the state's workforce, headed by electronic equipment and followed by chemicals. Nearly 10 percent of the nation's research dollars were spent in New Jersey research facilities and laboratories, while the resort industry emerged as a major factor in the state's economy. Accompanying these developments was the opening of the Garden State Arts Center and the completion of the Meadowlands Sports Complex, both of which helped to dispel the state's battered image. New Jerseyans continued to pack themselves into the center of a massive mega-lopolis that stretches from Boston to Washington, D.C. The state has come to epitomize urban sprawl, with its population density, housing shortages, water and air pollution, transportation gridlock, and urban crime and decay. Clearly, no matter how one charac-terizes it—as dormitory, garden, playground, work-shop, or, in the words of Senator Dick LaRossa, "one big city"—New Jersey is a multifaceted place.

In order to reverse the negative trends, Republican Thomas H. Kean (acting governor, 1973; governor, 1981–1989) signed the controversial income tax of 1976 to help alleviate dependency on property taxes. Previously, the state had collected its revenue from corporate and nuisance taxes, and since 1966 from the equally unpopular sales tax. Kean's commitment to higher education, open government, and environ-mental protection also signaled greater government intervention and larger budgets. Kean's administra-tion promoted an economic climate conducive to cre-ating more skilled jobs, but it also slashed industrial jobs, closed manufacturing plants, and squandered much-needed tax revenues. To combat the recession, in 1981 the legislature established the Department of Commerce and Economic Development to bring in new jobs and rebuild the state's crumbling infrastruc-ture. Governor Kean urged the creation of an infra-structure bank for New Jersey but the legislature voted it down.

Economic recession in the early 1980s precipitated increases in sales and income taxes during Governor Kean's stewardship, as New Jerseyans also experi-enced rising costs in health insurance and federal, state, and local taxes. These developments resulted in a doubling of unemployment, a precipitous fall in construction, plummeting real estate values, and a terrible decline in retail sales. State banks suffered from unpaid land and construction loans and had to be seized by federal marshals. Similar problems plagued the state's major insurance companies as well. The boom years of 1983–1988, however, saw the state budget double (from $5.5 billion to $11 bil-lion), property taxes soar 160 percent (reaching $9.7 billion), extensive construction of commercial and residential buildings, and a reduction in unemploy-ment from 7 percent to 3.5 percent.

The fastest growing areas of the state budget in-cluded aid for primary and secondary education, pe-nal incarceration, and health costs. Medicaid alone rose from $500 million to $1.2 billion, while school expenses climbed $1 billion from 1985 to 1990. An-other recession, with state revenues having been re-duced to a deficit of roughly $1 billion, coupled with a new constitutional mandate to balance the budget, forced the legislature to slash expenditures by $600 million and dip into the 1989 "undesignated" (sur-plus) funds of $400 million. Democratic Governor Jim Florio (1990–1994) was embarrassingly forced to admit a budget shortfall of $700–$800 million for the fiscal year 1991 and had to cope with a projected $1 billion deficit in the 1992 budget. In a doomed effort to help the poor and eliminate the budget deficit once and for all, Florio raised taxes by a record $2.8 bil-lion. His approval rating plunged below 20 percent.

Meanwhile, voter anger mounted against higher public spending and taxation, an outcry that Repub-lican gubernatorial candidate Christine Whitman best expressed and capitalized on. A former member of the New Jersey Assembly (1967–1977), she had come out of nowhere in a losing 1990 senatorial race against incumbent Democrat Bill Bradley but charged back to defeat the unpopular Governor Florio in 1994. Following her election Whitman claimed that she wanted to be a record-breaking budget cutter. She became the first woman governor of New Jersey and was the Republicans' only woman governor in the United States. Governor Whitman made good on her campaign promise to cut taxes by signing an across-the-board 5 percent income tax cut, the state's first income-tax reduction. She told the state assembly that "this tax cut is a down payment on my promise to cut income taxes by 30 percent for most New Jerseyans." With Republicans a majority in both chambers of the legislature, Whitman received a line-item veto to do as she pleased. Her pledges implied annual cuts of $600 million for three years from the $15 billion budget. She also had to reduce New Jersey's annual $1 billion structural deficit. The Re-publican experiment appeared to rest more on faith in a resurgent economy, which would raise tax revenues, than on any blueprint, but Whitman's efforts made her one of the most powerful governors in the country.

[Helen M. Kushner, ed., *New Jersey Spotlight on Gov-ernment,* 4th ed. (New Brunswick, N.J., 1983); Gerald M. Pomper, ed., *The Political State of New Jersey* (New Brunswick, N.J., 1986); Barbara Williams Prabhu, ed., *Spotlight on New Jersey Government,* 6th ed. (New Brunswick, N.J., 1992); Barbara G. Salmore and Stephen A. Salmore, *New Jersey Politics and Government* (Lin-coln, Nebr., 1993); Joel Schwartz and Daniel Prosser, eds., *Cities of the Garden State* (Dubuque, Iowa, 1977); Karen A. West, ed., *New Jersey Spotlight on Government,* 5th ed. (New Brunswick, N.J., 1985).]

TIMOTHY C. COOGAN

See also **SUPP:** Atlantic City; Newark.

NEW MEXICO is called the "land of enchantment" for its scenic beauty and rich history of three cultures—Native American, Mexican, and Anglo. It is the fifth-largest state in terms of size, but with a 1993 population of 1,616,483 (up 19 percent from 1980) it ranks only thirty-sixth in number of residents. The population, reflecting the history of settlement in the state, is 76 percent white, 38 percent Hispanic, 9 percent Native American, and 2 percent African American. In the 1990s about three-quarters of the population lived in urban areas, especially Albuquerque, Santa Fe, Las Cruces, Roswell, Farmington, and Rio Rancho. Rapid housing and office construction began in the 1970s in Santa Fe, Las Cruces, and especially Albuquerque. The latter, New Mexico's largest city, grew by more than 50 percent between 1970 and 1990.

Since 1970 the primary economic change in New Mexico has been the rise of the service industry and the decline of ranching, farming, and mining. By the 1990s services, concentrated in the state's urban areas, provided about 70 percent of New Mexico's gross product. The oil-boom days following the 1973 and 1979 oil embargoes led to short-term economic gains, but by the mid-1980s competition from new oil fields and the surplus of oil and natural gas in world markets had depressed this sector. Production of potash and uranium also declined. In 1995 the state government employed more people than any other single economic activity. Sharply increased defense budgets created or expanded military bases, nuclear energy research at Sandia National Laboratories and White Sands Missile Range, and space research. President Ronald Reagan's 1983 proposal to develop the Strategic Defense Initiative led to substantial expansion of defense-related research. State government and private business made a concerted effort to make the corridor between Albuquerque and Santa Fe a high-tech center of the Southwest. The area became noted for manufacture of military communication systems, silicon chips for computers, appliances, and telephone equipment. New Mexico's scenery, mild climate, rich history, and cultural attractions made the tourist industry an important part of the economy. In the 1970s and 1980s developers built resorts and improved services to areas such as Ruidoso, with its quarter-horse races and skiing; Red River, with its spectacular mountain scenery and skiing; and Santa Fe, with its outdoor opera and museums. A major issue for the 1990s was balancing the desire for more tourists and winter resorts with the need to protect natural resources.

[Calvin A. Roberts, *New Mexico* (Albuquerque, 1988); Marc Simmons, *New Mexico* (Albuquerque, 1988).]
ALFRED L. CASTLE

See also **SUPP:** Albuquerque.

NEW ORLEANS between 1970 and 1990 suffered a 26 percent loss of its white population to adjoining Louisiana parishes, despite the continuing attraction of its central area to U.S. and foreign tourists. During the same period the city's total population decreased from 593,471 to 496,938. In 1990 the city's population was 61.9 percent black, 34.9 percent white, and 6.7 percent other ethnic groups. The median income was $16,465, with 33 percent of households living on an annual income below $10,000. The city's political and business leaders sought to create jobs and raise tax revenue through increased tourism. The Louisiana World Exposition opened in 1984; after its close, the fair's New Orleans Convention Center continued to function, accommodating 7 million visitors each year, who spend $1.8 billion. The nearby Superdome, completed in 1975, is used for the New Orleans Saints professional football games and numerous other sporting and entertainment events. A shopping mall, the Riverwalk, and the Aquarium of the Americas were built along the Mississippi River to attract visitors, as well as a recreation park along the French Quarter riverfront. New Orleans's largest tourist attraction, the carnival activities leading up to Mardi Gras, underwent a significant change in December 1991, after a controversial city ordinance was passed that prohibited race and sex discrimination by carnival organizations that parade on the city streets. As a result, three of the oldest and most prestigious groups—Comus, Momus, and Proteous—withdrew from parading. Most carnival organizations abided by the ordinance. In addition to the Mardi Gras festivities, New Orleans also attracts crowds to its Jazz and Heritage Festival every spring. First held in 1970, the Jazz Fest makes its home at the Fair Grounds racetrack, and its audiences number about 250,000 people over the weeklong festival.

The local maritime industry has changed considerably since the 1970s, particularly the containerization by 1990 of most cargo and the subsequent loss of wages previously paid to longshoremen. The port of New Orleans also transferred some of its wharves from the Mississippi to the Industrial Canal and the Mississippi River–Gulf Outlet, but it remained second only to the New York–New Jersey port in total tonnage and was the acknowledged national leader in the movement of such bulk cargoes as grain, oil, and coal. Politics in New Orleans kept pace with the population changes. In 1977 Ernest N. ("Dutch") Morial was elected the first black mayor of the city. He was followed eight years later by another black mayor, Sidney Barthelemy, whose successor in 1994 was Marc Morial, son of Dutch Morial. The major problems that faced New Orleans in the 1990s were public housing, crime, and maintaining public services. In addition to the upturn in the depressed oil industry in the early 1990s and the increasing importance of tourism, the city pinned its hopes for future revenue beginning in 1992 on casino gambling boats and on construction of the world's largest land-based casino on the site of the Rivergate convention and exhibition center.

[Bethany Ewald Bultman, *New Orleans* (Oakland, Calif., 1994); Arnold R. Hirsch and Joseph Logsdon, eds., *Creole New Orleans: Race and Americanization* (Baton Rouge, 1992).]

JOY J. JACKSON

See also **SUPP:** Louisiana

NEWSPAPERS. By the early 1990s there were 9,000 newspapers published in the United States, about 1,600 of them dailies. Both their number and combined circulation of 60 million have changed little since the 1950s. Newspapers still receive the lion's share of dollars invested in advertising. In the mid-1990s most newspapers earned handsome profits, but the industry was gloomy because circulation had grown more slowly than the population, and papers were not attracting young readers. With increased competition for advertising money from television and magazines (usually three-quarters of a paper's income), some publishers tried to reach nonsubscribers with "shoppers," inserts filled with retail ads, while others changed content to match reader survey responses.

Other changes since the 1970s included the adoption in 1973 by journalists of a new voluntary code of ethics, and in several cities they published journals, including the *Columbia Journalism Review* and *American Journalism Review,* in which they criticized their own publications. The National News Council, which investigated complaints of unethical behavior against the largest newspapers and the wire services, was abandoned after eleven years in 1984, but a few publishers supported local versions. In 1995 newspapers employed fewer than 500,000 staff and other workers nationwide. The newspaper as a local institution

changed in 1982 when Gannett Company, the largest newspaper chain, launched *USA Today,* which quickly became the number two newspaper in the country. Like the *Wall Street Journal,* which has the highest circulation, *USA Today* utilizes satellites to print in several locales. These two national dailies are followed by the *Los Angeles Times* and the *New York Times,* both with circulations of more than a million, The *Washington Post,* the *New York Daily News,* and *New York Newsday* reported circulations in excess of 750,000. More than 100 others exceed 100,000. Smaller dailies received the Pulitzer Prize for Meritorious Public Service during the 1970s and 1980s, including the *Anchorage Daily News* (1976, 1989), the *Lufkin (Texas) News* (1977), the *Jackson (Miss.) Clarion-Ledger* (1983), and the weekly *Point Reyes (Calif.) Light* (1979).

The decades-long rush toward chain ownership abated in the early 1990s, in part because there were few privately owned dailies left to acquire. Only a handful of cities still supported competing dailies, leading many papers to avoid endorsing political candidates. Instead, many added op-ed pages, in which they publish columnists with diverse views. By the late 1980s computer terminals had replaced typewriters in newsrooms and offset printing was almost universal, which led to the increased use of color in photographs, illustrations, and maps. Technological improvements weakened the printing craft unions, causing the number of labor strikes to decline. The foreign-language press changed to serve the immigrants from Asia and Central America, and the *Miami Herald,* among others, prints editions in Spanish. The African-American press became more economically viable, thanks to increased advertising, and there was a trend toward consolidation. The *Afro-American* published editions in Washington, Baltimore, and other cities, while the *Chicago Daily Defender* acquired the *Michigan Chronicle* in Detroit.

[Newspaper Association of America, *Facts About Newspapers* (Reston, Va., 1994); Richard A. Schwarzlose, *Newspapers: A Reference Guide* (New York, 1987).]

JOHN D. STEVENS

NEW YORK CITY has changed very little geographically since 1975, although the borough of Staten Island initiated a plan of secession in the early 1990s. Demographically, however, there have been major changes; the city's population fell from 7,894,862 in 1970 to 7,071,639 in 1980, then rebounded to 7,322,564 in 1990. There were significant changes in the city's ethnic composition. The white population dropped from 4,972,509 (63 percent of total) in 1970 to 3,163,125 (43.2 percent) in 1990. The black population grew by 9 percent, reaching 1,847,049 in 1990. The Hispanic population grew by more 26 percent, to 1,783,511, making up 24 percent of the total population. In a change from post–World War II patterns, the biggest increase came from non–Puerto Rican Hispanics, whose numbers virtually duplicated Puerto Ricans by 1990, increasing 64 percent, to 886,748. Asians swelled from 115,830 in 1970 to 489,851 in 1990, a 63 percent increase. The 1980 census revealed the impact of the 1965 federal Immigration Act on New York City. Since 1970, 754,000 immigrants entered the New York–New Jersey metropolitan area. Of these, 116,500 (15 percent) came from Europe, traditionally the largest source of new city residents. In the 1970s, however, 168,000 (22 percent) came from Asia, with Hong Kong and India supplying the most. Of the 267,600 arrivals from North and Central America, Dominicans and Jamaicans accounted for 128,000. Newcomers from South America were led by Colombians, Ecuadorans, and Guyanans.

Despite the one-day stock-market crash in October 1987, New York remained the nation's economic and communications center. By 1990 the Manhattan central business district employed 2 million people in 600 million square feet of office space; more than 8 million more people worked in the greater metropolitan area, producing a gross regional product of $425 billion in 1985. A large force in the global economy, New York is the focus of major foreign investment in real estate and banking. Important accounting, advertising, and legal firms are based in New York. Beginning in the 1960s New York City changed from a manufacturing to a service economy. Although nearly a million persons worked in goods production and distribution in 1990, that figure was less than half the 1970 total. Corporate workers, management consultants, accountants, engineers, architects, and building and personnel service operatives became by 1989 the largest employment sector in the city. Gains were also made in entertainment, tourism, education, and research. The number of federal employees dropped from 106,000 to 76,000 by 1989, with further cuts in the early 1990s. In office work gender and race were major variables. Women were the overwhelming majority of secretaries, information clerks, and records processors. White women made up more than 60 percent of women clerical workers, down from 78.2 percent in 1970. Among computer operators, white workers declined from 84.2 percent in 1970 to 47.9 percent in 1990.

Following a fiscal crisis in the mid-1970s, during which the city faced bankruptcy, a period of prosperity emerged in the 1980s. More New Yorkers held jobs, household incomes rose, and housing improved. At the same time, inequality widened for blacks and Latinos and the population was afflicted with AIDS, drugs, and homelessness. The last of these social ailments provides a good example of the paradox of wealth: Single-room occupancy hotels housing the dependent elderly, deinstitutionalized mentally ill persons, and drug addicts were converted to luxury apartments and condominiums, pushing the former tenants into the streets. Similarly, the co-op conversion boom produced soaring property values and skyrocketing rents.

Local politics since the 1970s were characterized by mounting racial polarization. After Abraham Beame's single term as mayor, a coalition centered in the white neighborhoods of Queens and Staten Island brought three terms for Ed Koch, a neoconservative. Koch built a political coalition based on white, ethnic, middle-class voters and pursued policies promoting private investment and jailing of large numbers of criminals. By 1988 Democratic party liberals, disaffected by Koch's administration, nominated and elected the city's first black mayor, David Dinkins. Combining a resurgent black and Latino vote and a significant white vote, Dinkins barely defeated Republican Rudolph Giuliani. Four years later, after the bloom faded from the prosperous 1980s and following the ugly confrontation between blacks and Jews in 1991 in the Crown Heights section of Brooklyn, Giuliani narrowly defeated Dinkins by campaigning for reduced taxes and government spending, reversing affirmative action, and tougher law enforcement.

Widening economic and social gaps created an image of New York as a dual city, composed of prosperous and poor residents. Social disparity emerged in the 1989 "wilding" attack by a group of black teenagers on a female Wall Street investment banker in Central Park; social tensions later led to murders of black men by white mobs in Howard Beach in Queens and Bensonhurst in Brooklyn. Other indicators of poverty included a sharp increase in the number of female-headed households, low labor-force participation rates from virtually all subgroups of the population, mounting numbers of illegal immigrants unable to obtain the benefits of citizenship, and exclusion of blacks and Latinos from the rapidly growing and remunerative occupations of the postindustrial city. These groups were disproportionately represented in the informal economy that existed in sweatshops and petty criminal activities.

Such demographic and economic tensions were reflected in New York's cultural contributions. There was little change in performances at Lincoln Center, although jazz was newly represented. Broadway continued to produce elaborate musicals. The East and West Villages produced vanguard culture. Downtown, Joseph Papp's Shakespeare Festival remained the home of innovative theater. The Conversations with Writers series at the New School and "poetry slams" at the Nuyorican Theater reinvigorated public readings. Keith Haring and Jean-Michel Basquiat translated the visual language of city streets into paintings. Performance and conceptual art arose from the East Village. Punk music developed among self-consciously alienated art students in the Lower East Side and the new gallery district south of Houston Street, called Soho. West Indian immigrants popularized reggae music. New York was a major center of rap music, which combines storytelling over simple bass lines with distorted samplings of other musical artists.

[John Hull Mollenkopf, *A Phoenix in the Ashes: The Rise and Fall of the Koch Coalition in New York City Politics* (Princeton, N.J., 1992), and *New York City in the 1980s* (New York, 1993); John H. Mollenkopf and Manuel Castells, eds., *Dual City: Restructuring New York* (New York, 1991).]

GRAHAM RUSSELL HODGES

See also **SUPP:** New York State; World Trade Center Bombing.

NEW YORK STATE slipped from first in national population rankings to third by 1994, behind California and Texas, dropping from 18,241,391 in 1970 to 17,990,072 by 1990. The vast majority of New Yorkers lived in metropolitan areas, with only 1,605,000 persons living in rural areas. About 40 percent of New Yorkers live in New York City. The census of 1990 listed five cities with populations over 100,000, one less than in 1980. During the 1980s cities of 50,000 people showed declining populations. Hardest hit were Buffalo (–.083 percent), Rochester (–4 percent), and Syracuse (–4 percent). Much of New York was still rural; more than one-quarter of the state's total area was farmland and more than 180 villages had fewer than 1,000 people. Projections forecast continued slow population growth, reaching only 18,456,000 by 2010. In 1990 the population was 74 percent white, 16 percent black, 12 percent Hispanic, 4 percent Asian, and 3 percent Native American. Despite its stagnant population growth, New York remained among the most important states in the union. Although it placed thirty-eighth among "most livable states" in 1994 (*State Rankings, 1994: A Statistical View of the 50 United States*), it ranked second in Internal Revenue Service collections, at $109 million (10.1 percent of the national total). New York was first in federal corporate tax collections in 1991, second in social security contributions, and third in IRS individual liabilities, at $5,900 per person. In 1992 New Yorkers' annual pay averaged over $30,000, third in the nation.

New York State continued to emphasize public spending for education. Overall it ranked second in the nation in 1992 in annual appropriations for public schools and second and third, respectively, in public elementary and secondary school enrollment. Salaries for classroom teachers trailed only that of California. New York had the highest number of institutions of higher education and was first in annual appropriations for libraries. The state and New York City shared responsibilities for higher education; the State University of New York and City University of New York systems were the largest in the nation.

New York has been plagued by social problems. It ranked first in 1992 in total crimes and second in violent crimes, third in murders, and second in robberies. It suffered the highest rate of robberies per capita of any state in the nation. In 1993 New York had the third-largest prison population in the country. It employed nearly 67,000 state and local police and expended more than $3.5 billion on law enforcement. With almost 8,400 prisoners serving life sentences, New York reinstated the death penalty in 1995. Since the 1970s upstate New York has experienced rapid construction of prisons, employing erstwhile farmhands to guard inmates from inner cities. More than 70 percent of inmates come from New York City.

Economically, the state, led by New York City, moved from manufacturing to service industries, followed by finance, insurance, and real estate. New York State underwent deindustrialization, manifested by declines in iron, steel, textiles, and apparel manufacturing. Trade declined by 18 percent from 1975 to 1988. The proportion of New Yorkers employed in the total population was 46 percent in 1990, below the national average. Annual employment growth of under 2 percent has trailed national rates, as have start-ups of new firms. Agriculture remained the state's largest industry. New York led the nation in production of cottage cheese and cream cheese and was second in apples, tart cherries, fresh market sweet corn, maple syrup, and cabbages. New York ranked third in production of milk, ice cream, cheeses, grapes, cauliflower, and snap beans. The state's 48,000 farms employed 200,000 people.

New York's senators in 1995, Democrat Daniel Patrick Moynihan and Republican Alfonse D'Amato, were long-term officeholders. From 1975 until 1995 the Democratic party controlled the governorship. Hugh Carey served two terms from 1975 to 1983, and Mario Cuomo held office for three terms until Republican conservative George Pataki defeated him in 1994. Cuomo suffered from anti-incumbency sentiment, while Pataki campaigned for restoration of the death penalty and lower taxes. Much of state politics revolved around the relationship between New York City and the rest of the state. In many ways the city seems independent of the state. The city's giant bureaucracy was 42 percent larger than the state government. Moreover, the city's ethnic profiles and religious and political preferences differ sharply from upstate. These cleavages impede agreement on social issues, such as homosexual rights, abortion, welfare, and the death penalty. During the 1980s and 1990s, when state assistance replaced federal grants, New York, a problem-ridden city, was often forced to turn to the state for relief. Consequently, a cordial relationship between the city's mayor and the state's governor was required. In 1994 Republican Mayor Rudolph Giuliani endorsed Democrat Cuomo over Republican Pataki on the grounds that Cuomo would be better for the city.

In Albany, the state capital, the legislature shapes life in the cities. Reapportionment battles have restrained the power exercised by New York and other cities. Nonetheless, New York State led the nation in welfare and education assistance to cities. The state constitution enables state officials to intervene in matters of local government. Home rule has little basis in the constitution. The governor and state assembly control agencies affecting city dwellers, such as the Port Authority of New York and New Jersey, which constructs and manages tunnels and bridges in the city, and the Metropolitan Transportation Agency, which controls buses and subways.

State financing affects city expenditures. The state takes major responsibility for highways and bridges, environmental conservation, and prisons. New York City does have the power to tax personal income, business, and sales. The city and state share responsibility for social services. The city has a very large health care system, with an average hospital size of more than 400 beds. The city used to maintain this system alone, but after passage of the federal Medicare program in the 1960s, expenditures soared. In the early 1980s the state obtained a federal waiver of policy and took control of hospital revenues. Similarly, the state provides care for the mentally disabled. Following a court order in 1972, the state released tens of thousands of mentally disabled people from institutions. Using only drug therapy, the state in effect dumped patients onto the streets, creating a large component of its homelessness. Other state-city partnerships included housing, criminal justice, and child welfare. State and local expenditures for public welfare programs amounted to $18 billion in 1991.

The federal government is a critical part of state expenditures. Although federal activity on behalf of cities decreased, it still expended massive amounts in New York State. The federal government expended $77 billion in New York in 1991, the second highest in the nation. Direct payments to individuals for social security, Medicare, and other entitlement programs totaled $41 billion. Federal grants accounted for nearly a quarter of the state budget, and the federal government contributed almost 20 percent of the city budget. Still, the federal decline in expenditures dramatically altered the relationship between New York State and New York City. The process began in 1975 when the city's fiscal crisis alienated lenders, forcing it to the brink of bankruptcy. Preferring new state-authorized lending agencies to a federal bankruptcy judge, the city ceded power over major municipal policy to the Emergency Financial Control Board, dominated by the governor and his appointees. It was not until 1986 that the city government was able to regain autonomy. In the early 1990s the state economy showed signs of revival, although the 1992 election of Bill Clinton to the presidency did not bring a return of massive federal assistance. Upstate cities such as Buffalo, Syracuse, and Binghamton remained in the economic doldrums, whereas New York City exhibited a resurgent economy.

[Gary Alampi, ed., *Gale State Rankings Reporter* (Detroit, 1994); Gerald Benjamin and Charles Brecher, eds., *The Two New Yorks* (New York, 1988); Peter W. Colby and John K. White, eds., *New York State Today*, 2nd ed. (Albany, 1989); Edith R. Hornor, ed., *Almanac of the 50 States* (Palo Alto, Calif., 1994); Jerry Mumpower and Warren F. Ilchman, eds., *New York State in the Year 2000* (Albany, 1988).]

GRAHAM RUSSELL HODGES

See also **SUPP:** Buffalo; New York City.

NICARAGUA, RELATIONS WITH. As in Cuba in 1959 and Haiti in 1986, excesses of a despotic regime in Nicaragua compelled the United States to withdraw support from a longtime ally. During the 1970s the strongman of Nicaragua, Anastasio Somoza Debayle, a graduate of the U.S. Military Academy at West Point, N.Y., with many friends in Washington, D.C., could no longer control the country. Like Fulgencio Batista in Cuba and the Duvalier family in Haiti, the Somoza family not only had controlled political power but also used it to amass great wealth for itself and its close friends. What little economic progress occurred was concentrated in the capital city of Managua. The rest of the country was left to languish in poverty—ill-nourished, uneducated, and underemployed. Even Managua, devastated by an earthquake in 1972, came to be neglected by Somoza. Relief money sent from the United States and elsewhere to rebuild the city and aid its citizens disappeared or was diverted to other projects. Opposition to the dictatorial Somoza escalated from the mid-1970s until 1978, when the murder of popular journalist Pedro Joaquim Chamorro triggered a civil war. Sympathy within and outside Nicaragua turned toward the Sandinista National Liberation Front, which took its name from Augusto Sandino, the rebellious leader of the 1920s and early 1930s who had opposed the Nicaraguan government and its military supporter, the U.S. marines. Somoza and his henchmen left Nicaragua in 1979. The Sandinistas marched into Managua promising health care, literacy, agrarian reform, and elections within five years. Initially, relations between Washington and the Sandinista government were cordial. Simultaneously seeking aid from communist countries, Nicaragua's new rulers courted the administration of President Jimmy Carter, which responded with $8 million in emergency aid and $75 million in loans. The Sandinista leadership appeared to have learned from the Cuban example and avoided nationalizing all private enterprises or relying on one trading or ideological bloc.

The election of President Ronald Reagan in 1980 signaled a change in U.S. policy, which had emphasized human rights and tolerated some political pluralism in Central America. The new president was far less tolerant of a regime that openly adhered to Marxist principles. Exaggerated and often unsubstantiated accounts of Sandinista aid to leftist guerrillas in neighboring El Salvador provided justification as Reagan and his advisers became mired in a futile covert effort to dislodge the Sandinistas. The economy of Nicaragua and the prospect of a better life for the majority of the population declined sharply from 1981 to 1986, due in part to Sandinista mismanagement and a drop in prices for Nicaragua's agricultural products but also to the prolonged civil war promoted

by the United States and the trade embargo enacted in early 1985. Gradually, opposition to continued involvement in Nicaragua's affairs began to mount in the United States. Funds to the Contras, those fighting the Sandinistas, began to be withdrawn by Congress. Exposure in 1986 of a connection between continued aid to the Contras and sale of munitions to the government of Iran—both of which by then were illegal—created a political uproar in the United States.

In 1987 Central American governments moved to take the initiative in resolving the Nicaraguan civil war. Concerned with the threat of U.S. intervention, President Oscar Arias of Costa Rica proposed a peace plan for the entire region with specific proposals for Nicaragua. All Central American governments endorsed the plan, and seven South American countries and Mexico formed the Rio Group to support the initiative as well. Nicaraguan elections in 1990 resulted in defeat of the Sandinistas and the victory of Violeta Barrios de Chamorro, widow of the slain journalist, who immediately sought to deal with the troubled economy. Nicaraguans were weary of war but yearned for the unfulfilled promises of the revolution. By 1994 Chamorro was still trying to revive the economy and fulfill the promises. Meanwhile, many of the advances made by the Sandinistas in education and health had evaporated. Unemployment was high and the country remained tied to an external debt of $10 billion, a huge sum for a small country. An agreement with the International Monetary Fund cleared the way for $140 million in loans over the next three years as well as other foreign loans and aid. Nicaragua's economic future was by no means assured, because its export earnings were insufficient to meet its obligations. Continued economic uncertainty was accompanied by political squabbling that further hampered Chamorro's efforts. Such squabbling, however, provoked little concern in Washington. Democracy had been restored in Nicaragua, and the United States, for the first time in more than half a century, appeared ready to adhere to a strict policy of nonintervention in Nicaragua's internal affairs.

[E. Bradford Burns, *At War in Nicaragua* (New York, 1987); Anthony Lake, *Somoza Falling* (Boston, 1989); Neill Macaulay, *The Sandino Affair* (Durham, N.C., 1985).]

MARY COMMAGER

See also **SUPP:** Cuba, Relations with; Iran-Contra Affair.

NIH. *See* **National Institutes of Health.**

NOBEL PRIZES

NOBEL PRIZES. In 1975–1995, 109 U.S. citizens won or shared a total of sixty-nine Nobel Prizes. During this period, only one American—Holocaust survivor, author, and human rights advocate Elie Wiesel—received the Nobel Peace Prize (1986). The other American winners of the Nobel Prize were:

Literature: Saul Bellow (1976); Isaac Bashevis Singer (1978); Czeslaw Milosz (1980); Joseph Brodsky (1987); Toni Morrison (1993).

Economic Science: Milton Friedman (1976); Herbert A. Simon (1978); Lawrence R. Klein (1980); James Tobin (1981); George Stigler (1982); Gerard Debreu (1983); Franco Modigliani (1985); James M. Buchanan (1986); Robert M. Solow (1987); Harry M. Markowitz, William F. Sharpe, and Merton H. Miller (1990); Ronald Coase (1991); Gary S. Becker (1992); Robert W. Fogel and Douglass C. North (1993); John F. Nash and John C. Harsanyi (1994); Robert Lucas (1995).

Chemistry: William N. Lipscomb (1976); Herbert C. Brown (1979); Paul Berg and Walter Gilbert (1980); Roald Hoffmann (1981); Henry Taube (1983); R. Bruce Merrifield (1984); Herbert A. Hauptman and Jerome Karle (1985); Dudley R. Herschback and Yuan T. Lee (1986); Donald Cram and Charles J. Pedersen (1987); Thomas R. Cech and Sidney Altman (1989); Elias James Corey (1990); Rudolph A. Marcus (1992); Kary B. Mullis (1993); George A. Olah (1994); F. Sherwood Roland and Mario Molina (1995).

Physics: James Rainwater (1975); Burton Richter and Samuel C. C. Ting (1976); Philip W. Anderson and John H. Van Vleck (1977); Arno Penzias and Robert W. Wilson (1978); Steven Weinberg and Sheldon L. Glashow (1979); James W. Cronin and Val L. Fitch (1980); Nicolaas Bloembergen and Arthur L. Schawlow (1981); Kenneth G. Wilson (1982); Subrahmanyan Chandrasekhar and William A. Fowler (1983); Leon M. Lederman, Melvin Schwartz, and Jack Steinberger (1988); Norman Ramsey and Hans G. Dehmelt (1989); Jerome I. Friedman and Henry W. Kendall (1990); Joseph H. Taylor and Russell A. Hulse (1993); Clifford G. Shull (1994); Martin Pearl and Frederick Reines (1995).

Physiology or Medicine: David Baltimore, Howard M. Temin, and Renato Dulbecco (1975); Baruch S. Blumberg and D. Carleton Gajdusek (1976); Rosalyn S. Yalow, Roger Guillemin, and Andrew V. Schally (1977); Daniel Nathans and Hamilton Smith (1978); Allan M. Cormack (1979); Baruj Benacerraf and George D. Snell (1980); Robert W. Sperry and David H. Hubel (1981); Barbara McClintock (1983); Michael S. Brown and Joseph Goldstein (1985); Rita Levi-Montalcini and Stanley Cohen (1986); Gertrude B. Elion and George Hitchings (1988); J. Michael Bishop and Harold E. Varmus (1989); Joseph E. Murray and E. Donnall Thomas (1990); Philip A. Sharp and Richard J. Roberts (1993); Alfred G. Gilman and Martin Rodbell (1994); Edward Lewis and Eric Wieschaus (1995).

[Sharon McGrayne Bertsch, *Nobel Prize Women in Science* (Secaucus, N.J., 1993); Bernard S. Schlessinger and June H. Schlessinger, eds., *The Who's Who of Nobel Prize Winners: 1901–1990,* 2nd ed. (Phoenix, 1991).]

ELIZABETH V. BURT

NOISE POLLUTION is generally defined as unwanted sound produced by people and their activities, unwanted in that it interferes with communication, work, rest, recreation, or sleep. Unlike other forms of pollution, such as air, water, and hazardous materials, noise does not remain long in the environment. Its effects are both immediate in terms of annoyance and cumulative in terms of temporary and permanent hearing loss. Society has attempted to regulate noise since the early days of the Romans, who by decree prohibited the movement of chariots in the streets at night. In the United States, communities have for many years enacted ordinances against excessive noise primarily in response to complaints by residents. It was not until the late 1960s, however, that the U.S. government officially recognized noise as a pollutant and began to support noise research and regulation. Public laws leading to federal action against noise pollution include the National Environmental Policy Act of 1969, especially sections concerning environmental impact statements; the Noise Pollution and Abatement Act of 1970; and the Noise Control Act of 1972, which appointed the Environmental Protection Agency (EPA) to coordinate federal research and activities in noise control. The EPA received the assignment to establish federal noise-emission standards, identifying both major sources of noise and appropriate noise levels that would not infringe on public health and welfare.

The EPA's so-called Levels Document, which provided information concerning noise descriptors and safe noise levels, is the standard reference in the field of environmental noise assessment. In it the EPA established an equivalent sound level (Leq) and a day-night equivalent level (Ldn) as measures and descriptors for noise exposure. Soon thereafter most federal agencies adopted either the Leq, Ldn, or both, including levels compatible with different land uses. The Federal Aviation Administration (FAA) uses Ldn as the noise descriptor in assessing land-use compatibility with various levels of aircraft noise. Support for Ldn as the descriptor for environmental noise was provided in 1978 by Theodore J. Schultz, whose synthesis of many social surveys on noise annoyance showed a relation between Ldn and people highly annoyed by noise in their neighborhoods. The Schultz curve became a basis for noise standards.

As part of the effort to identify major noise sources in the United States, the EPA set about determining the degree to which noise standard could contribute to noise reduction. During the 1970s EPA-sponsored research on major noise sources led to regulation of the products that most affected the public, including medium and heavy trucks, portable air compressors, garbage trucks, buses, and motorcycles. Missing from the list was aircraft, which was considered the responsibility of the FAA. During the administration of President Ronald Reagan in the 1980s, the power of the EPA and its Office of Noise Abatement and Control was curtailed and most of its noise regulations rescinded, but efforts continued to curb noise pollution. The Department of Transportation maintains standards for highways, mass transit, and railroads, as well as aircraft. The environmental review process in accordance with the National Environmental Policy Act of 1969 remains the single most effective deterrent against noise pollution.

[Environmental Protection Agency, *Information on Levels of Environmental Noise Requisite to Protect Public Health and Welfare with an Adequate Margin of Safety* (Washington, D.C., 1974); Theodore J. Schultz, "Synthesis of Social Surveys on Noise Annoyance," *Journal of the Acoustical Society of America* 63 (August 1978).]

CARL E. HANSON

See also **SUPP:** Environmental Protection Agency.

NORTH AMERICAN FREE TRADE AGREEMENT

(NAFTA). The General Agreement on Tariffs and Trade (GATT), which went into effect in 1948 in the wake of World War II, sought to expand free trade by reducing tariffs between the twenty-three signatory nations. With the gradual privatization of state-run industries and economies, its membership expanded to ninety-six nations in 1988, and tariff barriers were reduced. A strong supporter of GATT throughout its history, the United States in 1986 began to urge that GATT move beyond the reduction of trade barriers and that its agenda include foreign investment, services, agriculture, and intellectual property rights. Many viewed this as an attempt to loosen environ-

mental and social regulations that might hamper access to resources throughout the world. While perhaps seeking to increase investment opportunities for corporate interests, the United States by the mid-1980s was clearly on the defensive economically. Once the leading creditor nation in the world, it had become the largest debtor nation and suffered from what some feared was a perpetual trade deficit.

Increasing competition from Pacific and European countries caused the United States to begin trying to assemble a dollar-dominated block in the American hemisphere. This desire led first to the Free Trade Agreement (FTA) with Canada, which went into effect on Jan. 1, 1989, and then to an expanded trilateral agreement with Canada and Mexico, the North American Free Trade Agreement, which went into effect on January 1, 1994. A multivolume, fifteen-pound document, NAFTA at its simplest level set up a schedule for the elimination of tariffs over a fifteen-year period. Given the earlier agreement between the United States and Canada, NAFTA dealt primarily with restructuring trade between the United States and Mexico and between Mexico and Canada. All tariffs between the United States and Canada would end by the year 1998; those between the United States and Mexico would be eliminated by 2008. The agreements, however, much like the expanded agenda for GATT, covered more than the elimination of trade barriers and led to divisive debate in all three countries. While few objected to freer trade, the opponents of the FTA with Canada and, later, NAFTA were many and vociferous. Concerns among Canadians in 1988 and Mexicans in 1992 reflected a lingering view of the United States as a powerful nation that might yet seek to swallow up or strangle its neighbors. While some critics employed a powerful emotional rhetoric reminiscent of the days when the United States was roundly condemned as the Colossus of the North, others focused on the perceived need to protect Canadian and Mexican sovereignty, which they saw as threatened by expanded U.S. investment in such crucial national resources as oil and in institutions such as banking. Given the unequal status between themselves and their powerful neighbor, these opponents argued, both Canada and Mexico risked becoming in effect economic colonies of the United States.

In 1988 Canadians voiced many of the same concerns expressed by labor leaders and environmentalists in the United States in the early 1990s. Because Canada was already part of GATT, Canadians questioned the necessity of the FTA and the benefit to

Canada of tying itself more closely to the largest debtor nation in the world. They argued that the movement of jobs from Canada to the United States, already a problem because of lower U.S. labor costs, would accelerate and that Canada's higher standards of environmental regulation and social programs would be threatened by U.S. investment and business practices. The debates over NAFTA that raged in all three North American countries in the early 1990s thus reflected not only old suspicions and prejudices but the confusion and uncertainty engendered by the end of the cold war, the increasingly global problems of overpopulation and pollution, and the growing interdependency of economies, as well as suspicion that the only ones who would benefit from the new agreements would be the transnational corporations, which many observers considered already too powerful and unregulated. By far the most emotional issue in all three countries was the effect of NAFTA on employment. While proponents of NAFTA stressed that implementation would ultimately create jobs, the fear of job loss inspired many opponents. The negotiations commenced and continued during a period of global recession and high unemployment. While the movement of jobs from Canada to the United States and from the United States to Mexico had preceded the FTA and NAFTA negotiations, labor groups in both the United States and Canada were unshakable in their opposition.

As the leaders of both Mexico and the United States sought to assuage the fears of those at home who opposed NAFTA, the fate of the pact had implications beyond the borders of North America in the early 1990s. When President George Bush and Mexican President Carlos Salinas de Gortari announced in June 1990 the possibility of a free trade agreement between Mexico and the United States, Bush also announced the Enterprise for the Americas Initiative, which envisioned a free trade block stretching from Alaska to Tierra del Fuego. This announcement preceded a dizzying number of new trading alignments within Latin America, including the agreement among Argentina, Brazil, Paraguay, and Uruguay in March 1991 to establish MERCOSUR, which pledged to integrate their economies by 1995, and numerous framework trade agreements between the United States and its southern neighbors. Most of these proposals received little attention, and public debate remained focused on the free trade agreement with Mexico.

Throughout the course of the NAFTA negotiations, which began in February 1991, more than economics was at stake. The creation of a multinational trading bloc represented a political as well as an economic objective. Correctly or not, Latin American leaders by the early 1990s had come to see the opportunity to move closer to the United States economically as a way to move their countries politically along a modern path of reform. At stake, then, was more than an economic reordering of the relationship among the three North American countries; achievement of a foreign policy objective—strengthening political ties throughout the hemisphere—was also on the line. NAFTA was approved by the U.S. Congress in November 1993. A complicated and cumbersome document largely unread by proponents and opponents alike, it included concessions made on all sides, because leaders in the United States, Mexico, and Canada sought to effect its passage, promote their own economies, and protect the frailest components of those economies.

[Marjorie Montgomery Bowker, *On Guard for Thee: An Independent Review of the Free Trade Agreement* (Quebec, 1988); Victor Bulmer-Thomas, Nikki Craske, and Monica Serrano, eds., *Mexico and the North American Free Trade Agreement: Who Will Benefit?* (New York, 1994); John Cavanagh et al., eds., *Trading Freedom: How Free Trade Affects Our Lives, Work, and Environment* (San Francisco, 1992).]

MARY COMMAGER

See also **SUPP:** Canada, Relations with; General Agreement on Tariffs and Trade; Mexico, Relations with; Trade, International.

NORTH ATLANTIC TREATY ORGANIZATION (NATO). The signing of the North Atlantic Treaty on Apr. 4, 1949, marked the end of a tradition of nonentanglement with European powers that had begun in 1800 with the termination of the Franco-American alliance of 1778. The treaty linked the United States with eleven other nations—Canada, Iceland, the United Kingdom, France, Belgium, the Netherlands, Luxembourg, Norway, Denmark, Portugal, and Italy. The proximate cause of this transformation in U.S. foreign relations was the Soviet communist menace to Western Europe. Initiative for the alliance came from Europe. In 1947 the administration of President Harry S. Truman had announced the Truman Doctrine, which established the principle of providing assistance to countries threatened by communist takeover, and the Marshall Plan, a program for the economic reconstruction of Europe that also included containment of communism as one of its goals. Worried that these measures did not provide sufficient security against communist subversion or Soviet pressures, however, the European nations sought a binding pledge from the United States. They received it in the form of Article 5 of the treaty, which stated that an attack on one member would be considered an attack on all. The allies in turn pledged to build their defenses, integrate their military forces, and prove through self-help and mutual assistance to be worthy of the U.S. commitment.

The alliance itself had little military significance in 1949. Its members assumed that the fact of U.S. adherence to the treaty would be sufficient to deter external attack and that a modest U.S. military assistance program would be sufficient to inhibit internal subversion. In 1950 the Korean War shattered these assumptions. If the Soviets were testing American resolve in a divided Korea, they might conceivably make their next move in a divided Germany. Fear of attack impelled the allies to expand the alliance into a military organization, under a Supreme Allied Commander in Europe (SACEUR) and in the Atlantic (SACLANT). A political headquarters was established in Paris in 1952. A vast military assistance program begun in the summer of 1950 was to raise the size of the ground forces to fifty divisions to cope with a potential Soviet invasion of the West. Greece and Turkey were brought into the alliance in 1952 to shore up the southeastern flank of NATO. West Germany entered the alliance in 1955 only after resistance from its neighbors, France in particular, had been overcome. From 1950 onward the purpose of the alliance was military rather than political. Throughout the 1950s and 1960s the SACEURs, beginning with General Dwight D. Eisenhower, were dominant figures, overshadowing the civilian secretaries-general. Although the drive to build up a large standing army waned in the 1950s, to be replaced by emphasis on nuclear weapons—tactical, intermediate, and by the end of the decade, intercontinental—the concern of the NATO allies remained centered on military security and U.S. authority remained self-evident.

By the late 1950s, however, there were clear signs of discontent among the allies, which gathered strength in the 1960s. Part of the problem was the increasing resentment of the U.S. nuclear monopoly as expanding economies in the European Economic Community generated a self-confidence that had been lacking earlier. At the same time Soviet technological achievements, epitomized by the Sputnik earth satellite in 1957, both stimulated interest of the allies in building their own nuclear weapons and cast

doubt on the support of the United States if its own cities were vulnerable to Soviet intercontinental ballistic missiles (ICBMs). Efforts on both sides of the Atlantic to shore up the alliance faltered in the face of a rising Soviet threat. An ambitious attempt to create a multilateral force in Europe, armed with nuclear weapons, collapsed in 1964 because of U.S. unwillingness to turn over control of the weapons to the allies. President Charles de Gaulle's France withdrew its military participation in 1966 but remained a member of the NATO alliance, and NATO's headquarters moved in the following year from Paris to Brussels.

In 1967 the Harmel Initiative, named for Belgium's foreign minister, reinvigorated the alliance by having NATO use détente as well as defense as a major objective. On the assumption that coexistence with the Soviet bloc was a reality, the NATO allies in the 1970s negotiated with the Soviet-controlled Warsaw Pact nations on such issues as reducing nuclear and conventional weaponry and accepting the postwar boundaries of East Germany and Poland. The periodic crises in the 1950s and 1960s over the status of West Berlin, which had led to the Berlin Wall and confrontation between Soviet and American tanks in 1961, seemed to have ended. There was still an uneasiness among the allies when détente did not prevent the Soviet Union from building up offensive nuclear weapons at a time when the United States was reducing its own defense effort. Chairman Leonid Brezhnev's Soviet Union was less volatile than that of Premier Nikita Khrushchev but was no less threatening. Europeans were particularly worried about intermediate-range ballistic missiles targeted on their cities. Soviet behavior induced the allies to follow a dual-track system of both increasing defenses and reviving détente. Although ICBMs based in the United States and Polaris missiles on U.S. submarines effectively neutralized Soviet missiles, European insecurity required deployment of U.S. cruise and Pershing II missiles in five European countries to ease their fears. The United States asked for major increases in NATO defense expenditures, and, in the administrations of Presidents Jimmy Carter and Ronald Reagan, committed itself to massive increases. The Soviet Union at first refused to accept mutual reductions, on the mistaken assumption that Western antinuclear public opinion would prevent the deployment of U.S. missiles. When President Mikhail Gorbachev came to power in the mid-1980s, however, he sought to deescalate the conflict; the Soviet economy could not withstand new burdens that would result from further military competition with the United States. Negotiations that had been interrupted in 1983 while the Soviets attempted to intimidate the West resumed in 1985.

The rush of events at the end of the 1980s—reunification of Germany and dissolution of the Warsaw Pact and of the Soviet Union itself—ended in NATO's achievement of its initial goal, removal of the communist menace. In the mid-1990s NATO's sixteen nations, including Spain since 1982, were seeking new functions for the organization. Until such could be found, the disarray in the former Soviet empire postponed any measures to terminate the Atlantic alliance.

[David P. Calleo, *Beyond American Hegemony: The Future of the Western Alliance* (New York, 1987); Lawrence S. Kaplan, *NATO and the United States* (New York, 1994); Stanley R. Sloan, *NATO's Future* (Washington, D.C., 1985).]

LAWRENCE S. KAPLAN

See also **SUPP:** Arms Race and Disarmament; Cold War; Eastern Europe, Relations with; Soviet Union.

NORTH CAROLINA. Since 1976 remarkable changes have occurred in North Carolina politics, especially in the movement toward a two-party system. Although Republicans have elected many key officials, they have yet to control the General Assembly. Since 1968 the state has voted Republican in every presidential race except 1976. First elected in 1972, U.S. Senator Jesse Helms has been repeatedly reelected. His strongest opponent was Governor James B. Hunt in 1984, whom he defeated in a mean-spirited and expensive campaign. Supporting other conservative Republican candidates with his National Congressional Club, Helms secured the election of two Senate colleagues—John East in 1980 and Lauch Faircloth in 1992. In 1972 James Holshouser became the first Republican elected governor since 1896; James G. Martin, elected in 1984 and 1988, became the second. The Republicans have usually controlled only three U.S. House seats, in the mountains and urban areas, but in 1994 eight of twelve congressmen elected were Republicans. Although the state legislature included only 10 Republicans in 1977, their numbers increased to 67 of 120 representatives and 24 of 50 senators in 1995.

Another important political development was the rise in importance of the black electorate. African Americans were elected mayors of Chapel Hill, Raleigh, and Charlotte and won more legislative seats (from three in 1977 to fourteen in 1991). The numbers of state and local offices held by African Americans increased from 247 in 1980 to 1,086 in 1992. Daniel T. Blue, Jr., was elected the first black speaker of the house in 1990, and Harvey B. Gantt ran a strong race against Senator Helms in 1992, receiving 48 percent of the vote. The black electorate benefited from a U.S. Supreme Court decision in 1986 that declared four North Carolina legislative districts in violation of the Voting Rights Acts of 1965 and 1982. In 1992 the legislature created two oddly shaped congressional districts with black majorities to assure the election of the first black candidates since 1901, Eva M. Clayton and Mel Watt. In addition, the political consciousness of women in North Carolina greatly increased. From 1973 to 1983 many women in North Carolina campaigned unsuccessfully for the legislature to ratify the Equal Rights Amendment. Regarded in the 1940s as a progressive plutocracy, in the 1970s North Carolina was called a "progressive paradox" or a "progressive myth," despite the political changes. Critics cited much evidence to show increasing conservatism, including the election of Senator Helms, the conviction of the Wilmington 10 for arson in 1972, and the acquittal of Ku Klux Klan defendants charged with killing Communist Workers Party members in Greensboro in 1979.

Developments in education were mixed. The state created a new university system, expanded community colleges, and tried to upgrade public schools. Higher education expanded in the 1960s, and rising enrollments created demands in the twelve state colleges for university status, but only campuses in Asheville, Charlotte, and Wilmington were placed in the University of North Carolina (UNC) system. The other nine campuses achieved status as regional universities. Because the fight for funds was fierce and the quality of education was threatened, Governor Robert E. Scott demanded and secured in 1971 a university system ruled by a board of governors. Thereafter the University of North Carolina, a system of sixteen institutions under Presidents William C. Friday and C. D. Spangles, achieved a very good national reputation. The five predominantly black state universities were not happy with this system. The National Association for the Advancement of Colored People brought suit to deny federal funds to the UNC system because it was racially segregated. At issue was more than money for the black students. After fighting the suit for years in the federal courts, the university system in 1981 agreed to a consent decree. It required the state to upgrade the black institutions and take steps to integrate all campuses. The state also created a system of community colleges. Starting in the 1960s as industrial education centers, these institutions grew into fifty-eight two-year technical and community colleges. Operating at first under local boards of trustees, they were brought under a state board of community colleges in 1981. Between 1975 and 1991 community colleges tripled their enrollments, serving more than 230,000 students in 1991–1992.

Public schools were not as successful as higher education, but the needs of gifted students were met partly by summer governor's schools in the 1960s and the creation in 1981 in Durham of the School of Science and Mathematics, which provides a free education for selected students at a residential campus and receives the most National Merit Awards in the state. Public schools have emphasized recruiting and retaining good teachers. Besides upgrading teacher certification standards, the state created the Center for the Advancement of Teaching, where the best teachers receive a week's intellectual stimulation and encouragement. In 1985 the legislature started funding a basic education program, providing smaller classes, teachers' aides, foreign language instruction in lower grades, and achievement testing. Complaining of the poor education of high school graduates, the university system offered many remedial courses. The system required all enrollees to complete a college preparatory curriculum. Despite these efforts, the public was shocked when the state's students received the lowest SAT scores in the nation in 1989 and low scores on standard essay tests in 1993.

North Carolina's economy has performed well since the end of the 1970s. Personal income (in constant dollars) rose from $66 billion in 1980 to $98 billion in 1992, a 3.3 percent increase per year; only four states exceeded this rate. There was little change, however, in the types of employment. Manufacturing, trade, and government were the largest employers in 1976; in 1990 services moved up to third place, increasing from 285,400 to 568,800 jobs. In manufacturing, textiles, apparel, and furniture remained the top three employers, but the machinery industry was growing rapidly. Two geographical areas led the economic growth—Charlotte-Mecklenburg and the Research Triangle—and both areas became regional airline hubs. Economic growth produced population growth, and between 1980 and 1990 Charlotte increased from 315,000 to 396,000 and Raleigh from 150,000 to 208,000. The major population trend was a 35 percent increase in Hispanics and a 250 per-

cent increase in Asians. The state population grew from 5.9 million to 6.6 million, an 11 percent increase.

The crime rate also increased, from 4,121 crimes per 100,000 people in 1985 to 5,889 in 1991. The increase prompted debate about the death penalty. Although the U.S. Supreme Court declared the state's death penalty unconstitutional in 1976 and the legislature enacted a new law in 1977, executions did not resume until 1984. The executions seemed to have little impact on the crime rate. A celebrated legal case in the 1980s involved the Charlotte television evangelists Jim and Tammy Bakker. The federal government prosecuted Jim Bakker for mail and wire fraud, resulting in his conviction and imprisonment. In 1994, for the first time in state history, the governor called a special session of the legislature to address the problem of crime.

An enthusiasm for sports swept the state. North Carolina collegiate teams won the men's NCAA basketball championship five times from 1982 to 1993—the University of North Carolina twice, Duke University twice, and North Carolina State once. The latter's coach, Jim Valvano, was released from his position because his program ran counter to the university system's emphasis on the academic success of athletes. The state's best-known sports figure was Michael Jordan. Charlotte investors established two professional teams—the Charlotte Hornets basketball team in 1988 and the Carolina Panthers football team in 1993.

[John L. Bell and Jeffrey L. Crow, *North Carolina* (Montgomery, Ala., 1992); Eric B. Herzik and Sallye B. Teater, comps., *North Carolina Focus* (Raleigh, 1981); Paul Luebke, *Tar Heel Politics* (Chapel Hill, 1990); North Carolina General Assembly, *North Carolina Manual* (Raleigh, 1977–1991).]

JOHN L. BELL

See also **SUPP:** Charlotte; Raleigh.

NORTH DAKOTA. Contrasts have always typified the state of North Dakota, such as the weather, which varies dramatically. The fourth driest year on record (1976, with 12.04 inches of precipitation) was followed by the wettest (21.67 inches). When weather fluctuates, so do harvests of wheat, the state's primary crop, ranging from 156 million bushels in 1970 to 328 million in 1981. Since the 1970s the economy fluctuated similarly. Wheat brought $1.45 per bushel in 1970 but rocketed to $4.82 in 1974, when, with good harvests and prices, federal government payments were 1.2 percent of total cash income for farmers. After the 1988 drought, however, federal payments were 23 percent of total income. Social and economic contrasts abounded. Although nicknamed the "Peace Garden State," during the 1960s and 1970s North Dakotans joked that if the state seceded from the union, it would be the world's third-largest nuclear power. In 1991 it ranked first in the percentage of eighteen-year-olds in college, but thirtieth in residents with bachelor's degrees and forty-eighth in teachers' salaries. In 1977 it was the first state to complete the total interstate highway mileage assigned in the Federal Controlled Access Highway System, and in 1985 it was the last to report an AIDS case. Although outraged when decreasing population led *Newsweek* to label North Dakota and other states "America's outback," residents proudly sported buttons proclaiming "40 Below Keeps Out the Riffraff!"

Although 1980 saw the first population gain since 1930 (from 617,761 in 1970 to 652,717), 1990 recorded a decline to 638,800. By 1990 the state's urban population (53 percent) exceeded the rural (47 percent). From 1970 to 1990 the largest city, Fargo, grew from 53,365 to 74,111, and the capital, Bismarck, grew from 34,703 to 49,256. Demographically, North Dakota remained homogeneous. In 1990 the three largest ancestral groups were Germans (51 percent), Norwegians (30 percent), and the Irish (8 percent). In contrast, only 4 percent were Native Americans, and Hispanics, African Americans, and Asian Americans accounted for less than 1 percent each. Native Americans have struggled economically, despite five tribal community colleges, military manufacturing contracts, and casino gambling on reservations. In 1990 half lived below the poverty line, one-fourth were unemployed, and per capita income was only 31 percent of the state average.

Since the 1970s the state has depended heavily on the federal government. Agricultural price supports stabilized the farm economy but also increased its vulnerability to federal policies. Farmers benefited enormously from Soviet purchases, which drove wheat prices to $4.82 per bushel in 1974. When President Jimmy Carter embargoed grain sales to the Soviets in response to their invasion of Afghanistan, farmers suddenly found themselves with bulging grain bins. Despite the dependence and vulnerability accompanying them, federal funds generally benefited North Dakota. In 1992 the state ranked eighth in the nation in per capita federal funds received. Although agriculture remained the core of the state's economy, it had changed dramatically. The propor-

tion of agricultural workers fell from 21 percent in 1970 to 10 percent in 1990, the number of farmers decreased from 43,000 to 29,000, and farms dropped from 45,500 to 33,000. The average farm size increased from 920 acres in 1970 to 1,224 acres in 1993. U.S. Air Force bases and Minuteman missile silo complexes were another example of federal dependence. In the 1980s the proportion of the labor force in the military was almost twice the national average.

North Dakotans continued to favor Republicans for president, but in the late 1980s most officials were Democrats. Voters regularly reelected U.S. senators of either party whose seniority brought federal dollars home. Senator Milton R. Young, a conservative Republican in office from 1945 to 1980, gained the nickname "Mr. Wheat" for his devotion to North Dakota's agricultural interests. The liberal Democratic Senator Quentin N. Burdick (1960–1992), Young's political opposite on almost every issue, earned similar distinction. National legislators continued to hold town hall meetings to gauge public opinion and keep voters informed. State politics retained a populist streak, with minimum voter registration procedures and high voter turnout. Permissive initiative and referendum requirements allowed direct participation in lawmaking, and citizens had sometimes restructured the tax system to the dismay of legislators.

Energy development was a veritable economic roller coaster after 1970. Production expanded of lignite, a soft, low-sulfur coal found close to the surface and ideal for strip mining. The construction of enormous lignite-powered electrical-generation plants, exporting electricity to neighboring states, caused a steady increase in tons of coal mined, from 5 million in 1970 to 32 million in 1992. Crude oil production was 22 million barrels in 1970 and remained stable until the late 1970s, when it increased dramatically. It peaked at 52.7 million barrels in 1984, then fell to 32.9 million by 1992, as the world price of crude oil collapsed. The reduction devastated western North Dakota, leaving many towns with rows of empty houses and abandoned businesses. On the other hand, North Dakotans prided themselves on their high quality of life. In 1991 the state had the lowest violent crime rate and the third-highest rate of church membership in the nation. The proverbial "good place to raise children," it had reasonable taxes, wide-open spaces, clean air, and friendly people.

[*North Dakota Centennial Blue Book, 1889–1989* (Bismarck, 1989); University of North Dakota, Bureau of Business and Economic Research, *Statistical Abstract of*

North Dakota, 1988, 3rd ed. (Grand Forks, 1988); Robert P. Wilkins and Wynona Huchette Wilkins, *North Dakota: A Bicentennial History* (New York, 1977).]

LARRY R. PETERSON

NPR. *See* **National Public Radio.**

NRA. *See* **National Rifle Association.**

NRC. *See* **Nuclear Regulatory Commission.**

NSF. *See* **National Science Foundation.**

NUCLEAR POWER, in physics, refers to energy produced by fission, when atoms are split, or by fusion, when two nuclei of a light atom are fused to form a single nucleus. The energy produced can be used for weapons or for peaceful purposes. The phrase is also used to designate those nations that have nuclear weapons. The nations that have declared they have nuclear weapons are China, France, the former Soviet Union, Great Britain, and the United States. The breakup of the Soviet Union in the early 1990s resulted in the addition of Byelarus, Kazakhstan, and Ukraine as nuclear-weapon states because the nuclear missiles and storage sites placed on their territory by the Soviet Union became the property of these newly independent states. All three have declared their intention to transfer their weapons to Russia. In addition, a number of nations, such as India, Pakistan, and North Korea, are believed to have the capacity to develop nuclear weapons within a few months. Others, such as Israel, are suspected of having developed one or more such weapons secretly.

Nuclear power also refers to plants and industry that generate electric power from nuclear sources. Nuclear power plants differ from hydroelectric plants, which generate electricity from the force of flowing water, and coal-, oil-, or gas-fired electric plants, which generate electricity from the heat drawn from burning fossil fuels. Nuclear power plants generate steam to drive electric turbines by circulating liquid through a nuclear reactor. The reactor produces heat through the controlled fission of atomic fuel. Normally the fuel for power reactors is slightly enriched uranium. In 1951 the U.S. Atomic Energy Commission built the first nuclear reactor to generate electric power. The increasing availability of uranium ore at that time and the resulting reduction in price of this essential fuel increased interest in commercial exploitation of the new technology. Nuclear reactors have several advantages over power generation using other fuels. Unlike fossil fuels, nuclear fuel does not foul the air and is not dependent on oil imports from unstable parts of the world. The rising costs of the world's diminishing coal, oil, and natural gas resources and the limitation on the number of hydroelectric power plants that can be built could be overcome by nuclear plants. The attraction of electricity generated by nuclear power was not limited to the United States. Industrial and some developing nations embarked on ambitious programs of their own. By 1966 nuclear power generators were being built or operating in five countries. By the beginning of the 1980s there were 100 nuclear power plants in the United States.

One of the by-products of nuclear power generation is plutonium, a material that can be chemically processed for use in nuclear weapons. The danger of such use by nonnuclear nations led to international safeguards under the 1968 Nuclear Nonproliferation Treaty. In Article III signatory nations agreed to inspections by the International Atomic Energy Agency (IAEA), "with a view to preventing diversion of nuclear energy from peaceful uses to nuclear weapons or other nuclear explosive devices." Most of the world's nuclear and nonnuclear nations signed this treaty. Iraq in 1992 and North Korea in 1994 were subjected to IAEA inspections that proved treaty violations in the former and raised serious suspicions about the latter. Both nations were signatories of the treaty, although North Korea announced its withdrawal some months prior to inspection. Iraq's nuclear-weapon production facilities were discovered as a result of a series of highly intrusive IAEA inspections and were subsequently destroyed by the United Nations.

When Congress passed the Atomic Energy Act of 1954, it approved President Dwight D. Eisenhower's Atoms for Peace program, which included commercial development of nuclear reactors for the purpose of generating electric power. During the 1960s electricity generated by nuclear power contributed 1 to 2 percent of the nation's energy total. Since then that percentage has grown steadily, surpassing the proportion from hydroelectric sources in 1984. By 1990 nuclear power amounted to one-fifth of the nation's total generation of electricity. By 1992 nuclear generation reached 619 billion net kilowatt hours, more than double the amount generated in 1979, when the Three Mile Island accident produced an adverse effect on U.S. development of nuclear power plants.

NUCLEAR REGULATORY COMMISSION

In reaction to the 1973 oil embargo, U.S. consumers temporarily used less energy, which diminished the rate of growth in electricity generation. As a result of this and other factors, such as higher construction costs, delays brought on by antinuclear protests, increased operating costs resulting from new federal regulations, and uncertainties about disposal of high-level radioactive waste, no requests for construction of new nuclear power plants had been received by the Nuclear Regulatory Commission since 1978. The level of generation was still rising, however, because plants started in the 1970s had gone on-line, and modernization after 1979 made power plants more efficient. The rising production trend was expected to continue until the beginning of the twenty-first century, then level off and begin to fall, unless more nuclear plants were built.

[Department of Energy, Energy Information Administration, *Annual Energy Outlook 1994* (Washington, D.C., 1994), and *1992 Energy Facts* (Washington, D.C., 1993); Daniel Deudney and Christopher Flavin, *Renewable Energy: The Power to Choose* (New York, 1983); Peter Mannfield, *World Nuclear Power* (New York, 1991).]

ROBERT M. GUTH

See also **SUPP:** Arms Race and Disarmament; Energy Industry; Energy Policy; Hazardous Waste; Nuclear Regulatory Commission; Strategic Arms Limitations Talks; Three Mile Island.

NUCLEAR REGULATORY COMMISSION (NRC). The attraction of nuclear power has been dimmed since its beginnings by the danger of accidents. Governments faced a dilemma between promoting what was for many years seen as the promise of clean and cheap power and the need to regulate commercial development to protect public safety and the environment. The Nuclear Regulatory Commission was created as the U.S. government's regulator. Established under the Energy Reorganization Act of 1974, it inherited licensing and regulatory authority from its predecessor, the Atomic Energy Commission. The NRC licenses and regulates the construction and operation of civilian nuclear reactors and the possession, use, processing, handling, and disposal of nuclear materials. It issues rules and standards to protect public health and safety and the environment from the dangers of commercial nuclear programs and inspects them for adherence to NRC rules. The five commissioners are appointed by the president (who also selects the chair) for five-year terms. A maximum of three commissioners may be of the same political party. The NRC's major program responsibilities are administered by the Offices of Nuclear Reactor Regulation and Nuclear Material Safety and Safeguards. Field operations are conducted from regional offices in Atlanta, Philadelphia, Chicago, Dallas, and San Francisco. NRC headquarters is in Bethesda, Md. The Office of Nuclear Reactor Regulation licenses construction and operation of nuclear reactors and seeks to ensure their safe and environmentally sound operation. Since the late 1970s, however, applications for new construction of nuclear power plants have dwindled to the point where safety of operations and environmental inspections and reviews have become the office's principal business. The Office of Nuclear Material Safety and Safeguards oversees uranium mines, mills, and recovery facilities for the proper processing, handling, transportation, storage, and prevention of theft and sabotage of nuclear materials. The Office of Nuclear Regulatory Research develops safety and environmental standards for the operation of nuclear facilities and management of nuclear waste. It sponsors research on which to base standards and to support the NRC's responsibilities for evaluating accidents and predicting risk.

Established to relieve tension between the development and regulation of nuclear power, the NRC found itself divided between responsibilities for safety and environmental protection and the profitability of the nuclear power industry. Public confidence in nuclear power was undermined by the Mar. 28, 1979, accident at the Three Mile Island nuclear plant near Harrisburg, Pa., in which a cooling-system failure of one reactor led to a partial exposure of its uranium core, threatening an explosion and wide release of radioactivity until the crisis was contained twelve days later. The NRC received scathing criticism for lax enforcement and poor preparation for emergencies from the commission investigating the accident. Inevitably more stringent regulation followed, leading to increased costs for new plants. Industry budgets had to deal with lengthening start-up times that were already seen as excessive and account for expensive cleanup in the event of another accident. As of 1995 no applications to build new commercial nuclear power plants had been received since the 1979 accident and projects for the construction of new plants were abandoned in the 1980s. The cost of electricity produced by earlier plants and those completed since the accident rose steadily into the 1990s and were projected to continue rising. Environmental concerns linked to fossil fuels may well drive costs of nonnuclear power generation up to the point where nuclear generation again may look commercially attractive.

[Philip L. Catelon and Robert C. Williams, *Crisis Contained: The Department of Energy at Three Mile Island* (Carbondale, Ill., 1982); Fred Clement, *The Nuclear Regulatory Commission* (New York, 1989); Union of Concerned Scientists, *Safety Second* (Bloomington, Ind., 1987).]

ROBERT M. GUTH

See also **DAH:** Atomic Energy Commission; **SUPP:** Energy, Department of; Energy Industry; Energy Research and Development Administration; Hazardous Waste; Nuclear Power; Three Mile Island.

NUCLEAR WASTE. *See* **Hazardous Waste.**

NURSING. Since the 1960s nurses have expanded their knowledge, practice, and independence. With congressional legislation authorizing Medicare and Medicaid, enormous numbers of people sought primary-care services. Aware that there were not enough physicians, Congress authorized federal funding to hospitals, clinics, and schools of nursing that offered training in ambulatory, primary care to nurses. In the ensuing years, certified nurse practitioners (CRNPs) developed specialties in pediatrics, geriatrics, and women's health, joining nurse-midwives, visiting nurses, and nurse-anesthetists who had practiced more independently than other nurses from the early years of the twentieth century. Nurses' roles in the acute care of hospitalized patients also enlarged. Advances in medical science and technology from World War II greatly increased the invasiveness of procedures and risk to patients of hospital care. Nurses and physicians worried about patients residing unobserved in semiprivate rooms, as patients utilized the coverage offered by health-insurance plans to avoid hospitalization in wards. Nurses responded by grouping their sickest patients in areas that could be more intensely monitored. The first such arrangements took the form of recovery rooms following surgery. Coronary-care units followed, and by the 1990s critical-care units existed for patients with almost every kind of organ dysfunction. Intensive nursing care gave these units their character, and critical care evolved as a specialty of expert nurses. The American Association of Critical Care Nurses, founded in 1969, began the journal *Heart and Lung* and rapidly became nursing's largest specialty organization.

The two major nursing fields started to merge in the 1990s. Hospitals began to hire nurse practitioners in specialties as substitutes for medical house staff residents. Clinical nurse specialists began to develop physical examination and diagnostic skills. Hospitals thus hired nurses to deliver medical services and often chose minimally trained substitutes to give nursing care. In the 1960s the American Nurses' Association and the National League for Nursing recommended the baccalaureate degree for beginning professional nurses. Community college and hospital program graduates were to be designated "technical nurses." Licensed practical nurses would continue to graduate from hospital and high school programs. State legislatures balked at passing such proposals, and by 1994 only North Dakota had passed the legislation. Although enrollments in programs that prepared registered nurses reached an all-time high of 257,983 in 1992 (from 230,803 in 1973), only 102,128 were baccalaureate enrollees, 132,603 were associate degree candidates, and 23,252 were hospital diploma program participants. Men comprised 12 percent of these enrollees, up from 7 percent a decade earlier. Meanwhile, graduate nursing programs were increasing. In 1973 eight doctoral programs in nursing enrolled 375 students. By 1992 fifty-four doctoral programs had 2,727 students enrolled. By the mid-1990s employers generally required nursing researchers, educators, and administrators to hold doctorates.

[Barbara Melosh, *"The Physician's Hand": Work Culture and Conflict in American Nursing* (Philadelphia, 1982); Susan M. Reverby, *Ordered to Care: The Dilemma of American Nursing* (New York, 1987).]

ELLEN D. BAER

See also **DAH:** Medical Education; Nursing; **SUPP:** Health Care; Physician Assistants.

NUTRITION. While the federal government continued its food-stamp and Women, Infants, and Children food-aid programs in the last quarter of the twentieth century, nutritional emphasis in the United States had changed since the 1970s. The government and scientific groups, such as the National Academy of Sciences, raised alarms about the effects of poor diets on health, while pharmaceutical companies promoted megavitamins and weight-reduction diets. Beginning in 1973 the Food and Drug Administration required exact nutrient labeling of all foods with added nutrients or nutritional claims. In 1977 the Senate Select Committee on Nutrition and Human Needs established quantitative goals for consumption of protein, carbohydrates, fat, fatty acids, cholesterol, sugars, and sodium. Nutritionists disagreed with some of the findings, and the U.S. Department of Agriculture

(USDA) found it impossible at the time to use the 1977 goals to revise its food guide, which had been in existence since 1916. The goals induced the department to pay more attention to health and to make more specific dietary recommendations to the public. Consequently, the department issued a series of dietary guidelines for maintenance of a healthy weight and a diet with a variety of foods, low in fat and cholesterol, and moderate in sugar, sodium, and alcoholic beverages.

Interest in promoting quantitative nutritional information prevailed. In 1990 Congress passed the Nutrition Labeling and Education Act, which required processed-food labels to state the amounts of daily intake of nutrients. The USDA had been working on the revision of its food guide for several years and issued its new food guide "pyramid" in 1992. This new daily guide and an accompanying brochure increased the categories of foods and drinks from four to six. The department recommended fats, oils, and sweets (sparingly); milk, yogurt, and cheese (two to three servings); meat, poultry, fish, dry beans, eggs, and nuts (two to three servings); vegetables (three to five servings); fruits (two to four servings); and bread, cereal, rice, and pasta (six to eleven servings). Of all the nutritional issues raised during this period, cholesterol received most attention from biomedical researchers. The Nobel Prize–winning (1985) cholesterol research of Doctors Michael S. Brown and Joseph Goldstein of the University of Texas Health Science Center in Dallas led to an understanding of the genetic involvement of cholesterol and ultimately to treatment for high blood cholesterol. Studies of cholesterol culminated in a 1985 conclusion by a conference sponsored by the National Institutes of Health that lowering blood cholesterol could prevent heart disease.

Consumption of excess fat also aroused concern. A 1991 survey of U.S. high school students by the Centers for Disease Control showed that a median of 69 percent reported eating two or fewer servings of high fat foods each day. The federal government established national health objectives for persons over two years of age to reduce fat in their diets and increase complex carbohydrate and fiber-containing foods. Meanwhile, the American Cancer Society listed among its goals a desire to bring up to 80 percent the proportion of teenagers eating no more than two servings a day of high fat foods. Thus, while Americans received more information about nutrition by the 1990s, the results seemed uncertain. One-third of all Americans were overweight, according to statistics released in 1994; reduction of fat consumption did not solve weight problems because sugars and carbohydrates also add weight to the consumer.

[J. Campana, "Participation in School Physical Education and Selected Dietary Patterns Among High School Students—United States, 1991," *Journal of the American Medical Association* 268 (Sept. 16, 1992); Susan O. Welsh et al., *USDA's Food Guide* (Hyattsville, Md., 1993); Jack Zeev Yetiv, *Popular Nutritional Practices* (Toledo, Ohio, 1986).]

RUTH ROY HARRIS

See also **SUPP:** Food, Fast; Health Food Industry.

O

OAKLAND, a major California urban area located on San Francisco Bay's east shore and the thirty-ninth largest city in the United States, had a population of 372,242 in 1990. African Americans made up 44 percent of the population and white residents one-third. The Asian (15 percent) and Hispanic (14 percent) communities have grown rapidly since the 1970s. Originally home to the Ohlone people, the area now comprising Oakland was included in an 1820 Spanish land grant given to Don Luis Maria Peralta. A supply and departure point for the 1849 gold rush, Oakland was chartered in 1852 and incorporated as a city in 1854. Selected as the western terminus of the first transcontinental railroad in 1869, the city grew as an industrial center in the early twentieth century. Attracting residents and businesses from across the bay following the 1906 earthquake, Oakland's growth accelerated during World War I and after the completion of the San Francisco–Oakland Bay Bridge in 1936. As a port for container ships and a railroad terminus, it serves as a link for Pacific trade. Although propelled by the World War II boom, Oakland has struggled since the 1960s. While manufacturing still accounts for one of every five jobs, plant closings and cutbacks cost the city 20 percent of its manufacturing jobs in the 1980s. Job growth was in the public sector and low-paying service and retail sectors. The local school system, suffering from inadequate resources, racial tensions, and mismanagement, was taken over by the state in 1989. Responding to neighborhood deterioration and declining public services, officials and residents initiated a variety of neighborhood organizations and development projects, such as Preservation Park. Oakland's troubles were compounded by the earthquake of 1989, during which the Nimitz Freeway collapsed, and wildfires in 1991. A center for African-American culture and politics, Oakland was the birthplace of the Black Panther Party in 1966. Since the 1970s African-American politicians have led the city government (Mayors Lionel Wilson and Elihu Harris) and represented Oakland in Congress (Democrat Ron Dellums). The city hosts a number of African-American museums and performing arts groups, as well as a variety of ethnic festivals. Oakland benefits from a temperate climate, striking natural features such as Lake Merritt, and ties to nearby cities through a complex of freeways, bridges, and the Bay Area Rapid Transit system.

[Beth Bagwell, *Oakland: The Story of a City* (Novato, Calif., 1982); Marilyn S. Johnson, *The Second Gold Rush: Oakland and the East Bay in World War II* (Berkeley, Calif., 1993).]

ERIC FURE-SLOCUM

See also **DAH** and **SUPP:** California; San Francisco; **SUPP:** Earthquakes.

OBSERVATORIES. In the first half of the twentieth century, U.S. astronomers were the world champions among builders of large telescopes. The 100-inch reflector at Mount Wilson Observatory, near Los Angeles, was a technological marvel when it opened in 1917. In 1948 a 200-inch reflector was completed at the Palomar Observatory outside San Diego. Astronomers continued to want larger telescopes to examine fainter and more distant celestial objects. Unfortunately, the technology of the 1950s through 1970s was not up to the task. Russian astronomers built a

236-inch telescope in the mid-1970s, but it proved too massive and unwieldy, and offered less-than-ideal performance. Later technology ushered in a new era of large-telescope building. In 1979 scientists at the University of Arizona and the Smithsonian Astrophysical Observatory completed the multiple-mirror telescope on Mount Hopkins near Tucson, Ariz. It combines six 72-inch mirrors into one instrument with the light-gathering power of a 176-inch telescope but the weight of the smaller one at Mount Wilson. Other new designs incorporate largely hollow, honeycomb (hexagonal) mirrors; very thin mirrors; or giant mirrors made from many smaller pieces. Simple, lightweight mountings controlled by computers can maintain the mirrors' precise optical shapes and keep the entire telescope pointed at a celestial target for hours at a time. By the year 2000 there should be at least ten telescopes around the world with apertures ranging from 250 to 630 inches. All but two will be built mainly by U.S. astronomers, although some will be located in other countries to study parts of the sky not visible from the United States. In 1991 the W. M. Keck Telescope atop Mauna Kea, Hawaii, became the world's largest at about 400 inches. A twin telescope (Keck II) was scheduled to open on the same site in 1996. Plans were drawn up in the early 1990s for the National Optical Astronomy Observatories to build two 300-inch reflectors, one each in the Northern and Southern Hemispheres, in the hope that astronomers could use these and other glass giants to solve cosmic mysteries.

[Kevin Krisciunas, *Astronomical Centers of the World* (New York, 1988).]

RICHARD TRESCH FIENBERG

See also **DAH:** Observatories, Astronomical; **DAH** and **SUPP:** Astronomy.

OCEANOGRAPHIC SURVEYS. Since the mid-nineteenth century oceanographic surveys for military, scientific, and commercial purposes by major countries of the world have proliferated, with the United States leading these efforts. Investigations have included the water masses, ocean floor, and ocean surface. Surveys by the U.S. Naval Oceanographic Office have covered a large portion of the major oceans. Since the 1970s massive data-gathering efforts have been made with great navigational precision. The U.S. military has employed satellites to measure ocean surface characteristics. Results are largely classified, although some of that data has been included in the maps and charts of the U.S.

Navy and the National Oceanic and Atmospheric Administration (NOAA). Information acquired by nonmilitary agencies and research groups has rivaled the amount collected by the military. In the mid-1990s academic researchers in the United States had available twenty-six research vessels and several research submarines as well as data from satellites of NOAA and the National Aeronautics and Space Administration. The U.S. Geological Survey published detailed bathymetric surveys (measurement of water depth) of much of the United States Exclusive Economic Zone, an area that extends 300 miles off the Atlantic, Gulf, Pacific, Alaskan, and Bering Sea coasts. Spatial locations are accurate to a few tens of meters. Data taken by the military services is deposited with the Defense Mapping Agency with offices in and near Washington, D.C. Federally funded civilian agencies or groups deposit their data at appropriate national archives, which include the National Geophysical Data Center (Boulder, Colo.), the National Oceanographic Data Center (Washington, D.C.), and the National Space Science Data Center (Greenbelt, Md.).

J. R. HEIRTZLER

See also **DAH:** Oceanographic Survey; **DAH** and **SUPP:** Oceanography.

OCEANOGRAPHY. Oceanographic science is divided into the subfields of physical, chemical, and biological oceanography and marine geology and geophysics. As an exact science oceanography began in the latter part of the nineteenth century when activities were directed at learning the depth of the oceans, their systems of currents and water masses, and major chemical and biological components. During World War II it became essential to understand the acoustic transmission properties of ocean waters for submarine warfare and to predict sea surface conditions for ocean ship traffic. In contrast, coastal oceanographic studies have always differed from deep-water oceanography because they are concerned with erosion and coastal damage. By the late 1950s a large amount of marine geophysical data had been collected, including measurements of the ocean floor's sediment thickness, magnetic field anomalies, and heat flow from the floor. With new knowledge about internal currents of the oceans, calculations of mass and energy balance could be made. The Global Positioning System, a method of determining one's latitude and longitude precisely by observing signals from U.S. Navy satellites whose orbits are accurately known, allowed a new precision (to a few dozen meters) in open-water navigation, and computers organized these data. It was possible to confirm theoretical ideas of sea floor spreading and continental drift.

In 1964 oceanographers initiated the Deep Sea Drilling Project, originally a cooperative endeavor between four U.S. oceanographic institutions. It was enlarged and sponsored by many U.S. institutions and several foreign governments. A large, specially equipped ship was used to drill holes of up to several kilometers in the ocean floors of the world. Drill cores were analyzed to determine ocean sediments and to reconstruct their history. This project, continued under the title of Ocean Drilling Project, has bored several thousand holes. Because ocean sediments have been laid down in a systematic manner and are less disturbed than sediments on land, core analysis has yielded much information on paleoceanography and paleoclimatology. Global change has been an important area of investigation since the 1960s, when man-made changes in the earth's atmosphere became evident. The oceans are believed to be an important sink (carbon is taken from the air by ocean surface water, which then sinks, thereby reducing carbon in the air) in the global carbon cycle, regulating the greenhouse effect. Oceanographers have also been observing a coupling of oceanic and atmospheric effects in the South Pacific called El Niño, which has far-reaching effects on fishing and climate.

In the 1970s oceanographers discovered geothermal vents at the axis of the midocean ridges. Ocean chemists and biologists found organisms there that receive nourishment directly from hydrogen sulfide rather than from photosynthetic processes. In another development, satellites that scan ocean color and temperature have enabled biologists to determine much about the biological productivity of the ocean surface layer. In the 1980s and 1990s an effort developed to coordinate oceanic cruises with special oceanic satellites. The cruises ensured temporal and global coverage (measuring all of the oceans at all times), while satellites recorded the variability of oceanic surface and atmospheric conditions. It was thereby possible to determine the elevation of the surface (accurate to a few centimeters), analyze ocean currents and their eddies, and learn details of the ocean floor as reflected in the shape of the ocean surface.

[National Research Council, *Oceanography in the Next Decade: Building New Partnerships* (Washington, D.C., 1992).]

J. R. HEIRTZLER

See also **SUPP:** Oceanographic Surveys.

OFFICE TECHNOLOGY evolved rapidly, beginning in the 1970s, and incorporated ever greater automation, principally through computers. The result was greater productivity as well as changes in work patterns. Offices have long relied upon telephones, copiers, and calculators, and when commercial computers appeared in the 1950s businesses were early customers for so-called mainframes, which are large devices that serve multiple users simultaneously and can store large quantities of data. Advancing technology has replaced mainframe computers in many offices. The first replacement was the minicomputer, smaller and less expensive than mainframes but still serving multiple users. In the 1980s microcomputers, also known as personal computers, supplanted mainframes and minicomputers. A personal computer generally has only one user, although advances in networks now allow users to communicate easily and share data. In 1977 Apple Computer introduced the first in a series of highly popular personal computers. International Business Machines (IBM), long the dominant maker of mainframes, launched its first personal computer in 1981. Although IBM computers have not captured a dominant share of the market, other companies copied IBM's technical standards. IBM-compatible computers and software prevail in U.S. offices today. Because of the large investment that companies have made in hardware, software, and employee training, IBM compatibles are likely to retain their market domination.

Early personal computers had only rudimentary capabilities, but engineers have radically improved the chip inside the device that serves as its processing unit. A typical computer on an office desk in the mid-1990s had more power than a 1960s-era mainframe. The wider availability of hardware also encouraged new software. A key example is the spreadsheet, developed for personal computers, which manipulates numerical data, such as in preparation of a budget. Spreadsheets can now accommodate text and graphics. The first spreadsheet was Lotus 1-2-3, which captured the lion's share of the market after 1982. Personal computers equipped with word-processing software and printers have virtually replaced typewriters. A computer can store an electronic copy of a document, making it easy to revise without retyping. Word-processing software frequently includes spell-checkers, which search for misspelled words and typographical errors. Another category of software attributable to the rise of personal computers is desktop publishing, in which an operator can produce a professional-quality document, such as a newsletter or book, that incorporates text, pictures, and graphics, without conventional printing equipment. Yet another type of office software is the database program, which stores information in retrievable fashion. Databases were available in some mainframes, but it was not until the advent of personal computers that software allowed searches for information that met wide specifications. The first database developed for personal computers was dBase, which became one of the most popular computer programs.

Another milestone in office technology was xerography, a copying process used in most photocopying machines. Xerox Corporation's 914 copier, the first xerographic office copier, appeared in 1959 and made seven copies per minute. Advances in computers and electronics breathed new life into the facsimile (fax) machine, developed early in the century. In the 1980s technology expanded the capability of fax machines, and industry-wide design standards ensured that virtually all fax machines could communicate with one another, transmitting pictures and text digitally over telephone wires. Developments in computers and telecommunications led to voice mail, answering machines shared by all telephones in offices that offer individualized messages for each phone, and electronic mail (E-mail), messages sent between computer users via a computer data network. Advances in miniaturization of electronic components made possible mobile devices, such as the laptop computer, the beeper, and the hand-held cellular phone. New techniques for mass-producing inexpensive communication satellites have encouraged companies to plan global satellite networks that allow executives to communicate with home offices at any time from any point on the planet.

[U.S. Congress, Office of Technology Assessment, *Automation of America's Offices* (Washington, D.C., 1985).]

VINCENT KIERNAN

See also **SUPP:** Communications Industry; Computers; Electronic Mail; Internet; Telecommunications.

OFFSHORE OIL and gas development in the United States since the mid-1970s has been shaped largely by tensions generated by the efforts of the federal government to reduce dependence on foreign oil on one hand and pressures from environmentalists and conservationists to reduce energy consumption, especially of fossil fuels, on the other. Except during the Arab oil embargo of 1973–1974 and the U.S. embargo on Iranian oil, in effect from 1979 to 1981, the trend in the industry has been toward low prices and oversupply of foreign crude oil. It was not until the oil shocks of the 1970s that there was an incentive to expand offshore exploration and production. With the low prices that have prevailed since 1986, expensive and labor-intensive recovery techniques have lost their economic feasibility. Since the 1970s U.S. energy policy has emphasized environmental protection and the conservation of U.S. reserves. The federal government has developed stringent environmental regulations governing the exploration and development of offshore crude oil fields in the lower forty-eight states and in Alaska. Opposition to offshore drilling is strong, especially in California, where there are large untapped offshore reserves. As early as 1975 California's State Lands Commission halted drilling of fifty-three offshore wells in the Santa Barbara Channel, and the National Energy Policy Act of 1992 came close to banning offshore drilling. Federal regulations imposed a leasing moratorium on sections of the Outer Continental Shelf and in the Arctic National Wildlife Refuge east of Alaska's Prudhoe Bay.

[Michael L. Godec and Khosrow Biglarbig, "Economic Effects of Environmental Regulations on Finding and Developing Crude Oil in the U.S.," *Journal of Petroleum Technology* 43 (1991).]

STEPHEN J. RANDALL

See also **DAH** and **SUPP:** Petroleum Industry; **SUPP:** Energy, Renewable; Energy Policy; Oil Crises.

OHIO entered the 1970s after three decades of economic and population growth, propelled by World War II and the postwar expansion of its large industrial sector. Employment peaked in 1967, however, and by the early 1990s had declined by more than 25 percent. Although Ohio's 1990 population of more than 10.8 million was slightly higher than it had been twenty years earlier, the state dropped in rank to seventh place, falling behind Texas and Florida. With the decline of the steel, automobile, and rubber industries, large industrial cities such as Cleveland, Akron, and Youngstown lost population. Only the state capital, Columbus, countered the downward urban trend, thanks in part to aggressive annexation of suburbs. Despite some gentrification—the return of middle- and upper-income persons to restored neighborhoods—Ohio's largest cities followed the national pattern of housing a disproportionate number of the poor and unskilled. Increasingly, jobs as well as people migrated to the suburbs, which now include retail and commercial centers that equal or even eclipse the older downtown core areas. Ohio's central cities responded by trying to revitalize downtown areas with office, retail, and residential construction. Success was mixed but certain entertainment and business activities remained uniquely situated in urban centers, ensuring continued vitality.

The quest for economic development has been a theme in state politics since 1970. Political leaders used incentives, such as tax concessions, employee training, and infrastructure improvements, to hold on to old industries while luring in new ones. These efforts did not completely reverse underlying trends, but there were notable successes, such as the decision of the Japanese carmaker Honda to locate most of its U.S. manufacturing in Ohio in the early 1980s. Much of this job growth occurred in rural and small-town areas where pressures for unionization and higher wage levels were weaker.

Historically, Ohio politics have followed moderately conservative lines, and pragmatic considerations have been important. Known as a bellwether Republican state in the early twentieth century, Ohio began to shift toward the Democrats in the 1940s, and by the 1970s and 1980s the Democratic Party was leading the state in the direction of liberal reform. During the administration of Governor John J. Gilligan (1971–1975), Ohio joined other industrial states in levying a personal income tax. With the support of organized labor, Gilligan used the increased revenue to improve state services. In 1972 the Democrats gained control of the state legislature, and Vernal G. Riffe, Jr., speaker of the Ohio House of Representatives (1975–1994), became a powerful figure in allocating state resources. The popular Republican governor of the 1960s, James A. Rhodes, returned to office with a narrow victory over Gilligan in 1974. Rhodes's decision to send National Guard troops to quell student unrest at Kent State University in 1970, which culminated in the deaths of four students, tarnished his record as the longest-serving governor in Ohio history (1963–1971, 1975–1983). Ironically, a tremendous expansion in public higher education was one of his greatest achievements as governor. In the 1970s and 1980s he also emphasized economic development, such as negotiations with Honda and other Japanese firms. Democratic Governor Richard F. Celeste, elected in the midst of the severe economic recession of the early 1980s, emphasized further liberal reform, supporting a move to allow state employees to strike and increasing state programs. A former Rhodes scholar and Peace Corps director, he injected a new style into Ohio politics.

Scandals involving his political backers, such as the Home State Savings collapse in 1985 and some political appointments, tarnished his overall record.

At the national level Ohio's political leaders were not as prominent in leadership as in earlier times. In 1973, during the Watergate crisis, Senator William B. Saxbe resigned to become the last attorney general in President Richard M. Nixon's beleaguered administration, a position he retained during part of Gerald R. Ford's presidency. John H. Glenn, the first U.S. astronaut to orbit the Earth, became the first Ohio senator elected to a fourth consecutive term in 1992. He had made little headway, however, in his unsuccessful bid for the 1984 presidential nomination. The more liberal Howard M. Metzenbaum retired from the U.S. Senate in 1994 after three terms. Supported by organized labor and liberal interest groups, he often challenged business corporations. Lagging population growth between 1970 and 1992 reduced Ohio's delegation in the House of Representatives from twenty-four to nineteen.

Compared to other states, Ohio's moderate politics usually did not place it in the forefront of progressive innovation, but changes since the 1970s have led Ohioans to expect more help from government in enhancing the quality of life. One such area of concern has been environmental protection. By the late 1960s lack of attention had given Ohio a national reputation for dirty air and water, best symbolized by the "death" of Lake Erie and the 1969 fire on the Cuyahoga River in Cleveland. The state legislature created the Ohio Environmental Protection Agency, and in 1972 a strip mining reclamation program. By the 1990s billions of dollars had been spent on cleanups. Air quality showed improvement, especially in the heavily industrial Upper Ohio Valley. Concern remained about hazardous waste dumps (subject to regulation through the federal Superfund program) and the quality of drinking water. Still, Lake Erie and the state's rivers had improved so substantially that they were once again viable resources. In 1974 Congress established Ohio's first national park, the Cuyahoga Valley National Recreation Area, 32,512 acres of scenic gorge and forest land located near the 4 million residents of the Cleveland and Akron metropolitan areas.

Education was another area of concern to Ohioans. In the post–World War II era, Ohio led the national average in rates of high-school graduation but lagged in college attendance, a predictable pattern in a state with a large blue-collar workforce. State support for elementary and secondary education increased after 1970, but much of the money continued to come from local property taxes, with a resulting disparity between wealthier and poorer districts. Proceeds from the state lottery, begun in 1974, were earmarked for education but represented a small part of the state's contribution. Teachers demanded higher salaries and in some communities defied the ban on strikes. Problems involving finances, declining student achievement, drugs, and violence were acute in urban districts, but few if any schools were immune from such woes. In the 1990s judicial remedies were introduced to address the problem of inequitable funding. Beginning in 1994 high-school graduation was denied any Ohio student who failed mandated examinations in mathematics, reading, writing, and citizenship. Meanwhile, like most other states, Ohio attacked its crime problem with a massive increase in prison construction. In 1990 a Republican former mayor of Cleveland who had worked actively to revitalize that city in the 1980s, George V. Voinovich, succeeded Governor Celeste. Voinovich promised to "do more with less" by maintaining and managing state programs efficiently, without major tax increases. Republicans looked forward to the prospect of other electoral gains, as leading Democrats retired and others faced questions regarding conduct in office. The Ohio legislature passed a more stringent ethics enactment in 1994.

[George W. Knepper, *Ohio and Its People* (Kent, Ohio, 1989); Carl Lieberman, ed., *Government and Politics in Ohio* (Lanham, Md., 1984); Leonard Peacefull, ed., *The Changing Heartland: A Geography of Ohio* (Needham Heights, Mass., 1990).]

JOHN B. WEAVER

See also **SUPP:** Cincinnati; Cleveland; Columbus; Rustbelt; Superfund; Toledo.

OIL CRISES. In 1973–1974 and 1979 the United States experienced shortages of gasoline and other petroleum products because of reduced domestic oil production, greater dependence on imported oil, and political developments in the oil-rich Middle East. Historically, the United States had supplied most of its own oil, but in 1970 U.S. oil production reached full capacity. Imported oil, especially from the Middle East, rose from 19 percent of national consumption in 1967 to 36 percent in 1973. The Arab-Israeli War of 1973 contributed to the first oil crisis. At that time, Saudi Arabia controlled 21 percent of the world's oil exports. After Egypt and Syria attacked Israel in October and the United States came

to Israel's aid, oil ministers from the five Persian Gulf states and Iran cut their monthly production by 5 percent to discourage international support for Israel. They banned oil exports to Israel's allies, including the United States, the Netherlands, Portugal, South Africa, and Rhodesia (Zimbabwe). World oil prices jumped from $5.40 per barrel to more than $17. Retail gasoline prices in the United States increased 40 percent, and consumers often faced long lines at service stations. To conserve gasoline and oil, President Richard M. Nixon reduced the speed limit on national highways to 55 miles per hour and encouraged people to carpool and to lower their house thermostats. It was Israeli victories and U.S. arrangement of Arab-Israeli negotiations and not domestic programs, however, that helped end the embargo in March 1974.

The Organization of Petroleum Exporting Countries (OPEC) continued to keep world oil prices high, which slowed the world economy. In 1973–1975 the U.S. gross national product declined by 6 percent and unemployment doubled to 9 percent. The economies of Europe and Japan also suffered, but the developing countries that lacked money to pay for expensive oil suffered most. In 1975 Congress established fuel-efficiency standards for U.S. automobiles to reduce energy costs and dependency on foreign oil. President Jimmy Carter urged additional steps. By the late 1970s the United States was exploring both old (coal) and new (solar, thermal, and wind) sources of energy.

A second oil crisis followed the collapse of the government of the shah of Iran and suspension of Iran's oil exports in December 1978. Iran was the world's second-largest exporter of oil. If buyers, including oil companies, manufacturers, and national governments had not panicked, however, this second oil shortage would not have been so severe. Gasoline prices rose, and people again waited in lines at service stations. These factors, combined with the hostage crisis in Iran, contributed to President Carter's defeat in the 1980 election. The worst of the second crisis was over by 1980. In late 1985 a drop in world oil prices (from $32 to $10 per barrel) gave American consumers a sense that the crisis had ended, but concerns about the increasing U.S. dependence on foreign oil remained in the 1990s.

[Daniel Yergin, *The Prize: The Epic Quest for Oil, Money, and Power* (New York, 1991).]

KENNETH B. MOSS

See also **SUPP:** Energy Industry; Energy Policy; Hostage Crises; Middle East, Relations with; Petroleum Industry.

OIL INDUSTRY. *See* **Offshore Oil; Oil Crises; Petroleum Industry.**

OKLAHOMA, the Sooner state, lies between the Midwest and South, the Great Plains and the arid Southwest. The rolling, tree-covered hills of its eastern and southern counties resemble the Ozark regions of bordering Missouri and Arkansas. As it follows an upward slope to the north and west the land becomes more level, the rainfall much lighter, and the trees and streams scarce. The western and panhandle counties are extensions of the Texas plains and Kansas prairies. The entire western half is one of the nation's leading producers of winter wheat and beef cattle, both increasingly capital-intensive industries. Agriculture in the eastern section tends to be more diverse but less demanding of heavy investment. One consequence is that per capita incomes are almost always higher in western than in eastern counties. Ironically, although both areas lost population, the western counties were most affected by a steady depopulation trend that began with the Great Depression and accelerated thereafter. In both cases the migrants generally preferred to stay close to home, which is why Oklahoma City, Tulsa, and other cities experienced slow but consistent growth between 1970 and the mid-1990s. During that period the state population increased from just over 2.5 million to 3.1 million. Its Native American population (252,089 in 1990) was the largest in the nation.

Those years also witnessed a continuation of the state's familiar pattern of boom and bust economic cycles. Massive grain sales to the Soviet Union and others pushed wheat and other grain prices to near-record levels during the 1970s. At the same time, the 1973 Arab oil embargo and insatiable energy demands propelled crude oil prices to unheard-of levels. At the decade's end unemployment was all but nonexistent in the state, per capita income for the first time reached the national average, public services expanded, and teachers and other public employees moved toward competitive salaries.

All of that changed abruptly in the mid-1980s. International oil prices dropped from a 1978 high of $42 per barrel to $30.90 in November 1985. Within seven months, they slid to $10.25. Grain prices took similar hits as the price of wheat plummeted in a matter of months from $5.60 per bushel to $2.70 by the summer of 1986. The effects were felt in every sector of the state's economy. Oil industry jobs evaporated by the tens of thousands. Family farms, many of them dating to the famous nineteenth-century land runs, disappeared. Merchants and others dependent upon the regular flow of oil and wheat money went bankrupt. Before it was over, auto dealerships, implement sellers, entire shopping malls, and several dozen state banks all had gone under. The collapse of one of those banks—Oklahoma City's Penn Square Bank—was the first domino to fall in a chain of bank failures that went on to claim as its final and greatest casualty what had been the nation's fourth-largest bank, Continental Bank of Illinois.

The economic disorder magnified and accelerated changes already transforming state politics. With rare exceptions, Oklahoma had been part of the Democratic Solid South since it entered the Union in 1907. This pattern remained unchanged until Oklahoma's electoral votes went to Republican Dwight D. Eisenhower in the 1950s and then Richard M. Nixon in 1960. Subsequent elections proved these were no temporary aberrations. Lyndon B. Johnson returned Oklahoma to the Democratic column in 1964 as part of his national landslide, but Johnson proved to be the only Democrat to win Oklahoma's electoral votes between 1952 and 1992, a record of Republican support exceeded only by that of Arizona. "Presidential Republicanism" quickly became gubernatorial and senatorial Republicanism. Sooners elected their first Republican governor in 1962 and voted Republican in the next three gubernatorial elections. The GOP also claimed seven of the ten races for U.S. Senate seats between 1968 and 1995. In the latter year Republicans held the governorship, both Senate seats, and five of six House seats.

The shift in party dominance owed much to the increasingly conservative national mood and to Oklahoma's economic dislocations. During the boom years, the state coffers were full. When the collapse came, the government suddenly was confronted with a staggering $350 million annual shortfall. Disaster was averted only by two bitterly fought tax increases recommended by a Republican governor (Henry Bellmon) and approved by Democratic legislatures. Taxpayers thereupon exercised their traditionally populist aversion to taxes and politicians and amended the constitution to limit legislative terms and require voter approval of nearly all subsequent tax increases.

In the 1970s and 1980s voters were further angered by a series of political scandals. The largest of these involved the state's county commissioners, who fell victim to a Justice Department probe that uncovered years of systematic corruption, primarily involving contracting kickbacks. In all, between 1977 and

1987, 246 sitting officials were convicted of federal crimes, and a number of others were convicted of state offenses, including two governors, a speaker of the state house, and several state legislators, whose misdeeds ranged from election rigging to narcotics trafficking.

[W. David Baird and Danney Goble, *The Story of Oklahoma* (Norman, Okla., 1994); David R. Morgan, Robert E. England, and George G. Humphreys, *Oklahoma Politics and Policies* (Lincoln, Nebr., 1991); Howard F. Stein and Robert F. Hills, eds., *The Culture of Oklahoma* (Norman, Okla., 1993).]

DANNEY GOBLE

See also **SUPP:** Oklahoma City; Oklahoma City Bombing; Tulsa.

OKLAHOMA CITY, capital of the state of Oklahoma, sprang into existence with the land run of April 22, 1889, when more than 10,000 settlers established a tent city on the site in one day. From the beginning its government was dominated by businessmen, who scored a coup in 1910 when they wrested the state capital from Guthrie. With the discovery of oil in 1928, Oklahoma City's economy came to rest primarily on oil-related activities and its politics controlled by oilmen, bankers, and merchants. Since the 1970s fluctuating international oil prices created a boom-and-bust economic cycle. In politics Republicans asserted their domination of the city, using the rising prosperity to attract voters and then blaming the decline on Washington and Oklahoma's long tradition of Democratic rule. The population in 1990 was 450,000: 74 percent white, 16 percent African American, 5 percent Hispanic, and 4 percent Native American. Oklahoma City was rather typical of the nation's medium-sized cities, except that the median household income did not place it in the top 500 of U.S. cities.

[Odie B. Faulk et al., *Oklahoma City* (Northridge, Calif., 1988).]

DANNEY GOBLE

See also **DAH** and **SUPP:** Oklahoma; **SUPP:** Oklahoma City Bombing.

OKLAHOMA CITY BOMBING (April 19, 1995), in which a bomb composed of a fertilizer called ammonium nitrate mixed with fuel oil destroyed the Alfred P. Murrah federal building in Oklahoma City, Okla., killing 168 people, including fifteen children in a day-care center. The building housed branches of federal departments including the Bureau of Alcohol, Tobacco, and Firearms, thought initially to be the target of the bomb. The worst act of terrorism in U.S. history, the blast sent Americans into mourning and deep apprehension over civil disorder. President Bill Clinton led a national day of sorrow on Sunday, April 23. For seventeen days after the explosion rescue teams from around the nation combed the rubble seeking survivors and excavating bodies, often under hazardous conditions. Shortly after the blast Federal Bureau of Investigation agents arrested Timothy McVeigh, a former U.S. Army sergeant with extreme right-wing views, as the principal suspect in the bombing. McVeigh, authorities believed, rented a truck in Kansas, filled it with the combustible mixture, and drove it to Oklahoma City. He allegedly parked the truck in front of the Murrah building, lit the fuse, and walked away; witnesses identified him at the scene. Federal authorities believed he acted to avenge destruction of the Branch Davidian cult in Waco, Tex., which took place on the same date two years earlier, and because he feared federal revocation of the constitutional right to carry guns. On Aug. 16 McVeigh and a friend from his time in the army, Terry Nichols, were arraigned in federal court under extraordinary security; both pleaded not guilty to charges that they had carried out the terrorist attack in Oklahoma City. Another army friend, Michael Fortier, under threat of indictment, testified to government officials against McVeigh and Nichols. Fortier reportedly was promised lesser charges in exchange for testimony. After eliminating leads concerning other unknown participants (John Does) in the bombing, federal investigators declared that McVeigh and Nichols acted alone and not in conspiracy with any organization. Attorney General Janet Reno announced that the government would seek the death penalty if the pair were convicted. McVeigh's extreme views directed media attention to conservative radio talk-show hosts and "citizen militias" vowing to execute federal agents infringing Second Amendment Rights, although all disavowed any connection with the bombing. Incredibly, one talk-show host blamed the government for the explosion while another, G. Gordon Liddy, advised on the best methods to assassinate federal agents. The FBI sought links between McVeigh and far-right militia groups. President Clinton called for stronger antiterrorist laws, although support for additional statutes was lukewarm among Republicans and civil rights proponents.

GRAHAM RUSSELL HODGES

See also **SUPP**: Militias; Oklahoma City; Terrorism; Waco Siege.

OLYMPIC GAMES. By the 1970s the Olympics had become the largest multisport event in the world and through satellite technology attracted a worldwide television audience. The 1972 Olympic Winter Games were held in Sapporo, Japan, the first Winter Games awarded to an Asian city. Unprecedented achievement and controversy occurred at the 1972 Summer Games in Munich, Germany. U.S. swimmer Mark Spitz won a record seven gold medals, while his teammates lost the first-ever Olympic basketball game in a controversial gold medal contest with the Soviet Union. A tragic event cast a pall over the Munich games when on Sept. 5, 1972, Palestinian terrorists kidnapped and murdered eleven members of the Israeli team. Competition was suspended for an entire day, although a call to discontinue the games was ignored by International Olympic Committee (IOC) President Avery Brundage of the United States. Amid tight security, in 1976 a thousand athletes from thirty-seven countries gathered for the Winter Games at Innsbruck, Austria. The Summer Games later that year in Montreal were mired in debt and reduced international interest in hosting the Olympics. In the summer of 1978 the United States Olympic Committee (USOC) moved its headquarters from New York City to Colorado Springs. The Amateur Sports Act, enacted by Congress in 1978, named the USOC the coordinating body of sports in the Pan American Games and the Winter and Summer Olympics and recognized national governing bodies for sports in these competitions.

At the 1980 Winter Games in Lake Placid, N.Y., U.S. speed skater Eric Heiden won an unprecedented five gold medals, and the U.S. hockey team won its first gold medal in twenty years with a dramatic final-round victory over the Soviet Union. Because of the Soviet invasion of Afghanistan, President Jimmy Carter called for a boycott of the 1980 Moscow Summer Olympics. For the first time in modern Olympic history, the United States, joined by sixty-one other boycotting nations, did not participate.

A turning point in the Olympics occurred in 1984 when the Los Angeles Summer Olympics, although boycotted by the Soviet Union and most other eastern bloc countries, produced a $225 million profit, largely because of the contributions of commercial sponsors. Joan Benoit won the first women's Olympic marathon, and the U.S. women's basketball team

claimed the first gold medal by the United States in that competition. The U.S. women's basketball team took the gold again in 1988, as did the men's basketball team in 1984 and 1992. Sprinter and long jumper Carl Lewis began his collection of Olympic gold medals by winning four in Los Angeles. He added two more gold medals and a silver medal in 1988 and claimed two more gold medals in 1992. Also at Los Angeles, Mary Lou Retton won the first gold medal in women's gymnastics. A highlight for the U.S. team during the 1984 winter competition, held in Sarajevo, Yugoslavia, was the gold medal victory in the men's figure skating competition by Scott Hamilton, who had begun ice skating as therapy for an intestinal disorder.

Four years later the games were held in Calgary, Alberta, Canada. For a decade Brian Boitano of the United States and Brian Orser of Canada had been figure skating rivals, and in 1988 both skaters presented exemplary performances, but Boitano edged out Orser for the gold medal. By the time of the 1988 Summer Olympics in Seoul, South Korea, professional athletes had become more visible in the Olympic movement. The IOC had decided to let professionals participate in the Olympic Games in an effort to attract the best athletes. Diver Greg Louganis became the second U.S. Olympian to achieve a "double-double," when he repeated his 1984 victories in springboard and platform diving at the Seoul Olympics. Louganis's springboard victory came a day after he accidentally hit and cut his head on the board during a dive, an event that gained significance in 1995, when Louganis revealed publicly that he was aware at the time that he was HIV-positive but did not inform the physicians who treated him. Also in 1988 Jackie Joyner-Kersee began her dominance of the heptathlon and made two additional Olympic appearances, winning two gold medals and a silver in the event.

The CBS television network paid $243 million for the rights to televise the 1992 Albertville Winter Games in France, while NBC paid a record $401 million to televise the 1992 Summer Olympics in Barcelona, Spain, the last time that summer and winter competitions were held in the same year. The IOC voted to separate the competitions by two years in order to generate more television revenue. In 1992 Kristi Yamaguchi became the first American woman since Dorothy Hamill to win an Olympic figure skating title. At the 1992 Summer Olympics in Barcelona the U.S. basketball team, composed of professional players (the "Dream Team"), won the gold medal.

Three-time gold medal winner Bonnie Blair became the leading gold medalist among American women when she won two more gold medals in speed skating at the 1994 Winter Games in Lillehammer, Norway. Tommy Moe became the first American downhill skiing gold medalist since Bill Johnson a decade earlier; he also won a silver medal in the super giant slalom. After two disappointing Olympic appearances, Dan Jansen, in his last Olympic race, finally reached the top of the medal podium, winning the 1,000-meter speed skating championship in Lillehammer. In an incident that attracted widespread attention in the weeks leading up to Lillehammer, U.S. figure skater Nancy Kerrigan was attacked during the Olympic trials and sustained a leg injury. The husband of rival U.S. figure skater Tanya Harding was later convicted of conspiring to injure Kerrigan. Because the USOC did not have evidence to implicate Tanya Harding, she was allowed to compete in Lillehammer. Kerrigan claimed her second singles silver medal, while Harding finished in sixth place. Harding was later implicated in the plot to injure Kerrigan and was expelled from the U.S. Figure Skating Association, thus ending her amateur career.

The 1996 centennial Olympics were awarded to Atlanta, Ga., and the 1998 Winter Games to Nagano, Japan.

U.S. gold medalists from 1984 to 1994 were:

Archery: Darrell Pace (1984); Jay Barrs (1988).

Boxing: Tyrell Biggs (1984); Mark Breland (1984); Paul Gonzales (1984); Steven McCrory (1984); Meldrick Taylor (1984); Jerry Page (1984); Frank Tate (1984); Henry Tillman (1984); Pernell Whitaker (1984); Andrew Maynard (1988); Kennedy McKinney (1988); Ray Mercer (1988); Oscar De La Hoya (1992).

Canoeing: Greg Barton (1988); Joe Jacobi and Scott Strausbaugh (1992).

Cycling: Connie Carpenter-Phinney (1984); Alexi Grewal (1984); Mark Gorski (1984); Steve Hegg (1984).

Diving: Greg Louganis (1984, 1988); Mark Lenzi (1992).

Equestrian: Karen Stives (1984); U.S. team jumping and three-day event team classification (1984).

Figure Skating: Scott Hamilton (1984); Brian Boitano (1988); Kristi Yamaguchi (1992).

Gymnastics: Mary Lou Retton (1984); Bart Conner (1984); Trent Diamas (1992).

Rowing: U.S. women's eight-oar team (1984).

Shooting: Pat Spurgin (1984); Matthew Dryke (1984); Edward Etzel (1984); Launi Meili (1992).

Skiing: Bill Johnson (1984); Phil Mahre (1984); Donna Weinbrecht (1992); Diann Roffe-Steinrotter (1994); Tommy Moe (1994).

Speed Skating: Eric Heiden (1980); Bonnie Blair (1988, 1992, 1994); Cathy Turner (1992, 1994); Dan Jansen (1994).

Swimming: Theresa Andrews (1984); Tracy Caulkins (1984); Tiffany Cohen (1984); Mary T. Meagher (1984); Carrie Steinseiffer (1984); Mary Wayte (1984); U.S. women's relay teams (1984, 1992); Janet Evans (1988, 1992); Nicole Haislett (1992); Summer Sanders (1992); Mike Barrowman (1992); Matthew Biondi (1984, 1988, 1992); Richard Carey (1984); George DiCarlo (1984); Steve Lindquist (1984); Pablo Morales (1984, 1992); Michael O'Brien (1984); U.S. men's relay teams (1984, 1988, 1992); Nelson Diebel (1992); Mel Stewart (1992).

Synchronized Swimming: Candy Costie (1984); Tracie Ruiz (1984); Kristen Bob-Sprague (1992); Karen and Sarah Josephson (1992).

Tennis: Zina Garrison (1988); Pam Shriver (1988); Ken Flach (1988); Robert Seguso (1988); Jennifer Capriati (1992); Gigi Fernandez (1992); Mary Jo Ferguson (1992).

Track and Field: Evelyn Ashford (1984, 1988, 1992); Joan Benoit (1984); Valerie Brisco-Hooks (1984); Benita Fitzgerald-Brown; Florence Griffith Joyner (1988); Jackie Joyner-Kersee (1988, 1992); Louise Ritter (1988); Gail Devers (1992); Gwen Torrence (1992); U.S. women's relay teams (1984, 1988, 1992); Alonzo Babers (1984); Al Joyner (1984); Roger Kingdom (1984, 1988); Carl Lewis (1984, 1988, 1992); Edwin Moses (1984); Joe DeLoach (1988), Steven Lewis (1988); Andre Phillips (1988); Mike Conley (1992); Mike Marsh (1992); Mike Stulce (1992); U.S. men's relay teams (1984, 1988, 1992); Quincy Watts (1992); Kevin Young (1992).

Wrestling: Ed Banach (1984); Lou Banach (1984); Bruce Baumgartner (1984, 1992); Jeffrey Blatnick (1984); Steven Fraser (1984); Randy Lewis (1984); David Schultz (1984); Mark Schultz (1984); Robert Weaver (1984); Kenneth Monday (1988); John Smith (1988, 1992); Kevin Jackson (1992).

Yachting: U.S. teams (1984, 1988, 1992).

[International Olympic Committee, *Olympic Charter* (Lausanne, Switzerland, 1992); U.S. Olympic Committee, *Legacy of Gold* (Clearwater, Fla., 1992).]

PAULA D. WELCH

See also **SUPP:** Sports, New; and individual sports.

OMAHA, founded on July 2, 1854, in the newly established Nebraska Territory at a ferry crossing on the Missouri River, was a frontier village when eastern capitalists selected it as the eastern terminus of the first transcontinental railroad, the Union Pacific, constructed between 1862 and 1869. Omaha, located across the Missouri River from Council Bluffs, Iowa, had no special natural advantages, but Omaha was at the start of the Mormon Trail and was the winter quarters for Mormon migrants heading for Utah in 1846–1848. Omaha served as the capital of the territory until 1867, when Nebraska became a state, and was incorporated as a city that same year. During the last quarter of the nineteenth century, the city became an important transportation and meat-packing center and overcame severe depression conditions in the 1890s. A symbol of Omaha's recovery was the highly successful Trans-Mississippi and International Exposition of 1898. Between 1900 and 1940 Omaha's population increased from 102,555 to 223,844, and the city endured social and racial tensions. In 1909 rioters drove several hundred Greek immigrants out of town, and in 1919 a mob estimated at 20,000 watched the brutal lynching of a suspected African-American rapist. A powerful political machine, headed by Thomas Dennison, dominated Omaha politics during the first thirty years of the twentieth century. The conservative business community fought hard but unsuccessfully to keep out unions. The economy surged following the outbreak of World War II, led by construction of a bomber plant that employed 20,000 workers. In the immediate postwar period the Strategic Air Command moved its headquarters to the Omaha area at Offutt Air Force Base. In the 1950s and 1960s new agribusiness endeavors contributed to the steady expansion of the private sector. Federal projects, especially highway construction, funneled great sums into Omaha. Although most of the packing plants closed in the 1960s, a large insurance industry flourished, and corporations established regional headquarters in Omaha. In 1990, with a population of 335,719, Omaha was the center of a metropolitan area of 639,580.

[Lawrence H. Larsen and Barbara J. Cottrell, *The Gate City: A History of Omaha* (Boulder, Colo., 1982).]

LAWRENCE H. LARSEN

See also **SUPP: Nebraska.**

OPEC. *See* **Middle East, Relations with; Oil Crises; Petroleum Industry.**

OPINION POLLS in the United States primarily involve measuring public views through surveys. Polling gained legitimacy after the 1936 presidential election, when three pollsters, including George H. Gallup, correctly predicted Franklin D. Roosevelt's victory. The *Literary Digest* incorrectly picked Roosevelt's opponent, basing its forecast on responses mailed in by 2 million Americans. The pollsters instead used scientific sampling, which established that predictions made from polling a small random sample, usually 1,200 people, can be equally or more valid than asking a million respondents. When pollsters incorrectly predicted the 1948 presidential election results, picking George Dewey over Harry S. Truman, it was not because samples were too small but because they were improperly drawn and thus not representative. The 1948 embarrassment led to procedures that resulted in increasing acceptance. Polling organizations now emphasize reliability, whether similar results would occur if the same survey was conducted repeatedly, and validity, whether the survey measured what it was designed to measure.

From its onset, polling raised concerns about the effect on voting and other public behavior. Some early critics argued that polls did not merely measure opinion but affected it. Later research found that while voters may be influenced by poll results early in a campaign, the effects decrease as election day nears. Many observers voiced concerns following the 1980 presidential election about exit polling, interviews conducted as people left voting sites, fearing that early reports of the results could affect voter turnout in later time zones. Although exit polls are still conducted, many feel that their impact has been exaggerated. Of greater concern during and since the presidency of Ronald Reagan (1981–1989) has been the inclusion of communication, polling, and media specialists in the White House who have become barriers between the president and the public. The combined expertise of these specialists, who favor nostalgic posturing, sound bites, and negative advertising, may be responsible for even lower voter turnout. After reaching new heights in the 1988 and 1992 presidential campaigns, negative ads and polls influenced by them became even more prevalent in the 1994 midterm elections when 70 percent of campaign budgets for national office went to media and polling consultants. "There's not a competitive race in the country that doesn't use a poll," Democratic pollster Mark Mellman said in 1994, adding, "You've got to point out the faults of your opponent or you'll get creamed." The marketing of modern politicians as though they were commercial products, using computerized mass mailings and phone banks, minimizes discussion of serious issues, dehumanizes politics, and devalues leadership. As of the mid-1990s neither the American people nor their elected representatives seemed prepared to question the impact of polling and negative advertising on the U.S. political system.

KATHLEEN B. CULVER

See also **DAH:** Public Opinion; **SUPP:** Campaigns, Presidential.

OPTICS, FIBER. *See* **Fiber Optics.**

OPTIONS EXCHANGES. In the increasingly complex U.S. financial markets, options are a major innovation. Option trading began in the United States in 1973 with the opening of the Chicago Board Option Exchange. The logic of the option market is simple but the dynamics are difficult for the average investor to understand. An option gives a purchaser the right to buy or sell a specified security (or commodity) during a particular time for a specific amount. An option is attractive to institutional investors who want to reduce risks by protecting against major price changes and market fluctuation. Options exchanges are in most major financial markets including those in New York, Chicago, Philadelphia, Minneapolis, Kansas City, and San Francisco. Options are sold on major stock indexes, bonds, foreign currencies, and commodities. The option buyer makes a calculated decision on what direction—up or down—the actual price change for the security or commodity will go. Buyers purchases "call" options if they want to buy during the specified period, or "put" options if they want to sell. Buyers pay close attention to the exercise price, that is, the price at which the stock can be bought (call) or sold (put). An exercise price determines when the option can be executed. Failure to reach the price on a put can result in a quick and severe loss. Options are different from futures contracts that obligate both buyers and sellers to purchases and prices at a later date. Although they are listed in the major financial newspapers along with stocks and mutual funds, options clearly are for sophisticated investors. The volume of options contracts grew dramatically with the development of more options offered along with investor education and confidence. Option volumes in 1995 were expected to exceed the previous record of 164 million contracts set in 1987.

[Merton H. Miller, *Financial Innovations and Market Volatility* (Cambridge, Mass., 1991).]

BRENT SCHONDELMEYER

See also **SUPP:** Banking and Finance; Financial Exchanges; Financial Services Industry; Wall Street.

OREGON. Although more than 90 percent of Oregon's 1994 population of 3,080,000 was white, minority groups have grown in numbers since the 1960s and have obtained greater political and economic opportunities. Hispanic Americans, once largely migratory workers, have settled as permanent residents and in the 1990s made up the state's largest minority. African Americans worked to obtain their civil rights through such organizations as the National Association for the Advancement of Colored People, the Urban League, and the Black United Front. Several Native-American tribes, including the Siletz, Grande Ronde, and Klamath, reorganized in order to obtain recognition from the federal government, which carries economic benefits. Support of public libraries and bookstores is far above the national average, and Oregonians have attained national and international distinction in literature and the arts. Don Berry published a trilogy of historical novels about the pioneer era including *Trask, Moontrap,* and *To Build a Ship,* while Ken Kesey received acclaim for *One Flew Over the Cuckoo's Nest* and *Sometimes a Great Notion,* both made into motion pictures. Ursula Le Guin was one of the world's most popular authors of science fantasy as evidenced by her winning all of the major awards in this genre. Sallie Tisdale is a recognized writer of nonfiction, and Barry Lopez is an internationally acclaimed essayist on science and the environment. In architecture, Pietro Belluschi founded the Northwest style, which uses regional materials to construct churches and residences that fit their natural surroundings.

Oregon became nationally known for its political progressivism in the 1960s and 1970s, when the legislature established the first system of statewide land-use planning in the United States, sought to preserve wild rivers, and created the Willamette River Greenway. The state was largely Republican in the first half of the twentieth century, then established a two-party system in which elections were closely contested. During the 1980s and early 1990s, Oregon politics became more conservative as voters became less willing to spend tax dollars. In 1990 a property tax limitation was adopted as a constitutional amendment, which had the effect of crippling government services. On the national scene Senator Bob Packwood was a proponent of tax simplification, while Senator Mark O. Hatfield was best known for championing a noninterventionist foreign policy. Liberal Democratic Governors Neil Goldschmidt (1987–1991) and Barbara Roberts (1991–1995) were able to accomplish little because of conservative strength in the state legislature. Oregon's economy depends on natural resources and the condition of the national economy. Agriculture, forest products, and tourism are the principle industries. Increasingly, manufacturing jobs have been replaced by lower-paying service and retail jobs. The state's economy grew during the years after World War II but plummeted between 1979 and 1982, primarily because of a near-collapse in the forest-products and construction industries. Recovery began in 1983, however, and since 1986 the state's employment growth has outpaced that of the nation as a whole.

[Gordon B. Dodds, *The American Northwest: A History of Oregon and Washington* (Arlington Heights, Ill., 1986).]

GORDON B. DODDS

See also **SUPP:** Portland.

ORGAN DONATION. *See* **Transplants and Organ Donation.**

ORGANIC FARMING coalesced as a movement in the United States in the 1940s with the work of J. I. Rodale of Emmaus, Pa., who followed the British agriculture botanist Sir Albert Howard in the belief that healthy soil produces healthy people. Rodale published a magazine dedicated to organic gardening and farming that drew subscribers ranging from home gardeners to truck farmers. Spurning synthetic fertilizers, he advocated natural soil-builders, such as composted organic materials and ground rock. He and his disciples reacted against synthetic pesticides, such as DDT, and livestock antibiotics, such as penicillin, which were just finding their way onto farms and into farm produce. After the publication of Rachel Carson's *Silent Spring* (1962), many Americans became concerned with human health and permanence. Thus, organic farming found many adherents in the late 1960s and the 1970s among both antitechnology members of the counterculture and environmentally concerned consumers. Synthetic agricultural chemicals, which had become a staple in U.S. agriculture in the post–World War II period, increasingly came under attack as scientists recognized many of them as carcinogenic. The back-to-basics philosophy of the environmental movement boosted the popularity of organic agriculture as a healthy alternative to the seemingly apocalyptic results of high technology.

For decades the U.S. Department of Agriculture (USDA) had advocated use of synthetic agricultural chemicals while bemoaning the loss of humus and topsoil. Responding to environmental concerns, petroleum shortages, and rampant inflation in the 1970s, the USDA began to advocate research into conversion of urban and industrial organic wastes into composted soil-builders that farmers could use to increase fertility and restore structure. The Organic Foods Production Act of 1990 called for federally funded pilot projects to help introduce organic techniques as supplements to chemical-intensive agriculture. Supporters maintained that organic farming would support family farms by lowering costs, increasing yields, and raising quality, as well as assisting farmers to conserve soil and other natural farm resources. By the mid-1980s organic techniques such as low-till and no-till farming, in which farmers leave crop residues in fields to increase humus and to decrease water and wind erosion, were common practice among cereal farmers in the Midwest.

Public awareness of these issues continued to grow. In the late 1980s there was a widely publicized controversy over Alar, a chemical sprayed on apples and other produce to enhance color and prolong shelf life, which had been linked to cancer in laboratory studies. The Environmental Protection Agency attempted to reconcile 1950s legislation prohibiting carcinogenic pesticide residues on food with the highly sensitive measuring devices of the 1990s. Projects such as Biosphere 1 and 2 experimented with a sustainable lifestyle in a closed ecosystem. Organic farmers hoped to tap into the antichemical sentiment that drove these activities by selling produce labeled "organically grown" in supermarkets. Initially organic farming was an attempt to preserve "good farming" practices in the face of a rapidly changing agriculture. In the 1990s organic farming techniques gained acceptance as a result of environmental regulation, rising energy prices, and consumer demand.

[Samuel P. Hays, *Beauty, Health, and Permanence: Environmental Politics in the United States, 1955–1985* (New York, 1987).]

DENNIS WILLIAMS

See also **SUPP:** Agriculture; Biosphere 2; Fertilizers; Health Food Industry; Hydroponics.

ORGANIZATION OF PETROLEUM EXPORTING COUNTRIES (OPEC). *See* **Middle East, Relations with; Oil Crises; Petroleum Industry.**

OZONE DEPLETION. Ozone, a denser form of oxygen that is designated by the chemical notation O_3

and that shields the Earth from excessive ultraviolet radiation from the sun, became a concern of environmentalists in the 1980s. As early as the 1950s scientists had detected substantial fluctuations in the amount of ozone in the atmosphere over Antarctica between summer and winter. In the 1970s some chemists, notably Sherwood Rowland and Mario Molina of the University of California, blamed the lower level of ozone over Antarctica in the winter on the rapidly increasing use of chlorofluorocarbons (CFCs), as refrigerants and propellants in aerosol cans and in the manufacture of plastic foam products. This charge was confirmed by the National Academy of Sciences in 1976. The process of depletion, as described by Rowland, involves the migration of the highly stable CFC molecules to the stratosphere, where, moved by global air circulation patterns, they collect over the Antarctic ice cap during the cold winter months and become fixed on polar stratospheric clouds that, because of their cold temperature, are isolated from the normal atmospheric circulation. When sunlight returns to Antarctica in early spring, the ultraviolet rays bring about a chemical reaction that in turn releases a chlorine-oxide free radical that precipitates a chemical chain reaction breaking up the oxygen molecules that form the ozone layer. A world that has been producing and releasing into the atmosphere 1 million tons of CFCs per year has seen a rise in the reservoir of these chemicals in the atmosphere from 0.8 parts per billion by volume in 1950 to 4 parts per billion in 1990. This accumulation is expected to continue to rise in the twenty-first century.

A greater sense of urgency about ozone depletion arose after scientists stationed in Antarctica reported in 1985 a virtual disappearance of ozone from the Antarctic stratosphere in winter. This announcement was confirmed by measurements taken in 1986 and 1987. The United Nations Environmental Program had registered concern about ozone depletion as early as 1977, and its administrators began negotiations that led in 1985 to the Vienna Convention, signed by twenty nations agreeing to take action to phase out the use of CFCs. In 1987 all major industrial nations signed the Montreal Protocol, agreeing to deadlines for ending the use of CFCs. These deadlines were advanced in an agreement, signed in Copenhagen by eighty nations, calling for the almost total elimination of CFCs, as well as methyl chloroform and carbon tetrachloride, by 1996. Major chemical companies around the world proposed as substitutes for CFCs another group of chemicals known as HCFCs. Although these chemicals also contain chlorine, the chemical responsible for ozone destruction, they also contain hydrogen, which speeds up their dissolution before they reach the stratosphere. Production of HCFCs is to be capped at the level of output achieved in 1996, and they are subject to a gradual phaseout beginning in 2004 and terminating in 2030.

Scientists have determined that the ozone layer in the stratosphere is diminishing worldwide at a rate of between 2 and 3 percent per year. In the late 1980s it was feared that an ozone "hole" comparable to that over the Antarctic might develop over the Arctic, but subsequent measurements have indicated that the risk is not as great; the Arctic does not become as cold as the Antarctic and warms sooner in spring, so there is less time for the ozone-destroying chain reaction created by chlorine free radicals to do its work. Scientists remain concerned, however, about the general reduction in the ozone layer, since it creates a risk of greater penetration of the lower atmosphere by ultraviolet radiation from the sun. They predict an increase in skin cancer because measurements in temperate latitudes in fact show increasing penetration by ultraviolet radiation.

[Seth Cagin and Philip Bray, *Between Earth and Sky: How CFC's Changed Our World and Endangered the Ozone Layer* (New York, 1993); F. Sherwood Rowland, "Stratospheric Ozone in the 21st Century: The Chlorofluorocarbon Problem," *Environmental Science and Technology* 25 (1991).]

NANCY M. GORDON

See also **SUPP:** Air Pollution.

P–Q

PACIFIC, TRUST TERRITORY OF THE. *See* **Trust Territory of the Pacific Islands.**

PACIFIC RIM, a region described as that bordering the vast Pacific Ocean—Asia, along with North and South America. Geologically the region contains four-fifths of the world's seismic activity. It is the region's economic activity, however, that has given the geological term currency in international business and in world politics, especially with regard to Asia. In sheer rate of economic growth the Asian countries in the Pacific Rim have begun to outperform those of all the rest of the world. Asian economies went from producing just 4 percent of the world's overall economic output in the 1960s to 25 percent in the 1990s. By the early 1990s U.S. exports to Asia exceeded those to Europe; transpacific trade had become more important than transatlantic. The region's economic growth was not confined to the economic miracle of Japan. This ferocious growth was led by the four "little dragons," Singapore, Hong Kong, South Korea, and Taiwan, which rapidly industrialized. Closely following in their wake were Indonesia, Malaysia, and Thailand, which initially provided inexpensive labor and undertook only industrial assembly operations but soon developed industries using the latest technology. Adding to the importance of the region was the increasing involvement of China in international trade as it reluctantly began to open its market of 1.1 billion consumers to outside trade. The Pacific Rim nations in 1989 formed the Asia-Pacific Economic Cooperation (APEC), and in 1994 this eighteen-nation group signed an accord to achieve "free and open trade and investment" in the region among its industrialized countries while giving its developing nations until the year 2020 to comply. The hope was that the agreement would transform the region into the world's largest free-trade area.

[Alexander Besher, *The Pacific Rim Almanac* (New York, 1991).]

BRENT SCHONDELMEYER

See also **SUPP:** China, Relations with; Japan, Relations with; North American Free Trade Agreement; Trade, International; Trade Agreements.

PACs. *See* **Political Action Committees.**

PAINTING. In the last third of the twentieth century U.S. painters occupied a prestigious place within the Western art world. Aided by growing public appreciation, art in general and painting in particular enjoyed a remarkable popularity. A uniquely American art is impossible, because the physical size of the country, the diversity of its population, and desire for freedom of expression works against conformity. A stunning array of styles has emerged, ranging from super-realism to the farthest reaches of the abstract. Viewers confront paintings that are variously material- or process-oriented, deliberately casual or overtly formal, political or apolitical, or contrived through craft-based mixed media. Whereas art lovers once had to visit institutions or studios to see original works, near the end of the twentieth century they needed only have access to the art walks that appeared in every major city during the 1970s and 1980s. An outgrowth of politics of the 1960s, street art brought the visual expressions of the poor and dispossessed to public attention.

Painters made a radical departure in expressing their understanding of urban subjects. Instead of the exalted roles accorded to people in the work of Robert Henri or the reverential stance toward the metropolis assumed by John Marin, street artists turned to such commonplace subjects as structural and street deterioration, garbage heaps, and haphazard human presence, all underneath the intrusive glare of commercial signs. With brilliant colors and bold forms they splashed their messages across framed canvases and murals, occasionally mixing the results with participatory theater in a fashion reminiscent of the composer John Cage's "happenings" in the 1950s. In similar fashion more mainstream artists scrutinized the forces within their own lives. The clarion call came from New York, where artists painted and sculpted soup cans, cigarette butts, comic book characters, and giant hamburgers. Aware of the role played by the media in shaping moods and attitudes, the first "pop art" practitioners challenged the notion that complexity (of theme, technique, content, execution) necessarily connotes seriousness of purpose.

The marriage of street art and pop art philosophies produced superrealism, a style characterized by excruciatingly detailed images achieved by colors applied with equal brightness across a canvas. As in the photorealism movement earlier in the century, superrealists paint from models and photographs. Superrealists strive to deliver pointed messages. One of the most compelling examples of this style is Jack Beal's *History of American Labor,* a four-panel commission for the General Services Administration building in Washington, D.C., which captures the optimism-turned-pessimism-turned-confusion experienced by workers in the face of labor trends (the fight for unions, the dominance and decline of same, and the subsequent allegiance to the old views of individual initiative and self-reliance) over the course of the twentieth century. Scattered amid the avant-garde paintings is a respectable showing of works in traditional styles. In any urban center at virtually any time viewers can see settings, thoughts, and issues in every style from baroque to cubism. A typical encounter could bring a side-by-side view of a realist, an expressionist, and a minimalist, all interpreting the same scene or idea.

If there is a thread running through the art annals of the United States it is the decided preference of Americans for figurative painting. Artists have expanded the conventions of figurative painting by using collages, photomontages, and found objects in their compositions. One of the most favored painters in the latter genre was Romare Bearden, an African American respected for provocative depictions of religious events, conjuring women, and not-so-placid garden scenes. An emerging element of importance was the push for egalitarianism in the arts. Although the idea is old, contemporary artists have challenged the exclusionary policies and economic controls practiced by galleries, although many artists benefited during the 1980s from the highly inflated climate created and sustained largely by such gallerists as Mary Boone. The feminist movement brought about intriguing developments in art. Such artists as Judy Chicago and Miriam Schapiro developed pattern painting, a style that features human forms, floral patterns, and an endless litany of nonobjective shapes arranged in configurations similar to wallpaper. Contrived through mixed-media designs of needlework, cloth, and other crafts associated with women, feminist paintings often appear under the guise of performance pieces written and choreographed by other feminist artists.

The interaction between artists and the ease with which artists moved among media continue to alter modern painting. Surfaces sculpted for texture and alternative views toward line, balance, and form hint of aesthetic vistas yet unexplored. The increasing popularity of art in public places could lead to greater intimacy between painters and viewers. All told, the painter of the future may be forced to abandon the garret and seek succor from the streets.

[Daniel M. Mendelowitz, *A History of American Art,* 2nd ed. (New York, 1970); Barbara Rose, *American Art Since 1900,* rev. ed. (New York, 1975); John Wilmerding, *The Genius of American Painting* (New York, 1973).]

EVELYN S. COOPER

See also **SUPP:** Folk Art; Graffiti; National Endowment for the Arts; Sculpture.

PALEONTOLOGY. Although the last dinosaur died 65 million years ago, the decades of the 1970s, 1980s, and 1990s can be called the dinosaur age. Some, although not all, of the interest in dinosaurs stemmed from the theory that the creatures may have been destroyed by a meteorite or comet that hit the earth. A large fossil crater underlying the Yucatán peninsula has been identified with a catastrophe at the end of the Cretaceous period, but some paleontologists defend the role of vulcanism as an alternative scenario for the extinction of the dinosaurs, and still other paleontologists suggest that such factors as climate change or disease killed off this group. Arguments as to whether birds are allied to or directly descended from dinosaurs have whetted the public's appetite for surprisingly sophisticated general discussions of the intricacies of evolution. The collection of dinosaur bones in the West has spurred at least one court case over ownership of the skeleton of a Tyrannosaurus rex, valued at several million dollars.

Invertebrates have not generated quite as much fervor as dinosaurs, but an account published in 1989 of bizarre fossil animals found in the Burgess Shale in Canada from the Middle Cambrian period (520 million years ago) reached the *New York Times* bestseller list. The book's commercial success was aided by reports of similar although slightly older Early Cambrian fossils found in China, Australia, Canada, and Greenland. These fossils have pointed up the problem posed by the abrupt appearance of skeleton-bearing animals at the base of the Cambrian. No adequate theory accounts for why or how some groups developed hard parts, while others, such as worms and jellyfish flourish without a skeleton. Progress has been made on the study of Precambrian fossils, forms older than 540 million years. The Ediacaran fauna first described in Australia in the 1950s has been recognized worldwide in rocks from 650 to 550 million years old. Some of the fossils may be allied to jellyfish, but others have no living counterparts. With one dubious exception, none of these early animals has a mineralized skeleton. They show no close relation to the atypical Early and Middle Cambrian fauna mentioned earlier, and it has even been suggested that some kinds formed a separate kingdom of organisms.

The low price of crude oil and its abundant supply since the mid-1980s resulted in reduced employment opportunities for paleontologists in the oil industry, especially micropaleontologists. Partly offsetting this loss was the Deep Sea Drilling Project (DSDP), the latest phase in drilling in the ocean for scientific results that began in the 1960s. The DSDP has achieved remarkable biostratigraphic precision in dating some microfossils, with some dated to intervals of 100,000 years and even less. At the same time, there has been a dramatic shift in the profession away from stratigraphic investigations. The emphasis in the 1990s was on evolutionary studies, spurred by the debate over "punctuated equilibrium," which suggests an abrupt appearance of new forms, versus gradual change; the problem of interpreting mass extinctions; and questions about predator-prey relationships. Pa-

leoecological studies and functional morphology systematic studies increased, while classic monographic systematic studies declined. New sections of the *Treatise on Invertebrate Paleontology*, which began in 1953, continued to be published, with paleozoologists producing new summary volumes of groups and revising previously published sections.

Studies of former plant life continued into the 1990s, including the search for ancestors of angiosperms; the coal-forming forests of the past were being interpreted with the ideas of modern ecology; and remarkably well-preserved fungi more than 300 million years old were added to the geologic record. Artifacts from the Precambrian, nine-tenths of the time of earth, were slowly yielding information on the origin and the early evolution of life. Team studies of the Archean (1983) and the Proterozoic (1992) periods clarified earlier hypotheses about early life and documented much of its course from the appearance of life 3,500 million years ago. Studies of other planets have emphasized the uniqueness of life on earth and its effect on the planet.

[Stephen Jay Gould, *Wonderful Life: The Burgess Shale and the Nature of History* (New York, 1989); J. W. Schof, ed., *Earth's Earliest Biosphere: Its Origin and Evolution* (Princeton, N.J., 1983); J. W. Schof and C. Klein, eds., *The Proterozoic Biosphere: A Multidisciplinary Study* (Cambridge, 1992).]

ELLIS L. YOCHELSON

See also **DAH** and **SUPP**: Archaeology and Prehistory.

PALESTINE LIBERATION ORGANIZATION (PLO). *See* **Israel-Palestine Peace Accords; Middle East, Relations with.**

PALESTINIAN AMERICANS. There have been four waves of Palestinian immigration to the United States. The first occurred following creation of the state of Israel in 1948, which made many Palestinians refugees. The second occurred in the early 1970s following the 1967 Arab-Israeli Six-Day War, when immigrants were fleeing the Israeli occupation of the West Bank and Gaza. The third wave was a result of the 1987 popular uprising (intifada) against the Israeli occupation. A fourth immigrant group arrived after the Gulf War of 1991, expelled from Kuwait and the Gulf region. Although Palestinian Americans have deep roots in Arabic culture and often maintain their language and customs, they have excelled in U.S. schools and universities. Notable Palestinian American academicians are the literary scholar Edward Said, the historian Walid Khalidi, and the writer Ibrahim Abu-Lughod. Palestinian Americans also have prospered as entrepreneurs, especially in the food, clothing, and electronics industries.

[Samia El-Badry, *Fitting In: An Analysis of Socio-Economic Attainment Patterns of Foreign Born Arab Americans and Other Nationalities in the United States* (Austin, Tex., 1987).]

SAMIA EL-BADRY
SAMAR SAKAKINI

See also **SUPP:** Arab Americans; Middle East, Relations with.

PALIMONY, a term derived from "alimony," is the legal action upholding oral agreements between unmarried couples to share property and earnings acquired while the couple shared the same abode. In 1976 Michelle Triola Marvin sued actor Lee Marvin, claiming that she abandoned her own singing career to serve as his companion, cook, and confidante and that in return he agreed to share his earnings. She eventually sued Marvin for close to $2 million for "services" as his "wife" and loss of her career. The California courts let her sue under the theory that the couple had an oral contract. In the end she won $104,000. Palimony is misnamed in that it implies the equivalent of alimony when unmarried couples break up. The legal basis of palimony suits where states allow them is an oral contract for services, other than sexual, provided during cohabitation.

PAUL FINKELMAN

See also **SUPP:** Marriage and Divorce.

PANAMA CANAL TREATY (1977). The genesis of the 1970s agreements between Panama and the United States lay in increasing Panamanian discontent over existing treaty relationships with the U.S. government. The 1903 Hay-Bunau-Varilla Treaty had granted "in perpetuity" to the United States a canal zone within which the United States could exercise "all the rights, power, and authority" of a sovereign state. Severe rioting in January 1964 led to twenty-one Panamanian deaths and considerable destruction of U.S.-owned property. In December of that year President Lyndon B. Johnson promised negotiations to abrogate the 1903 treaty. The following year Johnson and Panamanian President Marco Aurelio Robles announced agreement on a set of principles to guide subsequent negotiations. Draft treaties were completed and initialed by late June 1967, but leakage of the terms to the press stirred opposition in both countries and led to the shelving of the covenants.

An October 1968 coup in Panama brought to power Guardia Nacional Colonel Omar Torrijos Herrera. A chance conversation two years later between President Richard M. Nixon and Panamanian President Demetrio Lakas led to resumption of negotiations between the two countries. In May 1973 Panamanian Foreign Minister Juan Antonio Tack formulated a set of principles (similar to the Johnson-Robles principles of 1967) to undergird any U.S.-Panama agreement. Secretary of State Henry Kissinger signed a modified version of the Tack principles in 1974. The administration of President Gerald R. Ford could not obtain Pentagon support for the proposed treaties until the autumn of 1975. President-elect Jimmy Carter in January 1977 requested a review of negotiations and subsequently authorized a resumption on the basis of the Tack-Kissinger principles. Treaties following the terms of the 1967 principles were signed by Carter and Torrijos on Sept. 7, 1977.

The Panama Canal Treaty stated that the United States would maintain control of the waterway until Dec. 31, 1999, and Panama would assume a greater role in the canal's operation, maintenance, and defense. An increasing percentage of canal revenues would accrue to Panama during the transition period. A second agreement, the Neutrality Treaty, required Panama to keep the canal neutral and open to all nations, with the United States and Panama pledged to guarantee neutrality. A Carter-Torrijos "statement of understanding" was issued as a clarification of two articles of the Neutrality Treaty. Each country could act to defend the canal "against any aggression or threat," although this did not mean that the United States could intervene in Panama's internal affairs. Both treaties were approved by plebiscite in Panama on Oct. 23, 1977, but final congressional approval took two years. Republican Senator Dennis DeConcini of Arizona proposed an amendment to the Neutrality Treaty stating that in the event of the closure of the canal the United States and Panama independently had the right to take any necessary steps to reopen it, including use of force. With this amendment the U.S. Senate approved the Neutrality Treaty on Mar. 16, 1978, by a vote of 68 to 32. The Canal Treaty was ratified by the same margin on April 18. It contained an amendment introduced by the Senate leadership stating that nothing in either treaty would have as its purpose or would be interpreted as a right of intervention in the internal affairs of Panama. President George

Bush may have violated this amendment when he ordered the invasion of Panama in 1989 to capture General Manuel Antonio Noriega. Enabling legislation for the two treaties passed the House and Senate late in September 1979; both treaties went into effect on Oct. 1, 1979.

[William J. Jorden, *Panama Odyssey* (Austin, Tex., 1984).]

RICHARD W. TURK

See also **DAH:** Panama Canal; Panama Revolution; **SUPP:** Panama Invasion.

PANAMA INVASION (1989). The invasion of Panama by U.S. forces in December 1989 was designed in part to end the rule of General Manuel Antonio Noriega. A graduate of the Peruvian Military Academy in 1962, he had supported Colonel Omar Torrijos Herrera, the ruler of Panama, during an attempted coup against the latter in 1969. Noriega soon became head of the Panamanian military intelligence service and served Torrijos for a decade as chief of security. Two years after Torrijos's death in an airplane crash in 1981, Noriega became commander of the Guardia Nacional, renamed the Panama Defense Forces (PDF). Torrijos and subsequently Noriega aided the U.S.-sponsored Contras with arms and supplies in their struggle against the Sandinista regime in Nicaragua. Noriega's involvement with the Medellín drug cartel in the 1980s and the emergence of Panama as a money-laundering site proved far more lucrative than receiving U.S. support because of assistance to the contras.

In 1987 a feud between Noriega and his chief of staff, Roberto Diaz Herrera, led to Diaz's publicly charging Noriega with crimes and encouraged Panamanian opponents to demand Noriega's resignation. Noriega responded with arrests and brutality. Secret negotiations between Panamanian and U.S. representatives designed to facilitate Noriega's departure broke down. The U.S. Justice Department filed indictments against Noriega in federal court; soon afterward the U.S. government imposed a series of economic sanctions. The United States sent additional military forces to the Canal Zone in Panama, recalled its ambassador, and encouraged PDF officers to overthrow Noriega. An attempted coup in 1989 failed and led to executions. The media criticized President George Bush and Secretary of Defense Richard Cheney for failing to provide more support to the coup leaders. The U.S. military drew up plans for an invasion, which began when a U.S. serviceman died from gunfire outside PDF headquarters on Dec. 16, 1989.

Operation Just Cause began December 20 and lasted through December 24. The PDF numbered 5,000, augmented by 8,000 paramilitary troops organized in "dignity battalions." The 13,000 U.S. troops stationed in Panama were reinforced by an additional 9,000. Fighting centered around Noriega's headquarters in Panama City. Noriega took refuge with the papal nuncio (the Vatican's representative in Panama), but surrendered on Jan. 3, 1990. Twenty-three U.S. soldiers were killed during the invasion. Panamanian deaths—military and civilian—exceeded 500. U.S. public opinion supported the operation but many foreign governments did not. A new civilian regime took control in Panama and the country experienced severe economic problems and a troubled security situation for months afterward. Noriega became a federal prisoner in Miami on Jan. 4, 1990; he was tried and convicted in April 1992 of cocaine smuggling and imprisoned. Political and economic stability remained an elusive commodity in Panama; nationalist resentment against the United States surged, and by 1995 Noriega's adherents may have regained a degree of authority in Panama.

[Edward M. Flanagan, Jr., *Battle for Panama: Inside Operation Just Cause* (Washington, D.C., 1993).]

RICHARD W. TURK

See also **DAH:** Panama Canal.

PAN AM FLIGHT 103, a U.S. passenger jet, was destroyed by a terrorist bomb on Dec. 21, 1988, over Lockerbie, Scotland, killing 259 passengers and crew and 11 residents. The incident ignited a protracted international effort to bring the suspected Libyan perpetrators to trial and marked a shift from hijacking to sabotage in terrorist attacks against Western targets. Passengers included thirty-five foreign-study students from Syracuse University who were en route to New York from London's Heathrow Airport when their aircraft was "decapitated" by a plastic explosive concealed in a forward cargo bay. Relatives of the dead blamed U.S. authorities for failing to make public information warning of a terrorist attack on a flight originating in Frankfurt, Germany. Bomb experts later confirmed that the explosive, hidden in a radio cassette player inside a suitcase, had been smuggled aboard in Frankfurt. Because West German authorities had arrested members of the Popular Front for the Liberation of Palestine–General Command earlier in 1988 and found plastic explosives in their possession, it first was thought that Palestinians were behind the bombing. Speculation also centered on Tehran, presumably in retaliation for the accidental downing of an Iranian passenger jet by the USS *Vincennes* in the Persian Gulf in July 1988. In 1991, however, the United States and Scotland indicted two Libyan intelligence agents for the bombing of Pan Am Flight 103. For the first time in its history the United Nations Security Council ordered one nation, in this case Libya, to surrender citizens to another nation. When Libya refused, the Security Council imposed an air and arms embargo on the country. Intelligence sources in the United States believe Libyan leader Mu'ammar al-Gadhafi ordered the bombing in retaliation for a U.S. air raid on Tripoli in April 1986. That attack was in turn a response to Libya's alleged bombing of a West Berlin discotheque that targeted off-duty U.S. servicemen and women.

[Steven Emerson and Brian Duffy, *The Fall of Pan Am 103: Inside the Lockerbie Investigation* (New York, 1990).]

BRUCE J. EVENSEN

See also **SUPP:** Middle East, Relations with; Terrorism.

PARENTAL CHOICE IN EDUCATION. *See* **Education, Parental Choice in.**

PARENTHOOD, SURROGATE. *See* **Surrogate Parenthood.**

PARKS, NATIONAL. Of the 83.3 million acres in the National Park System in 1994, 50.4 million were in the fifty-four national parks and 2.06 million in the seventy-three national monuments. The remaining acres can be accounted for in other areas in the system—such as national seashores, national scenic trails, and national historic sites—that are not designated as national parks or national monuments. During the administrations of Richard M. Nixon, Gerald R. Ford, Ronald Reagan, and George Bush, national monuments were created by congressional action. President Jimmy Carter, acting under the powers assigned presidents by the Antiquities Act of 1906, created national monuments in Alaska by proclamation.

Between 1974 and 1994 fifteen areas that were formerly national monuments became national parks: Badlands, Biscayne, Channel Islands, Death Valley, Dry Tortugas, Gates of the Arctic, Glacier Bay, Great Basin, Katmai, Kenai Fjords, Kobuk Valley, Joshua Tree, Lake Clark, Saguaro, and Wrangell–St. Elias. The Theodore Roosevelt National Memorial park,

created in 1947, was redesignated a national park in 1978, and in 1988 the National Park of American Samoa was established. The two largest National Park Service areas in 1995 were Wrangell–St. Elias and Gates of the Arctic, both in Alaska. In 1977 the National Park Service classification system that divided units into natural, historical, and recreational areas was abolished because these categories became difficult to apply, as some areas contained multiple attributes. National parks and national monuments are often, however, classified informally according to their primary attributes.

The twenty-nine national monuments categorized as primarily natural areas are Aniakchak, Alaska; Chiricahua, Organ Pipe Cactus, Sunset Crater Volcano, Arizona; Devils Postpile, Lava Beds, Muir Woods, Pinnacles, California; Black Canyon of the Colorado, Gunnison, Dinosaur, Florissant Fossil Beds, Great Sand Dunes, Colorado; Craters of the Moon, Hagerman Fossil Beds, Idaho; Agate Fossil Beds, Nebraska; Capulin Volcano, El Malpais, White Sands, New Mexico; John Day Fossil Beds, Oregon Caves, Oregon; Congaree Swamp, South Carolina; Jewel Cave, South Dakota; Cedar Breaks, Natural Bridges, Rainbow Bridge, Timpanogos Cave, Utah; Buck Island Reef, Virgin Islands; Devils Tower, Fossil Butte, Wyoming.

The forty-three national monuments categorized as primarily historical areas are Russell Cave, Alabama; Cape Krusenstern, Alaska; Canyon de Chelly, Casa Grande Ruins, Hohokam Pima, Montezuma Castle, Navajo, Pipe Spring, Tonto, Tuzigoot, Walnut Canyon, Wupatki, Arizona; Cabrillo, California; Hovenweep, Yucca House, Colorado; Castillo de San Marcos, Fort Matanzas, Florida; Fort Frederica, Fort Pulaski, Ocmulgee, Georgia; Effigy Mounds, Iowa; Poverty Point, Louisiana; Fort McHenry, Maryland; Grand Portage, Pipestone, Minnesota; George Washington Carver, Missouri; Little Bighorn Battlefield, Montana; Homestead, Scotts Bluff, Nebraska; Aztec Ruins, Bandelier, El Morro, Fort Union, Gila Cliff Dwellings, Petroglyph, Salinas Pueblo Missions, New Mexico; Castle Clinton, Fort Stanwix, Statue of Liberty, New York; Fort Sumter, South Carolina; Alibates Flint Quarries, Texas; Booker T. Washington, George Washington Birthplace, Virginia.

The most significant service acquisitions between 1974 and 1994 were in Alaska. Under the Alaska Native Claims Settlement Act of 1971 the secretary of the interior was given the discretion to withdraw up to 80 million acres of Alaskan lands that would qualify as units operated by one of the following agencies: National Park Service, Forest Service, or Fish and Wildlife Service. In 1973 Secretary Rogers C. B. Morton recommended that 32.3 million acres be withdrawn for parks. Congress had five years to act on the secretary's recommendation, which would double the size of the lands administered by the Park Service. There was strong opposition from commercial interests and from hunters who urged Congress to create preserves that permitted sport hunting and trapping, rather than parks that prohibited those activities. Representative Morris K. Udall of Arizona drafted a bill that created national preserves but it was defeated in May 1978.

It appeared that the five-year limit for Congress to act would expire and the withdrawn areas would revert to public lands. On Dec. 1, 1978, President Jimmy Carter proclaimed fifteen new national monuments and made additions to two others. He proclaimed the withdrawn lands as monuments to allow Congress time to draft legislation concerning their status. In 1980 Congress agreed to an Alaskan lands bill, and on December 2 President Carter signed the Alaska National Interest Lands Conservation Act into law, redesignating seven monuments as national parks and increasing the acreage of the National Park Service by more than 47 million, much more than the 32.3 million Secretary Morton had recommended for withdrawal. Five of the seven parks were accompanied by national preserves, allowing sport hunting and trapping.

[Barry Mackintosh, *The National Parks: Shaping the System* (Washington, D.C., 1991); National Park Service, *The National Parks: Index 1993* (Washington, D.C., 1993).]

JON E. TAYLOR

See also **DAH:** Parks, National, and National Monuments; Park Service, National, and National Park System; **SUPP:** Park Service, National.

PARK SERVICE, NATIONAL. Crowding in the national parks has placed pressure on their resources and exacerbated the tension inherent in the National Park Service's dual mission of preservation and public enjoyment. A major construction program—Mission 66—to accommodate visitors in the 1950s and 1960s was followed by an era of environmental concern that greater use and related facility development jeopardized park values. In the mid-1970s, during the bicentennial of the American Revolution, the two dozen historical parks commemorating the Revolution benefited from an extensive development program. At Independence National Historical Park in Philadelphia, the Park Service reconstructed the house where Thomas Jefferson drafted the Declaration of Independence, installed elaborate exhibits at the site of Benjamin Franklin's house, and moved the Liberty Bell to a new pavilion outside Independence Hall. On July 4, 1976, President Gerald R. Ford spoke at Independence Hall and signed legislation making Valley Forge a national historical park.

Beyond routine protection, management, and upkeep, Park Service personnel engage in a range of more specialized activities, from erection of fire lines to control damage to surface artifacts (for example, during the 1977 fire at La Mesa in Bandelier National Monument, near Los Alamos, N.Mex.) to an ongoing program of cyclical prospecting—identifying vertebrate fossils at risk from damage by natural causes—in the John Day Fossil Beds, Badlands National Park, S.Dak. Wilderness preservation received an enormous boost with the Alaska National Interest Lands Conservation Act of 1980, which, with the addition of Denali and Wrangell–St. Elias and five other preserves, more than doubled the size of the National Park System.

Because the Park Service's funding and staffing had not kept pace with its growing responsibilities, the administration of President Ronald Reagan and Congress in the 1980s sought to slow the system's expansion. Rather than creating more parks, they backed the Park Restoration and Improvement Program, which allocated more than $1 billion over five years to resources and facilities in existing parks. Beginning in Reagan's second term the National Park Service sought a greater role in educating the public about American history and environmental values. The service also returned to a more expansionist posture, supporting such additions as Great Basin National Park, Nevada, and Steamtown National Historical Site, a railroad connection in Scranton, Pa. The latter was a costly venture and was much criticized as an example of "pork barrel" politics, casting into doubt the national significance of other proposed parks that seemed primarily driven by local economic-development interests. During the presidency of George Bush (1989–1993) the National Park Service leadership spoke out against such a "thinning of the blood" of the National Park System and sought to regain the initiative from Congress in charting its expansion.

In 1990 the Richard King Mellon Foundation made the largest single park donation yet: $10.5 million for additional lands at Civil War battlefields and at

Shenandoah National Park. In all, ninety-seven units were added to the National Park System between 1975 and November 1994, including the National Mall in Washington, D.C.; Canaveral National Seashore, Florida; recreation areas in rural pockets of New Jersey, Georgia, New York–Pennsylvania, Nebraska, West Virginia, and Minnesota and in Guam; and Wrangell–St. Elias National Preserve and Denali National Preserve, both in Alaska. Denali, the fourth largest unit in the system and site of North America's highest mountain, Mount McKinley, brings in more than fifty buses, each carrying approximately forty people, every day. In 1996 the system comprised 369 areas—80 million acres—featuring resources as diverse as the Grand Canyon and the Statue of Liberty.

[Barry Mackintosh, *The National Parks* (Washington, D.C., 1991).]

EDWIN C. BEARSS

See also **DAH:** Park Service, National, and National Park System; Parks, National, and National Monuments; **SUPP:** Conservation; Parks, National.

PATIENTS' RIGHTS, a movement that was an outgrowth of the movement for individual rights of the 1960s and 1970s that gave rise to the idea of a set of rights for protection of medical patients and succeeded in having those rights enacted into law in many states. Although medical and hospital patients in most states were beneficiaries of common-law rights well before the 1960s, these protections were limited to the right not be treated without consent, the confidentiality of statements made to a physician during treatment, the right to damages in event of malpractice, and, to some extent, the confidentiality of a patient's hospital records. An advance in patients' rights occurred in 1973 when the American Hospital Association (AHA) approved a bill of rights for adoption by member hospitals. It promised patients considerate and respectful care, the right to know hospital rules and regulations relating to patient conduct, the right to know the identity of the physician in charge of care, sufficient information to enable patients to make informed decisions with respect to their treatment, the right to obtain information concerning diagnosis and treatment as well as prognosis if medically advisable, the right not to be a subject of experiment, the confidentiality of clinical records, and the right to receive an explanation of the hospital bill.

Although the AHA represented almost all of the 5,300 nonprofit, general, and investor-owned hospitals in the United States in the 1990s, the bill of rights adopted by most of the association's members was of little or no legal value because it was voluntary. Nonetheless, it established public awareness of patients' rights and set the stage for a second advance that took place between 1975 and 1985, when one-third of the states enacted patients' rights statutes. Although these statutes varied, they all incorporated the AHA pledges and generally went beyond them to guarantee the right to prompt emergency attention, the right to examine one's clinical chart during the course of treatment and to obtain a copy of it, the right (within limits) to privacy during the hospital stay, the right to receive an itemized bill, and the right to receive information about financial assistance and free care. The most important aspect of these statutes was that they were enforceable. California, Colorado, Illinois, Maryland, Massachusetts, Michigan, Minnesota, New York, Pennsylvania, and Rhode Island were some of the states that enacted statutes. In most instances the statutes were also applied to nursing homes. The right to refuse treatment extended to psychiatric patients if they were competent. By the 1990s federal law required hospitals and nursing homes to advise patients of their right to refuse care and their right to execute living wills or to name proxies if they become unable to make life-and-death treatment decisions.

[George J. Annas, *The Rights of Patients,* 2nd rev. ed. (Totowa, N.J., 1992).]

JACK HANDLER

PDA. *See* **Pregnancy Discrimination Act.**

PEACE CORPS. As an idea, the Peace Corps originated with Democratic Representative Henry S. Reuss of Wisconsin and Senator Hubert H. Humphrey of Minnesota in the late 1950s. Both advocated sending U.S. volunteers into developing nations to help alleviate poverty, illiteracy, and disease. Democratic presidential candidate John F. Kennedy adopted the idea in 1960. The Peace Corps appealed to Kennedy's notion of service to country and humanity; it also had the potential for encouraging goodwill for the United States among developing nations. The Soviets and Chinese, in Kennedy's opinion, were far ahead of the United States in cultivating friendships among nations emerging from colonialism after World War II. He wanted the Peace Corps to counter communist aims in developing nations by demonstrating U.S. democratic values. President Kennedy moved quickly, appointing his brother-in-law, Sargent Shriver, to create the Peace Corps. Shriver built the agency in a matter of weeks. The president signed an executive order on Mar. 1, 1961, temporarily establishing the Peace Corps, and in September, Congress voted to create a permanent corps. Appointed its first director, Shriver worked to develop a system for recruiting, training, transporting, supplying, and caring for overseas volunteers. His drive helped the Peace Corps gain independent status from other U.S. foreign policy agencies. Although directors of the Peace Corps are political appointees and have changed the focus of the organization somewhat as presidential administrations changed, the Peace Corps has remained relatively free from use as a direct foreign policy instrument.

After the end of the cold war the Peace Corps' goals remained unaltered. It seeks to promote world peace and friendship through interaction of the volunteers with their hosts. Volunteers spend two years in a host country that requests Peace Corps help, aiding in whatever ways the host desires. Tasks range from teaching and community organizing to assistance in agriculture. The corps concentrates on small, personal projects and has three broad aims—providing trained workers for developing nations, promoting understanding of the United States and its values, and increasing volunteers' understanding of the perspectives and values of people in developing nations. Despite attacks, low funding, and internal problems the Peace Corps survives as a popular agency. Since 1961 it has sent more than 140,000 volunteers to ninety-nine nations. The agency cannot keep pace with demands for volunteers. Charges of cultural imperialism have been leveled, but the agency responds that it does not seek to replace traditional societies' values with those of the United States but rather to act as a bridge between cultures. The Peace Corps continues to receive bipartisan congressional support.

[Gerard T. Rice, *The Bold Experiment: JFK's Peace Corps* (Notre Dame, Ind., 1985).]

JOEL D. SHROCK

PEACE MOVEMENTS. U.S. citizens take part in peace movements for a variety of reasons. Some limit their commitment to specific antiwar activities, particularly during military conflicts. Others champion internationalism, supporting worldwide peace organizations. Many are pacifists, religious or secular. Some believe that large standing armies pose a threat to liberty and democracy. Many link peace to such other interests as feminism, socialism, civil rights, or environmentalism. With the end of the Vietnam War

in 1975 the broad coalition of peace activists who had come together to protest the longest conflict in U.S. history broke down once again into smaller groups addressing a range of concerns.

Protests against the nuclear arms race, which had been a focus of peace groups since the 1950s, intensified in the 1980s in response to the Ronald Reagan administration's buildup of the U.S. nuclear arsenal. In the early 1980s the nonviolent Livermore Action Group sought to close the Lawrence Livermore National Laboratory in California, which produced nuclear weapons. Such actions reinforced the wider nuclear freeze campaign, a movement that in November 1982 led to the largest voter referendum on any issue in U.S. history. More than 11.5 million Americans, 60 percent of those voting on the freeze issue, supported the measure. The freeze issue appeared on the ballot in states and localities across the country. Twelve state legislatures, 321 city councils, 10 national labor unions and international bodies endorsed the effort by the United States and Soviet Union to ban mutually the testing, production, and deployment of nuclear weapons. One result of the movement was the Intermediate-Range Nuclear Forces (INF) Treaty of 1988 with the Soviet Union.

Activists also linked the huge U.S. military budget with neglect of such human needs as education, health care, and housing for the poor, which led to ambitious campaigns against such costly projects as the B-1 bomber, the MX missile system, and the Strategic Defense Initiative ("Star Wars"). Peace groups were critical of U.S. military interventions in Grenada (1983) and Panama (1989), and to a lesser extent, in Somalia (1992), challenging the morality as well as the effectiveness of using military means to achieve political, economic, or even humanitarian ends. Although the brief Gulf War of 1991 elicited overwhelming public support in favor of halting Iraq's aggression against Kuwait, many peace activists criticized the George Bush administration for engaging in a war they believed was more about U.S. dependency on Middle East oil than about freedom for the citizens of Kuwait. Elsewhere, protests were aimed at the Reagan administration for its support of the Contras seeking to overthrow the Sandinista government in Nicaragua, where in 1990 U.S. peace organizations monitored free elections.

A unique aspect of the peace movement since the 1970s has been the surge of feminist involvement. Awareness generated by the 1975–1985 United Nations Decade for Women resulted in international networks concerned with global issues of war, economic crises, and the rights of women. In 1980 and 1981 women encircled the Pentagon to oppose war. New York State in 1983 witnessed the massive Women's Encampment for the Future of Peace and Justice sited next to the Seneca Army Depot, a nuclear weapons storage facility. The 1987 Mother's Day action at the Department of Energy's nuclear test site near Las Vegas enlisted thousands of women from throughout the country. As in the past, peace movements appealed most to middle-income women, clergymen, educators, college students and people in their twenties, and some business leaders. Geographically, their centers of strength were in college towns, the large metropolitan areas of the Northeast and Midwest, and along the West Coast.

[Charles Chatfield, *The American Peace Movement: Ideals and Activism* (New York, 1992); Barbara Epstein, *Political Protest and Cultural Revolution* (Berkeley, Calif., 1991); Charles F. Howlett, *The American Peace Movement: References and Resources* (Boston, 1991); Lawrence S. Wittner, *Rebels Against War: The American Peace Movement, 1933–1983* (Philadelphia, 1984).]

CHARLES F. HOWLETT

See also **SUPP:** Arms Race and Disarmament; Grenada Invasion; Gulf War of 1991; Haiti, Relations with; Human Rights; Nicaragua, Relations with; Panama Invasion; Somalia, Relations with; Strategic Defense Initiative; Women's Movement.

PEARL HARBOR FIFTIETH ANNIVERSARY (Dec. 7, 1991) commemorated the bombing of the Pearl Harbor naval base in Hawaii on Dec. 7, 1941, and U.S. entry into World War II with an address by President George Bush. Along with 2,000 veterans who survived the Japanese attack he hailed the 1,177 Americans who died aboard the USS *Arizona* on the "date which will live in infamy." A navy pilot who had enlisted after Pearl Harbor, Bush avowed that fifty years later he held "no rancor in my heart toward Germany or Japan." He praised Japan's recent acknowledgment of "responsibility" for starting the Pacific War. Scholarly conferences, including one at Hofstra University, also remembered Pearl Harbor in the United States. There were no commemorative events in Japan.

J. GARRY CLIFFORD

See also **DAH:** Pearl Harbor; **SUPP:** War Memorials.

PENNSYLVANIA. William Penn, the founder of Pennsylvania, sought to balance goals of justice, political equality, and tolerance of religious diversity and hoped to establish a divinely inspired commonwealth where people would respect differences and reject ideological extremes stridently proclaimed as undeniable truths elsewhere. Three centuries later the Pennsylvania novelist John Updike described the state as one of "mild, misty, doughy middleness" where moderates rule. The events of the late twentieth century support this dual image of diversity and moderation. Pennsylvania voters tended to hold moderate positions and cared most about bread-and-butter issues. Pennsylvania politicians therefore stood in the center with the voters, avoiding ideology and focusing on jobs and services to communities and individuals. Consistent with this concrete service orientation was the political tradition of helping one's friends and providing favors, which in turn has led to tolerance of a degree of corruption neither Penn nor Benjamin Franklin would have found acceptable.

Indicative of political moderation is the outlook of the state's governors and senators. Governor Milton J. Shapp, a Democrat, promoted a moderate liberal agenda from 1971 to 1979. During his two terms the state passed a sunshine law for open government, established the Department of Aging, expanded women's legal rights, removed children from adult jails, and greatly increased government support for the arts and for handicapped children. During the 1970s, however, nearly 300 public officials at all levels of government admitted to, were convicted of, or pleaded no contest to corruption. Democratic Congressmen Joshua Eilberg and Daniel J. Flood accepted bribes, Republican Congressman J. Irving Whalley demanded kickbacks from staff members, and Republican Senator Hugh D. Scott accepted illegal gifts of $10,000 annually from the Gulf Oil Corporation. There were fewer corruption scandals in the 1980s but the bizarre suicide of Republican State Treasurer R. Budd Dwyer was particularly shocking. Convicted of accepting a $300,000 bribe, Dwyer shot himself before television cameras during a 1987 press conference. By dying before his sentencing Dwyer ensured that his family would receive pension benefits of more than $1 million.

Republican Richard Thornburgh was governor from 1979 to 1987. Thornburgh, who would later serve as Attorney General in the George Bush administration, campaigned as a moderate who pledged to end corruption and administer progressive social programs. His progressive appeal was so successful that he won the votes of traditionally Democratic African-American voters. His gubernatorial campaigns stressed moderate themes. Democrat Robert P. Casey continued the tradition of two-term governors. In both his campaigns Casey emphasized that his administration would work with business leaders to preserve jobs and create new ones. The voting records of Pennsylvania's senators since 1980 are consistent with the theme of moderation. Republicans H. John Heinz and Arlen Specter were among the Republican senators most likely to oppose the conservative positions of the Ronald Reagan and Bush administrations. After Senator Heinz died in a 1991 plane crash, Democrat Harris Wofford defeated former Governor Thornburgh to fill the final three years of Heinz's term. Wofford proposed health care reform and an activist government to promote jobs.

Part of Pennsylvania's moderation is its willingness to embrace standards that are more symbolic than tangible. Pennsylvania joined most other states in reestablishing the death penalty, for example, but the state government nonetheless has hesitated to execute anyone. Another area of symbolic standards with little tangible policy impact is abortion policy. In the 1970s the Pennsylvania Catholic Conference lobbied legislators to enact pro-life policies. Overriding Governor Shapp's veto, the legislature passed an antiabortion bill so extreme that the Supreme Court ruled it unconstitutional. In the 1980s the Court began to expand the scope of abortion legislation that could be enacted by the states. The Pennsylvania chapter of the National Abortion Rights Action League (NARAL) and other pro-choice groups, however, organized to challenge the influence of the Catholic Conference. After *Webster* v. *Health Reproductive Services* (1989) allowed states to place restrictions on women obtaining abortions, the legislature approved some of the measures favored by the Catholic Conference. A federal judge struck down portions of the law but the state appealed. The Supreme Court ruled in *Planned Parenthood of Southeastern Pennsylvania* v. *Casey* (1992) that spousal notification was unconstitutional but upheld other provisions, including a twenty-four-hour waiting period, informed consent of one parent of pregnant teenagers, and various reporting requirements. Finally implemented in 1994, the law has had little impact on abortion practices.

Pennsylvania's economy in the last quarter of the twentieth century shifted from manufacturing to services. The city of Pittsburgh reflected the change by surviving the demise of its steel industry through the development of diversified services. The loss of higher-paying union manufacturing and mining jobs (only 27,000 of the latter remained in 1990) was enormous,

but creation of nonunion, low-paying service jobs was so great that Pennsylvania's unemployment figures were not significantly higher than national averages. At the beginning of the 1990s there were 1.5 million service and 1.2 million wholesale and retail trade jobs, compared with 1 million manufacturing jobs. Agriculture continued to be the largest single occupation in the state, with 800,000 people employed and 57,000 farms. The state's mushroom industry was the largest in the country. Still, the loss of manufacturing jobs brought considerable pain. There were also great regional disparities as many industrial counties of western Pennsylvania suffered high unemployment and declining populations at the same time southern counties outside Philadelphia thrived.

In 1992 the state's population stood at 12,009,361, with a higher proportion of elderly citizens than in most states. Nine percent of Pennsylvanians were African Americans. The Amish still drove their buggies. Ethnic neighborhoods existed both in the cities and towns. Mahanoy City, a typical anthracite (coal-mining) town of 5,200 residents, boasted a dozen churches and a half-dozen fire companies representing different ethnic groups. These traditional cultures continued to enrich Pennsylvanians as they encountered the challenges of modern society with its diversified economy.

[Paul B. Beers, *Pennsylvania Politics Today and Yesterday* (University Park, Pa., 1980); Philip Klein and Ari Hoogenboom, *A History of Pennsylvania,* 2nd ed. (University Park, Pa., 1980).]

ROBERT E. O'CONNOR

See also **SUPP:** Philadelphia; Pittsburgh; *Planned Parenthood of Southeastern Pennsylvania* v. *Casey*; Three Mile Island; *Webster* v. *Reproductive Health Services.*

PENSION PLANS. Usually involving employers or government or both, pension plans provide periodic payments to employees or their families after retirement or in the event of death or disability. In some cases, usually among the self-employed, these arrangements are individual. Plans may be funded through employer set-asides, deferred profit sharing, or employee savings. Social security, a federal pension program for most working Americans established by the Social Security Act of 1935, may augment employer or private pension plans. Separate government pension plans exist for federal, state, and local government employees and the military. Individuals may augment their pensions through individual retirement accounts (IRAs) as well as 40l(k) or other thrift plans. Such savings strategies are a growing segment of the U.S. retirement system, offering tax deferrals and the promise of increased pension income as individuals reach qualifying age.

In 1991, 68 percent of U.S. workers were covered by employer-provided pension plans (although only 53 percent of these elected to participate in such plans), compared to just 19 percent who were covered at the end of World War II. One consequence of increased participation in pension plans is that the age at which many Americans choose to retire is now less than sixty-five, an age that previously was considered early retirement. Inflation, which greatly increased during the 1970s, led to automatic increases in many pension plans, which, together with the increased longevity of senior citizens, threatened the stability of some pension funds.

ROBERT M. GUTH

See also **SUPP:** Cost of Living Adjustment; Set-Asides; Social Security.

PENTECOSTAL CHURCHES. The Pentecostal movement emerged out of small beginnings in 1901 in Topeka, Kans. It had nineteenth-century antecedents, especially among clusters of holiness advocates in Tennessee and North Carolina but its defining doctrinal tenet first was advanced by Charles F. Parham (1873–1929) in Topeka. At the turn of the century scattered groups of populist radical Protestants sought a religious experience they called "the baptism with the Holy Spirit." Parham concluded that such baptism would always be manifested by speaking in tongues. Pentecostals were radical evangelicals who accepted as biblical Parham's view that tongues speech evidenced Spirit baptism. Their general beliefs and practices closely paralleled those of many others in their religious subculture. Only gradually did a Pentecostal movement disentangle itself from related and similar movements in the contemporary popular religious culture.

In the 1990s Pentecostalism was found all over the world. Seventy-five percent of all Protestants in South America (regardless of denomination) subscribed to Pentecostal beliefs. In parts of Africa huge indigenous churches were essentially Pentecostal in belief and worship style, as was a large portion of the Christian community in China. In the United States the charismatic renewal in mainstream denominations since the 1960s brought emphasis on beliefs and practices usually associated with Pentecostalism. The

term generally is used to describe a movement that acknowledges Parham and the revival meetings his views influenced at the Azusa Street Mission in Los Angeles in 1906. Adherents believe all Christians should have an experience of baptism with the Holy Spirit and that tongues speech is the "uniform initial evidence" of this baptism. They hold this view in a larger theological context shaped by premillennialism, advocacy of divine healing, and expectation of the presence among them of the "gifts of the Spirit" listed in the New Testament. Pentecostals emphasize evangelism and some denominations sponsor a strong missionary presence abroad. Their focus on spiritual gifts usually resulted in distinctive styles of worship. They tend to be verbal and expressive of faith and may vent feelings in hand clapping, tears, shouts, falling, dance, song, tongues, and other responses to what they believe to be the Holy Spirit's presence among and within them.

Despite such commonalities Pentecostalism historically has been divided. The first division stemmed from the first decade of the movement when it attracted people from various backgrounds whose unity was rooted in the quest for a particular experience. It soon became evident that disagreement over the timing and understanding of baptism with the Holy Spirit was deep and abiding. Some believed that the experience of Spirit baptism was authentic only if it followed two definite, instantaneous experiences—conversion and sanctification. Others held that Spirit baptism followed conversion and that sanctification was progressive. In the mid-1990s the largest groups holding to three experiences are the Church of God in Christ, headquartered in Memphis, Tenn., and the Church of God in Cleveland, Tenn. The best-known denomination advocating two crisis experiences is the Assemblies of God.

Another division emerged in 1913 when a sizable group opted to follow teaching that denied the Trinity in favor of emphasizing Jesus' name. Known as Oneness or Jesus Only Pentecostals, this segment of Pentecostalism remained apart from the movement as a whole because of its anti-Trinitarian stance. It historically has divided along racial lines. Among larger Oneness groups are the Pentecostal Assemblies of the World headquartered in Indianapolis, Ind., and the United Pentecostal Church centered in St. Louis, Mo. The third division was along racial lines. During the brief heyday of the Azusa Street revival (1906–1908), blacks and Anglo-Americans sometimes shared leadership. The acknowledged head of the Azusa Street Mission was an African American, William Seymour, who expelled Hispanics from the mission. In general,

Pentecostalism comprises denominations that are primarily black, primarily white, or primarily Hispanic. The Church of God in Christ has been primarily black, for example, whereas the Assemblies of God is primarily white, with a sizable Hispanic membership organized in separate districts and generally served by separate schools and publications.

Over the years black Pentecostals, Oneness and Trinitarian, have had limited contact with one another. Trinitarian white Pentecostals met annually beginning in 1948 through the Pentecostal Fellowship of North America until that organization disbanded in 1994. In its place, in a display of interracial goodwill, black and white Trinitarian Pentecostals created the Pentecostal-Charismatic Churches of North America. Trinitarian Pentecostals worldwide have an opportunity every three years to gather in the World Pentecostal Conference.

Most U.S. Pentecostal denominations oppose the ecumenical movement and distance themselves from the National Council of Churches and the World Council of Churches. At the local level and in local causes Pentecostals often participate in ministerial associations and church councils. Although the charismatic renewal provides limited opportunities for relationships with some mainline Protestants, most Pentecostals nurture stereotypes of mainstream denominations as "dead" and "cold" with little to offer people who have discovered the "full" gospel. Pentecostalism of the late twentieth century demanded far less separation from the culture at large, such as amusements, sports, entertainment, and fashion, from adherents than the movement once did. This, together with an openness to popular culture and readiness to answer all questions, made Pentecostalism attractive. Growth in membership in the United States has been flat since the early 1980s, but in the non-Western world Pentecostalism continued to thrive.

[Robert Mapes Anderson, *Vision of the Disinherited* (New York, 1979); Edith L. Blumhofer, *Restoring the Faith* (Urbana, Ill., 1993); Harvey Cox, *Fire From Heaven* (New York, 1994).]

EDITH BLUMHOFER

See also **SUPP:** Fundamentalism; Millenarianism; Religion.

PERSIAN GULF WAR. *See* **Gulf War of 1991.**

PERSONAL ADS. Advertisements placed by young women who had been left "destitute of Fortune and Friends" appeared in the United States as early as 1790. The *Philadelphia Public Ledger* was the first publication to devote a separate department to classified advertising, and by the end of the nineteenth century newspaper ads placed by "young masseuses" were common, as were ads placed by lonely men in the frontier West who were seeking companionship and marriage. Personal ads have been the basis for such motion pictures as *Sea of Love* (1989) and *Loves Music, Loves to Dance* (1991) about serial killers who find their victims through the papers. In addition to growing numbers of newspaper and magazine "personals," cyberspace users can search for love among millions of people around the world on the Internet and on independent computer bulletin boards.

[Frank Luther Mott, *American Journalism,* 3rd ed. (New York, 1962).]

JOHN J. BYRNE

PERSONAL COMPUTERS. *See* **Computers.**

PERSONNEL ADMINISTRATOR OF MASSACHU-SETTS V. FEENEY, 442 U.S. 256 (1979), a Supreme Court case that considered whether a Massachusetts law giving veterans a lifetime preference in filling open civil service positions violated the equal protection clause of the Fourteenth Amendment. Helen B. Feeney was a civil servant who received higher grades on civil service examinations than male veterans. Because of the preference law, however, males repeatedly were promoted over her. Twice the federal district court declared the law unconstitutional. The state of Massachusetts, supported by the solicitor general of the United States, appealed to the Supreme Court. The Court in a seven-to-two decision sustained the law. A basic question was whether the effect of the preference classification was "purposeful discrimination." The law violated the Fourteenth Amendment only if the claimant could prove that the discriminatory purpose was because of, not merely in spite of, its adverse effect on the employment opportunities of women. The history of the Massachusetts law indicated that the statute created "a preference for veterans of either sex over women." The law affected adversely more women than men because until 1967 there had been a 2 percent quota on women in the military. Male nonveterans, however, suffered from this preferred treatment as much as female nonveterans. Although the lower court initially applied this principle to decide in favor of Feeney, after appeals by the state she lost. The case clearly stated that in gender-discrimination suits mere foreseeability of a law's consequences does not establish the needed discriminatory purpose. The case supported state assistance to veterans even if discrimination toward women was a result. It also established a greater burden of proof on plaintiffs.

[Bruce E. Rosenblum, "Discriminatory Purpose and Disproportionate Impact: An Assessment After *Feeney,*" *Columbia Law Review* 79 (November 1979): 1376–1413.]

TONY FREYER

See also **SUPP:** Affirmative Action; *Equal Employment Opportunity Commission* v. *Sears, Roebuck and Company*; Women's Movement; Women's Rights.

PESTICIDES are chemicals that destroy organisms that compete with human activity. Seventy percent of all pesticides used in the United States are employed in agriculture to control insects, weeds, and fungi. Other uses include lawn maintenance and disease control. Since the development of synthetic chemicals in the 1940s, the use of chemical pesticides has increased dramatically. Between the early 1950s and the 1990s, agricultural use of pesticides, by weight, increased 900 times. The use of pesticides produces many short-term economic benefits. Pesticides clear areas of pests and are easy to transport, store, and apply. Pesticides contribute to increased crop yields; the annual U.S. investment of $3 billion in pesticides leads to $12 billion in increased agricultural revenues. The U.S. Department of Agriculture estimates that without pesticide use and sophisticated storage and transportation technologies, food prices would be 30 to 50 percent higher.

Concern over the long-term costs of pesticide use has increased since the early 1960s, when the warnings contained in Rachel Carson's *Silent Spring* (1962) led to critical examination of pesticide use. Research in ecology, economics, and public health during the 1970s and 1980s demonstrated the detrimental effects of pesticides. Pesticide practices prevalent in the 1990s compromised the ecosystem in several ways. Many pesticides kill a variety of species in addition to the target organism. Application of pesticides can be inefficient, contaminating soil and water supplies. Populations of pests often develop genetic immunity to pesticides. By 1990 almost 500 insect pest species had developed genetic resistance to pesticides. Moreover, the concentration, and thus the potential for harm, of pesticides increases as they move through organisms up the food chain. The integrity of ecosystems suffers as pesticides interfere with ecological relationships between organisms. Humans, equally dependent on healthy ecosystems, are also harmed by exposure to pesticides.

In response to environmental and health concerns and decreased efficacy of chemical pesticides, the Environmental Protection Agency banned the use of several pesticides, including DDT in 1973 and ethylene dibromide in the early 1980s, although export to foreign countries is still legal. The Department of Agriculture supports research on alternative pest control strategies. Traditional methods of cultivation used prior to the advent of pesticides, such as crop rotation and crop diversity, were reemerging, and cross-breeding and genetic engineering were producing plants that are more resistant to specific pests. Biological controls include the use of bacteria, viruses, natural predators, pheromones that attract insects to traps, and development-arresting hormones. These techniques are combined through integrated pest management (IPM) programs that examine the ecological relationships of pests, crops, and other organisms and produce control strategies utilizing a variety of nonpesticide techniques to raise crop yields. Government policy in the 1990s, through subsidies and price supports, still favored chemical pesticide use and production. There was, however, also a clear movement to develop techniques that ultimately may make pesticides obsolete.

[Walter H. Corson, ed., *The Global Ecology Handbook* (Boston, 1990); G. Tyler Miller, Jr., *Environmental Science* (Belmont, Calif., 1991); Sandra Postel, "Controlling Toxic Chemicals," in *State of the World, 1988,* edited by Lester R. Brown, Linda Stark, and Edward C. Wolf (New York, 1988).]

DAVID W. CASH

See also **DAH** and **SUPP:** Agriculture; Ecology; Insecticides and Herbicides; **SUPP:** Environmental Movement.

PETROLEUM INDUSTRY. The embargo of oil exports to the United States by Middle East Arab nations in the aftermath of the 1973 Arab-Israeli War was the most dramatic catalyst in shaping the global and U.S. petroleum industry in the 1970s and 1980s. Nominal prices of crude petroleum and petroleum products rose dramatically from less than $5 per barrel in the late 1960s to almost $40 per barrel in 1980 before tapering off in the late 1980s and early 1990s to approximately $15 a barrel. The rapid rise of crude oil prices drove gasoline prices to unprecedented levels in the 1970s and 1980s, contributing in 1973 and again in 1979–1980 to long lines for consumers at the gas pumps. Between 1970 and 1980 U.S. gasoline prices increased from less than $.40 a gallon to almost $1.40 a gallon before declining in the mid-1980s to under $1. Such significant increases in prices did not derive primarily from a decline in world production levels, although U.S. production did vary over the 1970–1990 period, adding additional uncertainty to the market. U.S. crude oil production declined in the 1970s from approximately 9.6 million barrels a day in 1970 to 8.6 barrels in 1980, following an even sharper decline to 8.2 in 1976. In 1976 the United States also fell to third place among world producers, behind the Soviet Union and Saudi Arabia. After a brief recovery to 8.9 barrels in 1985, production declined again to 7.3 by 1990. The initial fear of international oil shortages contributed to a quadrupling of prices between 1972 and 1982 before rapidly declining in the mid-1980s. World production levels (including the United States) continued impressive levels of growth to 1980, rising from 45.8 million barrels a day in 1970 to 59.35 a decade later. They then declined slightly before surpassing 1970 levels by 1990.

In 1971 the administration of President Richard M. Nixon imposed price controls on oil as part of the president's larger anti-inflation program. This measure, however, contributed to higher levels of consumption at the same time that it discouraged domestic producers. With the 1973 international crisis over supplies, demand increased sharply with the result that independent refiners experienced difficulty obtaining adequate supplies. In 1973, responding to political pressure to remove price controls, the Nixon administration introduced a voluntary allocation system and abolished the import quotas established a decade earlier by the administration of Dwight D. Eisenhower. Both measures were designed to improve access to supplies of crude oil, although the long-standing tension remained between a policy that encouraged domestic production by restricting imports and thus reducing dependency on foreign oil and a policy that encouraged imports both to protect domestic reserves and also to encourage lower prices for domestic use.

In late 1973 President Nixon addressed this issue in his first major address on energy, in which he called for Project Independence to make the nation self-sufficient in oil by 1985. That goal was to be achieved by increasing domestic supplies, developing alternative sources of energy, and through domestic conservation. In 1975 the administration of President Gerald R. Ford and Congress instituted price and allocation controls in the Energy Policy and Conservation Act. The legislation provided that the controls would be phased out by mid-1979. The Ford administration also sought to reduce imports by reducing demand and stimulating domestic production, transporting oil from Alaska, leasing the outer continental shelf, and reconsidering the effects of environmental controls. In the same year the administration established the Strategic Petroleum Reserve to reduce dependence on foreign supplies of crude oil.

President Jimmy Carter's administration was even more strongly committed to energy self-sufficiency. The President's National Energy Plan in 1977 identified as goals the reduction of vulnerability to interruption of supply, promoting conservation, and shifting to renewable or inexhaustible resources. The administration proposed taxes to reduce demand and force consumers to pay the full cost of energy. Price controls were recommended to prevent windfall profits to producers from radical increase in prices. Even more than the initiatives under Nixon and Ford, the Carter policies were intended to shift consumption from imports to domestic sources and toward coal and nuclear energy and away from oil and natural gas. The Carter proposals resulted in the 1978 National Energy Act, which incorporated in broad outline the Carter proposals, although it tended to weaken them. The legislation provided for reduction of electrical generation by oil and natural gas and tax incentives to encourage conservation, but oil and gas price controls were not continued. There were no provisions to develop alternative energy sources and only limited resources were allocated to research and development on alternative energies. The 1980 Energy Security Act established the Synthetic Fuels Corporation to provide financial support to the private energy sector.

Such initiatives had little impact on imports from the Organization of Petroleum Exporting Countries (OPEC), which continued to increase. In 1973 the United States imported 1.2 billion barrels of crude oil, more than one half coming from the Americas, and almost 300 million barrels from the Middle East. In 1979 imports rose to 2.4 billion barrels. By that date, however, Africa was the leading source of supply with 900 million barrels, followed by the Middle East with 750 million barrels. The Americas had fallen back to slightly more than 400 million barrels.

Government regulation of the industry in the 1970s had a variety of objectives, including reducing import dependency, encouraging domestic production, and attempting to stabilize prices. Higher prices for domestic refined oil in the United States encouraged producers and refiners to process oil that at lower prices would have been uneconomical. One effect of feared oil shortages during the decade along with high demand and rising prices was to increase corporate profits, although there is debate among specialists whether the refining or producing sectors benefited more. One evaluation of twenty-four major firms indicated an increase of net income for those firms from $6.4 billion in 1971 to $9 billion in 1973, $11.4 billion in 1974, and $16.3 billion in 1980.

Oil shortages occasioned by the curtailment of Iranian supply because of the 1979 revolution in that country produced the second major oil shock within ten years and for three years drove prices to unprecedented levels. Although a reduction in prices after 1982 encouraged greater U.S. economic growth in the 1980s, there was a disincentive to continue the conservationist and alternative energy initiatives of the Nixon through Carter administrations. President Ronald Reagan's administration also was committed to free-market conditions to resolve national energy problems, with more exploitation of oil, natural gas, coal, and uranium on public lands. The Reagan administration deregulated oil prices, although it increased contributions to the Strategic Petroleum Reserve. The Reagan and George Bush administrations, with their emphasis on market forces and deregulation, abandoned the effort to establish a clear, long-term national oil and energy policy, assuming that supply and price were under control. One result was that oil imports by the 1990s were on the rise again. In 1985 total imports of crude oil had fallen to the 1973 level of 1.2 billion barrels, with a reduced dependency on the Middle East as a source of supply (fewer than 100 million barrels compared with more than 600 million from the Americas). In 1990 Middle East supplies constituted 600 million of the 2.2 billion barrels imported. The United States was again dependent on foreign supplies for half its oil requirements.

One of the most dramatic and significant developments of the mid-1980s in the oil sector was the collapse of world and domestic prices—the third oil shock following those of 1973 and 1979–1980. The crisis was stimulated in large part by the rift within OPEC, between Saudi Arabia and other OPEC producers over market share, with OPEC objectives shifting from price control to markets. OPEC also began to increase production in 1985–1986. One result was that in 1985 the price of West Texas Intermediate oil fell sharply to $10 a barrel from a high in excess of $31. The consequences of this price decline of course varied within the U.S. economy; for consumers the decline was a boon, while for producing regions of the United States where there was a heavy reliance on the industry for employment and revenues the collapse meant severe recession.

The Gulf War of 1991 rekindled concern over security of supply and led the Bush administration to inaugurate a national energy strategy. The main objective of the strategy was to reduce the importance of oil in the U.S. economy and, accordingly, mitigate the vulnerability of the United States to foreign oil supply disruptions. Legislation under that initiative passed Congress in October 1992, although the legislation dealt less with oil and gas than with electric utility reform and nuclear power and authorized more research and development funds for alternative fuels and conservation. With the victory of the Republicans at the polls in the 1994 midterm elections and the movement of Republicans into key committee chairmanships in Congress, it was anticipated that the highly conservationist orientation of the previous decade would come under challenge from the 104th Congress. Congress moved quickly to end restrictions on exports of oil from the Alaska North Slope and to implement some royalty relief for deepwater projects in the Gulf of Mexico. It was also anticipated that there would be a strong effort to take a conservative stance on environmental regulation and enforcement. In 1995 oil industry specialists predicted a shift of the industry focus away from the oil and gas sectors in the Gulf of Mexico to Alaska and California, where the main interest is crude oil production.

The dilemma that confronted the industry and government was tension between those goals and economic and security interests. The Arctic National Wildlife Refuge was considered to be the most promising area for oil development in the twenty-first century. Given the high demand for oil and oil products and declining levels of U.S. domestic production (from 9 million barrels a day in 1985 to a projected 5 million in 2000), the tension between environmentalism and economic interest promised to be the main issue of the next decades.

[Joseph P. Kalt, *The Economics and Politics of Oil Price Regulation* (Cambridge, Mass., 1981); Peter Odell, ed., *Oil and World Power: Background of the Oil Crisis,* 8th ed. (New York, 1986); Daniel Yergin, *The Prize: The Epic Quest for Oil, Money and Power* (New York, 1991); Daniel Yergin and Barbara Kates-Garnick, eds., *The Reshaping of the Oil Industry: Just Another Commodity?* (Cambridge, Mass., 1985).]

STEPHEN J. RANDALL

See also **SUPP:** Energy, Department of; Energy, Renewable; Energy Industry; Energy Policy; Energy

Research and Development Administration; *Exxon Valdez*; Gulf War of 1991; Middle East, Relations with; Offshore Oil; Oil Crises.

PHARMACEUTICAL INDUSTRY. A wide variety of effective, high-quality products for both human and veterinary use are produced by the U.S. pharmaceutical, or drug, industry, including nonprescription, over-the-counter drugs marketed directly to the public, as well as ethical drugs, which require a prescription and are therefore marketed to the medical profession. After the introduction of sulfa drugs in the 1930s and such antibiotics as penicillin in the 1940s, the drug industry grew rapidly and began to produce a host of new products that were effective in the prevention, treatment, and in some cases eradication of many deadly diseases. Drug therapy became important, widespread, and generally cost effective. The drug industry in the late twentieth century was a large, highly profitable, socially important, and politically powerful entity. As a result of these successes and some widely publicized failures, drug company activities are highly politicized.

The largest and most sophisticated multinational drug companies combine research and development with an elaborate network for distribution of information and products. Although most of these companies are in Western Europe, the United States, and Japan, the industry has become increasingly international. Sixty countries have an annual production of at least $100 million. Worldwide production doubled between 1975 and 1990, reaching $150 billion. Market growth proved nearly as robust during the same period; worldwide per capita consumption jumped from $17 to $29. Debate continued as the twentieth century drew to a close about the extent and appropriateness of the high profits of the industry, which were well above the average for all manufacturing industries as well as for Fortune 500 companies. In 1992 the U.S. drug industry's return on sales was 11.5 percent, four times the average of Fortune 500 companies. During the 1980s drug prices did not rise as fast as overall health care costs but exceeded significantly the rate of inflation.

By the end of the 1980s public concern over the cost of health care and growing interest in health care reform had increased markedly. This concern politicized federal agency and industry decisions. For example, the Food and Drug Administration responded to the AIDS epidemic by developing guidelines for an accelerated approval process. In 1987 Burroughs Wellcome marketed AZT, the first anti-AIDS drug approved in the United States. The company's decision to price a year's supply at $8,000 to $10,000 was widely criticized as a rapacious pricing strategy. Drugmakers typically have offered price breaks to large buyers, such as hospitals and health maintenance organizations (HMOs), but pharmacists often face huge markups—sometimes 1,000 percent—over prices paid by hospitals and HMOs. In the early 1990s retail pharmacists and others brought price-discrimination suits against drug manufacturers. Analysts doubted the pharmacists would prevail in court, arguing that the real intent behind such suits may have been to keep pressure on Washington to include some limits on differential pricing practices as part of health care reform.

Conservatives and industry spokespeople argued against government interference in the market, particularly through price controls, the most common form of intervention in other countries. They claimed that without high profits there would be little innovation. Liberals and consumer advocates pointed to the monopoly benefits of patent protection, evidence of oligopolistic behavior, and extensive government subsidization of research costs to back their claims that there should be price controls or profit limits set by the government.

Pricing decisions have always taken place within the context of patent laws, and in industrial countries patent protection usually lasts sixteen to twenty years from the date of application (seventeen years from the date of grant in the United States). During this period—part of which is taken up by testing and approval—the company has exclusive marketing rights. Once the patent expires a drug is much less profitable. Even when prices are high, companies may claim products are cost-effective by pointing to the cost of alternative methods such as surgery and other treatments. This tactic was used in defending the price of AZT. The industry estimated the annual cost of standard AIDS treatment at $43,000 and defended the $8,000 to $10,000 annual price tag for AZT as a comparative bargain. Since the 1950s debate over pharmaceutical profits has been tied to the question of whether there is competition in the drug industry or if high profitability is the result of monopoly or oligopoly. It is doubtful that any firm enjoys monopolistic status, but evidence suggests that some enjoy considerable market power. New products sometimes generate high profits for particular firms, industry profitability is high, and the market position of major firms has remained stable.

The largely cordial relationship between government and the drug industry began to change in 1959 with the congressional investigations known as the Kefauver hearings. Questions emerged about research practices, drug safety and effectiveness, and price disparities between brand-name drugs and generic equivalents. The Thalidomide disaster, widely publicized in 1961, heightened public concern. Although not approved for use in the United States, the sedative Thalidomide led to birth defects in 12,000 children worldwide. Such events led to a more complex approval process and stricter manufacturing guidelines in the attempt to ensure both the safety and efficacy of drugs.

Drug manufacturers have complained about such regulations as lengthy approval processes, claiming they prevent marketing of potentially beneficial drugs. Many new drugs, however, are "me too" drugs that are often essentially equivalent to existing drugs and are not necessarily more effective. The FDA replaced 308 of 348 new drugs brought to market between 1981 and 1988 in this category. The industry has often benefited from government policies. Pharmaceutical manufacturers have rightly noted that research and development is risky and expensive, but much of the risk associated with the research and development of new drugs is borne by university laboratories, small companies, and the National Institutes of Health (NIH). These organizations do much of the initial screening of compounds for possible therapeutic efficacy. Once a promising compound is discovered it can be sold or licensed to the large drug companies. While the research costs for many new drugs are not subsidized by government funds, the government does provide roughly half of all U.S. health-related research money, largely through the NIH. The NIH conducts drug-related research, and when promising compounds appear, companies bid for a license to market them. Consumer advocates claim that the licensing fees do not reflect the value of the research and that drug companies fail to pass on such savings to the public. The industry benefits from a variety of tax breaks. Large companies have long taken advantage of Section 936 of the U.S. Internal Revenue Code. Intended to promote economic development in Puerto Rico, Section 936 allows U.S. industries partial tax exemption on profits from operations in Puerto Rico and other U.S. possessions. In late 1995, citing concerns about "corporate welfare" and the budget deficit, Congress considered elimination of Section 936. These and other issues continued to be debated as consumer advocates and policy-makers addressed the rising costs of health care in the late twentieth century.

[Robert Ballance, Janos Pogany, and Helmut Forstner, *The World's Pharmaceutical Industries* (Brookfield, Vt., 1992); Milton Silverman, Philip R. Lee, and Mia Lydecker, *Pills and the Public Purse* (Berkeley, Calif., 1981).]

M. SEAN DONNELLY

See also **SUPP:** Acquired Immune Deficiency Syndrome; Bacteriology and Virology; Food and Drug Administration; Hospitals; Insurance; Medicine; National Institutes of Health.

PHILADELPHIA. Between the 1970s and 1990s the City of Brotherly Love moved from a period of racial divisiveness and financial crisis to a less turbulent era of accommodating social relations and financial stability. In the 1970s the flamboyant Mayor Frank L. Rizzo linked crime and race as tensions heightened in a city where the minority population would soon reach 40 percent. In the 1980s African-American Mayor W. Wilson Goode won acclaim for handling race relations well but received criticism for alleged administrative incompetence. In the early 1990s, Mayor Edward G. Rendell took office with broad support from every racial and ethnic group. Financial problems reached their peak in 1991 when the city borrowed $150 million at an effective interest rate of 24 percent in order to avoid bankruptcy. The state provided funding to the city, required Philadelphia to plan balanced budgets for five years, and created a financial oversight board with the power to stop state funding if the plans were not implemented. Philadelphia temporarily lost some of its freedom but began to reestablish a sound financial position.

Migration of many middle- and upper-income Philadelphians to the suburbs was one cause of Philadelphia's financial woes. The city lost 6 percent of its population from 1980 to 1990. An even bigger decline of 13 percent took place from 1970 to 1980. The 1990 population of 1,585,577 was down from more than 2 million in the 1960s. The metropolitan area had between 5 and 6 million residents in 1990.

The dominant Philadelphian in the 1970s was Mayor Rizzo. A former police commissioner, he inspired both affection and enmity. His supporters applauded his intention to take forceful measures to reduce crime. Opponents believed his statements exploited racial tension by defending police brutality directed at African Americans. Rizzo left office in 1979 after voters rejected a charter amendment that would have allowed mayors to serve more than two consecutive four-year terms. The dominant Philadelphian in the 1980s was Mayor Goode, the city's first African-American mayor, who served two terms. Despite campaign themes that emphasized good management, deepening fiscal problems and administrative difficulties marked the Goode years. Symbolic of these years and the most memorable event of the 1980s was the MOVE (Community Action Movement) tragedy of May 1985. In trying to evict MOVE, a radical commune living in a Philadelphia row house, the police dropped a bomb on the building. The ensuing fire killed eleven MOVE members, including children. Sixty-one adjacent buildings also burned down, leaving 250 people homeless. After winning the 1991 Republican primary, Rizzo (a former Democrat) suffered a fatal heart attack. Rendell, a white Democrat, defeated two black candidates to win the Democratic nomination. He defeated the Republican candidate, Joseph M. Egan, with two-thirds of the vote and focused on economic concerns, including efforts to keep Philadelphia's sports teams in the city.

[Russell F. Weigley et al., eds., *Philadelphia: A Three-Hundred-Year History* (New York, 1982).]

ROBERT E. O'CONNOR

See also **SUPP:** Pennsylvania.

PHILANTHROPY. Charitable giving has been the subject of more study since 1970 than at any time in U.S. history. This popular and scholarly attention, reflected in a spate of books, articles, and university courses on the subject, have enriched our understanding of a national characteristic often overlooked. One hotly debated issue for scholars studying the role of charity in national institutions is whether philanthropy preserves economic inequalities in a capitalist society. Critics of Western democratic capitalism see private philanthropy as one of the many ideological means by which the capitalist class maintains its privileged status. In Western societies of the past, religion supplied the dominant ideology by which the lower classes were reconciled to their fate on earth with the promise of heavenly rewards. In contemporary U.S. society such principles as equality of opportunity, economic growth, individual initiative, and the absolute value of private property integrate citizens into a belief system that makes the financial success of some and the failure of others appear natural, inevitable, even just. From this viewpoint, a commitment to philanthropy—as opposed, for example, to efforts to achieve a more equal distribution of wealth—serves the interests of the capitalist class.

Defenders of philanthropy, however, argue that the right to associate freely and to support formally such associations is a key to safeguarding American liberties. Conservatives may also find philanthropy, with its frequent progressive agenda, suspect, but they argue that volunteer associations provide a critically needed layer between citizens and government. The right of people to "vote their values" through charitable giving is viewed as essential in a pluralistic democracy. Another major issue is the public's lack of understanding of the important role philanthropy has played historically in shaping U.S. history. More universities, however, began studying charitable giving in order to understand its effect on the nation's past and present. Excellent programs in nonprofit management and philanthropy exist at Yale University, Indiana University, and the University of San Francisco, among others.

The range, extent, and growth of giving in the United States is astonishing. Donors gave an estimated $124.3 billion to charity in 1992, 6.4 percent more than in 1991. According to *Giving USA,* an annual report on U.S. philanthropy, donations outpaced inflation despite a weak economy from 1970 to the mid-1990s. Foundation giving represented nearly 6 percent of this total, corporate giving 4 percent, and individual giving and bequests 90 percent. These percentages have been remarkably stable since 1970. Giving by the nation's 22,000 active grant-making foundations ($8.7 billion in 1992) has increased more than other sources of contributions since 1990. The continuing importance of foundation giving lies in the ability to concentrate funds on selected projects, call attention to trends in social needs, and venture capital on unproven solutions to social problems. Formation of new foundations in the 1980s and early 1990s, as well as more openness and accountability among smaller nonprofit organizations, is a trend that should continue. Corporate giving continues to raise controversy. In an era of downsizing, corporate officers have reduced charitable budgets, putting emphasis on gifts that enhance the marketability of their products and advance their business agenda. Short of cash, many corporations emphasize cause-related marketing partnerships with prestigious nonprofits from major universities or human service groups such as the Red Cross. The connection between giving and corporate interest has increased criticism of this sector. Should corporations engage in philanthropy with the funds of stockholders? Is corporate philanthropy just a marketing tool?

Much scholarly attention has focused on characteristics of individual donors. Considering that 90 percent of total funds donated come from this source, scholars and nonprofit professionals have begun asking questions and offering data about who gives, why, and in what areas. Although such research is still relatively new, patterns are emerging. A comprehensive survey of giving for the period 1987–1989 by the Gallup Organization–Independent Sector showed that U.S. households gave an average of $734, up 31 percent from $562 two years earlier. Seventy-five percent of households—94.6 million—made charitable deductions in 1989, up from 71 percent in 1987. Among demographic groups showing substantial gains in giving were baby boomers born between 1946 and 1964 (86 percent gave), those with household incomes between $75,000 and $100,000 (92 percent gave), and African Americans (61 percent gave). The largest increases went to environmental, health, educational, and human services needs, while international causes and arts groups saw declines in giving. These trends continued without substantial change into the 1990s.

Surveys show that activities and attitudes strongly correlate with charitable giving. In 1990, 100 million adults volunteered time to charities, a substantial increase from the 80 million who volunteered in 1987. Volunteers gave an average of $1,022 in 1989, nearly three times the $357 average contribution for nonvolunteers. Employers and charities benefited by encouraging volunteerism among underrepresented groups, including African Americans, youths ages eighteen to twenty-four, and people with household incomes below $20,000. When asked to volunteer, people from these groups did so at rates similar to other demographic groups. Surveys by the Council on Foundations and the Independent Sector indicate that another key variable in charitable giving is religious worship and church membership. Perhaps 70 percent of the population attends churches, synagogues, or mosques. People who worship regularly make 70 percent of all contributions to charity and give more to nonreligious charities than do nonworshipers. In 1989 members of congregations gave an average 2.4 percent of household income to charity, compared to 0.8 percent from households with no formal religious connection. Motives for giving are complex. Surveys agree that giving correlates with identifiable attitudes and feelings. Citizens who believe that those possessing wealth are responsible for the less fortunate tend to give more; those with well-defined personal philanthropic goals or who are concerned about reinforcing traditional moral values tend to give more; those giving for religious reasons give more.

Americans continued to support charities in record numbers and record amounts despite the 1986 Tax Reform Act, under which Congress disallowed tax deductions to donors qualifying for itemization of deductions on their returns. Tax considerations can affect the timing and amount of gifts but are not more important than a host of other donor motives, including a sense of personal satisfaction; furthering activities of institutions from which the donor benefited; responding to the request of a friend, influential business associate, or employer; and creating a memorial to a family member.

The changing culture of philanthropy helps define the ethos of the country as a whole as well as its regions. Historians, philosophers, economists, and sociologists are interested in what attitudes, beliefs, values, and expectations shape giving and receiving of gifts. Scholars such as James Joseph and Michael O'Neill provided perspectives on how, why, and where ethnic and racial groups define and support communities. Solid information about trends among groups other than traditional Catholic, Protestant, and Jewish donors was still sketchy in the mid-1990s, but scholarly attention began focusing on African-American, Hispanic, Asian-American, Native American and other groups heretofore underexamined. Clearly traditional philanthropy, which tends to dictate solutions "from the top of society down," is less important. Complex social problems require sensitivity to multiculturalism, grass-roots community planning, and multisector (private, government, and nonprofit) funding.

With the return of Republican control of Congress in the 1994 elections and fewer public resources for a host of familiar programs in support of the arts, education, health, and welfare, the 1990s witnessed a renewed debate about philanthropy's role. Many conservatives argued that reduced government spending would be adequately replaced by private giving. With a slow-growth economy and lingering recession in key states, such as California, there was no likelihood that giving rates could keep pace with human needs. Indeed, the traditional debate about the proper mix of public sector and private sector responsibility for the welfare of the country was revived. Many, particularly in the charitable foundations sector, continued to feel that organized philanthropy is best limited to social research, development, and innovation with government remaining responsible for social maintenance. The outcome of the debate promised to help shape policy in important ways as the twentieth century drew to a close. Philanthropy in the United States continued to help characterize its society. It is not likely that voters will allow government to restrict free association of the right of donors to help shape their communities by expressing values through giving. For all the imperfections and its occasional waste, philanthropy will continue to help define the United States as a culturally distinct part of the world.

[Robert H. Bremner, *American Philanthropy* (Chicago, 1988); Robert A. Nisbet, *The Making of Modern Society* (New York, 1986); Michael O'Neill, *The Third America* (San Francisco, 1989); Burton A. Weisbrod, *The Nonprofit Economy* (Cambridge, Mass., 1988).]

ALFRED L. CASTLE

See also **DAH:** Philanthropy and Benevolence; **SUPP:** Volunteerism.

PHILIPPINE ISLANDS remained an important outpost for U.S. naval and air forces until the end of the 1980s. To preserve its bases the United States supported the dictatorship of Ferdinand Marcos until 1986 and then managed the transition to an unstable democracy headed by Corazon Aquino. By the early 1970s U.S. investments in the islands had been surpassed by Japanese and Taiwanese capital, and, as the cold war came to a close, U.S. strategic interest in the islands diminished. As Catholic clergymen and members of the elite became increasingly vocal in their criticism of the government in the mid-1970s, Marcos intensified state repression. The Philippine military killed at least 2,255 persons in extrajudicial executions known as "salvagings," and as many as 70,000 persons may have been imprisoned. Eager to avoid conflict during talks on the military bases, including Clark Air Force Base and the Subic Bay Naval Station, the administration of President Jimmy Carter refrained from criticizing the Philippine record on human rights. A new accord on the bases was signed in January 1979, and U.S. loans, foreign aid, and trade rights continued to support the Philippine economy.

President Ronald Reagan openly embraced Marcos, inviting him for a state visit and declaring him a major ally, but administration officials worried about growing opposition to Marcos within the Philippines. In 1983 opposition leader Benigno Aquino was assassinated at the Manila airport by military conspirators close to the Philippine president. In the following months the armed insurgency of the New People's Army (NPA), a Maoist organization, gathered strength throughout the country. The NPA initiated hundreds of raids against military garrisons and controlled large portions of the countryside and even some cities. In July 1985 analysts for the U.S. Central Intelligence Agency predicted that the NPA might seize power in five years, and in October Reagan sent Senator Paul Laxalt to Manila to express concern over the deteriorating situation. Two weeks later Marcos announced a presidential "snap election" to be held in February 1986. Aquino's widow, Corazon, led a united opposition ticket. On election day, news of widespread fraud incited massive street demonstrations. Catholic bishops denounced the election and called for civil disobedience. On February 22 two leading military officials, Fidel V. Ramos and Juan Ponce Enrile, defected, sealing themselves in a military camp in central Manila. Thousands rushed to the camp to protect Ramos and Enrile from army units loyal to Marcos, while other demonstrators seized broadcast stations and marched on the presidential palace. At Reagan's urging, Marcos fled to Hawaii on February 25.

The new government, headed by Corazon Aquino, maintained strong ties to the United States, allowing the United States to keep its military installations despite increasing opposition to the bases from Filipinos. The Aquino administration endured a string of unsuccessful military coups, the boldest of which, in December 1989, was suppressed with the help of planes dispatched by President George Bush. The end of the cold war coincided with negotiations to renew the bases treaty, and by 1991 it was evident that President Bush was unwilling to offer sufficient aid to gain approval of the treaty from the Philippine senate. In June the eruption of Mount Pinatubo destroyed Clark Air Force Base and damaged the naval station at Subic Bay, further diminishing their value. Unsatisfied with the proposed terms for renewal, the Philippine senate rejected the new treaty in September; the last U.S. forces left the Philippines in November 1992. Relations between the two countries remained cordial, although the United States closed many of its aid programs and consulates, reflecting the Philippines' diminished importance for U.S. foreign policy. In 1992 Filipinos elected Ramos, who had been endorsed by Aquino, to the presidency.

[David Wurfel, *Filipino Politics: Development and Decay* (Ithaca, N.Y., 1988).]

NICK CULLATHER

See also **SUPP:** Filipino Americans.

PHILOSOPHY in the United States since the 1960s has been characterized by diversity and pluralism in the subjects studied and the methods employed, by a significant increase in the number of its practitioners, by a growing influence within colleges and universities, and by a waning influence in the larger society. Analytic philosophy, which dominated philosophic thought in the United States in the middle of the twentieth century, remained important, but wider diversity was brought about by other approaches, such as continental European thought; renewed interest in pragmatists and other historical figures; applied philosophy, including ethics; and new voices espousing feminism, environmentalism, and animal rights. In the 1990s philosophy seemed secure within institutions of higher education; the membership of the American Philosophical Association, most of whom teach in a college setting, climbed from 2,888 in 1975 to 8,792 in 1990. Philosophers also found an audience outside their own departments, as nonphilosophers took up such subjects as semiotics, feminism, and rights and the study of European philosophers, such as Ludwig Wittgenstein, Friedrich Nietzsche, Jacques Derrida, Michel Foucault, and Martin Heidegger. Outside the academic world, however, the specialized and often highly technical studies published by philosophers found only a small audience. The broader audience that earlier read Ralph Waldo Emerson, William James, or John Dewey had largely vanished.

Analytic philosophy, with its analysis of language, concepts, and logic, appeared in the writings of such practitioners as W. V. O. Quine, Hilary Putnam, Donald Davidson, and Robert Nozick. Work in logic and the mathematical analysis of language contributed to the study of artificial intelligence. Philosophers were in the forefront of the effort to explore the meaning of the mind and intelligence in an era of increasingly more powerful computers. Other philosophers, however, such as Richard Rorty, who returned philosophy to its broadly humanistic roots and concerns, rejected the analytic goal of transforming philosophy into a science. Rorty, in his influential *Philosophy and the Mirror of Nature* (1979), urged his colleagues to put aside their epistemological and analytic interests in favor of participation in the "conversation" that constitutes culture. According to Rorty, the best one can hope for is not some absolute, scientifically determined truth that accurately mirrors nature and the "real world," but edification—the effort to find newer, better, and more productive ways of talking about human interests and problems. Phenomenology and existential philosophy were two European imports that contributed to this reorientation of philosophical thought. Not all philosophers were willing

to put aside analysis for edification, but Rorty's work helped spur on a diversification of philosophical approaches.

Pragmatism experienced something of a revival beginning in the 1970s. Often regarded as the most important contribution of the United States to philosophic thought, pragmatism was developed at the turn of the twentieth century by Charles S. Peirce, James, and Dewey. Such neopragmatists as Rorty and Richard J. Bernstein hark back to Dewey's broad philosophical outlook. Other scholars found in Peirce valuable logical insights and a well-developed theory of signs, or semiotics. Peirce, ignored for decades, was finally recognized as perhaps the greatest American philosopher. His seminal work in semiotics influenced such diverse fields as literature and anthropology. The revival of pragmatism was aided by the publication of modern scholarly editions of the works of James, Dewey, and Peirce.

The interrelated approaches of ethics, moral theory, and applied philosophy received renewed attention. Fields such as biomedical and business ethics brought philosophy out of the classroom into operating rooms and corporate board rooms. John Rawls's *A Theory of Justice* (1971) reconfigured debates in moral and legal theory. The study of rights moved beyond abstraction to the consideration of the rights of particular groups, such as the disadvantaged, the disabled, women, animals, and the environment. These discussions had more than scholarly impact; many philosophers sought to ground existing law or policy or to advocate expanding the concept of rights and legal protection to previously unprotected categories.

Philosophy became increasingly decentered as philosophers asked new questions and adopted new perspectives and standpoints. The philosophy of science, building on the work of Thomas S. Kuhn, raised serious questions about the objectivity of science. Feminist philosophy, as practiced by Alison Jagger and Sandra G. Harding, for example, challenged the patriarchical assumptions undergirding most philosophical work and asserted the importance of women's ways of knowing. African-American philosophers, such as Cornel West, sought to counter Eurocentrism with insights from an Afrocentric perspective. Animal rights advocates, such as Peter Singer and Tom Regan, asserted the rights of nonhuman sentient beings. Environmental philosophers adopted a biocentric perspective, putting nature rather than humanity at the center of philosophic vision. By asking new questions and challenging old assumptions, these new perspectives enlivened philosophic debate and made philosophy more relevant for previously marginal groups. Pluralism and fragmentation were characteristic of philosophy in the United States near the end of the twentieth century. While the analysis of concepts, language, and logic remained important, the weakening of the analytic tradition and the rise of new voices and perspectives encouraged philosophers to participate in a broader humanistic conversation that was often international in scope.

[John Rajchman and Cornel West, eds., *Post-Analytic Philosophy* (New York, 1985); John Rawls, *A Theory of Justice* (Cambridge, Mass., 1971); Richard Rorty, *Philosophy and the Mirror of Nature* (Princeton, N.J., 1979).]

DANIEL J. WILSON

PHOENIX. During and after World War II the Arizona capital became a major military and high technology center due to massive federal funding. Phoenix moved to the top of the urban hierarchy in the desert Southwest in the 1950s and secured its hold on that position during the next thirty years as a center of manufacturing, tourism, and agriculture. The mass production of air conditioners in the 1950s made Phoenix livable in summer as well as winter. The population was 789,704 in 1980, up from 439,170 in 1960 and 65,414 in 1940. By 1980 the city ranked as the ninth-largest in the nation. The boom continued during the 1980s, and Phoenix expanded in size and prominence. A combination of economic opportunities and amenities attracted newcomers, and political changes and cultural developments appeared to the satisfaction of many residents. As Phoenix became a sprawling, multicentered metropolis, however, it served as an example of the problems as well as the progress of the new urban United States. City services often lagged behind growth. Critics complained but few were heeded. In the late 1980s recession brought hardship to Phoenix but by 1992 another economic boom and population explosion was under way. In that year Phoenix was declared the eighth-largest city in the country with a population of more than 1 million; the metropolitan area contained more than 2 million. In the mid-1990s the major problem facing Phoenix was the conflict between the area's two most cherished values—growth and the good life. The challenge was to handle growth in ways that would improve the quality of life rather than harm it.

[Bradford Luckingham, *Phoenix: The History of a Southwestern Metropolis* (Tucson, Ariz., 1989).]

BRADFORD LUCKINGHAM

See also **SUPP:** Arizona; Sunbelt; Tucson.

PHOTOGRAPHY. During the final decades of the twentieth century photography became easy for unskilled practitioners. The cumbersome method introduced by Louis J. M. Daguerre in 1839 had given way to affordable 35-mm compact automatics. Photographic images in silver, color dyes, and printers' ink had spread around the world. Innovations in moving film made faraway events accessible through simultaneous broadcast. Professional photographers were typically in the forefront of technology and trends. To compensate for the disappearance of skilled portraiture and documentation in the wake of the 35-mm revolution, photographers turned to publishing and advertising. Their camera of choice was a 2¼-inch format equipped with motor drives and used with multiple lenses and sophisticated artificial lighting. Fine-art photographers devoted considerable energy to experimenting with equipment, format, film, and paper, and their subjects tended toward the eclectic. Since the late 1940s they have attempted to capture "private realities," a quest that drew inspiration from such sources as Eastern religious philosophies, psychoanalytic theory, and abstract expressionist painting. The popularity of this form in the United States stemmed from the postwar economic boom, the ability of former military personnel to attend art schools and colleges at federal expense, and the founding of the Institute of Design, the Western Hemisphere version of the Bauhaus, which advocated a "new vision" of interpreting common places in personal ways. New vision photographers experimented with equipment and format, frequently contriving a final image from collages, montages, and multiple exposures.

The straight tradition popularized by Edward Weston remained the dominant but far from the only style in professional photography in the late twentieth century. A gifted photographer, educator, and author, Minor White, encouraged his followers to reveal "things for what they are" as well as "for what else they are." His advocacy of the "equivalent image" produced a cultlike following in the 1960s that continued into the 1990s. White's influence led photographers with a mystic bent to seek spiritual oneness with nature. With large-format cameras they photographed such natural phenomena as gnarled trees, tumultuous ocean waves, and dew-tinged leaves and petals. Photographers like Walter Chappell and Paul Caponigro struggled to evoke the mystic divinity of nature itself. Aerialists like Bradford Washington went aloft to invest nature with stunning abstractions of shifting land masses and geometrical farmlands.

Photographers took to the streets in the 1950s and 1960s using handheld units to frame reality with sardonic or ironic twists. Like the painter Andy Warhol, these photographers opted for the vernacular and emblems of popular culture. Modern masters like William Klein, Garry Winogrand, and William Wegman chose human (and in Wegman's case, canine) interaction among artifacts, whereas Elliott Erwitt, who beginning in the late 1940s has taken pictures of everyday scenes from around the world, preferred symbols largely free of human encroachment, although one well-known sequence shows the world of humans from a dog's point of view. Bruce Davidson and Diane Arbus sought odd faces in out-of-the-way places and captured them with a dignity previously reserved for the wealthy and classically beautiful.

Underlying the achievements of all photographers since the 1970s were technological improvements in cameras. The single-lens reflex camera became smaller and more reliable, with large-format cameras revamped to fit the computer age. In 1972 the Polaroid camera was improved with the SX-70 system, which was in turn supplanted by the 600 system, featuring automatic focus, electronic flash, and battery together with high-speed color film. In the last quarter of the twentieth century both black-and-white and color-positive-and-negative film vastly improved in speed and resolution. Infrared film sensitive to light invisible to the human eye had wide use in science. In the 1990s both Agfa and Ilford marketed wide-latitude film that joined dye couplers with silver halides to form images.

Electronic cameras, introduced in the early to mid-1990s, became increasingly sophisticated and easy to use, producing high-resolution photos and spelling the end of film photographic processes in certain quarters, notably news coverage. In 1987 United Press International and Associated Press, the largest news wire services in the United States, began transmitting pictures electronically. Still-picture versions of camcorders or videocameras (which themselves gained wide use as observation and surveillance tools in prisons, hospitals, courts, schools, and banks and were employed to help diagnose injuries and perform such surgery as laparoscopy) came into being, and digital cameras enabled photographers to store pictures on computer chips, which can be downloaded and tinkered with on a personal computer, obviating the need for the darkroom. Despite industry predictions that digital cameras were poised to do to the traditional silver halide photography market what camcorders did to Super-8 home movies, their high

cost made acquisition prohibitive to the average consumer, although a camcorder could be converted into a digital camera for under $200. Digital imaging and computer manipulation of photos led to the use of faked and "enhanced" pictures in magazines, on television, and in newspapers. A 1994 *Time* magazine cover featured a digitally altered image of O. J. Simpson's mug shot, taken when he was arrested for the murder of his former wife and one of her friends. Among applications by the scientific community was the use in 1994 of digital image processing of conventional photographs to reveal detailed views of the sun's corona during an eclipse.

[Ian Jeffrey, *Photography: A Concise History* (New York, 1981); Beaumont Newhall, *The History of Photography: From 1839 to the Present,* 5th ed. (Boston, 1982); Johann Willsberger, *The History of Photography* (Garden City, N.Y., 1977).]

EVELYN S. COOPER

PHYSICIAN ASSISTANTS (PAs), persons trained, certified, and licensed to take medical histories, conduct physical examinations, and diagnose and treat medical problems under the supervision of physicians, thereby extending the capacity of physicians to provide care. In the mid-1990s there were more than 20,000 PAs practicing in the United States in all areas served by physicians, including primary care, internal medicine, surgery, geriatrics, psychiatry, and pediatrics. The creator of this profession was Eugene A. Stead, chairman of the Department of Medicine at Duke University in the mid-1960s. A 1959 Surgeon General's report indicated that the nation faced a shortage of medical personnel, particularly among such traditionally underserved populations as the rural and inner-city poor and elderly. Stead's idea was that returning medical corpsmen from Vietnam, with their experience treating illness and injury, could be trained to work in health care facilities in less time than that required to complete an entire medical and residency program. In 1965 four medical corpsman entered the first PA program under Stead's direction at Duke; thirty years later there were fifty-eight such programs throughout the United States.

The American Medical Association officially recognized the profession in 1971 and began working on the process of PA certification. PA training has not changed a great deal since. Most programs require two years and include intensive clinical rotations under physician supervision. Physician supervision continues throughout the careers of PAs, making them "dependent practitioners" along with nurses. PAs see patients with routine and minor complaints, freeing physicians to see more serious cases, and provide continuity for regular patients in settings with medical residents and interns whose positions turn over rapidly. Malpractice claims against PAs have been few; insurance analysts consider PAs low-risk providers because they are dependent practitioners. PAs work in virtually all health care settings, including rural communities in which they may be the only practitioners. All states except Mississippi license and regulate PA practice and most allow PAs to write prescriptions. Work opportunities are extensive. The American Academy of Physician Assistants claims six jobs for every graduating PA and the Department of Labor projects a 44 percent increase between 1990 and 2005. PAs are no longer an experiment but an important part of mainstream medical care.

[Gretchen E. Schafft and James F. Cawley, *The Physician Assistant in a Changing Health Care Environment* (Rockville, Md., 1987).]

SUSAN ANDREW

See also **SUPP:** Health Care; Hospitals; Medicine.

PHYSICS. In the last quarter of the twentieth century, physicists expanded the range and power of the laser, learned how to obtain controlled nuclear fusion for short intervals, manufactured several new transuranium elements, discovered that certain exotic mixtures could be superconducting at relatively high temperatures, formulated the theory of quarks, and found a series of massive nuclear particles to confirm the augmented theory of atomic nuclei. U.S. theorists took the lead in establishing and developing the nuclear theory that is now called "the standard model," and U.S. scientists won the majority of Nobel Prizes in Physics during this period.

Lasers, invented in the early 1960s, were commonplace by the 1980s, used in bar-code readers and compact disk players. In the 1970s physicists discovered how to make tunable lasers, which greatly increased the possible color range, and by 1980 lasers could be used to make individual atoms stand still. The first successful X-ray laser was built in 1984. These can be so powerful that they were studied both as weapons for destroying enemy missiles (as part of the now-defunct Strategic Defense Initiative) and as tools for the production of controlled nuclear fusion.

Meanwhile, physicists, notably at Princeton University, developed the tokamak, a donut-shaped magnetic enclosure in which ionized matter could be contained and heated to the very high temperatures necessary for nuclear fusion to take place. By 1977 they obtained temperatures of 27 million kelvins. (For fusion to take place, 100 million kelvins are required.) Within a few years the Princeton experiments reached 80 million kelvins, and by 1991 Princeton physicists sustained fusion for two seconds. In May 1994 the Princeton tokamak momentarily generated nine megawatts of power by transforming hydrogen isotopes into helium.

In 1972 a group of Americans won the Nobel Prize in Physics for their work on the theory of superconductivity, the phenomenon where, at very low temperatures, electrical resistance ceases. The next year physicists discovered that a combination of the elements niobium and germanium became superconducting at 22.3 K, about 2 degrees higher than the previous record. In the late 1980s, however, scientists unexpectedly found other combinations with much higher (but still very cold) temperatures—above 120 K—that still lacked electrical resistance.

The greatest success in theoretical physics was in the understanding of the particles that compose the atomic nucleus and their interactions. By the 1960s physicists knew that in addition to the protons, neutrons, and electrons that had been used to explain atomic nuclei for several decades, there was a confusing number of additional particles that had been found using electron and proton accelerators (popularly known as "atom smashers"). A pattern, called the eightfold way, was discerned by the California Institute of Technology physicist Murray Gell-Mann and the Israeli Yuval Ne'eman. Gaps were noticed, predictions of a new particle were made, and the particle (the so-called Omega-minus) was promptly discovered. To explain the pattern, Gell-Mann postulated the existence of some underlying but unobserved elementary particles that he called "quarks."

Quarks carry electrical charges similar to protons or electrons, but the amounts of the charges are one-third or two-thirds of the charge of the electron or proton. Gell-Mann postulated several different kinds of quarks, giving them idiosyncratic names such as up, down, and strange. Protons and neutrons are clusters of three quarks. Protons are made of two up quarks, each with a charge of plus two-thirds, and a single down quark with a charge of minus one-third, so the total is plus one. Neutrons are made of one up quark and two down quarks, so the total charge is zero. Another group of particles, the mesons, are made up of quarks and antiquarks. More massive particles, such as the ones found independently by Burton Richter at the Stanford Linear Accelerator and

Samuel C. C. Ting at Brookhaven National Laboratory in 1974, fit into the picture as being made from charm quarks. Two years later Ting and Richter shared the Nobel Prize in Physics. The masses of these particles, like the spectrum of the hydrogen atom used by Niels Bohr many decades earlier to elucidate the quantum structure of the outer parts of electrons, now provided a similar numerical key for understanding the inner structure of the atom. Six different "flavors" of quarks are required to account for these heavy particles, and they come in pairs: up-down, charm-strange, and top-bottom. The first member of each pair has an electrical charge of two-thirds and the second of minus one-third.

Meanwhile, Sheldon Lee Glashow at Harvard University, Steven Weinberg at the Massachusetts Institute of Technology, and Abdus Salam at Imperial College in London in 1968 independently proposed a theory that linked two of the fundamental forces in nature, electromagnetism and the so-called weak nuclear force. Their proposal, known as quantum field theory, involved the notion of quarks and required the existence of three massive particles to "carry" the weak force, two charged particles (W+ and W−) and one neutral particle (Z). These particles are short-lived, massive versions of the massless photons that carry ordinary light. All of these particles are called bosons, or more precisely, gauge bosons, because the theory explaining them is called a gauge theory. The name, which comes about for purely historical reasons, refers to a type of symmetry in which labels of the particles can be interchanged according to rules suggested by quantum mechanics, and the resulting forces (and gauge bosons) are found as a consequence of the symmetry requirements.

By 1972 indirect evidence for the existence of the Z particle was found in Geneva at the European Centre for Nuclear Research (CERN), and the 1979 Nobel Prize in Physics went to Glashow, Weinberg, and Salam. It was not until 1983 that the Z particle itself was found, also at CERN, and close on the heels of this discovery came the detection of the W particle. Carlo Rubbia, a Harvard colleague of Glashow and Weinberg and leader of the successful discovery team, remarked to them, "Now you won't have to give back the prize!" A year later Rubbia himself shared the Nobel Prize in Physics.

In January 1987 the Tevatron proton-antiproton accelerator at the Fermi National Accelerator Laboratory (Fermilab) in Illinois came into operation. Having narrowly missed out on some of the earlier discoveries, the Fermilab scientists were particularly keen to find evidence for the postulated top quark, the only one of the quarks not yet measured and a particle so massive that only the most powerful accelerators could produce enough energy to find it. Their search at last succeeded in 1995.

Along with the quarks and bosons, a third type of particle completes the present roster: the lepton, of which the electron, positron, and a group of neutrinos are the best known examples. The leptons and quarks provide the building blocks for atoms. The gauge bosons interact with the leptons and quarks, and in the act of being emitted or absorbed, some of the gauge bosons transform one kind of quark or lepton into another. In the standard model, a common mechanism underlies the electromagnetic, weak, and strong interactions. Each is mediated by the exchange of a gauge boson. The gauge bosons of the strong and weak interactions carry electrical charges, whereas the photon, which carries the electromagnetic interactions, is electrically neutral.

In its simplest formulation, the standard model of the strong, weak, and electromagnetic interactions, although aesthetically beautiful, does not agree with all the known characteristics of the weak interactions nor can it account for the experimentally derived masses of the quarks. Nuclear theorists hoped that the Superconducting Super Collider under construction in Texas in the late 1980s would provide data to extend and correct the standard model. They were highly disappointed when Congress cut off funding for this expensive atom smasher.

The standard model is one of the great achievements of the human intellect. It will be remembered—together with general relativity, quantum mechanics, and the unraveling of the genetic code—as one of the outstanding intellectual advances of the twentieth century. It is not, however, the "final theory," because too many constants still must be empirically determined. A particularly interesting development since the 1970s is the joining of particle physics with the astrophysics of the earliest stages of the universe. The early universe may provide the laboratory for exploration of the grand unified theories (GUTs) at temperatures and energies that are and will remain inaccessible in terrestrial laboratories.

[Frank Close, Michael Marten, and Christine Sutton, *The Particle Explosion* (New York, 1987); P. C. W. Davies, *The New Physics* (New York, 1989); Gary Taubes, *Nobel Dreams* (New York, 1986); Peter Watkins, *The Story of the W and Z* (New York, 1986); Steven Weinberg, *Dreams of a Final Theory* (New York, 1992).]

OWEN GINGERICH
S. S. SCHWEBER

See also **SUPP:** Astronomy; Cold Nuclear Fusion; Fermi National Accelerator Laboratory; Laser Technology; Superconducting Super Collider; Superconductivity.

PHYSIOLOGY. Advances in technology and microbiology contributed to the great strides taken by U.S. scientists in animal and plant physiology during the latter part of the twentieth century. Recognition of such accomplishments resulted in dominance of the United States in Nobel Prizes for medicine and physiology from 1975 to 1993; twenty-eight U.S. citizens won those awards during that period. U.S. progress in basic research helped combat serious diseases. In 1976 the Nobel Prize in physiology and medicine went to went to Baruch S. Blumberg and Daniel Carleton Gajdusek of the National Institutes of Health (NIH) for identification of the origin and dissemination of infectious diseases. That same year, by identifying interleukin-2, a protein factor promoting growth of human T cells in culture, Robert C. Gallo and his group at the National Institute of Allergy and Infectious Diseases opened the way for identifying human retroviruses. Also in 1976 J. Michael Bishop and Harold E. Varmus discovered the cellular origin of cancer-causing genes known as oncogenes, found in retroviruses, work that won them the Nobel Prize in 1989. There were also achievements in physiology affecting the heart. In 1980 Baruj Benacerraf and George D. Snell shared the Nobel Prize with Jean Dausset of France for their explanation of how cell structures relate to organ transplants and diseases. For clarification of the cholesterol metabolism, Michael S. Brown and Joseph L. Goldstein received the Nobel Prize in 1985. The U.S. Department of Agriculture also won recognition. In the 1940s and 1950s Nobelist (1983) Barbara McClintock experimented with corn and found that genes in corn chromosomes moved and could cause mutations in future generations of plants descending from the parent with mobile genes.

[I. Edward Alcamo, *Fundamentals of Biology,* 3rd ed. (Redwood City, Calif., 1991); Maya Pines, *Inside the Cell: The New Frontier of Medical Science* (Washington, D.C., 1978).]

RUTH ROY HARRIS

See also **SUPP:** Acquired Immune Deficiency Syndrome; Bacteriology and Virology; Cancer; Cardiovascular Disease; Clinical Research; Epidemiology; Genetic Engineering; Human Genome Project; Medicine; Microbiology; National Institutes of Health; Research Laboratories.

PITTSBURGH, the second-largest city in Pennsylvania, in 1970 represented the potential of post–World War II urban renewal for American cities. A twenty-five-year program, engineered by the partnership of Richard K. Mellon, a powerful Republican financier, and David L. Lawrence, mayor of Pittsburgh from 1945 to 1958 and the local Democratic party leader, cleaned the city's air and rivers, revitalized the downtown area, and rebuilt the infrastructure. Despite this renaissance, as the redevelopment was called, industry expanded slowly, the city lost population, and the metropolitan area's population barely increased. After 1970 Pittsburgh's steel industry collapsed, and electrical equipment, glass, and coal-mining corporations shuttered old plants. The steel industry was hampered by excess capacity, obsolete technology, and high labor costs. More than half the metropolitan area's manufacturing jobs disappeared, 90,000 in primary and fabricated metals alone. By 1990 manufacturing employed 12 percent of the labor force. Plant closings mirrored the decline in the number of corporate headquarters located in Pittsburgh, which dropped from third to eighth rank among U.S. cities in the number of Fortune 500 corporate headquarters.

As both young people entering the labor market and middle-aged workers left Pittsburgh in search of employment opportunities, the five-county metropolitan area by 1990 lost more than 300,000 residents from its 1950 population, a 12 percent decline; the population of the city of Pittsburgh plunged to 370,000, half the figure in 1950. Although the African-American community did not grow in absolute numbers, its proportion of the city's total population rose to more than 25 percent. Few Hispanic or Asian migrants came to the city.

Pittsburgh's leaders drew upon the earlier renaissance to address the economic challenge. Democratic Mayor Richard Caligiuri rebuilt the partnership with corporate leaders, encouraged office construction in the downtown business section known as the Golden Triangle, supported a light rail and subway system as well as a new airport, and cooperated with foundations to develop cultural facilities. Called Renaissance II, this redevelopment initiative supported a burgeoning banking, legal, and business services sector. Moreover, higher education and medical institutions generated growth from medical research, advanced technology, and health care businesses. In

1990 services employed one-third of the metropolitan area's labor force. With a low crime rate, affordable housing, and cultural amenities, Pittsburgh received the mantle of America's most livable city in the mid-1980s.

The service sector softened the city's precipitous industrial decline, but development across the region was uneven. In the 1990s older towns of the industrial river valleys remained depressed, while suburbs with interstate highway access, Pittsburgh's downtown and university districts, and the airport corridor flourished. Pennsylvania state programs, economic and community development organizations, and foundations struggled to help depressed mill towns and create a regional perspective that would allow Pittsburgh and communities in the metropolitan area to work together.

[John P. Hoerr, *And the Wolf Finally Came: The Decline of the American Steel Industry* (Pittsburgh, 1988); Stefan Lorant, *Pittsburgh* (Lenox, Mass., 1988).]

EDWARD K. MULLER

See also **SUPP:** Pennsylvania.

PLANNED PARENTHOOD OF SOUTHEASTERN PENNSYLVANIA V. CASEY, 112 Supreme Court 2791 (1992) is best known for what it did not do—overrule *Roe* v. *Wade* (1973). By 1992 five associate justices had been appointed to the Supreme Court by Presidents Ronald Reagan and George Bush, both of whom pledged to select judges committed to overturning *Roe,* which had legalized abortion. Reagan had named William Rehnquist, one of the original dissenters in *Roe,* as chief justice in 1986. *Webster* v. *Reproductive Health Services* (1989) and *Rust* v. *Sullivan* (1991) had upheld laws limiting access to abortion and seemed indicators of doctrinal shifts. The Pennsylvania Abortion Control Act at issue in *Casey* did not ban abortion, but the Court upheld all of the restrictions on abortion imposed by Pennsylvania except for mandatory husband notification. These included a twenty-four-hour waiting period, informed consent of one parent for pregnant teenagers, reporting requirements, and a state-scripted warning against the medical procedure. As a result of *Casey,* restrictions on abortion would no longer be judged by a strict scrutiny standard requiring a "compelling state interest," as did restrictions on other constitutional rights. Instead, an "undue burden" standard was substituted, allowing states to place restrictions on abortion unless they posed "substantial obstacles" to a woman's right of privacy recognized in *Roe.* For

Justices Sandra Day O'Connor, Anthony Kennedy, and David Souter, all appointed by Presidents Reagan and Bush, "the reservations any of us may have in reaffirming the central holding of *Roe* are outweighed by the expectation of individual liberty." Hence, *Casey* was a defeat for both sides on the abortion issue. It represented a victory for centrist judicial politics.

[Barbara Hinkson Craig and David M. O'Brien, *Abortion and American Politics* (Chatham, N.J., 1993).]

JUDITH A. BAER

See also **SUPP:** Abortion.

PLURALISM, a concept that recognizes and affirms racial, ethnic, and religious diversity within U.S. society, has been a prominent mode of thought in political science and philosophy since the 1950s, when scholars first argued that individual and group differences have a self-correcting and synergetic effect on a common national culture. Multiculturalism, which gained currency on college campuses in the 1980s, sought to replace a "patriarchal" and "ethnocentric" national history with a "curriculum of inclusion" that emphasizes the struggles and achievements of neglected social groups and societies. Pluralism, however, usually emphasizes commonalities among U.S. citizens that multiculturalism does not. While pluralism legitimizes diversity and difference, it also assumes the necessity for intergroup toleration and cooperation in the larger framework of society. In a pluralistic society self-identified groups maintain autonomy while assimilated within a common national identity. Pluralism is the attempt to make the United States what the philosopher Richard Rorty calls "a community of communities, a nation with far more room for difference than most." Pluralism maintains that the United States inherits a complex, commonly held political philosophy resting on the rules of law, contract, and property, encased in a federal structure of limited government, on citizen-based consent. Pluralism operates on the system of representative democracy and citizen-based rights, liberty, equality, reform, and progress. These ideas overarch and unite citizens of different ethnicities, social backgrounds, and religions, strengthening the position of the individual and collective society. They draw strength from tolerance and inclusion. Some political theorists seek pluralism's political authority and legitimacy in the different communities that bind individuals and groups on the basis of religion, race, ethnicity, and other differences. Other theorists emphasize the pluralist values of ethnicity, localism, religion, and kinship, relying on informal customs, folkways, and habits of mind to sustain liberty and to moderate invasive national laws or administrative regulations.

GILBERT T. SEWALL

See also **SUPP:** Curriculum; Multiculturalism.

POLICE. In the early 1990s, the United States had more independent police agencies than any other country. Estimates have been as high as 40,000, but contemporary estimates range from 20,000 to 25,000. These figures contrast with such countries as Ireland and Israel, which have single national police forces, and with those countries whose multiple forces are centrally coordinated, such as France and Great Britain. It is at least partly by design that the United States has neither a single national police force or a centrally coordinated system of multiple agencies. Local control of police appeared to be a guarantee against the acquisition of too much political power by police. The Federal Bureau of Investigation has some characteristics of a national police force, but its jurisdiction is limited by other federal police agencies, as well as by state and local police forces. Many critics use what they regard as the serious abuses of power by J. Edgar Hoover, who headed the FBI for forty-eight years (1924–1972), to argue against greater centralization.

In 1995 there were more than sixty federal agencies with law enforcement powers. The FBI, U.S. Marshals Service, Immigration and Naturalization Service, and Drug Enforcement Administration are in the Department of Justice. Within the Department of the Treasury are the Secret Service, Customs Service, and Bureau of Alcohol, Tobacco and Firearms. The police power of this last agency was brought to the attention of the American public by its 1993 raid on the Branch Davidian complex in Waco, Texas. Federal police agencies have specialized law enforcement functions, but their geographical jurisdiction extends throughout the United States. Although the jurisdictions of state and local agencies are limited to territory governed by state or local political authorities, they have general law enforcement powers within their territories. There are some legal extensions to the geographically limited authority of local police. Buffer zones can extend beyond city or county lines within which police have full authority, and officers often have the authority to engage in "hot pursuit" of a suspect across boundaries that would

normally define their jurisdiction. The Texas Rangers, founded in 1835, before Texas became a state, became the first state police force. Pennsylvania established a state police force in 1905, and the other states, except for Hawaii, have followed suit. The law enforcement powers of state police vary from one state to another. State National Guard units, normally federally controlled army or air force units, can also be used by the governors of states as domestic police agencies in times of emergency. Sheriffs are county officials, generally elected to office. Although the list of tasks typically performed by sheriff departments is long, responsibilities vary from one department to another. In addition to law enforcement, sheriffs usually have charge of county jails and can be officers of the county court, enforcing courtroom security and serving legal notices, such as warrants, subpoenas, and foreclosures. Sheriff departments sometimes receive criticism because of their connection to politics and frequent failure to uphold professional standards for recruitment and training.

Police departments have become more professional by raising recruitment standards, increasing recruit training, and using advanced technology and the results of specialized research. Scientific police work began in Europe, with development of fingerprinting and other modern methods of crime detection, and U.S. police departments began to adapt the European model to the United States in the early twentieth century. There has been an increase in use of technology, from the introduction of radio-dispatched patrol cars in the 1930s to the use of computerized databases in the 1990s. Many police agencies now require recruits to have college degrees, and a growing number of programs in criminal justice have attracted students hoping to pursue careers in police work. The professionalization of the police was in response not only to the technical demands of law enforcement but also to repeated discoveries of corruption in police departments. In New York City the 1972 report of the Knapp Commission, appointed to investigate the corruption allegations of Detective Frank Serpico, stated that 15,000 New York City police officers, half the members of the department, were taking illegal payoffs. In 1986 police officers in Boston were found to have been stealing and fixing police promotion exams, and officers in New York and Philadelphia were accused of participation in gambling and drug operations. The beating of Rodney King in 1991 by Los Angeles police officers led to widespread investigations throughout the country of police racism and excessive use of violence.

Since the early 1970s police departments have recruited more women and minorities through the efforts of progressive police leaders and because of the legal requirements for equal employment and affirmative action. Recruitment of minorities was part of attempts to improve relationships between police and communities. Such incidents as the videotaped beating of King dramatized the need for police who are both highly professional and committed to the welfare of people within their jurisdictions. After the riots following acquittal of the officers who beat King, former Philadelphia Police Commissioner Willie Williams was appointed the first African-American police chief in the history of Los Angeles.

[David H. Bayley, *Patterns of Policing: A Comparative International Perspective* (New Brunswick, N.J., 1995); Randy LaGrange, *Policing American Society* (Chicago, 1993).]

RICHARD W. MOODEY

See also **SUPP:** Crime; Federal Bureau of Investigation; Justice, Department of; Los Angeles Riots; Waco Siege.

POLISH AMERICANS. The arrival of Poles at the Jamestown colony in Virginia on Oct. 1, 1608, initiated the Polish presence in America. The London Company recruited Poles, most probably to manufacture pitch, tar, and soap. When the hard-working Poles were denied the vote in the Virginia House of Burgesses in 1619, they objected and won the franchise. Few Poles, however, reached the colonies before the American Revolution. Kazimierz Pulaski and Tadeusz Kościuszko were the earliest Polish political émigrés. Pulaski served as a volunteer in the Continental army from 1777 to 1778 and then was made a general and ordered to organize a cavalry corps; he was mortally wounded at the Battle of Savannah in October 1779. Kościuszko was appointed colonel of engineers in the Continental army in 1776, and his fortifications at Freeman's Farm (Bemis Heights), N.Y., ensured the American victory at Saratoga in 1777. A scattering of exiles and émigrés followed in the first half of the nineteenth century.

The character of Polish migration changed in 1854, when 150 Silesian peasants settled Panna Maria, Texas, near San Antonio. Driven by what was unavailable at home, especially after the Polish Insurrection of 1863, Poles came to the United States, according to Henryk Sienkiewicz, a Nobelist in literature (1905), "in search of bread and freedom." They planted urban villages in the midwestern indus-

trial states of Illinois, Michigan, Wisconsin, Ohio, Minnesota, and Indiana and in the Atlantic coast states of New York, Pennsylvania, New Jersey, Massachusetts, Connecticut, Maryland, Delaware, Rhode Island. Polish settlements were particularly dense in metropolitan New York, Chicago, Detroit, Philadelphia, Milwaukee, Buffalo, Pittsburgh, Cleveland, Minneapolis–St. Paul, Boston, and Baltimore. They labored in steel and linen mills, factories, and mines, while only 10 percent made their way into agriculture. Polish immigrants organized a complex community infrastructure between 1854 and World War II. More than 950 Roman Catholic and Polish National Catholic parishes, 585 parochial schools, national insurance fraternal organizations (Polish National Alliance, Polish Roman Catholic Union, Polish Women's Alliance, and Polish Falcons), a Polish language press, and athletic, cultural, social, and political clubs and organizations. The 1930 U.S. Census counted 3,342,198 Polish immigrants and their descendants.

During World War I (1914–1918), Polish Americans lobbied the administration of President Woodrow Wilson on behalf of Poland's independence. In the interwar period, the Polish-American community pursued domestic priorities. Citizens clubs helped members acquire citizenship and political recognition. During and after the Great Depression, Polish Americans voted for Franklin D. Roosevelt and his New Deal and joined labor unions. By 1945 they constituted nearly 10 percent of the Congress of Industrial Organizations. The outbreak of World War II in September 1939 altered the Polish-American community's development. Following the Soviet occupation of Poland in 1944, 190,771 political émigrés, soldier-exiles, and displaced persons entered the United States between 1949 and 1956. The Polish American Congress, founded in 1944, articulated postwar Polish-American concerns, including the socioeconomic advancement of Americans of Polish origin. Polish settlements in the United States declined after World War II, as educational levels rose and Polish Americans joined the exodus from inner cities. A limited ethnic revival occurred in the 1970s, a response to the blight of ethnic humor in the media. The election of Pope John Paul II in 1978 stimulated Polish-American pride, as did the creation of the Solidarity movement in Poland in 1980.

Most descendants of pre–World War I Polish immigrants became Americanized, but the appearance of a more liberal communist government in Warsaw in 1956 reopened direct migration from Poland, reinforcing declining Polish communities in the United

States. The Immigration and Naturalization Act of 1965 also shaped Polish migration to the United States. Between 1965 and 1990 there were 178,384 immigrants, along with 957,360 nonimmigrants, temporary visitors who claimed to be tourists but actually sought work. In addition, 35,131 Solidarity-era political refugees arrived in the 1980s. The arrival of more than one million immigrants, nonimmigrants, and refugees helped Polish-American communities survive. The 1990 U.S. Census recorded 9.4 million Americans of Polish descent.

A century ago peasants and unskilled laborers were the majority in the immigrant community. Since World War II, however, Polish Americans' income, education levels, and occupational mobility increased, as did their percentages in the professions, management, research and education, and in technical jobs. Americans of Polish origin who have achieved professional acclaim include Senator Edmund S. Muskie and Representative Dan Rostenkowski; Stanislaw Ulam (physics); Zbigniew Brzezinski (political science); Arthur Rubenstein, Liberace, and Bobby Vinton (music); Pola Negri, Gloria Swanson, and Charles Bronson (motion pictures); Nobel laureate Czeslaw Milosz and novelist Jerzy Kosinski; General John Shalikashvili; and baseball's Stan Musial and Carl Yastrzemski, while Polish Americans have played on every National Football League team.

Polish Americans in the 1990s were still concentrated in the states where their ancestors settled, but they joined the migration to the Sunbelt states. They are part of the American tapestry, but retain ties to their ancestral homeland. Polish Americans hailed the fall of communism in 1989 but remained anxious about Poland's security and lobbied for Poland's admission to the North Atlantic Treaty Organization and European economic and political associations.

[Andrzej Brozek, *Polish Americans, 1854–1939* (Warsaw, 1985); John J. Bukowczyk, *And My Children Did Not Know Me: A History of Polish-Americans* (Bloomington, Ind., 1987); Waclaw Kruszka, *A History of Poles in America to 1908* (Washington, D.C., 1905–1908), trans. and repr., James S. Pula, ed. (1993–1995); W. S. Kuniczak, *My Name Is Million: An Illustrated History of the Poles in America* (New York, 1978); Helena Znaniecka Lopata, *Polish Americans,* rev. ed. (New Brunswick, N.J., 1994); James S. Pula, *Polish Americans: An Ethnic Community* (New York, 1995).]

STANISLAUS A. BLEJWAS

POLITICAL ACTION COMMITTEES (PACs),
groups that collect monies from their members or politically like-minded citizens, represent a single interest group, such as a labor union, corporation, or industry, or such socioeconomic issues as abortion or the environment. PACs use their monies to influence the legislative and executive branches of government. Even foreign powers have PACs working in the halls of state legislatures and Congress. Participation in PACs is not always voluntary. Groups put pressure on the men and women who work for them by inviting them to participate either monetarily or as volunteers. The hidden message often is that those who give money to PACs will be looked upon favorably by the organization in the form of promotions and pay raises. PACs attempt to gain support for their interests by contributing to political campaigns, hoping that their favors will be returned once candidates reach office. Even when candidates eschew PAC money, the very existence and need for that money assures that, for the most part, only independently wealthy candidates can compete with those who take PAC money. The most insidious thing about PACs is that they continue to be part and parcel of a political process that assures that those with the most money will have the most access and influence in the system.

The origin of PACs can be traced to the American labor movement and the Congress of Industrial Organizations (CIO). The first political action committee was formed during World War II, after Congress prohibited the assets of organized labor from being used for political purposes. The CIO created a separate political fund in 1943 to receive and spend voluntary contributions and called it the Political Action Committee. After the CIO merged with the American Federation of Labor, a political action committee called the Committee on Political Education (COPE) was formed in 1955. Other PACs, such as the American Medical Political Action Committee (AMPAC) and the Business-Industry Political Action Committee (BIPAC), were formed in the 1950s and 1960s, but it was not until the reform legislation of the 1970s that the number of PACs began to increase significantly.

While labor unions formed PACs during the 1940s, corporations were not allowed to support candidates until the Federal Campaign Act (FECA) of 1971, which allowed corporations to use their money to set up PACs. In 1974 and 1976 FECA was amended, giving trade associations and corporations a new role in politics. As a result, FECA changed its guidelines for raising political money, sparking a tremendous growth in the number of PACs and the amount of money spent to influence the political system. Even though revisions in FECA set limits on the amount of money PACs could contribute to individual candidates and political campaigns ($5,000) and set a $1,000 limit on individual contributions per candidate per election, PACs were able to get around these limitations and still influence the political system. In fact, PACs often receive guidance from the lobbyists who work directly in the halls of state legislatures and Congress. While it is conflictive and often forbidden to have labor unions, for example, use their members' dues for political influence, there is no question that such arrangements are made.

Observers have argued for reform of the election process, insisting that PAC money should be eliminated or at least severely limited. Even where there are legal limits, individuals and groups have gotten around them by giving so-called "soft money" to political parties instead of directly to candidates. Officially, soft money is supposed to be used for party housekeeping, but in fact parties manage to pass on their cash to candidates. Gifts of soft money tend to obligate party managers to PACs and their political goals. In fact, the very existence of PACs since the 1970s has run up the tab on elections to the point that a single congressional contest may involve the expenditure of $1 million or more. For example, in 1974 approximately 600 PACs gave $12.5 million to congressional candidates. In 1988 the number of PACs had increased seven times (approximately 4,200 with $132 million in contributions to primarily incumbents). This increase raised public criticism of PACs and led to congressional proposals to eliminate them in 1991–1992, but no significant action was taken. According to the Center for Responsive Politics, there were 3,954 registered PACs in existence at the end of 1994, but only 3,001 were active.

[W. Lance Bennett, *The Governing Crisis: Media, Money, and Marketing in American Elections* (New York, 1992); William J. Keefe and Morris S. Ogul, *The American Legislative Process: Congress and the States,* 5th ed. (Englewood Cliffs, N.J., 1981); Frank J. Sorauf, *Money in American Elections* (Boston, 1988); F. Wertheimer and Susan Weiss Manes, "Campaign Finance Reform," *Columbia Law Review* 94 (May 1994).]

ALAN CHARTOCK

POLITICAL CARTOONS. The history of American political cartoons can be divided into three eras, defined by the medium in which the cartoons were presented to the public—as prints, in magazines, and in newspapers. In the first era, which spanned from the 1750s to the 1870s, most cartoons were sold as steel engravings or, after 1820, lithographs. During the second era, from the 1840s to the beginning of the twentieth century, most cartoons appeared in magazines, either as woodcuts or lithographs. This was the first golden age of the political cartoon, when Thomas Nast of *Harper's Weekly* and Joseph Keppler of *Puck* made the political cartoon a tool for reform. The third era dawned in 1884, when publisher Joseph Pulitzer began printing political cartoons on the front page of the *New York World.* Since then the political cartoon has become a staple of the editorial pages of daily newspapers. Important newspaper cartoonists of the late nineteenth century and the first half of the twentieth century include Homer Davenport *(New York Journal),* John T. McCutcheon *(Chicago Tribune),* Jay Norwood ("Ding") Darling *(Des Moines Register),* and Daniel Robert Fitzpatrick *(St. Louis Post-Dispatch),* the last three of whom received Pulitzer Prizes. The cartoons of Herbert L. Block ("Herblock"), who received the first of three Pulitzers in 1942, have appeared in the *Washington Post* since 1946.

Many critics regard the period from the mid-1960s to the mid-1990s as the second golden age of cartooning. The period began when Patrick Oliphant emigrated from Australia to the United States in 1964 to work for the *Denver Post.* Unlike his predecessors, who tended to support one political party or the other, Oliphant made fun of all politicians. His satiric cartoons, full of demeaning caricatures of well-known politicians, prompted a generation of Americans once again to regard the political cartoon as a tool of reform. Those who have followed in Oliphant's footsteps include Jeff MacNelly *(Richmond News Leader* and later *Chicago Tribune),* Mike Peters *(Dayton Daily News),* Tony Auth *(Philadelphia Inquirer),* Doug Marlette *(Charlotte Observer, Atlanta Constitution,* and later *New York Newsday),* and Jim Borgman *(Cincinnati Enquirer),* all of whom have won the Pulitzer Prize for Editorial Cartooning. None of these cartoonists' work, however popular, had the impact of Garry Trudeau's comic strip "Doonesbury," which began in 1970 and was the first comic strip to be awarded the Pulitzer for editorial cartooning (1975). Because of its treatment of such controversial content as abortion, "Doonesbury" has been "censored" with some frequency (that is, certain strips have not been included by some newspapers that routinely run the strip). By the mid-1990s "Doonesbury" was appearing daily in more than 1,000 newspapers.

[*The Best Editorial Cartoons of the Year* (Gretna, La., annually since 1972); Stephen Hess and Milton Kaplan, *The Ungentlemanly Art: A History of American Political Cartoons* (New York, 1975); Richard Samuel West, *Satire on Stone: The Political Cartoons of Joseph Keppler* (Urbana, Ill., 1988).]

RICHARD SAMUEL WEST

POLITICAL CORRECTNESS (PC). Originally a term of approval used by old-guard communists to mean toeing the party line, "political correctness" was resurrected in the 1970s and early 1980s by leftist writers and activists who used it in an ironic sense among themselves to mock the Left's tendency toward dogmatic adherence to "progressive" behavior and speech, particularly with regard to the politics of race, gender, sexual orientation, labor, the Third World, and the environment. The term entered general use, however, in the late 1980s, when neoconservatives adopted it as a disparaging description of what they believed was rigid adherence to multicultural ideals on college campuses. Allan Bloom's *The Closing of the American Mind* (1987) and Dinesh D'Souza's *Illiberal Education* (1991) became best-sellers indicting academic political correctness. Both writers argued that PC stifled intellectual creativity on campuses. Among their complaints was the substitution in the undergraduate curriculum of recent literature by women and minorities for the classics of Western civilization. Bloom and D'Souza regretted the fall from grace of the "DWEMs" (Dead White European Males), claiming that multicultural "diversity" and "pluralism" had achieved iconic status. The most freely satirized element of political correctness was the use of such euphemisms as "vertically challenged" for short, "differently abled" for handicapped, and "companion animals" for pets.

[William Bennett, *The Book of Virtues* (New York, 1994); Paul Berman, ed., *Debating P.C.* (New York, 1992); Allan Bloom, *The Closing of the American Mind* (New York, 1987); Dinesh D'Souza, *Illiberal Education: The Politics of Race and Sex on Campus* (New York, 1991).]

PATRICK ALLITT

See also **SUPP:** Conservatism; Curriculum; Multiculturalism.

POLITICAL PARTIES. *See* **Democratic Party; Republican Party; Third Parties and Independents.**

POLLUTION. *See* **Air Pollution; Noise Pollution; Water Pollution.**

POPULATION. *See* **Demographic Changes.**

PORNOGRAPHY, written or visual images intended to excite sexually. In the 1990s hard-core pornography was widely accessible and often depicted nonconsensual sexual intercourse in violent graphic images, whereas at the beginning of the twentieth century that which was merely "immoral" or "sensational," such as a hazy drawing of a seminude woman, was viewed as pornographic. Thus, historically a far broader range of literature and visual images was subject to legal governmental regulation, from erotic photographs to literary classics. A provision of the 1842 Tariff Act restricted "obscene" pictures and prints from entering the United States. The government became more interested in pornography during the Civil War, when soldiers began trading and collecting French postcards of pictures of nude and seminude women. The U.S. postmaster general in 1865 received a limited right to confiscate "obscene" materials in the mail. The Comstock laws of 1873 went further by making it illegal to sell or distribute through the mail a multitude of images in literature and art, as well as information on birth control or abortion.

From the 1870s through the mid-1930s, legal regulation of printed material and motion pictures was at its most restrictive. During this era the Supreme Court did not use arguments based on free speech and the First Amendment to challenge or modify obscenity laws and postal restrictions on literature or visual images. Until 1957 the Court accepted with only slight modification the British 1867 definition of "obscenity," which based censorship rulings on whether the written or spoken word (or visual representation) was intended to "deprave and corrupt those whose minds are open to such immoral influences, and into whose hands such a publication might fall." In effect, the Supreme Court upheld a definition of obscenity that created a standard for culture based on the lowest common denominator of acceptability—one that would not impair the moral development of children.

Before 1933 some novels that are now regarded as classics could not be distributed in the United States. The situation changed dramatically for literature in that year when federal judge John M. Woolsey, ruled that Irish author James Joyce's *Ulysses* was not obscene, arguing that the work should be taken as a whole, and prosecutors could not quote passages out of context as proof a book was obscene. On its first case against motion pictures in 1915, the Supreme Court ruled that the movie industry was a profit-inspired business, not an art form, and therefore subject to regulation. This allowed censorship by review boards before distribution of movies to the public by any state or local government that deemed it necessary or desirable. Beginning in 1934 the movie industry practiced rigorous self-regulation, through the Motion Picture Association of America and its Production Code, trying to avoid federal censorship.

At the turn of the century, censorship was popularly viewed as a device for social change. Groups such as the Woman's Christian Temperance Union joined vice societies to advocate censorship of literature and art. The American public has continued to support laws restricting the access of youth to pornographic films, as well as harsh action against anyone who creates or distributes child pornography. Like earlier reformers, Americans in the 1990s argued that censorship was necessary to protect children and family values. With *Miller* v. *California,* however, which was decided by the Supreme Court in 1973, the only adult pornography subject to governmental regulation became that which an "average person" deemed was without literary, artistic, political, or scientific value. The so-called LAPS test was weakened in 1987 when the court in *Pope* v. *Illinois* ruled that because community views varied, "reasonable person" should be substituted for "average person." Combinations of sex and violence soon began permeating not only low-budget pornographic films but mass-distributed movies, videos, and magazines, making violent portraits of adult sex readily available. By the 1990s pornographic materials were a $10 billion operation in the United States alone.

Late-twentieth-century adherents of the women's movement had divided opinions about pornography. Because of increasing violence against women, many feminists believed that pornography, especially images depicting violence against women or nonconsensual sex, are often harmful to female actors and, more broadly, to all women. This belief in the danger of pornography is based on the assumption that male viewers watch and read pornography as if it were a manual or an instruction guide to behavior, including relations between the sexes. Although the most extreme antipornography activists asserted that men learn to rape by watching and reading pornography, no study has proven a direct link, although many researchers have indicated that pornography diminishes male sensitivity to women's legal rights including the right to withhold consent to sex. Feminists Catharine MacKinnon and Andrea Dworkin oppose pornography both as "injurious speech," because it condones and encourages violence against women, and as a violation of women's civil rights. In the 1980s they successfully lobbied for ordinances in Minneapolis, Bellingham (Washington State), and Indianapolis. All were subsequently ruled unconstitutional on First Amendment grounds.

Anticensorship feminists who focus on the First Amendment argue that pornography should remain nonetheless a protected form of speech. Rejecting the idea that people respond to pornographic movies or books by trying to emulate the characters, they argue that pornography may serve as a safety valve, preventing violence against women by serving as a form of fantasy and as "safe sex." Some anticensorship feminists also doubt the efficacy of censorship and dislike its tendency to be used against such political minorities as homosexuals. They suggest that pornography's most objectionable images could be counteracted if feminist women and men produced their own pornography that challenged patriarchal and heterosexual notions about women's place in society. Anticensorship feminists point out that violence against women was a problem before pornography became as available and graphic as it has since the 1960s and conclude that banning pornography would probably not solve the physical abuse of women.

[Edward De Grazia, *Censorship Landmarks* (New York, 1969); Susan Gubar and Joan Hoff, eds., *For Adult Users Only: The Dilemma of Violent Pornography* (Bloomington, Ind., 1989); Susan Kappeler, *The Pornography of Representation* (Minneapolis, 1986); Laura M. Lederer, ed., *Take Back the Night* (New York, 1980); Lynne Segal and Mary McIntosh, eds., *Sex Exposed: Sexuality and the Pornography Debate* (London, 1992).]

ALISON M. PARKER

See also **DAH:** Censorship; **DAH** and **SUPP:** Freedom of the Press; **SUPP:** Prostitution; Women's Movement; Women's Rights.

PORTLAND, largest city in Oregon, located at the confluence of the Willamette and Columbia rivers, is named for Portland, Maine. Incorporated in 1851, the city has depended on trade throughout its history. The city tapped the wheat belt of the surrounding country to supply the California gold miners, then provided supplies to the miners of Idaho and Montana in the 1860s, as it did for Alaskan miners at the end of the nineteenth century. After the Civil War, the city drew the Columbia River and railroad wheat traffic of eastern Oregon and southeastern Washington. In 1905 the city sponsored the Lewis and Clark Centennial Exposition, and it profited from shipbuilding during World War I. The next boom came from the rebirth of shipbuilding under the leadership of Henry J. Kaiser's corporations during World War II. Substantial numbers of defense workers from many parts of the United States moved to Portland. To house the war workers, the new community of Vanport (between Portland and Vancouver, Wash.) was created, a town swept away by Columbia River floodwaters on Memorial Day 1948. During the 1970s and 1980s the city was substantially revitalized. Neighborhoods were preserved, a downtown transit mall was developed, and the city participated with regional governments to provide recreational, waste disposal, and mass transit facilities. Portland's principal industrial employers in the 1990s were wholesale and retail trades, services, and manufacturing, and the city has a vibrant artistic, literary, and musical life. Principal social problems that arose in the 1980s and 1990s included the decline in quality of the public schools because of voter insistence on cutting property taxes, the rise in the number of racial and ethnic gangs, and the loss of low-cost housing stock as neighborhoods began "gentrification." The city's population in 1990 was 437,319.

[Carl Abbott, *Portland: Gateway to the Northwest* (Northridge, Calif., 1985), and *Portland: Planning, Politics, and Growth in a Twentieth-Century City* (Lincoln, Nebr., 1983).]

GORDON B. DODDS

See also **DAH** and **SUPP:** Oregon.

POSTAL SERVICE, UNITED STATES. Since its establishment in 1970, the United States Postal Service (USPS), an independent agency of the executive branch of the government, has become a self-supporting corporation. Although the Postal Service is legislatively enjoined to achieve and maintain financial independence, unlike private corporations, it must provide cost-effective service and carry out federal policies. When the USPS sought to reduce costs during the 1970s and 1980s by consolidating services and closing local branches, public disapproval caused Congress to override such plans. As a self-sustaining corporation operating within the competitive private sector, the USPS strives for efficiency and innovation. It has computerized its operations; added Express Mail, an overnight service and the first new official class of mail since 1918; introduced Mailgrams, electronic messages delivered but not originating in writing; and in 1983 expanded the ZIP (Zone Improvement Program) code sorting system, first introduced in 1963 from five to nine digits. Despite competition from private-sector carriers, the USPS in the 1990s was the largest carrier of the world's mail (161 billion pieces annually), at rates lower than those of nearly all other letter carriers worldwide. The USPS achieves this standard even as its status as a federal agency imposes additional demands. The USPS must publicize and enforce legislation concerning interstate commerce, narcotics trafficking, business fraud, selective service registration, and the distribution of materials deemed pornographic. In 1992 there were 39,595 post offices, stations, and branches in the United States and possessions; in 1993 the USPS employed almost 780,000 employees, second only to the Department of Defense.

[United States Postal Service, *History of the U.S. Postal Service 1775–1981* (Washington, D.C., 1982).]

KERRY A. BATCHELDER

POST-STRUCTURALISM, an eclectic school of thought that significantly influenced literary and cultural theory in the 1970s and 1980s. It emerged as a reaction against the claims of 1960s French structuralism to scientific rigor, objectivity, and universal validity. Structuralism convinced many theorists that the key to understanding culture lay in the linguistic systemization of interrelationships in language. Building on the theories of the Swiss linguist Ferdinand de Saussure, the French anthropologist Claude Lévi-Strauss, and Russian Formalism, the structuralists found the clue to literary and cultural analysis in the phoneme, a unit of sound meaningful only because of its differences from other phonemes. Phonemes exemplify the elements in a cultural system that derive meaning from relations and contrasts with other elements. Structuralists determine meaning not by correlation to external reality but by analyzing its functions within a self-contained, culturally constructed code. Linguistic meaning is often established through binary opposition—the contrast of opposites, such as cold-hot and nature-culture. A critic who understands the underlying rules or "language" determining individual utterances will understand meaningful combinations and distinctions.

Post-structuralism was in part a reaction to structuralism's claim to comprehensive and objective exploration of every cultural phenomenon. This countermovement denied the objectivity of linguistic and cultural codes, language, and categories of conceptualization. It emphasized the instability of meanings, categories, and the inability of any universal system of rules to explain reality. The result was a radically nonhierarchical plurality of indeterminate meanings. Central to post-structuralist thought is Jacques Derrida's deconstructionism. Influential among literary critics at Yale University in the 1970s and 1980s, deconstructionism indicts the Western tradition of thought for ignoring the limitless instability and incoherence of language. The dominant Western logocentric tradition sought a transcendent center or primal guarantee for all meanings. Logocentric thinking, common since Plato, attempts to repress the contingency and instability of meaning. Thus, any privileging of some terms as central to truth is denied as being merely arbitrary (for example, male over female, white over black). In the United States, literary critics used post-structuralist analysis to challenge the boundary between criticism of literature's subjectivity and objectivity, while elevating figurative language and interpretation. For post-structuralists there is no God, Truth, or Beauty—only gods, truths, and beauties. In the early 1990s post-structuralism underwent an intense critique from a range of social critics. Aside from the obscurantism of the movement, it seemed ahistorical, dogmatic, willfully nihilistic, and unable to provide a critique of moral and social injustice. Perhaps a part of the hedonistic flight from social responsibility of previous years, the movement seemed to slow down.

[Jonathan D. Culler, *Structuralist Poetics: Structuralism, Linguistics, and the Study of Literature* (Ithaca, N.Y., 1975); Edith Kurzweil, *The Age of Structuralism: Lévi-Strauss to Foucault* (New York, 1980); Selden Raman and Peter Widdowson, *A Reader's Guide to Contemporary Literary Theory* (Lexington, Ky., 1993).]

ALFRED L. CASTLE

See also **SUPP:** Literature.

POST-TRAUMATIC STRESS DISORDER (PTSD)

is a psychological condition in people who have suffered threats to life or bodily integrity and feel helplessness or terror; the syndrome may also appear in people who have witnessed horrifying events and feel unable to escape or alter them. Features of PTSD include intrusive memories or thoughts about the event, efforts to avoid thinking about it, a general numbing of emotional responsiveness, and a constantly heightened level of arousal. Dissociation, a sense of detachment from the reality of surroundings, is a way people often cope with repeated trauma. The full syndrome may only develop over months or years. PTSD as the explanation for "hysteria" emerged in the research of French psychologist Pierre Janet and, early in his career, Austrian psychoanalyst Sigmund Freud. During World War I, PTSD was common in soldiers; it came to be called combat neurosis or, colloquially, "shell shock" or "battle fatigue." The concept was developed by American psychiatrist Abram Kardiner in his book *The Traumatic Neuroses of War* (1941). The American Psychiatric Association accepted PTSD in 1980 as an official diagnosis, largely in response to descriptions of returning Vietnam War veterans. The revival of the feminist movement in the late 1960s led to heightened awareness of domestic violence and abuse, whose victims are now recognized as often suffering a severe and persistent form of PTSD. The limits of the diagnosis, although not its fundamental validity, were still being debated as the twentieth century came to a close.

[Joel O. Brende, *Vietnam Veterans* (New York, 1985); Judith Lewis Herman, *Trauma and Recovery* (New York, 1992).]

WILLIAM IRA BENNETT

See also **SUPP:** Domestic Violence; Prisoners of War and Missing in Action; Psychiatry.

POVERTY, especially in its most tangible forms of hunger and homelessness, continued to plague the United States as the twentieth century drew to a close. Poverty challenges the belief that hard work will be rewarded, and that all U.S. citizens have equality of opportunity. Poverty is defined as either a relative measure of money or material goods of one person in relation to others or as an absolute measure of how a person can meet the minimum requirements for survival. The most commonly used, although widely disputed, measure of poverty in the United States is an absolute measure, known as the poverty line. This is an amount of money calculated by multiplying the Department of Agriculture's Economy Food Plan by three (assuming therefore that food constitutes one-third of a family's expenditures). Developed for purposes of research, the measure was never meant to mark eligibility for social programs. The poverty threshold in 1994 was $15,141 a year for a family of four. In that same year, and by that measure, 14.5 percent of Americans lived in poverty. The poverty rate was not evenly distributed throughout the U.S. population. In 1994 it was 11.7 percent among whites, 30.6 percent among African Americans, and 30.7 percent among Hispanics. Also of concern was that 21.8 percent of all children in 1994 were poor.

The first large-scale effort to confront poverty on a national basis in the United States was during the Great Depression of the 1930s, when as much as 25 percent of the workforce was unemployed. No longer were religious and voluntary associations, which had given charity to the "deserving" poor, able to provide for those out of work. The Great Depression also underlined the structural problems (epitomized by the stock market crash of 1929) creating poverty, as opposed to the wage earner's lack of morality or personal failings. The Social Security Act of 1935 introduced the nation to social insurance, unemployment insurance, and public assistance. During the early 1960s President John F. Kennedy helped focus the nation's attention on the 22.2 percent of the population (in 1960) living in poverty. During President Lyndon B. Johnson's administration (1963–1969), legislation collectively known as the War on Poverty increased federal spending for the poor and helped bring the poverty rate down to 12.1 percent by 1969. One of the philosophical innovations of this era was the concept of "maximum community participation" of the poor. The poor became community action workers and sat on boards of antipoverty agencies.

Throughout the 1970s and 1980s there was widespread disillusionment with antipoverty efforts and a disdain for welfare programs that many observers saw as sapping people's work ethic. Under the administration of Richard M. Nixon (1969–1974), spending for the poor increased, contrary to the public impression of that Republican president's policies. Ronald Reagan's administration (1981–1989), however, promoted a "new federalism" to reduce the federal role in providing for the poor. Programs for the poor remained, but with restricted eligibility. During the administration of Bill Clinton, the Republican Congress, in alliance with Republican governors, continued the effort to transfer the responsibility for the poor from the federal government to the states, over the objections of the Democratic minority and President Clinton.

In the 1990s Americans were still debating ways to battle poverty. Especially disturbing was the homelessness and lack of opportunity facing the inner-city poor. Measures such as eliminating the welfare program available in some states for single, chronically unemployed persons, limiting the duration of receipt of welfare, or tying eligibility to work training or educational programs were hotly disputed. The most radical of the new proposals was the elimination of the federal commitment to provide subsistence payments to poor children through the Aid to Families with Dependent Children program. Instead, states would be given smaller sums of money and be allowed to decide who would get benefits and how much they would get, and benefits would not go to children born to teenage mothers or to children born to women already receiving assistance. Self-help and empowerment again become key phrases in discussions of antipoverty efforts and were implemented by agencies such as Habitat for Humanity, which involved the poor in rehabilitating housing.

[Irene Glasser, *Homelessness in Global Perspective* (New York, 1994); Michael B. Katz, *The Undeserving Poor: From the War on Poverty to the War on Welfare* (New York, 1989); Sar A. Levitan, *Programs in Aid of the Poor,* 6th ed. (Baltimore, 1990); William Julius Wilson, *The Truly Disadvantaged: The Inner City, the Underclass, and Public Policy* (Chicago, 1987).]

IRENE GLASSER

See also **SUPP:** Reaganomics; Unemployment; Welfare.

POWs. *See* **Prisoners of War and Missing in Action.**

PREGNANCY DISCRIMINATION ACT (PDA), a 1978 amendment to Title VII of the Civil Rights Act of 1964, prohibits workplace discrimination on the basis of pregnancy. The issue arose in 1976 when the Supreme Court in *General Electric* v. *Gilbert* decreed that denial of benefits for pregnancy-related disability was not discrimination based on sex. This reasoning recalled past management decisions by which married women faced job discrimination and pregnant women were routinely fired. By 1977 women made up more than 45 percent of the labor force, but only one-quarter had insurance plans that allowed sick leave for pregnancy-related illness. Women's organizations, feminists, labor and civil rights advocates, and some right-to-life groups formed a coalition known as the Campaign to End Discrimination Against Pregnant Workers to seek legislative relief from the Court's decision. In 1977 the original PDA that Congress considered sought to prohibit discrimination against pregnant women in all areas of employment, including hiring, firing, seniority rights, job security, and receipt of fringe benefits. More controversial aspects of the bill required employers offering health insurance and temporary disability plans to give coverage to women for pregnancy, childbirth, and related conditions. Although major corporations already provided such benefits, business associations argued that pregnancy was a "voluntary condition," not an illness, and that the bill would raise insurance costs. A more critical problem arose when congressmen attached an antiabortion rider disallowing benefits for elective abortions. After considerable debate the House and Senate passed versions that permitted employers to choose to provide abortion benefits but ambiguously told employers that they could rate a first pregnancy "more or less favorably" than other disabilities. The law took effect on Oct. 31, 1978, affecting only those companies with disability plans, thus failing to cover some 60 percent of female workers. Since passage, states and feminist groups have disagreed over how it should be applied, whether to protect pregnant women or to treat them equally.

[Joyce Gelb and Marian Lief Palley, *Women and Public Policies,* rev. ed. (Princeton, N.J., 1987); Joan Hoff, *Law, Gender, and Injustice* (New York, 1991).]

GRAHAM RUSSELL HODGES

See also **SUPP:** Family and Medical Leave Act; *General Electric Company* v. *Gilbert;* Women's Movement; Women's Rights.

PRESIDENCY. The American presidency has undergone a major transition since the 1970s. The president has vastly greater power than any official to lead the citizenry by setting the national agenda and determining foreign policy. Far more than his predecessors, however, the contemporary president must negotiate with Congress, the judiciary, cabinet departments, and executive and independent agencies, all of which have become more assertive. The president also faces ever-greater pressure from an electorate increasingly less loyal to political parties, from special interest groups that are well-financed and from media that are investigative. The president's international influence has been eroded by the rise of other industrial nations and Third World countries. Further, although the United States has unrivaled military strength and the world's largest economy, in the post–cold war era the president's command of nuclear weapons and foreign aid is not as effective as before to resolve conflicts and align nations, and the public is reluctant to approve U.S. participation in international peacekeeping or nation-building operations.

President Franklin D. Roosevelt (1933–1945) established the modern presidency. He acted as chief legislative whip and established the executive office of the president by moving the Bureau of the Budget into the White House offices in 1939, thereby expanding federal authority. His administrators managed New Deal programs and a wartime economy, and he exercised extraordinary diplomatic-military authority through executive agreements and summit conferences. Presidents expanded their power in the next decades by using the Bureau of the Budget and Council of Economic Advisers to assess the costs of legislative programs and national economic policy, marshaling federal authority to enforce Supreme Court desegregation rulings and civil rights laws and commanding television time for addresses and press conferences to advocate policies. Notably, President Lyndon B. Johnson (1963–1969) focused his political-legislative skills on his Great Society's commitment to voting and social welfare rights.

Presidential power over foreign affairs grew even more markedly. Harry S. Truman (1945–1953) became the first president to send troops to fight a major war—in Korea—and to station them abroad—in Western Europe—without formal approval from Congress. President Dwight D. Eisenhower (1953–1961) unilaterally approved military and covert actions against foreign governments. President John F. Kennedy (1961–1963) denied Congress a role in crises over Cuba and Vietnam. President Johnson used an incident in the Gulf of Tonkin in 1964 to persuade Congress to authorize almost unlimited retaliation, which led to a decade of war in Vietnam. Mounting protest against the Vietnam War, which television brought graphically into American homes, forced Johnson to forgo a reelection bid in 1968.

Richard M. Nixon, a Republican with a "southern strategy," was elected president in 1968 by promising not only to end the Vietnam War but to maintain a "law and order" administration, to reduce executive branch intervention in economic and social welfare matters, and to appoint conservative Supreme Court judges who would not "legislate" from the bench. Despite these pledges, the Nixon presidency (1969–1974) proved to be as "imperial" as any other. It enlarged and delegated authority to White House staff, expanded the Bureau of the Budget in 1970 into an even more powerful Office of Management and Budget (OMB), and impounded congressionally allocated funds, a virtual line-item veto. In 1971 Nixon instituted wage and price controls, suspended international convertibility of the dollar, and imposed a surcharge on imports. At the same time he outspent Johnson's Great Society, becoming the only cold war president to spend more on human resources programs than defense. Under Nixon the White House dominated foreign policy. It expanded the Vietnam War by secretly bombing Cambodia, intensified the warfare in Laos, and vastly increased bombing of North Vietnam. He restructured the National Security Council (NSC) to rival the Department of State and authorized his NSC adviser to use secret diplomacy to destabilize other governments, opened relations with the People's Republic of China, and negotiated to conclude the Vietnam War. Nixon also established a tenuous détente with the Soviet Union.

Congress gradually reasserted its authority at home and abroad during the Nixon era. It refused to confirm two Supreme Court nominees (although Nixon did appoint four justices who greatly influenced

Court opinions) and passed the Budget and Impoundment Control Act of 1974, creating the Congressional Budget Office to counter OMB functions. In 1969 the Senate resolved that a national commitment to use U.S. forces or finances to aid another country required formal approval from Congress. In 1970 congress repealed the Gulf of Tonkin Resolution and prohibited use of past or present appropriations to finance U.S. combat in Laos, Cambodia, and North and South Vietnam after August 1973. The Case-Zablocki Act of 1972 mandated that the president report all executive agreements to Congress within sixty days. The War Powers Act of 1973, passed over Nixon's veto, limited the president's use of troops abroad without formal congressional approval to sixty to ninety days, although the law conceded the president's authority to commit troops initially. In 1983 the Supreme Court, in an unrelated case, ruled that legislative vetoes (that is, Congress's right to overturn executive branch action either by withholding approval or voting to disapprove) such as provided in the War Powers Act were unconstitutional. In addition, since 1973 every president has sent troops abroad with scant reference to the War Powers Act.

The Watergate scandal during Nixon's second term brought the presidency into disrepute. White House aides and other officials were convicted for sanctioning or covering up a break-in at Democratic National Committee headquarters during the 1972 presidential campaign, a grand jury named the president an unindicted co-conspirator, and the House Judiciary Committee voted impeachment articles. In August 1974 Nixon became the first president to resign the office. Watergate was the worst White House scandal in U.S. history because it violated civil liberties and the political process and produced enduring public cynicism about the presidency and politics, but it also created a framework for scrutinizing alleged presidential transgressions. This included investigation by congressional committees and special prosecutors and a unanimous Supreme Court ruling that the president's executive privilege does not reach to withholding evidence in a criminal proceeding.

The presidency in the decade following Watergate and the end of the Vietnam War appeared at least temporarily weakened. President Gerald R. Ford (1974–1977) lacked a national constituency when he assumed the office following Nixon's resignation, and he undercut his support by pardoning Nixon. Ford's successor, President Jimmy Carter (1977–1981), lacked congressional allies, and his call for zero-based budgeting won no favor with federal officials, but he was able to broker Middle East peace accords and gain passage of the Panama Canal Treaty in 1978. His presidency foundered on matters beyond White House control: an energy crisis; inflation; the Soviet invasion of Afghanistan; and a revolution and hostage-taking in Iran.

Ronald Reagan won the presidency in 1980 by promising to minimize the size and scope of the federal government and to restore marketplace freedom and offering a foreign-military policy to regain U.S. global primacy. He identified closely with his party and capitalized on resurgent Republicanism in the older South as well as in newer Sunbelt regions and on rising religious fundamentalism. His victory catalyzed growing opposition to higher taxes and social welfare payments, administrative agency rulemaking, judicial decisions giving legal status to socially based rights, and animus toward the Soviet Union and terrorism. Reagan used both old and new political devices to strengthen his presidential power. He galvanized popular support with media messages, and used OMB's fiscal analyses and oversight of agency budgets and legislative proposals to slash social welfare, reduce taxes, and increase military spending. His economic policies, dubbed "Reaganomics," led to record budget deficits that necessitated cuts in social programs, prevented new entitlements, and created policy formation by budget priority. Reagan speeded deregulation. During his eight-year presidency, he appointed more than half of all federal judges—although Congress in 1987 rejected his controversial Supreme Court nominee, Robert Bork, who favored recent Supreme Court decisions that narrowed individual rights.

In foreign affairs Reagan undertook a vast nuclear weapons buildup, deployed forces to Lebanon, invaded Grenada, bombed Libya, and approved extensive covert activity in Central America. After difficult summit meetings with Soviet leaders, he reversed course in 1987–1988 to effect the most significant nuclear arms reduction since the start of the cold war. His presidency was jolted by the revelation that NSC officials had broken the law and lied under oath to Congress while exchanging arms for hostages with Iran and supporting covert actions in Central America. Congressional and blue-ribbon panel investigations of the Iran-Contra scandal proved only that the president gave his aides license, not instruction, to violate the law.

The popular Reagan propelled Vice President George Bush into the White House in 1988. Bush's forceful foreign policies against dictators in Panama and Iraq raised his standing to extraordinary heights in 1991, but he lost reelection a year later to a relatively unknown Democrat, Governor Bill Clinton of Arkansas, whose campaign emphasized domestic issues and benefited from sharp criticism of Bush's economic policies by an independent presidential candidate, billionaire businessman Ross Perot. Despite initial difficulties, Clinton won passage of the North American Free Trade Agreement in 1993 and a sharply modified economic program that raised taxes on high incomes, reduced burdens on lower income groups, and slowed the growth of annual budget deficits, but also included only modest appropriations for education and job programs. Clinton also appointed two moderate Supreme Court justices, Ruth Bader Ginsburg and Stephen G. Breyer. Most significantly, however, after appointing his wife, Hillary Rodham Clinton, to head a task force on national health care reform, the president failed to gain necessary support for its complex proposal intended to guarantee health coverage for all Americans and to contain health care costs, which had risen to 14 percent of the gross national product.

The Clinton presidency achieved moderate success in foreign policy despite a setback in 1993 when eighteen U.S. soldiers, part of a United Nations mission in Somalia, were killed by rebel forces, leading to the withdrawal of U.S. troops. Nonetheless, the Clinton administration helped to broker historic accords, signed at the White House, that initiated mutual recognition between Israel, the Palestinian Liberation Organization, and Arab autonomy on the West Bank and Gaza Strip. In 1994 Clinton effected a successful military—and peaceful—intervention to restore a democratically elected government in Haiti. The Clinton administration also fostered negotiations in 1995 intended to end four years of raging civil-religious war among Croatians, Bosnian Muslims, and Bosnian Serbs in the former Yugoslavia.

The Clinton presidency suffered a sharp political decline when the Republicans, who promoted term limits for federal officials and vastly reduced federal commitment—and greater state control—over social welfare programs, swept the congressional elections in 1994 and gained control of both houses of Congress for the first time in forty years. The Republican victories shifted the initiative for legislation from the White House to Congress, which rejected term limits but by the end of 1995 had prepared an economic program that proposed a balanced budget within seven years, lower taxes for high-income earners, and greatly reduced federal expenditures but more latitude for state controls for entitlement programs, including welfare (Aid for Families with Dependent Children) and Medicare and Medicaid. As 1996 opened it was unknown whether the president would try to compromise with Congress or veto the legislation and seek a new political mandate in the presidential election in the fall.

Post-Watergate presidents seem subject to unrelenting investigation of their personal as well as political behavior by Congress, special prosecutors, newspapers, and TV and radio talk shows. By 1995 the branches of government were more separate than ever before. Congress was voting programs and agency administrators and federal judges were making decisions that showed little deference for White House policy. A better-informed public was ready to change parties because of issues. The president still had unrivaled power to command public and congressional attention with policy statements, whether from the Oval Office or on talk shows. He had assistants to draft legislation and form political strategy. The OMB could bargain with congressional budget committees. The president retained almost unlimited power in foreign policy crises and great latitude in general to advance the national interest, even by reversing course with former adversaries, as Nixon did with China and Reagan did with the Soviet Union. Although constraints on presidential authority induced more accountability, they did not weaken the presidency, but even with great power, future presidents may find it more difficult to effect solutions to such problems as crime, poverty, drug addiction, and racial antipathy, as well as civil-religious wars, human rights violations, and nuclear proliferation.

[Ryan J. Barrileaux, *The Post-Modern Presidency: The Office After Ronald Reagan* (New York, 1988); Fred I. Greenstein, ed., *Leadership in the Modern Presidency* (Cambridge, Mass., 1988); Richard E. Neustadt, *Presidential Power and the Modern Presidents: The Politics of Leadership from Roosevelt to Reagan,* rev. ed. (New York, 1990); Malcolm Shaw, ed., *The Modern Presidency: From Roosevelt to Reagan* (New York, 1987).]

ARNOLD A. OFFNER

See also **SUPP:** Budget, Federal; Campaigns, Presidential; Democratic Party; Deregulation; Iran-Contra Affair; Reaganomics; Republican Party; Special Prosecutors; Third Parties and Independents; War Powers Act; Watergate, Aftermath of.

PRESIDENTIAL SUMMITS. *See* **Summits, Presidential.**

PRESS, FREEDOM OF THE. *See* **Freedom of the Press.**

PRINTING INDUSTRY was the fastest-growing manufacturing industry in the United States in the 1980s, but that growth was slowed by the recession late in the decade and in the early 1990s. By the early 1990s there were 64,000 commercial printing shops in the nation, and many other businesses that provided related services. Computers and other technologies changed the printing industry, automating older mechanical printing crafts, such as typesetting and page layout. Known as "desktop publishing," computerized print-related software and equipment became accessible to businesses and individuals outside the printing industry. The roles of printers and customers began to overlap because writers, designers, and other clients could now handle much prepress production themselves. Word processing and graphics programs made it possible to create and manipulate text and graphics completely within offices or on home computers and bypass steps (such as typesetting copy) traditionally handled by skilled workers in the printing crafts. Laser printers and other new copying equipment offered high-quality duplication of desktop-created computer files and other documents. This trend accelerated in the 1990s, with the advent of "paperless" multimedia publishing. Such documents and publications exist only "on line" in electronic and digital form, are distributed via computer disks or telephone lines, and are viewed on computers rather than on paper.

Technology reduced the need for professional printing services and crafts. It created business opportunities within the printing industry. Demand for printing services was bolstered by desktop publishing, because its ease and low cost prompted people to create publications, business documents, and other printed material that formerly required offset printing and other professional services. Many commercial printers adapted by offering desktop publishing and complementary services and by investing in advanced technology that remained too expensive and complex for clients. Specialized shops formed to handle pre- and postpress operations, such as color processing. Printing firms managed mailings and databases. Printers developed the capability to produce the new forms of electronic multimedia publications. Other trends stimulated the need for high-volume, high-quality printing, and special production methods. Magazine advertising began to include imbed-

ded fragrances and other features that relied on sophisticated printing techniques. Targeted marketing and advertising prompted more flexible methods of high-volume printing that could create versions of a publication or document, including printing methods that could make changes to individual copies within a single press run. With increased environmental concern and regulation, the printing industry faced the need to develop less toxic inks and other chemicals, more effective methods of waste disposal, and cater to the desire of many users for recycled paper.

[Nancy Aldrich-Ruenzel, ed., *Designer's Guide to Print Production* (New York, 1990); Liane Sebastian, *Electronic Design and Publishing: Business Practices* (New York, 1992).]

JOHN TOWNES

See also **SUPP:** Computers; Office Technology; Publishing Industry.

PRISONERS OF WAR AND MISSING IN ACTION (POWs and MIAs), an important legacy of the Vietnam War, with ramifications for both American domestic politics and U.S. relations with Vietnam. By the terms of the Paris Peace Accords of 1973, which ended U.S. involvement in Vietnam, the Democratic Republic of Vietnam (North Vietnam) agreed to release all American POWs that it was holding. North Vietnam, although having acceded to the Geneva Convention of 1949, which classified prisoners of war as "victims of events" who were entitled to "decent and humane treatment," had insisted that the crews of U.S. bombers were guilty of "crimes against humanity," and returning POWs told stories of mistreatment by their captors. The emotions stirred by evidence of mistreatment were magnified by reports that not all POWs had been returned and that Americans were still being held captive. These impressions of an inhumane Vietnamese government (officially called the Socialist Republic of Vietnam following the North's victory of 1975, which reunified the country) were reinforced by the plight of "boat people" fleeing Vietnam and Vietnam's invasion of Cambodia in 1978. These events helped to solidify public and congressional support for nonrecognition of Vietnam and a trade embargo.

The United States made "full accountability" of MIAs a condition of diplomatic recognition of Vietnam. At the end of the war, 1,750 Americans were listed as missing in Vietnam (another 600 MIAs were listed in neighboring Laos and Cambodia). The United

PRISONS AND PRISON REFORM

States also insisted that Vietnam assist in the recovery of remains of MIAs who were killed in Vietnam and in the return of any individuals who might have survived the war. Of particular concern were the "discrepancy cases," where individuals were believed to have survived an incident (for example, bailing out of an aircraft and having been reportedly seen later) but were not among the returning POWs.

The POW and MIA controversy triggered a rigorous debate and became a popular culture phenomenon in the late 1970s and 1980s, despite Pentagon and congressional investigations that indicated there were no more than 200 unresolved MIA cases out of the 2,266 the Department of Defense still listed as missing and about a dozen POWs unaccounted for. (Approximately 300,000 North and South Vietnamese are still considered MIAs.) President Ronald Reagan, speaking before the National League of POW/MIA Families in 1987, stated that "until all our questions are fully answered, we will assume that some of our countrymen are alive." The Vietnam Veterans of America, which sent several investigating groups to Vietnam in the 1980s, helped renew contacts between the U.S. and Vietnamese governments. Accordingly, agreements were reached between Vietnamese authorities and representatives of the Reagan administration that resulted in cooperation in recovering the remains of American casualties. Several hundred sets of remains were returned to the United States beginning in the late 1980s. In addition, progress was made in clarifying "discrepancy cases." The question resurfaced in the 1990s about whether President Richard Nixon and Secretary of State Henry Kissinger had done all they could during peace negotiations to free servicemen "knowingly" left behind or whether they both were so desperate to get out of Vietnam that they sacrificed POWs. Both Nixon and Kissinger maintained that it was the "doves" in Congress at the time who prevented any effective military action to find out the truth about POWs when it was still possible to do so in the summer and spring of 1973. On Feb. 3, 1994, with the approval of the Senate and business community, President Bill Clinton removed the nineteen-year trade embargo against Vietnam, and the Vietnamese government cooperated with veterans groups in locating the remains of U.S. soldiers and returning remains to the United States for burial, including those of nine soldiers in October 1995.

[Frederick Z. Brown, *Second Chance: The United States and Indochina in the 1990s* (New York, 1989).]

GARY R. HESS

PRISONS AND PRISON REFORM. Since the 1970s the goal of U.S. prisons has changed from rehabilitation to punishment. Most efforts at prison reform before that decade had been to introduce presumably better methods of turning criminals into good citizens. Beginning in the first quarter of the nineteenth century, reformers have debated the merits of the Pennsylvania (solitary confinement) and Auburn (separate and silent) systems, both designed for rehabilitation, but by the 1970s a number of academic studies concluded that none of the programs for rehabilitation had been successful. The studies came at a time when the national political climate was becoming conservative, with an emphasis on punishing rather than reforming criminals. A radical prisoners movement combined with academic studies and political conservatism to discredit rehabilitation.

Inspired by the civil rights movement and aided by the greater willingness of courts to intervene in supporting rights of prisoners, prisoners had become politically active beginning in the late 1960s. They protested against what they saw as the unfairness of indeterminate sentences, which were a part of the emphasis on rehabilitation. Convicts served unequal amounts of time for similar crimes, depending on the judgment of "experts" as to whether they had reformed. Activists believed that the length of time served should be proportionate to the seriousness of the crime. Court decisions supporting religious freedom in prison for Black Muslims and the rights of prisoners to sue prison officials led to increased activism in the 1970s, as well as frequent resentment on the part of many prison officials and guards who felt they were losing authority and respect. Prison demonstrations and rebellions of this period were not just about better physical conditions but also about greater rights for prisoners. Events at California's Soledad prison in 1969–1970 led to the organization of supporters outside the prison, the Soledad Brothers Defense Fund. Lists of demands at Soledad were echoed by inmates at California's Folsom Prison later in 1970, and at New York's Attica in 1971. Soledad, Folsom, and Attica became symbols of a movement that activists, outside prisons as well as inside, believed would radically change the nature of prisons in the United States.

Prisons did change but not in the direction desired by activists. An ironic effect of prisoner opposition to indeterminate sentences provided support for a conservative movement to "get tough" on criminals. By the end of the 1970s both the activist movement and the goal of rehabilitation had greatly weakened. The

1980 riot in the New Mexico State Penitentiary at Santa Fe contrasted with the Attica riot of 1971. Both were bloody, but at Attica most of the killing was done by officers of the law, whereas at Santa Fe prisoners tortured and killed other prisoners. The Santa Fe riot symbolized the end of hopes for prisoner activism. Mandatory sentencing became the norm in many states, and in 1987 guidelines for mandatory sentences for federal crimes were approved by the House of Representatives. Sentencing guidelines were not implemented in support of prisoners' rights but were part of the movement toward making prisons simply places of punishment.

The more punitive approach to imprisonment did not reduce the national crime rate, but it had noticeable effects upon rates of imprisonment. Rates remained steady during the 1960s but rose sharply in the early 1970s. The United States had about three times as many inmates in the 1990s (almost 800,000) as in the 1970s and more prisoners per capita than any other industrial democracy. For every 100,000 people, the United States has 300 in prison. Canada has the next highest rate, at 100 per 100,000, while that of the Netherlands is the lowest, fewer than 50 per 100,000.

Rates of imprisonment are not inevitable consequences of natural forces but the results of policy. They explain historical changes in imprisonment rates in Great Britain and the United States in terms of changes in policies in both countries. Punitive policies in Great Britain resulted in a rapid rise in the rate of imprisonment in the nineteenth century until about 1878. After that time different policies resulted in decreasing rates until about 1930, when they began to rise again. U.S. policies since the 1980s have resulted both in an extraordinarily high rate of imprisonment and serious levels of overcrowding. While there is general agreement that overcrowded prisons are inhumane and dangerous, there is little agreement about what ought to be done. Public opinion in the 1990s continued to support stiff sentences for individuals convicted of serious crimes but opposed tax increases to construct more prisons. Legislators responded by passing punitive laws but refused to appropriate funds and legislate taxes necessary to support these laws humanely.

[William Selke, *Prisons in Crisis* (Bloomington, Ind., 1993); Michael Sherman and Gordon J. Hawkins, *Imprisonment in America: Choosing the Future* (Chicago, 1981); Larry Sullivan, *The Prison Reform Movement* (Boston, 1990).]

RICHARD W. MOODEY

See also **DAH:** Auburn Prison System; Crime; Pennsylvania Prison System; **SUPP:** Crime.

PRIVATE SCHOOLS. *See* **Schools, Private.**

PRIVATIZATION, a term coined in 1969 by Peter F. Drucker in *The Age of Discontinuity* (actually "reprivatization") at the time U.S. government officials first considered privatizing goods and services. Privatization of government services involves selling, leasing, or contracting to a private company a service or product that had previously been performed or produced by the public sector. Until the twentieth century, government provided few services that could even be considered for privatization. Policy for 150 years was dictated by the principles of Adam Smith's *Wealth of Nations,* published in 1776. Smith argued that the "invisible hand" of a free marketplace was the most efficient way to maintain a country's economy. Intervention by government in the marketplace, in the form of regulations, public services, or public projects, he wrote, serves as a drag on the economy. This view prevailed, resulting in a tiny federal government that until the early twentieth century financed its operations almost exclusively with tariffs (with the exception of the Civil War). While state and local governments offered more services than the federal government, their activities were also narrow by modern standards.

Around the turn of the century, however, opinion began to change with the growth of the Progressive movement. While most people agreed that a free marketplace was the most efficient way to run an economy, the Progressives pointed out that it was not the kindest or best way to run a country. Public intervention became acceptable for the sake of safety and health, the maintenance of living standards, land conservation, and other areas of public good that would go unheeded by the private sector. At the same time the need for public facilities became more obvious as the nation's economy and its cities grew. Public lighting, well-maintained streets, police departments, water and sewer systems, and other services became pressing needs that the public demanded.

President Franklin D. Roosevelt took the Progressive movement one step further with the New Deal beginning in 1933. Through massive federal intervention in the form of public projects, Roosevelt aimed to take the nation's economy out of the Great Depression. For the next fifty years, government at the federal, state, and local levels took on responsibilities to provide goods and services for the marketplace. This trend eventually reversed itself, but it did so slowly. In 1955 the Bureau of the Budget issued a statement discouraging federal agencies from producing any "product or service [that] can be procured from private enterprise through ordinary business channels." In 1964 Republican presidential candidate Senator Barry Goldwater of Arizona called for sale of the Tennessee Valley Authority to private companies. The idea was rejected, even by his Republican colleagues. By 1980, however, privatization was a plank in Ronald Reagan's domestic platform in his bid for the presidency.

As government spending soared in the 1980s, more and more people went back to Smith's view that the private sector was a more efficient way of providing services than the government. In an often cited case, the city of Phoenix allowed private companies in the late 1970s to bid against its Public Service Department for local trash collection. The department lost the right to serve two of the city's five districts. Stung by the loss, the department took steps to improve service and cut costs. It later regained the lost districts. In 1984 the President's Private Sector Survey, known as the Grace Commission, called for adoption of private management practices in federal government and the sale of selected government services. In 1987 the government sold its 85 percent stake in Conrail for $1.65 billion, considered the largest privatization in U.S. history. One year later the President's Commission on Privatization made seventy-eight recommendations to privatize the federal government including sale of Amtrak, the repeal of statutes giving the U.S. Postal Service a monopoly on delivering letter mail, and the sale of a $250 billion loan portfolio of housing, business, agricultural, and education loans. President George Bush continued Reagan's efforts by making it easier for local and state government to privatize through regulatory changes. Reagan and Bush pushed for a school voucher system in which schools would compete with each other for students, introducing market forces into public education. President Bill Clinton also adopted many privatization initiatives after his election in 1992 through his efforts to "reinvent government."

Privatization took hold in the early 1990s, especially on state and local levels. Indianapolis Mayor Stephen Goldsmith undertook to privatize services ranging from sewer billings to operation of city parks. His efforts were followed by other large-city mayors, including New York City Mayor Rudolph W. Giuliani and Chicago Mayor Richard M. Daley.

Many cities and towns adopted versions of school choice or hired private companies to manage public schools. States joined the wave of privatization, shedding public management of road construction and maintenance and operation of prisons, state parks, and recreational facilities. Critics of privatization say the efficiencies gained from private sector involvement versus public sector are minimal. They cite the massive spending and fraud by defense industries as examples of private sector inefficiency. Unions note that private companies often underpay employees and are less inclined to hire women and minorities or provide basic workers' rights. Critics also argue that in many cases, such as operation of prisons, greater public goals, such as reforming criminals, are sacrificed for the sake of saving money.

[John D. Donahue, *The Privatization Decision* (New York, 1989); "Privatization," *Congressional Quarterly Researcher* 2 (Nov. 13, 1992).]

ERIK BRUUN

See also **DAH:** New Deal; Progressive Movement; Public Ownership; Public Utilities; **SUPP:** Education, Parental Choice in; Schools, For-Profit.

PRIZEFIGHTING generally means professional boxing, but other less savory matches featuring individual sparring include professional wrestling, strong-man competitions, televised gladiator contests, and illicit no-holds-barred fights produced for credulous audiences. Immensely popular and a recognized Olympic sport, boxing is an attack event in which a fighter punches to hurt and disable his opponent. Gloves are worn to protect the knuckles, not the adversary's chin or brain, as one commentator noted. The most visible survival of eighteenth-century English "blood sports," professional boxing is a fast-moving, exciting, aggressive challenge between two highly skilled, physically fit men. Amateur boxing is a fast-growing and popular sport among men and women.

Boxing suffers from a poor public image. Loosely organized in the 1990s by three associations, the World Boxing Council, the World Boxing Association, and the International Boxing Association, prizefighting is actually barely regulated. There is no national commission; each state has its own codes, permitting badly damaged fighters to compete frequently under false names, merely by crossing state lines. Unsavory promoters control the careers of boxers through options on future fights and powerful influence over television appearances. Whereas in other professional sports, athletes merely appearing with gamblers or criminals risk banishment, boxing matches are held in gambling casinos with heavy wagering. Since the mid-1970s, in an effort to increase the number of champions, boxing officials have subdivided older weight classifications into thirteen classifications bounded by flyweight (112 pounds) to heavyweight (no weight limit) with subdivided categories such as super middleweight. Boxing has suffered from fixing scandals, sham championship tournaments, and several deaths from fight injuries. In 1983 the *Journal of the American Medical Association* urged banning boxing because of evidence of chronic brain damage from fights.

Despite its many woes, boxing has produced important champions. The most prestigious title, the heavyweight championship, has lately been dominated by black pugilists including the great Muhammad Ali, Joe Frazier, Larry Holmes, Evander Holyfield, and Mike Tyson. White challengers such as Gerry Cooney have often garnered considerable attention. Perhaps the most famous white boxer since the 1970s was not really a boxer at all, but actor Sylvester Stallone, who immortalized an underdog champion in his Rocky movies. Major heavyweight matches have included Ali's recapturing the title by knocking out George Foreman in 1974; Ali's 1975 conquest of Frazier in the "Thrilla in Manila"; Ali's recapture of the crown from Leon Spinks in 1978; and Holmes's victory over Ali in 1980. Tyson seemed invincible from 1986 until Buster Douglas upset him in 1990. Tyson was convicted of rape in 1992 and sentenced to prison; following his release in 1995, the twenty-eight-year-old Tyson planned to resume his boxing career. In 1994 the forty-five-year-old Foreman regained the championship he lost twenty years earlier. Other legendary boxers since the 1970s have included Sugar Ray Leonard, Marvelous Marvin Hagler, Roberto Duran, and Thomas "Hit Man" Hearns. In 1980 Duran beat Leonard for the welterweight championship; six months later Leonard conquered Duran when the latter conceded, stating *"no mas"* (no more), allegedly suffering from stomach cramps. Leonard won a third fight in 1989 and fought other important matches against Hearns. Physical disabilities have hampered champions and opponents. Ali contracted premature Parkinson's disease from head punches; Leonard suffered a detached retina.

[Thomas Hauser, *The Black Lights: Inside the World of Professional Boxing* (New York, 1986); Joyce Carol Oates, *On Boxing* (Hopewell, N.J., 1994).]

GRAHAM RUSSELL HODGES

See also **SUPP:** Olympic Games.

PRO-CHOICE MOVEMENT, initiated primarily by such feminist groups as the National Organization for Women in response to the antiabortion pro-life movement that developed after the Supreme Court gave abortion constitutional protection in 1973. Pro-choice was the language activists used to highlight the central place of women in the abortion debate. They believe that women should have control over their reproductive lives, as a legal fact and fundamental right, and that abortion should be available to all women. The pro-choice movement is one part of the larger movement for reproductive rights that also opposes policies such as welfare measures penalizing women for childbearing.

[Ruth Colker, *Abortion and Dialogue: Pro-choice, Pro-life, and American Law* (Bloomington, Ind., 1992); Barbara Hinkson Craig and David M. O'Brien, *Abortion and American Politics* (Chatham, N.J., 1993); Faye D. Ginsburg, *Contested Lives: The Abortion Debate in an American Community* (Berkeley, Calif., 1989).]

NANCY B. PALMER

See also **SUPP:** Abortion; *Griswold* v. *Connecticut;* Pro-Life Movement; *Roe* v. *Wade; Rust* v. *Sullivan; Webster* v. *Reproductive Health Services;* Women's Health; Women's Movement.

PRODUCT TAMPERING, the deliberate and intentionally harmful alteration of consumer products, first took place in the 1890s, the most famous incident being the poisoning of two bottles of Bromo Seltzer with cyanide of mercury, which resulted in one death. The modern age of "consumer terrorism" began in Chicago, Ill., in 1982, with the injection of poison into packages of the painkiller Tylenol. Immediately following these incidents, more than 270 tampering episodes were reported, involving over-the-counter pharmaceuticals and packaged drinks and foods. Congress responded by passing the Federal Anti-Tampering Act of 1983, which made it a crime to tamper with products or to make false claims of tampering. The legislation made convictions punishable by three years in prison and a $10,000 fine for an attempted tampering; twenty years in prison and a $100,000 fine if serious injury occurs; and life imprisonment if there is a death. The threat of tampering alone can result in five years in prison and a $25,000 fine. Nevertheless, product tampering became a major cultural phenomenon in the United States. Motives have included murder, extortion, stock market manipulation, insurance fraud, and serial mayhem. Incidents of product tampering have been followed by public hysteria, copycat cases, and hundred of false reports. In 1993 false reports were made in twenty-three states that syringes were found in cans of Pepsi-Cola.

[Henry Glowa, "Criminal Product Tampering," *Southwestern University Law Review* 17 (Summer 1988); Barry Logan, "Product Tampering Crime," *Journal of Forensic Sciences* 38 (July 1993).]

ROBERT KRAIG

See also **SUPP:** Consumer Rights and Protection.

PRO-LIFE MOVEMENT, a grass-roots movement that developed in reaction to the 1973 Supreme Court ruling in *Roe* v. *Wade* that gave constitutional protection to legalized abortion. While the goal of the movement is to overturn *Roe,* participants have used direct action and the language of the civil rights movement to obstruct abortion clinics by harassing personnel and clients. Since the launching of Operation Rescue in 1987 by Randall Terry and Joseph Scheidler, violence against clinics has escalated to the extent that the 1990s witnessed murders of doctors performing abortions as well as of clinic personnel.

[Faye D. Ginsburg, *Contested Lives: The Abortion Debate in an American Community* (Berkeley, Calif., 1989); Kristin Luker, "Abortion, Motherhood, and Morality," in *Women's America: Refocusing the Past,* 4th ed., Linda K. Kerber and Jane Sherron De Hart, eds. (New York, 1995).]

NANCY B. PALMER

See also **SUPP:** Abortion; Adoption; Pro-Choice Movement; *Roe* v. *Wade; Rust* v. *Sullivan; Webster* v. *Reproductive Health Services.*

PROSECUTORS, SPECIAL. *See* **Special Prosecutors.**

PROSTITUTION, the exchange of money for sex, is illegal in every state with the exception of thirteen of sixteen counties in Nevada. In those states, closely associated crimes include pandering, or procuring prostitutes, and pimping, or living off the earnings of prostitutes. Between 1975 and 1991 there were an average of 89,000 annual arrests in the United States for male and female prostitution. Prostitution is overwhelmingly an urban phenomenon, with arrests far greater in cities of more than 250,000 people. Unlike Nevada, where prostitutes are carefully regulated, or San Francisco, where neither police enforcement or prosecution is actively pursued, most cities use an unofficial policy of enforcement to confine sexual commerce to "red light" districts. Most Americans do not worry greatly about prostitution unless activity is nearby. Prosecution can be politically advantageous for local politicians, but it is usually inconsistently pursued. Raids often become symbolic gestures, an unintended, negative effect of which is to consolidate a prostitute's self-identity. Critics of current law enforcement policies also argue that prosecution and incarceration expenses should be applied to drug treatment and job training. In the politics of the United States, legalization of prostitution in the 1990s was as remote as it was in the 1890s.

An average of 62,000 women, but few "Johns," are arrested each year. Female prostitution is hierarchical and male dominated. At the top are call girls, available by appointment through a madam or high-class male pimps. Fees may run into thousands of dollars. A similar system involves escort services, through which customers may hire a woman (or a man) for companionship or sex. Escort services operate superficially within the law and may even advertise in newspapers and in telephone directories. Far below escort services are strip joints and massage parlors, functioning in tawdry, unsanitary conditions. A related activity is telephone sex, emerging from the threat of disease, particularly AIDS, by which a customer receives verbal stimulation of fantasies from a distant voice. At the bottom of the hierarchy are streetwalkers. Protected only by a pimp, streetwalkers charge little, accept nearly all customers, and perform their work in cars, alleys, or cheap hotels. New York City authorities estimate that one-third of street prostitutes carry the HIV virus, which causes AIDS. Streetwalkers are 10 to 20 percent of all prostitutes, but account for 90 percent of arrests; a disproportionate number of the detained are women of color.

Prostitution is a transaction superficially involving mutual choice. Young men still regard visits as rites of passage; older men ostensibly work out marital and sexual difficulties. Customers include disabled, single men unable to find legitimate sex partners. Women enter prostitution for myriad reasons, the fundamental nature of which is controversial. Divisions exist as to whether female prostitutes seek financial gain otherwise unavailable or are pushed into this life because of high unemployment, particularly among minority women. The belief that prostitutes are oversensual females is now invalidated, but a link with childhood sexual abuse at home is accepted. Prostitution is recurrently connected to other criminal activities, including credit card forgery and extortion. Little joy seems attached to the work, and interviews emphasize ancillary entertainment over sexual pleasure.

Despite disagreements within the feminist movement over whether prostitution should be legalized (women controlled by state) or decriminalized (permitting women to control this oldest of professions), the institution has entered politics. In 1973 Margo St. James, a San Francisco prostitute, organized COYOTE (Call Off Your Old Tired Ethics), urging decriminalization through the magazine *COYOTE Howls.* Priding itself as a union local, PONY (Prostitutes of New York) also favors decriminalization and works with United Nations groups to fight international trafficking in women and children. WHISPER (Women Hurt in Systems of Prostitution Engaged in Revolt) opposes prostitution, while other groups offer counseling to help young women quit the life. The political and legal impact of these organizations has been minimal. Still, the most significant organization at the street level is the exploitative control of the pimp.

The world of male prostitutes is more shadowy. The male prostitute is generally a lone individual, although connections with escort services are possible. Arrests of male prostitutes and their male partners are on the rise because law enforcement has become more gender-neutral while public acceptance of homosexuality is greater, permitting homosexual prostitutes more visibility, and because male prostitution, like female, may be linked to patterns of drug trafficking. Male prostitutes, like female, work in pornographic productions, strip houses, and phone sex.

The most notorious type is the child prostitute, who has left or been exiled from home, fleeing sexual abuse or other mistreatment or homes broken by a parent's drug or alcohol abuse. The AIDS epidemic has made child prostitutes more desirable for customers who believe incorrectly that children are less likely to pass on the disease. Increasing numbers of streetwalkers are runaway children. In New York City in the early 1980s, Eighth Avenue and Forty-second Street, adjacent to the Port Authority Bus Terminal, the arrival point for many runaway children, was known as the "Minnesota Strip," because of the many runaways enlisted and working there as prostitutes. In contrast to its ambiguous treatment of adult pornography, the Supreme Court grants no Constitution protection to child pornography, and police are especially vigilant toward child prostitution, because many of these children also work in child pornography media.

[Kathleen Barry, *Female Sexual Slavery,* rev. ed. (1994); Nanette J. Davis, ed., *Prostitution: An International Handbook on Trends, Problems, and Policies* (Westport, Conn., 1993); Judith Ennew, *The Sexual Exploitation of Children* (New York, 1986); Eleanor M. Miller, *Street Women* (Philadelphia, 1986); "Special Issue on Prostitution," *CQ Researcher* 3 (June 11, 1993); Samuel M. Steward, *Understanding the Male Hustler* (New York, 1991).]

GRAHAM RUSSELL HODGES

See also **DAH:** Mann Act; Prostitution; Sexual Attitudes; Venereal Disease; **SUPP:** Acquired Immune Deficiency Syndrome; Women's Movement.

PROTESTANTISM. All Christians believe that there is one God, that God is revealed in Jesus of Nazareth, the Christ, and that the purpose of the church is to worship God and live in the way of Christ. Historically, three different Christian faith communities—Roman Catholic, Eastern Orthodox, and Protestant—developed, each with a distinctive way of understanding and living out those beliefs. The word "protestant" was applied to Martin Luther and others who in the Reformation of sixteenth century Europe protested certain beliefs and practices of the Roman Catholic church. Protestants came to North America from Europe to gain religious and economic freedom. They helped shape the New World forms of capitalism and democracy as well as religion. Protestants were in turn changed and shaped by pioneer life, democracy, the federal form of government, capitalism, and slavery. The historic Protestant theological foundation rests on three "alones" and one "all." A person is saved (reconciled with God, others, and self) through God's grace (unearned love) rather than through human works, rituals, sacrifices, or beliefs (grace alone). Such grace is available to anyone through trust in God (faith alone). God is revealed in the Bible (Scripture alone). Every believer has equal access to God, especially by reading the Bible, without going through the priests and rituals of the church (the priesthood of all believers). Thus, Protestantism is a faith of freedom and a faith in freedom. There exists in its very nature, however, a paradox that hovers over the line between inclusion and exclusion. The doctrines of grace alone, faith alone, and the priesthood of all believers are inclusive. The doctrine of Scripture alone, however, is exclusive. If God is revealed in the Bible, then everyone has access to the one revealed truth. Those who do not choose to accept it are excluded by their own choice.

Protestants have never resolved the tension between the inclusive and exclusive dimensions of their faith. Sidney Mead described the United States as "a nation with the soul of a church." This soul was expressed politically in democracy and personal responsibility. It took form culturally in the ethic of hard work and personal morality. The United States was formed largely by this basic Protestant principle of individual freedom and responsibility, producing a new "social contract." Nonetheless, exclusion was built into this religious social contract because it existed primarily for white males and not even for all of them. Indentured servitude was a part of early U.S. life. Immigrant groups such as the Irish had to struggle against severe prejudice before being accepted into the contract. Native, African, Asian, and Hispanic Americans were both overtly and covertly omitted from the American dream. Although women of all races often worked as equal partners with men under harsh conditions, they had very few legal rights and their social position was severely circumscribed. The U.S. story, however, despite the marginalization of many people, was one of expansion and growth. Protestant churches, especially those that adapted to frontier conditions, participated in that growth. By 1960 approximately 60 percent of all U.S. citizens identified themselves as Protestant.

In 1993, according to the *Yearbook of American and Canadian Churches,* the largest Protestant religious groups in the United States were Baptist (33.5 million), Methodist (14.6 million), Pentecostal (10.1 million), Lutheran (8.3 million), Latter-day Saints (4.5 million), and Presbyterian (4.2 million). These and other groups were further divided into approximately 150 groups of associated churches, ranging in size from the 15 million members of the Southern Baptist Convention to the 420 members of the United Christian Church.

Since the 1960s, however, Protestantism has divided not along traditional denominational lines of theology but along the battle lines of social issues. Fewer Protestants think of themselves as Baptist or Methodist or Presbyterian. They identify themselves, consciously or unconsciously, as conservative or liberal, moderate or fundamentalist, charismatic or feminist, Native American or African American. Divisions have focused on issues of abortion, the cold war, consumerism, politics, race, television, family values, gambling, gender, and homosexuality. Religious differences have centered on such issues as inclusive (that is, not exclusively male) language, especially about God; prayer in public schools; biblical inerrancy; ecumenism; denominational control; church growth or lack of it; the role of women, especially in the ministry; and theology, especially specifically focused theologies such as liberation, feminist, and black.

These are all issues of inclusion and exclusion. Can women, homosexuals, fetuses/unborn children, eth-nic minority persons, or communists be included in the church and the social contract? Should those be excluded who do not believe the Bible is without error, or those who participate in politics, get divorces, have children out of wedlock, or believe in evolution? Who is excluded by the nature of those prayers, or by prayer itself? Denominations, as associations of churches with common beliefs and practices, once provided fairly clear lines of inclusion and exclusion. In the 1990s, however, they were more administrative than theological.

Protestantism also has been shaped by religious consumerism. People choose a congregation because it meets their current needs and beliefs, not because of its denomination. They "church shop" and pick the congregation with the best youth program, the newest music, or the most congenial preaching. Even after making their choice they may not know what, if any, denomination they have selected. They tend to choose large congregations rather than small ones, causing decline in older denominations that have many small churches.

Since the 1970s population has shifted from the Northeast and Midwest to the Sunbelt. The shift from rural areas to large metropolitan areas has continued. Such older mainline denominations as Methodists and Presbyterians were heavily invested in church buildings and institutions in the industrial Rustbelt and in declining agricultural areas. As in earlier periods of U.S. history, newer, more conservative groups, such as pentecostals, were able to respond more readily. They established congregations where the people went. They grew as the more established denominations declined. Many of the most noticed churches do not even belong to denominations but are "megachurches" founded by entrepreneurial ministers who use television and modern fund-raising to build independent ministries. A large pool of new members for Protestant churches is composed of former Roman Catholics who no longer feel comfortable with the Catholic hierarchical structure, theology, or certain Catholic social stances, especially abortion, celibate clergy, and the place of women in church leadership.

In the 1960s and 1970s, several formal denominational mergers took place. Many Protestants talked about an "ecumenical imperative" to overcome denominational differences and witness to the unity of Christ through the unity of the church. Interdenominational ecumenism has now become almost irrelevant, however, because denominations no longer provide religious and social identity. This new ecumenism operative in Protestantism is based on individual Christians or, in some cases, congregations, joining together around issues. This creates tensions within denominations as their members are no longer united by theology but divided by issues of biblical inerrancy, speaking in tongues, abortion, homosexuality, women in ministry, and so forth. Almost every denomination has two or more groups in constant conflict with one another over who controls the denominational administration, theological schools, and missions.

Protestants are still individualistic, but it is an individualism based more on experience, practice, and social stance than upon theology. Protestants are as informed in spiritual practice by popular psychology and television talk shows as they are by traditional Christianity or denominational programs and literature. Although Protestants cannot agree on who should be excluded, there is considerable agreement on who should be included. Few denominations and congregations have succeeded in becoming interracial, but many have admitted women to full positions of leadership, both lay and clergy. They are increasingly sensitive to other marginalized persons, such as the physically challenged. They have transformed orphanages into homes for abused children and created retirement facilities for the burgeoning elderly population. Conservatives, liberals, moderates, charismatics, and feminists join together across lines of exclusion to feed the hungry, strengthen families, encourage the addicted, and comfort those afflicted by natural disasters.

[Harold Bloom, *The American Religion: The Emergence of the Post-Christian Nation* (New York, 1992); Roger Finke and Rodney Stark, *The Churching of America 1776–1990* (New Brunswick, N.J., 1992); George W. Forell, *The Protestant Faith* (Englewood Cliffs, N.J., 1960); C. Eric Lincoln and Lawrence H. Mamiya, *The Black Church in the African American Experience* (Durham, N.C., 1990); Sidney E. Mead, *The Nation with the Soul of a Church* (New York, 1975).]

JOHN ROBERT MCFARLAND

See also **DAH:** Adventist Churches; African Methodist Episcopal Church; Afro-American Church; Baptist Churches; Church of Christ, Scientist; Congregational Churches; Cumberland Presbyterian Church; Disciples of Christ; Episcopal Church; Jehovah's Witnesses; Lutheranism; Mennonites; Methodists; Presbyterianism; Puritans and Puritanism; Quakers; Reformed Churches; Religion; **DAH** and **SUPP:** Latter-day Saints, Church of Jesus Christ of; Pentecostal Churches; Reorganized Church of Jesus Christ of Latter-day Saints; **SUPP:** African-American Religions and Sects; Fundamentalism; Millenarianism; Religion; Televangelism; Women in Churches.

PSYCHIATRY. Between 1900 and 1920 medicine rapidly redefined itself as scientific. Psychiatry lagged behind other specialties in this regard, partly because it was broadening its scope to include social issues rather than confining its attention to the mainly biological. Although they began their careers by focusing primarily on biological aspects of mental illness, some leaders of the field, including Adolf Meyer and Elmer E. Southard, went on to write and speak expansively about mental health. Even as psychiatry widened its focus, psychiatrists were losing status as specialists of medicine. They responded with an effort to strengthen their organization and tighten their standards. In 1921 the American Medico-Psychological Association was renamed the American Psychiatric Association, which became more active, and its journal became the *American Journal of Psychiatry*. In 1934 the American Board of Psychiatry and Neurology was founded to provide certification for practitioners specializing in their respective fields.

These developments were not much influenced by the emergence of psychoanalysis in Europe at the beginning of the twentieth century, although Sigmund Freud's visit to the United States in 1909 drew some attention, and a few American psychiatrists or neurologists began to experiment with psychoanalytic treatment. In the 1930s, however, an influx of European psychoanalysts fleeing the Nazis brought Freudian thought to the United States, and this group achieved considerable prominence. For a generation psychoanalysis was the dominant intellectual current in American psychiatry, and the two terms, psychiatry and psychoanalysis, became all but synonymous in training programs and in popular culture, although there continued to be a group of psychiatrists who managed mental hospitals, administered biological treatments, and espoused non-Freudian approaches.

The scope and authority of psychiatry (and psychology) were greatly enhanced during World War II. The discovery of high rates of psychiatric disorder in men between the ages of eighteen and forty-five being screened for the military heightened awareness of the problems treated by psychiatrists. Psychological management of the troops came to be seen as crucial to the war effort. Psychiatrists influenced criteria for induction and managed psychological responses to military experience, thus acquiring governmental recognition of their professional competence. Also in this period, both psychological and pharmacological developments were increasing the effectiveness of psychiatric treatments.

An antipsychiatry movement emerged in the 1960s and 1970s, led in part by disaffected psychiatrists and psychologists. Psychiatric practice was criticized as an insidious form of social control based on a pseudoscientific medical model. A few critics claimed that mental illness is an intellectual construct and that it represents a valid alternative to ordinary thinking and behavior. In this period the hold of psychoanalysis also began to wane. Research showed that its claims had been overly broad; biological treatments proved effective; and economic forces made long-term, labor-intensive treatment impractical for all but a few.

Since World War II the intellectual content of psychiatry appears to have been reinvigorated, with enormous advances in both biological and psychological knowledge. Nevertheless, in the mid-1990s it was one of the three lowest-paid medical specialties (along with primary care and pediatrics), and with the loss of the psychoanalytic mystique, it declined in public esteem. Psychiatry appeared to be entering yet another crisis. The effort to contain health care costs targeted psychiatric treatment, in part reflecting the success of psychiatry with the public; demand for mental health services was seen as being high and thus costly to insure. Benefits for such treatment were being curtailed, and there was pressure to shift much psychiatric care into primary practice (for example, by training primary practitioners to diagnose and treat depression). Some predicted that the number of practicing psychiatrists would diminish markedly by the early decades of the twenty-first century, although the demand for psychiatric services did not appear to be waning.

[Daniel Blain and Michael Barton, *The History of American Psychiatry* (Washington, D.C., 1979); Ralph Colp, Jr., "History of Psychiatry," in *Comprehensive Textbook of Psychiatry,* edited by Harold I. Kaplan and Benjamin J. Sadock, 5th ed., 2 vols. (Baltimore, 1989); Gerald N. Grob, *Mental Illness and American Society, 1875–1940* (Princeton, N.J., 1983).]

WILLIAM IRA BENNETT

See also **SUPP:** Mental Illness; Psychology.

PSYCHOLOGY. From 1975 to 1995 there was tremendous growth of interest in psychology and its applications in advertising, mental health, and the courts. The relationship between genetics and psychology addressed the enduring question of nature versus nurture (heredity versus environment). While the hereditarian chose the former explanation, the behaviorist chose the latter, but evidence from both areas shows there is a strong interplay between genes and environment in molding human personality and intelligence. Tensions developed between experimentalists and clinician practitioners, and by 1988 the differing viewpoints became so marked that academic and research-oriented psychologists broke away from the venerable American Psychological Association (now dominated by clinician practitioners) to found the American Psychological Society.

Many experimentalists have used materials and settings applicable to those in the real world. Experimental findings from the laboratories (the principles of learning and conditioning discovered by Ivan Pavlov and B. F. Skinner) have not only been used for what is considered the public good but also to influence consumer decisions. A considerable part of the billions spent each year in the United States on advertising pays for messages conveyed by persuasive techniques derived from psychological principles. Health psychology, developed to alleviate mental or physical illnesses, has brought parts of its terminology into everyday vocabulary. Perhaps the most notable discovery in this regard was the correlation between personality type and health. Interestingly, it was published not by psychologists, but by two cardiologists, Meyer Friedman and R. H. Rosenman, who in 1974 identified characteristic behavior patterns known as Type A and Type B personalities; Type A patterns are risk factors for coronary heart disease.

Since the 1970s practitioners of what is called forensic psychology have offered court testimony regarding competency of defendants, which has been used for and against the insanity defense. Expert testimony has been also been offered regarding the plausibility of witness or client testimony. Examples that have captured the public's attention include sexual abuse charges, brought up by adults after recovering memories of childhood incidents during therapy. Clinical psychologists have offered testimony documenting such repressed memories, but experimentalists have offered data suggesting that what is sometimes revealed are false memories implanted during therapy. This debate over memories recalled after decades of amnesia continues. In a 1994 landmark case, Gary Ramona won damages after his daughter accused him of sexual abuse based on recovery of repressed memories during therapy; the court's verdict, against his daughter's therapists and the medical center where they worked, considered that these memories were implanted.

Another controversial area has been the enduring question of nature versus nurture. Identical twins separated soon after birth have provided a laboratory for separating the effects of genetics versus upbringing and environment. Such evidence has been beneficial in terms of explaining and treating schizophrenia as well as severe alcoholism. Intelligence differences between groups have also been examined by correlating IQ test scores of identical versus fraternal twins (research resumed in 1994 by Richard Herrenstein and Charles Murray in *The Bell Curve*). The validity of this evidence, however, has been hotly debated. The debate has also raged over the origins of psychological traits, with some researchers pointing to environmental factors and others to genetics. In particular, a team led by Thomas J. Bouchard, Jr., at the University of Minnesota, concluded in a 1990 article in the journal *Science:* "The effect of being reared in the same home is negligible for many psychological traits." Most scientists suggest, however, that evidence supports that there is a strong interplay between genes and environment.

Because of the unusual range of phenomena studied by experimental psychologists, divisions exist among them, and psychology has evolved into fields that are too disparate to fit into a single theory. According to the American Psychological Association, psychology has branched into fifty-eight fields, grouped into the study of personality, development, social psychology, perception, neuroscience, motivation and emotion, cognition, psychometrics, psychopathology, and psychotherapy.

One of the most dramatic and productive changes has been the wedding of cognitive psychology to neuroscience. Cognitive psychology developed in the 1970s to study questions about mental life, and cognitive psychologists expounded theories to explain how people plan, think, remember, and make decisions. Neuroscience, which studies the physiology of the brain, is a much older study, dating to the seventeenth-century French mathematician and philosopher René Descartes. Late-twentieth-century technological advances changed much of what neuroscientists could examine. Techniques developed in the 1980s and early 1990s, such as positron emission tomography (PET) and magnetic resonance imaging (MRI), allow neurologists and psychologists to look into a brain and observe its functioning. Related developments came from other

quarters outside psychology. The partnership between cognitive psychology and computer science resulted in remarkable insights. A generation ago it seemed that the computer was the model for the mind, but that order has been reversed, with the mind as the model for the computer. Computer engineers began building computers to simulate aspects of human thinking (artificial intelligence).

[Howard Gardner, *The Mind's New Science: A History of the Cognitive Revolution* (New York, 1985); Henry Gleitman, *Psychology,* 4th ed. (New York, 1995); L. S. Hearnshaw, *The Shaping of Modern Psychology* (London, 1987); Morton Hunt, *The Story of Psychology* (New York, 1993).]

CHERI L. WIGGS

See also **SUPP:** Mental Illness; Psychiatry.

PUBLIC HEALTH SERVICE began in 1798 as the Marine Hospital Service, a program established within the Treasury Department for the care and relief of sick and disabled seamen. It was not until the 1870s that the service was formally organized as a national hospital system with a central headquarters in Washington, D.C., under the direction of a supervising surgeon (later known as the surgeon general). As the duties of the service grew in the late nineteenth century to include authority for quarantine, medical inspection of arriving immigrants, and operation of a hygienic laboratory, its name was changed to Public Health and Marine Hospital Service in 1902 and to Public Health Service (PHS) in 1912. The PHS assumed increasing responsibilities for public health. In 1930 its Hygienic Laboratory became the National Institute (later Institutes) of Health, which evolved into the nation's largest center for carrying out and funding biomedical research. A malaria control program during World War II grew into another PHS agency, the Centers for Disease Control and Prevention. In 1955 the service assumed responsibility for American Indians and Alaskan natives under the program now known as the Indian Health Service. In 1968 the Food and Drug Administration became part of the PHS. Four other PHS agencies are the Agency for Health Care Policy and Research, the Agency for Toxic Substances and Disease Registry, the Health Services and Resources Administration, and the Substance Abuse and Mental Health Administration. The PHS became part of the newly created Federal Security Agency in 1939. It was incorporated into the Department of Health, Education, and Welfare (now the Department of Health and Human Services) when the department was established in 1953. The service was directed by the surgeon general until 1968, when a reorganization placed it under the leadership of the assistant secretary for health. The surgeon general continues to play an important role as an adviser to the public on health matters. In the 1990s the PHS agencies reported to the secretary of health and human services.

[Bess Furman, *A Profile of the United States Public Health Service, 1798–1948* (Washington, D.C., 1973); Fitzhugh Mullan, *Plagues and Politics: The Story of the United States Public Health Service* (New York, 1989); Ralph Williams, *The United States Public Health Service, 1798–1950* (Washington, D.C., 1951).]

JOHN PARASCANDOLA

See also **DAH:** Public Health; **SUPP:** Centers for Disease Control and Prevention; Food and Drug Administration; Health and Human Services, Department of; National Institutes of Health.

PUBLISHING INDUSTRY. Book publishing in the United States is among the most stable industries, but since the 1970s it has undergone enormous changes from top to bottom. Mergers and acquisitions among the largest houses have, according to some critics, increased profits for "blockbuster" best-sellers but decreased the volume of worthy and important, if less popular, works of fiction and nonfiction. In the 1990s about 50,000 new titles were published in the United States each year, but only half the public bought books. Most sales were in nonfiction (83 percent, with biography and autobiography dominating). Only 17 percent of books purchased were fiction, poetry, and drama, with mysteries topping the fiction category. While large publishing houses dominate sales, approximately 3,000 publishers bring out more than three books a year. Most are specialty firms that place emphasis on editor-author relations. They rely on a large profit margin per title and print runs are in the thousands.

Despite corporate takeovers in the 1980s, including the acquisition of William Morrow by Hearst; the takeover of Crown, Knopf, Pantheon, and Ballantine by Random House; the purchase of Charles Scribner's Sons by Macmillan and subsequent purchase of Macmillan by Paramount, many traditions of the historically family-owned houses persisted. The proliferation of mergers may have been offset by startup firms. These new houses have continued to publish books of merit despite financial risk. Because large publishers concentrate on promoting potential best-sellers, many midlist titles—those that sell reasonably well in the long term—are available to smaller publishers.

The typical bookstore today looks radically different from what it did in the 1970s. It is likely part of a large chain, such as Walden Books, B. Dalton Booksellers, Crown, or Barnes and Noble. At the beginning of the 1990s, the Walden Books chain boasted 1,000 outlets and B. Dalton claimed 800. Superstores carrying tens of thousands of titles were rapidly proliferating. Inside the stores, paperback titles dominated. From 1980 to 1985, paperbacks jumped from 30 percent of all books in print to 40 percent, and sales jumped ahead of hardbacks. Consolidation in retail has not meant savings for the consumer—the average title in 1995 cost twice as much as it did in the late 1970s. Bookstores prominently display items like coffee mugs and t-shirts with "literary" figures on them, board games like Trivial Pursuit, designer bookmarks, clip-on reading lights, audiocassettes, and videocassettes.

The hardcover book has far from disappeared. In most bookstores hardcover titles from such perennial best-selling authors as James Michener, Robert Ludlum, and Stephen King are prominently displayed and usually deeply discounted. They sell millions of copies and can make huge profits for the publisher through the sale of rights to republish the book in serial form in magazines and in editions for trade paperbacks, mass-market paperbacks, large type, and book clubs. Income for big sellers also includes movie rights and adaptations to formats such as CD-ROM and audiocassette.

The book publishing industry has been influenced by radical changes in other media, including television, radio, and films. It faced competition in the 1990s for attention and money from media that did not exist or were in their infancy in the 1970s: video games, computer bulletin boards and information services, cable television, and videocassettes. One justification, and possible benefit, of the merger mania of the 1980s is that publishers were able to use the resources of parent companies that owned other media outlets. Once Time merged with Warner to become Time Warner in 1989, the magazine publishing, film, and broadcast divisions could provide marketing and management for Time-Life Books; Little, Brown and Company; and the Book-of-the-Month Club. As a result of mergers and the proliferation of media, authors and publishers began creating or adapting their work in different formats. Art Spiegelman's critically acclaimed *Maus* (1986), an account of the Holocaust told in comic book format, was released in CD-ROM with supplementary sketches, interviews, and other materials. Reference works like the *American Heritage Dictionary, Grolier's Encyclopedia,* and the *Hammond World Atlas* adapted their offerings to CD-ROM, sometimes combining print and CD-ROM versions in one package. An entirely new medium, CD-ROM books, emerged, enabling authors to combine photos, text, sound, and graphics in a multimedia format for readers interested in interactive experience. Although the staying power of such technologies is questionable, the Book-of-the-Month Club's decision to start carrying CD-ROMs shows the format's strength. (The club's first offering in May 1994 was "Poetry in Motion," which features eighteen poets reading and discussing their works.)

The combination of new formats and increasing influence of corporations dependent on earnings forecasts led the industry to promote books as never before. Publishing houses in the past resisted market research and other preliminaries to publicity, but with books increasingly seen as properties and commodities, houses put greater effort into publicizing their output. They sought displays in bookstores and eagerly arranged for authors to appear on television and radio talk shows before, during, and after a book's release. More attention went to cover art, which can determine the browser's decision to purchase.

Best-sellers, fueled by the increasing influence of superstores carrying tens of thousands of titles, retail chains, and discount chains, and the continuing influence of book clubs, helped the industry survive difficult times in the 1980s and early 1990s. In 1994 a record seventeen books sold more than one million copies, compared to nine in 1993. During the same year a record 183 books sold more than 100,000, compared to 157 in 1993. (In 1983 the top ten best-sellers sold only 4.3 million copies combined.) Most of the blockbusters were by longtime favorite authors, such as John Grisham, Tom Clancy, Danielle Steel, and Ken Follett, indicating the increasing importance of authors as "brand names."

Book clubs, notably the Time Warner-owned Book-of-the-Month Club (which includes both the above-named club and eight others, such as the History Book Club and the Quality Paperback Book Club), changed their operations during the 1980s. The Book-of-the-Month Club used to stress low prices, and the club and its eight "siblings" boasted 3.5 million members in 1993. In the 1990s, however, it could no longer compete with deep discounts by the chains. The club responded by stressing gift wrapping, book

searching, and an "800" number for easier ordering. Special-interest inserts in catalogs used market research to appeal to each customer's particular preferences, such as books about music.

Publishers continued to face problems, both economic and cultural, in the mid 1990s. The economic problems centered around competition for readers' attention from traditional and new media. Censorship remained a cultural issue, especially in schools, where more than 200 incidents of book banning in some form or another were reported in 1991. Among titles removed from school bookshelves were classics like *The Adventures of Huckleberry Finn.*

[Kenneth C. Davis, *Two-Bit Culture: The Paperbacking of America* (Boston, 1984); N. R. Kleinfield, "The Supermarketer of Books," *New York Times Magazine* (Nov. 9, 1986); Walter W. Powell, "The Good Books Business: The Perils of Publishing, Part 2," *New Republic* (Sept. 15, 1986); John Tebbel, *Between Covers: The Rise and Transformation of Book Publishing in America* (New York, 1987).]

JEFFREY M. MERRON

See also **DAH:** Book Publishing; **SUPP:** CD-ROM Technology; Communications Industry; Freedom of the Press; Magazines; Newspapers.

PUERTO RICAN AMERICANS. Although Puerto Ricans began migrating to the United States soon after the turn of the twentieth century (2,000 from 1900 to 1909), it was not until the 1940s that they did so in large numbers (151,000 from 1940 to 1949). Puerto Ricans settled in major cities, including New York, Chicago, Boston, and Philadelphia, as well as such smaller cities as Albany and Buffalo, N.Y.; Cleveland; Hartford, Conn.; and Worcester, Mass. There was a decrease in the number of migrants in the 1960s (145,000), but that trend reversed in the 1970s, although some 160,000 mainland residents returned to Puerto Rico during that decade. In 1994 Puerto Ricans and those of Puerto-Rican descent in the United States numbered close to 3 million.

Studies of the Puerto Rican population in the United States have commonly treated it either as a divided nation or as an ethnic minority. The first conceptualization considers the migratory experience within the context of international capitalism. Expanding urban industry absorbed surplus labor from the "colony" during and after World War II. Shrinking economic opportunities on the mainland beginning in the 1960s halted the flow and eventually resulted in return migration, a phenomenon peculiar to Puerto Ricans because of their status as U.S. citizens since 1917. In the 1970s and 1980s, however, a "brain drain" occurred in Puerto Rico because of limited employment opportunities in certain fields for overqualified individuals, causing many in search of more competitive salaries and higher standards of living to move to U.S. cities. The second scholarly construction treats migrants as an ethnic minority being integrated into mainstream American culture. It emphasizes the conditions Puerto Ricans encountered when they arrived and explains their adaptation in terms of the available resources and social-service programs. This interpretation attributes return migration either to the failure of Puerto Ricans to adapt to the host country and their desire to seek refuge among family and friends on the island or to the inability of U.S. agencies to provide the necessary wherewithal for integration.

Government officials on both the mainland and the island have considered migrants and return migrants as a problem. In U.S. cities the first wave of Puerto Ricans became the target of much discrimination because of skin color, level of education, and cultural differences. The second and third generation reacted by developing "cultural" traits that would ensure survival. Gang violence, later connected to drug use, was one of the coping strategies stereotyped by sensational and insensitive media. Equally recognizable has been ghettoization, social marginalization, unstable household income, and high levels of unemployment and high school dropout rates. On the island a large number of Puerto Ricans rejected the first wave of return migrants. Most natives' understanding of and sympathy for the mainland experience was limited. To them, *nuyoricans* seemed aggressive, lacking in culture, and, probably most important, unable or unwilling to speak Spanish. The sources of conflict did not disappear and the situation became more manageable in the late 1980s only because it was more familiar.

On their part, migrants and their descendants have created a distinctive culture by appropriating elements from the societies of origin and destination. In every large U.S. city Latin markets provide ingredients for a diet in which indigenous and African food conforms to more American tastes. Church and community organizations promote traditional religious and social rituals, such as christenings or young women's fifteenth-birthday celebrations, and coordinate the commemoration of important U.S. events, such as the birthday of Martin Luther King, Jr., or Independence Day. Salsa, the Afro-Latin rhythm born in Spanish Harlem, became a popular staple of the U.S. commercial music world. Moving comfortably among constituencies and the larger American public, Puerto-Rican educators, politicians, and civil servants reinforced and even institutionalized these rich cross-cultural contributions.

[José Hernández Alvarez, *Return Migration to Puerto Rico* (Berkeley, Calif., 1967); Center for Puerto Rican Studies, *Labor Migration Under Capitalism: The Puerto Rican Experience* (New York, 1979); Luis Nieves Falcón, *El Emigrante Puertorriqueño* (Rio Piedras, P.R., 1975).]

TERESITA MARTÍNEZ-VERGNE

See also **SUPP:** Education, Bilingual; Hispanic Americans; Puerto Rico.

PUERTO RICO. The world rise in oil prices in 1973–1974 shattered Puerto Rico's industrial model, known since the 1940s as Operation Bootstrap. Based on external capital investment, it had raised per capita income but had not significantly lowered unemployment. The oil crisis brought a sharp decline in Puerto Rico's industrial production, increased unemployment, and brought a marked increase in migration to the mainland United States. To reduce unemployment, the Commonwealth of Puerto Rico generated public-sector jobs at enormous expense, resulting in a disproportionately high growth of government compared to other sectors of society. To stimulate the stagnant economy of the island, Puerto Rico, with support from U.S. corporations, petitioned Congress for revisions in the tax code to encourage corporations to reinvest their earnings. The subsequent changes in 1976 resulted in a noticeable influx of capital to banks already established in Puerto Rico and an expansion of pharmaceutical and electronics companies. Apparel and other labor-intensive industries benefited much less, and the much-needed increase in employment thus fell short of what was predicted.

Meanwhile, Puerto Rican politics changed markedly. After the pro-statehood New Progressive Party (PNP) defeated the pro-Commonwealth Popular Democratic Party (PPD) for the first time in 1968, a two-party system became firmly entrenched. Between 1972 and 1992 each party won three elections. The Puerto Rican Independence Party (PIP) maintained its 5 percent share of the voters throughout this period. Political discussions revolved around whether islanders should reform the Commonwealth, become a state of the Union, or aspire to independent status. A December 1991 referendum asked Puerto Ricans whether future votes on the status of the island must offer the choices of statehood, commonwealth, and independence. (A choice would have to carry more than 50 percent of the vote to win.) Had the voters approved, any direct "yes" or "no" vote on statehood would have been prohibited. To most people's surprise, the proposal was defeated. In November 1993 the voters chose to retain the island's commonwealth status by a slim 2 percent margin over statehood. The option of independence received 4.4 percent of the vote. Some analysts concluded that these two referenda indicated that the average voter was much less interested in changing the island's relationship with the United States than were the leaders of the PNP and PIP.

In November 1994 Puerto Ricans turned down two propositions. One proposed increasing the number of judges on the Commonwealth Supreme Court; the other limited the right to bail. The statehood party supported both amendments. Against all predictions both proposals were defeated. One of the most publicized political events in Puerto Rico during the last quarter of the twentieth century concerned the death in 1978 of two young pro-independence Puerto Ricans at what is known as the Cerro Maravilla. Accused of sabotaging communication towers, they were killed by policemen in what seemed an execution. Legal action was taken against those involved.

Puerto Rico's population increased from 2,722,000 in 1970 to an estimated 3,621,000 in 1993. Because of the mainland's sagging economy in the 1970s, more Puerto Ricans returned home than left the island. In the 1980s the normal pattern of a net outmigration to the mainland resumed. The migrants of that decade were wealthier and better educated than those of previous years. Estimates in 1990 stated that 2.7 million Puerto Ricans lived on the mainland. In 1980, 43 percent of the mainlanders resided in New York. By 1990 that figure was down to 39.8 percent, as migrants moved to such states as Florida, Massachusetts, Connecticut, and Pennsylvania. If the trend of overall population growth among mainland Puerto Ricans continues, by the year 2010 there will be more Puerto Ricans living on the mainland than in Puerto Rico. One possible reason for migration is the several natural disasters that struck Puerto Rico beginning in the late 1970s. In 1979 Hurricane David and Tropical Storm Federico left 4 people dead and millions of dollars in damages. In 1985 torrential rains from Tropical Storm Isabel caused floods and left 500 dead. In 1989 Hurricane Hugo left at least 50,000 people homeless and caused 7 deaths; damages were in the hundreds of millions of dollars. In

1994 a prolonged drought forced authorities to ration water for almost three months in the northeast. Rationing in areas of low rainfall continued into 1995.

[Arturo Morales Carrión, *Puerto Rico: A Political and Cultural History* (New York, 1983); James L. Dietz, *Economic History of Puerto Rico* (Princeton, N.J., 1986); Edwin Meléndez and Edgardo Meléndez, eds., *Colonial Dilemma: Critical Perspectives on Contemporary Puerto Rico* (Boston, 1993).]

MAYRA ROSARIO

See also **SUPP:** Hurricanes; Puerto Rican Americans.

PULITZER PRIZES, endowed by newspaper publisher Joseph Pulitzer following his death in 1911, are awarded each May by the president of Columbia University on the recommendation of the Pulitzer Prize Board for meritorious work done during the preceding year in journalism, letters, and music. The prizes, each $3,000 (except for the meritorious public service award, which is a gold medal) have varied over the years but in 1995 numbered fourteen in journalism, six in letters, one in music, and four fellowships of $5,000. Three fellowships are awarded to Columbia University graduates for travel and study abroad, and one is for specialization in drama, music, literary, film, or television criticism. The journalism prizes began in 1917 with awards for reporting and editorial writing. Since then the prizes have included awards for meritorious public service by a newspaper (1918), editorial cartooning (1922), correspondence for Washington or foreign news coverage (1929), spot news photography (1942), national reporting (1942), international reporting (1942), feature photography (1968), criticism and commentary (1970), feature writing (1979), explanatory journalism (1985), and specialized reporting (1985). Sometimes a citation award (1938) is given for work in more than one year and includes journalists as well as novelists, composers, photographers, and even press cartographers (1945).

Since 1917 Pulitzer Prizes have been given for works of letters in history of the United States. Twice the award for history has included diaries—C. Vann Woodward's *Mary Chestnut's Civil War* (1982) and Laurel Thatcher Ulrich's *A Midwife's Tale: The Life of Martha Ballard, Based on Her Diary, 1785–1812* (1991). Other letters awards since 1917 have gone to an American author for a distinguished biography or autobiography. One recipient was John F. Kennedy for *Profiles in Courage* (1957). Since 1918 a prize has been given annually for the best work of fiction by an American author and dealing with American life. Recipients have ranged from Edith Wharton (*The Age of Innocence*, 1921) to Toni Morrison (*Beloved*, 1988) and Alice Walker (*The Color Purple*, 1983). An exception occurred in 1977, when the overseeing board could not agree with the fiction jury about awarding the prize to Norman Maclean for *A River Runs Through It*, and no award was given that year. The poetry prize, established in 1922, has been awarded to Robert Frost (1924, 1931, 1937, 1943), Carl Sandburg (1951), Robert Penn Warren (1958, 1979), Sylvia Plath (1982), and Rita Dove (1987). In 1962 the category of general nonfiction was added and that award has gone to authors such as Studs Terkel (*The Good War*, 1985) and Neil Sheehan (*A Bright and Shining Lie: John Paul Vann and America in Vietnam*, 1989). Prizes have been given since 1918 for drama, preferably an original play and one dealing with American life. Receiving the award twice or more were Eugene O'Neill (1920, 1928, 1957), Robert Sherwood (1936, 1941), Tennessee Williams (1948, 1955), Edward Albee (1967, 1975), and August Wilson (1987, 1990). An award in music has been given since 1943 to an American composer, including a special posthumous award to ragtime composer Scott Joplin in 1976.

[J. Douglas Bates, *The Pulitzer Prize: The Inside Story of America's Most Prestigious Award* (New York, 1991).]

BETTY HOUCHIN WINFIELD

PURE FOOD AND DRUG MOVEMENT. The 1980s was a decade of retrenchment for the pure food and drug movement, the effort of individuals and organizations to ensure the healthfulness of food and drugs. It was a decade of frustration for activists, partly because of conservative leadership in national politics. Nonetheless, significant public action took place. Democratic Representative John Dingell of Michigan, chairman of the Committee on Energy and Commerce, led an effort in Congress to bolster regulation of food and drugs. He exposed inadequate safeguards against the spread of the AIDS virus through the nation's blood supply and the virtual corruption by drug manufacturers of the Food and Drug Administration's generic drug approval process. Despite Dingell's public committee hearings, tainted blood infected between 12,000 and 20,000 people with the AIDS virus during the decade.

The election to the presidency of Governor Bill Clinton of Arkansas in 1992 released the pent-up energies of pure food and drug activists. There followed such an outpouring of reform proposals that the Clinton administration publicly urged activists to let up. One area of concern in the 1990s was the nation's program of meat inspection, which is under the jurisdiction of the U.S. Department of Agriculture. In 1993–1994 an outbreak of illness, affecting 1,672 people, with 19 deaths, occurred because of inadequately inspected meat. This seemed merely the tip of an iceberg, and in 1993 some statisticians predicted that 8 million people would be stricken with food-borne illnesses each year and 9,000 would die annually.

Among the movements in the area of food and drugs is the Pure Food Campaign (PFC). Founded in 1992 under the leadership of Jeremy Rifkin, it fights against the use of bovine somatotropin, or bST, a genetically engineered hormone to increase milk production in dairy cows. The Food and Drug Administration approved the hormone late in 1993, and within months many dairy herds were given it, with marked increases in milk yields. The PFC also opposes genetically engineered vegetables, which Rifkin dubbed "Frankenfoods." The PFC also opposed food irradiation, a proposed method for killing bacteria in meat and poultry.

[Herbert Burkholz, *The FDA Follies* (New York, 1994); Elizabeth Amy Poyck, Marshall Alexander Smith, and Alison Toledo, "Federal Food and Drug Act Violations," *American Criminal Law Review* 26 (Spring 1993).]

ROBERT KRAIG

See also **SUPP:** Acquired Immune Deficiency Syndrome; Agriculture, Department of; Consumer Protection and Rights; Food and Drug Administration; Genetic Engineering; Product Tampering.

PYRAMID SCHEMES are frauds that pay a hierarchy at the top of the triangle out of investments made by those at the bottom. Often confused with legitimate multilevel marketing, pyramids are felonies in most states. In most scenarios, a pyramid is set up by a few people offering a seemingly attractive product or service. They recruit people to sell that product but require an investment for participation. Those investors are then encouraged to recruit still more participants. In legitimate multilevel marketing, profit comes from sales to actual customers. With pyramids, most of the money comes from cash investments of recruited participants and product sales to those recruits, often required. Eventually, the pool of recruits dries up, leaving latecomers unable to recoup their investments. Since the mid-1970s, regulators have unearthed large pyramid schemes, although investigators admit that most go undetected. Many that slip through the cracks involve small numbers of investors bilked by con artists who move from state to state. One popular small operation involves a plane scenario. A "pilot" sits atop the pyramid, the next level has two "copilots," the third level four "flight attendants," and the fourth and bottom level eight "passengers." Each passenger pays an entry fee, usually a few thousand dollars. The money is given to the pilot, who "jettisons" with huge profits. The plane then breaks into two new pyramids, with each copilot now sitting as the pilot. The new flight attendants then recruit fresh passengers, usually friends and relatives, and the scheme continues until it collapses under its own weight.

[Joseph Bulgatz, *Ponzi Schemes, Invaders from Mars, and Other Extraordinary Popular Delusions and the Madness of Crowds* (New York, 1992).]

KATHLEEN B. CULVER

QUALITY CIRCLES, a term used in the field of human resources management that refers to the technique of motivating workers by allowing them input into decisions concerning the production process, thereby increasing productivity and profits. Originat-
ing in Japan in 1962, quality circles were introduced in the United States in the early 1970s. By the mid-1990s thousands of manufacturing plants, banks, hospitals, and government agencies had implemented quality circles. A circle typically consists of three to twelve employees from a given department and a representative of management. The circle meets on a regular basis on company time to examine a limited range of issues related to the department, identify and analyze problems, and propose solutions. The focus of the circles is on improving both the quality of the product and the production process. The underlying premise is that productivity will increase because the person best able to decide the most efficient way to do a job is the person who does it for a living. Another premise is that if employees have greater control over the product, they will be more committed and effective workers.

[David Hutchins, *Quality Circles Handbook* (New York, 1985).]

JACK HANDLER

QUOTAS. *See* **Affirmative Action; Civil Rights Movement.**

R

RADIO. When radio first appeared in the United States in the early 1920s, it created an entirely new medium of entertainment—a "theater of the mind." By the 1930s listening to the radio became the most common home activity of families. All network programming was planned around the family. Women were offered daily dramatic serials during mornings and afternoons, nearly all sponsored by manufacturers of soap or detergent products ("soap operas"). Children were served adventure shows in the late afternoons. News and commentary programs followed. From 7:00 P.M. on, dramas and variety shows were broadcast for the entire family. Programming by and large was controlled by four national networks: the Radio Corporation of America's (RCA) National Broadcasting Company, with two networks (NBC-Red and NBC-Blue); the Columbia Broadcasting System (CBS); and the Mutual Broadcasting System (MBS). Because RCA owned two networks, the Federal Communications Commission ordered it to divest one, which it did in 1943, with NBC-Blue becoming the American Broadcasting Company.

Radio produced its own celebrities, few of whom could duplicate their successes in motion pictures. Jack Benny, Fred Allen, George Burns and Gracie Allen, Major Bowes, and Fanny Brice became extensions of virtually every U.S. family during radio's "golden age." For a time the most popular program featured a ventriloquist, Edgar Bergen, whose inability to keep his lips from moving doomed his attempts in later years to translate his show to television. It was the overwhelming popularity of Bergen and his dummy, Charlie McCarthy, a show that attracted one-third of all radio listeners, that may have prevented a national panic on Halloween of 1938. That night actor Orson Welles, whose "Mercury Theater on the Air" attracted a mere 3.6 percent of the national radio audience, broadcast a dramatization of the science-fiction book *War of the Worlds* by British author H. G. Wells that caused a near panic among the audience. A newspaper headline next day related that "Radio War Terrorizes U.S."; another read, "Panic Grips Nation as Radio Announces 'Mars Attacks World.'" The program demonstrated the power of radio's possible manipulation of the public's imagination.

Radio has had a marked effect on politics and reporting. President Franklin D. Roosevelt, whose voice rivaled those of the actors of the day, mobilized support for his New Deal in the 1930s by taking his message directly to the electorate via radio in "fireside chats." In the 1940s he used them to arouse the nation's patriotic ardor. When war came, first to Europe, then to the United States, radio was brought into the living rooms of Americans with on-the-scene reports from such correspondents as Edward R. Murrow, Walter Cronkite, William L. Shirer, Howard K. Smith, and Eric Sevareid.

With the advent of television—and concurrent development of the transistor—following World War II, radio was transformed into a portable jukebox, with networks becoming little more than headline news services. Independent stations appealing to niche audiences developed—stations with music appealing to older listeners, stations aimed at teenagers, and stations directed at ethnic minorities. With the emergence of new stations on the FM band by the 1970s, the niches were themselves partitioned. Stations were classified as "contemporary," "adult," "album-oriented," "urban," or described by a dozen other tags. FM broadcasting, with its superior fidelity, overtook established AM stations, in numbers and popularity. Between 1975 and 1995 FM stations in the United States nearly doubled to 5,000, and AM stations declined from 4,700 to 4,200.

With broadcasting companies downgrading their radio networks to insignificance, independent syndicators in the 1970s began providing special programming. A program hosted by Los Angeles disc jockey Casey Kasem, featuring a "countdown" of the top forty songs of the week, became the first program to attract a sizable national audience since radio's heyday in the 1930s and 1940s. In the mid-1970s a program syndicator, Westwood One, achieved a dominant position, eventually purchasing Mutual and NBC radio and signing Kasem to a long-term, multimillion-dollar contract. Its success was attributed to cost efficiencies achieved by distributing programs via satellite rather than by land lines. In 1980 Sony introduced the Walkman, a transistorized radio-cassette player that provided concert-hall sound in a package weighing only a few ounces. Demand became so great that a year after its introduction, there was still a month-long wait at many retailers. Ironically, competition with Walkman-type devices in the 1980s came from hefty portable players, or "boom boxes," that could blast the sound of popular radio stations through entire neighborhoods.

Because of the inferior tone quality of AM, many radio stations on that band turned to all-news and all-talk formats, where high fidelity was of little importance. News stations rehashed summaries of the day's events every twenty minutes—presumed to be the average length of an automobile commute. Indeed, all radio programmers recognized that most of their audiences listened in cars, so frequent traffic reports also became obligatory.

Initially, talk shows appealed to middle-aged audiences that appeared to delight in airing their personal problems through call-ins to station hosts, but in the early 1990s two utterly dissimilar national talk-show personalities, Howard Stern and Rush Limbaugh, rose to national prominence, overhauling the medium in the process. Stern's scatological satires made him the most listened-to personality on the air—even as federal regulators fined stations he appeared on for broadcasting obscene material. Limbaugh's humorous conservative broadcasts similarly caught on and produced a host of imitators. He and his cohorts were widely credited with helping the Republican party win a majority in both houses of Congress in 1994.

[Erik Barnouw, *A History of Broadcasting in the United States,* 3 vols. (New York, 1966–1970).]

LEW IRWIN

See also **SUPP:** Music Industry; National Public Radio; Talk Shows; Television; Voice of America.

RADON. *See* **Air Pollution.**

RAINBOW COALITION, a group developed within the Democratic Party during the 1984 presidential election. Led by African-American civil rights activist Jesse Jackson, it attracted blacks, Latinos, Asian Americans, American Indians, and poor whites. As the coalition's spokesperson (and candidate for president in the Democratic primaries), Jackson criticized the administration of President Ronald Reagan and called for cuts in defense spending, strengthening of affirmative action, and federal assistance for urban workers and farmers. Although he received 3.3 million votes in 1984 and 6.8 million in a second presidential bid in 1988, the coalition's alliance fragmented, its influence greatly diminishing by 1992. That year Jackson did not enter the presidential race. Perhaps in recognition that electoral campaigns could not fulfill its larger purpose, the coalition in 1993 turned to an outreach program for inner-city youth.

[Sheila Collins, *The Rainbow Challenge: The Jackson Campaign and the Future of U.S. Politics* (New York, 1986).]

JILL WATTS

RALEIGH. Founded in 1792 as North Carolina's first permanent capital, Raleigh evolved in the nineteenth century as a center of government, higher education, printing, and railroad transportation. In addition to the capitol, the state established a prison; an institution for the deaf, dumb, and blind; and a hospital for the insane. Raleigh's phenomenal growth, making it the state's second largest city after Charlotte, began in the 1960s, after the creation of the nearby Research Triangle Park. This 6,800-acre park attracted about eighty research institutions 35,000 employees and promoted the growth of scores of businesses outside the park. Expanding state government services, retailing, air transportation, and manufacture of electronics and textiles sustained the growth. The airport became a regional hub in 1987 and a gateway to Europe in 1988. A twenty-block state office complex employed more than 10,000 workers. North Carolina State University's student enrollment grew from

17,000 in 1975 to 27,500 in 1995. The city's population mushroomed from 47,000 in 1940 to 208,000 in 1990.

Since the early 1970s Raleigh has experienced rapid change. A political revolution in 1975 gave control of city government to a pro-growth faction that annexed large areas and expanded the city's infrastructure. Notable were completion of a beltline and a new reservoir. A major project was the revitalization of the downtown, which had been adversely affected by the opening of outlying malls and shopping centers. By 1994 successful revitalization encompassed a pedestrian mall, a civic center, a city market, high-rise offices and hotels, improved housing, and a state museum of history. The 1993 city elections resulted in the election of a Republican mayor—the first in a century. African Americans, about one-fourth of the population, have become better integrated. City and county schools merged in 1976 to provide more effective desegregation, and the city pledged itself to the hiring of more black police and firemen. Raleigh elected a black mayor in 1973 and a black sheriff in 1978. Plans for the future include an outer beltline to ease traffic congestion, better crime control, and sustained economic growth, partly through development of an additional 755-acre campus at North Carolina State University that will permit research support of private industry.

[Moses N. Amis, *Historical Raleigh from Its Foundation in 1792* (Raleigh, 1902); David Perkins, ed., *The News & Observer's Raleigh: A Living History of North Carolina's Capital* (Winston-Salem, N.C., 1994); Steve Stolpen, *Raleigh: A Pictorial History* (Norfolk, Va., 1977).]

JOHN L. BELL

See also **SUPP:** North Carolina.

RAPE as a political and social issue was transformed by the women's movement of the 1960s and 1970s. Rape is now increasingly interpreted as a crime of violence and control against women rather than a pathological sexual act that they invite. Activists have created rape crisis centers to help victim-survivors and their close friends and family. Following a comprehensive overhaul of rape law in Michigan in 1974, states revised their statutes and legal practices. Although reform has been uneven, state legislatures and court rulings have modified the definition and proof needed to establish rape. Shield laws now prevent all or much of a victim's previous sexual history from being introduced in court. Requirements for witnesses, use of physical force by the rapist, evidence of resistance, and prompt complaint have been dropped in most states. Rape under the law now includes nonconsensual sex with spouses. It also includes such sex with acquaintances, since the vast majority of victims are raped by men they know, not by strangers. Some jurisdictions provide advocates to help women when reporting rape, gathering medical evidence, and meeting prosecutors. Although some research suggests that convictions are now easier to obtain, others find that juror and judicial attitudes block convictions. Rape remains statistically contentious. Estimates for lifetime chance of rape for women range from 5 to 25 percent. In the 1990s date rape on campuses and elsewhere appeared to be endemic, but some argued that its extent has been overblown. Celebrated cases involving William Kennedy Smith, Mike Tyson, John Wayne Bobbitt, and the gang rape of a jogger in New York City's Central Park raised public awareness and controversy.

[Julie A. Alison and Lawrence S. Wrightsman, *Rape: The Misunderstood Crime* (Newbury Park, Calif., 1993); Carole Goldberg-Ambrose, "Unfinished Business in Rape Law Reform," *Journal of Social Issues* 48 (1992): 173–185.]

AMY FRIED

See also **SUPP:** Domestic Violence; Rape Crisis Centers; Women's Movement.

RAPE CRISIS CENTERS started in 1972, when the first such service opened in Washington, D.C.; twenty years later there were more than 550 centers. Their origin lay in the commitment of the women's movement's to "personal politics," which redefined problems experienced by individual women as public issues. Rape crisis centers, like women's health clinics and battered women's shelters, were designed for empowering and serving women. Centers counsel victim-survivors, provide information about medical and legal procedures, and act as advocates in hospitals and police stations and with prosecutors. At the outset centers were staffed by community volunteers with erratic funding. In the 1990s many were run by universities or local governments and employed professional counselors.

AMY FRIED

See also **SUPP:** Rape; Women's Rights.

RAPID TRANSIT. In the prosperous decade of the 1950s, the United States traveled a different road than most other nations in developing a transportation system, building an interstate highway system satisfying the needs of individual automobile owners across the country. Although other countries also invested in highways, they put considerable resources into public transportation systems such as subways and aboveground trains. For Japan and several European countries, these investments ultimately paid off in what are known as "bullet trains," trains capable of reaching speeds greater than 150 miles per hour, whisking people quickly between cities. Environmental and energy concerns, combined with the problem of traffic congestion in many cities, piqued interest among transportation and public planning officials in deploying the high-speed trains in the United States, but the U.S. transportation system generally relied upon automobiles.

Most public planning experts consider mass transit—everything from buses and subways to aboveground trains, trolley cars, and light rail systems—as the best way to transport people at the least expense, including such nonfinancial "expenses" as pollution and depletion of energy sources. Mass transit prevailed in many U.S. cities before World War II. After 1945 Americans began moving in droves to suburbs. This, combined with the postwar prosperity that raised incomes for working Americans, led to the boom in individual automobile ownership and a decline in urban mass transit systems and passenger train service. Environmental and energy concerns did not stop the postwar automobile boom because gasoline was inexpensive. Passenger train travel dwindled until no private companies were involved in the business; instead, the federal government subsidized Amtrak, which provided passenger trains. Federal, state, and local governments also subsidized bus services, subways, and elevated trains for transporting people in city and suburban areas. Such services, however, generally were associated with poor people, and most working Americans outside of major cities preferred their cars for travel. More cars meant more miles; the number of automobile miles driven increased from 901 billion in 1970 to 1,525 billion miles in 1990, and further increase at the same rate appeared likely.

Public planners looked to high-speed bullet trains as a good alternative to the highway system and to airplanes for long-distance travel, and environmentalists supported them because they lowered energy and pollution costs. Amtrak and several states—including Texas and Florida—announced bullet-train initiatives. Proponents of high-speed trains gained an interesting and powerful ally in defense industry contractors, who hoped to switch their production facilities to building high-speed trains as a way of replacing defense spending cutbacks following the end of the cold war. Even with the defense industry's support, however, development of high-speed trains in the United States seemed doubtful in the 1990s. Texas dropped its plans after the airline industry expressed opposition to the idea. The cost makes many of the projects prohibitive. Supertrains and light rail systems such as those in Portland, Oregon, and Los Angeles require new tracks, which could cost up to $100 million per mile in cities. Also, the federal government's budget deficit and conservative attacks on spending threatened subsidies for public transportation.

[Brian J. Cudahy, *Cash, Tokens, and Transfers: A History of Urban Mass Transit in North America* (New York, 1990); George W. Jernstedt, *Give the City Back to People: New Mobility Can Make Our Cities a Joy Again* (Bolivar, Pa., 1994).]

THOMAS G. GRESS

See also **SUPP:** Transportation, Department of; Transportation Industry; Urban Living.

REAGANOMICS is the broad term used to describe President Ronald Reagan's economic policy during the 1980s. It was outlined in a document presented to Congress shortly after the 1980 election, entitled *America's New Beginning: A Program for Economic Recovery.* The program called for budget reforms to cut the rate of growth in federal spending; a series of steps to cut personal income taxes and business taxes; a far-reaching program of regulatory relief; and a commitment to a monetary policy for restoring a stable currency and healthy financial markets. Based largely on the principles of supply-side economics, the program was designed to lift the nation's economy out of its deepest recession since the Great Depression by reducing the federal government's economic role. By shifting federal revenues to a less restricted private sector through tax reduction, President Reagan expected to reinvigorate the economy. At the same time he hoped to reduce, or even eliminate, the federal deficit, a task made more difficult by another political goal—increasing defense spending.

With assistance from the Republican minority and a cadre of conservative Democrats, many of Reagan's congressional initiatives were passed. Although the nation remained mired in recession for the first two years of his administration, a robust recovery soon turned into the longest peacetime economic expansion in U.S. history, ending only in 1990. More than

18 million jobs were created during the economic expansion from 1983 to 1990, unemployment fell, and inflation dropped from 12.5 percent in 1980 to 4.4 percent in 1988, but the growth came at a price. Unable to cut federal spending, Reagan oversaw a tripling of the federal debt to $2.7 trillion and a quadrupling of the annual trade deficit to $137 billion. The legacy of Reaganomics is a matter of intense debate. In 1980 George Bush, an unsuccessful presidential candidate in the Republican primaries, dubbed Reagan's policies "voodoo economics." Bush and others were skeptical about whether Reagan could cut taxes, increase defense spending, and balance the budget. Critics charge that government spending cuts came at the expense of the poor and that tax cuts almost exclusively benefited the wealthy, increasing the gap between rich and poor. Reagan's economic policies, they add, unleashed a "decade of greed" and rampant speculation that led to the 1987 stock market crash and the 1990 recession. Further, they say, the federal deficit will serve as a drag on the nation's economy for generations. Reagan's supporters say that virtually all sectors of the economy benefited from his economic policies, that he reduced the rate of federal spending growth, and that the federal debt as a percentage of the nation's gross national product decreased. They add that the Democratic majority in Congress thwarted Reagan's efforts to make deeper cuts in federal spending and eventually undermined his tax policies with tax reforms in 1986 and 1990.

[Lou Cannon, *President Reagan: The Role of a Lifetime* (1991); "The Real Reagan Record," *National Review* (Aug. 31, 1992).]

ERIK BRUUN

See also **SUPP:** Balance of Trade; Black Monday Stock Market Crash; Financial Exchanges; Stagflation; Supply-Side Economics; Unemployment; Wall Street.

REAL ESTATE INDUSTRY. Real estate includes land, buildings, water, and other property physically or legally connected to them. While property values and the pace of construction have always fluctuated, they became especially volatile between the 1960s and 1990s, a fact that affected many aspects of national life. The estimated nationwide median price of a new house increased from $23,400 in 1970 to $122,900 in 1990. The value of land and other properties also rose. Development and construction increased markedly. Despite slowdowns and regional differences, values and activity continued upward until a dramatic decline in the late 1980s. A combination of social and economic conditions created this situation, among them a surge in the demand for housing among the large generation born after World War II. Real estate markets also reflected population movements from depressed rural and industrial communities to fast-growing metropolitan areas and rural resorts. Increasing retail, recreational, and other commercial activity prompted development of shopping centers, resorts, and office complexes. In addition, financing became more available to home buyers and commercial real estate ventures through government and the private sector. New federal income tax deductions in 1981 stimulated investment in real estate.

As a result, real estate became increasingly speculative. Instead of purchasing homes as residences and long-term investments, more individuals bought and sold housing essentially because it was a general trend, not a universal motivation for people buying housing, and to capitalize on rapidly rising prices. Real estate developers invested in ambitious development projects, often using elaborate financing. They developed large tracts for new housing and other purposes while renovating older sites and structures and giving them new identities, as with the conversion of old factories and railroad stations into theme shopping complexes. Individuals and businesses profited from these trends. Jobs were created, communities and neighborhoods revitalized, but the loss of open land and local character, plus other environmental, social, and economic issues, sparked controversy. Rising property values made it difficult for longtime, but less affluent, residents to remain in some rapidly changing neighborhoods. An increasing number of young people could no longer afford housing. As the economy entered a recession in the late 1980s real estate activity declined significantly, with wide-ranging consequences. The shift first became noticeable in the South and Southwest around 1985 and in other regions over the next several years. Many individuals and investors had overextended themselves. A surplus of new homes appeared, and costly ventures such as suburban malls became unprofitable. All this occurred when many savings and loan institutions were collapsing. Lenders became more stringent about financing and repayments. The Tax Reform Act of 1986 removed real estate investment incentives. In this environment foreclosures, bankruptcies, high vacancy rates, and other real estate failures became more common. Although the situation began to improve in 1992, the mood had shifted from aggressive optimism to caution and conservatism.

RECREATION

[Steve Lohr, "Banking's Real Estate Miseries," *New York Times* (Jan. 13, 1991); Martin Mayer, *The Builders: Houses, People, Neighborhoods, Governments, Money* (New York, 1978); Lawrence J. White, *The S&L Debacle* (New York, 1991); Suzanne Woolley, "A Firm Footing At Last," *Business Week* (Dec. 27, 1993).]

JOHN TOWNES

See also **SUPP:** Banking and Finance; Housing; Savings and Loan Crisis.

RECREATION. The first emigrants from Europe to settle on the northeastern seaboard of what would become the United States brought with them a distinctive view of the place of work and recreation in life. Traditional recreation, such as dancing (between men and women), gambling, some sports, and smoking tobacco (except at dinner), were banned in New England at one time or another, and a work ethic was embraced in its stead. Puritans, Quakers, and other radical Protestant groups regarded idleness as a source of vice while honest toil characterized members of God's elect. While the Puritans never comprised a majority in the colonies, their values with respect to work and recreation proved widely influential. Even in Puritan New England, however, adults often enjoyed dining, riding, moderate exercise, and even alcoholic beverages.

The nineteenth century saw a mixed attitude toward work and recreation. The work ethic characterized the urban industrial order that emerged in England during the mid-1700s and arrived in the United States in the early 1800s. By that time the industrial revolution was well under way and with it "clock time" to regulate the work schedule. Many religious leaders believed factory work provided discipline, and they often advocated long hours of work while criticizing recreation and play. Nevertheless, many entertainments, including music, minstrel shows, the circus, and theater became popular in the early nineteenth century, while participatory and professional sports flourished during the century's second half. Universities and colleges included athletics in their extracurricular activities and the Young Men's Christian Association (YMCA), founded in London in 1844 and introduced to the United States in 1851, soon developed a program based on athletics and physical recreation. The Young Women's Christian Association (YWCA) was established in Great Britain in 1855, and its first program in the United States opened in Boston in 1866. While one of the goals of the YWCA in the 1990s was to empower women, partly through programs in sport, physical education, and recreation, athletics in the late nineteenth century was still strongly male oriented. Although vigorous physical activity was commonly thought to be unsuited to the female constitution, athletics gradually became part of women's recreation. Women played croquet and lawn tennis after the 1860s, and sex-segregated sports appeared in progressive women's colleges, such as Vassar, by the end of the century.

Concern for the continuing education of adults brought about the lyceum movement, founded in 1826 to bring public lecturers to communities to speak on a range of topics including history, philosophy, science, women's rights, temperance, prison reform, and the abolition of slavery. This movement was concomitant with efforts by labor to reduce the workday from twelve to fourteen hours down to ten. Increased free time was not to be spent in recreation, however, but in intellectual cultivation that would make one a more responsible citizen. The growing exploitation of natural resources led to concern for the nation's natural heritage. In 1864 Congress set aside in California the Yosemite Valley and the Mariposa Grove of Big Trees (later Sequoia National Park) as wilderness areas. Yellowstone (in Wyoming, Idaho, and Montana) became the first national park in 1872. Interestingly, the initial purpose of parks and other wildlife areas was not recreation, but the preservation of wildlife and natural areas as part of the nation's heritage. Central Park in New York City, the first municipal park in the United States, was established in 1856. The need for safe play space for children in cities, especially in poor districts, culminated in the playground movement. The Boston Sand Garden, opened in 1885, was the earliest response to this need. The New York Society for Parks and Playgrounds set up small playgrounds in the city in 1889 and 1891, while the Outdoor Recreation League founded the Seward Park playground in 1893.

The recreation movement visible by the end of the nineteenth century is usually described as a humanitarian reaction to urban circumstances. Reformers first attempted to improve working conditions and unhealthy living conditions and to prevent social disorders by providing modest outlets for recreation. Their efforts constituted a form of social control, as wholesome recreation was presumed to redirect impulses that led to delinquency and crime. Access to public and commercial recreation programs and facilities has increased greatly since World War II. Concern for physical fitness and assistance for individuals with physical, mental, or emotional disabilities expanded markedly during the 1950s and 1960s. Subsequently, the recreation movement suffered setbacks because of economic recessions that led to reduced budgets to support recreation programs. Nevertheless, losses in public recreation were more than compensated for by gains in commercial and consumer-oriented recreation. Consumer spending on recreation rose from about 3 percent of income early in the twentieth century to just under 5 percent by 1929. Although it has shown minor fluctuations over time because of economic conditions, recreation spending in the United States has remained about 7 percent since World War II. Much of this spending is directed at the media, including books, magazines, films, and television, but also toward tourism, such fashionable forms of exercise as jogging, tennis, aerobics, and membership in exclusive sports clubs. These latter forms of recreation commonly represent personal expressions of taste and status.

Drinking and gambling were frequent components of male recreation in colonial America. Although both have been opposed at times by social movements that achieved success, such as Prohibition and efforts to outlaw gambling, alcohol use in the 1990s was a common part of the recreation of both men and women, while legalized gambling was one of the fastest growing industries in the United States. In addition, since the 1960s the recreational use of drugs, including marijuana, cocaine, amphetamines, barbiturates, and various hallucinogens, experienced a phenomenal increase, peaking at 24.3 million users in 1979. Largely a middle-class phenomenon, recreational drug use dropped to a low of 11.4 million users in 1992, although it was suspected to be on the rise again.

Several conflicting trends characterized recreation in the early 1990s. After decades of declining influence, the work ethic reappeared; the leisure age predicted in the late 1960s never arrived. At the same time recreation seemed increasingly a commodity: people work hard not necessarily because it is satisfying, but to purchase recreation, spending some $500 billion per year in the process. Most of recreation continued to take place in the home, although the videocassette recorder (VCR), home computer, and access to multichannel cable television meant that the content of recreation was changing. After the neglect of the 1980s, concern over the environment was intensifying, although the carrying capacity of many national parks and other wilderness areas was being reached or exceeded. While expenditures on public facilities rose only modestly, commercial recreation enterprises were among the fastest growing in the economy.

[Gary Cross, *A Social History of Leisure Since 1600* (State College, Pa., 1990); Foster Rhea Dulles, *A History of Recreation,* 2nd ed. (New York, 1965).]

GARRY E. CHICK

See also **SUPP:** Fitness, Physical; Parks, National; Sports, New.

RECYCLING. The term "recycling" was virtually unknown before the 1970s, although within industry it has been practiced for many years, in some cases centuries. The first American paper mill, built near Philadelphia in 1690, used rags as its raw material. Rags continued to be the basis of paper manufacture until the development of the sulfite process for making wood pulp in the mid-nineteenth century. By the twentieth century, the use of scrap material in industry was common. Scrap dealers in metal have been part of the industrial scene for many years; the metal in "junk" cars has been reprocessed ever since World War II, and many of the parts are remanufactured for sale to repair shops.

National consciousness about recycling is a product of the environmental movement, which can be dated from 1970, the first year Earth Day was celebrated and the year the federal Environmental Protection Agency (EPA) was established. The environmental movement focused attention on the problem of both industrial wastes, notably chemicals seeping into the ground and affecting drinking water, and solid waste, the trash generated by households ending up in the municipal dump or landfill. By 1990 the amount of what the EPA called municipal solid waste amounted to 180 million tons per year and was rising. Under the Resource Conservation and Recovery Act, first passed by Congress in 1976 and reauthorized several times after, the federal government sponsored recycling to restrict the growth of landfills. In 1989 the EPA set a national goal of 25 percent recycling by 1995, that is, the diversion of at least 25 percent of material that would otherwise become municipal solid waste and the reprocessing of it to make other consumer items.

The definition of recyclable material remains in dispute. The EPA includes only material in the municipal solid waste stream, otherwise known as postconsumer waste. The U.S. Bureau of Mines, however, includes industrial scrap in its definition of recyclables, as well as junk cars and other metal products that never end up in landfills. Because of this diversity of meanings, figures on recycling are unreliable. The principle recycled commodities are various metals, paper products, old automobile tires, used automobile batteries, and textiles and chemicals, including plastics. The most recycled material is steel, largely because its magnetic property makes it easy to recover from mixed trash. Three-fifths of the steel used in the United States is recycled, and half of steel products made in the United States is produced from scrap steel and iron. One-third of scrap steel and iron is postconsumer, largely "tin" cans, much of which has been recycled since the late 1980s. Aluminum, primarily in the form of aluminum beverage containers, is substantially recycled. The economic incentive is strong because recycled aluminum costs much less than "virgin" aluminum. The bottle deposit laws in many states have promoted the recycling of aluminum cans; Oregon passed the first such law in 1971. Scrap copper sells for a high price, so significant quantities are recycled. About one-third of copper manufactures is composed of recycled scrap copper.

Paper products are the largest single item (by volume) in municipal solid waste; about 40 percent is recycled. The major difficulty in paper recycling is the many forms in which paper appears—newspaper, corrugated boxes, advertising material, packaging, and writing paper. Corrugated boxes can be and often are reprocessed into new corrugated material. Nearly 50 percent of newsprint is recycled. The major problem in recycling paper is the need to de-ink it first; the paper industry is slowly increasing the number and capacity of its de-inking plants. Automobile tires and automobile batteries have been banned from landfills since the late 1980s. Batteries are reprocessed through the original manufacturers. The United States generates about one old tire per inhabitant per year, and they have proved a problem because, while barred from landfills, when stored above ground they are breeding grounds for rodents and insects. Many truck tires and some auto tires are retreaded; more recently many tires have been shredded and incorporated into road asphalt. Tires contain petrochemical material, and some old tires are burned as fuel.

Some textiles are recycled in the form of clothing shipped to Third World countries. Others are reconstituted as wipe cloths for industry. Most toxic chemicals are reprocessed by the chemical industry, particularly since congressional legislation in the 1970s held manufacturers liable for any residual chemicals found in the ground. Polymer chemicals, the basis of the plastic containers widely used in the twentieth century, are increasingly recycled. The first two-liter plastic bottle was produced in 1978, and as more and more states have passed bottle deposit laws, these have been remanufactured rather than discarded. Two types of plastic are suitable for recycling: PET, used in soda bottles, and HDPE, used in milk jugs. PET can be remanufactured as soda bottles and has many fiber applications; HDPE can be made into many products, such as fences and park benches.

Postconsumer recyclables are collected through municipal recycling programs mandated in many states. Minnesota had the highest recycling rate in 1994 at 38 percent, followed by New Jersey, Washington state, Massachusetts, and Maine. The principal barriers to increased recycling have been the uncertain quality of the material collected and the difficulty of marketing it. In many cases industry is not equipped to use recycled material. Still, the demand is growing, particularly as governments require that the products they purchase contain recycled material. Consumer attitudes toward recycling are gradually becoming more favorable.

[David R. Powelson and Melinda A. Powelson, *The Recycler's Manual for Business, Government, and the Environmental Community* (New York, 1992).]

NANCY M. GORDON

See also **SUPP:** Environmental Business; Environmental Movement; Environmental Protection Agency; Waste Disposal.

REED V. REED, 404 U.S. 71 (1971), a Supreme Court case that represented a departure from sixty years of sex discrimination doctrine. Previously, the Supreme Court had consistently affirmed the ruling in *Muller* v. *Oregon* (1908), in which the Court ruled that "protective" labor laws for women were justified by physical differences between the sexes. The Court subsequently went further, invoking this precedent to uphold laws whose primary effect was to restrict women's work opportunities, such as a prohibition on women bartenders (*Goesaert* v. *Cleary*, 1948) and even laws that had nothing to do with work, such as restrictions on women's jury service (*Hoyt* v. *Florida*, 1961). Lower courts followed this lead. Opinion after opinion stated that sex was a reasonable basis for classification, whatever the specific issue. Sex-based discrimination received only the minimal scrutiny, in contrast to those cases involving constitutional rights or racial discrimination, which receive strict scrutiny. The receptivity to individual rights under Chief Justice Earl Warren did not extend to women's rights, but this was not entirely the Court's fault. Years of undeviating leniency to sex discrimination had dried up the flow of appeals, so that the Court had to wait until the reemergence of the feminist movement for new litigation and an opportunity to reconsider the issue.

Reed v. *Reed* marked the first time the Court used the equal protection clause of the Fourteenth Amendment to invalidate a state statute on the grounds of sex discrimination. *Reed* is a decision whose importance stems far more from its historical interest than from its effect on public policy or doctrine. The case presented a factual situation unlikely to arise often. An Idaho law gave automatic preference to men over equally qualified women in appointing the administrator of a dead person's estate ("qualification" being defined as relationship to the deceased by blood or marriage). Cecil and Sally Reed, who were divorced, both applied to become administrator of their deceased son's estate. Cecil was appointed and Sally sued. The state argued that administrative convenience (removing the need to choose among applicants) and family harmony (removing the potential for conflict) provided rational bases for the law. The Supreme Court disagreed. The short, unanimous opinion implicitly accepted the rational basis test as the appropriate standard for sex discrimination cases but found the necessary reasonableness lacking. "To give a mandatory preference to members of either sex," the Court declared, "is to make the very kind of arbitrary legislative choice forbidden by the equal protection clause." *Reed* did not change constitutional doctrine on sex discrimination; that development had to wait for later cases. In effect, the Court distinguished this case from the precedents and opened the door for what would become a new tier or level of scrutiny in sex discrimination cases with *Craig* v. *Boren* (1976). The decision's impact on future rulings was unclear, both because few laws were as arbitrary as Idaho's and because *Reed* was decided by only seven justices.

[Judith A. Baer, *The Chains of Protection: The Judicial Response to Women's Labor Legislation* (Westport, Conn., 1978), and *Women in American Law: The Struggle Toward Equality from the New Deal to the Present* (New York, 1991); Joan Hoff, *Law, Gender, and Injustice* (New York, 1991).]

JUDITH A. BAER

See also **SUPP:** *Craig* v. *Boren;* Women's Movement; Women's Rights.

REFUGEES. Between 1946 and 1993 the United States admitted 2,855,087 refugees for permanent resettlement. During this period both the annual numbers and national origins of refugees have varied dramatically. During the decade following World War II, more than 90 percent of refugees came from European countries; after 1960 the geographic composition changed. Migration from Cuba rose and continued into the 1990s. Large-scale resettlement of Indochinese refugees began in 1975 and continued into the mid-1990s but at lower annual levels. Admission of refugees from countries in Eastern Europe and the Soviet Union increased during the 1970s and again during the 1990s with the dismantling of communist governments. Other groups that resettled in the United States from the 1970s to the mid-1990s included Iranians, Afghans, and Ethiopians.

The mechanisms for admitting refugees to the United States have also undergone significant changes since World War II. A common theme throughout U.S. refugee policy, however, was a focus on the selective admission of refugees for permanent resettlement in the United States. Only in recent years has the role of the United States as a country of asylum emerged as an important policy consideration. Moreover, until 1980 and the passage of the Refugee Act, U.S. refugee policy was intertwined with and often constrained by immigration procedures.

In 1875 Congress passed the first immigration legislation, specifying reasons for denying the entry of aliens. Prior criminal convictions were grounds for exclusion, but political refugees were the exception to this law. Alien criminals were defined as "persons who are undergoing a sentence for conviction in their own country of felonious crimes, other than political or growing out of or the result of political offenses." Political refugees were also excepted from the requirements of the Literacy Act of 1917. In 1921 legislation was passed regulating not only the moral and political character of aliens seeking admission to the United States but the number and national origins of immigrants. A system of quotas for each country was instituted that favored countries in northwestern Europe, restricted immigration from southern, eastern, and central Europe, and effectively banned Asians. Between 1921 and 1946 aliens seeking entry to the United States as political refugees were admitted primarily within the limits of annual quotas for the country of origin. Policy during this period reflected isolationist currents in U.S. foreign policy and public sentiment. During the years just prior to U.S. entry into World War II, for example, special legislation for the admission of European refugees, including children, was routinely defeated in Congress.

The aftermath of World War II revealed to U.S. government officials the problematic connection between political stability and displaced populations.

Between 1946 and 1965 the relationship between U.S. foreign policy and refugee policy and programs was strengthened. The ineffectiveness of immigration policy for dealing with refugee resettlement was also made clear. The McCarran-Walter Act, passed over President Harry S. Truman's veto in 1952, served to reinforce the quota system and made no provisions for the demand for refugee migration to the United States. The postwar period was thus characterized by special presidential initiatives and legislation for the resettlement of Europeans. For example, more than 40,000 refugees were admitted under the Presidential Directive of 1945, nearly 410,000 aliens under the Displaced Persons Act of 1948, and 189,000 refugees under the Refugee Relief Act of 1953.

In 1956 President Dwight D. Eisenhower used the Immigration and Nationality Act for the temporary admission of individual aliens in order to admit approximately 31,000 Hungarians involved in the uprising of November 1956. Special legislation was then required to "adjust" their temporary parolee status to permanent resident or immigrant status. The mechanism was also used for admission of Cubans beginning in 1959 with the fall of Fulgencio Batista's government in Cuba. Cubans arriving initially were admitted as temporary visitors, whereas from 1960 until 1980 Cubans were paroled into the United States. As with the Hungarians, it was necessary for Congress to pass special legislation in order for Cubans to be granted U.S. immigrant status. Between 1967 and 1993, 512,000 Cubans became permanent residents under the Cuban Adjustment Act of 1966.

Support from Congress and the executive branch for the revision of immigration and refugee policy culminated in amendments to the Immigration and Nationality Act in 1965, which had eliminated the national quota system and established numerical limits for annual immigration from the Eastern and Western hemispheres, respectively. Immigrant visas were distributed according to a system that emphasized family reunification. Within that system, 10,200 annual visas were allocated for refugees, a recognition of the responsibility of the United States for refugee resettlement. The connection of refugee policy to foreign policy interests, however, remained consistent with the cold war. Refugees were defined as aliens who "because of persecution or fear of persecution on account of race, religion, or political opinion may have fled (1) from any Communist or Communist-dominated country or area and (2) from any country within the general areas of the Middle East . . . or . . . are uprooted by catastrophic natural calamity." Because political persecution was tied to communism, the U.S. definition was not consistent with the 1967 United Nations Protocol Relating to the Status of Refugees, ratified by the United States in 1968.

The limitations of the 1965 legislation for meeting the need for refugee resettlement became clear. Demand for refugee migration from the Soviet Union during the 1970s exceeded available visas; between 1972 and 1980, 53,500 Soviet émigrés were paroled in the United States. The parole authority was also used for the admission of refugees fleeing Indochina after 1975. Again, special legislation was passed to permit these and other groups to achieve immigrant status, and approximately 175,000 refugees became immigrants under the Indochinese Act of 1977 and another 139,000 under the Refugee-Parolees Adjustment Act of 1978, which included refugees from Indochina as well as such areas as Chile, Uganda, and Romania.

The Refugee Act of 1980 sought to disentangle U.S. refugee policy from the constraints of annual immigration admissions. The category for refugees within the family reunification–based system was replaced with a consultation process between Congress and the executive branch to set annual levels of refugee admissions. In 1993 the annual ceiling for refugees admissions was 132,000 allocated by geographic region as follows: Asia, 7,000; East Asia, 51,000; Eastern Europe, 2,725; Soviet Union, 49,775; Latin America and the Caribbean, 4,500; Near East and south Asia, 7,000; unallocated, 10,000. The 1980 act removed the requirement for flight from a communist country, making the U.S. definition of a refugee consistent with the UN protocol. Under the act aliens within the United States can apply for asylum. Aliens granted refugee status may apply for adjustment to permanent resident (immigrant) status after one year in the United States. Between 1980 and 1990, 778,000 aliens received permanent resident status. Of these, 44,000 or 5.6 percent were aliens granted political asylum. From 1991 to 1993 more than 365,000 refugees received permanent resident status; 45,000 or 12.3 percent were granted political asylum.

The extent to which refugee policy continues to serve foreign policy interests is an important consideration. Between 1981 and 1990, 90 percent of refugees and those seeking political asylum who were granted permanent resident status came from communist countries; 150,000 refugees were admitted from Eastern Europe, nearly 643,000 from Indochina and China, and 113,000 from Cuba. In 1993, 94 percent of the 56,000 applications for refugee status of persons from Eastern European countries and areas comprising the former Soviet Union were approved by the Immigration and Naturalization Service; 89 percent of applications from persons from Vietnam, Cambodia, and Laos were approved. Requests for refugee status from aliens from noncommunist countries such as El Salvador and Haiti have not been approved in such proportions. For example, between 1981 and 1990, just under 1,400 refugees from El Salvador were granted permanent resident status; from 1990 to 1993 the number was 2,800. Between 1991 and 1993, 32,000 applications for asylum were filed by El Salvadorans. The approval rate was 13 percent. A low proportion of applications from Haitians was approved during the early 1990s. In 1993 the figure was 10 percent.

Questions about refugee policy for different national groups have arisen concerning the government's response to Central American refugees and U.S. support for the government of El Salvador during the 1980s. During the 1990s similar concern arose about the strikingly different policy for Cuban and Haitian refugees. The unsympathetic response to requests for asylum led to an increase in undocumented immigrants from Central America and Haiti. Since the mid-1980s credible estimates of the number of undocumented El Salvadorans residing in the United States range between 300,000 and 500,000, many of whom applied for asylum; in 1992 between 50,000 and 100,000 undocumented Haitians were estimated to be residing in the United States.

[Peter H. Koehn, *Refugees from Revolution* (Boulder, Colo., 1991); Gil Loescher and John A. Scanlan, *Calculated Kindness* (New York, 1986); Robert W. Tucker, Charles B. Keely, and Linda Wrigley, eds., *Immigration and U.S. Foreign Policy* (Boulder, Colo., 1990); Aristede R. Zolberg, Astri Suhrke, and Sergio Aguayo, *Escape from Violence* (New York, 1984).]

ELLEN PERCY KRALY

See also **DAH** and **SUPP:** Immigration; **SUPP:** Asian Americans; Cuba, Relations with; Cuban Americans; Eastern Europe, Relations with; El Salvador, Relations with; Haiti; Latin America, Relations with; Soviet Americans.

REFUGES. *See* **Wildlife Refuges and Sanctuaries.**

RELIGION. For most of American history a Judeo-Christian heritage shaped public discourse. The dominant culture paid little attention to Native American or world religions. A change in immigration laws in 1965 opened the way for an influx that has changed the religious landscape. By the mid-1990s temples and mosques were scattered across the United States rather than confined to coastal cities, as Middle Eastern and Asian religions gained adherents. The resulting pluralism challenged both traditional religious communities and public institutions, raising issues of intolerance and harassment. Cultural tensions related to religious pluralism were influenced by several factors. First, people whose understanding is molded by Judeo-Christian thinking expressed alarm about cultural loss. While most of them did not advocate intolerance, they did advocate prayer in schools. Second, increasingly violent religious tensions abroad often raised fears in the United States. Americans cherish religious freedom. Tensions over pluralism found their source in ritual and social dimensions rather than in the experiential and ethical.

U.S. politics have often been marked by religious debates. Most conservative Protestants identify with the Republican party, while many Catholics and liberal denominations choose the Democratic party. By the 1990s, however, traditional party alignments were breaking down. Since the 1970s religious activists have fought over abortion, homosexuality, prayer in public schools, and creationism in the school curriculum. Polls taken from 1975 to 1995 indicate that the percentage of Americans who identified with a church or synagogue was fairly stable, ranging from 71 percent in 1975 to about 69 percent in 1995. While the percentage of Protestants and Catholics declined slightly, Jews remained at a constant 2 percent of the twenty-year period. Gallup polls pointed to a modest increase (3 percent over twenty years) in the number of Americans who identified with non-Western religions and to a similar increase in those surveyed who claimed no religious attachment at all. Attendance at religious services was a different matter, as were the churchgoing habits of regular attendees. While many churches abandoned all but Sunday morning worship, for example, some offered Saturday evening options. In any one week, however, more Americans found their ways to houses of worship than the citizens of other Western nations.

[Catherine L. Albanese, *America, Religions and Religion,* 2nd ed. (Belmont, Calif., 1992); Stephen L. Carter, *The Culture of Disbelief: How American Law and Politics Trivialize Religious Devotion* (New York, 1993).]

EDITH BLUMHOFER

See also **SUPP:** African-American Religions and Sects; Asian Religions and Sects; Catholic Church;

Cults; Freedom of Religion; Fundamentalism; Islam; Jews, American; Judaism; Latter-day Saints, Church of Jesus Christ of; Native American Church; Pentecostal Churches; Protestantism; Reorganized Church of Jesus Christ of Latter-day Saints; Televangelism.

RELIGION, FREEDOM OF. *See* **Freedom of Religion.**

REORGANIZED CHURCH OF JESUS CHRIST OF LATTER-DAY SAINTS (RLDS), the second-largest group tracing its heritage to the Mormon prophet Joseph Smith, Jr. (1805–1844), whose three sons succeeded him as RLDS president and sought to define the institution as somewhere in the middle between Mormonism and Protestantism. In 1978 Wallace B. Smith, the great-grandson of Joseph Smith, Jr., became president. He increasingly moved the church into mainstream Protestantism and in 1984 pressed for the ordination of women. In the same year the church opened its communion service to nonmembers. By the late 1980s the RLDS, based in Independence, Mo., had a worldwide membership of about 240,000 (90 percent in North America) and had abandoned many of their Mormon doctrines and practices in favor of greater ecumenism.

[Richard P. Howard, *The Church Through the Years*, vols. 1 and 2 (Independence, Mo., 1992–1993); Roger D. Launius, *Joseph Smith III: Pragmatic Prophet* (Urbana, Ill., 1988).]

ROGER D. LAUNIUS

See also **SUPP:** Church of Jesus Christ of Latter-day Saints.

REPRODUCTIVE TECHNOLOGY, broadly defined, includes any medical intervention in the processes of conception, pregnancy, and birth. More commonly, the term refers to techniques used by a third party (physician, donor, or both) to assist in the human processes of conception and gestation, usually in cases of infertility, where reproductive organs do not function normally. Artificial insemination (AI), in which sperm from a donor is injected, usually by a doctor, into a woman's uterus just before ovulation, was first performed in the United States in 1884. The first sperm bank opened in 1950 at the University of Iowa, and the first major commercial sperm banks opened in 1971 in New York City and Minnesota. In 1980 one California sperm bank gained national attention by seeking donations of sperm from Nobel Prize win-

ners. The age of so-called "test-tube babies" began in 1978 in England with the birth of Mary Louise Brown, who was conceived by the process of in vitro fertilization (IVF), in which a physician combines a woman's egg with sperm in a petri dish and then introduces the resulting early embryo into the mother's uterus. The first IVF clinic in the United States was opened in Virginia in 1981. The year 1978 also marked the first birth by a surrogate mother whose services were contracted for by an infertile couple through an intermediary. A surrogate agrees to bear a child (conceived by AI or IVF) and then to relinquish it at birth. In the mid-1980s two new processes were developed: gamete intrafallopian transfer (GIFT) and zygote intrafallopian transfer (ZIFT), in which the insertion of the gametes (egg and sperm) or the zygote (fertilized egg) into the fallopian tubes approximates the natural process of conception more closely than IVF.

None of these procedures has been introduced without controversy, and several individual cases have received tremendous media coverage. The birth of Louise Brown caused an international sensation. When a surrogate mother refused to surrender her child to its father and his wife in 1986, the ensuing legal battle over "Baby M" made headlines. Although the federal government does not fund research involving human embryos, it has left legislative decisions about reproductive technology to individual states. By 1994 ten states had laws mandating medical coverage for infertility treatments, and fifteen states had passed legislation regulating contracts and compensation in surrogacy arrangements. The legal, ethical, medical, social, and psychological implications of reproductive technologies have been hotly debated. Advocates argue that medical science has expanded the range of options for infertile couples, offering them the possibility of having children genetically related to at least one of the parents. Opponents point to the high cost of IVF and question the use of limited medical resources for such purposes. Feminists are concerned that reproductive technology reinforces the pronatalist bias in U.S. society, thereby stigmatizing those who choose to remain childless. They point out that reproductive technology is generally available only to heterosexual married couples and not to people in nontraditional relationships. Another concern is that this technology may lead to the commercialization of reproductive processes and products (that is, surrogacy, sperm, eggs, and embryos) and the removal of reproductive control (and possibly of reproduction itself) from women. Opponents fear that reproductive technology is one more step toward genetic engineering and warn that, with embryos in petri dishes, Aldous Huxley's brave new world of mechanically produced life may be dangerously close to reality.

[Dianne M. Bartels, Reinhard Priester, Dorothy E. Vawter, and Arthur L. Caplan, eds., *Beyond Baby M: Ethical Issues in New Reproductive Technologies* (Clifton, N.J., 1990); Elaine Hoffman Baruch, Amadeo F. D'Adamo, Jr., and Joni Seager, eds., *Embryos, Ethics, and Women's Rights: Exploring the New Reproductive Technologies* (New York, 1988).]

ELIZABETH WATKINS

See also **SUPP:** Fertility; Surrogate Parenthood; Women's Health.

REPUBLICAN PARTY. With the exception of Jimmy Carter's one term as president (1977–1981), Republicans dominated the presidency from 1968 until 1992. This record stood in striking contrast to the previous thirty-six years, when only one president, Dwight D. Eisenhower, carried the Republican banner. On all other levels of competition since the 1970s—party registration, seats in Congress, governorships, and state legislatures—Republicans as a rule ran behind the Democrats, although the discrepancy varied with each category and from year to year. In the 1980s the party undertook a shift to the ideological right, leading to virtual disappearance of a familiar force in American politics—the liberal Republican. Republican gains at the start of the 1970s stemmed as much from problems of the Democrats as from broad approval of Republican policies. The Republicans did profit from an end to the once "solid" Democratic South, at least in presidential politics. While southern Democrats continued to dominate on a reduced scale in state and local contests, a solid Republican South emerged in presidential races. Republican planners in the early 1970s hoped for a "southern strategy." More important to Republican fortunes was the Democratic association with the Vietnam War and its consequences in the late 1960s and early 1970s—demonstrations and riots, youth rebellion, emergence of a radical left—all of which divided the Democrats and seemed to challenge revered American principles.

In turning in 1968 to a centrist presidential candidate, Richard M. Nixon, Republicans sought to end their internal divisions of the 1960s. Brought into office in a close contest, the ticket of Nixon and Governor Spiro T. Agnew of Maryland overpowered the Democrats four years later with 61 percent of the popular vote. Democratic candidates Senator George McGovern and Sargent Shriver won only Massachusetts and the District of Columbia. Although Nixon had initially been elected on a law-and-order southern strategy campaign, desegregation continued in the southern states, albeit at times with little assistance from the president. His record on social and economic programs was mixed, but it contained more than expected by either conservatives or liberals. While he abolished the Office of Economic Opportunity, he proposed a family assistance plan, which failed to pass Congress, and supported proposals for environment control and consumer protection. Nixon was the only post–World War II president whose budgets, from 1970 through 1975, contained more spending on human resource programs than for defense.

Nixon's most visible achievements were in foreign affairs, where moves to reverse twenty years of hostility with the People's Republic of China and to pursue détente with the Soviet Union surprised liberals and caught rightist critics off guard. While the war in Vietnam continued through his first term, Nixon's plan of Vietnamization steadily reduced the U.S. commitment. By 1972 he could claim that peace was within sight. Although no viable peace was achieved, the margin of victory occurred because of the division of the opposition and a perception of the Democrats as the party of disorder and of McGovern as the candidate of the radical left. Nixon's victories brought factions within the Republican party together after Barry Goldwater's defeat by Lyndon Johnson in 1964. Republicans elected 192 members of the House of Representatives in 1968 and again in 1972, the largest number since 1956 and the largest until the 1990s. Between 1970 and 1992 in the House, only in 1972 did the margin by which Democrats outnumbered Republicans drop beneath fifty, and the number frequently stood at 100 or more. During the Nixon years the party had a deficit of at least ten seats in the Senate.

Rather than build on their gains, Republicans squandered them in the scandals of the early 1970s. First came the problems of Vice President Agnew, who, faced with charges of receiving bribes, pleaded no contest and resigned in October 1973. Nixon was by this time deeply involved in the Watergate affair, illegal activities against the Democrats and efforts to hide the truth. The Watergate tapes—secret recordings in the Oval Office—revealed that Nixon had obstructed justice by participating in efforts to conceal the origins of the scandal and repeatedly lied about the Watergate cover-up from June 1972 to August 1974. Rather than face impeachment and likely removal from office, he resigned on Aug. 9, 1974. The Watergate scandal went beyond the president. Republicans faced charges ranging from arrogant and mean-spirited behavior to shadowy fund-raising and various forms of illegal activity. Several government officials went to prison. The political fallout was immediate. The Republicans lost five Senate seats in 1974, leaving Democrats in control, 60–37. The Democratic margin in the House grew from 49 to 147. Republicans controlled legislatures in only five states, and whereas in 1970 they outnumbered Democrats in governorships by thirty-two to eighteen, in 1975 there were thirty-six Democratic governors to thirteen Republicans. Lopsided Democratic majorities in Congress held up in the election of 1976. Republicans could take encouragement from the fact that in the 1976 presidential election Gerald R. Ford, who replaced Agnew in 1973 and thus was on hand to serve out the final two and a half years of Nixon's presidency, came close to being elected over Carter.

After 1976 the Republicans did not stay down long. Changes in party procedure, economic thought, and the political climate helped produce a comeback in the 1980s. The Republican National Committee shifted fund-raising from large contributors to direct mailings and use of computer technology, acquiring substantially larger sums of money and a broader base. Several forces combined to produce an enlarged ultraconservatism, the New Right. First came the appeal in the nation, if not the world, of supply-side economics, the thesis that prosperity depended upon sharp reduction of taxes, especially in the highest brackets. Many people concluded that a divided and guilt-ridden America had become impotent in the aftermath of the Vietnam War, a charge seemingly made unchallengeable in the humiliating hostage crisis with Iran that began in 1979. Because Carter was president at the culmination of this post-Vietnam syndrome, blame was laid at his feet. Republicans continued to mobilize white voters in the South and Southwest, conspicuously through politicization of the religious right—white evangelicals disturbed with reform movements that favored affirmative action in the workplace and educational institutions, abortion, feminism, and homosexual rights. While strongest in the South, the religious right showed strength in other states.

The 1980s marked the high point of Republican domination during the post–World War II era. Ronald Reagan defeated Carter in 1980 by nearly 10 percent of the popular vote and Republicans won control of the Senate for the first time since 1954. Despite gaining thirty-three seats in the House, they could come no closer to the Democrats than fifty-one. A man of strong feelings rather than intellect, Reagan was a superb communicator who emerged as spokesman of neoconservative ideas—hostility to social programs, freedom of economic enterprise (expressed mostly in lower taxes), traditional values, and patriotism expressed in U.S. military power. Inspired by a tax cut (with no corresponding reduction in government spending) and by the admonition that it was proper, even American, to seek personal gain, the economy began a long surge. Interest rates and inflation went down. Massive increases in military spending and the president's skirmishes with foreign adversaries such as the dictator of Libya were indications that America "was back." Seemingly every Republican (and some Democrats) signed on to the program of nationalism and conservatism; scarcely anywhere could one find anyone who wore the label of liberal Republican. The high point came in the election of 1984 when the ticket of Reagan and George Bush defeated Walter Mondale and Geraldine Ferraro with 59 percent of the popular vote; the Democrats won only Minnesota (Mondale's home state) and the District of Columbia.

The scope of the Republican victory in 1984 was illusory. Republicans retained control of the Senate but made a disappointing gain of only fourteen seats in the House, leaving Democrats with a margin of eighty-one seats. The erosion of Republican power began. Democrats recaptured the Senate in 1986 and established a ten-seat margin that would carry into the 1990s. The majority in the House grew and by 1991 had reached 100. Republicans did narrow Democratic domination of governors' races. By Reagan's second term, however, it was possible to charge that the benefits of Reaganomics, as the economic program was called, had gone largely to the wealthy. The boom of the 1980s rested on borrowed money, leading to soaring budget deficits and a trade deficit that for a single year passed $150 billion. Reagan's popularity continued to befuddle opponents, but his presidential style came under criticism, notably in the Iran-Contra affair, a drawn-out scandal that raised constitutional questions about the conduct of foreign policy within the White House.

If the Reagan revolution was not fully a Republican revolution it continued to promote party fortunes in retaining the presidency in 1988. Victory of the Republican ticket of Vice President Bush and Senator Dan Quayle (by 54 to 46 percent) rested on the same coalition that had elected Reagan: the South, Great Plains, Rocky Mountain area, California and key industrial states, white Protestants (notably evangelicals), and partial support of white Catholics. Out of conviction or expediency, the Bush administration pledged more conservatism, more Reaganism. Encouraged by unexpected developments in foreign affairs, the new president received a high approval rating, and at one juncture it passed even that of Reagan. In speed and apparent fullness of victory, the Gulf War of 1991 dazzled the American people. Republicans claimed that the collapse of communism and of the Soviet Union, which occurred during 1989–1991 also were victories of Presidents Reagan and Bush. Bush's fall from grace, if more gradual than the rise, was equally profound. Problems that appeared earlier in the 1980s caught hold—budget and trade deficits, plant closings, and increasing unemployment. Conservatives who had claimed that growth in the 1980s had come from diminished government activity could not now urge more government involvement. In Governor Bill Clinton and Senator Al Gore the Democrats in 1992 offered young opponents who promised something new for the nation. Entry into politics of Ross Perot, an eccentric and appealing billionaire, complicated the political picture. Perot's message that something was seriously wrong in Bush's America did not bode well for the incumbent Republican. On the surface the defeat of Bush and Quayle was devastating—less than 38 percent of the popular vote and more reduction of Republican strength in Congress. The magnitude of the loss was offset by the size of the Democrat victory—Clinton and Gore received only 43 percent of the popular vote.

Ending twelve years of Republican control of the presidency did not end the contest for party leadership and direction. The party reevaluated the wisdom of being identified as a rightist organization with narrowly defined social and economic positions. An immediate problem of the mid-1990s was how the party would treat the religious right, a group that pledged votes, vigor, and money but that angered some Republicans and showed signs of producing diminishing returns. If the Republicans had received their best marks in managing world affairs, they had to answer charges that they were a party of whites, a nativist group in a nation increasingly immigrant, a party whose policies favored an economic elite. Debates in Congress over post–cold war foreign policy, health care, and crime reinforced this view. By the 1994 midterm elections, the most conservative Republicans at the state and national level had won the battle

to redefine the party. Rallying around their "Contract with America," they marched to an astonishing partisan victory at the polls. Playing to the anxieties of Americans about big government and higher taxes, and perceptions of President Clinton's ambivalence and weakness as a leader, the Republican party gained its first Senate majority in eight years, its first majority of governors since 1970, and its first House majority in thirty years and only the second since 1930. Not a single Republican incumbent senator, governor, or House member was defeated. The formerly Democratic "Solid South" left Republicans with 16 of 28 southern and border senators, 7 of the 14 southern governorships, and 73 of 139 southern representatives. When the dust cleared, control of Congress and of the Republican party was in the hands of Majority Leader Robert J. Dole in the Senate and Speaker Newt Gingrich in the House. Many pundits predicted that the long-awaited national party alignment had taken place—from Democratic dominance to Republican—not unlike the shift that had taken place in 1930 and 1932. It remained to be seen how valid that assessment would be—if the remarkable Republican gains of 1994 would be far-reaching.

[Sidney M. Milkis, *The President and the Parties* (New York, 1992); A. James Reichley, *The Life of the Parties: A History of American Political Parties* (New York, 1992).]

Ross Gregory

See also **SUPP:** Democratic Party; Iran-Contra Affair; Reaganomics; Supply-Side Economics; Watergate, Aftermath of.

RESEARCH LABORATORIES exist in nearly every sector of the U.S. economy, straddling the boundaries separating government from private enterprise, the academic sector from the corporate, and the civilian from the military. During the cold war, U.S. laboratories became vital sources of economic, military, and intellectual power, producing new consumer goods and weapons. The cold war's sudden conclusion, as well as globalization of the economy and increased pressure from foreign and domestic competition, dramatically altered the political economy in which such laboratories flourished. In the early twentieth century, corporations and philanthropies separated research from teaching and created the first industrial and private research laboratories. After World War II the U.S. military created a new technical order by maintaining such wartime weapons laboratories as Los Alamos in New Mexico and the Johns Hopkins University Applied Physics Laboratory in

Maryland and by establishing new research laboratories, such as the Lincoln Laboratory at the Massachusetts Institute of Technology. By the 1990s corporations and the federal government were reassessing the role that laboratories might play in the new global economy. All agreed that the products of research laboratories were essential for economic competitiveness, but few agreed on who should support these powerful but fragile institutions.

In 1990 one-sixth of the nation's scientists and engineers were employed in more than 700 federally funded laboratories, including sixty-five Department of Defense and Department of Energy institutions, which had annual budgets ranging from $15 billion to $21 billion, depending on who and what is counted. The armed services research institutions expanded during the 1980s under President Ronald Reagan's vast and expensive arms buildup. Furthermore, Reagan's Strategic Defense and Computing initiatives pumped billions into corporate and university-based research organizations. With the end of the cold war, military research institutions were forced to justify their cost, and collaboration between weapons laboratories and the commercial sector became an essential part of economic planning, as was the once unthinkable—the elimination or combination of one or more of the Department of Defense's weapons laboratories to reduce costs. Academic laboratories and their university sponsors were especially hard hit by the decline in military support. Indirect overhead money from government contracts, at rates greater than 50 percent of a contract's value, were important sources of university funding. Increasingly, basic research, the strength of the American university, was viewed as a luxury rather than a necessity.

Corporate research laboratories also underwent a massive change during the 1970s and 1980s. The breakup of American Telephone and Telegraph (AT&T) in 1984 affected the research done at Bell Laboratories, famous for invention of the transistor and a tradition of allowing researchers to pursue their own ideas. By the mid-1990s Bell Lab managers were intent on harnessing the laboratories' research to the needs of AT&T's operating divisions. IBM's Thomas J. Watson Research Center began emphasizing research for securing that firm's market share in the volatile computer market. Competitive pressures also forced corporate research laboratories to demonstrate their market value. The 1980s also witnessed a new phenomenon—the growth of research consortia in which industrial, government, and university scientists and engineers worked together to develop new,

basic technologies. Perhaps the best known was Sematech, devoted to semiconductor manufacturing technology.

[Stuart W. Leslie, *The Cold War and American Science: The Military-Industrial-Academic Complex at MIT and Stanford* (New York, 1993); U.S. Congress, Office of Technology Assessment, *Federally Funded Research: Decisions for a Decade* (Washington, D.C., 1991).]

MICHAEL AARON DENNIS

See also **SUPP:** Think Tanks.

RESEGREGATION. *See* **Schools, Resegregation of.**

RESOLUTION TRUST CORPORATION. *See* **Savings and Loan Crisis.**

RETAILING INDUSTRY. Since the late 1970s sales revenues in the retail trade in the United States seemed to indicate robust growth, but several sectors of the industry were hit hard by poor sales, changing trends, and consolidation by retailers such as Wal-Mart. Mass-merchandise discounters, led by Wal-Mart, became the nation's dominant institutions, while specialty stores catering to individual consumer tastes grew in popularity. Several enterprises, including gasoline service stations, automotive dealers, food stores, and drugstores, underwent steady consolidation. The number of service stations, for example, fell by 28 percent, from 176,465 million in 1977 to 105,334 in 1992. Smaller retail stores went out of business or merged into larger national chains as it became difficult to compete in price and provide employees with competitive wages and benefits. Retail trade was relatively stagnant in 1977 when there were 1.8 million retail establishments. By 1992 the number had grown 17 percent, to 1.5 million. Total retail sales grew 171 percent, from $700 billion in 1977 to $1.9 trillion in 1992.

Virtually every facet of the U.S. economy grew more slowly from 1977 to the mid-1990s than in previous decades. With factories closing, unions declining, and the economy switching from industry to lower-paying services, consumers had to shop in stores—usually Wal-Marts and Kmarts—that offered the cheapest prices on basic goods. Workers able to take advantage of the service sector's highest salaries—lawyers, doctors, executives—had more money to spend on expensive goods, helping the growth of specialty stores.

The predominant trend, however, was the growth of

discounters. Between 1987 and 1992 discounters increased their number of stores 16 percent, from 58,000 to 67,000, with sales increasing 49 percent, from $69.3 billion to $103.4 billion. By comparison, conventional department stores such as Macy's suffered and their number of stores fell by 2 percent, from 24,000 to 23,000, while sales increased only 7 percent, from $47.7 billion to $51.3 billion. Epitomizing the trend was Arkansas-based Wal-Mart, which became the nation's top retailer, both in number of stores and sales. Founded in the early 1960s by Sam Walton, the company expanded from a chain located mostly in small towns in the South and Midwest to a national chain with a presence in large suburban markets and cities. The store relied on folksiness and the small-town common touch by using store greeters and such promotions as gerbil races in its pet departments. At the same time it became a leader in using technology to make the company more efficient, allowing it to keep prices as low as possible and still ring up profits that impressed Wall Street. It spent billions installing such devices as price scanners and computers that tracked inventories and took care of administrative details such as payrolls. It built its own satellite system, which allowed store managers scattered throughout the country to stay in contact with company headquarters in Bentonville, Ark. Such innovations allowed Wal-Mart to stay ahead of its main competitor, Kmart, founded in 1962, which had a bigger national presence during the 1960s and 1970s. Wal-Mart overtook it, however, as Kmart suffered from poor merchandise, bad management, and a poorly designed diversification scheme that led it into bookstores, sporting goods outlets, and a home materials supply company.

By the mid-1990s, however, Wal-Mart ran into its own problems, as it had difficulty maintaining the same rapid pace of revenue and profit growth. It also faced its toughest competition from Target, a division of Minneapolis-based Dayton Hudson Stores, Inc. Target attracted shoppers with more upscale stores but still featured low prices on basic goods. The company showed strong growth during the 1990s and was one success story that Dayton Hudson, which also owned ailing department stores, could boast of. The growth of Wal-Mart and Target caused many smaller, independent retailers, especially in the small towns where Wal-Mart expanded in the 1980s, to go out of business. Such retailers usually could not compete and found their customers leaving traditional downtown stores to shop in new Wal-Marts at the edges of towns.

Technology became more important for all U.S. retailers in the 1990s. Stores and chains adopted Wal-Mart technology to make themselves more efficient. Products such as computers and software, as well as televisions, videocassette recorders, and stereo systems, recorded strong sales and helped such companies as Best Buy, Circuit City, and Blockbuster Entertainment become staples of the suburban shopping center and strip mall. Technology, however, challenged traditional retailers by allowing consumers to buy goods without going into stores. At the lowest end of the technological spectrum, mail-order houses such as L. L. Bean and Lands' End flourished by sending catalogs to consumers. The late 1980s saw the emergence of cable television networks dedicated to selling goods twenty-four hours a day. The two most prominent were the Home Shopping Network and QVC. By 1995 merchandising had moved onto the global computer network known as the Internet, with companies accessing the computer network system to sell to consumers. Many observers predicted that the Internet would become a huge source of commerce, but problems with sending credit card numbers through the system plagued the medium.

[Robert Spector and Patrick D. McCarthy, *The Nordstrom Way* (New York, 1995); Sandra S. Vance and Roy V. Scott, *Wal-Mart: A History of Sam Walton's Retail Phenomenon* (New York, 1994).]

THOMAS G. GRESS

See also **SUPP:** Home Shopping Networks; Mail-Order Industry; Malls, Shopping.

RHODE ISLAND, which began as a colony in 1636 based on the separation of church and state and religious freedom, by 1905 was the first state to have a Roman Catholic majority (61.7 percent in 1990). Whites overwhelmingly dominated the state's 1990 population of 1,003,464 (91.4%), while African Americans made up only 3.9 percent of the population. From its earliest days, Rhode Islanders had to scratch and scramble to create a productive economy. Having a tiny coastal state without an exploitable hinterland, natural resources, large scale agriculture, or population, its people have had to live by their wits. In the colonial era they turned to ocean commerce, privateering, slave trading, and smuggling, after the American Revolution to the China trade, and then to manufacturing in the nineteenth century. The twentieth century brought extended economic difficulties. While most of the United States suffered through the Great Depression from 1929 to 1940, Rhode Island's

RHODE ISLAND

depression began early in the 1920s and, except for the respite of World War II, lasted until the late 1950s. While Rhode Island shared in the general prosperity of New England from the 1960s to the mid-1980s, the state was particularly hard hit by the recession of the early 1990s. Unemployment exceeded both U.S. and New England levels as regional hard times tended to exaggerate conditions in the state. The largest civilian employer of Rhode Islanders, Electric Boat, a builder of submarines, reduced its workforce as defense contracts shrunk after the end of the cold war. The state's privately insured but corrupt credit union system collapsed in 1991, plunging the state into a deepened economic and political crisis.

Ranked as the nation's sixth-largest industrial center in 1900, Rhode Island steadily deindustrialized since then. Manufacturing, which employed 52 percent of the workforce in 1947, employed only 20 percent in 1993. In the 1980s manufacturing jobs fell by another 34,200; half of the remaining manufacturing jobs were in the jewelry industry. Of the twenty-one companies that employed 1,000 or more workers in 1941, only two remained in 1991. Several significant manufacturing concerns were based in Rhode Island, including Hasbro, one of the world's largest toy manufacturers, and GTECH, the world's largest supplier of on-line lottery systems. From being the first urban industrial state, Rhode Island began developing a postindustrial economy in the 1960s and 1970s. The population shifted out of the old industrial centers, and by 1990 nearly four times as many Rhode Islanders were employed in the service sector as in manufacturing. The leading economic enterprises became tourism, business and health services, and education. Rhode Island's recovery from the economic depression of 1990–1993 was slowed by the decline of defense employment, both in terms of defense manufacturing and by the withdrawal of the remaining naval vessels. The electronics industry that the state had hoped to build upon was hard hit in all of New England, and in 1993 the U.S. government ordered sharp restrictions on the fishing industry in order to permit depleted stocks to recover. When the U.S. Navy withdrew most of its operations from Newport after 1973, the city found its economic salvation in the tourist industry. Narragansett Bay remained a major asset and tourism continued to grow. Education constituted a significant "export" industry. While in the 1990s the state produced about 9,800 high school graduates each year, its colleges and universities awarded nearly 16,000 degrees, and most of the college students were from other states and nations.

After the Democratic party's capture of the state government in 1935, Rhode Island entered a period of one-party rule. Democratic domination was so pronounced that by the mid-1960s Rhode Island had the least interparty competition of any New England state, and the Republicans were so weak that they failed to offer even token candidates for more than half of the seats in the state's general assembly. In 1974, however, the first Republican to be elected mayor of Providence since 1938 won over a divided Democratic party. The first Republican U.S. senator since 1938 was elected in 1976, and the first Republican U.S. representative since 1940 won in 1980. By 1993 the minority party held half of Rhode Island's congressional delegation and three of five general state offices. Two significant factors promoted the waning of Democratic power—the rise of independent voting and the decline of ethnicity. Voters cast off party loyalty, allowing mavericks and Republicans to capture many important offices. Until the 1960s the four ethnic groups—Yankee, Irish, Italian, and French-Canadian—each representing about 20 percent of the population, dominated all the general state offices, the legislature, the mayoralties, and the congressional delegation. The Democratic party in particular had been built on a carefully balanced ethnic coalition, and it depended on ethnic loyalties to sweep the elections. Beginning in the 1960s, however, the old ethnic neighborhoods started to break up and the people scattered to the suburbs. Providence, which had 40 percent of the state's population in 1950, had only 15 percent by the 1990s. Consequently, individuals of small ethnic groups were elected by a public that cared little about ethnicity. For example, in 1992, in the most Catholic state in the Union, three of the five general state officers were Jewish, including the governor.

In the seventeenth century Rhode Island was tagged "Rogues' Island" by the neighboring Puritan colonies, which regarded the lack of a state church as wicked. In the last quarter of the twentieth century the state experienced such a stream of corruption in high and low places that "Rogues' Island" seemed a fitting name. Rhode Island suffered the embarrassment of seeing two consecutive chief justices of the state supreme court driven from the bench because of corruption. Revelations of corrupt and unethical practices embraced a former governor and three speakers of the state house and a number of legislators, mayors, and public officials. In the 1980s the mayors of Providence, North Providence, Pawtucket, and Cranston were charged with crimes and only one escaped conviction. Beginning in 1991 Rhode Island suffered a local version of the savings and loan scandal that hit several states in the 1980s. The failure of many banks and credit unions tied up one-third of the resources of the state's depositors and triggered a political uprising and major reforms in government.

[Patrick T. Conley, *An Album of Rhode Island History, 1636–1986* (Norfolk, Va., 1986); George H. Kellner and J. Stanley Lemons, *Rhode Island: The Independent State* (Woodland Hills, Calif., 1982); William G. McLoughlin, *Rhode Island: A History* (New York, 1978).]

J. STANLEY LEMONS

RICHMOND V. J. A. CROSON COMPANY, 488 U.S. 469 (1989), a Supreme Court case that considered whether the constitutionality of set-asides, affirmative action programs for minority businesses, permitted by a standard of strict scrutiny under the Fourteenth Amendment's equal protection clause should continue. Since 1942 Congress had approved legislation requiring businesses with federal contracts to draw up action plans for hiring minority workers. Until *Croson*, however, the Court had not questioned this practice. In 1983 the Richmond, Va., city council instituted a set-aside to remedy past discrimination by requiring prime contractors to whom the city awarded construction contracts to subcontract at least 30 percent of each contract's dollar amount to minority business enterprises. Prime contractor J. A. Croson Company did not comply with the program, whereupon the city awarded the contract to another company. Croson challenged the city's 30 percent quota as a violation of the Fourteenth Amendment's equal protection clause. The city responded that the quota merely copied federal policy guidelines. In a six-to-three vote, the Court decided in favor of Croson, signaling the Court's increased willingness to limit the states' use of quotas as a remedy for past discrimination.

TONY FREYER

See also **SUPP:** Affirmative Action; Set-Asides.

RIGHT-TO-DIE MOVEMENT. *See* **Euthanasia.**

RIOTS. The English Riot Act of 1715 made it a felony for twelve or more persons to gather together and disturb the peace. As part of the common law practiced in the American colonies and the United States, a riot could consist of as few as three persons, assembled for a common purpose, who behaved so as to cause observers to fear disturbance of the peace. Most events characterized as riots, however, involve more people, and sociologists and social psychologists now treat riots as instances of "collective behavior" or "crowd psychology." The common law definition of a riot allows public officials to break up even a peaceful assembly, if participants behave in such a way as to cause observers to fear disruption of civic peace. Whether actions of publicly assembled people cause a riot depends very much on point of view. The Boston Massacre of 1770 occurred when British troops fired into what they regarded as a rioting crowd, and the Boston Tea Party of 1773 was, to British authorities, another riot. From a later American perspective these were not unfortunate breaches of civic peace but events leading to the revolutionary war. When people protest against injustice they often view their action as a legitimate uprising, while those against whom the protest is directed are likely to define it as a riot.

The Constitution was a compromise between those who favored democratic self-government and those who feared that democracy would degenerate into mob rule. The First Amendment guarantees the "right of the people peaceably to assemble, and to petition the Government for a redress of grievances." Freedom of assembly establishes legitimacy of peaceful demonstrations, but it is widely held that crowds are more irresponsible than the individuals they comprise. From the perspective of those in authority, crowds must be kept under control. A riot is not just a failure to keep the people under control, but it is also an occasion for using force to gain control. The right of people to assemble is balanced by the right of authorities, established in common law, to declare an assembly a threat to civic peace.

One of the worst waves of riots was occasioned by the military draft during the Civil War. The Conscription Act of 1863 not only required men to fight for a cause in which many did not believe, but allowed any man drafted to avoid service by finding a substitute or paying $300. There were riots across the country, but the worst were in New York City in July 1863, where there were many poor Democrats who both sympathized with the South and resented the ability of the rich to buy out of military service. It took four days and a combination of police, militia, army, navy, and West Point cadets to quell the rioting.

The history of labor unions has been punctuated by civil disturbances. The weapon of unions has been the strike, and strikes have often resulted in violence. Workers struck against the Carnegie Steel Company in Homestead, Pa., in 1892, and the company hired Pinkerton detectives to protect the strikebreakers brought in by the company. The battle between strikers and detectives led the governor to call in the state militia, which broke the strike. Strikers often engage in picketing to publicize their grievances, discourage the public from patronizing the business being struck, and prevent strikebreakers from taking their jobs. Both strikes and picketing have resulted in court decisions and legislation to protect workers, owners, and the peace. The courts have usually frowned on protecting civil disorder or violence, most recently in the case of protesters outside of abortion clinics.

Veterans, impoverished by the Great Depression, marched on Washington, D.C., in 1932 and camped out in fields and government buildings. They were supporting passage of a bill to grant them immediate payment of their World War I bonus. After the bill was defeated in Congress approximately 2,000 of the 15,000 veterans refused to leave the capital, and some government officials feared that the veterans would disturb the peace. When attempts by local police to remove the veterans resulted in four deaths, Army Chief of Staff General Douglas McArthur, on orders from President Herbert Hoover, sent in U.S. troops, which set fire to the camps and drove the "bonus marchers" from the city.

The unpopular and undeclared Vietnam War, and the use of the draft to provide soldiers for it, was the occasion for many antiwar demonstrations. In the summer of 1968 civil rights and antiwar protesters joined in a march outside the Democratic National Convention in Chicago. One of the reasons for emphasis on nonviolence in the civil rights and antiwar movements in the 1960s was to make it more difficult for officials to declare a march or demonstration a riot. In Chicago, however, city and party officials viewed the march as a potential riot, and Mayor Richard J. Daley sent in busloads of police. Protesters and sympathizers described what happened as a police riot, claiming the protest peaceful and nonviolent until police attacked. Defenders of the police argued that television cameras recorded only violence of the police, not provocations of demonstrators.

A 1968 report of the National Advisory Commission on Civil Disorders identified white racism and resulting feelings of hopelessness and powerlessness on the part of African Americans as the cause of race riots during the 1960s. The same reasoning could be applied to actions taken by members of the American Indian Movement, who occupied Alcatraz in San Francisco Bay in 1969, and Wounded Knee on the Pine Ridge Reservation in South Dakota in 1973. Different factors, however, were identified as the causes behind the disturbances in Los Angeles during the summer of 1992, when Hispanics and Koreans as well as African Americans took to the streets. The actions followed the acquittal of white police officers who had beaten Rodney King, a black man. The beating was videotaped and shown so often on national television that many Americans, white as well as black, saw the acquittal as a miscarriage of justice. It was argued that the beating was only an occasion for the rioting, the latter being an expression of frustration on the part of poor racial groups in Los Angeles. According to this argument, the Los Angeles uprising of 1992 had more to do with class than with race. The difficulty Americans had in categorizing what happened in Los Angeles in 1992 demonstrates the continuing debate in the United States over what distinguishes a riot from legitimate protest over injustice.
[Robert Gooding-Williams, ed., *Reading Rodney King, Reading Urban Uprising* (New York, 1993); Barbara Salert, *The Dynamics of Riots* (Ann Arbor, Mich., 1980).]
RICHARD W. MOODEY

See also **DAH:** Draft Riots; Race Riots; **SUPP:** Alcatraz; American Indian Movement; Los Angeles Riots; Wounded Knee.

RLDS. *See* **Reorganized Church of Jesus Christ of Latter-day Saints.**

ROBBERIES. The United States experienced a boom in bank robberies in the 1990s, and in 1991 banks reported the greatest number in U.S. history. Los Angeles accounted for 20 percent of the robberies, with an average take of $3,000 and 85 percent of thieves caught. While robbers lacked the drama and flair of such bandits from earlier eras as Bonnie Parker and Clyde Barrow or Willie "The Actor" Sutton, the new generation brought about the reinstitution of past practices. A holdup that netted $434,000 drove a Wells Fargo bank to post a $10,000 reward, a practice unknown since the 1890s. Automatic teller machines (ATMs) brought theft increases. With more than 77,000 ATMs nationwide early in the 1990s, they became prime sites for small robberies. In some cases, hackers were able to crack computer codes and steal cash. In rare instances, thieves removed entire machines, opened them, and stole their contents.

While law enforcement officers were successful in tracking down most bank robbers, they were less successful with armored car robberies, solving only one-third of 340 armored car heists between 1988 and 1992. The nation's largest open-road armored car robbery, in which thieves netted $10.8 million, remains unsolved. The theft occurred June 26, 1990, outside a convenience store in Henrietta, N.Y. In January 1993, in nearby Rochester, N.Y., thieves held up a Brink's depot, escaping with $7.4 million. Authorities arrested four men, alleging that most of the money was funneled to the Irish Republican Army. In what may have been the largest cash theft in history, owners of Revere Armored Car, Inc., were charged in 1993 with stealing as much as $40 million from client businesses and banks over three years. Attempts to have charges dismissed because the government failed to preserve the company's records failed in 1994.

The Isabella Stewart Gardner Museum in Boston was the site of the biggest art heist in history on Mar. 18, 1990. Thieves stole thirteen pieces worth an estimated $200 million, including five works by Degas, a Vermeer, a Manet, and three Rembrandts. The thieves made their way through the museum, slicing paintings out of frames. On Sept. 15, 1993, a 1960s radical surrendered in one of the nation's most infamous robbery cases. Katherine Ann Power turned herself in to police twenty-three years after driving the getaway car in a small-time robbery that turned deadly. A student and Vietnam protester, Power was involved in a plot to rob a Boston bank on Sept. 23, 1970. While she waited in the car, an accomplice killed Boston police officer Walter Schroeder, father of nine children. Power fled, living as a fugitive in various cities before settling in Oregon in 1977 under the name Alice Metzinger. Unable to overcome her conscience, she surrendered to authorities and began serving an eight-to-twelve-year sentence in September 1993.

[Keith Middlemas, *The Double Market: Art Theft and Art Thieves* (Farnborough, Eng., 1975); Debra Weyermann, *The Gang They Couldn't Catch* (New York, 1993).]

KATHLEEN B. CULVER

See also **SUPP:** Crime; Crime, White-Collar.

ROBERTS ET AL. V. UNITED STATES JAYCEES,

468 U.S. 609 (1984), a case in which the Supreme Court ruled that the states may forbid sex discrimination not only in public accommodations but also in private associations whose membership is restricted. The Civil Rights Act of 1964 exempted private clubs from its coverage, but by the 1980s California and Minnesota had extended their bans on sex discrimi-

nation to cover these groups. Minnesota's law led to a confrontation between the local and national organizations of the Junior Chamber of Commerce (the Jaycees), which encouraged members to participate in community activities, including running for office. Membership is open to any eligible person who pays the dues, and the Jaycees have welcomed all races, religions, and nationalities since it was founded in 1920. Until 1984, however, only males between the ages of eighteen and thirty-five could be full members. Women began demanding Jaycee membership in the 1970s, arguing that exclusion denied them equal professional and civic opportunities. Some local chapters began admitting women, and when the national organization threatened to revoke the charters of the Minneapolis and Saint Paul chapters, the case ended up in the Supreme Court. The justices ruled unanimously that, in light of the Jaycees' traditionally inclusive membership, they "have demonstrated no serious burden on their male members' freedom of association." *Roberts* did not ban all sex discrimination in private associations; it held only that the Constitution did not bar the states from prohibiting sex discrimination in a group like the Jaycees. Nevertheless, one month after the decision, the national organization voted to admit women.

[Judith A. Baer, *Women in American Law* (New York, 1985–1991).]

JUDITH A. BAER

See also **SUPP:** *Rotary International* v. *Rotary Club of Duarte.*

ROBOTICS is the science of designing and building independent mechanical devices that perform actions in place of human beings. Karel Čapek coined the term in his 1921 play *R.U.R.* in which robots wage and win war against humans. The word is derived from the Czech word *robat,* meaning "compulsory service" or "compulsory labor." Popular culture generally depicts robots as simulating the movements, speech, and appearance of humans, an image that has raised public concern about the possibility of conflict between humans and robots. In a wildly popular series of science fiction novels and short stories relating to robots, the writer Isaac Asimov in 1950 proposed three immutable laws governing the behavior of robots: a robot may not injure a human being or, through inaction, allow a human being to come to harm; a robot must obey orders except where orders would conflict with the first law; and a robot must protect its own existence as long as such protection does not conflict with the first or second law. Other writers adopted his three rules of robotics.

The reality of robotics has been both more mundane and more far-reaching. Robotic devices have proved useful in a variety of applications, and robotics has drawn on—and stimulated—advances in artificial intelligence, because of the interrelatedness of the fields. The most common application for robotics is in industry. The Robotic Industries Association defines an industrial robot as a reprogrammable, multifunctioning manipulator designed to move materials, parts, tools, or specialized devices through variable programmed motions for the performance of a variety of tasks. In 1961 the first of three prototype machines was installed in the General Motors Turnstedt plant in Trenton, N.J.; the machines quenched hot parts produced by a die-making process. PUMA (Programmable Universal Machine for Assembly) is a computer-controlled robot arm developed in the 1970s that grew out of pioneering research by Massachusetts Institute of Technology researcher Victor Scheinman with financial support from General Motors. Since then, robots have been designed for a wide range of industrial tasks, including welding, inspecting parts, painting, gluing, and drilling. In most cases robots perform the same task over and over with little variation but with greater accuracy than humans would produce for such repetitive work. Robots also have been employed in assembling devices or objects from an array of pieces, but such robotic systems require more advanced technology than those performing repetitive tasks. The robot must be able to sort components, picking the proper ones, placing them precisely, and fastening them properly. Such an application demands the highest level of sophistication in several areas, such as robot vision and sensation of torques and touch.

Mobile robots offer new opportunities for exploring places that are either inaccessible or unsafe for humans to visit directly, such as other planets and deep undersea. Such robots are controlled through teleoperation, in which a distant human reviews data gathered by the robot and directs its activities in response. Dante, a semiautonomous, eight-legged robot built at Carnegie Mellon University, descended part way into Mount Erebus, a volcano in Antarctica, in 1993; the test demonstrated how teleoperated robots could explore Mars or other planets. Robots have also played a key role in exploration of the sea floor and objects on it, such as the wreck of the *Titanic;* images from the robot were beamed to schools around the United States via satellite. Advances in miniaturiza-

tion, originally developed for manufacturing semiconductors, promise to speed the creation of ultrasmall robots, using components called microelectromechanical systems, which are no bigger than one millimeter. These systems could be used to devise small robots for use in applications such as surgery.

[Tom Logsdon, *The Robot Revolution* (New York, 1984).]
VINCENT KIERNAN

See also **SUPP:** Artificial Intelligence; Cybernetics.

ROCKEFELLER COMMISSION REPORT (1991). The National Commission on Children, created by Congress in 1987, began its deliberations two years later and presented its report in 1991. Chaired by Senator John D. (Jay) Rockefeller IV of West Virginia, the committee was broadly based and included representatives of all levels of government, business and civic leaders, and child welfare administrators. Its purpose was to "assess the status of children and families in the United States and propose new directions for policy and program development." The resulting assessment was bleak: one in five children lived in poverty, two out of five were at risk for failure in school, one out of four was being raised by a single parent, and millions were involved in sexual promiscuity, drug and alcohol abuse, and crime. The commission recommended early intervention, support through government programs and workplace benefits, and a general shoring up of families. It gave more attention to moral development than had reports of previous years. Most controversial among the recommendations were a proposed $1,000 per child tax credit and a proposal that employers provide unpaid parental leave for births, adoptions, and other family emergencies. The commission proposed new federal spending of $52 to $56 billion annually, which gave rise to substantial public criticism and an uncertain future for the commission's recommendations.

[National Commission on Children, *Beyond Rhetoric: A New American Agenda for Children and Families* (Washington, D.C., 1991).]
ELLEN GRAY

ROCK MUSIC. *See* **Music, Rock and Roll.**

***ROE* V. *WADE*,** 410 U.S. 113 (1973), which established a woman's constitutional right to choose to have an abortion, set one of the most controversial precedents in the history of the Supreme Court. By a vote of seven to two, the Court invalidated Texas and Georgia laws prohibiting abortion except when necessary to save the mother's life. "Jane Roe" was the pseudonym of Norma McCorvey, a pregnant woman who challenged the Texas statute. The law prevented her from terminating the pregnancy (she gave her daughter up for adoption), but her case won that right for other women. Justice Harry Blackmun's majority opinion relied on the right of privacy recognized eight years earlier in *Griswold* v. *Connecticut.* "This right," he declared, "is broad enough to encompass a woman's decision whether or not to terminate her pregnancy." The Court acknowledged that the right to choose an abortion based on a private decision between a woman and her doctor was not absolute. Like all rights it could be infringed if government had a compelling interest in doing so.

Texas had advanced two justifications for abortion laws: protecting the mother's health and preserving prenatal life. The Court ruled that each interest became compelling at a different stage of pregnancy. No restrictions were justified in the first trimester (three months). Concern for maternal health justified appropriate regulations, but not prohibition, in the second trimester, when abortion became more risky than going to term. The question of prenatal life was more complex. If, as many people believe, human life begins at conception, the state has not only the power but the duty to protect the constitutional rights of the fetus. *Roe* concluded that "the word 'person' as used in the Fourteenth Amendment does not include the unborn." The state's interest in "potential life" became compelling, however, when the fetus could survive outside the mother's body. Since viability occurred at approximately the end of the sixth month, a state could prohibit third-trimester abortions—except when necessary to save the mother's life.

Although *Roe* was not based on the equal protection clause, it was a victory for women's rights. The need for reproductive choice, regardless of the exact judicial rationale, is indicated by the fact that 1.5 million elective abortions are performed in the United States every year. The Court's opinion, however, received widespread criticism even from those who were positive or neutral about the result. The justices evinced little awareness of the considerable differences between birth control, the issue in *Griswold,* and abortion. If Justice Harry Blackmun emphasized the possible devastating effect of unwanted pregnancy, he did not explain why bearing an unwanted child was worse than many other things government forces upon individuals. *Roe* also did not

explain why, if no legal, medical, or philosophical consensus exists on when life begins, a state cannot decide that it begins at conception. The public reaction to *Roe* v. *Wade* made reproductive choice one of the country's most debated issues and even inspired presidential selection of justices expected to overturn *Roe.* Decisions upholding indirect restrictions have weakened the impact of *Roe.* In practice only adult women who have access to abortion and can afford it have the right to choice.

[Judith A. Baer, *Women in American Law* (New York, 1991); Joan Hoff, *Law, Gender and Injustice* (New York, 1991).]

JUDITH A. BAER

See also **DAH:** Woman's Rights Movement; **SUPP:** Abortion; *Griswold* v. *Connecticut*; *Planned Parenthood of Southeastern Pennsylvania* v. *Casey*; Pro-Choice Movement; Pro-Life Movement; *Rust* v. *Sullivan; Webster* v. *Reproductive Health Services;* Women's Movement; Women's Rights.

ROMAN CATHOLICISM. *See* **Catholic Church.**

ROTARY INTERNATIONAL **V.** *ROTARY CLUB OF DUARTE,* 107 Supreme Court 1940 (1987), upheld the second of two state laws prohibiting sex discrimination in private associations. This decision involved a California statute similar to the Minnesota law upheld in *Roberts* v. *United States Jaycees* (1984). Like *Roberts*, the case represented a conflict between a local chapter and its parent organization. Two Supreme Court justices had to recuse themselves from the case—Harry A. Blackmun because he was a member of the Rotary and Sandra Day O'Connor because her husband was a member. Rotary, it was clear, was not a private club. It describes itself as "inclusive, not exclusive" and, like the Jaycees, works to remove racial, religious, and cultural barriers— among males. The difference between *Rotary* and *Roberts* was that the Rotary has always been a less political and more selective group than the Jaycees. Rotary does not take positions on public issues, and local chapters determine their own admissions procedures (the international organization recommends selection committees). In rejecting Rotary International's claim that the state law violated the constitutional right to privacy recognized in *Griswold* v. *Connecticut,* the Court emphasized "factors such as size, purpose, selectivity, and whether others are excluded from critical aspects of the relationship." A year later, the Court, in *New York State Club Association* v. *New York,* upheld an ordinance banning sex discrimination in even the most elite "city clubs."

[Judith A. Baer, *Women in American Law* (New York, 1991).]

JUDITH A. BAER

See also **SUPP:** *Roberts* v. *United States Jaycees.*

RURAL LIVING. Many Americans have believed rural living to be remote, obsolete, and deprived. The rapid mechanization of farming in the twentieth century has meant combination of farms into ever-larger entities, sometimes known as agribusiness, with ever-fewer Americans working on farms. The boundaries between rural and urban actually no longer exist, however, because rural residents have imported more mass-society patterns of dress, food, and leisure. Agrarian society is increasingly subject to urban patterns of consumption. This melding of what hitherto were different ways in living is reflected in the U.S. Bureau of the Census definition of "rural" as non-metropolitan. "Rural," by census definition, does not refer to making a living on farms but to people who live outside cities and metropolitan areas. The rural population, so defined, increased slightly between 1970 and 1990, from 53,565,000 to 61,656,000, to 24.8 percent of the national population. Statistically, rural Americans are among the nation's poorest citizens. Rural states rank near the bottom in collections by the Internal Revenue Service, federal payments to individuals, state and government income, gross production, and per capita income. Rural states generally have more people below the poverty level and higher dropout rates among high school students. Some compensation can be found in that rural locations have increasingly attracted minor and low-paying, nonunionized industries and residue enterprises, such as prisons, landfills, and nuclear waste receptacles. Rural life is also undeniably safer than city living. Maine, Wyoming, Vermont, North Dakota, and South Dakota had only sixty-one murders combined in 1991. These states ranked near the bottom in virtually all crime statistics, including robberies and aggravated assaults, despite very low expenditures for police and penitentiaries.

Americans feel deep nostalgia for rural America. Garrison Keillor's radio show *Prairie Home Companion* spoke to urbanized America's longing for a romanticized version of rural simplicity. States such as Montana and Idaho have attracted wealthy real estate investors seeking refuge from the stress of urban life. Ironically, services for such elite made rural life emulate the rest of the nation, with the introduction of satellite and cable television, automated banking, computer modems, fast food restaurants, sports centers, and rapid mail delivery. By the early 1990s such developments curtailed the isolation of national parks. Thus, rural areas now offer all comforts of urban living for those who can afford them.

[Gary Alampi, ed., *Gale State Rankings Reporter* (Detroit, 1994); Janet M. Fitchen, *Endangered Species, Enduring Places: Change, Identity, and Survival in Rural America* (Boulder, Colo., 1991).]

GRAHAM RUSSELL HODGES

See also **SUPP:** Urban Living.

RUSSIANS. *See* **Soviet Americans.**

RUSTBELT, an economic region of the United States concentrated in the formerly dominant industrial states of Illinois, Indiana, Michigan, Ohio, and Pennsylvania. By the 1980s the Rustbelt became what the Dust Bowl was to an earlier generation—the symbolic name for a devastating economic change. The 1984 Democratic presidential candidate, Walter Mondale, is generally credited with the origin of the term. During the campaign, the former vice president from Minnesota attacked the economic policies of incumbent President Ronald Reagan, stating that the Republican president was "turning our great industrial Midwest and the industrial base of this country into a rust bowl." The media, however, repeated and reported the notion as "Rustbelt" and the phrase stuck. It described the declining industrial heartland, especially the steel- and automobile-producing regions in the Northeast and Midwest. The phrase became synonymous with industrial decline in the once dominant U.S. heavy manufacturing and steel industries.

The Rustbelt has indefinite boundaries, although in 1979 Joel Garreau dubbed the same general region "the Foundry." Both terms—"Foundry" and "Rustbelt"—aptly characterized the region's economic history and its underpinnings. With readily available coal, labor, and inland waterways, the region was ideal for steel manufacturing. Moreover, the automotive industry—a major buyer of steel—developed nearby. The U.S. steel industry, however, underwent decline and lost its world dominance. The U.S. worldwide market share of manufactured steel went from

20 percent in 1970 to 12 percent by 1990. U.S. employment within the industry dropped from 400,000 to 140,000 over the same period. Starting in the late 1970s, steel factories began closing. Among the hardest hit communities was Youngstown, Ohio, where the closure of three steel mills starting in 1977 eliminated nearly 10,000 high-paying jobs. Also hard hit were foundries in Buffalo, N.Y., Johnstown, Pa., and Pittsburgh, where the last outmoded steel plant closed in the late 1980s. While steel is produced in thirty-five states, the large steel plants in the Rustbelt were particularly hard hit because their large open-hearth furnaces were unprofitable and outdated. Many were sulfur-burning, coal-fired steel plants, which had difficulty meeting stringent environmental regulations on smokestack emissions. Layoffs occurred even as worldwide demand for steel grew. New demand often was met with lower-cost and sometimes higher-quality steel produced abroad, particularly in Japan. The steel industry rebounded by developing low-cost, highly automated minimills, which use electric arc furnaces to turn scrap metal into wire rod and bar products, but the minimills employ fewer workers.

The region was the nation's industrial heartland with large, densely populated urban areas. Those cities, which began showing signs of decline, had initially served as the melting pot for early European migration and the destination point for a tremendous migration of African Americans north to join the industrial workforce following World War II. With the industrial decline, however, thousands of well-paid, benefit-laden, blue-collar jobs were permanently lost. Families left the Rustbelt and relocated to the Sunbelt and the West, seeking jobs and better living conditions. The black populations in the Chicago and Pittsburgh metropolitan areas declined, reversing the earlier northern migration patterns from the Deep South. The population shift meant fewer congressional representatives from the region following the 1990 reapportionment.

[Richard Florida, *The Breakthrough Illusion: Corporate America's Failure to Move from Innovation to Mass Production* (New York, 1990); Joel Garreau, *The Nine Nations of North America* (Boston, 1981).]

BRENT SCHONDELMEYER

See also **SUPP:** Illinois; Indiana; Michigan; Ohio; Pennsylvania; Pittsburgh.

***RUST* V. *SULLIVAN*,** 111 Supreme Court 1759 (1991). Congress enacted a law in 1970 that supported family-planning services by making available federal funds under Title X but forbade the use of federal funds for abortions. Over a fifteen-year period the Department of Health and Human Services (HHS) so regulated use of the funds under the law, but in 1986 HHS tightened regulations, attempting to limit the ability of clinics to provide information about abortions. Two years later, with the strong support of President George Bush, HHS imposed a gag rule upon clinics and their physicians, prohibiting references to abortion in family-planning programs. The first issue in *Rust* was whether the 1970 law could be construed to allow the gag rule even though Congress had not granted federal authorities such power. The second was whether the regulations including the rule violated freedom of expression guaranteed by the First Amendment and the due process of law protected by the Fifth Amendment. On both issues the Court decided in favor of the government. Conceding that the intent of Congress was ambiguous, the Court nonetheless held that it should defer to the judgment of those charged with applying the law. Regarding the second issue, the Court found that discussion of abortions could occur outside the federal program and thus there was no violation of either the First or Fifth Amendment. *Rust* affected 4,500 facilities serving nearly 4 million women and raised the question of whether the government could impose free-speech restrictions on other institutions receiving Title X funds. It marked a further limit of a woman's right to an abortion since the Court's landmark decision of *Roe* v. *Wade* (1973). The impact of the decision declined, however, when the administration of President Bill Clinton lifted the gag rule in 1993.

[David Garrow, *Liberty and Sexuality: The Right to Privacy and the Making of* Roe v. Wade (New York, 1994).]

TONY FREYER

See also **SUPP:** Abortion; Contraception; *Roe* v. *Wade; Webster* v. *Reproductive Health Services.*

S

SACRAMENTO, the major urban center of California's Central Valley, is located at the confluence of the American and Sacramento rivers. The region has been a crossroads of trade and commerce since its earliest habitation. John A. Sutter, a German-speaking Swiss adventurer, arrived in Sacramento in 1839 and built a fort as a frontier outpost for the Mexican government. The gold rush that began in 1848 led the following year to the platting of the city of Sacramento, which became the state capital in 1854. It was briefly the western terminus of the Pony Express in the early 1860s and of the first transcontinental railroad, which was completed in 1869. Located at the lower end of one of the world's highest-volume watersheds, Sacramento experienced its first flood in 1849. Completion of the Shasta Dam on the Sacramento River in 1949, Folsom Dam on the American in 1956, and Oroville Dam on the Feather in 1968 led to extensive development on the flood plains. A major flood in 1989, which eclipsed all previous runoffs, and local flooding in January 1995 caused local, state, and federal agencies to reassess land use patterns. The completion of Interstate Highways 5 and 80 in the 1960s reaffirmed Sacramento's role as a transportation hub. Several factors shielded the local economy from the problems that beset other regions of California after the cold war. In the 1990s housing and land prices were one-third lower than in the San Francisco Bay area, approximately eighty miles to the southwest. Local, state, and federal government employment provided a stable, albeit declining, share of the job market. With many institutions of higher learning, including community colleges, California State University, Sacramento, and the University of California, Davis, the region has a well-educated labor force. Since the 1970s data processing centers, high-tech manufacturing companies, biotechnology enterprises, and financial services companies were created in or relocated to Sacramento. The city's population increased from 275,741 in 1980 to 366,500 in 1990, when the Sacramento–Yolo County Consolidated Metropolitan Statistical Area had a population of nearly 1.5 million in 1990. From its inception in 1839, when Sutter arrived with a party that included ten Hawaiians, one Belgian, one German, and one Irishman, Sacramento has had a multicultural population. Like the state of California, but at a much slower pace, Sacramento has experienced increased ethnic diversity since the 1970s. In 1989 a national news magazine listed Sacramento as one of the ten best places to live in the United States. Among its amenities are its colleges and universities, a symphony, an opera company, a ballet, many theater companies, and the American River Parkway, which extends more than thirty miles upstream from the Sacramento River to Lake Folsom.

[Robert L. Kelley, *Battling the Inland Sea: American Political Culture, Public Policy, and the Sacramento Valley, 1850–1986* (Berkeley, Calif., 1989); Joseph A. McGowan, *Sacramento: Heart of the Golden State* (Woodland Hills, Calif., 1983).]

GREGG M. CAMPBELL

See also **DAH** and **SUPP:** California.

SAINT LOUIS, located in eastern Missouri, experienced a major population decline from its 1950 high of 856,796 residents to only 396,385 in 1990. Old legislation prevented the city from expanding beyond its 1876 limits, but the metropolitan area continued to advance, to 2.5 million in 1990. Beginning in the 1970s Saint Louis promoters touted an urban renaissance that included an extensively restored railroad station that is also a stylish shopping center. New sports facilities were built, including Busch Memorial Stadium, and the Saint Louis Zoo remains a major tourist attraction. The first parts of a new light rail system were opened to much acclaim. A comprehensive freeway binds much of the metropolitan area. Many old neighborhoods vanished, however, and urban decay, which began after World War II, was a depressing reality in the 1990s. School desegregation was far from complete, although 47 percent of the city's population was African American. For many years the largest city in Missouri, in 1990 Saint Louis fell behind its traditional rival, Kansas City.

[James Neal Primm, *Lion of the Valley: A History of St. Louis* (Boulder, Colo., 1981).]

LAWRENCE H. LARSEN

See also **SUPP:** Kansas City; Missouri.

SALARIES. *See* **Wages and Salaries.**

SALT. *See* **Strategic Arms Limitation Talks.**

SAMOA, AMERICAN, an unincorporated trust territory of the United States in the southern Pacific and consisting of seven islands of the Samoa group. American Samoa approved its first constitution in 1960, but the Samoans rejected the idea of electing their own governor until 1977, when Peter Tali Coleman won office. The Fono, American Samoa's legislature, is bicameral, with the senate made up of *matai* membership and elected representatives in the house. Since 1970 American Samoa has had an official representative in the U.S. Congress. In the 1960s American Samoa saw major changes, receiving congressional funding for roads, schools, and a hospital; economic development in tourism and fisheries; and an experimental television broadcast system in the schools. These efforts and subsequent programs brought about a more Westernized lifestyle than is evident in Western Samoa, along with dependence on U.S. aid. Tuna canning and tourism remained the major industries of American Samoa. Outmigration from the islands is a crucial factor in the economy; in the 1990s there were more Samoans living outside than within American Samoa, and large Samoan communities existed in Hawaii and California. The 1990 population of American Samoa was 46,773, but it is estimated that more than 60,000 American Samoans lived in the United States. As U.S. nationals, American Samoans travel extensively between Samoan communities "abroad" and the home islands. This escape valve has alleviated the problem of jobs for graduates of the islands' high schools and the Community College of American Samoa. Samoans in the United States nonetheless faced the same problems as other immigrant groups, including the breakdown of traditional authority and kinship roles.

[Frederick Koehler Sutter, *Amerika Samoa* (Honolulu, 1984).]

KAREN M. PEACOCK

SAN ANTONIO, located in south-central Texas, was the tenth-largest city in the United States in 1995. Its culture is strongly influenced by a predominantly Hispanic population and a strong Mexican heritage. San Antonio's historical sites, such as the Alamo, as well as the lovely River Walk along the San Antonio River and family amusement parks, have helped make the city the state's leading tourist center. San Antonio also became a major livestock and agricultural center, but no single factor has shaped modern San Antonio as much as its close ties with the U.S. military. Almost from its beginning as a Spanish outpost in 1718, the city's economy benefited from the military, a relationship that continued well into the twentieth century. By the 1980s San Antonio contained Fort Sam Houston, a fixture in the city since 1879, and Lackland, Kelly, Brooks, and Randolph air force bases. More than 44,000 military personnel lived in San Antonio in the early 1990s and about 35,000 civilians worked for the military. The city experienced a surge of growth in the 1970s and 1980s not only because of the military but also because of an expanding service sector, including health care, thanks to the South Texas Medical Center and the University of Texas Health Center. San Antonio's population in 1990 reached 935,933, a 43 percent increase from its 1970 population of 654,153. The 1995 decision by the Defense Base Closing and Realignment commission to shut down Kelly Air Force Base posed real problems for the city's future prosperity because the closing eliminated 13,000 civilian jobs.

[John L. Davis, *San Antonio: A Historical Portrait* (Austin, Tex., 1978); David R. Johnson, John A. Booth, Richard J. Harris, eds., *The Politics of San Antonio: Community, Progress, and Power* (Lincoln, Nebr., 1983).]

ROBERT B. FAIRBANKS

See also **SUPP:** Texas.

SANCTUARIES. *See* **Wildlife Refuges and Sanctuaries.**

SAN DIEGO, a Pacific port and southern California city located near the border of Mexico's Baja (Lower) California. Occupied by Native Americans, called Kumeyaay, the area was first visited by Europeans when Juan Rodríguez Cabrillo entered the harbor in 1542. Sebastian Vizcaíno gave the city its name in 1602 to honor San Diego de Alcalá, a Spanish Franciscan brother. The region remained unsettled until 1769, when Gaspar de Portolá, governor of Baja California, and Father Junípero Serra founded a military post and mission. During Mexican rule (1821–1846) San Diego became a civilian pueblo occupying the site known today as Old Town. The Mexican War in 1846–1848 brought Americans into the area, and San Diego made a peaceful transition to U.S. control in 1850, the year the city was incorporated. William Heath Davis founded New Town three miles south and close to San Diego Bay in 1850, but the site did not become successful until promoted by Alonzo E. Horton in 1867. By 1872 major businesses and the courthouse had moved to New Town and the first water company was formed in 1873. Arrival of the Santa Fe Railroad in 1884 set off a boom, and although growth slowed during the 1890s, San Diego, with its ideal climate and sandy beaches, continued to prosper well into the twentieth century. San Diego Bay, a natural deepwater harbor, is headquarters for the U.S. Eleventh Naval District and a base of operations for a number of military installations. The San Diego Zoo, Old Globe Theatre, Sea World, Mission Bay Aquatic Park, the Cabrillo National Monument, and a new convention center made tourism a major part of the city's economy. Trends in the 1990s were toward transborder activities and an emphasis on information and high-tech industries, including aerospace, electronics, and biomedical research. The city's population increased from 334,387 in 1950 to 1,110,549 in 1990. It is the seat of San Diego County, which numbered 2,498,016 in 1990.

[Iris H. W. Engstrand, *San Diego: Gateway to the Pacific* (Houston, 1992).]

IRIS H. W. ENGSTRAND

See also **SUPP:** California.

SAN FRANCISCO in the mid-1990s was still one of the most cosmopolitan cities in the United States. Although surpassed in population in 1989 by its Bay Area neighbor San Jose, it remained a center for Pacific Rim finance and trade and a city noted for ethnic and cultural diversity. The fourteenth-largest city in the United States in 1990, and part of the fourth most populous metropolitan area, San Francisco boasted a population of 723,959 that year. From 1970 to the early 1990s its Asian and Pacific Island communities grew from about 13 percent to almost 30 percent of the population. The Hispanic community also expanded (primarily Mexican and Central American immigration), while white residents decreased to about half the population and African Americans to 11 percent.

Known as a liberal city, San Francisco has been an important site for a succession of political and countercultural movements, from the general strike of 1934 to the Beat Generation in the 1950s to the hippies of the 1960s who were drawn to the Haight-Ashbury section and large civil rights and antiwar demonstrations in the 1960s and early 1970s. In the 1990s there was a sizable gay and lesbian community, about 20 percent of the adult population, centered around the Castro district. Voters have elected Democratic mayors since 1963, with John Shelley, Joseph L. Alioto, George Moscone, Dianne Feinstein (the city's first female mayor, later elected to the U.S. Senate in 1992), and Art Agnos heading the city through the end of the 1980s. From his election in 1964 until 1983, the prominent liberal Phillip Burton served San Francisco in the U.S. House of Representatives. Building on a tradition of neighborhood politics and environmentalism, slow-growth movements opposed (with mixed success) local freeway projects and the continued construction of high-rise office buildings in the downtown district. An increasingly strained city budget in the 1980s, however, and the election in 1991 of conservative Democrat and former police chief Frank Jordan as mayor illustrated the many tensions facing the city's liberal politics.

San Francisco's manufacturing sector and seaport business began declining in 1970, but finance, insurance, high-technology, medical science, real estate, transportation, fashion, and low-paying service jobs gained increasing importance in the area's economy. The arts, entertainment, and tourism also played an important role. The city is known for its temperate climate, natural beauty, geographic compactness, abundance of restaurants, and eclectic mix of Victorian, Mediterranean, and postmodern architecture. Tourists and residents enjoy such local attractions and amenities as Golden Gate Park, the cable cars, Fisherman's Wharf, Chinatown, and the Bay Area Rapid Transit (BART), along with an array of museums and national sports teams. San Franciscans have encountered serious challenges since the 1980s. Despite the city's relatively high average income, by 1990 up to 7,000 residents were homeless. More than 7,000 people died in the 1980s of Acquired Immune Deficiency Syndrome (AIDS), the highest per capita rate in the United States. Other shocks included the 1978 murders of Mayor Moscone and gay city supervisor Harvey Milk, the 1989 Loma Prieta earthquake, and a statewide recession in the early 1990s. As San Francisco's population and economy declined relative to that of the surrounding South Bay and suburbs, its role as a hub city diminished, but it was likely to retain its standing as a global city.

[Richard Edward DeLeon, *Left Coast City: Progressive Politics in San Francisco, 1975–1991* (Lawrence, Kans., 1992); William Issel and Robert W. Cherny, *San Francisco, 1865–1932: Politics, Power, and Urban Development* (Berkeley, Calif., 1986).]

ERIC FURE-SLOCUM

See also **SUPP:** California; San Jose.

SAN FRANCISCO EARTHQUAKE (Oct. 17, 1989).

At 5:04 P.M., shortly after a nationwide television audience tuned in to a World Series baseball game in San Francisco, the biggest earthquake since the great one of 1906 ripped northern California. Under the Santa Cruz Mountains, sixty miles southeast of the city, a section of the San Andreas fault had broken. As the earthquake vibrations raced outward they collapsed many buildings in small cities such as Santa Cruz and Watsonville near the epicenter and, to the surprise of many experts, also severely shook the low-lying and waterlogged soils near San Francisco Bay with devastating results. Falling buildings, bridges, highways, and other objects killed sixty-three people, most of them caught in cars under the collapsing Cypress Viaduct, a double-deck freeway on Interstate Highway 880 in Oakland, across the bay from San Francisco. In addition a section of roadway in the Bay Bridge connecting San Francisco and Oakland fell in, closing that vital span for a month. The quake injured at least 3,757 people, damaged 18,000 homes and 2,500 businesses, and left 12,000 people homeless. The cost of damage was $6 billion. Geologists refer to the event as the Loma Prieta Earthquake, after a mountain in the rugged region where it started. They place its magnitude at 6.9 to 7.1 and calculate that it ruptured twenty-five miles of fault, at depths from two to twelve miles. Some of the seismic waves may have bounced off deeper layers in the earth's crust and come up in the San Francisco area, possibly explaining why damage was so severe more than fifty miles from the source. Although the earthquake was large, it was far smaller than the 1906 San Francisco quake, which broke 250 miles of the fault and, with a magnitude of 8.0, released about thirty times more energy than the Loma Prieta quake.

[George Plafker and John P. Galloway, eds., *Lessons Learned from the Loma Prieta, California, Earthquake of October 17, 1989*, United States Geological Survey Circular 1045 (1989); State of California Office of Planning and Research, *Competing Against Time: Report to Governor George Deukmejian from the Governor's Board of Inquiry on the 1989 Loma Prieta Earthquake* (North Highlands, Calif., May 1990).]

CHARLES PETIT

See also **DAH:** San Francisco Earthquake; **SUPP:** Earthquakes; Oakland; San Francisco.

SAN JOSE,

city in California, was organized in 1777 seven miles below the southern tip of San Francisco Bay in the fertile Santa Clara Valley, but not on navigable water. Despite serving as a depot for gold seekers and incorporation in 1850, it languished until acquisition of railroad connections in 1864. Improved transportation enhanced San Jose's role as an agricultural market, and by 1900 the city had 21,000 inhabitants. Over the next forty years it grew gradually, acquiring important agribusiness concerns. During World War II, under the innovative San Jose Plan, local businesses cooperated to obtain war contracts. The population reached 95,280 in 1950. During the second half of the twentieth century, tremendous growth occurred in San Jose and surrounding Santa Clara County, with the city reaching a population of 204,106 in 1960. The population more than doubled in the next decade, as the economy became more diversified. Electrical plants, military bases, and aerospace activities helped fuel the expansion, as did the rise of computer manufacturing in Silicon Valley. In 1990 San Jose was the eleventh-largest city in the United States with 782,248 people.

LAWRENCE H. LARSEN

See also **SUPP:** California; Silicon Valley.

SANTA CLARA PUEBLO V. MARTINEZ, 436 U.S.

49 (1978). In 1968 Congress enacted the Indian Civil Rights Act, applying certain provisions of the Bill of Rights to Native American tribal governments. Congress left principal responsibility for enforcing the law to tribal authorities. In criminal cases the act

gave federal courts only a habeas corpus remedy. Over the years, however, federal judges developed an implied power to grant declaratory or injunctive relief or other civil remedies. As a result of this implied authority federal judges reviewed many policies of the tribal governments. A female member of the Santa Clara Pueblo tribe married a Navajo and had seven children. The Santa Clara Pueblo denied membership to the woman's children based on a tribal ordinance excluding children of female but not male members who married outside the tribe. Children excluded under the tribal ordinance could neither vote nor hold secular office and were not permitted to remain on the reservation in event of the mother's death or to inherit their mother's house or interest in communal lands. The mother asked the federal district court to enjoin enforcement of this gendered ordinance. The district court decided in favor of the mother on the merits, employing an implied jurisdiction to issue an injunction. The representative of the Santa Clara Pueblo appealed, arguing that the Indian Civil Rights Act did not authorize civil actions in federal court for relief against a tribe or its officials. Upon appeal, the Supreme Court through Justice Thurgood Marshall's opinion decided in favor of the tribe and held that the district court possessed no implied jurisdiction. The decision established strong tribal autonomy, except where Congress explicitly provided for federal judicial review.

[Catherine A. MacKinnon, *Feminism Unmodified: Discourses on Life and Law* (Cambridge, Mass., 1987); Susan Sanders Molander, "Case Notes: Indian Civil Rights Act and Sex Discrimination," *Arizona State Law Journal* 1 (1977).]

TONY FREYER

See also **SUPP:** Native Americans; Women's Rights.

SAVINGS AND LOAN CRISIS. One of the most dramatic financial stories of the 1980s was the collapse of hundreds of savings and loan institutions (S&Ls, also known as "thrifts") that had became insolvent in the wake of federal deregulation of the industry. As mandated by law, the government stepped in to protect the federally insured depositors of the failed thrifts, at a cost of billions of dollars. Traditionally, S&Ls had provided savings accounts and long-term residential mortgages and had been restricted by government regulation from offering most other types of financial services. With the failure of many S&Ls in the Great Depression, the Federal Savings and Loan Insurance Corporation (FSLIC) was created in 1934 to protect depositors' money. This system worked well in an environment of stable or falling interest rates, but the industry faced severe pressure from rising interest rates in the late 1960s and throughout the 1970s. S&Ls were forced to pay higher short-term rates to attract and keep deposits but could not increase revenue from the long-term, fixed-interest-rate home mortgages they had issued. In 1966 Congress placed a limit on the interest S&Ls could pay on deposits, setting it slightly higher than the rate allowed to banks. This limitation hurt S&Ls in the 1970s as investors began to shift money to higher-paying Treasury bills and newly created money market mutual funds. At the same time, most S&Ls continued to be prohibited from issuing adjustable-rate home mortgages.

Congress attempted to address these problems through a process of deregulation that started in 1980, when the Depository Institutions Deregulation and Monetary Control Act began to phase out interest-rate ceilings on deposits, allowed S&Ls to compete with banks in offering interest-paying checking accounts, and raised federal insurance on deposits to $100,000 per account. Problems continued and in 1981 for the first time the S&L industry as a whole was unprofitable. The Garn–St. Germain Depository Institutions Act of 1982 extended deregulation by authorizing S&Ls to issue adjustable-rate mortgages, permitting up to 40 percent of assets to be invested in nonresidential real estate loans and up to 10 in commercial loans and generally easing net worth and ownership requirements to give S&Ls more flexibility. Concurrently, several states liberalized their own regulation of state-chartered S&Ls, even as these non–federally chartered institutions still qualified for FSLIC deposit insurance.

The S&L industry grew dramatically. Assets soared from $686 billion in 1982 to $1.1 trillion in 1985. In the same period assets held in the traditional home mortgage market fell from 64.7 percent to 38.1 percent. Much of the increased asset base came from large (usually $100,000) deposits gathered nationally by "money brokers," such as Wall Street securities firms. Certain S&Ls, especially in Texas, Florida, Colorado, Arizona, and California, used their new powers to invest heavily in commercial real estate and even riskier investments, such as the high-paying, low-credit-rated "junk bonds" issued by Wall Street firms in the 1980s. The lavish personal expenditures and flamboyance of some S&L executives, many of whom were new to a traditionally low-key industry, garnered public attention. The fundamental problem that brought down many of these high-flying S&Ls was their inordinate exposure to high-risk and unsound investments that in the Southwest turned sour after oil prices plummeted in the mid-1980s. The high rates of interest paid to depositors and the fact that deposits were federally insured were a formula for disaster. Ultimately, government would be liable for the greed and excess of a certain part of the S&L industry.

As early as 1985 officials of the Federal Home Loan Bank Board (FHLBB), which regulated S&Ls, were aware of these problems and began to try to deal with them. They were hindered for several years by the failure of Congress to support them and by intervention of lawmakers on behalf of specific S&Ls. Still, quicker action by the FHLBB would not have eliminated the bad loans and investments already on the books of S&Ls. To close insolvent institutions required increased capitalization of the FSLIC insurance fund. Congress in 1987 approved a limited increase, inadequate to make much of a dent in the problem. Less money for the FSLIC meant fewer bad S&Ls could be closed, and House Majority Leader Jim Wright of Texas intervened on behalf of a group of Texas S&L owners. The FSLIC requested $15 billion in additional funds but received less than half that amount. The most celebrated case of successful lobbying to thwart federal regulators was that of the "Keating Five." Charles H. Keating, Jr., enlisted the aid of five senators—Alan Cranston of California, Dennis DeConcini and John McCain of Arizona, Donald W. Riegle, Jr., of Michigan, and John Glenn of Ohio—on behalf of his troubled Lincoln Savings and Loan. Keating contributed a total of $1.4 million to the campaign funds of these senators and was able to keep going until 1989, when Lincoln closed at an estimated cost to taxpayers of $2.5 billion. He later served a prison term for securities violations, and the five senators, particularly Cranston, were reprimanded by their colleagues.

Faced with limited congressional cooperation, the FHLBB in 1988 began to close insolvent S&Ls by arranging for their acquisition by outside investors; 205 S&Ls were disposed of in this fashion. The full dimensions of the problem, however, required the attention of President George Bush and Congress, which led in 1989 to the Financial Institutions Reform, Recovery, and Enforcement Act (FIRREA). This sweeping legislation authorized initial borrowing of an additional $50 billion to support the cleanup and established a new agency, the Resolution Trust Corporation (RTC), to carry out this task. The FHLBB was abolished and regulation of the remaining healthy S&Ls was lodged in the Office of Thrift Supervision in the Department of the Treasury. The FSLIC was merged into the Federal Deposit Insurance Corporation, which insured commercial bank deposits. Higher insurance premiums, much tighter net worth requirements, and restrictions on lending and investment practices were placed on S&Ls. This caused additional institutions that had not been greatly involved in the excesses of the 1980s to be closed or merged with banks. By 1995 the RTC had sold or merged 747 insolvent thrifts, leaving a smaller but presumably healthier industry. The cost to taxpayers under FIRREA was $180 billion, significantly higher than the initial expectations when the RTC was created but ultimately less than other estimates, which ranged as high as $500 billion. In any case, the savings and loan crisis was a sobering experience that raised many questions about business, government, and politics in the United States in the late twentieth century.

[Edward J. Kane, *The Gathering Crisis in Federal Deposit Insurance* (Cambridge, Mass., 1985); Lawrence J. White, *The S&L Debacle* (New York, 1991).]

JOHN B. WEAVER

See also **SUPP:** Banking and Finance; Corruption, Political; Deregulation; Junk Bonds; Real Estate Industry; Reaganomics.

SBA. *See* **Small Business Administration.**

SCANDALS. Political, financial, and sexual misconduct by government and business leaders, entertainers, and other well-known figures has occurred in every period of U.S. history. Since the 1970s, however, instances in which private misconduct becomes public scandal have increased dramatically with the burgeoning numbers and intensified scrutiny of news media as well as changing attitudes toward what constitutes "scandalous" behavior. As in the past, scandalous political behavior tends to involve blatant financial corruption such as taking bribes. In the early 1970s, however, the definition of political scandal took on new dimensions with the Watergate cover-up, in which revelations of the abuse of constitutional powers led for the first time to the resignation of a sitting president, Richard M. Nixon. Similarly, members of the Ronald Reagan administration involved in the Iran-Contra scandal of the 1980s were found to have subverted the democratic process for political ends. The 1980s also were marked by financial scandals in the private sector, chief among them the Wall Street insider-trading scandal, which resulted in prison terms for two of the market's most prominent figures, Ivan Boesky and Michael Milken; and the savings and loan debacle, in which some 2,000 deregulated thrift institutions failed because of the rampant greed of directors such as Charles H. Keating, Jr., who went to prison.

Scandals involving adultery and other forms of sexual misconduct have become far more frequent than in the past. Public figures, whether Hollywood stars or U.S. presidents, were once largely protected from exposure of their illicit affairs by journalists and public relations staffers. In the 1980s, however, even the most legitimate news organizations began to justify exposure of such activities as indicative of dishonesty or hypocrisy, as in the cases of the televangelists Jim Bakker and Jimmy Swaggart and of Senator Gary Hart, whose 1984 presidential campaign was derailed when he prevaricated about having an extramarital affair. Changing public mores fueled by the concerns of women also played a role by expanding the moral and legal definition of sexual misconduct to include date rape and sexual harassment and intensifying both censure of and criminal penalties for spousal abuse. Public discussions of these issues were carried on in large part through such widely publicized scandals as the rape trials of Senator Edward Kennedy's nephew, William Kennedy Smith, who was found innocent, and the heavyweight boxing champion Mike Tyson, who was convicted; the Hill-Thomas hearings in 1991 and sexual harassment charges against Senator Robert Packwood of Oregon in 1994–1995; and the 1995 trial of football star turned actor O. J. Simpson, who was acquitted of murdering his ex-wife after an earlier conviction for abuse during their marriage.

While the controversies surrounding these events have forced Americans to reevaluate their moral, religious, and political values, critics worried that the intense media coverage of these and literally hundreds of more minor scandals had created a "culture of scandal" that encouraged an unhealthy degree of public mistrust and cynicism. In an increasingly competitive media landscape, however, it seems a culture of scandal is here to stay.

[Sissela Bok, *Lying* (New York, 1978); Suzanne Garment, *Scandal: The Culture of Mistrust in American Politics* (New York, 1991); George C. Kohn, *Encyclopedia of American Scandal* (New York, 1989).]

JEFFREY M. MERRON

See also **SUPP:** Abscam Scandal; Celebrity Culture; Corruption, Political; Crime, White-Collar; Housing and Urban Development (HUD) Scandal; Iran-Contra Affair; Iraq-gate; Junk Bonds; Korea-gate; Savings and Loan Crisis; Sexual Harassment; Televangelism; Thomas Confirmation Hearings; Watergate, Aftermath of; Whitewater.

SCHOOLING, HOME, which refers to parents educating their children at home instead of sending them to a school, advanced from an eccentricity in the 1960s to a national movement by the 1990s. Home schooling was once a mainstay of education on the American frontier but never enjoyed great popularity in established urban areas. By the mid-1850s religious and political leaders, fearing negative consequences of radical individualism, placed great hope in a universal system of compulsory, public education that would provide the "engine of democracy" for the nation. Over the next century Americans learned, however, that their increasingly bureaucratized educational system could not prevent social ills. By the 1960s a small number of parents had turned to the family as the means of teaching children. While a census is impossible by virtue of the informal, noninstitutional nature of home schooling, the movement has experienced remarkable growth. According to the U.S. Department of Education, the number of children educated at home grew from 15,000 in the early 1970s to 300,000 by the early 1990s. Home-schooled children are most numerous in the West and South. The typical home-schooling family is economically prosperous and white, and at least one parent has some college education. In nine of ten such households the mother does most of the teaching. The average length of home education is one year.

Home-schooling families tend to subscribe to one of two rationales. The vast majority of parents—85 percent in one study—educate children at home for religious reasons. They want their children to learn doctrine that is denied in public schools and that in many cases also reflects a conservative political and social perspective. Other parents doubt that a child's intellectual growth and creativity can flourish in the rigidly structured, bureaucratic setting of most public schools. Home-schooled children perform better on standard tests than children in schools, but critics cite concerns about the social development of children isolated from peers. Researchers disagree as to whether home-schooled children have lower or higher self-esteem than children in school. The home-schooling movement has been marked by legal confusion as to whether children can be excused from school, what must be taught at home, and who is qualified to teach in the home. Home schooling is now legal in all fifty states, but there are no national standards for instruction. Within each state standards often vary from school district to district.

[Jane Van Galen and Mary Anne Pitman, eds., *Home Schooling: Political, Historical, and Pedagogical Perspectives* (Norwood, N.J., 1991); Alfie Kohn, "Home Schooling," *The Atlantic Monthly* 261 (April 1988); Anne Pedersen and Peggy O'Mara, eds., *Schooling at Home: Parents, Kids and Learning* (Santa Fe, N.Mex., 1990).]

PAUL S. VOAKES

See also **DAH** and **SUPP:** Education; **SUPP:** Education, Parental Choice in.

SCHOOLS, COMMUNITY, are committed to broad education and characterized by home, school, and community collaboration to achieve learning. Beginning in the mid-1960s, thousands of small alternative schools sprang up across the United States and Canada. They varied widely in programs and policies, but common factors were a disenchantment with conventional schooling, a desire to reform education, and the belief that schools should be controlled by the population served, including students, parents, teachers, and community members. The National Coalition of Alternative Community Schools was formed in 1976. Community schools include rural schools that serve as community centers, featuring educational and social programs; others are independent neighborhood schools meeting academic, social, and cultural needs of children of African Americans, Hispanic Americans, Latino Americans, Native Americans, and Asian Americans. The New York State Community School Program organized public inner-city schools as sites for the delivery of social services to needy children and their families. Community schools described as "integrative" have sought to bring disabled students into the regular school program. Corporate community schools created partnerships among business executives, educators, and community leaders to establish and operate business-sponsored elementary schools in inner cities. Their goal is to reform urban public education by setting standards and demonstrating instructional methods and school management that can be used across the country.

[Mary Leue, *Challenging the Giant* (Albany, 1992); Heleen Owen, "Community Schools and Service Integration in New York," *Equity and Choice* 6 (1990).]

MARY DEANE SORCINELLI

See also **SUPP:** Education.

SCHOOLS, FOR-PROFIT. The idea of schools for profit is rooted in the growing discontent with public schools that began in the 1960s, but an experiment in performance contracting, the hiring by public schools of private companies to provide instruction with remuneration dependent on student achievement, was deemed ineffective in a 1972 government report. Responding to widespread calls in the late 1980s for broad educational reforms, media entrepreneur Christopher Whittle and businessman John Golle offered for-profit school plans to redesign U.S. schools. In May 1991 Whittle announced the Edison Project, a plan for a multibillion-dollar chain of 150 to 200 private schools, which he declared would provide better instruction at lower per-pupil cost than public schools. A year later Whittle hired Benno C. Schmidt, Jr., president of Yale University, to head the project. After failing to raise sufficient capital, the project was scaled back, focusing instead on obtaining management contracts with existing schools or to winning public funds to establish new schools. In March 1994 Massachusetts became the first state to award charters for the project to operate schools. Meanwhile, Golle started Education Alternatives, Inc. (EAI), in 1986. His first schools, which opened in 1987, did not make money, so he turned to managing public schools. Following mixed results in Miami, Fla., and Duluth, Minn., EAI gained a $133 million contract to operate nine inner-city schools in Baltimore. At the end of its second year of operation, EAI showed significant positive changes in parent involvement, facilities maintenance, and student performance on standardized tests. Supporters of for-profit schools envision positive changes resulting from incentive management. Detractors declare dismay at the money-making and believe proliferation of private schools would further undermine the public schools and widen the existing chasm in educational quality between children from affluent and less-well-off families. Teachers' unions almost universally oppose for-profit schools.

[Kenneth Jost, "Private Management of Public Schools," *CQ Researcher* (Mar. 25, 1994); Myron Lieberman, *Privatization and Educational Choice* (New York, 1989).]

MYRNA W. MERRON

See also **DAH** and **SUPP:** Education.

SCHOOLS, MAGNET. A desire to help multicultural communities achieve academic excellence has led to the establishment of magnet schools in urban districts throughout the country. They differ from regular or zoned schools in three ways—by emphasizing a special core curriculum or special method of instruction, voluntary enrollment and open access beyond the geographic attendance zone, and by promoting student and parental involvement. In some big cities magnet schools have effected markedly reduced levels of racial, ethnic, and socioeconomic isolation in elementary and secondary schools.

[Mary Haywood Metz, *Different by Design: The Context and Character of Three Magnet Schools* (New York, 1986); Inger Morton, *Improving Urban Education with Magnet Schools* (New York, 1991).]

MARY DEANE SORCINELLI

See also **SUPP:** Education; Schools, Community.

SCHOOLS, PRIVATE. Enrollment in private elementary and secondary schools in the United States rose to nearly 6.4 million students in 1965, fell to 5 million during the 1970s, and since then has fluctuated between 5 and 5.7 million (approximately 10 to 13 percent of the total school population). Much of the decline was in Catholic schools, which in 1965 accounted for almost 90 percent of students in private schools but by 1990 enrolled only about 55 percent. The number of Catholic schools fell from a record 13,292 in 1965 to 8,587 in 1990 as Catholic migration to the suburbs and increased Catholic enrollment in public schools closed many inner-city schools. A growing number of non-Catholic religious schools, 11,476 by 1990 (46 percent of private schools), offset the Catholic school decline. Still, they only enrolled 31 percent of private school students, with approximately 4,483 nonsectarian institutions serving the rest. Nonsectarian schools frequently addressed particular educational concerns: preparatory schools provided rigorous training for college, military academies stressed discipline, and Waldorf and Montessori schools offered alternative educational philosophies. The increased number of non-Catholic religious schools came largely from growth of evangelical Christian academies. These academies responded to the concerns of parents about societal problems (drug abuse, violence, and sexual promiscuity) and the apparent unfriendliness of public schools toward Christianity, which critics attributed to an advancing secular humanist ideology. For similar reasons a rapidly increasing number of families—estimated in the 1990s at about 300,000—engaged in home schooling.

Private preschools also experienced a boom. Whether run by churches, employers, or entrepreneurs, these centers responded to the increased demand for child care created when growing numbers of women entered the labor force out of economic necessity or personal preference. The U.S. Department of Education study "A Profile of Child Care Settings" estimated that between 1976 and 1990 the number of child care centers increased from 18,307 serving 897,700 children to 55,960 serving 3.8 million.

Critics of the public schools proposed such reforms as tuition tax credits and school vouchers to enable private schools to compete for government funds, thereby increasing educational options for families and pressuring public schools to operate more efficiently. This "school choice" proposal gained national attention when President Ronald Reagan advocated it in 1981 and when President George Bush included it in the America 2000 Excellence in Education Act that he introduced in 1991. The religious nature of many private schools led to protests that school choice, besides undermining public education, would violate church and state separation. (Since the 1940s the U.S. Supreme Court has rarely allowed religiously affiliated private schools to have access to public funds.) President Bill Clinton consequently excluded school choice measures from his version of America 2000, the Goals 2000: Educate America Act of 1994. Nonetheless, several states—including California, Minnesota, New York, and Wisconsin—adopted or tested school choice programs.

[James C. Carper and Thomas C. Hunt, eds., *Religious Schooling in America* (Birmingham, Ala., 1984); Peter W. Cookson, *School Choice* (New Haven, Conn., 1994); Abbie Gordon Klein, *The Debate Over Child Care, 1969–1990* (Albany, N.Y., 1992).]

ALFRED LINDSAY SKERPAN

See also **SUPP:** Education; Education, Cooperative; Education, Experimental; Schooling, Home.

SCHOOLS, RESEGREGATION OF. In the landmark case *Brown* v. *Board of Education of Topeka* (1954), the Supreme Court decided school segregation was immoral and unconstitutional. Forty years later the desegregation of U.S. public schools remained unfinished. Even after court-ordered desegregation, a school district could remain segregated through what is termed "resegregation." School resegregation is the process that separates students by racial or ethnic groups within desegregated schools. Resegregation may result from allocating elementary students to separate classrooms or sorting them within classrooms according to ability. In junior and senior high schools, tracking or homogeneous grouping by ability reduces opportunities for cross-racial contact. Students of color may be disproportionately selected and removed from the classroom for special, compensatory, or bilingual education. Disciplinary policies may contribute to disproportionate suspension or expulsion of students of color. To reduce resegregation, schools have looked to alternatives. Recommendations have included assessing and assigning students to groups based on different and richer kinds of information standards; organizing instruction to encourage heterogeneous classrooms; and advocating cooperative learning as a model for mixed-ability grouping. Such techniques appear to have a positive effect on both race relations and achievement. Other measures include encouraging interracial contact in extracurricular activities and discipline that emphasizes keeping students in school rather than suspending them.

[Janet Eyler et al., *Resegregation* (Nashville, 1982).]

MARY DEANE SORCINELLI

See also **DAH:** *Brown* v. *Board of Education of Topeka;* Busing; Integration; **SUPP:** Civil Rights Movement; Education, Cooperative; Educational Testing.

SCHOOLS, SINGLE-SEX. Before the American Revolution most formal schooling was all-male. The common school movement of the mid-nineteenth century eliminated almost all single-sex primary schooling, while female seminaries and, later, colleges exposed women to some advanced subjects pursued by men in all-male colleges. High schools and some colleges and universities offered coeducational instruction by the late nineteenth century. Private schools and colleges have been virtually the only single-sex schools in the twentieth century, and large numbers of them became coeducational for financial reasons and as a result of the women's movement in the 1970s and 1980s. In 1986 only 6 percent of colleges and universities and 24 percent of private schools were single sex. In the 1980s proponents of the remaining women's colleges often argued that single-sex schooling best enables women to learn.

[David Tyack and Elisabeth Hansot, *Learning Together: A History of Coeducation in American Schools* (New Haven, Conn., 1990).]

CHRISTINE A. OGREN

See also **DAH:** Academies; **DAH** and **SUPP:** Colleges and Universities; **SUPP:** Coeducation; Colleges, Women's.

SCIENCE MUSEUMS. The first public science museum was the Ashmolean Museum, founded at Oxford University in England in 1683 and based on the natural history collections of the scholar, Elias Ashmole, and created to educate and entertain the English public. In the United States the Franklin Institute in Philadelphia (founded 1824) and the American Institute of New York (1828) were among the first organizations to hold exhibitions of scientific developments. For many years only natural history science museums existed, such as the Smithsonian Institution (1846), American Museum of Natural History (1869), and Chicago's Field Museum of Natural History (1893), which served as depositories for rich collections of specimens ranging from plants and animals to geological materials and human artifacts. By 1969 two different types of science museums existed—the traditional natural science museum with its collections for viewing and the science museum that incorporated science and technology with participatory activities. Oskar von Miller was the first person to create exhibits that were participatory in nature, with the establishment in 1903 of the Deutsches Museum in Munich, Germany. He called the exhibits "experimental exhibits." Almost all modern day science and technology museums emulated this style, including the National Air and Space Museum, which is part of the Smithsonian and opened in 1976. The majority of science and technology institutions are not involved in research, but are more involved in the hands-on interpretation of science. The traditional natural science museum is deeply involved in research and the care of collections, and are storehouses for the world's natural treasures.

Many science museums had their beginnings in world fairs. The first major international exhibition of a world fair of science was the 1851 Exhibition of the Industry of All Nations, better known as the Crystal Palace Exhibition and sponsored by the Royal Society of Arts in London; a similar exhibition with the same name was held in New York City in 1853. The well-known Museum of Science and Industry in Chicago occupies the sole surviving building from the 1893 World's Columbian Exhibition; it opened as a museum during the Century of Progress International Exhibition (1933–1934). The participatory science movement in the United States began in the 1970s, and by the 1990s there were 23 major science and technology centers and some 260 smaller institutions. The first major science and technology museum that did not house collections was the Exploratorium in San Francisco, which opened its doors in the early

1970s after a European tour of science museums by its founding director, Frank Oppenheimer. During his tour he had the opportunity to visit the Deutsches Museum and to bring back the museum's hands-on philosophy. The exhibits created at the Exploratorium proved to be so successful that Oppenheimer and his associates published a two-volume manual called *The Cookbook,* the first guidebook on building interactive exhibits. Many of the Exploratorium's exhibits have been copied and are in use by the majority of science centers that have been created since the early 1970s. These museums are constantly seeking ways to involve visitors. Science museums in the United States are a very diverse group. Many have gone through major additions, such as the Saint Louis Science Center (1959), which, in addition to pre-Columbian North American Indian artifacts, has modern interactive exhibits on the world we live in and the environment. Discovery Place in Charlotte, N.C. (1981), has a living rain forest and in 1991 added an omnimax theater and a large planetarium. Planetariums, such as Adler Planetarium (1930) in Chicago have also added interactive science exhibits. The California Museum of Science and Industry (1880) in Los Angeles houses exhibits on aerospace and computer-aided design and manufacturing. The Oregon Museum of Science and Industry (1944) in Portland has exhibits on earthquakes, computers, and electricity. Zoos, aquariums, and national parks have also added small science museums to their exhibit areas.

[Victor J. Danilov, *Science and Technology Centers* (Cambridge, Mass., 1982).]

FREDA H. NICHOLSON

See also **DAH:** Exhibition of the Industry of All Nations; Field Museum of Natural History; Science, Popularization of; Smithsonian Institution; World's Columbian Exposition; **SUPP:** Museums.

SCIENCE TELEVISION. Popular awareness of science in the United States is often linked to the launch of *Sputnik,* the first artificial satellite, by the Soviet Union in 1957. That event was covered on television by newscaster Walter Cronkite with the help of a blackboard and rudimentary animation and helped launch his career as America's first broadcast science journalist. Cronkite later became the narrator for the first network science shows, *21st Century* and *Universe.* In the early 1960s the British Broadcasting Corporation (BBC) launched a second channel with a mandate to develop popular science programming. The result was the forty-five-minute weekly series

Horizon, which began as a live studio-based show with filmed segments but soon developed into a documentary series with each episode shot entirely on film and devoted to a single science theme. American public television's first science programs were explicitly modeled on the BBC example. In 1974 Boston-based producer Michael Ambrosino recruited several *Horizon* producers and created the one-hour weekly Public Broadcasting System series *NOVA,* the longest-running science documentary series in the United States, reaching 25 million viewers a month. In 1980 astronomer Carl Sagan attracted an enormous audience with his lavishly produced thirteen-part series *Cosmos,* which set the stage for a decade of multipart science series backed by major corporations and featuring glossy production style and spectacular animation. In the 1990s cable-television stations, such as the Discovery Channel, broadened the range of outlets for science programming. Audience research has shown that certain subjects, notably archaeology, paleontology, and astronomy, consistently draw many viewers. Some subject areas, such as chemistry or theoretical physics, are notoriously difficult to present in the type of "story" format demanded by television viewers. Outstanding science programs for children are *Newton's Apple* and *3-2-1.*

EVAN HADINGHAM

SCIENTIFIC FRAUD. In the late 1970s and 1980s the media called attention to incidents in which scientists falsified research data or plagiarized the work of others. Although cases of fraud have been recorded throughout the history of science, disclosures of these new incidents suggested that many research universities had failed to investigate charges of fraud and that individuals who made charges (sometimes called "whistle-blowers") were frequently singled out for retaliation. In 1985 Congress required research institutions to develop an administrative process for handling reports of fraud in connection with biomedical and behavioral research supported by the Public Health Service. The new federal Office of Research Integrity was established in the Department of Health and Human Services to develop regulations and provide oversight for institutional reviews. In 1987 the National Science Foundation authorized its inspector general to develop similar regulations. The effort to devise regulations and procedures has been complicated by disagreement over definitions of fraud or misconduct in science, conflicts regarding division of labor between federal agencies and research institutions, and complexities of fact-finding and due process. The first case of scientific fraud to receive attention in a federal court involved a research scientist, Dr. Stephen E. Breuning, formerly at the Western Psychiatric Institute of the University of Pittsburgh Medical School. Dr. Breuning in 1988 pleaded guilty to two charges of providing false reports involving federally funded research, for which he was sentenced to a fine and community service. A central issue in discussions of scientific fraud is the extent to which the research environment contributes to misconduct. Although many scientists believe that fraud is rare, incentives such as the pressure to publish have been cited. Several research institutions therefore have developed guidelines that not only describe procedures for investigating charges of fraud but also address such issues as credit for contributions, exchange of materials or data, dissemination of preliminary research results, and peer review.

[Alexander Kohn, *False Prophets* (New York, 1986); National Academy of Sciences, Committee on Science, Engineering, and Public Policy, *Responsible Science: Ensuring the Integrity of the Research Process,* 2 vols. (Washington, D.C., 1992–1993).]

ROSEMARY CHALK

See also **SUPP:** National Science Foundation.

SCULPTURE. The late 1960s saw the rise of minimalism as the dominant art form in sculpture. Minimalism can be viewed as a logical extension and exploration of the ideas of late modernist sculpture produced by such artists as David Smith. Late modern sculpture was pushing toward a purified non-illusionistic form expressed through basic geometric structures. The pioneering minimalists, Donald Judd, Robert Morris, Dan Flavin, and Carl André, reduced their sculptures to essentials, removing the artist's touch. Judd's metallic boxes were factory fabricated according to his specifications. André's modular work used presized timbers and bricks. Minimalists dispensed with pedestals and bases, hoping to achieve engagement between viewer and art object without the artifice of illusion a formal "frame." If the ends of minimalism seemed simple enough, the means were multifaceted and intellectually charged. It explored notions of time and space, measurement, mathematics, proportional systems, and perceptual psychology. Minimalists included Beverly Pepper, Richard Serra, and southern California artists Robert Irwin and Larry Bell. Minimalism achieved acceptance in the 1970s, when it influenced the Inter-

national style of architecture favored by corporate America, but many artists felt constrained by the purity of minimalism. They could not ignore the social issues that were gripping the country—the Vietnam War, pollution, sexism, racism, and consumerism. Four movements followed minimalism, ushering in the postmodern era: process art, conceptual art, earth art, and performance art.

Eva Hesse, Jackie Winsor, and Hans Haacke were important process artists. Hesse created soft, organic hanging works that were rich with generative and sexual metaphor. She allowed materials and techniques to influence her sculpture and, in contrast to the minimalists, used such fragile and malleable materials as cheesecloth and latex. Winsor subjected her meticulously self-constructed cubes to fire and explosives. Haacke used the cube to create self-contained "weather boxes" that addressed the relation between nature and culture. In response to the increasing commercialism of the art world, conceptual artists focused on ideas behind their sculpture. Artists such as Sol LeWitt, Robert Morris, and Joseph Kosuth expressed their ideas through temporary installations. LeWitt's *All Variations of Incomplete Open Cubes* (1974) was an investigation of the mental possibilities of permutation. Morris's *Steam Cloud* (1969) represented an attempt at deobjectification. As early as 1965, with *One and Three Chairs,* Kosuth investigated the relation between language and visual art. His text-object sculpture continues to influence artists who often make reference to semiotics and linguistics.

Earth art is exemplified by *Spiral Jetty,* constructed in Utah's Great Salt Lake by Robert Smithson in 1970. Prompted by environmental concerns, large-scale earthworks were created throughout the 1970s with the aid of heavy machinery and complex engineering. Walter de Maria's *Lightning Field,* completed in 1977, and Michael Hiezer's *Double Negative* (1970) are striking examples of what was accomplished by earth artists. Prominent women sculptors of earth art include Alice Aycock, Nancy Holt, and Ana Mendieta. Influenced by sacred architecture, Holt was known for her precise celestial orientations. By the late 1970s many sculptors turned to performance art. Seeking to engage their audiences, Laurie Anderson, Chris Burden, and Bruce Nauman often used film or video. Performance art verges on theater but it also illustrates the interdisciplinary nature of contemporary art. Burden, known for his masochistic performances, created such politically charged installations as *The Reason for the Neutron Bomb* (1979).

Impressive public sculptures were commissioned throughout the 1970s and 1980s. Some commissions were publicly acclaimed, such as Isamu Noguchi's 1975 design for Hart Plaza in Detroit, while others, such as minimalist Serra's site-specific *Tilted Arc,* installed in Federal Plaza in New York City, met with negative criticism; *Tilted Arc* was removed in 1989. Maya Lin's abstract design for the Vietnam War Memorial in Washington, D.C., dedicated in 1982, so disappointed conservative critics that a figurative sculptural grouping of three soldiers by Frederick Hart was added.

The pluralistic sculpture of the 1980s was known as new image art. Minimalism had lost momentum and sculptors returned to figurative and metaphorical subjects borrowed from art history and science, appropriating it in surprising ways. The sculpture of Nancy Graves derived from study of taxidermy and fossils. Joel Shapiro constructed minimal stick figures from modules similar to those of André. Scott Burden's rock chairs seemed to be both natural rock formation and functional furniture. Jonathan Borofsky and Siah Armajani created multilayered sculptures that elude precise meaning. In the late 1980s Duane Hanson and John DeAndrea made hyperrealist sculpture. Countering it were the colorful and active neoexpressionist wall assemblages of Judy Pfaff and the brooding abstract bronzes of Julian Schnabel. The 1990s were characterized by variety, exemplified by exhibitions at New York City's Whitney Museum, in which the sculpture ranged from the sardonic pop-inspired objects of Jeff Koons to the elegant abstract pieces of Martin Puryear and the socially poignant installations of Jenny Holzer.

[Richard Armstrong and Richard Marshall, eds., *The New Sculpture, 1965–1975: Between Geometry and Gesture* (New York, 1990); Robert Atkins, *Art Speak: A Guide to Contemporary Ideas, Movements, and Buzzwords* (New York, 1990); Lucy Lippard, *Overlay: Contemporary Art and the Art of Prehistory* (New York, 1983); Daniel Wheeler, *Art Since Mid-Century: 1945 to the Present* (New York, 1991).]

PETER C. SUCHECKI

See also **SUPP:** Architecture; Painting.

SDI. *See* **Strategic Defense Initiative.**

SEALING AND WHALING. For centuries sealing and whaling were accepted means of extracting wealth from the sea. After Earth Day in 1970, however, U.S. citizens began to see these practices as cruel and un-

necessary. Environmental groups that opposed sealing and whaling effectively used the media to gain support in the United States, where few people earned their livings from either pursuit. Sealing had long been an important livelihood on the northeast and northwest coasts of North America. On the Pribilof Islands in the Bering Sea, Aleuts working for private companies in 1867–1910 and then the federal government in 1910–1984 harvested adolescent male fur seals for the fashion industry. The government discontinued the harvest in 1984 when protests against sealing and the fur industry intensified. The harvesting of harp seal pups on the other side of the American subcontinent created a storm of protest. Young harp seals have beautiful, almost pure white coats that serve as excellent camouflage on ice floes against natural predators. Each spring, fishermen from Newfoundland seeking to supplement their meager incomes headed out to the ice floes to gather seal pelts, which involved clubbing the animal on the head and removing the skin. The killing spawned criticism from environmentalists who noted that furs were luxury items and that continued harvesting of the young threatened the species. Television crews filmed the appalling scenes of slaughter. Although harvesting of young seals was a minor problem in the long list of environmental crises facing the global community, the undeniable appeal of baby mammals made it a headline issue that fueled the growth of the environmental and animal rights movements.

Whereas protest against sealing revolved around the animals' appearance, protest against whaling depended largely on the rarity, intelligence, and awe-inspiring presence of whales. By the 1970s most whale species were approaching extinction. Environmental groups, such as Greenpeace and the American Cetacean Society, undertook an ambitious plan to educate U.S. citizens, harass whalers, and challenge the International Whaling Commission (IWC), which had worked ineffectually for decades to maintain whale stocks. In 1972 Congress passed the Marine Mammal Protection Act, which in conjunction with other legislation required the Commerce Department to restrict imports from any country that pursued any policy that harmed worldwide stocks of seals, whales, or dolphins. Throughout the 1970s and 1980s the United States was one of the leaders in pushing the IWC to action. U.S. resolve was crucial in halting most whaling.

[Briton Busch, *The War Against the Seals* (Kingston, Ont., 1985); Richard Ellis, *Men and Whales* (New York, 1991).]

KURK DORSEY

SEATTLE is located in the western part of Washington State, on Puget Sound 120 miles inland from the Pacific Ocean. With a 1994 population of 531,400 and 2.5 million more in the three-county Consolidated Metropolitan Statistical Area, Seattle is the largest city and leading commercial center of the Pacific Northwest. Its traditional economic base has rested on forestry, fishing, and transpacific trade, but during World War II the city became a center of the aircraft industry. Native Americans, including the chief for whom the city was named, had villages along the shore before the first Euro-Americans settled there in 1851. Fishing, timber cutting, and the milling of lumber destined for California were early industries as the village spread along Elliott Bay. Several early developments helped assure a permanent role for Seattle. The city acquired the territorial (later state) university in 1861, and a substantial business district was rebuilt after a fire in 1889 destroyed wooden buildings and piers. After becoming the terminus of the Great Northern Railway in 1893, Seattle emerged as a taking-off point and provision supplier for prospectors headed for the Klondike gold rush in 1897; the physical expansion of the city was made possible when hills were leveled early in the twentieth century to fill tideflats and ravines. A vital labor movement, highlighted by a citywide general strike in 1919, gave Seattle a radical reputation, but it also helped create a population of emerging middle-class homeowners and few extremes of rich and poor.

A growing identity and self-assurance followed World War II, but Seattle entered the 1970s suffering from a severe recession after the dominant Boeing Company experienced reverses common to the cyclical aircraft industry. Prosperity returned as Boeing and the area diversified. Container shipping facilities revitalized water-borne commerce, and an electronics and computer software industry emerged. The city struggled to offset the growth of burgeoning suburban areas and maintain a viable downtown while also seeking to strengthen neighborhoods. A covered stadium, an aquarium, a convention center, an art museum, and an underground bus tunnel were built downtown. Culturally, Seattle in the 1990s was marked by increasing ethnic diversification and influence, although the dominant white population remained three-fourths of the total; many newcomers arrived from small Asian nations. A popular youth culture of "grunge" dress and music became nationally influential. Seattle's reputation for surrounding natural beauty, increasing cultural and recreational amenities, and a casual lifestyle made the city attractive to visitors and potential residents even as officials wrestled with major transportation difficulties, educational inequities, and emerging crime problems.

[Murray Morgan, *Skid Road: An Informal Portrait of Seattle* (Seattle, 1982); Roger Sale, *Seattle Past and Present* (Seattle, 1976).]

CHARLES P. LEWARNE

See also **DAH:** Puget Sound; Seattle World's Fair; **DAH** and **SUPP:** Washington, State of.

SELF-HELP MOVEMENT is a vast collection of mostly small, local groups of people loosely linked through national newsletters or associations. These groups seek to reach, through mutual support, such goals as physical, mental, and spiritual enhancement; the ability to cope with loss or social stigma; upgrading occupational status; improving interpersonal relations; and achieving competence in specialized activities. Although physicians, social workers, therapists, clergy, and other professionals often initially form and convene self-help groups, their continued involvement is usually limited. Groups have not been the only vehicle through which self-help activities have been undertaken. With the development and growth in popularity of videocassettes and personal computers, along with books, magazines, and recordings, entrepreneurs have created a huge and thriving industry of self-help materials that consumers can use by themselves. This trend appears to have diminished the need for groups, making self-help less a grassroots social movement and more a vast sea of isolated individuals seeking personal change.

[Alfred H. Katz and Eugene I. Bender, *The Strength in Us: Self-Help Groups in the Modern World* (New York, 1976); Stephen Starker, *Oracle at the Supermarket: The American Preoccupation with Self-Help Books* (New Brunswick, N.J., 1989).]

NORMAN GEVITZ

SEMICONDUCTORS. The electrical conductivity of this class of solids is less than that of conductors but greater than that of insulators. Highly refined semiconducting elements such as silicon and germanium can be made more conductive by adding trace impurities, a process called doping. Electron-rich or electron-deficient elements produce negative (n-type) or positive (p-type) semiconductors that, when joined together, create one-way gates for electric current (diodes). More complex electrical junctions lead to devices that can amplify weak electrical signals (transistors), store electric charges (electronic memory), or convert electric energy to light (solid-state lasers and photodiodes).

Invention of the junction transistor in 1948 produced a revolution in the military and consumer electronics industries and allowed for the development of fast and efficient electronic computers. In little more than a decade transistors replaced bulky and inefficient vacuum tubes. Breakthroughs in technology enabled the coupling of diodes and transistors into integrated circuits and computer processing chips. Computer chips containing more than a million switches (bits) per square millimeter were commonplace by the 1990s, and three-dimensional stacks of these chips permitted densities exceeding one billion switches per cubic inch. Because electrical signals cannot travel faster than the speed of light, the increasing speeds at which computers processed information were linked to development of high-density microchips.

In addition to use in computers and consumer electronics, semiconductor devices find wide application in solar energy and in light-sensing, where large arrays of microscopic detectors (charge-coupled devices, or CCDs) produce highly sensitive, high-resolution video cameras and astronomical telescopes. Miniaturized chemical detectors also are possible by depositing thin reactive films onto semiconductors, with applications ranging from detecting polychlorinated biphenyl (PCB) vapors in office buildings and drug levels in the blood to monitoring hydrogen levels in the cabin of a space shuttle.

[Alan M. Litke and Andreas Schwarz, "The Silicon Microstrip Detector," *Scientific American* (May 1995); Gary Stix, "Toward 'Point One,'" *Scientific American* (February 1995); Ken Zweibel, "Thin Film Photovoltaic Cells," *American Scientist* (July-August 1993).]

DAVID K. LEWIS

See also **DAH** and **SUPP**: Computers; **SUPP**: Computer Industry.

SERIAL KILLINGS. According to the National Institute of Justice, serial killings, or serial murders, are series of two or more murders committed as separate events, usually but not always by one offender acting alone over a period of time ranging from hours to years. Often the motive is psychological, with the offender's behavior and the evidence reflecting sadistic, sexual overtones. Law enforcement officials estimate that in the 1990s there were between thirty and fifty serial killers active at any given time in the United States. Records of serial killings in the fif-

teenth and sixteenth centuries and the murders by Jack the Ripper in nineteenth-century England attest that the practice is not new, nor are serial killings strictly a U.S. phenomenon. The former Soviet Union bred a number of serial killers, although their existence did not become manifest until the collapse of communism in 1990. Andrei Chikatilo, a schoolteacher and factory procurer from the small coal-mining town of Shakti, holds the modern record—fifty-two known killings, mostly children under the age of twelve. The largest number of serial killers, however, have been North American. Although victims of serial murders are few in comparison with other murders, the twentieth century saw a marked increase in serial killings. Serial murders are committed by members of all races and both genders, acting in pairs or even in gangs, but the greatest number are committed by single white males. A small percentage of serial murderers act because of greed or the possibility of gain. Curiously, the number of female killers with such purposes is almost triple that for female serial killers who act for other reasons. Serial killings, once recognized, receive great attention from the media. Among the most notorious serial killers of the second half of the twentieth century are Ted Bundy, who raped and murdered women in several states in the 1970s and 1980s (executed in 1989); Albert DeSalvo, known as the Boston Strangler; New York's David Berkowitz, known as Son of Sam; Wayne Williams of Atlanta; Richard Ramirez of southern California; and Jeffrey L. Dahmer, who by his own admission tortured, killed, and dismembered men and boys in Milwaukee and was convicted in 1992 of killing fifteen. Sentenced to fifteen consecutive life terms, Dahmer was himself bludgeoned to death in prison in 1994.

[David Lester, *Serial Killers* (Philadelphia, 1995); Michael Newton, *Hunting Humans* (Port Townsend, Wash., 1990); Joel Norris, *Serial Killers* (New York, 1988).]

ROBERT M. GUTH

See also **DAH** and **SUPP**: Crime.

SET-ASIDES, a form of affirmative action used by governments in contracting government business, including programs that typically designate a percentage of government contracts or funds (either for services or construction of public works) for minority-owned businesses. In 1977 Congress passed a law that directed 10 percent of federal public works funds to minority-controlled businesses. The Public Works Employment Act defined these businesses as ones in which 50 percent of the business was held by African Americans, Hispanics, Asian Americans, Native Americans, Eskimos, or Aleuts. Set-asides are adopted in the belief that government support for minority-owned businesses will help overcome traditional economic disadvantages minorities have faced and promote economic development in minority communities. Like affirmative action programs generally, set-aside programs are controversial. Opponents claim that they constitute reverse discrimination and are not cost efficient, because contracts go to businesses that may not have been the lowest bidder or the most qualified.

Constitutional challenges to set-aside programs have met with mixed results. In *Fullilove* v. *Klutznick* (1980) the Supreme Court upheld the 1977 federal program, finding it did not violate the equal protection clause of the Fifth Amendment or Title VI of the Civil Rights Act of 1964 because it was a legitimate exercise of Congress's spending power. In *City of Richmond* v. *J. A. Croson Company* (1989), however, the Court struck down a municipal set-aside program, stating that the Fourteenth Amendment authorizes Congress, not state and local governments, to create remedies for racial discrimination. This decision called into question the constitutionality of similar programs in twenty-two states. In 1993 the Court permitted contractors in Jacksonville, Fla., to file suit against that city's program, which was modeled after the 1977 federal statute *(Northeastern Florida Chapter of the Associated General Contractors of America* v. *City of Jacksonville).* Signaling a new level of skepticism about all such programs, in 1995 the Court held that the federal government must be subject to the same "strict scrutiny" as state and local governments when attempting to remedy discrimination. In *Adarand Constructors, Inc.* v. *PENA* the Supreme Court rejected a federal set-aside program established in the Small Business Act to aid "socially disadvantaged individuals."

[Kent Greenawalt, *Discrimination and Reverse Discrimination* (New York, 1983).]

KATY J. HARRIGER

See also **SUPP:** Affirmative Action; *Richmond* v. *J. A. Croson Company.*

SEXUAL HARASSMENT, the most common and often most subtle form of sexual abuse experienced by women in the United States, was frequently trivialized as unimportant until the Senate confirmation hearings of Clarence Thomas for the Supreme Court in October 1991. The testimony of Anita Hill, who worked for Thomas while he was director of the Equal Employment Opportunity Commission (EEOC), was met with sexist responses by senators who supported President George Bush's nomination of Thomas and gave sexual harassment prominence as a serious issue. By the mid-1990s the United States led the industrialized world with respect to sexual harassment legislation and guidelines, according to a 1992 report by the International Labor Organization. The Thomas confirmation hearings prompted such concern among women across the United States that in 1992 an unprecedented number ran for political office and won. Twenty-one obtained state executive office and 1,374 entered state legislatures. Eleven women ran for the U.S. Senate, several of them opposing men who had supported Thomas; five won, as did one female incumbent. Twenty-nine women (twenty-two of them new members) won in races for the House of Representatives, for a total of forty-eight. Also significant during the 1992 elections was the fact that a variety of sexual accusations became major issues in state and national races involving several male politicians. In 1993, for the first time in American history, a president had to take sexual harassment charges into consideration when making appointments to office. That same year the U.S. Navy issued guidelines to prevent sexual harassment within its ranks following the embarrassment, firings, and resignations caused by the Tailhook incident of 1991, when drunken naval aviators assaulted female officers at the aviators' annual convention.

In its broadest sense, sexual harassment is the unwanted imposition of sexual requirements in the context of a relationship of unequal power. As more technically defined by the 1980 guidelines of EEOC, sexual harassment can be any behavior that has the "purpose or effect of unreasonably interfering with an individual's work performance or creating an intimidating or hostile or offensive environment . . . [including] unwelcome sexual advances, requests for sexual favors, and other verbal or physical conduct of a sexual nature." Despite this inclusive federal definition, during the presidency of Ronald Reagan (1981–1989) the EEOC under Thomas did not make the enforcement of sexual harassment a top priority. It is estimated that anywhere from 30 to 70 percent of all working women will experience or have experienced some type of sexual harassment. (Figures for sexual harassment vary dramatically because there have been no national statistical studies that controlled for type of job—blue-collar, pink-collar, or white-collar female workers—let alone women in professional or executive positions.) In the mid-1970s surveys indicated that women in factories and the military experienced more sexual harassment than pink- or white-collar clerical personnel. A 1981 study of federal government workers indicated that 42 percent had been sexually harassed. In 1986 the Association of American Colleges documented that one-third of tenured female faculty members at Harvard University and half of untenured ones reported being sexually harassed. This same study estimated that as many as 40 percent of all undergraduate women and 29 percent of female graduate students had been harassed by faculty members. On most campuses, however, the 40 to 60 percent of female students who report being sexually harassed say that it is by other students. In 1986 the United Nations Ad Hoc Groups on Equal Rights for Women reported that half the women interviewed had been victims of sexual harassment on the job. A 1990 Defense Department study substantiated that two-thirds of female military personnel had endured such abuse.

Two types of sexual harassment are recognized under U.S. law. First, there is quid pro quo harassment—being fired or forced to quit for not complying with sexual demands. The second type is more subtle and occurs when the harassment becomes a pervasive condition of work, that is, constitutes a hostile work environment but for which dismissal or demotion is not necessary to prove employment discrimination. This type of sexual harassment was not recognized as sex discrimination under Title VII of the 1964 Civil Rights Act until the U.S. Supreme Court decision in *Meritor Savings Bank* v. *Mechelle Vinson* in 1986. Before *Meritor* the 1980 EEOC guidelines prohibited sexual harassment under various circumstances, including the creation of an "intimidating or hostile or offensive environment." The *Meritor* case marked the first time the Supreme Court attempted to interpret these guidelines, although they had been variously used between 1980 and 1986 by lower courts.

Because hostile work-environment harassment began to be recognized as actionable only in the late 1980s, so much confusion remained at the federal circuit court level in the early 1990s that the Supreme Court granted certiorari to resolve discrepancies between districts over how to determine the level of harm and employer liability. In the summer of 1993 the New Jersey Supreme Court took up this challenge to set standards that both employees and employers could understand and which the latter could enforce. In *Lehmann* v. *Toys 'R' Us, Inc.* (1993), the New Jersey court in a detailed decision outlined four stan-

dards. First, a plaintiff has a cause for action when "he or she alleges discriminatory conduct that a reasonable person of the same sex in the plaintiff's position would consider sufficiently severe or pervasive to alter conditions of employment and to create intimidating, hostile or offensive working environment," and that the plaintiff need not be the direct target of harassing conduct. Second, in cases of supervisory sexual harassment the cumulative effect of incidents and not just single incidents will determine whether the employer "will be held strictly liable for equitable damages and relief," regardless of whether such discrimination is intentional or unintentional. Third, in cases where supervisors act as the employers' surrogates or abuse their authority, employers will be vicariously liable under the principles of agency law for compensatory damages that exceed equitable relief. Fourth, employers will not be held liable for punitive damages unless they authorize, approve, or participate in creating an offensive working environment. *Lehmann* set forth the most logical set of tests and reasoned standards for state and federal courts to follow in deciding sexual harassment cases for the remainder of the 1990s.

[Joan Hoff, *Law, Gender, and Injustice,* rev. ed. (New York, 1994); Catharine MacKinnon, *Sexual Harassment and Working Women* (New Haven, Conn., 1979); Jane Mayer and Jill Abramson, *Strange Justice: The Selling of Clarence Thomas* (Boston, 1994).]

JOAN HOFF

See also **SUPP:** *Meritor Savings Bank* v. *Mechelle Vinson;* Tailhook Incident; Women's Movement; Women's Rights.

SEXUALITY. In the aftermath of the "sexual revolution" of the 1960s, Americans remained deeply ambivalent in their attitudes toward sex as the twentieth century neared its close. Despite their insatiable appetite for sexual images, manifested in the explosion of sexually oriented advertising, movies, videos, and talk shows, Americans had difficulty talking about sexual attitudes and practice and continued to cling to puritanical notions that relegated sexual matters to the privacy of the marital bedroom. In many respects, technology surged into the twenty-first century while attitudes remained frozen in the past.

This ambivalence toward sexuality inhibited much-needed scientific research into post–sexual revolution changes in sexual attitudes and practice. Without major support from either government or private foundations, research was conducted on a limited scale in sex clinics, specialized academic fields, and popular literature. Following the controversial *Kinsey Report* of the 1950s, researchers William H. Masters and Virginia C. Johnson pushed back the boundaries of sexual research in the 1970s by moving from the interviews Alfred C. Kinsey had employed to direct observation of sexual activity. From their Saint Louis institute, Masters and Johnson recorded sexual interplay of married couples in order to develop therapeutic methods for enhancing the desired responses. While they pioneered controversial methods for recording sexual response, their aim was conservative. Believing that human beings thrive in long-term, heterosexual, monogamous relationships, Masters and Johnson focused on achieving a working sexual relationship within marriage by curing dysfunction. Reflecting their emphasis on marriage, they explained a great deal about sexual response in middle and old age, offering information about the aging process designed to preserve sexual response in aging couples.

One of the most important areas of sex research to emerge from academe was in the field of cognitive development. In 1987 social scientists Lisa A. Serbin and Carol H. Sprafkin proposed a developmental model using schema theory to show the relationship between cognitive and sexual development. According to schema theory, our most basic cognitive development is linked to sexual identification. Beginning with pink and blue blankets in the nursery, infants are sexually marked. This early identification forms our most basic schema for sorting information. Serbin and Sprafkin identified differing developmental patterns in boys and girls. Because male sex organs are visible and more easily manipulated, boys reach the level of cognitive development needed to understand their sexual organs much earlier than girls. For boys, cognitive development is achieved at the same age as sexual maturity; whereas in girls, there is a five- or six-year gap between physical maturity and the cognitive development needed to understand their sexual organs. Serbin and Sprafkin suggested that this gap could account for the high rates of teenage pregnancy in the United States. In showing the relation between sexual and cognitive development, developmental theory can aid realistic sex education programs that take into account the stages of sexual development.

In other fields, scientific inquiry was polarized along the lines of the nature-versus-nurture debate. Research in the physical sciences, especially cell development, endocrinology, and brain function, stressed biological differences between male and female sexual development, whereas social scientists emphasized the importance of social and cultural conditioning in shaping human sexuality. This debate created a paradox wherein the physical sciences catalogued differences between men and women while social sciences noted similarities. In grappling with this paradox, researchers sought to understand the interaction between nature and nurture in the development of human sexuality. After twenty-five years of debate, the consensus suggested that biology (nature) physically determines male and female forms while culture (nurture) inscribes those forms with socially constructed, communally enforced gender roles to order sexual relations. Thus, while nature determines, nurture governs.

This principle was borne out in the 1990s by the most extensive survey of sexual practice in the United States since Kinsey. In 1987 the National Health and Social Life Survey (NHSLS) began as a response to the AIDS epidemic. Initially intended to survey the sexual practice of 20,000 Americans, the study was significantly scaled back when it lost government funding in 1991. Carrying on with private funds, the NHSLS surveyed more than 3,500 individuals. The results of the NHSLS survey contradicted results of popular surveys, suggesting that sexual practice was more conservative than what was described by the *Hite Report,* the *Janus Report,* and *Redbook* and *Playboy* magazines. While noting the dramatic change in sexual openness driven by popular culture, the NHSLS survey concluded that sexual attitudes are formed by social groups, sexual practice is prescribed by social norms, the choice of sexual partners is limited to individuals within social networks, and sexual events are scripted by social convention.

While Americans were less promiscuous and more convention-bound than reported by the popular surveys, the NHSLS report noted significant changes in sexual behavior after the 1970s. Americans were having more sexual partners over their lifetimes, but they tended to have one partner at a time and generally remain faithful to that partner while the relationship lasted. In refuting the myth of widespread promiscuity, the study asserted that only a few had many partners, while many had a few partners. Marriage remained the most popular institution for regulating sexual relations, although cohabitation was widely practiced as a precursor of marriage. Fewer women were virgins when they married, although the survey noted a slight increase in the number of male virgins. Americans were engaging in sexual activity both earlier and later in life and arrived at the peak of sexual activity in their twenties. In sum, the report concluded that Americans were having their first sexual experience at an earlier age, were marrying later, divorcing more, and having more sexual partners in the course of their lives.

[Paul R. Abramson and Steven D. Pinkerton, eds., *Sexual Nature, Sexual Culture* (Chicago, 1995); Robert T. Michael, John H. Gagnon, Edward O. Laumann, and Gina Kolata, *Sex in America: A Definitive Survey* (Boston, 1994); Paul A. Robinson, *The Modernization of Sex* (New York, 1976); Lisa A. Serbin and Carol H. Sprafkin, "A Developmental Approach: Sexuality from Infancy through Adolescence," in James H. Geer and William O'Donohue, eds., *Theories of Human Sexuality* (New York, 1987).]

MARIAN YEATES

See also **DAH:** Sexual Attitudes; **SUPP:** Marriage and Divorce; Sexual Orientation; Sexually Transmitted Diseases.

SEXUALLY TRANSMITTED DISEASES (STDs),

formerly known as venereal diseases and now called sexually transmitted infections (STIs) or reproductive tract infections (RTIs), are a major health problem in the United States. Twelve million new cases of STDs occur each year, two-thirds of them among persons under age twenty-five. At that rate one American in four will acquire an STD at some time in his or her life. Until the early 1980s only five STDs—syphilis, gonorrhea, chancroid, lymphogranuloma venereum, and granuloma inguinale—were widely recognized. By the mid-1990s more than fifty organisms and syndromes were known to be transmitted sexually. With the possible exception of acquired immune deficiency syndrome (AIDS), none of the STDs on this expanded list is "new"; rather, advances in medical technology have permitted more accurate diagnosis of many of these infections. Still, there was a large increase in the incidence of STDs in the latter decades of the twentieth century. Changes in sexual mores increased the number of years in which individuals are sexually active. Many sexually active persons have several sexual partners (on average, adults have seven partners during their lifetimes), which raises their chances of encountering someone infected with an STD. Moreover, most people with multiple partners are not consistent users of condoms, which can substantially reduce the risk of infection. Some diseases, including chlamydia (the most common STD), gonorrhea, and syphilis, are caused by bacteria and can generally be cured easily with antibiotics if diagnosed early. STDs caused by viruses, however, such as genital herpes, human papilloma virus (HPV, or genital warts), hepatitis B, and human

immunodeficiency virus (HIV), the last of which causes AIDS, cannot be cured and can be passed on to sexual partners even when no symptoms are present. STDs have a disproportionate effect on women, because women become infected more easily than men, infections are harder to diagnose in women, and the complications of infection are more severe in women. Thousands of women each year become infertile or experience life-endangering fallopian-tube pregnancy (ectopic pregnancy) as a result of STD infection. Infected women can transmit an STD to their offspring during pregnancy or childbirth with devastating results. STDs exact a huge financial cost. The costs of just three diseases—chlamydia, gonorrhea, and herpes—are estimated at $5 billion annually.

[Allan M. Brandt, *No Magic Bullet: A Social History of Venereal Disease in the United States Since 1880* (New York, 1987); Patricia Donovan, *Testing Positive: Sexually Transmitted Disease and the Public Health Response* (New York, 1993).]

PATRICIA DONOVAN

See also **SUPP:** Acquired Immune Deficiency Syndrome.

SEXUAL ORIENTATION. A person's erotic, romantic, and affectional attraction to the other sex, the same sex, or both is referred to as sexual orientation. An individual who is attracted to the other sex is referred to as heterosexual or straight. A person attracted to the same sex is called homosexual, gay (a term more often applied to men), or lesbian if she is a woman. One who is attracted to both men and women is bisexual. The term "sexual preference" is sometimes used instead of "sexual orientation" but may be misleading because it implies conscious preference or choice. Sexual orientation is a part of sexual identity, a sense of self that also includes how one identifies in terms of gender. Identity as male or female is relatively independent of sexual orientation. Homosexuality is not synonymous with transsexuality; lesbian women do not believe themselves to be or wish to be men and gay men do not have a female gender identity. Sexual fantasies, sexual behavior, and the gender of the person with whom one falls in love are not always consistent and may change over a lifetime. A woman may live happily in a monogamous marriage for many years, never questioning her heterosexuality. Later she may fall in love with a woman and begin to develop a lesbian identity. Heterosexual men in prison may engage in sexual behavior with men because of the absence of female partners (referred to as situational or circumstantial homosexuality). When no longer imprisoned they may choose women partners exclusively. Such men identify as heterosexual although their lifetime behavior patterns might be considered bisexual.

Scientific concepts of sexual orientation have evolved since the late nineteenth century, when the terms "sexual inversion" and "homosexuality" were introduced by John Addington Symonds and Havelock Ellis. In the late 1940s Alfred C. Kinsey and his colleagues developed the concept of a bipolar continuum of sexual orientation ranging from exclusive heterosexuality to exclusive homosexuality, now known as the "Kinsey Scale." Prior to this many scholars regarded heterosexuals and homosexuals as distinct categories and bisexuals as homosexuals repressing their true identities and/or trying to "pass" as heterosexual. Since Kinsey, others have proposed more complex models to describe and quantify variability in sexual orientation. For example, homosexuality and heterosexuality may be seen as independent dimensions—a person high on both is bisexual, a person low on both is asexual; and persons high on one scale and low on the other are homosexual and heterosexual, respectively.

In 1956, at the annual meeting of the American Psychological Association, Evelyn Hooker presented a paper documenting normal psychological adjustment patterns in nonclinical samples of male homosexuals. Prior to this time, with the exception of Ellis and Kinsey's work, there was little scientific literature that was not founded in a pathological model for understanding homosexuality. Hooker's work was largely overlooked until 1967, when Stanley Yolles, director of the National Institute of Mental Health, appointed a task force on homosexuality. Its final report was issued in October 1969, six months after the Stonewall riots in New York City marked the beginning of the gay liberation movement. In addition to recommendations regarding further research, the report included recommendations related to social policy and others related to treatment and prevention. The former were welcomed positively by the organizing gay community, whereas the latter were less welcomed.

Despite growing evidence to the contrary, psychopathological explanations of homosexuality were still widely believed, particularly among psychoanalysts, but in 1973 the American Psychiatric Association removed homosexuality from its *Diagnostic and Statistical Manual of Mental Disorders*. Many psychiatrists, particularly those whose work was based in

psychodynamic theory, remained opposed to "normalizing" homosexual behavior, citing writings of psychoanalysts reporting on homosexuality as a psychopathological condition that could be "cured" for at least some proportion of individuals through psychoanalytic techniques. As a compromise, in 1980 the term "ego-dystonic homosexuality" was included in the *Manual*. Further debate led to the removal of this term in 1986 and inclusion of a statement in a more neutral manner that some individuals may wish to change sexual orientation.

Attitudes toward homosexuality underwent many changes in the last decades of the twentieth century as a result of increased understanding of sexual orientation, further questioning of psychodynamic theory, and activism for gay and lesbian rights. Many psychoanalytically trained psychiatrists, however, still view homosexuality as psychopathological. Some religious and political groups also maintain that homosexuality is pathological or immoral. In the 1990s discrimination against homosexuals was common, and there were vocal groups on both sides of the issue regarding the acceptance of homosexuality as an alternate lifestyle or its condemnation as a perversion, sin against God, or transgression against society. Most professionals today question the ethics of using therapy to try to change a trait that is not a disorder and is such an important aspect of an individual's identity. In general, interventions to change sexual orientations of homosexuals have led to reduced sexual behavior and self-esteem rather than creating or enhancing attraction to the other sex.

Many theories about the etiology of sexual orientation have been put forward. Sigmund Freud did not view homosexuality as a mental illness but suggested that homosexual men tended to have weak or absent fathers and domineering mothers, seductive mothers, or unresolved oedipal feelings. Later psychoanalysts adopted a more pathological view. Others suggested homosexuality was caused by seductive other-sex parents, seduction by older persons of the same sex, rape (for lesbianism), or insufficient heterosexual opportunities during development. There is, however, little empirical support for these psychoanalytic and social environmental theories. Early gender nonconformity (sissy behavior in boys and tomboyism in girls), especially in the extreme, may be indicative of a predisposition toward homosexuality, but the cause of the gender nonconformity remains a question.

Later studies highlighted the potential role of biological factors in sexual orientation. These include findings suggesting genetic causes of homosexuality, reports of neuroanatomical and neuropsychological differences in the brains of homosexuals compared to heterosexuals, and evidence that the prenatal hormone environment may affect the relative masculinization/demasculinization or feminization/defeminization of the brain and thus influence behavioral development. By the 1990s, however, many experts thought nature (biological determinism) versus nurture (environment or social determinism) arguments overly simplistic. Sexual orientation appears to result from the interaction of nature and nurture, each influencing the other at critical periods. Likely to develop in stages, sexual orientation appears to be formed by complex interactions of biological, psychological, social, cultural, and circumstantial factors with multiple developmental pathways possible.

[Alan P. Bell, Martin S. Weinberg, and Sue Kiefer Hammersmith, *Sexual Preference: Its Development in Men and Women* (Bloomington, Ind., 1981); Richard Green, *The "Sissy Boy Syndrome" and the Development of Homosexuality* (New Haven, Conn., 1987); Dean H. Hamer and Peter Copeland, *The Science of Desire: The Search for the Gay Gene and the Biology of Behavior* (New York, 1994); Simon LeVay, *The Sexual Brain* (Cambridge, Mass., 1993); David P. McWhirter, Stephanie A. Sanders, and June M. Reinisch, eds., *Homosexuality/Heterosexuality: Concepts of Sexual Orientation* (New York, 1990).]

STEPHANIE A. SANDERS

See also **DAH:** Sexual Attitudes; **SUPP:** Gay and Lesbian Movement; Psychology; Sexuality.

SHIPPING INDUSTRY. *See* **Merchant Marine.**

SIDS. *See* **Sudden Infant Death Syndrome.**

SILICON VALLEY, located around Santa Clara and San Jose, California, is the home of many key U.S. corporations specializing in advanced electronic and information technologies. First called "Silicon Valley" in 1971 by a local newsletter writer, Donald C. Hoefler, the "Valley" became the center of technologies that many believed would revolutionize computers, telecommunications, manufacturing procedures, warfare, and even U.S. society itself. The name came to symbolize a type of high-risk business characterized by rapid success or failure, extensive job mobility, and informal behavior, traits thought by some to be the wave of the future. The location of such high-tech research, development, and manufacturing in an area once known as the "prune capital of America"

was not coincidental. Stanford University in nearby Palo Alto provided a research-oriented institution active in engineering and electronics. In 1951 Stanford established a research park where companies could build facilities and conduct research in cooperation with the university, the first such enterprise in the country.

If there was a founder of Silicon Valley it was William Shockley, an English-born physicist who worked on early concepts of the transistor at Bell Laboratories before World War II and became director of Bell's Transistor Physics Research Group. A restless person whose inquisitive mind and entrepreneurial aspirations did not find satisfaction in the larger corporation, he became a visiting professor at the California Institute of Technology in 1954 and the following year founded Shockley Semiconductor Laboratories just south of Palo Alto in the north end of Silicon Valley. Shockley's business acumen did not equal his skills in science and engineering. In 1957 eight of his engineers created Fairchild Semiconductor, supported by Fairchild Camera and Instrument. Their departure established a mobility that would characterize careers in Silicon Valley and elsewhere in electronics companies where employees shunned ties of corporate loyalty in favor of personal fulfillment and financial reward. Fairchild Semiconductor later lost employees as well. In 1968 Robert Noyce, Gordon Moore, and Andrew Grove left to establish Intel. Another Fairchild employee, W. J. Sanders III, founded Advanced Micro Devices soon thereafter. In the early 1970s one survey found forty-one companies in Silicon Valley headed by former Fairchild employees. This pattern continued into the 1980s with such companies as National Semiconductor, Atari, Apple Computer, LSI Logic, and Cypress Semiconductor having all or part of their origins in Silicon Valley.

To many observers the California location was central to the success and, later, the problems of Silicon Valley. The popular image of California, with its promise of individual and professional renewal, played a part, as did the cultural climate of the 1960s, which criticized large organizations for suppressing personal expression. The moderate climate of Silicon Valley combined with a pool of educated talent from California universities, and a largely nonunion work force attracted investors and corporations. Publicity about Silicon Valley in the 1970s generated discussion about options for U.S. industry, especially in electronics. The Valley to a degree represented a shift in political and economic power from the older industrialized Northeast and Midwest to the Pacific Coast. The rise of Silicon Valley occurred at a time when many electronics companies were affected by changes in financial markets and availability of capital. During the 1950s and early 1960s much of the Valley relied on military contracts, but this dependence declined as commercial and then personal markets for computers emerged. Investors hoping for a very high rate of return increasingly were willing to risk supporting these companies even if as many as 25 percent would fail after a few years. Demand for capital increased as the size of electronic components such as memory chips decreased. With smaller size came the need for more sophisticated and costly technologies in manufacturing. By the late 1980s companies estimated they needed as much as $1 billion to establish a manufacturing facility for the latest generation of semiconductors. Observers of investment practices and corporate strategies began to worry that this reliance on venture capital had created a pattern in U.S. business that stressed short-term profits rather than longer-term concerns about product development and competition from foreign corporations. Silicon Valley's success and the boost it gave to California's image and economy led such states as Oregon, Michigan, Texas, Colorado, New York, and Minnesota to invite or promote advanced electronic firms. In the 1990s, however, Silicon Valley remained the major indicator of the health of the industry.

Products such as memory and logic chips, microprocessors, and custom-made circuits are expensive to manufacture, subject to price-cutting in the market, and have a short product life (sometimes two years or less) before the next generation appears. Their sale depends on the health of important segments of U.S. industry, including computers, telecommunications systems, automobiles, and military contractors. Silicon Valley and its counterparts elsewhere in the United States thus are subject to cycles of boom and bust. The latter occurred in 1984–1986, when many of the Valley's companies found themselves with surplus products after a drop in the U.S. personal computer market. Companies had to lay off workers and some went out of business. Foreign competition, especially from Japan, was perhaps the greatest cause of problems for Silicon Valley. Business and political leaders debated whether or not trade policy needed to defend the interests of U.S. electronics firms more aggressively and whether U.S. companies should receive government funding to make them more competitive in the international market. Silicon Valley had begun to worry about

Japanese competition by the late 1970s. In 1981 U.S. companies controlled 51.4 percent of the world's semiconductor market; Japan's share was 35.5 percent. Within seven years the figures were virtually reversed, with Japan at 51 percent and the United States 36.5 percent. U.S. companies charged their Japanese counterparts with dumping semiconductors onto the U.S. market at low prices to undercut U.S. manufacturers while Japan kept much of its home market closed. The Semiconductor Industry Association, representing many companies in Silicon Valley urged bilateral agreements to open Japan's market. The first of these was signed in 1986 and a second followed in 1992. By the early 1990s it appeared that U.S. industry had started to recover some of the ground lost to Japan.

Meanwhile, the lure of Silicon Valley was lessened by several factors. New technologies, the ascent of successful electronic-component manufacturing elsewhere in the United States, and foreign competition moved attention away from Silicon Valley. People learned that the manufacturing of electronic components was not as environmentally clean or safe as some thought; the growth of the Valley led to traffic congestion and air pollution; and in the early 1990s California's economy experienced a serious recession. Silicon Valley remained a center of research, development, and manufacturing in the electronics industry but its symbolic role as a frontier of industrial and social organization was no longer certain.

[Tom Forester, *High-Tech Society* (Cambridge, Mass., 1987); Robert Teitelman, *Profits of Science* (New York, 1994).]

KENNETH B. MOSS

See also **SUPP:** California; Computer Industry; Computers.

SINGLE PARENTHOOD. *See* **Family.**

SKIING. During the 1980s skiing reached a peak of popularity as a recreational activity, and U.S. downhill skiers excelled on the international competitive circuit. Phil Mahre won World Cups from 1981 through 1983, Tamara McKinney won the women's World Cup in 1983, and the United States earned an unprecedented three gold medals in skiing at the 1984 Winter Olympics, including Bill Johnson's victory in the men's downhill. Weakened by injuries, the 1988 U.S. Olympic ski team gave a disappointing performance, but the sport's recreational popularity continued to rise as technological improvements in equipment made skiing safer. Lift-ticket sales increased from $51.4 million during the 1984–1985 season to more than $1 billion in 1986–1987, but sales declined to $900 million by 1989, partly because the price of an all-day lift ticket rose. Other alternatives to traditional skiing included snowboarding, mogul skiing, ski dancing, tree skiing, bordercross (a variation on snowboarding that is like a slalom but with five skiers on the course at once), aerial freestyle skiing, and heli-skiing. A turnaround in U.S. competitive alpine skiing fortunes occurred at the 1994 Winter Olympics in Lillehammer, Norway, capped by the efforts of Tommy Moe, who became the second American to capture the gold medal in the downhill. Diann Roffe-Steinrotter won a gold medal in the women's Super-G alpine skiing event.

[Ralph Hickok, *The Encyclopedia of North American Sports History* (New York, 1992); Richard Needham, *Ski: Fifty Years in North America* (New York, 1987).]

DAVID P. MCDANIEL

See also **SUPP:** Olympic Games; Sports, New.

SKINHEADS. *See* **White Supremacists.**

SKYSCRAPERS. *See* **Architecture.**

SLANG, informal language of a highly picturesque and metaphorical nature, is often ingenious and amusing. It is usually created as a more convenient, more private, or more entertaining means of communication than anything available in the standard language. Its terms are only temporary but are widely dispersed during their popularity. Gradations between slang and standard English are often difficult to distinguish, because language is a living entity, constantly taking in new members and dismissing old ones. Terms such as "show off," "chisel," "bootlegger," "racketeer," "movie," and "OK" had risen from slang to standard English by the 1950s, and some of the slang of the 1960s, 1970s, and 1980s such as "dude," "online," and "boom box" achieved standard usage by the 1990s. Most slang, such as the language of citizens band radio users in the 1970s or "Valley girls" in the 1980s, faded before reaching acceptability. The improved communications systems of the twentieth century shortened the time it takes for slang terms to reach acceptance and caused the regional character of slang to decline. In the 1920s and 1930s slang of national currency was created and disseminated by radio, motion pictures, and nationally syndicated comic strips and gossip columns. The coming of television in the 1950s and cable TV in the 1980s added a still more powerful means of disseminating slang.

Little slang was used in the United States before the great westward movement of the nineteenth century. Freed from the conventionality of eastern settlements, pioneers expressed their exuberant optimism and individualism in dazzling extravagances. The humorous literature of the Old Southwest introduced such terms as "rambunctious," "skedaddle," "shebang," "galoot," "stewed," and "woozy." The books of Mark Twain are rich repositories of the slang of the mid-nineteenth-century Middle and Far West.

The objects, actions, and ideas described with slang are in some ways constant. Each generation's subcultures produce hundreds of new terms related to sex, alcohol (and more recently drugs), and bodily parts and functions. At any given time a society's slang also reflects the popular preoccupations of its culture. Slang of the early 1940s reflected a nation at war and was drawn mostly from the military. The beginning of the Space Age in the 1950s added such terms as "in orbit," "blast off," "countdown," and "A-OK." In the 1960s society's fascination with the hippie counterculture increased the slang of drug use, radical politics, and rock music ("far out," "freaked out," "strung out," "bummed out"). The 1980s saw the emergence of another counterculture, an urban, African-American youth culture that found its expression in rap music and the spread of its slang soon followed ("homey," "hood," "dissed"). Slang terms, like standard terms, undergo shifts in meaning. In the 1940s "dope" referred to a stupid person; by the 1960s dope was an illicit drug, usually marijuana, and by the 1990s dope had become an adjective meaning "excellent."

[Paul Dickson, *Slang! The Topic-by-Topic Dictionary of Contemporary American Lingoes* (New York, 1990); H. L. Mencken, *The American Language* (New York, 1963); Tony Thorne, *Dictionary of Contemporary Slang* (New York, 1990).]

PAUL S. VOAKES

See also **DAH:** Slang, American; Slang, Military.

SMALL BUSINESS ADMINISTRATION (SBA), founded in 1953 to assist small companies, particularly those serving military interests, traces its roots to 1932, when President Herbert Hoover established the Reconstruction Finance Corporation to provide loans for small businesses during the Great Depression. Ten years later President Franklin D. Roosevelt created the Smaller War Plants Corporation to bolster the ability of small companies to secure military contracts during World War II. The corporation was disbanded in 1946 but reinstated as the Small Defense Plants Administration during the Korean War. President Dwight D. Eisenhower and Congress then consolidated the Small Defense Plants Administration and the Reconstruction Finance Corporation into the SBA, which also took on responsibilities of the Office of Small Business in the Department of Commerce. SBA's initial role called for keeping an inventory of businesses that could serve a military purpose in peacetime, provide disaster relief, and offer loans and technical assistance. The agency oversaw a lending program for veterans who wanted to start or expand small businesses. The Equal Opportunity Act of 1964 expanded the SBA's role to include programs to assist minority-owned businesses. President Richard M. Nixon added a minority set-aside program known as the Philadelphia Plan, which allocated a share of federal procurement contracts for minority small businesses. Enterprises owned by women, the disabled, and Vietnam veterans benefited from set-asides. In the 1990s the SBA assisted businesses specializing in high technology, environmental resources, and exports. Its constituency comprises 21.5 million companies with fewer than 500 employees, or 99 percent of all businesses in the United States, but directly serves only 1 percent of such businesses. Small businesses accounted for all of the job growth in the nation from 1987 to 1992 and are considered the engine for the national economy. Employing 54 percent of the workforce, they account for half the gross national product.

ERIK BRUUN

See also **SUPP:** Enterprise Zones; Environmental Business; Minority Business; Set-Asides.

SMOKING. In 1900 per capita consumption of cigarettes among U.S. adults was forty-nine per year. By the mid-1960s per capita consumption stood at more than 4,300. The rise of cigarette smoking was characterized by consolidation of a major industry as well as by increased advertising and consumption. Since release of the surgeon general's *Report on Smoking and Health* in 1964 there has been a revolutionary change in attitudes and behavior regarding smoking in the United States. The report reviewed and evaluated epidemiological studies that began to appear in the 1940s and 1950s implicating cigarettes as a serious cause of lung cancer, heart disease, and other ill-

nesses. At the time of the report almost half of adult Americans were cigarette smokers. By 1994 the percentage of smokers in the general population had fallen to 26 percent, although it had begun to rise among high school students, particularly young women.

The surgeon general's report touched off a debate about controlling or restricting cigarettes. Congress the next year passed the Federal Cigarette Labeling and Advertising Act, requiring cigarette packages to be labeled "Caution: Cigarette Smoking May Be Hazardous to Your Health." By 1970, as the harmful effects of smoking were increasingly documented, Congress mandated a stronger label: "Warning: The Surgeon General Has Determined that Cigarette Smoking Is Hazardous to Your Health." Congress banned cigarette advertisements from television and radio. In 1984 Congress passed legislation requiring four rotating warning messages on cigarette packages. In 1986 the surgeon general released a report on the detrimental effects of passive (secondary) smoke. A 1993 report by the Environmental Protection Agency named environmental tobacco smoke (ETS) as a Class A carcinogen. In 1994 the FDA announced that nicotine was an addictive substance and congressional hearings accused the tobacco industry of secretly manipulating the nicotine level of cigarettes to keep smokers hooked.

Evidence of the harmful effects of cigarette smoke for nonsmokers has led since the late 1970s to increased restrictions on smoking in the workplace and public spaces. By the late 1980s more than forty states had restricted smoking in public places and thirty-three had legislated prohibitions on smoking on public transportation. The General Services Administration restricted smoking in its 6,800 buildings throughout the United States. In 1988 Congress directed domestic airlines to ban smoking on flights of two hours or less; in 1990 this ban was extended to all domestic flights. A few U.S. airlines have banned smoking on international flights.

Despite the dramatic decline in numbers of Americans who smoke and the increasing stigmatization of smokers in U.S. society, cigarettes continue to cause serious health effects. In the early 1990s cigarettes were associated with 30 percent of cancers, 21 percent of deaths from coronary artery disease, and 82 percent of deaths from chronic obstructive pulmonary disease. Since 1982 lung cancer has become the leading cause of cancer deaths among women, surpassing breast cancer—the epidemiologic result of the rise in smoking among women from the 1940s to the 1960s. The total economic cost of smoking-related disease is estimated at $60 billion a year. According to the

American Cancer Society, smoking causes 400,000 deaths each year in the United States. Conservative estimates from a 1995 study indicate that smoking by pregnant women annually causes at least 19,000 miscarriages, 32,000 low-birth-weight babies, 14,000 babies requiring intensive care at birth, 1,200 cases of sudden infant death, and 3,100 deaths of children by the age of one month from complications caused by tobacco smoke. As the U.S. market has declined since the mid-1970s the United States tobacco industry has worked diligently to open new markets abroad; critics also have charged the industry with targeting teenagers in its domestic advertising campaigns. In July 1995 President Bill Clinton proposed that the Food and Drug Administration regulate the sale and advertising of cigarettes to minors.

[Robert L. Rabin and Stephen D. Sugarman, eds., *Smoking Policy: Law, Politics, and Culture* (New York, 1993); Robert Sobel, *They Satisfy: The Cigarette in American Life* (New York, 1978); Susan Wagner, *Cigarette Country* (New York, 1971).]

ALLAN M. BRANDT

See also **DAH** and **SUPP:** Tobacco Industry.

SOCCER, the most popular sport in the world, earned little interest in the United States until the nation hosted the 1994 World Cup. Held every four years, that championship is the most-watched single-sport event. The fifty-two games of World Cup '94 broke all previous records, attended by 3.5 million and watched on U.S. television by 4.5 million households. Organizers hoped that U.S. interest in the World Cup would translate into success for the newly formed Major League Soccer (MLS), the country's first serious outdoor professional soccer. Slated to begin in April 1996, MLS has twelve teams competing in a six-month season in ten cities.

In a nation saturated with baseball, basketball, football, and hockey leagues, professional soccer has had a difficult time earning the recognition it has found abroad, despite a long history of the sport in the United States, dating from collegiate teams in the 1800s to formation of ethnic (for example, Scottish, Irish, Portuguese, and Brazilian) teams in major cities in the last two decades of the nineteenth century. Professional organizations have included the American Football Organization (1884), the first governing body for soccer in the United States; the United States Football Association (1913), which was recognized by the Zurich-based Fédération Internationale de Football Association; the Professional American Soccer League (1933); and the North American Soccer League (1968). Nonetheless, Americans have never caught the fever that leads to ecstatic victory celebrations in South America or mass crowd frenzy and violence in Great Britain. Although it is generally called "football" internationally, soccer does not resemble U.S. football, which is more closely associated with rugby. Because the clock virtually never stops and only the referee knows the official time, play stoppages are close to nonexistent in soccer. The game continues when penalties are committed and player substitutions are much less frequent than in football or basketball.

In 1975 the U.S. Cosmos signed Brazilian Edson Arantes do Nascimento, better known as Pele, who eventually scored 1,280 goals in 1,362 matched (400 goals is considered phenomenal for a player). His skill and star quality spurred children to flock to the sport in record numbers. According to a sports marketing group, soccer in 1993 was the fourth most popular sport for youths under eighteen and second only to basketball for those under twelve. Total soccer participation increased 8 percent from 1992 to 1993, when 16.4 million Americans played the game, 4.2 million of them adults. Increased interest led to the 1988 awarding of World Cup '94 to the United States, a move derided internationally because the country did not yet have a bona fide professional outdoor soccer league, and its national team had not even qualified for the Cup since 1950. The U.S. team did make the 1990 Cup but critics remained unconvinced about the prospects for 1994. In addition to the commercial success of World Cup '94, played by twenty-four teams in nine cities, the U.S. team fared better than it had since 1930. The team upset the favorite, Colombia, 2–1, aided in part by Colombian player Andres Escobar's mistaken deflection that sent the ball into his own goal. A pall was cast over the victory when Escobar was shot to death upon return to Colombia and officials announced that a fan irate about his mistake was responsible. Still, the victory wiped away previous U.S. failures in World Cup participation, and promoters reported a surge in demand for a professional outdoor league. The Major Indoor Soccer League, many of whose stars (Steve Zungal and Preki of Yugoslavia and Tatu of Brazil) came from outside the United States, enjoyed mixed success in the 1990s after being beset by disorganization and falling fortunes during the previous decade.

[Michael L. LaBlanc and Richard Henshaw, *The World Encyclopedia of Soccer* (Detroit, 1994); Christopher Merrill, *The Grass of Another Country* (New York, 1993); Gary Rosenthal, *Everybody's Soccer Book* (New York, 1981).]

KATHLEEN B. CULVER

SOCIAL SECURITY

SOCIAL SECURITY is the largest, costliest, and most successful domestic program in the history of the United States. Through its 1,300 local branches, ten regional headquarters, and central offices in Baltimore and Washington, the Social Security Administration issues 500 million checks a year. Officials deal with old-age and survivors benefits, assess the needs of disabled workers, and provide eligible senior citizens with hospital insurance and supplemental medical insurance under Medicare. The administration's error rate is under 3 percent—a remarkable achievement for any bureaucracy. Beginning in the 1980s fear arose because of the program's imminent bankruptcy, but a majority of Americans continued to express considerable confidence in the system. Social security, Democratic Senator Bill Bradley declared in 1983, is "the best expression of community that we have in this country today."

Social security was designed to enable ordinary people to cope with the "risks" associated with loss of wages. Although Americans now tend to view it as a program for the elderly, its New Deal architects perceived old-age dependency in the context of family networks that changed with the generations. As Franklin Delano Roosevelt told Congress in 1934, "If, as our Constitution tells us, our federal government was established among other things, 'to promote the general welfare,' it is our plain duty to provide for the security upon which welfare depends. . . . Hence I am looking for a sound means which I can recommend to provide at once security against several of the great disturbing factors of life, especially those which relate to unemployment and old age. . . . These three objectives—the security of home, the security of livelihood, and the security of social insurance—are, it seems to me, a minimum of the promise that we can offer to the American people."

The Social Security Act of Aug. 14, 1935, largely met Roosevelt's expectations by mounting a two-pronged attack on old-age dependency. A federal-state partnership was established under Title I, which gave men and women over sixty-five years of age assistance if deemed eligible. (Because no national guidelines were established, southern states managed to circumvent the spirit of the provision and maintain racial discrimination. Still, procedures were established to enable applicants to appeal; this made old-age assistance a right, not a gratuity.) To reduce old-age poverty, employers and employees were expected to contribute 0.5 percent each (for a total of 1 percent) of the first $3,000 of an employee's salary for a retirement pension. The 1935 act dealt with the needs of younger citizens as well. Titles III and IX established a mechanism for unemployment compensation. Title IV launched what would eventually become Aid for Families with Dependent Children; Title X assisted the blind. Under Title V states received money for crippled children, rural public health services, and vocational rehabilitation; the U.S. Public Health Service received training funds under Title VI. The Social Security Board was authorized (Title VII) to evaluate programs. Although Title XI gave Congress "the right to alter, amend, or repeal any provision of this Act," President Roosevelt knew his program was safe: "We put those payroll contributions there so as to give the contributors a legal, moral, and political right to collect their pensions and unemployment benefits. With those taxes in there, no damn politician can ever scrap my social security program."

In 1939 Title II benefits were extended to widows and other family members of contributing workers. Whereas private insurance would have required an increase in taxes on grounds of equity, no new Federal Insurance Contribution Act (FICA) taxes were levied, showing a social-welfare orientation. Disability provisions were added in the 1950s, medicare in 1965. The 1972 amendments combined assistance provisions into a supplemental security income program, which established the nation's first poverty floor. That same year automatic cost-of-living adjustments were added. As its creators envisioned in the depths of the Great Depression, by the mid-1970s nearly every worker paid taxes on his or her wages. In principle, nearly all U.S. citizens were eligible for entitlements at some point in their lives. President Gerald Ford (1974–1977) first confronted the fiscal problems associated with expanding social security. To strengthen the system, President Jimmy Carter (1977–1981) adjusted benefit schedules and imposed steep tax increases. Although the 1983 amendments shored up financing of the retirement program, public confidence in the system's future remained shaky. The disability insurance program remains volatile; neither experts nor policymakers seem able to define "disability" in a consistent manner.

[W. Andrew Achenbaum, *Social Security: Visions and Revision* (New York, 1986); Martha Derthick, *Agency Under Stress: The Social Security Administration in American Government* (Washington, D.C., 1990); Eric R. Kingson and Edward D. Berkowitz, *Social Security and Medicare: A Policy Primer* (Westport, Conn., 1993).]

W. ANDREW ACHENBAUM

See also **DAH:** Medicare; New Deal; Social Security; Taxation; **SUPP:** Medicare and Medicaid.

SOMALIA, RELATIONS WITH. Somalia, in north-eastern Africa, is one of the few African states composed largely of people from the same ethnic group. Almost all Somalis are Muslim and most are pastoral herders. The people are divided into six clan-families of varying size. Historically these clans frequently fought each other. The British and the Italians conquered the Somalis in the nineteenth century and divided them into two colonies, which were combined in 1960, when Somalia gained independence. Many Somalis still live across the country's western border in Ethiopia. In 1969 the government was overthrown by the military led by Mohammed Siad Barre. During the 1970s Barre courted the Soviet Union, from which he acquired considerable military aid. In 1980 he switched sides and allied with the United States, which also poured in military aid. As the cold war ended Somalia lost its attraction as an ally. Partly because of reduced aid from the United States, Barre was overthrown in 1991. His ouster allowed clan rivalries, which his dictatorial rule had held in check, to erupt into civil war. The large number of weapons introduced during the cold war made the conflict especially devastating. The war and severe drought destroyed Somalia's economy, and thousands starved. In response to televised scenes of starving children the international community sent aid, which the war prevented from reaching its intended recipients. The United Nations in December 1992 introduced troops from several nations, under the command of the United States, to see that the food reached the starving people. This food mission initially succeeded, but when its commanders also tried to settle the civil war, troops were caught in a chaotic situation. Thirty U.S. soldiers lost their lives in the course of the conflict, the worst incident being an October 1993 army ranger raid in which eighteen U.S. soldiers were killed and their bodies paraded through the streets of Mogadishu, the capital city. The bloody exchanges caused the American public to demand a withdrawal of U.S. forces in early 1994. Other UN troops remained until U.S. marines helped evacuate them in March 1995. After more than two years and $2 billion the UN operation left Somalia with no government or administration and controlled by heavily armed rival clans.

R. L. WATSON

See also **SUPP:** Africa, Relations with.

SON-OF-SAM LAW. Adopted in New York State in 1977 as a response to the public outrage over profits made by convicted serial killer David Berkowitz (also known as "Son of Sam") for selling his story to a publishing house, the law required publishers to deposit money owed to persons either convicted of a crime or who confessed to having committed a crime in a fund used to compensate their victims. In *Simon and Schuster, Inc.* v. *Members of the New York State Victims Board* (1991) the Supreme Court struck down the New York law because it violated the First Amendment.

KATY J. HARRIGER

SORORITIES. *See* **Fraternities and Sororities.**

SOUTH AFRICA, RELATIONS WITH. U.S. interest in South Africa did not become sustained until the 1880s, after discovery of vast deposits of diamonds and gold in the briefly independent Boer Republics of Transvaal and the Orange Free State. U.S. mining engineers such as John Hays Hammond worked closely with British imperialist Cecil Rhodes in his pursuit of mineral wealth in South Africa. In the 1899–1902 war between Great Britain and the Boer Republics the U.S. government remained technically neutral but gave strong unofficial support to the victorious British. In subsequent years the United States gradually improved its relations with the white South Africans. After establishment as a Dominion of the British Commonwealth in 1910, the Union of South Africa bolstered its intense racial discrimination against the majority African population. Despite lingering dislike for Great Britain among many of the Dutch-descended Afrikaners (Boers), the Union of South Africa fought on the British and U.S. side in World Wars I and II. By the 1940s most Americans had come to see South Africa as a dependable ally and beacon of European civilization on a generally unenlightened continent, an amiable relationship personified by the South African military and political leader Jan Smuts.

After World War II relations gradually became difficult. The electoral defeat of Smuts in 1948 dismayed the U.S. government, especially because it came at the hands of the anglophobic Nationalist (later National) Party, the primary goal of which was to establish an even more rigid form of racial segregation and inequality known as apartheid. For a while the Nationalists' fervent anticommunism and total support for the U.S. position in the developing cold war proved more important than U.S. concerns about befriending the emerging antiracist Third World. The 1950 South African agreement to sell its extremely valuable uranium ore exclusively to the United States and Great Britain brought intimacy, despite diverging views of domestic race relations. U.S. trade and investment in South Africa expanded dramatically after World War II and continued to increase until the 1980s. Meanwhile, however, desegregation in the United States brought pressure to condemn Pretoria. U.S. administrations, especially that of President Jimmy Carter (1977–1981), distanced themselves at least rhetorically from South African practices. By the 1980s a vocal movement on college campuses and elsewhere demanded institutional divestiture of South African securities. In 1986, overriding the veto of President Ronald Reagan, Congress responded to public pressure by passing economic sanctions against South Africa. The release of African National Congress leader Nelson Mandela from prison in 1990 and his election as president of South Africa in 1994 in the nation's first all-races election led to the cancellation of those sanctions and much warmer relations between the United States and South Africa.

[Thomas Borstelmann, *Apartheid's Reluctant Uncle: The United States and Southern Africa in the Early Cold War* (New York, 1993); William Minter, *King Solomon's Mines Revisited* (New York, 1986); Thomas J. Noer, *Cold War and Black Liberation* (Columbia, Mo., 1985).]

THOMAS BORSTELMANN

See also **DAH:** African-American Relations; **SUPP:** Africa, Relations with.

SOUTH CAROLINA. The decline of agriculture in South Carolina has been one of the most important developments since the 1960s. As late as 1960 more than half the state's cotton was picked by hand. Over the next twenty years mechanization eliminated tens of thousands of jobs in rural counties. By 1990 only about 2 percent of South Carolinians lived on farms. Cotton is no longer king, and farmlands are being converted into timberlands. The decline of agriculture has had an effect on state government in which for nearly a century politicians from rural counties dominated the legislature. In 1973 the 100th General Assembly adjourned, the last in which representation was allocated by counties. The house of representatives and senate were reapportioned into single-member districts. Coupled with the federal Voting Rights Act of 1965, this change transformed South Carolina politics. The South Carolina Democratic party, which dominated the state for a century after Reconstruction, suffered serious losses in the 1994 elections. Republicans won all but one statewide constitutional office and control of the state house of representatives.

Nearly a half century after a school desegregation case in Clarendon County that would eventually become part of the landmark *Brown* v. *Board of Education* decision of 1954, South Carolina was a far different place from what it was even in the 1950s. African Americans were regularly elected to local and county offices and to the U.S. House of Representatives. Racial issues no longer played a major role in political campaigns, but politics had begun to take on racial characteristics, with African Americans supplying a core of voters for Democratic candidates and urban and suburban whites a core for Republicans. A panel of citizens was appointed in 1991 to study the structure of South Carolina government. Although initial reform efforts were unsuccessful, state agencies were reorganized and the executive branch given more authority. Many observers saw restructuring as the first step toward overhaul of every facet of state government. Education is a major issue and reform measures, the most important of which was the Education Improvement Act of 1984, have improved opportunities for all schoolchildren.

The closing of military installations made new jobs a pressing need and attracting industry a goal of the state's leadership. Since 1975 South Carolina has attracted a significant number of foreign corporations, including Michelin, which located its U.S. headquarters in the state. The stretch of Interstate 85 from the North Carolina line to Greenville is sometimes referred to as "UN Alley" because of the number of non-American companies located there. Nevertheless, there was increasing concern for the effect of new industries on land and water resources. This concern was especially pressing with regard to the tourist industry, which has been big business in the state since the 1950s. With a semitropical climate and relatively inexpensive land, South Carolina has been a developer's dream. Along the coast sleepy family beaches such as Myrtle Beach have grown into major tourist destinations. Barrier islands south of Charleston, such as Kiawah and Hilton Head, are playgrounds and retirement communities for wealthy outsiders. The state's attempts to manage coastal development in an orderly and environmentally sound manner have run afoul of federal court decisions. The U.S. Supreme Court in *Lucas* v. *South Carolina Coastal Council* ruled that the state, in forbidding construction on threatened beachfront property, had, in effect, seized the plaintiff's property without due process of law. The property owner was entitled to financial compensation from the state for the loss of the use of his property. As the billions of dollars in damage caused by Hurricane Hugo in 1989 graphically illustrated, there was a real need for the state to act.

In 1992 there were 3,603,227 South Carolinians, 69 percent of whom were white, 30 percent African American, and less than 1 percent Hispanic.

[Walter B. Edgar, *South Carolina in the Modern Age* (Columbia, S.C., 1992); Charles F. Kovacik and John J. Winberry, *South Carolina: The Making of a Landscape* (Columbia, S.C., 1989).]

WALTER B. EDGAR

See also **SUPP:** Charleston; Hurricanes.

SOUTH DAKOTA. The population of South Dakota grew by only 5 percent from 1970 to 1990, reaching a total just under 700,000, with residents about equally divided between rural and urban areas. The limited productivity of the land and a somewhat inhospitable climate restricted population growth to a rate supported by selective economic diversification. Occupations related to agriculture, tourism, mining, lumber, and wildlife industries plus federal assistance sustained the residents. The state's Native American population enrolled on its nine reservations was 75,400, nearly 4 percent of all Native Americans reported in the 1990 census. Since 1970 a renaissance in traditional American Indian culture, a revival in tribal governance, and the improvement of economic circumstances were the factors that led to the increase in the number of Native Americans living on or near the reservations.

When an experiment with state-sponsored socialism in 1917–1925 left South Dakota with several profitable tourist spots but also a $40 million debt, the state shifted away from its undiversified economy to federal support. Between 1952 and 1992 federal contributions to annual state expenditures rose from 20 percent to 39 percent. Federal support of farming and ranching—South Dakota's primary industry—reached a record $436 million in 1991–1992. Tourism flourished, especially at the Badlands National Park and the Mount Rushmore National Memorial, and brought in approximately $380 million per year. Low unemployment resulted from the presence of the U.S. Army Corps of Engineers along the Missouri River, the U.S. Forest Service overseeing the timberlands and grasslands, and Ellsworth Air Force Base. Thrifty fiscal management and administrative efficiency have been the hallmark of state officials since the 1970s. Legislators and administrators operated with constrained budgets to maintain a surplus while consolidating agencies and functions. By the mid-1970s

officials had merged 3,300 school districts into 200, consolidated 1,000 rural schools into fewer than 50, and collapsed 160 agencies into 16 departments. A cumbersome judicial system was replaced with a supreme court of five judges, thirty-six circuit judges for eight districts, and magistrate courts limited to criminal and minor civil matters. Officials modernized law enforcement under the attorney general and Department of Public Safety and replaced game wardens with conservation officers under a wildlife, parks, and forestry department.

By substantial majorities South Dakota voters have resisted economic improvements at the expense of ecological integrity. Instead of attracting manufacturing and chemical or nuclear-waste-disposal plants, South Dakotans have taken an interest in "clean" businesses. Because the state has no income tax and maintains a regressive tax system, banking giant Citicorp moved its credit card operations to Sioux Falls in 1981, and Gateway Computers, one of the largest mail-order suppliers of personal computers in the United States, established itself at North Sioux City and Sioux Falls. *Money* magazine in 1992 designated Sioux Falls as the most desirable urban center in the United States, not merely because of limited taxation but because of clean air, a network of roads and highways linked by bridges across the Missouri, and easy air transportation. The state's institutions of higher learning—sixteen colleges and universities serving 700,000 people—are fewer in number as compared to a generation earlier. During the 1980s Huron College became a vocational school, owned first by British and then Japanese investors. The state college campus at Springfield was converted into a prison, as was Yankton College.

Native Americans in South Dakota have flourished since the 1960s because of a new generation of political and cultural leaders. On each reservation an elected, constitutional government has been encouraged and empowered by Congress. The Indian Civil Rights Act of 1968 protected the national constitutional rights of individuals while it required tribal approval for state governmental intervention in jurisdiction rightly claimed by the tribes. The Indian Self-Determination and Education Act of 1975 consolidated previous efforts to affirm federal responsibility, encouraged tribal leaders to govern functions previously under the purview of the Bureau of Indian Affairs, and invited tribal participation in governing education, with the Tribally Controlled Community College Act of 1978 assuring federal grants. Since 1970 tribal leaders have reduced unemployment rates in some places by more than 80 percent with new occupational opportunities in the transportation and construction industries, livestock and agricultural production, wildlife management, and bingo operations and gambling casinos free from state taxation (under the National Indian Gaming Act of 1988).

[Herbert T. Hoover, *The Yankton Sioux* (New York, 1988); Herbert T. Hoover and Karen P. Zimmerman, *South Dakota History: An Annotated Bibliography* (Westport, Conn., 1993); Herbert T. Hoover and Larry J. Zimmerman, *South Dakota Leaders* (Lanham, Mo., 1975).]

HERBERT T. HOOVER

SOUTHEAST ASIAN AMERICANS is a term that encompasses several national and ethnic groups, the largest of which includes former citizens of the Philippines, Vietnam, Laos, Cambodia, and Thailand. Filipino Americans, numbering 1,406,770 in 1990, were the largest group. The 1990 census enumerated 614,547 Vietnamese Americans, 149,014 Laotian Americans, 147,411 Cambodian Americans, 91,275 Thai Americans, and 90,082 Hmong Americans (an ethnic group from Vietnam). Before 1975, when the first wave of Southeast Asian refugees arrived in the United States following the fall of the governments of South Vietnam, Laos, and Cambodia to communist forces, few immigrants from those countries settled permanently in the United States. During the 1950s fewer than fifty-five people emigrated per year, and during the 1960s the total gradually increased from about 100 at the beginning of the decade to 1,000 toward its end. Vietnamese constituted the greatest number, totaling 18,000 by 1974 as compared with fewer than 300 from Laos and Cambodia. Immigration from Vietnam, Laos, and Cambodia was, of course, linked to U.S. involvement in the Vietnam War and to Asian exclusion laws that prevailed until 1965. Many immigrants arrived between the 1960s and 1974 as spouses of U.S. servicemen in South Vietnam or as students, often under U.S. government sponsorship. They were distributed throughout the country, with 18 percent of Vietnamese living in California in 1974 and 7 percent in Texas. The immigration and settlement pattern changed dramatically in 1975 with the first wave of refugees, who greatly outnumbered the earlier arrivals, and the second wave, which reached a peak in 1980. Refugees, as opposed to immigrants, were individuals who arrived under the Indochina Migration and Assistance Act of 1975 and the Refugee Act of 1980.

The communist victory in Phnom Penh and Saigon in April 1975 triggered the flight of thousands of Cambodian government officials, military officers, and others together with their families and a massive and chaotic evacuation of Vietnamese government and military personnel. Many of the Cambodians sought refuge in Thailand, from whence some left to join the Vietnamese exiles as refugees in the United States. Laotian refugees were not allowed to enter under the provisions established for the first wave. Vietnamese, comprising 95 percent of the first group, and Cambodian refugees, more than 130,000 by August 1975, were taken to Guam, Thailand, the Philippines, Wake Island, and Hawaii, where they were processed by the Immigration and Naturalization Service before being transported to receiving centers in California, Arkansas, Florida, and Pennsylvania. The refugees were registered with voluntary agencies that found sponsors to help locate housing, clothing, food, and jobs and enroll children in school. The 1975 Refugee Assistance Act helped ease the burden of resettlement.

Because of the war's devastation, the Vietnamese government's persecution of minorities, particularly ethnic Chinese, the brutality of the Pol Pot regime in Cambodia, and the flight of Hmong and lowland Laotians, the flow of refugees continued. "Boat people," the majority of whom were ethnic Chinese, endured great privation at sea, were preyed upon by pirates, and were turned away on the beaches of Malaysia, Indochina, the Philippines, and Hong Kong. Totaling 500,000, perhaps as many as half perished. The numbers climbed throughout the late 1970s, with 20,400 arriving in the United States in 1978, 80,700 in 1979, and 166,700 in 1980. China took in 250,000 Sino-Vietnamese. Half of the refugees worldwide resettled in the United States, 761,000 by 1985, with Canada, Australia, and France admitting 100,000 each.

Policy initially was to disperse refugees throughout the United States ostensibly to minimize economic and cultural disruption in host communities and facilitate assimilation. Kin and ethnic isolation proved difficult and unpopular, and refugees moved to warm states like California. About 30,000 Hmong had settled in Fresno between 1980 and 1986, largely in response to appeals from leaders. The need for familial and cultural support in a strange and sometimes hostile environment compelled reexamination of policy and led to a strategy better accommodated to the desires of refugees, including recognition that ethnic clustering could yield beneficial results. The largest numbers of Vietnamese, Laotian, Cambodian, Thai, and Hmong Americans lived in California, according to the 1990 census, but many Vietnamese Americans lived in Texas, Laotian Americans in Washington and Minnesota, Cambodian Americans in Massachusetts and Washington, Thai Americans in New York and

Texas, and Hmong Americans in Minnesota and Wisconsin. Despite government assistance in alleviating problems of resettlement and refugee efforts directed at self-sufficiency, significant numbers continued to show economic and social need.

Refugees in the first wave were generally well-educated and skilled, proficient in English, and from wealthy social groups, whereas refugees of the second wave tended to be less educated and skilled, with limited English, and from poorer social groups. In 1980, among Vietnamese Americans, 76 percent of men and 63 percent of women age twenty-five to twenty-nine had completed high school as compared with 87 percent of white men and women students. For Southeast Asian Americans as a whole (excluding Filipino Americans), 3 percent were employed as managers in 1987, 22 percent were service workers, and 58 percent blue-collar laborers. Southeast Asian Americans established themselves through retention and adaptation recalling their long history in Indochina of resisting and receiving invaders and in keeping with their syncretic religious and world views. The family and extended kinship are foundations of the community, and families pool resources to bring other members from Southeast Asia. Changes are under way within the family structure because of the greater freedom of children in the United States and because more women are employed outside the household, which raises their standing. Catholic churches, Buddhist temples, and business districts provide points of convergence for the community and ways of linking Southeast Asian American communities within the wider American society. A goal of the Vietnamese Buddhist temple in Los Angeles, for example, is to promote cultural and religious dialogue between Vietnamese and other Americans.

In what some observers have described as a coming to terms with the Vietnam War, Congress in 1978 passed the Amerasian Homecoming Act, which provided for immigration of American-Vietnamese children born between January 1962 and January 1976 and certain of their family members. Often abandoned by their American fathers and ostracized by the Vietnamese, Amerasians were a sharp reminder of a war and a past that many had hoped to forget. They came to the United States poorly educated, were ambivalently received, and searched for identities. By 1989, 22,000 Amerasians had been admitted to the United States.

[James M. Freeman, *Hearts of Sorrow: Vietnamese-American Lives* (Stanford, Calif., 1989); David W. Haines, ed., *Refugees as Immigrants: Cambodians, Laotians, and Vietnamese in America* (Totowa, N.J., 1989); Paul James Rutledge, *The Vietnamese Experience in America* (Bloomington, Ind., 1992).]

Gary Y. Okihiro

See also **SUPP:** Filipino Americans; Japanese Americans.

SOVIET AMERICANS. The entry of more than 243,000 émigrés from areas within the former Soviet Union between 1981 and 1993 represents the second large wave of Russian/Soviet immigration to the United States. Between 1881 and 1920, 3.2 million people, the majority of them Jewish, came to the United States from areas of the former Soviet Union. Between these two eras immigration of both Soviet Jews and non-Jews was at very low levels. Public displays of anti-Semitism and lack of opportunities for social and economic advancement increased pressure on the Soviet government to allow the emigration of Soviet Jews during the late 1970s. The U.S. government responded by admitting more than 50,000 refugees from the Soviet Union, the majority of whom were Jews, between 1972 and 1980. Since 1980, 96 percent of immigrants to the United States from areas within the Soviet Union have entered as refugees. Since the late 1980s Soviet refugee streams have included increasing numbers of non-Jews as well as Jews. During the 1990s refugee arrivals from areas within the former Soviet Union ranged between 40,000 and 60,000 per year. For 1993 Congress authorized the admission of 49,775 Soviet refugees.

The communities of Russian and Soviet émigrés within the United States reflect each of these waves of large-scale migration. Between 1970 and 1990 the size of the U.S. population that had been born in the Soviet Union declined from 463,500 to 334,000, reflecting the aging of immigrants who entered at the turn of the century. Nearly two-fifths of the 1990 U.S. population of persons born in czarist Russia or the Soviet Union had entered in the previous ten years.

Since 1992 the U.S. Immigration and Naturalization Service has reported immigration from specific areas in the former Soviet Union. Of the 58,600 immigrants admitted from the former USSR in 1993, 31.3 percent were born in Ukraine, 20.6 percent in Russia, 10.7 percent in Armenia, and 8 percent in Belarus. More than half of recent Soviet immigrants are women and 30 percent are under the age of twenty, indicating the important role of the family in emigration.

As with other groups, Soviet émigrés are concentrated in specific geographic areas in the United States. In 1990, 48 percent of this population resided in the Northeast and 27 percent in western states; among Soviet immigrants arriving during the 1980s, 36 percent settled in California. The New York metropolitan region had the largest number of Soviet- and Russian-born people, and large communities of émigrés were formed in the Los Angeles–Long Beach area. Settlement of Soviet Jewish immigrants was aided in large part by private Jewish organizations in metropolitan areas throughout the United States. Results of survey research on resettled Jewish populations, moreover, indicate that Soviet Jewish émigrés to the United States expressed strong religious identities similar to Soviet émigrés to Israel.

Descendants of earlier waves of Russian immigration have been characterized by high levels of education and occupation. In the 1990 census half of the Russian-ancestry male population reported either professional specialties or executive, administrative, or managerial occupations; among Russian-ancestry women, 40 percent were in these occupations. These levels are significantly higher than those for other ancestry groups. Recent immigrants also have been distinctive in levels of education and occupation. Among Soviet immigrants admitted to the United States in 1993, one-third of those reporting occupations listed professional, executive, administrative, or managerial occupations. Occupations among recent Soviet Jewish immigrants are estimated to be proportionally even higher. Estimates for immigrants aided by the Hebrew Aid Society in 1989 suggest that two-thirds of Soviet Jewish immigrants were in professional, scientific, technical, and white-collar occupations prior to migrating.

[Stanley Lieberson and Mary C. Waters, *From Many Strands: Ethnic and Racial Groups in Contemporary America* (New York, 1988); Rita J. Simon, ed., *New Lives: The Adjustment of Soviet Jewish Immigrants in the United States and Israel* (Lexington, Mass., 1985).]

ELLEN PERCY KRALY

See also **SUPP:** Immigration; Jews, American; Refugees; Soviet Union, Relations with.

SOVIET UNION, RELATIONS WITH. Between the 1970s and 1990s relations between the United States and the Soviet Union experienced change unexpected in either scope or pace. At the end of the 1960s the two nations were opposing one another in a struggle for ideological domination of Indochina. Washington's prestige in the Third World was plummeting. Criticism of U.S. policies spread in Europe and relations within the U.S.-led North Atlantic Treaty Organization (NATO) were increasingly strained. At home the

Vietnam War provoked divisions within society. The economy suffered, inflation mounted, and social justice issues languished as the war diverted money and attention from the Great Society programs so optimistically unveiled just a few years before. In contrast, the Union of Soviet Socialist Republics (USSR) appeared to be in an improving position. Its economy, somewhat revived by the reforms of former Communist Party First Secretary Nikita Khrushchev, was producing increased amounts of industrial and agricultural goods. The administrative turmoil and political uncertainties stirred by Khrushchev had quieted since the accession of Leonid Brezhnev to the chief party post in 1964. The supremacy of the will of the Soviet Union over its satellites in Eastern Europe and its own alliance system, the Warsaw Pact, had been unchallenged—despite a certain degree of noncooperation on the part of Romania—since 1968, when the Soviets crushed Czech moves for democratic reform and independence from that alliance.

By the close of 1991, however, the former Soviet empire in Eastern Europe had come apart, the Warsaw Pact was dissolved, and the prestige of communism and Moscow as its leader in world affairs had fallen sharply. Economic and environmental crises were spreading throughout a fragmented country. Protests against mismanagement, misrule, and worsening living standards were turning into ethnic wars. The United States, if still troubled by persistent social and racial problems and a stagnant economy, seemed more self-confident. Moreover, its stature as a world leader had been reasserted by the Gulf War of 1991 that restored Kuwait's independence from Iraq. How this reversal of fortunes came about continues to be the subject of much inquiry by historians. Although some analysts have assigned substantial credit or blame to individual statesmen, consensus suggests the causes are multiple, rooted not only in individual decisions and national philosophies but also in factors ranging from technology to the environment, from economics to chance. Moreover, if economic and military pressures had much to do with the deterioration of the Soviet Union, subsequent developments have shown that those same forces also harmed the United States. The latter may have outlasted the Soviet Union, enabling it to claim victory in the cold war. Nevertheless, the toll levied on the U.S. economy, social programs, and capacity for future world leadership was considerable.

Domestic unrest and the untenable position of the United States in Vietnam at the beginning of the 1970s had much to do with diplomatic initiatives that altered Soviet-U.S. relations and affected the course of the cold war. Confident that the United States was weakening, the Brezhnev leadership expanded the Soviet role in Africa, South America, the Middle East, and Central Asia, ultimately invading Afghanistan in 1979. Activism in the Third World dictated an easing of tensions in Europe. An equilibrium had been achieved over the previous decades as both East and West became more comfortable with—or at least accustomed to—the de facto division of the continent. Unlike his predecessors, Brezhnev suspected that victory over capitalism did not rest solely on class struggle but also on technical knowledge as the determinant of new modes of production. It was in this area that the Soviets and their allies most seriously trailed the West. A relaxation of tensions might permit increased trade with the West, including the acquisition of machine tools and improved technologies. Such information also was necessary because China and its leader, Mao Zedong, increasingly challenged Soviet leadership of the communist world. Indeed, incidents along the Chinese border and the necessity of stationing more troops there emphasized the value of reducing confrontation in the West, lest the Soviets be confronted with simultaneous crises on borders more than 2,000 miles apart.

China also loomed large in the thinking of President Richard M. Nixon, who took office in January 1969. Because of his credentials as a strong anticommunist cold warrior, Nixon was one of the few U.S. politicians who could take the initiative in opening relations with the People's Republic of China without facing the criticism of being "soft" on communism. Nixon also saw the value of playing off China and the Soviet Union against one another. The Chinese, although mistrustful, also saw the utility of improving relations with the United States because they feared a Soviet preemptive air strike against their northern nuclear sites. Cautious approaches led to Nixon's visit to Beijing in February 1972 and U.S. rapprochement with the largest communist nation in the world. U.S.-China contacts did not pass unnoticed in Moscow, which consequently shifted to a more accommodating stance in disarmament talks that had proceeded desultorily since 1968. In May 1972 Nixon traveled to Moscow to sign the Strategic Arms Limitation Treaty (SALT I).

Thus was inaugurated a period of Soviet-U.S. relations known as détente, or relaxation of tensions, but the relaxation both desired did not conceal that the two nations interpreted détente differently. Soviet leaders believed history was evolving in the direction of communism and saw détente as a process that would allow that to happen with as few military en-

counters as possible. This arrangement, called "peaceful coexistence," did not imply any socialist retreat or even acceptance of a static situation. In particular the Soviets were willing to accept détente in Europe as long as they were able to continue expanding their role in the Third World. For U.S. leaders détente meant a way, other than traditional containment, to urge the USSR into behavior more like that of Western industrialized nations. The United States, too, thought time was on its side and that emerging countries, if left to themselves, would evolve toward democracy and industrial capitalism.

The SALT I arms agreement was modest, primarily limiting to two the number of antiballistic missile (ABM) systems each power could deploy. This proviso assured that neither power could launch a "safe" nuclear first strike, because neither could wipe out its opponent's retaliatory power or protect itself from a retaliatory strike, maintaining the possibility of mutually assured destruction (MAD) that had militated against outbreak of nuclear war between the superpowers. As for offensive weapons, the number of strategic missile launchers each possessed would be frozen for five years. In short, SALT I produced no reduction of armaments, just a reduction in their expansion to a rate acceptable to the strategic plans and economies of both powers. SALT I did, however, indicate that negotiation was possible. Other contacts were opened and in the summer of 1972 the Soviets arranged extensive grain purchase contracts with the United States. U.S. farmers cheered but consumers did not when it was discovered the Soviets had quickly and quietly purchased at prices subsidized by U.S. taxpayers more grain than warranted by national reserves, thus elevating bread prices in the United States. Disarmament talks continued. In November 1974 Brezhnev and President Gerald R. Ford agreed at a summit meeting in Vladivostok to limits on strategic missile launchers and a sublimit on multiple, independently targeted reentry vehicles (MIRVs). As construction of ABM systems was proving technologically difficult, both were willing to reduce such systems to one per country.

Arms reduction and other discussions stimulated by détente involved some alteration in the U.S. diplomatic posture toward the Soviet Union. Since 1947 the United States had followed a policy of containment, which by the 1960s had come to mean primarily the encirclement of the Soviet Union with military bases and nuclear weapons. Only limited effort had been expended on comprehensive negotiations. A diplomatic stalemate had resulted, with only isolated breakthroughs. Through détente and a concept known as linkage, Nixon and his national security adviser and later secretary of state, Henry Kissinger, attempted to move negotiations along a broader front than in the past by tying progress in one area to progress in another. The United States still wished to contain the Soviet empire but saw a need for new approaches at a time when Soviet prestige in the Third World was mounting and economic and political support for an active U.S. foreign policy and military role was waning. The United States also wanted help in leaving Vietnam and for the Soviets to restrain themselves in the Third World. In return, Nixon and Kissinger offered recognition of strategic parity, access to Western trade and technology, and some willingness to tolerate the record of the USSR and its satellites on human and democratic rights.

Détente and linkage had only minor influence on events outside Europe. The Soviets continued to press for advantage in the Third World, and the West endeavored to retain a strong influence there. In the Middle East, both the United States and the Soviet Union placed troop contingents on highest alert during the Yom Kippur War of 1973. The success of the Israelis in defending themselves against Egyptian-Syrian attack strengthened the U.S. position in the region, as did Egyptian expulsion of Soviet advisers. In Africa, by contrast, the success the Soviets and Cubans experienced in supporting Marxist-Leninists in Angola in the mid-1970s demonstrated the weakness of U.S. influence in that area. If détente faltered on the periphery it succeeded in Europe by temporarily facilitating the efforts of West German Chancellor Willy Brandt to improve relations between his country and Eastern Europe. Brandt already had achieved treaties with Poland and the Soviet Union. In 1972, with the Soviets and the West reaching agreements over access to Berlin, the East and West German governments signed what came to be called the Basic Treaty—each entered the United Nations the following year with approval of both superpowers. In 1973 Brezhnev and Nixon signed an agreement renouncing nuclear warfare between their countries and promising to try to prevent it among themselves.

Aside from armament limitation the 1975 Helsinki Accords were the major achievement of détente, but even these were very much a part of the cold war. A key Soviet goal had long been separation of the United States from its European allies and promotion of East-West understanding in Europe without U.S. involvement. Moscow also wanted formal acceptance of European borders arising from World War II. To this end, in the spring of 1968 the Soviets proposed a conference solely of European states. Their heavy-handed actions in Czechoslovakia a few months later, however, strengthened the resolve of European NATO members not to be separated from their Canadian and U.S. friends. Eventually, foreign ministers of thirty-five nations, including all NATO partners, gathered in Helsinki in 1973 to initiate what has now become the larger Conference on Security and Cooperation in Europe (CSCE). In time the CSCE talks led to a tripartite statement of principles signed by the participants in 1975. Basket I dealt with security matters and essentially confirmed the status quo in Europe; Basket II called for cooperation on environmental, technological, and economic problems; and Basket III contained a statement of human rights that the signatories promised to protect. The Soviets initially considered the Helsinki Accords a triumph for their side because it confirmed the status quo in Eastern Europe. The West paid little attention or criticized the accords as an abandonment of Eastern Europe by the United States, its will and economy weakened by the Vietnam experience. In response the Ford administration tried to link U.S. acquiescence to Soviet and satellite promises to better human rights. These promises would be taken by East European reformers as a rallying point and leverage tool with which to demand transformation of their governments.

The election of Jimmy Carter to the U.S. presidency in November 1976 brought to the White House a novice in international affairs. For advice he turned to two able individuals of differing views, Secretary of State Cyrus Vance and national secretary adviser Zbigniew Brzezinski. Interested in arms control, Vance believed in strengthening détente and hoped for cooperation from younger Soviet officials who were not as dogmatically Marxist as the aging Brezhnev generation. He also worried that China might use the United States for its own ends, worsening Soviet-U.S. relations, and did not want Third World issues to dominate the Soviet-U.S. agenda. Brzezinski saw little use in trying to reach agreement with the Soviets or in waiting for them to assume a more cooperative stance. They needed to be countered everywhere, change in Kremlin attitudes was not to be expected, and the aid of the Chinese should be enlisted in challenging Moscow. According to Brzezinski the contest was a total one and compromise or concession a mistake.

Without serious challenge the Soviets and Cubans aided seizures of power by communist or pro-Soviet groupings in Angola, Ethiopia, Afghanistan, Cambodia, Grenada, and Nicaragua. Although they viewed the Carter regime as ineffectual, Soviets were angered by their exclusion from the Camp David talks wherein Carter achieved a breakthrough in fostering Israeli-Egyptian agreement. Meanwhile, Soviet successes and the nudgings of the Chinese, who indeed wanted to use the Americans against the Soviets, turned the U.S. electorate and Carter himself away from the views of Vance and toward Brzezinski's more traditional cold warrior tactics of confrontation.

Despite Soviet adventurism in the Third World and changing U.S. attitudes, détente still held possibilities for arms control. Although the European states of NATO were wealthier than those of the Warsaw Pact, they disliked the notion of sacrificing domestic programs for additional military expenditures. Efforts to achieve a mutual and balanced force reduction of conventional forces went nowhere, and in the late 1970s both sides determined to modernize their intermediate-range nuclear forces (INF) in the European theater. Discussions regarding long-range missiles made some headway. A SALT II treaty signed in June 1979 by Carter and Brezhnev upheld the agreements reached at Vladivostok and placed a sublimit on seaborne forces (but not seaborne launchers). It also postponed the possibility of the intercontinental ballistic missiles (ICBMs) of either side being vulnerable to attack, thus preventing either power from considering a preventive first strike. By this time, however, anti-SALT forces were strong in the U.S. Senate, where conservatives resented Carter's successful negotiations for the eventual relinquishment of control over the Panama Canal. Specious controversy arose over a brigade of Soviet troops that actually had been in Cuba for many years and represented no reinforcement of Soviet arms there. Doubts mounted over Brezhnev's assurance that the Soviet Backfire bomber, which had many performance characteristics of a strategic bomber, was not adaptable to intercontinental use. Any prompt ratification of SALT II became impossible.

Benefits anticipated by the Soviets from the granting of most-favored-nation trading status by the United States at the beginning of the détente period in return for settlement of old World War II lend-lease debts failed to materialize. Almost immediately Senator Henry M. Jackson of Washington, a noted cold war hawk, demanded revocation of an exit tax imposed by the Soviets on émigrés, intended to reimburse the cost of education provided by the state. His amendment to a trade bill forced the Soviets to cancel their tax. Jewish immigration from the USSR became a substitute for ideological confrontation. The United States soon pressed the USSR to double the number of Jews it would allow to emigrate. Legislative restrictions were placed on Export-Import Bank loans, to be lifted only if the Soviets removed restrictions on emigration by all nationalities according to a schedule approved by the United States. Brezhnev and his advisers interpreted such legislative notions as meddling in Soviet civil affairs. Their annoyance with Carter mounted when he responded to the deployment of new Soviet missiles aimed at Europe by pressuring NATO allies to accept installation of Pershing and cruise missiles, both of which posed serious defensive problems for the Soviets.

While the value of détente was being questioned by both superpowers the dangers of ethnic factionalism and rising Islamic fundamentalism in Afghanistan led to Soviet military intervention in December 1979. The U.S. reaction was perhaps more severe than the Kremlin anticipated. Branding the USSR an aggressor nation, Carter imposed a grain embargo and declared that U.S. athletes would not participate in the summer Olympic Games to be held in Moscow. Détente was at an end and a renewed arms race appeared likely. This possibility seemed confirmed by the election as president of Ronald Reagan, an old-style cold warrior who characterized the Soviet Union as the "evil empire," but even he had to continue some form of arms negotiations. The U.S. proposal that both sides eliminate nuclear weapons in Europe was rejected by the Soviets. Their campaign to persuade European governments to resist deployment of new U.S. intermediate-range missiles failed; the Soviets then withdrew from both intermediate- and long-range missile talks. Further cooling of relations flowed from sympathy in the United States for the Solidarity movement in Poland. The United States imposed economic sanctions against that country when the Soviet Union pressured the Polish military into seizing power in Warsaw in 1981. By the end of 1983 U.S.-Soviet relations were at their lowest point in years.

During that year the Soviet Union was adjusting to new leadership. Brezhnev, too old and feeble to attempt any new policy orientation, had died in November 1982. His successor, Yuri Andropov, appeared aware that the USSR's expansionism in the Third World and its search for absolute security might be negatively affecting attitudes in Washington. Moreover, unrest in Poland and economic conditions in Russia were becoming increasing problems. At the end of August, Soviet fighters shot down a Korean jetliner that had strayed into Soviet airspace. Soviet spokesmen first denied responsibility then asserted that the airliner was serving as a spy plane. Reagan and the world harshly chastised the Soviets for wantonly taking civilian lives.

In the early years of containment the United States was content to "hold the line" while hoping for internal changes in the Soviet Union. Now it began to exert more pressure. U.S. troops were sent to Grenada in 1983 ostensibly to protect U.S. medical students; as a result, the island's government passed from the hands of Marxists to pro-Westerners. U.S. aid also was secretly funneled to the Contras opposing the Sandinista regime in Nicaragua as part of the Reagan Doctrine of supporting forces opposing pro-Soviet regimes throughout the world. The president traveled to China and reaffirmed what had been a weakening relationship there. Most notably, Reagan generally increased the U.S. defense budget and military forces. He also proposed in March 1983 the Strategic Defense Initiative (SDI). Although the Soviets protested that a new outer space defense against ballistic missiles violated the 1972 ABM treaty, the Americans forged ahead with research. The Soviets could ill afford to fall behind in the new arms race. If that race put severe strains on the United States, which markedly increased its national debt, it spelled near-disaster for the Soviets, who had fewer reserves and a less developed economy. Moreover, the death of Andropov in February 1984 and the succession of the geriatric Konstantin Chernenko meant a lack of strong leadership when it was most needed.

By the time the dynamic Mikhail Gorbachev became the first secretary of the party after Chernenko's death in March 1985 it was clear that a new course was necessary. As part of his new thinking, Gorbachev decided to reduce expenditures associated with Soviet commitments overseas, in Afghanistan where fruitless warfare continued, and even in Eastern Europe. Gorbachev's initiatives to achieve troop and arms reductions took Washington by surprise, but Reagan's genuine fear of nuclear war and his wish to make a historic contribution to the peace process meant Soviet offers would be favorably received. After months of negotiation and several summit meetings, an INF treaty was signed in December 1987. It entailed not just a limitation on deployments but an actual reduction in armaments. SDI remained a roadblock as well as an incentive for further talks regarding strategic missiles. Meanwhile, the Soviets announced a withdrawal of troops from Afghanistan, a process that was completed in February 1989.

Gorbachev's willingness in 1989 to allow East European countries to choose their own political paths, followed by his acquiescence to German reunification, had more to do with Soviet economic and political issues than with U.S. relations. It did, however, have the effect of wiping out many of the old quarrels that had contributed to the cold war and facilitating what Gorbachev understood his country badly needed to restructure its economy—more trade and investment from the West. During the Gulf War of 1991 he even reluctantly abandoned former Arab friends and aligned the USSR with the United States. Gorbachev's foreign policy and military cutbacks partially stimulated the failed August 1991 conservative coup that shifted governing power in the USSR to other leaders, such as the more radical Boris Yeltsin and heads of various republics who desired independence for their regions. They would declare the end of the Union of Soviet Socialist Republics as of Dec. 31, 1991. Ironically its demise occurred at probably the friendliest point in U.S.-Soviet relations since World War II. The cold war was over, but its legacy in placing stress on both the USSR and the United States would be felt for years to come.

Multiple issues remained to be resolved between the United States and the successor states to the Soviet Union. Sharp debates arose between Russia, the largest of the republics, and the United States despite mutual desire for good relations. How much financial aid would the United States provide for the reconstruction of the new Russia? To what extent would Russia welcome private U.S. investment? What role should the United States play in the dismantling of antiquated Soviet nuclear weapons and plants? Differing views were strongly held on the possible expansion of NATO to include former Soviet satellite states, on the treatment of crises in the Balkans, and on the extent of Russian and U.S. influence in the other successor republics. A half decade of such controversies firmly demonstrated that the road to true harmony in U.S.-Russian relations would require long traveling.

[Warren I. Cohen, ed., *The Cambridge History of American Foreign Relations,* vol. 4, *America in the Age of Soviet Power, 1945–1991* (New York, 1993); Walter LaFeber, *America, Russia and the Cold War, 1945–1991,* 7th ed. (New York, 1993); Don Oberdorfer, *The Turn: From Cold War to a New Era: The United States and the Soviet Union, 1983–1990* (New York, 1991).]

JONATHAN E. HELMREICH

See also **DAH:** Arms Race with the Soviet Union; Berlin Wall; Cuban Missile Crisis; Missiles, Military;

Russia, U.S. Relations with; **DAH** and **SUPP:** Cold War; North Atlantic Treaty Organization; Strategic Arms Limitation Talks; Summit Conferences; **SUPP:** Afghanistan, Invasion of; Arms Race and Disarmament; China, Relations with; Eastern Europe, Relations with; Gulf War of 1991; Strategic Defense Initiative; Summit Conferences, Presidential.

SPACE PROGRAM. The U.S. civil space program went into something of a holding pattern after completion of Project Apollo in December 1972. For the next decade the major program of the National Aeronautics and Space Administration (NASA) was the development of the Space Transportation System, a reusable space shuttle that was supposed to be able to travel back and forth between the Earth and space more routinely and economically than the spectacular but expensive series of missions that had followed the Apollo 11 moon landing on July 20, 1969. Between the autumn of 1969 and early 1972, NASA leaders worked to convince President Richard M. Nixon that the shuttle was an appropriate follow-on project to Apollo. They were successful on Jan. 5, 1972, when the president issued a statement announcing the decision to "proceed at once with the development of an entirely new type of space transportation system designed to help transform the space frontier of the 1970s into familiar territory, easily accessible for human endeavor in the 1980s and 1990s." The shuttle became the largest, most expensive, and most highly visible project undertaken by NASA after its first decade, and it has continued to be a central component of the space program.

The space shuttle that emerged in the early 1970s consisted of three primary elements: a delta-winged orbiter spacecraft with a large crew compartment, a fifteen-by-sixty-foot cargo bay, and three main engines; two solid rocket boosters (SRBs); and an external fuel tank housing the liquid hydrogen and oxidizer burned in the main engines. The orbiter and SRBs were reusable. The shuttle was designed to transport up to 45,000 pounds of cargo into near-Earth orbit for a planned space station, to be located 115 to 250 miles above the earth, and to accommodate a flight crew of ten (although seven would be more common) for a basic space mission of seven days. For its return to earth, the orbiter was designed to have a cross-range maneuvering capability of 1,265 miles to meet requirements for liftoff and landing at the same location after only one orbit. This capability satisfied Department of Defense require-

ments for a shuttle that could place in orbit and retrieve reconnaissance satellites.

NASA began developing the shuttle soon after the president's announcement with the goal of flying in space by 1978, but because of budgetary pressure and technological problems the first orbital flight was delayed until 1981. There was tremendous excitement when *Columbia,* the first operational orbiter, took off from Cape Canaveral, Fla., on Apr. 12, 1981, six years after the last U.S. astronaut had returned from space following the Apollo-Soyuz Test Project in 1975. After the two-day test flight, the nation watched with excitement as the shuttle landed like a conventional airplane at Edwards Air Force Base in California. The first flight was a success, and both NASA and the media proclaimed the beginning of a new age in space flight, an era of inexpensive and routine access to space for many people and payloads. Speculation abounded that within a few years shuttle flights would take off and land as predictably as airplanes and that commercial tickets would be sold for regularly scheduled "spaceline" flights.

As it turned out, the shuttle program provided neither inexpensive nor routine access to space. By January 1986 there had been only twenty-four shuttle flights; in the 1970s NASA had projected more flights than that for every year. Although the system was reusable, its complexity, coupled with the ever-present rigors of flying in an aerospace environment, meant that turnaround time between flights was several months instead of several days. Missions were delayed for all manner of problems, and it took thousands of work hours and expensive parts to keep the system performing. Observers began to criticize NASA for failing to meet expectations. Analysts agreed that the shuttle had proven neither cheap nor reliable, both primary selling points, and that NASA should not have used those arguments in building a political consensus for the program. By 1985 there was general agreement that the effort had been both a triumph and a tragedy. An engagingly ambitious program had developed an exceptionally sophisticated vehicle, one that no other nation on earth could have built at the time. At the same time, the shuttle's much-touted capabilities had not been realized. Criticism reached its height following the tragic loss of *Challenger* and its crew of seven in an explosion during a launch on Jan. 28, 1986. Pressure to get the shuttle schedule more in line with earlier projections had prompted NASA workers to accept operational procedures that fostered shortcuts and increased the opportunity for disaster, although that was not the entire reason for the explosion. Several investigations followed the accident, the most important being the blue-ribbon commission mandated by President Ronald Reagan and chaired by William P. Rogers. It found that the *Challenger* accident resulted from a poor engineering decision, an O-ring used to seal joints in the SRBs that was susceptible to failure at low temperatures.

Following the *Challenger* accident, the shuttle program went into a two-year hiatus while NASA redesigned the SRBs and revamped its management. James C. Fletcher, NASA administrator between 1971 and 1977, was brought back and given the task of overhauling the agency. NASA invested heavily in safety and reliability programs and restructured its management. Most important, engineers added a way for the astronauts to be ejected from a malfunctioning shuttle during launch. Another decision resulting from the accident was to increase the use of expendable launch vehicles. The space shuttle finally returned to flight on Sept. 29, 1988, with the launch of *Discovery*. Through April 1993 NASA launched an additional thirty shuttle missions without an accident. Each undertook scientific and technological experiments ranging from deployment of space probes, such as the *Magellan* Venus radar mapper in 1989 and the Hubble Space Telescope in 1990 to the continued *Spacelab* flights in 1991 for the European Space Agency (which NASA had undertaken in 1983) and a dramatic three-person extravehicular activity (EVA) in 1992 to retrieve a satellite and bring it back to earth for repair. Through all these activities, a good deal of realism about what the shuttle could and could not do began to emerge.

In addition to the shuttle, the space program initiated a series of spectacular science missions in the 1970s. Project Viking was the culmination of an effort begun in 1964 to explore Mars. Two identical spacecraft were built, each consisting of a lander and an orbiter. Launched on Aug. 20, 1975, *Viking 1* landed on July 20, 1976, on the Chryse Planitia (Golden Plains). *Viking 2* was launched on Sept. 9, 1975, and landed Sept. 3, 1976. One of the scientific activities of the project was an attempt to determine whether there was life on Mars, but the Viking landers provided no clear evidence for living microorganisms in soil near landing sites. One of the most important space probes undertaken by the United States was initiated because the Earth and all the giant planets of the solar system were due to gather on one side of the sun in the late 1970s. This geometric lineup made possible close observation of all planets in the outer solar system (with exception of Pluto) in a single

flight, which was called the Grand Tour. The flyby of each planet would bend a spacecraft's flight path and increase velocity enough to deliver it to the next destination, which would occur through a complicated process known as gravity assist (something like a slingshot effect), thereby reducing the flight time to Neptune from thirty years to twelve. Project Voyager was a satellite reconnaissance in which two Voyager spacecraft were launched from Kennedy Space Center in 1977 to photograph Jupiter and Saturn. As the mission progressed, with achievement of all objectives at Jupiter and Saturn in December 1980, flybys of the two outermost giant planets, Uranus and Neptune, proved possible—and irresistible. *Voyager 1* and *Voyager 2* explored all the giant outer planets, including their rings and magnetic fields and forty-eight of their moons.

The $2 billion Hubble Space Telescope project received much media attention in the early 1990s. A key component of the telescope was a precision-ground 94-inch primary mirror shaped to within microinches of perfection from ultralow-expansion titanium silicate glass with an aluminum-magnesium fluoride coating. The telescope was launched from the space shuttle in April 1990, and the first photos provided much better images than pictures of the same target taken by ground-based telescopes. Controllers then began moving the telescope's mirrors for better focus, and although focus sharpened, the best image still had a pinpoint of light encircled by a hazy ring or "halo." Technicians concluded that the telescope had a spherical aberration, a mirror defect one twenty-fifth the width of a human hair that prevented Hubble from focusing all light to a single point. Many observers believed the spherical aberration would cripple the forty-three-foot-long telescope, and NASA received much criticism, but scientists found a way to work around the abnormality with computer enhancement. Because of difficulties with the mirror, NASA launched *Endeavour* in December 1993 on a mission to insert corrective lenses on the telescope and to service other instruments. During a weeklong mission *Endeavour*'s astronauts conducted a record five space walks and completed all programmed repairs. The images returned afterward were more than an order of magnitude better than those obtained before.

During the 1980s plans were put forth for a new generation of planetary exploration. The Reagan administration called for a permanently occupied space station in 1984. Congress made a down payment of $150 million for space station *Freedom* in the fiscal year 1985 NASA budget. From the outset both administration officials and NASA intended *Freedom* to be an international program. Partners abroad, many with their own rapidly developing space capabilities, could enhance the effort. NASA leaders pressed forward with international agreements among thirteen nations to take part, but almost from the outset *Freedom* was controversial. Debate centered on costs versus benefits. The projected cost of $8 billion had tripled within five years. NASA pared away at the budget, and in the end the project was satisfactory to almost no one. In the late 1980s and early 1990s a parade of space station managers and NASA administrators, each attempting to rescue the program, wrestled with *Freedom* and lost. In 1993 the international situation allowed NASA to include Russia in the building of an international space station, a smaller and cheaper successor to *Freedom*. On Nov. 7, 1993, a joint announcement was made by the United States and Russia that they would work with other international partners to build a station for benefit of all. Even so, the space station remained a difficult issue as policymakers confronted competing national programs. Even more troubling for the space program was the ambitious Space Exploration Initiative (SEI), which would return people to the moon by the year 2000, establish a lunar base, and, using the space station and the moon as bases, reach Mars by 2010. The price tag was estimated at $700 billion over two decades. Congress refused to fund SEI despite lobbying by Vice President Dan Quayle as head of the National Aeronautics and Space Council, an advisory group to President George Bush. Although the president castigated Congress for not "investing in America's future," members believed such a huge sum could be better spent elsewhere. "We're essentially not doing Moon-Mars," Senator Barbara Mikulski of Maryland declared bluntly.

By 1993 the highly successful *Magellan* mission to Venus had provided data about that planet. The *Galileo* mission to Jupiter had become a source of concern because not all systems were working, but it also returned useful data. The ill-fated *Mars Observer* reached its destination in 1993 but was lost as a result of an onboard explosion. Thus, as the U.S. space program approached the last years of the twentieth century its reputation had been tarnished by debates about the space station and SEI, the initial failure of the Hubble Space Telescope, and the deficiency of *Galileo*, to say nothing of the *Challenger* accident. The fate of the space station program was undecided in 1994, on the twenty-fifth anniversary of the first moon landing,

but both it and the stillborn Space Exploration Initiative pointed up the difficulty of building a constituency for large science and technology programs.

[Roger E. Bilstein, *Orders of Magnitude: A History of the NACA and NASA, 1915–1990* (Washington, D.C., 1989); Wernher von Braun, Frederick I. Ordway III, and Dave Dooling, *History of Rocketry and Space Travel*, 3rd ed. (New York, 1986); Roger D. Launius, *NASA: A History of the U.S. Civil Space Program* (Melbourne, Fla., 1994); Howard E. McCurdy, *Inside NASA: High Technology and Organizational Change in the U.S. Space Program* (Baltimore, 1993); Walter A. McDougall, *The Heavens and the Earth: A Political History of the Space Age* (New York, 1985).]

ROGER D. LAUNIUS

See also **DAH:** Astronautics; National Aeronautics and Space Administration; **SUPP:** Astronomy; *Challenger* Disaster; Hubble Telescope.

SPECIAL PROSECUTORS. When a prosecutor who would ordinarily be responsible for a given case has, or is perceived to have, a conflict of interest in its investigation and prosecution, a special prosecutor may be appointed. Special prosecutors are used in state and municipal government for investigations of public corruption but their prominence in U.S. history arises largely from their use in national politics. Calvin Coolidge appointed special counsel to investigate the Teapot Dome scandal of the 1920s, and special prosecutors appointed by President Richard M. Nixon figured prominently in the investigation of the Watergate scandal of the early 1970s. Watergate helped institutionalize use of special prosecutors at the national level. After Nixon dismissed Special Prosecutor Archibald Cox, public outcry forced him to appoint a successor, Leon Jaworski. Congress then began debating proposals that provided for independent special prosecutors. The Ethics in Government Act of 1978 arranged for judicially appointed independent counsel to investigate allegations of criminal misconduct against high-ranking executive officials. The act's provisions remained controversial throughout their existence. Opponents argued that appointment of independent prosecutors was an unconstitutional violation of the doctrine of separation of powers. In *Morrison* v. *Olson* (1989) the Supreme Court ruled that such arrangements were constitutional. Between 1978 and 1992, the year Congress failed to reauthorize the Ethics Act, its provisions were invoked in cases involving members of the Jimmy Carter and Ronald Reagan administrations. The most prominent and controversial of these involved the Iran-Contra scandal. In response to allegations of misconduct by President Bill Clinton in the Whitewater scandal, Republicans dropped their opposition to the provisions and they were reauthorized in 1994.

[Katy J. Harriger, *Independent Justice: The Federal Special Prosecutor in American Politics* (Lawrence, Kans., 1992).]

KATY J. HARRIGER

See also **DAH:** Teapot Dome Oil Scandal; Watergate; **SUPP:** Iran-Contra Affair; Scandals; Whitewater.

SPECIES, INTRODUCED. As humans settled in North America over the past 15,000 years, they brought with them a variety of species novel to the environment. Many introduced, or exotic, species, such as wheat, potatoes, cattle, pigs, and horses, were brought to the United States intentionally. Many organisms, however, have been unintentionally introduced, traveling in the holds of ships or planes, hitching rides on imported produce, or escaping from captivity. Both intentional and unintentional introductions can leave unforeseen and destructive economic and ecological effects. Although most introduced species are poorly adapted to a novel ecosystem and die out, some thrive. Arriving in an ecosystem that evolved without them, introduced species frequently have no predators. Native species may not have the defenses necessary to ward off a novel predator. Introduced species can outcompete native species and drive them to extinction or change an ecosystem by altering relationships within it.

The results of introductions of species, intentional and unintentional, are often dramatic. The ecosystems of Hawaii, which evolved in isolation, have been devastated by the introduction of exotic species. Since the arrival of Polynesians 1,000 years ago and Europeans 200 years ago, many of the islands' native plant, bird, and insect species have become extinct because of competition and predation by rats, cats, sheep, goats, and other introduced organisms. In the 1990s there were three times as many introduced species of plants on the islands as there were native plants. In an effort to produce domestic silk, the caterpillar of the gypsy moth was imported to the United States in the nineteenth century. Moths escaped in 1869 and spread throughout the country because they had few natural predators or parasites. Their effect reached a climax in the 1980s, but the insects continue to cause widespread damage to hardwood forests throughout North America. In 1890 European starlings were released in New York City by a birding enthusiast who wanted to establish in the United States all birds from William Shakespeare's writings. The population of these opportunistic and aggressive birds quickly increased as they displaced native cavity-nesting birds, and their range now includes most of North America.

In 1956 the African species of honeybee that had been imported into Brazil escaped from captivity and established colonies and hybridized with the European species of honeybee, itself an introduced species essential for the production of honey and pollination of fruit trees. Africanized honeybees began migrating north and crossed into Texas in October 1990. The Department of Agriculture predicted that the Africanized species will have substantial negative effects on U.S. agriculture. One of the most celebrated cases of an introduced species causing economic damage was the unintentional introduction of the Mediterranean fruit fly, or Medfly, in the 1970s in California. Imported on foreign produce, these small flies caused widespread fruit and vegetable damage. The spread of the Medfly spurred an eradication campaign in California that highlighted the pros and cons of pesticide use.

An introduced species that began causing widespread economic and ecological disruption in the 1990s was the zebra mussel, believed to have been released from the ballast of a European tanker in the Great Lakes in 1988. The mussel population exploded, displacing native mollusks, blocking water pipes and dam outlets, disrupting fisheries, and destroying native aquatic ecosystems. The projected cost to control the zebra mussel invasion is $5 billion by the year 2000. The urgency of the situation provoked Congress to pass the Nonindigenous Aquatic Nuisance Prevention and Control Act of 1990. Near the end of the twentieth century there were thousands of introduced species living in the United States. The Department of Agriculture estimated that introduced species were the primary factor in the population decline of approximately 225 of the nation's 660 endangered or threatened species.

[Marcia Barinaga, "Entomologists in the Medfly Maelstrom," and Mark H. Crawford, ed., "Africanized Bees Near Texas Border," *Science* 247 (1990); Allen Hammond, *World Resources Institute Environmental Almanac* (Boston, 1994); John Ross, "An Aquatic Invader Is Running Amok in U.S. Waterways," *Smithsonian* 24 (1994).]

DAVID W. CASH

See also **SUPP:** Ecology; Endangered Species; Pesticides.

SPEECH, FREEDOM OF. *See* **Freedom of Speech.**

SPERM BANKS. *See* **Reproductive Technology.**

SPIES AND SPYING. *See* **Espionage, Industrial; Intelligence, Military and Strategic.**

SPORTS, NEW. During the 1970s and 1980s a number of new sports appeared on the U.S. scene as a result of popular concerns about health and fitness and commercial promotion of nontraditional activities. These sports tend to be fast-paced, highly individualistic, and aggressive. Hang gliding began to flourish in California with development of a rigid and easily controllable wing design. The first soaring association, the Peninsula Hang Glider Club, organized in December 1971, became the U.S. Hang Gliding Association in 1973. It holds twelve regional meets each year leading to a national championship. Paragliding, a cross between hang gliding and skydiving that originated in Europe in the mid-1980s, was adopted in the United States in the mid-1990s. Other subspecies of skydiving included skysurfing (like skydiving except that the jumper has a board attached to his or her feet that facilitates stunts), and BASE jumping, which involves leaping from *b*uildings, *a*ntennae, *s*pans, and *e*arth.

Frisbee games such as freestyle and Ultimate came into their own during the 1970s. Freestyle is an individual sport in which players are judged on their style and tricks while throwing and catching. Ultimate is a seven-player team sport played on a sixty-by-forty-yard field with thirty-yard end zones. The disk must be passed from player to player and a catch made in the end zone is worth one point. Bicycle sports such as cyclo-cross and trail-bike riding also became competitive events. Riders traverse difficult terrain and at least once must carry their bikes across a body of water. Cyclo-cross peaked in the early 1970s and has since declined, while the noncompetitive mountain biking remained popular. Like many sports, competitive freestyle skiing grew out of a recreational activity, in this case the stunts and tricks performed by downhill skiers known as "hot-dogging." The first meet was held in 1971 and two years later devotees formed the National Freestyle Skiers Association. Inclusion of freestyle skiing as a demonstration sport at the 1988 Winter Olympics represented the coming of age of this entertaining activity.

Perhaps the most grueling of new sports, the triathlon, began in Hawaii in 1978, when on a whim several men decided to compete in the Waikiki Roughwater Swim, the Around Oahu Bike Race, and the Honolulu Marathon all in the same day. Their efforts inspired the Hawaii Ironman Triathlon (in which both sexes participate). After portions of the event were televised in 1982, the popularity of the sport increased dramatically. By the 1990s an estimated 750,000 triathletes took part in 2,000 races worldwide. In 1994 triathlete Karen Smyers won her fifth consecutive national women's championship. Sailboarding became a competitive sport in the early 1980s. A sailboard is essentially a surfboard with a pivoting mast and a triangular sail of sixty square feet. Competitions among riders of these wind-driven boards involve course racing, slalom, and freestyle. The United States Boardsailing Association, organized in 1980, governs this sport. Other new sports since 1970 include arena football, indoor soccer, roller blading, jet-ski boating, parasailing, Wally ball, and ski orienteering. They represent the U.S. public's insatiable desire for varied competitive and recreational activities.

[Ralph Hickok, *The Encyclopedia of North American Sports History* (New York, 1992); Thomas C. Jones, *The Great American Sports Book* (Geneva, Ill., 1990).]

DAVID P. MCDANIEL

See also **SUPP:** Aerobics; Fitness; Marathons; Olympic Games; Skiing; Tennis; individual sports.

SSC. *See* **Supercolliding Super Conductor.**

STAGFLATION, a term referring to transitional periods when the economy is simultaneously experiencing the twin evils of inflation and high unemployment in the early stages of stagnation, a condition many economists as late as the 1950s considered atypical of the U.S. economy. Stagflation occurs when the economy is moving from an inflationary period to a recessionary one. If the economy goes through an overheated period in which prices rise because of increases in wages, machinery, credit, and/or natural resources, the reaction of business firms is to produce less and charge higher prices. The term first came into use in the mid-1970s, when inflation soared to 12 percent and the unemployment rate nearly doubled to 9 percent. This inflation was caused by the quadrupling of oil prices by the Organization of Petroleum Exporting Countries (OPEC), increases in the price of raw materials, and the lifting of government-imposed wage and price controls. At the same time, the economy went into recession. In 1980–1981 the country entered a period of stagflation so severe that a new term, "slumpflation," was used. After years of double-digit inflation the Federal Reserve Board (FRB), under Paul Volcker, raised interest rates to record levels of 20 percent to induce a recession and break the inflation cycle. Subsequently the FRB pursued a monetary policy designed to head off significant increases in inflation, but in 1994–1995 seven FRB increases in short-term interest rates failed to moderate economic growth. This led to speculation that in a global economy, domestic monetary policy may not be as effective in controlling either stagflation or slumpflation as previously thought.

ERIK BRUUN

See also **DAH:** Inflation; **SUPP:** Banking and Finance; Federal Reserve System; Oil Crises.

STARK **INCIDENT.** On May 17, 1987, an Iraqi fighter plane attacked the U.S. frigate *Stark* in the Persian Gulf and killed thirty-seven of the crew. The vessel was on patrol to demonstrate freedom of navigation in international waters during the Iran-Iraq War. Claiming the attack was a mistake, Iraq paid the United States $27 million in compensation, but the attack and a U.S. decision two days later to protect eleven Kuwaiti oil tankers triggered congressional debate over both U.S. foreign policy and the dangers facing U.S. forces in the Persian Gulf before the 1991 war against Iraq.

[George P. Shultz, *Turmoil and Triumph: My Years as Secretary of State* (New York, 1993).]

KENNETH B. MOSS

See also **SUPP:** Gulf War of 1991; Iran-Iraq War; Middle East, Relations with.

STAR WARS. *See* **Strategic Defense Initiative.**

STATE, DEPARTMENT OF. The Constitution empowers the president to appoint diplomats and consuls to represent the United States abroad. Since 1789 their work has been directed by the Department of State. For much of the nineteenth century, appointments to the diplomatic and consular services were used to reward political contributors and the party faithful. The 1890s witnessed the first lasting steps to end this arrangement and to base appointments on demonstrated merit. By the time the United States entered World War I not only had the consular service and that portion of the diplomatic corps below the rank of ambassador or minister been taken out of politics, but the foundations and structural outline for a career foreign service had been put into place.

Appointments now were made to the services only after examination and incumbents were not turned out of office when the other political party captured the White House. The State Department's operations and its links with the field foreign service were systematized, primarily through development of the geographic bureaus, which have been the basis for much of the department's organization ever since. In 1924 the Rogers Act, drafted in the State Department, merged the diplomatic and consular services into the Foreign Service of the United States. Many of the reforms of prior years, such as appointment only after competitive examination, were given statutory authority.

In the 1990s, there were approximately 4,700 Foreign Service officers (FSOs) working at some 250 diplomatic and consular offices abroad as well as at the State Department in Washington, D.C., in four major areas: political reporting and analysis; economic reporting and analysis; consular affairs (primarily handling visa applications and assistance to U.S. citizens); and administration. Even before the Rogers Act, the proportion of chiefs of mission coming from the career service had reached 50 percent. In the decades that followed, and particularly with the great increase in the number of nations after World War II, roughly a 70:30 ratio came to prevail. From the 1960s to the mid-1990s about 70 percent of such appointments went to career FSOs and 30 percent to political appointees. That ratio was slightly more favorable for FSOs under President Jimmy Carter (75:25) and slightly less favorable under Ronald Reagan (67:33). Some commentators have observed that the United States is the only major country that chooses large numbers of its envoys from outside its career service and that both Republican and Democratic presidents have dealt in "bought commissions" for ambassadorial appointments. Others note that in some instances a president may need to appoint to a foreign capital a person in whom he has confidence or with whose views he is in agreement. This sentiment is by no means new, as illustrated by Woodrow Wilson's letter, four months into his presidency, to a State Department official: "Every day, I feel more and more keenly the necessity of being represented at foreign courts by men who easily catch and instinctively themselves occupy our point of view with regard to public matters."

Since the Rogers Act, changes in the organization of the Foreign Service have demonstrated an almost continuous effort to adapt the foreign affairs machinery to changing circumstances. The Foreign Service Act of 1980, for example, created a Senior Foreign Service for older officers, fostering the advancement of younger FSOs. A principal problem for the State Department has been that it has not been alone in representing the nation abroad, much less in helping the president formulate and conduct foreign policy. The State and Commerce departments have clashed over certain issues involving foreign trade promotion since the Commerce Department was created in 1903, and since World War II foreign affairs agencies have proliferated. One observer counted sixty-one in 1971 and a study in 1993 found eighty-seven. At the typical U.S. embassy abroad fewer than 20 percent of the personnel are State Department people. At home, the department has had to contend in policy planning matters not only with a much enlarged Defense Department but with agencies traditionally domestic in their orientation, such as the Departments of the Treasury and Agriculture, as foreign and domestic questions have become more intertwined.

The State Department's chief competitor in Washington, D.C., has been the National Security Council (NSC), created in 1947 by the National Security Act. Particularly since the John F. Kennedy administration (1961–1963), the NSC has built a large staff to contend with State for the ear of the president and his staff. Several presidents have relied more on the national security adviser than the secretary of state, and they have appointed strong and articulate academics to the former post, such as Kennedy's McGeorge Bundy, Richard Nixon's Henry Kissinger, and Jimmy Carter's Zbigniew Brzezinski. An example of a president bypassing the secretary of state occurred in the summer of 1980, when Secretary of State Edmund Muskie and other State Department officials learned only from newspaper accounts that President Carter had two weeks earlier issued a directive revising the U.S. nuclear war strategy; by contrast, the Defense Department and the NSC had taken part in the decision.

During the Ronald Reagan (1981–1989) and George Bush (1989–1993) administrations, the secretary of state's role vis-à-vis the national security adviser was strengthened, primarily because of the forcefulness of Secretaries of State Alexander Haig, George P. Shultz, and James Baker. Yet even Secretary Shultz felt obliged in 1986 to cable all U.S. ambassadors with a warning not to bypass him by communicating directly with the national security adviser. It is clear that the traditional concept of a State Department serving the president as the only agency for foreign policy development, as well as having nearly total responsibility for official contacts and relations with other nations, has not been a viable one since at least the late 1940s. Critics frequently have called upon the State Department to coordinate the activities of the various foreign affairs agencies, a task more easily said than done.

Another problem for the State Department has been its lack of a domestic constituency. During the first years of the twentieth century, department officials were able to mobilize support from the business community for their work on behalf of promoting foreign trade and reforming the consular and diplomatic services. Most of this support was soon diverted to the Commerce Department's commercial attachés. Other agencies, such as the Departments of Defense and Agriculture, have developed powerful domestic pressure groups lacking in the Department of State.

Social changes in the United States and the world also have left their marks on the State Department and Foreign Service. Among these are changes in the roles of women. Increasingly, wives of FSOs have demonstrated a strong desire for careers of their own, yet traditionally they have acted as unpaid hostesses and until 1972 were even included as an element in their husbands' annual performance evaluations. In 1978 the department established the Family Liaison Office, which received legislative sanction in the Foreign Service Act of 1980, to help with careers for spouses. The 1980 act also provided for retirement and survivor benefits for divorced spouses. Women Foreign Service officers likewise gained ground. As late as 1971 a woman FSO was expected to resign if she married and women were routinely assigned to consular rather than to diplomatic work. Also in 1971 the first sex discrimination suit was filed against the department. *Palmer* v. *Shultz* (1985) held that the department did not discriminate but was reversed the next year, resulting in cancellation of the 1989 foreign service examination while the department worked to take corrective action as prescribed by the court.

Concern that the Foreign Service contained too small a proportion of minorities and women led to concerted efforts to recruit and retain persons from both groups. Hence, the department has pursued affirmative action, as it did in the early twentieth century for white male Democrats from the South in order to create the fact and the image of greater political diversity in the foreign service. By the late 1980s and early 1990s the department's efforts were achieving results. From 1987 to 1993 women and minorities eligible for promotion were advanced at rates slightly higher than other eligible FSOs. The push for affirmative action did not slacken with the advent of the Bill Clinton administration and its advocacy of a government that "looks like America." Meanwhile, with much less attention, the composition of the service also has been changing in terms of the college background of officers, with a pronounced decline in the proportion possessing Ivy League degrees and a significant rise in the fraction of alumni from state universities.

Another development greatly affecting the Foreign Service has been the growing incidence of terrorism directed at U.S. embassies abroad, of which the Iranian hostage situation of 1979–1981 was only the most prominent and dramatic. By 1981 the State Department was offering a two-day seminar on how to avoid and survive terrorist attacks, and by early 1983 some 15 percent of the department's expenditures were used to protect U.S. personnel and facilities. In 1986 the Bureau of Diplomatic Security was established at State, and in that same year Congress voted to provide U.S. government employees taken hostage by terrorists cash payments of not less than half the worldwide average per diem. The reference by Secretary of State John Foster Dulles (1953–1959) to Foreign Service officers as "soldiers in the front line trenches of our foreign policy" was taking on additional meaning in the last quarter of the twentieth century.

[Barry M. Rubin, *Secrets of State: The State Department and the Struggle Over U.S. Foreign Policy* (New York, 1985); Andrew L. Steigman, *The Foreign Service of the United States: First Line of Defense* (Boulder, Colo., 1985); Richard Hume Werking, "Department of State," in Donald R. Whitnah, ed., *Government Agencies* (Westport, Conn., 1983).]

RICHARD HUME WERKING

See also **SUPP:** Commerce, Department of; Defense, Department of; Hostages, Middle East; Terrorism.

STOCK MARKET. *See* **Financial Exchanges; Options Exchanges; Wall Street.**

STOCK MARKET CRASH OF 1987. *See* **Black Monday Stock Market Crash.**

STRATEGIC ARMS LIMITATION TALKS (SALT). From November 1969 until June 1979, the United States and the Soviet Union negotiated limitations on their strategic nuclear arms. Two sets of agreements

were reached—the SALT I accords signed at the first summit meeting of President Richard M. Nixon with Soviet leader Leonid I. Brezhnev in Moscow in May 1972, and the SALT II Treaty signed at the only summit meeting between President Jimmy Carter and Brezhnev, in Vienna in June 1979. These were the first substantial arms control agreements between the two countries. Originally proposed by the United States in December 1966, the Soviet Union equivocated until May 1968, when the Soviets had numerical strategic parity in sight. A planned opening of SALT at a summit meeting in September 1968 was derailed by the Soviet-led Warsaw Pact occupation of Czechoslovakia in August. With the defeat of the Democrats in the 1968 presidential election, SALT had to await a new administration and its review of defense and foreign policies. The delay of the opening of SALT from fall 1968 to late fall 1969 had one significant adverse effect; during that year the United States successfully tested and developed deployable MIRV (multiple, independently targeted reentry vehicle) warheads for its strategic missiles—five years ahead of the Soviet Union. As a result, the negotiations placed no restrictions on MIRV technology, seriously undercutting the value of the SALT I and SALT II agreements limiting strategic offensive arms.

Two SALT I accords were reached in January 1972—the Antiballistic Missile (ABM) Treaty, which severely limited ABM defenses, and the Interim Agreement on the Limitation of Strategic Offensive Arms, which froze the total number of strategic missile launchers pending further negotiation of a more comprehensive treaty limiting strategic missiles and bombers. (A separate agreement on measures to avert accidental use of nuclear weapons had been concluded in September 1971.) The ABM Treaty, of indefinite duration, restricted each party to two ABM sites, with 100 ABM launchers at each. (In the only later amendment to the treaty, a 1974 protocol, the two parties agreed to forgo one of those sites, so that each was thereafter limited to a single deployment location.) Further constraints included a ban on the testing and deployment of land-mobile, sea-based, air-based, and space-based systems. Only fixed, land-based ABM systems could be deployed at the one allowed site. The Soviet Union kept its existing ABM deployment around Moscow. The United States completed its deployment at a site for defense of intercontinental ballistic missile (ICBM) launchers near Grand Forks, S.Dak., but in 1975 mothballed the complex as too expensive. The ABM Treaty was a solid achievement in arms limitation, although agreement was facilitated by doubts on both sides as to the cost-effectiveness of available ABM systems. While the treaty headed off a costly and useless ABM deployment race, it did not have the desired effect of also damping down deployment of strategic offensive missiles, especially because MIRVs were not constrained.

The Interim Agreement froze the level of land- and sea-based strategic missiles (permitting completion of launchers already under construction). The Soviet Union had a quantitative advantage with 2,348 missile launchers to 1,710 for the United States. This was, however, offset in two important ways. First, neither strategic bombers nor forward-based nuclear delivery systems were included, and the United States had a significant advantage in both categories. Second, although the Soviet Union had more missile launchers and deployed missiles, the United States had a larger number of strategic missile warheads and by 1972 had already begun deploying MIRV warheads. Overall, the Interim Agreement placed only modest limits on strategic missiles. In contrast to the ABM Treaty, it was not significant as an arms control measure.

SALT II was the name given to the follow-on negotiation of a treaty to replace the SALT I Interim Agreement. These talks lasted from November 1972 to June 1979. The SALT II Treaty provided equal levels of strategic arms (2,400, to be reduced over time to 2,200, strategic delivery vehicles) and included strategic bombers as well as strategic missiles. Intended to be in effect for ten years, during which a third SALT negotiation for further reductions was envisaged, the SALT II Treaty fell afoul of the collapse of the Soviet-American détente of the 1970s after the Soviet occupation of Afghanistan in 1979 and was never ratified. Its major constraints, however, were formally observed by both sides until 1986, and for all practical purposes even after the dissolution of the Soviet Union.

In 1982, under the administration of President Ronald Reagan, a new series of negotiations, the Strategic Arms Reduction Talks (START), succeeded SALT. In July 1991 the START I Treaty was signed in Moscow by President George Bush and Soviet President Mikhail Gorbachev. In January 1993 the START II Treaty was also signed in Moscow, by Bush and Russian President Boris Yeltsin. The treaties involved increasingly substantial reductions, but even so, START I brought the level of strategic warheads down only to about the SALT II level, and START II down to the SALT I level.

The SALT process was a success in demonstrating that adversaries could reach arms limitation agreements, but owing to the very cautious and conservative approaches of both sides, the limitations on strategic offensive arms were unable to keep up with the military technological advances given precedence by the two countries. The ABM Treaty, buffeted mainly by revived U.S. interest in President Reagan's Strategic Defense Initiative (SDI) of 1983, survived the decade before the SDI was abandoned. It remained an effective arms control agreement. Pursuant to the SALT I agreements a Standing Consultative Commission (SCC) was established to resolve questions regarding the meaning of and compliance with the SALT agreements. It was also stipulated that there would be no interference with the use of national technical means of verification, such as observation satellites. SALT thus helped at least to stabilize, if not greatly reduce, the military balance. The SALT process and the agreements reached, while causing some friction and disagreements, contributed to the overall political détente of the 1970s. While not sufficient to sustain that détente, the SALT process helped ensure that even under renewed tension the risk of nuclear war remained low.

[John Newhouse, *Cold Dawn: The Story of SALT* (New York, 1973); Gerard C. Smith, *Doubletalk: The Story of SALT I* (New York, 1980); Strobe Talbott, *Endgame: The Inside Story of SALT II* (New York, 1979); Thomas W. Wolfe, *The SALT Experience* (Cambridge, Mass., 1979).]

RAYMOND L. GARTHOFF

See also **SUPP:** Arms Race and Disarmament; Cold War; Soviet Union, Relations with; Strategic Defense Initiative.

STRATEGIC ARMS REDUCTION TALKS (START). *See* **Arms Race and Disarmament.**

STRATEGIC DEFENSE INITIATIVE (SDI), known to its critics as "Star Wars," was introduced in 1983 by President Ronald Reagan as a new and highly effective program to protect the United States from nuclear attack. SDI would have employed infrared detectors and exotic weapons, such as high-powered lasers to identify, track, and destroy incoming ballistic missiles. Traveling at the speed of light, a satellite-based laser beam could engage an enemy missile soon after launch. According to President Reagan, SDI would safeguard the nation, making nuclear weapons "impotent and obsolete." Despite its attraction, the proposal evoked immediate opposition. Critics questioned the legality of SDI because space-based antimissile weapons were prohibited by the 1972 ABM (antiballistic missile) Treaty. Moreover, they claimed that the system would require many major technological breakthroughs and would be prohibitively expensive (estimates ran as high as $1 trillion). They also claimed that SDI would be vulnerable to many countermeasures, and the immensely complex computer code required for battle management could never be tested and was unlikely to work. The administration argued that all the technical problems could be overcome with an aggressive research program, which was legal under its interpretation of the ABM Treaty. During the Reagan administration and that of George Bush (from 1981 to 1993), Congress funded the program at levels substantially below administration requests. As technical difficulties arose, the program was modified to emphasize more conventional weapons such as small heat-seeking rockets ("brilliant pebbles"). President Bill Clinton's first secretary of defense, Les Aspin, promoted theater missile defenses by substituting ground-based missile defense systems for space-based ones. In effect this proposal put an end to SDI, a course made easier by the collapse of the Soviet Union and the end of the cold war.

[Steven Anzovin, ed., *The Star Wars Debate* (New York, 1986); Robert M. Lawrence, *SDI: A Bibliographic and Research Guide* (Boulder, Colo., 1987).]

LEO SARTORI

See also **SUPP:** Arms Race and Disarmament.

STRIKES. Since the late eighteenth century, workers have used strikes, or organized work stoppages, to secure union recognition and better working conditions, wages, and benefits from employers. In the 1980s, however, fundamental changes both in the structure of the U.S. economy and in labor practices severely undercut the efficacy of the strike as a pressure tactic, resulting in fewer and shorter strikes involving substantially fewer workers. In 1974 the Department of Labor reported 424 strikes at businesses with 1,000 or more employees, involving nearly 1.8 million workers. After 1981 strikes numbered fewer than 100 annually, dropping as low as 35 in 1993.

The strength and militancy of the union movement declined as global competition, deregulation, and other factors forced massive layoffs and plant closures in such bastions of organized labor as the steel and automobile industries. Workers were increasingly displaced in heavy industry by automated manufacturing. The automobile industry relocated plants to southern states, where unionization was traditionally opposed, or to such countries as Mexico. These developments resulted in dramatic changes in the U.S. workforce as higher-paying, unionized industrial jobs gave way to lower-paying, generally nonunionized service-sector work. As late as 1960, for example, 30 percent of all U.S. employees were union members. By 1994 membership had dropped to 15.5 percent. The movement showed no appreciable growth as baby boomers and women joined the workforce and boosted employment to record levels. Employers increasingly turned to part-time employees or independent contractors who generally received none of the benefits provided by union contracts. Job growth occurred in small entrepreneurial companies, usually technology firms where unions had never existed.

The most dramatic setback suffered by labor was the 1981 strike by the more than 11,000-member Professional Air Traffic Controllers Organization (PATCO). The controllers, who were federal employees, struck for higher wages, shorter hours, better retirement benefits, and better equipment, saying that such changes would improve air safety. President Ronald Reagan responded by dismissing all the striking controllers and replacing them with supervisors, nonunion controllers, and military controllers. Reagan, who led a Screen Actors Guild strike in 1960, said he respected the right of workers in the private sector to strike but that the government had to "provide without interruption the protective services which are government's reasons for being." He pointed to the no-strike oath each controller had signed as a condition of federal employment. Reagan's position was reminiscent of the stance taken by his political hero Calvin Coolidge, who as governor of Massachusetts in 1919 opposed a strike by Boston police, stating that "there is no right to strike against the public safety by anybody, anywhere, anytime." The PATCO strike did massive damage to the labor movement. The strike was not honored by other airline unions, and the air traffic control system was rebuilt with little apparent effect upon public safety.

Perhaps the most serious consequence of the strike for labor was that the firing of the controllers encouraged private employers nationwide to thwart other strikes by hiring "replacement workers" even when the strike involved skilled employees. One prominent labor action involving replacement workers was the 1994–1995 Major League Baseball strike. Minor league and replacement players were brought into spring training in 1995, although the strike ended just prior to opening day. No agreement had been reached between owners and the Players' Association as the 1996 season approached. The city of Decatur, Ill., known as a union town, endured two strikes and a lockout in the 1990s. On July 12, 1994, 3,000 members of the United Rubber Workers went on strike at six locations of Bridgestone-Firestone. The Japanese owners of the company hired 2,300 replacement workers in February 1995, and the union accepted the company's contract offer and ended its strike in August, in a decision union members said was aimed at forestalling a union decertification election. Other strikes in the 1990s included that of nine of ten unions that went on strike against the *New York Daily News* in 1990; the union and British publisher Robert Maxwell, who bought the failing paper from the Tribune Company of Chicago, reached a contract agreement in the summer of 1991. On June 20, 1994, the United Auto Workers (UAW) struck eleven plants of Caterpillar, the world's leading maker of earth-moving and construction equipment. It was the tenth strike in three years by 10,000 UAW members, who had an average of twenty-four years on the job.

Deregulation weakened unions in industries where they had previously been the strongest, such as airlines, trucking, and railroads. Management engaged unions in negotiations over "give backs," including wage concessions and work rules. From the union-side, the negotiations shifted to job security, health insurance, and seniority. The agreements often changed unions' relation to management. Sometimes the agreements gave unions seats on boards. In other cases, particularly in the airline industry, unions became owners. Organized labor's strength shifted to the public sector, where 7.1 million workers (federal, state, and local) were union members in 1994, 38.7 percent of total public sector employment. Federal and often state laws restricted strikes by public sector employees. Out of forty-five major strikes in 1994 only eight involved public-sector employee unions. Of those disputes, five involved education. Labor's political clout waned. Traditionally, organized labor supported Democratic congressional and presidential candidates, but election of Republican majorities in both houses of Congress in 1994 undercut what little ability labor had to protect hard-won bargaining rights under federal law. President Bill Clinton did manage to sidestep Congress in 1995 by issuing an executive order barring federal agencies from granting contracts in excess of $100,000 to companies that permanently replaced striking workers.

Indicative of labor's troubles and attempts to revivify the movement was the forced resignation in 1995 of longtime AFL-CIO president Lane Kirkland. After the first contested election for the presidency in the union's history, he was succeeded by reform candidate John J. Sweeney, who campaigned on a record of aggressive organizing in the service sector as president of the Service Employees International Union. A new generation of union leaders called for a return to civil disobedience and confrontational tactics to stem the decline of unionism in the United States, but the increasingly international nature of the U.S. economy made the success of such efforts uncertain.

[David Brody, *Workers in Industrial America,* 2nd ed. (New York 1993); Charles B. Craver, *Can Unions Survive?* (New York, 1993); William Winpisinger, *Reclaiming Our Future: An Agenda for American Labor* (Boulder, Colo., 1989); Robert H. Zieger, *American Workers, American Unions,* 2nd ed. (Baltimore, 1994).]

BRENT SCHONDELMEYER

See also **SUPP:** Air Traffic Controllers Strike; Automobile Industry; Aviation Industry; Baseball Strike of 1994–1995; Labor Unions.

STYLE. *See* **Fashion and Style.**

SUBMARINES. Because neither light nor radar can penetrate water to any appreciable extent, a submerged submarine is very hard to locate. The ships are very quiet in order to avoid detection by sonar. All these factors make submarines the least vulnerable of any ship to attack. Modern missile-carrying submarines are nuclear-powered and can stay submerged for months. Submarines are used as launch platforms for submarine-launched ballistic missiles (SLBMs); the long range of these missiles gives the submarine a large operating area. SLBMs are the most numerous component of the U.S. strategic triad, which also includes land-based intercontinental ballistic missiles (ICBMs) and strategic bombers. Beginning with the Poseidon missile (1970), all U.S. SLBMs have carried multiple warheads, dubbed multiple independently targeted reentry vehicles (MIRVs). The most modern U.S. submarine, *Trident,* carries twenty-four Trident C-4 or D-5 missiles, each loaded with eight warheads. The Soviet Union had more submarines but fewer total warheads. In 1988 the United States had 6,600 warheads on thirty-two submarines and the Soviet Union 3,400 warheads on sixty-three submarines. Both forces have been reduced under the terms of the first Strategic Arms Reduction Talks Treaty (START I). Once the January 1993 START II agreement was implemented the United States planned to download its missiles in order to maintain a force of about 1,700 warheads on eighteen submarines. Early SLBMs were fairly inaccurate in large part because of uncertainty in the location of the submarine. The accuracy was greatly improved with the introduction of the global positioning system (GPS). Signals emitted from satellites in orbit enable the missile's computers to calculate its position with very high precision. With GPS guidance, the Trident missile is estimated to be accurate to within 100 meters, as good as that of the most accurate ICBMs.

[Thomas B. Cochran et al., *Nuclear Weapons Databook*, vols. 1 (Cambridge, Mass., 1984) and 4 (New York, 1989).]

LEO SARTORI

See also **SUPP:** Arms Race and Disarmament.

SUBSTANCE ABUSE, the improper consumption of harmful chemicals, includes excessive or habitual drinking of alcohol; use of such illegal drugs as cocaine, heroin, and marijuana; improper use of medications such as tranquilizers, stimulants, and steroids; and less common practices such as inhaling fumes of cleaning fluids. Cigarette smoking is also referred to as substance abuse in some contexts, especially since a 1994 FDA advisory committee voted unanimously that "the amount of nicotine delivered by currently marketed cigarettes [is] likely to lead to addiction in the typical smoker." In addition to direct physical and emotional harm, substance abuse is frequently cited as an important factor in crime, family strife, and other social problems. Substance abuse has been a concern throughout the nation's history but became prominent after 1960. Developing a national consensus or effective strategy to deal with it has proved difficult, because of contradictory beliefs about drugs and alcohol. As a result, government policies have shifted a number of times.

People use alcohol and drugs for a variety of reasons. Alcohol produces pleasurable sensations and a sense of escape from reality; certain drugs can heighten awareness and stimulate energy, while others can dull the user's consciousness and offer a sense of relaxation. The difference between use and abuse depends on many factors, including legitimate benefits, detrimental physical and psychological effects, and circumstances of the user. Distinctions may reflect religious and other values, social beliefs, and interpretation of scientific research. There are varying degrees of abuse. Addicted people have extreme physical and psychological needs and can suffer withdrawal. Others are not addicted but habitually misuse substances and find it difficult to stop. Many people abuse substances only on rare occasions, such as drinking too much at a party.

In the nineteenth century cocaine and opium were widely sold and used in medications, nonmedicinal "health tonics," and other products. Concern about their addictive qualities and other effects increased, and local and state governments passed laws limiting use. The federal government established drug policies with the Harrison Act of 1914. This initiative ended common use of opiates and other narcotics except for medical purposes. Although alcohol was not considered to be in the same category as narcotics, liquor became a focus of controversy and many localities restricted or banned it. The Eighteenth Amendment made liquor illegal nationally in 1920. The amendment was repealed in 1933 but concern remained, and liquor continued to be regulated and remained illegal in some localities. Ironically, drinking gained social acceptance during and after Prohibition and was further encouraged by advertising, movies, and customs such as the cocktail party. Drug abuse became an increasing problem throughout the twentieth century, especially among the poor. A criminal economy developed to supply illegal narcotics. Addicts stole money or engaged in other illicit activities to obtain money for drugs. New tranquilizers, stimulants, and prescription medications led to problems among middle- and upper-income groups.

After 1960 the nation entered a period of social and political upheaval, and drugs became an important part of a larger national polarization of values and lifestyles. Early in that decade a small group of nonconformists known as hippies emerged, most visibly in the San Francisco area. The use of drugs was central to their spiritual exploration and free-spirited hedonism. Most hippies disapproved of liquor and depressant narcotics because they dulled the senses. They favored drugs that they believed heightened perception and expanded spiritual consciousness. Among these were marijuana, which is usually inhaled from pipes or smoked in cigarettes, and more powerful drugs known as psychedelics, such as LSD (lysergic acid diethylamide), which caused hallucinations and other vivid and bizarre mental experiences. The hippies' unusual, flamboyant lifestyle attracted increasing national attention and spread to other communities. Many young people, and some older ones, adopted the music, clothing, and attitudes of this new movement, often called the counterculture.

Problems associated with the proliferation of drug use soon became evident. While many users had no apparent ill effects from drugs like LSD and marijuana, others suffered frightening emotional experiences and long-lasting traumas. Some users even killed themselves. Warnings were raised by scientists about genetic damage and other long-term harm. Many users were continually under the influence of drugs and some turned to new, particularly dangerous substances such as "speed" (methamphetamine), a stimulant that caused erratic behavior and serious physical damage. The drug-related deaths of such popular cultural figures as rock musicians Janis Joplin and Jimi Hendrix focused attention on the dangers of substance abuse. At all levels of government, officials tried to update existing drug laws and policies to reflect the changing situation. Federal drug-control authority expanded and became more flexible. The Bureau of Narcotics was established in the Treasury Department in 1930. In 1968 the bureau was moved to the Justice Department and was combined with other agencies into the new Bureau of Narcotics and Dangerous Drugs, which in 1975 became the Drug Enforcement Administration. The efforts of federal agencies active in drug-law enforcement led to the Controlled Substances Act of 1970, which established classifications and penalties for types of drugs. The government also became active in prevention programs. The Community Mental Health Centers Act of 1963 provided drug-abuse treatment. State and local authorities revised their laws.

Drugs proliferated and the illegal markets that supplied them became more pervasive. Controversies continually arose over strategies to control drugs. Some observers believed that all drugs were dangerous and that the best way to control them was through stringent laws and vigorous enforcement. Others contended that many illegal drugs were harmless and should be legalized. There were shades of opinion between these extremes. One debate was whether to concentrate on drug education and treatment or on enforcement. People who disapproved of marijuana nevertheless believed it was improper to punish otherwise law-abiding citizens who used it. Others countered that so-called "soft drugs" such as marijuana led users to more dangerous hard drugs such as heroin. It was also contended that trying to stop trade in controlled substances was a losing battle and that it would be more effective to legalize but tightly regulate drugs, as had been done with alcohol after

Prohibition. Opponents of legalization argued that making drugs more available would only increase drug abuse. Despite widespread public support for fighting drug-related crime, efforts to strengthen enforcement also raised objections that such actions would erode civil liberties and hinder drug-related scientific research.

Drugs affected foreign policy because much of the supply of heroin, cocaine, and other hard drugs originated in other nations, especially in Latin America and Asia. Treaties encouraged international cooperation in the fight against drug trafficking. Coordination proved difficult to achieve. In 1969 a federal anti–drug smuggling initiative called Operation Intercept offended the government of Mexico in part because extensive searches of vehicles at the U.S.-Mexico border caused traffic delays.

As the 1970s progressed stronger psychedelic drugs such as LSD went out of fashion and the generation that had embraced the hippie ethic became more conservative. Marijuana lost much of its divisive symbolism. Although it remained illegal and was disapproved by a majority of citizens, many people used it as a recreational drug and nonusers became more tolerant. Oregon and other states "decriminalized" marijuana, reducing the penalties for possession of small amounts. Use began to level off and declined after 1979. New types of recreational drug abuse emerged, including medical depressants known as downers. Cocaine resurfaced after many years of obscurity. Although it was considered a recreational drug with a glamorous image when it reappeared, this view of cocaine quickly changed because of the drug's side effects.

After the 1960s the drug problem in low-income inner-city communities began to increase. This trend escalated in 1985 when a concentrated form of cocaine known as crack appeared. Because crack is immediately addictive it became associated with increasing violence. The lucrative market for cocaine and heroin also stimulated the growth of domestic gangs and international crime organizations. Drugs began to spread the fatal disease AIDS through the use of unsanitary hypodermic needles. As drugs became more closely linked with violence, the scope of activities and amount of money allocated to enforcement and treatment programs increased dramatically. The U.S. military began to try to control international drug trafficking, and public and private groups launched education and treatment programs. First Lady Nancy Reagan became the spokesperson for a nationwide educational campaign to discourage drug abuse among young people based on the motto "Just say no." By 1988 the federal budget reached $10 billion for the "war on drugs." That year Congress passed the Anti-Drug Abuse Act, which included the Office of National Drug Control Policy to oversee prevention, enforcement, and treatment, with a director referred to as the nation's "drug czar."

As the war on hard drugs raged the prevailing view of alcohol changed markedly. People became critical of alcoholism, drinking among young people, and other social problems created by alcohol abuse such as family violence and drunk driving. A 1973 report by the National Commission on Marijuana and Drug Abuse (a joint congressional and presidential committee) emphasized the similarities between alcohol and other drugs. The view of alcoholism as a biological disease among people susceptible to becoming dependent on liquor gained increasing acceptance. The parallel between drugs and alcohol was reinforced by psychological theories that all addictions stem from common emotional and mental patterns regardless of the substance. The same parallel between tobacco and other drugs began to be drawn, a view that was bolstered in 1994 when the FDA asserted that nicotine is an addictive substance.

Despite setbacks the push to bring the problem of substance abuse under control achieved some success. Many alcoholics and drug abusers joined self-help groups such as Alcoholics Anonymous or checked into rehabilitation clinics and other treatment programs, a trend that became known as the twelve-step recovery movement. By the late 1980s statistics indicated that fewer people were using illegal drugs or drinking excessively. Stringent laws and awareness campaigns against drunk driving changed the social habits of many citizens. Smoking and other forms of tobacco consumption were on the decline overall and smoking was banned or restricted in many locations. Popular culture and attitudes shifted from messages that condoned or encouraged substance abuse to emphasis on moderation or abstinence. By the early 1990s sobriety had become as fashionable as indulgence once had been. Nevertheless, substance abuse remained a widespread problem. In the early 1990s there were signs of a new cycle of abuse, with a resurgence in the use of tobacco, marijuana, and LSD among young people. The issues surrounding use and abuse of chemical substances were becoming more complex. Advances in medical research were expanding the level of knowledge about the human brain and psyche. Popularly accepted theories about alcoholism and other addictions were challenged and new forms of treatment developed. A new generation of psychiatric drugs was emerging, such as the antidepressant Prozac, which offered the ability to control emotions and behavior in increasingly subtle and powerful ways. These drugs added to the basic social questions and debate about the role that chemical substances should have in shaping human behavior.

[John C. Burnham, *Bad Habits* (New York, 1993); H. Wayne Morgan, *Drugs in America* (Syracuse, N.Y., 1981); Stanton Peele and Archie Brodsky, *The Truth About Addiction and Recovery* (New York, 1991); Elaine Shannon, *Desperadoes, Latin Drug Lords, U.S. Lawmen, and the War America Can't Win* (New York, 1989).]

JOHN TOWNES

See also **DAH:** Drug Addiction; Prohibition; **SUPP:** Food and Drug Administration; Smoking; Tobacco Industry.

SUBURBAN LIVING. American suburban life is unique in several respects: affluent and middle-income citizens live in areas far from their workplaces, in houses they own, and with yards that by urban standards are enormous. The first suburbanites left urban problems far behind, but this was no longer true in the 1990s. Between 1950 and 1980, suburban living markedly increased. By 1980 two-thirds of the nation's housing units were for single-family living in a single dwelling surrounded by an ornamental yard. Dependence on the automobile surrounded bucolic suburbs with massive ropes of highways. One-time minor roads became the main streets of suburbs. Near or along the roaring corridors are strips of fast-food chains, inexpensive motels, quick-stop gas stations, and malls. Long considered centerless, suburbs after 1980 were reshaped by construction of corporate headquarters, in flight from high taxes and congestion in city cores. Suburbs offered parking and open space.

The original uniformity of suburbs gave way to extraordinary diversity. The most dynamic growth areas in the nation, suburbs since the mid-1970s turned into a broad patchwork of inner suburbs, office parks, retail centers known as edge cities, and large suburban cities. Nor are they exclusively white and middle-income. The racial character of suburbs changed dramatically between 1980 and 1990. The black suburban population increased by one-third, from 5.9 million to 8 million. The Hispanic population rose from 5.1 million to 8.7 million (a 69.3 percent increase) and the Asian population from 1.5 million to 3.5 million (125.9 percent). Rapid changes within suburbia were not without problems. Construction produced housing gluts, which combined with the economic recession of the late 1980s to induce record mortgage defaults. Central city problems of drug and alcohol abuse, petty property crime, and family violence reappeared in the suburbs. In 1990 one-third of poor Americans lived in the suburbs. Politically, suburban residents regard themselves as less and less connected to the welfare of urbanites and the fiscal condition of city governments. Through reapportionment, suburban communities gained larger political power in state legislatures and Congress. Increased power allows suburbanites to ignore urban problems in allocation of federal resources, sustaining a fallacious belief in separate destinies, urban and suburban.

[Kenneth T. Jackson, *Crabgrass Frontier* (New York, 1985); Anthony Towns, *New Visions for Metropolitan America* (Washington, D.C., 1994).]

GRAHAM RUSSELL HODGES

See also **SUPP:** Urban Living.

SUDDEN INFANT DEATH SYNDROME (SIDS), sometimes referred to as crib death, is a medical term for the decease of an apparently well infant and describes a death that remains unexplained after all known and possible causes have been ruled out through autopsy, investigation of the scene, and review of the child's medical history. SIDS was first identified as a separate medical entity and named in 1969. SIDS causes the death of 7,000 infants each year in the United States. It occurs most frequently in the third and fourth months and is the most common cause of death in children between their first week and first birthday. SIDS more frequently affects males than females, non-Caucasians than Caucasians, and infants in poverty than those in higher-income situations. Most at risk are infants born prematurely, infants whose mothers smoked during pregnancy or after delivery, children with a history of severe apnea (periods of rapid breathing followed by periods of not breathing), and those whose siblings have died of SIDS. Deaths usually occur during sleep and are more likely during cold months. The cause of SIDS is unknown. Theories include an unidentified birth defect, stress in a normal baby caused by infection or other factors, and failure to develop. Scientists have explored the nervous system, brain, heart, breathing and sleep patterns, body chemical balances, autopsy findings, and environment. It is likely that SIDS, like many medical disorders, will prove to have more than one explanation. There are many popular misconceptions about the cause of SIDS, including belief that

the child has suffocated in its bedclothes or inhaled its own vomit. Because no definitive cause can be found and because parents are totally unprepared for such a loss, the death often causes intense feelings of guilt.

JACK HANDLER

SUICIDE. *See* **Euthanasia.**

SUMMIT CONFERENCES, PRESIDENTIAL, denote personal diplomacy at the highest levels of government. They are based on the assumption that U.S. presidents, possessing the ultimate power over questions of peace and war, can in direct conversations with other heads of state resolve disagreements too long protracted, perhaps dangerously, by lesser officials. For that reason well-publicized exchanges between national leaders, even when they achieve nothing, offer reassurance to a troubled world that current conflicts, however bitter, exist far below the threshold of war. Presidential summitry implies that the country's interests, power, and prestige are directly engaged in the issues of the day. There were occasions before the dramatic events of the late 1930s when presidents participated in international gatherings or conferred privately with leaders of other countries, but those occasions scarcely passed as summit conferences, which supposedly address troublesome international issues head-on. Formal or ceremonial state visits had slight diplomatic significance, or perhaps none at all.

It is not strange, therefore, that the experience of the United States in summitry began with Franklin D. Roosevelt's efforts to influence the course and consequences of World War II. At the Atlantic Conference aboard the *Augusta* off Newfoundland in August 1941, Roosevelt and British Prime Minister Winston Churchill framed the Atlantic Charter to define their wartime goals. At Casablanca in January 1943 Roosevelt and Churchill agreed on basic war plans, and Roosevelt proclaimed the Allied goal of unconditional surrender. In late November 1943 Roosevelt conferred with China's Chiang Kai-shek in Cairo and then continued on to Tehran for his first tripartite summit with Churchill and the Soviet leader Joseph Stalin. Early in December he returned to Cairo for a minor summit with Churchill and President Ismet Inönü of Turkey. At Yalta in February 1945 Roosevelt held his second and final summit with Churchill and Stalin. President Harry S. Truman terminated the wartime tripartite summits at Potsdam in July and

August of 1945. With the emergence of the cold war, summit conferences with the Soviet Union were rendered elusive by Washington's demands that the Kremlin first abandon its objective of advancing world revolution, discard its aggressiveness, and appear ready to fulfill any international agreements by demonstrating its good faith.

Churchill used the term "summit" in calling for a conference at the highest level in the spring of 1953. Denying that the USSR was prepared to fulfill one or more of the country's established requirements, President Dwight D. Eisenhower refused for two years to attend a summit with the Soviet leaders. Retreating under domestic and world pressure, Eisenhower attended the Geneva Big Four Conference of July 1955. Despite its outward display of cordiality, the Geneva summit achieved very little. In November 1957 Kremlin leaders launched a crusade for another summit. The Eisenhower administration demanded that any future summits have adequate preparation, an agreed-upon agenda, and reasonable assurance of success. It was also decided to seek the approval of regional allies, usually registered in a presummit foreign ministers conference. Soviet leaders argued that presummit conferences eliminated the possibility of diplomacy among equals. Again with considerable reluctance, Eisenhower attended the Paris summit of 1960 only to face an angry Nikita Khrushchev, who quickly terminated the conference because of the president's refusal to apologize for sending spy planes across Soviet territory.

For President Richard M. Nixon summitry became symbolic of his effort to advance the spirit of détente between the United States and the communist powers. His summitry began with his trip to China in February 1972—a spectacular media event. His Moscow summit with Soviet leader Leonid Brezhnev in late May 1972 marked the high point of official Soviet-American cordiality during the cold war. In addition to the SALT I Treaty on nuclear weapons, the two leaders signed a variety of lesser agreements to extend the interests binding the two countries together. The two succeeding Nixon-Brezhnev summits, in Washington and Moscow, were anticlimactic. Both countries had reached the outer limits of successful coexistence. Nixon's East-West summits never overcame the doubts and antagonisms that characterized the cold war. President Ronald Reagan's four summits with Mikhail Gorbachev, beginning with the Geneva summit of November 1985 and ending with the Moscow summit of May 1988, marked the beginning of the end of the cold war itself. President George Bush's summit with Gorbachev at Malta in December 1989 continued that trend into the post–cold war era.

Noted critics of summitry, such as British diplomat Harold Nicolson and former U.S. ambassador George F. Kennan, warned that diplomacy among heads of states would lack the time and knowledge that professionals could bring to the task. In practice the summits scarcely engaged those present in diplomacy. Such gatherings permitted an exchange of views, extensive socializing, and photo opportunities in abundance, interspersed occasionally with the signing of agreements prepared laboriously by professional diplomats over long periods of time. Thus, summitry was designed less to settle disputes then to publicize agreements already reached. In personalizing such agreements, summits enabled those attending to exaggerate their achievements and thereby enhance their stature as world leaders. Presidents, responding to global expectations, possessed the authority to make concessions not permitted to those obligated to defend established policies. In practice, however, successive presidents refrained from exercising their special prerogatives as heads of the nation's foreign policy establishment. Still, their presence at the summits was a reminder that presidents, not others, carried the responsibility for the country's external policies. Summits invariably reflected the political, military, and diplomatic realities of the time with little capacity to change them. If presidents on occasion chose to be their own secretaries of state, they seldom revealed that proclivity at the summits.

[Elmer Plischke, *Summit Diplomacy: Personal Diplomacy of the President of the United States* (Westport, Conn., 1974), and *Diplomat in Chief: The President at the Summit* (New York, 1986).]

NORMAN A. GRAEBNER

See also **DAH:** Atlantic Charter; Cairo Conferences; Casablanca Conference; Geneva Conferences; Paris Conferences; Potsdam Conference; Summit Conferences; Tehran Conference; Yalta Conference; **DAH and SUPP:** China, Relations with; Cold War; Soviet Union, Relations with; Strategic Arms Limitation Talks; **SUPP:** Arms Race and Disarmament.

SUNBELT, comprising the states of the South and Southwest, is a term coined to describe both the warm climate of these regions and the rapid economic and population growth that have been characteristic since the 1960s. The Sunbelt stretches approximately from Virginia south to Florida and west to California but also includes western mountain states, such as Colorado and Utah, that have experienced similar economic growth. Historically, most of the nation's population and economic power has been based in the Northeast and upper Midwest. The Southeast had a smaller population, a less robust economy, and hot, humid summers that many northerners considered uncomfortable. Much of the Southwest was settled later and remained sparsely populated well into the twentieth century because of its remote location and an inhospitable desert climate that regularly reached triple-digit temperatures in summer. With the advent of air conditioning, however, year-round comfort became possible in both regions.

A shift from northeastern dominance was evident by the early 1970s. The term "New South" came into use to describe economic progress and social changes in the Southeast. California and oil-rich Texas were established as thriving economies, and newer regions of prosperity were emerging throughout the West. This pattern intensified in following decades as many states in the North lost population and industries. Domestic and international businesses were attracted to the Sunbelt for many reasons, including lower non-union wages and energy costs, state policies favorable to business, and, in the West, proximity to the increasingly important Pacific Rim nations. A national emphasis on developing domestic fuel sources in the early 1970s stimulated growth in Texas, Colorado, and other states. Many newcomers were attracted by the lifestyles and natural beauty of Sunbelt states. Southern and western states gained increasing political and economic power. All six winners of U.S. presidential elections between 1964 and 1992 were from the Sunbelt. Southern culture and values became influential, such as the nationwide popularity of country and western music. Hispanic cultures of the Southwest and Florida gained prominence.

The Sunbelt also faced difficult issues, including social problems that many people hoped to escape by moving there. Despite areas of prosperity the Southeast continued to have many sections of poverty. Texas and other energy-oriented states experienced a steep, if temporary, economic decline in the mid-1980s because of a fall in oil prices. California suffered serious economic recession and social stresses in the late 1980s and early 1990s, which caused a significant migration of businesses and residents to other nearby states. The impacts of growth and development became matters of urgent concern, as many Sunbelt communities experienced suburban sprawl, congestion, and pollution, along with an erosion of

their regional characteristics and identities. These trends provoked many controversies, which continued into the 1990s. Some people opposed the changes, but others saw them more positively as signs of progress and prosperity. Nationally, experts predicted that the economic growth and increasing influence of the Sunbelt marked a permanent change in the demographic, economic, and political structure of the nation.

[Donald J. Bogue, *The Population of the United States: Historical Trends and Future Projections* (New York, 1985); Charles Reagan Wilson and William Ferris, eds., *Encyclopedia of Southern Culture* (Chapel Hill, N.C., 1989).]

JOHN TOWNES

See also **SUPP:** Entries on individual states and cities.

SUPERCONDUCTING SUPER COLLIDER (SSC), a federally financed project abandoned in 1993 that would have been capable of accelerating subatomic particles to energy levels forty times that previously achieved by researchers. For reasons of national prestige and international economic competitiveness the Ronald Reagan administration in 1982 encouraged U.S. high-energy scientists to devise a challenging national accelerator project. Physicists responded with plans for the most ambitious particle accelerator ever attempted, a superconducting super collider. It was to be a proton collider far more energetic than existing ones, employing the superconducting magnetic technology recently developed at the Fermi National Laboratory in Illinois. The primary justification for the machine was a search for particles known as Higgs bosons. The machine was to produce 40 TeV protons (where 1 TeV, or tera-electron volt, is 1 trillion electron volts). This determined the size (a fifty-four-mile-long ring) and the projected cost ($4.4 billion). Federal funding for the machine required justification. Support from the Texas congressional delegation and the promise of $1 billion toward the project from the state of Texas led to the decision to build the accelerator in Waxahachie, Tex., rather than near Fermilab. In the autumn of 1993 the House of Representatives, faced with a more than doubled price tag, voted overwhelmingly to kill the project. By then $2 billion had been spent, the superconducting magnets had been tested, one-third of the ring had been excavated, and two teams of a thousand physicists and engineers from around the world were working out detailed designs of the two enormous particle detectors to observe and analyze proton collisions in the TeV energy range.

SUPERCONDUCTIVITY

[Daniel J. Kevles, *The Physicists: The History of a Scientific Community in Modern America,* 2nd ed. (Cambridge, Mass., 1995); James Trefil, "Beyond the Quark: The Case for the Super Collider," *New York Times Magazine* (Apr. 30, 1989); Steven Weinberg, *Dreams of a Final Theory* (New York, 1992).]

See also **SUPP:** Fermi National Accelerator Laboratory; Superconductivity.

SUPERCONDUCTIVITY. An electrical conductor becomes superconductive when, at low temperatures, its resistance to electric current decreases to zero. A solid in its superconducting state repels magnetic materials. The most important use of superconductive materials is in construction of electromagnets capable of producing high magnetic fields. The phenomenon was discovered in 1911 by Heike Kamerlingh Onnes, who noted that electrical resistance of frozen mercury suddenly drops to zero at temperatures below −269° C, or 4.2 kelvins (4.2 degrees above absolute zero). Repulsion of magnetic materials by superconductors was described by Walther Meissner and R. Ochsenfeld in 1933. In 1957 the physicists John Bardeen, Leon N. Cooper, and John R. Schrieffer presented a theoretical description of the behavior of electrons in superconductors, for which they received the Nobel Prize in 1972.

Thirty-six elements and hundreds of alloys are superconductive, most at very low temperatures. J. Georg Bednorz and K. Alex Muller in 1986 reported a lanthanum-barium-copper oxide that becomes superconductive at about −240° C (33 K). They received the 1987 Nobel Prize in Physics. This set off an immense international effort to produce composites in which the transition to superconductivity occurs at even higher temperatures. The effort was successful and by the mid-1990s materials that are superconductive at temperatures above −145° C (128 K)—the boiling temperature of commonly available liquified nitrogen—were available. The search continued for superconductive materials that do not require cooling.

Superconductors have found wide application despite the need for cooling to low temperatures. High-field electromagnets make possible such medical diagnostic techniques as magnetic resonance imaging, the related nuclear magnetic resonance spectroscopy widely used by chemists to identify molecules, and accelerators used by nuclear physicists. Applications envisioned for the future include smaller and more efficient electrical motors and generators, magnetically levitated trains, and controlled nuclear fusion.

[Paul C. W. Chu, "High-Temperature Superconductors," *Scientific American* 273 (September 1995).]

DAVID K. LEWIS

See also **SUPP:** Fermi National Accelerator Laboratory; Magnetic Resonance Imaging; Physics; Superconducting Super Collider.

SUPERFUND, officially the Comprehensive Environmental Response, Compensation, and Liability Act of 1980, began as a $1.6 billion, five-year program created by Congress to expedite cleanup of the nation's worst hazardous waste sites. National concern over the release of hazardous wastes buried beneath the residential community at Love Canal in western New York State prompted its passage. The term also refers to the Superfund Amendment and Reauthorization Act (SARA) of 1986, which comprehensively revised the original act and added $9 billion to the fund. In response to a 1984 tragedy in Bhopal, India, in which 3,000 people died and hundreds of thousands were reported to be affected by exposure to deadly methyl isocyanate gas that leaked from a Union Carbide plant, Congress included provisions in SARA requiring corporations to inform host communities of the presence of dangerous materials and to develop emergency plans for dealing with accidental releases of such materials. From the beginning Superfund met with harsh, and often justified, criticism. President Ronald Reagan's commitment to reduce government regulation of industry undermined the effectiveness of the legislation. At the end of five years the money was gone, and only 6 of the 1,800 hazardous waste sites identified at that time had been cleaned up. Another 18,000 suspected sites remained to be investigated. Caution over a Superfund provision holding a single polluter financially liable for the cleanup of wastes created by many polluters caused additional delays. The Environmental Protection Agency's focus on the legal process rather than on the actual cleanup routinely prevents polluters who are willing to restore a site from doing so because the legal issues are not resolved to EPA's satisfaction. Such delays can postpone cleanups for five to ten years. Many believe that Superfund's fundamental problems cannot be overcome without a legislative overhaul.

[Michael D. LaGrega, Phillip L. Buckingham, and Jeffrey C. Evans, *Hazardous Waste Management* (New York, 1994); Robert A. Taylor, "$1 Billion Later, Toxic Cleanup Barely Begun," *U.S. News & World Report* (Apr. 22, 1985); WMX Technologies, "Superfund Reform," *Views on Responsible Environmental Management* 2 (Winter 1994).]

JOHN MORELLI

See also **SUPP:** Bhopal Explosion; Environmental Protection Agency; Hazardous Waste; Love Canal.

SUPPLY-SIDE ECONOMICS, based on the premise that high tax rates hurt the national economy by discouraging work, production, and innovation, represented a major shift in U.S. economic thinking and policy in the 1980s. Supply-side theory was far from new, its basic ideas dating back to the early-nineteenth-century works of Jean-Baptiste Say and David Ricardo. It had been ignored in the United States since the New Deal, however, because of the demand-side theories of the British economist John Maynard Keynes, who believed in raising income and reducing unemployment by expanding demand even if the government does so through deficit spending. Supply siders, as they were dubbed, argued that high tax rates hurt the national economy because high taxes discourage work and encourage nonproductive investments in tax shelters or outright tax avoidance. Their recommendation was to cut taxes, particularly those of high income groups. In the 1980s supply siders found an audience looking for an alternative to deficit-oriented, demand-side policies. The idea was popularized by Arthur B. Laffer, who said that cutting taxes would increase government revenues. With lower tax rates there would be more incentives for business and for individuals to work and less reason to avoid taxes. There would be more jobs, a more productive economy, and more government revenues.

This theory fitted nicely into the conservative political agenda because it meant smaller government and less interference with the economy. Supply-side economics dominated the administration of President Ronald Reagan, who instituted major tax cuts in 1981 and 1986, reducing the top U.S. rate from 70 percent to roughly 33 percent. Deficits soared to record levels, which many supply siders attributed to the failure at the same time to adopt a balanced budget amendment that would control federal spending. Thus, in the view of some advocates, supply-side theories remained untried. The legacy of supply-side economics has been more political than economic. In the mid-1990s Republican House Speaker Newt Gingrich observed that supply-side economics has "relatively little to do with economics and a great deal to do with human nature and incentives." It contributed to the larger debate about the respective roles of government, individuals, and incentives in U.S. society as the nation faced a global economy.

[Victor A. Canton, Douglas H. Joines, and Arthur B. Laffer, *Foundations of Supply-Side Economics* (New York, 1983); Federal Reserve Bank of Atlanta, *Supply-Side Economics in the 1980s* (Westport, Conn., 1982).]

BRENT SCHONDELMEYER

See also **SUPP:** Budget, Federal; Conservatism; Gramm-Rudman-Hollings Act; Laffer Curve Theory; Reaganomics.

SUPREME COURT. In 1969 Chief Justice Earl Warren retired from the Supreme Court, bringing to an end the "Warren revolution," a period of unprecedented judicial activism in protection of personal rights ranging from the landmark *Brown* v. *Board of Education of Topeka,* 347 U.S. 483 (1954), which fueled the civil rights movement of the 1950s and 1960s, to *Miranda* v. *Arizona,* 384 U.S. 436 (1966), which protected citizens from arbitrary police interrogation. While many observers expected the Court of Warren Earl Burger (1969–1986), with four justices including the chief justice appointed by President Richard M. Nixon, to undo the Warren revolution, matters did not turn out that way. No important Warren Court decision was overruled; some were narrowed but others were not only applied but expanded.

During the Warren Court years, a new activism in protection of personal rights became the judicial hallmark. Strict scrutiny became the primary legal tool to broaden individual rights by reinterpreting the First Amendment, the procedural guarantees of the Bill of Rights (incorporated into the Fourteenth Amendment), the equal protection clause of the Fourteenth Amendment. For the most part the Burger Court continued this liberal jurisprudential trend, but it did more than merely confirm Warren Court jurisprudence. It reintroduced substantive due process to protect personal rights—a doctrine not employed widely since the first quarter of the twentieth century, under which due process was employed to review the reasonableness of laws. The outstanding example was the decision in *Roe* v. *Wade,* 410 U.S. 113 (1973), which ruled that there was a constitutional right to an abortion during the first three months of pregnancy. The right was based on the constitutional right of privacy that had been recognized by the Warren Court. *Roe* was as activist as any Warren Court decision—based on "policy" judgments that led to recognition of a new right not enumerated in the Bill of Rights.

The Burger Court also substantially expanded other women's rights. While it never declared sex a suspect classification under the Fourteenth Amendment, it did establish a "middle" or "heightened" level scrutiny test for sex discrimination cases as the result of three decisions between 1971 and 1976. In the first of these rulings, *Reed* v. *Reed,* 404 U.S. 71 (1971), the Supreme Court invalidated for the first time in its history a statute on the grounds of sex discrimination. In the second, *Frontiero* v. *Richardson,* 411 U.S. 677 (1973), the Court came within one vote of declaring sex a suspect classification. In the third, *Craig* v. *Boren,* 429 U.S. 190 (1976), the Court ruled that "classification by gender must serve important governmental objectives and must be substantially related" to the achievements of these objectives. This new standard has been applied to cases involving women since 1976.

The Burger Court also aided the cause of desegregation of public schools with its decision in *Swann* v. *Charlotte-Mecklenburg Board of Education*, 402 U.S. 1 (1971), which vested broad remedial power in the courts to ensure desegregation, including extensive busing. The *Brown* principle was also expanded to uphold affirmative action programs. As Justice Sandra Day O'Connor, the first woman justice to sit on the Court, later concluded, "We have reached a common destination in sustaining affirmative action against constitutional attack." The same was true in other areas, including the First Amendment, reapportionment, and equal protection. In all these areas the Warren principles remained. The Burger Court dealt with other crucial constitutional issues. *United States* v. *Nixon*, 418 U.S. 683 (1974), brought the Court into the Watergate scandal by ruling that the president could not retain subpoenaed tapes by claiming executive privilege. Its decision led directly to the first resignation of a U.S. president.

Under Chief Justice William H. Rehnquist (1986–), the Court reflected the rightward tilt in U.S. politics affirmed in the 1994 midterm congressional elections, in which Republicans gained control of Congress for the first time since the 1950s. Under the leadership of this conservative activist the Court began to shape a new constitutional case law undoing some of the work of its predecessors. A definite change in direction was manifested in the Rehnquist Court's decisions on civil rights and criminal law. In *Richmond* v. *J. A. Croson Company,* 488 U.S. 469 (1989), the Court struck down a Richmond, Virginia, affirmative action plan, known as set-asides, under which prime contractors awarded city contracts were required to subcontract at least 30 percent of each contract to minority business enterprises. Set-asides represented a form of affirmative action introduced by the Nixon administration, but the Rehnquist Court ruled that the Fourteenth Amendment required strict

scrutiny of all race-based action by state and local governments. Without proof of intentional discrimination by the city, the Richmond plan could not be upheld. The argument that the city was attempting to remedy discrimination, as shown in the disparity between contracts awarded in the past to minority businesses and the city's minority population, was rejected. The Burger Court, in *Fullilove* v. *Klutznick*, 448 U.S. 448 (1980), had sustained federal works programs that set aside 10 percent of the value of contracts for businesses owned by blacks and other minorities. In *Adarand Constructors* v. *Peña* 115 S.Ct. 2097 (1995), however, five justices of the Rehnquist Court cast grave doubt on the continued validity of *Fullilove*. Although neither the federal construction program involved in the case or federal affirmative action in general was declared unconstitutional, strict scrutiny was for the first time applied to federal as well as state affirmative action programs, casting doubt on the validity of many such programs.

Other Rehnquist Court decisions shifted the burden of proof in civil rights cases, holding that plaintiffs, not employers, had the burden of proving that a job requirement shown statistically to screen out minorities was not a "business necessity." Employers were permitted to show by only a preponderance of the evidence rather than by clear and convincing evidence (a higher burden of proof) that refusals to hire were based on legitimate and not discriminatory reasons. The Rehnquist Court also refused to invalidate a death sentence imposed upon a black defendant despite a detailed statistical study that showed black defendants who killed white victims were far more likely to receive the death penalty than white defendants. The Court stressed that there was no proof that the decision-makers in this particular case acted with discriminatory purpose.

From 1973 to 1989 the Supreme Court struck down most attempts by states to place restrictions on women's constitutional right to abortions. In *Webster* v. *Health Reproductive Services,* 492 U.S. 490 (1989), the Rehnquist Court upheld restrictions on abortions but refused to overrule the fundamental right to abortion declared in *Roe*. In *Planned Parenthood of Southeastern Pennsylvania* v. *Casey,* 112 S. Ct. 2791 (1992), the Rehnquist Court again declined to overrule *Roe,* although it did uphold a variety of other restrictions on abortion.

Rehnquist Court decisions also marked the beginning of a trend in favor of property rights. For the first time in years, the Court began to stress the constitutional prohibition against taking property without compensation. Noteworthy in such cases was the Court's use of heightened scrutiny to review the merits of land-use regulations in deciding whether a challenged regulation required judicial invalidation in the absence of compensation. Indeed, the Court implied that claims of unconstitutional takings (whether by acquisition or regulation) fall into a particularly sensitive constitutional category comparable to that of freedom of speech. As the chief justice stated in a 1994 case, "We see no reason why the Takings Clause . . . should be relegated to the status of poor relation." The Court's decisions on takings without compensation signaled a tilt in favor of property rights and away from the strong preference given to personal rights by the Warren and Burger courts. Nonetheless, significant Warren Court criminal-procedure decisions remained a part of Rehnquist Court jurisprudence. The key Warren criminal trilogy—*Gideon* v. *Wainwright*, 372 U.S. 335 (1963); *Mapp* v. *Ohio*, 367 U.S. 436; and *Miranda* v. *Arizona*, 384 U.S. 436 (1966)—continued to be followed, although some of their doctrines were narrowed. When the Rehnquist Court struck down New York City's legislative apportionment in *Board of Estimate* v. *Morris*, 489 U.S. 688 (1989), it relied on the Warren Court's one-person, one-vote principle.

By the end of the Court's session in 1995 a conservative majority began to assert itself in a series of five-to-four decisions. Thus, it ruled that race cannot be the primary factor in redrawing congressional districts, held against Kansas City's ambitious court-ordered program for desegregating schools, permitted Boston's St. Patrick's Day parade organizers to exclude homosexuals from participating, upheld drug-testing of student athletes, limited lawsuits by prisoners protesting prison conditions, decided that the University of Virginia violated the free speech rights of students when it denied funding for a Christian student newspaper, and similarly found that Ohio could not prevent the Ku Klux Klan from erecting a cross in a public park.

[David P. Currie, *The Constitution in the Supreme Court: The Second Century, 1888–1986* (Chicago, 1990); Robert McCloskey, *The American Constitution*, 2nd ed. (New York, 1994); David M. O'Brien, *Storm Center: The Supreme Court in American Politics*, 2nd ed. (New York, 1990); William H. Rehnquist, *The Supreme Court: How It Was, How It Is* (New York, 1987); David G. Savage, *Turning Right: The Making of the Rehnquist Court* (New York, 1992); Bernard Schwartz, *The Ascent of Pragmatism: The Burger Court in Action* (Reading, Pa., 1990), *A History of the Supreme Court* (New York, 1993), and *Decision: How the Supreme Court Decides Cases* (New York, 1996);

James F. Simon, *The Center Holds: The Power Struggle Inside the Rehnquist Court* (New York, 1995); William M. Wiecek, *Liberty Under Law: The Supreme Court in American Life* (Baltimore, 1988).]

BERNARD SCHWARTZ

See also **DAH:** *Brown* v. *Board of Education of Topeka;* Gideon Case; *Miranda* v. *Arizona;* **SUPP:** *Craig* v. *Boren; Frontiero* v. *Richardson; Planned Parenthood of Southeastern Pennsylvania* v. *Casey; Reed* v. *Reed; Richmond* v. *J. A. Croson Company; Roe* v. *Wade;* Watergate, Aftermath of; *Webster* v. *Reproductive Health Services.*

SURGERY since the 1960s has undergone a revolution. Treatments have been devised for conditions previously thought beyond the surgeon's reach, such as replacing failed organs or unblocking clogged arteries. Technological advances have allowed surgeons to shrink the size of incisions and hasten recovery time. In some cases surgery has been replaced by other treatments. Transplantation of human organs was the most exciting advance. Early attempts were stymied because the recipient's immune system mounted an attack against the foreign organ. In 1954 Joseph E. Murray performed the first successful human kidney transplant in Boston. He avoided the problem of rejection by taking the donor kidney from the patient's identical twin brother. In 1990 he won the Nobel Prize for his work on kidney transplantation. Thomas E. Starzl performed the first human liver transplant in 1963. Until immunosuppressant drugs began to be developed in the 1960s, surgeons tried to stave off rejection by disabling patients' immune systems, which left recipients vulnerable to infection. The advent of drugs that diminish but do not shut down immune response made possible more than 10,000 kidney transplants and 3,000 liver transplants in the United States each year.

The first experimental heart transplant in the United States was performed at Stanford University soon after Christiaan Barnard's groundbreaking operation in South Africa in 1967. The procedure, however, was not widely accepted until introduction of the immunosuppressant drug cyclosporine in 1984. Ten years later 2,300 heart transplants were being performed in the United States annually, and by the mid-1990s 77 percent of heart-transplant recipients were still alive two years later. Transplants of bone marrow, corneas, bone, and heart valves also were performed. In 1987 research groups in the United States, Mexico, and Germany transplanted fetal brain tissue into brains of people with Parkinson's disease, but the procedure remained controversial. Many sick people cannot be helped because there are not enough suitable organs. Artificial body parts are more readily available. In the 1990s artificial implants included pacemakers (electrical devices that help the heart beat at a steady rate), eye lenses, heart valves, joint replacements, hearing aids, and penile prostheses. The first artificial heart was implanted in a human patient in 1982, but repeated experiments show that these devices can sustain life only for a limited time. They are used only to keep people alive while they wait for a suitable donor organ.

The era of open-heart surgery began in 1953 when John H. Gibbon of Philadelphia used a heart-lung machine to do the work of heart and lungs while those organs were temporarily stilled by anesthesia. In the 1990s the most common cardiac operation was coronary artery bypass, first performed in 1967. To improve blood flow to the heart surgeons remove a length of a blood vessel from elsewhere in the body (usually the leg or chest) and use it to carry blood past a narrowed or blocked coronary artery. In 1971, 24,000 of these operations were performed in the United States; by 1992 the number had soared to 468,000 each year. No sooner did coronary artery bypass surgery catch on than a clever surgeon learned how to unclog coronary arteries without cutting open the patient's chest. The Swiss surgeon Andreas Gruntzig introduced balloon angioplasty to the United States in 1979. In this procedure the surgeon threads a catheter through the blood vessel to the blockage. There, a balloon on the catheter tip is inflated to stretch the constricted area and break up the obstruction. More than 300,000 of these procedures were performed in the United States each year in the mid-1990s, but one study found that more than half the patients who had balloon angioplasty needed either coronary-artery bypass surgery or repeat angioplasty within a three-year period. Researchers began developing other less invasive ways to reopen clogged vessels, such as using lasers to burn away fatty deposits. Drugs also helped people relieve the symptoms of coronary artery disease without undergoing surgery.

Doctors used to call upon surgeons when they needed to know what was amiss inside the body. Computer imaging techniques have made exploratory surgery almost obsolete but have increased medical costs. Computerized axial tomography (CAT) was introduced to the United States in the mid-1970s. It involves using a computer to generate cross-sectional views of the body that are clearer and more detailed than those made by conventional X-ray techniques. Magnetic resonance imaging (MRI) came in the mid-1980s. MRI uses electromagnetic waves to produce detailed images of the body in any plane. A few state-of-the-art operating rooms include an MRI device that can repeatedly scan the patient during an operation. Sensors attached to surgical instruments allow surgeons to see exactly where they are in the body.

There were also major advances in the use of endoscopes, tubes to view the inside of the body. Nineteenth-century surgeons attempted to see inside the body using rigid telescope-like tubes. By the 1930s the invention of semiflexible gastroscopes allowed doctors to examine the stomach visually. In the 1960s flexible endoscopes with fiber-optic viewing made it possible to inspect the inner reaches of the body. Surgeons began using endoscopes to perform laparoscopic or "band-aid" surgery. Traditionally, major procedures required an incision large enough for the surgeon's hands and tools. In laparoscopic surgery endoscopes with tiny cameras transmit an image of the body cavity to a video screen and allow surgeons to operate with tiny instruments inserted through incisions of five to ten millimeters. U.S. surgeons first used laparoscopy in 1988 for gall bladder removal. Five years later more than 85 percent of gall bladder operations in the United States were performed laparoscopically. Surgery for gallstones, appendicitis, perforated ulcers, and hernias can be done this way. Laparoscopic surgery causes less tissue damage, is less painful, requires a shorter hospital stay, and speeds recovery. It is not perfect, however, because surgeons cannot rely on sense of touch, and the tiny incisions restrict the range of movement of operating instruments. In 2 percent of cases complications occur and the surgeon has to open up the patient.

Surgery has been changed by the realization that lasers, originally developed for military use, could help surgeons perform bloodless operation on parts of the body too delicate for conventional instruments. A laser produces a narrow beam of intense energy that can cut through tissue. In 1964 a laser beam was used to stop abnormal bleeding in the retina. Thirty years later lasers were used in many eye operations, particularly to repair retinal tears, and were also used to seal bleeding arteries in peptic ulcers, destroy early malignant tumors, reopen blocked fallopian tubes, and remove tattoos and skin blemishes. Microsurgery was another advance made possible by technological innovations. Surgeons use a specially designed pedal-operated microscope, tiny instruments, and delicate stitches to work on minute nerves, blood vessels, or other structures. Ophthalmologic surgeons pioneered microsurgical techniques but today the most celebrated use of microsurgery is reconstructive. Surgeons have been able to reattach severed fingers, toes, penises, and limbs.

Cataract removal is the most commonly performed operation in the United States. Nearly 2 million of these operations are carried out each year, and in 90 percent of cases the patients go home immediately following the procedure. This was not always the case. Until the 1950s cataract operations were agonizing. Patients had to spend two weeks lying in a dark room in the hospital with their heads held in place by sandbags because movement could tear out the stitches. Improvements in stitches, bandages, and painkillers made it possible for patients to recover at home. Large incisions and stitches are no longer required because ophthalmologists can use ultrasound to break up the cataract and remove it in fragments through minuscule cuts that heal themselves and artificial lenses that fold for insertion.

Advances in treatment of cancer show the changing role of surgery. In the case of breast cancer, surgery is used less extensively and usually paired with such adjunct treatments as radiation and chemotherapy. Until the 1960s radical mastectomy (complete removal of the affected breast, chest and underarm lymph nodes, chest muscle, and additional fat and skin) was the standard treatment for breast cancer. In the 1950s surgeons began reporting that simple mastectomy (removal of internal tissue from the affected breast) and radiation could be just as effective. Today surgeons often recommend lumpectomy (removal of cancerous tissue) or quadrantectomy (removal of affected tissue plus a wedge of surrounding tissue) and radiation.

Methods for evaluating surgical outcomes also changed. Researchers now use clinical trials to determine what surgical interventions are most effective and whether procedures that are technically successful improve the patient's quality of life. These measures assess not only traditional procedures but innovations that sound like science fiction. Scientists are experimenting with technology that may allow surgeons to operate on patients that are miles away. Although the potential for new procedures seems limitless, the money to pay for them is not. Surgeons soon may be faced with not only deciding whether an operation is medically feasible but whether it is economically sound.

[W. F. Bynum and Roy Porter, *Companion Encyclopedia of the History of Medicine* (New York, 1993); Charles B. Clayman, ed., *The American Medical Association Encyclopedia of Medicine* (New York, 1989); John Duffy, *From Humors to Medical Science: A History of American Medicine* (Urbana, Ill., 1993); Knut Haeger, *The Illustrated History of Surgery* (New York, 1988); Ira M. Rutkow, *Surgery: An Illustrated History* (St. Louis, Mo., 1993).]

PETA GILLYATT

See also **SUPP:** Cancer; Cardiovascular Disease; Chemotherapy; Clinical Research; Computerized Axial Tomography; Heart Implants; Hospitals; Laser Technology; Magnetic Resonance Imaging; Medicine; Transplants and Organ Donation.

SURROGATE PARENTHOOD. A surrogate parent is one who bears a child for someone else to raise. While the term "surrogate father" may describe a sperm donor, "surrogate parent" usually refers to a woman who is artificially inseminated by a man whose wife is infertile. In rarer cases the woman may be implanted with a fertilized egg and carry the child to term for another couple. The infertile couple generally pays a fee, typically $10,000, to the surrogate mother in addition to medical costs. While informal surrogacy arrangements are referenced as far back as the Bible, in the United States the controversial practice of surrogacy contracts and the emergence of surrogate parenting clinics began in the mid-1970s. As of 1988 it was estimated that 2,000 children had been born to surrogate mothers. Until the 1988 "Baby M" court case in New Jersey, the practice received little public attention or scrutiny. Since then reneged surrogacy agreements and complex developments in infertility treatment have routinely commanded the media spotlight. In the Baby M case, the birth mother, Mary Beth Whitehead, kept the baby against the terms of a surrogacy contract with the Sterns. After a protracted court trial, custody was given to the Sterns, although Whitehead was granted visitation rights. While the majority of surrogate parenting arrangements proceed without legal complication, in rare cases the contracts go awry, with devastating consequences to the surrogate, the would-be parents, and the child. In 1993 the California Supreme Court became the first court to uphold a surrogacy contract, and by 1994 a few other states had passed legislation to uphold such contracts. On the other hand, at least ten states had passed legislation declaring surrogacy contract unenforceable. While new technologies and the fluctuations of human intent continued to raise controversy, as of 1995 there was no legal consensus regarding the validity of surrogacy contracts.

SUSTAINABILITY

[Martha A. Field, *Surrogate Motherhood: The Legal and Human Issues* (Cambridge, Mass., 1988); Amy Z. Overvold, *Surrogate Parenting* (New York, 1988).]

Anne C. Weiss

See also **SUPP:** Fertility; Reproductive Techniques.

SUSTAINABILITY, a central premise of the environmental movement, expresses the idea that societies that overexploit natural resources and destroy ecosystem integrity cannot be maintained indefinitely and therefore must make their economic and social goals compatible with the limits to growth established by the natural environment itself. By the late 1980s sustainable development had transformed debates about socioeconomic growth worldwide and become the stated goal of virtually all international development agencies. The term also is associated with preserving ecosystem viability and biological diversity.

[Donella H. Meadows, *Beyond the Limits* (Post Mills, Vt., 1992); World Commission on Environment and Development, *Our Common Future* (New York, 1987).]

Bron R. Taylor

See also **SUPP:** Bioregionalism; Conservation Biology; Environmental Business; Environmental Movement.

T

TAILHOOK INCIDENT (1991). The Tailhook Association, named for the arresting gear on carrier-based aircraft, is a private group of navy and marine aviators that has worked closely with the U.S. Navy hierarchy. During the association's 1991 annual convention in Las Vegas, eighty-three women, many of them naval officers, alleged that they had been sexually assaulted passing through a hotel hallway filled with male officers. Secretary of the Navy H. Lawrence Garrett III and Chief of Naval Operations Admiral Frank B. Kelso II attended the convention, but both said they witnessed no improper behavior. A subsequent navy investigation was indecisive, and on June 18, 1992, Secretary Garrett asked the Defense Department's inspector general to take control of the inquiry. The next week several female victims, led by navy Lieutenant Paula A. Coughlin, a helicopter pilot and aide to Rear Admiral John W. Snyder, Jr., brought charges. They described their mistreatment in interviews with newspaper and television reporters. On June 26 Secretary Garrett resigned. Members of Congress criticized the pace of the investigation, the commitment of investigators, and the stonewalling of Tailhook members whose memories of the incident could not be refreshed. In July the Senate Armed Services Committee approved 1,126 promotions for navy and marine officers only after the committee had been assured that those officers had not attended the convention. The 1993 defense appropriation barred the Tailhook Association from receiving federal funds. In April 1993 the Defense Department's Inspector General accused 140 officers of indecent exposure, assault, and of lying under oath. About fifty were fined or disciplined. Accusations in more prominent cases did not lead to court-martial convictions or even demotions. On Feb. 8, 1994, a navy judge ruled that Admiral Kelso had misrepresented his activities at the convention and had tried to manipulate the subsequent investigation. Denying these charges, Kelso decided to retire two months early with a full pension, in return for a tribute from Defense Secretary John J. Dalton that stated Kelso was a man of the "highest integrity and honor." During that same week Coughlin announced her resignation, saying her career in the navy had been ruined because she had chosen to bring charges. Commenting on these two distinctly different career endings, Democratic Representative Pat Schroeder of Colorado concluded that the investigation of Tailhook had been "mishandled from its tawdry beginning to its embarrassing finale." Coughlin sued the Tailhook Association and received a monetary award in a September 1994 out-of-court settlement (the amount was not disclosed). Her negligence suit against the Hilton Hotels Corporation and the Las Vegas Hilton Corporation, which claimed that inadequate security was provided during the convention, went to trial in October, and she received $6.7 million in damages, a decision that set the stage for other lawsuits against Hilton.

[Congressional Quarterly, "Tailhook," *Congressional Quarterly Almanac* 48 (1992).]

IRWIN N. GERTZOG

See also **SUPP:** Sexual Harassment; Women in Military Services.

TALK SHOWS. Television talk shows have been a staple of viewers since Sylvester L. (Pat) Weaver, Jr., produced *Today* starring Dave Garroway, Jan. 14,

1952, on NBC. Because they are the least expensive type of show to produce, they are the bread and butter of daytime television. More than 4,000 interview programs are broadcast daily throughout the United States, ensuring that most of the 192 million television sets in the United States are tuned in to at least one such show. More than 1.7 million guest bookings occur each year. Talk shows are either syndicated, such as Donahue (with host Phil Donahue), aired on any station that buys the program, or network programs such as *The Tonight Show,* aired on one network. Types of telecasts are talk shows (*Face the Nation* and *Meet the Press*); talk-variety (*Tonight* and *The Late Show with David Letterman*) in which celebrities make up the majority of guests; talk-service programs (*Charlie Rose, The Oprah Winfrey Show,* and *Donahue*) in which bookings relate to controversial issues; and talk-religious shows (*Oral Roberts*), which are geared to an audience of a specific religious persuasion. Interview techniques vary from the straight one-on-one interviews of William F. Buckley's *Firing Line* to Larry King's discussions with call-in viewers to telephone interviews with guests in remote locations. The longevity of this type of program depends on the personality of the celebrity in charge. The longest-running talk show in prime time is *The Tonight Show,* which premiered Sept. 27, 1954, on NBC with Steve Allen as host. He was succeeded by Ernie Kovacs and then by Jack Paar and guest hosts. Johnny Carson and Ed McMahon made their debut as host and co-host on Oct. 2, 1962, and gathered the largest talk-show viewing audience on Dec. 17, 1969, with the televised wedding of Tiny Tim, a bizarre celebrity of the day, and his bride, Miss Vicki. Carson relinquished the host chair to Jay Leno in May 1992. Talk shows can be educational, enlightening, entertaining, and even serve the political process. Both John F. Kennedy and Robert F. Kennedy appeared with Jack Paar on *The Tonight Show*; both before and after their election in 1992, President Bill Clinton and Vice President Al Gore made extensive use of popular talk shows.

[Richard Mincer and Deanne Mincer, *The Talk Show Book* (New York, 1982).]

JOHN J. BYRNE

See also **SUPP:** Radio; Television.

TAYLOR V. LOUISIANA, 419 U.S. 522 (1975), a Supreme Court decision that represents an early judicial response to the reemergence of feminism in the late twentieth century. Ironically, the defendant, Billy Taylor, who won this early male sex discrimination case, was accused of rape. The Supreme Court sustained Taylor's claim that a state law infringed on his right to a jury trial by exempting women from jury duty. In Louisiana women could be called for jury service only if they filed a written declaration of their willingness to serve. As a result most Louisiana juries, including the one that convicted Taylor of kidnapping, were all-male. Louisiana's practice was similar to one that the Court had unanimously upheld in *Hoyt* v. *Florida* (1961), a decision that sustained the Florida law as a reasonable concession to women's family responsibilities. As a result of the *Hoyt* decision a woman accused of murdering her husband could be tried by a jury almost certain to consist entirely of men. The Court had implied acceptance of states' exclusion of women from grand juries as recently as 1972, but *Taylor* ended special treatment for women, invalidating all remaining state laws restricting jury duty on the basis of gender. The Court quoted from an earlier case: "Who would claim that a jury was truly representative of the community if all men were intentionally and systematically excluded from the panel?" but defendants had no right to a "representative" jury or even one that included both women and men despite the Sixth Amendment, which "affords the defendant in a criminal trial the opportunity to have the jury drawn from venires [a jury pool] representative of the community." Since *Taylor* jury duty has been a responsibility shared equally by men and women.

[Judith A. Baer, *Women in American Law* (New York, 1991).]

JUDITH A. BAER

TEACHER CORPS. The Higher Education Act of 1965 created the Teacher Corps after Senators Gaylord A. Nelson of Wisconsin and Edward M. Kennedy of Massachusetts proposed the legislation and President Lyndon B. Johnson gave the idea a name. During its seventeen-year life the corps conducted more than 650 projects in cities, small towns, and rural areas, focusing on educational innovation. The first broad concern of the Teacher Corps was to improve education for the disadvantaged. In the mid-1960s policymakers likened it to the Peace Corps—idealistic young people would bring energy and commitment to schools in blighted urban areas and poor rural communities. The corps encouraged graduates of liberal arts colleges and members of minority groups to join. The perspectives of these nontraditional teachers led to curricular innovation in individual instruction and multicultural education. A second innovation was in teacher training. After eight weeks of training, interns spent two years engaged simultaneously in university study, work-study in the schools, and work in communities, which included after-school recreation activities, home visits, and health programs. During its last years the Teacher Corps was more concerned with in-service training for teachers already in schools, focusing on professional development and innovations among veteran teachers. Cooperation among educators was important to the Teacher Corps. The Department of Health, Education and Welfare provided funds. At the state level college and university teachers instructed interns and consulted with local schools. School districts and community groups used the interns. Controversy surrounded the Teacher Corps from the beginning. The corps threatened the traditional rights of the states in educational matters, and issues of trust and authority simmered beneath the surface of relations between teachers and interns, school districts and universities, the national office and local educators. Community groups were concerned about being shuffled aside. By the late 1970s the mission of the corps became difficult to define, its varied constituents hard to satisfy. In an effort to cut back federal involvement in education, President Ronald Reagan officially eliminated the corps as part of the 1981 Education Consolidation and Improvement Act and it ceased operations in 1983.

[Ronald G. Corwin, *Reform and Organizational Survival: The Teacher Corps as an Instrument of Educational Change* (New York, 1973).]

CHRISTINE A. OGREN

See also **SUPP:** Education; Education, Department of; Education, Experimental.

TEACHER TRAINING in the United States began in 1794, when the Society of Associated Teachers was formed in New York City to establish qualifications for teachers in that city. The Free School Society, established in 1805, also in New York City, began training teachers using public funds and organized a teacher-training course. In 1885 Brown University began to offer students courses in pedagogy, establishing one of the first university-level departments of education. When the study of teaching methods was recognized as a valid program in the twentieth cen-

tury, the certification standards for teachers were raised throughout the United States. By the end of the twentieth century, almost all U.S. teachers received preservice training in institutions of higher education with programs that complied with state guidelines for certification. These institutions usually have separate schools or departments of education and prospective teachers are education majors. Nearly every teacher holds a bachelor's degree, and the vast majority have additional credits, with more than half holding one or more advanced degrees. Many states require graduate education for permanent certification. Education students must take courses in pedagogical techniques, and prospective secondary teachers need a specified number of credit hours in the specific subject they plan to teach. Training includes a student teaching requirement, a period of classroom teaching under the supervision of a certified teacher. States vary in their course content and credit requirements. Critics of teacher training programs cite an overemphasis on methods and psychological studies, the neglect of academic subjects, the need for accountability to ensure that training and certification are based less on academic credits and more on ability to function in the classroom, and the lack of uniform requirements among states. *A Nation at Risk,* the 1983 report of the National Committee on Excellence in Education, appointed by President Ronald Reagan, alerted the American public to the need to attract high-quality teaching candidates and to improve their training. By the mid-1990s most states offered alternative routes to certification to mid-career people and liberal arts graduates via programs that provide on-the-job supervision.

MYRNA W. MERRON

TELECOMMUNICATIONS. Beginning in the 1870s the Bell Telephone Company dominated the nation's phone network, known as the Bell System, including long-distance service under its subsidiary, American Telephone & Telegraph (AT&T). In the late 1960s, however, AT&T faced pressure from the U.S. government to break its protected monopoly. In 1969 government regulators allowed MCI Communications to sell long-distance service and connect with the AT&T network. In 1984 a federal court decision allowed AT&T to retain its long-distance service and manufacturing and research operations but forced the company to divest itself of the seven regional Bell operating companies, the so-called Baby Bells, and agree to purchase equipment from other companies besides its subsidiaries. The implications of the divestiture of AT&T in 1984 were far-reaching. At first there was confusion as customers began paying phone bills to both a local phone company and a long-distance company. Soon consumers adjusted to a variety of long-distance companies, such as AT&T, MCI, and Sprint, and many companies began to sell phone equipment to consumers.

By the mid-1990s new technologies had rapidly changed the telecommunications market. The expanded use by the 1980s of fiber-optic cable in network systems enabled companies to transmit telephone calls by digital technology, which conveys information about the transmitted signal through a numerical code rather than representing it, as is done with analog technology. This change resulted in improved clarity on phone lines, but in the mid-1990s as many as half the phones in the United States still relied on analog technology to send a signal between the network system and the home or office. For computers and fax systems to use analog technology, it was necessary to provide them with a modem, which converts the digital message into audio signals. Increasingly, some argued that telephones did not need to rely on traditional network systems and that a radio signal or even a satellite transmission could be used, which was the basis of the expanding mobile and cellular phone business. Between 1990 and 1992 the number of cellular phones in the United States increased from 4 million to 9 million. In fact, because of the accelerating integration of technologies related to computers, telephones, and cable television, and other entertainment media seemed uncertain by the mid-1990s. Companies that provided the network system for telephones wanted changes in U.S. laws that would enable them to carry entertainment shows into homes in order to challenge cable television. During the early and mid-1990s a number of agreements and mergers between telecommunications and entertainment companies occurred that reflected new technological capabilities. Likewise, the regional Bell companies wanted Congress to revise existing laws so that they could compete directly against AT&T and other companies in the manufacture of telecommunications equipment.

[Irwin Lebow, *Information Highways and Byways: From the Telegraph to the 21st Century* (New York, 1995); Steven Lubar, *InfoCulture: The Smithsonian Book of Information Age Inventions* (Boston, 1993).]

KENNETH B. MOSS

See also **DAH:** Telephone; **SUPP:** Communications Industry; Computers; Fiber Optics; Internet; Office Technology.

TELEVANGELISM. The propagation of the Christian gospel over the airwaves, dubbed "televangelism," is a natural extension of evangelicalism's exploitation of communications technology. Throughout U.S. history evangelicals (those who interpret the Bible literally and who believe in the centrality of the conversion, or "born-again," experience) have been pioneers in mass communications, from George Whitefield's open-air preaching in the eighteenth century to Charles G. Finney's use of newspapers in the nineteenth century to the radio programs of Aimee Semple McPherson and Charles Fuller early in the twentieth century. When Billy Graham emerged as a cultural phenomenon after World War II, he turned first to radio and then to television.

Because of changes in television, evangelists gained even larger audiences in the 1970s. The Federal Communications Commission (FCC) mandated that all local stations allocate time to religious broadcasting. Network policy forbade local affiliates to accept money for such programming. With increased independence of local stations, however, and with the blessing of the FCC, stations began accepting money for religious broadcasts. Evangelists seized upon the opportunity, recognizing that they could draw in donations that would pay for the inexpensive airtime available on Sunday mornings. The nature of religious programming changed dramatically. Whereas religious broadcasts once had been dominated by the staid liturgies of Roman Catholicism and mainline Protestantism, evangelicals, drawing on the long evangelical tradition of mixing religion and entertainment, translated the gospel into what some critics said was show business. The "electronic church" took many forms: the pentecostal and healing emphasis of Kathryn Kuhlman, Oral Roberts, and Ernest Angley; the positive-thinking messages of Rex Humbard, Robert Schuller, and Robert Tilton; the inimitable theatrics of Jimmy Swaggart; the conservative politics of James Robison and Jerry Falwell; and the talk-show format of Pat Robertson and, later, Jim and Tammy Faye Bakker, whose programs were modeled after Johnny Carson's *Tonight Show.* Televangelism thus became profitable. Many televangelists received millions every year, far exceeding the budgets of some denominations. Robertson's ability to garner audiences turned his network, the Christian Broadcasting Network (CBN), into a formidable organization that provided the foundation for his campaign for the Republican presidential nomination in 1988.

By the middle of the 1980s scandal caught up with many of the televangelists. Bakker's flamboyant lifestyle led to financial improprieties that eventually sent him to prison but did not bar him from returning to television upon his release at the end of 1994; Swaggart was caught in dalliances with a prostitute in Louisiana; and Roberts declared that God would "take [him] home" unless God's people ponied up $4.5 million to save his flagging empire. Early in the 1990s Tilton was reeling from an ABC news exposé that cast serious doubts on his integrity. The effect of the scandals was a sag in ratings and revenues. Many of the larger televangelist organizations cut back on operations but the proliferation of cable television beginning in the early 1990s opened the doors for new televangelists and new networks.

[Quentin J. Schultze, *Televangelism and American Culture: The Business of Popular Religion* (Grand Rapids, Mich., 1991).]

RANDALL BALMER

See also **DAH:** Evangelism, Evangelicalism, and Revivalism; Finney Revivals; **SUPP:** Fundamentalism; Pentecostal Churches; Protestant Churches; Religion.

TELEVISION. At the end of the twentieth century television was the primary leisure activity of most Americans and their most likely source for news. The medium had changed markedly since the mid-1970s, when three national networks, ABC, CBS, and NBC, dominated television; 87 percent of all TV stations were affiliated with a network. In the evening, when most Americans watched television, 90 percent of all sets were tuned to a network program. The networks fought for first place in audience ratings. Because advertisers sponsoring programs paid more for large audiences, high ratings meant millions of dollars. The networks spared no expense to lure viewers.

Network rivalries were fierce in the mid-1970s. ABC, long the weakest of the three networks in terms of popular programming and affiliates, gradually achieved parity with CBS and NBC, winning younger viewers with situation comedies like *Happy Days* and *Three's Company.* The latter's sexually teasing qualities, apparent in another ABC hit, *Charlie's Angels,* about three female private detectives, encouraged imitation by CBS and NBC. ABC also poured resources into its long-dormant news division, which by the 1980s enjoyed an equal rating with its competitors. ABC also benefited from television sets equipped to receive ultra high frequency (UHF) channels 14 through 83, relying on UHF stations for affiliates. In 1967 just under half of all viewers had sets equipped to receive UHF; eight years later the number was 90 percent. UHF ultimately undermined all three networks; UHF stations began operations with-

out network affiliation. "Independent stations" increased from 13 percent in 1975 to 39 percent in 1987. They began counterprogramming, especially in the early evening, with game shows and other entertainment to compete with the network news shows. Availability of stations unaffiliated with ABC, CBS, or NBC encouraged formation of a fourth network, Fox, in 1986.

The three original networks underwent changes in ownership in 1986. General Electric purchased NBC, Capital Cities purchased ABC, and the investor Lawrence Tisch bought CBS. To their dismay the new proprietors found themselves in a cost squeeze. In the 1970s inflation had allowed networks to pass along to advertisers higher production expenses. Sponsors, affected by the inflation psychology, did not protest. A decade later, with inflation falling, demand for national time softened; the networks no longer enjoyed a seller's market. Although programming costs continued to rise, advertisers refused to make up the increases. Even network news divisions, sources of industry pride, had to lower expenses. Staffs were cut and domestic and overseas bureaus pared or shut. Each network looked for cheaper programming, including more news shows. Despite lavish salaries awarded a few newscasters, news programs such as CBS's *48 Hours* cost less than entertainment series. The networks produced the news shows and did not have to share their profits with independent producers in Hollywood. Despite reductions in operating expenses the three networks' woes worsened; profits fell 50 percent between 1984 and 1988. By the mid-1990s Fox emerged as a serious rival of the big three. Like ABC in the 1970s, Fox succeeded with comedies like *The Simpsons* and *Married . . . With Children,* as well as a sexy dramatic series, *Beverly Hills 90210,* which appealed to the younger viewers coveted by advertisers. In 1994 Fox outbid CBS for the rights to telecast National Football League games, which the latter network had aired since the 1950s. A year later Fox led CBS in many large TV markets.

Cable television proved the greatest blow to the networks' oligopoly. Cable required a monthly fee to enhance reception but offered many more choices in programming. In a typical viewing area in the 1980s a noncable household had seven channels; a cable household thirty-three. In the 1990s experts predicted as many as 500 cable channels might eventually be available. Cable systems had entered some areas to improve reception, not choice, as early as 1949, but the Federal Communications Commission (FCC) and local governments, which regulated underground wiring connecting households to cable, discouraged the new system until the mid-1970s. Over the next years government oversight relaxed. Households with cable increased from 15 percent in 1975 to 60 percent in 1994. It was not until the late 1980s that the networks recognized cable's threat. Earlier they had started cable channels but their involvement was half-hearted; their emphasis remained over-the-air broadcasting.

Meanwhile, the Public Broadcasting System (PBS), established in 1967 and partly supported by federal and state sources, lost viewers and programming to cable outlets emphasizing culture. The Cable News Network (CNN) established a small but devoted following and was boosted by the Gulf War of 1991 and the sensational murder trial of O. J. Simpson four years later. In 1992 CNN programs combined with radio talk shows to assist the independent presidential candidacy of the Texas billionaire Ross Perot, initially ignored by the networks. Democratic nominee Bill Clinton similarly used "alternative media," including the all-music MTV channel.

Communication satellites benefited cable TV. In the mid-1970s several companies, including independent stations in Atlanta, New York, and Chicago, began relaying signals off satellites and making them available to cable companies across the country. Pay-cable outlets led by Home Box Office offered recently released and uncut feature films together with original programming. In late 1993 more than one-fourth of all households with television sets received one or more pay cable outlets. The videocassette recorder (VCR) delivered another blow to the networks. Sales of VCRs began in the early 1980s and by the mid-1990s four out of every five households with televisions had VCRs. Although some owners used VCRs to tape network shows to watch later, many more rented feature films, especially on weekends, which greatly reduced TV viewing. The effects of cable and VCRs were clear by the early 1990s. The network share of evening prime time fell to 60 percent. In 1980 three-fourths of viewers tuned to network evening newscasts; by 1992 that share had fallen almost to half.

One response to cable, seen at NBC in the early 1980s, was to make programs more "realistic," more like uncut movies on pay channels, with explicit treatment of sex and violence. Relaxed standards in feature films and popular music inspired this new realism. Being frank about sex and violence on television, however, infuriated parents, members of Congress, and conservative pressure groups, who accused the networks of contributing to a decline of national morality. In 1992 Vice President Dan Quayle condemned the TV series *Murphy Brown* for having the title character give birth out of wedlock. Relatedly, the news divisions were anxious to boost their programs' appeal and compete with many more channels. Network newscasts began to mimic local stations, which had never taken their responsibilities as seriously as had the networks. Especially at CBS, less attention was devoted to international and national news and more to human interest stories and segments on helping viewers cope with medical and financial matters. News programs competing against entertainment shows in the evening began to imitate the "tabloid" or sensational programs aired by Fox and independent producers.

[Ken Auletta, *Three Blind Mice* (New York, 1992); James L. Baughman, *The Republic of Mass Culture* (Baltimore, 1992).]

JAMES L. BAUGHMAN

See also **SUPP:** Advertising; Cable News Network; Music Television; Radio; Science Television; Talk Shows; Televangelism.

TELEVISION, SCIENCE. *See* **Science Television.**

TENNESSEE. Experiencing steady growth throughout its 200 years, Tennessee in 1970 had a population of 3,925,164; by 1990 that figure had grown to 4,877,187, an increase of more than 24 percent. The population became concentrated in urban areas, and many rural counties suffered substantial declines. Crockett, Obion, and Gibson, in the northwestern part of the state, lost substantially, as did the middle counties of Lawrence, Lewis, and Lincoln. Most eastern counties remained stable or reflected gains. Cheatham, Montgomery, Wilson, Sumner, Rutherford, and Williamson—all in close proximity to Nashville—each grew 20 percent or more in the 1980s. Among the cities, Memphis, with a population of 610,337, remained the state's largest, while Nashville's growth of 7.2 percent pushed the capital city's population to a half million. Knoxville, just ahead of Chattanooga, lost 5.7 percent, with a 1990 population of 165,121.

Industry expanded as well. Nissan Motor Manufacturing Company opened a $300 million truck-assembly plant near Murfreesboro in the 1980s; by 1994 it was worth $1.2 billion and manufactured trucks, buses, and Sentra passenger cars. By 1994 Japanese companies had invested $4.7 billion in Tennessee, and more than half of the 114 Japanese-owned operations were related to the automobile. Agriculture remained an important industry; principal crops were corn, tobacco, cotton, wheat, and soy beans. Beef cattle and dairying were also important. The number of farms continued to decline as construction of automobile and other plants led increasing numbers of Tennesseans to give up farming in order to take more lucrative jobs in factories. Many moved to the towns and cities. Others continued to raise crops and livestock on the farms while commuting to nearby plants for their principal incomes.

The expansion of industry and increasing population brought changes in politics. Traditionally part of the Democratic solid South, Tennessee in the 1990s was substantially a two-party state. During the 1970s and 1980s, Republicans, concentrated primarily in the eastern counties and the major cities, battled Democrats on an about-even basis. Republicans held the office of governor for twelve years between 1970 and 1990, both U.S. Senate seats for six years, and won the state's electoral votes in four of the six presidential elections through 1992. Democrat Ned Ray McWherter served two terms as governor but Republicans returned to power in the landslide of 1994. That year, even as native son Al Gore, a Democrat, served as U.S. vice president, they elected the governor, both U.S. senators, and five of the nine congressmen. Democrats retained control of the state legislature immediately after that election but within a few months lost the senate because of defections to the Republicans.

Tennessee is known as the country music capital of the world, and the "Nashville sound" means to millions not only country music but Western and religious music as well. In the literary field, Alex Haley, a Henning native and retired sailor, in 1976 published the most successful book ever written by a Tennessean. His *Roots,* translated into twelve languages and adapted for a television film seen in twenty-eight countries, gained new respect for the heritage of African Americans. By the mid-1990s, however, the state had not come to grips with the needs of state-supported education. In urging the legislature to build more schools, Governor John Brown in 1873 referred to his state as "third in ignorance"; Tennessee's rank was not much improved 100 years later. Although Governor Lamar Alexander's "better schools program" and Governor McWherter's increase in the sales tax kept the program respectable, educators and tax reformers alike argued that only a state income tax would place the state's educational program on a par with that of other states. In higher education the state in the 1970s authorized a medical school at Johnson City and several two-year colleges, but Tennesseans serving on a nationwide panel in 1993 to study offerings at 3,400 colleges and universities joined with other members in a highly critical statement of their own state's programs. They called on administrators to concentrate on improved academic offerings and the strengthening of values. Some of the trauma of racial integration during the 1960s continued into the next two decades, but schools were no longer segregated, although African Americans continued to experience job discrimination.

As in the country as a whole, crime and health care were major issues by the early 1990s. Problems of overcrowding, violence, idleness, and filth in the prisons resulted in the federal government's taking temporary control in 1982. After six new prisons accommodating 1,000 prisoners each were opened, the system was returned to state control in 1993. In the following year, more than a third of a billion dollars went into operating the prisons. In health care, TennCare was substituted for Medicaid. With federal approval the plan enabled the state to use federal money to purchase health care from providers for uninsured workers and Medicaid recipients. The controversial plan, begun early in 1994, was designed to expand health care and save money at the same time.

[Robert E. Corlew, *Tennessee: A Short History* (Knoxville, Tenn., 1989); William F. Fox and Patricia A. Price, *An Economic Report to the Governor of the State of Tennessee on the State's Economic Outlook* (Nashville, 1993).]

ROBERT E. CORLEW

See also **SUPP:** Memphis; Nashville.

TENNIS. In the late 1960s tennis began to undergo great changes, in part because of improvements in technology. For nearly one hundred years after the introduction of tennis in the United States during the 1870s, the best tennis rackets were made from wood but that changed with invention of the steel racket, which first appeared in the United States in 1967. Other innovations involving new materials followed. Aluminum rackets appeared in 1968 and graphite and fiberglass rackets during the 1970s. In 1976 Prince Manufacturing introduced an oversized racket with a head more than 50 percent larger in surface area than conventional models. During the 1970s and 1980s wood and metal rackets gave way altogether to new synthetic materials and conventional head sizes disappeared in favor of oversized and new intermediate, midsized heads. Rackets in use in the 1990s were simultaneously larger, lighter, and stronger than older wood or metal rackets. Another significant innovation appeared in the United States in 1987. Called the "widebody" because of the thickness of the racket head, this racket generates greater power than older designs. By the mid-1990s it had not yet gained wide acceptance among professional men players but was almost universally used by professional women players.

Competitive techniques and styles of play were greatly affected by the new racket technology. The two-handed backhand, popularized during the 1970s by Bjorn Borg, Jimmy Connors, and Chris Evert, proved to be ideally suited to the new, larger racket heads and became a staple of the competitive game; in 1970 none of the world's top ten men or women used the stroke, but five of the top men and six of the top women did in 1992. The greater power and flexibility of the two-handed shot made the backhand an offensive weapon for more players. In general, the newer rackets made it possible to hit harder with less effort and, consequently, increased the rewards for offensive tactics. The new racket technology was clearly responsible for a greater reliance on power in both women's and men's competitive tennis in the 1990s.

Tennis also underwent major economic changes. Until the late 1960s the sport's most prestigious competitions were open exclusively to amateurs. The arrival of Open tennis in 1968 led to the establishment of money prizes for all world-class tournaments. Since then the amount of prize money has increased dramatically. In 1969 the world's top male player, Rod Laver, earned a total of $124,000; in 1993 Pete Sampras won $4.1 million and Steffi Graf $2.8 million. Financially, tennis became one of the elite professional sports; *Forbes* magazine placed nine tennis players on its list of the world's forty highest-paid athletes in 1991. In 1993 Ivan Lendl led all men players in career prize money, with total earnings of $21 million, while Martina Navratilova led all women with $19.4 million. The professionalization of competitive tennis changed the careers of players. In the amateur era, players were typically young, and few players could afford to play full-time for more than a few years after college because of the difficulty of earning a living as a tennis player under the rules governing amateur status. After the advent of Open tennis, the mean age of competitive players rose sharply, as many found they could earn more playing tennis than in other careers. At the same time increasing prize money brought about the intensive training

of young players. Junior competitions and training programs proliferated, and tennis academies were established where promising young players could live and train year-round. This more intensive training made many teenage players more advanced technically than young players of the past. Consequently, another feature of the Open era was the entry of small numbers of gifted players into adult competition at very young ages.

Tennis has long been one of the most international of sports, but the growing prize money and publicity of the Open era increased its geographic extent. During the 1990s the rankings of the world's top players for both men and women have consistently included citizens of more than twenty different countries, but the United States remains the single most important source of world-class players. At the end of 1991 there were seventeen Americans ranked among the world's top 100 men, and twenty-five Americans among the top 100 women; no other country had even half as many players in either group. The sport's champions have also been Americans in disproportionate numbers. Between 1970 and 1993 six American men—Stan Smith, Jimmy Connors, Arthur Ashe, John McEnroe, Jim Courier, and Pete Sampras—held the world's top ranking in ten of twenty-four years, and Ivan Lendl, a naturalized American, added another three. In the same period Americans Billie Jean King, Chris Evert, and Tracy Austin held the top women's ranking in a total of eight years, while Martina Navratilova, a naturalized American, added another seven. Tennis enjoyed a remarkable growth in popularity in the United States during the 1970s. An estimated 10 million Americans played the sport in 1970 but that number more than tripled to 32–34 million in 1974–1978. After a period of declining popularity during the 1980s, interest in the sport revived and an estimated 23 million Americans played during 1993.

[Bud Collins and Zander Hollander, eds., *Bud Collins' Modern Encyclopedia of Tennis* (Detroit, 1994).]

DAVID W. GALENSON

TERRORISM uses low levels of violence or intimidation for political ends. U.S. terrorist groups have been racist (Ku Klux Klan, Black Panthers), nationalist (Puerto Rican Liberation Army), opposed to a strong central government (Posse Comitatus), antiwar (Weathermen, Symbionese Liberation Army), and xenophobic and anti-Semitic (neo-Nazi skinheads). From 1985 to 1993 there were five to ten terrorist incidents in the United States annually, mostly bombings and arson, with about the same number of suspected and prevented incidents. The first incident of international terrorism against the United States occurred just before the Algeciras Conference in 1904, when the Moroccan chief Ahmed ibn-Muhammed Raisuli kidnapped Ion Perdicaris, a naturalized American citizen, from his villa near Tangier. Secretary of State John Hay telegraphed the U.S. consul-general in Tangier demanding "Perdicaris alive or Raisuli dead." The public acclaimed the tough handling of the incident, but an unpublished part of the telegram had warned the consul to avoid force without specific instructions.

The Department of State has kept statistics on international terrorism since 1968. The data show that U.S. citizens and property have been the most frequent targets of terrorism—about 20 percent of all international incidents in 1985 and more than 40 percent in 1990. In 1975 American citizens suffered 36 percent of the casualties from international terrorism; in 1985, 21 percent; and in 1990, only 5 percent. U.S. casualties peaked at 386 (271 fatalities, 115 wounded) in 1983, when on October 23, 241 marines died when a member of the Islamic Jihad drove a truck loaded with dynamite into the barracks at the Beirut International Airport. The level of terrorism has been directly related to U.S. foreign policy. There were, for example, some 160 terrorist attacks worldwide within six weeks of the start of the Gulf War in January 1991. The most significant international terrorist act against the United States was the seizure of the U.S. embassy in Tehran, Iran, on Nov. 4, 1979. Fifty-two Americans were held for 444 days with the collusion of the Iranian government. They were released on Jan. 20, 1981, in return for the $6 billion in Iranian assets frozen in U.S. banks. The event helped defeat Jimmy Carter in the 1980 presidential election. The worst incident of international terrorism within the United States was the Feb. 26, 1993, bombing in New York City of the World Trade Center, the tallest building in the nation's most populous city. Six people were killed and more than 1,000 injured by explosives equal to 1,500 pounds of TNT.

The U.S. government has demanded the extradition of terrorists, trained foreign antiterrorist forces, launched air strikes, and enforced trade sanctions against states that support terrorism. It also has traded weapons to Iran for hostages kidnapped in Lebanon and reportedly paid $3 million to Sheik Mohammed Hussein Fadlallah, who organized the 1983 bombing of the marine barracks, not to attack U.S. interests in Beirut again. International terrorism accounted for

fewer than 2,000 deaths during 1970–1979 and just over 4,000 fatalities during 1980–1989. Terrorism has been more frightening and dangerous than these statistics indicate, however, because terrorists have targeted civilians and attempted to destabilize governments.

[Walter Laqueur, *The Age of Terrorism* (Boston, 1987); John L. Scherer, ed., *Terrorism* (Minneapolis, 1986– , quarterly); U.S. Department of State, *Patterns of Global Terrorism* (Washington, D.C., annually); Alexander Yonah, ed., *Terrorism: An International Journal* (New York, 1977–1991, quarterly).]

JOHN L. SCHERER

See also **SUPP:** Beirut Bombing; Fundamentalism; Hostage Crises; Oklahoma City Bombing; White Supremacists; World Trade Center Bombing.

TEXAS. The Lone Star State achieved a new level of prosperity and recognition in the 1970s. During that decade Texas not only grew at a tremendous pace but caught the imagination of Americans as never before. This success grew out of a series of developments that began in World War II, when massive government spending for defense injected needed capital into the state's economy and boosted industrial development, particularly in aircraft manufacturing, petrochemicals, and shipbuilding as well as oil and natural gas. Oil production increased after the war with the growing popularity of the automobile. High oil prices precipitated by the Arab oil embargo of 1973 sent profits skyrocketing and brought even greater prosperity to the state. The rapid migration to Texas of people eager to take part in its expanding economy set off a building boom that provided more job opportunities and lured even more workers from the stagnating North. Between 1950 and 1980 the population of Texas doubled from 7 million to 14 million. Some 58 percent of that growth during the 1970s came from migration from other states. Many factors other than the oil economy were responsible for that growth; the state particularly benefited from the expansion of manufacturing, tourism, transportation, international trade, and the continued military buildup begun during World War II and necessitated by the cold war. Growth of the computer and electronics industries after 1960 made an even greater impact on the state's economic health. A number of companies established regional offices and some national corporations such as American Airlines relocated their headquarters to Texas.

The postwar transportation revolution played a significant role in the state's expansion. Improvement of commercial aviation and construction of new airports in Texas, including the massive Dallas–Fort Worth International Airport in 1974, helped make the state more accessible. The interstate highway system initiated in the 1950s and cheap fuel costs lessened the state's isolation and helped attract manufacturers. Low taxes and a probusiness, antiunion climate also did not hurt. The importance of the automobile to the state's development is illustrated by the fact that Texas has more than 220,000 miles of municipal and rural highways. The growing use of air conditioning in the 1950s and 1960s for home and car also lured newcomers to the state by making the hot summer days more tolerable.

The country's ongoing defense buildup continued to have a major impact on Texas. The Manned Spacecraft Center in Houston (which opened in 1963), the aircraft and high-tech industries of north Texas, and the presence of military posts throughout the state played a critical role in stimulating the economy. Texas thus evolved from one of the nation's most rural states to one of its most urban. By 1990 it had three of the ten largest cities in the United States—Houston, Dallas, and San Antonio. Texas contained 298 municipalities with a population of at least 5,000, and more than 80 percent of its residents lived in urban areas. Its total 1990 population was 16,986,510. Demographic changes occurred in the 1980s. Population increased by 19 percent during the decade, with Hispanic Americans accounting for more than 45 percent of that growth. The African-American population also rose at a more rapid rate than Anglos, and there was a significant influx of Asian Americans. Indeed, Texas attracted unprecedented numbers of legal and illegal immigrants and became a much more ethnically diverse state than ever before. The economy also underwent changes in the 1980s. The oil boom that gave Texas one of the nation's healthiest economies during the 1970s soured in the 1980s as the price of oil plummeted from $40 a barrel in 1981 to $18 a barrel in 1992. The state suffered from banking failures in the 1980s, losing 163 banks between 1987 and 1988, and the building boom of the 1970s came to an abrupt halt. An economy that once depended on oil, natural gas, and cotton increasingly relied on high-tech industries and the service sector, including tourism, health, and education.

The state has experienced both political and social transformation. At the beginning of the twentieth century, white males in the Democratic party controlled the state and minorities had few rights or op-

portunities. For example, the Texas legislature approved a poll tax in 1902 and later barred blacks from the Democratic primary. The state also passed Jim Crow segregation laws and showed little tolerance of African Americans or the growing number of Mexican Americans streaming into the state. Change occurred, however, when the Supreme Court's *Smith* v. *Allwright* decision (1944) voided the state's white Democratic primary and gave the state's large minority populations the opportunity to participate more fully in politics. The civil rights movement of the 1950s and 1960s that led to the Voting Rights Act of 1965 further strengthened the political hand of the state's minorities. By 1978 the Texas House of Representatives included fourteen African Americans and seventeen Mexican Americans. In 1980 almost 1,000 Mexican Americans held public office in local government although the number of African Americans remained below 200. Despite sending prominent liberals to the U.S. Senate after World War II, such as Lyndon B. Johnson and Ralph Yarborough, Texas voters retained their conservative tendencies even during the presidencies of John F. Kennedy and native son Johnson. The election of Republican William P. Clements in 1978 as governor signaled the rise of a two-party system in Texas. The Democrats, however, reclaimed the governor's mansion in 1982 with the election of Mark White. Eight years later Texas voters selected another Democrat, Ann Richards. Under her administration women and minorities gained unprecedented opportunities to participate in the state's government and development. Texans supported Jimmy Carter, a Sunbelt Democrat, for president in 1976 but voted Republican in the next three presidential contests. Indeed, in 1992 Bill Clinton became the first Democrat in the history of the United States to lose Texas and win the presidency. Two years later Republican George W. Bush, son of the former president, beat Ann Richards for state governor. Meanwhile, Republican Kay Bailey Hutchison in 1993 became the first woman to represent Texas in the U.S. Senate. Her election marked the first time Texas had two Republican senators since 1875. This victory, along with the defeat of Clinton in Texas a year earlier, clearly suggested the growing strength of the Republican party in a state that historically had been Democratic.

[David G. McComb, *Texas: A Modern History* (Austin, 1989); Robert S. Maxwell, *Texas Economic Growth, 1890 to World War II* (Boston, 1981); Char Miller and Heywood T. Sanders, eds., *Urban Texas: Politics and Development* (College Station, Tex., 1990); David Montejaño, *Anglos and Mexicans in the Making of Texas, 1836–1986* (Austin, 1987).]

ROBERT B. FAIRBANKS

See also **SUPP:** Austin; Dallas; El Paso; Fort Worth; Galveston; Houston; San Antonio; Sunbelt.

TEXTBOOKS constitute the de facto curriculum in many disciplines. American history, especially at the secondary level, where 85 percent of the nation's students take courses before graduation, is a controversial area because of disputes over content and interpretation. U.S. history texts include the study of continental geography, political history, economic development, social history, and diverse cultures. Private corporations provide textbooks to state and local governments for a profit, an arrangement that differs from most industrialized countries, where the national government creates the curriculum and publishes textbooks. The total domestic market for instructional materials was an estimated $5 billion in 1992, of which more than $2 billion represented elementary and high school materials.

Changes in textbooks since 1970 have been particularly considerable in U.S. history and social studies, as social history, revisionism, and multiculturalism influenced curriculum composition. Publishers expended considerable effort to make texts redress earlier omissions. Still, as state-level controversies of the late 1980s and early 1990s in California and New York indicated, textbook publishers remained beset by special-interest groups, including ethnic activists, feminists, the disabled, environmentalists, homosexuals, and religious groups, all desiring favorable and prominent treatment. Such pressures make it difficult for publishers to balance academic integrity against market requirements. Several federal court cases in the 1980s reflect the perennial disputes over textbook censorship, content, and interpretation. Challenges have arisen over biology, health, literature, and history texts. Three significant federal cases originated in local complaints that textbooks promote secular humanism (*Smith* v. *Board of School Commissioners of Mobile County,* 1986), atheism (*Mozert* v. *Hawkins County Public Schools,* 1987), and the theory of evolution (*Aguillard* v. *Edwards,* 1987).

Textbooks remain useful and efficient devices for learning in all formal subjects. Offering organized, convenient sequences of ideas and information, they structure teaching and learning. In the 1990s schools at all levels began to experiment with CD-ROMs and other video technologies as curriculum supplements.

The classroom use of CD-ROM reference works, electronic atlases, and on-line databases was growing, but it was not certain that such media would supplant textbooks in the future.

[Philip G. Altbach et al., *Textbooks in American Society* (Albany, N.Y., 1991); Joan Del Fattore, *What Johnny Doesn't Know: Textbook Censorship in America* (New Haven, Conn., 1992).]

GILBERT T. SEWALL

See also **SUPP:** American Studies; Cultural Literacy; Curriculum; Education; Multiculturalism.

THEATER. Profound changes began to occur in theater during the 1960s, establishing patterns that prevailed into the 1990s. The major development was decentralization of the professional theater, which provided careers for artists outside New York City and made professional theater accessible to audiences throughout the United States. Theaters were most often established as not-for-profit operations, heavily dependent on local and federal support. The regional shift occurred because rising production costs in New York discouraged risk taking and admission prices gradually increased (in 1994 Broadway theater tickets reached a high of $75). By the early 1990s, 300 not-for-profit professional theaters were playing to more than 16 million people annually. Despite the demise of forty theaters between 1980 and 1993, largely the result of economic pressure, in the early 1990s not-for-profit theaters were a $366 million industry.

One interesting result of the spread of American theater was transference of successful productions by regional theaters to New York (and national or international recognition), beginning with the Washington, D.C., Arena Stage production of Howard Sackler's *The Great White Hope* in 1976. Since then major American plays have frequently originated outside New York: David Mamet's *Glengarry Glen Ross* (Chicago's Goodman Theatre, 1984), Marsha Norman's *'night, Mother* (American Repertory Theatre in Cambridge, Mass., 1983), Herb Gardner's *I'm Not Rappaport* and *Conversations with My Father* (both presented first at the Seattle Repertory Theatre), and all of the plays by African-American playwright August Wilson, beginning with *Ma Rainey's Black Bottom* (Yale Repertory Theatre, 1984). Sixteen of the seventeen Pulitzer Prizes in drama (1976–1993) went to plays developed by not-for-profit companies. The winner of the 1992 prize, Robert Schenkkan's *The Kentucky Cycle* was seen first in Seattle in 1991. The

1993 winner, Tony Kushner's *Angels in America,* received the prize several weeks before its Broadway opening, after development in London, San Francisco, and Los Angeles.

A residual effect of the socially committed, aesthetically radical theater artists of the late 1950s and early 1960s, and in opposition to theater epitomized by Broadway, was an avant-garde theater centered in the Off-Broadway and Off-Off-Broadway districts and in major cities throughout the country. This avant-garde theater paralleled the winding down of the Vietnam War. Stimulated by the English-born director Peter Brook and the Polish national Jerzy Grotowski, it sought to strip away old conventions and reach what Brook and Grotowski called a "holy" core or essence. Experiment led to changes in style and structure and encouraged new topics and such cross-disciplinary hybrids as dance-theater, performance art, docudrama, environmental theater, guerrilla theater, and New Vaudeville. Eschewing conventional plots and characters, director-playwrights Richard Foreman, Lee Breuer, and Robert Wilson emerged in the 1970s, and such ensembles as Mabou Mines and the Wooster Group turned from polemic to self-reflective visionary and aural images. In the 1980s a more conservative atmosphere encouraged radical artists—for example, Eric Bogosian, Laurie Anderson, Karen Finley, Spalding Gray, and Anna Deavere Smith—to explore social and political issues in more personal ways. The controversial authorial voice of stage directors, which began in the 1970s, intensified in the work of JoAnne Akalaitis, Meredith Monk, Elizabeth LeCompte, Anne Bogart, and Peter Sellars.

All the while there was an expansion of demographics on stage and in the audience. The voices of African Americans, Latinos, Asians, gays, and women, in the past on the fringe, reached the centers of theater. Previously marginalized artists moved into positions of considerable visibility. Pulitzer Prizes were won by Beth Henley (*Crimes of the Heart,* 1981), Marsha Norman (*'night, Mother,* 1983), and Wendy Wasserstein (*The Heidi Chronicles,* 1989), raising by half the number of Pulitzers in drama awarded to women since their inception in 1918. The African-American director George C. Wolfe became producer of the New York Shakespeare Festival, a major not-for-profit theater established by Joseph Papp (1921–1991). In 1993 the National Endowment for the Arts appointed as its head actress Jane Alexander, the first artist to hold this post.

Commercial theater since the early 1970s, despite unwillingness to experiment and despite soaring production costs, has enjoyed considerable prosperity, with long runs of spectacular musicals, many imported from abroad, such as *Cats, Les Misérables, Phantom of the Opera, Miss Saigon, Sunset Boulevard,* and others with small-cast plays. Major figures included playwright Neil Simon, whose *Lost in Yonkers* (1991) won the Pulitzer Prize, and composer-lyricist Stephen Sondheim, who continued to be the most original American creator of musical theater. Playwrights who first gained attention in the 1970s, such as John Guare, Terrence McNally, and August Wilson, became major voices in the theater by the late 1980s. By the mid-1990s, however, despite productions dealing with controversial subjects *(Kiss of the Spider Woman, Angels in America),* Broadway continued to be dominated by musical revivals *(Guys and Dolls, Crazy for You, She Loves Me, Joseph and the Amazing Technicolor Dreamcoat, My Fair Lady, Damn Yankees, Show Boat).*

[C. W. E. Bigsby, *Modern American Drama, 1945–1990* (New York, 1992); Mary C. Henderson, *Theater in America: 200 Years of Plays, Players, and Productions* (New York, 1986); Don B. Wilmeth and Tice L. Miller, *Cambridge Guide to American Theatre* (New York, 1993).]

Don B. Wilmeth

THEME PARKS. The origins of the theme park trace back to late-nineteenth-century beach clubs, such as those along Coney Island in Brooklyn, N.Y., where people drank, socialized, and watched musical productions in pavilions. Mechanical rides were added to these resorts and to picnic parks that were developed by trolley companies to build weekend and holiday use of local transit systems. By the 1930s these areas had developed into amusement parks. In 1955 Walt Disney built the first amusement theme park, Disneyland, in Anaheim, Calif., where he combined fantasy with rides, food, and shows in a safe, clean, family environment. In the 1990s there were ten major types of theme park: multi-theme, such as Disneyland and Six Flags Great Adventure (N.J.); water theme, such as Water Country USA (Va.); holiday and Santa Claus theme, such as Holiday World (Ind.); imaginary character theme, such as Dogpatch USA (Ark.) and Sesame Place (Pa.); movie theme, such as Disney-MGM Studios (Fla.) and Universal Studios (Fla.); musical theme, such as Dollywood (Tenn.) and Opryland USA (Tenn.); marine life theme, such as Marineland (Fla.) and Sea World (Fla.); historic theme, such as The Old Country (Va.); western theme, such as Frontier City (Okla.); and animal and nature theme, such as Busch Gardens' The

Dark Continent (Fla.) and Waimea Falls Park (Hawaii). The largest theme park in the world is Walt Disney World in Lake Buena Vista, Fla. With almost 28,000 acres, it is twice the size of Manhattan and admits more than 20 million visitors each year.

[American Automobile Association, *The AAA Guide to North America's Theme Parks* (New York, 1992).]

JOHN J. BYRNE

THINK TANKS are policy-oriented research organizations that have proliferated in twentieth-century America, but no precise count or unambiguous definition exists for such organizations. They perform studies that result in policy recommendations; they usually publish their findings; they may undertake research for a client on a grant or contract basis or initiate their own studies; and most, not all, have nonprofit status. Their work frequently is of an interdisciplinary character in contrast to the more traditional disciplinary studies of university scholars. Think tank examples include the Rand Corporation, Brookings Institution, American Enterprise Institute, Hudson Institute, and such newer entities as the Heritage Foundation and the Cato Institute. The creation of think tanks came in three waves. The earliest ones were established in the Progressive Era as part of the movement to bring efficiency to government. A second wave came after World War II when many think tanks such as the Rand Corporation were set up to advise the federal government, especially in defense. In the 1970s a third wave emerged that reflected a political policy or ideological orientation. Think tanks engage in dialogue with one another and are often cited or referred to by government officials or by political protagonists, although their effect on policy remains a matter of debate. In their number, variety, and intellectual vitality, think tanks are a U.S. phenomenon, and they contribute to the dynamism, openness, and pluralism of the nation's policymaking process.

[Joseph C. Kiger, ed., *Research Institutions and Learned Societies* (Westport, Conn., 1982); Bruce L. R. Smith, *The Advisors* (Washington, D.C., 1992), and *The Rand Corporation* (Cambridge, Mass., 1966); James Allen Smith, *The Idea Brokers* (New York, 1991).]

BRUCE L. R. SMITH

THIRD PARTIES AND INDEPENDENTS. The decline since 1960 in identification among the electorate with either the Republican or Democratic parties contributed to a proliferation of minor parties and two of the most successful independent presidential

tickets in U.S. history. Third parties in the United States have always been quite diverse in goals and organization. With the exception of Alabama Governor George Wallace's American Independent party in the presidential election of 1968, the only aspect such parties have had in common is their failure to influence the electoral process. Wallace's party exemplified the third party as protest vote, and his strength at the polls (13.5 percent of the total) inspired the administration of Richard M. Nixon to adopt rhetoric and policies specifically designed to capture Wallace's traditionally Democratic followers for the Republican party. Wallace competed in the Democratic primaries in 1972 but was shot in an assassination attempt, and the party he founded faded into obscurity.

Most third parties are ideologically based, and purity of doctrine is more important than pragmatic efforts to build a campaign organization and establish a coalition of voters. The Marxist parties—Socialist Workers, Communist, Socialist Labor, Workers World, Socialist—are cases in point. All remained active through the 1980s, but none received more than one-tenth of 1 percent of the votes cast, in part because state laws make it difficult for third-party candidates to qualify to be on ballots. The Libertarian party has achieved greater success on the far right of the political spectrum. Emphasizing individual freedom, an unregulated market economy, and voluntarism (even to the extent of opposing the power of taxation), the Libertarians have contested most national and many state offices. Their presidential candidate in 1980, Ed Clark, received just over 1 percent of the vote, and the 1992 candidate, Andre Marrou, .28 percent. A few minor parties focus essentially on a single issue, much like interest groups. The Prohibition party continued to field presidential candidates, although it drew only a few thousand votes per election and only 985 votes in 1992. The Citizens party, founded by Barry Commoner in 1969 and similar to the Green parties in Europe, qualified for federal matching funds in 1984 but attracted only 72,000 presidential votes. The Right-to-Life party, which opposes abortion, has received even fewer votes.

Far more impressive than third parties has been a series of independent candidates. Former Democratic Senator Eugene McCarthy drew almost 1 percent of the vote nationally in the 1976 presidential election. Republican John Anderson qualified for federal matching funds in 1980, initially while contesting his own party's primaries and then as an independent in the general election. He spent almost $15 million on the campaign and captured 6.6 percent of the popular

257

vote. In 1990 maverick Republican Lowell Weicker won the governorship of Connecticut as an independent, while Bernard Sanders of Vermont ran as an independent for the U.S. House of Representatives and became the first Socialist elected to Congress since World War I. In the 1992 presidential campaign Texas billionaire Ross Perot ran as an independent and captured almost 19 percent of the popular vote (the best third-party showing since Theodore Roosevelt ran as a Progressive in 1912), even though he dropped out of the race for ten weeks in midsummer. Perot created a tightly controlled campaign organization, designed primarily to obtain signatures to qualify him for the ballot in every state. He spent tens of millions of his own dollars on lengthy network television "infomercials," $3 million on election eve alone. He was also the first third-party candidate to be included in televised presidential debates. Perot's success illustrated both widespread disaffection with the major parties and the crucial importance of money in politics.

[Earl R. Kruschke, *Encyclopedia of Third Parties in the United States* (Santa Barbara, Calif., 1991); Frank Smallwood, *The Other Candidates: Third Parties in Presidential Elections* (Hanover, N.H., 1983).]

KEITH IAN POLAKOFF

THOMAS CONFIRMATION HEARINGS (1991). President George Bush's nomination of Clarence Thomas in July 1991 to succeed Associate Justice Thurgood Marshall on the Supreme Court proved controversial from the beginning. Opponents argued that Thomas was minimally qualified and had done a poor job of enforcing civil rights laws as director of the Equal Employment Opportunity Commission (EEOC). Despite the fact that the Senate Judiciary Committee sent the Thomas nomination to the floor with no recommendation on Sept. 27, 1991 (the committee split seven to seven), it appeared that Thomas would be confirmed in a close vote by the full Senate. Then, shortly before the Senate was to act, news was leaked that Anita Hill, a former employee of Thomas, had accused him of sexual harassment during his directorship of the EEOC, forcing the Senate Judiciary Committee to reopen its hearings.

On the weekend of Oct. 11–13, 1991, millions of Americans watched the televised hearings, during which Hill accused Thomas of repeated unwanted sexual advances and the use of graphic sexual language in the office. Eighty-four percent of the public reported watching at least one hour of the hearings. More than half (52.4 percent) thought the reopened hearings were "an orchestrated campaign to discredit

the nominee's character" (*Los Angeles Times* poll). Ultimately, Thomas and his supporters were able to save his nomination by using hearsay and innuendo against Hill, thus taking advantage of the fact that Senate hearings do not adhere to standard courtroom procedures, such as burden of proof or rules of evidence. Republican Senators Alan Simpson, Orrin Hatch, and Arlen Specter were especially aggressive in questioning Hill. Thomas indignantly defended himself from what he called a "high-tech lynching of an uppity black." His reference to "lynching" galvanized much support among African Americans. With his white wife visible behind him throughout the hearings, Thomas evoked an earlier era of black persecution. Democrats on the committee demonstrated no strategic plan for questioning witnesses or, like Senator Edward Kennedy, were reduced to ineffectual roles because of their own sexual history. For many Democratic senators, the Thomas vote became an issue of racial loyalty rather than qualifications, ideology, or even sexual conduct. One study showed that a moderate Democratic senator from a state that was one-third black was two-thirds more likely to support Thomas's nomination than a similar senator from a state that had no blacks, but hundreds of African-American women took out a full-page ad in the *New York Times* protesting the "racist and sexist treatment" of Hill and expressing their "vehement opposition to the policies represented by the placement of Clarence Thomas on the Supreme Court." Ultimately, the confirmation of Thomas squeaked through the Senate by a vote of fifty-two to forty-eight, the closest margin for a Supreme Court appointment in more than 100 years.

Although public support for Thomas was about the same before and after the hearings, it would be wrong to overlook the political and social impact of this event. First, it heightened awareness of sexual harassment of women in the workplace because of Hill's testimony. Second, the perception that Hill was unfairly treated by the all-male Judiciary Committee contributed to the political "year of the women" in 1992, when an unprecedented number of women were elected at all levels of government. Third, the Senate came under attack for its status as an all-white, mostly male institution that was "out of touch" and "just didn't get it." By 1994 the Senate was less white, less male, and more sensitive to gender-related issues, in part because of the Thomas confirmation hearings.

[John C. Danforth, *Resurrection: The Confirmation of Clarence Thomas* (New York, 1994); Jane Mayer and Jill

10

Abramson, *Strange Justice: The Selling of Clarence Thomas* (Boston, 1994); Timothy M. Phelps and Helen Winternitz, *Capitol Games: The Inside Story of Clarence Thomas, Anita Hill, and a Supreme Court Nomination* (New York, 1993).]

DAVID T. CANON

See also **SUPP:** Sexual Harassment; Women in Public Life, Business, and the Professions.

THREE MILE ISLAND, site of the worst nuclear power program mishap in the history of the United States, is located in the Susquehanna River near Harrisburg, Pennsylvania. The event, which could easily have become a major disaster, shook public confidence in nuclear technology. The seven-day emergency began on Mar. 28, 1979, at Unit 2, one of two nuclear power plants built on the island in the early 1970s. The plant's operators initially mishandled the accident, and the resulting emergency was poorly managed by technical experts as well as state and federal officials responsible for public safety. The seriousness of the accident became clear, however, when both Governor Richard L. Thornburg of Pennsylvania and President Jimmy Carter visited the stricken plant while its operators were still struggling to resolve the menacing situation. A combination of faulty design and human error caused the problem. An overheated reactor core whose protective coolant was largely gone resulted in reactor temperatures as high as 4,300 degrees and the accidental release of radiation into the atmosphere. The event could have led to core temperatures so high (5,200 degrees) that the core would have melted through its base, resulting in unprecedented damage to the containment structure. Although a nuclear meltdown had never occurred, there was little doubt that such an event could have caused a release of deadly radiation into the atmosphere many times greater than the fallout created by the atomic bomb exploded at Hiroshima in the final days of World War II. The population around Three Mile Island and possibly—depending on prevailing winds—hundreds of miles away would have been in deadly peril. Government analysts calculate that, at the height of the crisis, the Three Mile Island reactor was within approximately one hour of a meltdown. The lessons learned at Three Mile Island led to stricter supervision and design modifications that, together with the prospects of high cleanup costs, such as those incurred at the stricken Pennsylvania plant, made earlier profit expectations unrealistic. Thus, the accident had a strong negative effect on the nuclear power industry's plans for building new plants.

[Philip L. Cantelon and Robert C. Williams, *Crisis Contained: The Department of Energy at Three Mile Island* (Carbondale and Edwardsville, Ill., 1982); Fred Clement, *The Nuclear Regulatory Commission* (New York, 1989); Daniel F. Ford, *Three Mile Island: Thirty Minutes to Meltdown* (New York, 1982); Mike Gray and Ira Rosen, *The Warning: Accident at Three Mile Island* (New York, 1983); President's Commission on the Accident at Three Mile Island, *The Need for Change: The Legacy of Three Mile Island* (Washington, D.C., 1979).]

ROBERT M. GUTH

See also **SUPP:** Nuclear Power; Nuclear Regulatory Commission; Pennsylvania.

TIANANMEN SQUARE PROTEST (Apr. 15–June 4, 1989) began in Beijing, China, as peaceful prodemocracy demonstrations by students calling for political liberalization and an end to official corruption. The protests in the square and at gathering places in other Chinese cities soon escalated into massive demonstrations involving people from all walks of life. In June the government used heavily armed troops to crush the movement. Soldiers killed more than 1,000 protesters and bystanders, many of them workers, and a much larger number were injured. These acts of repression horrified many Americans, who watched the movement unfold on television and sympathized with the protesters. President George Bush responded by imposing minor diplomatic sanctions against the Chinese regime.

[Jeffrey N. Wasserstrom and Elizabeth J. Perry, eds., *Popular Protest and Political Culture in Modern China: Learning from 1989* (Boulder, Colo., 1992).]

JEFFREY N. WASSERSTROM

See also **SUPP:** China, Relations with.

TIMBERLANDS. The use of fire by Native Americans had altered American forests by the time of European arrival, and European settlers accelerated forest change. The expansion of agriculture cleared vast areas of forest, and Europeans employed wood for a multitude of purposes—for houses, of course, not to mention roads (for a while), ships, tools, and many other items. In the mid-1990s forests in the United States covered 70 percent of the area that was forested in the early seventeenth century. Seventy percent of America's timberland is east of the Mississippi, where hardwood forests predominate. Nearly three-fourths of U.S. timberland is privately owned.

Nonindustrial private owners hold half of all timberlands; what one might describe as industrial forests account for 14 percent of U.S. forests. National forests, subject to careful rules, comprise most of the federal land. The bulk of timber harvested in the nation comes from privately owned land. Forest conservation programs have reversed forest loss. In the 1920s timber growth nationally was about half the rate of harvest. Annual forest growth in the 1990s was more than three and one-half times the 1920 rate, and the ratio of timber growth to harvest was 1:1.33. The rehabilitation of America's forests is one of the world's greatest conservation success stories. Changing public attitudes toward the purposes of forests have generated pressure for changes in the use of public forests, away from timber to recreation, wildlife, and ecosystem management. Timber production increasingly is concentrated on privately owned forest lands.

[Douglas S. Powell et al., *Forest Resources of the United States: 1992* (Fort Collins, Colo., 1994); Michael Williams, *Americans and Their Forests* (New York, 1989).]

HAROLD W. WISDOM

TIMES BEACH, a town in Missouri, came to national attention in December 1982, when Environmental Protection Agency (EPA) officials received laboratory reports indicating that soil samples taken from the town's dirt roads contained dioxin, a toxic chemical by-product, in concentrations hundreds of times higher than levels considered safe for human exposure by the Centers for Disease Control. The EPA had investigated sites where a contractor hired by Times Beach had sprayed waste automotive oil onto dirt roads to control dust. The contractor, a waste hauler named Russell Bliss, had disposed of industrial sludge from a defunct chemical company by mixing it with the waste oil. The EPA purchased all property in Times Beach and permanently evacuated its 2,000 residents. The buyout was the first under the Superfund program.

[Linda Garmon, "Times Beach: The Long Road to Recovery," *Science News* (Apr. 23, 1983); Michael Posner, "Anatomy of a Missouri Nightmare," *Maclean's* (Apr. 4, 1983).]

JOHN MORELLI

See also **SUPP:** Environmental Protection Agency; Hazardous Waste; Missouri; Superfund.

TOBACCO INDUSTRY. Despite decades of turmoil caused by medical evidence that tobacco use creates a health hazard, in the mid-1990s the tobacco industry still maintained its important position in the U.S. economy. The industry enjoyed political and social approval during the first half of the twentieth century, although its pricing policies and advertising practices sometimes drew public ire. After the Supreme Court broke up the American Tobacco Trust in 1911, six corporations—American Tobacco, R. J. Reynolds, Philip Morris, Brown and Williamson, Liggett and Myers, and P. Lorillard—dominated cigarette manufacturing. Cigar, pipe, and chewing tobacco manufacturers likewise tended toward concentration, led by U.S. Tobacco. In 1946 the Supreme Court upheld lower court findings that cigarette manufacturers had tacitly fixed prices, albeit through collusion rather than formal agreement. Beginning in the 1950s the Federal Trade Commission (FTC) regularly issued cease-and-desist orders against tobacco manufacturers for misleading advertising, which made health claims in such slogans as "A Treat Instead of a Treatment" and "Not a Cough in a Carload." Despite such interventions cigarette smoking was encouraged by the government and even the Red Cross during both world wars and was adopted by many Americans as chic, convenient, and socially acceptable. Movies, advertising, and Prohibition promoted increased use of tobacco products. In 1920 the industry sold 298,590 metric tons of tobacco (or 11.3 grams per adult per day); by 1950 that number had risen to 511,880 (12.7 grams per adult per day). Increased use of cigarettes accounted for most of the growth. More than half of men and about a third of women smoked regularly in 1950.

Medical studies regarding the safety of cigarette smoking threatened tobacco's economic and political status. During the early 1950s British and U.S. physicians, together with organizations like the American Cancer Society, began to publicize epidemiological studies showing a long-suspected association between cigarette smoking and cancer as well as heart disease and other ailments. Newspapers and magazines such as the *Reader's Digest* published articles condemning smoking, producing the first national health scare. As a result, in 1953 and 1954 both tobacco stock prices and cigarette consumption declined. Manufacturers responded in several ways: exporting to other markets, producing filter-tip cigarettes, and launching new advertising and public relations campaigns. Exports climbed after 1955, from 15 million cigarettes to 25 million ten years later; they increased more rapidly after 1970. The popularity of filter tips grew because smokers thought they were safer than regular cigarettes. Before 1953 just one brand of filtered cigarettes was sold in the United States, but each of the major companies put at least one brand on the market in 1953 or 1954; market share grew from 1 percent in 1950 to 19 percent in 1955. The industry spent $38 million on television, magazine, and newspaper advertising in 1954. It promoted filtered cigarettes, although not all filters were effective and some, such as one made of asbestos, were harmful.

Forbidden by a 1911 antitrust order to form a trade association, cigarette manufacturers engaged a New York public relations agency, Hill and Knowlton, which advised company presidents to recruit public relations firms, growers, and warehouses to create the Tobacco Industry Research Committee (TIRC). TIRC's mission was to provide research money for study of issues related to smoking and cancer and to conduct a public relations program. TIRC representatives insisted that because a clinical link between smoking and lung cancer had not been proven (which was true) more research should be conducted. In 1958 the Hill and Knowlton agency created the Council for Tobacco Research, responsible for scientific research only, and the Tobacco Institute, the industry's lobbying and public relations arm.

The 1964 U.S. surgeon general's *Report on Smoking and Health* created a second national health scare. Based on more than 4,000 published studies on tobacco use, the report indicated that without question smoking was hazardous and that the problem warranted remedial action. Two-thirds of the adults in a government survey that year said they believed smoking caused lung cancer, up from two-fifths the previous year. This widespread and growing belief brought a threat of federal regulation but neither the FTC or the Food and Drug Administration took decisive action, and the U.S. Department of Agriculture continued to provide subsidies to tobacco farmers. Congress divided on the issue of tobacco and health, usually to the industry's benefit. The first hearings on smoking and health took place in 1957, when a House committee found that the FTC had not adequately reacted to deceptive advertising about filters. After the surgeon general's report Congress in 1965 passed the Cigarette Labeling and Advertising Act, which required that all cigarette packages and advertisements contain the warning label "Caution: Cigarette Smoking May Be Hazardous to Your Health." Critics found the warning weak because it said "may be" rather than "is" and because it did not include warnings about lung cancer or other diseases.

The industry opposed any label but accepted the 1965 version; ironically, the label later provided legal protection for the industry, which could prove that after 1965 smokers had been aware of potential risks associated with tobacco use but chose to smoke anyway.

Congressional investigation of cigarette advertising and an aggressive campaign that used the Federal Communications Commission's Fairness Doctrine to gain free air time for antismoking messages led manufacturers in 1970 to remove all cigarette ads from television and radio, while Congress continued to fund research on how to grow more and better tobacco. Revenue from tobacco taxes made it difficult for Congress to be decisive about regulating cigarette smoking. In 1964 annual federal taxes on cigarettes totaled $2 billion; state taxes brought in well over $1 billion.

Despite growing criticism of the industry, tobacco manufacturers never acknowledged that their products were harmful or addictive, although they offered filter tips and took steps to lower the amounts of tar and nicotine in cigarettes. Tobacco remained a legal product and tobacco interests gained exemptions from such measures as the Consumer Product Safety Act, the Fair Packaging and Labeling Act, the Hazardous Substances Act, and the Toxic Substances Control Act. During the 1980s tobacco corporations diversified by purchasing less controversial companies, such as Nabisco and General Foods, which helped protect stock prices. Exports, especially to Asia, continued to rise. Fifty years after the first major health scare the tobacco industry was valued at $50 billion and had 50 million consumers worldwide.

A wave of civil lawsuits against the tobacco industry also reflected smokers' concerns; between the mid-1970s and 1995 more than 400 unsuccessful lawsuits were filed. The companies responded with a no-compromise legal strategy. They defended every claim regardless of cost through trials and appeals. Tobacco attorneys outspent and outlasted plaintiffs who ran out of money or died while litigation lingered. In 1994, however, the first class-action suits were brought against tobacco companies, including a suit by sixty law firms in five states. The suit represented up to 40 million smokers and 50 million former smokers claiming to be addicted or damaged or both by tobacco products. The solidarity of the tobacco companies against lawsuits and regulation was shattered in March 1996, when the Liggett Group (the fifth-largest company but with only a 2 percent market share) agreed to settle its part of the suit. Liggett agreed to payments for an antismoking campaign, not to oppose new government regulations, and to make the first damage payments ever by a tobacco company. Shortly thereafter, two former Philip Morris employees confirmed charges against the tobacco companies of manipulation of nicotine levels to keep smokers hooked. Other class-action suits were pending as well, including one against Philip Morris involving 60,000 flight attendants who said they were forced to inhale secondary smoke in airline cabins before smoking on airplanes was banned. In February 1994 the state of Florida decided to sue the tobacco companies for the Medicare costs it incurred in treating smokers; West Virginia, Minnesota, and Mississippi filed similar suits.

[John C. Burnham, *Bad Habits* (New York, 1993); A. Lee Fritschler, *Smoking and Politics,* 4th ed. (Englewood Cliffs, N.J., 1989); Robert L. Rabin and Stephen D. Sugarman, eds., *Smoking Policy: Law, Politics, and Culture* (New York, 1993); Robert Sobel, *They Satisfy: The Cigarette in American Life* (Garden City, N.Y., 1978); Susan Wagner, *Cigarette Country* (New York, 1971); Thomas Whiteside, *Selling Death* (New York, 1971).]

KAREN S. MILLER

See also **SUPP:** Advertising; Environmental Protection Agency; Food and Drug Administration; Smoking; Substance Abuse.

TOKYO ROUND. *See* **General Agreement on Tariffs and Trade.**

TOLEDO, the fourth-largest city in Ohio in the 1990s, began as a French trading post (1680) and fortification (1700). Ceded to the British in 1763, it was incorporated into the U.S. Northwest Territory in 1787, but permanent settlement did not begin until after the War of 1812. Canals and railroads helped establish Toledo as a major inland port and center of industry on the Maumee River estuary at the western end of Lake Erie. In 1835 the city was claimed by both Ohio and Michigan, in the so-called Toledo War, and the dispute was settled by Congress, which awarded the city to Ohio (and the Upper Peninsula to Michigan). During the Progressive Era in the early twentieth century Toledo won national recognition for urban reform through the works of Mays Samuel "Golden Rule" Jones and Brand Whitlock. Historically, Toledo has been a major producer of glass and automotive products, but these industries declined, and from 1970 to 1990 employment in the Toledo metropolitan area decreased markedly. During this same period population declined from 383,062 to 332,943. Toledo

has experienced other problems. A 1967 race riot caused extensive property damage, injuries, and arrests. Public schools were closed for several weeks in 1976 and 1978 because of teacher strikes. In July 1979 a bitter dispute between the city government and police and firemen led to a two-day general strike and costly arson fires. The mood of those years was caught by John Denver's satiric 1973 song "Saturday Night in Toledo, Ohio." In the 1980s and 1990s Toledo sought to emphasize its strong medical, cultural and higher educational institutions. New downtown buildings and the Portside festival marketplace along the Maumee was indicative of business leaders' commitment to the city.

[Morgan Barclay, *Toledo: Gateway to the Great Lakes* (Tulsa, Okla., 1982); Melvin D. Berger, *Toledo: Focused for the Future* (Chatsworth, Calif., 1991).]

JOHN B. WEAVER

See also **DAH:** Toledo War; **DAH** and **SUPP:** Cincinnati; Cleveland; Columbus (Ohio); Ohio.

TORNADOES are products of thunderstorms of unusual power. Major thunderstorms extend from the ground up through the jet stream to the stratosphere. They often produce a double vortex, the upper vortex turning in a direction opposite to the circular motion of the lower. The latter normally stretches from the bottom of the storm cloud to the ground and commonly has a funnel-like shape. The typical tornado is in contact with the ground for only about six miles, and its path may be no more than 500 feet wide. Tornadoes typically travel at about thirty miles per hour but can move as rapidly as sixty miles per hour, with wind speeds exceeding 250 miles per hour. Although tornadoes can occur anywhere in conjunction with thunderstorms, they are most common in the central United States as a result of the topography. The west-to-east flow of air across the United States is interrupted by the Rocky Mountains, which pushes the air currents up; they fall suddenly when they reach the Great Plains. If moisture-laden air is pulled in from the Gulf of Mexico and meets the high dry air over the plains, that confluence creates the conditions for a tornado. The average number of tornadoes in the United States ranges between 700 and 800 a year, but in some years, notably 1973, 1982, 1990, and 1992, the total has exceeded 1,000. In 1992 a total of 1,300 were recorded, the greatest number since 1950, when records were first kept. Texas generally has the most tornadoes, followed by Oklahoma and Kansas. Fatalities have tended to be higher in the Deep South and generally total fewer than 100 per year. The year 1974 was an exception; 350 people died on April 3–4 in Alabama, Georgia, Tennessee, Kentucky, and Oklahoma. Tornadoes cause one-fifth of natural disaster losses each year in the United States. The National Severe Storms Forecast Center, in Kansas City, Mo., is responsible for issuing warnings of approaching tornadoes. It bases its predictions on meteorological conditions in combination with unusual patterns on the weather radar. Although the approach of a tornado can be forecast only 50 percent of the time, warnings have been important in reducing the death toll.

[Joe R. Eagleman, *Severe and Unusual Weather* (Lenexa, Kans., 1988).]

NANCY M. GORDON

See also **SUPP:** Disasters, Natural and Environmental.

TOURISM, one of the leading industries in the United States in the 1990s, generated more than $300 billion per year in transportation, lodging, eating and drinking, and amusement and recreation services, and more than 10 million people were employed in these services. Half of the tourist trade consisted of domestic travelers touring the United States and half of foreign visitors coming to this country. When U.S. citizens go on vacation 31 percent choose to visit cities, with Washington, D.C., and New York City the favorite choices, while 26 percent favor the oceans and beaches. Twenty-two percent visit small towns, 10 percent favor the mountains, while the remainder go to lakes, streams, and other places. Each year 1.3 billion trips are taken, 500 million of which are to visit friends and relatives, 500 million to pursue other pleasure, and the rest traveling for business and to attend conventions. Collectively, U.S. families enjoy 900 million vacation trips and 770 million weekend trips. Since the 1980s several factors have favored domestic travel, including expansion of international terrorism, the decline in the U.S. dollar that makes travel abroad more expensive, and the low price of gasoline.

While Florida's Disney World is the most popular vacation spot, attracting 22 million visitors per year, California is the number-one state for domestic travel. After California and Florida, U.S. travelers spend most of their vacation money in New York, Texas, and Illinois, while the fewest dollars are spent in South Dakota, North Dakota, Delaware, Vermont, and Wyoming. During the winter Florida is by far the most popular destination of U.S. tourists, followed by Hawaii, Colorado, California, and Nevada. In Wash-

ington, D.C., the top sites visited are the Holocaust Museum, the National Air and Space Museum, the National Gallery of Art, and the National Museum of Natural History. The White House on a busy day attracts 7,000 people—compared to 4,000 per day who tour Graceland, Elvis Presley's house in Memphis, Tenn. The travel industry is the top employer in thirty-nine states. California and Florida have the highest budgets for tourism and receive the greatest benefits, while Kansas, North Dakota, and Nebraska spend the least, $1 million per year. More than $168 million a year is spent for network travel advertising.

In the early 1990s tourism became the country's leading source of foreign currency. In 1990 foreign visitors spent $43 billion on vacations in the United States, $450 million more than Americans spent abroad. In 1992 foreign visitors spent $53.8 billion. Each year sets a new record. By the mid-1990s more than 50 million foreign tourists were expected to arrive and spend more than $61 billion. In 1993 for the first time overseas visitors exceeded the total visitors from Canada, which, along with Mexico, is the greatest single source of the U.S. tourist trade. Most visitors to the United States coming for pleasure are from the United Kingdom, Germany, France, Japan, China, Korea, Brazil, Venezuela, and Argentina. Japan's 4 million yearly tourists do not comprise the greatest number of visitors but they spend the largest amount of money in the United States—$13.8 billion. Overseas travelers spend six times more per person per day on a one-trip basis in this country than domestic travelers.

The average stay of foreign visitors of almost three weeks is five times longer than the average domestic vacation of four nights. One in every seven hotel rooms in the United States each night is rented to a visitor from overseas. Tour operators have increased overseas promotions so that foreign visitors have exceeded the previous year's total each year since the late 1980s. Hotels and restaurants provide bilingual clerks and waiters, and airports have signs in several languages advising passengers of delays. The bombing of the World Trade Center in New York City and the murders of foreign tourists in Florida have not stopped the massive influx. The most frequently visited place for first-time visitors from abroad is New York City, where foreigners make up 22 percent of the city's 25 million yearly visitors and where they spend $1.6 billion a year for shopping. The Disney parks are next in attendance, and the number-one destination of all visitors to the United States is Disney World. One attraction for foreign visitors is shopping at malls. The average visitor to this country spends $539 per capita on gifts and souvenirs and malls have developed their own promotional material for tourists. Sawgrass Mills, an outlet mall just west of Fort Lauderdale, Fla., attracts the most foreigners. Nearly half of its 18 million annual visitors come from abroad, making it the second-largest tourist attraction in Florida.

[Peter E. Tarlow and Mitchell J. Muehsam, "Wide Horizons: Travel and Tourism in the Coming Decades," *The Futurist* (Sept.-Oct. 1992).]

JOHN J. BYRNE

See also **SUPP:** California; Florida; New York City; Parks, National; Recreation; Theme Parks; Washington, D.C.

TOWER COMMISSION. Appointed by President Ronald Reagan in November 1986, the Tower Commission investigated and reported on allegations involving arms sales to Iran in exchange for U.S. hostages in Lebanon and the diversion of money from arms sales to the Nicaraguan contras in violation of congressional legislation. Headed by former Senator John Tower, the commission was charged with explaining events surrounding these allegations and proposing changes in the National Security Council (NSC) to prevent any such action in the future. Its report, released in February 1987, concluded that members of the NSC staff were responsible for the secret diversion of funds and that President Reagan was out of touch with the actions of his own White House. It exonerated Vice President George Bush who later as president unsuccessfully tried to appoint Tower as secretary of defense. A House-Senate investigation confirmed much of the Tower Report, but after an eight-year investigation Special Prosecutor Lawrence E. Walsh concluded that although neither Reagan nor Bush knew of the diversion of money to the contras or violated any criminal statutes, Bush was aware, contrary to his earlier claims, of the arms-for-hostages deal.

[Harold Hongju Koh, *The National Security Constitution: Sharing Power After the Iran-Contra Affair* (New Haven, Conn., 1990); President's Special Review Board, *The Tower Commission Report* (New York, 1987).]

KATY J. HARRIGER

See also **SUPP:** Iran-Contra Affair; Nicaragua, Relations with.

TOXIC SHOCK SYNDROME (TSS), a rare, sometimes fatal disease that caused widespread panic among women during the early 1980s when the Centers for Disease Control (CDC) and other public health organizations linked the growing number of cases of TSS with the increasing popularity of high-absorbency tampons. First identified in 1978, the earliest reported cases of TSS occurred among seven children. All were linked with the presence of *Staphylococcus aureus*. Symptoms of the disease include vomiting, diarrhea, high fever, and sunburnlike rash. A dramatic upsurge in cases reported to the CDC occurred in 1980, when 890 cases were reported, 812 of which were among women whose illness coincided with the start of their menstrual periods. Fatalities among early TSS patients were around 8 percent. This striking association of TSS with menstruating women stimulated careful epidemiological analysis. When information collected by the Utah Department of Health suggested that a particular tampon brand, Rely, had been used by many women with TSS, a detailed study was devised by the CDC in September 1980 to examine tampon brand use. This study found that 71 percent of a test group of women with TSS had used Rely tampons. On Sept. 22, 1980, Procter and Gamble recalled all Rely tampons on the market and all tampon manufacturers subsequently lowered the absorbency of their tampons. The Food and Drug Administration began requiring that all tampon packages carry information on TSS advising women to use tampons with the minimum absorbency needed to control menstrual flow and to change tampons frequently. Although cases of menstrually related TSS fell off dramatically after 1984, the overall number of cases is suspected to have risen as the staphylococcal bacteria that produces the deadly toxin spread to more people. By the 1990s only about half of the cases of staphylococcal toxic shock syndrome were connected with menstruating women in part because of the increased use of sanitary napkins in the wake of the TSS scare. TSS has been reported in men, children, and older women and in conjunction with surgery, influenza, sinusitis, childbirth, and intravenous drug use; a wound, abscess, boil, cut, or even an insect bite; and use of a contraceptive sponge, cervical cap, or diaphragm.

[Maria E. Donawa et al., "Toxic Shock Syndrome: Chronology of State and Federal Epidemiologic Studies and Regulatory Decision-Making," *Public Health Reports* 99 (1984); Elizabeth W. Etheridge, *Sentinel for Health: A History of the Centers for Disease Control* (Berkeley, Calif., 1982).]

SUZANNE WHITE-JUNOD

See also **SUPP:** Centers for Disease Control and Prevention; Epidemiology.

TRADE, BALANCE OF. *See* **Balance of Trade.**

TRADE, DOMESTIC. Between 1970 and 1995 the U.S. domestic economy went from being manufacturing based to information and service based. Partly as a result of this change, and primarily as a result of competition from abroad, U.S. industry spread throughout the globe. Many everyday consumer products, such as cars, personal computers, and home electronics, were manufactured both overseas and in the United States, making the definition of "domestically produced" a highly subjective one. The difficulties underlying understanding of the new domestic economy became evident when in the 1980s many Americans reacted to a large foreign trade deficit by encouraging citizens to "buy American." During this period many articles appeared in the popular press explaining that most Honda (a Japanese firm) automobiles purchased in the United States were actually made in Ohio, while many personal computers made by U.S. companies such as Compaq, Apple, and IBM were manufactured wholly or in part by overseas firms. In 1994 the Federal Trade Commission (FTC) accused the Boston-based shoemaker New Balance of deceiving customers by labeling its shoes "Made in the USA" even though the soles were imported from Asia. A competitor, Hyde, which produced Saucony shoes, agreed to use the phrase "Made in the USA of domestic and imported components."

Large U.S. manufacturing firms, primarily automakers and other producers of durable goods, suffered from imports during the last quarter of the twentieth century. In the 1970s and 1980s foreign firms had the advantage of much cheaper labor, but their labor costs began rising and U.S. costs were declining because of the increasing weakness of U.S. labor unions. The competitiveness of foreign manufacturers, however, increased in terms of shipping goods, as the slow, expensive ships of former times gave way to huge and efficient container vessels. The once-considerable costs of communication began to lessen with computer and satellite technologies. The decline of large manufacturing firms in the United States led to a resurgence in small businesses (firms with fewer than 500 employees). In the early 1990s small businesses provided 56 percent of private sector employment and represented fully half of the gross national product. Few small companies engaged in manufacturing but those that did prospered, producing 37.4 percent of the nation's total manufacturing output in 1986. Meanwhile, larger manufacturers were downsizing plants, with pre-1970 plants av-

eraging about 650 employees and post-1970 plants averaging only about 250 workers.

The primary cause for the growing importance of small businesses in domestic trade was their ability to adapt to rapidly changing conditions. As new technologies, such as personal computers, fax machines, and computer networks, became cheaper, smaller firms were better able to compete with larger companies. CAD, CAM, and CAE (computer-aided design, manufacturing, and engineering) became standard for both small and large companies. Enhanced communications and networking enabled small companies to cooperate and allowed larger corporations to subcontract work more easily. These changes were most evident in the automobile and computer industries. The big three automakers—General Motors, Ford, and Chrysler—lost their domestic dominance in the 1970s and 1980s as high-quality, inexpensive, and fuel-efficient imports from Japan attracted consumers. Because of the energy crises of 1973 and 1979 the federal government stipulated fuel-efficient cars. At the same time Detroit failed to anticipate the importance of imports and when it became evident failed to react swiftly. It was not until the late 1980s and early 1990s that U.S. automakers, due in part to cooperative design agreements with Japanese automakers, U.S.-Japanese trade agreements, and real declines in gasoline prices, were able to recover some of their market share.

Domestic industries responded to the fast-changing global economy in an inconsistent fashion. Demand for electronic components was strong in the early 1990s but that industry gained, especially by cutting its workforce. Manufacturing in the United States in the mid-1990s was dependent on growth in five industries: automobiles, housing, computers, health care, and environmental equipment. Computers were the fastest-growing industry between 1973 and 1988, health care equipment between 1987 and 1994. Still, in 1991 the gross domestic product of the United States was $6 trillion, the largest in the world. Despite ups and downs throughout the late 1970s, 1980s, and early 1990s domestic trade grew in a fairly consistent pattern. Manufacturing nearly tripled in income during this period, from $317.5 billion in 1975 to $873.8 billion in 1992. Agricultural income more than doubled, from $46.5 billion in 1975 to $95.6 billion in 1992. Transportation tripled from $48 billion in 1975 to $144.8 billion in 1992. The most dramatic change occurred in communications, where income quadrupled, from $26.8 billion in 1975 to $98.6 billion in 1992. Other developments indicated continued strength for domestic trade. The North American Free

Trade Agreement, linking the Canadian, Mexican, and U.S. economies, went into effect on Jan. 1, 1994, providing for elimination of many tariffs by the year 2005. A trend toward business deregulation that began with the administration of President Ronald Reagan (1981–1989) continued to remove barriers for interstate commerce.

[Mansel G. Blackford, *A History of Small Business in America* (New York, 1991); Barry Bluestone and Bennett Harrison, *The Deindustrialization of America* (New York, 1982).]

JEFFREY M. MERRON

See also **SUPP:** Agriculture; Automobile Industry; Balance of Trade; Commerce, Department of; Communications Industry; Economic Indicators; Foreign Investment in the United States; Manufacturing; North American Free Trade Agreement; Real Estate Industry; Retailing Industry; Small Business Administration; Trade, International; Trade Agreements; Transportation Industry.

TRADE, INTERNATIONAL. Between the 1970s and the mid-1990s the U.S. post–World War II dominance of world trade came to an end. Major changes in transportation, finance, corporate structures, and manufacturing restructured the global economy, erasing the significance of international economic boundaries. This process was painful for some and profitable for others. The uncertain and uneven impact of trade liberalization contributed to anxiety, controversy, and political divisiveness. Whole industries in the United States were largely eliminated, unable to compete effectively against cheaper and often better imports. In labor-intensive industries, such as textiles, shoes, and assembly work, the competition came from low-wage developing countries; in the automobile, steel, and electronics industries it came from technological innovators abroad who developed new products and efficient manufacturing.

The United States continued to be the world's largest internal economic market, but this did not isolate the United States from international trade, as it willingly imported goods and services and eagerly exported goods and know-how. The United States sought a role in the global economy, as evidenced by the North American Free Trade Agreement (NAFTA) and major revisions in the General Agreement on Tariffs and Trade (GATT). NAFTA, which became effective in January 1994, created a major regional trading block including Canada, the United States, and Mexico. This far-reaching agreement reduced tariffs

over a fifteen-year period, eased cross-border transportation, and opened Mexico to U.S. and Canadian investments, even in banking and state-owned energy monopolies. Labor unions opposed NAFTA, asserting that corporations would transfer jobs and plants to Mexico because of lower wages and lax environmental regulations. GATT negotiations were protracted. Revisions were negotiated by three presidents—Ronald Reagan, George Bush, and Bill Clinton—who supported cutting tariffs among 123 nations. The GATT agreement known as the Uruguay Round reduced tariffs by 40 percent, cut agricultural subsidies, extended patent protection, and set out rules on global investment. Disputes were to be resolved by the World Trade Organization (WTO), a powerful arbitration board that would decide whether a nation's domestic laws violated the agreement. Proponents estimated that the latest revisions to GATT, when they become fully effectively in 2004, would create jobs and pump up to $100 billion annually into the U.S. economy. (This figure represents less than 2 percent of the nation's total economic output.) Opponents said decisions by the WTO would violate U.S. sovereignty and environmental protection laws.

The arguments for trade liberalization through NAFTA and GATT were the classic economic arguments of comparative advantage originally articulated by the early nineteenth-century British economist David Ricardo. The idea was simple—nations should specialize in products they can produce cheaper or better. Deciding what products that would mean for the United States was problematic. The last U.S. trade surplus (U.S. exports exceeding imports) occurred in 1975, when the nation enjoyed a $12.4 billion surplus. By 1984, however, the United States was posting $100 billion-plus trade deficits each year, reaching a record $166 billion in 1994. The trade deficit is a summary statistic for a more complicated set of relationships that includes country-to-country deficits and surpluses and differences between economic sectors. In 1993, for example, the United States ran a trade surplus of $12.8 billion for foods, feed, and beverages but had large deficits in automotive vehicles ($50 billion) and consumer goods ($79.4 billion).

U.S. productivity lost its advantage when other industrializing nations used new technologies and lower wages to gain access to the vast U.S. market, outcompeting domestic manufacturers. A television-addicted nation sat glued in front of foreign-produced sets. The last U.S. television factory—operated by Zenith Electronics Corporation in Springfield, Mo.—

closed in 1992, leaving more than 1,300 workers jobless when production shifted to Mexico. Japan cut into several consumer markets—electronics, cameras, computers, automobiles. Japanese brand names became household words: Sony, Mitsubishi, Toyota, Nissan, Honda, Hitachi, Mazda, Sharp, Canon, Panasonic. The United States turned to quotas to stem Japanese imports. Japan responded by opening plants in the United States that employed U.S. workers but still diverted dollars abroad. ·

Labor unions urged the public to "buy American," but identifying the products was far from easy. A car "made in America" contained components built in more than a dozen countries on three continents and ultimately assembled in a U.S.-based factory. Was the car American made? A General Motors executive in 1952 testified before Congress: "What is good for the country is good for General Motors." The reasoning no longer held as GM moved jobs and facilities to East Asia or to Mexican plants along the U.S. border. Displaced from well-paying jobs, U.S. workers and managers found reentering the workforce difficult. Even in a growing economy, new jobs paid less. The Census Bureau found that workers who left or were laid off between 1990 and 1992 saw their weekly wages fall 23 percent when they regained employment, often without health insurance and other benefits.

The international economy developed an infrastructure of transportation, financing, and communications that made the movement of money, information, and goods easier and cheaper. Corporations moved money around the world to finance trade, protect against currency fluctuations, or to seek higher returns on investments. Meanwhile U.S. individual and institutional investors looked overseas for investments, often financing enterprises that competed against U.S.-based companies. Huge amounts of capital that otherwise might have been invested in domestic companies found its way abroad into emerging markets in Eastern Europe, Latin America, and the Pacific Rim. Money could be moved instantaneously around the world. Capital's loyalties were not to governments or domestic economies but to the best rate of return. Development of global finance introduced volatility into world financial markets. This new world economic order in effect placed increased burdens on the United States to stabilize or prop up other economies. The Mexican economy collapsed in December 1994 under a severe currency devaluation, leaving the U.S. government and the International Monetary Fund to come up with loan guarantees to stabilize the economy. This bailout fol-

lowed a 1982 collapse in Mexico and South America wherein the U.S. government intervened to bail out U.S. banks with substantial loans in the region. U.S. financial intervention was selective, however, as little assistance was provided the former republics of the Soviet Union when they experienced a currency collapse in 1994.

Making the United States competitive internationally was easier to advocate than accomplish. It put pressures on corporations to reduce employment and improve production. Competition stimulated corporations to undertake organizational change based on ideas in an influential book by Michael Hammer and James Champy, *Re-Engineering the Corporation* (1993). The authors offered a harsh critique of the modern business companies: "Inflexibility, unresponsiveness, the absence of customer focus, an obsession with activity rather than result, bureaucratic paralysis, lack of innovation, high overhead—these are the legacies of one hundred years of American industrial leadership." In their business manifesto the authors urged corporations to reinvent themselves through a "fundamental rethinking and radical redesign of business processes." Typically, "reinvented" companies had fewer employees and fewer managerial levels and used technology to achieve improved performance. Some observers believed the United States needed a "national industrial policy," whereby the government would undertake measures to stop the deindustrialization resulting from corporations moving jobs and capital abroad. Individuals favoring a national industry policy pointed to Japan, where the powerful Ministry of International Trade and Industry worked closely with business. Economists, however, questioned government's ability to pick industrial winners and whether the industrial policies of Japan, France, and Germany were as successful as portrayed, noting that the two European countries were also losing manufacturing jobs.

Problems created in the United States by trade liberalization remained largely unaddressed by the mid-1990s. For the public, trade liberalization was complicated and confusing, with contradictions that were difficult to explain or accept. If trade agreements were good for the nation, why were jobs lost and industries hurt? In 1994 the United States displaced Japan as the world's most competitive economy, based on an annual index by the World Economic Forum. The international economy subjected the U.S. labor force to new economic pressures—job insecurity, stagnant wages for nonskilled labor, and fewer company-sponsored benefits, particularly health insurance. U.S. wage rates were substantially lower than those in Germany and Japan, but within the United States something else occurred—a long-term trend of widening income inequality between the nation's rich and the poor and middle classes. Between 1989 and 1994 the share of income earned by the top 5 percent of Americans increased from 18.9 percent to 21.2 percent, while that earned by the middle 50 percent of Americans fell from 49.3 percent to 46.8 percent. The middle class, accustomed to higher wages and rising living standards in the post–World War II economic boom, found the going tough. Major corporations, even while making record profits, reorganized, eliminating jobs of well-paid middle managers. Meanwhile, the domestic economy was transforming itself, moving from an industrial age to the information age, one for which many workers were ill prepared. The questions were how many high-tech, well-paying jobs could the economy realistically create and how could those stuck in low-wage jobs in the growing service section support themselves and their families.

[John J. Accordino, *The United States in the Global Economy* (Chicago, 1992); Donald B. Bartlett and James B. Steele, *America: What Went Wrong?* (Kansas City, 1992); Michael Hammer and James Champy, *Re-Engineering the Corporation* (New York, 1993); Paul R. Krugman, *The Age of Diminished Expectations* (Cambridge, Mass, 1990).]

BRENT SCHONDELMEYER

See also **SUPP:** Balance of Trade; Foreign Investment in the United States; General Agreement on Tariffs and Trade; International Monetary Fund; North American Free Trade Agreement; Trade, Domestic; Trade Agreements; Wages and Salaries.

TRADE AGREEMENTS. When two or more nations wish to establish or modify economic relations and set tariffs on international commerce they enter into a trade agreement. Any authorized government official may negotiate such an agreement but all participating governments must formally ratify the proposed treaty before it becomes effective. As a result, domestic political forces and interest groups exert considerable influence over the provisions of any trade agreement. The United States negotiated few trade agreements in the eighteenth and nineteenth centuries. Domestic political pressures determined how high or low import taxes (tariffs) would be. From the earliest debates in the First Congress, some political leaders favored low tariffs designed to raise revenue while others favored much higher rates to protect domestic producers from foreign competition.

Lower rates generally prevailed through the 1850s but protectionist tariffs were sponsored by the dominant Republican party during and after the Civil War. To encourage particular types of trade within the forbiddingly high post–Civil War tariff structure some leaders favored bilateral trade agreements in which each nation agreed to reduce rates in return for reciprocal reductions.

In the 1870s the United States signed a reciprocal trade agreement with the then-independent Hawaiian government that gave Hawaiian sugar exporters tariff-free access to the U.S. market. In the early 1890s Secretary of State James G. Blaine negotiated reciprocal trade agreements that softened the effect of the highly protectionist McKinley Tariff Act of 1890, but the 1894 Wilson-Gorman Tariff Act made such agreements impossible. With the exception of the Underwood Act, which passed in 1913 but never went into effect because of World War I, protectionist rates remained until the Great Depression, when it appeared that the nation's high import duties were not only detrimental to world trade but also might be harmful to the domestic economy. The Reciprocal Trade Agreements Act of 1934 permitted reduction of trade barriers by as much as half in return for reductions by another nation. In the late 1930s and 1940s U.S. negotiators arranged a great number of bilateral trade agreements.

Concessions to one nation through bilateral negotiations were often extended to all others through the most-favored-nation principle. Many international agreements included a clause stating that the parties would treat each other in the same way they did the nation their trade policies favored the most. If in bilateral negotiations the United States agreed to reduce its import duties on a particular commodity, that same reduction was automatically granted to imports from any nation with which the United States had a most-favored-nation arrangement. The high tariff walls surrounding the United States were gradually chipped away through bilateral agreements that established much lower rates for all its major trading partners.

The next step was to move negotiation to a multinational setting. When a proposed international trade organization proved unpopular with Congress after World War II, officials tied their hopes to the General Agreement on Tariffs and Trade (GATT), the world's first major multinational trade agreement. GATT resulted from negotiations involving twenty-three nations in 1947. In subsequent decades it served as the primary trade agreement for the noncommunist world and underwent numerous revisions and extensions.

Through eight formal rounds of negotiations, tariff rates on industrial goods dropped to an average of only 4 percent. Multinational negotiations proceed in much the same way as the bilateral negotiations that preceded GATT. A supplier enters into discussions with its primary customer and each side offers incentives it hopes are mutually beneficial. Once such an agreement has been reached it extends to all signatories of the multinational agreement through most-favored-nation provisions. Since 1934 U.S. trade negotiations have been an executive responsibility, but Congress has maintained a strong interest in both procedures and outcomes. In the 1960s and 1970s it called upon the U.S. Tariff Commission to identify "peril points," where reduction of specific duties might cause serious damage to U.S. producers or suppliers. Other federal legislation provided for relief measures if increased imports cause injury to a domestic industrial sector.

The world's acceptance of more liberal trade agreements has had different effects on U.S. producers. Most likely to benefit are those engaged in the nation's traditionally export-oriented agricultural sector. Production costs are relatively low in the U.S. heartland, so a freer market tends to benefit domestic agricultural exporters. At the same time, labor-intensive industries, such as textiles, electronics, and automobiles, have suffered from the gradual reduction of import restrictions. U.S. wage rates range far higher than comparable rates in certain countries that have built very efficient textile mills and fabrication plants for electronic devices and appliances. The recovery of the U.S. auto industry in the 1990s, however, demonstrated that increasing the use of industrial robotics and automated assembly lines can help undermine the cost advantage of foreign manufacturers. As more liberal trade agreements promote competition among producers, each nation is likely to develop stronger and weaker economic sectors that complement those of its global trading partners. The ultimate trade agreement is one in which all national barriers disappear. The European Union (formerly the European Economic Community) represents an approximation of that goal, as does the 1993 North American Free Trade Agreement (NAFTA) among the United States, Canada, and Mexico. NAFTA cancels all major barriers to exchange of goods and services among the participants, leaving the GATT structure in control of imports and exports outside the free trade area.

[Ricardo Grinspin and Maxwell A. Cameron, eds., *The Political Economy of North American Free Trade* (New York, 1993); Joseph A. McKinney and M. Rebecca Sharpless, eds., *Implications of a North American Free Trade Region* (Ottawa, Ont., 1992).]

JOHN M. DOBSON

See also **DAH:** Reciprocal Trade Agreements; Tariffs; **SUPP:** European Community; Foreign Investment in the United States; General Agreement on Tariffs and Trade; North American Free Trade Agreement; Trade, Domestic; Trade, International.

TRANSPLANTS AND ORGAN DONATION. The first successful human organ transplant, in 1954, was a kidney donated by a young man to his identical twin. Since then transplantation has rapidly become a major part of medical care. By the 1990s there were transplant programs for kidneys, hearts, lungs, livers, and pancreases. Dramatic improvements in understanding the human immune system and ability to control immune responses vastly improved the success rate of transplants. Recipients receive organs that are antigen-matched to their own immune systems. Antirejection drugs have fewer side effects. Supply and distribution of donor organs is coordinated nationally.

Between 1980 and 1990, 102,879 organ transplants were performed in the United States. The vast majority (81,283) were kidney transplants. While such established forms of transplant experienced substantial growth, others went from being experimental to relatively common. There were twenty-six liver transplants in 1981 and 2,656 by the end of the decade. Although transplants increased dramatically, demand increased even more. Between 1987 and 1991 waiting lists for every type of organ increased—for kidneys, there was a 67 percent increase. The majority of patients receive transplants from cadavers. Depending on the quality of the organs, a single cadaver can provide many organs; consequently, identifying and obtaining consent from every possible donor is essential. Twenty-one percent of the kidneys transplanted in 1991 were from living donors. With other organs living donation is rare, although there are programs to transplant segments of liver and, more recently, lung.

There has been a chronic shortage of transplant organs in the United States despite a number of programs aimed at increasing the available supply. In 1968 a congressional committee drafted a Uniform Anatomical Gift Act, which allows adults to donate their bodies after death for transplantation and was adopted in some form by every state by 1973. All fifty states and the District of Columbia have some form of donor card associated with driver's licenses. In the early 1980s it was hypothesized that in some cases health care professionals were failing to offer families the opportunity to donate organs because of fear of legal liability. In response, required request laws, which protect health care professionals from liability and require that they ask families of eligible donors to donate organs, were enacted. By 1989 required request laws had been adopted by most states and were linked to Medicare reimbursement and hospital accreditation. Such legislation increased awareness of transplantation but did not result in more donated organs.

As transplant programs developed and expanded so did formal and informal mechanisms for obtaining, sharing, and allocating organs. In 1977 the United Network for Organ Sharing (UNOS) was established to coordinate the distribution of kidneys nationally and to maintain a registry of persons awaiting transplant. UNOS was granted the federal contract to establish the Organ Procurement Transplant Network, mandated by Congress as part of the Omnibus Budget Reconciliation Act of 1986. All transplant centers were required to join the newly established network and abide by its rules. Only one organ procurement organization is allowed to function in each of the eleven national regions. Nevertheless, the shortage of organs persists.

The first kidney transplant raised questions about whether the chances of success were great enough to justify the risks; similar concerns were later expressed about living donations of liver and lung tissue. The difficulty of deciding who will receive a particular organ is exacerbated by the shortage of supply, which has raised questions about the policy prohibiting a donor from designating a recipient. Presumed consent laws and programs allowing payment for donation are being examined for their potential effect on the number of donated organs and on the values underlying donation. The question is constantly being raised of whether there are undiscovered potential donors who might increase supply. Specific groups being considered include anencephalic infants, non-heart-beating cadaver donors, and unrelated living donors. Such possibilities, however, necessarily raise concerns about risks to society, families, and donors.

[Rick Hanson, *Spare Parts: Organ Replacement in American Society* (New York, 1994).]

BETH A. VIRNIG

See also **SUPP**: Cardiovascular Disease; Medicine; Surgery.

TRANSPORTATION, DEPARTMENT OF. In a message to Congress in March 1966, President Lyndon B. Johnson outlined a proposal for a unified transportation authority, and in October Congress established the Department of Transportation (DOT). In April 1967 President Johnson activated the new department, which was headed by a cabinet-level secretary of transportation. The new department, which brought together about 90,000 employees from more than thirty formerly separate agencies, was given responsibility for federal investments in transportation and for creating an economical, efficient, and safe national transportation system, taking into account environmental standards and national defense. It did not take over the regulatory activities of the Civil Aeronautics Board (dissolved in 1984), the Interstate Commerce Commission, or Federal Maritime Commission. In 1981, however, the Maritime Commission, renamed the Maritime Administration, was transferred by Congress to DOT. Officials responsible for the nation's overall system of transportation report to the secretary of transportation, as do the administrators of nine special operating divisions, most of which are devoted to specific modes of transportation. Responsible for the general transportation system are a deputy secretary, a general counsel, and assistant secretaries for budget and programs, policy and international affairs, governmental affairs, public affairs, and administration. The nine operating divisions are the United States Coast Guard, Federal Aviation Administration, Federal Highway Administration, Federal Railroad Administration, National Highway Traffic Safety Administration, Urban Mass Transportation Administration, Saint Lawrence Seaway Development Corporation, Research and Special Programs Administration, and Maritime Administration. Although the administrators of these divisions report to the secretary of transportation, they are appointed by the president and must be confirmed by the Senate.

Railway transportation was in crisis in the late 1960s, and DOT participated in the creation of the National Railroad Passenger Corporation (Amtrak), established in 1971, and Consolidated Railroads (Conrail), established in 1976 primarily as a freight carrier. Both were chartered by the federal government as quasi-public, profit-making corporations. They have not been profitable, however, and have required federal subsidies. In 1987 the federal government sold its shares of Conrail stock as part of President Ronald Reagan's privatization program. Amtrak, however, through a combination of rate hikes, cost cutting, and effective marketing, managed to reduce its reliance on federal subsidies. The secretary of transportation is one of the nine members of the Amtrak board.

A related but autonomous agency is the National Transportation Safety Board (NTSB), established by the same act that created DOT. NTSB is a five-member board, appointed by the president, that reports directly to Congress. It is responsible for investigating accidents involving all forms of transportation, taking over investigations formerly carried out by the Civil Aeronautics Board and the Interstate Commerce Commission. In practice, much of the initial accident investigation is carried out by the operating division within DOT that has jurisdiction over the mode of transportation involved in the accident.

[Robert C. Lieb, *Transportation: The Domestic System,* 2nd ed. (Reston, Va., 1981); Roy J. Sampson, Martin T. Farris, and David L. Shrock, *Domestic Transportation: Practice, Theory, and Policy,* 5th ed. (Boston, 1985).]

RICHARD W. MOODEY

See also **SUPP:** Transportation Industry.

TRANSPORTATION INDUSTRY. The United States always has been a mobile society, and this trend accelerated in the 1970s even though the future did not look bright for most U.S. transportation industries in that decade. The automobile industry rapidly lost market share to Japan, and energy crises in 1973 and 1979 made drivers wait in long lines to buy gas that had more than doubled in price by the end of the decade. Congested roads around major urban areas frustrated commuters. The greatest achievement of the 1970s and 1980s was the completion of the Interstate Highway System, a network of 45,493 miles of superhighways that was begun when President Dwight D. Eisenhower signed the Federal-Aid Highway Act (also known as the Interstate Highway Act) of 1956. By the late 1980s the system supported 20 percent of the nation's traffic and 49 percent of truck-trailer traffic.

Commuters continued to favor the car into the 1990s but commuting patterns shifted dramatically. In the early 1970s most commuters drove from suburban houses to jobs in the city. Twenty years later many commuters traveled from suburb to suburb or to newly created "edge" cities, where many companies

had relocated because of lower taxes and greater convenience for workers. Inexpensive computers and fax machines enabled companies to disperse from city centers and also enabled some workers to "telecommute." This trend was reflected in the number of workers working at home, which rose from 2,179,863 in 1980 to 3,406,025 in 1990, an increase of more than 56 percent. Another trend was the twenty-four-hour, time-shifted workday. Increasingly workers went to and returned from work at irregular hours, creating around some cities all-day rush hours. These changes resulted in greater congestion around urban areas as commuters resisted carpooling because it was not convenient and gas prices were reduced. While the percentage of all commuters traveling by car, truck, or van rose only 2 percent between 1980 and 1990, the percentage of commuters traveling alone increased by 9 percent; in 1990, almost three out of every four (73 percent) commuters rode to and from work by themselves. The percentage of commuters carpooling dropped from 19 percent in 1980 to 13 percent in 1990 and all forms of public transportation declined in popularity. The one bright spot for urban commuters, however, was the resurgence in light-rail trolley systems. San Diego, Portland, Sacramento, Buffalo, and Denver all had systems operating by the mid-1990s and many other cities were planning them.

Passenger railroad service did not rebound from a lengthy decline despite the establishment in 1971 of Amtrak, a national railroad that covered 24,000 miles in forty-five states by the 1980s. Although aided by government subsidies, the railroad could not compete with automobiles and airlines. Long-distance rail fares often were more expensive than airline fares, and the safety of the system was called into question with several derailments resulting in deaths in the 1990s. The country's aging track system limited trains to relatively slow speeds. In late 1994 Amtrak announced severe cutbacks in long-distance routes, and the company's future looked poor.

The airline industry, however, continued to grow. The airplane manufacturing industry, dominated by Boeing and McDonnell-Douglas, was one of the few businesses in which the United States remained technically and economically superior worldwide, with the companies ranking first and seventh in exports in 1992. Deregulation of the airline industry in the late 1970s led to the formation of scores of new airlines, many offering inexpensive fares and shuttle service along the Northeast corridor (Boston–New York–Washington) and between San Francisco, Los Ange-

271

les, and San Diego. One of the first and most successful of these airlines, People's Express, succeeded for a short time but then went out of business. Deregulation resulted in a greater concentration among airlines, with three major carriers—United, American, and Delta—dominating domestic service in the mid-1990s, although these were being challenged by new "no frills" carriers like Kiwi and Southwest. Meanwhile such giants as Pan Am and Eastern Airlines went out of business. The U.S. airline industry remained the dominant world player, boasting a fleet of 4,000 large jets carrying more than 450 million passengers a year. The future of the U.S. aviation industry was uncertain. There was wide agreement by the 1990s that the air traffic control system was outdated and that major airports had reached their carrying capacity limits. The reliability of the air traffic control system was first questioned in 1981 after President Ronald Reagan fired 11,500 striking controllers. The Federal Aviation Administration and the airlines developed new technologies, including computer systems, radar signaling devices on planes, and automated control systems. It was hoped these would result in a great reduction in the number of air-traffic controllers needed. Despite technological advances and statistics showing that air travel was one of the safest means of transport, safety concerns rose to the forefront in the 1980s and 1990s. While the number of fatalities declined steadily from 2.2 per 100,000 passenger hours in 1975 to 1.3 per 100,000 passenger hours in 1991, deregulation and the aging air traffic control system resulted in reduced maintenance requirements and more congestion on the ground in centers designated as "hubs" by the remaining major airlines.

[Brad Edmondson, "Alone in the Car," *American Demographics* (June 1994); Stephen B. Goddard, *Getting There: The Epic Struggle Between Road and Rail in the American Century* (New York, 1994); Mark H. Rose, *Interstate: Express Highway Politics, 1939–1989*, rev. ed. (Knoxville, 1990); Anthony Sampson, *Empires of the Sky: The Politics, Contests and Cartels of World Airlines* (New York, 1984).]

JEFFREY M. MERRON

See also **SUPP:** Aircraft Development and Transport; Air Traffic Controllers Strike; Automobile Industry; Rapid Transit; Transportation, Department of.

TREASURY, DEPARTMENT OF THE, established in 1789, consisted in 1995 of sixteen departmental offices and eleven operating bureaus: the Customs Service (established in 1789); U.S. Mint (1792); Internal Revenue Service (1862); Bureau of Engraving and Printing (1862); Office of the Comptroller of the Currency (1863); Secret Service (1865); Bureau of the Public Debt (1919); Financial Management Service (1920); Federal Law Enforcement Training Center (1970); Bureau of Alcohol, Tobacco, and Firearms (1972); and the Office of Thrift Supervision (1989). The Treasury Building in Washington, D.C., was declared a national historic landmark on Oct. 18, 1972. Secretary of the Treasury Salmon P. Chase's Civil War office, the office used by President Andrew Johnson for six weeks in 1865, and the Cash Room were restored with private funds.

The secretary of the Treasury is the chief adviser to the president on fiscal and financial affairs and plays a key role in the formulation and execution of domestic and international economic policy. Since 1970 the Treasury Department has played a central role in important international events. The Treasury, with support from other U.S. agencies, developed comprehensive proposals for reform of the international monetary system after the collapse in the early 1970s of the Bretton Woods system (the world payments system of fixed exchange rates for major currencies centered on the dollar and its convertibility into gold). It took the lead in the Smithsonian Agreement of 1971 (a last attempt to realign fixed rates and bolster the Bretton Woods system); revision of the articles of the International Monetary Fund in the mid-1970s, the basis for a new system of management of floating exchange rates; and the Plaza Accord of 1985 (the first substantive effort by the United States, United Kingdom, France, Germany, and Japan to coordinate their economic policies, including exchange rate policies). Through the Office of the Assistant Secretary for International Affairs, the Treasury Department was also the architect of the U.S. government's yen-dollar talks and two other bilateral financial consultations with Japan in the 1980s aimed at liberalizing Japan's capital markets.

Treasury played a key role in the major tax reforms of the 1970s and the 1980s. Significant peacetime U.S. tax reforms took place during the administration of President Ronald Reagan (1981–1989), when the economic and legal staffs of the Office of the Assistant Secretary for Tax Policy helped draft the Economic Recovery Tax Act of 1981 and the Tax Reform Act of 1986. The staffs also played a key role in the formulation of the deficit reduction bills passed in 1990 and 1993. The Treasury Department also administered the revenue sharing program, an initiative of President Richard M. Nixon's administration that distributed $82.6 billion among 39,000 states, cities, and other general-purpose local governments between the program's enactment in 1972 and its repeal in 1986.

The Office of the Assistant Secretary for Economic Policy participated actively in the formulation of the four phases of wage and price controls (Aug. 15, 1971–Apr. 30, 1974); studied the impact of changes in the financing and benefit structure of the Social Security Trust Fund and provided input for the major reforms enacted in 1983; analyzed the hospital cost containment proposal of President Jimmy Carter's administration in 1980 and President Bill Clinton's health care reform proposal of 1993–1994; and analyzed the deficit reduction packages of the George Bush and Clinton administrations.

The U.S. government securities market is the largest and most liquid securities market in the world. Sales of Treasury securities to the public raise funds to cover the shortfall between the government's receipts and expenditures and to refinance debt. The public debt amounted to $371 billion on June 30, 1970. On Sept. 30, 1994, it was $4.7 trillion. More than half that amount, $2.7 trillion, was in marketable securities held by private investors. Nonmarketable Treasury securities, including U.S. savings bonds, and marketable debt held by government accounts and the Federal Reserve System, make up the rest of the public debt.

The Office of the Under Secretary for Domestic Finance, which develops the legislative and regulatory financial institutions policy for each presidential administration, developed the Financial Institutions Reform, Recovery, and Enforcement Act of 1989, which addressed the savings and loan crisis. The Fiscal Assistant Secretary's Office manages the government's cash balances. The Office of the Under Secretary for Enforcement oversees the government's second largest law enforcement complement. The Internal Revenue Service (IRS), the largest bureau of the Treasury Department, collects more than $1 trillion each year in tax revenue. Although income taxes account for the bulk of this amount, the IRS also collects corporate, excise, and estate and gift taxes. Electronic filing of tax returns was initiated in 1986, and passage of the Taxpayer's Bill of Rights in 1988 strengthened protections for individual taxpayers. The Bureau of Engraving and Printing produced U.S. paper money only in its Washington, D.C., plant until 1991, when it opened a second currency facility in Fort Worth, Texas. The savings and loan crisis of the 1980s led to

the creation of the Office of Thrift Supervision in 1989, replacing the Federal Home Loan Bank Board.

[Mark Walston, *The Department of the Treasury* (New York, 1989).]

ABBY L. GILBERT

See also **SUPP:** Banking and Finance; Budget, Federal; Savings and Loan Crisis.

TRIALS. Between 1975 and 1995 Americans were fascinated, indeed obsessed, with famous trials and trials of the famous. This interest must be seen as part of a long tradition of public fascination with trials, facilitated in the modern era by radio and then television, making law a spectator sport. The most prominent political trials of the era were in connection with the Iran-Contra affair, in which officials of President Ronald Reagan's administration, including national security advisers John M. Poindexter and Robert C. McFarlane and National Security Council aide Lt. Col. Oliver North, conspired illegally to sell arms to the government of Iran and use the money to aid the contras, right-wing guerrillas in Nicaragua. A federal jury in April 1990 found Poindexter guilty on five counts of perjury, including lying to Congress and conspiracy. North was convicted of destroying documents, misappropriating money for personal use, and obstructing a congressional investigation. Lesser defendants were convicted on a variety of counts. The Poindexter and North cases were subsequently dismissed by federal judges because key evidence came from congressional hearings. All defendants claimed they were acting with the support of President Reagan but he denied any knowledge of the illegal activities. Before leaving office President George Bush pardoned six former officials who remained convicted of or were faced with charges, including McFarlane and former Secretary of Defense Caspar Weinberger.

The longest and costliest criminal case in U.S. history was the McMartin-Buckey child abuse trial. Police in 1983 began to investigate allegations of sexual abuse of children at a Los Angeles County day-care center, which led to the arrest of seven people, although only two, Peggy McMartin Buckey and Raymond Buckey, faced trial, which took place in an atmosphere of hysteria supported by questionable police activities, grandstanding by publicity-seeking prosecutors, and media coverage of dubious objectivity. The children in the case accused the defendants of wholly impossible or utterly fantastic acts, including taking them for airplane rides in the middle of their preschool classes and practicing satanic rituals not witnessed by any of the other children in the school. During the trial one prosecutor quit, complaining about the coaching of child witnesses and expressing doubt about the credibility of the initial adult witness, who subsequently died from alcoholism. On Jan. 18, 1990, a jury acquitted the defendants on fifty-two counts and remained deadlocked on twelve other charges against Raymond Buckey. In his retrial on those counts in July 1990 the jury deadlocked again. In January 1991 the presiding judge declared a mistrial and dismissed all remaining counts. The judge noted the case had "poisoned everyone who had contact with it."

Beginning in the 1970s notable cases involved serial killers. In January 1989 the state of Florida executed Theodore R. "Ted" Bundy for the 1978 murder of twelve-year-old Kimberly Leach. By the time of his death Bundy had been linked with as many as forty murders, mostly of young women, in Washington, Colorado, and other western states as well as in Florida. Jeffrey L. Dahmer was arrested in July 1991 by Milwaukee police. He confessed to seventeen murders beginning in 1978, mainly of gay and/or non-white men and teenage boys. Evidence of necrophilia and cannibalism added to the already gruesome details of the trial. Dahmer pleaded not guilty by reason of insanity to fifteen counts of murder, but a Wisconsin jury determined he was legally sane and sentenced him to fifteen terms of life imprisonment. On Nov. 28, 1994, an inmate at Columbia Correctional Institution in Portage, Wis., murdered Dahmer.

The nation's war on drugs led to a few high-profile trials. In 1983 federal agents arrested the automobile executive John Z. DeLorean on drug trafficking charges, accusing him of selling drugs to obtain money to start his own company. After a twenty-two-week trial and twenty-nine hours of deliberation a Los Angeles jury acquitted him in the belief that the government had entrapped him and that federal agents were seeking to gain political support for the war on drugs. The federal government was only marginally more successful in its prosecution of the mayor of Washington, D.C., Marion S. Barry, arrested on Jan. 18, 1990, on various drug-related charges. Barry was filmed buying and smoking $60 worth of crack cocaine. After a six-week trial Barry was convicted on only a single misdemeanor count of possession; he was acquitted on one count and the jury deadlocked on twelve others. Complicating the case were allegations, which the jury apparently believed, that the George Bush administration had tar-geted Barry because he was black. Some jurors believed the government may have entrapped him by using a friend who had become an informant to lure him into a hotel room where she offered him crack cocaine. After serving less than two years Barry was released. In 1994 he was reelected mayor of Washington, D.C.

A more successful case was the federal prosecution of General Manuel Antonio Noriega, the former head of the government of the Republic of Panama. After the invasion of Panama in 1989 federal officials removed Noriega to Florida and charged him with international drug trafficking. Noriega's trial began in September 1991 and ended when a jury convicted him on eight of ten counts of cocaine trafficking, racketeering, and conspiracy. Noriega wanted to present evidence that the Central Intelligence Agency (CIA) had been involved in drug trafficking to raise funds to aid anticommunist guerrillas in Central America. The court accepted the government's contention that national security required the defense not to discuss the CIA's involvement with Noriega or his longtime role as a CIA informant.

The 1980s and 1990s saw a number of other high-profile trials. In connection with the Wall Street insider-trading scandal of the mid-1980s the arbitrageur Ivan F. Boesky agreed in 1986 to pay $100 million in fines, settled civil suits for $50 million, and served two years of a three-year prison term for violation of securities laws, while the wealthy stockbroker Michael Milken began a prison sentence in 1991 for illegal stock and bond manipulations. Child and spousal abuse became a national issue with the case of Joel B. Steinberg and Hedda Nussbaum in New York City. Charged with murdering the couple's six-year-old adopted daughter, Lisa, Steinberg was convicted in January 1989 after Nussbaum, whom he had battered for years, testified against him. In 1993 the actress Mia Farrow and the director Woody Allen traded accusations in highly publicized hearings over custody of their children. A Florida jury in 1991 acquitted William Kennedy Smith of rape in a highly publicized trial. Smith was the nephew of Senator Edward M. Kennedy, the late Senator Robert Kennedy, and the late President John F. Kennedy. The case against Smith was never strong and some commentators believed the prosecutor may have proceeded with it to avoid charges of favoritism. At the same time as the Smith case, an Indiana jury convicted Michael Tyson, the heavyweight boxing champion of the world, of raping a beauty queen contestant, Desiree Washington. After serving nearly three years in jail

Tyson was given a hero's welcome in Harlem, New York, in June 1995.

Televised court proceedings meanwhile reached new heights of sensationalism with the 1993–1994 trial of Lyle and Erik Menendez, who admitted killing their parents with shotguns. The brothers claimed their father had emotionally and sexually abused them and thus justified the murders. The presiding judge ultimately declared mistrials when the jurors could not decide between verdicts of first-degree murder and a lesser charge. In a class by itself was the 1994–1995 trial in Los Angeles of one of the nation's greatest football players, O. J. Simpson, for the murder of his ex-wife, Nicole Brown Simpson, and her friend Ronald L. Goldman. The live televised proceedings were followed by millions of viewers and engendered a frenzy of media coverage. The trial raised issues about race (Simpson was black, his ex-wife and her friend were white), domestic abuse (Simpson had frequently abused his wife during their marriage), and the role of money in the U.S. system of justice (the bill for Simpson's defense ran into the millions of dollars). Sloppy police work called into question the legitimate use of DNA evidence, and police racism became a key issue when one of the prosecution's chief witnesses, Los Angeles police detective Mark Fuhrman, was revealed on audiotape to be a vicious racist who boasted of planting evidence in cases involving African-American suspects, thus bolstering defense allegations that crucial evidence had been planted to frame Simpson. In a verdict that shocked many observers who had thought the evidence against Simpson was overwhelming despite the failings of the L.A. Police Department, the jury took only three hours to find Simpson not guilty.

Trials always have been part of U.S. life but took on a new role in the late twentieth century. In a popular television show, *The People's Court,* a retired California judge heard disputes that ordinarily would be settled in small claims court. One cable television network, *Court TV,* devoted all of its programming to televised trials. The line between entertainment and life in the world of law increasingly blurred. In the glare of publicity caused by cameras in the courtroom and the emerging celebrity status of defendants and attorneys, it was not at all clear that justice was being achieved.

PAUL FINKELMAN

See also **SUPP:** Corruption, Political; Crime, White-Collar; Domestic Violence; Iran-Contra Affair; Los Angeles Riots; Scandals; Serial Killings; Wall Street.

TRUST TERRITORY OF THE PACIFIC ISLANDS. Captured by U.S. forces during the Pacific campaigns of World War II, some 2,000 Micronesian islands became the Trust Territory of the Pacific Islands (TTPI) in 1947, a United Nations strategic trusteeship administered by the United States. The TTPI included the Marshalls, Ponape (later Pohnpei), Truk (Chuuk), the Northern Marianas, Yap, and Palau. Initially administered by the U.S. Navy, the islands came under civilian control of the Department of the Interior in 1951, with the exception of Saipan (Northern Marianas), which reverted to the navy soon thereafter. A high commissioner appointed by the president held the chief executive office in the TTPI, which comprised six districts: Marshalls, Pohnpei, Marianas, Yap, and Palau. In 1966 the Congress of Micronesia was created and three years later its Joint Committee on Future Status began the long process of negotiating with the United States over the question of self rule. Micronesia was far from unified in its quest for self-government, and in 1972 the Marianas initiated separate talks that in 1975 led to creation of the Commonwealth of the Northern Marianas (CNMI), made up of Saipan, Rota, Tinian and the tiny Northern Islands. This arrangement is comparable to the status of Puerto Rico. Further fragmentation occurred when the Marshalls and Palau, both concerned that they might be forced to share their economic potential with less wealthy neighbors, held their own negotiations. In 1978 Pohnpei, Kosrae, Chuuk, and Yap approved the constitution that created the Federated States of Micronesia (FSM). The Republic of the Marshall Islands (RMI) and the FSM in 1986 moved into free association with the United States. The fifteen-year agreements arranged by Micronesian and U.S. negotiators gave the new entities control over internal and external affairs, guaranteed U.S. financing for the island governments, and put defense matters under U.S. control. Because of the conflict between U.S. military interests and the nuclear-free provisions of their constitution, citizens of the Republic of Palau (Belau) voted in repeated referenda without reaching the 75 percent approval required by Palauan law to accept the free-association compact. In 1993, having amended the 75 percent requirement of the constitution to a simple majority, Palau approved the compact. On Oct. 1, 1994, the agreement took effect, and the world's last trusteeship ceased to exist.

[P. F. Kluge, *The Edge of Paradise: America in Micronesia* (Honolulu, 1993); Arnold H. Leibowitz, *Defining Status: A Comprehensive Analysis of United States Territorial Relations* (Boston, 1989).]

KAREN M. PEACOCK

TUBERCULOSIS

See also **DAH:** Guam; Trust Territory of the Pacific; **DAH** and **SUPP:** Samoa, American.

TUBERCULOSIS, cited by the National Institute of Allergy and Infectious Diseases (NIAID) as the leading cause of death by disease in the United States in the nineteenth century, appeared to be vanishing by the mid-1970s. The decline brought a decrease in tuberculosis programs and research. NIAID, the major tuberculosis research center of the National Institutes of Health, gradually reduced its research through the 1970s. New York and New Jersey, for example, closed tuberculosis sanatoriums and hospital wards, transferred tuberculosis care to local clinics and community care on an outpatient basis, and decreased money for programs. Physicians attributed the disappearance of tuberculosis to the combination therapy of streptomycin, isoniazid, and PAS (para-aminosalicylic acid) and possibly with one or more other newer drugs. They believed that a short period of such therapy eliminated the contagious nature of persons infected with the disease, but some experts worried that the monitoring of drug therapy among outpatients in a community-based setting was far more lax than that for hospitalized patients.

Early warnings of the disease's resurgence came from the American Lung Association, the leading lobbying and support organization for tuberculosis research. Predicting an epidemic, the association's president in 1979 urged Congress not to abolish programs. By 1985 the long decline in tuberculosis cases was over. In 1989 the number of cases in New York City alone increased 68 percent from those recorded in 1980 with a high incidence in females aged twenty-five to forty-four. Researchers connected the rise to multidrug resistance, emergence of the human immunodeficiency virus (HIV) and its development into the acquired immunodeficiency syndrome (AIDS), and the discovery that short-term drug treatment did not eradicate the contagion. Some blamed the resurgence on the difficulties of organizing health services to diagnose, treat, and prevent the disease. Others pointed to lack of new drugs to combat multidrug-resistant tuberculosis and absence of a successful vaccine.

AIDS increasingly played a part in tuberculosis expansion. The correlation of tuberculosis with AIDS increased from 2.5 percent of all AIDS sufferers in 1984 to 17.42 percent in 1992 according to twenty-eight major metropolitan health departments in the United States. Tuberculosis hospitalizations associated with AIDS doubled between 1988 and 1992. By 1995 the World Health Organization announced that tuberculosis was the leading cause of death worldwide among HIV-infected people. To curb the rise, the American Thoracic Society and the Centers for Disease Control and Prevention (CDC) jointly published guidance on diagnosis, treatment, prevention, and control. In the early 1990s a voluntary group of thirty-four scientists and public health officials issued *The Tuberculosis Revival,* urging that close observation of outpatient drug therapy be required. Acknowledging tuberculosis as a public health concern, the CDC in 1992 counted 26,673 active cases in all the states, a 20 percent increase over cases reported in 1985. The disease was affecting all societal groups but hurting the poor and minorities the most. Nevertheless, experts considered tuberculosis preventable and curable, especially if caught early and monitored. In response to the rise in tuberculosis, NIAID increased research support from seven projects and $514,000 in 1979 to more than 100 projects and $28 million in 1994. Thus, the effort continued to wipe out this disease in the United States and the rest of the world.

[National Institute of Allergy and Infectious Diseases, *Tuberculosis: Resurgence of an Old Problem* (Bethesda, Md., 1993); Frank Ryan, *The Forgotten Plague: How the Battle Against Tuberculosis Was Won and Lost* (Boston, 1993).]

— Ruth Roy Harris

TUCSON, the second-largest city in Arizona, takes its name from a Papago Indian village across the Santa Cruz River at the base of the Stjukshon mountain, or present-day Sentinel Peak. Situated in the lower Sonora Desert basin, Tucson is surrounded by the Santa Catalina and Santa Rita mountains, which serve as natural fortifications against unchecked urban sprawl. In 1700 Jesuit missionary Eusebio Francisco Kino founded San Xavier del Bac Indian Mission, and the Spanish established the Presidio de San Augustin de Tuguison in 1775. Tucson became part of U.S. territory with the Gadsden Purchase in 1853 and served as the capital of Arizona Territory from 1867 to 1877. The Southern Pacific Railroad reached Tucson in 1880 and the city was incorporated in 1883.

Following World War II the city experienced rapid growth, and since the 1960s the former Spanish settlement turned southwestern metropolis nearly doubled in size and quadrupled in diversity. The 1970 population figure of 262,933 grew to 405,390 residents by 1990, with the metropolitan area claiming 660,880 inhabitants. Through booster campaigns and individual initiative, Tucson's economy in the 1990s embraced every pursuit from agriculture to state-of-the-art electronics. The accelerated growth and development threatened a dwindling water supply; in 1980 Tucson was depleting water tables by four to five feet per year. The Central Arizona Project began supplying Colorado River water to Tucson in 1991. Although conservation strategies were put into place, the availability and cost of water remained a widespread concern. Both as a result of its traditional political liberalism and mass awareness of the water issue, Tucson is one of the most environmentally conscious cities in Arizona. The first city to offer municipally supported recycling, Tucson is home to both the Biosphere experiment and many national environmental groups.

With its eclectic appearance and scenic setting, Tucson offers activities for every taste and pocketbook. Wilderness enthusiasts enjoy the reaches of Mount Lemmon, the mysteries of Sabino Canyon, and vast stretches of desert graced with towering saguaros. Wealthy tourists and celebrities favor the amenities of the many expensive resorts, while more modest spenders patronize the Desert Sonora Museum and the "Old Town" restaurants and movie set that has served as the site for more than 200 feature-length films. The University of Arizona is at the center of cultural life in Tucson. In recent years, Arizona's second-largest university has sponsored ground-breaking medical and agricultural research. Since the late 1970s the university faculty has included such critically acclaimed writers as Native American authors Leslie Marmon Silko and N. Scott Momaday. Although Tucson suffered in the recession of the late 1980s, prosperity and optimism returned in the 1990s. While elected officials plotted new economic strategies, residents reaffirmed their long-standing desire to avoid the traffic congestion and rampant modernity of their historic rival, the capital city of Phoenix.

[Nat de Gennero, ed., *Arizona Statistical Abstract: A 1990 Handbook* (Tucson, 1990); C. L. Sonnichsen, *Tucson: The Life and Times of an American City* (Norman, Okla., 1982); Henry P. Walker, *Historical Atlas of Arizona* (Norman, Okla., 1979).]

EVELYN S. COOPER

See also **DAH** and **SUPP:** Arizona; **SUPP:** Phoenix; Sunbelt.

TULSA, city in northeastern Oklahoma, was part of Indian Territory and was settled by the Talasi band of Creek Indians who journeyed from their native Alabama to the banks of the Arkansas River in 1832. Other settlers arrived after the railroad in 1882, and the city became a transportation center. Discovery of oil in the area led to Tulsa's rapid growth early in the twentieth century, which continued during World War II, when several large industries were established there. Once known as the "oil capital of the world," Tulsa in the 1990s was headquarters for more than 1,000 energy-related corporations that accounted for 10 percent of total employment. The boom-and-bust of international oil prices had a sobering effect upon the city. After a few years of rapid rise and fall, the city's population steadied at 367,302 in 1990. Among the more notable qualities of Tulsa's population is that 5 percent are at least one-quarter Indian and 8 percent define themselves as Native American. The city's white population (80 percent) and African-American population (14 percent) grew with the rise of the oil industry in the 1920s, aircraft production in the 1940s and 1950s, and manufacturing and electronics firms. Tulsans regard themselves as different from other Oklahomans, and that view is often seconded by others, particularly those in Oklahoma City. Oklahoma has grown more conservative while traditionally Republican Tulsa has become more independent and moderate in its own politics. Another difference is that Tulsa prides itself on its cultural life, which includes opera, ballet, and theater companies and a symphony orchestra together with the Thomas Gilcrease Institute of American History and Art and the Philbrook Museum of Art.

[Angie Debo, *Tulsa: From Creek Town to Oil Capital* (Norman, Okla., 1943).]

DANNEY GOBLE

See also **DAH** and **SUPP:** Oklahoma City; Oklahoma.

U

UFOs. *See* **Unidentified Flying Objects.**

UNEMPLOYMENT. Few economic indicators are as important politically as unemployment. A rise in unemployment can bring down a presidency, while a decline in unemployment is welcome news, a sign that prosperity may be just around the corner. To be unemployed, a person must not have a job, must be able to take a job if one were offered, and must have actively looked for work in the preceding four weeks. To be considered employed, one must work for pay or profit or work at least fifteen hours without pay in a family-run business. The labor force is defined as the sum of the employed and unemployed, and the unemployment rate is the number of unemployed divided by the labor force. The unemployment rate is controversial because the definition of unemployment excludes "discouraged workers," persons who do not have jobs and are not actively seeking them because they believe that a job search would be fruitless; this exception makes the unemployment rate seem lower than it actually is.

Economists distinguish between frictional, seasonal, structural, and cyclical unemployment. Frictional unemployment refers to normal turnover of workers in any dynamic capitalist economy. Seasonal unemployment occurs because production varies over the year. Thus, for example, unemployment between 1976 and 1986 was 20 percent higher on average in January and February than in October. Structural unemployment refers to a mismatch between workers and jobs. The mismatch can be spatial—for example, entry-level jobs may go begging in suburbs because

unemployed youths in central cities cannot get to them—or it may be skill-based. Together, frictional and structural unemployment define a natural rate of unemployment, one to which the economy tends in the long run. The natural rate usually ranges between 4 and 5 percent, but it has risen since the 1970s. This rise is partly due to the changing composition of the U.S. labor force. Minorities make up an increasing part of the labor force but have higher unemployment rates than average. In 1993 the unemployment rate for black males ages sixteen to nineteen was 40.1 percent, approximately six times the national average of 6.8 percent. Structural unemployment has also worsened since 1970. Cyclical unemployment arises during a recession and can be combated by fiscal or monetary policy. During the recession of the early 1980s the unemployment rate peaked at 9.7 in 1982. Most unemployed workers are covered by unemployment insurance, which provides benefits that vary with previous earnings and are normally paid for up to twenty-six weeks, although they can be extended if unemployment in a state is unusually severe or if Congress votes an extension. Unemployed workers may also be eligible for a variety of government programs that provide training for new employment opportunities, for example, the programs established by the 1982 Job Training Partnership Act.

There is no accepted theory of unemployment. Some economists believe that all unemployment is voluntary, because there are always job openings, even in a recession. Instead of taking such jobs, the unemployed rationally choose to wait for better offers. Other economists, influenced by John Maynard Keynes, hold that unemployment arises because wages are too high in terms of demand and supply. Wage "stickiness" has been attributed to the tendency of companies to pay efficiency (higher than market-clearing) wages in the belief that highly paid workers are more loyal and more productive. The insider-outsider theory posits that the employed (insiders) resist wage cuts, which lower their incomes but make more jobs available to the unemployed (outsiders). Insider-outsider theory is popular in Europe, where many countries experienced double-digit unemployment rates through the 1980s.

[Bruce E. Kaufman, *The Economics of Labor Markets and Labor Relations* (New York, 1989).]

ROBERT A. MARGO

UNIDENTIFIED FLYING OBJECTS (UFOs). The U.S. Air Force examined thousands of reports of UFOs since the first sighting in 1947 until 1969, since when no U.S. agency has claimed to be involved in investigating UFOs. During that period the air force investigated 12,618 reports, of which 701 were unexplained. Investigations found nonextraordinary causes (for example, birds, weather balloons, and marsh gases) for 95 percent of reported sightings, some of which were hoaxes. Thus far, no one has convincingly proved the existence of UFOs. The great majority of scientists discount the possibility that UFOs are extraordinary phenomena. Those who believe otherwise have various theories, ranging from alien visitors from outer space to symbols of deep religious belief to near-death experiences. UFOs became part of popular culture because of many black-and-white amateur films and low-budget science fiction motion pictures that contributed to the cult status of UFOs and because of the success of two major Hollywood films, *Close Encounters of the Third Kind* (1977) and *E.T.: The Extra-Terrestrial* (1982), both of which remain on the list of all-time favorite movies. A special telephone line offers callers tips regarding UFO sightings, alien abductions, and extraterrestrial anatomy. The Center for the Study of Extraterrestrial Intelligence attempts to contact UFOs by broadcasting sounds allegedly made by UFOs, by flashing lights, and by trying to establish telepathic contact. Each year at the University of Wisconsin, a conference is held for people who believe they have been abducted by extraterrestrials or have been through episodes involving UFOs. In 1993 folk-rock star Richie Havens and ALOID and the Interplanetary Invasion, a band billing itself as "the world's first UFO rock group," performed at a UFO convention in New York City.

They believed that entertainment was the best way to inform the public about UFOs.

[Robert T. Rood and James Trefil, *Are We Alone?* (New York, 1981); Dennis Stacy, "The Omni Open Book Field Investigator's Guide: Part Two," *Omni* (April 1995); Pamela Weintraub, "Let the Project Begin," *Omni* (November 1994).]

JOHN J. BYRNE

UNIONS. *See* **Labor Unions.**

UNITED KINGDOM, RELATIONS WITH. Strong ties have long existed between the United States and the United Kingdom: a common language, culture, and legal system as well as a political alliance forged in the crucible of two twentieth-century world wars. The so-called special relationship, however, is not one between equals. Since the end of World War II the United States has dominated the relationship politically, economically, and militarily.

In the 1980s the countries were led by like-minded leaders, Prime Minister Margaret Thatcher and President Ronald Reagan. Their mutual relationship was singular, a striking convergence of ideologically driven conservatives who shared similar domestic agendas and a common foreign policy. Both led domestic political revolutions—supply-side economics, increased defense spending, privatization, deregulation, and an overall conservative agenda. Reagan was the Great Communicator, Thatcher the Iron Lady. The two were great friends. In 1982 the United States tried to mediate a dispute between Great Britain and Argentina over territorial control of the Falkland Islands, located in the south Atlantic Ocean. When mediation failed, the United States supported Great Britain by quietly providing logistical support and military intelligence during the three-month conflict. Reagan and Thatcher's mutual trust had great effect, particularly with regard to the Soviet Union. In 1984 Thatcher became the first Western political leader to meet with Mikhail Gorbachev before his ascension to the Soviet presidency. As Thatcher told the world, "We can do business together." That assessment shifted Western political rhetoric from East-West confrontation to conciliation and support for internal democratic reform in the Soviet Union. Reagan adopted Thatcher's view, largely abandoning his own harsh depiction of the Soviet Union as the "focus of evil in the modern world." The collapse of the Soviet Union, however, lessened U.S. military need for a trusty friend in Europe. Thus, U.S. relations with

Great Britain began to focus more on trade and economic issues.

Within the United Kingdom the focus shifted toward development of an "ever closer union" with the other nations of the European Community. The long-ruling Conservative party split over the issue of Europe. Thatcher, who wanted to keep Great Britain an island apart, was forced to resign in November 1990. She was replaced by Conservative John Major, who wanted the nation to be "at the heart of Europe." In 1991 the United Kingdom approved the Maastricht Treaty on political union and a common currency among democratic European states, although it opted out of some provisions. Tensions continued over the extent to which the United Kingdom would be part of a United States of Europe. Meanwhile, the larger political interests of the United States focused on Japan and Germany—two huge economies that affected international trade and currency-exchange rates.

Politically the United States retained a keen interest in Northern Ireland. Americans claiming Irish heritage numbered 44 million in 1995, compared to 5 million residents of Ireland and Northern Ireland. The United States pressured Irish nationalists to call a cease-fire in August 1994 and maintained consistent pressure on both the Irish Republic and the United Kingdom to reach a political settlement in the long-standing war. The Republic of Ireland pressured the Irish Republican Army (IRA) to halt its military terrorist campaign so that Sinn Féin, the IRA's political wing, could join all-party talks to create a new governmental structure for Northern Ireland. In 1995 Bill Clinton became the first U.S. president to visit Northern Ireland and urged the embattled Protestant and Catholic communities to "take risks for peace."

In the 1980s and 1990s Americans were eager consumers of such cultural exports as British rock music and BBC television productions and remained entranced with the continuing melodrama of the British royal family, especially the marital travails of Charles and Diana, prince and princess of Wales.

[Geoffrey Smith, *Reagan and Thatcher* (New York, 1991); Margaret Thatcher, *The Downing Street Years* (New York, 1993).]

BRENT SCHONDELMEYER

See also **SUPP:** European Community; Falklands War.

UNITED NATIONS (UN). The United States played a key role in the founding of the United Nations and maintained a strong if sometimes troubled relationship with the organization throughout the United Nations' first fifty years. The United Nations had its beginnings in a meeting between British Prime Minister Winston Churchill and President Franklin D. Roosevelt on Aug. 14, 1941, four months before U.S. entry into World War II. This meeting produced the Atlantic Charter, pledging "the final destruction of the Nazi tyranny" and proposed a postwar "establishment of a wider and permanent system of general security." In February 1945 Roosevelt met with Churchill and the Soviet leader Joseph Stalin at Yalta in the Soviet Crimea. There, even before the war's end, it was agreed to proceed with a United Nations Conference and draw up a UN Charter. Roosevelt believed that through the United Nations he could build a peaceful world and predicted that "the Crimean Conference . . . spells the end of the system of unilateral and exclusive alliances and spheres of influence and balances of power." He soon had misgivings about Stalin, however. On the day Roosevelt died, April 12, 1945, he asserted "that the spirit of Yalta was being betrayed by the Soviets." Thirteen days after Roosevelt's death the United Nations Conference convened in San Francisco. Two months later, on June 25, the delegates unanimously approved the UN Charter, and on July 28 the U.S. Senate ratified it by a vote of eighty-nine to two. The United Nations came into being on Oct. 24, 1945, with the approval of the required majority of the fifty-one participating nations.

An early concern was finding a permanent home for the new organization. The initial site of meetings was London, where the first General Assembly convened in January 1946. Several other European cities sought to have the UN headquarters, including Paris, Geneva, and The Hague. On Mar. 21, 1946, the Security Council moved into temporary quarters in the United States, the gymnasium on the Bronx Campus of Hunter College in New York City, while the search for a permanent home continued. When classroom space was needed by Hunter, the Security Council moved to the Sperry Gyroscope plant at Lake Success on Long Island and the General Assembly convened on the site of the 1939 New York City's World's Fair in Flushing Meadow, Queens. Then Robert Moses, New York's dynamic builder of bridges, tunnels, parks, and roads, suggested a permanent home in the Turtle Bay area of midtown Manhattan, six blocks of slaughterhouses and slums along the East River. The real estate entrepreneur William Zeckendorf put the parcels together, and on Dec. 11, 1946, John D. Rockefeller, Jr., offered to give $8.5 million to buy the site. The General Assembly accepted the offer by a vote of forty-six to seven. The UN complex, comprising a thirty-nine-story Secretariat building, a General Assembly hall, and a conference building for the Security Council on eighteen acres of land, was designed mainly by Wallace K. Harrison, one of the architects for Rockefeller Center. With the work completed in less than six years, the United Nations settled into its own complex in 1952, but a number of the specialized agencies occupied the old League of Nations sites in Geneva, with others in Vienna.

From the beginning, the UN atmosphere was quarrelsome because of the burgeoning cold war between the United States and the Soviet Union, both permanent members of the UN Security Council, which deliberates questions of peace and war. In 1946, only days after the election of the first UN Secretary-General, Trygve Lie of Norway, Stalin announced a new Five Year Plan for Soviet economic development that emphasized armaments rather than consumer goods. Stalin declared that the Soviet Union had to defend itself against "all kinds of eventualities" because "no peaceful international order is possible." Supreme Court Justice William O. Douglas described the speech as "the declaration of World War III." On Mar. 5, 1946, Winston Churchill, in company with President Harry S. Truman, delivered the address in which he described the Soviet takeover of Eastern Europe as an "iron curtain" that had descended across the Continent. Stalin declared the address "a call to war with the Soviet Union."

In those early years the pattern was set for the next four decades. The General Assembly, to which all member nations belonged, had no authority other than to recommend. The authority of the Security Council, which held the powers of peace or war or other punitive measures, was consistently blocked by the Soviet Union, which had veto power by virtue of its being a permanent member of the Security Council. After the United States joined with eleven other nations to form the North Atlantic Treaty Organization (NATO) to deter communist aggression, in April 1949, NATO nations had to resort to Article 51 of the UN Charter, which sets forth "the inherent right of individual or collective self-defense," when they decided to intervene militarily.

The first real test of the United Nations came with the Korean conflict in 1950. In an emergency meeting, the Security Council granted President Truman the authority to conduct a "police action" to counter North Korea's attack on South Korea. This approval was possible only because of the absence of the Soviet Union, which at the time was boycotting the Security Council in an attempt to force it to seat the communist People's Republic of China. On July 7, 1950, the Security Council set up a unified UN command with soldiers from fifteen nations under General Douglas MacArthur. Through the persuasion of the U.S. ambassador to India, Chester Bowles, India introduced in the UN General Assembly a cease-fire resolution on Dec. 3, 1952, that was adopted by fifty-four nations. President-elect Dwight D. Eisenhower, en route to the United States from Korea, a few days later sent an open message heard around the world asking General MacArthur to meet him in New York City at the president's residence at Columbia University to plan a strategy to end the war. This psychological warfare strategy worked. Talks began between the UN Command and the North Koreans at Panmunjom at the thirty-eighth parallel on Apr. 27, 1953. So began the process that finally brought the armistice on July 27, 1953. Ironically, Secretary-General Lie was a victim of the armistice process when the Soviets charged that during the negotiations he had sided with the United States. The effectively ostracized Lie resigned in April 1953 and was succeeded by Dag Hammarskjöld, a member of the Swedish cabinet. Lie warned his successor that "the task of Secretary-General is the most impossible job on earth."

The Middle East was a concern of the United Nations from its inception. On Nov. 20, 1947, the UN General Assembly adopted a resolution that ended the British mandate in Palestine and, against Arab wishes, partitioned the country into an Arab state and a Jewish state. Jerusalem, in which the holy places of the three great religions were located, was to be under international administration. Immediately the Arab delegation marched out of the assembly and announced they would not be bound by this decision. Not dissuaded, the Provisional State Council in Tel Aviv proclaimed the birth of Israel at midnight, May 14, 1948. Within eleven minutes President Truman had announced recognition of Israel. The president's action cut off a UN move for a temporary trusteeship. Full-scale war, which immediately erupted between Israel and its Arab neighbors, was ended in January 1949 by a cease-fire negotiated by Dr. Ralph Bunche, a member of the UN Secretariat. Bunche returned to New York an international hero and became the first African American to be awarded the Nobel Peace Prize. In May 1949 Israel was admitted to the United Nations.

The United Nations emerged as a strong moral force during the Suez crisis of 1956, with the establishment of the use of UN peacekeepers. On July 26, 1956, Egypt seized the Suez Canal, which had been built by the French and was of great commercial importance to both France and Great Britain. Over the objections of the UN Security Council, those two countries, joined by Israel, launched an armed attack against Egypt. With the support of both the United States and the Soviet Union, the United Nations intervened by sending in a UN Emergency Force numbering 6,000 men, known as Blue Helmets, to supervise a cease-fire and the withdrawal of troops. In retrospect, this must be viewed as one of the most significant UN military interventions in its first half century.

The growth of Third World countries and their entry into the United Nations in large numbers after 1960 made it increasingly difficult for the United States to control votes in the General Assembly. (From 51 nations in 1945, UN membership grew to 185 by 1995.) These primarily poor nations paid an extremely small part of total UN operating costs, which bothered some Americans, even though the United States was often in arrears in its own dues payments. As the former British, French, Portuguese, German, Belgian, Dutch, and Italian colonies in Africa and elsewhere emerged as nations, many were taken over by regimes backed by the Soviets, thus increasing resistance in the UN General Assembly toward the U.S.-led Western alliance.

In 1961, Secretary-General Hammarskjöld personally led UN Swedish troops into the seceding Katanga portion of the Congo, with the full support of President John F. Kennedy, in an effort to stop the fighting. Hammarskjöld was killed in a plane crash during the operation and was posthumously awarded the Nobel Peace Prize for 1961. Despite the presence of 20,000 Blue Helmets, it took until 1964 to achieve a cease-fire. The United Nations did not intervene with a major military force again until the 1992 operation in Somalia.

During the 1960s the United Nations, led by Hammarskjöld's successor, U Thant of Burma, was ineffectual in dealing with the escalating conflict in Vietnam. U Thant did, however, succeed in sending the Blue Helmets to Cyprus to keep Greeks and Turks from conflict on that newly independent island. Another notable accomplishment was the General Assembly's 1968 approval of the Treaty on Nonproliferation of Nuclear Weapons.

The United Nations continued to play a role in events in the Middle East. Blue Helmets had occupied outposts between Egypt and Israel since the 1956 Suez emergency. In 1967, however, Egypt demanded their withdrawal. To the consternation of Great Britain and the United States, U Thant complied. A few weeks later the Six-Day War broke out between Israel and Arab forces (Egypt, Jordan, and Syria), and continued sporadic fighting led eventually to the Yom Kippur (or October) War of 1973. Cease-fire agreements in 1974 established a UN peacekeeping force and buffer zone between the two armies.

In December 1971, Kurt Waldheim of Austria succeeded U Thant as the fourth secretary-general of the United Nations; in 1982 Waldheim was forced to resign in the face of allegations that he had been a member of the Nazi party during the Third Reich. He was succeeded by Javier Pérez de Cuéllar of Peru, who presided over the General Assembly's 1987 adoption of a resolution with terms for ending the Iran-Iraq War, which had raged since 1980. In 1988 the Nobel Peace Prize was awarded to UN peacekeeping forces. By the end of 1991, the last day for Pérez de Cuéllar as secretary-general, peace was also coming to civil war–ravaged El Salvador, in part due to both U.S. and UN efforts.

When Iraq invaded Kuwait on Aug. 2, 1990, President George Bush, a former U.S. ambassador to the United Nations, immediately asked for UN action. For the first time Arab nations did not vote as a block and, with Russian and American support, the United Nations authorized "all necessary means," which meant force to repel the invasion of Kuwait. UN forces led by the United States swiftly defeated the Iraqi army, and the now greatly enhanced Security Council appeared to have become what Roosevelt had envisioned—the heart of the United Nations. The Gulf War of 1991 was the third time the United Nations was an important instrument of the president of the United States during an international security crisis, just as it had been for Truman in 1950 and Eisenhower in 1956.

Boutros Boutros-Ghali, a former Egyptian diplomat and law professor, became the sixth secretary-general in 1991. Peacekeeping clearly had become the chief business of the United Nations in the post–cold war era. In its first four decades the Security Council had authorized only thirteen peacekeeping missions. In its fifth decade, 1985–1995, twenty were authorized. In 1995 alone the United Nations operated seventeen peacekeeping missions with 73,000 troops and police. During this era there were successful missions in Cambodia, Mozambique, and Haiti. A mission in December 1992 to end famine in Somalia was flawed, however, because it failed to impose political order despite the presence of 38,000 Blue Helmets, 25,000 of them from the United States. From March 1992 to October 1995, 20,000 UN peacekeepers also failed to stop the slaughter, known as ethnic cleansing, in the former Yugoslavia, the "safe areas" never being made safe. While the United States provided minimal air cover, it did not contribute ground soldiers to this effort.

The UN failure in Bosnia, combined with the desire of NATO to play a post–cold war role, set the stage for U.S. Secretary of State for European Affairs Richard Holbrooke to broker an agreement in Dayton, Ohio, among the Serbs, Croats, and the Bosnian government in October 1995. Signed in Paris in December 1995, the accord withdrew the UN from Bosnia and replaced them with a NATO-directed force of 60,000, including 20,000 Americans. (Russian personnel outside of NATO were also included.) In 1993 the United Nations established in The Hague an eleven-member war crimes tribunal; under the Dayton agreement the parties were to send indicted war criminals to The Hague for trial. The replacement of UN forces did not spell the end of peacekeeping as a basic mission of the United Nations but rather a failure in this instance without the dominant force of the United States.

From the beginning, UN policies were affected by the atrocities committed during World War II. It almost immediately appointed a human rights commission, which, under the leadership of Eleanor Roosevelt, issued the 1948 United Nations Universal Declaration of Human Rights. Since then the United Nations has endorsed other human rights treaties or covenants that the U.S. Senate has yet to ratify: the Convention on the Elimination of All Forms of Discrimination Against Women; the American Convention on Human Rights; the International Covenant on Economic, Social, and Cultural Rights; and the International Convention on the Elimination of All Forms of Racial Discrimination. The United Nations also sponsored four international conferences on women between the 1970s and 1995.

Although the primary mission of the United Nations was to eliminate "the scourge of war," the preamble of its charter also states its purpose "to promote social progress and better standards of life in larger freedom" and "to employ international machinery for the promotion of the economic and social advancement of all people." On these grounds the UN specialized agencies were created. The International Labor Organization (ILO) of 1919 was revived. Added were the Food and Agriculture Organization (FAO), World Health Organization (WHO), and United Nations Educational, Scientific, and Cultural Organization (UNESCO). In all, by the 1990s there were nineteen specialized agencies with combined budgets far exceeding the operation of the United Nations itself (save for peacekeeping missions) and with more employees than the UN Secretariat. Clearly it had become a bureaucracy requiring reform. In the case of UNESCO, the United States withdrew from the organization in 1984 after a scathing critique of it by U.S. Ambassador Jeane Kirkpatrick. Still, there were some remarkable accomplishments among the specialized agencies. In 1980, for example, WHO announced global eradication of smallpox, and global eradication of polio was expected by the year 2000.

As leaders from 140 countries gathered in New York City in October 1995 to celebrate the fiftieth anniversary of the United Nations, there was a clear need for change and reform. The possible addition of states as permanent members of the Security Council remained a subject of dispute, as was the bloated UN bureaucracy. Yet for all its troubles, the world organization domiciled in New York proved its worth in its first fifty years; surely the world would have been a much more ugly, less satisfying place without it.

[Sidney D. Bailey, *The United Nations: A Concise Political Guide*, 3rd. ed. (Lanham, Md., 1995); William Jacobs, *Search for Peace: The Story of the United Nations* (New York, 1994); David Evan Trant Luard, *The United Nations: How It Works and What It Does* (New York, 1994); Stanley Meisler, *United Nations: The First 50 Years* (New York, 1995).]

R. GORDON HOXIE

See also **DAH:** North Atlantic Treaty Organization; United Nations Conference; United Nations Declaration; **SUPP:** Bosnia-Herzegovina; Gulf War of 1991; Middle East, Relations with; North Atlantic Treaty Organization; Somalia; Soviet Union, Relations with; State, Department of.

UNIVERSITIES. *See* **Colleges, African-American; Colleges, Women's; Colleges and Universities; Free Universities.**

URBAN LIVING. Between 1970 and 1990 the urban population of the United States grew from 150 million to 187 million, or from 73.6 percent to 75.2 percent of the total. Major cities (more than 2.5 million people) slipped from 6.92 percent to 5.46 percent. Major metropolitan areas lost or gained slightly in population during the same years. Greater New York dropped 0.4 percent annually, while Chicago posted only a 0.4 percent annual gain; by contrast Los Angeles grew by 2.1 percent per year. The biggest increases occurred in such Sunbelt cities as Tampa–Saint Petersburg, Orlando, Miami, and Houston. Many urban dwellers left for the suburbs. Among the forty-four metropolitan areas in 1990 with more than 1 million residents, the suburbs of forty-two gained population; the central cities of eighteen lost, weakening the power of cities in state legislatures and Congress.

Urban problems spiraled in the 1980s. Population losses translated into job flight to the suburbs, which captured more than 95 percent of new metropolitan manufacturing jobs from 1976 to 1980. One study of urban decline demonstrated that between 1960 and 1989, eighteen of the seventy-seven largest American cities lost employed residents. Pittsburgh, Newark, Saint Louis, Louisville, Buffalo, Cleveland, and Detroit lost more than one-fourth of employed residents. Lower-income people became increasingly concentrated in central cities. Because poverty begets social problems, the 1980s saw sharp increases in urban crime, drug use, unemployment, and births out of wedlock. Social plagues included severe illnesses such as AIDS. All these problems translated into higher costs for police and fire protection, judicial systems, jails, and public hospitals. Expenses translated into higher property and other taxes.

Cities remained centers for intellectual activities, cultural endeavors, and specialized retail facilities, including high-fashion stores, symphonies, medical centers, and institutions of higher learning. Cities still are the nodes for technology, transportation, and housing for low-income workers and newly arriving immigrants. Cities have experienced revivals as highly educated, upwardly mobile young people flooded into their core areas. Attracted by inexpensive housing and services, many such returned urbanites gentrified decaying neighborhoods with refurbished housing, restaurants, and stores. The economic uniformity of these "yuppies," as they were sometimes disparagingly called, also undercut the pluralism of cities. At worst, they forced long-term residents, especially the aged, from their homes and indirectly caused an increase in homelessness. Homosexuals have also concentrated in formerly decaying downtown areas; in addition to well-known gay neighborhoods like Greenwich Village in New York City and the Castro District in San Francisco, communities have arisen in Los Angeles, Houston, Seattle, Denver, Cincinnati, and Saint Louis.

[Anthony Downs, *New Visions for Metropolitan America* (Cambridge, Mass., 1994).]

GRAHAM RUSSELL HODGES

See also **DAH:** Cities, Growth of; Urban Structure; **SUPP:** Crime; Demographic Changes; Housing; Poverty; Suburban Living; Unemployment; Urban Renewal and Development.

URBAN RENEWAL AND DEVELOPMENT. In the 1950s and 1960s the federal government poured billions of dollars into massive "urban renewal" projects in an attempt to revitalize disintegrating U.S. cities. These projects, while sometimes creating successful public institutions, such as performing arts complexes and civic centers, typically involved razing vast sections of the affordable-housing stock and displacing poor and elderly residents, whose housing alternatives were then often limited to bleak-looking public-housing high rises. By the early 1970s the term "urban renewal" had taken on distinctly negative connotations, and policymakers began to search for new approaches to the problem of urban revitalization in an era of increasing scarcity, austerity, and privatization.

With the passage of the Housing and Community Development Act of 1974, which established the Community Development Block Grant program (CDBG), privatization emerged as the central thrust of federal urban-improvement policy. This act brought "revenue sharing" to the nation. It empowered the federal government to issue block grants to local governments for a wide range of improvement projects. Since then the federal government has affected central-city revitalization through a tangle of programs, especially those administered by the Department of Housing and Urban Development (HUD). These include Section 8 and Section 810 of the 1974 Housing and Community Development Act, which set up a national demonstration program with the help of HUD. Block grants were intended primarily for private and public housing rehabilitation and located in low- and moderate-income areas. Urban renewal, model cities, water and sewer line subsidization, open-space procurement, and housing rehabilitation were subsumed by these block grants.

President Jimmy Carter advanced three different urban policies during his tenure, specifically, a $16 billion "economic stimulus" package in 1977, the enactment of the Urban Development Action Grants

(UDAG) program, and a new emphasis on "targeting" aid to distressed cities. This package represented a 25 percent increase in intergovernmental aid to big cities. During the Carter years, $3.5 billion was awarded in direct financial assistance to central-city government as a kind of bonus revenue sharing. UDAG, which fostered central-city revitalization, provided a new and more flexible form of urban renewal in which federal assistance could sweeten development deals negotiated between local government and private builders. UDAG targeted communities with declining populations and large per-capita income disparities, poverty populations, and blocks of substandard houses. It also provided capital for developments that promised increases in jobs and local tax bases. (In 1979, $487 million in federal grants were matched by $2.86 billion in private investment.) By 1980 nearly 700 grants across 400 cities had been authorized, totaling $1.3 billion. Cities with these funds established some 160,000 temporary construction jobs, retained 92,000 old jobs, and created 200,000 permanent openings.

The Carter program also stressed a "new partnership" among various levels of government, the private sector, neighborhoods, and voluntary associations, but Congress proved unwilling to extend the antirecessionary measures of 1977. Carter's new partnership was mostly symbolic. Its $12 billion in proposals contained nothing for the Community Service Administration (successor organization to the Office of Economic Opportunity), only $40 million to AC-TION to initiate an "urban volunteer corps," and a mere $15 million for a HUD program of small grants to neighborhood groups.

During Carter's presidency, antirecessionary fiscal assistance, the Comprehensive Employment and Training Act (CETA), and local public works were all phased down or cut out. Taken together, Carter's last two budgets (1979 and 1980) failed to achieve either general welfare reform or enactment of the more limited but equally critical youth employment idea. Nor did the programs ensure that needy central-city residents got the jobs created or retained by subsidies to private capital. Neighborhood revitalization was promoted by the Neighborhood Housing Services (NHS) program, a joint effort between HUD and the Federal Home Loan Board, and by urban homesteading, in which city-owned houses were distributed for little or no money to individuals who agreed to renovate and reside within them. Neither program, however, went very far toward combating urban decay.

By 1979, 86 percent of all cities with more than 50,000 people had created revitalized neighborhoods, but this typically was manifested in gentrification, a more benign form of urban renewal marked by trendy restaurants, boutiques, and overpriced specialty stores. Cynically attacked by critics as "private urban renewal," "reinvasion," or "reverse blockbusting," successful gentrification usually was followed by a substantial bidding-up of property values. For example, UDAG grants were awarded in 1980 to build department-store and office space in downtown Detroit and luxury harborside housing and a downtown office and shopping complex in Baltimore. This process of "devitalization," some economic critics claimed, produces no real active street life. Gentrification rehabilitates the cream of a city's older housing stock but in such a way that only upper-income residents benefit, meanwhile displacing longtime residents.

In the 1980s the administration of President Ronald Reagan emphasized placing urban redevelopment in the hands of the private market and relying on state rather than federal intervention to solve urban ills. Reagan's National Urban Policy Report of 1982, put out by HUD, outlined the Republican urban philosophy of New Federalism, which called for more revenue sharing and the creation of "enterprise zones"—areas excluded from many locally imposed taxes, zoning restrictions, and other regulations—to attract new businesses to impoverished areas. In 1984 Reagan's second Urban Policy Report recognized the problems of particularly distressed cities of the Rustbelt/Frostbelt. The limited amount of federal funding earmarked for urban growth and other local development was increasingly divided between tax incentives for large corporate projects and small-scale ancillary projects, such as street lighting and neighborhood spruce-up projects. While UDAG money under Republican supervision continued to finance new development that attempted to fill the gaps created by abandoned housing, it was parceled out stingily (from 1981 to 1985 UDAG funding fell from $440 million to $235 million), presaging its total demise by decade's end. Federal housing assistance and job training funds also fell precipitously. The Reagan administration halted virtually all government-subsidized rental-housing construction and instead began issuing vouchers for families, another policy in keeping with the trend toward "privatizing" housing subsidies. Responding to these Republican-initiated strategies, the U.S. Conference of Mayors in 1985 called for the protection of urban-directed programs, such as general revenue sharing, urban development action grants, subsidized housing, mass transit assistance, student loans, and jobs programs.

During the presidency of George Bush, Secretary

of Housing and Urban Development Jack Kemp continued to emphasize enterprise zones as the keystone of federal urban policy. Under Bush, states and localities that offered the most favorable incentive programs were given preferential treatment in determining enterprise zone eligibility. While commendable, Kemp's priorities for HUD—employment, home ownership, revitalized inner cities, and care for the homeless—were never fully pursued, however. President Bill Clinton, like his Republican predecessors, also relied on privatization as the solution for urban renewal. His presidency saw the implementation of many economic-growth initiatives set forth by the country's mayors, including stronger community-assistance programs, targeted fiscal assistance to cities in direst need, summer-jobs initiatives and training programs for inner-city youth, a crackdown on discriminatory "redlining" by lending and insurance institutions and other forms of housing discrimination, and the enforcement of a revitalized Community Reinvestment Act.

[John A. Jakle and David Wilson, *Derelict Landscapes: The Wasting of America's Built Environment* (Savage, Md., 1992); Michael H. Lang, *Gentrification and Urban Decline: Strategies for America's Older Cities* (Cambridge, Mass., 1982); John H. Mollenkopf, *The Contested City* (Princeton, N.J., 1983); Donald B. Rosenthal, ed., *Urban Revitalization* (Beverly Hills, Calif., 1980); Jon C. Teaford, *The Rough Road to Renaissance: Urban Revitalization in America, 1940–1985* (Baltimore, 1990); Morris Zeitlin, *American Cities: A Working Class View* (New York, 1990).]

TIMOTHY C. COOGAN

See also **SUPP:** Housing; Housing and Urban Development, Department of; Urban Living.

URUGUAY ROUND. *See* **General Agreement on Tariffs and Trade.**

USDA. *See* **Agriculture, Department of.**

UTAH, a state of 84,916 square miles of diverse geographic features—desert basins, broad plateaus, deep canyons, prehistoric dry lake beds, river valleys, salt flats, and the Wasatch and Uinta mountains, with the state's highest point, Kings Peak, at 13,528 feet—had a population of 1,722,850, in 1990, a 17.9 percent increase since 1980. Eighty percent of Utah's land is under the stewardship of the federal government. Utah's native people include the nomadic Shoshone, Paiute, and Ute, from which the state received its name, which means "home on the mountaintop." All three groups adapted to the region's extremely harsh conditions by living in caves or in portable brush lodges and by gathering seasonal harvests of wild plants as well as hunting, fishing, and trapping.

Economically, Utah mirrored the nation during the hardship years of the Great Depression and the subsequent economic upsurge generated by the demands of World War II. Between 1980 and 1990 the state's economy, like those of many other states, shifted away from the production of goods and toward the production of services. The energy boom of the 1970s became an energy bust of the 1980s. With a decline in mining and construction, and only modest gains in manufacturing, the employment growth in the service-producing industries accounted for 97 percent of all new jobs in the 1980s. In 1990 approximately 80 percent of all nonagricultural workers were employed in the service-producing industries. In the 1980s fewer than 13,000 families farmed, compared with a maximum of 132,000 in 1910. Despite this decline, land values and rural ways continued to reflect strong sentiments and preferences, evidenced in the vitality of state and county fairs at which livestock, rural, and home exhibits were avidly patronized. Tourism became a major part of Utah's economy during the last quarter of the twentieth century, thanks to the state's ski areas, five national parks, six national monuments, and two national recreation areas. By 1991 visits to Utah's 45 state parks had exceeded 5 million. A 1986 government study showed that approximately 11 million people visited the state each year, which increased to 14 million in the early 1990s, and that 50,000 Utahans were employed in the tourism industry. In the 1990s tourism accounted for $2.9 billion in revenue annually.

Utah's innovations in scientific research include the first artificial heart implant in Barney Clark in 1982 and the pioneering of artificial eyes, ears, and arms. The state saw the first renal transplant in 1965. Continued progress in thoracic surgery led to teams of surgeons doing heart transplants in four Utah hospitals, and the 90 percent survival rate in the 412 transplants performed from 1985 to 1992 was one of the best in the country. Among the products developed and produced in Utah in the last quarter of the twentieth century were computers, electronic devices, aircraft, rockets, and computer software. LDS Hospital had become a world model for the most sophisticated system of using computers in total patient care.

The Church of Jesus Christ of Latter-day Saints (LDS), whose membership numbered more than 8 million on a worldwide basis in 1991 and made up some 70 percent of Utah's population at the same time, continued to play a prominent role in the economic, political, and social life of the state. Economically, its building programs, educational institutions, and other activities were major sources of employment, and the businesses it operated, such as the Deseret Book Company, the *Deseret News,* and the broadcasting facilities of Bonneville International Corporation, provided employment and an important tax base. The racial climate in Utah improved after the LDS church announced in 1978 that the priesthood was open to "all worthy male members of the Church . . . without regard to race or color." This had an immediate effect upon the status of blacks in the church and doubtless that of all African Americans residing in Utah. Professional basketball franchises also improved Utah's racial climate. After the American Basketball Association's Los Angeles Stars moved to Salt Lake City in 1970 and changed their name to the Utah Stars, many of their black players were popular not only because of their athletic ability but also for their individual contributions to the community. In 1979 the National Basketball Association's New Orleans Jazz relocated to Salt Lake City and became the Utah Jazz. The popularity of the NBA elevated some Jazz players to celebrity status, and they were looked upon as role models on and off the court.

After World War II there was an expansion of the state's cultural institutions, such as the Utah Symphony Orchestra, the Mormon Tabernacle Choir, and Ballet West. The Sundance Institute, established by actor-director Robert Redford in 1981, gained international recognition for developing and exhibiting films.

[Dean L. May, *Utah* (Salt Lake City, 1987); Richard D. Poll, ed., *Utah's History* (Provo, Utah, 1978); Allan Kent Powell, ed., *Utah History Encyclopedia* (Salt Lake City, 1994).]

KAREN MARY SHREEFTER

UTOPIANISM. The lure of utopia (the Greek word *outopos* (literally "no place") has been strong throughout American history, especially in a land that so long boasted a western frontier. Many were experiments in social engineering; most of the utopian communities that flourished in the eighteenth and nineteenth centuries had religion at their core, such as the Protestant monasticism of the Ephrata Colony; the belief in Christ's second appearing for the Shakers; the postmillennialism of Oneida; and the transcendentalism of Brook Farm and Fruitlands. Others, notably New Harmony in Indiana, the Fourier Phalanxes, and the Icarian communities were socialist. All shared an aspiration to show the wider world how to organize society. After an attenuation of utopian fervor in the latter half of the nineteenth century, the utopian impulse revived somewhat in the twentieth. Some communities, like Estero, founded in Florida in 1900, were based on pseudoscientific notions, while others, like the Hutterites in the Dakotas and Canada and the Society of True Inspiration in eastern Iowa, sought to perpetuate a particular lifestyle derived from religious principles. The late 1960s saw another flowering of utopian communities; nearly all of them, from Total Loss Farm in Vermont to the various communes on the West Coast, were strongly identified with the counterculture of that era.

[Robert Fogarty, *Dictionary of American Communal and Utopian History* (Westport, Conn., 1980).]

RANDALL BALMER

See also **SUPP:** Communes and Communitarian Groups.

VEGETARIANISM, the practice of subsisting on a diet composed primarily or wholly of vegetables, grains, fruits, nuts, and seeds, with or without eggs and dairy products, was endorsed in the United States in 1838 by the American Health Convention. It enjoyed a rebirth with the counterculture of the 1960s. Still, in 1971 only 1 percent of U.S. citizens described themselves as vegetarians. By 1992 the number had jumped dramatically to 7 percent. Half of all vegetarians abstain from meat for health reasons and 15 percent are most concerned about animal welfare. In 1991 the National Restaurant Association endorsed vegetarianism, encouraging restaurants to carry vegetarian dishes because one-third of restaurant patrons had indicated they would order them if offered.

[Waverley Lewis Root and Richard de Rochemont, *Eating in America: A History* (New York, 1976).]

JEFFREY M. MERRON

See also **SUPP:** Animal Rights Movement; Health Food Industry; Nutrition.

VENEREAL DISEASES (VD). *See* **Sexually Transmitted Diseases.**

VERMONT. After World War II, but particularly starting in the 1980s, Vermont's political and economic landscape was transformed. Locally owned marble, granite, and machine tool companies that early in the twentieth century had surpassed agriculture as the prime source of income, were absorbed by international conglomerates, only to decline in favor of other industries, notably electronics. In 1880 the Vermont Marble Company was the state's largest employer; in 1980 it was IBM. Tourism also flourished: at peak season more people were employed on Vermont's ski slopes than in farming. In 1990 there were 2,381 dairy farms, down 8,000 from 1948, and while the size of individual herds increased, there was a significant decrease in acreage. The 263,000 cows in 1948 produced 1.2 billion pounds of milk as compared to the 167,000 cows that produced 2.1 billion pounds in 1990. A federal program to curb overproduction, the "whole herd buyout," ran from 1983 to 1984 and from 1986 to 1987 and attracted many Vermont farmers who, after accepting buyouts, sold their land to developers. As an incentive to retain land in agriculture, the state imposed a use tax in 1980, as distinguished from market value property tax.

The emergence of a two-party system in the state, with the rise of the Democratic party in the early 1960s, brought marked changes. Since Philip H. Hoff in 1962 became the first Democratic governor in 109 years, the governor's office has rotated between the parties. After 1970 both houses of the state assembly had occasional Democratic majorities. In 1974 the first Democratic senator since the founding of the Republican party was elected. In 1995 the Vermont congressional delegation consisted of Republican Senator James M. Jeffords, Democratic Senator Patrick J. Leahy, and independent socialist Representative Bernard Sanders—respectively Protestant, Catholic, and Jewish. The old power structure had disappeared. The gender barrier was breached in 1984, when Vermont elected its first woman governor, Madeleine M. Kunin, who served three terms.

Recent anthropological and historical studies that substantiate an Abnaki Indian presence in northwestern Vermont since 9000 B.C. kindled assertions of aboriginal rights and land titles. Unsuccessful in securing federal tribal recognition, the Abnaki Tribal Council has looked to the state for support. A lame-duck governor's executive order in 1976 accorded the Abnaki tribal status, but it was revoked by his successor the following year. Another temporary victory was won in 1989, when a Vermont court recognized the Abnaki claim to "unextinguished fishing rights" by dismissing charges of fishing without a license against the chief and other tribe members. In 1992 a higher court reversed the decision by concluding that a series of historical events, "the increasing weight of history," had extinguished aboriginal rights.

Showing a 14 percent population gain over the preceding decade, the 1970 census was the first since 1830 to record a more than 10 percent increase in residents, and the 1980 census showed 15 percent growth. A sluggish economy and state regulations restricting development contributed to slower growth during the 1980s, but gains remained substantial at 10 percent; in 1990 the state's population stood at 563,000. The cause of population growth was the interstate highway system, especially the interstate into Canada built in the 1960s. Having long promoted a pastoral retreat from urban life, Vermont became accessible to 40 million urban dwellers within a three-hour drive. Farms, hillsides, and roadsides were converted to vacation uses, including ski resorts and associated developments. Beginning in 1970 the state began to redirect its policies from reversing rural depopulation to preserving rural identity and landscape. Popularly known as Act 250, the legislation mandated permits for developments of more than 10 acres, with burden of proof for ecological soundness of a proposal resting upon the developer. In 1984 the statewide planning provision of the act was repealed, but four years later the legislature passed Act 200 to facilitate "growth management" by encouraging towns to develop plans. Opponents of Acts 250 and 200 alleged that the permit process had become so cumbersome and expensive that it inhibited sound development. A second source of opposition came from property owners organized for repeal of land management legislation as a denial of property rights and local control. During the early 1990s the administrators of land management legislation made accommodations to these sentiments. Vermonters in favor of more strict compliance with the two acts, however, could take heart: in June 1993 the entire state was designated an "endangered place" by the National Trust for Historic Preservation, becoming the first state so designated. The 1990 census figures show that despite Vermont's population growth in the 1980s, Vermont remained a white state of small towns. Asian-Pacific Islanders, American Indian, and African-American populations grew, but their numbers remained very small.

[Madeleine Kunin, *Living a Political Life* (New York, 1994); Harold A. Meeks, *Time and Change in Vermont: A Human Geography* (Chester, Conn., 1986); Joe Sherman, *Fast Lane on a Dirt Road: Vermont Transformed, 1945–1990* (Woodstock, Vt., 1991).]

SAMUEL B. HAND

VETERANS AFFAIRS, DEPARTMENT OF. In 1987 President Ronald Reagan threw his support behind a movement to raise the Veterans Administration, an independent government agency since its creation in 1930, to a cabinet-level department, and in 1988 he signed a bill creating the Department of Veterans Affairs (VA). In 1989 the secretary of veterans affairs became the fourteenth member of the president's cabinet. The VA is the second-largest cabinet-level department of the government; only the Department of Defense is larger. The VA is responsible for administering a wide variety of benefits for military veterans and their dependents. Within it are the Veterans Health Services and Research Administration, the Veterans Benefits Administration, and the National Cemetery System. Their heads and the general counsel for the VA are appointed by the president and confirmed by the Senate. Health benefits administered by the VA include hospitals, nursing homes, and outpatient medical and dental care. More than half the practicing physicians in the United States received part of their training within the health care system administered by the VA. There is a Prosthetics Assessment and Information Center, and programs include vocational as well as physical rehabilitation. The VA oversees military pensions, compensation for disabilities and death, and insurance and loans for veterans. The GI Bill of 1944 provided housing and educational benefits for World War II veterans, and benefits have been continued for veterans of the Korean and Vietnam Wars, all administered by the VA.

[Donald R. Whitnah, ed., *Government Agencies* (Westport, Conn., 1983).]

RICHARD W. MOODEY

VICE PRESIDENCY. The office of the vice president of the United States continued carrying a mixed legacy as the United States approached the end of the twentieth century. While the conception of its duties and its process of selection were flawed, the vice presidency has more or less performed the function the framers of the U.S. Constitution intended and has not—as some critics feared—led the nation into deep trouble. Choosing the vice-presidential candidate, and thus a vice president, remains above all an instrument for assisting in election of the president. The presidential candidate made the selection in every race between 1976 and 1992, as a rule picking someone with an appeal different from his. While traditional geographic and ideological "ticket balancing" remained alive—as in Jimmy Carter's selection of Walter Mondale in 1976—other considerations took on importance. Because Americans after the mid-1970s preferred presidential candidates (other than incumbents) from outside the ranks of national elective officeholders, running mates were insiders from Capitol Hill. Of the ten major party vice-presidential candidates between 1976 and 1992, all had served in Congress, seven of them in the Senate.

Recent years have seen innovations in the selection process. Mondale's choice in 1984 of the first woman, Geraldine Ferraro, acknowledged a changing political climate and created a new form of ticket balancing. George Bush's naming of Dan Quayle, a little-known senator with seemingly not much to offer the ticket or the nation, provoked much puzzlement, concern, and ridicule. Bill Clinton seemed to defy conventional logic in 1992, when he picked Senator Albert Gore, producing a ticket of two white males of similar age and ideology, both Baptist and both from southern states. Gore, however, enhanced an image that Clinton wished to project, and as a popular insider was strong in areas where Clinton was weak. None of these choices challenged the proposition that a vice-presidential candidate's responsibility was to help elect a president, nor did Ronald Reagan's selection in 1980 of Bush, a "moderate" balance to Reagan's conservatism and a candidate who could help the ticket in Texas, a critical state.

The people who have held the office—and who have run for it—since the 1970s generally have been capable, experienced individuals of sober judgment. The most apprehension arose from the candidacy of Quayle, who seemed ill-equipped and ill-prepared for the job despite several years in Congress. Recent presidents have made a point of having their vice presidents at important meetings and giving them special assignments. The issue of temporary succession came up twice during the presidency of Ronald Reagan, first when Reagan was shot on Mar. 30, 1981, and rushed into surgery, leaving it unclear as to who was in charge. When Reagan had surgery again in July 1985, he signed a transfer of power to the vice president for the period of his operation. For all the effort to promote the visibility of recent vice presidents, there is little to suggest they have had a major impact on policy. Indeed, Bush proudly asserted that he was not "in the loop" of decisions about the unpopular Iran-Contra episode. The most encouraging sign of change came with the Clinton administration in the mid-1990s. Clinton treated Gore as an equal partner during the election of 1992, and the two often campaigned together. Upon taking office Gore represented the new administration on environmental issues, operated behind the scenes in key congressional votes, and in 1993 presented the administration's case in a heralded debate with Ross Perot on the North American Free Trade Agreement. Projecting a refreshing self-confidence on most aspects of policy, Gore had a promising start.

Despite the persistence of jokes about its impotence and suggestions that it be changed, even abolished, the vice presidency remains firmly established in the U.S. government. Critics continue to insist that the vice president become more active and that the office serve as a training ground for the presidency. The process of selection, flawed—even risky—as it is, remains entrenched in party politics and is unlikely to change. The best the nation can hope for is that in choosing a running mate, the presidential nominee will give more heed to expertness in governance and less to politics, with the people making anyone pay who does not. Experience since the 1970s, and more broadly since 1945, has affirmed that in picking a running mate a presidential nominee probably is choosing a future presidential candidate. This proved true even of the most ridiculed of recent vice presidents, Quayle, whose national book tour in 1994 catapulted him into a potential presidential candidacy (before illness ruled it out).

[The Twentieth Century Fund, *A Heartbeat Away: Report of the Twentieth Century Task Force on the Vice Presidency* (New York, 1988); Jules Witcover, *Crapshoot: Rolling the Dice on the Vice Presidency* (New York, 1992).]

Ross Gregory

See also **SUPP:** Presidency.

VIDEO GAMES are electronic games played on "closed platform" game consoles—hand-held portables, cartridge players that connect to a television set or arcade systems—that can only run software from publishers who have paid fees to the system manufacturer. In contrast, personal computers are an "open platform" system: PC software publishers do not pay system manufacturers. Video games emerged in the early 1970s with the development of the microprocessor. The first game released in the United States was Atari's Pong, which approximated Ping-Pong. The game systems of the early 1980s—Atari, Intellivision, ColecoVision—seem primitive compared with the first Nintendo Entertainment System (NES), released in 1985, which used an eight-bit processor. The NES was soon surpassed by the sixteen-bit Super Nintendo Entertainment System (SNES), Sega Genesis, and Sega CD, a CD-ROM player that connects to the Genesis system. Since the mid-1970s the video game industry has been dominated by two manufacturers, Nintendo and Sega. In 1994 more than one-third of American homes had a video game system, the video arcade had become a teen gathering place in malls nationwide, and the industry projected annual sales of $7 billion. The popularity of video games was paralleled by controversy over their purported health risks and benefits. One measure of a game's success is its "addictiveness," and parents are encouraged to monitor the content and duration of children's play. In late 1993 a U.S. Senate subcommittee addressed concerns about violence in video games, resulting in industry-generated ratings. Video games are growing increasingly realistic. Both Sega and Sony released CD-based systems with thirty-two-bit processors in 1995, and Nintendo was expected to release a sixty-four-bit-system in 1996. Further developments are likely to include interactive "movies" for multiple players delivered via fiber-optic cable networks, and virtual reality games.

[Steven A. Schwartz, *Parent's Guide to Video Games* (Rocklin, Calif., 1994); David Sheff, *Video Games: A Guide for Savvy Parents* (New York, 1994).]

CAROL GASKIN

See also **SUPP:** CD-ROM Technology; Fiber Optics.

VIETNAM. *See* **Prisoners of War and Missing in Action.**

VIETNAM WAR MEMORIAL. The Vietnam Veterans Memorial was dedicated on the Washington Mall in November 1982. Maya Ying Lin, a Yale University architecture student who won the national design competition, erected two elongated, tapered walls of black granite that joined at the higher ends at a 125-degree angle to form an open "V." The back sides of the walls were landscaped to be even to the ground. Open front sides sloped downward into the earth to a depth of ten feet where the wings meet. The names of the 57,939 American men and women dead or missing in action in the war were etched, chronologically, in white on the polished granite. At the dedication, veterans and family members read the names of the dead in alphabetical order, which required more than three days. The organizers of the Vietnam Memorial intended their project as a symbol of reconciliation. Their nonpolitical memorial would not comment on the rightness or wrongness of the Vietnam War. By focusing simply on those who served and died, the organizers hoped to conciliate the war's supporters and opponents. Their choice of a site across from the Lincoln Memorial meant, as one veteran put it, that "no one could ignore it." The wall's stark design offended some conservatives and veterans groups, who agitated for a more heroic memorial. As a compromise, sculptor Frederick Hart prepared a statue of three U.S. soldiers—one black, one white, and one Eurasian—as a counterpoint to the abstract simplicity of the wall. Since its unveiling, the Vietnam Memorial has been the third most-visited site in Washington.

[Wilbur J. Scott, *The Politics of Readjustment: Vietnam Veterans Since the War* (New York, 1993).]

J. GARRY CLIFFORD

See also **SUPP:** Prisoners of War and Missing in Action; War Memorials.

VIGILANTES. On the U.S. frontier of the nineteenth century, vigilantes were self-appointed groups of property owners organized to keep order and put down illegal activity. Vigilante committees were organized when citizens found law enforcement absent or inadequate. By the turn of the century, as law enforcement increased, most committees disbanded. The term "vigilante" has since been used to describe actions by groups or individuals who take the law into their own hands or punish real or perceived wrongdoings outside the legal system. Dissatisfaction with law enforcement or the legal process remains the principle motive. Typically that dissatisfaction is shared by other individuals who see vigilante actions as heroic. Among the many cases receiving media coverage in the late twentieth century was that of Bernard Goetz. His 1984 shooting of four black youths, who he believed were attempting to rob him in a New York City subway car, gained Goetz national celebrity status. Admirers provided bail when he was arrested and letters of support from victims of similar crimes appeared in the press. In the early 1990s attention focused on a vigilante incident dating back to 1923, when a large group of white attackers torched the black-populated town of Rosewood, Fla. The invasion was caused by a questionable accusation that a black man had assaulted a white woman in nearby Sumner and that the assailant was a Rosewood resident. When he could not be found, a group of Sumner men took it upon themselves to resolve the matter. In May 1994 the state of Florida paid $2 million to nine of the survivors, the first time in U.S. history that a state awarded damages to citizens for failing to properly defend them. Additional compensation was set aside for scholarships for the descendants of residents. Both the Goetz and Rosewood cases illustrate vigilantism in its modern meaning—unlawful retribution by private citizens.

ROBERT M. GUTH

VIOLENCE, DOMESTIC. *See* Domestic Violence.

VIOLENCE AGAINST WOMEN BILL was introduced in Congress in January 1991 by Senator Joseph Biden of Delaware. Biden, chairperson of the Senate Judiciary Committee, and the cosponsors were motivated by the high incidence of assaults, aggravated assaults, murders, and rapes committed against women. In 1991 an estimated 4 million women were victims of domestic violence, with 20 percent of all assaults that were reported to the police occurring in the home. The bill was made part of the Violent Crime Control and Law Enforcement Act and was signed into law on Sept. 13, 1994, by President Bill Clinton. The act authorized $1.6 billion to be spent over six years on the creation of rape crisis centers and battered women's shelters and authorized additional local police, prosecutors, victim advocates, and a domestic violence hotline; funds were also made available to train judges who hear domestic violence cases. Provisions of the act expanded rape shield laws, created offenses for interstate spousal abuse, and allow women who are victims of gender-based crimes to sue those responsible in federal court. Under the latter section of the act victims have to prove the crime was not random and was motivated by animus toward their gender, a finding similar to that required to prove racially motivated crimes. Por-

tions of the act not originally part of the Violence Against Women Bill include restrictions on gun purchases for persons guilty of domestic abuse; safeguards to protect the confidentiality of information kept by state motor vehicle bureaus, with the aim of preventing stalkers and other criminals from finding their victims; and increased penalties for hate crimes in which the victim is targeted on the basis of race, gender, religion, or sexual orientation. An eleventh hour Republican effort to remove domestic violence provisions from the act, on the grounds that funding them constituted government waste, was defeated narrowly in the House of Representatives and by a cloture vote ending a filibuster in the Senate.

[Congressional Caucus for Women's Issues, *Update* (September-October, 1994); U.S. Senate, Majority Staff of the Committee on the Judiciary, *Violence Against Women: A Week in the Life of America* (Washington, D.C., 1992).]

IRWIN N. GERTZOG

See also **SUPP:** Domestic Violence; Women's Rights.

VIRGINIA. Beginning in the 1960s the state of Virginia increasingly reflected national patterns in society and politics. Its black population ended a long relative decline and held at just under 19 percent in the censuses of 1970, 1980, and 1990. Meanwhile, residents of Asian ancestry increased from a negligible number at the time of the 1965 Immigration Act to a figure approaching 4 percent of all Virginia residents by the 1990s. The state's total population grew from 4,648,494 in 1970 to 5,346,818 in 1980 (a 15 percent increase) and to 6,187,358 in 1990 (a 16 percent increase). Net in-migration accounted for fully half the growth in each decade, and by 1990 only 54 percent of all residents were Virginia natives. Such developments illustrated significant changes in Virginia's recent history, as the state had been a large exporter of people throughout the nineteenth century and well into the twentieth. Virginians lived increasingly in urban or suburban areas. The city of Virginia Beach offers one measure; by 1990 it had grown to a population of 393,069, the nation's thirty-seventh largest. The core cities of Norfolk, the state's port city and adjacent to Virginia Beach, and Richmond, the state capital, each lost between 15 and 20 percent of their population between 1970 and 1990. Nonetheless the urbanization of northern and eastern Virginia proceeded rapidly. The counties bordering Richmond—Henrico and Chesterfield—displayed massive growth. Some largely rural counties, such as Prince William and Loudoun, found themselves ab-

sorbed into metropolitan Washington, D.C. Others, mostly in the southern and western parts of the state, lost population as rural residents moved to urban areas.

Political changes dating from the 1960s continued over the ensuing decades. In 1964 the Twenty-fourth Amendment ended the poll tax as a condition of voting in federal elections, and in a 1966 case that arose in Virginia the U.S. Supreme Court struck down the tax in state elections as well. The Supreme Court rendered decisions that forced reapportionment in elections to Congress and to the Virginia state legislature. These changes led to the defeat of long-term incumbents, such as U.S. Senator A. Willis Robertson and U.S. Representative Howard W. Smith. The newly reapportioned legislature enacted a sales tax in 1966, and in 1969 a Republican, A. Linwood Holton, won the governorship, breaking the stranglehold of rural white Democrats on Virginia politics. Republicans won again in 1973 with former Democrat Mills E. Godwin, Jr., and in 1977 with John N. Dalton, but Charles S. Robb retrieved the state executive office for the Democrats in 1981. Gerald L. Baliles and L. Douglas Wilder held it for the Democrats in 1985 and 1989, but the Republican candidate, George F. Allen, won in 1993. In legislative races Republicans and Democrats faced each other as equals in the 1990s. As late as 1975 the hundred-member Virginia House of Delegates included only seventeen Republicans, but by 1994 the number was forty-seven. Meanwhile, Virginia became a Republican state in presidential elections. As early as 1948, although President Harry S. Truman took the state that year, Virginia Democrats had begun to abandon their party in presidential elections. Black Virginians abandoned the Republican party and embraced the Democrats, but were swamped by the stream of white voters heading in the other direction, who together with many new residents voted Republican. From 1952 through 1992 the Democratic presidential candidates won Virginia's electoral votes only in 1964.

In terms of race and gender, Virginia politics in the 1990s differed greatly from the 1960s. In the late 1960s, for the first time since the 1880s, black candidates won election to the state legislature, and the number of women, most of them white, increased slowly as well. By the 1994 session thirteen of the legislature's 140 members were black and sixteen were women. Meanwhile, after the 1985 elections, Mary Sue Terry began the first of two terms (eight years) as state attorney general. L. Douglas Wilder, after sixteen years in the state senate, was elected lieutenant governor in 1985 and in 1989 became the first African American elected governor of any state. The declining significance of race in Virginia politics can be seen in the fact that while a majority of white voters pulled the Republican lever, Wilder's victory depended on the support of far more whites than blacks. As for the judiciary, in 1983 John Charles Thomas became the first black justice of the Virginia Supreme Court, and in 1988 Elizabeth B. Lacy became the first female justice. In 1986 James Randolph Spencer became Virginia's first black federal judge, and in 1989 Rebecca Beach Smith became the first woman appointed to such a position. After the 1992 elections Virginia's congressional delegation, like the state legislature, was no longer all white and all male. Robert C. Scott became only the second African American to win a seat from the Old Dominion, 104 years after John Mercer Langston's election in 1888, and Leslie L. Byrne became the first woman ever elected to Congress from Virginia, although Byrne lost her bid for reelection in 1994.

Major changes occurred in higher education in Virginia in the last decades of the twentieth century. Such changes were related to public finance, numbers of students, the racial desegregation that came to Virginia in the 1950s and 1960s, and expansion of opportunities for women. The 1966 legislature inaugurated a statewide system of community colleges. By the 1990s three universities—Virginia Polytechnic Institute and State University, Virginia Commonwealth University, and George Mason University— each enrolled more than 20,000 students, as did Northern Virginia Community College. The University of Virginia was not far behind. Before the 1950s only one public institution of higher education in Virginia (now known as Virginia State University) admitted black students; by the 1990s blacks attended every school, although the numbers were still well below the African-American percentage of Virginia residents. Women were first admitted to the University of Virginia as undergraduates only in 1970; by the 1990s men and women attended in almost equal numbers. Although women had begun attending law school there in 1920, they comprised 10 percent of the total number of law students only after congressional enactment of Title IX in 1972. By the 1990s women comprised one-third of each graduating class. In the 1990s the state reversed a quarter-century-long trend and trimmed its spending on higher education; those budget cuts drove up tuition costs.

Virginia's economy made major shifts between the 1970s and the 1990s. The reduction of the U.S. military in the 1990s meant the loss of thousands of military-related jobs, from the Radford Arsenal to the Newport News Shipbuilding and Drydock Company. Agriculture, although still a large part of the economy, continued to decline in relative importance, while tobacco became less important among agricultural commodities. Tourism remained a major industry; Virginia's beaches and mountains as well as its shrines to the colonial era, the American Revolution, and the Civil War—Colonial Williamsburg, the Blue Ridge Parkway, George Washington's Mount Vernon—were among the leading attractions. Manufacturing—electronics and transportation equipment, textiles and apparel, paper and printing—increased only 16 percent and dropped from first to fourth in total employment between 1970 and 1990. Services rocketed from fourth to first; jobs in trade climbed from third to second; employment in government slipped from second place to third. In the same twenty-year period, the per capita income of Virginians rose from 94 percent to 105 percent of the national average.

In the 1990s Virginia had a growing population that was increasingly urban, a diverse economy, and a two-party political system. Virginians as different as tennis player Arthur Ashe and evangelist Jerry Falwell had an effect on people far from Old Dominion. Students from foreign countries came to Virginia for college and university educations, foreign investment in Virginia mounted, and Virginia governors went overseas in quest of export markets for the state's products.

[Frank B. Atkinson, *The Dynamic Dominion: Realignment and the Rise of Virginia's Republican Party Since 1945* (Fairfax, Va., 1992); Thomas C. Parramore, Peter C. Stewart, and Tommy L. Bogger, *Norfolk: The First Four Centuries* (Charlottesville, 1994); Marie Tyler-McGraw, *At the Falls: Virginia and Its People* (Chapel Hill, N.C., 1994); Peter Wallenstein, "'These New and Strange Beings': Women in the Legal Profession in Virginia, 1890–1990," *Virginia Magazine of History and Biography* 101 (April 1993).]

PETER WALLENSTEIN

See also **SUPP:** Virginia Beach.

VIRGINIA BEACH, a resort city of hotels, casinos, and beaches in Princess Anne County, Va., and located on Chesapeake Bay. First developed in 1880, Virginia Beach was incorporated as a town in 1906 and became an independent city in 1952. During and after World War II the Hampton Roads region, with its naval and shipbuilding facilities, ballooned in employment and population, but the number of residents of Virginia Beach had reached only 8,091 in 1960. In 1959 the city of Norfolk annexed a large portion of Princess Anne County, and to thwart further annexation political leaders and residents of Virginia Beach and what remained of the county initiated a merger, ratified by referendum in 1962 and approved by the Virginia legislature the same year. The new city of Virginia Beach became a reality on Jan. 1, 1963. With an area of 256 square miles—more than four times that of Norfolk or Richmond, the cities with the largest populations in the state—Virginia Beach had ample room to grow. By 1970 it ranked third among Virginia cities with 172,106 residents. Its population grew by 52 percent in the 1970s and another 50 percent in the 1980s. By 1990, with 393,069 residents, it had become Virginia's most populous city and the thirty-seventh largest in the nation. By 1990 the city's population was 80 percent white, 14 percent black, and 4 percent Asian. Virginia Beach borders Norfolk International Airport and it contains First Landing State Park. Military installations in the city include the Oceana Naval Air Station, and facilities for higher education include the Virginia Beach campus of Tidewater Community College.

[Stephen S. Manfield, *Princess Anne County and Virginia Beach: A Pictorial History* (Norfolk, 1989); Thomas C. Parramore, Peter C. Stewart, and Tommy L. Bogger, *Norfolk: The First Four Centuries* (Charlottesville, 1994).]

PETER WALLENSTEIN

See also **SUPP:** Virginia.

VIRGIN ISLANDS. By the 1970s economic and social change was under way in the U.S. Virgin Islands—Saint Thomas, Saint Croix, and Saint John. The once-dominant sugar industry ceased production in 1966, and within a few years virtually all other agriculture had disappeared, except for a few small-scale fruit and vegetable farms on Saint Croix. Agriculture and commercial fishing gave way to tourism, especially on Saint Thomas and Saint John, and to petrochemical and aluminum production on Saint Croix. Displaced native farmers and fishers resented the influx of migrants from the U.S. mainland, Puerto Rico, and other Caribbean islands who came to take the new industrial and tourist-related jobs. These arrivals helped swell the population from 63,000 in 1970 to 102,000 in 1990. High-living tourists, mostly white, incurred the wrath of natives influenced by the contemporary U.S. and Caribbean black power movement. A wave of violent crimes against tourists broke out during the administration (1971–1975) of the first elected governor of the U.S. Virgin Islands, Republican Melvin H. Evans, a native black physician. Eight persons, seven of them white, were murdered at Fountain Valley Golf Club on Saint Croix in September 1972, a crime for which five members of the Nation of Islam were convicted. More than a dozen other whites died during the next two years in apparently racially motivated crimes on Saint Croix. The situation was less tense on Saint Thomas and Saint John, but all the islands suffered drastic reductions in tourist revenues due to publicity about the crimes.

Governor Evans lost his reelection bid in 1974 and was succeeded by Cyril E. King of the populist Independent Citizens Movement (ICM). The new legislature, however, was composed of nine Democrats, five ICM members, and one Republican, which set the pattern for the next dozen years, with the ICM controlling the governorship, the Democrats dominating the legislature, and the Republicans marginalized. Attempts to restructure the territorial government failed as island voters rejected four proposed constitutions during the 1970s and 1980s, leaving the 1954 Organic Act in force. The propensity of territorial legislators to vote themselves hefty salary increases made voters leery of constitutional changes that would create a local bureaucracy to replace federal civil servants in the administration of the islands. Democrat Alexander A. Farrelly was elected governor in 1986 and soon launched a study of the territory's public administration needs, hiring Marion S. Barry, Jr., mayor of Washington, D.C., as a consultant. In 1989 it was revealed that $260,000 was squandered on lavish living by Washington city employees sent to advise Farrelly on personnel policy. Despite the scandal, the governor was reelected for another four-year term in 1990.

As the crime wave subsided, the tourist industry revived, although racial tensions remained beneath the surface and gave rise to sporadic outbreaks of violence throughout the 1980s, especially on Saint Croix. In 1989 Hurricane Hugo devastated that island. Saint Thomas and Saint John largely escaped the effects of the hurricane, and their sheltered waters continued to provide a prime playground for visiting yachts. In the early 1990s large cruise ships annually disembarked more than 1 million visitors at Saint Thomas, and increasing numbers of ecotourists were attracted to the surrounding coral reefs and the national park that covers two-thirds of the adjacent island of Saint John. In 1995 Hurricane Marilyn swept through the islands, causing damage amounting to more than $800 million and leaving more than half the structures on Saint Thomas destroyed or seriously damaged.

[Isaac Dookhan, *A History of the Virgin Islands of the United States* (Kingston, Jamaica, 1994); Earle B. Ottley, *Trials and Triumphs: The Long Road to Middle Class Society in the U.S. Virgin Islands* (Saint Thomas, 1982); Ralph M. Paiewonsky and Isaac Dookhan, *Memoirs of a Governor: A Man of the People* (New York, 1990).]

NEILL MACAULAY

VIROLOGY. *See* **Bacteriology and Virology.**

VIRTUAL REALITY refers to computer-generated, three-dimensional simulations that allow a participant to experience and interact with a setting or situation. In the most advanced forms of virtual reality, a participant wears a large headset that incorporates high-resolution video displays and audio speakers. The headphones provide the participant with the visual and auditory sensations of being immersed in the simulation. The participant also wears a special glove or body suit studded with sensors that monitor all movements by the participant. Data from the sensors are fed back into the computer, which modifies the simulation accordingly. For example, a simulation might include the image of an object in front of the participant. If the participant moves toward the object, the virtual reality system will change the participant's apparent angle of viewing the object. If the participant moves a hand to lift the object, the display is revised accordingly. In a more theoretical sense, virtual reality systems allow a participant to experience, navigate through, and manipulate cyberspace, a hypothetical area filled with imaginary structures and objects. The term "cyberspace" is often regarded as a synonym for virtual reality; the writer William Gibson first used it in his 1984 novel *Neuromancer*. By the mid-1990s virtual reality technology was limited to simulating the senses of sight and hearing. Virtual reality systems provided, for example, little or no sensation of weight when the participant is supposed to be carrying an object.

Computers have often been used to produce simulations, such as those used to train airline pilots. The advent of inexpensive but powerful computers, combined with the development of sophisticated computer graphics techniques, has enabled virtual reality systems to operate more quickly and to generate more detailed simulations, adding to the reality of the experience. A major use for virtual reality technology is likely to be entertainment; it can provide consumers with a choice of exotic, surreal, or breathtaking experiences without the need to take any physical risk. Virtual reality technology also can be employed for more serious ends. Astronauts at the National

Aeronautics and Space Administration used virtual reality devices as part of their training for the 1993 space shuttle flight, during which they repaired the flawed Hubble Space Telescope. Experts at the Department of Energy use a virtual reality version of a nuclear weapon in a shipping container to train emergency workers to handle trucking accidents involving such weapons. Another application of virtual reality technology is telepresence, or giving the participant a sensation of being in a distant location. Telepresence systems allow a physician in a hospital to perform emergency surgery on a soldier by remote control while the soldier is still on the battlefield, rather than having to wait for the soldier to be transported to the hospital. Telepresence can also be used to operate robotic rovers on the moon or on Mars for scientific purposes or for profit-making entertainment ventures.

[Michael Heim, *The Metaphysics of Virtual Reality* (New York, 1993); Howard Rheingold, *Virtual Reality* (New York, 1991).]

VINCENT KIERNAN

VOICE OF AMERICA (VOA) is a multilingual radio broadcasting service begun in 1942 and administered since 1953 by the United States Information Agency (USIA), known from 1978 to 1982 as the International Communications Agency. The agency is an organization responsible for the dissemination of U.S. policy and information to foreign countries. In administering the VOA, the director of the USIA reports to the secretary of state and the president of the United States. Under its congressionally mandated charter, the VOA seeks to broadcast reliable news stories, present a balanced view of U.S. culture, and report on U.S. policy. Programming is intended for non-U.S. audiences, and under provisions of the Smith-Mundt Act (1948) and a clarifying amendment in 1972 programs may not be broadcast within the United States without congressional approval. VOA broadcasts have been blocked by communications services in some countries, which have criticized its programming as anticommunist propaganda, but the agency has continued to receive support from Congress and U.S. presidents into the early post–cold war years. Voice of America continued its work in the 1990s with programs ranging from the promotion of democracy to the war on drugs. Its programs reach an estimated 130 million people. In 1983 VOA established the International Broadcast Training Center in Washington to train broadcasters from developing countries and to demonstrate the value of a free press. In

1985 VOA founded Radio Marti for broadcasting to Cuba, and in 1990 it expanded efforts to deliver uncensored news to that nation with the establishment of TV Marti. In 1987 VOA began programming aimed at drug addiction and narcotics trafficking.

[Holly Cowan Shulman, *The Voice of America: Propaganda and Democracy, 1941–1945* (Madison, Wis., 1990); Thomas C. Sorensen, *The Word War: The Story of American Propaganda* (New York, 1968).]

KERRY A. BATCHELDER

VOLCANOES are mountains with a central tube from which molten material from deep within the earth can spew under the appropriate conditions. Volcanoes have existed for geologic eons but many are no longer active. The number of volcanoes worldwide in the mid-1990s viewed by earth scientists as active, that is, that could possibly erupt, was about 500. Volcanoes are usually located at the junction of the earth's lithospheric plates. In the United States, most active volcanoes are located in the state of Hawaii, which consists of a group of islands formed by earlier volcanic eruptions, or in Alaska; a relatively inactive zone occurs on the West Coast of the continental United States. The two principal volcanoes in the United States are Mauna Loa and Kilauea on Hawaii Island in the Hawaiian island chain. Mauna Loa is the world's largest volcano. Its most recent eruptions occurred in 1975 and 1984. Kilauea is in almost continuous eruption, notable events occurring in 1977, 1984, 1986, and 1990. Alaskan eruptions occurred in 1986, involving an unnamed volcano on Augustine Island in Cook Inlet, 180 miles southwest of Anchorage; in 1989, when Mount Redoubt, along Cook Inlet 115 miles southwest of Anchorage, erupted; and in 1992, when Mount Spurr erupted. Although not in the United States, Mount Pinatubo in the Philippines, which erupted in 1991, had a significant cooling effect on U.S. climate for several years as a result of the ash projected into the stratosphere. Eruptions in the lower forty-eight states are rare but certainly not unknown. The eruption of Mount Saint Helens in Washington State in 1980 was widely publicized. Despite dire predictions, and the fact that a minor eruption occurred in 1990, the area surrounding Mount Saint Helens has largely recovered from the effects of the 1980 eruption. Two volcanic observatories exist in the United States. One was established on Kilauea in 1912, the second oldest in the world. (The oldest is in Italy on Vesuvius.) Following the eruption of Mount Saint Helens in 1980, an observatory was established there.

[Robert W. Decker, *Mountains of Fire: The Nature of Volcanoes* (New York, 1991); Alwyn Scarth, *Volcanoes* (College Station, Tex., 1994).]

NANCY M. GORDON

See also **SUPP:** Alaska; Hawaii; Mount Saint Helens.

VOLUNTEER ARMY. Throughout most of its history, the United States has relied on volunteers to fill the ranks of its military forces, resorting to conscription only for brief periods in times of great peril. The cold war marked a departure from that tradition. Beginning in 1948 the drafting of young males—a system known as Selective Service—became the preferred means of sustaining the military establishment. By the late 1960s, however, perceived inequities in the draft and opposition to the Vietnam War had undermined the legitimacy of the Selective Service system. To undercut the antiwar movement, President Richard M. Nixon in 1972 announced that he would abolish the draft. Although Selective Service legislation remained on the books and eighteen-year-old U.S. males continued to register for the draft, monthly draft calls were reduced to zero. The military establishment created by this shift in policy was known as the All-Volunteer Force or the Volunteer Army. Throughout the 1970s efforts to attract recruits in the quantity and quality required achieved only mixed success, and these difficulties prompted critics to question the feasibility of relying exclusively on volunteers. In the 1980s, however, recruiting methods and the quality of recruits improved. Several factors contributed to that turnaround: improved pay and benefits; skillful marketing of the armed forces; expanded career opportunities for women; and the fading memory of Vietnam. By the late 1980s and early 1990s, a string of U.S. military successes—most notably in the Gulf War of 1991—seemed to vindicate Nixon's decision to revert to the volunteer tradition.

[William Bowman et al., *The All-Volunteer Force After a Decade* (New York, 1986); John Whiteclay Chambers, *To Raise an Army* (New York, 1987); Richard Halloran, *Serving America: Prospects for the Volunteer Force* (New York, 1988).]

ANDREW J. BACEVICH

See also **SUPP:** Draft.

VOLUNTEERISM, broadly defined as socially beneficiary activities by individuals and groups that are noncompulsory and not profit oriented, has become more significant since the 1970s, with increasing numbers of people contributing time and expertise to community organizations, mutual aid societies, and social welfare programs. As a national phenomenon volunteerism dates back to World War I, when Herbert Hoover and others encouraged individuals and especially businesses to cooperate in such wartime activities as food rationing and price controls. When volunteerism failed during the Great Depression its reputation diminished, only to be temporarily rescued during World War II. In addition to being associated with national cooperation efforts, volunteerism since the nineteenth century has denoted the unpaid philanthropic, social service, and political work of American women. The recession of the early 1970s and the subsequent ebbs and flows of the national economy led to an increasing reliance on technology, which resulted in a greater need for more highly trained workers. Unemployment plagued the economy, straining public assistance and social service programs. When the great numbers of children born in the decade following World War II entered the workforce in the 1970s, jobs were often unavailable for them. The jobs that were available often required training that traditional educational institutions could not provide.

Volunteerism became one solution to these many social challenges. A few government programs supporting volunteer activity had been created in the 1960s, most notably the Peace Corps, Volunteers in Service to America (VISTA), the Foster Grandparents Program, and the Retired Senior Volunteer Program (RSVP). These programs set the stage for President Richard M. Nixon to inaugurate a major national volunteer force. In 1971 a new governmental agency, ACTION, was created to coordinate the existing programs and encourage participation on a national level. At the same time a nongovernment agency, the National Center for Voluntary Action, was created by Congress to centralize and promote volunteerism throughout the country. Older workers, who were increasingly encouraged to make way for younger employees by taking early retirement, were targeted as an important volunteer pool for community-based and public-sector social programs. Volunteerism by the young was emphasized as a solution to the need for both service to the community and specialized training not provided by the educational system. Since the 1970s "service learning" components have been incorporated into elementary, high school, and college curricula.

Aimed at decentralizing government welfare functions, the federalist policies of Presidents Ronald Reagan and George Bush in the 1980s continued the trend of the previous decade. Both administrations heralded community volunteerism as the ideal solution to social problems, and Reagan and Bush believed that cuts in government social services would stimulate voluntary community service. The leaders of many volunteer organizations, however, stated that voluntary efforts could not compensate for federal cuts. Volunteerism was also a significant concern of President Bill Clinton, who emphasized community service, the integration of education with labor needs, and grass-roots organizing against crime and other social problems. In 1993 Congress passed President Clinton's plan allowing students to repay federal college loans through community service. In the 1990s volunteer labor became an entrenched sector of the economy wherein volunteers engaged in "co-production" along with traditional public- and private-sector providers.

[Susan J. Ellis and Katherine H. Noyes, *By the People: A History of American Volunteers* (San Francisco, 1990); Jon Van Til, *Mapping the Third Sector: Voluntarism in a Changing Social Economy* (New York, 1988).]

JULIET NIEHAUS

See also **DAH:** ACTION; **SUPP:** Peace Corps.

W–Z

WACO SIEGE (1993). The deaths of four federal agents and seventy-eight members of the Branch Davidian religious group during a fifty-one-day siege of their commune headquarters outside Waco, Texas, provoked widespread controversy over the use of force in dealing with dissident sects. A botched and bloody attempt on Feb. 28, 1993, to arrest the group's leader, David Koresh, on a weapons charge led to stalemate until U.S. Attorney General Janet Reno ordered the use of force on Apr. 19 to end the standoff. Fire engulfed "Ranch Apocalypse," killing seventy-two, including Koresh and seventeen children. Although some surviving members of the sect were tried for manslaughter and found not guilty, they were convicted of lesser charges and received extremely harsh sentences.

[Martin King and Marc Breault, *Preacher of Death: The Shocking Inside Story of David Koresh and the Waco Siege* (New York, 1993); Dick J. Reavis, *The Ashes of Waco: An Investigation* (New York, 1996); James D. Tabor and Eugene V. Gallagher, *Why Waco?: Cults and the Battle for Religious Freedom in America* (Berkeley, Calif., 1996).]

BRUCE J. EVENSON

WAGES AND SALARIES. From the end of World War II to 1973, average wage and salary earnings in the United States, adjusted for inflation, more than doubled for men working in full-time, year-round employment, from $15,257 to $30,578 (in 1987 constant dollars). This favorable situation reflected U.S. dominance in global markets and a large base of high-wage manufacturing jobs. The pattern in wages and salaries since 1973 has been much slower growth and significant declines for certain groups within the population. Young males (ages 25–34) with a high school education or less have seen the greatest drop in earnings, as many manufacturing jobs disappeared because of foreign competition and greater productivity. In 1973, 64 percent of such persons earned annual incomes of $20,000 or more (1987 dollars); by 1986 the percentage was down to 40 percent. Before the 1980s the difference in earnings between college-educated and non–college-educated persons had been narrowing, as the first wave of the baby-boom generation born after World War II flooded into higher education and then the job market. Since 1980, however, the gap has steadily widened. Men with at least a four-year degree represented the only group in manufacturing to see an increase in real earnings between 1973 and 1986. Productivity gains were much slower to translate into job reductions in the service sector of the economy.

For women the change in wage and salary patterns was different. The increasing proportion of married women working full-time caused average female earnings to rise at a faster rate than male earnings since 1973. The shift from manufacturing to service-sector employment was of relatively greater advantage to women. Although they continued to earn less than men, the difference was shrinking, from a ratio of women's to men's earnings of 57 percent in 1973 to 85 percent in 1993. While educational level became a more powerful determinant of income level, even women with five years of college education earned only 69 percent of what was earned by men with the same amount of schooling. Another group whose salaries became the object of much public attention in the 1980s was that of corporate business executives. Their average incomes rose dramatically. In 1980 the ratio of a chief executive officer's (CEO) salary to that of a factory worker was 42:1. By 1991 this ratio had risen to 104:1, far higher than in other industrial countries. The average CEO earned more than $1 million in salary plus other forms of compensation.

For some commentators the image of a "vanishing middle class" emerged out of this economic data. The most rapidly growing segments of the population were families making less than $20,000 or more than $50,000 a year. While per capita income continued to increase after 1973, this was largely because of more women entering the labor force and a lower birth rate, trends expected to level off and thus have less impact on income levels. Stagnation of wages and salaries was identified as a key factor behind public resistance to higher taxes, the large federal budget deficit, and low rates of personal savings. Proposed solutions ranged from immigration restriction to improved education and job training.

[Frank Levy and Richard Michel, *The Economic Future of American Families: Income and Wealth Trends* (Washington, D.C., 1991); Lawrence Mishel and Jared Bernstein, *The State of Working America, 1994–1995* (Armonk, N.Y., 1994).]

JOHN B. WEAVER

See also **SUPP:** Poverty; Unemployment.

WALL STREET. No other street or location in the United States evokes the idea of money, financial power, and capitalism as does Wall Street, the financial district of capitalism, and that was never more true than during the 1980s and early 1990s, when a series of "bull" markets sent stock and bond prices on an upward spiral, doubling or tripling prices and encouraging Americans to invest. Interestingly, however, by this time New York City's Wall Street no longer was the epicenter of the nation's finance; there were also financial markets in London, Frankfurt, Tokyo, and Sidney. Smaller exchanges appeared in Western and Eastern Europe and in Latin America, all attracting money away from Wall Street. Computers, fax machines, and electronic wire transfers made location largely irrelevant. In minutes, trades and deals could be executed and money moved anywhere. Because of world differences in time, it also became possible to trade around the clock. A sign that every street in the world was becoming a competitor to Wall Street was the loss of occupants in prestigious buildings on "the street"; office vacancies were said to amount to eight empty buildings as large as the Empire State Building.

All the while there were new kinds of investors, new products, and new rules. Perhaps the greatest factor in change was the tremendous influx and influence of institutional money in all its configurations—public and private pension funds, corporate treasuries, and mutual funds. The mutual funds took on strength during bull markets, profoundly changing investing while enriching millions of middle-class Americans who previously had shied away from taking market risks. Everything seemed to be changing. Consider what happened with mutual funds in the 1980s and early 1990s. First offered in Boston in 1924, such investments initially had attracted little investor interest because growth was hampered by a legality—the "prudent man" rule obligated investment managers to preserve capital and avoid risks. It was a play-it-safe approach in which investing was done with an eye to not losing money rather than to achieving growth. Quantitative economic research developed ideas about managing portfolios of risk. Investments could be grouped and managed so that losses in one investment likely would be offset by gains in others. This key development—assisted by the growing ability to number-crunch data—liberated money managers. Mutual funds offered a convenient way for middle-income investors to obtain part of the riches being generated in financial markets at home and abroad in emerging markets. For investments of as little as $50 or $100, investors could buy into diversified portfolios. As stocks soared, mutual funds swelled, with millions of Americans moving money out of passbook savings and certificates of deposits. More money meant more funds. In 1980 there were roughly 500 mutual funds, with a total asset value of $135 billion. By 1995 there were about 5,300 mutual funds with $2.2 trillion in assets. One-third of U.S. households owned part of at least one fund.

The funds of the Boston-based Fidelity Investments firm illustrates the vast growth of mutual funds. Founded in 1946, the firm grew into a financial powerhouse. By 1994 it managed assets of nearly $300 billion, making it comparable to some of the largest banks. Its Magellan Fund, managed by Peter Lynch, generated double-digit returns and grew into the nation's largest mutual fund. Lynch himself became a star, writing best-selling books on investing, making television appearances, and finding his opinions regularly quoted by financial writers. It was, of course, difficult for fund managers to outperform the market. Lynch's successes, as well as the even greater investing success of Warren Buffett, an Omaha investor who ran Berkshire Hathaway, called into question the prevailing academic theory about Wall Street, called the efficient market theory (EMT), which claimed that Lynch and Buffett's methods of examining company performance and prospects in hopes of finding an undervalued stock were worthless. EMT maintained that a stock could neither be overpriced nor underpriced; each day the market correctly set a stock's price because the price reflected all the information about a company known that day. A popular book by Burton Malkiel, *A Random Walk Down Wall Street*, introduced EMT to the general public in the early 1970s.

EMT became the accepted gospel as classic market economics regained exalted status in political, academic, social, and economic circles, but holes in EMT began to pop open. The *Wall Street Journal* ran a six-month contest comparing the performance of four stocks selected by investment professionals to four stocks—expected to represent EMT—selected by throwing darts at a stock table pinned to a dart board. The experts, however, beat the dart board, albeit by a narrow margin. Meanwhile, Lynch, Buffett, and other investment managers, such as John Neff and John Templeton, punched more holes in the EMT by repeatedly outperforming the market by large margins. Nonprofessionals also gave EMT fits. A group of sixteen Illinois women—ages forty-one to eighty-seven and known as the Beardstown Ladies—created an investment strategy that generated an annual return of 23 percent between 1983 and 1994, outperforming the Standard & Poor's 500 index for the same period.

The flow of money into mutual funds helped sustain a strong bull market that started in October 1990 and by spring 1995 had become the third longest such market in Wall Street history. It was exceeded only by the six-year bull market from 1924 to 1929 and the five-year market from August 1982 to August 1987. The market of the early 1990s pushed the Dow Jones Industrial Average (DJIA) ever upward. Quoted in points instead of dollars, the index reflects the closing stock prices of thirty widely held companies. The companies represented one-fifth of the New York Stock Exchange's total value. In November 1972 the Dow Jones broke the 1,000-point barrier, although it collapsed during the recession associated with the oil embargo imposed by the Organization of Petroleum Exporting Countries. It was not until 1987 that the DJIA broke 2,000. The 3,000 barrier was broken in 1991 and the 4,000 and 5,000 barriers in 1995.

Wall Street became populated by aggressive, take-no-prisoners business school graduates attracted by the prospect of getting rich. Much money was made in corporate takeovers in which bankers, accountants, attorneys, and management made big fees and substantial bonuses. Buffett regularly criticized chief executives who "possess an abundance of animal spirits and ego" that send them hunting for deals. "When such a CEO is encouraged by his advisers to make deals," Buffett said, "he responds much as would a teenage boy who is encouraged by his father to have a normal sex life." He added: "It's not a push he needs." Often the deals left companies awash with debt, forcing them to divest holdings, fire employees, or plunge into bankruptcy to protect themselves from creditors. James Grant, writer of an influential New York investment newsletter, noted at the time (like Buffett employing a sexual metaphor) that "the 1980s are to debt what the 1960s were to sex."

Unfortunately, the market craze had a darker side. The get-rich mentality of the 1980s led some Wall Streeters to engage in criminal practices such as insider trading. The scandals of the decade landed some of the nation's best-known financiers in jail, including Michael Milken, who had pioneered the use of junk bonds in corporate takeovers, and Ivan Boesky, who specialized in securities arbitrage. Prosecutors snared a *Wall Street Journal* reporter who was trading stocks based on information gathered from a broker who was a source for stories. The scandals provided grist for a movie, *Wall Street* (1987), directed by Oliver Stone, in which a character similar to Milken and Boesky proclaimed that "greed is good."

The stock market's upward climb was not without fast and dangerous falls. One of those was the Oct. 19, 1987, market crash, known as Black Monday. That day the exchanges almost broke under the trading volumes. The DJIA plunged a record 508 points—a 22.6 percent decline. It was the largest single-day decline in percentage terms in stock market history. The crash, which unregulated computer-directed sell orders helped accelerate, left investors wary, but they surprised observers of the market, who expected smaller investors to cash out. Instead, money was shifted into less aggressive stock investments, where the cash stayed while investors waited for the market to improve. Eventually the markets shrugged off the losses. Volume grew from 26.2 billion shares in 1982 to 103.4 billion shares in 1992. Much trading shifted from the New York Stock Exchange (NYSE) to the National Association of Securities Dealers Automated Quotations (NASDAQ). In 1983 the NYSE had 55 percent of the 39.5 billion shares traded on the U.S. exchanges, with NASDAQ responsible for 40 percent and the American Stock Exchange for 5 percent. By 1992 NASDAQ's share percentage had increased to nearly half. The tradition-bound NYSE found itself challenged by NASDAQ, which advertised itself as "the market for the next hundred years." Advertisements featured NASDAQ's stellar stocks, many of them high-technology companies that went public during the 1970s and 1980s, including Microsoft, the software corporation; Apple Computer, maker of the Macintosh computer; and Intel, whose microprocessors powered personal computers.

Throughout these years of change there was a dropping away of government and exchange rules, known as deregulation. The abolition of rules was international. In 1973 a nearly forty-year period of fixed rates for currency exchanges under the Bretton Woods Agreement of 1944 ended when major Western governments allowed currencies to be traded against each other. Supply and demand would determine the value of each currency. Freely traded currencies opened up a whole new arena for markets in which to speculate or protect against changes in currency values. Trading currencies—the U.S. dollar, Japanese yen, German mark, French franc, English pound—linked what previously were largely separate and isolated financial markets across the world. A second and this time internal U.S. deregulation occurred in 1975, when Congress forced the New York Stock Exchange to end its 183-year-old practice of fixed brokerage commissions, a reform that the Securities and Exchange Commission and others both inside and outside the exchange had pushed for years. Announced on May 1, the decision was dubbed Mayday—the international distress-call signal. For some brokerages it was just that, but others like the new brokerage house of Charles Schwab thrived. Schwab established a brokerage that offered no financial advice, merely trades at rock-bottom prices. Interestingly, the first office opened in San Francisco, not on Wall Street.

A landmark in U.S. financial deregulation was the elimination in the early 1980s of Regulation Q, established by the Federal Reserve in 1933, which had limited the interest rates banks could pay on deposits. In 1966 the regulation had been extended to savings and loans. With its termination in 1982, banks and thrifts found they had to pay higher interest to attract depositors. Savers woke up to rates, looking harder at where they deposited money. Banks and thrifts had to compete for business—paying more for deposits and earning less.

The 1980s and early 1990s saw a constant expansion of new investments, and in the early 1990s a novelty known as derivatives began to raise questions. It was not easy to understand, even for professionals. In 1994 and 1995 professionals who invested heavily in derivatives, investment instruments tied to interest rates, incurred large losses when rates rose. Wealthy Orange County in southern California filed for protection from bankruptcy in 1994 because of $1.3 billion in losses in its investment in derivatives. A twenty-eight-year-old British trader in Singapore lost $1.5 billion in 1994, pushing the 233-year-old House of Baring Bank in London into bankruptcy. Also in 1994 a government bond trader at Kidder Peabody was accused of fabricating $350 million in phony profits to boost his year-end bonus; Kidder claimed it was unaware of what was going on, but was so damaged by the deals that it was sold to another brokerage. Losses resulted in calls for new regulations, although the general experience was that regulations never could keep abreast with innovations. Moreover, Wall Street regulations only encouraged trading in other markets, often those abroad.

[Marshall E. Blume, Jeremy J. Siegel, and Dan Rottenberg, *Revolution on Wall Street: The Rise and Decline of the New York Stock Exchange* (New York, 1993); Paul Gibson, *Bear Trap: Why Wall Street Doesn't Work* (New York, 1993); Michael Lewis, *Liar's Poker: Rising Through the Wreckage on Wall Street* (New York, 1989); Joseph Nocera, *A Piece of the Action: How the Middle Class Joined the Money Class* (New York, 1994).]

THOMAS G. GRESS
BRENT SCHONDELMEYER

See also **SUPP:** Banking and Finance; Black Monday Stock Market Crash; Crime, White-Collar; Deregulation; Financial Exchanges; Financial Services Industry; Junk Bonds.

WARD'S COVE PACKING COMPANY V. ATONIO, 490 U.S. 642 (1989), briefly redefined the nature of the disparate-impact theory of employment discrimination. Since 1971 courts had been following the standards of the *Griggs* v. *Duke Power Company* case for disparate-impact situations. If a plaintiff could show that an employer action harmed a protected group then the employer had the burden of proving that its actions were a business necessity. The *Ward's Cove* case was widely regarded as shifting the burden of proof to employees, making it harder to prove discrimination. The *Ward's Cove* plaintiffs (nonwhite employees) sued the Alaskan salmon canning company on the basis of a disparate impact theory, providing statistical evidence on the disparity in the racial composition of jobholders in skilled and in unskilled cannery work, thereby establishing a prima facie case. The Supreme Court held that the plaintiffs had to do more than show disparate impact; they had to prove the specific relationship between employer practices and a discriminatory outcome. In addition, employers no longer had to prove that their actions were based on business necessity; a less stringent "business justification" standard would suffice as a defense. Critics argued that the reasoning and conclusion in this case, and other recent Supreme Court decisions of the 1980s, eroded civil rights. The outcry stimulated civil rights groups to seek substantive legislative amendments, an effort that ultimately succeeded with the passage of the Civil Rights Act of 1991. That legislation overturned the decision, restoring the *Griggs* standards for disparate-impact suits.

[Vincent J. Apruzzese, "Selected Recent Developments in EEO Law: The Civil Rights Act of 1991, Sexual Harassment, and the Emerging Role of ADR," *Labor Law Journal* 43 (June 1992).]

GILBERT J. GALL

See also **SUPP:** Civil Rights Act of 1991; *Griggs* v. *Duke Power Company.*

WAR MEMORIALS. The Minuteman Statue, Liberty Bell, Tomb of the Unknowns, U.S.S. *Arizona* Memorial, Rough Riders Monument, Holocaust Memorial, and Vietnam War Memorial are all artifacts that reflect the importance of conflicts in American memory. The National Park Service maintains in pristine condition the memorials and sites of the American Revolution and Civil War. The American Battle Monuments Commission preserves the cemeteries, landscapes, and memorial chapels of Americans who died in the two world wars. Smaller conflicts, such as the Korean War and the War of 1812, have fewer shrines. Belated recognition of African Americans and women killed in war suggests that earlier memorials were a reflection of American prejudice as well as sacrifice.

[James M. Mayo, *War Memorials as Political Landscape* (New York, 1988).]

J. GARRY CLIFFORD

See also **SUPP:** Vietnam War Memorial.

WAR POWERS ACT (1973), officially the War Powers Resolution. According to the Constitution, the president as chief executive is also commander-in-chief of U.S. armed forces, but the Constitution explicitly assigns to Congress the authority to declare war. Rather than distinguishing clearly between the authority to initiate war and the authority to wage it, this effort to distribute war-making authority has fostered ambiguity and political controversy. In practice, chief executives have employed the U.S. military without congressional mandate virtually as a matter of routine throughout much of U.S. history, especially during the cold war. The purposes for which presidents have deployed U.S. forces range from a show of force to minor hostilities to large-scale warfare. Although such actions have not been uniformly popular, the existence of a consensus regarding U.S. foreign policy generally muted any complaint about presidents exceeding their constitutional prerogatives.

That consensus collapsed with the Vietnam War. Presidents Lyndon B. Johnson and Richard M. Nixon cited the Tonkin Gulf Resolution of August 1964 as congressional authorization for involvement in Vietnam and escalation of the U.S. role in the war. The conflict proceeded without benefit of any formal declaration of war, becoming increasingly unpopular as it dragged on. Within the federal government, opposition to the war was lodged in the Congress. Critics attributed the costly U.S. involvement in the Vietnam War to a failure to prevent successive presidents from usurping authority that rightly belonged to the legislative branch. This perception provoked calls for a reassertion of congressional prerogatives to check future presidential adventurism. Such thinking culminated in passage of the War Powers Resolution of November 1973, which was passed despite President Nixon's veto. The resolution directed the president to consult with Congress prior to introducing U.S. forces into hostilities; it required the president to report to Congress all nonroutine deployments of military forces within forty-eight hours of their occurrence; and it mandated that forces committed to actual or imminent hostilities by presidential order would be withdrawn within sixty days unless Congress declared war, passed legislation authorizing the use of U.S. forces, or extended the deadline. The sixty-day time limit could be extended to ninety days if the president certified that additional time was needed to complete the withdrawal of U.S. forces.

Heralded as a congressional triumph, the War Powers Resolution proved to be of limited use. Presidents continued to insist that the resolution was an unconstitutional infringement on executive authority. Time and again they circumvented or disregarded its provisions: Gerald Ford in 1975 at the time of the *Mayaguez* operation; Jimmy Carter in 1980 with the Desert One hostage rescue attempt; Ronald Reagan in 1983 with the intervention in Grenada and in 1986 with the air attack on Libya; and George Bush with the 1989 invasion of Panama. Even the U.S. military response to the Iraqi invasion of Kuwait in August 1990 was launched without benefit of congressional mandate. President Bush relied on executive authority in ordering the U.S. buildup of 500,000 troops in the Persian Gulf. When it came to legitimizing his action, the president showed more interest in securing the endorsement of the United Nations Security Council than of the U.S. Congress. It was only when U.S. forces were in place and the decision to use force had effectively been made that Bush consulted Congress, even then acting less for constitutional than for political reasons. On Jan. 12, 1991, Congress narrowly passed a resolution authorizing Bush to do what he clearly intended to do anyway—forcibly eject Iraqi troops from Kuwait. When four days later Operation Desert Storm began, the usefulness of the War Powers Resolution seemed more problematic than ever and the goal of restoring a division of war-making powers appeared ever more elusive.

ANDREW J. BACEVICH

See also **DAH:** War, Declaration of; War and the Constitution; War Powers of the President; **SUPP:** Grenada Invasion; Gulf War of 1991; Panama Invasion.

WASHINGTON, D.C., or the District of Columbia, came of age in a political sense during the mid-1970s, a time of high expectations. In 1973 Congress approved the Home Rule Act, giving the 700,000 residents the right to elect local officials, including a mayor and city council. Since 1874 congressional committees, often run by avowed southern segregationists, had controlled the nation's capital, to the detriment of the large African-American population. While the Home Rule Act continued Congress's control over the city's budget and laws, the new era ushered in opportunities for local politics and perhaps eventually statehood. By 1976 social changes begun in the late 1950s had created a polarized city. Many middle-class families, white and black, moved to the suburbs of Maryland or Virginia. The remaining white residents—who made up 30 percent of the population—generally were wealthy liberals who lived west of Rock Creek Park in the city's northwest quadrant. Middle-class blacks lived between the park

and the Anacostia River. East of the Anacostia the residents were predominantly poor and black. The races and classes rarely mixed, either in social or business settings. The district's story had become a tale of five cities: the federal city of government and monuments that attracted millions of tourists; the international city of embassies and diplomats; white neighborhoods of lawyers, journalists, and government officials; stable black communities of physicians, clerks, and government officials; and poor black neighborhoods.

Could a new political system, dominated by African Americans, bring the classes and races together and lift the poor? Marion Barry, Jr., promised to do just that in 1978 when he won a slim victory in the crucial, three-way Democratic primary and then scored a landslide in the general election to become the city's second mayor under home rule. He cut a dashing figure as a former civil rights activist, appealing to white liberals and the city's underclass. The city's African-American elite rejected him, but they were a minority. In his first term, he opened the doors of the District Building to the entire city and brought services to people who had been neglected for years. After 1982, when Barry was elected to his second four-year term, the nation's capital experienced a commercial real estate boom that created local millionaires and transformed the central business area. Pennsylvania Avenue—between the Capitol and the White House—was rejuvenated. Investors from Toronto to Tokyo bought high-priced ground in America's capital city. The downtown blossomed with new restaurants, hotels, and nightclubs. The revenues from the building boom, however, were never applied to the city's pressing problems of poverty, a dismal school system, and high infant mortality. Barry instead used the money to create a bloated bureaucracy and wasted millions of dollars. His administration never "took the boards off" public housing, as he had promised. Public housing complexes festered and became breeding grounds for drugs and violence, just as Barry cut funds for the police department.

By the late 1980s the U.S. capital city had earned the infamous label "murder capital." More people were killed in proportion to the population in the District of Columbia than in Detroit, Miami, or New York. Drug gangs fought over the right to control sections of the city that were awash in crack cocaine. In 1991, 489 were slain. It was a murder rate essentially in black, not white: few whites were killed, and fewer than five murders occurred in white neighborhoods.

As the city succumbed to crack, so did Mayor Barry, by then in his third term. His drug habit was no secret. Metropolitan police had covered up for him for years, but in 1989 a team of local police and federal agents conducted an investigation and set up a "sting" operation to catch Barry in the act. On Jan. 18, 1990, they made a videotape, later shown around the world, of Barry drawing on a crack pipe. Convicted of one misdemeanor count of possession, he was sentenced to a six-month jail term.

The District of Columbia suffered but there was hope once again in the election of 1990, which brought Sharon Pratt Dixon to office as mayor. A sparkling and articulate African-American utility executive, she was accepted on Capitol Hill as a "breath of fresh air" but had a difficult time governing. She ran up deficits, alienated supporters, and couldn't keep professional football's Washington Redskins from moving to the suburbs. Meanwhile, in the early 1990s the district's more prosperous blacks began streaming out of the city because of high crime and poor schools, leaving it with fewer taxpayers and role models. Hispanic immigrants from Central America began taking up residence in the Adams Morgan and Mount Pleasant neighborhoods, and Korean merchants took over inner-city stores. The city began to take on an ethnic tone, but the population had plummeted to 570,000. The failure of local government to control spending and deliver services seemed to be holding back the city's progress. Toward the end of 1994 and throughout 1995 Congress began taking back power that it had given to the district in the Home Rule Act twenty years before. It installed a federal control board to take control of the city's purse strings. Meanwhile, Barry staged a miraculous comeback by returning from jail and running successfully for mayor in 1994, which only served to deepen the city's crisis and inflame Congress. Statehood for the District of Columbia was all but dead.

[Constance McLaughlin Green, *Washington: A History of the Capital, 1800–1950* (Princeton, N.J., 1976); Harry S. Jaffe and Tom Sherwood, *Dream City: Race, Power, and the Decline of Washington, D.C.* (New York, 1994).]

HARRY S. JAFFE

WASHINGTON, STATE OF. Two events in 1974 served as harbingers of what would prove the predominant factor in the life of Washington in the modern era. Host to two previous world's fairs in Seattle in 1909 and 1962, Washington opened its third fair in Spokane in 1974. The theme for Expo '74 was the effect of human beings on the environment. Earlier

that year Judge George Boldt of the federal district court in Tacoma made what proved to be a landmark ruling in *United States* v. *Washington,* declaring that the state's Native American peoples were entitled to fish at all of their "usual and accustomed places," borrowing a phrase from treaties enacted in the 1850s. Indeed, the treaties used language stipulating that incoming American settlers could fish "in common with" Indians, from which Judge Boldt determined that the Native Americans' modern-day descendants were entitled to one-half of all of the harvestable catch. No event in Indian-white relations for the previous one hundred years superseded this decision in importance. A century or more of grievances originating in broken promises had led to a sequence of Indian demonstrations and counter-demonstrations along the banks of the Nisqually and Puyallup rivers in western Washington. This agitation, including occasional violent encounters between Indian and white fishermen and fisheries officials of the state of Washington, was brought to a crisis when the federal Department of Justice joined the Indians and sued the state. Not only were the tribes' treaty rights reaffirmed by Judge Boldt's decision (upheld by the Supreme Court in 1979), the one-half set-aside for native fishermen enhanced the competition among white commercial interests and sports fishermen for a resource increasingly recognized as being in rapid decline.

Developments in Washington during the previous forty years were the telling influence in this story. Dams built on the Columbia and Snake rivers and their many tributaries, plus increased urbanization, and particularly suburbanization in the Puget Sound lowlands, severely affected the environment. So critical had the situation become that by 1993 the Snake River salmon were on the verge of being listed as an endangered species.

The Spokane World's Fair and the Boldt decision served as more general indicators of the state of Washington's evolving environmental consciousness. The state's timber stands—the principal source of industrial employment from the time of American settlement in the 1840s until the late 1930s—became as much an environmental battleground as had the state's rivers and streams, and several concerns also brought an era of limits to the timber industry. One was the loss of scenic quality because of the clear-cutting of timber on privately held land—and more particularly the state's several national forests. Another was the damage to watersheds that such practices engendered. A third, emerging in the early

1990s, involved the northern spotted owl's survivability. Similarly, the environmental consequences of the Hanford Project near Richland in eastern Washington, site of the Manhattan Project's World War II plutonium facility, became a major public issue in the early 1980s. The Washington Public Power Supply System, an ambitious nuclear power plant consortium, defaulted on $2.25 billion in bond payments in 1983 because of large cost overruns associated with the construction of five nuclear power plants. This development, the largest municipal bond default in American history, soon was compounded by the end of the cold war and, accordingly, the diminished need for plutonium. Thousands of layoffs led to an economic crisis in the Richland area, the capital of Washington's nuclear industry. The state's evolving environmental consciousness, however, proved to be that locale's economic savior as federal, state, and community support for cleaning up the waste left from forty years' worth of nuclear production resulted in what is now the most expensive public works project in the state's history. In fiscal year 1994 alone, the federal government invested $1.6 billion in the clean-up effort, which was estimated to require decades to complete.

Concurrently, Washington from 1970 to 1990 developed a sizable tourism and hospitality industry, which surpassed the old staples of fishing and logging as a source of employment. An "attraction economy" of ski resorts, wineries, national parks, and modern museums supplanted the world of "wigwam" incinerators of sawmill waste and purse seine fishing nets. Washington proved to be an attractive destination for permanent residents as well as tourists. Population growth in the largest cities continued unabated, as did a few of the more rural areas, such as the San Juan Islands, an appealing destination for retirees from other regions, especially California. Seattle was regularly listed in the popular press as one of the nation's "most livable" cities.

Washington's population in 1970 stood at 3.4 million. By 1993 it was estimated to be 5.2 million. A leading factor in this growth was the great expansion of the Boeing Company's production of airplanes from 1985 to 1990 plus the emergence of a robust high-technology sector lead by the Microsoft Corporation. Despite repeated attempts to diversify the economy after the aerospace busts of the early 1970s and the 1980s, the most important factor in the economic health of the state remained the economic fortunes of Boeing.

The state of Washington's coming of age since the 1970s was reflected in the maturing of its arts and cultural scene. A particularly noteworthy and trend-setting arts phenomenon with its roots in Washington was the Art in Public Places program, resulting from legislation passed in 1974. Although this program engendered its share of controversy, many pieces of modern art were placed in Washington's schools and urban settings. Two of the nation's most respected architects earned commissions for the design and construction of the state's flagship cultural enterprises. A new downtown version of the Seattle Art Museum, credited to postmodernist Robert Venturi, opened in 1992. Charles Moore, also a postmodernist, won an international design competition for the new Washington State History Museum in Tacoma, for which ground was broken in December 1993.

The best-known development in Washington since 1970 was the volcanic eruption of Mount Saint Helens on May 18, 1980, which killed sixty people and reinforced in the minds of residents and observers how the natural environment of Washington continues to serve as a principal factor in shaping events in the state.

[Robert E. Ficken and Charles P. LeWarne, *Washington: A Centennial History* (Seattle, 1988); Carlos Schwantes et al., *Washington: Images of a State's Heritage* (Spokane, 1988).]

DAVID L. NICANDRI

See also **SUPP:** Environmental Movement; Mount Saint Helens; Nuclear Power; Seattle.

WASTE DISPOSAL. Societies have always had to deal with waste disposal, but what has been defined as waste, as well as its ultimate destination, has varied greatly over time. Large-scale waste disposal is primarily an urban issue because of the waste disposal needs of population concentrations and the material processing and production-type activities that go on in cities. Waste is often defined as "matter out of place" and can be understood, as the noted sanitary engineer Abel Wolman wrote, as part of a city's metabolic processes. Cities require materials to sustain their life processes and need to remove wastes resulting from consumption and processing to prevent "nuisance and hazard." Well into the nineteenth century, many U.S. cities lacked garbage and rubbish collection services. Cities often depended on animals such as pigs, goats, and cows, or even buzzards in southern cities, to consume slops and garbage tossed into the streets by residents. In the middle of the century, health concerns stimulated such larger cities as New York to experiment with collection, often by contracting out. Contractors and municipalities often discarded wastes into nearby waterways or placed them on vacant lots or the city fringe.

Rapid urbanization in the late-nineteenth century increased the volume of wastes and aroused concern over nuisances and hazards. Garbage had been viewed as a nuisance, but the public health movement, accompanied by widespread acceptance of anticontagionist theory, emphasized the rapid disposal of organic wastes to prevent epidemics. Municipalities were driven to consider collection, usually setting up their own services, granting contracts, or allowing householders to make private arrangements. By the late nineteenth century, cities were relying on contractors, although there were shifts between approaches. Cities apparently preferred contracting to municipal operation because of cost as well as the absence of a rationale for government involvement in a domain with many private operators.

During the first half of the twentieth century, municipal control over collection gradually increased to between 60 and 70 percent, largely for health and efficiency reasons. Just as they had moved from private to public provision of water because of concerns over inability of the private sector to protect against fire and illness, cities began to question leaving waste removal to contractors. Contractor collection was often disorganized, with frequent vendor changes, short-term contracts, and contractor reluctance to invest in equipment. Municipal reformers concluded that sanitation was too important to be left to profit-motivated contractors. Initially, responsibility went to departments of public health, but as the germ theory of disease replaced anticontagionism, control over the function shifted to public works departments. Garbage collection was increasingly viewed as an engineering rather than a public health problem, and municipal concern shifted from health to fire hazards and the prevention of nuisances such as odors and flies.

Changes in both composition of wastes (or solid wastes, as they were now called) and collection and disposal methods occurred after World War II. A major fraction of municipal solid wastes before the war had been ashes, but as coal was displaced by heating oil and natural gas, ashes became less important. The solid wastes generated by individuals did not decrease, however, because there were sharp rises in the amount of nonfood materials, such as packaging and glass. Another change occurred in regard to disposal

sites. Before the war cities had disposed of wastes in dumps, on pig farms (a form of recycling), by ocean dumping, or by incineration; a few cities used garbage reduction or composting. For nuisance and health reasons, cities found these methods unacceptable, and in the decades after 1945, they adopted the so-called sanitary landfill method of waste disposal, which involved the systematic placing of wastes in the ground using a technology such as a bulldozer or a bull clam shovel. The sanitary landfill, or tipping, had been widely used in Great Britain before the war. It was developed in the late 1930s by Jean Vincenz, director of public works in Fresno, California. Vincenz used the sanitary landfill to deal with solid wastes at army camps during the war. Public works and public health professionals and municipal engineers viewed the technique as a final solution to the waste disposal problem. Between 1945 and 1960 the number of fills increased from 100 to 1,400.

A further development, starting in the late 1950s, involved a rise in private contracting. Firms that provided economies of scale, sophisticated management, and efficient collection absorbed smaller companies and replaced municipal operations. Sharp rises in the costs of disposal as well as a desire to shift labor and operating costs to the private sector also played a role. In the 1980s private contracting grew rapidly because it was the most cost-effective method available.

In the 1960s the environmental movement raised questions about solid waste disposal and the safety of sanitary landfills, both in terms of the environment and health. Environmental regulations were strengthened by states in the 1950s, while the federal government followed with the Solid Waste Act in 1965 and the Resource Conservation and Recovery Act in 1976. Higher standards for landfills raised costs. Increasingly, society sought disposal methods such as recycling that were protective of health and environmentally benign. By the last decade of the twentieth century, as new techniques for utilizing recycled materials and controlling waste generation developed, society seemed on its way to a more sustainable balance; the tendency of Americans to consume ever-increasing amounts of goods, however, dampened the rate of improvement.

[Martin V. Melosi, *Garbage in the Cities: Refuse, Reform, and the Environment, 1880–1980* (College Station, Tex., 1981); William Rathje and Cullen Murphy, *Rubbish! The Archaeology of Garbage* (New York, 1992).]

JOEL A. TARR

See also **SUPP:** Hazardous Waste; Recycling.

WATERGATE, AFTERMATH OF. The term "Watergate" has resonated in America's collective consciousness since the scandals and crimes committed during the 1972 presidential election campaign by members of President Richard M. Nixon's administration became public. The exposé published by the *Washington Post,* which revealed that the burglary of National Democratic Party headquarters on June 17, 1972, at the Watergate apartment-office complex in Washington, D.C., was committed by employees of the Committee to Reelect the President, arguably encouraged investigative journalism and accentuated the adversarial relationship between government and media. Congress acted quickly after the Senate Watergate hearings in 1973 by enacting laws limiting executive control over foreign policy, notably the War Powers Act of 1973, passed in November over President Richard M. Nixon's veto shortly after what came to be called the "Saturday Night Massacre," when Nixon fired Special Watergate Prosecutor Archibald Cox. Congress enacted campaign finance reforms, conflict-of-interest legislation, stronger freedom of information statutes, and protection of privacy laws. The Ethics in Government Act of 1978 provided for judicially appointed special independent prosecutors to investigate executive wrongdoings.

The Iran-Contra affair of 1985–1986 during President Ronald Reagan's administration—with a similar cast of characters, embattled presidential aides, televised congressional hearings and special prosecutor—evoked a sense of Watergate déjà vu, although this time Congress stopped short of impeaching a popular president. The suffix "-gate" became a descriptive label to denote political scandals: "Koreagate" involved bribes of members of Congress by South Korean agents in 1976–1978; "Billygate" referred to President Jimmy Carter's brother Billy and his connection to the Libyan government; and "Iraqgate" concerned secret and illegal loans to Iraq by the administrations of Reagan and George Bush before the Persian Gulf War of 1991. Other terms that emerged during the Watergate investigations and hearings—"smoking gun," "dirty tricks," "enemies list," and "stonewall"—have remained in political parlance.

Political analysts noted a "post-Watergate morality," a new set of expectations about the ethical behavior of public officials. Remembrance of past transgressions led to watchful surveillance. Law schools offered more courses on legal ethics. Public-interest organizations such as Common Cause tripled in membership. In 1977 the House and Senate passed new codes of conduct for its members on financial disclosure, imposed limits on outside income, and added new restrictions on campaign fund-raising. States passed similar laws. Private as well as public morality of government officials came under scrutiny, such as when a special prosecutor was appointed to investigate a presidential aide accused of cocaine use. As the media investigated the sexual behavior of presidential candidates and Supreme Court nominees, some people reportedly shunned public office lest they endure the media circus and public exposure mandated by post-Watergate reforms. Whether a healthy concern for public ethics had become an obsession, Watergate irrevocably changed political mores in the United States.

Debate continues over whether Watergate was a constitutional crisis or a personal aberration. Investigations in the aftermath of Watergate exposed assassination plots by the Central Intelligence Agency and other abuses of power by presidents before Nixon. Defenders of Nixon made it seem that his greatest crime was in getting caught. It became less clear which Watergate offenses Nixon alone had perpetrated (obstruction of justice) and which had become routine during an arrogant, imperial presidency. A conservative interpretation thus depicted Watergate as more scandal than crisis, a morality play in which Nixon's liberal enemies in the press and Congress harried the president from office over minor offenses. A British historian called Watergate "the first media Putsch in history, as ruthless and anti-democratic as any military coup by bemedaled generals with their sashes and sabers." The liberal interpretation downplayed the media story and depicted Watergate as raising "weighty questions of governance, especially concerning the role of the presidency and its relation to other institutions in the governmental apparatus." Liberals advocated a number of campaign financing reforms and limitations on presidential power, including a special prosecutor mechanism to prevent future Watergates, none of which has operated very effectively. Conservatives contended that the system worked without the need for additional safeguards. By contrast, radical historians characterized Nixon's 1974 resignation and subsequent pardon by President Gerald Ford as "an inexpensive expiation" that prevented a fundamental reevaluation of the American national security state and reinforced a two-tier system of justice that does not hold top U.S. politicians accountable for illegal or unconstitutional actions.

A 1987 Gallup Poll asked Americans what major events had most affected their thinking. Only 5.9 percent listed Watergate, placing it behind the Vietnam War, Ronald Reagan's presidency, and the Great Depression. Apparently, most Americans remember Watergate more as a frothy scandal than as a serious constitutional crisis. Nixon's later efforts at political rehabilitation reflected the continuing ambiguity of Watergate. In televised interviews in 1977, he claimed he "did not commit a crime, an impeachable offense," although "I did let down our system of government." His memoirs, published the following year, asked for public acceptance and public sympathy. Watergate, he predicted, would get only a footnote when future historians assessed his foreign policy triumphs. With more books on foreign affairs, international trips, op-ed pieces, the opening of the Nixon Library in 1990, his advice solicited by Presidents Reagan, Bush, and Bill Clinton, Nixon seemed to achieve the status of elder statesman before he died in 1994, but his Gallup Poll approval rating in 1990 had risen to only 38 percent (from 24 percent in 1974), indicating that Watergate remained "the spot that will not out." The eulogies at Nixon's funeral notwithstanding, the subsequent publication of diaries by key individuals involved in Watergate and documentaries commemorating the twentieth anniversary of Watergate reminded everyone that Nixon was the first president to resign because of a constitutional crisis.

[Stephen E. Ambrose, *Nixon: Ruin and Recovery* (New York, 1991); Katy Harriger, *Independent Justice* (Lawrence, Kans., 1991); Godfrey Hodgson, *All Things to All Men: The False Promise of the Modern American Presidency* (New York, 1980); Joan Hoff, *Nixon Reconsidered* (New York, 1994); Stanley Kutler, *The Wars of Watergate: The Last Crisis of Richard Nixon* (New York, 1980); Tom Wicker, *One of Us: Richard Nixon and the American Dream* (New York, 1991).]

J. GARRY CLIFFORD

See also **DAH:** Nixon, Resignation of; Watergate; **SUPP:** Iran-Contra Affair; Iraq-gate; Korea-gate.

WATER POLLUTION. Widespread water pollution in the United States, including contamination of major rivers and large portions of lakes and estuaries, was primarily a product of three nineteenth-century trends—natural resource exploitation, industrialization, and urbanization. Although development of natural resources, especially lumbering and mining, caused the despoliation of many lakes and rivers, urbanization and industrialization were the primary causes of water pollution. Effluents generated by cities and factories produced widespread contamination of waterways and municipal water. Water pollution increasingly posed a threat to human health in the last decades of the nineteenth century as cities constructed sewer systems discharging millions of gallons of untreated sewage per day into rivers and lakes. By 1904 about 28 million people lived in cities with sewers, but only 1.1 million had their sewage treated. Deaths from such waterborne diseases as typhoid fever rose sharply in cities whose water supplies came from nearby rivers and lakes.

In the early 1890s biologist William T. Sedgwick directed an interdisciplinary group in Massachusetts for clarifying the relation of typhoid fever to sewage. By 1905 thirty-six states had enacted legislation protecting drinking water, with enforcement by state boards of health; most laws, however, were weak. In 1912 concern over pollution and health led Congress to assign the Public Health Service (PHS) to investigate "the diseases of man and conditions influencing the propagation and spread thereof, including sanitation and sewage and the pollution, either directly or indirectly, of the navigable streams and lakes of the United States." The PHS investigations focused on the effects of sewage and industrial waste on stream quality, the assimilative characteristics of streams, and the measurement of pollution. In 1914 the PHS set the first water quality standards for interstate commerce, based on bacterial methods of water analysis. Reduction of waterborne disease, however, was accomplished primarily through water and sewage treatment. Experiments in the 1890s showed how slow sand and mechanical filters could treat sewage-polluted waters used for drinking. Many inland cities then installed filters, resulting in an impressive decline of typhoid fever as well as other waterborne diseases. Advances were also made in sewage treatment methods, but implementation proceeded at a much slower rate because sewage treatment benefited primarily downstream cities.

In the 1920s the PHS undertook investigations regarding industrial wastes, especially where they contributed to drinking water problems, but all action to control water pollution in that decade was at the state level. The Pennsylvania Sanitary Water Board, created in 1923, established a widely emulated classification scheme to balance environmental quality and industrial progress, protecting streams used for drinking water but designating others for waste disposal. Conservation groups such as the Izaak Walton League protested this approach, because waste disposal affected recreational use of waterways. As regulation lagged, pollution of waterways accelerated. During the 1930s, President Franklin D. Roosevelt created the Water Planning Committee of the National Resources Board and the Special Advisory Committee on Water Pollution Control. Under New Deal programs, the federal government aided in the construction of 1,165 new municipal sewage treatment plants, while the population served by sewage treatment increased from 21.5 million in 1932 to more than 39 million in 1939. While some federal officials and conservation organizations pushed for federal water control, Congress balked and so left power in state hands. By World War II water quality had improved in river basins with treatment plants. The war exacerbated the problem because of emphasis on production. Not only were such traditional industries as metals, food, and petroleum expanded without attention to pollution control, but many new substances capable of producing long-lasting environmental damage were produced. Among them were rayon, artificial rubber, the chlorinated hydrocarbons (DDT, chlordane, endrin, and others), and synthetic detergents.

Congress approved the Water Pollution Control Act in 1948. It kept standards enforcement at the state level but provided federal technical assistance, research, and comprehensive planning, and matching funds to localities for construction of sewage treatment plants. Although it provided for $27 million annually for five years, only $8.5 million was actually allocated under the program. In 1956 Congress approved the Federal Water Pollution Control Act Amendments, which maintained the "primary responsibilities and rights of the states" to control water pollution while providing them with assistance. In 1960 President Dwight D. Eisenhower vetoed legislation that would have increased federal grants for sewage treatment facilities by $90 million annually. In 1961, however, President John F. Kennedy persuaded Congress to approve the Federal Water Pollution Control Act Amendments, which extended federal enforcement to coastal and interstate waters and provided $570 million over six years for construction.

The Water Quality Act of 1965 marked a new direction for water pollution control. It redefined the federal effort as being one "to establish a national policy for the retention, control, and abatement of water pollution." It established water quality standards, to be set by the states, for interstate waters. If the states failed to establish them, they were to be developed by the Department of Health, Education, and Welfare (HEW). The act created the Federal Water Pollution Control Administration within HEW. It provided that pollutant discharges resulting in "sub-standard" interstate water quality would be subject to federal proceedings. The Clear Waters Restoration Act of 1966 provided new funds for construction and research. The 1965 and 1966 legislation, however, relied on state standards, which were prey to delays by poorly funded state programs. A more effective approach was required.

The Federal Water Pollution Control Act Amendments of 1972 (commonly known as the Clean Water Act) marked a major shift in policy by moving control to the federal government. Passed over President Richard M. Nixon's veto, the act sought complete elimination of pollutant discharges (zero discharge) by the mid-1980s. It called for industry's implementation of the "best practicable" water control technology by mid-1977 and the "best available" technology by mid-1983. Municipalities had to offer secondary treatment or better by mid-1977 and "best practicable" treatment by mid-1983. The act was amended in 1977, 1981, and 1987 to extend deadlines, permit "innovative and alternative" technologies in meeting effluent standards, and allow for state management of nonpoint pollution, such as urban runoff. Issues of groundwater pollution remained. The constant generation of new chemicals and suspicions about older ones such as chlorine, plus the ability to detect ever smaller amounts of pollutants, suggest that concerns over water pollution will be an issue long into the future.

[Earl Finbar Murphy, *Water Purity: A Study in Legal Control of Natural Resources* (Madison, Wis., 1961); Philip V. Scarpino, *Great River: An Environmental History of the Upper Mississippi, 1890–1950* (Columbia, Mo., 1985); Joel A. Tarr, *The Search for the Ultimate Sink: Urban Pollution in Historical Perspective* (Akron, Ohio, 1996).]

JOEL A. TARR

See also **DAH:** Sanitation, Environmental; **SUPP:** Hazardous Waste; Public Health Service; Recycling; Waste Disposal.

WEAL. *See* **Women's Equity Action League.**

WEATHER SATELLITES, robotic spacecraft that observe changes in terrestrial weather patterns, play a key role in weather forecasting. The satellites are credited with sharply reducing deaths from hurricanes and other violent weather. The first weather satellite, TIROS I, was launched in 1960 and functioned only eighty-nine days. TIROS (an acronym for Television and Infrared Observation Satellite) recorded television images of cloud patterns below, enabling meteorologists to track the movement of weather patterns and fronts with new accuracy. Since then, weather satellites have grown much more durable and can register more data, including wind speeds, atmospheric and surface temperatures, water temperatures, wave heights, and height of the polar ice caps. Weather satellites have been fielded by the United States, the Soviet Union and Russia, the European Space Agency, Japan, India, and China. The U.S. government operates separate weather satellite programs for civilians and the military.

Weather satellites fall into two types. A geostationary satellite remains parked over a given point of the Earth's equator, allowing it to keep continuous watch over a large portion of the Earth from an altitude of 22,000 miles. A polar-orbiting satellite flies at a much lower altitude—about 500 miles—in an orbit that carries it nearly over the Earth's north and south poles. Such a satellite views a much smaller portion of the Earth than a geostationary satellite but can make more detailed observations. Also, the polar-orbiter's orbit is designed so that the sun is at the same angle on every orbit, eliminating the confusion of shifting shadows on the Earth's surface below. For civilian weather forecasting the U.S. government typically has maintained two geostationary satellites and two polar-orbiting satellites in orbit at all times, but satellite weather forecasting ran into a snag in 1989, when the GOES-6 failed in orbit. A replacement, GOES-8, was to have been launched on a space shuttle mission, but the *Challenger* shuttle explosion interrupted all shuttle launches. The replacement was further delayed until 1994 by technical problems with the instruments on the satellite, the first of an improved model of geostationary spacecraft. To fill the gap a European weather satellite was repositioned over the Atlantic Ocean to provide coverage of the eastern United States. The new line of geostationary satellites does not have to spin to remain stable; its two principal instruments can operate simultaneously rather than taking turns, and its instruments gather more data than previous models.

[William James Burroughs, *Watching the World's Weather* (New York, 1991); P. Krishna Rao et al., eds., *Weather Satellites: Systems, Data, and Environmental Applications* (Boston, 1990).]

VINCENT KIERNAN

See also **SUPP:** Weather Satellites.

WEATHER SERVICE, NATIONAL. In the late twentieth century the National Weather Service (NWS) increased its computerization of ground and upper-air data and thereby enhanced its forecasting and climatological services. The excellent Doppler radar for tornadoes and other severe weather was a leading example, but technological advance was plagued by slow and allegedly faulty manufacturing of equipment and huge cost overruns by private companies. Also seemingly retarding progress was mismanagement within the National Aeronautics and Space Administration, which sponsored development of weather satellites for the NWS that included the Geostationary Operational Environmental Satellites (GOES) and Landsat series. Public users of forecasts and other data continued to criticize errors in this inexact science. In federal court Delta Airlines pilots, rather than air traffic controllers, who used NWS forecasts on the thunderstorms, received blame for negligence (misuse of NWS data) in landing during a thunderstorm crash at Dallas–Fort Worth in 1985. Meanwhile, the NWS impressed Congress as being a sound operation. Budget cutbacks in the 1980s and threats of privatization were apparently ended in 1994. The service even sought increased funding, particularly for personnel but also to develop better technology for tracking hurricanes as well as predicting wind shear and microbursts at airports.

[Donald R. Whitnah, *A History of the United States Weather Bureau* (Urbana, Ill., 1961), and "National Weather Service," in *Government Agencies* (Westport, Conn., 1983).]

DONALD R. WHITNAH

See also **SUPP:** Weather Satellites.

WEBSTER V. REPRODUCTIVE HEALTH SERVICES, 492 U.S. 490 (1989), marked a significant change in the Supreme Court's approach to abortion rights and demonstrated the influence of President Ronald Reagan's appointments to the Court. Appointing conservative judges, particularly those opposing *Roe* v. *Wade* (1973), was a top priority of the Reagan administration, which went to unprecedented lengths to ensure the ideological acceptability of judicial candidates, subjecting them to a stringent legal "litmus test" before their nominations went to the Senate. During Reagan's first term only one Supreme Court vacancy occurred, which he filled with Sandra Day O'Connor. Her consistent votes to uphold abortion restrictions, and the government's frequent appearance as an amicus curiae (third party) in these cases, were reflected in the Court's changed attitude toward parental consent laws. Nonetheless, the Court did not overrule *Planned Parenthood* v. *Danforth* (1976), which had invalidated a consent law. *Planned Parenthood* v. *Ashcroft* (1983) even sustained a regulation including a "judicial bypass" (a provision al-

313

lowing a minor to obtain permission from a judge if her parents refused consent). The Court continued to invalidate restrictions on adult access to abortion. As late as 1986, *Thornburgh v. American College of Obstetricians and Gynecologists* reaffirmed the principle of abortion rights and struck down most of a Pennsylvania law that imposed various obstacles to abortion.

When Chief Justice Warren Burger, a member of the *Roe* majority, retired in 1986, Reagan promoted William Rehnquist to the chief justiceship, and replaced him with Antonin Scalia, an appeals court judge of impeccable conservative credentials. Lewis Powell's retirement in 1987 and the appointment of Anthony Kennedy further eroded the support for *Roe*. When Reagan left office in 1989, only four justices committed to abortion rights remained on the Court: Harry Blackmun, William Brennan, Thurgood Marshall, and John Paul Stevens. The reversal of *Roe v. Wade,* a long-awaited conservative victory, seemed within reach. Anti-choice activists (those opposed to a woman's right to choose an abortion, also known as pro-lifers) put increased pressure on state legislatures to forbid abortion outright.

Webster came to the Court from Missouri, a stronghold of the anti-choice movement. The Missouri legislature had tried to limit abortions ever since *Roe*; both *Planned Parenthood v. Danforth* and *Planned Parenthood v. Ashcroft* were Missouri cases. A third Missouri law, passed in 1986, began, "The general assembly of this state finds that the life of each human being begins at conception." Among this statute's provisions were a ban on abortions in public facilities or by public employees, a requirement that all abortions after sixteen weeks of pregnancy take place in a hospital, and mandated "viability" testing after twenty weeks. Reproductive Health Services, a clinic, joined a class-action suit asking a federal court to declare the law unconstitutional. The plaintiffs won in the lower courts. William Webster, the state's attorney general, obtained Supreme Court review. The Justice Department filed an amicus curiae brief urging the Court to overturn *Roe v. Wade*. The decision was a clear warning that women were in danger of losing the right to choose abortion. *Thornburgh*'s five-to-four vote to invalidate restrictions became a five-to-four vote to sustain them. *Webster* did not allow states to forbid abortion, although journalists who covered the Court reported that in internal court discussions, Rehnquist almost succeeded in getting *Roe* overturned. His plurality opinion, joined by White and Kennedy, minimized the need to follow precedent in constitutional cases and dismissed the possibility that "legislative bodies, in a nation where more than half the population is women," would "enact abortion regulations reminiscent of the dark ages." The plurality described the law's preamble a "value judgment" without coercive effect and ruled that *Roe*'s viability testing provision "permissibly furthers the state's interest in protecting potential human life." Since testing was required well before the end of the sixth month, the plurality of justices eviscerated the "trimester" framework of *Roe*. Justice O'Connor concurred in the opinion but disavowed much of the wording, while Justice Scalia's sarcastic opinion accused the plurality of attempting to "prolong this Court's self-awarded sovereignty over a field where it has little proper business." Justice Blackmun's dissent was equally passionate: "I fear for the future. I fear for the liberty and equality of millions of women."

Webster was a victory for opponents of abortion. The Court extended the state's power to regulate, hinted that new laws limiting abortion would receive sympathetic consideration, and accepted three new cases for the next term, but the predicted rush by state legislatures to pass new antiabortion laws did not materialize. Only nine states and one territory had done so by the end of 1991, the first full legislative year after *Webster*; only three of these laws forbade most early abortions. Two events in 1992—the Court's weak but explicit reaffirmation of abortion rights in *Planned Parenthood v. Casey* and the election of Bill Clinton, a Democrat, to the presidency—indicated that the anti-choice movement may have gone as far as it could.

[Barbara Hinkson Craig and David M. O'Brien, *Abortion in American Politics* (Chatham, N.J., 1993).]

JUDITH A. BAER

See also **SUPP:** Abortion; *Planned Parenthood of Southeastern Pennsylvania v. Casey;* Pro-Choice Movement; Pro-Life Movement; *Roe v. Wade;* Supreme Court.

WEEA. *See* **Women's Educational Equity Act.**

WEIGHT CONTROL seeks to promote good health and prevention of obesity, which carries such attendant risks as cardiovascular disease and diabetes. In the mid-1990s more than 30 million adult Americans were overweight and the number was increasing. To reduce further incidence, the risks of obesity were being emphasized to promote better health care in the home and in the workplace. Attempts were made to improve the quality of school meals, to reduce the fat content of "fast foods" eaten daily by millions of Americans, and to discourage advertisement of other foods contributing to obesity. By encouraging physical activity and improved diet, obesity can be prevented in many cases.

[Reva T. Frankle and Mei-Uih Yang, *Obesity and Weight Control* (Rockville, Md., 1988); Albert J. Stunkard and Thomas A. Wadden, eds., *Obesity: Theory and Therapy,* 2nd ed. (New York, 1993).]

PETER H. WRIGHT

See also **SUPP:** Eating Disorders; Fitness, Physical; Food, Fast; Health Food Industry.

WELFARE in the United States generally refers to the complex of social insurance programs such as social security, disability insurance, Medicare, and public assistance programs of two varieties: in-kind programs, such as food stamps, the Special Supplemental Food Program for Women, Infants, and Children (WIC), and Medicaid; and income maintenance programs, such as Aid to Families with Dependent Children (AFDC), generally known as welfare, and General Assistance (GA), relief provided by the states. In the years since these programs came into being, social welfare policy has been constantly debated and adjusted. Public assistance of the 1990s had its roots in the Social Security Act of 1935. The Great Depression shattered many of the myths about the ability of the United States to provide full employment to all citizens, and the ability of people to "pull themselves up by their own bootstraps." Although private assistance was available from voluntary organizations and from churches, these services could not meet the great need in the 1930s. In the 1960s the Great Society programs of President Lyndon B. Johnson's administration were established. Welfare reform in these years consisted of extending AFDC to families with unemployed fathers, authorizing work training, and adding social services to move people off the welfare rolls. The trend of poverty and welfare programs also was to increase benefits to the elderly. There were new in-kind programs, such as housing subsidies, public housing units, and nutritional programs. In 1970 Congress made food stamps available at no cost to families below the poverty line, mostly welfare recipients, and at a small price to those just above the poverty line, the so-called working poor.

Most of the increase in welfare spending during the last quarter of the twentieth century was in the AFDC program. In addition to loosened eligibility, participation rates among the eligible rose sharply. One reason for the increase was worsening economic conditions for black Americans due to the mechanization of southern agriculture, which pushed blacks northward into cities where automation and deindustrialization were greatly reducing the number of factory jobs. Another reason for higher participation rates was the "feminization of poverty," due to the increasing divorce rate, increased out-of-wedlock births, continuing gender discrimination in employment, and increased activity by welfare rights organizations. The overall poverty rates declined in 1960–1986. By some accounts white poverty decreased by 38 percent, black poverty by 26 percent. Child poverty, although dropping precipitously between 1960 and 1974 (from 27 percent to 15 percent), subsequently increased to 21 percent in 1986. The rise in female-headed households was largely responsible for this trend.

Although always controversial, welfare became a political target in the mid-1970s, when large-city and federal deficits increased tremendously. The "welfare state" was characterized as out of control. In many states General Assistance was the first program cut through "welfare reform," because it was the program whose recipients were most "employable." Young single people who were not parents, regardless of their skills or prospects for finding or holding a job providing a living wage, were cut from the GA rolls. Despite talk of job training or retraining, very few of these individuals went into the workforce. They were more likely to end up in homeless shelters, whose numbers were growing. Other public assistance benefits slipped between the mid-1970s and the mid-1980s. The maximum AFDC benefit dropped by one-third and the combined AFDC and food stamp benefits dropped by one-fifth.

In the 1980s major welfare cuts were enacted during the administration of President Ronald Reagan. Supplemental Security Income (SSI), granted to people of any age unable to work for at least one year because of disabilities since the 1960 and 1965 amendments to the Social Security Act, was withdrawn from 200,000 recipients. People with mental disabilities were particularly vulnerable to being ruled ineligible. AFDC sustained a large cut. By 1983, 408,000 people lost eligibility, and 299,000 lost their benefits. The average dollar loss to an AFDC family was $1,555 per year, and the savings to federal and state governments were $1.1 billion. Between 1982 and 1985 total funds spent on unemployment insurance went down 6.9 percent, food stamps went down 12.6 percent, child nutrition programs were cut 27.7 percent, housing assistance 4.4 percent, and low-income energy assistance 8.3 percent. Only WIC was increased.

Welfare policy was criticized by both political parties, by conservatives and liberals, and by other groups. One conservative argument is that welfare is antilibertarian. This criticism is based on the assumption that welfare redistributes income. Conservatives also state that welfare has failed to end poverty, crime, and lack of education. A third argument is that welfare costs too much, given the lack of significant results. Another is that the federal role in welfare programs is too great and constitutes "social engineering." Another argument is that welfare erodes family values. Liberal arguments against welfare claim that it has failed to reduce economic inequality, that welfare programs cannot counteract the distributive injustice resulting from a capitalist system, and that welfare does not promote collective responsibility, but provides scapegoats for workers who have been able to find employment.

A feminist criticism of welfare is that while gender has been a fundamental organizing principle of the welfare system, it has been largely invisible. When gender is brought into view, it becomes apparent that there is a double standard for men and women: welfare policy accepts the premise that women, particularly mothers, should be at home and supported by men. The alternatives offered to women are dependence on the state through AFDC or independence through work. Because programs to train and employ AFDC recipients have never been wholeheartedly supported by sufficient funding and private sector cooperation, and because backing in the larger society in the form of equal job opportunities for women, equal pay, and high-quality affordable day care have been slow in coming, it can be surmised that as a society, Americans prefer to keep women dependent. The stigmatizing of recipients makes welfare an unattractive alternative to being supported by men. Therefore, it can be argued, the welfare system in the United States functions to keep women dependent on men and men dependent on work.

In the public discourse on welfare, a distinction is made between the "deserving" and "undeserving" poor. Throughout welfare history there has always been a preoccupation with such groupings. The deserving poor are those who "through no fault of their own" have fallen from a higher economic level to a

temporary and reluctant dependency on the state. The undeserving are characterized as dependent by nature, having different values and aspirations than productive Americans, and lacking morality, restraint, and decorum. There is also a racial element in these characterizations, with the undeserving poor most often assumed to be African American. There are still other presumed shortcomings of the welfare system. One is that public assistance grants are too small to permit a decent standard of living and do nothing to get recipients out of poverty. By design these programs do not allow recipients to build equity of any kind, and therefore it is extremely difficult for them to improve their situation. Public assistance recipients (less so for recipients of social insurance) are stigmatized in U.S. society. Prior to the passage of the Family Support Act of 1988, only twenty-eight states had AFDC-UP (Aid to Families with Dependent Children–Unemployed Parent [father]) programs. Elsewhere, families with two parents were ineligible for assistance, which encouraged fathers to desert wives and children so they could obtain assistance. Even three years after the passage of that act only 7.1 percent of AFDC recipients received benefits based on unemployment in a two-parent family. Another criticism is that AFDC and other public assistance programs are bureaucratized, overregulated, and hence inefficient. Further, there are loopholes in eligibility. It is possible to be very poor with no real prospect of work and still be ineligible for assistance. Potential recipients can be denied benefits in some states until the sixth month of pregnancy with their first child; if they are under eighteen and not in school; if their income has dropped within two months from a level at which they would be ineligible; or if there is a stepfather living in the home, regardless of his willingness to support the applicant child.

Although welfare is usually discussed in terms of the altruistic and moral purposes that this set of programs serves, or fails to serve, historical analysis shows the expansions and contractions of welfare benefits in functional terms. Some researchers assert that the two principal functions of welfare are maintaining civil order and enforcing work. The assistance programs begin or expand during times of widespread unemployment and civil unrest and decrease when order is restored to provide an incentive for work.

[Linda Gordon, ed., *Women, the State, and Welfare* (Madison, Wis., 1990); Michael B. Katz, *In the Shadow of the Poorhouse: A Social History of Welfare in America*

(New York, 1986), and *The Undeserving Poor: From the War on Poverty to the War on Welfare* (New York, 1989); Frances Fox Piven and Richard A. Cloward, *Regulating the Poor: The Functions of Public Welfare* (New York, 1971); William J. Wilson, *The Truly Disadvantaged: The Inner City, the Underclass, and Public Policy* (Chicago, 1987).]

ELLEN GRAY

See also **SUPP:** Budget, Federal; Cost of Living Adjustment; Health Care Reform; Medicare and Medicaid; Poverty; Unemployment.

WEST BERLIN DISCO BOMBING. On Apr. 5, 1986, a bomb killed two U.S. soldiers and a Turkish woman and injured more than 200 others in a West Berlin discotheque popular with U.S. military personnel. U.S. and German intelligence sources linked the bombing to the Libyan government of Mu'ammar al-Gadhafi. Already worried about a wave of anti-American terrorist actions by groups from Syria, Iran, and Libya, President Ronald Reagan ordered air strikes against Libyan targets, including Gadhafi and his family, on Apr. 14, 1986, to signal a tough U.S. policy toward terrorism. Nevertheless, Libya continued to support terrorist organizations, although its role in terrorist incidents in Europe decreased.

[Brian L. Davis, *Qaddafi, Terrorism, and the Origins of the U.S. Attack on Libya* (New York, 1990); George P. Shultz, *Turmoil and Triumph: My Years as Secretary of State* (New York, 1993).]

KENNETH B. MOSS

See also **SUPP:** Terrorism.

WEST VIRGINIA remained near the top or bottom of every social and economic ranking from the 1970s to the mid-1990s. With few exceptions the state was dominated by the Democratic party. In the presidential contest of 1980 Jimmy Carter carried West Virginia over Ronald Reagan by 33,000 votes; in the same year Democrat John D. Rockefeller IV won a second term as governor by defeating Republican Arch A. Moore, a popular two-term governor (1969–1977). Although the state legislature went Democratic by a huge margin in 1980, Republicans Michael "Mick" Staton, a South Charleston banker, and Cleve Benedict, a Greenbrier County farmer, capitalized on national trends to win congressional seats, creating a split state delegation of two Republicans and two Democrats; two years later, however, the delegation became solidly Democratic and remained so through the 1994 elections. In 1984 President Ronald Reagan carried the state, while Moore

regained the governorship for an unprecedented third term over Democrat Clyde See. That year, Rockefeller reportedly spent $11 million of his own money to win the U.S. Senate seat vacated by Jennings Randolph; in 1990 he won reelection. Rockefeller joined a stalwart among West Virginia politicians, Robert C. Byrd, in the Senate. Since entering Congress in 1953 as a U.S. representative, Byrd had been the state's most durable vote-getter. As Democratic majority leader and chairman of the Senate Appropriations Committee, he steered hundreds of millions of federal dollars into the state as well as several thousand federal jobs. In the early 1990s he was instrumental in securing the establishment of a large Federal Bureau of Investigation fingerprinting facility at Clarksburg.

In the 1988 presidential election Democrat Michael Dukakis carried the state handily over George Bush; four years later Bill Clinton won over President Bush, although third-party candidate Ross Perot received 109,000 votes. In state politics Democrat Gaston Caperton, a Charleston insurance executive, won the governorship in 1988 over Arch Moore; in the same election former Republican Congressman Cleve Benedict was elected agriculture commissioner to break the Democratic monopoly on state elective offices. Caperton was reelected in 1992. The state's political scene was rocked in 1990 when former Governor Moore received a seventy-month prison term after pleading guilty to extortion, mail fraud, tax evasion, and obstruction of justice. The Democratic president of the state senate was sentenced to federal prison on unrelated corruption charges. In 1994 the director of the state lottery went to prison.

After the state's population fell from 1,949,000 in 1980 to 1,793,000 in 1990, West Virginia lost one of its congressional seats. The population drop stemmed from decreased economic activity. Per capita income of $15,065 in 1992 placed the state forty-ninth in national rankings. The poverty rate among whites was the highest in the nation. Coal production, one of the state's mainstay industries, rose from 121.6 million tons annually in 1980 to 171.2 million in 1990, but the number of mining employees fell from 55,500 to 28,900. Attempts by conservatives to enact right-to-work legislation failed in the legislature, but union membership plummeted nonetheless. The state had one of the nation's lowest high school and college graduation rates. Aside from the usual mining and industrial fatalities, floods in 1985 devastated river valleys. The floods resulted from a tropical storm that swept through the southeastern United States from the

Louisiana coast. The West Fork River at Clarksburg crested at 18.5 feet—11 feet above flood stage. An estimated forty-four people in eight counties lost their lives and many citizens incurred staggering property losses. In an outpouring of public support, all fourteen of the state's television stations participated in a telethon featuring prominent West Virginians, including Governor Moore, Senator Rockefeller and wife, the supersonic pilot Charles "Chuck" Yeager, and the astronaut Jon McBride. The popular singer John Denver helped in the effort to raise funds for flood relief. Despite its troubles, West Virginia in the mid-1990s continued to enjoy one of the nation's lowest crime rates.

[Otis K. Rice and Stephen W. Brown, *West Virginia: A History,* 2nd ed. (Lexington, Ky., 1993).]

PAUL D. CASDORPH

WETLANDS. The term "wetland" refers to any of an array of habitats, including marshes, bogs, swamps, estuaries, and prairie potholes, in which land is saturated or flooded for some part of the growing season. According to the U.S. Fish and Wildlife Service, wetlands contain water-loving plants (hydrophytes) and hydric soils. Since 1780 human activity has destroyed more than half the wetlands of the United States—more than 60 acres per hour. Wetlands serve many ecological and practical purposes. They provide habitat and breeding sites for fish, shellfish, birds, and other wildlife and help maintain biological diversity (biodiversity). They reduce the effect of floods by diverting and storing floodwaters; provide protection from storm waves and erosion; recharge ground waters; and improve water quality by filtering out sediments, excess nutrients, and many chemical contaminants. Wetlands provide recreational, research, and aesthetic opportunities, such as fishing, boating, hunting, and observing and studying wildlife. Wetlands comprise only 5 percent of the land surface of the contiguous forty-eight states, or 104 million acres, but they are extremely productive, exceeding even the best agricultural lands and rivaling rain forests in quantity and diversity of plant and animal life. More than half of the saltwater fish and shellfish harvested in the United States and most of the freshwater sport fish require wetlands for food, reproduction, or both. At least half of the waterfowl that nest in the contiguous states use the midwestern prairie potholes as breeding grounds. Wetland-dependent animals include bald eagles, ospreys, beaver, otter, moose, and the Florida panther.

The value of wetlands was not recognized until the mid-1970s. Before then, most people considered wetlands to be wastelands. They were destroyed by draining, ditching, diking, or filling so they might be used for other purposes, primarily agriculture and development. Early legislation, such as the Swamp Lands acts of 1849, 1850, and 1860, allowed fifteen states on the Mississippi River to "reclaim" wetlands for cultivation. By the middle of the twentieth century, accumulating evidence, including U.S. Fish and Wildlife wetlands inventories in 1954 and 1973, made clear that destruction of wetlands was causing declines in fish and waterfowl. Federal, state, and local laws—notably the federal Clean Water Act of 1972 and amendments in 1977—attempted to regulate destruction. Development, agriculture, and increasing pollution still threaten U.S. wetlands. One-third of wetland losses occurred in midwestern farmbelt states. All but three states (Alaska, Hawaii, and New Hampshire) have lost more than 20 percent of their wetlands. Biologists and economists agree that preserving wetlands is less expensive than attempting to restore damaged wetlands. There is still controversy regarding whether it is possible to restore wetlands and how scientists might measure restoration. The economic and biological feasibility of restoration is hotly debated when a developer seeks permission to build on a wetland, thus destroying it, and offers (or is required) to attempt to rehabilitate a second, already degraded site in return. Many biologists feel that because a degraded site cannot be fully restored, it may not be acceptable to allow this trade-off in any but the most desperate circumstances.

[Council of Environmental Quality, *Environmental Trends* (Washington, D.C., 1989); National Research Council, *Restoration of Aquatic Ecosystems: Science, Technology, and Public Policy* (Washington, D.C., 1992).]

SUSAN J. COOPER

See also **SUPP:** Environmental Movement; Environmental Protection Agency; Fish and Marine Life; Wildlife Refuges and Sanctuaries.

WHALING. *See* **Sealing and Whaling.**

WHITE-COLLAR CRIME. *See* **Crime, White-Collar.**

WHITE SUPREMACISTS. Since World War II the number of whites who profess belief in racial equality has steadily increased, but there continue to be many Americans who proudly proclaim their belief in white supremacy. White supremacist organizations in the United States tend to be short-lived, but new organizations always take the place of those that die. The best known of these groups is the Ku Klux Klan (KKK), a name that a number of organizations have used. A group of ex-Confederate soldiers, who were mainly interested in amusing themselves with pranks and practical jokes, started the first Klan in Pulaski, Tenn., in 1866. It grew rapidly in the former Confederate states, but was breaking up into separate groups by the time it was suppressed by the federal government under legislation passed in 1871. Since then there have been several periods when a number of new Klans sprung up, a large group after World War I and smaller ones in the 1960s during the civil rights movement and still again in the late 1970s and 1980s. In the 1990s there were numerous Klans active under a variety of names. A partial list of other white supremacist groups in the 1990s includes the American Nazi Party, Nazi Skinheads, Posse Comitatus, Aryan Nations, The Order, the National Alliance, Populist Party, Liberty Lobby, White Patriot Party, the John Birch Society, and the Church of Jesus Christ Christian. These groups varied in the degree to which they advocated armed violence as a means to realize their goals. Many white supremacists are Identity Christians, who believe that white "Aryans" are the only true descendants of the Israelites, God's chosen people.

[Mark S. Hamm, *American Skinheads* (Westport, Conn., 1993); James Ridgeway, *Blood in the Face: The Ku Klux Klan, Aryan Nations, Nazi Skinheads, and the Rise of a New White Culture* (New York, 1990).]

RICHARD W. MOODEY

See also **DAH:** Ku Klux Klan; **SUPP:** Militias.

WHITEWATER, a scandal involving charges against President Bill Clinton and his wife, Hillary Rodham Clinton. Scandals have bedeviled modern U.S. presidents as much as failed foreign policies and budget deficits. Watergate forced Richard M. Nixon from the White House, and the Iran-Contra scandal stained Ronald Reagan's final term. Both scandals originated in the White House and involved constitutional questions about abuse of executive power. Although Whitewater raised questions about the actions of President Clinton and his aides during his White House tenure, the scandal had its origins in a 1978 Arkansas land development deal. The issue was whether he, while Arkansas governor, and his wife, a Little Rock lawyer, used political influence with state banking officials for the benefit of a partner in the land development deal in return for campaign contributions and other financial favors from the partner. The Clintons' partners in the Whitewater Development Corporation were a longtime friend, James McDougal, and his wife, Susan. After investing in Whitewater, McDougal bought a Little Rock savings and loan known as Madison Guaranty. Under McDougal's stewardship Madison apparently dispensed loans to board members and prominent Arkansas politicians, with the loans sometimes only partially repaid or not repaid at all. McDougal also threw a fund-raiser in 1985 at Madison to help Clinton repay campaign debts undertaken in his successful run for governor the previous year.

Madison was poorly run, and federal regulators eventually declared it insolvent, but one of the main Whitewater charges was that Governor Clinton in 1985 appointed a new state banking commissioner specifically to protect McDougal. The banking commissioner's actions allegedly kept Madison from being shut down in 1985, increasing the savings and loan's loss when federal regulators finally closed it in 1989. After Clinton became president, congressional Republicans arranged hearings about the matter, with Republican Senator Alfonse D'Amato spearheading the probe. The scandal took on darker dimensions when Clinton's deputy White House counsel, Vincent Foster, apparently in charge of the Clintons' taxes and Whitewater files, committed suicide in July 1993. In 1994 Clinton legal confidant Webster Hubbell, a partner of Hillary Clinton's in a Little Rock law firm, pleaded guilty to fraud charges resulting from false billings he made while with the firm. The billings were discovered as part of the Whitewater investigation. Meanwhile, in 1994 independent prosecutors Robert B. Fiske and then Kenneth W. Starr began looking into contacts between White House and Treasury Department officials over Whitewater; no criminal charges were brought, but a top Treasury official, Roger Altman, resigned the same year. In 1995 the independent prosecutor scrutinized the actions of White House aides and of Susan Thomases, a New York lawyer who was a close friend and adviser to Hillary Clinton. Republicans, gaining strength from their congressional election victories in 1994, initiated Senate hearings that continued into 1996.

[Robert L. Bartley, ed., *Whitewater: From the Editorial Pages of the* Wall Street Journal (New York, 1994).]

THOMAS G. GRESS

WILDFIRES have shaped the landscape of America since long before the arrival of humans. Those fires were all caused by lightning, and lightning is still a major cause of wildfires, particularly in the West. In the twentieth century, governments at all levels tried to suppress wildfires. In the second half of the century, the environmental movement introduced the notion that wildfires were ecologically beneficial, and in 1972 the National Park Service adopted, experimentally, a policy of letting some wildfires burn; in 1976 the policy was adopted generally and became known as the "let-burn" policy. In 1978 the U.S. Forest Service adopted the same policy. Most such fires, designated "prescribed fires," burned less than 100 acres. In years of drought, however, there were major problems. In 1977, 175,000 acres of California wilderness burned in the Marble Cone fire. In 1979 wildfires in California, Oregon, Idaho, Montana, and Wyoming burned more than 600,000 acres. In 1981 a swamp fire in Florida consumed 300,000 acres. Three years later 250,000 acres of Montana forest and range burned, and in 1987, 200,000–300,000 acres in Oregon burned. The worst wildfire season since World War II came in 1988; more than 6 million acres burned, 2.2 million of them in Alaska. Fires around Yellowstone National Park were shown on television and had a major public effect. As drought in the West persisted, wildfires continued to pose major risks. Yosemite National Park closed temporarily in 1990 because of a nearby wildfire. In 1991 a wildfire raced through a residential section of Oakland, Calif., killing at least twenty-four people. In 1993 a spectacular wildfire in the brushland north and south of Los Angeles burned the houses of many celebrities and caused nearly $1 billion in damage. In 1994 more than fourteen firefighters were killed fighting wildfires in Colorado and elsewhere in the West; acreage burned again exceeded one million acres.

[Stephen J. Pyne, *Fire in America: A Cultural History of Wildland and Rural Fire* (Princeton, N.J., 1982).]

NANCY M. GORDON

WILDLIFE REFUGES AND SANCTUARIES. The first wildlife refuge in the United States was a 3.5-acre area on Pelican Island, Fla., designated by President Theodore Roosevelt in 1903 as a breeding refuge for such shore birds as pelicans, herons, and egrets. By 1993 the U.S. Fish and Wildlife Service administered 500 refuges encompassing 90 million acres in the National Wildlife Refuge System, with an additional 2.1 million acres of wetlands designated for 174 waterfowl production areas. Elements of society supporting the federal wildlife refuge system have been quite diverse. Conservation organizations such

as the National Audubon Society, sport hunting clubs such as the Boone and Crockett Club and Ducks Unlimited, and scientific associations have supported the refuge system. Extinction of the passenger pigeon in 1914 persuaded sport hunters and conservationists like Roosevelt to take steps to deal with declining waterfowl populations. Most people blamed decreasing numbers on the meat and apparel markets, which traded waterfowl and other game animals as commodities. In 1934 the federal government began purchasing private property with money collected from duck stamps, which were fees imposed on waterfowl hunters. Previously such refuges as the National Elk Refuge in Jackson Hole, Wyo., were acquired by philanthropists and donated to the federal government. Other refuges were established by nongovernmental organizations, such as the National Audubon Society and Nature Conservancy. States and municipalities also created refuges to facilitate public recreation on state lands as well as to benefit wildlife populations.

Scientific interest in nongame animals and ecosystem management increased throughout the twentieth century. Refuges became field laboratories in addition to game reservoirs. Prior to the 1960s refuge managers worked to protect game populations important to hunters and wildlife observers. Perhaps one of the more famous examples of protecting game animals at the expense of others is that of Aldo Leopold, known for his books *Game Management* (1933) and *A Sand County Almanac* (1949) and who pushed the wolf population on the Kaibab Plateau (in Arizona and Utah) to extermination in an effort to increase the deer population. This policy resulted in a deer overpopulation that led to a massive natural die-off from starvation. After the 1960s, drawing on such examples, managers focused on ecosystem health rather than the well-being of particular species.

[Laura and William Riley, *Guide to the National Wildlife Refuges* (Garden City, N.Y., 1979).]

DENNIS WILLIAMS

See also **DAH:** Bird Sanctuaries; Conservation; **SUPP:** Conservation Biology; Ecology; Endangered Species.

WINE AND SPIRITS INDUSTRY has grown in size since the 1970s, despite a growing public awareness during the late 1980s and 1990s of the dangers of excessive alcohol consumption, and its products have improved in quality. The number of wineries burgeoned, especially in California but also in Oregon and Washington, and these wineries, particularly those that employed European vinifera, were producing ever-better wines. Wineries also sprung up elsewhere in the United States, but they rarely used local grapes; instead they imported grapes and their juices, sometimes frozen, for their winemaking activities and thus did little for production of truly local wines. Although American wines continued to improve in taste and longevity, they were not extensively marketed in the Far East, and their prices remained relatively high, often exceeding those for well-known European wines. Bourbon continued to be the most significant contribution of the United States to the spirits industry. Small and exclusive distilleries produced superior whiskeys that commanded respect and ever-higher prices throughout the world.

[Barbara Ensrud, *American Vineyards* (New York, 1990); Harold Grossman and Harriet Lembeck, *Grossman's Guide to Wines, Beers, and Spirits*, 8th rev. ed. (New York, 1995).]

COOPER P. SPEAKS

WISCONSIN. The "Rustbelt" phenomenon—the decline of the traditional heavy goods manufacturing economy—took its toll in Wisconsin beginning around 1970, as it did in the neighboring western Great Lakes and upper Mississippi River states. Major industrial firms such as Allis-Chalmers ceased to exist; others moved away or expanded only out-of-state or cut back their Wisconsin workforce and output; and a few survived by adjusting their product lines. The resulting decline in well-paid employment, both managerial and production, proved devastating to organized labor and by the mid-1990s was probably not complete. There was, however, some recovery of employment in manufacturing (printing, publishing, and papermaking were strong), and employment increases in service fields left the state with a below-average unemployment level for the region and nation—although the new jobs generally paid lower rates than the lost jobs.

From the 1970s to the 1990s less dramatic but important changes occurred in dairying, for a century the backbone of the state's agriculture. Income from dairying fell, although the state remained a leading milk producer and especially a producer of milk products such as cheese. Milk prices remained flat while government regulations and mechanization raised production costs. The result was declining numbers of farms and farmers, an increase in average farm size, and a concern over the impact of such technology as bovine growth hormone. The state's other major farm products, such as processed vegetables

and fruits, remained stable. Private and government tree farming was important to the northern half of the state, but lumbering remained modest. Despite periodic efforts, especially in copper, the state's mining production was small. The strength of financial institutions—banks, insurance companies, and securities firms—contributed to the economy's survival in the 1970s and 1980s.

The effect of a major convulsion in industry and a continuing decline in farming was felt in politics. From the pre–Civil War decade to the mid-twentieth century, Wisconsin was dependably Republican. Early in the twentieth century, the La Follette Progressives reinforced that bias, while adding a commitment to the use of state government for the general welfare, especially in regulation, taxation, and social programs. Despite the creation by the La Follette Progressives of their own party in the 1930s, Republicans resumed ascendancy before World War II and remained dominant for a decade thereafter. With new leadership and the help of organized labor and distressed farmers, the Democrats became fully competitive with the Republicans beginning in 1957–1958, dominating the state assembly and sharing the governor's office, the nine-member delegation to the U.S. House of Representatives, the two U.S. Senate seats, and presidential electoral votes. By the mid-1990s, Wisconsin's politics were centrist. Radical positions on social and cultural issues—abortion, race, ethnicity, lifestyle, education, crime, and gambling—were neither partisan nor sustainable. Overall the state's politics were moderate, and two post–World War II governors regarded as moderates—Republicans Walter J. Kohler, Jr. (1951–1957), and Warren Knowles (1965–1971)—were acknowledged to have been highly successful. Conversely, three governors who failed of reelection—Republican Vernon W. Thomson (1957–1959) and Democrats John Reynolds (1963–1965) and Anthony Earl (1983–1987)—were apparently perceived as out of the mainstream on social and economic issues. Republican Tommy Thompson (1987–), who stressed economic development, sought consensus with Democratic legislators on many statewide issues.

Economic development had bipartisan support. Democrats tilted toward organized labor, marginal farmers, and minorities but supported initiatives to control spending, limit taxes, and adjust the three major sources of state and local revenue—the income tax, sales and excise taxes, and the property tax, which until the 1990s produced roughly equal amounts of revenue. Democrats launched the selective sales tax in 1962, cut a property tax on business, and acquiesced in the Republican initiative to reduce income taxes and phase out the inheritance tax, all departures from La Follette Progressive traditions. In 1995 the governor and legislature adopted measures to provide two-thirds of local public school funding by 1997, in order to reduce the pressure on local property taxes. Growing public dissatisfaction with school performance, especially in inner cities, brought approval of extensive school choice and other reforms.

Since about 1970 Wisconsin has sought business expansion, especially by changes in administrative and regulatory rules, tax relief, and loans and grants. It was difficult to focus business recruitment because of the state's location, climate, and limited natural resources. One exception was renewed emphasis on tourism, especially to offset declines in heavy industry and agriculture and depression in small towns and the northern cutover. Wisconsin has had an above-average tourist appeal since the late nineteenth century, owing to its varied scenery, abundant lakes and rivers, broad temperature ranges, and a corresponding recreational and vacation appeal to residents of Chicago, metropolitan Milwaukee, and Minneapolis–Saint Paul. These factors were still in play in the mid-1990s but with a changed emphasis. The lakes of southeastern Wisconsin had been converted from resorts and cottages to all-year residences. Central and northern Wisconsin lost some of their "mom and pop" resort culture but acquired additional summer residents from all three metropolitan areas. The north retained its fishing and hunting allure and added a skiing and snowmobiling clientele. To such traditional tourist attractions as the Wisconsin River Dells and the Door County peninsula were added the unique House on the Rock near Madison, the Victorian mansion of beer baron Frederick Pabst in Milwaukee, and the annual July fly-in of more than 2,300 planes held by the Experimental Aircraft Association at Oshkosh. Big league sports teams are another attraction. The major ones in Wisconsin are the Green Bay Packers, an original National Football League team; the Milwaukee Brewers, an American League baseball team since 1970; and the Milwaukee Bucks of the National Basketball Association, who play in the Bradley Center, a $73 million gift in 1990 from heirs to the Allen-Bradley fortune. Tourism was promoted along four themes: the ethnic settlements along the Lake Michigan shore on the east; the Fox-Wisconsin River route diagonally across the state; the Lac du Flambeau in the Chippewa Indian reservation area; and architect Frank Lloyd Wright's heritage,

especially his studio-school, Taliesin, near Spring Green.

In 1987 the state legislature and the electorate approved a dramatic break with the past by authorizing a state lottery and limited gambling. Two considerations led to this step—expectation of property tax relief and competition for tourist dollars. Lottery receipts disappointed taxpayer hopes, and the four greyhound racetracks had varying profitability. Because gambling did not develop exactly as legislators and voters had expected, there was little disposition to expand it in the mid-1990s. As a consequence of federal legislation, however, the state's Native American population—39,387 in 1990—qualified for seventeen casino gambling operations that since 1991 dramatically improved the economic status of the tribal organizations.

Despite economic problems, the state continued to show a stable growth pattern. The incidence of unemployment was, however, highly uneven. Black migrants from the South since World War II disproportionately settled in the heavy goods industrial centers—Milwaukee, other Lake Michigan cities, and Madison and the Rock River Valley—which were most heavily hit by the Rustbelt phenomenon. Unemployment and underemployment among young black males, especially in Milwaukee, increased welfare dependency and impeded family formation and stability. In metropolitan Milwaukee stubborn residential segregation complicated the economic and social consequences of black unemployment, especially in public schools, and led to some outmigration. Hispanic migrants to the state, smaller in numbers, later in time, and handicapped by language but not as much as blacks by color, experienced problems similar to those of blacks in the same industrial centers. The state's population (4,891,769 in 1990) showed declining growth: 11.8 percent in 1960–1970; 6.5 percent in 1970–1980; and 4.0 percent in 1980–1990. In 1990, 92.2 percent of residents were white, compared with 98.8 percent in 1950. Outmigration, chiefly for jobs and a milder climate, was offset by black and Hispanic inmigration and post–World War II increases in Native Americans to the highest level in history, three times their 1940 numbers. In 1990 blacks constituted 5 percent of the population, Hispanics 1.9 percent, and Native Americans 0.8 percent. The Native American increase was due to state and federal assistance programs and migration to urban areas, some of it seasonal. Improvements in tribal self-government, following reversal in 1973 of the experiment in the 1950s in defederalization with the Menominee, brought two developments in the 1980s—the Indian casino gambling boom, a significant contributor to employment and to tribal coffers, and a more aggressive tribal effort to enforce broad hunting and fishing rights, guaranteed by land cession treaties of the mid-nineteenth century and enforced by federal courts.

Post-secondary education in the state was dominated by two systems reorganized in the 1960s and 1970s. Vocational, technical, and adult education, a Progressive Era program, became regional rather than local, with more state funding and a junior college role; eventually, the program had almost half a million enrollees annually. The University of Wisconsin system resulted from merger of the university's four four-year campuses, its two-year centers, and its extension unit with the nine campuses of the Wisconsin State University cluster. One of the largest systems in the nation, it enrolled more than 150,000 students in the 1993–1994 academic year. The Madison campus retained its preeminence in the biological and physical sciences, chemical engineering, computer science, sociology, and economics. Since the Vietnam era protests, which culminated in the Mathematics Research Center bombing of 1970 that involved one fatality, the Madison campus has lost some of its reputation for student radicalism.

[Robert C. Nesbit and William F. Thompson, *Wisconsin: A History,* 2nd rev. ed. (Madison, Wis., 1990); Wisconsin Legislative Reference Bureau, *State of Wisconsin Blue Book* (Madison, Wis., 1853–).]

FREDERICK I. OLSON

See also **SUPP:** Milwaukee; Rustbelt.

WOMEN IN CHURCHES. Since colonial times women have made up more than half the membership of American churches. In the Society of Friends, for example, women had leadership roles in congregations and as traveling missionaries as early as the seventeenth century. In the nineteenth century Catholic nuns pioneered in the founding of schools, hospitals, and orphanages. Protestant women led revivals and founded home and foreign missionary societies. New religious movements, such as the Shakers and Christian Science, were founded by women. Social reform movements, such as abolitionism, prison reform, temperance, and the suffrage movement were led by Christian women. Women also began to demand the right to be ordained. At the first women's rights convention, held in 1848 at Seneca Falls, N.Y., the delegates called for women's ordination. In 1853 the Congregationalists ordained the first woman to the

ministry, Antoinette Louise Brown Blackwell. Methodists, Lutherans, and Episcopalians created orders of deaconesses in the late nineteenth century to channel women's desire for ministry. It was not until 1953 that the Methodist and Presbyterian churches voted to ordain women. The growing numbers of women ministers and theological professors brought women's issues into theology and seminary education. Many churches revised their liturgies to use gender-inclusive language for human beings, but female imagery for God became a source of controversy in most churches.

[Rosemary R. Ruether and Rosemary S. Keller, *Women and Religion in America,* 3 vols. (San Francisco, 1981).]

ROSEMARY RADFORD RUETHER

WOMEN IN MILITARY SERVICE. Major changes in the status of women in the military occurred during the last three decades of the twentieth century. In 1975 Congress ended the prohibition on female matriculation at the military academies. The creation of an all-volunteer force in 1973 prompted the services to recruit more women. Whereas prior to 1967 no more than 2 percent of each service could be women, more than 10 percent of each service was female by the early 1990s. In the early 1970s most occupational specialties were opened to women. By 1994, 91 percent of all army career fields and 67 percent of all positions were accessible to women, and they constituted 12.9 percent of the active army. These changes called attention to imbalances in the rights and responsibilities of service personnel, and several landmark court cases leveled the playing field. In *Frontiero* v. *Richardson* (1973) the Supreme Court held that male spouses of female service personnel were entitled to the same benefits as those received by female spouses of servicemen, even when the servicewomen were not the chief sources of financial support for their spouses. The decision in *Crawford* v. *Cushman* (1976) forbade dismissal of a woman because she became pregnant. The *Owens* v. *Brown* (1978) decision allowed servicewomen to be assigned to ships other than hospital or transport ships. In 1981, however, the Supreme Court said that Congress had not violated women's rights by excluding them from the draft (*Roskter* v. *Goldberg,* 1981). The Court held that women's ineligibility for combat justified exclusion from the draft.

Several events in the 1980s and early 1990s prompted reconsideration of women's combat roles. The invasion of Panama in December 1989 marked the first time in modern U.S. military history that women soldiers engaged in combat. In the Gulf War of 1991 women made up more than 7 percent of the 540,000 troops deployed to the region. They received the same $110 a month imminent danger pay as servicemen. Thirteen women were killed. In May 1991 Democratic Representatives Patricia Schroeder of Colorado and Beverly Byron of Maryland succeeded in amending the 1992 defense authorization bill to remove combat restrictions on women air force and navy pilots. A second amendment to the bill established a fifteen-member presidential commission (Commission on the Assignment of Women in the Armed Forces) to study women's roles in the military and report its recommendations to the president by Nov. 15, 1992. The commission of nine men and six women was chaired by retired Air Force General Robert T. Herres and called for few changes. It voted eight to seven to retain the prohibition on flying combat missions, ten to zero to exclude women from land combat units, and eleven to three to continue ineligibility for the draft. The panel voted eight to six to allow women to serve on all combat ships except submarines and amphibious vessels. Secretary of Defense Richard Cheney said he would allow the incoming administration of President Bill Clinton to respond to the report. On Apr. 28, 1993, Secretary of Defense Les Aspin ordered the armed services to drop most of their restrictions on women in air and naval combat. He also ordered the navy to draw up legislation for Congress to permit assignment of women to ships on combat missions.

[Martin Binkin and Shirley J. Bach, *Women in the Military* (Washington, D.C., 1977); Judith Hicks Stiehm, *Arms and the Enlisted Woman* (Philadelphia, 1989); Carol Wekesser and Matt Polesetski, eds., *Women in the Military: Current Controversies* (San Diego, 1991).]

Irwin N. Gertzog

See also **SUPP:** *Frontiero* v. *Richardson;* Tailhook Incident.

WOMEN IN PUBLIC LIFE, BUSINESS, AND THE PROFESSIONS. The 1970s witnessed the most energetic feminist activism since suffrage, a new women's movement committed to a redefinition of social roles for both men and women. The new feminist credo urged that women play a larger public role and men take on more private responsibility for family care. In 1950, 34 percent of women worked for pay; by 1970 that figure had grown to 43 percent. In the two decades that followed the growth rate was even steeper. By 1990, 57.5 percent of all women worked outside the home. Employment of married women with children younger than six rose sharply from 14 percent in 1951 to 30.3 percent in 1970 to 59 percent in 1990. Two-thirds of them were working full time. Until 1991 African-American women consistently worked at rates higher than white women. In that year the median earnings for all women who worked full time and year round increased to 70 percent of those for men, up from 60 percent in 1971. Black women's median earnings rose in that period from 52 percent to 62 percent of those for men.

Economic participation resulted primarily from pressure on family incomes, and working women in 1990 continued to concentrate in clerical, service, and sales work, as well as the historically female professions of teaching, nursing, library service, and social work, but feminist activism for enforcement of laws protecting job rights and enactment of legislation prohibiting sex discrimination in education permitted women to pursue more occupations. Between 1975 and 1990 women doubled their ranks in executive and managerial jobs (from 5.2 to 11.1 percent) and more entered the historically male professions and occupations. Between 1970 and 1991 the proportion rose from 4.7 to 19 percent of lawyers; 12.1 to 18.1 percent of physicians; and 2.7 to 14 percent of police officers. Although engineering remained virtually unbreached (women made up 8.2 percent of engineers in 1991), women advanced in most of the sciences, from less than 10 percent in 1973 to more than 25 percent by 1991. In 1988, 47 percent of Fortune 1000 companies reported women on boards of directors, up from 13 percent in 1976. In 1982 women owned 25 percent of U.S. firms (mostly sole proprietorships), and in 1987 receipts from women-owned firms accounted for 14 percent of the U.S. total.

As women claimed a full public role they sought political positions at every level with the support of new national and local feminist political organizations. In 1971 women occupied 4.5 percent of the seats in state legislatures; by 1993 the proportion had grown to 20.4 percent. Seven women held mayoralties in 1971; twenty years later there were 151. From fifteen women in the 92nd Congress (1971–1973) numbers climbed slowly to thirty-two (three senators and twenty-nine representatives) on the eve of the 1992 election. With that election Congress expanded to fifty-four women members, forty-eight in the House and six in the Senate. The latter included the first African-American woman senator, Carol Moseley Braun of Illinois; in the House there were nine African-American women, one Asian/Pacific-

American woman (Patsy Mink of Hawaii), and three Latinas. Women obtained a fairer share of places in the judiciary. By 1970 only six women had ever been named to the federal district and circuit courts; by 1992 they composed 13.4 percent of federal judicial officers and a year later two of the nine Supreme Court justices, Sandra Day O'Connor and Ruth Bader Ginsburg. By the 1990s the legitimacy of women in politics and the workforce was beyond question. The assumption by men of a larger responsibility for family life was slow to emerge, however, and women continued to face the burden of meeting the frequently conflicting demands of their private and public roles.

[Cynthia Costello and Anne J. Stone, eds., *The American Woman, 1994–1995: Where We Stand* (New York, 1995).]

CYNTHIA HARRISON

See also **SUPP:** Affirmative Action; Equal Employment Opportunity Commission; Equal Pay Act; Family Leave Act; Pregnancy Discrimination Act; Sexual Harassment; Women in Churches; Women in Military Services; Women's Equity Action League; Women's Movement.

WOMEN'S COLLEGES. *See* **Colleges, Women's.**

WOMEN'S EDUCATIONAL EQUITY ACT (1974) was passed as part of the Special Projects Act contained in the Education Amendments of 1974. The purpose of the act is to promote educational equality for women in the United States, an equality that Congress had mandated two years before in Title IX of the 1972 Education Act Amendments. The act also authorized federal grants to develop and evaluate curricula and textbooks; to promote educational equity for disabled women and girls; to help unemployed women and female drop outs; and to encourage women to develop math and science skills. The congressional appropriation in 1991 to achieve these goals was about $2 million.

[U.S. Department of Education, *Women's Educational Equity Act Program: Report of Activities, 1988–1992* (Washington, D.C., 1992).]

IRWIN N. GERTZOG

WOMEN'S EQUITY ACTION LEAGUE (WEAL), founded in Ohio in 1968 and headquartered in Washington, D.C., draws its members largely from the ranks of professional women and has taken a conser-

vative stand on the issue of abortion to distinguish itself from the larger, more liberal National Organization for Women (NOW). WEAL developed from a small, volunteer organization into a national society of thousands of members. In 1970 it initiated the first sex-discrimination case on behalf of women in educational institutions, which led to the hiring of more female faculty. WEAL set up a tax-exempt fund to support lawsuits and to monitor implementation and enforcement of Title IX legislation of the 1972 Education Act Amendments dealing with academic discrimination and economic equity. It also sought to remove gender as a factor in insurance ratings and joined the fight to pass the Pregnancy Discrimination Act of 1978. Initially dependent on federal funds, the organization was able to secure grants from the Ford Foundation after 1980. WEAL published *WEAL Washington Report, Better Late Than Never: Financial Aid for Older Women*, and newsletters on issues of concern to women including executive and legislative actions and court decisions.

[Joyce Gelb and Marian Lief Palley, *Women and Public Policies,* rev. ed. (Princeton, N.J., 1987).]

GRAHAM RUSSELL HODGES

See also **SUPP:** Women in Public Life, Business, and Professions; Women's Educational Equity Act; Women's Movement.

WOMEN'S HEALTH. During the 1960s and 1970s the women's movement publicized and politicized the experiences of women as medical providers, investigators, and patients, as well as the objects of research. Feminist health activists argued that notions of female inferiority undergirded medical theory, research, and practice. Threatened with a sex discrimination class-action suit in 1970, medical schools dramatically increased enrollment of women medical students. Nonetheless, the gendered concentration of women physicians in such fields as pediatrics and primary care continued. Self-help groups and alternative clinics, such as the Feminist Women's Health Collective of Los Angeles sought to demystify medical knowledge and expose medical sexism. *Our Bodies, Ourselves* (1975), written by the Boston Women's Health Book Collective, became the "bible" of the feminist health movement. By the 1990s the National Women's Health Network, a coordinating lobby group founded in 1975, represented 500 women's health organizations. Activists worked with such groups as the National Abortion Rights Action League to demand legal reform in the name of equal rights. Instead, the Supreme Court in *Roe* v. *Wade* (1973) ruled that abortion was governed by the right to privacy and that the state could not intervene until the fetus was "viable"—a term that has shifted in meaning with improving medical technologies. Access to abortion, especially by poor women, was severely limited by the Hyde Amendment (1976) and such legal decisions as *Maher* v. *Roe* (1977), *Webster* v. *Reproductive Health Services* (1989), *Rust* v. *Sullivan* (1991), and *Planned Parenthood of Southeastern Pennsylvania* v. *Casey* (1992). In addition, the training of doctors qualified to perform abortions declined dramatically in the 1980s as did the number of counties with clinics or hospitals providing abortion services.

In the 1960s the feminist health movement was made up mainly of white middle-income women who shared a liberal integrationist view; with the establishment of black, Latina, and Native American health groups a broader movement embraced class, racial, and ethnic diversity and the resulting heterogeneous perspectives on women's health issues. Debates over women's choice and state control have been exacerbated by new reproductive technologies, especially in vitro fertilization, embryo transfer, sophisticated prenatal tests, and the contraceptives Norplant and Depo-Provera. The feminist health critique encouraged greater use of birthing centers and patient consent forms and more open public discussions about sexuality, breast cancer, mental illness, surrogate motherhood, and eating disorders.

Risks of sterility, disease, and death were recognized in the high-estrogen pill, the synthetic hormone DES, the Dalkon Shield and other intrauterine devices, and high-absorbency tampons. Fear of legal action led some companies to exclude women from jobs exposing them to chemicals harmful to their reproductive capacities, raising complex issues of civil rights and gender discrimination. In 1991, however, the Supreme Court in *Automobile Workers* v. *Johnson Controls* ruled in favor of women's, not fetal, rights, saying that employers could not discriminate against fertile women by excluding them from jobs that might harm a fetus. In the 1980s activists increased public awareness of the absence of women subjects in long-range studies of diseases, such as heart disease, that affect both men and women, as well as the lack of resources devoted to research of diseases, such as breast cancer, that primarily affect women. In response to calls for new categories and methods of research, Congress in 1993 passed legislation requiring scientists of the National Institutes of Health to include women in research designs and analyses.

[Rima D. Apple, ed., *Women, Health, and Medicine: A Historical Handbook* (New York, 1990); Flora Davis, *Moving the Mountain: The Women's Movement in America Since the 1960s* (New York, 1991).]

NAOMI ROGERS

See also **SUPP:** Abortion; *Automobile Workers* v. *Johnson Controls;* Cancer; Childbirth; Contraception; Eating Disorders; *Planned Parenthood of Southeastern Pennsylvania* v. *Casey;* Reproductive Technology; *Rust* v. *Sullivan;* Toxic Shock Syndrome; *Webster* v. *Reproductive Health Services;* Women's Movement; Women's Rights.

WOMEN'S MOVEMENT. The reemergence of the women's movement in the United States in the late 1960s is commonly referred to as the second wave of feminism, which serves to distinguish it from the period more than a century earlier when women first organized around demands for full citizenship. While this modern wave of feminism changed during its first three decades, the demand for greater equity and self-determination for women in the United States remained its core. Through its many struggles and achievements, the women's movement remained a salient force for social justice and equity in the 1990s. The roots of the second wave lay in large-scale structural changes that occurred in the United States after 1960. Demographic change, including a rapidly falling birth rate, increased longevity, a rising divorce rate, and an increase in the age at which people married, radicalized the expectations of girls and women. They flooded into the full-time labor force, stayed in school longer, secured college and postgraduate degrees in increasing numbers, and linked their newfound sexual freedom with the desire to control their own reproduction.

What women found as they emerged from the relative shelter of wife and mother roles, however, was a society reluctant to accept them as full and equal participants. This contradiction variously produced disappointment, outrage, anger, and finally a social movement determined to acquire for women full rights of citizenship. The earliest organized forms of second-wave feminism were modeled on the civil rights movement's successful challenge to racial injustice in the United States. Many early activists in the women's movement had participated in the civil rights and antiwar movements or in the New Left politics and counterculture of the 1960s. The organizing lessons learned and the contacts developed served as the basis for their own attempts at change.

The ideology of the movement was diverse from

the beginning, but there were underlying themes common to all those who sought to improve women's status. One was that of sexism—the notion that there are political and social institutions as well as deep-seated cultural attitudes that discriminate against women, denying them the opportunity to reach their fullest potential. A second theme was the goal of individual self-determination—the claim that women should be free to choose their own paths in life, perhaps helped by but not constrained by men or other women. Finally, perhaps the most widely publicized theme was that the "personal is political," the conviction that the only way to change women's individual problems in the form of battering, rape, low-paying jobs, unfair divorce laws, discriminatory education, or degrading notions of femininity is through political organizing and political struggle.

Organizations and small groups appeared in the late 1960s and the 1970s as feminists grappled with the difficult question of how to act on these themes and insights. The largest and most structured of the new feminist organizations, the National Organization for Women (NOW), founded in 1966, fought legal and legislative battles in an unsuccessful attempt to secure passage of the Equal Rights Amendment, intended to eliminate discrimination against women in education and the labor force and safeguard women's reproductive freedom. In contrast, the small, loosely organized consciousness-raising groups typical of the early women's liberation movement held intimate discussions in which women explored their struggles to become more assertive and to resist a socialization process that had taught them to be passive and self-denigrating.

Some feminists believed that street protests were the most effective way to communicate feminism's message to large numbers of people. Direct-action tactics included protests at the Miss America pageant in 1968; the hexing of the New York Stock Exchange by women dressed as witches; the Women's Strike for Equality on Aug. 26, 1970, involving more than 100,000 women throughout the country; and, later, huge demonstrations to assert women's right to abortion. Other activists worked for a feminist vision of change by organizing alternative institutions. Rape hot lines and battered women's shelters were established; women's health clinics, food stores, publishers, a symphony orchestra, art galleries, bookstores, banks, and bars provided outlets for creative energies and entrepreneurial skills. Although there was much disagreement within the movement about which of these disparate tactics was most effective, their combined effect was staggering. They touched the lives of

millions of Americans and began to transform the ways people thought about and acted toward women.

In the 1990s the women's movement faced new challenges and problems. Despite substantial gains in many areas over thirty years, sexist attitudes and behavior endured. The gap between women's and men's incomes narrowed but persisted, with women earning approximately 25 percent less than men regardless of education. Abortion rights, while guaranteed, came under renewed attack and in some states were eroded. Sexual harassment was a recognized crime but continued to compromise women's full equality. More women were running for and winning elective office than ever before but in 1994 women constituted only 10 percent of the Congress. Many women earning their own incomes had to work a "second shift" because they remained responsible for most or all of their families' care, even in two-earner households. These and other concerns shaped the ideological debates within feminism at the end of the twentieth century. The women's movement continued to contain within itself a plethora of differing analyses and opinions concerning women and social change.

One such debate focused on the issue of sexual violence. Feminists were divided about the role of pornography in engendering and encouraging the sexual violence rampant in the United States. Many who believed that pornography was a major cause of woman-centered violence called for strict regulation or outlawing of pornography as a violation of women's civil rights. Other feminists were concerned about the difficulty of defining pornography, claiming that the real causes of violence against women are complex and rooted deep within our culture and social institutions. They argued that pornography is a form of free speech—however abhorrent—that must be tolerated in a democratic society. Disagreements were apparent as well on the question of how to define and punish such problems as sexual harassment, date rape, and marital rape. Some questioned the legitimacy of a "battered woman defense," giving women victims of systematic violence the right to strike back against their abusers. While all feminists agreed that gender-based crimes against women, including violent acts against lesbian women, were a virulent form of sexism that must be eradicated, they differed in their analyses of and remedies for these problems.

Another debate divided "difference" feminists from "equality" feminists. Difference feminists stressed that women resemble one another and differ from men in fundamental ways. They focused on the value of presumed feminine characteristics, claiming women's greater empathy, cooperation, intuition, and care and posited these as superior to those thought to characterize men. Although they frequently pointed to socialization rather than biology as the source of sex differences, these feminists believed women's characteristics are shared by all women and difficult if not impossible to alter. Equality feminism, in contrast, rejected the view that there are basic social and psychological differences between women and men. It focused on eliminating barriers to fulfilling individual potential. Equality feminism defined social justice in a gender-neutral fashion, anticipating a future that would provide women and men with opportunities to exercise individual choice on a wide range of issues, including reproduction, education, employment, legal rights, sexual orientation, and personal relationships. It rejected the traditional idea that women's differences from men are inherent or can ever be legitimately used to justify either sex's exclusion from any aspect of society or social life. The political ramifications of difference and equality feminism were many. They divided feminists who advocated special provisions for women in the labor force and the law from those who wanted equal treatment for women and men. One practical aspect of this debate concerned the appropriate remedy for the persistent disadvantages of women in the labor force. When compared to men, women earned less, were promoted less frequently, and continued to be segregated in "female" occupations. Most harmful of all was the pattern of interrupted work histories that characterized large numbers of women as they continued to drop out of the labor force in order to almost single-handedly rear children and care for their homes.

Insisting on preserving women's special relationship to home and children, difference feminists addressed women's disadvantaged position in the workforce with such solutions as the "mommy track." This special arrangement of part-time work enables female lawyers, for example, to spend more time at home without forgoing their law practices. Women retain their relationships with firms even though the ability to qualify as partners is delayed and salaries are considerably lower than are those of full-time lawyers. Equality feminists, however, rejected such special protections. Their search for remedies focused rather on finding ways to equalize men's and women's responsibilities for home and child care. Many equality feminists believed that parental leaves of absence from work when children are young or ill, expanded availability of low-cost and high-quality day care, and greater participation of men in fairly

dividing responsibilities for housework and child rearing were the only real solutions to women's dual-workload problem. By the middle of the 1990s, however, neither difference nor equality feminists had been able to exercise the political power necessary to resolve women's continuing disadvantages in the labor force.

The ideologies of difference and equality separated feminists with respect to strategies for building the movement itself. Difference feminists tended to be wary of coalitions, especially those with men. They were generally pessimistic about the possibility of changing what they saw as men's essentially intractable sexist attitudes and behavior and frequently claimed that only women can understand and fight women's oppression. As a result, feminists influenced by a difference model tended to be separatist, inward looking, and focused on what they saw as women's inevitable victimization. Their activism often took the form of trying to shield women from sexism, especially by separating them from its sources. Thus, one of their primary goals was the creation of all-women environments that were considered safe spaces, such as those at women's music festivals or retreats.

The ideology of equality feminism, in contrast, concentrated on eradicating sexism by removing its causes. For many equality feminists this included working in coalition with men to change their attitudes and behavior toward women. They focused on issues that could unite women and men of different social classes and races, such as the disproportionate poverty of U.S. women and their children, federal funding for abortions, and the need for day care. Their goal was to change those aspects of the society that engender sexism. They fought for fair laws and nonsexist legislation and staged large demonstrations and protests to create a broad-based, diverse, and effective movement for ending sexism.

The difference and equality debate raged within academic institutions. The establishment of women's studies courses and programs in almost every institution of higher education in the country was unquestionably one of the women's movement's most significant achievements. These programs and the women's centers with which they were often associated on college campuses altered the way scholars and students thought about issues of gender. Reversing a situation in which women and their contributions to history, science, and society were almost entirely ignored, women's studies courses educated millions of young people about the importance of both women and men to our cultural heritage and contemporary world. Despite their success, women's studies programs faced an identity crisis in the 1990s. On one side, equality feminists argued that the subjects of women and gender should be integrated into the curriculum and not require separate courses or programs. To them the primary goal of women's studies programs was to facilitate that integration. In contrast, difference feminists claimed that only an independent women's studies curriculum could fulfill the continuing need for courses dedicated to women's unique place in and approach to the world. Thus, feminists celebrated the many accomplishments of women's studies programs even as they disagreed about the strategy that should be adopted by such programs.

The women's movement remained a forum for debate, with issues, strategies, and tactics subject to controversy. While such diversity may have confused a public looking for simple definitions or perplexed those who wanted to know, finally, "What do women want?" its multifaceted nature was the movement's strength. The women's movement had room for everyone who agreed that sexism has no place in a society dedicated to social justice. The most important contribution of the women's movement of the late twentieth century was to improve women's lives by reducing obstacles to the full expression of their desires and choices. Feminists contributed to the wider society as well, because their activism was an important element in the continuing struggle for a more equitable and just society for all.

[Alice Echols, *Daring To Be Bad: Radical Feminism in America, 1967–1975* (Minneapolis, 1989); Sara M. Evans, *Born for Liberty: A History of Women in America* (New York, 1989); Jo Freeman, *The Politics of Women's Liberation* (New York, 1975); Victor R. Fuchs, *Women's Quest for Economic Equality* (Cambridge, Mass., 1988); Arlie Hochschild, *The Second Shift* (New York, 1989); bell hooks, *Ain't I A Woman? Black Women and Feminism* (Boston, 1981); Wendy Kaminer, *A Fearful Freedom: Women's Flight from Equality* (New York, 1990); Kristin Luker, *Abortion and the Politics of Motherhood* (Berkeley, Calif., 1984); Susan Schechter, *Women and Male Violence* (Boston, 1982); Carol Tavris, *The Mismeasure of Woman* (New York, 1992).]

JOAN D. MANDLE

See also **SUPP:** Abortion; Affirmative Action; Comparable Worth; Contraception; Domestic Violence; Ecofeminism; Equal Employment Opportunity Commission; Equal Pay Act; Equal Rights Amendment; Family; Family Leave Act; Gay and Lesbian Movement; Marriage and Divorce; Pornography; Pregnancy Discrimination Act; Pro-Choice Movement; Pro-Life Movement; Rape; Rape Crisis Centers; Sexual Harassment; Violence Against Women Bill; Women in Churches; Women in Public Life, Business, and the Professions; Women's Educational Equity Act; Women's Equity Action League; Women's Health; Women's Rights; Women's Studies.

WOMEN'S RIGHTS. The demands of U.S. women for equal rights reached a high point during the 1960s and 1970s as they sought to alter their political, social, and economic status. The modern women's rights movement was known as the feminist movement or the women's liberation movement. It was also known as the second wave of feminism in acknowledgment of the nineteenth-century activism for women's rights that led in 1920 to passage of the Nineteenth Amendment, which gave women the right to vote. Feminists in the 1960s were responsible for placing the issue of women's inequality on the public policy-making agenda. Women formed such groups as the National Organization for Women (1966), the Women's Equity Action League (1968), and the National Women's Political Caucus (1971) to give greater force to their demands for equality. Women's rights advocates generally agreed on a common set of goals. For the most part, they believed in equal employment opportunity, equal pay for equal work, an end to sexual harassment in the workforce and educational institutions, more equitable divorce and child-custody laws, and greater concern with violence against women. Most also supported pay equity or comparable worth, reproductive rights (including abortion), and greater domestic autonomy. They believed that many of these reforms would occur when the numbers of women at all levels of government increased.

Early successes of the women's rights movement included the 1963 Equal Pay Act, the 1964 Civil Rights Act, laws prohibiting discrimination in educational and credit opportunities, and Supreme Court decisions expanding the civil liberties of women. In 1972 Congress sent the Equal Rights Amendment to the states for ratification; despite approval from more than half the states it failed to obtain the necessary two-thirds needed by 1982. Subsequent gains included the Civil Rights Restoration Act of 1987, the Civil Rights Act of 1991, the Family and Medical Leave Act of 1993, and the Violence Against Women Act of 1994. Victories in state legislatures included laws establishing greater protection for battered women and victims of violent crime, reform of rape statutes, and laws providing for more equitable distribution of marital property following divorce, made necessary by the negative impact of no-fault divorce laws on women. At the same time, many states placed restrictions on women's constitutional right to obtain abortions and often interpreted no-fault divorce laws in ways that harmed women's economic status.

For all their successes, women's rights advocates in the 1990s regarded the battle as far from over. While advocates won many victories in the 1960s and 1970s, a backlash against women's rights occurred in the 1980s and violence against women spread. In the 1990s women continued to be paid less than men and were underrepresented in government, corporations, and educational institutions; access to abortion clinics diminished; and families headed by single women were among the poorest in the nation.

[Nancy E. McGlen and Karen O'Connor, *Women, Politics, and American Society* (Englewood Cliffs, N.J., 1995); Susan Gluck Mezey, *In Pursuit of Equality: Women, Public Policy, and the Federal Courts* (New York, 1992); Sheila Ruth, ed., *Issues in Feminism,* 3rd ed. (Mountain View, Calif., 1995);Virginia Sapiro, *Women in American Society,* 3rd ed. (Mountain View, Calif., 1994).]

SUSAN GLUCK MEZEY

See also **SUPP:** Abortion; Affirmative Action; Civil Rights Act of 1991; Civil Rights Restoration Act of 1987; Comparable Worth; Domestic Violence; Equal Pay Act; Equal Rights Amendment; Family Leave Act; Marriage and Divorce; Pregnancy Discrimination Act; Rape; Sexual Harassment; Violence Against Women Bill; Women in Public Life, Business, and the Professions; Women's Equity Action League; Women's Health; Women's Movement; Women's Studies.

WOMEN'S STUDIES. Between the late 1960s and early 1990s hundreds of U.S. colleges and universities developed interdisciplinary women's studies courses, majors, undergraduate and graduate programs, departments, and research institutes. Not confined to the United States, women's studies extended a presence internationally, especially in Canada, New Zealand, Australia, and the Netherlands and subsequently in Kenya, Great Britain, Vietnam, Russia, India, Italy, and Poland. The regional and institutional diversity of their settings imparted great variety to women's studies enterprises. Much of the impetus behind the work of women's studies founders was compensatory. In virtually every field, research and teaching was male-dominated or reflected unduly the experiences and perspectives of men. New knowl-

edge about women was needed to redress the bias, but when research and publication of vast new bodies of knowledge about women's history, literature, art, music, sociology, politics, economics, religion, and science failed to alter in any substantial way the ordinary workings of disciplines, it became clear that feminist scholarship was an insufficient catalyst for change. Some feminist scholars initiated a fundamental questioning of masculine investments in the existing disciplinary forms and the inherent limitations of those forms, encouraging an interdisciplinary approach for women's studies teaching and research.

Achievements of women's studies programs in their first twenty-five years included the founding of such influential journals as *Signs* and *Feminist Studies;* the sorting out of challenging teaching methods; the involvement of a wide range of faculty and students; self-criticism about issues of race, class, sexual orientation, and other differences among women; the scrutiny of the gender biases of knowledge-making itself; and practical participation in public policy governing gender relations. Administrators of women's studies typically preferred loosely structured interdisciplinary programs over departmental organization. At the 1994 National Women's Studies Association conference, program directors argued that institutional weakness characterized programs without tenured faculty and where the principal focus of activity is undergraduate teaching. Few Ph.D. programs in women's studies existed in the United States by the mid-1990s; the highest degree achieved by most women's studies majors was the master's degree.

Debates within women's studies in the 1990s addressed the departmentalization, professionalization, and fund-raising necessary to secure viable programs into the twenty-first century. They distinguished between monodisciplinary feminist research and interdisciplinary women's studies scholarship. Some observers questioned the continued viability of the term "women's studies" for a field that also analyzed gender, masculinity, and cultural aspects of sexuality. Others questioned whether women's studies should describe itself as an interdisciplinary field or as an interdisciplinary method. It remained to be seen whether women's studies would transform traditional approaches to knowledge or whether it would succumb to the same theoretical and political differences that fragmented the women's movement in the 1990s.

[Judith A. Allen, "Feminist Critiques of Western Knowledges," in K. K. Ruthven, ed., *Beyond the Disciplines: The New Humanities* (Canberra, 1992); Catharine R. Stimpson, *Women's Studies in the United States* (New York, 1986).]

JUDITH A. ALLEN

See also **SUPP:** Colleges and Universities; Colleges, Women's; Curriculum; Multiculturalism; Women's Movement.

WOODSTOCK (1969 and 1994). Near the end of the 1960s, with the anti–Vietnam War and counterculture movements peaking in strength, a series of rock music festivals crisscrossed the United States, especially in 1969. The Woodstock Music and Art Fair was the high point of the festivals and, many would argue, of the decade as well. From 400,000 to 500,000 people crammed onto a farm in Bethel, N.Y., near Woodstock, to camp, listen to music, and commune with nature. The festival attracted many of the top musicians and bands of the 1960s, including Janis Joplin, Jimi Hendrix, Joan Baez, Santana, The Who, Joe Cocker, and Crosby, Stills, Nash, and Young. The festival also attracted many of the era's favorite recreational drugs, including marijuana and LSD, although the latter sometimes came laced with toxic substances. Added to the mix of music and drugs, heavy rains turned the farmland into acres of mud and led thousands to shed their clothes. A benevolent chaos and anarchy ruled the festival, with many attendees cutting down the gates surrounding the farm to avoid the eighteen-dollar ticket charge. For many in the counterculture and antiwar movement, Woodstock represented the best of the 1960s. Reality, however, tarnishes the myth. For all of its antiestablishment underpinnings, a corporate and government presence constantly hovered over the festival. Organizers later said that their main goal was to make money from the festival; Warner Brothers had cameras present and produced an Academy Award–winning movie, while Atlantic Records recorded the festival for a multi-record set. When food and water ran out, helicopters ferried in those supplies along with medicine—the same type of helicopters that ferried soldiers and munitions during the Vietnam War, the target of much of the counterculture's wrath.

Woodstock organizers staged a reunion concert in Saugerties, N.Y., in August 1994. This festival was openly corporate, with Pepsi, Häagen Dazs ice cream, and MCI among the sponsors. It was also expensive: advance tickets cost $135 each; those attending found a Häagen Dazs ice cream bar selling for $3 dollars and a cup of Pepsi for $2 while an official program cost $15. This second concert's music lineup was geared toward the tastes of baby boomers' children, with "alternative" rock and punk bands such as Green Day, Nine Inch Nails, and Porno for Pyros as the headliners. On the other hand Bob Dylan performed this time, while several Woodstock I performers showed up, including Cocker, Santana, and Crosby, Stills, and Nash. Moreover, two stalwarts of the original festival—drugs and mud—reappeared. Many concertgoers used marijuana and LSD, despite the efforts of a large security force to confiscate the contraband, but there was less drug use than in 1969. Heavy rains left the more than 300,000 people in attendance covered with muck.

[Joel Makower, *Woodstock: The Oral History* (New York, 1989); Robert Stephen Spitz, *Barefoot in Babylon: The Creation of the Woodstock Music Festival, 1969* (New York, 1979).]

THOMAS G. GRESS

See also **SUPP:** Music, Rock and Roll; Music Festivals.

WORLD'S FAIRS are one-time international expositions that feature exhibits showcasing developments in science, technology, industry, and the arts. Held in cities, they typically run for six months, from spring to fall. Exhibitors include governments, corporations, and large private organizations. The Crystal Palace Exhibition held in London in 1851 began the modern era of international expositions. Staged to demonstrate the superiority of British industry, it housed exhibits of machinery, art, and crafts and attracted more than 6 million visitors. Since the Crystal Palace world's fairs have become more than demonstrations of industrial progress and have acquired symbolic purposes. The Philadelphia Centennial Exposition of 1876 commemorated the anniversary of the Declaration of Independence. The 1893 World's Columbian Exposition at Chicago celebrated the anniversary of the discovery of America. In 1915 the San Francisco Panama-Pacific International Exposition honored the opening of the Panama Canal and the city's recovery from the earthquake of 1906.

Fairs held in the United States during the 1930s helped visitors cope with the Great Depression. In 1933–1934 Chicago's Century of Progress International Exhibition took shape around the theme of scientific and industrial progress since the city's founding. It marked the first time that such firms as General Motors constructed pavilions to display their products. The 1939–1940 New York World's Fair, billed as "The World of Tomorrow," drew more than 44 million visitors. It introduced television and promoted suburban living and pollution-free, automated factories. World War II and its aftermath precluded international expositions until the late 1950s. The United States did not host a postwar world's fair until the

1962 Century 21 Exposition in Seattle. The inspiration for this fair came in part from the cold war; after the Soviet Union launched *Sputnik* in 1957, U.S. leaders and scientists wanted to demonstrate the nation's scientific prowess. The Seattle fair featured the 605-foot Space Needle, a monorail, an amusement park, and many exhibits. In 1964–1965 the New York World's Fair drew more than 51 million visitors, offered striking pavilion architecture, and pioneered audiovisual display techniques. It included 200 buildings and the Unisphere, a 140-foot-high stainless steel globe signifying "Peace Through Understanding." In response to the ecological crisis of the 1970s the United States hosted three fairs dealing with energy conservation and the environment: Spokane (1974), Knoxville (1982), and New Orleans (1984). The Bureau of International Expositions, which since 1928 has overseen world's fairs, authorizing dates and enforcing exhibition standards, authorized three events through the year 2000: Expo 96 in Budapest, Hungary; Expo 98 in Lisbon, Portugal; and Expo 2000 in Hanover, Germany.

[John E. Findling and Kimberly D. Pelle, eds., *Historical Dictionary of World's Fairs and Expositions, 1851–1988* (Westport, Conn., 1987); Robert W. Rydell, *World of Fairs: The Century-of-Progress Expositions* (Chicago, 1993).]

ANDREW FELDMAN

See also **DAH:** Centennial Exposition; Century of Progress International Exhibition; New York World's Fairs; Panama-Pacific International Exposition; Seattle World's Fair; World's Columbian Exposition.

WORLD TRADE CENTER BOMBING. On Feb. 26, 1993, Islamic terrorists exploded a car bomb in the underground garage to the World Trade Center in New York City, killing six people and injuring more than 1,000. Federal authorities soon arrested Sheik Omar Abdel Rahman, a blind fundamentalist Islamic cleric implicated in the assassination of Egypt's Anwar el-Sadat a decade earlier, and nine co-conspirators. Following a nine-month trial, during which a Federal Bureau of Investigation informant who had infiltrated the group provided secretly videotaped evidence, Rahman and his followers were convicted of plotting to blow up the United Nations, FBI offices, highway tunnels, and the George Washington Bridge, in addition to the World Trade Center. Sheik Rahman and El Sayyid Nosair received life sentences and the other conspirators prison terms ranging from twenty-five to fifty-seven years. Notwithstanding

Rahman's claim that the trial was part of the "American war against Islam," U.S. Attorney Mary Jo White denied any "prosecution of Islam or any other religion" and hailed the sentences as "strong and appropriate."

[Laurie Mylroie, "The World Trade Center Bomb," *National Interest* 42 (Winter 1995–1996).]

J. GARRY CLIFFORD

See also **SUPP:** Middle East, Relations with; Terrorism.

WORLD WIDE WEB, also called WWW, the Web, or W3, is an information environment that links computers around the globe to form a literal web of machines distributing hypermedia—text, images, audio, video, and computational services—on the Internet. The WWW uses a standard set of protocols and conventions, which makes it easy for anyone on the Web to roam, browse, and participate in electronic exchanges. According to late 1995 estimates, 18 million people use the WWW at tens of millions of sites, or computers connected and serving hypermedia on the Web. The WWW uses the Hypertext Transfer Protocol (HTTP) as its core communications protocol on the Internet. Documents are written in Hypertext Markup Language (HTML), which controls the formatting and presentation of the hypertext on each Web site. Hypertext allows users to make selections and navigate further into the text through keywords and interrelated links that can point to hypertext documents contained on one isolated Web site or another site around the globe. The World Wide Web project was begun in 1989 by Tim Berners-Lee at CERN, the European Particle Physics Laboratory, who formed the World Wide Web Consortium—an industry consortium run by the Laboratory for Computer Science at the Massachusetts Institute of Technology—to develop common standards for the evolution of the Web.

[Graphics, Visualization, and Usability Center, *Fourth WWW User Survey* (Atlanta, 1995); Ed Krol, *The Whole Internet User's Guide and Catalog* (Sebastopol, Calif., 1992).]

MICHAEL REGOLI

See also **SUPP:** Internet.

WOUNDED KNEE. The confrontation between Native Americans and U.S. authorities at Wounded Knee in 1973 emerged out of a long history. The incident was also influenced by the civil rights activism of the 1960s and the growth of confrontational politics, especially on behalf of racial minorities. The radical American Indian Movement (AIM), formed in 1968, provided leadership in the seizure of Alcatraz Island in November 1969 and the occupation of the Bureau of Indian Affairs (BIA) building in Washington, D.C., in November 1972. The small Indian settlement of Wounded Knee on the Pine Ridge Sioux Reservation in South Dakota was significant as the site of a mass grave resulting from the last "battle" of the Indian wars of the nineteenth century, a brutal episode revisited in Dee Brown's best-selling *Bury My Heart at Wounded Knee* (1971). Pine Ridge also signaled a division in Native American ranks between largely urban militants and the more conservative tribal leadership of the Oglala Sioux. On Feb. 27, 1973, some 200 armed men, most belonging to AIM, seized the village at Wounded Knee by taking eleven elderly hostages and destroying seven Indian homes, two churches, and a museum. The action was designed to publicize Indian grievances and challenge the elected local tribal head, Richard Wilson. Only the government's decision to place U.S. marshals on the road to Wounded Knee prevented these two groups of Native Americans from attacking one another. Even so, the government's action produced a military standoff and a crisis. While a full-blown shootout did not transpire in the seventy-day siege, exchange of gunfire did lead to the deaths of two Indians and serious injury to a federal marshal. The end came on May 8, 1973, with agreement that the insurgents would lay down their arms and the government would discuss grievances. Charges against AIM leaders were either dropped or rejected in court; a judge dismissed charges against AIM leaders Russell Means and Dennis Banks in 1974. The disagreement among the Oglala Sioux did not end, nor did friction between AIM and the government. A shootout at Pine Ridge in June 1975, which killed one Indian and two FBI agents, led in 1977 to a controversial trial and a life sentence for murder for AIM leader Leonard Peltier. The episode and its aftermath gave Wounded Knee new meaning to Native Americans and produced a broadened awareness of Indian problems. Before and after the Wounded Knee standoff, the administration of President Richard M. Nixon increased the BIA budget and supported reform legislation that led to passage of the Indian Self-Determination and Educational Assistance Act of 1975.

[Peter Matthiessen, *In the Spirit of Crazy Horse* (New York, 1983); Wilcomb E. Washburn, ed., *History of Indian-White Relations* (Washington, D.C., 1988).]

ROSS GREGORY

See also **SUPP:** American Indian Movement; Native Americans.

WYOMING, the least populated of the fifty states, with a 1990 population of 453,588 and a land area that is ninth largest, with 97,104 square miles. Sixty-five percent of the state's population lived in areas defined as urban. The Great Plains extend into the eastern part of the state, the land rising to mountains and high plateaus in the west. Winter temperatures can fall as low as minus sixty degrees, although humidity is extremely low. Brisk winds add to the generally harsh climate. Vast distances separate the towns and cities. Because of the small and homogenous population, the state has been characterized as a "small town with a long main street."

Natural resource exploitation, livestock raising, irrigation farming, and tourism have been the main industries. Manufacturing is almost nonexistent, even in the larger towns. Oil and coal, along with trona (a source of sodium compounds discovered in 1938) and uranium (discovered in 1918 but not produced until the 1950s), have made Wyoming susceptible to economic booms and busts. Wyoming's economy was locked into two decades of stagnation until 1973, when the Arab oil embargo caused energy prices to rise dramatically. By the mid-1970s oil exploration had brought hundreds of new workers to Wyoming, but the coal industry experienced the greatest growth. The industry practically died in the 1950s when the railroads switched from coal-burning locomotives to diesels. Public utilities began building coal-fired plants across the country, including plants in Wyoming at Rock Springs, Kemmerer, Glenrock, and Wheatland during the 1970s, which brought thousands more workers to the state. During the decade the population soared from 320,000 to 469,000. By the 1990s, 98 percent of the state's electricity was provided by steam-powered plants.

The coal beds in Wyoming, estimated to underlie 40 percent of the land area, are often close to the surface, making strip mining practical in most areas. More than 96 percent of the coal is subbituminous with a relatively low heat content. Nonetheless, it contains sulfur, making it a more acceptable fuel for meeting clean air standards. The area of greatest expansion in coal production was the Powder River Basin in northeastern Wyoming. For example, the state's total production in 1974 was just 20 million tons. In 1992 the Black Thunder Mine near Gillette was producing 28.6 million tons annually. Coal production in

Wyoming was greater than in any other state from 1989 (171 million tons) to 1995 (263 million tons).

The mineral boom of the 1970s brought with it increasing demands for government services and local amenities. The small ranching communities could not provide enough facilities to accommodate all of the new arrivals. In 1969 the state had adopted a severance tax on minerals, and with increasing prices and production of minerals, the tax raised hundreds of millions of dollars by the late 1970s. Some of the funds were directed back to local communities in order to build new water and sewer systems, streets, schools, and jails.

In the 1980s energy prices declined and pushed Wyoming into its worst economic depression. The population fell 3.4 percent from 1980 to 1990. By the early 1990s the state's economy was stagnant and, except for some resort towns, most places continued to lose population. Tourism flourished, however, especially at Yellowstone National Park, Grand Teton National Park, and Devil's Tower National Monument (generating approximately $1.5 billion in revenue annually in the 1990s), but it did not offset the loss of highly paid jobs in the minerals sector. Jackson Hole, nationally renowned for the beauty of the nearby Tetons and for outdoor sports, grew rapidly, causing housing prices to inflate to West Coast levels. The federal government controlled 46.5 percent of the state's land in 1993. Although many residents resented the federal presence, a substantial number relied on federal assistance, particularly in the livestock, tourism, and mineral industries.

Republicans have dominated politics for much of Wyoming's history, but party affiliation has been less important than strong personalities and constituent service. Although Republicans have dominated the state legislature, the governors from 1974 to 1993 were Democrats. During the early 1970s Wyoming voters kept Democrat Gale McGee and Republican Clifford Hansen in the U.S. Senate. McGee sought reelection in 1976 but lost to rancher and businessman Malcolm Wallop. In 1978 Hansen, a former governor, retired from the Senate to his Jackson Hole ranch. His successor was Alan K. Simpson, the son of former governor and senator Milward Simpson. Democrat Teno Roncalio retired in 1978 after five terms in Congress. Republican Richard Cheney, former chief of staff to President Gerald R. Ford, succeeded Roncalio in Wyoming's only seat in the U.S. House of Representatives; he was reelected every two years until 1989, when he resigned to accept the post of secretary of defense. Cheney's successor, Republican

Craig Thomas, went on to the Senate in 1995 after Wallop retired. Democrat Ed Herschler was first elected governor in 1974 and was the first governor to be elected to three terms. He retired in 1986 and was replaced by another Democrat, Michael J. Sullivan, who served two terms. The Democrats lost the governorship to Republican Jim Geringer in 1994, when Sullivan ran unsuccessfully against Thomas for Wallop's Senate seat. That same year the one seat in the House was won by Republican Barbara Cubin, the first woman elected to Congress from Wyoming.

[Loren Jost, ed., *Wyoming Historical Blue Book,* 3rd ed. (Cheyenne, Wyo., 1990); T. A. Larson, *History of Wyoming* (Lincoln, Nebr., 1979); Clynn Phillips et al., *Wyoming Data Handbook* (Cheyenne, Wyo., 1991); Phil Roberts et al., *Wyoming Almanac,* 3rd rev. ed. (Laramie, Wyo., 1994).]

PHIL ROBERTS

YUGOSLAVIA. *See* **Bosnia-Herzegovina.**

ZOOLOGY is the study of the structure, function, and ecology of animals. Throughout the eighteenth and nineteenth centuries, zoological study in the United States focused on identifying and classifying the abundant and diverse animals found on the North American continent. Researchers such as John James Audubon undertook massive cataloging efforts, identifying and describing animal natural history. During this time a parallel effort was also made in the field of botany. At the end of the nineteenth century, zoology evolved into a more integrative science, encompassing the fields of natural history, morphology (the study of the structure of animals), and physiology (the study of the functions in animals). As advances were made in genetics in the early twentieth century, zoology began to focus on that area. The fields of ecology, comparative anatomy, embryology (fetal development), cytology (cell development), parasitology (parasite biology), systematics (classification of organisms), and protozoology (microorganism biology) all were part of the overarching field of zoology.

The discovery of DNA, the molecule that transfers genetic information in all organisms, in the 1950s brought molecular biology to a central position in the field of biology, which it continued to dominate for the rest of the century. Throughout the 1960s, 1970s, and 1980s, as interest in molecular biology increased, interest in whole organisms and morphology decreased. In the 1970s the effort to integrate the branches of zoology gained ground, partly in response to the growing interest in ecology. By studying the ecology of animals, zoologists joined their understanding of the molecular biology of animals with their understanding of how animals fit into the larger picture of ecosystems and environments. Articles in zoology journals focused on the roles animals play in their ecosystems and on how they interact with their environment, as zoologists studied the interrelationships among animals, plants, microorganisms, and physical factors.

The trend toward a more ecological approach was grounded in increased concern over environmental degradation during the 1980s and 1990s. As zoologists noted the precipitous decline in animal populations in the wild, they sought to explain the reasons for the decline and to develop methods to reverse it. In the years since the passage of the Endangered Species Act in 1973, zoologists have played a central role in the research necessary for the implementation of the act. Zoologists have also studied species extinction. The threat to global biodiversity has caused alarm among biologists, and efforts have been undertaken to document which animals are threatened, which animals have become extinct, and the causes of the decline in biodiversity. Ironically, this concern has created a need to catalog animals that parallels the early zoological efforts in the eighteenth and nineteenth centuries in the United States. E. O. Wilson, a Harvard University biologist and an expert on biodiversity, called for a major effort to identify, classify, and catalog the millions of species that remain unknown, arguing that the effort to protect the world's habitats and thus animal diversity must begin with a comprehensive knowledge of which animals live where.

Although cataloging has become one area of increased zoological interest, the major thrust has been on the interaction between animals and their environments. A specific area of this research that is gaining in prominence is the investigation of the influence of human activity on animals. Changes in the environment caused by pollution, habitat destruction, climate change, and hunting all affect animal survival. Examination of these influences is increasingly falling into the domain of zoologists. In addition to identifying how human activity affects animals, zoologists study ways of remediating human impacts. Zoos have begun making captive breeding programs a priority among their activities. These programs will permit the restoration of endangered animals into the wild. Zoologists play a key role, not only in understanding the reproductive biology and ecology of animals, but in determining the most effective methods of reintroduction. Issues like species extinction are extraordinarily complex. The integration of the expertise of many fields is essential for solving the problems that affect the world's animals. Zoologists therefore collaborate with botanists, soils experts, land and water resource specialists, atmospheric scientists, and policymakers in their joint effort to understand and maintain the earth's biological resources.

[Keith R. Benson and Brother C. Edward Quinn, "The American Society of Zoologists, 1889–1989: A Century of Integrating the Biological Sciences," *American Zoologist* 30 (1990); C. Leon Harris, *Concepts in Zoology* (New York, 1992); E. O. Wilson, *The Diversity of Life* (Cambridge, Mass., 1992).]

DAVID W. CASH

See also **DAH** and **SUPP:** Ecology; **SUPP:** Endangered Species; Species, Introduced.

ALPHABETICAL LIST OF ENTRIES

ALPHABETICAL LIST OF ENTRIES

INDEX

Numbers in boldface refer to the main entry on the subject. Museums are listed under "Museums"; orchestras under "Orchestras"; legal cases, other than Supreme Court cases, under "Legal cases"; and Supreme Court cases under "Supreme Court cases." Titles of radio programs appear under "Radio programs" and titles of television programs and shows under "Television programs."

A

A. H. Robins, **1:**157a
Aaron, Hank, **1:**70b
AARP. *See* American Association of Retired Persons (AARP)
Abbas, Mahmoud, **1:**336b
Abbott Laboratories, **1:**316b
ABMs. *See* Antiballistic missiles (ABMs)
Abnaki Tribal Council, **2:**290a
Abortion, **1:3a–6a,** 200b
 Catholic Church opposition to, **1:**101a
 children's rights and, **1:**116a
 Christian conservatives and, **1:**154b
 clinics harassed by pro-life movement, **2:**146a
 and Food and Drug Administration, **1:**255b
 and genetic engineering, **1:**281a
 Harris v. *McRae* (1980), **1:**292b
 as issue in Minnesota politics, **2:**37a
 as issue in presidential campaign of 1984, **1:**94b
 laws, **2:**181a
 legislation in Pennsylvania, **2:**111a
 not discussed in presidential campaign of 1976, **1:**93b
 and pregnancy discrimination Act, **2:**137b
 and privacy, **1:**287b
 rights, **2:**327b, 329b–330a
 and Supreme Court, **2:**240b, 313b–314b
 and Women's Equity Action League, **2:**325b
Abourezk, James, **1:**40b, 362a

Abruzzo, Ben, **1:**66a
Abscam scandal, **1:6a–b,** 151b, 159a, 165b
Abu-Lughod, Ibrahim, **2:**104a
Academic freedom, **1:6b–7a**
Academic research, **1:**7a
Accidents, **1:7a–b**
 alcohol as cause of, **1:**60b
Accounting
 firms in New York City, **2:**72a
 jobs in, **2:**8a
Achille Lauro, **1:7b–8a**
Acid rain, **1:8a–b,** 31b, 201b, 215a, 224a
Acquired Immune Deficiency Syndrome (AIDS), **1:8b–11b,** 64a,b, 104a, 296b; **2:**16b, 17a, 59a
 activists' pressure on health care system, **1:**298a
 in Africa, **1:**19a–b
 benefit concerts for, **1:**74a
 in California, **1:**92b
 as cause of death, **1:**181b, 367b
 and dance, **1:**174b
 and drug use, **2:**233b
 and Food and Drug Administration, **1:**255b, 256a
 and gay liberation, **1:**274b
 identification of virus, **2:**29b
 international conferences, **1:**10a
 as metaphor for gay writers, **1:**372a
 in New York City, **2:**72b
 and prostitution, **2:**146b
 pure food and drug movement, **2:**156a
 in San Francisco, **2:**188a
 and sexuality, **2:**202b, 203a,b
 and tuberculosis, **2:**276a–b

Acreage Reduction Program, **1:**243a
Act for Better Child Care (1990), **1:**114b
ACTION, **2:**298b
ACT UP (AIDS Coalition to Unleash Power), **1:**10b, 256a, 274b
Acupuncture, **2:**19b–20a, 66b
ADA. *See* Americans with Disabilities Act (ADA)
Ada County, Idaho, **1:**315a
Adams, Abigail, **1:**247a,b, 376b
Adams, John, **1:**278a; **2:**49b
 on language, **1:**205a
Adams, Oscar, **1:**33b
Adams County, Colo., **1:**183b
Addiction, **2:**232a–b
Adena culture, **1:**41a–b
Adler, Mortimer J., **1:**207a; **2:**58b
Administrative convenience, **2:**167a
Adoption, **1:11b–13b,** 236b, 262b
 laws for assistance, **1:**116a
 See also Foster care
Adoption Assistance and Child Welfare Act (1980), **1:**12b, 262b
Advanced Micro Devices, **2:**205b
Advertising, **1:13b–15a**
 and direct mail, **1:**187a
 firms in New York City, **2:**72a
 infomercials, **2:**5a
 in magazines, **2:**3b
 of mail-order business, **2:**4b
 in newspapers, **2:**71a
 as outlet for photographers, **2:**123b
 psychology applied to, **2:**150a
 tobacco industry, **2:**260b, 261b
Aerobics, **1:15a–b**

INDEX

in Virginia, **2:**295a
in Wyoming, **2:**333b
Agriculture, Department of (USDA),
   1:28a–29a, 222b
   alternative pest control strategies, **2:**114b
   Economy Food Plan, **2:**136b
   food guide, **2:**85b–86a
   genetically modified plants regulation,
      1:79b
   Germplasm Research Information
      Network, **1:**84b
   and introduced species, **2:**224b
   and organic farming, **2:**99a–b
   and pesticides, **2:**114a–b
   pure food and drug movement, **2:**156b
   and State Department, **2:**227a,b
   subsidies to tobacco farmers, **2:**261a
   and subsidization, **1:**243a
Ahmadiyya Muslims, **1:**336a
AIDS. *See* Acquired Immune Deficiency
   Syndrome (AIDS)
AIDS and Its Metaphors (Sontag), **1:**377b
AIDS Clinical Trial Network, **1:**10b
AIDS Medical Foundation (AMF), **1:**9b
AIDS Research, Office of, **1:**11b
Aid to Families with Dependent Children
   (AFDC), **1:**5a; **2:**137a, 140b, 210b,
   315a,b
   in California, **1:**90b
Aid to Families with Dependent Children-
   Unemployed Parent (AFDC-UP),
   2:316b
*Aiiieeeee: An Anthology of Asian-American
   Writers* (ed. Chin), **1:**371a
Ailey, Alvin, **1:**174a
AIM. *See* American Indian Movement
   (AIM)
Airbus Industrie, **1:**29b
Aircraft and air transport, Honolulu center
   of, **1:**303b
Aircraft industry, **1:29a–30b; 2:**271b
   in Fort Worth, **1:**262a
   in Seattle, **2:**198a
   in Tulsa, **2:**277b
Air force bases in North Dakota, **2:**82b
Air Force Special Weapons Center
   (Kirkland Air Force Base), **1:**35b
Airline Deregulation Act (1978), **1:**30b
Airline industry, **2:**271b–272a
   deregulation, **1:**184a; **2:**271b
   and strikes, **2:**231a
Air pollution, **1:30b–32b,** 222b, 223a
   concern in California, **1:**90b
   indoor, **1:**32a
Air traffic control, **2:**230b, 272a
Air traffic controllers strike (1981), **1:32b,**
   356b; **2:**272a
Air transport, **1:29a–30b**
Akalaitis, JoAnne, **2:**256a
Ak-Chin Pima; **2:**63a
Akron, Ohio, **1:**138b; **2:**90b
   golf in, **1:**285a
Alabama, **1:32b–34a**
   tornadoes in, **2:**263a
Alabama Democratic Conference, **1:**33a
Alabama New South Coalition, **1:**33a
Alar, **2:**99b
Alaska, **1:34a–35a**
   abortion legalization, **1:**4a
   North Slope of, **1:**216b–217a

oil spill (1989), **1:**232b–233b
volcanoes in, **2:**297b
wetlands of, **2:**318b
and wildfires, **2:**320a
Alaska, Gulf of, **1:**232b–233b
Alaska National Interest Lands
   Conservation Act (1980), **1:**35a;
   2:107a,b
Alaska Native Claims Settlement Act
   (1971), **1:**34b; **2:**106b
Alaska Permanent Fund, **1:**34b
Albania, **1:**197b
Albany, N.Y., **2:**74a
   Puerto Ricans in, **2:**153b
Albee, Edward, **2:**156a
Albuquerque, N.M., **1:35a–b; 2:**70a
Alcalá, San Diego de, **2:**187a
Alcatraz, **1:35b; 2:**178a
Alcatraz Island, **2:**333a
Alcohol
   advertising, **1:**14b
   as cause of accidents, **1:**60b
   minimum drinking age, **1:**160a
   and recreation, **2:**165a
Alcohol, Drug Abuse, and Mental Health
   Administration, **1:**295b
Alcohol, Tobacco and Firearms, Bureau of,
   2:35a, 272b
   law enforcement powers of, **2:**129a
   office in Oklahoma City, **2:**94b
Alcohol abuse and alcoholism, **2:**16b, 21a,
   151a, 232a–234b, 320b
   Native Americans and, **2:**63b
Alcohol Abuse and Alcoholism Institute,
   2:58b
Alcoholics Anonymous, **2:**234a
Alcorn University, **2:**40a
Alcott, Amy, **1:**285b
Alcott, Louisa May, **1:**376b
Alegría, Ricardo, **2:**58a
Aleuts, **2:**197b
   business development assistance, **2:**38b
   set-asides and, **2:**200a
Alexander, Jane, **2:**57b, 256a
Alexander, Lamar, **1:**206b; **2:**251a
Algeria; **2:**33a
   hostage crisis mediation, **1:**306b
Ali, Muhammad, **2:**145a
Ali, Noble Drew, **1:**335b
Aliens, **2:**167b, 168b
   See also Illegal aliens; Refugees
Alimony, **2:**11a
Alioto, Joseph L., **2:**187b
Allen, Fred, **2:**159a
Allen, George F., **2:**294a
Allen, Gracie, **2:**159a
Allen, Ivan, **1:**283a
Allen, James B., **1:**361a
Allen, Marcus, **1:**23b
Allen, Paul, **1:**147a
Allen, Richard, **1:**20a
Allen, Steve, **2:**246a
Allen, Woody, **2:**274a
Allende, Isabel, **1:**370a
Allende, Salvador, **1:**131a, 326a
Allergy and Infectious Diseases Institute,
   2:58b
Alliance Airport, **1:**262a
Alliance for Progress, **1:**211b
Alliance Industrial Center, **1:**262a

Allican language, **1:**244a
Allis-Chalmers, **2:**321a
Allison, Bobby, **1:**34a
All-volunteer force (AVF), **1:**194a–b
Almanac Singers, **1:**73b
Alpha Delta Pi, **1:**263a
Altair, **1:**145a, 147a,b
Alternative Medicine (NIH), **2:**59a
Alternatives, Inc. (EAI), **2:**192b
Altman, Robert A., **1:**165b
Altman, Roger, **2:**319b
Altman, Sidney, **2:**76a
Alton, Tex., disaster, **1:**191b
Aluminum
   production in Saint Croix, **2:**295b
   recycling of, **2:**166a
Alurista, **1:**371a
Alvarez, Luis W., **1:**282a
Alzheimer's disease, **1:36a**
   altered genes and, **1:**310b
Amahl and the Night Visitors (opera,
   Menotti), **2:**49b
Amalgamated Clothing and Textile
   Workers' Union, **1:**273b
Amateur Sports Act (1978), **2:**95a
Ambassadors, U.S., **2:**227a
Ambrosino, Michael, **2:**195b
Amendment to the Social Security Act
   (Kerr-Mills program) (1960), **2:**15b
Amerasian Homecoming Act (1987), **1:**50a;
   2:215a
America 2000 Excellence in Education Act
   (1991), **2:**193b
American Academy of Physician
   Assistants, **2:**125a
American Airlines, **1:**30b; **2:**272a
American Anti-Vivisection Society,
   1:39a
American Association of Critical Care
   Nurses, **2:**85a
American Association of Retired Persons
   (AARP), **1:**26a, **36a–37a**
   Modern Maturity, **2:**4a
American Association of University
   Professors (AAUP), **1:**6b
American Association of University
   Women, **1:**129b–130a
American Basketball Association, **2:**288a
American Battle Monuments Commission,
   2:305a
American Board of Psychiatry and
   Neurology, **2:**149b
American Broadcasting Company (ABC),
   1:142b; **2:**249a,b
   Baseball Network, **1:**70a, 71b
   baseball on, **1:**69b
   radio network, **2:**159a
American Buddhist Society and
   Fellowship, **1:**52b
American Cancer Society, **2:**260b
   and fat consumption, **2:**86b
American Cetacean Society, **2:**197b
American Challenge, The (Servan
   Schreiber), **1:**229a
American Civil Liberties Union (ACLU),
   1:232a
American Clinical and Climatological
   Association, **1:**128a
American College of Obstetricians and
   Gynecologists, **1:**113b

INDEX

Delaware City, Del., **1:**178b
Delaware Medical Center, **1:**179a
Delaware River, **1:**178a–b
Delbruck, Max, **1:**64a
Delco Electronics, **1:**321b
DeLillo, Don, **1:**370a
DeLoach, Joe, **2:**96b
DeLorean, John Z., **2:**274a
Delors, Jacques, **1:**230a
Delta Air Lines, **1:**30b; **2:**272a
Delta State, **2:**39b–40a
Del Tredici, David, **2:**51b
Dementia, **2:**16b
D'Emilio, John, **1:**274a
DeMille, Cecil B., **2:**43a, 44a
Democracy as human right, **1:**312b
Democratic Farmer-Labor party
(Minnesota), **2:**37a
Democratic Leadership Council, **1:**181a
Democratic National Committee, **1:**180b
Democratic National Convention (1968),
2:178a
Democratic party, **1:179a–181a**
energy policy and, **1:**219b
national headquarters in Watergate,
2:310a
Rainbow Coalition, **2:**160b
and religion, **2:**169b
in Rhode Island, **2:**176a
in South Carolina, **2:**212a,b
in West Virginia, **2:**317a
in Wisconsin, **2:**321b–322a
in Wyoming, **2:**334a
Democratic South, **2:**171a, 173b
Democratic Steering Committee, **1:**149b
Democratic Study Group, **1:**152b
Demographic changes, **1:181a–183a**
Demographics
African Americans, **1:**21b
in Alaska, **1:**34a
in Arizona, **1:**43a
in Arkansas, **1:**44b
in California, **1:**92b
cities, **2:**284b–285a
in Colorado, **1:**137b
delegate selection and, **1:**180a
in Detroit, **1:**186b
in Illinois, **1:**317a
in Indiana, **1:**321a
in Iowa, **1:**330b–331a
in Kansas, **1:**347a
in Kentucky, **1:**350b
in Las Vegas, **1:**358a–b
in Los Angeles, **1:**378b
in Louisiana, **1:**380a
in Maine, **2:**5b
in Massachusetts, **2:**13b
in Memphis, **2:**21a
in Miami, **2:**26a
in Milwaukee, **2:**35b
in Minneapolis, **2:**36a
in Minnesota, **2:**37b
in Mississippi, **2:**40a
in Nebraska, **2:**64a
in Nevada, **2:**65a
in Newark, **2:**67a
in New Hampshire, **2:**67a
in New Jersey, **2:**68b
in New Orleans, **2:**70b
in New York City, **2:**71b–72a

in North Dakota, **2:**82a
in Oakland, **2:**87a
in Ohio, **2:**90b
in Oklahoma, **2:**93a
in Omaha; **2:**97a
in Oregon, **2:**98b
in Pennsylvania, **2:**111b
in Philadelphia, **2:**118b
in Phoenix, **2:**123a
in Pittsburgh, **2:**127b
in Puerto Rico, **2:**155a
in Raleigh, N.C., **2:**160b
in Rhode Island, **2:**175b
in Tennessee, **2:**250b
in Texas, **2:**253b
in Tucson, **2:**277a
in Tulsa, **2:**277b
in Vermont, **2:**290a
in Virginia, **2:**293b
in Virginia Beach, **2:**295b
in Washington State, **2:**308a
Deng Xiaoping, **1:**117a,b
De Niro, Robert, **1:**338b
Denmark
and European Community, **1:**228a,
229a,b
and NATO, **2:**78b
Dennison, Thomas, **2:**97a
Denny, Reginald, **1:**379b
Dental Research Institute, **2:**59a
Dentistry, **1:183a–b**
Denver, Colo., **1:183b–184a**
Denver-Boulder-Greeley Consolidated
Metropolitan Statistical Area, **1:**137b
desegregation and, **1:**185b–186a
light-rail trolley system, **2:**271b
Denver, John, **2:**262b, 318a
Denver Center for the Performing Arts,
1:184a
Denver County, Colo., **1:**183b
Denver International Airport, **1:**138a
aviation disaster near, **1:**190a
Denver Post, **2:**132b
Denver Public Library, **1:**184a
Denver Tech Center, **1:**184a
Department of Education Organization Act
(1976), **1:**206a
Department of Energy Organization Act
(1977), **1:**214a, 219a
Department stores, **2:**175a
Depository Institutions Deregulation and
Monetary Control Act (1980), **1:**67b,
240a–b; **2:**189b
Depression (medical), **2:**17a, 21a
drugs for, **2:**22a
Deregulation, **1:184a–b**
and financial exchange rules, **2:**304a
Derivatives, **2:**304b
Derrida, Jacques, **2:**122a, 135b
DES. *See* Diethylstilbestrol (DES)
DeSalvo, Albert, **2:**199b
Desegregation, **1:184b–186a; 2:**240a
in Atlanta, **1:**283a
and football, **1:**257a
and Nixon, **2:**171b
Raleigh, N.C., **2:**160b
in Saint Louis, **2:**186a
in South Africa, **2:**212a
Deseret Book Company, **2:**288a
Deseret News, **2:**288a

Desert One hostage rescue attempt, **2:**306a
Desert Shield. *See* Gulf War (1991)
Desert Storm. *See* Gulf War (1991)
Desktop publishing, **2:**89b, 141a
Des Moines, Iowa, floods, **2:**249a
Des Moines Register, **2:**132b
Des Moines River, **1:**249a
Destructuralism. *See* Post-structuralism
Détente, **1:**130b–131a; **2:**217a–219a, 229a–
b, 236a
use by NATO, **2:**79b
Detroit, **1:186a–b; 2:**27b, 285a
Arab Americans in, **1:**40b
Polish Americans in, **2:**130b
sculpture in, **2:**197a
Detroit Metropolitan Airport, aviation
disaster near, **1:**190a
Deukmejian, George, **1:**90a
Deutch, John, **1:**106a
Devers, Gail, **2:**96b
Devil's Tower National Monument, **2:**334a
Dewey, George, **2:**97b
Dewey, John, **1:**170a; **2:**122a,b
Dharma Realm Buddhist Association,
1:52b
Diabetes, **2:**314b
altered genes and, **1:**310b
prevention, **2:**17b
Diabetes and Digestive and Kidney
Diseases Institute, **2:**59a
*Diagnostic and Statistical Manual of
Mental Disorders,* **2:**21b
Dial, **1:**376b
Diamas, Trent, **2:**96a
Diamond, David, **2:**49b
Diamond Head Crater, **1:**304b
DiCarlo, George, **2:**96b
Dickhoff, Robert Ernest, **1:**52b
Dickinson, Emily, **1:**377a
Dick-Read, Grantley, **1:**113a
Dickson, William Kennedy Laurie, **2:**43a
Dictionary of Cultural Literacy, The (Hirsh,
Kett, and Trefil), **1:**170a
Didion, Joan, **1:**91a, 377b
Diebel, Nelson, **2:**96b
Diebenkorn, Richard, **1:**91b
Diethylstilbestrol (DES), **1:**255b; **2:**326a
Dieting, **1:**200a
Dietz, Robert S., **1:**281b
Difference feminists, **2:**327b–329a
Different, Not Dumb (Marek), **1:**374a
Digital Equipment Corporation (DEC),
1:144b–145a, 146b
expert computer system, **1:**49b
restructuring, **1:**145b
Digital imaging, **2:**124b
Digital sound, **1:**243b
Dillinger, John, **1:**239a
Dillon, Douglas, **1:**276b
Diners Club, **1:**160b, 161a
Dingell, John, **2:**156a
Dinkins, David, **2:**72b
Dioxin, **1:**223b, 224a; **2:**260a
Diplomacy and summit conferences,
2:236b
Diplomatic corps, **2:**226a–b
Diplomatic Security, Bureau of, **2:**228a
Direct mail, **1:186b–187a**
Directorate of Science and Technology,
1:105a

INDEX

Dirty tricks (Watergate), **2:**310a
Disability
    disabled employees, **1:**237b–238a
    and education, **1:**116b, 203a, 204a
    insurance, **2:**315a
    reduced income grants under Reagan,
        1:298a
    rights movement, **1:187b–188b**
Disarmament, **1:45a–49a**
Disaster Relief and Assistance Act (1974),
    1:188b
Disasters
    Bhopal disaster. *See* Bhopal disaster
    Challenger. See Challenger disaster
Disasters, natural and environmental,
    1:188b–189b
    Alaska oil spill (1989), **1:**232b–233b
    Galveston hurricane (1900), **1:**271a–b
    insurance and, **1:**323b, 324a
    in Puerto Rico, **2:**155a–b
Disasters, nonenvironmental, **1:189b–192a**
Disc jockeys, **1:**192a
Disco dancing, **1:**174b
Discos, **1:192a**
Discount stores, **2:**174b–175a
Discover Card, **1:**161a, 246b
Discovery Place (Charlotte, N.C.), **2:**195a
Discovery space shuttle, **1:**107a; **2:**222a
Discrimination
    and disabilities, **1:**187b–188b
    and fraternities and sororities, **1:**263a
    and gay liberation, **1:**274b
    and homosexuality, **2:**204a
    against Korean Americans, **1:**353b
    sex-based classifications, **1:**160b
Diseases
    and genetic engineering, **1:**279b–281a
    identification of genes involved in,
        1:310a–b
    and water pollution, **2:**311b
    See also Bacteriology and Virology;
        Epidemiology
Disney, Walt, **1:**250b
Disparate-impact theory, **2:**304b–305a
Displaced Persons Act (1948), **1:**317b;
    2:168a
District of Columbia. *See* Washington, D.C.
Diversity. *See* Multiculturalism; Pluralism
Divided government, **1:**150b, 151a
Divine, Father, **1:**169a
Diving into the Wreck (Rich), **1:**377b
Divorce, **2:10a–11b**
    effect on housing markets, **1:**307b
    increase in rate of, **2:**11a
    no-fault, **2:**330a
    rate, **1:**351a
    result of, in families, **1:**237a
Dixon, Sharon Pratt, **2:**307a
DNA (deoxyribonucleic acid), **1:**63a,b
    molecules, **1:**279b
    testing and genealogy, **1:**275b
    and zoology, **2:**334b
Dobelle, William, **1:**80a
Dobelle Institute (New York), **1:**80a
Docking, Robert, **1:**347b
Doc Martens boots, **1:**238b
Documentaries, **2:**195b
Dodd, Christopher, **1:**153a
Dodsworth (film), **2:**44a
Dole, Elizabeth H., **1:**356a

Dole, Robert, **1:**347b; **2:**173b
    presidential campaign of 1976, **1:**93b
    presidential campaign of 1988, **1:**94b
Dolphins, **2:**197b
Domenici, Pete V., **1:**337b
Domestic terrorism, **1:**239b
Domestic violence, **1:192a–194a,** 237a
Dominguez, Francisco Atanasio, **1:**137a
Dominican Republic
    Columbus quincentenary, **1:**139a
    immigrants from, **1:**301b, 319b
    U.S. relations with, **1:**359a
Dominicans, **1:**320a
    in New York City, **2:**72a
Domino, Fats, **2:**52a
Donahue, Phil, **2:**246a
Don Juan (film), **2:**44a
Donor's Offspring, **1:**243a
Donovan, Raymond, **1:**356a
Doolittle, Hilda. *See* H. D.
Doomsday Syndrome, The, **1:**221b
"Doonesbury," **2:**132b
Door County, Wisc., **2:**322a
Doping, **2:**197b
Doppler radar, **2:**313b
Double Eagle II (balloon), **1:**66a
Douglas, Buster, **2:**145a
Douglas, Ellen, **2:**39b
Douglas, William O., **1:**221a, 266b, 287b;
    2:282a
Douglas County, Colo., **1:**183b
Douglass, Frederick, **1:**20b
Dove, Rita; **2:**156a
Dover Air Force Base, **1:**178b
Dow Jones Industrial Average, **1:**244b–
    245a; **2:**303a,b
Downsizing
    corporate, **1:**178b
    industry, **2:**265a–b
    military, **1:**178a
Down's syndrome, **1:**242b; **2:**16b
Down These Mean Streets (Thomas),
    1:371a
Draft, **1:**177a, 194a–b
Drag, **1:**274a
Drexel, Burnham, and Lambert, **1:**364b
Drexel Burnham, junk bonds, **1:**345b
Drifters, **2:**52a
Drinker, Philip, **1:**80a
Driver education, **1:**170b
Drogoul, Christopher P., **1:**334a
Drop City, **1:**141a
Drought of 1980s, **1:194b–195b**
Drucker, Peter F., **2:**143b
Drug abuse. *See* Substance abuse
Drug Abuse Institute, **2:**59a
Drug czar, **2:**234a
Drug Enforcement Administration, **2:**233a
    and Federal Bureau of Investigation,
        1:239b
    law enforcement powers of, **2:**129a
Drugs
    in Jacksonville, **1:**339a
    in New York City, **2:**72b
    Operation Intercept, **2:**233b
    psychedelic, **2:**232b, 233b
    recreational use of, **2:**165a
    in Washington, D.C., **2:**306–307a
Drugs, pharmaceutical
    and endangered species, **1:**214a

experimental, **1:**128b
patents, **2:**117b
pricing, **2:**117b
psychiatric drugs, **2:**234b
research and development, **2:**118a
testing, **2:**241a
therapy, **2:**117a
treatment for mental illness, **2:**21b, 22a
Drunk driving, **2:**234a
    legislation in Kentucky, **1:**350a
Dryke, Matthew, **2:**96a
Drystad, Joanell, **2:**37a
D'Souza, Dinesh, **2:**133a
Duarte, José Napoleon, **1:**212a
Du Bois, W. E. B., **1:**278a
Dubs, Adolph, **1:**17a
Duchenne muscular dystrophy, **1:**310b
Ducks Unlimited, **2:**320b
Duffey, Joseph D., **2:**58a
Dukakis, Michael S., **1:**180b; **2:**67b, 317b
    presidential campaign of 1988, **1:**94b,
        95a
    presidential elections of 1988, **2:**14a
Duke, David, **1:**381b
Duke Power Company, **1:**287a
Dulbecco, Renato, **2:**76a
Dulles, Allen, **1:**105a
Dulles, John Foster, **2:**228a
    Egypt, **2:**30b
    Iron Curtain and, **1:**199a
Duluth, Minn., **2:**37b
    and for-profit schools, **2:**192b
Dumas, Henry, **1:**374a
DuPage County, Ill., **1:**316b
Du Pont, Pierre S., IV, **1:**178b
Duran, Francisco Martin, **1:**54a
Duran, Roberto, **2:**145a
Durenberger, David, **2:**37a
Durham, N.H., **2:**67b
Duryea, Frank, **1:**61b
Duval County, Fla., **1:**339a
Duvalier, François ("Papa Doc"), **1:**291b
Duvalier, Jean-Claude ("Baby Doc"),
    1:291b
Dworkin, Andrea, **2:**134a
Dwyer, R. Budd, **2:**110b
Dye, Pete, **1:**285a
Dyer Act (1919), **1:**239a
Dylan, Bob, **1:**74a; **2:**52b, 331a

E

E. F. Hutton, **1:**77b
E. I. du Pont de Nemours & Co., **1:**178b,
    224a
    negative connotation of chemistry,
        1:109a
Charles and Ray Eames Collection of
    Design, **1:**367a
Earl, Anthony, **2:**321b
Earnhardt, Dale, **1:**62a
Earth art, **2:**196b
Earth-based spirituality, **1:**200b
Earth Day (1970), **1:**221a, 222b; **2:**165b,
    197a
Earth Day (1990), **1:**222a
Earth First!, **1:**221b–222a
Earthquakes, **1:197a–b**
    in California, **1:**324a; **2:**87b
    Loma Prieta (1989), **2:**188a,b

G

INDEX

INDEX

Kroger Company, **1:**122a
Krone, Julie, **1:**305a
Krugman, Paul, **1:**260a
Kucinich, Dennis, **1:**127b
Kuhlman, Kathryn, **2:**248b
Kuhn, Bowie, **1:**69a, 70b
Kuhn, Thomas S., **2:**122b
Ku Klux Klan, **2:**34b, 80b, 241a, 319a
   and Asian Americans, **1:**51a
   in Georgia, **1:**283a
   intimidation of African Americans in
      public housing, **1:**308b
   and terrorism, **2:**252b
Kunin, Madeleine M., **2:**289b
Kuniyoshi, Yasuo, **1:**251b
Kurds, **1:**289b
Kushner, Tony, **1:**11b, 372a; **2:**256a,b
Kusner, Kathy, **1:**304b
Kuwait
   and Gulf War, **1:**288a–290a
   Iraq invasion of, **1:**333b; **2:**32b

L

Labor, Department of, **1:355a–356a**
   affirmative action, **1:**16a
   Wage and Hour Division of, **1:**237b
Labor-Management Relations and
   Cooperative Programs, Bureau of,
   1:355b
Labor Statistics, Bureau of, **2:**7b, 9a
Labor unions, **1:**126b, **356a–357a**
   and Democratic party, **1:**180a
   and garment industry, **1:**273a,b
   in Idaho, **1:**316a
   "Made in the USA" defined, **2:**267a
   opposed to NAFTA; **2:**266b
   and political action committees, **2:**131b
   and racial discrimination, **1:**328b
   and riots, **2:**177b–178a
   and strikes, **2:**231a,b
   teachers, **2:**192b
   See also Strikes
Labov, William, **1:**368b
Lac du Flambeau, **2:**322a
Lackland air force base, **2:**186b
La Cucaracha (film), **2:**44a
Lacy, Elizabeth B., **2:**294b
Ladies' Professional Golfers Association
   (LPGA), **1:**285b
Laemmle, Carl, **2:**43a
Lafayette, La., **1:**380a
Laffer, Arthur B., **1:**357a; **2:**239a
Laffer curve theory, **1:357a–b**
Lafitte, Jean, **1:**271a
La Follette Progressives, **2:**321b, 322a
LaGuardia Airport aviation disaster, **1:**190a
Laird, Melvin R., **1:**177a
Lakas, Demetrio, **2:**104b
Lake County, Ill., **1:**316b
Lake Erie, **1:**224a; **2:**91b
Lake Merritt, **2:**87b
Lake Michigan, **2:**322b
Lake Placid, N.Y., **2:**95a
Lamaze, Ferdinand, **1:**113a
Lamm, Richard D., **1:**137b
Lamont-Doherty Earth Observatory
   (Columbia Univ.), **1:**80a
Lancaster bombers, **1:**175a
Landfills, **2:**309b

See also Waste disposal
Land Management, Bureau of, **1:**201b;
   2:65b
Land management legislation, **1:**214a
   in Vermont, **2:**290a
Landon, Alf M., **1:**347b
Land preservation, **1:**213b
Landrieu, Mary, **1:**381b
Lands' End, **2:**175b
Lang, Eugene M., **1:**204b
lang, k. d., **1:**274b
Langer, Bernhard, **1:**285a
Languages
   death of, **1:**368b
   ecology, **1:**368b
   Reader's Digest poll on swearing, **2:**7a
Laos refugees, **2:**169a
Laotian Americans, **1:**50b; **2:**214a,b
   in Garden City, Kans., **1:**319b
Laparoscopic surgery, **2:**242b
La Raza Unida, **2:**25a
LaRossa, Dick, **2:**69a
Lasagna, Louis, **1:**10b
Las Cruces, **2:**70a
Laser technology, **1:357b–358a; 2:**125a
   and arms control, **2:**229a
   and fiber optics, **1:**243b
   printers, **2:**141a
   and surgery, **2:**242b
Lasky, Jesse L., **2:**43a
Last Days of Mankind, The, **1:**221b
Las Vegas, Nev., **1:358a–b; 2:**65a
   disaster in, **1:**191a
   and gambling, **1:**272b
Latch-key kids, **1:**236a
Late Great Planet Earth, The (Lindsey),
   2:35a
Latham, Woodville, **2:**43a
Latin America
   debts of countries, **1:**360a–b
   and drug traffic, **2:**233b
   refugees from, **2:**168b
   U.S. relations with, **1:358b–360b**
Latin-American immigrants
   influence on Catholic Church, **1:**101b
   in Los Angeles, **1:**379a
Latinos
   birthrates and, **1:**181b
   in theater, **2:**256a
   writers, **2:**370b–371a
Latter-day Saints, Church of Jesus Christ
   of, **1:360b–361b; 2:**148a, 170a
   and genealogy, **1:**275a
   in Utah, **2:**287b–288a
Latvia independence, **1:**133a
Laurent, Robert, **1:**251b
Laver, Rod, **2:**252b
Lawrence, David L., **2:**127b
Lawrence, Ernest O., **1:**240b
Lawrence, Mass., **1:**319b
Lawrence Livermore National Laboratory,
   2:109b
Laxalt, Paul, **2:**121b
Laying Waste (Brown), **1:**382a
LBOs. *See* Leveraged buyouts (LBOs)
LDS. *See* Latter-day Saints, Church of
   Jesus Christ of
Leadbelly, **1:**73b
Lead poisoning, **1:**224b–225a
League of Arab States, **2:**31a

League of Conservation Voters, **1:**222a
Leahy, Patrick J., **2:**289b
Leavitt, David, **1:**372a
Lebanese Americans, **1:361b–362a**
Lebanon, **1:362a–b**
   U.S. forces in, **2:**139b
Lebow, Fred, **2:**9b
LeCompte, Elizabeth, **2:**256a
Lederman, Leon M., **1:**241a, 317a; **2:**76a
Led Zeppelin, **2:**52b
Lee, Spike, **2:**46a
Lee, Yuan T., **2:**76a
Lee Teng-hui, **1:**118b
Legal cases
   Aguillard v. *Edwards* (1987), **2:**255a
   *Equal Employment Opportunity
      Commission* v. *Sears, Roebuck and
      Company* (1986), **1:226a–b**
   Morgan v. *Hennigan* (1974), **1:**84a
   Mozert v. *Hawkins County Public
      Schools* (1987), **2:**255a
   Smith v. *Board of School Commissioners
      of Mobile County* (1986), **2:**255a
   See also Supreme Court cases
Legal Defense and Educational Fund
   (LDF), **2:**56b
Legal profession, **1:362b–363b**
   firms in new York City, **2:**72a
   jobs in, **2:**8a
Legionnaires' disease, **1:**64a,b, 104a, 224b,
   363b–364a; 2:29a–b
Legislative veto, **1:**150b
Le Guin, Ursula, **1:**369a; **2:**98b
Lendl, Ivan, **2:**252a,b
Lend-Lease Act (1941), **1:**198b
Lennon, John, **1:**103a, 164a
Leno, Jay, **2:**246a
Lenzi, Mark, **2:**96a
Leonard, Elmore, **1:**369a
Leonard, Glen M., **1:**361a
Leonard, Sugar Ray, **2:**145a
Leopold, Aldo, **1:**153b, 221a; **2:**320b
Leopold Center for Sustainable Agriculture,
   1:330b
Lesbians
   and sexual orientation, **2:**203b
   writers, **1:**371b
   See also Gay and Lesbian movement
Let It Bleed (Rolling Stones), **2:**52b
*Letters on the Equality of the Sexes and the
   Condition of Women* (Grimké), **1:**376b
Leuprolide acetate, **1:**242a
Levees, **1:**249b
Levels Document, **2:**76b
Leveraged buyouts (LBOs), **1:364a–b**
Levi, Edward H., **1:**346a
Levi-Montalcini, Rita, **2:**76a–b
Lévi-Strauss, Claude, **2:**135b
Lewis, Bernard, **2:**58b
Lewis, Carl, **2:**95b, 96b
Lewis, Edward, **2:**76b
Lewis, Jerry Lee, **2:**52a
Lewis, Randy, **2:**96a
Lewis, Sinclair, **2:**44a
Lewis, Steven, **2:**96b
Lewis and Clark Centennial Exposition
   (1905), **2:**134b
Lewiston-Auburn, Maine, **2:**5a
LeWitt, Sol, **2:**196b
Liability insurance, **1:**323b–324a

N

INDEX

Outdoor Recreation League (New York), 2:164b
Outsider art. *See* Folk art
Outward Bound, 1:207a
Oven Fork, Ky., disaster at, 1:190a–b
Owen, Robert, 1:140b
Owens-Illinois, 1:364b
Oxen Hill, Md., 1:244a
Ozarks, 1:44b; 2:40a
  bioregion, 1:80b
Ozick, Cynthia, 1:369b
Ozone depletion, 1:31b–32a, 223b; 2:99b–100b
Ozzie and Harriet (Television), 1:236a

P

P. Lorillard, 2:260b
Paar, Jack, 2:246a
Pabst, Frederick, 2:322a
Pace, Darrell, 2:96a
Pacific Far East Line, 2:23a
Pacific financial exchange, 1:244a
Pacific Islanders
  in San Francisco, 2:187b
  in Vermont, 2:290b
Pacific Northwest Festival, 2:53b
Pacific Rim, 2:101a–b
  finance and trade in, 2:187a–b
Pacino, Al, 1:338b
Packwood, Robert, 2:98b, 191a
PACs. *See* Political Action Committees (PACs)
Paffenbarger, Ralph S., Jr., 1:249a
Page, Jerry, 2:96a
Paglia, Camille, 1:238b
Pahlavi, Mohammad Reza (shah), 1:46b, 306b; 2:32a
Paideia proposal, 1:207a
Paid Land Diversion Program, 1:243a
Paine, John Knowles, 2:49a
Painting, 2:101b–102b
Paiute, 2:287a
Pakistan
  Baghdad Pact (1955), 2:32a
  and foreign aid, 1:258b
  immigrants from, 1:319a
  and nuclear power, 2:83a
Palau. *See* Trust territory of the Pacific Islands
Paleontology, 2:102b–103b
Palestianian Americans, 2:103b–104a
Palestine Liberation Front (PLF), 1:7b
Palestine Liberation Organization (PLO), 2:31a
  in Lebanon, 1:362a
  peace accord with Israel, 1:336b
Palestinian Intifada, 2:31a
  Palestinian emigration to the United States, 2:103b
Palestinian-Israeli peace accord, 1:336a–337a; 2:140a
Palestinians, 2:31a
  immigrants, 1:319a
  in Lebanon, 1:362a
  terrorism, 2:31a, 95a
Palimony, 2:104a
Palm Beach County, Fla., 1:249b
Palmer, A. Mitchell, 1:239a

Palmer, Arnold, 1:285a
Palmer, Daniel D., 2:19b
Palmer, Robert, 2:49b
Palmer Hydrological Drought Index, 1:195a
Palo Alto, Calif., 2:205b
Palomar Observatory, 2:87b
Pan Am, 1:30b; 2:272a
Panama
  Contadora, 1:360b
  treaty under Carter, 1:359b
Panama Canal Treaty (1977), 2:104a–105a, 139b
Panama Defense Forces, 2:105a
Panama invasion (1989), 1:99b, 358b, 360a; 2:105a–b, 306a
  censorship, 1:103b–104a
  criticized by peace groups, 2:109b
  press during, 1:103b–104a
  women and, 2:323b–324a
Pan-American Games, 1:323b; 2:95a
Pan-Americanism, 1:360b
Pan Am Flight 103, 2:105b–106a
Panasonic, 2:267a
Pan-Atlantic Steamship Corporation, 2:22b, 23a
Pantheon, 2:152a
Paper
  acid, 1:365b
  manufacturing, 2:9a, 165b
  recycling of, 2:166a
Papp, Joseph, 2:73a, 256a
Paragliding, 2:225a
Paraguay, 1:360b; 2:78a
Paramilitary groups, 1:127a
Paramount, 2:44a, 152a
  television programming, 1:142b
Parasailing, 2:225b
Parasitology, zoology and, 2:334b
Paredes, Américo, 2:58b
Parenthood, surrogate. *See* Surrogate parenthood
Parham, Charles F., 2:112a
Pari-mutuel betting. *See* Off-track betting
Paris Peace Conference (1919), 1:198a
Park, David, 1:91b
Park, Tongsun (Park Tong Sun), 1:351b, 352a
Park Chung Hee, 1:351b, 352a
Parker, Horatio, 2:49a
Parkinson's disease, 2:17a, 242a
Park Restoration and Improvement Program, 2:107b
Parks, Gordon, 2:46a
Parks, national, 2:106a–107a, 164b, 165a
  in California, 1:90b
Parks, Rosa, 1:185a
Parks, state
  in Indiana, 1:322a
  in Utah, 2:287b
Parks and playgrounds, 2:164b
Park Service, National, 1:201b, 327b, 328a; 2:107a–108a
  in Nevada, 2:65a
  role in historic interpretation and preservation, 2:47b
  visitor centers, 2:47b
  and war memorials, 2:305a
  and wildfires, 2:320a
Park System, National, 2:106a

Parochial schools, 1:101b
Parole, 1:163a
Parolees. *See* Refugees
Partch, Harry, 2:49b, 51b
Particle accelerators, 1:240b; 2:237b
Parton, Dolly, 2:56a
Parton, Sara Willis, 1:376b
Party politics, 1:151a–b
Pasco County, Fla., 1:249b
Passaic, N.J., 2:68b
Passamaquoddy, 2:63a
Passenger pigeons extinction, 2:320b
Pasteur Institute, 1:11a
Pataki, George, 2:74a
PATCO. *See* Professional Air Traffic Controllers Organization (PATCO)
Patent and Trademark Office (PTO), 1:280a
Patents, genetically engineered organisms, 1:78a
Paterson, N.J., 2:68b
Pather Panchali (film), 2:45b
Patient Self-Determination Act (1991), 1:175a
Patients' rights, 2:108a–b
  final care determination, 1:297a
Patriot missiles, 1:289a
Patriot movement, 2:34b
Pattern-and-practice suits, 1:225b
"Patterns" (Lowell), 1:377a
Patton, Charley, 2:39b
Patz, Etan, 1:115a
Paul, William, 1:11b
Paul Quinn College, 1:173a
Paul VI (Pope), 1:100b
Pay-cable outlets, 2:250a
PCBs. *See* Polychlorinated biphenyls (PCBs)
Peabody Hotel (Memphis), 2:21a
Peace Corps, 2:108b–109a, 298b
Peaceful coexistence, 2:217b
  See also Détente
Peace Garden State. *See* North Dakota
Peace Mission Movement, 1:169a
Peace movements, 2:109a–110a
Pearl, Martin, 2:76a
Pearl Harbor, 1:198b
Pearl Harbor Fiftieth Anniversary (1991), 2:110a
Pearl Jam, 2:54b
Pease Air Force Base (N.H.), 2:33b, 67b
Pedersen, Charles J., 2:76a
Peete, Calvin, 1:285b
Pei, I. M., 1:138b
Peirce, Charles S., 2:122b
Pele (Soccer player). *See* Arantes do Nascimento, Edson
Pelican Island, Fla., 2:320a
Pelikan, Jaroslav, 2:58b
Pelli, Cesar, 1:138b
Peltier, Leonard, 1:37a; 2:333a
Pelton, Ronald, 1:326b
Peña, Federico F., 1:137b, 183b
Pendergast, Thomas, 1:349a
Peninsula Hang Glider Club, 2:225a
Penn Central, 1:122a
Pennsylvania, 2:110a–111b
  Asian Indian Americans in, 1:51b
  aviation disaster in, 1:190a
  and immigration, 1:319b; 2:214b

INDEX

INDEX

INDEX

INDEX

INDEX

DICTIONARY OF AMERICAN HISTORY